UNITED STATES HISTORY:
SEARCH FOR FREEDOM

WE THE PEOPLE

UNITED STATES HISTORY:
SEARCH FOR FREEDOM

Richard N. Current   University of North Carolina at Greensboro

Alexander DeConde   University of California, Santa Barbara

Harris L. Dante   Kent State University, Kent, Ohio

Scott, Foresman and Company

Library of Congress Catalog Card Number 72-93709
ISBN-0-673-03300-7

Copyright © 1974 Scott, Foresman and Company, Glenview, Illinois.
Philippines Copyright 1974 Scott, Foresman and Company.
All Rights Reserved.
Printed in the United States of America.
Some of the material in this book was previously published in
    United States History, Copyright © 1967 Scott, Foresman and Company.

Regional offices of Scott, Foresman and Company are located
in Dallas, Texas; Glenview, Illinois; Oakland, New Jersey;
Palo Alto, California; Tucker, Georgia; and Brighton, England.

AUTHORS

RICHARD N. CURRENT

Richard N. Current is Distinguished Professor of American History at the University of North Carolina at Greensboro. He has taught at colleges and universities in nine states and also at the University of Munich, Germany; the University of Oxford, England; and the University of Chile, Santiago. Dr. Current received his A.B. degree from Oberlin College, his M.A. degree from Fletcher School of Law and Diplomacy at Tufts University, and his Ph.D. degree from the University of Wisconsin. He has written many historical books, including *Daniel Webster and the Rise of National Conservatism; The Lincoln Nobody Knows;* and *Three Carpetbag Governors.* Dr. Current is a past member of the board of editors of the *American Historical Review* and is at present a councilor of the Society of American Historians, Inc.

ALEXANDER DE CONDE

Alexander DeConde is Professor of History at the University of California, Santa Barbara. He has also taught at Stanford University, Whittier College, Duke University, the University of Michigan, and elsewhere. He received a B.A. degree from San Francisco State College and M.A. and Ph.D. degrees from Stanford University. Dr. DeConde has written extensively in the field of American diplomatic and political history. His books include *The American Secretary of State: An Interpretation; Entangling Alliance: Politics and Diplomacy Under George Washington; A History of American Foreign Policy; Half-Bitter, Half-Sweet: An Excursion into Italian-American History;* and *Student Activism: Town and Gown in Historical Perspective* (ed.). Dr. DeConde has received two Guggenheim Fellowships and two Fulbright Awards in American studies.

HARRIS L. DANTE

Harris L. Dante is Professor of History and Education at Kent State University, Ohio, where he teaches courses in social studies education and the history of United States education. He holds B.A. and M.A. degrees from the University of Illinois and a Ph.D. degree from the University of Chicago. Dr. Dante gained both high-school and college teaching experience in Burlington, Iowa, and has taught at the University of Chicago. Active in the National Council for the Social Studies, he has served two terms on that organization's board of directors and in January 1973 became president. Dr. Dante has written articles for many historical and educational publications, including the *Journal of the Illinois State Historical Society* and *Social Education.*

CONTRIBUTING AUTHOR

Elston Coleman
Social Studies Teacher
Englewood High School
Chicago, Illinois

EDUCATIONAL CONSULTANT

Daniel Powell
Associate Professor of Education
University of Illinois at Chicago Circle

Editorial Vice-President: Betty Ryan
Executive Editor: Alice Kay

Editorial Development: Nora Whitford
          with Janet Kanter, Ida M. Fisher, Betty Rand, Ann Ladky, Ann James,
          Virginia Munzer, Jane Rogers, Kathleen G. Manatt, and Sharon Grodsky
Designers: Thomas Gorman, Daniel Smith
Picture Editors: Denise Tamayo, Sheryl Bailey, Shirley Sklencar
Production Staff: Philip O'Neil, Nancy Huelsman, Adele McGann

TEXT ACKNOWLEDGMENTS

Pages 183, 314, 413, 483, and 631 (chart), adapted from "American Business Activity Since 1790," 43rd edition, April 1972. Reprinted by permission of The Cleveland Trust Company, Cleveland, Ohio.

Page 203, from *The Emancipation of the American Woman* (original hardcover edition: *The Better Half*), by Andrew A. Sinclair. Copyright © 1965 by Andrew A. Sinclair. Reprinted by permission of Harper & Row, Publishers, Inc., and Elaine Greene Ltd.

Page 402, from *The Melting-Pot*, by Israel Zangwill. Copyright 1910 by The Macmillan Company.

Page 414, from *The Jungle*, by Upton Sinclair. Copyright 1905, 1906 by Upton Sinclair.

Page 421 (left), excerpts from Remarks of Senator George G. Vest (1887), *Congressional Record*. Page 421 (center), excerpt from Carrie Chapman Catt, President's Annual Address (1902), the National American Woman Suffrage Association. Page 421 (right), from *Are Women People?* by Alice Duer Miller from *Up From the Pedestal*, edited by Aileen S. Kraditor. Reprinted by permission of Denning Duer Miller.

Page 461, from *Woman Suffrage and Politics*, by Carrie Chapman Catt and Nettie Rogers Shuler. Copyright 1923 by Charles Scribner's Sons. Reprinted by permission.

Page 489 (left), from *Vital Speeches of the Day* (February 10, 1936). Reprinted by permission. Page 489 (center), from *After the New Deal, What?* by Norman Thomas. Copyright 1936 by Norman Thomas, renewed 1964 by Norman Thomas. Reprinted by permission of The Macmillan Company. Page 489 (right), from *The Roosevelt I Knew*, by Frances Perkins. Copyright 1946 by Frances Perkins. Reprinted by permission of The Viking Press, Inc., and Laurence Pollinger Limited.

CONTENTS

UNIT 1 — The Path to Independence, 1492–1783 — 12
- Chapter 1   Prelude to Independence — 18
- Chapter 2   The American Revolution — 40

UNIT 2 — Establishing a New Nation, 1783–1815 — 64
- Chapter 3   The New Republic — 68
- Chapter 4   The Federalist Era — 91
- Chapter 5   The Jeffersonians — 112

UNIT 3 — Life in a Growing Nation, 1815–1850 — 132
- Chapter 6   The Early National Years — 136
- Chapter 7   Jacksonian Democracy — 158
- Chapter 8   Manifest Destiny — 185

UNIT 4 — Division and Reunion, 1850–1877 — 212
- Chapter 9   Two Ways of Life — 216
- Chapter 10   A Divided Nation — 239
- Chapter 11   The Civil War — 260
- Chapter 12   Restoring the Union — 282

UNIT 5 — Problems of an Industrial Nation, 1877–1900 302
- Chapter 13 The Rise of Industry 306
- Chapter 14 The Agricultural Revolution 326
- Chapter 15 The Politics of Discontent 344
- Chapter 16 The Gilded Age 366

UNIT 6 — The Rise of a World Power, 1900–1920 386
- Chapter 17 The Changing Society 390
- Chapter 18 The Progressives 408
- Chapter 19 Foreign Involvement 429

UNIT 7 — The Time Between the Wars, 1920–1941 454
- Chapter 20 Postwar Politics 458
- Chapter 21 The New Deal 478
- Chapter 22 Years of Hope and Despair 498
- Chapter 23 From Isolation to War 517

UNIT 8 — Hot and Cold Wars, 1941–1960 536
- Chapter 24 The Global War 540
- Chapter 25 Period of Adjustment 564
- Chapter 26 The Eisenhower Years 585

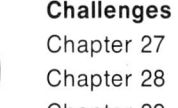

UNIT 9 — Challenges of the Space Age, 1960–1972 608
- Chapter 27 New Hopes and Old Realities 612
- Chapter 28 Global Turmoil 632
- Chapter 29 People or Machines? 651

Reference Section 673
- Atlas of the Modern World 674
- The Declaration of Independence 685
- The Constitution of the United States of America 687
- Presidents, Vice-Presidents, and Secretaries of State 708
- Bibliographies 710
- Acknowledgments 716
- Index 720

ECOLOGY FEATURES

27	The Land as It Was
121	Plant and Animal Resources
149	Land and Water Resources
299	The Civil War and Population Dynamics
317	The Sad Tale of the Cities
415	The Conservation Movement
463	The Flivver: Anatomy of a Pollution Cure
579	Oh Strange New World
667	The Earth as Guinea Pig

ART AND LEISURE FEATURES

43	Leisure: The Colonial Period
127	Leisure: The Early Nation
237	Leisure: At Midcentury
349	Leisure: The New Industrial Era
401	Leisure: The Good Old Days
404–405	Art: The Turn of the Century
475	Leisure: The Roaring Twenties
506–507	Art: The 1920's and 1930's
604–605	Art: The 1940's and 1950's
617	Leisure: Recent Times
668–669	Art: The 1960's and 1970's

SPECIAL FEATURES

21	The Indians
37	Beyond the Southern Frontier
79	The California Missions
103	The People of the United States, 1790
177	The Treaty of New Echota
227	The Know-Nothings
249	Slavery: Three Views
284–285	Reconstruction: Two Views and Two Reactions
353	The Rise of Jim Crow
402	The Immigrants
421	Women's Suffrage: Three Views
435	Involvement in Mexico
489	The New Deal: Three Views
493	A New Deal for the Indians
543	A Study in Hysteria
603	Transforming Puerto Rico
625	A New Look at the Melting Pot

MAPS AND CHARTS

Page	Title
16–17	European Exploration of North America
21	Indian Tribes and Ways of Life
25	British Possessions in North America, 1763
51	American Revolution, 1775–1776
55	American Revolution, 1777–1779
59	American Revolution, 1780–1781 (inset, Yorktown Campaign)
75	Western Land Claims and Cessions, 1776–1802
76	The Land Ordinances, 1785 and 1787
85	The Structure and Powers of the Government
87	Amending the Constitution of the United States
103	National Origins and Religions, 1790
107	Presidential Elections, 1796–1802
116	Westward Expansion, 1803–1807
143	The Cumberland Road (National Road)
147	Missouri Compromise of 1820
153	United States, 1819
155	Presidential Elections, 1816–1828
179	Presidential Elections, 1832–1844
183	Business Activity, 1800–1850 (detail, 1820–1828)
189	Population Growth, 1790–1850
196–197	The Mexican War, 1846–1848
198	United States, 1853
209	Railroads in Operation, 1850
217	Ten Largest Cities, 1840–1860
219	Immigration to the United States, 1820–1870
233	Abolition of Slavery, 1800–1865
247	Presidential Elections, 1848–1860
261	Resources of the Union and the Confederacy
276	Civil War, December 1862
277	Civil War, December 1863
278	Civil War, March 1865 (detail, Appomattox Campaign)
297	Presidential Elections, 1864–1876
309	Railroads in Operation, 1890
314	Business Activity, 1850–1898 (detail, 1884–1894)
324	Population Growth, 1850–1900
346	Presidential Elections, 1880–1888
381	United States Possessions in 1899
384	Presidential Elections, 1892–1900
392	Population Growth, 1900–1920
402	Immigration to the United States, 1870–1920
413	Business Activity, 1898–1920 (detail, 1910–1920)
423	Presidential Elections, 1904–1916
436	Europe, 1914
440–441	World War I, 1914–1918
442	World War I, Meuse-Argonne Campaign
452	Europe, 1922
467	Presidential Elections, 1920–1932
483	Business Activity, 1920–1941 (detail, 1932–1940)
499	Population Growth, 1920–1940
525	Presidential Elections, 1936–1940
546–547	World War II, European Theater, 1939–1942
550–551	World War II, European Theater, 1943–1945
553	World War II, Pacific Theater, 1941–1943
555	World War II, Pacific Theater, 1943–1945
571	Europe, 1952
582–583	Korean War, 1950–1953
587	Presidential Elections, 1944–1956
595	Immigration to the United States, 1920–1970
615	Presidential Elections, 1960–1972
631	Business Activity, 1941–1971 (detail, 1960–1971)
653	Population Growth, 1940–1970
674–675	The World
676	North America
677	South America
678	Europe
679	Asia
680	Africa
681	Oceania
	United States
682	Relief
683	Political
684	Alaska and Hawaii

The manner of their fishing.

UNIT ONE 1492–1783

The Path to Independence

Our nation is moving toward two societies, one black, one white—separate and unequal.
—*Report of the National Advisory Commission on Civil Disorders*

Give me your tired, your poor, your huddled
  masses yearning to breathe free,
The wretched refuse of your teeming shore,
Send these, the homeless,
  tempest-tossed to me:
I lift my lamp beside the golden door.
—*Inscription on the Statue of Liberty*

The Indian wars of the past should rightly be regarded as the first foreign wars of American history. As the United States marched across this continent, it was creating an empire by wars of foreign conquest just as England and France were doing in India and Africa. Certainly the war with Mexico was imperialistic, no more or less than the wars against the Sioux, Apache, Utes, and Yakimas. In every case the goal was identical: land.
—Vine Deloria, Jr., *Custer Died for Your Sins*

Three views of the United States: Is any one of them accurate? Just looking at the nation as it is today won't give you the answer. To know what the United States is and where it is going, you first must know where it has been. And where it has been is the content of American history.

American history begins with the tribes of people who started coming from Asia some 25,000 years ago. Many scientists believe that for thousands of years there was a land bridge across the present Bering Strait. They think that Asians crossed it while hunting for animals or fleeing from enemies. These men, women, and children then moved southward, eventually peopling both the North and South American continents. They had many names for their tribes, but other people came to call them Indians.

European migration to America started thousands of years later with colonizers from western Europe. They brought their ways of life with them to the New World. They changed the land and people, but the land and people also changed them.

As they land at Roanoke, English explorers come face to face with members of the Croatoan tribe. Sir Walter Raleigh began colonies on the swampy Virginia coast in the 1580's, but they failed disastrously.

The first lasting colonies were Spanish. Most of them were in South or Central America, but some were in North America. Large parts of these former Spanish colonies are now within the United States.

In America, the Spaniards conquered huge Indian empires, set up colonial governments, and tried to re-create Spain in America. The Spaniards at first used Indian slaves to do most of the mining and farming in New Spain. Many Indians died from the harsh conditions of slave life, however, and many escaped.

Few Spanish women came to the colonies; hence most of the male colonists married Indian women. In time, their Spanish-Indian children formed a new people, *mestizos,* who blended Indian and Spanish cultures.

African slave labor was introduced into the Spanish colonies in 1502. For the most part the Africans were brought to the islands in the Caribbean Sea, the so-called West Indies. The Africans came from a number of nations and tribes, with different languages and cultures. On the islands, people from different areas were thrown together. Since they were usually unable to speak the same language, it was difficult for them to plan together to resist enslavement. On the plantations where they worked they were forced to give up many of their old customs and to adopt European ways. As a result, much from their native cultures was lost.

The English and French started colonies during the hundred years after the Africans began coming to the New World. England's settlements were founded along the eastern coast of North America, and France's to the north, west, and south of England's. Both countries also started important colonies in the West Indies.

The experiences of the English and French as colonists differed from those of the Spaniards. The English at first searched for gold and tried to enslave the Indians. Since they found little gold and they were unsuccessful in their attempts at enslaving the Indians, they soon abandoned this pattern and set up farming communities. The English colonies usually were made up of European families.

There was far less intermarriage with the Indians and quite a bit more warfare. Instead of incorporating the Indians into their communities, the English often pushed them out of the areas in which they were living or killed them. The French usually set up fur-trading posts or fishing villages, and they depended on the Indians for help in trapping for furs or catching fish. Indian tribes often allied with the French or Spanish against the English. (But there were other tribes that allied themselves to the English.)

Other Europeans, notably the Dutch and Swedes, also started settlements on the East Coast. These did not last as separate colonies but became parts of English America. People from other countries came to the colonies as immigrants, rather than to start their own colonies. The Scotch-Irish, Germans, Scots, French Protestants, Irish, Finns, Italians, Poles, and many others were all found in the English colonies.

The earliest colonists did not look at themselves as a new people. Those from England, for example, thought of themselves simply as English people who happened to be living in North America. The English who stayed at home looked upon the colonists in the same way. As time passed, however, the colonists began to feel that they had become different, as indeed they had. By 1750, they usually considered the people of Britain and other European nations as foreigners, and those people often referred to the colonists as "Americans."

New ways of life were developing in the New World. For this there were two main reasons. One was that the Americans were a mixture of nationalities. "What is the American, this new man?" asked a French nobleman, Michel Guillaume Jean de Crèvecoeur, in his book, *Letters from an American Farmer,* published in 1782. He noted that in America a man might have an English grandfather, a Dutch wife, and a French daughter-in-law. "Here individuals of all nations are melted into a new race of men," Crèvecoeur said, "whose labor and posterity will one day cause great changes in the world."

A second reason for the development of a civilization that was distinctive and new was the physical environment of the colonies. Here lay great forests to be cleared and abundant land to be cultivated. The first pioneers along the coast faced many hardships and dangers. In time they developed farms and villages and later mills and towns and cities, with many of the social, religious, and political institutions common to European communities. As more and more colonists arrived and as they moved farther and farther inland, they went through a similar process of pushing out the Indians, clearing the forests, and re-creating European civilization.

By 1783, a new republic of thirteen states had arisen from the thirteen English colonies on the eastern coast of North America. The way of life in these states was mainly based on ideas and customs that had been brought from the British Isles and western Europe. American society was primarily a branch of European civilization. Yet, in the course of years, a sense of "Americanness" had appeared. The development of this sense and the achievement of independence provide two of the main themes of American history in these formative years.

Greenland
ERIC THE RED, 982
ERICSON, 1000
JOHN CABOT, 1498
Hudson Strait
HUDSON, 1610
Labrador
Hudson Bay
CARTIER, 1534-36
Newfoundland
JOHN CABOT, 1497
Hudson cast adrift
St. Lawrence R.
Stadacona (Quebec)
Hochelaga (Montreal)
CHAMPLAIN, 1603-09
L. Champlain
L. Superior
L. Huron
L. Michigan
L. Ont.
L. Erie
HUDSON, 1609
Columbia R.
JOLIET AND MARQUETTE, 1673
LA SALLE, 1681-82
Missouri R.
ATLANTIC OCEAN
Colorado R.
Ohio R.
Arkansas R.
Mississippi R.
VERRAZANO, 1524
CORONADO, 1540-42
DE SOTO, 1539-41
Death of De Soto
Death of Narvaez
PONCE DE LEON, 1513
CABRILLO AND FERRELO, 1542-43
Rio Grande
CABEZA DE VACA, 1536
MOSCOSO DE ALVARADO, 1542-43
COLUMBUS, 1492
San Salvador
Culiacán
Gulf of Mexico
Cuba
Hispaniola
NARVAEZ, 1528
Compostela
"NORTH SEA" (CARIBBEAN SEA)
982–1513
1514–1602
1603–1682
DRAKE, 1577-80
"SOUTH SEA" (PACIFIC OCEAN)
PREPARED BY UNIVERSAL MAP, INC.

EUROPEAN EXPLORATION OF NORTH AMERICA: 982-1682

Note: Present-day place names are used in these descriptions to help locate the areas of exploration.

Eric the Red, a Norse seaman, discovered Greenland in 982 and set up a colony there. The tales of his deeds were narrated by several generations of Scandinavians before being written down.

Leif Ericson left his father's colony in Greenland and sailed along the coast of North America in 1000. He landed three times: at *Helluland,* or land of flat stones; *Markland,* or woodland; and *Vinland,* or vineland. Some scholars identify these sites as Newfoundland, Nova Scotia, and Massachusetts.

Christopher Columbus sailed August 3, 1492, from Palos, Spain. Land (the Bahamas) was sighted on October 12. After island-hopping in the Caribbean Sea, Columbus returned to Spain, saying that he had reached Asia. He made three additional trips.

John Cabot (Giovanni Caboto), was backed by English merchants who hoped to break the Arab hold on the spice trade. His single ship reached "newfounde land" in June 1497. The next year, with his son Sebastian, he explored the New England coast.

Giovanni da Verrazano, of Florence, was sent by Francis I of France to find a strait through the New World. His search, in 1524, led him into New York harbor, which he explored.

Henry Hudson, an Englishman, first tried to sail northeast around Russia to the Orient, but decided in 1609 to cross the Atlantic. He claimed New York harbor for his Dutch sponsors and sailed north on the river that now bears his name. In 1610, sailing under the English flag, he found a great bay, where his mutinous sailors left him to die.

Juan Ponce de León tried to explore Florida in 1513 but was stopped by Indians. The Spanish king promised that he could be governor if he conquered Florida. Returning in 1521 with 200 well-armed soldiers, Ponce de León again failed to defeat the Indians; he himself died of an arrow wound.

Pánfilo de Narváez led Spaniards to Florida in 1528. Disease, starvation, and Indian fighting reduced his army of 400 to 4. The survivors crossed the Gulf of Mexico to Texas. Two of them, **Alvar Núñez Cabeza de Vaca,** and **Estavanico,** a black, crossed the Southwest to join other Spaniards in Mexico in 1536.

Hernando De Soto and 600 Spanish nobles in 1539 successfully invaded Florida. Searching for Indian treasure, they traveled north to the Carolinas, then west to Texas. The search failed, but De Soto did claim for Spain much of the Southeast. After he died in 1542, about 300 of his men, led by **Luis de Moscoso de Alvarado,** managed to reach Mexico.

Francisco Vásquez de Coronado, a Spanish noble, spent his fortune searching for the legendary Seven Cities of Gold. His expedition (1540–1542) was led by an Indian who hoped to exhaust the Spanish plunderers and avenge the killing of his people.

Juan Rodriguez Cabrillo, a Portuguese navigator sailing for Spain, and **Bartolomeo Ferrelo** explored the West Coast. Their failure (1542–1543) to find a transcontinental river convinced the Spanish to give up the search for such a passage.

Sir Francis Drake, trying to escape with his pirate ship, landed on the California coast in 1579. He brazenly planted the English flag, although the Spanish held many prior claims to California. Drake returned to England by sailing west across the Pacific.

Jacques Cartier, searching for the Northwest Passage, opened the vast Northeast interior to French settlement. On voyages in 1534 and 1535 he explored the St. Lawrence River Valley.

Samuel de Champlain first came to Canada in 1603. He returned twice, staying the second time to govern the fur-trading posts he had set up. He explored northern New York (Lake Champlain) and the St. Lawrence River Valley, "founding" Quebec in 1608 on the site of an Indian village.

Louis Joliet, a French subject born in America, and **Jacques Marquette,** a Jesuit priest, first sighted the Mississippi River in 1673. They went down the Mississippi as far as Arkansas, where they were turned back by Indians. They already realized that the "great river" was not a route to the Pacific.

La Salle (the French noble Robert René Cavelier) gave the name Louisiana, after Louis XIV of France, to the land he explored. In 1682, with 23 Frenchmen and 18 Indians, he went down the Illinois and Mississippi rivers to the Gulf of Mexico.

Prelude to Independence

CHAPTER 1

1492–1763

A Secotan farming village in North Carolina.

When did the history of the United States begin? Was it the day thousands of years ago when an Asian hunter first stepped onto the North American continent in Alaska? Did it start in 1492 when Columbus landed in the West Indies? Or did it begin in 1607 with Jamestown, the first permanent English colony in America?

No matter. Sooner or later someone would have found the North and South American continents and started settling them. The "when" of United States history often is not as important as the "how" and "why."

COLONIZATION BEGINS

Six hundred years before the founding of Jamestown, an expedition led by the Norse explorer Leif Ericson landed on the northeastern coast of North America. Its travels led to no lasting consequences, for Europe was not yet ready to respond. In the next five centuries, however, Europe underwent remarkable changes. When Christopher Columbus "discovered" the New World in 1492, he touched off one of the largest colonization movements in history.

The changes going on in Europe amounted to a kind of reawakening. People had begun to take more and more interest in the world about them. They tried to control natural forces by means of science and invention rather than prayer or magic. Among the new inventions were guns, windmills and water mills, the printing press, and the mechanical clock. Especially important for overseas exploration were the compass and the *astrolabe,* a device for finding the latitude by sighting a star.

Well-organized nations with strong kings or queens were coming into existence. The rulers had the support of merchants, who began to form a new "middle class" between the nobles who held the land and the serfs who worked it. Towns increased in size and

On this map of Spain's holdings in Mexico, published in 1555, west is at the top. European colonization of North America came in two major thrusts—by the Spanish pushing north and by the British and French pushing west. The Spanish brought horses with them, and such animals transformed the lives of the western Indians. Silver mining *(background)* became a major business in New Spain.

number as they became centers of trade. Commerce reached out from Europe to distant places in East Asia. Merchants brought costly items of trade—jewels, glass and chinaware, silks and other fine cloths, drugs, perfumes, and spices—to Europe all the way from Japan, China, India, and neighboring islands of East Asia.

The trade routes lay partly over seas and partly over land. They were controlled at certain points by Arab, Italian, or other merchants. These middlemen took such a large profit that prices were excessively high by the time the goods reached the British Isles and other parts of western Europe. Both the merchants and the rulers of these nations hoped to find new routes, entirely by sea, that they could control.

Columbus was looking for such a route when, with the backing of Queen Isabella and King Ferdinand of Spain, he sailed westward over the uncharted Atlantic Ocean. When he sighted land, he thought he had reached one of the islands of East Asia. On three later voyages he looked for a passage by water to the Pacific. In the next hundred years, other explorers sailing under the flags of various nations kept up the search. They never discovered the kind of passage they were seeking (since one did not exist), but they revealed most of the outlines and much of the interior of the North and South American continents.

On the basis of Columbus's discoveries, Spain at first claimed all of the New World. Soon it agreed to share the part now known as Brazil with Portugal. In the sixteenth century, Spain began founding colonies and building an empire in North and South America.

Other nations, among them England, challenged the Spanish claim to a monopoly of the New World. Because of its success, England rather than Spain was to be the "mother country" of the United States.

England Versus Spain

England based its claim to a share of the New World on the explorations it had sponsored. For many years, however, England was too weak to make good its claim against the opposition of Spain, which in the sixteenth century was the greatest power in the world.

The Spanish monarchs ruled a huge empire in Europe as well as in the New World. After the Protestant Reformation began, they became the champions of the Roman Catholic Church. (The Reformation protested against and tried to reform certain practices of the Church of Rome. In time, Roman Catholic leaders started their own reforms and tried to win back people who had joined Protestant churches.) Bitter religious wars were fought, but Europe remained divided between Roman Catholic and Protestant nations.

England became a Protestant nation after King Henry VIII broke away from the Church of Rome. He set up the Church of England (the Anglican Church) and declared himself its head. His daughter Elizabeth I, who ruled from 1558 to 1603, defended the church and the government against the Roman Catholics at home and abroad. At home the Roman Catholics plotted to put Mary "Queen of Scots" on the throne. Abroad, the Spanish king, Philip II, encouraged the plotters and threatened to attack England.

Elizabeth dealt with the threat at home by having Mary put to death. Abroad, she carried on an undeclared war against Spain. English seamen roved the waters of Spanish America, capturing treasure ships and attacking towns. After Elizabeth made an alliance with the Dutch, who were revolting against Spanish rule, Philip II declared war on England.

In 1588 he sent a large fleet, the "Invincible Armada," to invade and conquer

The Indians

No one knows how many Indians once lived in the area that is now the United States. Historians' estimates of the Indian population at the beginning of European exploration range from a low of 840,000 to a high of 12 million. The Indians made up hundreds of tribes, many with separate languages.

Variations in climate, land, and resources affected tribal life-styles. Some tribes, like the Hopi and Zuñi, were primarily agricultural. Others, including the Shoshone, gathered plants, seeds, and roots and caught small animals for food. Many of the northeastern tribes farmed, hunted, and fished. In the Pacific Northwest, where fish were plentiful, there was little need to practice agriculture, for the rivers, lakes, and ocean held plenty of food.

Social and political organization varied. Among the Hopi and Zuñi, for example, families were organized into clans. Relationships were traced through the women, who owned the crops and houses. Political activities were directed by male religious leaders.

Perhaps the most far-reaching Indian political organization was the League of the Iroquois, composed of the Mohawk, Oneida, Onondaga, Cayuga, Seneca, and Tuscarora tribes. In these Six Nations, political power rested with the female leaders of *ohwachiras,* groups of related families. These women appointed men as delegates to the ruling council of the League. The League council did not interfere in a tribe's internal affairs, but it did intervene in serious disagreements among tribes. The Six Nations sometimes united against common enemies.

All of the North American tribes were greatly affected by European and African immigration. By the nineteenth century, Europeans called the Choctaw, Chickasaw, Creek, Cherokee, and Seminole the "Five Civilized Tribes," because their culture reflected European notions of "civilization." Most Indians valued some of the introductions from the Old World, including iron tools, horses, oxen, and guns. But with these additions and others, Indian cultures lost some of their unique qualities.

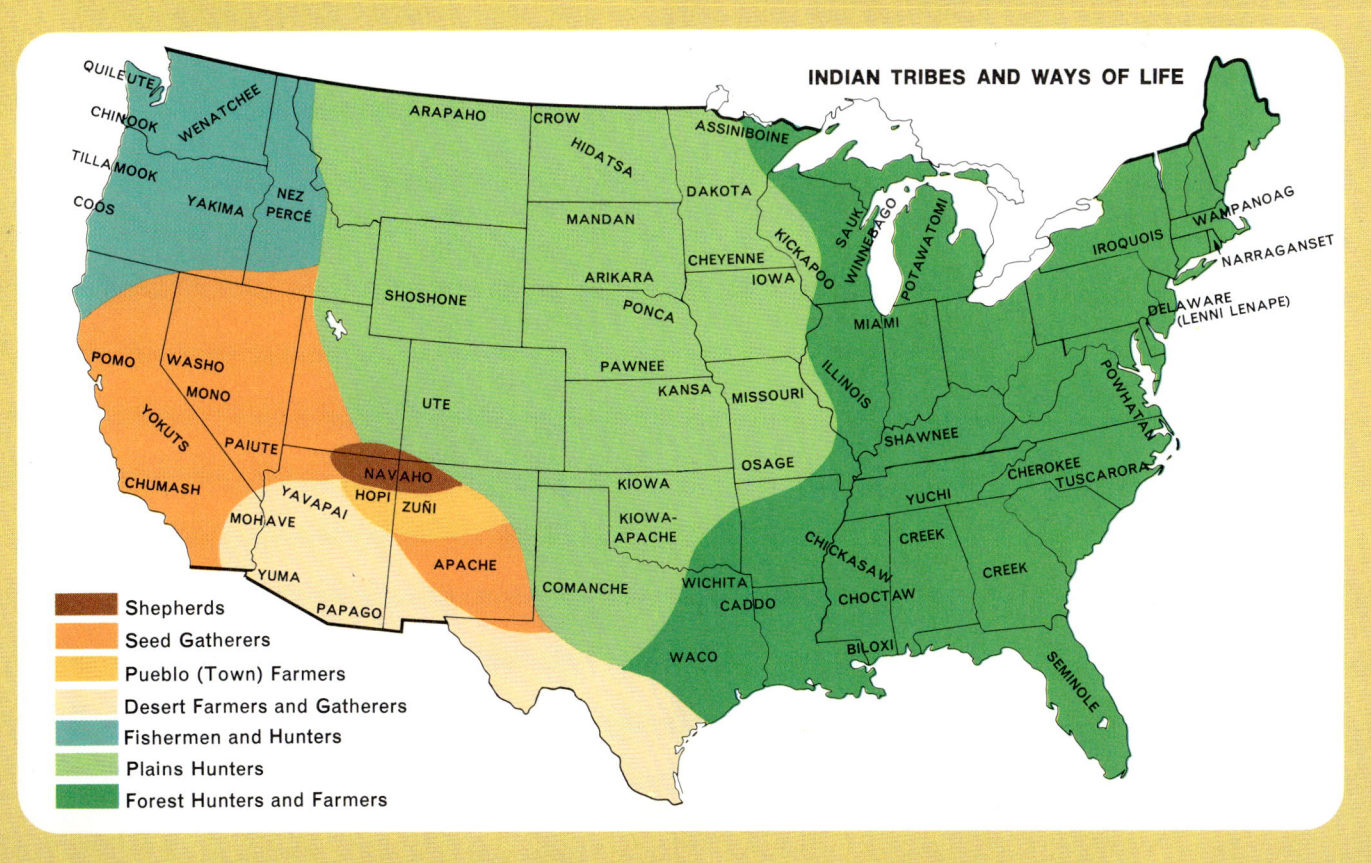

INDIAN TRIBES AND WAYS OF LIFE

- Shepherds
- Seed Gatherers
- Pueblo (Town) Farmers
- Desert Farmers and Gatherers
- Fishermen and Hunters
- Plains Hunters
- Forest Hunters and Farmers

England. The English were ready with a large number of small, fast, highly maneuverable ships. After the Armada arrived, a terrible storm arose. The storm helped the English, for it sank or scattered most of the Spanish fleet. England, now the strongest sea power, could set up colonies of its own in North America.

Colonization's Appeal

In his book *Utopia* (1516) the Englishman Sir Thomas More described life on an imaginary island in the New World. Here there were no poor and no rich. All the people lived comfortably, but they had only contempt for wealth itself. Everyone worked, but no one had to work too hard. Peace and happiness prevailed. (As a result, the term *utopia* has come to mean an ideal society.)

The imaginary life in *Utopia* contrasted sharply with English life in More's time. Many landowners were making their farms into sheep pastures because more money could be made from wool than from grain. The farm tenants were forced from the land, and many roamed around in gangs begging and stealing.

While most people were poor and in many cases growing poorer, the wool growers, dealers, and manufacturers prospered. Great merchants exported woolens and other goods to foreign nations. Some of the merchants formed companies to share the expenses, risks, and profits in large trading ventures. Often the company shareholders made fantastic profits from a single voyage.

The merchants adopted a theory of trade that eventually came to be known as *mercantilism*. They claimed that a country was strongest and most prosperous when exports were greater in value than imports. According to this theory, the government should encourage sales to foreign nations and discourage purchases from them.

The idea of starting colonies in North America fitted well into the mercantilist theory. Colonies would become places to send the poor and the unemployed, to sell manufactured goods, and to get raw materials that would otherwise have to be bought from foreign lands. The colonial trade would increase business for shipowners and raise tax money for the government.

Colonies would also be places of refuge for religious and political minorities. Not all the English people were satisfied with the established church, the Church of England. Roman Catholics objected to it, as did many Protestants. The Puritans wished to simplify the services—to "purify" them by making them less like the Catholic. The Quakers and other groups wanted complete independence of worship. According to the laws, however, everyone was required to follow the practices of the established church and to pay taxes to support it.

During the seventeenth century, there was a continual struggle between the Parliament and the monarch. Under James I, the government persecuted the Puritans and other Protestant dissenters. These groups got control of Parliament and, in the 1640's, fought a civil war, executed Charles I, and set up a dictatorship under Oliver Cromwell. In 1660, the monarchy was restored, with Charles II on the throne. Finally, in the Glorious Revolution (1688–1689), Parliament deposed James II, who had become a Roman Catholic. Parliament then brought in James's daughter Mary and her husband William, both Protestants, as rulers.

During this troubled period, first one group and then another looked to North America as a place to find safety. At the same time, the people in power looked to North America for lands with which to reward their friends and followers. Thus religious, political, and economic conditions in England promoted an interest in colonies in the New World.

Thirteen English Colonies

According to English law, the monarch was the owner and ruler of all new lands that English people discovered or settled. The government did not, however, start colonizing projects. These were left to individuals, partnerships, or companies.

The promoters of colonies generally had patriotic or religious goals as well as profits in mind. They expected to sell or rent land to settlers and engage in colonial trade. First, they had to get from the monarch a grant of land and a charter allowing them to start a colony and govern the colonists. Next, the promoters had to bring together ships, supplies, and people and send them to North America. This was an expensive business.

There was a good deal of quarreling and confusion about the promotion of colonies. Kings and queens awarded land grants and colonial charters one after another. Sometimes the boundaries overlapped, and sometimes the people receiving the land gave parts of it to others. Sometimes charters, after having been awarded, were changed or revoked. Nevertheless, companies and "proprietors," either individuals or groups, established lasting colonies. Grants made to two groups of merchants led to the beginnings of Virginia and Massachusetts. Grants to various proprietors resulted in the founding of Maryland, the Carolinas, New York, Pennsylvania, Delaware, and New Jersey. Settlers moving out from Massachusetts

Most of the early French settlers in North America made their living by trapping or fishing. They traded or exported dried codfish and valuable beaver pelts to other colonists and Europe.

formed Rhode Island, New Hampshire, and Connecticut, all of which eventually managed to get separate charters. A group of trustees acting in the name of charity set up the last of the mainland colonies, Georgia.

The appearance of New Amsterdam reflected the Dutch heritage of the colony's people.

In the period from 1607 to 1733, thirteen English colonies were set up on the North American continent. (Still others appeared on islands in and near the Caribbean Sea.) The promoters did not make the money they had hoped, and colonization proved more or less a failure as a business enterprise. Still, it was a success in the making of new societies.

GROWING COLONIES

The early arrivals from England were impressed by the almost unbroken forest they found in North America. With the animals and birds it sheltered, this forest furnished plenty of food, fuel, and building material.

The English colonists often tried to buy the land they wanted from the Indian tribes. Since their ideas of land ownership differed, the Indians and the English did not really agree on the terms. Many of the Indians signed treaties thinking they would still be able to use the land that they had "sold" to the colonists. When the colonists tried to force the Indians off the newly purchased land, war resulted.

During the colonial period there was continual war between one tribe or another and the colonists. The Europeans had better weapons than the Indians, and they usually won the battles. Also, the tribes rarely united to fight the colonists, for many of them were traditional enemies. Slowly, as tribes were defeated and as more colonists arrived from Europe and Africa, the colonial population moved inland.

Differences in physical environment from north to south contributed to the development of three fairly distinct regions, each with its own forms of economic life. In New England, the farms were small and fairly self-sufficient. Shipbuilding, fishing, and shipping became important industries. In the middle, or "bread," colonies (New York, New Jersey, Pennsylvania, and Delaware), farms were larger and more productive. Much grain, flour, and meat were sold to other colonies and to overseas markets. In the South, there were large plantations as well as modest-sized farms, where tobacco, rice, and indigo were produced for export.

Colonial Population Growth

The colonies needed workers to develop their economic resources. The Old World contained thousands eager to get a new start in life in the colonies, but most people were too poor to pay the fare across the ocean. To bring laborers to the colonies, a system of "indentured" servitude developed. Men and women signed contracts, called indentures, to work as servants for a period of four to seven years. The contracts were sold to land-

British Possessions in North America, 1763

Thirteen original colonies
All others

TYPE OF COLONY AND DATE

1642	1691	1715
CORPORATE	ROYAL	PROPRIETARY

COLONY	TYPE			FIRST SETTLEMENT	DATE
VIRGINIA	1606	1624		JAMESTOWN	1607
NEW HAMPSHIRE	1622	1679		RYE	1623
MASSACHUSETTS	1629	1691		PLYMOUTH	1620
MARYLAND	1632	1691	1715	ST. MARY'S	1634
RHODE ISLAND	1644			PROVIDENCE	1636
CONNECTICUT	1662			HOUSE OF HOPE	1633
NORTH CAROLINA	1663	1729		ALBEMARLE SOUND	1650
SOUTH CAROLINA	1663	1729		ALBEMARLE POINT	1670
DELAWARE	1664			FORT CHRISTINA	1638
NEW JERSEY	1664	1702		FORT NASSAU	1623
NEW YORK	1664	1685		FORT ORANGE / FORT AMSTERDAM	1624
PENNSYLVANIA	1681	1692	1694	NEW GOTHENBERG	1643
GEORGIA	1732	1753		SAVANNAH	1733

PREPARED BY UNIVERSAL MAP, INC.

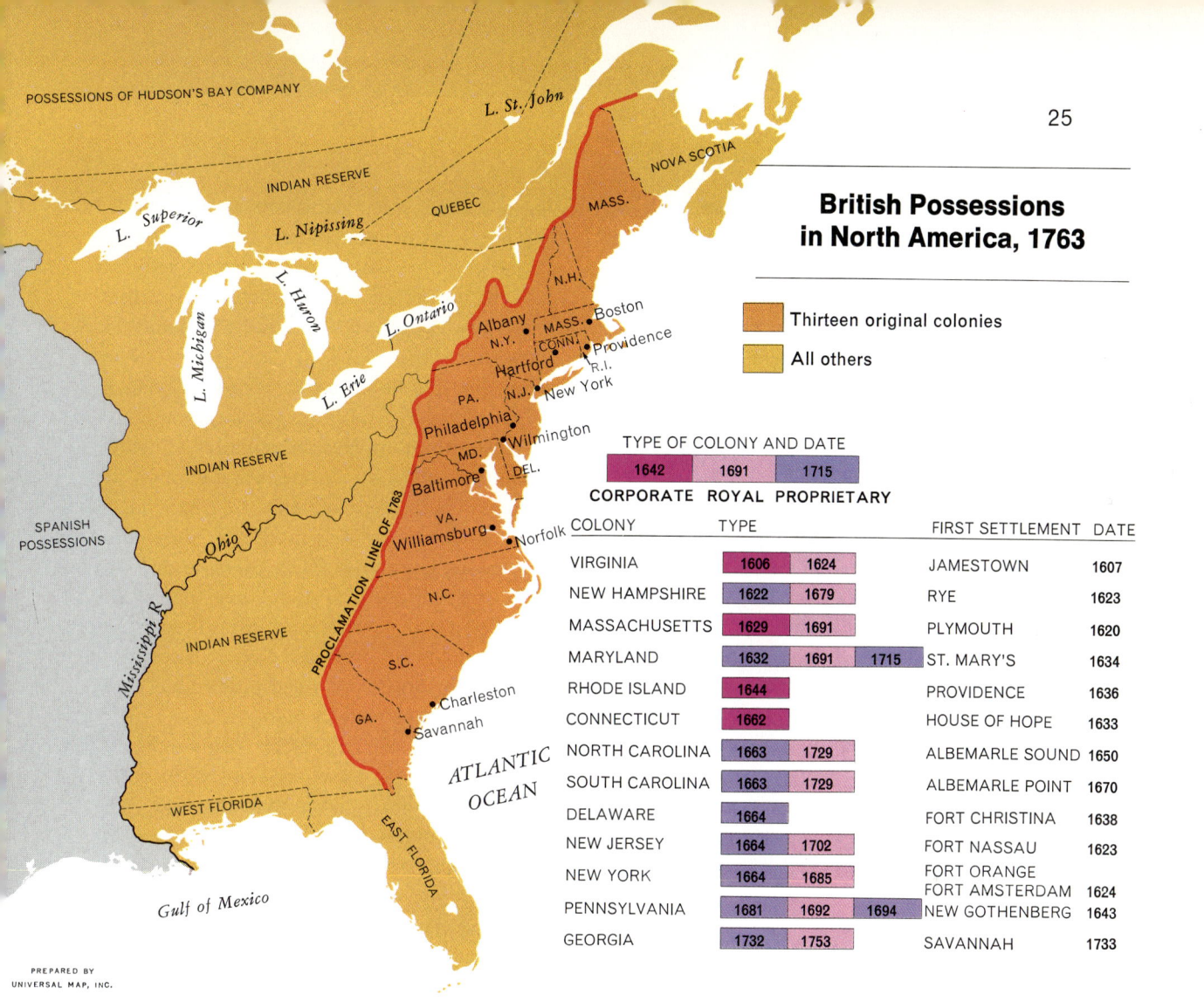

holders who needed workers, and thus money was provided to pay for the ocean passage.

The landholder had to care for the servants during their terms of service. At the end of their terms they were free, and if they could make enough money, they too might obtain land and servants.

Most indentured servants went to the middle colonies. At first, many also went to the South. In 1619, however, a Dutch ship docked at Jamestown and left twenty Negroes there. For a time these and other blacks who were brought in were held in temporary servitude like white servants, but gradually more and more Negroes began to be kept as permanent slaves.

Indentured servants continued to arrive in the colonies, some even after the Revolutionary War, but after 1700, slaves rapidly replaced indentured servants on the tobacco plantations. In the rice fields of South Carolina and Georgia, Negro slavery was the rule from the start. In New England and the middle colonies, some black slaves were used as household servants or as farmhands, but they were much less numerous than in the South.

During the eighteenth century many colonists came from France, Germany, and Ireland. Those from France were chiefly Huguenots, Protestants who had been denied freedom of worship at home. Those from Germany were Catholics and Protestants who had suffered from French invasions of their nation. Those from Ireland were Presbyterians whose ancestors had come from Scotland. When they disagreed with economic and religious policies, these so-called Scotch-Irish began to leave Ireland by the thousands.

The colonial population grew fast, partly because of heavy immigration and partly because of a high birth rate. By 1775, the total population was more than three million. Better than 60 percent of the people were either immigrants or descendants of immigrants from England and Wales. There were more than 500,000 Africans in the colonies, 90 percent of them slaves. The rest of the people came from various European nations.

A Nation of Farmers

In the colonies at least 90 percent of the people made their living chiefly by farming. Some also depended on industries, and these, too, were closely related to the natural resources.

Farming methods in both the colonies and Europe were crude. The farmer used a hoe, a pick, or a wooden plow drawn by oxen to break the ground. He or she sowed by hand, harvested with a sickle or scythe, and threshed grain by flailing it or having oxen trample it.

Colonial farmers gave less attention to fertilizing and conserving soil than did European farmers. In North America, land was generally rich and plentiful, but labor was scarce; thus it paid to economize on labor rather than on land. Despite their more careless methods, colonial farmers produced more than their European counterparts.

In New England the typical farm was so small a family could take care of it. The women grew vegetables, milked cows, tended pigs and poultry, helped harvest, and did most of the home manufacturing, such as weaving and candlemaking. The men cared for orchards, cattle, and horses and tended the fields, growing hay and corn. New Englanders were discouraged from growing wheat because of a plant disease, and they came to depend on the middle colonies for wheat.

In the middle colonies, especially Pennsylvania, the typical farm was larger and better tilled than in New England. It yielded crops not only for home use but also for export. Many Pennsylvania Germans used the careful farming methods they had learned in Germany. With their large holdings, they needed all the labor they could get. The farm women and girls often toiled in the fields as well as doing their usual work. The farms also used indentured servants, women as well as men.

The leading export crop in Virginia, Maryland, and North Carolina was tobacco. Its cultivation quickly wore out the soil, and many growers acquired larger plantations in order to gain reserve supplies of fresh land. The labor was simple and repetitive, the kind that slave gangs could easily be forced to do.

In South Carolina and Georgia, it was profitable to use slaves. Part of the year they waded in flooded fields along the river bottoms to cultivate rice. In other seasons they tended indigo plants and helped make blue indigo dye.

On farms and plantations everywhere there was a good deal of manufacturing. Families made their own yarn, cloth, clothes, shoes, candles, and soap, as well as bread, butter, cheese, and other foodstuffs. Some farmers operated sawmills, and many fished.

Lumbering, fishing, fur trading, iron making, and shipbuilding developed into large and specialized industries, especially in the middle colonies and New England. These industries often employed many workers.

In the cities, such skilled craftsmen as cobblers, carpenters, candlemakers, weavers, tailors, wheelwrights, tinsmiths, and black-

The land as it was

To the first English settlers, America was trees. Even before they sighted land, the early voyagers to the colonies could sometimes smell the fresh forest scent. When they stepped ashore they entered a land with rich and seemingly endless resources. The good soil, minerals, and inland waterways had barely been touched. The forests and waters teemed with animal life. The land had a long growing season and good rainfall.

The Indians, scattered but numerous at the start of colonization, were soon decimated by European diseases and by battles. Many bands had cleared patches of land where they cultivated a variety of crops, including corn, beans, squash, and tobacco. Indian farming techniques were soon copied by the colonists.

First the Indians cleared the land by girdling or cutting the trees and burning the underbrush. Then they planted seeds between the stumps, in soil enriched by the ash. Some tribes—and some colonists—would use fish as fertilizer, but often the land went unfertilized. The colonists also neglected the European practice of planting clover to enrich the soil.

Though the colonists borrowed the Indians' farming techniques, they retained European notions of landownership. Unlike the Indians, who would use a patch of land for a few years and then move on to another patch, the colonists stayed put. Once they had cleared an area, they viewed it as their own. They did not give up this land but worked a field again after allowing it to lie fallow. To make up for the low yield from overworked fields, they acquired more land. The colonists had draft animals like horses and oxen, and thus were able to farm extensively.

The territory that later became the United States included almost 2 billion acres, nearly half of it in forest. The same colonists who were awed when they first saw the forest soon came to regard it with less friendly eyes. The forest held animals that would prey on their livestock; it also concealed the whereabouts of Indians. Moreover, England needed timber, for its woods were almost depleted. Thus the colonial period was one in which the forest receded under the relentless fall of the axe.

smiths appeared. Master craftsmen were much like the owners of small businesses. They worked, but they also hired journeymen and apprentices to help them. These employees hoped to become master craftsmen with shops of their own.

Overseas Trade

Before the colonial period ended, Americans were making more than half the manufactured goods they used. However, they had to import heavy machinery, fine tools, and fancy furniture and cloth from Britain.

The colonists had to find ways to pay for these imports. Gold and silver coins were scarce, and Britain refused to let the colonies mint money. In their own dealings the people often resorted to barter. They also made payments with beaver skins, warehouse certificates for tobacco in storage, or paper currency. None of these circulated as money outside the colonies. The colonists had to sell goods abroad in order to get the foreign money or credit with which to pay for the imports they wanted.

In selling abroad, the colonists were limited by British law. They could send their tobacco, furs, timber, naval supplies, and certain other listed items only to Britain. They could not, however, export any fish, flour, wheat, or meat to the British Isles or British West Indies, for these would compete with similar products from Britain.

A large direct trade in the listed items arose between the colonies and Britain. To dispose of the other products, colonial merchants looked to other markets. In the French, Dutch, and Spanish islands of the Caribbean the products were exchanged for coins and for sugar, molasses, and other West Indian produce. Some of this was taken to Britain and used, along with foreign money, to help pay for goods that the mainland colonies imported from Britain.

Another pattern of indirect or "triangular" trade developed with southern Europe. Colonial ships with cargoes of fish and other products would go to southern Europe. They exchanged their cargoes for wine and money, took these to Britain, and then returned home with British manufactured goods.

The slave trade often took a triangular form. Colonial ships took rum and other supplies from New England to the Guinea coast of Africa. From Africa the ships transported slaves to the West Indies, and from there returned to the home ports with sugar, molasses, and cash. The "middle passage," from Africa to the West Indies, was gruesome. Many of the captives, chained together and closely packed in the holds of the ships, died of disease and were thrown overboard. Still others fought their captors or committed suicide rather than become slaves.

On some voyages only a third of the captives survived the crossing. The survivors were fattened up and trained in the West Indies. Most of them stayed in the islands, but about 10 percent were shipped to the North American mainland, to be sold to tobacco and rice planters.

SOCIAL AND INTELLECTUAL LIFE

Most of the social and intellectual habits of the colonists came from England. From England came the language, the system of weights and measures, and the money calculations in pounds, shillings, and pence. With the language came folklore, literary and scientific knowledge, and ideas of education and law.

Most colonists read the King James version of the Bible, first published in 1611. Their religious ideas came largely, but not entirely, from English interpretations of the Christian faith.

The colonists also brought from England their ideas of the proper relation of person to person in society. Few people believed in complete social equality. Most of them took for granted distinct social classes, with an upper class of landholding gentry and a titled aristocracy or nobility at the top. In the colonies, however, social classes developed along somewhat different lines than in England.

Social Distinctions

Though some aristocrats were promoters of colonies, few of them settled in North America as colonists. Some of the gentry became settlers, but the great majority of the European colonists were originally of the middle or lower classes. The African immigrants were originally of many classes, for most of them had come as slaves after being taken prisoner in battle.

In North America those colonists who became great landholders or wealthy merchants formed a kind of aristocracy. Beneath them in the social order was a large middle class, much larger than that in England. It was made up of merchants, shopkeepers, craftsmen, and farm owners. Lower yet was a class that included indentured servants, other farm laborers, and unskilled town workers. Though free blacks were found in the upper and middle classes, the majority of the blacks, who were slaves, were at the very bottom of the social order.

The colonists were quite aware of belonging to one class or another. The differences were clearly marked by clothing and personal appearance. Farm people wore plain homemade clothes and shoes, while the wealthy dressed in fancy clothes, buckle shoes, and powdered wigs.

Nevertheless, except for the slaves, people in the colonies had more chances to improve their economic and social standing than did people in England or other European nations at that time. Social mobility—movement up and down in society—was characteristic of the colonies. A person who gained wealth was likely to be accepted as a social equal by those who were already rich. His or her children and grandchildren tended to think of themselves as born aristocrats.

Women were more respected and had somewhat greater freedom in the colonies than in England. However, they had far less freedom than did colonial men. Single women were supposed to obey their fathers or brothers and married women their husbands. Nor did women have the same chances as men to improve their social and economic standing. A woman's place in society depended on that of her father or husband. Unless she was a widow, a woman usually could not own property or sign contracts. Divorces were rarely granted.

Because it was believed that woman's place was in the home, women had few opportunities to work outside the family farm or business, except as servants, governesses, or seamstresses. A widow, however, often carried on her husband's work, and so there were female planters, merchants, printers, and shipowners.

Children, whether free or slave, had definite places in society, depending on their ages and the family's social standing. Relatively few spent much time in school. Some boys were apprenticed to master craftsmen and in this way learned skilled trades.

It was most important to be able to do the farm work well, and this was usually learned at a parent's side, not in a classroom. The children might churn butter, pound grain, hoe the garden, feed the poultry, and carry water or lunches to the field workers. At harvest time, like everyone else, they helped gather the crops.

Among the slaves, the greatest social distinctions were based on jobs or skin color. The greatest prestige on large plantations was to be a house servant. Some supervised the work of other slaves, and many slaves were craftsmen. Light-skinned slaves were often given special treatment. They were more likely to be sent to school or to be trained as house servants than darker slaves.

Most slave men worked in the fields. Slave women worked in the fields most of the time and also did the housework and home manufactures. They were encouraged to produce slave children, and some were used as wet nurses.

Since slaves were regarded as property, they had no legal rights. They could not legally marry, and slave families were often broken up by the sale of family members. Because slaves could not move upward in society, many chose to move "outward" by escaping, joining Indian tribes, or plotting rebellions.

Religion

The religions were brought from Europe, but they formed a new pattern in North America. In each European nation there was a state church, usually Catholic or Protestant, and the people were required to follow its practices and contribute to its support, whether they agreed with it or not. In the colonies, by contrast, there were a number of religious groups, none of them completely dominant over the others.

True, the Church of England was the established church in several colonies, and the people had to pay taxes to support it. In fact, however, the Church of England kept its privileged position only in Virginia, Maryland, and parts of a few other colonies. Even in those places other denominations eventually were allowed to worship as they pleased.

The Puritan, or Congregational, church had been established in Massachusetts, Connecticut, and New Hampshire. In the early years, other religious groups were not allowed to set up churches of their own. By the end of the colonial period, however, this policy had been changed.

To visitors from Europe, the number of religious groups in the colonies seemed unbelievable. Actually, this variety was not surprising, given the number of nationalities found in the colonies. Many of the religious groups got their start with members of state churches from the old country. The Anglicans, Congregationalists, Quakers, and Baptists represented the variety of belief among English Protestants. The Presbyterians were often from Scotland, the Lutherans and Moravians from Germany or the Scandinavian countries, and the Dutch Reformed from the Netherlands.

The great majority of the people were Protestants, but there were some Catholics and Jews. Most of the Catholics were English, Irish, or German. Many of them settled in Maryland, which was founded by a Catholic proprietor, Lord Baltimore, to provide a haven for Catholics. The first Jews in the colonies had come from Spain and the Netherlands by way of Brazil. Most of them settled in New Amsterdam (later New York) and Rhode Island, where the laws allowed them a certain measure of freedom to practice their beliefs. By 1720, the majority of the Jews were from Germany.

Many of the Protestants were Calvinists.

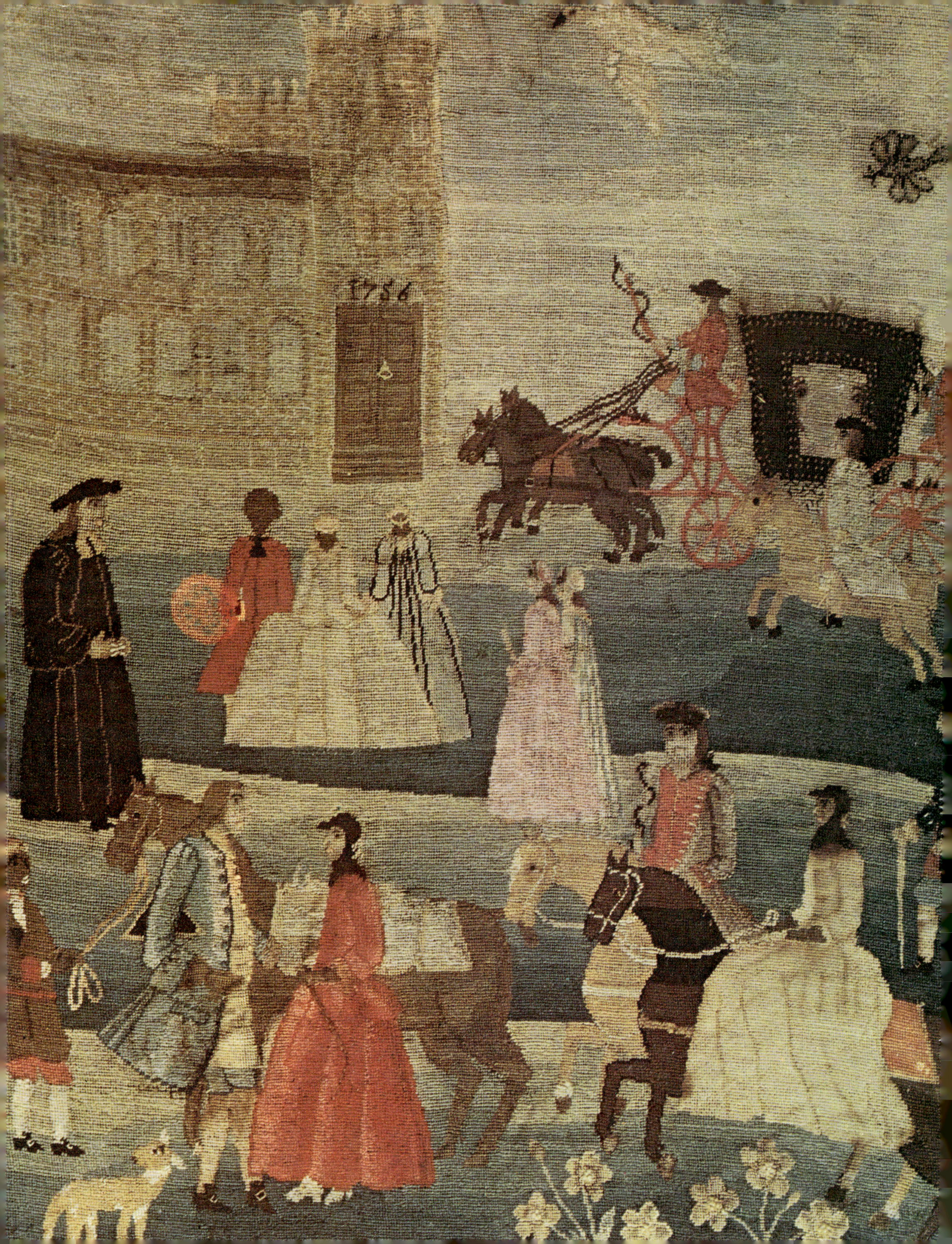
1756

Their beliefs were based on the teachings of John Calvin, a French theologian. He had taught that, from birth, each soul is predestined for either salvation or damnation. He had also insisted upon hard work and strict morality.

Such Calvinist or Puritan attitudes dominated the lives of most New Englanders in the early days. As life gradually became easier, however, many Puritans and other Protestants began to take religion less and less seriously.

This trend was reversed by the Great Awakening, a series of revivals during the 1730's and 1740's. The revivalists tried to turn people back to the strict Puritan faith of their ancestors.

The Great Awakening spread throughout the colonies but was most effective in the back country of the South. On the whole, it failed to revive old-fashioned Calvinist doctrines, but it was important in spreading other denominations. Thousands became members of Baptist and "New Light" Presbyterian churches. Long after the revivals ended, they were having some effect in encouraging denominationalism.

In the colonies, more than anywhere else at the time, there came to be a tolerant attitude toward religious differences. Tolerance seldom extended to Catholics and Jews, but more and more Protestants let each other worship as they pleased.

Intellectual Development

By the 1750's, the language spoken in the thirteen colonies was becoming the "American dialect." The people had added to and changed English, the mother tongue of most of the colonists. Words from many languages, such as *squash* from an Indian tongue, *prairie* from French, and *boss* from Dutch, were part of the dialect. New words, such as *snow-plow* and *bull-frog*, had been formed by combining old ones. The language also retained a number of expressions, such as *catercorner* and *fall* (for *autumn*), that were going out of use in England.

Many English people thought the Americans were barbarians. Actually they took great pains to keep learning alive. Massachusetts in 1647 required each town to make sure that boys and girls were taught to read and write, so that they might read the Bible. Every town of a hundred or more families was supposed to have a Latin grammar school (high school) for boys. In other colonies, many children learned to read and write in private or church schools or at home from tutors or parents. Slave children were rarely sent to school, and few were taught to read and write. Some colonial schools set up separate classrooms for Indian children, but this was not typical.

Girls' education consisted mainly of housekeeping, some reading and writing, and needlework. Upper-class girls were trained to be charming, and so studied French, dancing, painting, and music. Further education for women was strictly opposed. It was thought to be against God's will for women to study and dangerous for their health because their brains were supposedly weak.

By 1763, there were three thousand male college graduates in America. Six colonial colleges were open: Harvard, William and Mary, Yale, the College of New Jersey (Princeton), King's College (Columbia), and the College of Philadelphia (University of Pennsylvania). All but the last two had been founded primarily to train ministers.

Most books and magazines were imported from England, but some books were published in the colonies, especially in and near Boston. Weekly newspapers appeared in all the colonies except New Jersey and Delaware, which were well enough supplied from New York City and Philadelphia. After 1750, several monthly magazines were printed in the colonies, though none had a very long career. Yearly almanacs contained a variety of reading matter in addition to weather data. The most famous of these was *Poor Richard's Almanack,* published by Benjamin Franklin. It was full of popular sayings that stressed Puritan virtues.

GOVERNING THE COLONIES

England's government was both *constitutional* and *representative.* Its constitution was made up of unwritten customs and written documents that limited the powers of the monarch and guaranteed certain rights to the people.

One constitutional document was Magna Charta, signed in 1215. Originally it did no more than assure special privileges to the nobility and make the monarch subject to the law. In the course of time, however, it came to mean that the people as a whole, not just the nobles, had rights that the monarch must respect.

The representative part of the English government was the Parliament, consisting of the House of Lords and the House of Commons. The House of Lords included titled nobles and certain church officials. The House of Commons was an elective body chosen by the relatively few men who were allowed to vote. Together, the two houses were supposed to represent the interests of the nation and the empire.

Laws for England and the colonies were made, according to ancient custom, by the monarch and the Parliament. After about 1720, however, the initiative in both making and carrying out laws fell to a group of parliamentary leaders. They formed a cabinet with a prime minister at the head. The prime minister, rather than the king or queen, began to act as the real head of the British government.

A Lax Government

In governing the colonies, Britain's main concern was to achieve mercantilist aims. Mercantilism required the colonies to concentrate upon producing those goods that the homeland could not produce.

To carry out these aims, Parliament, from 1660 on, passed a series of laws on shipping, trade, manufactures, and money. The shipping laws, or Navigation Acts, provided that all goods shipped to or from the colonies must be carried in either English or colonial ships. The trade laws required that tobacco and other listed items be sent only to Britain and prohibited other products, such as meat, grain, and flour, from being sent there. The Hat Act, the Iron Act, and other manufacturing laws were intended to prevent the rise of industries that would compete with those in Britain. The currency laws prohibited the colonies from issuing paper money.

The English government did increase its authority over some of the individual colonies. Originally, all of them had been either *corporate* (that is, founded and largely governed by companies) or *proprietary* (founded and largely governed by proprietors). Gradually most became *royal* colonies that were supervised directly by the monarch and Parliament. After 1752, eight of the thirteen were royal colonies.

In the royal colonies, the British government appointed governors and other officials, and in all the colonies it appointed royal officials, such as customs collectors. Many of these people did a poor job of governing. Moreover, there was no single office in Britain in charge of the colonies. Each department administered laws in the colonies as well as in Britain. Because of confusion and inefficiency, it would have been hard to enforce the laws in the colonies even if the British government had consistently wished to do so.

From about 1713 on, the government rarely tried to enforce the laws. The government leaders believed that Britain would be better off if the colonies were not strictly controlled. The prime minister, Sir Robert Walpole, reasoned that if the colonists increased their business, they would be able to buy more from British merchants. As a result, the government followed a policy of *salutary neglect;* that is, for the good of the country, the government did not fully enforce the laws.

Colonial Assemblies

The colonial charters had given certain powers of government to the companies and proprietors who founded colonies. They also guaranteed the rights of English people to the colonists. On the basis of the charters, the founders of colonies came to allow some of the male colonists to elect representatives to assist in colonial government. Most of the people, however, could not vote.

The first elected assembly appeared in Virginia in 1619. The stockholders of the Virginia Company in England, who had been making laws for the colony, authorized the election of a general assembly. It came to be called the House of Burgesses and met in Jamestown. The next assembly appeared in Massachusetts, in 1630. By then, a majority of the stockholders of the Massachusetts Bay Company lived in the colony. These "freemen" met four times a year as a General Court to approve laws for Massachusetts. Later, some nonstockholders were made freemen, and the freemen began to send representatives to the General Court instead of going in person.

In all the colonies the same general pattern of government arose. In each, there was a governor and a two-house legislature. In the royal colonies the governor was appointed by the English authorities; in the proprietary colonies, by the proprietors with the approval of the monarch. In the corporate colonies he was chosen by the colonial legislature. The upper house of the legislature usually was the governor's council, and its members were chosen in the same way as the governor.

The lower house was elected. Less than

one-tenth of the people had the right to vote or hold office. Women were not allowed to do so at all. In some colonies, only those men who belonged to the established church could vote or hold office and, in all colonies, only men who owned a certain amount of property had these rights. There were many property owners, however, especially in New England. Hence, in the colonies, a greater proportion of the men enjoyed political rights than in England.

In the colonies it early became the rule that a representative must live in the district from which he was elected. In England a member of Parliament need not live in the town or borough that he represented.

Gradually, each colonial assembly assumed the power to pass certain kinds of laws for its colony. The governor could veto the laws, and the London authorities could reject them. Sometimes, to keep the governor from using his veto, an assembly would threaten not to pay him. Sometimes, to get around the London authorities, an assembly passed a rejected law in a slightly different form. As time went on, each colonial legislature came to consider itself as supreme within its colony as Parliament was in England.

Colonies at Odds

No colony was willing to give up any of its powers to England or the other colonies. Even when the thirteen faced common problems, they did not like to cooperate with each other. The greatest problem involved relations with the Indians. There was constant fighting along the edge of European settlement, where colonists were taking over Indian lands or vying for control of the fur trade. Different tribes allied themselves to groups of colonists—British, Spanish, Dutch, and French. When these colonists fought, their Indian allies often joined in.

In 1643, people in Massachusetts, Plymouth, New Haven, and Connecticut formed

At New England town meetings, each man had the right to be heard and to vote. At this meeting, it appears that hot tempers have disrupted democratic debate.

the New England Confederation, a kind of military alliance. It proved ineffective when the worst Indian conflict of colonial times, King Philip's War, broke out in 1675. In three years of fighting, King Philip (also known as Metacomet), a leader of the Wampanoag tribe, and his followers tried to regain control of lands in New England.

In later years, as population increased and settlements spread, people of different colonies came into closer contact. Roads were improved and intercolonial trade grew. The postal service was extended and speeded up. By about 1750, postriders carried the mails from Maine to Georgia. Nevertheless, each colony continued to act as though it were quite independent of the rest.

In 1754, at the call of the British government, delegates from seven colonies and representatives of the League of the Iroquois met in Albany, New York. The British government wanted the colonists to discuss ways to improve relations with the Iroquois and to strengthen colonial defenses. As a delegate, Benjamin Franklin proposed what became known as the Albany Plan of Union. According to this plan, "one general government" would be set up for the colonies. The monarch would appoint a president general, and the colonial assemblies would elect a grand council. The colonies would keep their separate governments but would allow the new general government to direct war making and relations with the Indians.

The colonial assemblies did not approve of Franklin's plan, and it never went into effect. The English colonists would not be ready to cooperate in government until after a great war with the French and their Indian allies had been fought and won.

INTERNATIONAL RIVALRIES

From the beginning, Britain had to deal with other European nations in North America. The Dutch, after founding New Netherland in the Hudson Valley, remained at odds with New England for half a century. After defeating the Dutch in three wars, the English finally took New Netherland in 1664 and renamed it New York.

The Spanish had the oldest and largest empire in the New World, but most of their holdings—including Texas, Mexico, and California—were far from Britain's. Only on the southern frontier, where Spain held the Floridas, was there opportunity for conflict. Here, from time to time, the English and Spanish fought.

The most serious threat to British America came from the French. France's empire in North America was almost as old as Britain's. The French had started their settlement at Quebec in 1608, a year after the founding of Jamestown. Eventually, French forts, towns, and trading posts were scattered along the St. Lawrence Valley, around the Great Lakes, and down the Mississippi Valley to the Gulf of Mexico.

Vast as it was, the North American continent was not big enough to accommodate the British and French in peace. By 1750, they had fought three wars. Yet the French and their Indian allies remained a threat to the British colonies and their Indian allies.

This danger was, oddly enough, a help to Britain in its dealings with its colonies. After a tour of the colonies in 1748–1749, a Swedish professor, Peter Kalm, wrote:

I have been told by Englishmen . . . that the English colonies in North America, in the space of thirty or fifty years, would be able to form a state by themselves, entirely independent of Old England. But as the whole country which lies along the seashore is unguarded and on the land side is harassed by the French, in times of war these dangerous neighbors are sufficient to prevent the connection of the colonies with their mother country from being quite broken off. The English government has therefore sufficient reason to consider the French in North America as the best means of keeping their colonies in due submission.

Conflict

Trouble arose between the French and British colonies for several reasons. The French were Catholics and the British mostly Protestants; fanatics on each side feared for the future of their religion. The French and the British also competed for the fur trade of the Indians, and they disputed the ownership of the Ohio country—the territory between the Great Lakes and the Ohio River. This territory was important to the French because it provided the shortest route between their colonies of New France (Canada) and Louisiana. The British looked to this land as a future home for their growing colonial population.

Still another reason for conflict in America was the British and French struggle for power elsewhere in the world. Whenever

Beyond the Southern Frontier

Rivalries among the Spanish, French, and British shaped the early history of the areas south and west of the thirteen British colonies. The Spanish claimed the territory that is now Florida but were unable to maintain colonies against raids by the English. They set up small towns and forts on the east coast and limited their colonizing efforts to converting the Indians. But British settlers in South Carolina and Georgia continually raided Florida towns for slaves and harassed the Spanish settlers. Finally, in 1762, the British captured Havana in Cuba and traded it to Spain for Florida.

The British were more successful in Florida than the Spanish had been. Wealthy investors lured settlers with attractive offers. For example, Dr. Andrew Turnbull persuaded 1,500 persons to leave Italy, Greece, and Minorca and set up a colony at New Smyrna. As roads were built, the east coast became prosperous.

During the development of Florida and the British colonies, France controlled most of what is now Louisiana. By 1699 the French had set up the colony of Biloxi. Louis XIV was more interested in the possibility of gold and silver in the region than he was in colonization. No treasure was found, however. To rid itself of the burden of maintaining settlements in Louisiana, the French government gave trading rights to Antoine Crozat, a rich merchant. Unsuccessful, in 1717 he gave his rights to the Company of the West. This company advertised the Louisiana wilderness as a paradise and lured thousands of Europeans. Although New Orleans began to grow rapidly, the rest of Louisiana did not. Income from trade was so small that the French government had to support the colony.

After defeat in the French and Indian War, Louis XV of France gave New Orleans and all of Louisiana west of the Mississippi to Carlos III of Spain. Louis gave the French settlements east of the river, except New Orleans, to Britain.

This gift did not please the French colonists in Louisiana. In 1766, a mob of settlers took over New Orleans, expelled the Spanish governor, and prevented his return for ten months.

This view of a prosperous colony in Biloxi was used to promote immigration to the settlements.

France and Britain went to war, their colonies and their Indian allies became involved. The first three wars between the French and the English colonies (King William's War, 1689–1697; Queen Anne's War, 1702–1713; and King George's War, 1744–1748) began in Europe and spread to North America.

The fourth and final war was different. It began in North America and then spread to Europe and even to India. To Americans, this war seemed much more important than the earlier three, and they thought of it as their own war. They called it *the* French and Indian War (1754–1763). Europeans, however, remembered it as the Seven Years' War (1756–1763).

The French and Indian War

To enforce their claim to the Ohio country, the French began building a line of forts from Lake Erie to the junction of the Allegheny and Monongahela rivers. The British government told the colonial governors to stop the French. The acting governor of Virginia (which claimed the Ohio country as part of the colony) sent a force to head off the French and build a fort of its own. The French drove off the Virginians, completed the fort, and named it Fort Duquesne. When relief troops arrived from Virginia, they were beaten and forced to surrender (July 4, 1754). Thus began the French and Indian War.

In the following years there was fighting all over the Ohio country and along the frontier. General Edward Braddock tried to retake Fort Duquesne in July 1755, but he was killed and his force defeated, in part because he tried to use European methods of warfare.

The war had started badly for the British, even though the population of the British colonies was fifteen times that of the French. The British colonists lacked enthusiasm for the war, except when their own homes were endangered. When the British government asked the colonies for soldiers and supplies, the assemblies seldom responded quickly or adequately. Many New England merchants made money from the war by selling supplies to the French.

At first the British government also had poor leadership. Then in 1757, Prime Minister William Pitt was given special war powers. He reorganized the war effort. The war reached a turning point when the British and the Americans captured Fort Duquesne in 1758.

The decisive battle of the war was fought in 1759. The English general James Wolfe brought an army up the St. Lawrence River, led the men to the heights above Quebec, and surprised a larger French force led by the Marquis de Montcalm. Wolfe quickly won the battle, but both he and Montcalm lost their lives.

Not until 1763 was a peace treaty signed. The French then gave New France and most of their claims east of the Mississippi River to Britain. They yielded the rest of their claims on the continent to Spain. Nothing was left of the French empire in North America but a few islands in the West Indies and in the Gulf of St. Lawrence and a strong French heritage in the former colonies.

Problems of Peace

The war doubled Britain's territory in North America. To govern and defend all this land would be a complicated and expensive task. The war also left Britain with a huge national debt. It would be difficult enough to pay this debt without the added cost of administering an enlarged empire.

British landowners and merchants, who were influential in Parliament, objected to paying new taxes. They thought it only fair that the colonists should pay part of the cost of their own defense. Government leaders agreed. They remembered the half-hearted support that many colonists had given to the war, as well as the illegal trade that some had carried on with the enemy.

British leaders now felt that the policy of salutary neglect had been a mistake. They decided that control over the colonies ought to be tightened up, smuggling stopped, and all customs duties collected. To help enforce the laws and defend the colonies, land and naval forces ought to be stationed there permanently, even in peacetime. To raise more money, taxes ought to be imposed directly on the colonists. Such were the lessons that the British leaders learned from the French and Indian War.

Quite different, however, were the lessons that leading colonists learned. From their war experiences they had gained confidence in themselves as soldiers and had developed a low opinion of British military ability. Now that the French were no longer dangerous neighbors, they felt little need for British protection. Certainly they were in no mood to submit quietly to new taxes or to any new controls.

The postwar problems of the empire were bound to lead to serious trouble between the mother country and the colonists.

A Look at Specifics

1. What important changes were taking place in Europe about the time of Columbus's voyages?

2. What mistaken notions of the New World were held at least until Magellan's voyage of 1519?

3. List the basic ideas of mercantilism.

4. Describe indentured servitude.

5. How did the social standing of colonial women differ from that of colonial men?

6. What were some important sectional differences among the colonies?

7. How did the colonial assemblies control the colonial governors and avoid control by the London authorities?

8. Which European countries rivaled Britain for control of North America? Which rivals were eliminated during the colonial period?

A Review of Major Ideas

1. What events in Europe led to the colonization of North America?

2. How did the British colonists earn a livelihood? How were they affected by the mercantilist system?

3. How did the American colonies differ from Britain in social structure and religion?

4. How did self-government in the various colonies develop under British rule?

5. How did the rivalries between Britain and other European nations affect the thirteen colonies? How did the French and Indian War affect the relationship between Britain and the colonies?

For Independent Study

1. Some historians have suggested that the abundance of land in the United States was a major factor in the growth of democracy and the development of a nation of small farms. Considering the experience of other frontier populations, such as the Australians, Argentinians, or Cossacks in czarist Russia, do you believe this notion is sound? Explain your answer.

2. One historian has said, "In a number of ways what Americans would be for generations to come was settled in the course of those first hundred years." Discuss this statement.

3. Compare the political institutions that developed in the British, French, and Spanish colonies of North America in the mid-eighteenth century. Which country permitted its colonists to achieve the greatest degree of self-government? Why?

4. How do you explain that, despite the different circumstances under which they were founded, the thirteen British colonies had developed similar governments by 1750?

The American Revolution

CHAPTER 2
1763–1783

The Boston Massacre.

Since the end of World War II, more than sixty new countries have appeared in the world. Most of them had been European colonies in Asia or Africa. Although the majority won their independence by peaceful means, some were able to become separate nations only by fighting wars of independence. In this they were like the British colonies in North America in 1776.

The American Revolution was the first great movement by which a colonial people broke away from an empire. In many ways it was a model for the revolutions that were to come. It was led not by the poorest and most miserable of the colonists, but by some of the most able, best-educated, and most successful people in the colonies.

NEW BRITISH POLICIES

George III was twenty-two when, in 1760, he became king of England. His mother had advised him: "George, be a king." For nearly half a century his great-grandfather George I and then his grandfather George II had sat upon the throne without exercising real power. Both of them had been more German than English. During their reigns, the Whig party had governed Britain and the empire through Parliament and the cabinet.

The new king followed his mother's advice. Although he did not abolish the system of parliamentary government, he tried to control it. Disputes often arose between the king and Parliament, and the treatment of the colonies became inconsistent.

Unpopular Legislation

After the French and Indian War, the British government began its new colonial policy. The first big change came in the Royal Proclamation of 1763, which was a response to Pontiac's Rebellion that same year. Indians under the Ottawa chief Pontiac had attacked settlers along the frontier, from

Detroit to Pennsylvania. The king's proclamation forbade settlement west of the Appalachian Mountains. By keeping colonists out of the Indian country, the king intended to prevent further troubles with the Indians. To the colonists, however, the proclamation seemed an attempt to deprive them of western lands.

Several acts of Parliament were also passed to control the colonists. The Sugar Act of 1764 was designed to stop illegal trade and to raise money. It was applied toward molasses, which was used in making rum.

Previously, a duty of sixpence a gallon was supposed to be collected on any molasses brought from the French West Indies to the colonies. Colonial merchants seldom paid the duty, for they usually gave the British customs officials a bribe, averaging about a penny a gallon. At this rate, molasses from the French West Indies was cheaper than the duty-free molasses that came from the British West Indies.

The Sugar Act reduced the duty on imported molasses from six to three pennies, but it also provided for strict enforcement of the law. Ships of the royal navy were now to be stationed permanently in North American waters to watch for smugglers. When caught, lawbreakers were to be tried in the navy's courts by judges appointed and paid by the British government. In the past, juries in local courts usually had sympathized with smugglers. With good reason, colonial merchants feared the destruction of their profitable trade with the French West Indies.

The Currency Act of 1764 prohibited the colonies from issuing paper money. Its purpose was to keep colonial debtors from trying to pay their English creditors in paper currency, which was worth less than silver. Its effect would be to discourage business in the colonies, since they were always short of coin and needed paper money to carry on business.

Under the terms of the Quartering Act of 1765, any colony in which British troops were stationed was required to provide living quarters and certain supplies for the soldiers. This law was intended to make the colonists support the troops that were sent among them. The colonists, however, could see no reason for the presence of the army. Troops had not been kept in North America before 1754, when there was danger from the French and their Indian allies. Why should troops be kept in North America now that the danger had been eliminated?

Suspicious colonists thought that the new policy deprived them of their rights to be taxed only by their own elected representatives and to be tried only by a jury of their equals. The colonists also feared that the new policy would end their prosperity. When a business depression came, they blamed it on the Sugar Act and the Currency Act.

At first, the colonists only grumbled about the laws and evaded them as best they could. After the passage of an even more unpopular law, however, they resorted to strong words and violent deeds.

The Stamp Act

The Stamp Act of 1765 put a tax on legal documents and on newspapers, almanacs, and other items. Each of these had to bear a stamp to show that the tax had been paid. The law was designed to raise money to defend the colonies. It was not intended to provoke those colonial leaders—the lawyers and publishers—who could best arouse their fellow colonists. Yet this was the effect of the law.

Members of the colonial legislatures soon assembled to discuss the Stamp Act. The Virginia House of Burgesses adopted resolutions that said that the General Assembly had the "*sole exclusive* Right and Power to lay Taxes" on the people of the colony. The Massachusetts assembly proposed that all of the colonies send delegates to a congress, or convention, to agree upon joint action.

Nine colonies sent representatives to the Stamp Act Congress, which met in New York in September 1765. It drew up resolutions granting "all due subordination" to Parliament but denying its right to tax the colonies. The congress asked the king and Parliament to repeal both the Stamp Act and the Sugar Act. The congress also called upon the people to back up these demands by refusing to buy British goods.

Merchants in New York, Philadelphia, and Boston refused to import from Britain. Mobs in these and other places took more forceful steps. They attacked stamp collectors and made them resign before they had succeeded in selling any stamps. Groups known as Sons of Liberty, with Samuel Adams of Massachusetts and Patrick Henry of Virginia among the leaders, were formed to organize the resistance to the law.

The colonists argued that the law violated the English constitution. One of the rights guaranteed by the constitution, they said, was "That no man can justly take the Property of another without his Consent." By taxing the colonists, the British government was taking some of their property. The colonists could consent to this only through their elected representatives. Since the colonists elected no representative to Parliament, its members had no right to tax them.

All this talk of "taxation without representation" made little sense to most people in England, who took a different view of their constitution. True, the colonies sent no representatives to Parliament, but neither did Ireland nor certain areas of England. This did not mean that these places were unrepresented. They were "virtually" represented by members from other places, who looked out for the interests of the parts of the empire as well as the whole.

The idea of "virtual" representation made no sense to most Americans. They were used to actual representation by men elected from the localities that they were supposed to represent. Of course, few colonists really wanted to elect their own members of Parliament. They would not have enough members to prevent undesirable laws, and yet their presence would give Parliament the right to make laws for the colonies.

In 1766, with business starting to feel the effects of the colonists' refusal to buy British goods, Parliament decided to repeal the Stamp Act. First, however, it passed the Declaratory Act, which said that Parliament had full power to make laws "to bind the colonies and people of America . . . in all cases whatsoever."

External Taxes

The British authorities in London assumed, incorrectly, that the Americans objected to "internal" taxes like the Stamp Act but would be willing to accept "external" taxes. Accordingly, in 1767, Parliament imposed the so-called Townshend duties on colonial imports of lead, paint, paper, glass, and tea. Like the stamp duties, these were

Leisure

In the colonial period, few people had much spare time. Wealthy colonists often had time to spend in preparing musical programs, boating, picnicking, or hunting. Women with leisure might read, paint, or do decorative needlework like "The Fishing Lady" *(below)*, which illustrates some leisure activities of colonial aristocrats.

The Fishing Lady, Courtesy, Museum of Fine Arts, Boston

intended to raise revenue. Unlike the stamp taxes, they were to be collected before the goods entered the colonies. In that sense, they were external.

The Townshend duties caused no such uproar as the Stamp Act, but they seemed equally unconstitutional to the colonists. As John Dickinson explained in his *Letters from a Farmer in Pennsylvania* (1768), Parliament could levy external duties, but only to regulate trade, not to raise revenue. Once again, merchants agreed to import no goods from Britain, and the Sons of Liberty threatened violence to all who failed to cooperate.

Soon the British government further angered the colonists. The colonial assemblies had not fully obeyed the Quartering Act, and Parliament singled out the New York assembly for punishment. In 1767, it refused to recognize any of the assembly's actions until full support should be provided for the British troops quartered in the colony. By punishing only one of them, Parliament had hoped to divide the American colonies, but the others quickly expressed their sympathy with New York.

That same year the government appointed a special board of British customs commissioners. It was to be located in Boston instead of London to assure the collection of duties and to better deal with smuggling. The commissioners soon made themselves unpopular, ordering sudden raids and seizing ships on technicalities. Every seizure meant money for the commissioners, since they received one-third of the value of the cargo.

To protect the commissioners, troops were sent to Boston. The local Sons of Liberty, under Samuel Adams, made life miserable for the soldiers standing guard in front of the custom house. On March 5, 1770, a jeering crowd led by Crispus Attucks, a black seaman, threw rocks and snowballs at the ten men on duty, as crowds often had done before. This time the soldiers started firing. Several in the crowd, including Attucks, were killed, in what Americans afterwards called the Boston Massacre.

Already, merchants in Britain were demanding repeal of the Townshend duties because they were hurting business. In 1770, Parliament repealed all the duties except the one on tea. Parliament hoped that this one would raise some money as well as remind the colonists of the powers that had been claimed in the Declaratory Act.

COLONIAL COOPERATION

From about 1770 to 1773, good feelings prevailed between the colonies and Britain. True, there were occasional incidents, as in 1772, when Rhode Islanders burned a British patrol ship after it had run aground near Providence. Also, the more radical colonial leaders, such as Samuel Adams, continued to insist on the colonists' rights and to de-

Paul Revere's engraving shows the coffins of the men who died in the Boston Massacre. The *Boston Gazette* printed other inflammatory pictures and stories to arouse colonial sympathy and anti-British feeling.

nounce Parliament's tyranny. Most people, however, were content to enjoy the prosperity that came with the reopening of trade.

Now that the colonies were less troubled by Britain, they began to give more attention to their complaints against each other. Connecticut, for example, claimed land in northeastern Pennsylvania. While resisting Connecticut's claim, Pennsylvania quarreled with Virginia over some territory in the Ohio Valley.

The most serious trouble took place in North Carolina. Settlers in the Carolina foothills objected to the actions of their own colonial assembly. They charged that the assembly was run by eastern planters who passed unfair taxes and denied the rights of local self-government. In a brief, small-scale civil war in 1771, militiamen from the east defeated the westerners in the Battle of Alamance. This left the westerners so bitter that many of them continued to oppose the easterners even after the struggle with Britain had been renewed. On the whole, however, the renewal of the dispute with the British brought about closer cooperation and greater unity among the colonies than had ever before existed.

The Tea Act

The East India Company was a great corporation that controlled the government as well as the commerce of Britain's possessions in India. In 1773 it found itself in serious financial trouble, and Parliament passed the Tea Act to help it.

This law allowed the company to sell tea directly to retailers in North America, paying only the Townshend tea tax. In the past, the company had paid various taxes in Britain and had sold its tea only to British merchants. They in turn sold it to American merchants, who then distributed it among retailers in the colonies. Under the new law,

Flourishing trades and commerce contributed to Boston's rapid growth.

Two rowdy colonists, having tarred and feathered an unfortunate royal tax collector, "offer" him some tea. This cartoon shows the degree of bad feeling stirred up by British plans to enforce the hated Tea Act of 1773. Although the violence of the "Boston Tea Party" at first threatened to divide colonial opinion, Britain's harsh reaction changed the climate. All the colonies protested angrily, united to boycott tea, and rallied to support the blockaded Bostonians.

with the merchants' profits and most of the taxes removed, the company would be able to undersell all competitors. The colonists, who had a reputation as great tea drinkers, were expected to swallow the Townshend tax along with the cheap tea.

The reaction in North America surprised the British authorities. American tea dealers, of course, protested against the unfair competition from a giant corporation. Tea drinkers also resented the new law, for they considered it a trick to make them accept taxation by Parliament. The colonists vowed to use none of the company's tea. When its tea ships arrived in colonial ports, angry crowds made them either turn back or leave their cargo, unsold, in warehouses. Women formed anti-tea leagues, some of which later became the Daughters of Liberty. In Boston harbor, the followers of Samuel Adams, disguised as Indians, boarded the ships and threw the tea into the harbor.

As punishment for the "Boston Tea Party," the British government struck at the Bostonians with four laws that became known as the Intolerable Acts (1774). One closed the port of Boston to all shipping except military supplies and shipments of food and fuel cleared by customs officials. Another decreased the power of the Massachusetts assembly and restricted the right of the people to hold town meetings. A third limited the power of the colony's courts. It provided that customs officers and other royal officials, when accused of murder while carrying out their duties, could be tried in Britain. The other authorized the quartering of troops among the people as well as in the barracks that the colony had provided.

Still another British measure that Americans saw as a threat to their interests was the Quebec Act of 1774. It set up a civil government and drew boundaries for the province of Quebec, which had been ruled by a military governor since 1763. The new Quebec government was to have no elected assembly; it was to include certain features of French law; and it was to favor the Catholic Church. The boundaries were to include the area west of the Appalachian Mountains and north of the Ohio River. Britain intended to provide for Quebec an orderly government that would be acceptable to the French settlers of the province. The British colonists, however, looked upon it as another attempt to halt representative government in North America and to discourage people from taking up land in the west.

By singling Massachusetts out for punishment through the Intolerable Acts, Parliament had hoped to isolate it from the other colonies. After the passage of these laws and then the Quebec Act, however, the other colonies came to the support of Massachusetts. They stiffened their resistance to British authority, and they were soon to be better united than before.

The First Continental Congress

Revolutions do not just happen. They must be led and organized. In the colonies, people like Patrick Henry and Samuel Adams, extreme opponents of British policy, were the early leaders of what was to become the American Revolution. At first, the colonial assemblies were centers of resistance. Then delegates from nine of the assemblies met in the Stamp Act Congress. A number of people enrolled in local groups like the Sons of Liberty. Still later, committees of correspondence were formed.

Local committees of correspondence had appeared in 1772. Samuel Adams had persuaded the towns of Massachusetts to appoint correspondents to keep in touch with each other and agree upon united action. These committees, drawing up statements of rights and grievances, kept alive the anti-British feeling in New England.

Intercolonial committees of correspondence began in 1773. Patrick Henry and other Virginians set up a committee for their colony and suggested that the other colonies do the same. Thereafter, the colonies had a network of committees through which to coordinate their plans. After the passage of the Intolerable Acts and the Quebec Act, these committees arranged for an intercolonial congress to be held.

The Continental Congress, with delegates from all the colonies but Georgia, met in Philadelphia for the first time in September 1774. From the start, the delegates were divided. Moderates were willing to let Parliament regulate colonial trade so long as it did not try to raise revenue by taxation. The more extreme members, however, had moved beyond that position. They wished to deny Parliament any power of legislating for the colonies.

On behalf of the moderates, Joseph Galloway of Pennsylvania proposed a plan to reform the empire. His plan was something like the one that Benjamin Franklin had presented at Albany twenty years earlier. A council, to represent all the colonies, was to have a veto over acts of Parliament; but Parliament was to have a veto over the actions of the colonial council. This plan was defeated by one vote.

Moderates and extremists agreed on a statement of grievances, to be sent in a petition to the king. It denied that Parliament had any authority over the colonies, but said that the colonists would nevertheless abide by Parliament's acts if they were confined to legitimate regulations of trade. The statement assured the king of the Americans' "allegiance to his majesty" and their "affection" for their "fellow subjects" in Britain.

Responding to the demands of the extremists, the majority approved a set of resolutions that a convention in Suffolk County, Massachusetts, had passed. The Suffolk Resolves called upon the people to prepare military defenses against a possible attack by the British troops in Boston.

The majority also decided that all trade with Britain should be stopped. They agreed on nonimportation, nonexportation, and nonconsumption of any goods to or from Britain. To see that the agreement was enforced, they formed the Continental Association, with members in each colony.

Finally, when the delegates adjourned, they agreed to meet again the following spring. Thus they viewed the Continental Congress as a continuing body, not a temporary organization.

British Reaction

"The New England Governments are in a State of Rebellion," George III exclaimed in November 1774. "Blows must decide whether they are to be subject to this Country or Independent." Not only New England but also the middle and southern colonies, at the Continental Congress, had defied the mother country and had declared what amounted to economic war.

The British policy makers faced a dilemma. If they gave in to the demands of the Continental Congress, they would have to recognize the colonies as practically independent. On the other hand, if they rejected the petition from the colonists, they would probably have to fight a full-scale war.

During the winter of 1774/75, Parliament debated over the treatment of the colonies. Some members favored giving in to them. Others insisted that if the colonies were to be kept subordinate within the empire, Samuel Adams and others of his kind would have to be taught a lesson.

Twice before, Parliament had backed down in quarrels with the colonies. It had repealed the Stamp Act and, with one exception, the Townshend duties. This time, it did not back down. It refused to repeal the Intolerable Acts.

Instead, Parliament passed the Conciliatory Propositions. These suggested that the colonies avoid parliamentary taxation by taxing themselves "for contributing their

The Battle of Lexington was the first skirmish of the Revolutionary War. On the morning of April 19, 1775, a band of 40 minutemen met a column of 700 British soldiers on the village green at Lexington, Massachusetts. The battle was of no military significance, but the spirit of Lexington became a symbol of the Revolution. Over the years, as the details of the event became hazy, some Americans began to glorify the stand of the minutemen. Notice that each of these three illustrations *(right)* depicts the same landscape. Drawing a few months after the battle, Amos Doolittle showed the minutemen breaking ranks and running from the fire of the superior British forces. No shots were returned by the colonists. Fifty-five years later, the artist Pendleton included several minutemen returning the redcoats' fire, and only a few Patriots fleeing the battle. But in 1886, 111 years after the event, Henry Sandham painted "The Dawn of Liberty" with a steadfast line of minutemen firing away at the royal troops. *Left:* A minuteman prepares to leave his home and join his company.

The Battle of Lexington, by Amos Doolittle, 1775. The Connecticut Historical Society

The Battle of Lexington, by Pendleton, 1830

The Dawn of Liberty, by Henry Sandham, 1886

proportion to the common defence." The propositions did not say how much the "proportion" of each colony would be. Presumably, this would be left for Parliament to decide.

The Conciliatory Propositions did not suit the discontented colonists. They could see little difference between being taxed by Parliament and being forced to tax themselves at Parliament's request. The propositions said nothing about the Intolerable Acts and the other laws that troubled the colonists. In any case, the British offer came too late. By the time it was received in North America, the first shots of the Revolutionary War had been fired.

INDEPENDENCE

Time and again throughout history, a war undertaken for one purpose has been carried on for other, quite different, purposes. This was true of the Revolutionary War. At the beginning, the aim of the colonists was only to uphold their idea of the British Empire. After the first year of fighting, however, the aim was changed to independence.

By 1775, many Americans looked upon the British Empire as a kind of federation of peoples. Each group had its own legislative body, and all groups were tied together by loyalty to the monarch. For the colonists to assert their complete independence, they had only to announce that they were breaking the connection with the British crown. This they did with the Declaration of Independence in 1776.

They were not unanimous, however, in making the final break. All along, some Americans had been unwilling to resist the powers of Parliament. At the end these people could not bring themselves to give up their loyalty to the king. John Adams of Massachusetts, who helped lead the revolt, estimated that about a third of the people actively supported the war, another third secretly or openly opposed it, and the rest were indifferent.

Revolutions usually are carried out by a determined minority, and apparently the American Revolution was no exception.

Early Battles

During the winter of 1774/75, New Englanders began to prepare for a possible attack from the British troops in Boston. "Minutemen," ready to fight on a minute's notice, drilled in militia companies. Guns and gunpowder were collected and stored for emergency use.

On April 18, 1775, a force of 700 British soldiers left Boston to march the eighteen miles to Concord. They intended to seize the arms and ammunition that had been collected there. During the night, hard-riding American horsemen warned the people in the villages and on the farms. When the redcoats reached Lexington, on the way to Concord, colonial militiamen were waiting for them on the village green. A British officer ordered the militiamen to disperse, when suddenly shots rang out. Who fired the first shot, nobody knows, but some militiamen were killed and others were wounded.

The British moved on to Concord and found that the Americans had removed most of the powder supply. After burning what was left and fighting off an American attack, the British started to march back to Boston. All along the way, they faced the gunfire of Americans hidden behind trees, rocks, and stone fences. Before the day was over, the British had suffered 273 casualties (killed, wounded, or missing), about three times as many as the Americans.

In the weeks that followed, militiamen came from all over New England to fight the British in Boston. In the Battle of Bunker Hill, which was fought on Breed's Hill on June 17, 1775, the British attempted to break the siege. After two unsuccessful attacks, the British advanced a third time. The Americans, their ammunition almost gone, were forced off the hill in bitter hand-to-hand fighting.

For the British, this victory was both costly and incomplete. Their losses were 226 killed and 828 wounded, compared with the Americans' 100 killed, 267 wounded, and 30 captured. The siege had not been broken. Both sides now realized that they had a hard and bloody war on their hands.

The Declaration of Independence

In May 1775, the second Continental Congress had met in Philadelphia, with delegates again from twelve colonies. This congress did not confine itself to adopting resolutions. It also acted as a central governing body for the colonies.

Within the colonies, the assemblies took charge of government. They defied the gov-

1775–1776

April 19, 1775 Battles of Lexington and Concord. British victories. The British sent troops to seize rebel military supplies at Concord. A small force of minutemen met them at Lexington. Fighting began, and the minutemen retreated. The British went on to Concord and destroyed the supplies. On the return march to Boston, the British suffered heavy casualties.

May 10 and 12, 1775 Capture of Forts Ticonderoga and Crown Point. American victories. The capture of these strategic forts in New York gave the Patriots artillery and other supplies needed for the siege of Boston.

June 17, 1775 Battle of Bunker Hill (Breed's Hill). British victory. The British tried to dislodge Patriot troops from a hill overlooking Boston. The Patriots withdrew, but the British suffered heavy casualties.

September 12–December 31, 1775 Invasion of Quebec. British victory. The Patriots hoped to get Quebec to join the rebellious thirteen colonies and prevent the British from using the city as a base. The Patriot assault on Quebec failed.

February 27, 1776 Battle of Moore's Creek Bridge. American victory. The British planned to join forces with Loyalists in the South, but the Patriots defeated the Loyalists.

March 17, 1776 Siege of Boston. American victory. The Patriots forced the British to evacuate the port of Boston.

June 28, 1776 Battle of Charleston. American victory. Unable to unite with the Loyalists, the British tried but failed to set up a southern base at Charleston.

August 27, 1776 Battle of Long Island. British victory. The British and the Patriots fought to occupy New York City. The Americans retreated through New Jersey.

December 26, 1776 Battle of Trenton. American victory. The Patriots needed a spectacular win to raise morale. They surprised and captured the British garrison.

American Revolution

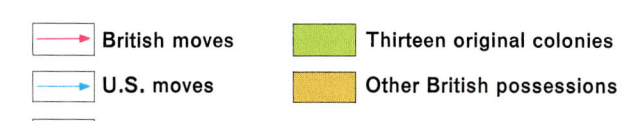

- → British moves
- → U.S. moves
- × Battles
- Thirteen original colonies
- Other British possessions

ernors and other royal officials, who sooner or later stopped trying to reestablish British authority.

Even though the congress and assemblies were acting as independent governments, most Americans still hesitated to declare independence. In July 1775, the congress sent another petition to King George III and issued the "Declaration of the Causes and Necessity of Taking up Arms." This blamed the troubles on the king's ministers rather than on the king himself. In choosing resistance, the Americans said they had no "ambitious designs of separating from Great Britain, and establishing independent states."

Nevertheless, just one year later, the congress adopted a much different declaration. This one concluded that "these United Colonies are, and of Right ought to be Free and Independent States." What accounted for the change in war aims?

First, the Americans received no satisfaction from the British government. The king did not even answer their petition. Instead, he proclaimed that the colonies were in rebellion. Parliament voted to send 25,000 additional troops to North America and passed a law prohibiting trade with the colonies.

Second, the Americans desperately needed foreign aid in order to win even a limited war—one waged only to correct grievances within the empire. To get the aid they needed, they would have to act as an independent people, with full power to make treaties and alliances with foreign countries. Thus, fighting the war caused a change in war aims.

Third, the Americans found that they had to make terrible sacrifices in order to carry on the struggle. The costs would be out of proportion to the benefits unless some grand objective were sought.

Fourth, a powerful pamphlet, *Common Sense,* helped many Americans make up

A colonist sets fire to a grain crop that is ready for harvesting. Farmers sometimes aided the Patriot cause by burning crops or hiding goods that might be useful to the advancing British army.

their minds. It was first published in January 1776 by Thomas Paine, an Englishman who had come to North America less than two years earlier. He argued that it was common sense for this great continent to cut itself loose from a small island that was no more fit to govern it than a satellite was to rule the sun.

After much debate, the congress appointed a committee in June 1776 to draft the Declaration of Independence. The group, which included Benjamin Franklin and John Adams, left most of the writing to one member, Thomas Jefferson of Virginia.

Jefferson based the declaration on the ideas of John Locke, an English philosopher. According to Locke, people had originally created government in order to protect their rights to life, liberty, and property; whenever the existing government failed to do its job, the people could abolish it and create a new one. Jefferson changed the emphasis of Locke's theory by stressing human rights rather than property rights. He wrote:

We hold these truths to be self-evident; that all men are created equal, that they are endowed by their Creator with certain unalienable Rights, that among these are Life, Liberty and the Pursuit of Happiness.

He also listed the ways in which King George III had stepped on the rights of the colonists, thus giving them grounds to abolish British rule and set up independent governments. In his original draft, Jefferson had included the institution of slavery as one of the grievances against George III. But pressure from other southern colonists caused him to remove this statement from the final draft.

On July 2, 1776, the congress passed a resolution dissolving "all political connexion" between the colonies and Britain. On July 4, 1776, the congress adopted the Declaration of Independence written by Jefferson to emphasize this resolution. Henceforth, the United Colonies were known as the United States.

In Philadelphia and elsewhere in the new nation, cannon were fired and church bells were rung to celebrate the news of independence. Not all the people rejoiced, however. A large minority remained loyal to the king. They called themselves Loyalists, but the Patriots called them Tories.

Directing the War

The second Continental Congress directed the American war effort—the raising of supplies, money, and soldiers, and the planning of military campaigns. Yet the congress had no power to impose taxes or to draft soldiers; it could only make requests to the states and leave the taxing and drafting to them.

From the beginning there was a shortage of war materials in America. There were many gunsmiths but not enough to make the needed guns. Some states offered bounties to encourage the making of arms and ammunition. The congress set up a government arsenal for manufacturing them at Springfield, Massachusetts. American troops occasionally captured equipment from the British. For most of its military supplies, however, the United States had to rely on imports, especially from France.

Even when materials were available, it was hard for Americans to find the means to pay for them. Cash was scarce, and the states disliked taxing their people. As a result, the congress often got supplies directly from farmers or manufacturers and paid for them with certificates of indebtedness—promises to pay later—or with paper money. This currency was issued in such large quantities that it became practically worthless. To meet the costs of war, the congress had to borrow more and more from foreign countries.

Support for the Revolution came from several sources. Many non-English immigrants supported the Patriots rather than the Loyalists. Since they had come from other countries, they did not feel as bound to England as those whose roots were there. Moreover, the colonial aristocracy was primarily English. For some, fighting England was also a way to fight the aristocracy.

There were blacks in every major battle from Lexington on. George Washington, as commander in chief of the American forces, at first was reluctant to let blacks fight. Thus many slaves fought on the side of the British, who promised them freedom. (Some did gain freedom in this way, but others were sent to the West Indies and kept in slavery.) However, continued British recruitment of blacks persuaded Washington to change American policy, and many blacks finally supported or fought on the Patriot side. They hoped that an independent United States would abolish the slave trade, end slavery, and upgrade the social standing of blacks.

Some women fought in the war, and others acted as spies. Most women aided the war effort by carrying the burden of two jobs. They filled the vacuum created by the absence of men on farms and in family businesses as well as doing their usual work. Women supplied large quantities of food and clothing for the army. Throughout the colonies, they raised money for the war effort, and at least one group attacked hoarders.

The Indians were split by the war. Most tribes, however, fought against the colonists. The Royal Proclamation of 1763, which limited the colonists to the east side of the Appalachians, had helped win them to the side of England in the conflict.

Many Tories helped and even fought alongside the British. The Patriots themselves generally disliked regular military service, though they were willing enough to oppose the enemy whenever troops approached their homes. Fortunately, the United States was to receive military and naval support from abroad.

To encourage men to enlist, the states offered bounties, usually in the form of land. Several states resorted to the draft. The men served in militia units that remained under state control. In addition, the congress raised a regular force of volunteers, the Continental Army. In June 1775, it appointed George Washington as commander in chief of the army and of all the state militia.

Washington, then forty-three, had early favored independence. He had gained military experience in the French and Indian War, and he had qualities of character that made him a natural leader. During the Revolutionary War, he did not have a free hand in planning strategy, for the congress often interfered with his plans. Nevertheless, more than any other person, he was responsible for keeping the Patriot armies in the field and leading them to victory.

IMPORTANT VICTORIES

In waging war, the United States faced serious disadvantages. The population of the United States was less than a third the size of Britain's, and many of the Americans opposed the war effort. The economic resources of the Americans were even smaller in proportion to those of the British. The governments in the United States were newly organized, and control was divided. The United States had no navy except what it could hastily put together, while Britain was the strongest sea power in the world.

Yet the Americans had the advantage of fighting on their own soil. The British had to carry the war to them, at a distance of three thousand miles and more. Moreover, the people of Britain were divided, and most of them showed little enthusiasm for the war. The British were reluctant to join the army,

1777–1779

January 3, 1777 Battle of Princeton. American victory. The Patriots defeated the British and cleared most of New Jersey.

July 5, 1777 Fort Ticonderoga. British victory. The British, on their way from Quebec to Albany, recaptured the fort.

August 6, 1777 Battle of Oriskany. American victory. A second British force, heading for Albany, besieged Fort Stanwix. On the way to help the fort, Patriots fought off an attack.

August 16, 1777 Battle of Bennington. American victory. The British went to Bennington for supplies but had to leave without them.

September 11, 1777 Battle of Brandywine. British victory. The Patriots merely slowed the British on their way to Philadelphia.

October 4, 1777 Battle of Germantown. British victory. The British beat back the Patriots near Philadelphia.

October 17, 1777 Battle of Saratoga. American victory. The British defeat at Saratoga, New York, ended the invasion from Quebec.

June 18, 1778 Evacuation of Philadelphia. The British, hearing reports of a French fleet, left for New York City.

June 28, 1778 Battle of Monmouth. A draw. The Patriots attacked the British. After some success, the Patriots were forced on the defensive, but the British withdrew.

July 4, 1778 Capture of Kaskaskia. American victory. To stop raids in the West, the Patriots sent troops to several posts, including Kaskaskia and Vincennes.

December 29, 1778 Battle of Savannah. British victory. The British defeated a force of local militia and occupied the city.

February 23, 1779 Battle of Vincennes. American victory. After recapturing Vincennes, the British were forced to surrender it.

American Revolution

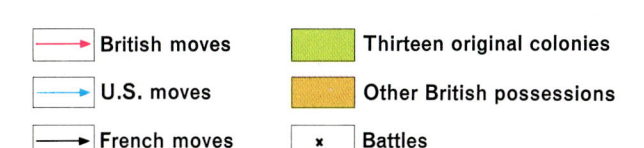

- → British moves
- → U.S. moves
- → French moves
- Thirteen original colonies
- Other British possessions
- × Battles

and the government had to hire mercenaries from Germany. A total of 30,000 mercenaries, more than half of whom were Hessians, fought in the colonies.

Saratoga

During the first year of the fighting, the Patriots took the initiative on several fronts. When the British forces sailed away from Boston in March 1776, they abandoned their last foothold on American soil. Before long, however, they reappeared. That summer, hundreds of ships and an army of 32,000 soldiers—the largest war-making expedition that Britain had ever sent abroad—arrived in New York harbor. Henceforth, the Patriots were to be on the defensive.

The commander of the newly arrived British army, General William Howe, offered the American rebels a choice of surrendering with a royal pardon or facing what he thought was an unbeatable force. Certainly, Washington's army was no match for Howe's army in numbers, training, or equipment. Nevertheless, commissioners from the congress rejected Howe's offer.

When Howe's troops landed, they routed Washington and his soldiers from Long Island and Manhattan Island. Slowly and stubbornly, the Americans retreated through New York and New Jersey, across the Delaware River, and into Pennsylvania. On Christmas night, 1776, Washington daringly recrossed the Delaware and surprised and scattered the Hessians at Trenton. Later he drove off the redcoats at Princeton. By the year's end, though the Patriots had given up a great deal of ground, Howe was a long way from the grand triumph that he had been anticipating.

The next year, Howe captured the American capital, Philadelphia. Washington set up winter camp at Valley Forge, nearby, and the congress took refuge in York, Pennsylvania.

Although Howe held both New York and Philadelphia, the two largest cities in the United States, he controlled only a small part of the country as a whole. He had won additional battles, but he was as far as ever from a decisive victory. Another British general, however, was about to suffer a major defeat.

General John Burgoyne, with an army of British regulars, Canadians, German mercenaries, and Indian allies, had invaded the United States from the province of Quebec. Burgoyne easily took Fort Ticonderoga. Then he began to run into trouble. At Bennington, New Hampshire militiamen caught one of his detachments and cut it to pieces. In other engagements he lost more and more troops. Finally, on October 17, 1777, he was surrounded at Saratoga, New York, and had no choice but to surrender all that was left of his army, about 5,000 soldiers.

The victory at Saratoga was a great turning point in the war. It led to an alliance between the United States and France.

Help from France

From the beginning of the controversy between the colonies and Britain, the French government had closely watched events in North America. The French remembered their defeat by Britain in 1763, and they were eager to avenge it. They assumed that Britain would be weakened if it should lose a part of its empire. Thus they were glad to help the Americans break away.

The Revolutionary leaders knew well the French point of view. Even before the Declaration of Independence, the congress had appointed a secret committee to seek foreign

Guerrilla troops under Francis Marion cross the Pee Dee River to attack British forces. Cooperation between Marion's small band and regular troops helped to break British control of the South. The guerrillas staged hit-and-run attacks on supply posts, roads, and river crossings. These attacks cut off British troops and made them vulnerable to attack by Patriot forces led by General Nathanael Greene.

aid, and it had sent an agent to France. The French and Spanish kings were willing to furnish supplies but insisted on doing so secretly, in order to keep the British from learning about it. The French set up a fake trading company that sent millions of dollars worth of munitions to the Americans.

After the Declaration of Independence, the Americans hoped for French recognition of the United States government and additional aid. Benjamin Franklin went to France to seek a treaty for these purposes. He received an enthusiastic welcome from the French people, but the government was cautious. It gave new grants and loans to the United States but delayed making a treaty. The French leaders wanted to see whether the Americans actually had a chance of winning the war.

Then came the news of the victory at Saratoga. In London, the news caused Parliament to make another peace offer. It granted most of the American demands, including the end of parliamentary taxation and the repeal of the Intolerable Acts. In Paris, the French leaders saw that they must act promptly. If the Americans and British were to reconcile, France would lose the chance to disrupt the empire. In 1778, American representatives signed a treaty of friendship and commerce and a treaty of alliance with France. Soon France was at war with Britain.

The French alliance brought needed naval support to the Americans. The congress controlled only a few warships, though it commissioned hundreds of privately owned vessels to prey on British commerce. The French navy was no match for the British navy as a whole, yet a French fleet was to gain a temporary and local advantage in American waters.

Yorktown

After the defeat at Saratoga, the British adopted a cautious war plan. Sir Henry Clinton, who replaced General Howe in the spring of 1778, abandoned Philadelphia and marched his troops back to New York. Washington followed with his army and remained nearby to keep an eye on Clinton.

Soon Clinton invaded the southern states. He assumed that Loyalists were numerous in the South and that they would welcome and help the British.

Approaching from the sea, the British took Savannah and later Charleston. A number of Loyalists joined the invaders, whom Clinton had left under the command of Lord Cornwallis. The combined forces fought far into the back country. The farther they went, however, the more resistance they met from Patriot militiamen. At King's Mountain, South Carolina, in 1780 the Patriots killed, wounded, or captured a force of more than a thousand Loyalists.

To deal with Cornwallis and his followers, Washington sent General Nathanael Greene to the Carolinas. Greene, a blacksmith from Rhode Island, was probably the finest American officer other than Washington himself. At first, Greene used hit-and-run tactics and avoided a pitched battle. Finally, when he thought his army was ready, he took up a position at Guilford Courthouse, North Carolina. Cornwallis attacked on March 15, 1781. Though he drove Greene from the field, he lost so many troops he decided to abandon his effort to conquer and hold the Carolinas.

After this battle, Greene and Cornwallis moved in opposite directions. Greene headed south, to try to retake Charleston and Savannah. Cornwallis left for Virginia, hoping to conquer it, but he soon retreated to the relative safety of the seacoast. At Yorktown, Virginia, he began building a fort while waiting for the British navy to reinforce or rescue his troops.

Washington, still watching Clinton's army in New York City, learned that a French fleet under Admiral de Grasse was sailing for Chesapeake Bay. After conferring with the French army commander, General de Rochambeau, Washington decided to try and trap Cornwallis at Yorktown. Washington and Rochambeau marched many of their troops to the head of Chesapeake Bay and then transported them by ship to the James River. This army of more than 15,000, nearly half of whom were French, hemmed in Cornwallis on the land side. De Grasse's fleet, larger than any the British could send to the scene in time, prevented escape by sea. Cornwallis and his 7,000 soldiers were helpless as the much larger French and American forces began to close in. On October 19, 1781, he surrendered.

PEACE

Despite its victory at Yorktown, the United States had not yet definitely won the war in 1781. Other British forces remained on United States soil and continued to occupy important seaports. The British soon recovered complete control of American waters. Britain was far from beaten, and it could have gone on fighting, had it wished to do so.

King George III wanted to continue the war, but other government leaders were ready to consider peace. The war had become more and more unpopular with the British people. Besides, it had driven the former colonies into an alliance with Britain's rival, France. By letting the colonies go and granting them generous terms, perhaps Britain could draw them—as independent states—back to friendly relations with the mother country.

Peace making, however, was no longer a simple matter of negotiations between the British and the Americans. The American Revolution had broadened into a general war. Not only the United States and France but also Spain and the Netherlands were fighting against Britain.

Trouble with France

In 1779, the congress had appointed John Adams to represent the United States at a peace conference, if and when one should

1780–1781

May 12, 1780 Siege of Charleston. British victory. The Patriots were besieged and finally forced to surrender.

August 16, 1780 Battle of Camden. British victory. The Patriots tried to go on the offensive but were routed by the British.

October 7, 1780 Battle of King's Mountain. American victory. The tide turned in the South as the Patriots defeated the Loyalists.

January 17, 1781 Battle of Cowpens. American victory. The British attacked the southern Patriots but suffered heavy casualties.

March 15, 1781 Battle of Guilford Courthouse. British victory. The Patriots were defeated, but the British suffered heavy losses and finally withdrew.

May 21–October 19, 1781 Yorktown campaign. American victory. The Patriots (George Washington) and the French (Comte de Rochambeau) planned a joint attack against the British in New York. But when Comte de Grasse notified Washington that he was bringing the French fleet from the West Indies (Aug. 13) to Chesapeake Bay, Washington decided to head south. The French and Patriot troops pretended to be preparing an attack on Staten Island but sneaked through New Jersey.

De Grasse set up a naval blockade off Yorktown (Aug. 30) and landed his troops. The Patriots (Marquis de Lafayette) were blockading the British (Lord Cornwallis) from the land side. The British fleet (Admiral Thomas Graves) appeared, and action followed. The British fleet withdrew to New York for repairs (Sept. 10).

De Grasse sent ships up Chesapeake Bay to bring Washington's and Rochambeau's troops to Yorktown (Sept. 14–24). The combined forces besieged Cornwallis, who was forced to surrender (Oct. 19) when the British fleet failed to return in time.

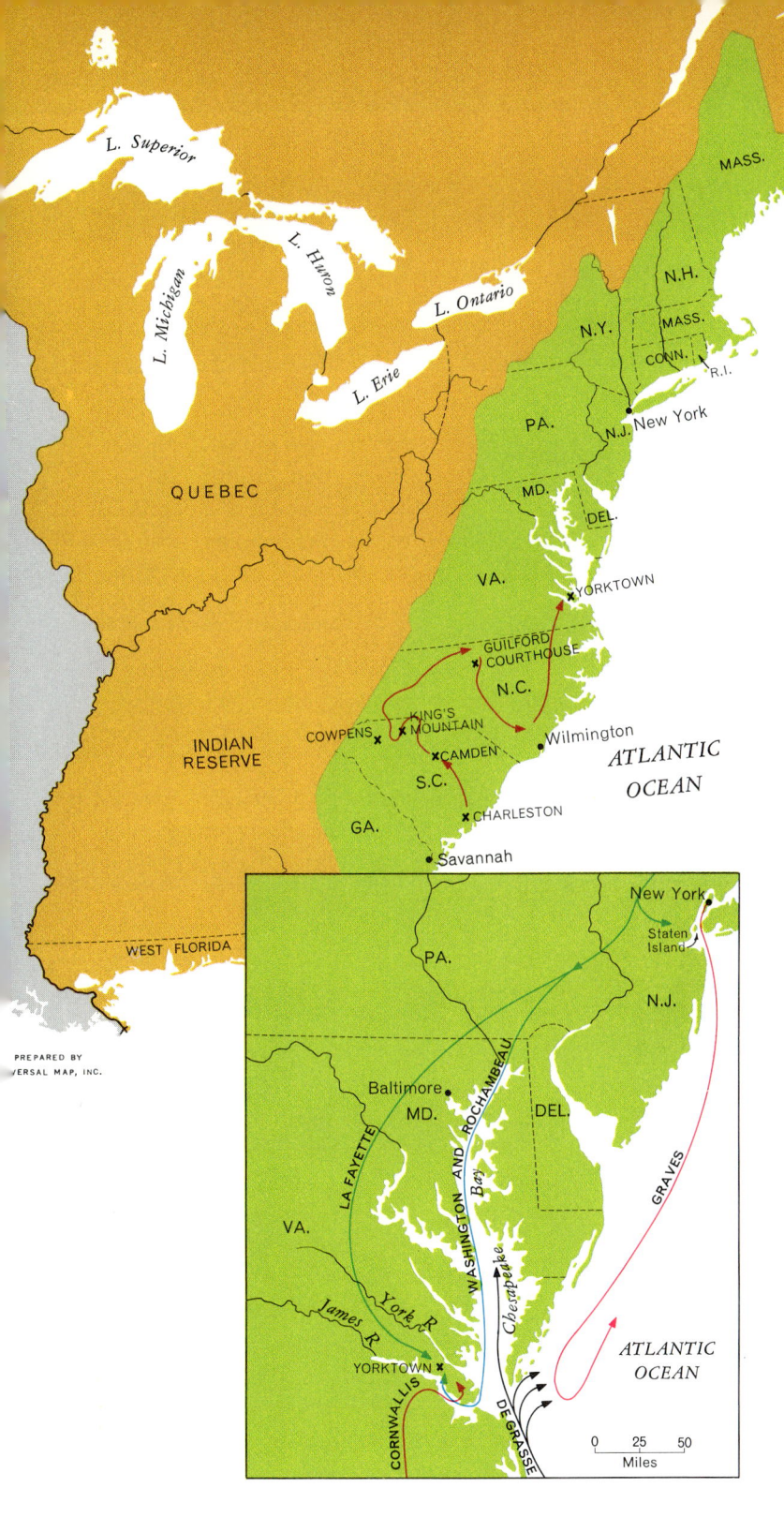

meet. Adams was bound by the 1778 treaty of alliance with France, which stated that neither of the two countries would "conclude either truce or peace with Great Britain without the formal consent of the other first obtained." He had instructions from the congress to enter into no negotiations unless Britain first recognized the United States as "sovereign, free, and independent." He also was told to insist upon boundaries that would give the United States the territory between the Appalachian Mountains and the Mississippi River.

After arriving in France, Adams argued with the French leaders. They wanted to control American policy, and they found that they could not control Adams. Through the French minister in the United States, they used their influence in the congress to get a new peace delegation with a new set of instructions. Adams left France for the capital of the Netherlands, where he was to serve as the American minister.

The congress appointed a commission that included Adams, Benjamin Franklin, and John Jay, the American minister to Spain. It was directed to demand the recognition of independence, but it no longer had to insist upon particular boundaries. Instead, it was to proceed "as circumstances may direct." Moreover, the commission was to keep in close touch with the French government and follow its advice.

In the spring of 1782, while Adams and Jay were elsewhere, the British government sent a man to Paris to talk informally with Franklin. To the British agent, Franklin suggested "necessary" and "desirable" terms. His necessary terms included both independence and the Mississippi boundary. He thought it desirable for Britain to cede its remaining possessions in North America to the United States as a means of bringing about true "reconciliation."

When Jay arrived from Spain, he objected

By 1778, the Revolution was one theater of a world war. At right, a British 90-gun ship batters a French ship of the line in a 1782 battle for control of strategic ports in the West Indies. That same year, British ships and shore batteries had to fight off a renewed Spanish attack on Gibraltar.

to continuing the conversations with the British. The communications from the British government were addressed not to official representatives of an independent nation, the United States, but to "persons" from "colonies or plantations." Franklin agreed to end the conversations.

Franklin had kept the French government informed of what was going on, but Jay was becoming suspicious of both France and Spain. His experiences in Spain had been less than reassuring. The Spanish government had refused to officially receive him as the minister from the United States, let alone negotiate a treaty with him.

True, Spain had gone to war, but not for American independence. It had hoped to recover some possessions that had been lost in earlier wars with Britain.

Though Spain had no alliance with the United States, it had one with France. In 1779 the two powers had agreed to make no separate peace. Thus France was bound to Spain, while the United States was bound to France.

Jay feared that France might try to get concessions for Spain from Britain. The three powers might agree to divide the territory from the Appalachians to the Mississippi between Britain and Spain. When Jay learned that a secret mission was leaving Paris for London, he thought his suspicions were confirmed. Franklin was much less worried than Jay. Actually, though Jay was mistaken about details, he was correct in thinking that the French government was considering separate negotiations with Britain. Such negotiations would have violated the terms of the American alliance and would have lessened the bargaining power of the United States.

Treaty with Britain

On his own initiative, Jay suggested to Britain that separate negotiations be opened between the British and the Americans. When Adams returned to Paris from the Netherlands, he approved what Jay had done, and Franklin was willing to go along with the idea. The British hoped this was a chance to break up the alliance between France and the United States.

Even though the British had not yet recognized them as representatives of a sovereign nation, the three Americans soon began secret negotiations with British representatives in France. The Americans no longer told the French government what they were doing. Before the end of 1782, a preliminary treaty had been drawn up between the United States and Britain.

The American diplomats had of course disregarded their instructions from the congress, but technically they had not violated the terms of the alliance with France. According to those terms, the United States was to make no peace without France. The preliminary treaty did not in itself provide for peace. By its own words, the preliminary treaty was not to take effect until a final treaty, with the approval of France, had been made.

When the French foreign minister protested to Franklin about the American action, Franklin admitted that they had perhaps seemed disrespectful, but he assured him that they held the French king and his government in high regard. He said:

The English, I just now learn, flatter themselves they have already divided us. I hope this little misunderstanding will therefore be kept a secret, and that they will find themselves totally mistaken.

After thus playing upon French fears of losing its American ally, Franklin coolly asked for a new loan for the United States from the French government.

Despite his protest, the French foreign minister was probably as much pleased as annoyed by the Americans' separate negotiations. He was getting tired of Spain's stalling, and he now had an excuse to hold the final negotiations, whether Spain got what it wanted or not. He was eager to keep the friendship of the United States, and France promptly granted the new loan that Franklin had requested.

Spain as well as France at last agreed to a general settlement. On September 3, 1783, in Paris, Britain and the United States signed a final treaty. The terms of the Treaty of Paris were essentially the same as those of the preliminary treaty. Britain recognized the independence of the United States. Though it did not cede its remaining possessions in North America, it did agree to boundaries that gave the United States all the territory southward from present-day Canada to present-day Florida and from the Atlantic Ocean to the Mississippi River.

From the Indian point of view, the treaty was grossly unfair. Even though many tribes had allied themselves with the English, the British government made no provision for them in the treaty. Much of the territory that Britain handed over to the American negotiators was actually in Indian hands. Some tribes, particularly members of the Six Nations, refused to stop their fighting until the United States recognized their land claims.

From the American point of view, the treaty had certain defects. Some of its boundary descriptions were vague, and it contained unpopular articles concerning debts owed to British creditors and the return of Loyalists' property. Worst of all, the treaty made no provision for American trade with the British Empire.

For the time being, however, the American people had good cause to rejoice. Before the end of 1783, the British forces sailed away from New York City. George Washington rode into the city at the head of a column of soldiers. The United States government was now in control.

A Look at Specifics

1. What advantages did the colonists enjoy as members of the British Empire?

2. What was the purpose of the Stamp Act of 1765?

3. For what purpose were the Sons of Liberty organized?

4. What was the American interpretation of the right of representation in government?

5. Why did the British believe the colonists would accept the Townshend duties? Why did John Dickinson think they were unconstitutional?

6. What laws did the British pass in response to the Boston Tea Party? What effect did these laws have on the colonies?

7. In what ways was the British government looking at the colonies from the standpoint of the empire as a whole?

8. How many people were estimated by John Adams to have supported the American Revolution? How many people opposed it?

9. Why is *Common Sense* by Thomas Paine considered an important document?

10. How did the ideas of John Locke contribute to Jefferson's political thought? How did Jefferson change the emphasis of Locke's ideas?

11. Why was Britain willing to let the colonies become independent even though it was not yet defeated militarily?

A Review of Major Ideas

1. How did the British attempt to tighten their control over the thirteen colonies between 1763 and 1774? Why? What was the basis of the colonists' opposition to the measures taken by the British?

2. What attempts did the British make to compromise with the colonists? Why did the colonists refuse to accept the British compromise proposals?

3. What events caused the colonies to declare their independence from Britain?

4. What advantages and disadvantages did the United States have in waging war with Britain?

5. Despite its difficulties with France and Spain, how was the United States able to negotiate a favorable treaty with Britain?

For Independent Study

1. Some historians have said that the Declaration of Independence was basically propaganda. Analyze the document and decide if the charges against King George were true, false, or exaggerated. The colonists had a great deal of trouble with Parliament, and yet there is little mention of this in the document. Why might the delegates have avoided blaming Parliament?

2. Why were the thirteen colonies not joined by the British West Indies and the remaining British-held possessions in North America in the rebellion against British rule?

Unit Review

Examining the Times

1. How did the rivalries between Britain and other European nations affect the development of the thirteen colonies? The establishment of the United States of America?

2. How did British rule affect the colonies before 1763? After 1763?

3. What led to the rebellion of the thirteen colonies? How did the colonists justify their rebellion against British rule?

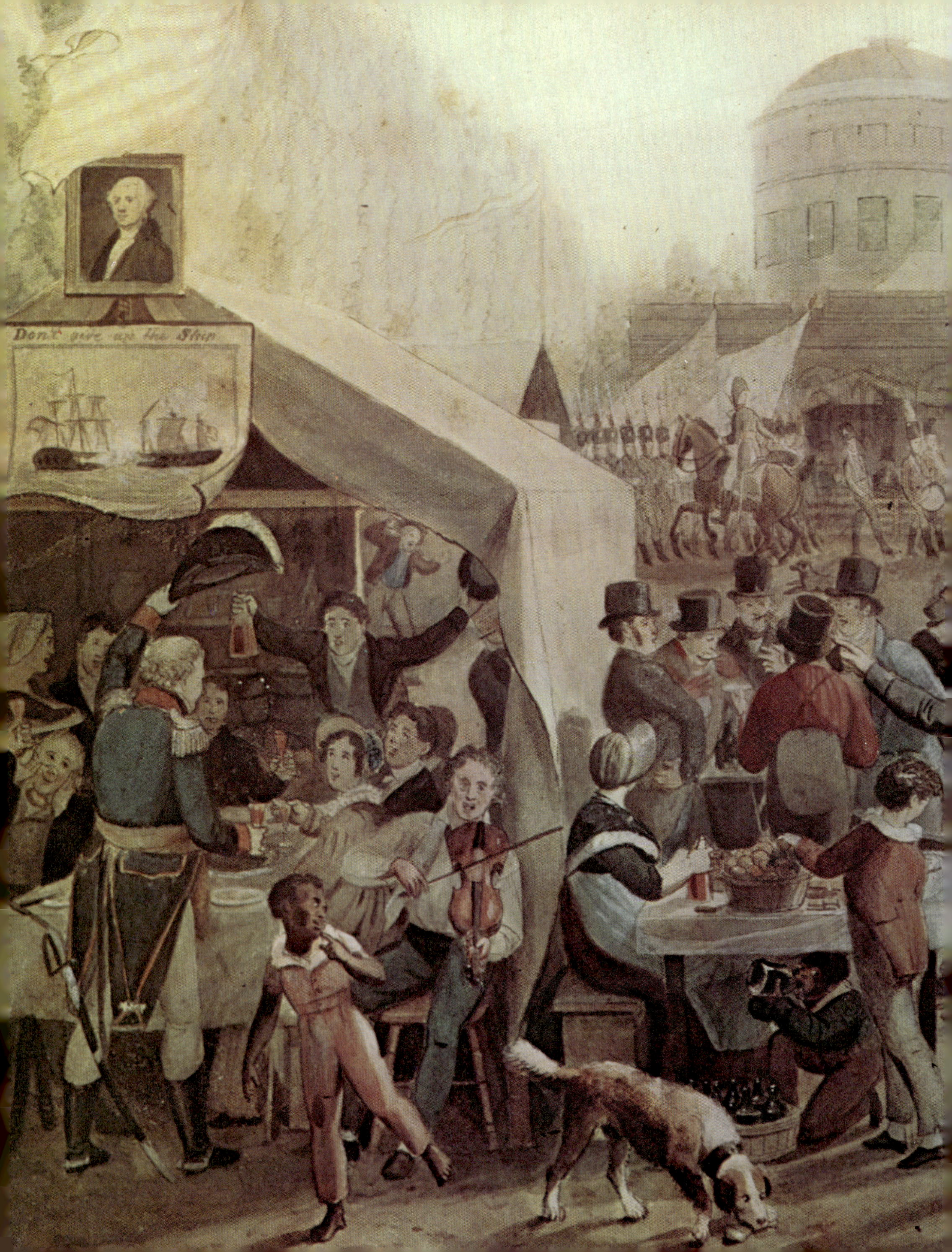
Don't give up the Ship

UNIT TWO   1783–1815

Establishing a New Nation

The American Revolution was not an isolated event. Just as the fighting of the Revolutionary War involved the major European powers, the consequences of the war were felt on both sides of the Atlantic.

Between 1783 and 1815, the most important European developments began in France. There, during the 1780's, people became more and more dissatisfied with the government and society, both of which were controlled by the Bourbon royal family and wealthy landholders. This discontent led to the French Revolution. It began in 1789 when a representative assembly, the Estates General, put limitations on the king's power and set up a constitutional monarchy. After this relatively mild beginning, the revolution became radical. In 1792 its leaders deposed the king and proclaimed France a republic. In the reign of terror that followed, the king, the queen, and hundreds of other men and women were put to death. Finally, in 1799, the revolutionary experiment ended; a young soldier, Napoleon Bonaparte, seized control of French affairs. He made himself dictator and later, in 1804, emperor of France. Then he tried to make himself master of all Europe. From 1791 on, France was continually involved in wars. Its chief enemy was Britain. At first Britain fought to prevent the spread of French revolutionary ideas. Later it tried to stop Napoleon's drive to dominate the European continent and the British Isles. At last, in 1815, Britain and its allies ended Napoleon's threat by defeating the French in the Battle of Waterloo.

The American Revolution had had a great impact on France. In helping American revolutionaries, the French government had spent so much money that it found itself practically bankrupt. It was this financial crisis that led the government to call the Estates General, the first step in the French Revolution. Important leaders of the revolution were inspired by the principles of the American Declaration of Independence. The French, in 1789, adopted their own Declaration of the Rights of Man, which included similar ideas. "Men are born and remain equal in rights," the French declaration said. "The aim of every political association is the protection of the natural and imprescriptible rights of man."

A good way of looking at the American and French revolutions would be as parts of a broad movement that affected people in many countries. In the 1780's, for instance, encouraged by the example of Britain's North American colonies, colonists rebelled, unsuccessfully, in Peru, Colombia, Ecuador, and Venezuela. One reason for their failure was that—unlike the North Americans, who received help from France—the isolated Latin American rebels fought without aid. But the democratic ideals of the time continued to spark colonial revolts. These ideals were summed up in the slogan of the French Revolution—*liberté, égalité, fraternité* (liberty, equality, and brotherhood).

Not all the supporters of democracy proposed, as yet, that the right to vote be given to every person. Women, for example, were not usually thought to have the same rights as men. But democrats all felt that no group of people, simply because they were born into the ruling class, should be allowed to govern the rest of the human race. The democrats believed that the people should form a real *community,* a society in which all had an interest in the welfare of others and an opportunity for their own advancement.

Originally, the word *fraternité* implied the ideal of community, but soon it came to mean something else. During the French Revolutionary and Napoleonic wars, the French government emphasized the need for all the people to be loyal to the nation. *Fraternité* began to signify this kind of loyalty, that is, *nationalism.*

Of course, nations had existed before, and the people of each of them had been expected to obey the monarch. The new type of nationalism, however, aroused and involved the people in a way that the old-fashioned patriotism never had. European monarchs, for example, had fought their wars with small bands of hired professional troops. By contrast, the American states and the Continental Congress relied upon citizen-soldiers in the Revolutionary War. The French revolutionary leaders went even further. They passed a law in 1793 known as the *Levée en Masse.* It declared that every French man, woman, and child was "in permanent requisition for the service of the armies." This, the first national draft in modern history, proved highly effective. Henceforth, all French people owed their highest loyalty to the nation and were required, if called upon, to die for it.

The new kind of nationalism spread to other countries, especially to some of those Napoleon conquered. Leaders in those countries passed conscription laws and aroused a national spirit in order to drive out the French invaders and regain national independence. *Fraternité,* in the form of nationalism, became a unifying force in a number of countries besides France.

The ideas of *liberté* and *égalité* led to divisions within countries, including France. Advocates of these ideas—called "democrats"—were opposed by members of the old order, who were known as "aristocrats."

The French Revolution and the European wars accompanying and following it provide a background for Latin American history of that period. In these years the black people of Haiti overthrew the French regime on their island and set up a republic. In other parts of Latin America, the Spanish American colonists refused to recognize the French regime that seized control of Spain in 1808. Led by Simón Bolívar and José de San Martín, the colonists started their own revolutionary wars, which would take some twenty years to complete.

In the United States in this period, the major developments were the adoption of the Constitution, the strengthening of the national government, the rise of political parties, the beginning of neutrality, the purchase of the Louisiana Territory, and the fighting of two wars. These events developed in response, wholly or partly, to events in Europe, and all of them reflected the spirit of the times.

The influence of nationalism can be seen in several developments in the United States. The Constitution of 1787, replacing the Articles of Confederation, created a stronger central government. This was further strengthened, during the 1790's, by the economic policies of Alexander Hamilton. Even though wars with France and Britain produced serious divisions within the United States, they, too, stimulated nationalism.

Differences of opinion over foreign policy, as well as over Hamilton's economic program, helped create two national political parties. The leaders of the emerging parties agreed, at first, that the United States should stay out of the wars raging in Europe. Hence the government adopted a policy of neutrality in 1793. And President George Washington, in his Farewell Address of 1796, argued that the United States should not get involved in European quarrels. The policy failed to work perfectly, but neutrality was, on the whole, fairly well maintained. It proved advantageous to the American people, for during most of the period from 1783 to 1815 they prospered.

American ships roamed the seas, opening United States commerce to the world. Much of their trade was carried on in the Western Hemisphere, primarily with the French, Spanish, and British colonies in the West Indies. The start of the China trade in 1784 brought American merchants in touch with the Spanish and Portuguese colonies along the coast of South America, with the Spanish colony of California, and with Russian America. Some Americans continued to take part in the slave trade, selling black human beings from the Guinea coast of Africa to planters in the West Indies. The United States also fought a brief war with the Barbary pirates of North Africa, who were attacking ships in the Mediterranean and Atlantic.

The conflicts among the European nations provided opportunities for the United States to grow and prosper. The country enlarged not only its commerce but also its territory. For years after 1783, Britain occupied United States soil in the Ohio country, and Spain disputed the American claim to territory in the Floridas. Because of the war in Europe, Britain in 1794 and Spain in 1795 made treaties with the United States and recognized American claims to sovereignty over territory as far west as the Mississippi River. Again, because of the requirements of war in Europe, France in 1803 sold to the United States the vast territory known as Louisiana. This action doubled the area of the country and prepared the way for its growth as a great continental power.

The New Republic

CHAPTER 3
1781–1789

Country court in session, 1804.

You are the leader of a guerrilla movement. For the last six years you have been fighting to get rid of the colonizing power that governs your people. Despite overwhelming odds, you have just won independence. Your followers are now in control throughout the new nation.

What do you do now? Do you set up a new government, or do you think government is unnecessary? If you think government is necessary, what kind will you set up? Under your leadership, will peaceful change be possible? Will each section of the nation be treated fairly? Will the life of the average person be changed for the better with your group in control?

These are the kinds of questions that the leaders of the American Revolution faced after the battle of Yorktown. The decisions they made in the next nine years were to provide examples for other countries that would later overthrow colonial rule.

A LOOSE ASSOCIATION

In the second Continental Congress, Americans had created a central government. But this body was designed only to meet an emergency. It had no legal basis. Therefore, in June 1776, Congress appointed a committee to draft a constitution.

State Constitutions

While the Continental Congress worked on a government for the nation, people in the thirteen colonies started remodeling their governments. The new state governments resembled the old colonial governments, and all were based on written constitutions.

In some cases, temporary state legislatures, busy with wartime problems, drew up constitutions and put them into effect. In other states, the constitutions were written by special conventions that submitted their work to the voters. These constitutions went into effect only after the voters had approved them.

Since the state constitutions grew out of a common heritage, they were alike in many ways. All tried to protect personal liberties by listing them in declarations of rights. In addition, all attempted to protect citizens from unjust rule by the executive.

Each state had an elected governor with clearly limited powers. The writers of the state constitutions deliberately planned for a weak executive branch. Although Americans of the Confederation era spoke of separating and balancing powers among the legislative, executive, and judicial bodies, in fact they gave the legislature the greatest power. The legislatures, almost all composed of two houses, were elected by the eligible voters.

The new state governments were generally conservative. They did not establish complete democracy. All states had property qualifications for voting and higher ones for holding office. None granted every free white male citizen the right to vote, but all granted the right to vote on terms more generous than in the colonial period. In some states, many people could easily meet the property qualifications.

Few states allowed free blacks to vote, and none permitted slaves to do so. Although Indians were not specifically barred from voting, few could meet the property or citizenship requirements. Women were not given the vote except in New Jersey, and the legislators there soon revoked the right. Even if a state constitution did not limit the right to vote or hold office, state and local laws sometimes did. For instance, although the constitutions did not include religious qualifications, the laws in some states forbade Catholics, Jews, or nonbelievers in Christianity from holding office. Despite their limitations, the new state governments started the American people on the road to local self-government.

The Confederation

The Articles of Confederation were drawn up in 1776 by a committee led by John Dickinson of Pennsylvania. They were amended by the second Continental Congress and finally, in November 1777, were sent to the states for approval.

The Articles set up a loose form of government that did not limit the *sovereignty,* or basic independence, of the states. The authors of the Articles deliberately created a weak government, which they called a firm league of friendship.

The new confederation would have a Congress composed of delegates appointed by the states. The Congress would maintain an army and navy, conduct foreign relations, make treaties, declare war, and handle Indian affairs. Each state delegation, regardless of the state's size, would have one vote. In minor matters, Congress would govern by simple majority vote. In larger issues, such as those affecting war and peace, it could act only if nine of the thirteen states approved.

Under the Articles, the states retained all powers except those expressly delegated to the central government. Congress had no power to tax. To obtain funds, Congress had to ask the states for them. The states were supposed to contribute in proportion to the value of their improved lands.

Congress would have a president, but he would not be a true executive officer. He would mainly preside over meetings of Congress. The Articles did not provide for national courts, except for those to deal with specific disputes between states. Each state was obligated to honor the laws and judicial decisions of every other state.

This loose union of states, the Articles said, was to be perpetual. It would be almost impossible to change this constitution, for any amendment required approval of all the states.

The second Continental Congress insisted on ratification of the Articles as written. Within a few months most of the states accepted them. The other states refused to ratify unless the Articles were changed.

The source of difficulty was a clause that said "No state shall be deprived of territory for the benefit of the United States." This clause would protect the claims of seven states to the lands between the Appalachian Mountains and the Mississippi River.

Maryland, one of the six states without western lands, refused to accept the Articles unless the clause were removed. With the support of other "landless" states, Maryland argued that the western lands should belong to all Americans rather than to individual states. All the states had fought for this territory; therefore, all should profit from it.

Despite the arguments, the need for union during the war was so great that by February 1779 all the states but Maryland had ratified the Articles. Maryland's refusal meant the Articles could not go into effect.

In October 1780, New York and Virginia,

Far from being typical, this eighteenth-century farm exhibits the kind of prosperity that many Americans sought.

which had the largest land claims, accepted a congressional resolution that satisfied the landless states. The resolution said that the western lands should be sold for the benefit of the whole nation and that the territory should be formed into states.

Several months later, the landed states, led by Virginia, surrendered most of their western claims. On March 1, 1781, Maryland ratified the Articles, and the nation's first constitution went into effect.

A NEW SOCIAL ORDER

So important were the social changes in the American Revolution that some historians have talked about *two* revolutions. One gained freedom from Britain, and the other changed the social system at home.

Before the Revolution, the upper class in the colonies had consisted of a landholding gentry, many of whom had inherited their wealth. During and after the Revolution, many other Americans for the first time felt free of the restrictions that had limited their social standing for life. These people wanted to keep their newly found personal freedom and were willing to experiment with a new social order where advancement was open to all—at least to all white males—regardless of birth.

Abolishing Aristocracy

In colonial times, the use and ownership of land often determined a man's political rights and his place in society. For example, his right to vote and to hold office usually depended upon the amount of property he owned. Americans who wanted to build a social democracy therefore worked to change the property laws to discourage large inherited holdings of land.

The reformers also attacked other symbols of the old order, such as hereditary titles and honors. Many of the state constitutions prohibited the new governments and their officials from creating, granting, or accepting titles of nobility. The Articles of Confederation also forbade officials to accept such titles from foreign governments.

Loyalist Losses

Historians have estimated that one-fourth to one-third of the people stayed loyal to Britain during the Revolution. Although most aristocrats were Loyalists, most Loyalists were *not* aristocrats. In wealth, education, and social standing they differed little from the average Patriot.

From the British point of view the Loyalists had been faithful subjects and valuable allies. Fifty thousand of them had fought with the British armies, and others had given food, supplies, and information to the British. The Patriots, however, thought of the Loyalists as traitors who had turned against friends and neighbors.

During the Revolution, the Patriots had dealt harshly with Loyalists. In 1777, the Continental Congress urged the states to seize and sell Loyalist property to help pay for the war. All the states eagerly took Loyalist land and other forms of wealth. Eighty thousand Loyalists left the country to avoid persecution by angry Patriots.

After the war, British authorities tried to help the Loyalists. The peace treaty of 1783 required Congress to ask the states to settle the Loyalists' claims. Congress did so, but the states ignored the request. Many Patriots had become landowners by buying Loyalist property. Partly because of the influence of these new landowners in state legislatures, the Loyalists were unable to recover their property. No payment was made to them, and some Americans even suggested that Loyalists should not be allowed to return to the United States.

Nonetheless, some Loyalists did return. Like those who had remained in the country throughout the Revolution, they gradually accepted independence. They, too, began to profit from the changes it brought.

Slavery

The Revolution also affected black slaves. Although many Americans were opposed to any change in the institution of slavery, some Patriots attacked both the slave trade and slavery.

The African slave trade had started in the 1440's. Explorers brought Africans from the Guinea coast—the long coastline from present-day Mauritania to Namibia (South-West Africa)—to work in the fields of Portugal. When the Spanish and Portuguese began settling in South America in 1502, they brought slaves to the New World.

Most of these slaves were purchased from African slave traders on the Guinea coast and taken to the West Indies. Those who survived the crossing were kept in the islands for a while to get used to the climate, diseases, and work methods in the New World. Of the 5 million Africans who survived the Atlantic crossing before 1800, probably only one-tenth were taken to the North American mainland.

The slave trade had been the subject of debate in colonial assemblies for many years. Some legislatures had abolished the trade, only to have their laws vetoed in England. In general, those who profited from the trade, whether in England or the colonies, wanted to see it continued. After independence, states began prohibiting the trade. Within ten years every state but Georgia and South Carolina had outlawed it. The traffic in

By the mid-1700's, slave traders from France, Portugal, England, and the Netherlands had separate slave pens in Africa. As blacks were captured, they were

human beings continued illegally for many years, but the laws did limit it.

The campaign against slavery itself was far more difficult. In the North, where slaves were few, defenders of slavery were scarce. Vermont abolished slavery in 1777, Pennsylvania in 1780, and Massachusetts in 1783. During the Confederation period, slavery lost ground everywhere in the North.

In the South the situation was different. Though many important southerners were opposed to slavery, most southern whites considered it profitable and necessary. For example, George Washington and Thomas Jefferson spoke out against slavery but

herded into the pens. When a boatload had been "collected" in a single pen, the captives were shipped to the West Indies or the United States.

owned many slaves themselves. James Madison said that slave labor allowed him the free time to carry on his public career. Some southern states, such as Virginia and Maryland, permitted *manumission,* or the freeing of a slave by his or her master. In addition, the codes governing slave life were eased in some ways.

Both northerners and southerners worried about the consequences of freeing the slaves. A year after slavery was outlawed in Massachusetts, some whites agitated to keep free blacks out of Boston. They claimed that if Negro workers were allowed in the city, they would compete for the jobs of lower-class whites. This agitation did not keep free blacks out of Boston, but it reduced the number living there.

Church and State

Religious discrimination was common in the colonies. Every colony allowed freedom of worship, but this freedom mainly benefited Protestants rather than Catholics or Jews.

In most colonies there had been established churches—churches supported by taxes paid by all the people, regardless of their religious beliefs. In New England, except Rhode Island, the established church was Congregational. In the South, government supported the Anglican church.

Some Patriots favored freedom of religion and believed that worship should be a private matter. To them, religious freedom also included a person's right to deny support to any church. Others went even further, saying that they had the right to be nonbelievers if they so chose. They wanted to separate church and state.

Many Americans wanted this separation because they saw it as an important step toward social democracy. Soon after the Revolution, a number of states ended public support for religious groups. In some places, however, the last ties were not cut until years later.

In December 1785, the Virginia legislature passed a noteworthy law, the Statute of Religious Liberty. It said that "no man shall be compelled to frequent or support any religious worship, place, or ministry whatsoever," and that all people were free to think as they desired in matters of religion.

Public Education

Schools at all levels suffered in one way or another during the Revolutionary War. Some were abandoned, others lost students and financial support, and many were swept clean of teachers with Loyalist leanings.

Some Patriot leaders worked to establish a system of public education open to both the rich and the poor. Beginning in 1779, Thomas Jefferson urged the state of Virginia to set up a public school system. He proposed elementary education for white boys and girls, secondary schooling for some white boys, and a liberal university education for the most gifted white boys, especially those who gave promise of becoming leaders in society. The bill failed, however, to pass the legislature.

In constitutions, laws, and legislative resolutions, the states supported the concept of expanding the education system at public expense. The number of private colleges increased, and a few public schools were set up; some actually opened their doors in the 1780's. Unfortunately, most states did not get beyond the talking or planning stage. Americans of the Confederation era did not have the money or the will to build public schools.

PLANNING FOR ORDERLY GROWTH

Congress's western lands' resolution of October 1780 established a policy that affected the nation's growth for the next hundred years. In the past, most countries had treated settlements beyond national boundaries as colonies. Americans of the Confederation era, many of whom were crossing the mountains to settle in the West, rejected the colonial idea. They decided that their rapidly growing settlements should be governed not as colonies, but as territories that would some day become states equal to all other states.

Surveying and Selling the Land

When the Revolutionary War began, only a few thousand colonists lived west of the Appalachian Mountains. During and after the war, settlers swarmed into the area. By 1790, some 120,000 were living there.

To profit from this rapid western settlement, the central government had to set up a system for selling the land and creating new states. A committee headed by Thomas Jefferson worked out the Land Ordinance of 1785, which provided for the survey and sale of western lands. This ordinance divided the Northwest (the area northwest of the Ohio River and east of the Mississippi River) into six-mile-square townships. A township would contain thirty-six sections, each one mile square. Four sections were to be set aside for the federal government and one for the support of public schools. The other sections were to be sold for not less than a dollar an acre in public auctions at land offices in the Northwest.

The ordinance was designed to bring money to the national government rather than to make settlement easy. It did not permit the sale of less than one section (640 acres). A person therefore would have to have at least $640 in order to buy directly from the government land offices. Few pioneers could bring together that much money. Thus the terms favored speculators, who often formed private companies to buy government lands.

Several land companies wanted even greater advantages than they had under the Ordinance of 1785. They tried to get Congress to suspend the ordinance. Because the government wanted money immediately, Congress gave in to the speculators.

The most successful speculative group was the Ohio Company, formed in Boston in 1786 by veterans of the Revolutionary War. In the summer of 1787, Congress agreed to sell a vast tract of land to the Ohio Company at bargain prices. Although Congress reserved some sections for educational and other purposes, 1.5 million acres went to the Ohio Company for less than nine cents an acre.

Once the members of the Ohio Company owned the land, they wanted to be sure that they could use it for profit. Without government support this would be difficult.

Tribal Rights and Claims

Even though Congress had set up a system for surveying and selling the land, it still did not own the land. The states, to be sure, had given up their colonial claims to western lands. The Indian tribes had not, however, given up their rights to most of the lands between the Appalachian Mountains and the Mississippi River. Before land could be sold, the Indian title to it had to be "extinguished." Congress would follow the British practice of requiring formal, written treaties to transfer the land.

Many Indian tribes were forced to cede their land to the United States government. Some, however, voluntarily gave up their territory because their hunting grounds no longer provided enough game for the tribe. Some of the Cherokee in Georgia, for instance, gave up their lands before 1800 and moved west. Many more tribes ceased to rely on hunting and became farming communities. These tribes rarely agreed willingly to give up their land, and they ceded it only when forced. Not until 1848 were the last lands east of the Mississippi ceded.

A common way to extinguish the Indian title to tribal lands was this: American pioneers would settle in areas that were closed to them by treaty and by law. When the tribes tried to remove them by force, the pioneers would fight back. Often the United States Army was called in to put down the "Indian uprising." With better weapons and greater numbers behind them, the pioneers invariably won. The losing Indians

Western Land Claims and Cessions, 1776–1802

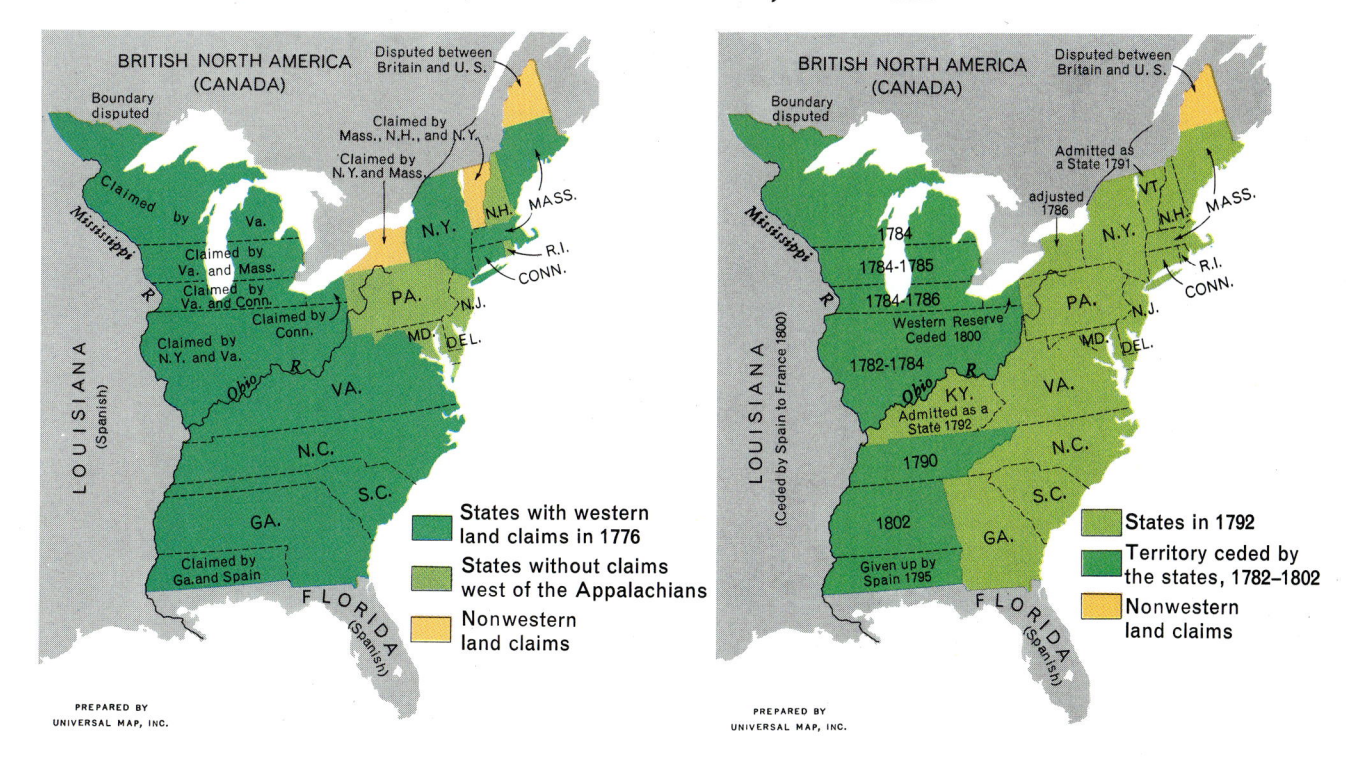

The Land Ordinances, 1785 and 1787

The Territory Northwest of the River Ohio *(left)* was commonly known as the Northwest Territory. It was set up by Congress in 1787 under the Northwest Ordinance. That law provided for government in the territory and outlined the steps through which a part of the area could become a state. Two years earlier, the Land Ordinance of 1785 had provided for the survey and sale of western lands as a source of immediate income for the Confederation government. This public land was divided into townships six miles square. Section 16 of each township was set aside for support of education, and four additional sections were set aside for the government. Even before the Northwest Ordinance was passed, land-hungry squatters had moved west, made clearings, and built crude dwellings.

The two land ordinances set precedents for further territorial development. Later laws changed some of the procedures set up under these ordinances, such as the system for numbering the sections.

The plats below show how townships and sections were described, as provided in the Land Ordinance of 1785. Plat A shows townships in relation to the base line and principal meridian. The township shown in dark green is described as Township 3 North, Range 3 East. Plat B is an enlargement of Township 3 North, Range 3 East, showing how the 36 sections of a township were numbered. (A section is a square mile, or 640 acres.) Plat C is an enlargement of Section 32, showing how the section might be subdivided.

An American Log-House

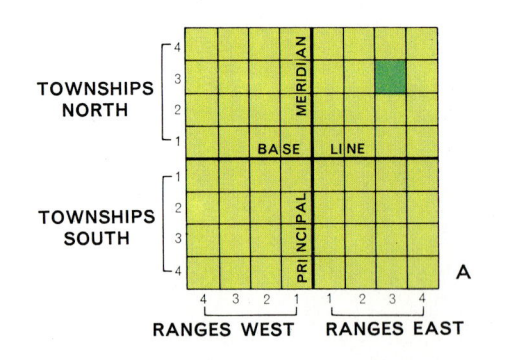

would then make a treaty giving up the section of land in question.

Some treaties were made with Indians who did not truly represent their tribes. In most tribes there were a few people who were willing to sell tribal lands for their own personal gain. The men who were called "chiefs" by the government were not always the true leaders of their tribes.

Moreover, the central government's role was limited. The Articles of Confederation gave Congress control over relations with those Indians "not members of any state." A number of states exceeded their powers by signing treaties or waging war with Indians who lived beyond their borders. Congress was powerless to stop them.

The Northwest Ordinance

In July 1787, Congress passed an important law, the Northwest Ordinance. It set up the Northwest Territory. It also provided a system of limited self-government under which statehood could be reached in three stages.

In the first stage, Congress would choose officials who would govern the entire Northwest Territory. They would put into effect those laws from the thirteen states that they thought suitable.

In the second stage, when the Northwest Territory had a population of five thousand free adult males, the eligible voters could elect a legislature that would share power with appointed officials. The legislature could, at this stage, send a nonvoting delegate to Congress. Neither the legislature nor the territorial officials could interfere with the personal freedoms of the people, which were protected by a bill of rights. However, not all would have the right to vote. No women were allowed to vote, and only those men who owned at least fifty acres of land could vote.

The law called for dividing the Territory into no fewer than three and no more than five states. When any part of the Territory had a free population of 60,000 or more, it became a territory. In this, the third stage, it could write a constitution and apply for statehood. Congress would then admit it to the Union as a state on an equal footing with the original thirteen states.

The Northwest Ordinance prohibited slavery in the entire Territory. This provision had the effect of keeping slavery south of the Ohio River. Some of the local communities also prohibited free blacks from settling within their boundaries, although this was not part of the Northwest Ordinance.

Like most other land laws enacted after 1763, the Ordinance of 1787 required fair treatment of the Indian tribes in the area. Lands could be acquired only by purchase or treaty, except in "just and lawful wars authorized by Congress." The actual practice, as usual, differed from the letter of the law. The Miami, Shawnee, Wyandot, and Delaware had been pushed into the Northwest Territory by other tribes and by European and African settlers arriving on the East Coast. Now they were to face a flood of settlers crossing the Appalachians and taking their land.

FOREIGN AFFAIRS

Under the Articles of Confederation, only the Congress was to carry on relations with foreign governments. It could send and receive ambassadors and negotiate treaties and alliances. However, it lacked effective power in foreign relations, for it could not make the states comply with the treaties it made.

Foreign nations were aware of the weakness of the Confederation government. Since they doubted that the loose union truly was a nation, they showed little respect for it. They interfered in American politics and tried to manipulate the new government.

Trouble with Britain

The Confederation government's most serious diplomatic problems were with Britain. British leaders demanded harsh treatment of the former colonies. The British government prohibited trade with Americans in the British West Indies. It also required that most products going to its ports be carried in English ships. These actions particularly hurt New England towns where shipbuilding and trade were important.

Many Americans were unhappy with Britain's treatment. The states would not, however, follow a common policy toward Britain, and the Confederation government had no way to force the British leaders to change their policies.

In 1785 the Confederation government sent John Adams to London to negoriate a commercial treaty with Britain. The British would make no treaty, and they refused to send a minister to the United States.

Adams also tried to deal with violations of the peace treaty of 1783. Both the United States and Britain were guilty of some violations. The British, for instance, had carried away American property and slaves.

The Americans, in turn, refused to repay millions of dollars that had been loaned to them before the Revolution. The Confederation Congress tried to uphold the repayment provision of the treaty, but some of the states passed laws forbidding state courts to help collect the debts. Congress had no power to force the states to honor the treaty. It was equally helpless in trying to carry out the treaty provisions dealing with Loyalists.

The unpaid debts and mistreatment of Loyalists gave the British an excuse to keep military and trading posts in the Northwest. In the peace treaty, Britain had promised to give up these posts.

Some Englishmen believed that their government had been foolishly generous by granting the Northwest to the United States. Others argued that the treaty violated Britain's obligations to its Indian allies in the territory. British commanders feared an Indian uprising if the area were to come under American control. The British government therefore told its officials in North America not to deliver the posts to the Americans.

The presence of British soldiers on United States soil angered many Americans. Many westerners were convinced that British agents from the posts supplied Indians with arms and supported raids on pioneer settlements. Yet the Confederation government could not make Britain honor the treaty.

Difficulties with Spain

Relations with Spain were about as bad as those with Britain. There were three major issues: use of the Mississippi River, the southern boundary, and trade policy. Each of these issues affected a different section of the country.

Westerners depended on using the Mississippi River to get their produce to eastern markets. Since Spain owned Louisiana and the Floridas, it controlled the last two hundred miles of the Mississippi. In 1784, it closed the river to Americans. Westerners demanded that Congress force Spain to reopen the river.

At the same time, disagreement arose about the southern boundary. The peace treaty with Britain had set the boundary between the United States and West Florida at the 31st parallel. The Spaniards argued rightly that they were not bound by the Anglo-American peace treaty. They established military posts far north of the 31st parallel and also armed the Indians in that area.

In Congress, delegates from the Northeast represented trading interests and were not greatly concerned about the problems of western settlers. What they wanted most was a commercial treaty that would allow Americans to trade in Spanish ports.

The California Missions

Although the Spanish had claimed territory in California in the 1500's, they made no effort to settle it until the mid-eighteenth century. Then their claim was endangered by Russia and Britain. In 1767, Carlos III of Spain authorized a colonizing expedition to California.

Fifteen Franciscan priests left New Spain to spread the Christian faith and to "civilize" the California Indians. They dedicated their first mission, San Diego de Alcalá, in 1769. In the next fifty years, twenty other missions were set up, mostly by Father Junípero Serra and Father Fermín Francisco de Lasuen.

Besides teaching Christian doctrine and the Spanish language, the Franciscans taught the Indians irrigation methods and trades. The Indians under mission control raised a variety of crops and livestock. Many of the missions were quite prosperous. They were able to trade their hemp, hides, wine, and oil for clothing and tools from New Spain. At its peak in about 1834, the mission population included 31,000 Indians. (The total California Indian population at the time was about 300,000.) The missions owned 750,000 head of cattle and laid claim to millions of acres of land.

The effects of mission life on the Indians have been widely debated. Some historians have defended the Franciscans, saying that the priests educated many of the Indians, that the work load was light, and that discipline was mild. They also say that the Indians entered mission life willingly and were not forced to join the Catholic Church.

Other historians accuse the Franciscans of abusing their power. They argue that the priests showed little respect for the Indians' culture and operated a system of forced labor and harsh punishment.

In the early nineteenth century, the Spanish colonies rebelled, and California became part of Mexico. In 1833, the Mexican government secularized the missions. It gave the Indians half the mission lands, livestock, and tools, as well as some rights of citizenship. Many Indians left the missions. A few stayed to continue farming the land, but many lost their holdings to dishonest administrators and speculators.

Indians at the Carmel mission line up to greet members of a visiting French scientific expedition.

Spain sent a special representative to the United States to negotiate the issues. The resultant treaty was not ratified by Congress. It aroused strong disagreement between the sections and even threatened to break up the loose confederation.

CRITICISM OF CONFEDERATION

The failures in foreign policy helped those who wanted a stronger national government. Many Americans saw that they could have an effective foreign policy only if the Confederation government had more power. At the same time, internal problems also led to criticism of the government.

Financial Failures

When the United States became independent, the people did not become as prosperous as they had expected. Instead they faced years of financial troubles. There was some economic growth, but from 1783 to 1787, the United States suffered from an economic depression. This struck New England especially hard.

In financing the war, Congress had run up a large public debt. It had also tried to pay some of the war costs by issuing paper money that was not backed by gold or other forms of wealth.

The states also issued uncounted sums of paper money. This paper currency fell rapidly in value, becoming worthless. At the end of the war, most states refused to accept the paper money in payment of taxes. In effect, because they now refused to redeem it, Congress and the states had used paper money as though it were a tax to finance the war.

After the war, Congress tried to raise money to pay its remaining debts at home and abroad by asking the states for it. Between 1781 and 1786, the payments sent by the states to the national treasury usually could not even pay the government's run-

Primitive though it may seem, this hotel kitchen is equipped with the most up-to-date conveniences of the early 1800's.

ning expenses, let alone its debts.

The states, too, had come out of the war with large debts. They tried to pay wartime debts by raising taxes.

Most states directly taxed land and buildings. Some states had import duties, and others had excise taxes. The taxes, especially import duties, led to conflict and misunderstanding. Some states treated the boats, barges, and ships of other states as if they were foreign. In some cases one state might refuse to trade with another state.

As the depression grew worse, seven states issued more paper money. As before, this money fell in value. Nonetheless, some state legislatures made this money *legal tender* (that is, they passed laws requiring that it be accepted for debts). In Rhode Island, merchants and creditors nevertheless refused to accept payment in paper money. Creditors found the situation intolerable. They wanted to strengthen the power of the national government in financial matters.

Even before all of the states had adopted the Articles of Confederation, Congress had struggled with its lack of financial power. It tried to amend the Articles to increase its taxing powers. Various states blocked ratification, and the Congress continued to limp along with little power.

The failure to amend the Articles of Confederation pointed up one of their major defects—the need for unanimous consent by the states for any amendment.

Shays's Rebellion

While the amendments were under consideration, farmers who could not pay their taxes or their private debts saw the courts take their property and sell it. The situation was particularly bad in New England.

Farmers there believed that their welfare was being sacrificed to add to the wealth of creditors in Boston and other towns. In several areas, mobs of poor farmers rioted in protest.

In western Massachusetts, Daniel Shays, a former captain in the Continental Army, led farmers in a revolt known as Shays's Rebellion. In 1786 he organized and trained his followers, many of them war veterans armed only with sticks and pitchforks. He announced a program that demanded cheap paper money, tax relief, a *moratorium* (legal delay) on payment of debts, and the abolition of imprisonment for debt. Shays's followers used force or threats of violence to prevent collection of debts. They invaded county courts and broke up sheriffs' sales of seized property.

The creditors asked Congress to help put down the revolt, but Congress had no money to pay for troops. Neither did the state. Finally, wealthy Boston merchants agreed to provide funds, and they got the governor to call out the state militia. In January 1787, these troops attacked the rebels and killed 3, wounded 1, and captured about 150, including Daniel Shays.

Although Massachusetts had crushed the rebellion, people with property continued to fear for their safety. The rebels were tried and sentenced to death but were later pardoned. The state gave in to the farmers' demands by granting tax relief and allowing postponement of debt payments. More important, Shays's Rebellion convinced many people in various parts of the country that only a strong national government could keep mobs from gaining control of state governments. These people decided to try to change the Articles.

A Special Convention

The movement for change in the first constitution grew out of efforts by several states to cooperate on problems they could not handle alone. Representatives from Maryland and Virginia met at Mount Vernon in 1785 to try to settle a quarrel over the use of the Potomac River, which formed a boundary between the two states. After agreeing on uses of the Potomac, they decided to discuss other interstate problems. They invited all the states to a conference at Annapolis, Maryland, in September 1786.

Only five states sent delegates to the Annapolis conference. With such small representation, the meeting was not able to do anything about interstate problems. It did prepare a report asking the Confederation Congress to call a special convention of delegates from all the states to discuss amendments to the constitution. The convention would meet in Philadelphia on May 14, 1787, and would report its results to Congress.

Congress was slow to back the convention. In February 1787, it invited all the states to Philadelphia, explaining that the sole purpose of the convention was to revise the Articles. All but Rhode Island responded favorably and chose delegates.

SETTING THE STAGE

Some Americans were satisfied with the existing state of affairs and doubted the need for the convention. Also, a large number of Americans distrusted the convention delegates. They were afraid that the delegates would establish a strong central government controlled by an aristocracy.

The Delegates

The state legislatures or governors appointed seventy-four delegates to the convention at Philadelphia. Of these, nineteen failed to appear. Those who did attend made up an outstanding group of Americans.

The delegates came from twelve states and from practically every geographic or political division within the states. Social and economic groups did not receive broad representation. All of the delegates were white men, mostly Protestants of English descent. None came from the poor, the debtors, or the working class. They were mostly lawyers, merchants, and plantation owners.

Many were leaders in their own states. Forty-two of them had served in the Continental Congress. Nearly all had held some important public position or had served in the state legislatures. Many had read widely and knew much about law, history, and politics. About half had graduated from college—a remarkable achievement in the 1780's.

Nationalists in Command

Poor weather and bad roads made travel difficult, especially for delegates from New England. By May 25, the delegations from seven states had arrived, and the necessary quorum was finally present. The sessions were called to order at Philadelphia's State House—known to later generations as Independence Hall—where independence had been declared.

The South had the largest representation at the convention. Southern delegates were also most regular in attendance and most influential in debate. Fourteen of them worked throughout the convention and signed the Constitution. New England's representation was smaller, and only six New Englanders signed the Constitution. A few others from the area refused to sign it.

Delegates who favored a strong central government—called nationalists—held private meetings before the sessions opened to plan how to replace the Articles. Therefore, when the convention opened, the nationalists took command.

At the start, the nationalists arranged to elect George Washington as presiding officer. To encourage free debate, the delegates moved to keep the convention's proceedings secret. To prevent the intrusion of public pressure, they closed the doors and stationed armed guards outside and inside the hall.

Important Decisions

Committees did most of the work at the convention, and debate most often revolved around committee reports. In the committees and in the convention, about a dozen men made the key decisions.

James Madison, who combined leadership, youth, hard work, intelligence, and learning, was in this group. During the convention, he made notes on the proceedings. These notes were published more than fifty years after the convention.

Benjamin Franklin, who was famous as a statesman and scientist, was also at the meeting. Although Franklin was too old to be as active as Madison, he gave dignity to the convention.

The most important delegate was George Washington, who was a national hero. His participation helped reassure those Americans who feared the results of the convention. Washington seldom spoke or took part in the proceedings, but he was almost always present. Like Franklin, he took a moderate position on most issues.

Randolph's Plan

On May 29, when the convention at last met for its main business, Governor Edmund Randolph of Virginia spoke to the group. He noted the defects of the Articles of Confederation and then proposed fifteen resolutions to correct them.

His first resolution went directly to the core of the issue. He proposed that the delegates forget their instructions to revise the Articles and, instead, draw up a new constitution. The delegates at first reacted to this idea with silence. Then heated debate broke out.

The nationalists realized that public sentiment was against them. They also knew that they might not get another chance to write a new constitution. They would have to plan a national government that was so much better than the existing one that the voters would be willing to adopt it.

Washington urged the delegates to do what they believed to be right, even if their plans should turn out to be unacceptable to the voters. "If to please the people," Washington said, "we offer what we ourselves disapprove, how can we afterwards defend our work? Let us raise a standard to which the wise and honest can repair."

Many of the delegates apparently took his advice. Randolph's resolution to set up a new government passed. It was after the adoption of this resolution that the gathering became a constitutional convention. The delegates themselves, not the people or their elected representatives, made the decision to draw up a new constitution. In this they went beyond their instructions.

A NEW PLAN OF GOVERNMENT

The delegates now faced the problem of working out a plan of government that they themselves could accept. They had to devise a government that would not favor large states over small states or one section over another.

Two Plans

The Virginia plan was proposed by the nationalists. It would set up a strong, unified central government that would operate directly upon the people rather than upon the states. It would have its own officers and agencies to carry out its laws and duties.

The source of government power would be a national legislature. There also would be an executive officer and a system of national courts.

Under the Virginia plan, the states with the largest free population would control the national legislature. The legislature would set the limits of its own power as well as the power of the states. The large states therefore favored the plan.

Delegates from the small states feared that the Virginia plan would destroy their independence. They wanted all the states to be represented equally in the national legislature. Such representation would prevent the large states from controlling national affairs and would at least suggest that the states were independent. The small-state delegates wanted the states to control the central government. These ideas were the basis of the New Jersey plan.

With some changes, the New Jersey plan would keep the main features of the Articles of Confederation. It would strengthen the Congress by allowing it to regulate commerce among the states and raise money with taxes. It also would make acts of Congress and all treaties the supreme law of the land, regardless of laws within the states.

The Virginia and New Jersey plans offered the convention two choices: a strong, centralized union or a loose association of states tied more firmly than before. Both plans would keep republican government—rule through elected representatives. In both plans the legislature would have the greatest power.

Compromise

Faced with these choices, the delegates debated. When neither side would give in, the convention deadlocked.

This alarmed Benjamin Franklin. If the convention failed, he warned, "mankind may hereafter . . . despair of establishing Governments by human wisdom and leave it to chance, war and conquest." Franklin's comments influenced the delegates, and they worked to settle their differences.

Representatives from Connecticut presented the plan that brought the two sides together. They suggested that there be a two-house legislature. The lower house, the House of Representatives, would be elected by the eligible voters. States would be assigned representatives according to population. The upper house, or Senate, would be chosen by the legislatures of the states. Each state, regardless of population or wealth, would have two senators. This plan, the Great Compromise, was adopted by the convention.

The delegates now turned to sectional differences. Northerners wanted slaves to be included in the population when figuring a state's share in payment of direct taxes. But they did not want the slaves counted toward representation in the House. They also wanted the Congress to have the power to set up tariffs and regulate trade. Southerners, who owned most of the slaves, wanted the slaves counted toward representation, but not for direct taxation. Also, southerners feared that if the Congress had power over tariffs and trade, it might put export taxes on their crops, stop the slave trade, and make commercial treaties that injured the South.

By compromise, it was decided that three-fifths of the slaves would be counted for purposes of representation and direct taxation. The Congress was allowed to regulate commerce but not to levy export taxes. The Congress was prohibited for twenty years from ending the foreign slave trade. The new Constitution gave the President the power to make treaties, but two-thirds of the Senate, rather than a simple majority, had to approve them. Acting as a group, the states in one section would be able to veto a commercial treaty that they did not favor.

New Powers

As more compromises were reached, the Constitution took shape. The kingpin clause

The Structure and Powers of the Government

The Constitution of the United States provides for three separate branches of the national government and gives certain broad powers to each. Abuses of power by any one branch are controlled by a system of checks and balances.

SEPARATION OF POWERS

The top chart shows how each branch of the new government was organized in 1789. Each branch has grown, but the basic structure is the same.

Legislative. Among other things, Congress is empowered to tax, to regulate commerce, to declare war, and to make all the laws necessary to carry out its specified powers and duties.

Executive. As chief executive, the President serves as commander in chief of the armed forces, makes treaties, suggests programs to Congress, signs or vetoes bills, executes laws, and appoints many national officials.

Judicial. The Supreme Court and lesser courts try cases that come under their jurisdiction. They also hear appeals on cases from lower courts. The function that takes up the least amount of the Supreme Court's time but arouses the most interest is that of determining the constitutionality of federal, state, and local laws.

CHECKS AND BALANCES

The bottom chart shows how the system of checks and balances works. Each branch participates in and checks the affairs of the other two branches.

Many checks and balances may be traced to specific clauses in the Constitution; others have developed through interpretation. For example, *judicial review,* the power of the courts to determine the constitutionality of federal laws, was established through interpretation in the case of *Marbury* v. *Madison* (1803).

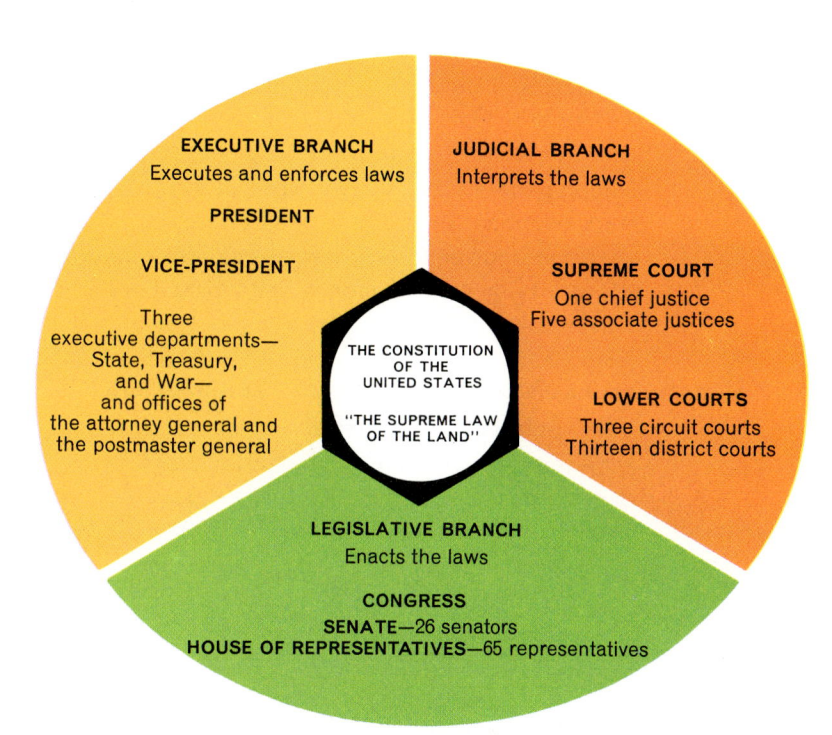

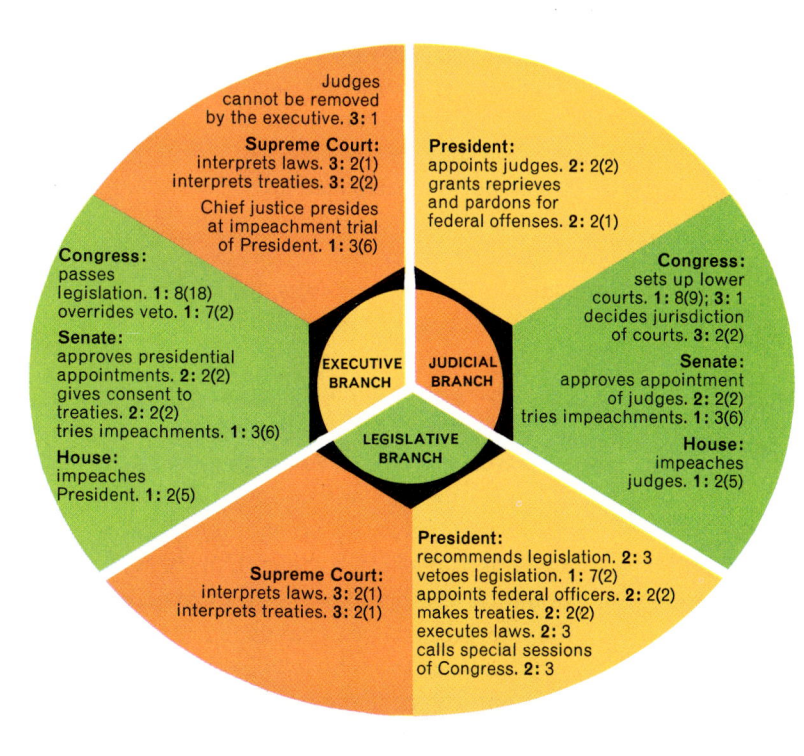

EXECUTIVE BRANCH
Executes and enforces laws
PRESIDENT
VICE-PRESIDENT
Three executive departments—State, Treasury, and War—and offices of the attorney general and the postmaster general

JUDICIAL BRANCH
Interprets the laws
SUPREME COURT
One chief justice
Five associate justices
LOWER COURTS
Three circuit courts
Thirteen district courts

LEGISLATIVE BRANCH
Enacts the laws
CONGRESS
SENATE—26 senators
HOUSE OF REPRESENTATIVES—65 representatives

THE CONSTITUTION OF THE UNITED STATES "THE SUPREME LAW OF THE LAND"

EXECUTIVE BRANCH

Judges cannot be removed by the executive. **3:** 1
Supreme Court: interprets laws. **3:** 2(1) interprets treaties. **3:** 2(2)
Chief justice presides at impeachment trial of President. **1:** 3(6)

Congress: passes legislation. **1:** 8(18) overrides veto. **1:** 7(2)
Senate: approves presidential appointments. **2:** 2(2) gives consent to treaties. **2:** 2(2) tries impeachments. **1:** 3(6)
House: impeaches President. **1:** 2(5)

JUDICIAL BRANCH

President: appoints judges. **2:** 2(2) grants reprieves and pardons for federal offenses. **2:** 2(1)

Congress: sets up lower courts. **1:** 8(9); **3:** 1 decides jurisdiction of courts. **3:** 2(2)
Senate: approves appointment of judges. **2:** 2(2) tries impeachments. **1:** 3(6)
House: impeaches judges. **1:** 2(5)

LEGISLATIVE BRANCH

Supreme Court: interprets laws. **3:** 2(1) interprets treaties. **3:** 2(1)

President: recommends legislation. **2:** 3 vetoes legislation. **1:** 7(2) appoints federal officers. **2:** 2(2) makes treaties. **2:** 2(2) executes laws. **2:** 3 calls special sessions of Congress. **2:** 3

in the new Constitution (*Art. 6, para. 2*) was basic to holding the Union together. It said that the Constitution and the laws and treaties made under it would be the "supreme Law of the Land."

The new Constitution granted certain specific powers to the central government. Among these was exclusive control over foreign relations. In addition, the Congress was given the power to levy taxes, regulate commerce, fully control money, and pass laws "necessary and proper" to carry out its responsibilities (*Art. 1, sec. 8*). The Constitution took from the states some of the powers that could best be exercised by the national government. At the same time, certain powers were to be shared by the national and state governments.

The new Constitution did not recognize the claim of any state to independence. It was a plan for a nation, not a loose association of states.

Provisions for Change

The delegates wrote a brief, general document—one that did not attempt to spell out all the powers of government. They left it to Congress, the President, and the courts to add to what they had written and to interpret what was not entirely clear.

The delegates provided two ways of proposing amendments and two ways of ratifying them. These provisions made amendment difficult but not impossible.

The amending process was important in the development of democracy. For example, the right of black Americans, women, and young people to vote has been granted in amendments to the Constitution.

Since the process of amendment is difficult, Americans often have had to take advantage of the broad wording of the Constitution to bring about change. Particularly when they have thought it unlikely that an amendment might be adopted, Americans have changed the Constitution by having the courts interpret it. Within the design of the original Constitution, the people of the United States have taken a republican government with limited democratic features and made it into a government that is basically democratic.

Checks and Balances

The delegates created a government with checks and balances. Each branch—legislative, executive, and judicial—would have specific powers. At the same time, each branch would have enough power to stop abuses of power by the other branches. When power was used properly, the whole government would be in balance and would work in an orderly way.

As a result of their experiences under British rule, the delegates feared the abuse of power by the executive. At the same time, they thought of democracy as mob rule that would lead to control by dictators.

Several features of the new government showed the influence of these beliefs. For example, the Constitution gave the voters a direct part only in the election of representatives to the House. The state legislatures, not the voters themselves, would choose the senators. The delegates made the selection of the executive—the President—even more indirect. The President was to be chosen by electors who had been appointed by the state legislatures or by the voters.

The powers given to the President were limited. Still, despite the controls on the presidency, it became a position of considerable power.

The courts were also to be removed from control by the voters. With the consent of the Senate, the President would appoint judges to the national courts. They would hold office for life.

Practically all of the delegates wanted a supreme national court, but they disagreed

Amending the Constitution of the United States

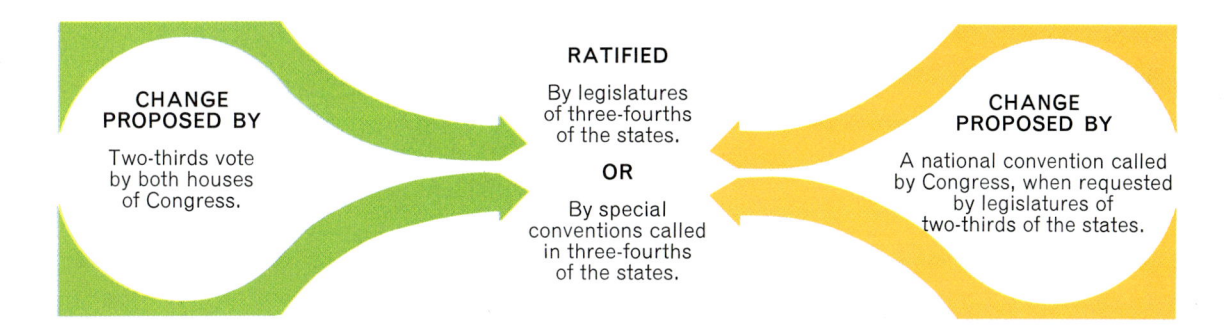

CHANGE PROPOSED BY Two-thirds vote by both houses of Congress.

RATIFIED By legislatures of three-fourths of the states. OR By special conventions called in three-fourths of the states.

CHANGE PROPOSED BY A national convention called by Congress, when requested by legislatures of two-thirds of the states.

The writers of the Constitution provided for flexibility in government by including a process for changing the Constitution. They wanted any amendments to become part of the Constitution itself. The formal process of amending the Constitution has two steps—proposal and ratification. Thus far, all amendments to the Constitution have been proposed by Congress, but some people have attempted to use the other method of proposing amendments. Congress decides which method of ratification will be used at the same time it approves an amendment. Only one amendment has been ratified by special conventions.

on its powers. Some wanted to give the Supreme Court a veto over laws it considered unconstitutional; others did not. When the Constitution was completed, it did not specifically give the Court such a veto.

After all of the compromises had been agreed upon, a committee polished the language. When this final draft went to the convention, only forty-two delegates were still present. Few were fully satisfied with the package of compromises, but only three delegates refused to approve it. On September 17, 1787, thirty-nine delegates signed the Constitution.

FIGHTS OVER RATIFICATION

Three delegates to the Philadelphia convention immediately brought the new Constitution to the Confederation Congress. Ten days after the convention had ended, Congress sent the Constitution to the states.

Since the people of Rhode Island were opposed to a stronger union, the state refused to call a ratifying convention. In the other states the legislatures held elections for delegates to the ratifying conventions. These elections were contests for or against the Constitution, for the delegates were chosen on the basis of their attitudes toward the new document.

In the elections, the voters sometimes split into groups over local issues. Most of the time, though, they voted on the basis of economic, class, or sectional interests. Most merchants, plantation owners, lawyers, doctors, and people with property and education were nationalists. They called themselves Federalists and supported the new Constitution. Owners of small farms, frontiersmen, debtors, and the uneducated and the poor were generally Antifederalists. They opposed the new plan.

Federalists

Federalists had many advantages in the ratification battle. They had a positive program that they believed could overcome difficulties facing the nation. They had better organization and greater resources than did the Antifederalists. Most of the newspapers and many highly respected citizens favored the Federalist position on ratification.

Even the method of electing delegates to the state conventions favored the Federalists. Delegates were to be elected in the same way as representatives to the state legislatures. This meant that people from the coastal areas would be overrepresented. Property qualifications for voting also assured Federalists of heavy representation.

Despite these advantages, the Federalists knew that public opinion was not on their side. To overcome this, they began a campaign of persuasion in newspapers and pamphlets. The Federalists admitted that the Constitution had flaws, but they also argued that it was the best plan of government that the nation's finest minds could produce.

For ten months, Federalists pleaded for support of ratification. Alexander Hamilton, James Madison, and John Jay published a series of essays that examined the Constitution and explained the Federalist point of view. These essays were later published as a book called *The Federalist.*

The Federalist was not an objective view of the Constitution. The authors were careful to point out, however, that the Constitution was federal as well as national. They tried to show that the powers of the government would be shared between the states and the central government. They insisted that the central government had to be strong enough to insure survival as a nation. The Federalists argued for a government that would have independent powers to tax and to act directly on the people.

Antifederalists

Nearly all of the Antifederalists believed that the Constitution would give too much power to the central government. Critics said that the Constitution would cripple good government, destroy state sovereignty, and take away the rights of the people.

Antifederalists argued, for example, that

A parade in New York urges ratification of the Constitution by that state.

the "necessary and proper" clause (*Art. 1, sec. 8, para. 18*) would allow the central government to take away the powers of the states. They also insisted that the government's independent powers of taxation could drain the states of their sources of revenue.

Of all the Antifederalist arguments, the strongest was the statement that the proposed Constitution had no bill of rights. The writers of the Constitution had discussed including such a bill. They had decided it was unnecessary because all the state constitutions in some way guaranteed personal liberties to free citizens. The Antifederalists pointed out, however, that the central government would have sovereignty of its own and would operate directly on the people. Without a bill of rights to restrain it, that government might some day take away basic human freedoms.

The Antifederalists also wrote in defense of their ideas. The *Letters of a Federal Farmer,* published in October 1787, was one of the most influential Antifederalist works. Its author, Richard Henry Lee, presented most of the standard Antifederalist arguments. They reflected the common fear of the Antifederalists that the new government would be controlled by the rich—the upper classes. Lee's essays were moderate in tone and won a wide audience.

The Antifederalists had strong arguments, great concern about democracy, and, probably, majority sentiment on their side. However, they were not as effective as the Federalists in swaying public opinion. At a time when the nation needed a positive program, their stand was defensive and negative.

Ratification

Several states acted promptly. Delaware, Pennsylvania, and New Jersey ratified the

Constitution in December 1787, Georgia and Connecticut in January 1788, and Maryland in April 1788. South Carolina became the second large state to approve, in May 1788.

Elsewhere, Federalists and Antifederalists fought closer battles. In Massachusetts, after a hard struggle, the Federalists won. In February 1788, that state voted for ratification. On June 21, 1788, New Hampshire became the ninth state to ratify, making official the adoption of the Constitution. Nonetheless, the nation's fate was still in doubt. Four states, where about 40 percent of all Americans lived, still had not ratified it. Without two of those states, Virginia and New York, it seemed unlikely that the new Union could succeed.

Virginia at the time had the largest population and the greatest influence in the Union. The Antifederalists fought and lost their best battle in Virginia. On June 25, 1788, that state became the tenth to ratify.

On the Fourth of July, many people celebrated the ratification with parades and bonfires. In Providence, Rhode Island, however, mobs of farmers attacked the merrymakers; in New York, rioting broke out between Federalists and Antifederalists.

New York was a key state. The Antifederalists had a large majority in the ratifying convention. Yet New York City threatened to secede if the state did not ratify the Constitution. Finally, on July 26, New York's convention approved the Constitution by a narrow margin.

The Constitution had needed the backing of these major states before it could really go into effect. North Carolina and Rhode Island continued to be Antifederalist strongholds. North Carolina did not give approval until November 1789, nor Rhode Island until May 1790.

A New Government

Now that the Constitution had been ratified, people turned their attention to the election of members of the new Congress. As critics of the Constitution had foreseen, the first Congress included few Antifederalists. When the first Congress assembled, almost a month late, many friends of the Constitution were among its members.

The presidency, too, was entrusted to a friend of the Constitution. In accordance with the Constitution, the electors voted for two persons. The one with the largest vote, if a majority, was to be President. The one with the next largest vote was to be Vice-President. As expected, George Washington was a unanimous choice. John Adams of Massachusetts came in second.

At noon on April 30, 1789, Washington rode alone in a four-horse carriage to Federal Hall in New York City. There, on a balcony, the state's highest judge administered the oath of office. Afterwards he cried, "Long live George Washington, President of the United States!" The crowd below shouted the same words, and the cannon roared.

A Look at Specifics

1. How did the Virginia Statute of Religious Liberty change church-state relations?

2. In the Northwest Ordinance, what provision did Congress make for acquiring land from Indian tribes?

3. What economic conditions in New England led to Shays's Rebellion?

4. What important powers did Congress lack under the Articles of Confederation? Why was it unable to enforce its laws?

5. Which groups tended to be Federalists? Antifederalists?

6. What were some of the major arguments for ratification of the Constitution presented in *The Federalist?*

7. What arguments did the Antifederalists use in opposing ratification?

8. What sectional conflicts were reflected in the drafting of the Constitution?

9. How did the procedure for ratifying the Constitution differ from that required to amend the Articles of Confederation?

A Review of Major Ideas

1. What were some of the achievements of the United States under the Articles?

2. Discuss the ways in which the Revolution brought about social changes in the United States.

3. In what ways did the backgrounds and attitudes of the convention delegates contribute to the Constitution's development?

4. In what ways was the central government under the Constitution stronger than that under the Articles of Confederation?

For Independent Study

1. "The government under the Articles of Confederation was the only kind of authority that Americans would have accepted at the time." Oppose or defend this statement.

2. How did the Constitution emerge as a balance between state and national sovereignty? Is this balance a problem today?

3. The United States has become a great power under a written constitution. Britain has attained greatness with a body of laws and traditions that is often called an "unwritten constitution." What are the advantages of a written constitution over an unwritten one? The disadvantages?

4. "As in any other revolution, the radicals who successfully won independence for the United States were replaced within a few years by a conservative, strong-arm government led by the military." Oppose or defend this statement.

The Federalist Era

CHAPTER 4
1789–1801

Time and distance—these were probably the greatest assets the new United States had. The nation had time for its people and leaders to learn how to govern. The country also was far enough away from Europe so that it did not become a battleground in Europe's many wars.

The nation had other assets, of course, but most of its resources were untapped or undeveloped. In 1789, when George Washington became President, there were fewer than 4 million people in the thirteen states. Most people ate regularly and well, but they were far from being rich. With a new government in control, Americans hoped the nation would enter a period of stability and prosperity.

WASHINGTON'S ADMINISTRATION

President Washington and the members of the first Congress knew that their actions would set precedents for the future. Therefore, they were careful as they applied the basic ideas of the Constitution to existing situations. Gradually, the outlines of the new government began to fill in.

The Machinery of Government

The first Congress soon found that the Constitution did not clearly provide for executive departments. It referred to them vaguely but said nothing about how many or what kinds they should be. Assuming that it had freedom to act, Congress quickly created three executive departments—state, treasury, and war. It also set up the offices of the attorney general and the postmaster general. The persons heading these departments and the major executive offices soon came to be regarded as the President's *cabinet,* or group of chief advisers.

The judicial system, too, required action by Congress before it could work. The Constitution said:

Pennington Mills in Baltimore, Maryland, 1804.

The judicial power of the United States, shall be vested in one supreme Court, and in such inferior Courts as the Congress may from time to time ordain and establish.

In September, Congress passed the Judiciary Act of 1789. It created a supreme court of six members, three circuit courts, and thirteen district courts. This law also outlined which kinds of cases were to be heard in each kind of court. It gave the state courts original jurisdiction in cases involving the Constitution, the laws, and the treaties of the United States. This meant that the state courts were at the base of the federal judicial system. In effect, this act distributed the nation's judicial power between the central government and the states.

The Constitution did not say that a case could be appealed from a state court to a federal court. Federalists in Congress assumed that this right was implied in the Constitution. In the Judiciary Act, therefore, they established the principle of judicial review of state legislation.

The Bill of Rights

During the struggle over ratification, the Federalists had realized that the greatest weakness in the Constitution was the lack of a bill of rights. The delegates had not been opposed to such a bill. They had thought it unnecessary because the national government would have only the powers listed. In several states, however, including Virginia and New York, the outcome of the fight for ratification had hinged on including a bill of rights. Federalists won some people to their side by promising amendments to the Constitution that would clearly protect the personal liberties of free citizens.

In the state ratifying conventions, dozens of amendments were proposed to protect individual rights. Under the leadership of James Madison, Congress went through the proposals and reduced them to twelve

Prisons carried on some businesses. Newgate *(opposite)* had a copper mine. Unfair trial and unjust imprisonment were guarded against through four amendments in the Bill of Rights.

amendments. In September 1789, they were submitted to the states. Three-fourths of the states ratified ten of the amendments but rejected two of them. In December 1791, the ten amendments became part of the Constitution.

Since the Bill of Rights (as these amendments came to be called) limited the central government and not the states, it added strength to the federal features of the Constitution. The first eight amendments listed individual rights, such as freedom of religion, speech, and press, and the right to trial by jury. The Ninth Amendment stated that the listing of rights in the Constitution was not complete or exclusive. The Tenth Amendment said:

The powers not delegated to the United States by the Constitution, nor prohibited by it to the States, are reserved to the States respectively, or to the people.

The lingering distrust between the nationalists and the supporters of states' rights could be seen in the debate over the Tenth Amendment. Some supporters of states' rights wanted to place the word *expressly* before the word *delegated.* They felt that this would more clearly shift the emphasis of the Constitution away from nationalism. Their effort failed, but the Tenth Amendment still marked a retreat from the strong nationalism of the Philadelphia convention.

STRENGTHENING THE GOVERNMENT

Washington at first tried to organize a nonpartisan administration. But party politics soon developed. Washington appointed Federalists to most of the government posts, and

A Prospective View of Old Newgate, Connecticut's State Prison.

The subterranean Vault, over which this place is built was wrought about the middle of the 17th Century for the purpose of obtaining Copper Ore. the opening into those Gloomy Caverns is a Desent of 35 feet, from thence Desending in various Serpentine Directions 75 Yards, opens to the Well is in depth 74 feet from the Surface to the Water.

1. The Commandant's apartment 2. the Guard Room 3. the work shop 4. the store for Nails 5. the Bake house 6. the Cole house 7. the Smiths shop 8. the Well 9. the gate for Entrance 10. the Pickets & inclosure of the Prison 11. the path leading from the work shop to the Caverns

The Connecticut Historical Society

these people formed the core of the first national political party.

Alexander Hamilton

Many of the basic ideas of Washington's government came from Alexander Hamilton, the secretary of the treasury. Hamilton was young, brilliant, and thirsty for power. He had definite views on politics, economics, and foreign affairs, and he also had plans for putting his ideas into practice.

Hamilton, though born poor in the British West Indies, had developed aristocratic tastes and ideas. Through his marriage to Elizabeth

Schuyler, a member of a wealthy New York family, he had finally joined the aristocracy of wealth that he had long admired.

Hamilton believed that the common people were ignorant and incapable of governing. He admired the British aristocracy, based on a hereditary nobility. He insisted that the British system of government was the best in the world. He wanted to entrust political power to men of intelligence, education, and wealth. Men of property, he reasoned, would have a selfish interest in the government. Since their property would need government protection, they would support and defend the Constitution.

Hamilton's Program

With Washington's support, Hamilton developed a program designed to gain the respect of foreign nations for the new government. Hamilton's program was designed to strengthen the nation's economy, political system, and foreign policy.

In January 1790, Hamilton presented his plan to the House of Representatives. He pointed out that the United States would have to be fair to its creditors if it were to be able to borrow in the future. Its credit would depend on how faithfully it paid its existing debts. He recommended that the national debt be *funded* at face value. This meant that the government should take in its various certificates of indebtedness and replace them with government bonds bearing one dependable rate of interest. The money for this funding would come from import duties and excise taxes—taxes on goods produced within the country.

Hamilton also recommended that the government *assume,* or take over the payment of, the debts that the states had acquired during the Revolutionary War. Hamilton hoped to strengthen the national government by making the state governments financially dependent upon it. Also, he wanted holders of either state or national bonds to become strong supporters of the national government.

Establishing Credit

Most members of Congress liked the idea of funding the public debt to improve the nation's credit. They felt that the foreign debt should be paid in full. But many objected to replacing domestic loan certificates, many of them worthless, with new bonds promising to pay the same amount in sound new dollars.

Hamilton and his friends argued that the foreign and domestic debts could not be divided. They insisted that national honor required payment of the entire public debt at face value. When the debate subsided, Congress passed the funding bill that Hamilton had proposed.

Unfortunately, some speculators knew beforehand of the plans to fund the debt. They were able to buy outstanding certificates at low prices from people who thought they had become worthless. The speculators made huge profits.

Hamilton's proposal to assume the states' debts met stiffer opposition. States with large or unpaid debts liked the idea of having the national government take over their payment. States that had repaid most of their debts opposed the plan. They did not want to pay federal taxes to help states that had not taken care of their own debts.

Virginia, which had repaid most of its debt, led the opposition. The struggle increased the distrust between northern and southern states. To avoid a sectional split, Hamilton asked Thomas Jefferson, the secretary of state, to persuade fellow Virginians to accept a political deal. In exchange for votes from the South in favor of assumption, Hamilton offered northern votes in Congress for locating the national capital on the Potomac River. The Virginians were eager to have the capital in the South, and so Jefferson agreed to the deal. Hamilton's assumption bill passed in July 1790.

A National Bank

Another feature of Hamilton's program was the Bank of the United States, modeled after the Bank of England. Private individuals would own four-fifths of its stock and the national government would own one-fifth. The bank would operate under a charter from the central government and would be given all of the government's banking business. The bank would be able to issue banknotes that would circulate as paper money.

At the time, there were few banks in the nation, and most of them were unstable. Hamilton argued that a national bank was needed to provide banknotes that had a set value. He said that the bank would give the government a safe place to deposit federal funds, increase government income by paying for its charter, and stabilize the price of government bonds by purchasing them at proper times.

Hamilton had three basic reasons for wanting the bank. First, the bank would benefit the merchants and bankers who would control it, and it would be another tie between the wealthy class and the national government. Second, by allowing the government to engage in the banking business, Congress would broaden the power of the central government. Third, this enlarging of national powers would weaken the power of the states.

Nothing in the Constitution specifically authorized Congress to create a bank. The only basis could be found in the "elastic" clause (*Art. 1, sec. 8*), which allowed Congress to enact such laws as were "necessary and proper" for carrying out the powers of government. When the bank bill reached Congress, James Madison and others fought against it on the grounds that it was unconstitutional and that it would benefit only the wealthy. Nonetheless, Congress passed the bill, and it went to the President.

Washington, too, wondered if the bank bill violated the Constitution. He asked his department heads for their opinions. Hamilton, of course, argued for the bank. He pointed out that the government had power to coin money and collect taxes. A bank, he said, was "necessary and proper" to execute these powers. Jefferson opposed the bank. Washington accepted Hamilton's advice and, in February 1791, signed the bank bill. The Bank of the United States began operating under a charter that ran for twenty years.

Taxation

The new government's main source of money was the sale of public lands. To pay for funding and assumption, the national government needed still more money. Hamilton favored two kinds of taxes to raise more money: a tariff on imports and an excise tax on distilled liquors, such as whiskey.

Through the tariff, Hamilton also hoped to encourage American industry. The tariff would raise the price of foreign manufactured goods. Hamilton believed that if these prices went high enough, Americans would buy goods made in the United States rather than imports.

In the summer of 1789, Hamilton's supporters managed to get a tariff through Congress, but its rates were lower than those requested by Hamilton. Nonetheless, it produced some of the revenue the government required.

In December 1791, Hamilton explained his ideas for the encouragement and protection of industry. In his Report on Manufactures, he pointed out that America's new industries suffered from shortages in experienced labor and in capital. Without the government's help, they could not be expected to compete with the established industries of Europe.

"Christening the Baby" (left) and "Inside of the Old Lutheran Church" (right) hint at the importance of religion in the lives of most Americans in the late eighteenth and early nineteenth centuries. The practice of *christening*, or baptizing, a child within the first year of its life is still an important religious tradition in many Christian churches. In the late eighteenth century a number of new sects developed, among them the Methodist and Baptist churches. In some of these churches, adult baptism was practiced and dunking, or total immersion in the baptismal waters, was required. These new branches of the Christian faith were most popular with the working class. In the South, many slaves became members of Baptist or Methodist churches.

Hamilton urged Congress to set up protective tariffs and establish bounties for new industries. He asked Congress to give bonuses for improvements in goods, reward inventors, and allow needed raw materials to enter the country duty free. Congress would not accept all of Hamilton's proposals, but in May 1792 it passed a tariff act that included some of his recommendations.

Testing the Government

In March 1791, Congress had passed the tax on distilled liquors. Hamilton had intended this tax to have a political as well as an economic impact. He wanted to use it to assert the direct power of the national government over individuals. Such power had previously belonged only to the states.

Almost from the day the tax was passed, it aroused opposition. The farmers in the back country of Pennsylvania, Virginia, and North Carolina had difficulty moving their crops to market, and so they commonly made part of their crops into whiskey. They then transported this whiskey over mountain trails to country towns, where they sold it or bartered it for supplies. To many farmers, Monongahela rye whiskey was as good as money. The excise tax went as high as 25 percent of the price, and it hit the western distillers hardest.

In 1794, farmers in four counties of western Pennsylvania refused to pay the tax. Their attack on the tax collectors started the Whiskey Rebellion. Hamilton viewed this uprising as a chance to test the power and strength of the national government.

Under the Constitution, Congress had the power to use the militia "to execute the laws of the union" and to "suppress insurrections." Congress therefore authorized the President to call out state militia to end the uprising. In this first test of federal law, no one knew if the states would remain loyal to the Union and respond to the President's request.

Four states, including Pennsylvania, provided troops. An army of some 13,000 men, headed by Hamilton and accompanied part of the way by the President, marched on Pennsylvania's western counties. At the approach of this force, opposition vanished. The troops captured a few rebel leaders, whom Washington later pardoned.

The government had triumphed against its first rebels, and the farmers now paid the tax. As Hamilton had foreseen, few now doubted the power of the federal government to make the people obey its laws. But Hamilton and the Federalists paid a price for this victory. Many Americans, particularly westerners, condemned the use of such great force to stop a few farmers. These critics turned to political action to oppose the government and Hamilton's policies.

Jeffersonians Versus Hamiltonians

Several years before the outbreak of the Whiskey Rebellion, people inside and outside the government began grouping into two national parties. Those who followed the leadership of Hamilton and Washington became known as Federalists. Their opponents, led by Thomas Jefferson and James Madison, were called Republicans.

Hamilton and Jefferson differed over how the United States should develop. Their ideas were reflected in their parties.

While Hamilton dreamed of a United States that was an industrial giant, Jefferson hoped the country would remain a nation of small farmers. The Hamiltonians thought the government should encourage business and industry by granting special privileges. The Jeffersonians were opposed to this idea.

Many of the Hamiltonians were merchants, bankers, and manufacturers from the New England states and the coastal areas, and wealthy farmers and southern plantation owners. Jeffersonians were mostly craft workers, frontier settlers, or owners of small farms in the South and West.

Jefferson favored a more democratic form of government than the British system that Hamilton admired. He thought that most men were capable of self-government, and he wanted to lower the voting qualifications so that more men could vote.

As members of the Republican party, the Jeffersonians pushed for a strict interpretation of the Constitution, with most of the power residing in the states and little given to the central government. They opposed Hamilton's efforts to broaden the powers of the national government. The Republicans also were more concerned with civil liberties, such as freedom of speech and the press. The Hamiltonians, as Federalists, sponsored laws to restrict these freedoms.

Although Federalists and Republicans differed over many issues, they divided with greatest bitterness over foreign policy. Federalists believed that the nation would be best served if the government tied itself closely to Britain. Republicans generally favored a policy of close political and economic cooperation with France.

The French Revolution, which had started in 1789, strengthened party feelings in the United States. At first, most Americans were in sympathy with the revolt in France, and many even praised it. Then, in April 1793, the revolutionaries beheaded King Louis XVI and declared war on Britain, the Netherlands, and Spain. Republicans rejoiced because France had become a republic and was fighting Britain, America's old enemy. They celebrated French victories and wore the tricolored cockade, a hat symbolic of the French republic. The Federalists were horrified by the violence in the French Revolution. They defended Britain and denounced France.

FEDERALIST DIPLOMACY

As secretary of state, it was Thomas Jefferson's job to plan the government's foreign policy. Hamilton feared that Jefferson and James Madison would drive the country to war against Britain. Determined to prevent this, the secretary of the treasury interfered with the conduct of foreign affairs. He tried to get Washington to follow his, not Jefferson's, ideas in dealing with France and Britain. At times he negotiated privately with the British.

As a result, Jefferson decided, in 1792, to resign. He said he could not stand Hamilton's tampering with foreign affairs. Hamilton also spoke about leaving. Washington asked both of them to stay so that the government could remain unified. Both Jefferson and Hamilton agreed to stay in the President's cabinet.

As the end of his term approached in 1792, Washington made plans to retire. Fearing that party differences might break up the Union unless Washington served a second term as President, both Hamilton and Jefferson begged him to reconsider. Jefferson told Washington, "North & South will hang together, if they have you to hang on."

Others also pleaded with Washington, and no one would run against him. He easily won reelection. Although Republicans made a party contest out of the balloting for Vice-President, John Adams also was reelected.

A Policy of Neutrality

In his second term, Washington devoted much of his time to foreign relations. One of his first decisions in the new term concerned American policy in the war between France and Britain. He turned to his cabinet members for advice. All the advisers agreed that the President should adopt a policy of neutrality. Washington made this the official policy in a proclamation that he issued on April 22, 1793. It said that the United States was at peace with both France and Britain, and it warned Americans not to act hostilely toward either country.

The overthrow of the French monarchy raised other policy questions. Washington asked his advisers if the American treaties with France were still in effect and if he should receive a minister from the French republic. Again Hamilton and Jefferson differed. Hamilton wanted to suspend the treaties and refuse to recognize the republican government of France. He wanted to use the French Revolution as an excuse to end the alliance with France.

Jefferson argued that the treaties were still legally binding and that the President should recognize the French republic. This time Washington followed Jefferson's advice.

The new French minister was a rash young man known as "Citizen" Edmond C. Genêt (the French revolutionaries used "citizen" in place of "mister"). As soon as he arrived in the United States, Genêt meddled in American politics. He appealed directly to the people, rather than to the heads of the government. He insulted Washington and enraged the Federalists. He did not ask for military aid under the terms of the French alliance, but he did demand assistance that would have violated American neutrality. His disregard for American neutrality became intolerable, and Washington demanded that the French government recall him. Genêt's misconduct also forced the government to clarify its neutrality policy. The Neutrality Act of 1794, which prohibited foreign warships from being fitted out in United States ports, was the result.

Jay's Treaty

Meanwhile, the United States was brought to the verge of war with Britain. During the European war, France had opened ports in its Caribbean colonies to American shipping. These ports had previously been closed to foreigners. France opened them because it needed supplies. The British were destroying most French shipping, and only neutral ships could get through.

The profits were good, and Americans quickly built up a flourishing trade in these ports. Since this trade helped France, the British decided to stop it. Beginning in June 1793, Britain issued three executive orders which said that Britain would not allow in time of war a trade that was prohibited during peace. In enforcing this policy, British naval officers seized United States ships and cargoes and imprisoned the seamen.

Newspapers in the United States played up these captures. Anti-British feelings became so strong that it was difficult to follow Washington's policy of neutrality. The difficulty increased when word reached the capital of British actions in the Northwest.

The troubles stemmed from Washington's efforts to conquer the Indians in that region. American military expeditions in 1790 and 1791 failed, in part because British officials had provided the Indians with supplies. The British also had promised the tribes that they could recover lands settled by Americans at

The couple *(center)* are doing a religious dance, probably of Yoruba (West African) origin. Slaves had little leisure.

the time of the Revolutionary War. This promise enraged Americans.

Americans had other grievances. British troops still held the northwest posts on American soil and the British government still refused to make a commercial treaty. Together these grievances brought on a crisis between the United States and Britain.

Many Americans started preparing for war, much to the alarm of Hamilton and other Federalists. To head off a war, in April 1794 Hamiltonians persuaded the President to send John Jay, the chief justice of the United States, on a special mission to London. Jay was able to get a commercial treaty, which he signed in November 1794. When details of the treaty reached the United States, Republicans called it a sellout to Britain. The treaty granted few of the things that Jay had been told to get from Britain, such as payment for the Caribbean captures and generous trade privileges.

Republicans tried and failed to defeat Jay's Treaty in the Senate. In the House of Representatives, they attempted to withhold the funds necessary to carry out the provisions of the treaty.

Although the treaty had shortcomings, it kept the peace at a time when war with Britain might have split the Union. Because of it, the British finally left the northwest posts. In addition, the willingness of Britain to make a treaty with its former colonies was at least a small victory for American diplomacy.

Though few Americans realized it at the time, Jay's Treaty had a great influence on the defeat of the Indian tribes in the Ohio country. During the treaty negotiations, Britain told its troops in the northwest posts to prepare to evacuate. When the Miami, Shawnee, Chippewa, Potawatomi, and Ottawa fought American troops in the Battle of Fallen Timbers (August 1794), their British allies gave them no help. The American soldiers burned the cornfields, killed the fruit trees, and destroyed the villages. The following June the defeated tribes signed the Treaty of Greenville. In it they gave up their rights to most of Ohio, part of Indiana, and scattered sites, including those that became Detroit, Vincennes, and Chicago.

Agreement with Spain

While Jay was negotiating in London, Spain broke with Britain and became an ally of France. Because Jay's mission seemed to draw the United States closer to Britain, Spain feared an attack by Anglo-American forces on its North American colonies. Spain also thought that American pioneers might invade Louisiana and Florida. Its ministers decided to purchase American good will.

In 1794, Spain asked the United States to negotiate its grievances. Washington sent Thomas Pinckney, the minister in London, to Madrid. In October 1795, he and the Spaniards signed the Treaty of San Lorenzo (Pinckney's Treaty). So pleased were American leaders with the agreement that the Senate approved it unanimously.

The treaty gave the United States unrestricted navigation of the Mississippi River and the right to deposit goods in warehouses at New Orleans for reloading on ocean-going vessels. It also set the boundary of West Florida at the 31st parallel. Spain promised that it would not promote Indian attacks against Americans, and the United States promised to keep Indians in its territory from striking at Spanish lands.

The new national government had made important diplomatic gains. It had done so, in part, because Spain and Britain were preoccupied with their policies in Europe. The Jay and Pinckney treaties freed American soil from the British and the Spanish for the first time since independence.

France's Interference

When the French learned of Jay's Treaty, they became angry. They considered it pro-British and anti-French. They said it violated the French-American treaties of 1778. Therefore, the French interfered in American politics to try and prevent Jay's Treaty from going into effect.

The French made a distinction between the American people and their Federalist government. They portrayed Washington's administration as a slave to British policy while most Americans favored French friendship. The French ministers to the United States publicly supported Republicans in elections, put pressure on senators to defeat the treaty, and tried to get the American people to oppose that agreement.

This interference in American politics enraged Washington. It made him determined to support the British treaty. The tensions over foreign policy also prompted Washington to announce his decision to retire. For some time, he had been tired and disappointed with abusive politics. However, the French meddling convinced Washington that his nation needed a warning. He decided to give it in the form of a farewell statement, which he issued through the newspapers in September 1796.

Washington's Farewell Address came to be one of the most influential statements on foreign policy ever made by an American. The President began by announcing that he would not be a candidate for a third term. He warned against "foreign influence," stressed faithfulness to existing agreements, and said " 'tis our true policy to steer clear of permanent alliances with any portion of the foreign world." He defended his own policies and denounced French meddling.

Federalists praised the Farewell Address; Republicans called it political propaganda; and the French disliked it. The French minister threw his weight into the presidential campaign on the side of Thomas Jefferson, the Republican candidate. He said that only a victory by Jefferson would end the possibility of war with France.

The French minister's interference did Jefferson more harm than good. John Adams won the nation's first contested presidential election, in 1796. Though Jefferson gained the vice-presidency, Federalists retained control of the government. It seemed likely that there would be no basic change in American policies.

AVOIDING AN ALL-OUT WAR

In the period between Adams's election and his inauguration, tension with France increased. The French government recalled its minister and refused to receive America's new minister to France.

Two days before Adams was to take office, the French government published a decree that amounted to a declaration of limited war against United States commerce. France justified the action by saying that Jay's Treaty had violated the French alliance.

The "XYZ" Affair

As soon as Adams became President, he called Congress into session to deal with the crisis. At his request, Congress approved a special mission to France. The commissioners were Charles C. Pinckney, the minister to France; John Marshall, a Virginia Federalist; and Elbridge Gerry, a Massachusetts Republican. They were to offer shipping and trade concessions similar to those in Jay's Treaty. In return, Adams wanted France to resume diplomatic relations, respect American rights at sea, and release the United States from the treaties of 1778.

Pinckney, Marshall, and Gerry met in Paris in October 1797, but Charles Maurice de Talleyrand-Périgord, the French minister of foreign relations, refused to officially receive them. Through secret agents, he demanded a bribe of $250,000 merely for negotiating. Since the commissioners had no money to pay a bribe, they rejected Talleyrand's proposals.

After months of waiting, the commissioners finally ended their mission. Their dispatches telling of their treatment reached Philadelphia before they did. The story convinced Adams that he could not deal with the French government except through force. In March 1798 he explained the mission's failure and asked Congress for authority to arm merchant ships and take other defensive measures.

Refusing to believe the President's story the Republicans accused Adams of seeking war. They demanded to see the commissioners' dispatches. Adams substituted the letters *X, Y,* and *Z* for the names of Talleyrand's agents and sent the dispatches to Congress. A short time later the dispatches were published. Now even some Republicans turned against France, and Federalists talked openly of war.

An Undeclared Naval War

The "XYZ" dispatches made Adams temporarily popular. Congress responded to his requests by authorizing naval action against French sea raiders. It also created the navy department, voted money for new warships,

The People of the United States, 1790

The population grew rapidly in the years before the 1790 census. It is estimated that the British colonies gained 1 million people between 1760 and 1775, primarily because of a high birth rate and the influx of immigrants.

The colonists were encouraged to marry and to marry early. Since considerable labor was needed to make a farm productive, a big family was considered a necessity. Families of ten or twelve children were common, and those of twenty or twenty-five were not unusual. The country had a high death rate among infants and young children, however. Even in well-settled areas, as many as one-third of the children died before the age of five.

Life was hard for adults as well as for children. Many marriages ended early with the death of one partner. Second marriages were often entered into shortly after the funeral, for marriage was in many ways an economic necessity. Third and fourth marriages were not uncommon.

During the Revolutionary War, population growth slowed. This was partly due to fatalities of war (approximately 100,000), the departure of many Loyalists, and a lower birth rate. Some of these losses were offset by continued immigration and by British and German troops who decided to stay after the war.

As peace was restored, the population began to grow rapidly again. Most Americans favored unlimited immigration, and political leaders encouraged it. Also, the slave trade increased.

By 1790, the United States was still a nation with a young population. For example, the median age of white males was 16.

At the time of the first census in 1790, western New York and Pennsylvania were considered the most promising areas in which to settle. Both had fertile, reasonably priced land to offer, and both were less crowded than many of the New England and southern states. A large number of Americans were moving west in 1790. By that year, the non-Indian population of the territory of Tennessee, for example, had grown to approximately 70,000.

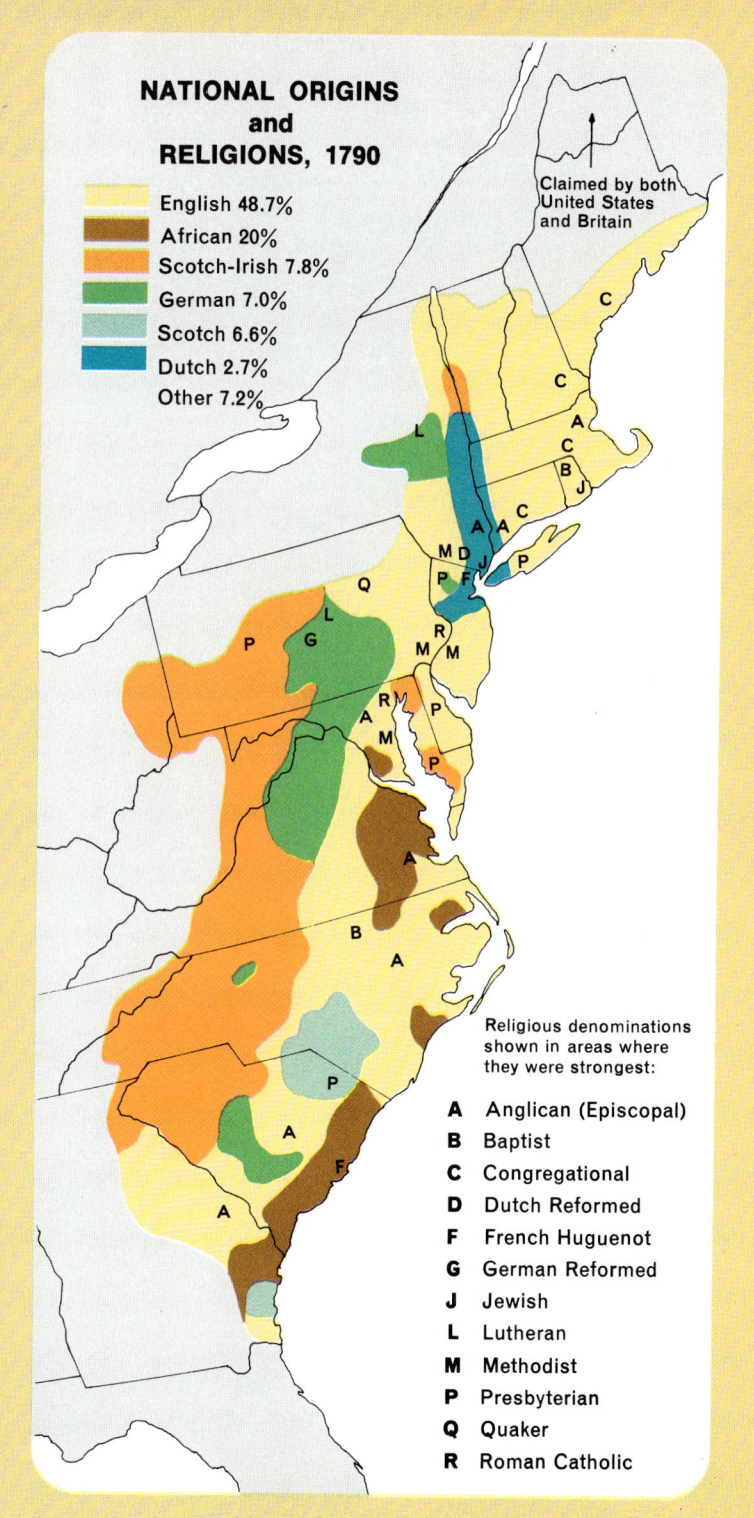

NATIONAL ORIGINS and RELIGIONS, 1790

- English 48.7%
- African 20%
- Scotch-Irish 7.8%
- German 7.0%
- Scotch 6.6%
- Dutch 2.7%
- Other 7.2%

Religious denominations shown in areas where they were strongest:

- **A** Anglican (Episcopal)
- **B** Baptist
- **C** Congregational
- **D** Dutch Reformed
- **F** French Huguenot
- **G** German Reformed
- **J** Jewish
- **L** Lutheran
- **M** Methodist
- **P** Presbyterian
- **Q** Quaker
- **R** Roman Catholic

and authorized increases in the army. Washington came out of retirement to command a new army that was to be organized by Alexander Hamilton.

Since Republicans in Congress were not in favor of a declaration of war against France, Adams placed the nation in a state of half war. Neither country declared war, and neither authorized attacks or the capture of private property by warships. The United States Navy fought primarily to protect commerce. It attacked only French warships and *privateers,* privately owned vessels that were armed to raid commerce.

The new United States Navy performed well. By the winter of 1798, it had stopped the attacks in American coastal waters and forced the French back to their bases in the West Indies. At some risk, the navy then based most of its ships in the Caribbean, where several battles were later fought.

Unpopular Laws

The undeclared war disturbed many Federalists. The extremists among them wanted a full-scale war against France as an excuse to expand the nation's frontiers and to draw the United States closer to Britain. (Hamilton wanted to invade Louisiana and Mexico, which belonged to Spain, France's ally.) They thought that a war would provide the opportunity to crush the Republican party and other political opposition.

The Federalists tried to destroy their opponents with four laws, known as the Alien and Sedition Acts. President Adams signed the first of these laws, the Naturalization Act, in June 1798. This law raised the residence requirement for citizenship from five years to fourteen years and limited the freedom of action of aliens. Since most immigrants had become Republicans, this law struck at one source of the opposition's strength.

The Alien Friends Act gave the President

The United States frigate *Constellation* captures the French frigate *L'Insurgente* (Feb. 9, 1799) in an important battle in the undeclared naval war. The Americans fought mainly to protect their commerce.

the power to deport aliens whom he considered dangerous. This was aimed at alleged French agents in the United States. A third law, the Alien Enemies Act, would apply only in case of invasion or declared war. It permitted the President to arrest or deport aliens from enemy countries in order to preserve public safety.

Topping off their repressive program, the Federalists passed the Sedition Act. It provided for fines and imprisonment for conspiracies against the government and for scandalous statements about the Congress or the President. This law struck at native Americans as well as at foreigners.

Although the work of extreme Federalists, the Alien and Sedition Acts won broad support in the party. Not one prominent Federalist opposed their enactment. Adams did not deport any foreigners under the alien laws, but his administration did enforce the Sedition Act.

The Republican leaders saw in the Alien and Sedition Acts a trend toward unjust rule, which they felt they had to resist and expose. Late in 1798, Jefferson expressed his opposition in a set of resolutions adopted by Kentucky's state legislature. Madison wrote a set of similar resolutions, which the Virginia legislature approved.

These Kentucky and Virginia resolutions declared the Alien and Sedition Acts void and unconstitutional because the federal government had exercised powers not specifically delegated to it. The resolutions said that a state could judge for itself when the national government exceeded its constitutional power. When the central government went too far, the states could rightfully *nullify,* or declare illegal, all offending laws. The resolutions called on all the states to take similar action against the laws, but none did so. As a strong expression of the states' rights view of the Union, these resolutions were important long after the Federalist era.

Peace with France

Most Americans did not want war. Republicans were opposed to it, and extreme Federalists were unable to gain majority support for war even within their own party.

Yet the naval battles and the news of widespread anti-French feeling in the United States alarmed Talleyrand. War would offer no direct benefits to France and would ruin the plans of French officials to get Louisiana back. Therefore, Talleyrand made peaceful overtures to the United States. The French government repealed decrees against United States shipping, restrained its privateers in the West Indies, and told some Americans that it wanted peace.

President Adams had broken with the extreme Federalists as a result of a quarrel with Hamilton. Consequently, he had lost much of his enthusiasm for war. He accepted Talleyrand's offer to negotiate a peace with honor, and in 1799 he sent a second mission to Paris. This action deepened the split in the Federalist party, for the extremists had insisted that the French overtures were meaningless and had urged their rejection.

The commissioners—three reliable Federalists—met in Paris in March 1800. After long negotiations with a French commission, the Americans agreed to the Treaty of Mortefontaine. It was signed in September 1800. Despite strong resistance by extreme Federalists, the Senate finally approved the treaty after Adams left office.

The treaty ended the undeclared war, freed the United States from its first entangling alliance, cleared the way for Napoleon Bonaparte to regain Louisiana, and helped weaken the influence of the Federalist party. Adams always defended his decision for peace and his missions to France. "They were," he later wrote, "the most disinterested and meritorious actions of my life."

THE ELECTION OF 1800

By the end of John Adams's term, the Federalist party had ceased to be an effective national organization. The party split into two groups, with one wing following Adams and the other following Hamilton.

The difficulties within the party had begun almost as soon as Adams became President. In his inaugural address, Adams had pledged to continue Washington's policies. He had also kept Washington's cabinet, which proved to be a mistake. Most of the cabinet officers were Hamilton's friends, and they secretly went to Hamilton for advice on almost all matters of policy.

When Adams discovered that Hamilton was controlling the cabinet officers, he reacted against the extreme wing of the party. Extreme Federalists predicted that the party would be so deeply divided by Adams's action that the Republicans would win the coming election.

Hamilton Versus Adams

Despite the party split, John Adams was the Federalist choice for President in 1800. Jefferson was the Republican candidate, as he had been four years earlier.

Hamilton decided to work secretly against Adams. In the New York elections, Hamilton tried to fill the state legislature with men who were personally loyal to him. Since the legislature would choose New York's presidential electors, Hamilton could in this way influence the presidential election. But the Republicans defeated Hamilton's Federalist candidates.

The defeat in New York had several important political consequences. It assured Jefferson of the state's twelve electoral votes, made Aaron Burr of New York the Republican choice for the vice-presidency, and prompted Adams to rid his cabinet of "Hamilton's spies."

Strife within the Federalist party became bitter. Hamilton decided to attack the President directly. In autumn 1800, he wrote a long letter, intended for private circulation among Federalists, in which he tried to show that Adams was unfit for the presidency. A copy fell into Burr's hands, and he had it published as a pamphlet.

Most Federalists were shocked. Friends of Adams rushed out pamphlets of their own attacking Hamilton. These attacks merely made the situation worse. Federalist chances for victory now seemed lost.

A Federalist Defeat

While the Federalists fought among themselves, Jefferson hailed the strife as "wonderful." The Republicans never let up in their attacks on Adams. They denounced him as an aristocrat who favored monarchy. They attacked unpopular administration measures, such as the Alien and Sedition Acts, and stressed the peace issue. They claimed that they had forced Adams to send his second mission to Paris, and that they, not he, had "saved the country from war."

Federalists charged that Jefferson would disrupt the Union through his nullification doctrine, as stated in the Kentucky and Virginia resolutions. They said that he would force French ideas on Americans. They also claimed that a vote for a deist like Jefferson would be a vote against God.

Despite the split in their ranks, Federalists fought hard to regain the ground lost in the New York elections, and they did reasonably well. Nevertheless, the Republicans won the presidency and gained majorities in both houses of Congress. Federalist leadership in

PRESIDENTIAL ELECTIONS: 1796-1812

In the charts illustrating presidential elections, the winning candidate is always listed first. Because political parties were not well developed prior to 1796, the elections of 1789 and 1792 are not included. The party listed here as Republican was founded by Jefferson and Madison. It later was known as the Democratic-Republican and, after 1828, as the Democratic party. The present Republican party was not founded until 1856.

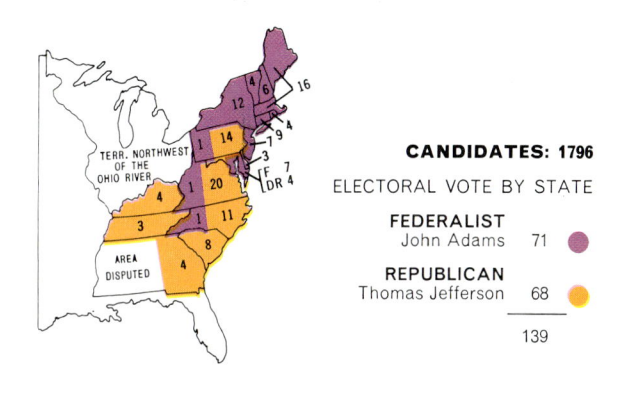

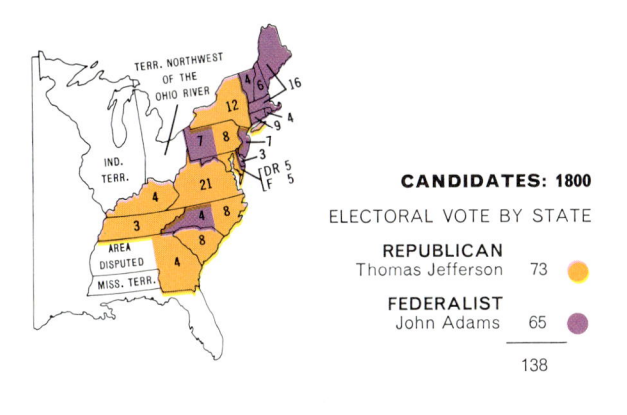

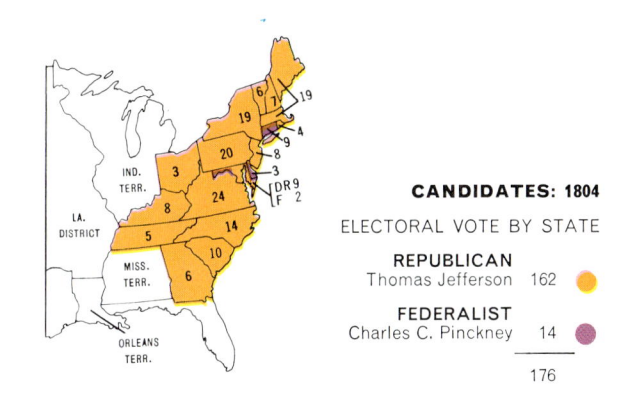

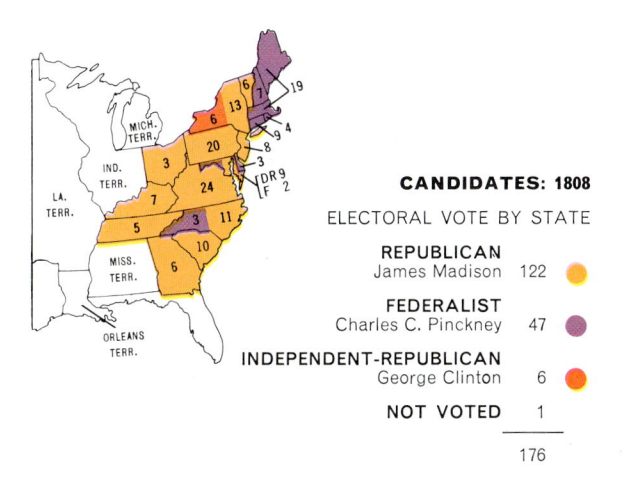

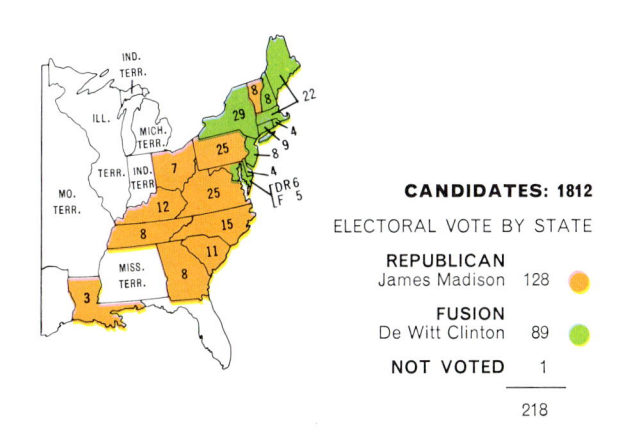

CANDIDATES: 1796

ELECTORAL VOTE BY STATE

FEDERALIST
John Adams 71

REPUBLICAN
Thomas Jefferson 68

139

CANDIDATES: 1800

ELECTORAL VOTE BY STATE

REPUBLICAN
Thomas Jefferson 73

FEDERALIST
John Adams 65

138

CANDIDATES: 1804

ELECTORAL VOTE BY STATE

REPUBLICAN
Thomas Jefferson 162

FEDERALIST
Charles C. Pinckney 14

176

CANDIDATES: 1808

ELECTORAL VOTE BY STATE

REPUBLICAN
James Madison 122

FEDERALIST
Charles C. Pinckney 47

INDEPENDENT-REPUBLICAN
George Clinton 6

NOT VOTED 1

176

CANDIDATES: 1812

ELECTORAL VOTE BY STATE

REPUBLICAN
James Madison 128

FUSION
De Witt Clinton 89

NOT VOTED 1

218

national affairs had been overthrown.

Adams had come close to victory. In states other than New York, he ran stronger in 1800 than he had run four years earlier. The switch of a few hundred votes in New York City would have given him the election.

Decision in the House

Accustomed to power, the Federalists were bewildered by their loss. Many were convinced that a revolution similar to the one in France would follow and destroy the nation. One thing consoled them. Jefferson and his running mate, Burr, had received the same number of electoral votes.

At that time each of the electors simply voted for two persons. The one who received the highest number of votes became President, and the one with the second highest total became Vice-President. According to the Constitution, in the case of a tie the election would be decided by the House of Representatives. Each state would have one vote, and the balloting by states would decide who would be President.

The decision on the election of 1800 was to be made by the existing Congress, where the Federalists held control, not in the newly elected House where the Republicans would have a majority. Everyone knew that the Republicans had intended Jefferson to have the presidency. Nonetheless, some of the Federalist leaders talked about making Aaron Burr President. Hamilton, who considered Burr "the most unfit and dangerous man" in politics, opposed this plan.

In February 1801, when the balloting in the House took place, the Federalists almost succeeded in giving the presidency to Burr. Finally, after thirty-six ballots, Jefferson was chosen President. The Twelfth Amendment, which was adopted in 1804, made impossible another such vote for the presidency. It required separate ballots for the President and the Vice-President.

TECHNOLOGICAL CHANGE

During Washington's and Adams's administrations, there were a number of developments in technology that would in time greatly change the nation. Most of these were already having an effect on American life by the time Adams left office.

The Factory System

The factory system developed earliest in England, in cloth manufacturing. There, spinning and weaving machines were brought together in mills or factories. English methods of manufacturing cloth were jealously guarded secrets. The British passed laws forbidding the export of machinery and the emigration of skilled cloth workers.

A number of Americans attempted to build spinning mills but were unsuccessful. State legislatures offered bounties to anyone who could set up such a factory. The first spinning mill in the United States was finally set up in 1791, at Pawtucket, Rhode Island, with the help of Samuel Slater, a mechanic from England. Lured by the bounties, he had memorized the plans of English textile machinery and had disguised himself as a farmer in order to emigrate to the United States.

The use of machinery powered by water brought workers together in fairly large factories. Previously, most workers had labored alone or with a few others at home or in small shops. Many continued to do so.

Shoemakers, for example, still made shoes by hand. In shoemaking centers like Lynn, Massachusetts, the work became highly specialized. Each person concentrated on cutting out a particular piece or making a particular stitch. Generally, these people did their work at home. A merchant provided them with material, collected the processed pieces, and paid for the labor. The merchant then arranged for finishing and selling the shoes.

These ready-made shoes did not have graded sizes or differences between lefts and rights. They were used primarily by sailors and by slaves. Most people still made their own shoes or had them made to order.

The arrangement by which a merchant put out materials and collected the work from homes or shops is known as the "putting-out" system. It was also used in the manufacture of cloth. The merchant provided cotton or wool for spinners and thread or yarn for weavers. This system continued, in some instances, to the middle of the nineteenth century.

Most families, especially on the farms, still produced the larger proportion of the goods they needed for their own use—from soap to shoes, from candles to cloth. However, the putting-out system and household manufactures were giving way to the factory system and factory-made products.

Mass Production

A one-time Massachusetts farm boy, Eli Whitney, invented a system of mass production using standardized and interchangeable parts. In 1798, the government needed thousands of muskets, and it needed them in a hurry, for it expected an all-out war with France. In those days, skilled gunsmiths made weapons one at a time, each a little different from any other. There were not enough gunsmiths in the entire world to produce the needed muskets quickly enough.

Whitney had a plan for making identical guns and producing them with great speed. He designed a separate machine to turn out each part. The parts produced by one machine would be identical and would fit together interchangeably with other parts made by machine. Whitney contracted with the government to deliver 10,000 finished guns in two years. Though he was late in filling his contract, he proved the value of his new technique. Afterward, other manufacturers would use the same system for producing such things as clocks, farm implements, and sewing machines.

A Cotton Gin

In the United States, cotton was first grown along the coast and on the offshore islands of Georgia and South Carolina. This was a very fine quality cotton. Its long fibers could be easily separated from the smooth black seeds. But "sea-island" cotton required a constantly warm and moist atmosphere and could not be grown successfully more than a few miles from the coast.

There was also "upland" cotton, which had shorter fibers. It would thrive in almost any place where the growing season was long enough and the autumn rainfall was not too heavy. But fuzzy green seeds stuck to the fibers, making them hard to clean.

By 1793, cotton planters were looking for a "gin" (short for "engine") to clean upland cotton. The legislature of Georgia even offered a prize for a satisfactory one. Eli Whitney was serving as a tutor on the Georgia plantation of Catharine Greene. Whitney and, according to some historians, Mrs. Greene soon devised a practical machine. It

The toll gate on the Baltimore-Reisterstown Road is now Pennsylvania Avenue and Fulton Avenue in Baltimore.

consisted of a bin with slats on one side, a roller with wire teeth, and a revolving brush. As the roller turned, the teeth pulled the fibers between the slats, leaving the seeds behind. The brush, revolving in the opposite direction, swept the fibers off the teeth. Using water power, a gin could clean a thousand pounds of green-seed cotton a day. Someone doing the work by hand could clean only a pound or two a day. The cotton gin was to have a profound influence on the nation's development, for it made slavery profitable.

Improved Transportation

Although transportation was neither good nor rapid, it was better than it had been in colonial times. Water transportation was the easiest form to develop. Travelers or traders moved inland most easily on navigable streams.

Before 1800, a number of canals had been built in England. Some Americans hoped to follow the English example. Though distances were greater and the terrain was rougher in the United States, by the early 1800's a number of short canals were in use. Most of them were owned and built by private companies.

So were "turnpikes." These were toll roads that got their name from a common type of tollgate—a horizontal pole, or pike, which turned on a post at one end to open or close. Most of these roads were surfaced with crushed rock and laid out as straight and level as possible, crossing streams by means of wooden or stone bridges. The first turnpike, begun in 1792, connected Philadelphia and Lancaster, sixty miles away. Other companies went into the business, and soon toll roads radiated from each of the eastern cities to surrounding towns.

Turnpikes made traveling easier and faster. Other roads were little more than two tracks, often deeply rutted and dusty when not muddy. They skirted around tree stumps and went right through shallow streams.

A Look at Specifics

1. What did the Judiciary Act of 1789 accomplish? What principle did it establish?

2. In what respects was the Tenth Amendment to the Constitution a concession to supporters of states' rights?

3. Why did Hamilton want to entrust political power to men of property?

4. What ideas did Hamilton promote in his Report on Manufactures?

5. Why did the whiskey tax arouse strong opposition from frontier farmers?

6. What effect did Jay's Treaty have on the Indians in the Ohio country?

7. Why was Spain willing to negotiate a treaty with the United States in 1794?

8. What advice did Washington give to the nation in his Farewell Address?

9. How did Congress respond to the publication of the "XYZ" dispatches?

10. What economic, social, and sectional differences tended to distinguish Federalists from Republicans?

11. Why did the extreme Federalists want an all-out war with France?

12. What were the provisions of the Virginia and Kentucky resolutions?

A Review of Major Ideas

1. How did the work of the first Congress help shape the Constitution?

2. What led to the formation of political parties during Washington's administration?

3. How did Hamilton's legislative program improve the nation's economy and strengthen the national government? Why did many people criticize his program?

4. Explain how the Federalist and Republican parties differed in economic policy, constitutional interpretation, political philosophy, and foreign policy.

5. Describe the diplomatic accomplishments of Washington's administration.

6. What political developments brought about the end of the Federalist era?

7. What contributions to the nation were made by the Federalists?

For Independent Study

1. The historian Carl N. Degler has said that "almost all of the Hamiltonian program was enacted in the early 1790's and, from the vantage point of retrospect, this was most fortunate; for of the two contending economic programs, the Federalists' was the more far-sighted. The laissez-faire... [society] of Jefferson would have been neither a strong nor a prosperous nation for long." Do you agree with this statement? Give reasons for your answer.

2. Is the advice given in Washington's Farewell Address as applicable today as it was in 1796? Why?

3. In general, Hamilton's broad interpretation of the Constitution has gained greater acceptance than has Jefferson's strict interpretation. What reasons can you suggest to explain this development?

4. Could the need for maintaining a strong national defense ever justify the passage of such laws as the Alien and Sedition Acts? Has the Congress passed laws similar to them in later periods of the nation's history?

5. Was the invention of the cotton gin essential to the continuation of slavery in the South? Explain.

The Jeffersonians

CHAPTER 5
1801–1816

"Mad Tom in a Rage," a Federalist view of Jefferson.

Revolution, revolution, revolution. Most politicians running for President insist that their administrations will bring about revolution in government. Once in power, however, a President finds it is not easy to make radical changes in the government.

Thomas Jefferson believed that his election marked the beginning of a revolution in American politics. In time this view became the legend that Jefferson had overthrown the aristocratic Federalist system and replaced it with his own democratic system. Later generations would look upon him as the father of American democracy and a founder of the Democratic party.

A landed, slaveholding aristocrat, Jefferson can hardly be considered a democratic man of the people. Since his narrow victory in 1800 did not lead to great changes, it cannot be considered a real revolution. Yet there is no doubt that the Jeffersonians did bring to the national capital some innovative ideas about how the American federal system should operate.

JEFFERSONIANS IN CONTROL

When the Jeffersonians took office, they found the machinery of government in good working order. The nation was at peace, and the people were prosperous. Both political parties, despite their differences, were committed to supporting the Constitution. The new President had time to think and to plan before he took any action.

Jeffersonian Ideas

Both parties favored a republican form of government, one in which the people ruled through their elected representatives. Unlike the Federalists, the Republicans disliked aristocracy. Their beliefs were more democratic. Though they did not think that *everyone* should be allowed to vote, they did want all male property owners to have this privilege.

The Republicans thought the ideal society would be composed of small farmers and shopkeepers. They generally opposed the development of great cities like those in Europe, which they thought were corrupt.

The Jeffersonians opposed government aid to business and disliked bigness in government. They wanted to limit the power of government and keep the number of government jobs at a minimum. They were convinced that power tended to corrupt those who used it.

In his inaugural address, Jefferson tried to heal some of the wounds of the campaign. He appealed to the people for unity, saying "every difference of opinion is not a difference of principle.... We are all Republicans, we are all Federalists." He also said that his would be a "wise and frugal government" that would leave people "free to regulate their own pursuits of industry and improvement." He pledged "honest friendship with all nations, entangling alliances with none."

A Partisan Administration

Jefferson, unlike George Washington, considered himself a partisan President. With his inauguration, the government of the United States passed from the hands of one political party to those of a rival party. Jefferson acted quickly to appoint loyal Republicans to jobs with power.

James Madison, whose ideas were similar to his own, became secretary of state. The new secretary of the treasury was Albert Gallatin of Pennsylvania. Gallatin had defended the farmers who took part in the Whiskey Rebellion, and he had opposed Hamilton's program.

In other appointments, Jefferson moved slowly. He did not remove Federalists, but whenever there was an opening, he gave the job to a Republican. By the time he had completed eight years in office, all the government jobs were held by members of his party. Though the laws had not changed, people with a different philosophy of government were administering and interpreting the laws as they saw fit.

Changing the Hamiltonian Program

Although Jefferson and Madison were determined to rid the government of abuses by their predecessors, they accepted most of the Hamiltonian program. They built their own program on that framework.

The Republicans wished to relieve the people of internal taxation and reduce the public debt. The only way they could do this was by cutting public services and running the government more economically. A large number of government employees lost their jobs when Congress repealed all of the internal taxes. This action left the national government dependent on import duties and land sales for revenue.

Jefferson and his fellow Republicans believed that the public debt, wars, armies, and navies were sources of corruption. Albert Gallatin therefore tried to reduce the debt by cutting the budget of the armed forces. The administration trimmed the size of the army and navy and kept only a few warships in commission.

These reductions reflected Jefferson's fear that a large standing army would threaten civilian government. He did not consider the navy a threat, but he saw no reason why Republican farmers should pay taxes to protect a few Federalist shippers. He believed that trade and commerce should be kept subordinate to agriculture. Gallatin's economies were so successful that within eight years he had lowered the public debt from 83 million dollars to 57 million dollars.

The Louisiana Purchase

Shortly after Jefferson became President, he heard rumors that Spain had ceded Louisiana back to France. Louisiana extended from the Mississippi River to the Rocky Mountains and included the important seaport of New Orleans. France had given the region to Spain at the end of the French and Indian War.

The rumors troubled Jefferson because France was much stronger than Spain. If France regained New Orleans, he said, the United States must marry itself "to the British fleet and nation."

In October 1802, Spain turned Louisiana over to France. At the same time, the Spanish official in charge of New Orleans ordered the warehouses there to stop allowing Americans to deposit their goods. Without this right of deposit, Americans could not go on sending exports to world markets by way of the Mississippi River.

Jefferson saw that the situation could lead to a war against Spain or France, for the Federalists were demanding that the United States take New Orleans by force. He decided to try to purchase New Orleans and the Floridas, which at that time were thought to be part of the Louisiana cession.

In January 1803, he sent James Monroe to France. Monroe was told to work with the American minister, Robert R. Livingston, in attempting to buy the city of New Orleans and the Floridas. The men were authorized to offer as much as 10 million dollars for the land. In return, the United States would guarantee to France the free navigation of the Mississippi as well as the ownership of Louisiana west of the river. Monroe and Livingston were told that if the negotiations with France should fail, they were to seek an alliance with Britain.

Before Monroe arrived in Paris, Napoleon approached Livingston and offered to sell all of Louisiana. His reasons were complex but understandable.

Napoleon had lost 50,000 French troops in the fight to end a rebellion of former slaves in Haiti. This fighting had delayed the French occupation of Louisiana. In addition, Napoleon expected to go to war against England in the spring of 1803. He decided to give up his plan for an empire in North America. To keep Louisiana out of British hands and to realize some profit from it before Americans claimed it for their own, Napoleon offered to sell Louisiana for 25 million dollars.

Although Livingston and Monroe had no authority to spend that much, they realized they had stumbled onto a bargain. They decided to act on their own without delay. After haggling over the price, they signed a treaty for the purchase of Louisiana, dated April 30, 1803. The United States agreed to pay 15 million dollars, or about three cents an acre, for this vast land in the heart of North America.

The proposal raised another problem: Jefferson thought he lacked the legal power to buy Louisiana and to bring its people into the Union. He believed this could be done only through a constitutional amendment. His advisers insisted that he could accomplish all that was necessary through the President's power to make treaties. Jefferson saw the need for a quick decision and he finally accepted their advice.

The Federalists fought the treaty in the Senate, saying that France did not truly own the territory and therefore had no right to sell it. Nonetheless, in October 1803, the Senate approved the treaty. In December, France transferred the territory to the United States.

Explorers

The Indians, French, Spanish, and British had explored and settled in the Louisiana Territory, but few people in the United States knew much about the region. Jefferson wanted to learn more about the territory. He named two army officers, both familiar with

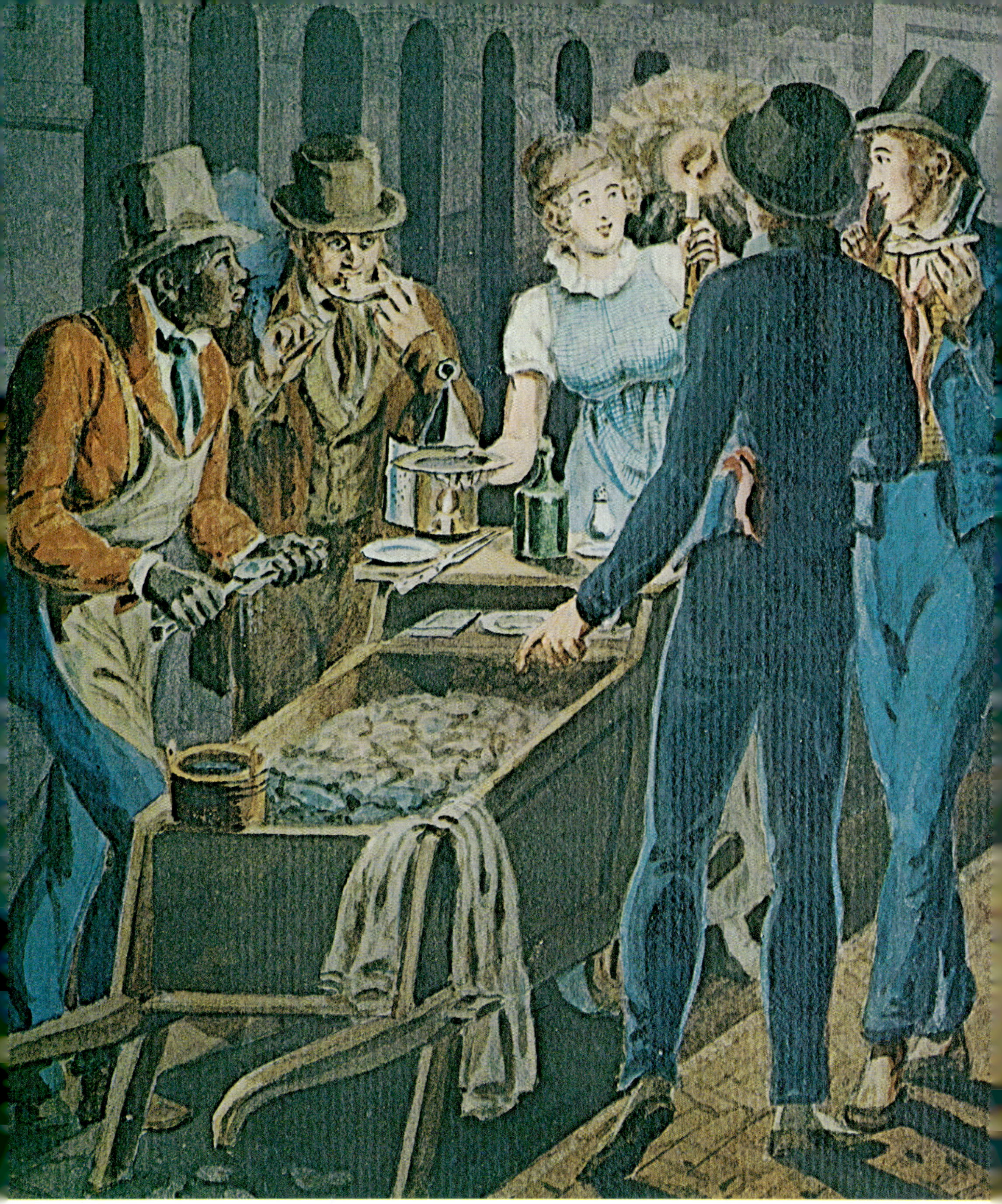

Westward Expansion, 1803–1807

Legend:
- United States, 1803
- Louisiana Purchase, 1803
- Spanish
- Claimed by Britain, Russia, Spain, and U.S.
- Route of Lewis and Clark, 1804–1806
- Route of Pike, 1805–1806
- Route of Pike, 1806–1807

PREPARED BY UNIVERSAL MAP, INC.

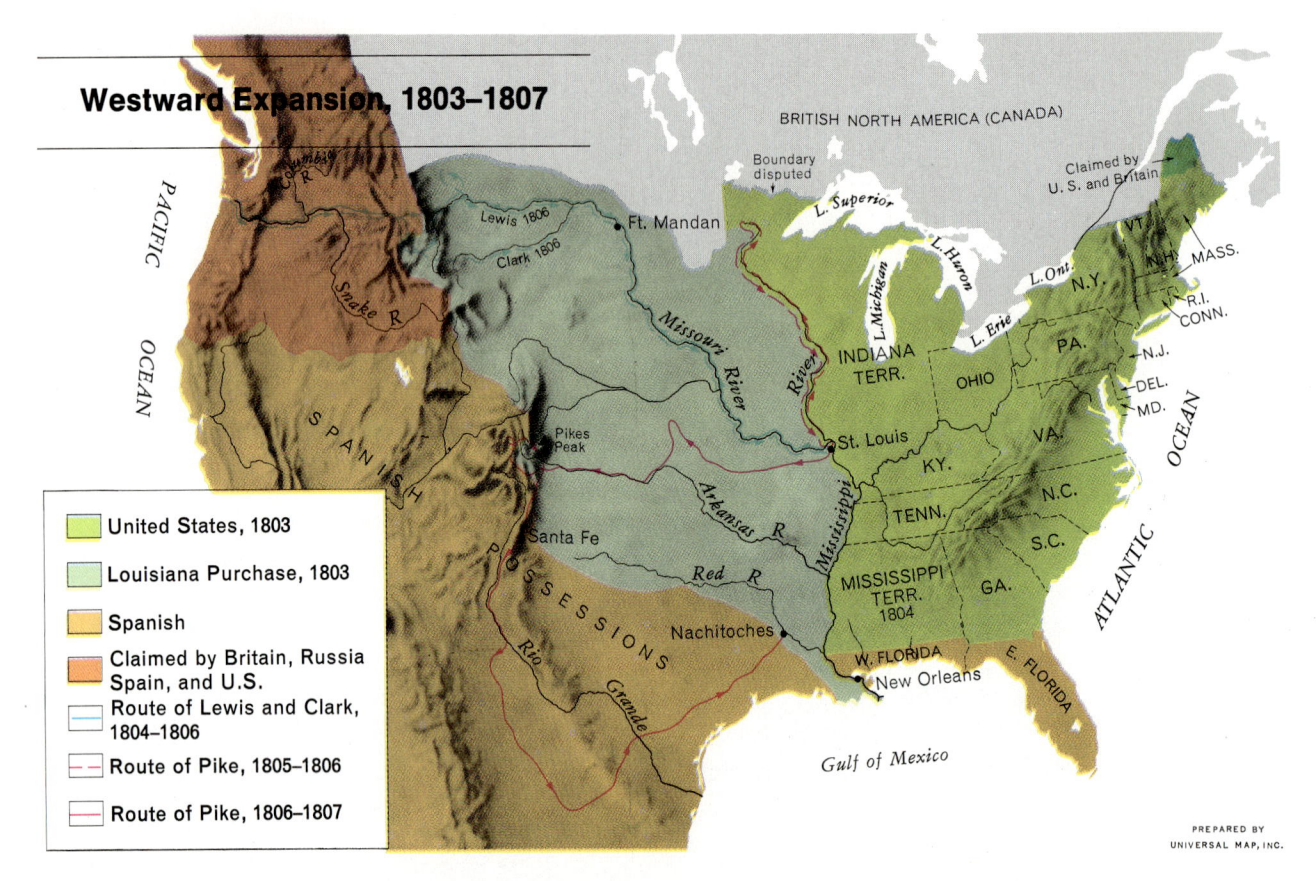

survival in the wilderness, to lead an exploration of the area. One was his private secretary, Captain Meriwether Lewis. The other was Lieutenant William Clark, a former Indian fighter.

Lewis and Clark carefully chose and trained the men for their expedition. They started up the Missouri River in May 1804. Part of the time they were led by Sacajawea, a Shoshone. She had been enslaved by the Mandans after a tribal war and wanted to return to her tribe. Cutting through the Rocky Mountains, the expedition moved westward along the Snake and Columbia rivers, into the Oregon country. Finally, in November 1805, the explorers sighted, as Clark described it, "this great Pacific Ocean which we have been so long anxious to see."

The expedition camped for the winter on the Pacific shore, hoping to be picked up by a passing boat. No boats came by, and the expedition returned overland, splitting in two for a time while the men explored different areas. They arrived in St. Louis in September 1806, where they found that everyone had given them up for dead. They had kept careful records of what they had seen and done. Their expedition strengthened the claim of the United States to the Oregon country and marked land and river routes for settlers who were to come later.

Another noted American explorer of the Louisiana Territory was Lieutenant Zebulon Montgomery Pike. In the fall of 1805, he led a group trying to find the true source of the Mississippi River. Although Pike did not find what he was looking for, he brought back useful information about the area explored.

In the summer of 1806, Pike led an expedition seeking the headwaters of the Arkansas and Red rivers. He explored what is now Colorado and New Mexico. In Colorado, Pike discovered the peak that now bears his name. On his return, Pike described the Great Plains as a desert, unsuitable for use as farmland.

The Northern Confederacy

Most Americans were pleased with the purchase of Louisiana. Some Federalists, however, feared that New England's influence would diminish. Extremists among them preferred to have New England leave the Union and form a separate northern confederacy rather than face a future of shrinking political power.

If such a confederacy were to succeed, it would have to include New York as well as the New England states. Alexander Hamilton, still powerful in New York, rejected the scheme. The plotters then turned to Vice-President Aaron Burr, whose future in the Republican party appeared bleak. In 1804, Burr agreed to run with Federalist support for governor of New York. Although Burr did not openly support the confederacy plan, many people assumed he was in favor of it.

Hamilton urged friends to vote against Burr, who he said could not be trusted in high office. Burr discovered that Hamilton was working against him. After he lost the election, he blamed Hamilton for the defeat and challenged him to a duel. Hamilton accepted and fell before Burr's bullet at Weehawken, New Jersey, on July 11, 1804. He died the next day. Vice-President Burr fled to Washington, where he finished out his term, but his political career was ruined.

With the Federalist loss in New York, the plot for a northern confederacy collapsed. The party's power had been greatly weakened. In the election of 1804, Jefferson carried every state but Connecticut and Delaware. His running mate was George Clinton, the former governor of New York.

A STRONG SUPREME COURT

During the early years of the United States, the courts had played a minor role in the national government. By the middle of Jefferson's first term, however, the Supreme Court began to become a strong check on the actions of the states and of other branches of government. The person most responsible for this change was John Marshall, the nation's fourth chief justice.

John Marshall

John Marshall was chief justice of the United States from 1801 to 1835. Like Jefferson, he was a Virginian; but like Hamilton, he was a staunch Federalist. He had been with George Washington's army at Valley Forge during the terrible winter of 1777/78, when the soldiers were suffering for want of supplies. That experience impressed on him the need for a strong national government.

Marshall was appointed chief justice in January 1801, in the closing weeks of the Adams administration. His appointment was one of the crowning achievements of John Adams's term as President. During his thirty-five years on the Supreme Court, Marshall delivered hundreds of opinions. In all of them he took a broad view of the Constitution. In general, the effect of his decisions was to limit the powers of the separate states and to enlarge the powers of the national government. He greatly irritated the Republicans, who favored a weak judiciary.

Overruling Congress

Marshall's first important decision was the case of *Marbury* v. *Madison* (1803). In it he established the Court's right of *judicial review*. He said that the Court had the power to review laws and decide whether or not they were constitutional.

The facts of the case were these: Shortly before the end of his presidential term, John

Adams signed a paper appointing William Marbury as a justice of the peace in the District of Columbia. When Jefferson became President, this document had not yet been delivered, and Marbury could not take office. Marbury asked Secretary of State James Madison to give him the commission, but the secretary of state refused. Marbury turned to the Supreme Court and requested a special kind of court order (a writ of mandamus) directing Madison to deliver the appointment paper to him.

Giving the Court's opinion, John Marshall said that Madison really ought to give the commission to Marbury. However, he went on to say that the Court could not issue the kind of order that Marbury had requested. True, Congress had provided for this in the Judiciary Act of 1789, but Congress had exceeded its powers. The Constitution specified the kinds of cases over which the Court should have jurisdiction (*Art. 3, sec. 2*), and this was not one of them. Therefore the clause of the Judiciary Act of 1789 regarding writs of mandamus was unconstitutional.

By rejecting a specific power that Congress had given, Marshall seemed to be reducing the authority of the Supreme Court. At the same time, however, he was asserting a general power that was far more important—the power to overrule Congress.

Not for more than half a century was the Supreme Court again to declare unconstitutional any part of an act of Congress. Meanwhile the Court upheld a number of acts of Congress, and it overruled a number of acts of state legislatures.

Reviewing a State Law

The Constitution restricts the states in various ways. Among other things, it forbids them to pass any law "impairing the obligation of contracts," (*Art. 1, sec. 10, para. 1*). The Supreme Court had to decide what this prohibition meant, and it gave a partial answer in the case of *Fletcher* v. *Peck* (1810).

The case grew out of certain land grants made by the legislature of Georgia. A later legislature, in 1796, repealed the law that authorized the grants. Some of the grantees, who thus had their land taken away from them, appealed to the Supreme Court. Their lawyers claimed that the grant of lands was essentially a contract between the state of Georgia and the grantees. They said the state had therefore violated the Constitution by impairing the obligation of the contract. The attorneys for the state of Georgia argued that some of the legislators had been bribed to pass the law granting the lands. They said that the later legislature therefore had a perfect right to undo what the previous one had done.

In the Court's decision, Marshall held that a land grant was indeed a contract. He said that even though there had been corruption, it was unconstitutional for Georgia to repeal the law making the grant. This was the first time the Court had struck down a state law on the grounds that it was inconsistent with the federal Constitution.

JEFFERSON'S SECOND TERM

Thomas Jefferson could look back on the results of his first term with satisfaction. The American people were contented, his party was stronger than it had been four years earlier, and the Louisiana Purchase was viewed as a great achievement. Jefferson told a friend, "Other nations view our course with respect and anxiety."

In Jefferson's second term, everything changed. Difficulties soon arose from the renewed war between Britain and France. In 1805, the British said they would not allow

Well-to-do women had the time and money to engage in activities like this painting class. Most American women, however, worked from sun to sun.

neutral ships, including those of the United States, to trade with Britain's enemies. British naval cruisers began capturing United States ships that were carrying goods to French or Spanish ports, especially those in the Caribbean.

In European waters, Britain blockaded territory under French control. Napoleon then threw a "paper" blockade—one that he could not really enforce—around the British Isles. Napoleon also tried to keep British goods out of Europe. Britain struck back with a series of orders prohibiting neutral trade with Europe. This was a serious blow to the United States.

Protests Over Impressment

As a result of its victories at sea, the British fleet was in control of the oceans. Most of America's trade went to British ports, and most of the nation's grievances went against Britain. The bitterest feelings were caused by *impressment*—naval recruiting by force. The British used "press" gangs to force men into their navy. Impressed sailors often deserted. Many of them entered service on United States merchant ships, where the pay was higher and the living conditions better.

British naval officers searched for deserters on neutral ships in ports and at sea. The British government claimed that sailors born in Britain were still British subjects even if they had become American citizens. "Once an Englishman, always an Englishman." So the British navy often took British-born—and sometimes even American-born—citizens of the United States. In 1806, Jefferson protested the impressment of Americans, but Britain would not retreat on the issue.

A clash at sea a short time later made Americans angrier than ever. In June 1807, the British ship *Leopard* hailed the United States ship *Chesapeake* off the coast of Vir-

The Watercolor Class, Courtesy of The Art Institute of Chicago

ginia. The Americans refused to allow the British to search for deserters. The British fired upon the *Chesapeake,* killing three United States sailors and wounding others. A search party boarded the *Chesapeake* and took off four alleged deserters. One proved to be a deserter, and the British hanged him. The other three were United States citizens.

The *Chesapeake* was a United States warship, not a privately owned merchant vessel. Americans considered the attack on it as an attack on their country. Many clamored for war. In negotiations later the British apologized and offered to make amends, but they refused to give up impressment.

An Embargo

Jefferson thought that economic pressure would force Britain and France to respect American rights. He wanted to stop all United States trade with Britain and France. Jefferson thought that if these nations could no longer get raw materials and foods from the United States, they would come to terms over neutral rights.

In December 1807, Congress passed Jefferson's Embargo Act. It prohibited United States ships from leaving for foreign ports. Later laws gave the national government broad power to enforce this law. The Embargo Act appeared to be impartial, but in practice it helped Napoleon. Since Britain had already destroyed France's overseas commerce, the embargo had the effect of denying American supplies only to Britain.

The embargo misfired. It caused greater hardship in the United States than in Britain. Seaports, especially those in New England, suffered from a financial depression. Moreover, Napoleon took advantage of the embargo. He said that since American-owned ships could not leave port legally, those in European harbors must be British ships in disguise. He seized the American merchant ships in Europe.

Both the Republicans and the Federalists denounced the embargo. Because of the strong public reaction, the Federalists saw a chance to win in the election of 1808. Their party spirit was revived, and they fought hard. Though they made some gains, James Madison, Jefferson's secretary of state, was elected President.

Just before Jefferson left office, Congress repealed the Embargo Act. At the same time, it passed the Nonintercourse Act. This law banned American ships from British and French ports and closed United States ports to ships from Britain and France. However, it allowed the President to open trade with whichever nation agreed to respect American rights.

MADISON IN COMMAND

James Madison was the third Virginian to be elected President. His two terms in office were dominated by the issues of neutral rights and impressment. At first, Madison continued Jefferson's policy of economic pressure. But as his first term drew to a close, the United States entered a second war with Britain.

Economic Pressure

Six weeks after taking office, Madison got the British minister in Washington to agree to a satisfactory settlement of United States grievances. Madison then lifted the Nonintercourse Act as it applied to Britain. However, the British foreign secretary repudiated the agreement, and Madison again put the policy of nonintercourse into effect against Britain.

Like the embargo, nonintercourse put an unbearable burden on United States commerce. In 1810 Congress replaced this policy with Macon's Bill No. 2. This law reopened United States trade to the world, but barred British and French warships from United

Plant and animal resources

The first colonists in the United States used whatever plants and animals they could find. Within a short time, however, they began importing familiar Old World species. Wheat, cows, and horses were brought from Europe; peanuts and other foods, from Africa.

John Bartram was named the royal botanist for the colonies by King George III. He explored widely, collecting seeds and plants for use by the colonists. His son William joined him on explorations into Florida and also became a well-known naturalist. William Bartram's book *Travels,* published in 1799, became a basic reference book on American botany.

Other Americans experimented with new varieties of plants and animals. At his home, Monticello, Thomas Jefferson grew Tuscany rice, having smuggled the seed out of Italy. Jefferson also introduced the Merino sheep and the Calcutta hog to American farming. By breeding these animals with similar animals, he tried to improve the quality of livestock in the United States.

The activities of the Bartrams and Jefferson were notable in part because they were so unusual. The typical treatment of plants and animals was much more destructive. Many early pioneers were fur trappers who ruthlessly pursued beavers for their pelts. The destruction of these small animals injured the total environment. Beaver dams created ponds that eventually filled with silt and became meadows. And before they silted up, beaver dams helped prevent floods.

Another animal that faced slaughter was the passenger pigeon, which numbered in the billions during the colonial period. It was eventually rendered extinct by hunters.

The importation of species from other countries inevitably included a few pests. Certainly the microorganisms that caused European diseases drastically affected the human population of the Americas. The Hessian fly threatened the growth of wheat until new strains of the grain were perfected about 1790. The pests that destroyed American chestnut and elm trees, however, were not imported until the late nineteenth and early twentieth centuries.

States waters. It permitted the President to apply nonintercourse to one belligerent if the other agreed to respect American rights.

Since Macon's Bill No. 2 favored Britain, Napoleon had to convince Madison that he was ready to respect United States rights. He succeeded, and in February 1811, Madison applied nonintercourse only against Britain. Many Americans expected war.

Fighting on the Frontier

Grievances against the British on the frontier contributed to the expectation of war. For more than ten years, the United States had been acquiring Indian land by making questionable treaties with individual tribes. Many tribes fought to save their land from the advancing pioneers. Before Jay's Treaty was signed, the British had supported this resistance. After the treaty, the British no longer supported the Indians. However, anti-British feelings had become strong in the United States. Many westerners believed rumors that the British in Canada were encouraging Indian attacks on frontier settlements.

Indian resistance actually stemmed from the land policies of the American government. In September 1809, William Henry Harrison, governor of the Indiana Territory, had made treaties at Fort Wayne with several tribes. These agreements opened millions of acres of rich farmland to pioneers and forced the Indians to move westward.

Most Indians disliked these treaties, by which they lost the use of their land. Two Shawnees—the chief Tecumseh and his brother Tenskwatawa, the Prophet—tried to unite all of the tribes against the advancing whites. (Free blacks were not allowed to settle in the Indiana Territory.) Tecumseh urged his people to surrender no more land to the whites. He told Harrison that the whites "have driven us from the sea to the lakes—we can go no farther."

Westerners believed that British plotting was behind Tecumseh's resistance and his plan of Indian confederation. On November 7, 1811, about a thousand of Harrison's troops defeated Tecumseh's forces in a battle at Tenskwatawa's village on Tippecanoe Creek. Harrison's soldiers found weapons in

Death of Tecumseh

the village that had been made in Britain. This discovery increased support for war against Britain.

The War Hawks

The leaders of the Twelfth Congress were young men who had replaced the leaders of the Revolutionary generation. They came from the West and South and were nationalists and belligerent patriots. Although they did not form a majority in Congress, or even among the Republicans, they controlled important committees. They considered impressment a national disgrace and demanded war against Britain. They became known as "war hawks."

The war hawks argued that the only way to end the Indian troubles on the Northwest frontier was to conquer Britain's possessions in Canada. Since the United States lacked a strong navy, an attack on Canada would also be the easiest way to strike at the British.

Southerners, too, wished to expand the nation and at the same time injure Britain. The southerners favored an invasion of Florida, which belonged to Britain's ally, Spain.

President Madison and his secretary of state, James Monroe, sided with the war hawks. However, Federalists and moderate Republicans resisted the war. New England Federalists thought that war against Britain would be a national tragedy. They considered Napoleon the nation's true foe.

When the British learned that Americans were seriously preparing for war, they relaxed their restrictions on United States commerce. This action came five days too late. On June 18, 1812, unaware of Britain's action, Madison had signed a declaration of war against Britain.

War

In his war message to Congress, Madison insisted that the United States must defend its neutral rights against Britain's violations. Impressment was at the top of the list of United States grievances. Madison did not give much attention to Indian troubles, and he said nothing about American hopes to gain Canada and the Floridas.

Despite Madison's emphasis on freedom of the seas, many representatives from states that had been injured by impressments and ship captures voted against war. While the people from the New England and Middle Atlantic states had suffered, they also had profited from overseas trade. War would destroy this source of income.

The Federalists were convinced that the French had violated United States rights as badly as the British. Many other Americans believed that the United States had as good cause for war against France as against Britain. A proposal for war against France lost by only four votes in the Senate.

Opposition to the War

The people of the United States were unprepared for war in 1812. Bitter party feelings and sectional jealousies divided them and weakened the war effort.

New England Federalists were most opposed to the war. They looked upon the war as the Republican party's fight rather than the nation's. They called it "Mr. Madison's War." Some New England Federalists discouraged enlistments, withheld money from the government, and supplied British troops with provisions. Some even swore their loyalty to King George.

In Congress, the Federalists refused to support taxes, loans, and other measures for the war program. They hinted that the Republicans had gone to war to help Napoleon.

The depth of public feeling about the war could be seen in the presidential election of 1812. Some politicians said that the only party division was between those who wanted peace and those who wanted war. In New York, antiwar Republicans nominated DeWitt Clinton, and Federalists supported him. Clinton carried every state north of the Potomac River except Vermont and Pennsylvania. Madison, with the solid support of the South and West, won reelection. But Federalist strength in Congress was doubled.

The greatest organized opposition to the government came from New England late in the war. In December 1814, a convention of New England states met secretly in Hartford, Connecticut, to discuss their grievances. Saying that the war violated states' rights, extreme Federalists wished to threaten secession. Moderate Federalists gained control, however, and the Hartford Convention merely denounced Madison's conduct of the war. It also proposed amendments to the Constitution to safeguard New England's position in the Union. Many Americans considered the convention treasonable and, as a result, the Federalist party suffered.

The Invasion of Canada

Madison and his advisers wanted an early peace. They knew that the nation was divided and unprepared. However, the war hawks wanted a swift victory in Canada before any peace was settled. They believed the conquest would be cheap, "a mere matter of marching."

Canada, with a population of less than a million, was weak. It was easy to attack from the United States and difficult for British sea power to defend. Moreover, Americans expected the French Canadians to aid them rather than the British.

Logically, the United States soldiers should have marched on Montreal in order to isolate the Great Lakes. Instead, in the summer of 1812, the United States sent its inadequate forces in three directions. One force struck by way of Detroit, another moved across the Niagara River, and the third pushed forward from Lake Champlain.

General William Hull marched from Detroit with two thousand soldiers, lost a skirmish, retreated, and, without firing a shot, surrendered the fort at Detroit to the British. The invasion across the Niagara River failed when citizen soldiers from New York refused to fight outside their own state. They watched from across the river while the British killed or captured United States regulars. The third group of invaders was to strike at Montreal from Plattsburgh on Lake Champlain. The troops marched north about twenty miles, but they, too, refused to leave the state. The commanding general then marched the troops back to Plattsburgh.

The Americans received no assistance from the French Canadians. Nowhere did they make the gains they had expected to make. Before the end of 1812, Americans tried and failed to retake Detroit. In 1813, Canadians hurled back two more invading armies.

Naval Successes

Americans fought well on water during the early part of the war. Until the spring of 1813, the United States Navy had only sixteen ships.

When the fighting began, the British could spare only a few warships for duty in United States waters. Most of its eight hundred ships were needed in the European war against Napoleon. This made it possible for the American frigates and sloops-of-war to win a number of individual duels with British warships. These battles had little effect on the outcome of the war.

In the spring of 1813, the British sent more ships to North America and tightened its

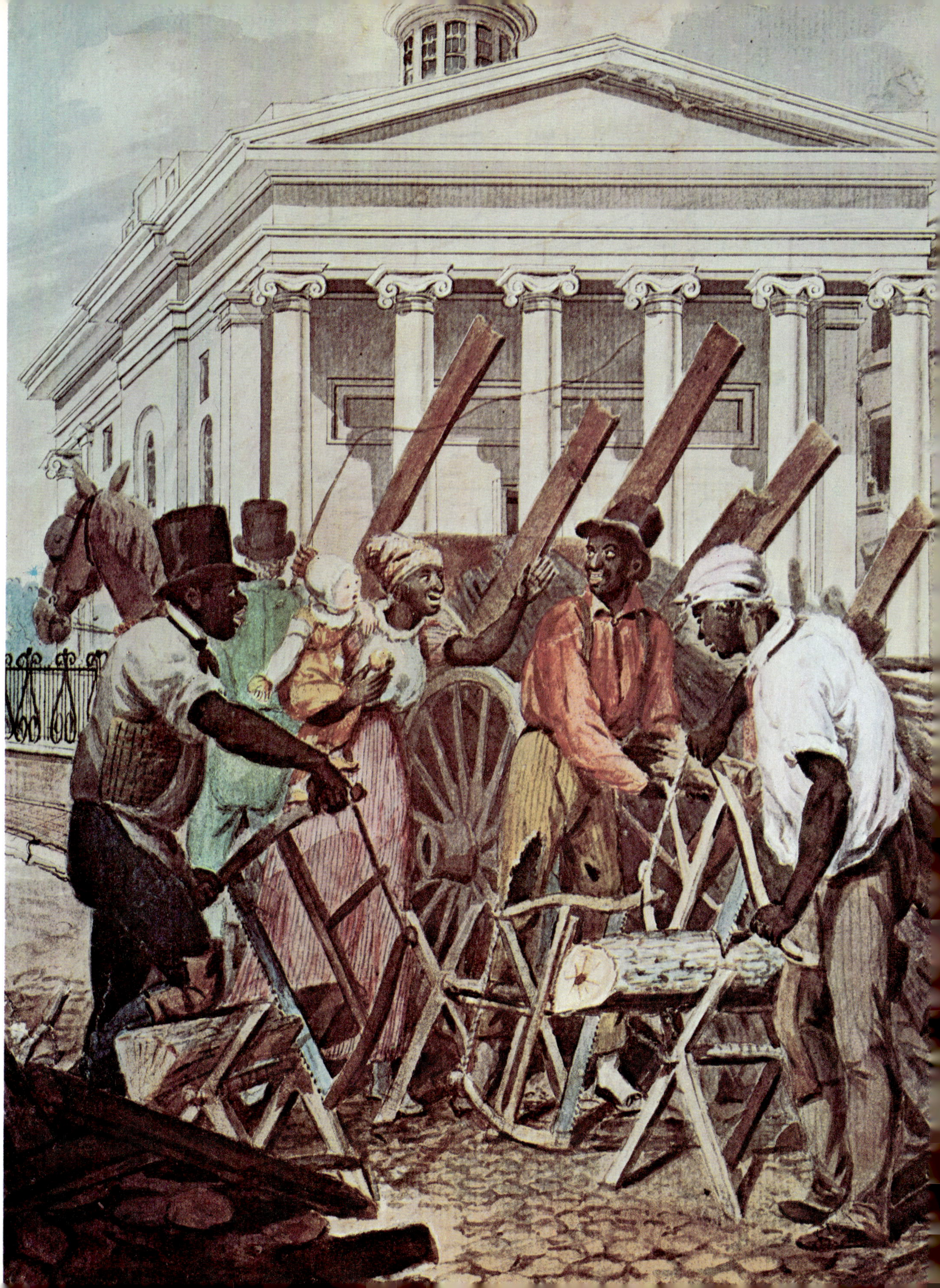

blockade of United States ports. By 1814, most American warships were unable to get out of port, and United States commerce was swept from the seas.

The most notable naval victory for the United States took place on Lake Erie in 1813. There, Captain Oliver Hazard Perry manned vessels with inexperienced sailors and Kentucky riflemen and went after the British. Perry's victory left Lake Erie under United States control.

The British forces abandoned Detroit. General William Henry Harrison pursued and overtook them on the Thames River in what is now Ontario. Here Harrison won the Battle of the Thames. It was here, too, that Tecumseh, who had become a general in the British army, was killed. His death led to the breakup of the Indian confederation and opened the way for further United States expansion in the Ohio Valley.

The British Invasion

The war took an especially bad turn for the United States in 1814. In Europe, Napoleon had been forced to abdicate and go into exile. Britain could now concentrate its full might against the United States. Britain tightened its blockade of the Atlantic coast and shipped thousands of veteran troops to its possessions in North America.

Up until this time, the British had simply defended their North American colonies against attacks by the United States. Now they planned to invade the United States. They were going to strike southward from Lake Champlain, raid Chesapeake Bay, and hit New Orleans.

The British sent ten thousand disciplined troops to gain control of Lake Champlain. A United States naval squadron met the British on the lake at Plattsburgh and forced them to retreat to Montreal. This battle saved New England and New York from invasion.

At the same time, an army of four thousand British soldiers landed near Chesapeake Bay and marched toward Washington. About seven thousand poorly trained United States militiamen made a stand at Bladensburg, Maryland. In the face of the British attack, the militia broke and ran. The British then marched into Washington, and President Madison and other officials fled to Virginia.

To retaliate for the burning of York (later known as Toronto) by United States troops in 1813, the British burned most of the government buildings in Washington. With the city of Washington partially in ruins, the British army headed for Baltimore.

Guarding the way to Baltimore was Fort McHenry. On September 13, 1814, the British ships stood offshore and bombarded the United States fort. Francis Scott Key, an American lawyer, was inspired by the fort's resistance to write the words to the "The Star-Spangled Banner." Set to the music of an old ballad, Key's song later became the national anthem.

After the unsuccessful assault on Baltimore, the British withdrew to Jamaica. Except for the burning of Washington, which enraged the people of the United States, the thrust accomplished nothing.

NEGOTIATING A PEACE

An unusual feature of the War of 1812 was that peace efforts were begun before the fighting had started. These early efforts failed because neither nation would change its position on the issue of impressment.

In November 1813, the British foreign secretary offered to start peace talks. Madison quickly accepted the offer. The President appointed five Americans to meet with a British commission in the Flemish town of Ghent, then occupied by British troops.

Since it took many weeks for letters and reports to cross the Atlantic Ocean, the United States commission was given wide

Leisure

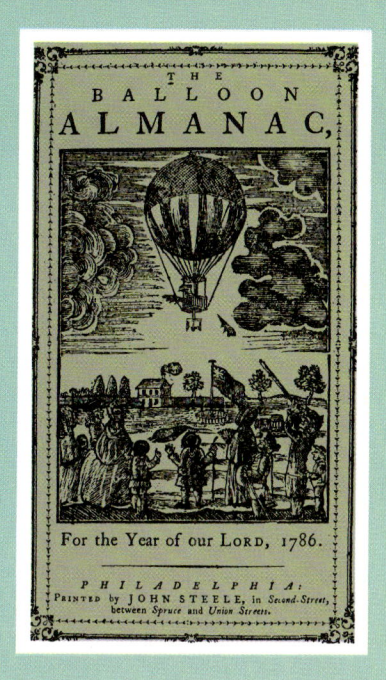

The theater and home entertainments were typical leisure activities of the wealthy. In the late nineteenth century, ballooning became the rage. For many Americans, however, the country fair was the only entertainment outside the home.

Franciscan missions were set up with *presidios*, or military garrisons, responsible for representing Spanish civil authority. Mission San Carlos Del Rio Carmelo was built on a typical plan. Living quarters and a church surrounded a central courtyard. Fields and pastures were in outlying areas, some relatively far from the mission.

powers. Fortunately, the American commissioners were exceptionally able. The three British commissioners, however, were neither distinguished nor powerful. Britain regarded the negotiations at Ghent as a sideshow. It sent its finest diplomats to the Congress of Vienna, where the European peace negotiations were being conducted. Peace talks in Ghent began on August 8, 1814.

A Satisfactory Peace

Secretary of State James Monroe had told the United States commissioners that if Britain would not abolish impressment, "the United States will have appealed to arms in vain." Britain refused to give up impressment; however, the issue had lost its fire. With the end of the war in Europe, the royal navy needed fewer sailors, and it stopped impressing them from United States ships. President Madison let the issue drop. The American representatives were told to seek a peace treaty that restored territory and diplomatic relations with Britain to their prewar standing.

At first, the British peacemakers made drastic demands. For instance, they insisted that the United States give up territory in the Northwest to form an independent Indian "buffer state." Rejecting the British demands, the Americans threatened to break off negotiations. Finally, the British government accepted the American outline as the basis for a peace settlement. On Christmas Eve, 1814, the commissioners signed the Treaty of Ghent.

The peace treaty provided for both sides to give up any territory gained in the war. It also called for fair treatment of the Indians who had fought on either side in the war and for the settlement of boundary conflicts by commissions composed of Americans and Englishmen.

Although the United States had not done well militarily, its diplomats gained a satisfactory peace. They were men with diplomatic skill, but their success was largely due to British disinterest. The British wished to be free to deal with European questions. They did not want to be bogged down in a continuing military campaign in North America in search of complete victory.

Mission San Carlos Del Rio Carmelo, by Oriana Day. Published by permission of the M. H. de Young Memorial Museum, San Francisco

Jackson's Victory

It would have been difficult for Britain to have a complete victory, as military developments in the South proved. General Andrew Jackson, with the aid of the Cherokees, campaigned against Britain's Indian allies. In the Battle of Horseshoe Bend in March 1814, his troops defeated the Creek Confederacy, the most powerful group of Indians in the South. Under the treaty that followed, the Creeks surrendered large tracts of land in the Mississippi Territory, more than half their lands. This rich land later became the heart of the cotton country.

Because of his victories against the Creeks, Jackson was given the responsibility for meeting the British thrust against New Orleans. He believed the British might strike at Florida and seek to use Pensacola as a base. On his own authority, he invaded Florida and captured Pensacola. Then he marched his troops to New Orleans.

At the same time the treaty was being signed at Ghent, the British were landing an army near New Orleans. On Christmas Day, Sir Edward Pakenham took command. He planned to attack New Orleans, capture it, and use it to gain favorable terms in negotiations. Neither he nor anyone in the United States knew of the peace treaty.

Since Pakenham was slow in preparing his assault, Jackson had time to throw up defenses. He placed his army—made up of about five thousand Tennessee and Kentucky white militiamen, Louisiana Creoles, blacks, and pirates—behind a dry canal. Then Jackson's troops built high mud breastworks, reinforced with sugar barrels.

The Battle of New Orleans began at dawn on January 8, 1815. Pakenham attacked head-on with about eight thousand disciplined soldiers. Jackson's troops held their fire until the redcoats were at close range. Then they slaughtered the invaders. The British were forced into hasty retreat, leaving behind 700 dead—including Pakenham himself—1,400 wounded, and 500 to be captured by the Americans. The United States suffered only 8 dead and 13 wounded.

Jackson's victory brought joy to many Americans. News of the battle reached Washington in February 1815, about a week before news of the peace treaty reached the people. Many Americans incorrectly thought that the United States had humbled Britain and forced it to make peace. The Battle of New Orleans could have no effect on the negotiations at Ghent, but it made a national hero of Andrew Jackson.

Consequences of the War

On the day the Treaty of Ghent arrived, the President quickly sent it to the Senate, where it was unanimously approved. The Senate's action showed the deep desire for peace. The Federalist press critized the treaty, but it was one of the most popular ever negotiated by Americans. Although the United States gained none of its war objectives, the treaty ended a needless war.

The War of 1812 did have a number of important consequences. It weakened the Indian power east of the Mississippi and opened the way to expansion and settlement by United Staes pioneers.

The war and the peace that followed aroused a spirit of patriotism. New England's influence in national affairs declined, and the South and West lent new color to American life. The people of the United States seemed to feel a new sense of unity. Albert Gallatin wrote, "They are more American; they feel and act more like a nation."

This nationalism also helped United States industry. Even though the Jeffersonians did not favor government support of business, their foreign policies encouraged the growth of manufacturing. By cutting off imports of English textiles, Jefferson's embargo of 1807 and the War of 1812 had stimulated the growth of spinning mills in the United States. By 1815, there were more than a hundred such mills, mostly in New England.

Instead of putting their money into shipbuilding, investors backed the financing of factories. The chief increase in national wealth at the end of the war came from expanding manufacturing.

The peace of Ghent also marked a turning point in the relations of the United States with other nations. Up to that time, the new nation either had been involved in or had been affected by Europe's rivalries. After 1815, Americans began to pay more attention to domestic than to foreign affairs. They entered a long period of relative isolation from the international politics of Europe.

The people concentrated on developing the United States. Many of the proposals suggested in Hamilton's Report on Manufactures were finally made law (by a Republican Congress, no less). In 1816, Congress passed a protective tariff and chartered the second Bank of the United States.

In the presidential election of 1816, Secretary of State James Monroe, the Republican candidate, easily defeated Rufus King, the Federalist choice. Most of the opposition to Monroe, a Virginian, came from voters in the New England states.

A Look at Specifics

1. What themes did Jefferson emphasize in his first inaugural address?

2. How did Jefferson's tax program reflect his philosophy of government?

3. Why did Jefferson wish to limit the size of the armed forces?

4. Why were many New England Federalists displeased with the Louisiana Purchase?

5. What was John Marshall's view of the powers of the national government? What were the main effects of the decisions made by the Supreme Court during his years as chief justice?

6. Why were Americans embittered over the *Chesapeake* affair?

7. What was the purpose and effect of the Nonintercourse Act? What was the purpose of Macon's Bill No. 2?

8. Why did the views of the war hawks appeal to both the Northwest and the South?

9. Why did many Americans think it would be easy to conquer Canada.?

10. What were the final terms of the Treaty of Ghent?

A Review of Major Ideas

1. Discuss the basic principles of the Jeffersonian program.

2. What circumstances led to the purchase of Louisiana?

3. How did the Jefferson and Madison administrations attempt to defend American neutral rights during the war between Britain and France? Why were these attempts unsuccessful?

4. What grievances led the United States to declare war on Britain in 1812? Why was the nation divided over the war?

5. In what respects did the United States become more unified as a result of the war?

For Independent Study

1. Should the political changes in 1800 be considered a revolution? Give evidence to support your answer.

2. As secretary of the treasury, who do you think was more aware of the problems of a growing nation: Alexander Hamilton or Albert Gallatin? Why?

3. Neutral rights at sea is a subject that has troubled the United States in other eras. Report on at least one of these historical situations.

4. "The War of 1812 should never have been fought; but if the United States were going to fight, it fought at the wrong time and against the wrong country." Oppose or defend this statement.

Unit Review
Examining the Times

1. What circumstances accounted for the rise of the Federalist party? For its decline?

2. What domestic and international problems of the nation under the Articles of Confederation led some leaders to favor a stronger central government? What provisions did the new Constitution make for dealing with these problems?

3. What important precedents did the first four Presidents set that helped strengthen the growing nation?

4. What events from 1783 to 1815 tended, in the long run, to strengthen nationalism in the United States? What, if any, developments between 1783 and 1815 tended to discourage nationalism?

HOTEL.

Post Office.

UNIT THREE 1815–1850

Life in a Growing Nation

The end of the War of 1812 in the United States coincided with the end of Napoleon's rule in Europe. While 1815 brought increased independence for the United States, that year also marked the start of a reactionary period in Europe.

The ruling classes of Europe were glad to be rid of Napoleon. They looked upon his rule as a natural result of the French Revolution, which they viewed as an outbreak of mass insanity. They were determined both to prevent future revolts and to change Europe back to what it had been in the past. In other words, they stood for *reaction*—a return to past conditions.

At the Congress of Vienna in 1815, the five great powers—Russia, Prussia, Austria, Britain, and France—made a peace settlement. They restored the monarchies that Napoleon had overturned, they put old ruling families back on the thrones, and they divided European territory among themselves.

The great powers formed an alliance known as the Concert of Europe. The members were supposed to cooperate in preventing revolutions and wars. At times, however, some of the members encouraged revolts. For example, Britain, France, and Russia backed the Greeks when they rebelled against the Ottoman (Turkish) Empire. In 1830, Greece won independence.

In a series of revolts the people of Spain's colonies in South America overthrew colonial rule. In this they were helped by Britain, which had commercial reasons to want these peoples to be free. By 1826, Mexico and all of Spain's former colonies in South America were independent.

While the great powers supported freedom for the colonies of other nations, they tried to extend their own colonial empires. For example, by midcentury, Britain had gradually extended its control over the entire subcontinent of India.

In the early 1800's, when it had an unfavorable balance of trade with China, Britain tried to reverse the balance by shipping opium to China. By the 1830's many of the people had become opium addicts, and the Chinese government wanted to end the shipments. The British used force. In the Opium War that followed (1839–1842) the Chinese lost. While the European powers did not carve China into colonies, they gained considerable influence over China's affairs.

European powers were also becoming interested in Africa. A number of European explorers started making their way into the interior. The British took over the Cape Colony from the Dutch in 1806. The French colonized Algeria in 1830.

Despite their support of selected rebellions, all of the great powers passed laws at home to stamp out what the rulers considered to be dangerous ideas. These laws limited or prohibited freedom of speech, of the press, and of political association.

While the governments were trying to maintain the existing state of affairs, the development of the factory system was making great changes in economic and social conditions. This development (sometimes called, rather inaccurately, the Industrial Revolution) had begun in England in the early 1700's and had spread throughout Europe and to the United States by the early 1800's. New machines, powered by water or by steam, were being used more and more in manufacturing. The machines were placed in factories, which were located where power was available. Workers were drawn from the countryside to tend the machines. A new class, composed of factory workers, grew up; and a new class of factory owners, or industrial capitalists, arose also.

Both the workers and the capitalists had grounds for discontent. In the growing mill towns, life was hard, dirty, and disagreeable. The factory laborers, many of them children, generally were overworked and underpaid. Craftsmen and women who continued to make goods by hand objected to the factory system. It often produced the same goods more cheaply and thus forced them to lower their prices. Though the capitalists were better off, they also had cause for complaint. Their political influence was not equal to their wealth, nor was it equal to the political influence of the great landowners. Even in 1815, most mill owners and shopkeepers could not vote.

In 1815, few Europeans thought that much could be done to improve society or government. By about 1830, however, the mood of the people began to change. More and more of the workers, capitalists, and others came to believe in social and political progress. They began to feel that poverty and suffering could and should be lessened. They began to think that governments could and should respond more to the will of the people, or even be completely democratic.

The new faith in progress took various forms. There were many different kinds of reformers, and the disagreements among them made it difficult for them to cooperate effectively.

Humanitarianism was simply a strong sympathy for the poor and unfortunate and an urgent desire to help them. *Political liberalism* was the belief that governments should regulate life as little as possible, leaving individuals fairly free to pursue their own concerns. *Democratic radicalism* had two main ideas: first, that the purpose of government should be "the greatest good to the greatest number," and second, that "every man ought to count for one and none for more than one." *Socialism,* in its most common form, included several ideas: that the workers should own and operate the factories and other means of production; that each should contribute according to his or her abilities and should share in the output according to individual needs; and that the workers should run the government as well as the economic system.

In France and other European countries the reformers could make little headway by peaceful means. They turned to violence, but they were not much more successful. In July 1830, the French workers rebelled and overthrew the king, who was soon replaced by another king.

In 1845 and 1846, the failure of the potato crop in Ireland led to terrible famines and some riots. Several hundred thousand people died of starvation or disease. Many of those who survived would work from then on to overthrow British rule. Eventually millions of the Irish left their homeland, some for Britain or the continent but most for the United States.

The year 1848 brought trouble throughout Europe. Another revolution in France led to the establishment of a new republic, which proved to be short-lived. That same year, revolutions were also attempted in Italy, Prussia, and Austria, but none of them proved successful.

In Britain, the reformers did not stage a revolution, though they resorted to rioting at times. They achieved some political reform by peaceful means. The radical democrats continued to insist upon even greater reform. In 1848 they presented to Parliament a great "charter"—a petition with thousands of signatures—which demanded, in vain, that all men be allowed to vote.

Social reformers in Britain gained some of their objectives through legislation. A law of 1833 abolished slavery throughout the British colonies. By 1850, other laws had changed practices in the British Isles. For instance, the death penalty was no longer imposed for petty crimes, and owners of mills and mines were required to make at least some provision for the safety of their employees.

In the United States, there were reform movements similar to those in Europe. Reform was largely an international cause. But Europeans and Americans faced different problems in attempting to bring about reforms. In the United States, the reformers did not have to fight an entrenched aristocracy. They were able to extend what democracy they had. Though poverty and suffering were less widespread in the United States, there existed a social evil as bad as, if not worse than, any in Europe—slavery. American social reformers therefore had at least as much to do as the European reformers.

Reform in the United States was largely a sectional matter. Both the factory system and the reform spirit were far more common in the North than in the South. Slavery persisted in the South alone. The economic and social differences resulted in political controversies between the sections. These were intensified by the spread of antislavery feeling in the North and proslavery feeling in the South. The controversy was also intensified by territorial expansion, as the North and the South contended for the control of new territories in the West.

In the United States, reform did not lead to revolution as it did in several European countries, but by 1850 it was threatening to bring civil war.

The Early National Years

CHAPTER 6
1815–1828

The city of Washington, D.C., in 1833.

Americans have often been torn between loyalty to one state or section and loyalty to the nation as a whole. As a result, one of the main themes in United States history has been the conflict between sectionalism and nationalism.

After the War of 1812 the spirit of nationalism grew stronger than before. Evidence of this can be seen in constitutional law, foreign policy, domestic politics, and even literature. At the same time, strong sectional feelings were also developing, but they were based primarily on economic differences.

THE ERA OF GOOD FEELINGS

Soon after he took office in 1817, President James Monroe visited New England. Monroe was a Virginian and a Jeffersonian. Although the Federalists in New England had strongly opposed Jefferson and Madison, Monroe was now received with great enthusiasm. A Federalist newspaper in Boston commented that an "era of good feelings" had begun with Monroe's inauguration. This phrase was repeated in other parts of the United States, and Monroe's presidency (1817–1825) came to be known as the Era of Good Feelings.

Political feelings seemed good because there was no longer a strong opposition party. The Federalist party was on the verge of disappearing altogether. Despite the appearances of political harmony, however, there was a good deal of discontent beneath the surface. Much of the discontent was based on conflicts between the sections.

The Northeast

The Northeast was well on its way to becoming an industrial center. In this area, and especially in New England, many streams provided good water power. Even during colonial times, water mills had been set up to grind grain, saw lumber, or operate iron forges. Now they were used to power factory machinery. By the early 1800's, many people in the Northeast were skilled in the use of machines.

The region also had two other important assets: money to invest in factories or mills and plenty of unskilled workers to operate the machines. The workers came, first, from the less prosperous farms of the section and, later, from the immigrant ships that put in at northeastern ports.

During this period, the mills and factories in the Northeast never provided a livelihood

The Book Bindery, M. and M. Karolik Collection, Museum of Fine Arts, Boston

Women bind books in a New England factory. In the early 1800's, unmarried farm women were becoming part of the factory labor force. Often they lived in dormitories provided by the employers.

for all the people, or even for most of them. The majority continued to live and work on farms. Nevertheless, the industrial interests were starting to give the Northeast its special character as a section.

The Northwest

Before the War of 1812, settlers in the Northwest Territory battled with the Indians for control of the land. During the war, United States victories broke the power of the tribes in the region. As a result, the federal government forced new treaties upon the tribes, compelling them to give up more and more land.

Once the Indians had been defeated, pioneers rushed to take up land. They headed to the Northwest by two main routes. One route included the Ohio River and its tributaries; the other, the Erie Canal and the Great Lakes.

Most of the Northwest was heavily wooded, but in Illinois much of the land was already treeless. This was the grand prairie, covered with tall wild grass. The early pioneers had never seen anything quite like this growth, and they avoided it. They found that much of the land was wet and marshy. Where it was dry, the tough sod was hard to break with a wooden plow. Before long, however, determined settlers began to drain and plow the prairie land and to grow rich crops on the fertile black soil.

The Northwest was primarily a land of farms and farmers. The great majority of the people first lived and worked on relatively small farms. Many were subsistence farms, producing a variety of things for the use of the farm family only. In time, most of the farms became commercial operations, specializing in certain crops and producing these for sale. The chief products were corn, wheat, pork, mutton, and beef.

The use of machinery was beginning to increase the production on farms. New tools were most widely used in the Northwest. Many farmers there could afford the equipment. Also, the grain fields were flat enough and broad enough to allow the farmers to use machines easily and economically.

Plowing became easier and faster as

wooden plows were replaced after 1819 by plows made of cast iron. The new ones were made with several parts, which could be replaced individually if broken. Planting was aided by the introduction of horse-drawn harrows and grain drills. Harvesting was improved even more by horse-drawn mowing machines and hay rakes.

The South

In colonial times, the leading southern crops had been tobacco and rice. After independence, both crops continued to be produced, and new crops appeared—hemp in Kentucky, sugar cane in Louisiana. Most important of all, cotton became a big crop in most of the southern states.

Once the cotton gin had been invented, cotton cultivation spread rapidly over Georgia and both the Carolinas. Soon it began to spread westward, to the area then called the Southwest.

Cotton growing gave new life to slavery. Political leaders like George Washington and Thomas Jefferson had once expected slavery to die out because tobacco growing had seemed less and less profitable. As cotton cultivation spread throughout the South, slavery spread with it.

Tobacco and cotton cultivation quickly wore out the soil. Many farmers abandoned their farms and moved west. Migrating southerners looked first to Alabama and then to territory farther west. "*The Alabama Fever* rages here with great violence," a North Carolina planter wrote in 1817, "and has carried off vast numbers of our citizens. . . . if it continues as it has done, it will almost depopulate the country." The westward movement did almost depopulate some parts of the Carolinas, just as it did some parts of New Hampshire and Vermont. The older states gained population slowly, while the newer ones grew with amazing speed.

As a rule, the earliest pioneers in the Southwest, like the ones in the Northwest, worked their own small farms and were nonslaveholders. Some of them prospered, bought slaves and additional lands, and became large plantation owners themselves. Others sold their original clearings, moved farther west, and pioneered again. From the already settled states also came planters migrating with slaves and money. They either bought up the partially improved lands or bid for large tracts at the government land offices.

Not that the South was ever made up of plantations alone. There were cotton, sugar, tobacco, and rice plantations, all of them worked by slaves. But the great majority of southerners never owned any slaves. Countless small farms in the region were tilled not by slaves but by the farm families. These small southern farms produced more corn,

Pioneer farm families settled in heavily wooded areas of the Northwest *(above)* and cleared land by burning. They built houses and "snake fences" of rough logs.

Illinois farmers *(below)* sow grain after plowing the heavy prairie sod. Slaves on a Louisiana plantation *(opposite)* harvest sugar cane.

mules, and oxen than the farms of the Northeast and the Northwest together.

The South also had some industries, and it had a few sizable cities—New Orleans, Charleston, and Baltimore. Shortly after the War of 1812, many southerners expected cotton mills to spring up in the South, since the section had plenty of water power as well as raw material. However, cotton raising seemed more profitable than cotton manufacturing. It made more money than any other southern crop. Cotton and slavery, more than anything else, would cause the South to become increasingly different from the Northeast and Northwest.

A Protective Tariff

After the War of 1812, many Republicans began to favor policies they had once opposed. They now wanted protective tariffs, a national bank, and federal spending for improved transportation.

The aim was to create a "home market." Tariffs supposedly would encourage the growth of industries and industrial towns, which would buy the products of farms and plantations. A national bank would provide credit and currency so that payments could be made easily throughout the entire country. Improvements in transportation would make it possible to rapidly ship both farm products and manufactured goods. Henry Clay, one of the leading backers of such measures, referred to them as the "American System." Clay and other leaders believed that the system would be good for all the people.

In 1816, the protectionists carried through Congress the highest tariff yet passed. This law had the support of many congressmen from both parties and all sections. Some southerners voted in favor of it. They expected that many cotton factories would be built in the South. Some northerners voted against it. Merchants in Boston and other seaports, who made a living by importing and selling foreign products, opposed protective tariffs because these would cut down on imports.

Trade

At one time, foreign trade had been divided among a number of Atlantic seaports, from Savannah and Charleston northward. These ports were especially numerous in New England. After the War of 1812, most of the smaller ports fell into disuse, and the larger ones grew bigger and busier than ever. The leading ports on the Atlantic were Boston, Philadelphia, Baltimore, and, above all, New York. The largest city in the United States, New York had a fine natural harbor and good access to inland markets.

The first line of *packets*—fast sailing ships—between the United States and Britain began operating from New York in 1819. The packets carried passengers, mail, and light freight on a regular schedule, making the trip in three weeks when winds were favorable.

The first steam-powered ship to cross the ocean was the *Savannah,* in 1819. It left from Savannah, Georgia, and took nearly a month to make the crossing. It used sails to supplement its paddle wheels.

Most imports were landed at New York and, from there, distributed to the rest of the nation. High-grade cloth, iron and steel products, china and earthenware, wines and liquors, exotic fruits, sugar and molasses, coffee, cocoa, and tea were the main imports. Most exports went out through New York, but in the export trade, New Orleans ran a close second and occasionally took first place. This was to be expected, for tobacco, cotton, and other southern products made up two-thirds of all American exports. The other third was mainly grain, flour, and meat.

The foreign trade of the United States involved most nations of the world. Still, as in colonial times, Britain remained by far the

Southern plantations grew tobacco, cotton, and other crops for American and European markets. The idealized drawing of a prosperous tidewater plantation *(above)* shows the main house, outbuildings, mill, and dock. In the Northeast, whaling grew into an industry after 1825. Besides producing millions of barrels of whale oil, whaling stimulated many other businesses, including shipbuilding. A page from a whaler's logbook *(below)* details the pursuit and capture of a whale.

biggest supplier of foreign goods and by far the best customer for American products.

Money Problems

Much of the domestic trade was really a part of the foreign trade. It arose from the gathering of products to be exported and from the distribution of goods that had been imported. This trade was often handicapped by the lack of a sound, uniform, and plentiful money supply.

Though a mint had been founded in Philadelphia in 1792, gold and silver coins of the United States were rarely seen for many years thereafter. Until the great discoveries in the Far West, little gold or silver was mined in the United States. Most of the cash that Americans used consisted of foreign coins, but there were never enough of these coins to meet the needs of trade.

In the cities and larger towns, stores had begun to specialize in groceries, dry goods, hardware, or other lines. In the villages and smaller towns, there were general stores full of miscellaneous merchandise. Wandering through the countryside were peddlers. Some traveled on foot and carried packs containing pins, needles, combs, jewelry, clocks, and other lightweight items of some value. Other peddlers drove wagons.

In dealing with peddlers and country storekeepers, the customers often paid in kind—exchanging their own produce, such as fresh eggs, for their purchases, such as tea or coffee. This custom of bartering continued for many decades because of the scarcity of money.

In place of coins, banknotes were circulated as paper money. These amounted to nothing more than promises to pay cash. They had no government backing, and they were not *legal tender* (that is, they did not have to be accepted in payment of debts). They were issued by banks that sprang up in great numbers after the War of 1812. Often these banks issued more in notes than their cash on hand would safely allow them to do. If too many holders of the notes suddenly presented them for payment, such banks had to close, and their notes became worthless. So varied were the state banknotes that it was hard for an uninformed person to know their real value.

From 1816 to 1836 there was also a national bank, the second Bank of the United States, which had branches in the principal cities. The second Bank of the United States, like the first one (1791–1811), was chartered by Congress. It held a monopoly of the federal government's banking business but also served the general public. Its own banknotes were dependable, well known, and acceptable everywhere. From 1819 on, it made a practice of collecting state banknotes and presenting them to the issuing banks for payment. This action forced the state banks to be more careful than they had been in issuing notes.

Transportation

Private corporations could afford to construct toll roads only through areas where traffic would be heavy. If improved highways were to be run long distances through thinly settled country, the national or state governments would have to finance at least part of the construction.

In 1803, Congress had provided that part of the money from the sale of western public lands might be used for building roads. With such money, from 1811 to 1818 the federal government constructed a toll highway, the Cumberland Road. It extended across the Appalachians from Cumberland, Maryland, to Wheeling, in what is now West Virginia, thus connecting the Potomac River with the Ohio River. A few years later, a private corporation got financial aid from the Pennsylvania government to extend the Philadelphia-Lancaster turnpike to Pittsburgh.

The Delaware and the Susquehanna rivers were thus connected with the Ohio. Between 1825 and 1838, the federal government extended the Cumberland Road, or National Road, westward to Illinois. The Illinois and Missouri governments subsequently carried it on across the Mississippi River.

The National Road and other turnpikes were busy and profitable. Over them moved long lines of stagecoaches, freight wagons, and private carriages. Nevertheless, overland freight rates were too high for the hauling of bulky products, such as grain, flour, or lumber. It was much cheaper and easier to transport goods by water than by land.

Water transportation was given a big boost by Robert Fulton's invention of the steamboat. Fulton had been interested in boats since he was a boy in Pennsylvania. When he was twenty-one, he went to England to work as an engineer. Fulton began to experiment with steam-powered ships, first in England and then in France. After twenty years abroad, he returned to the United States.

In the summer of 1807, Fulton made a test run with the *Clermont,* an American sailboat equipped with an English-built engine and a paddle wheel on each side. He went up the Hudson River from New York City to Albany and back, a distance of approximately three hundred miles, at an average speed of nearly

A peddler *(above)* displays his goods at a prosperous farmhouse. Such peddlers sold housewares from their wagons and brought news to sparsely populated areas. Construction of the Cumberland Road *(below)* was welcomed by pioneers living west of the Ohio River who wished to promote the growth of their section. Road traffic, which moved at about 6 miles per hour, soon grew heavy. New coach and freight companies, such as the National Line, the June Bug Line, and the Shake Gut Line, sprang up.

The Cumberland Road

(NATIONAL ROAD)

- Built by the federal government, 1811–1818
- Built by the federal government, 1825–1838
- Built by Illinois and Missouri after 1840

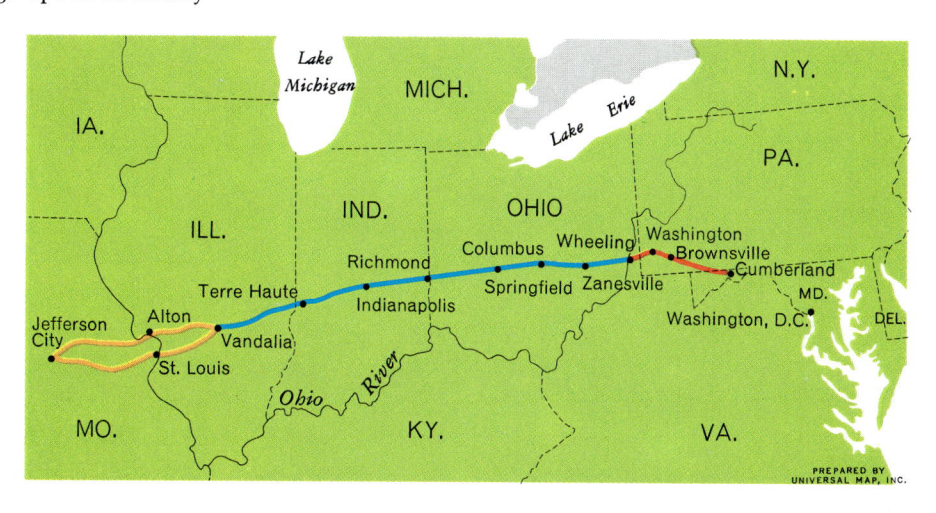

five miles an hour. "The power of propelling boats by steam is now fully proved," Fulton boasted to a friend. Other inventors had tried out steamboats before, but none of these boats had gone so far or so fast.

Soon companies were formed to operate steamboats on the Hudson and other rivers. In 1811, the *New Orleans,* the first steamboat to operate west of the Appalachians, traveled from Louisville to New Orleans. The boat then plied back and forth regularly between New Orleans and Natchez.

A special kind of steamboat was developed for the Mississippi and its tributaries. These rivers were shallow and had suddenly changing currents, shifting sand or mud bars, and submerged tree trunks and roots. The typical Mississippi boat had a flat bottom, a powerful high-pressure engine, and large paddle wheels on each side of the boat or one paddle wheel that extended the width of the boat at the stern.

The larger and faster a boat, the more profitable it would be, and so both the size and the speed of boats were increased. The early flatboats, which were poled upstream, had taken almost four months to go from New Orleans to St. Louis. The first steamboats made the same journey in less than four weeks. The emphasis on speed often led to races in which boats exploded or ran aground. Nevertheless, as one southerner of the time wrote, "wealth rolls up in the cities as a result of the speedy and cheapened transportation."

New waterways also had an impact on sectional development. The canal age began in earnest on July 4, 1817. Governor De Witt Clinton of New York presided over ceremonies at which the first shovelful of earth was dug for the Erie Canal. The route ran from the Hudson River up the Mohawk River and on to Lake Erie. Eighty-three locks and many aqueduct bridges were necessary to carry the canal through hills and across

On the Erie Canal in the 1830's, mules walking on towpaths alongside the waterway pull the boats and barges. In the locks *(center)*, water levels are raised or lowered so that boats can go from one level of the canal to another.

valleys. By October 1825, Clinton's "big ditch"—4 feet deep, 40 feet wide, approximately 350 miles long—was completed.

The Erie Canal proved an immediate success. Its prosperity encouraged the state of New York to build several branches and inspired the states of Ohio and Indiana to construct waterways from Lake Erie to the Ohio River. Freight and passengers could then go by water, with several boat changes, all the way from New York through the Great Lakes to Chicago, or down the Ohio and Mississippi rivers to New Orleans.

Through the Erie Canal, New York City had the best access of any city to the trade of the interior. The cities of Baltimore and Washington hoped to compete by means of the Chesapeake and Ohio Canal. Along with the federal government, these cities contributed money to a private company that began construction in 1828. The company intended to tunnel through the mountains, but it never got beyond Cumberland.

Government Land Policy

When the first settlers arrived west of the Appalachians, practically all the land was claimed by the federal government. In accordance with the land laws, the government first surveyed the "public domain," then opened land offices and offered lands for sale to the highest bidders.

At the time the great migration began, after the War of 1812, the minimum price was $2 per acre and the minimum purchase was 160 acres. A person would have to pay at least $320 for a farm even if there were no competitive bidding. But the buyer could get a farm and begin to live on it by paying one-fourth down—$80 in cash—and the rest in three annual installments.

This sounded easy, but many settlers found that they could not complete the payments. A business depression began in 1819, and many feared the loss of their land if they were held to their debts. Congress changed the land law in 1820. The new land law eliminated installment purchases but reduced the minimum price to $1.25 and the minimum purchase to 80 acres. Now a buyer would need at least $100 in cash, but with that sum he or she could make an outright purchase of a small farm.

SECTIONAL DISAGREEMENTS

As the sections became more distinctly different, jealousy and disagreement came out in the open, usually in Congress. Much of the discontent on the part of northerners was based on a belief that the South unfairly dominated national politics. After all, three Presidents in a row had been Virginians.

Northerners complained that the nation was being ruled by a "Virginia dynasty." They also pointed out that the slave states were overrepresented in Congress and in the electoral college because of the "three-fifths clause" of the Constitution (*Art. 1, sec. 2, para. 3*). This clause provided that three-fifths of the slaves (even though they could not vote) should be counted in determining the number of congressional representatives and presidential electors a state should have. Hence the vote of a man in a slave state carried more weight than the vote of a man in a free state.

Controversy in Congress

Certain northern politicians hoped to revive the Federalist party and make it a broad northern party by playing upon northern suspicion and jealousy of the South. An opportunity seemed to present itself when Missouri applied for admission to the Union as a slave state. There were, at that time, eleven free states and eleven slave states. If Missouri should be admitted with slaves, the balance would shift. In the Senate the slave states would have a majority of twenty-four to twenty-two, though in the House the free states would continue to have a majority. Some northern congressmen, for reasons of both politics and principle, rigorously opposed the admission of Missouri as a slave state.

When a bill to enable Missouri to become a state was being discussed in Congress, a representative from New York, James Tallmadge, Jr., proposed an amendment. It provided that no more slaves should be brought into Missouri and that those already there should gradually be set free. After a heated debate, the Tallmadge amendment passed the House, but it failed to pass the Senate.

While the House and the Senate were arguing over Missouri, a bill was brought up to admit Maine as a free state. Maine was a part of Massachusetts, and Massachusetts had given its permission for separate statehood, but on the condition that Congress should give its approval before March 4, 1820. The southerners in Congress said, however, that they would refuse to admit Maine unless the northerners would agree to admit Missouri as a slave state.

The Missouri advocates claimed that Congress had no constitutional right to tell a state, when it applied for admission, whether or not it could have slavery. They said that Missouri would be the equal of any other state once it entered the Union. It could then decide on its own "domestic institutions" just as South Carolina or New York could. The "anti-Missourians" replied that Congress could impose conditions on the admission of a state and that it had done so in the past. By prohibiting slavery in the Northwest Territory, for example, Congress had imposed freedom as a condition for the admission of any state from that territory.

The Missouri Compromise

A compromise was gradually worked out. First, the Senate agreed to combine the bills for admitting Missouri with slaves and Maine without. Then the Senate adopted an amendment proposed by Senator Jesse B. Thomas of Illinois. The Thomas amendment prohibited slavery, not in the state of Missouri, but in the rest of the Louisiana Purchase to the north of latitude 36°30' (the southern boundary of Missouri). By this amendment, Thomas hoped to make the compromise more acceptable to the "anti-Missourians" in the House.

In the House the speaker, Henry Clay, secured the passage of the amended Maine-Missouri bill after dividing it into separate bills. Still a third step was necessary, however, before the controversy ended. The Missouri constitution, though permitting slaves to be brought in, forbade free Negroes to enter the state. It conflicted with the provision in the federal Constitution that "The citizens of each state shall be entitled to all privileges and immunities of citizens in the several states" *(Art. 4, sec. 2, para. 1)*. This meant that citizens of New York were entitled to the same privileges as citizens of Missouri, including the privilege of moving to and living in Missouri. Negroes were citizens in New York and a few other states. This Missouri constitution would deprive black citizens of privileges and immunities guaranteed them by the Constitution.

Clay took the lead in arranging a settlement. He simply resolved to admit Missouri

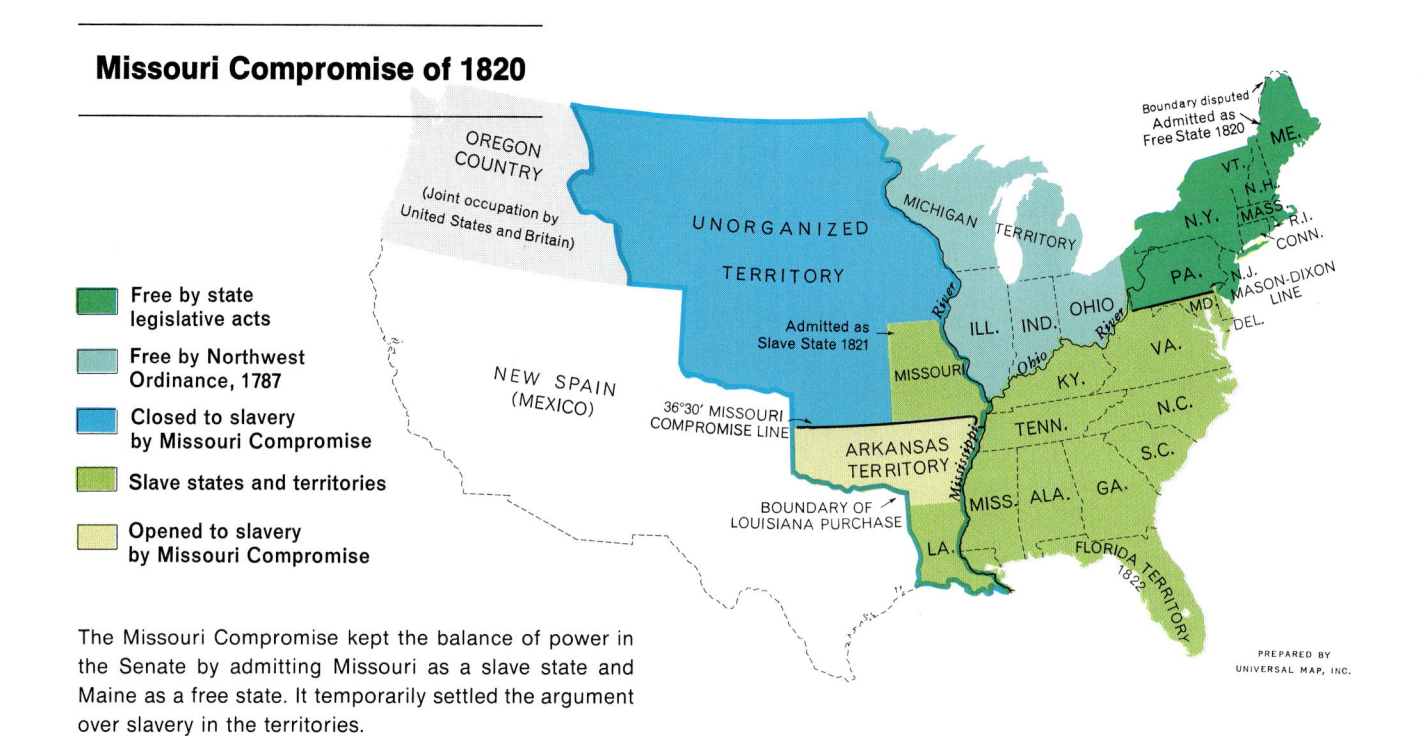

Missouri Compromise of 1820

Legend:
- Free by state legislative acts
- Free by Northwest Ordinance, 1787
- Closed to slavery by Missouri Compromise
- Slave states and territories
- Opened to slavery by Missouri Compromise

The Missouri Compromise kept the balance of power in the Senate by admitting Missouri as a slave state and Maine as a free state. It temporarily settled the argument over slavery in the territories.

---

on the condition that the offending clause should never be interpreted so that it infringed on the privileges and immunities of citizens of any state. Obviously, the Clay resolution did not mean very much. Yet both houses of Congress passed it and, having done so, agreed to let Missouri in.

Before the Missouri Compromise, the Mason-Dixon Line (the southern boundary line of Pennsylvania) and the Ohio River had come to form the boundary between freedom and slavery. The Missouri Compromise extended this boundary westward across the Louisiana Purchase territory.

A Court Case

National and sectional interests also were influenced by Supreme Court decisions. Still headed by John Marshall, the Court made decisions that favored the growth of business and put the national government's concern over that of the states.

The case of *Dartmouth College* v. *Woodward* (1819) arose from a quarrel between the president and the trustees of the college. The trustees dismissed the president, and he then obtained from the legislature of New Hampshire a new charter that converted Dartmouth into a state school, with himself as its president. Dartmouth's original charter had been granted by King George III, before the Revolution. The college trustees, through their attorney, Daniel Webster, maintained that this charter was a contract that the state had no right to break.

When the case came before the Supreme Court, Webster reminded Marshall and the associate justices that they had already decided, in the case of *Fletcher* v. *Peck*, that "a *grant* is a contract." Webster proceeded to argue that "a grant of corporate powers and privileges is as much a *contract* as a grant of land." The Court decided in favor of the original college trustees.

This decision meant that private colleges and other nonprofit corporations would be safe from the arbitrary interference of state governments. At the time it also seemed to mean that business corporations would be free from government control. In this respect, the decision was favorable to the growth of business.

The Nation Over the States

Time and again one state or another asserted powers that came into conflict with powers claimed by the federal government. In such cases, Marshall and his associates decided in favor of the federal government and against the state.

The case of *McCulloch* v. *Maryland* (1819) involved the second Bank of the United States, which had been founded in 1816. Like the first Bank of the United States, it was a corporation that was chartered by the federal government. The Bank had its main office in Philadelphia and branches in other cities throughout the country.

In the business depression of 1819, many people found themselves unhappy with the Bank. The state of Maryland tried to drive the Baltimore branch out of business by imposing a heavy tax upon it. When the head of the Baltimore office refused to pay the tax, the state threatened him with imprisonment, and he appealed the case to the Supreme Court.

The Court was faced with two basic questions. Was it constitutional for Congress to charter the Bank? If so, was it constitutional for a state to tax one of the branches?

Marshall pointed out that the Constitution authorized Congress to pass all laws "necessary and proper" for carrying out the specified powers of Congress, such as the power to lay and collect taxes. A bank, he said, was "necessary and proper" for such purposes. In answering the second question, he observed that the power to tax was the "power to destroy." If a state could tax agencies of the federal government, it could destroy them and thus destroy the Constitution itself. In short, Marshall decided that Congress could set up a bank and that the states could not impose taxes upon it.

The case of *Gibbons* v. *Ogden* (1824) arose from a dispute over the use of steamboats on the Hudson River. The inventor of the steamboat, Robert Fulton, and the promoter, Robert Livingston, had secured from the state of New York a charter that gave them the sole right to carry passengers on the river to and from New York City. Fulton and Livingston authorized Aaron Ogden to operate ferryboats between New York and New Jersey. The federal government, through an act of Congress, gave a license to another man, Thomas Gibbons, and he went into business in competition with Ogden. When Ogden sued Gibbons in the New York courts, the judges decided in Ogden's favor and ordered Gibbons to quit the business. Gibbons then appealed to the Supreme Court.

In deciding this case, Marshall and his fellow judges had to interpret the commerce clause of the Constitution. It says that Congress shall have power to regulate commerce among the states (*Art. 1, sec. 8, para. 3*). The Constitution does not define the word *commerce,* nor does it say whether Congress has the exclusive power to regulate it. The judges had to decide whether "commerce" included navigation and whether congressional laws to regulate it took precedence over state laws.

Marshall reasoned that the authors of the Constitution had used the word *commerce* in a broad sense; they had intended to include the operation of boats as well as the buying and selling of goods. The regulatory power of Congress, he concluded, was "complete in itself." Therefore, the law of New York, granting a steamboat monopoly between New York and New Jersey, must give way to the law of Congress. This decision, by forbidding the states to restrict interstate com-

Land and water resources

Not all the land in the United States was rich. After two centuries of continuous European settlement, even good land and water resources had deteriorated.

Europeans in America used water for irrigation and to power water wheels, as well as for drinking, cleaning, and shipping. The rapidly flowing rivers in the Northeast, with their many falls, gave that region of the country a head start in using water to power industrial machines. Irrigation was most often practiced in the rice fields of the Southeast and the mission lands of Spanish California.

Though water was often abundant, it was rarely pure. Water-borne diseases were common killers even in the early colonial period. Locating a source of drinking water was a part of every pioneering venture. Once an area advanced beyond its pioneer state, the water quality steadily declined. Sewage and pollution caused important problems even at the beginning of industrialization.

Land resources received the most attention in the Southeast. Unlike the soil in the Northeast, which had always been stony and thin, the soil in the Southeast had once been extremely fertile. But continual farming of tobacco and cotton had worn out the soil.

Two of the most important advocates of scientific farming were John Taylor and Edmund Ruffin of Virginia. Taylor conserved his own soils by using compost as fertilizer, reducing the production of tobacco, and rotating corn and wheat crops. Ruffin studied European soil discoveries and carried on experiments in soil chemistry. He advocated contour plowing, crop rotation, and methods of draining and fertilizing the land. He published a newspaper, *The Farmer's Register,* and wrote several books expounding his views.

Every development was not necessarily an improvement. The curved plow invented by Thomas Jefferson and the cast-iron plow made by Charles Newbold in 1797 made plowing easier but also tore away underlying roots that helped prevent soil erosion.

merce, also helped prepare the way for the economic growth of the nation.

Harsher Controls on Blacks

During the Era of Good Feelings, many slaves and free blacks started to face greater obstacles because of their race. As white planters became more dependent on maintaining the institution of slavery, they tightened the slave codes, which regulated the behavior of slaves. In some quarters, slavery was praised as a "positive good," where once it had been viewed as a necessary evil.

There were occasional rumors that slaves were planning to revolt, and these, too, helped bring harsher controls. The most notable plot of the 1820's was that planned by Denmark Vesey, a free black in Charleston. After his plans for a massive insurrection were revealed by a slave, he and thirty-five other blacks were tried and hanged. The plot led to laws isolating slaves from free blacks.

Though the slave codes were limited to the South, blacks in the North did not fare much better. Their rights were often disregarded. Like free southern blacks, they lived with the fear that they might be kidnaped and sold into slavery. Attempts to improve their lot sometimes met with violence.

ENLARGING THE UNITED STATES

When Napoleon sold Louisiana to the United States, the boundaries were not defined. The purchase treaty merely said that France was transferring the territory with the same boundaries it had had. But what were they?

It was commonly supposed that Louisiana consisted of all the land between the Mississippi River and the Rocky Mountains and from the Gulf of Mexico to Canada, a British possession. President Jefferson argued that the purchase also included the part of West Florida between the Mississippi and Perdido

The woodcut at right was part of a handbill titled "Dreadful Riot on Negro Hill." The verse on the handbill was a fictitious account of a Boston riot in the late 1820's. Blacks and immigrants were often the victims of riots in the 1830's. Little was done to protect victims or to prosecute rioters.

rivers. In 1810 and again during the War of 1812, people from the United States seized parts of West Florida, and the federal government extended its jurisdiction to include them. Spain, however, continued to claim all of West as well as East Florida. In addition, it disputed the southwestern boundary of the Louisiana Purchase.

Invasion of the Floridas

The American desire for the remainder of Florida had been one of the causes of the War of 1812. This territory was important because of the richness of the land and because of its location. Whoever controlled Florida could interfere with trade on the Mississippi and other rivers flowing into the Gulf of Mexico. The territory was important for still other reasons. Runaway black slaves frequently headed south to Spanish Florida and freedom. Indian raiding parties from Florida often attacked American settlements to the north.

In 1818, Andrew Jackson and a small army pursued a band of Seminole Indians into Florida. He did not stop until he had seized the fort of St. Marks, the town of Pensacola, and every other important Spanish post except St. Augustine. He captured two British traders, tried them on charges of supplying and inciting the Seminoles, and had them put to death. He later said he was sorry he did not also hang the Spanish governor of the territory.

Already famous as the "hero of New Orleans," Jackson was hailed by many Americans. Most of President Monroe's cabinet advisers felt, however, that Jackson had exceeded his orders and had unnecessarily complicated relations with Spain. All but one of the cabinet members thought he should be censured.

The Spanish government was outraged. It demanded that Jackson be punished and an indemnity be paid to Spain. At first, the British government also took offense but before long decided that the two victims of Jackson's hasty justice had deserved their fate. Britain refused to support Spain, and Spain was too weak to risk war without a powerful ally.

A Treaty with Spain

Monroe's secretary of state, John Quincy Adams, had been negotiating with Luis de Onís, the Spanish minister to the United States. They were trying to settle the existing disagreements between the two nations.

Adams used the Jackson incident to strengthen his hand in the bargaining with Onís. As secretary of state, Adams replied to the Spanish demands not by apologizing but by accusing. He said that the Spaniards were to blame for the trouble in Florida by failing to live up to their obligations. In Pinckney's Treaty of 1795 the Spaniards had promised to restrain the Indians and prevent raids across the border. Adams demanded that the Spanish government punish the Spanish officials in Florida for their negligence and pay the United States for the expenses of Jackson's expedition!

Adams went on to demand that Spain either place a force in Florida to protect the territory or cede it to the United States. He hinted that if Spain should refuse to do either of these things, the United States would simply take Florida.

Spain's other American colonies were fighting for their independence, and Spain was in no position to defend Florida. In 1819, Onís agreed to a treaty. By its terms, Spain ceded all of Florida to the United States. Spain also agreed on a definite southwestern boundary for the Louisiana Purchase and gave up its vague claim to the Oregon country. The United States abandoned its equally vague claim to a part of Texas (which some Americans thought was part of the Louisiana Purchase). The two nations agreed that Spain would not have to pay damages to American citizens who had suffered losses because of Spanish ship seizures in earlier years. Instead, the United States promised to reimburse its citizens for these losses up to a total of 5 million dollars.

The Adams-Onís Treaty of 1819 went into effect in 1821. It was a "transcontinental treaty" that drew a line between Spanish and American possessions all the way from the Gulf of Mexico to the Pacific Ocean.

The Northern Border

The desire of Americans for Canada as well as for Florida had contributed to bringing on the War of 1812. In 1817, the Rush-Bagot Agreement between the United States and Britain was signed in Washington. The two nations agreed to partial and gradual disarmament on the Great Lakes and Lake Champlain, thus reducing fear of invasion on both sides.

Another agreement, made in London in 1818, defined part of the boundary between the United States and Canada. This boundary was set at the 49th parallel from the Lake of the Woods to the crest of the Rocky Mountains. The area beyond the Rockies—the Oregon country—was left "free and open" for settlement by both British subjects and American citizens for ten years. The new boundary gave a new northern limit to the Louisiana Territory.

Reaching Beyond the Borders

Throughout United States history, private citizens and companies have greatly influenced foreign policy. After the War of 1812, some American citizens settled or explored in regions far beyond the United States borders. In time, their settlements would be the bases on which the United States claimed the territory for its own.

American whaling ships began appearing off Russian America in about 1820. Their action prompted the Russian government to ban their presence. This led to a treaty that set the boundary between Russian America and the Oregon country at 54° 40'.

In the Oregon country, American fur traders set up posts. The British had granted a monopoly in the fur trade to the Hudson's Bay Company, and the Americans tried, without much success, to compete with that huge company.

In 1820 the first Protestant missionaries from New England arrived in Hawaii. Although few in number, these Americans strongly influenced the development of the islands.

Also in this period, Americans began settling in Texas. In 1821 the newly independent Mexican government began making large grants of land to Americans. The first were given to Moses Austin and his son Stephen. Mexico made the grants on the condition that the grantees would bring in Roman Catholic families from the United States to settle on the land. They would be expected to develop farms and defend the frontier.

FOREIGN POLICY

In a message to Congress on December 2, 1823, President Monroe announced an important policy. It was a policy of America for Americans and Europe for Europeans. It did not yet have a name, but thirty years later

United States, 1819

- United States, 1819
- Claimed by U.S. and Britain
- 1816 Date of admission to the Union

TERRITORIAL GROWTH OF THE UNITED STATES

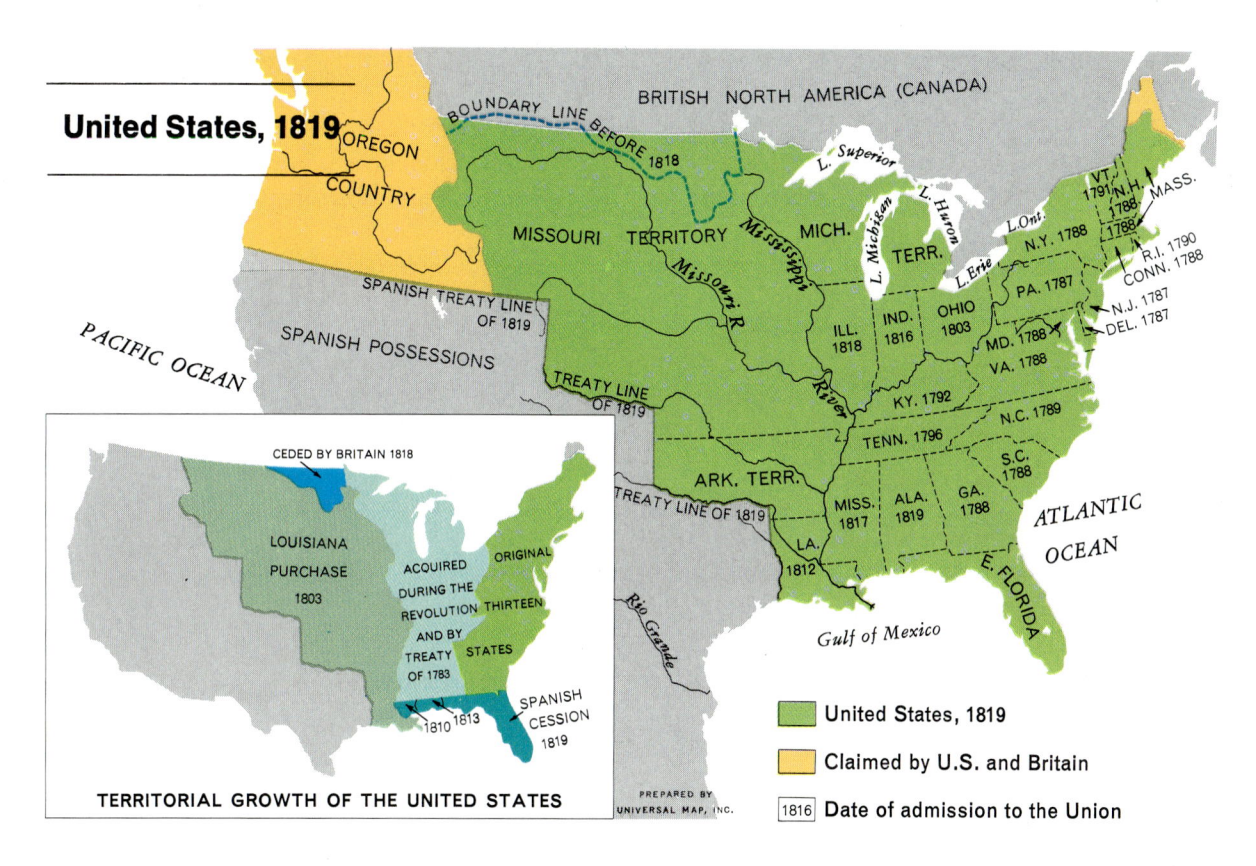

people began calling it the Monroe Doctrine. Although Monroe made the first official statement of the policy, he was expressing ideas that were already widely held. The background for Monroe's announcement lay in a number of European actions toward the Western Hemisphere.

European Threats

Starting in 1810, several colonies in Latin America rebelled against Spanish rule, declared themselves independent, and set up their own governments. During the wars for independence, the American people generally favored the rebels and supported their cause in a number of ways.

The United States government wanted to recognize these new countries but had to wait until the Adams-Onís Treaty went into effect before it was wise to do so. In 1822, President Monroe agreed to send ministers to Argentina, Chile, Peru, Colombia, and Mexico.

Early in 1823, it looked as if four members of the "Holy Alliance," a group of conservative monarchies, might send troops across the Atlantic to try to recover these former colonies for Spain. Russia, Austria, and Prussia had authorized France to invade Spain and put a Bourbon king back on the Spanish throne. After France had done so, many people in both Europe and America wondered if the European allies would next intervene in Spanish America.

Another threat came from Russia, which claimed territory on the Pacific coast of North America. Russian explorers had landed in Alaska in 1741. For years afterward the Russians carried on a fur trade with the Aleut Indians. In 1799 the czar authorized the creation of the Russian-American company, which started settlements in Alaska and along the Pacific coast as far south as New Ross, California (near San Francisco). It even tried to get a foothold in Hawaii.

In 1821 the czar ordered non-Russian ships to stay south of the 51st parallel along the Pacific coast. Secretary of State John Quincy Adams strongly objected to the czar's order. It would interfere with American whalers and fur traders as well as strengthen the Russian territorial claims. Adams saw the order as an effort to enlarge the jurisdiction of Russian America, and he repeatedly protested to the Russian government.

Another supposed threat came from Britain. Adams feared that the British wanted Cuba, which still belonged to Spain. Like Jefferson and others before him, Adams did not want to see Cuba transferred from a weak nation like Spain to a strong nation like Britain. He thought that Cuba would eventually free itself from Spanish control and become part of the United States.

Monroe's Announcement

Britain did not agree with its European allies on the treatment of Spanish America. Of course, Britain did not entirely agree with the United States, either. The British wished to see the Spanish empire reestablished, provided the Spaniards would give them special trading privileges. The British did not want the French to intervene, for that would probably lead to French domination.

In the summer of 1823, the British prime minister, George Canning, proposed to the United States minister in London, Richard Rush, that their nations act together. Canning suggested that the two governments make a joint statement. In it they would warn the Holy Alliance not to intervene and would promise never to take any additional American territory for themselves. Rush was ready to accept Canning's proposal on one condition: Britain must first agree to recognize the new Latin American nations. When Canning refused to promise recognition, Rush wrote home for instructions.

After hearing from Rush, President Monroe asked for advice. Former Presidents Jefferson and Madison urged him to authorize the joint statement. Secretary of State Adams disagreed. Adams opposed the joint statement for two reasons. First, he hoped the United States eventually would get Cuba, Texas, and other territory. Second, such a joint statement would make it seem to the world as if the United States were only trailing along after Britain. Adams felt that it would be more dignified and honorable for the United States to speak out on its own.

By the time Monroe spoke out, in December 1823, the British had lost interest in making a joint statement with the United States. The French minister to Britain had assured Prime Minister Canning that France really did not intend to intervene in Spanish America by force of arms.

Monroe directed his message to all the powers of Europe, including Britain. He said that the United States would oppose attempts by European powers to regain old colonies or to acquire new ones, to interfere with independent nations, or to extend a European system of government and diplomacy in North or South America. He also said that the United States would not interfere in the "internal concerns" of Europe.

Important Consequences

By his statement, President Monroe did not frighten off the powers of Europe. True, the new nations of Latin America kept their independence, and others later gained theirs. The United States was able to maintain Monroe's principles, to the extent that it did, largely because the powers of Europe disagreed among themselves.

The long-range effects of Monroe's message were extremely important. Later leaders of the nation repeated and elaborated upon

PRESIDENTIAL ELECTIONS: 1816-1828

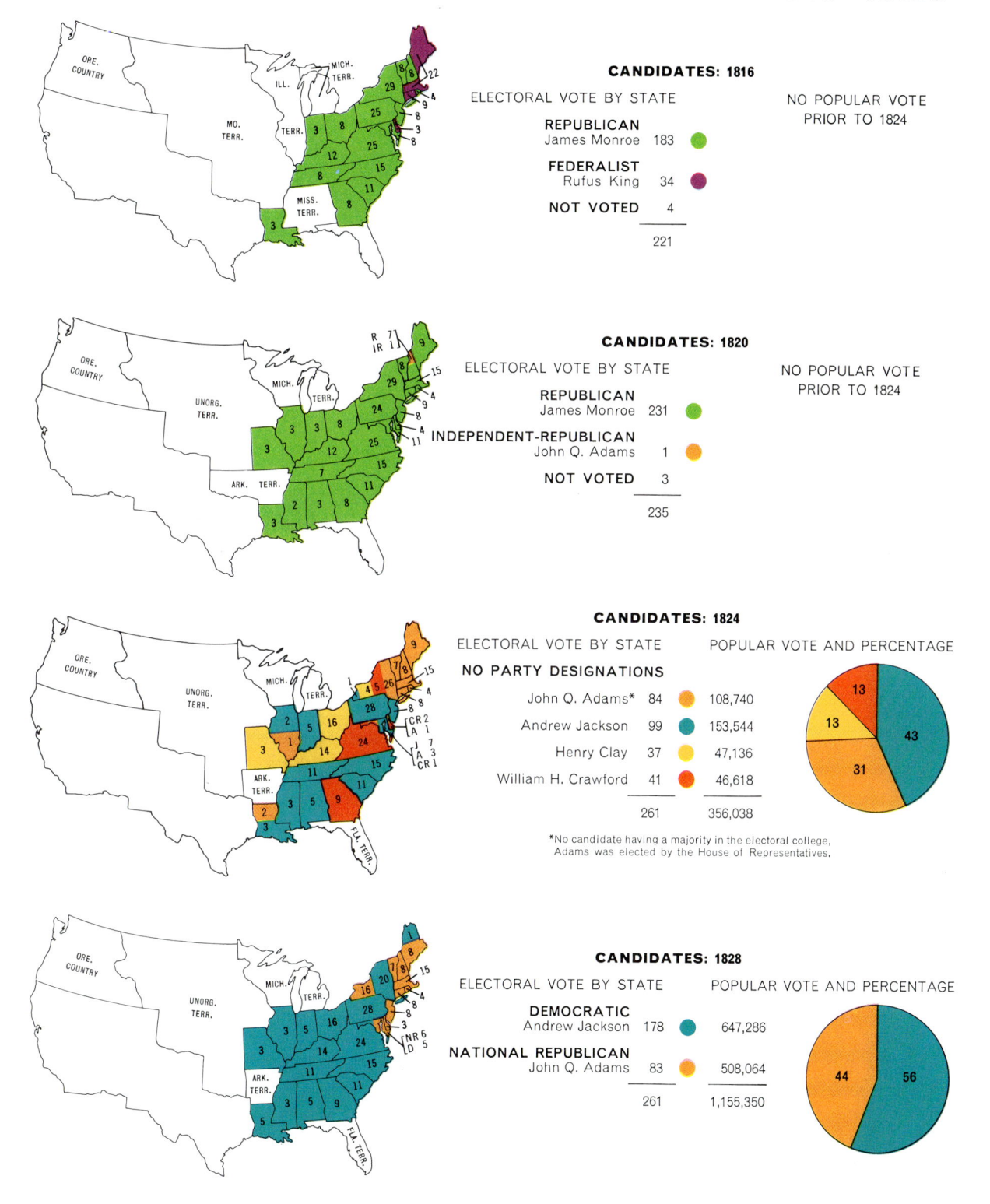

CANDIDATES: 1816

ELECTORAL VOTE BY STATE

REPUBLICAN
James Monroe 183

FEDERALIST
Rufus King 34

NOT VOTED 4

221

NO POPULAR VOTE PRIOR TO 1824

CANDIDATES: 1820

ELECTORAL VOTE BY STATE

REPUBLICAN
James Monroe 231

INDEPENDENT-REPUBLICAN
John Q. Adams 1

NOT VOTED 3

235

NO POPULAR VOTE PRIOR TO 1824

CANDIDATES: 1824

ELECTORAL VOTE BY STATE — POPULAR VOTE AND PERCENTAGE

NO PARTY DESIGNATIONS

John Q. Adams* 84 — 108,740
Andrew Jackson 99 — 153,544
Henry Clay 37 — 47,136
William H. Crawford 41 — 46,618

261 — 356,038

*No candidate having a majority in the electoral college, Adams was elected by the House of Representatives.

CANDIDATES: 1828

ELECTORAL VOTE BY STATE — POPULAR VOTE AND PERCENTAGE

DEMOCRATIC
Andrew Jackson 178 — 647,286

NATIONAL REPUBLICAN
John Q. Adams 83 — 508,064

261 — 1,155,350

it. In time, the United States grew strong enough to make it dangerous for other powers to seek territory or political influence in the Western Hemisphere.

GREATER POLITICAL ACTIVITY

After the War of 1812, the number of voters and elective offices increased, and so political parties became more important. It was up to them to bring large masses of people together and provide them with definite political goals. It was also up to the parties to organize the state and national governments and give central direction to the many elected officials.

Nominating Candidates

Since the Constitution does not provide for political parties, it does not provide a way for parties to nominate candidates for office. From 1796 to 1816, the representatives and senators of each party in Congress got together in two separate *caucuses* (party meetings) and named the presidential candidates. In 1820, when President Monroe ran for reelection, he did not need a caucus to renominate him because no other Republican was seeking the nomination. The Federalist party had no caucus because it had practically ceased to exist.

If the caucus system were to be revived in 1824, the man named by the Republican caucus would win. No new party had appeared to take the place of the Federalist party, and so the Republican candidate would have no opposition. Nomination would amount to election.

To some the idea of a caucus seemed unfair and undemocratic. Members of the House and the Senate were not elected for the purpose of naming a President. A demand arose to overthrow "King Caucus."

In 1824, King Caucus was overthrown. A nominating caucus met, but only about a third of the Republicans in Congress were present. The man they picked, William H. Crawford of Georgia, did not have the field to himself. Three other candidates, Andrew Jackson, Henry Clay, and John Quincy Adams, were nominated in new ways—by the state legislatures or by mass meetings in the various states.

Of the four presidential candidates, none won a majority in the electoral college. The House of Representatives had to choose between the two highest, Jackson and Adams. The followers of Jackson, the great military hero of the War of 1812, thought the House of Representatives ought to choose him, because he had received more popular votes and more electoral votes than Adams. Nevertheless, Clay threw his support to Adams, and the House chose Adams.

After his election, Adams named Clay as his secretary of state. In those days the office of secretary of state was looked upon as a stepping stone to the presidency. The angry Jacksonians charged that there had been a "corrupt bargain" between the two men, with Clay agreeing to make Adams President now and Adams promising to make Clay President later. No doubt Adams had agreed to support Clay in the future, but there was nothing corrupt about the agreement.

The Jacksonians were determined to win the next election, and they immediately began to prepare for it. Indeed, Adams's term as President might be viewed as one long battle over the election of 1824. Adams was a nationalist who wanted to see the nation flourish. He suggested much (more roads and canals, a national astronomical observatory), but accomplished little.

By 1828, there were again two parties. The more conservative Republicans, who had picked up many of the old Federalist doctrines, were now called National Republicans (later to be known as Whigs). They supported President John Quincy Adams for reelection. The Republicans who upheld the doctrine of states' rights and represented the agricultural interests were called Democratic-Republicans or Democrats. They offered Andrew Jackson as their candidate. But there was still no regular system for making nominations. They were made by state legislatures or by local mass meetings.

The election of 1828 had some of the characteristics of a "grudge fight." Certainly it was a dirty campaign. The Jacksonians accused the conscientious and puritanical Adams of waste, extravagance, and all kinds of misdeeds as President. The Adamsites accused Jackson of even worse crimes, including murder and adultery. They said he had shot some of his own soldiers in cold blood during the War of 1812 and had knowingly lived for a time with another man's wife. The charges and countercharges, false though they were, aroused the interest of the voters and brought them to the polls in unprecedented numbers. Jackson, with 56 percent of the popular vote, easily defeated Adams.

A Look at Specifics

1. Why was Monroe's period as President called the Era of Good Feelings? In what way is this title inaccurate?

2. Why did industry develop most rapidly in the Northeast?

3. How did the federal government aid in the building of turnpikes?

4. Why did many northern politicians oppose the admission of Missouri as a slave state?

5. What was Henry Clay's role in achieving the Missouri Compromise?

6. What were the "slave codes"?

7. How did Chief Justice John Marshall interpret the use of the word *commerce* in the Constitution?

8. What were the main features of the Monroe Doctrine?

9. Why was the United States able to uphold the principles of the Monroe Doctrine in the early nineteenth century?

A Review of Major Ideas

1. What developments made the sections increasingly dependent upon each other?

2. How did improvements in transportation both contribute to national unity and increase sectional feelings and specialization?

For Independent Study

1. The Missouri Compromise was the first attempt to settle the question of the expansion of slavery into the territories. Do you agree with Jefferson's observation that the drawing of a geographical line would tend to strengthen sectional differences, or do you think that the reasoning of the Compromise was sound and conceivably could have settled the matter permanently? Explain.

2. Before 1823, the United States attempted to keep itself free from entangling alliances. The Monroe Doctrine, however, reflected a willingness to become involved in the affairs of Latin America. Did the doctrine indicate a substantial change in United States foreign policy, or was it a new interpretation of old principles? Explain.

Jacksonian Democracy

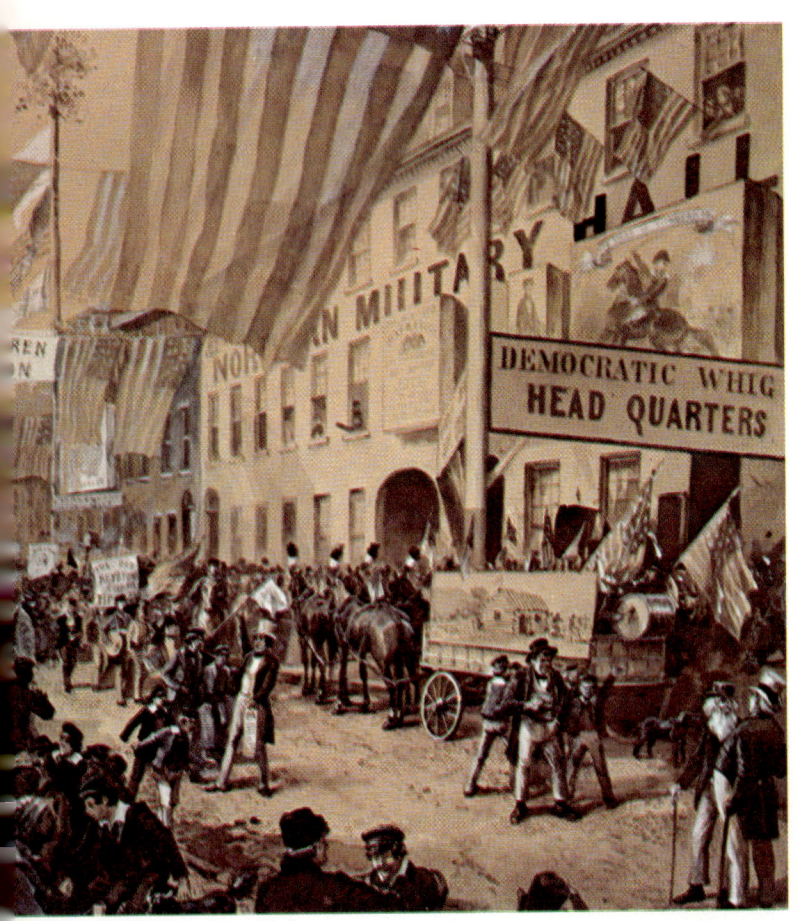

CHAPTER 7
1828–1840

Preparing a preelection parade, 1840.

Modern Americans usually think of their President as a powerful person who can greatly influence their daily lives. The early Presidents, however, were not viewed in such a light. Because the national government's powers were limited, the President could not act in many areas. During the terms of Andrew Jackson, this started to change, and the American presidency began to be a much more powerful office.

Jackson was a popular hero who ushered in a period and style of government that came to be called "Jacksonian democracy." His election in 1828 came after twenty-five years of reforms that led to greater participation in politics by more Americans.

CHANGES IN GOVERNMENT

The original state constitutions did not provide for political equality. With few exceptions, they did not allow women, blacks, Indians, or white men without a specified amount of property to vote or hold office. In some states there were also restrictions on holding office for Catholics, Quakers, Jews, and members of other religious groups.

At the time these constitutions were adopted, a great many men owned their farms and could therefore vote. There were few workers in towns and cities, and many of them were skilled craftsmen who owned their businesses or other property and also could vote. With the growth of industry, however, it appeared that the time might come when large numbers of people would be factory workers who owned no taxable property. These people would have no political rights under the existing constitutions. As a result, reformers began working to broaden the voting rights.

The new states that were forming in the West set some examples for those in the East. The western settlers were roughly equal in social and economic opportunity, and it seemed natural to make them more equal in political opportunity as well. When Ohio joined the Union in 1803, its constitution gave the vote to all white men. As other new states were formed, their constitutions usually did the same.

The older eastern states became concerned about their loss of population to the western states. If they were to keep people at home, they would have to grant more political rights.

New State Constitutions

The eastern states began, one by one, to hold conventions for drawing up new constitutions. In some states, there was strong opposition to removing the property qualifications. When the Massachusetts convention met in 1820, Daniel Webster argued that men with property ought to have more influence in government than men without it. He said "power *naturally* and *necessarily* follows property" and "property as such should have its weight and influence in political arrangement." Some people believed that if the poor were given political power, they would use it to pass laws depriving the rich of some of their wealth.

Despite the resistance, changes were made. In Massachusetts the new constitution, adopted in 1821, restricted the vote to taxpayers but lessened the influence of the rich. In New York the property requirement for voting was abolished.

In a few northern states, blacks benefited from the extension of the vote. Generally, however, they were bypassed. In Pennsylvania, the right to vote was taken from all black men at the same time it was given to more white men. The Pennsylvania constitution adopted in 1838 added the word "white" as a qualification for voting.

The legislatures in some states did not give equal representation to all parts of the state. The parts that had been occupied the longest had more representatives in proportion to population than did the newly occupied areas.

When a constitutional convention met in Virginia in 1829, delegates from the western counties demanded fair representation. In the revised constitution of 1830 these counties gained seats in the House of Burgesses. Nevertheless, the *tidewater,* or coastal, counties continued to be overrepresented.

In a number of states the new constitutions allowed voters to elect more officials than before. The first constitutions had provided for the election of only the legislature, the governor, and a few other state officials. The rest of the officials were appointed by the governor or the legislature. The revised constitutions, however, provided that most of the high officials should be chosen by the voters.

The new constitutions also affected national politics. The writers of the national Constitution had provided for an "electoral college" to choose the President. Each state legislature was to choose electors, who would then meet to cast the votes for President. The only way the voters could influence the choice of a President was in selecting state legislators. As time went on, this indirect method gave way to more direct methods. By 1800, six of the sixteen states allowed the voters to help choose the presidential electors. After 1828, in only one state—South Carolina—did the legislature still pick the presidential electors.

The New Politics

When Jackson took over the presidency in 1829, he believed that the government officeholders considered themselves a privileged group. They seemed more concerned with their own welfare than with the people's interests. He thought that their jobs should belong to the people and that most ordinary people were fit to hold them.

Some of Jackson's followers spoke more cynically. They said the government jobs should be used to reward those who had helped put the political party into power. One of the Jacksonians declared: "To the victors belong the spoils."

Accordingly, President Jackson began to remove officeholders and replace them with his followers. He did not remove nearly so many, however, as his opponents claimed. During his two terms he replaced only about one-fifth of the total number. Many were removed for good reason, and the proportion removed was no greater than that under Jefferson. Nor did he appoint illiterates to positions requiring special knowledge, as his critics also charged.

If the common man was fit to govern, then no one should hold a particular job very long. Instead, it ought to be passed around among several men. Following this kind of reasoning, the Jacksonians favored "rotation in office."

The granting of government jobs in return for political support sometimes led to serious abuses. Despite its evils, the spoils system had some desirable and democratic implications, at least in the beginning. It gave more people than before a chance to hold government jobs. It meant also that a party could get the support of enthusiastic job seekers at election time. As a result, the party could win elections without depending heavily on rich individuals and corporations for campaign funds, as is now often the case.

Increased Voter Interest

Only about 27 in 100 white men had voted in the presidential election of 1824, but in 1828 about 55 in 100 did so. The proportion of voters remained approximately the same in the elections of 1832 and 1836. Then it jumped again in 1840, with more than 78 in 100 voting.

This remarkable increase was due only in

Despite the chaos around them, jurors listen to legal arguments in a rural court. In most regions, the pioneers quickly set up courts and legal practices and usually abided by the courts' decisions. Many disputes centered around ownership of property.

part to the changes in voting laws. It was also caused by the activity of political parties. Elections became more exciting and aroused more popular interest than in earlier years.

The angry divisions over the outcome of the election of 1824 had led to new party activity. The political parties that had disappeared in the "Era of Good Feelings" reappeared in slightly different form.

The election of 1828 was preceded by a bitter, and dirty, presidential campaign that was in many ways a personality contest. John Quincy Adams was a brilliant man who had great ideas for the United States. He had, however, a cold manner that put people off. Andrew Jackson had a reputation as a national hero, and his election was no great surprise.

Jackson was so popular that he easily won reelection in 1832. Then, in 1836, he picked his Vice-President, Martin Van Buren, to succeed him. The Whigs (formerly the National Republicans) put three candidates in the field—William Henry Harrison, Daniel Webster, and Hugh L. White. Van Buren, with Jackson's backing, defeated them all.

New Party Procedures

During the Age of Jackson, the revitalized political parties became somewhat more democratic. An important change was the start of national nominating conventions to choose the candidates for President and Vice-President.

The convention system was introduced in time for the election of 1832. It was first used by the earliest third party in United States history—the Anti-Masonic party. This party opposed a secret fraternal organization called the Society of Freemasons. Feeling against the Masons had become strong when, in 1826, a man named William Morgan mysteriously disappeared from his home. Morgan had written a book in which he accused the Masons of horrible deeds. Morgan's friends believed that Masons had kidnaped and murdered him in order to keep the book from being published. The excitement over Morgan's disappearance spread.

Since President Jackson was a Mason, some of his opponents tried to use this against him. They organized the Anti-Masonic party. In 1831 they held a convention in Baltimore to nominate a presidential candidate for the election of 1832. The National Republicans and the Democrats then picked up the idea of the nominating convention and held meetings of their own.

The idea behind the convention system was democratic. Party members in local meetings elected delegates to state conventions. These, in turn, sent delegates to the national convention. In practice, professional politicians came to dominate the proceedings. Nevertheless, many more people were able to take part than had been able to do so under the caucus method.

JACKSON'S POLICIES

Unlike John Quincy Adams, Andrew Jackson had no definite program to propose to Congress. Jackson had run on his record as a military hero. The voters had no way of knowing how he would stand on questions of policy once he was in office.

In some ways, President Jackson proved to

be an advocate of states' rights rather than national powers. For example, he vetoed a bill to give federal aid for the building of the Maysville road in Kentucky. Even though this route was intended to form a branch of the Cumberland (National) Road, Jackson doubted whether the government could constitutionally finance an improvement lying entirely within a single state. Nevertheless, Jackson strongly upheld the national authority in a feud with South Carolina about the tariff laws.

The Tariff of Abominations

In 1828 a bill was introduced for raising the tariff on many imports, including raw wool. This bill did not entirely please New England manufacturers, since it would add to the cost of some of their raw materials. Yet many of the New England representatives and senators voted for the bill, and it passed.

Southerners called the tariff of 1828 the "tariff of abominations." The cotton growers of South Carolina were especially bitter. The state was not very prosperous, and many people were abandoning their exhausted lands for farms in the Southwest. Most South Carolinians, however, blamed their troubles on the tariff. Certainly the tariff, which raised the prices of imported goods, made their troubles even worse.

Calhoun's Theory

Some South Carolinians demanded that their state secede from the Union. This demand was a challenge for John C. Calhoun. He was the outstanding leader of his state and the Vice-President of the United States. He wished to eventually become President. He needed to find a way to satisfy his fellow South Carolinians without antagonizing the rest of the country.

Calhoun answered this challenge with the theory of nullification. According to this theory, which he began to work out in 1828, the separate states were sovereign. By ratifying the Constitution, they had given certain powers to the federal government, but they had given up none of their sovereignty. They alone could decide whether or not Congress was exceeding the powers that had been granted to it.

In deciding the constitutionality of acts of Congress, the states could use the same procedure they had used to ratify the Constitution. That is, if the voters of a particular state felt that an act of Congress were unconstitutional, they could hold a convention and "nullify" the act. So far as that state was concerned, the law would then be null and void.

If people in other states believed that the law in question should be upheld, they could add a constitutional amendment giving Congress the power to pass such a law. The amendment would overrule the nullifying state. That state would then have to yield unless, as a last resort, it chose to secede. It could secede by holding another convention and repealing the ordinance by which it had once ratified the Constitution. According to Calhoun, secession, like nullification, was a legal and constitutional process.

The legislature of South Carolina published Calhoun's theory, together with a denunciation of the tariff, in *The South Carolina Exposition and Protest* (1828). Calhoun wrote the document, but he kept this a secret because he was running for reelection. Calhoun hoped that Jackson, if he were elected President, would try to lower the tariff. But Jackson as President did nothing to lower it.

In 1832, a new tariff law was passed, but it made only slight changes. Since it did not satisfy Calhoun or his followers in South Carolina, they held a convention and adopted a "nullification ordinance." It declared that all the tariff acts, especially those of 1828 and 1832, were "null, void, and no law, nor binding upon this state."

Jackson issued a proclamation denouncing nullification as both unconstitutional and unpatriotic. "The laws of the United States must be executed," he said. He prepared to execute them by using the army and the navy. His supporters in Congress introduced a "force bill" giving him authority to use force, if necessary, against South Carolina.

Another Political Compromise

Henry Clay took the lead in bringing about a compromise. He sponsored a bill to lower the tariff by yearly stages. After ten years the rates would be about the same as they had been in 1816. When Congress passed this tariff, it also passed the force bill, which was to take effect only if South Carolina continued to defy federal law.

The South Carolina convention met again. First, it repealed its ordinance nullifying the tariff laws. Second, it adopted an ordinance nullifying the recently passed Force Act.

Calhoun and his followers boasted that they had saved their state from both the injustice of the tariff and the danger of invasion. True, they had brought about a gradual tariff reduction. But they also had failed to get nullification accepted by the rest of the country.

Calhoun continued to proclaim his theory of nullification and secession. He also turned more and more to developing a sense of solidarity throughout the South, in the hope that the section as a whole would support his theory.

Meanwhile, the United States had survived

Courtesy of The Art Institute of Chicago

Volunteer fire companies like those in Charleston *(above)* existed in many cities in the 1840's. Some functioned as social clubs. But with the growing number of fires and riots in cities at this time, many people became convinced that professional fire and police departments were needed. The woodcarving of a Kentucky preacher *(left)* was done in 1850.

the worst sectional crisis it had yet faced. Temporarily at least, the sense of national unity was strengthened as a result of the nullification attempt.

Indian Policy

When it came to Indian policy, Jackson sometimes took a states' rights stand. Like many other westerners, Jackson disliked and distrusted Indians. The Indians disliked and distrusted him, too, with reason. Jackson's two terms as President were marked by constant fighting with the tribes.

The government's, and especially Jackson's, aim in this period was to remove all Indians living in the area east of the Mississippi. Explorers had described the area west of the Mississippi as the "Great American Desert," unsuitable for farming. Thinking that white settlers would never want this arid land, government leaders decided it would be the perfect spot to put the Indians. Thus the government would end the seemingly endless cycle by which white settlers moved into Indian territory, fought over it, defeated the tribes, negotiated a treaty, pushed the tribes out, settled, filled up the territory, and moved toward more Indian land. By locating the Indians on land that no whites wanted, the leaders thought they would be giving the Indians a permanent territory. At the same time they would be getting rid of the tribes in areas that whites wanted for themselves.

The Bureau of Indian Affairs, which had been set up as part of the War Department in 1824, was expanded in 1832. Under Jackson, the BIA directed the signing of ninety-four treaties by which tribal peoples gave up some of their lands.

In the North, most of the tribes had already been moved west of the Mississippi. The last stand of the northeastern tribes was the Black Hawk War, in 1832. Led by the Sauk chief, Black Hawk, the Sauk and Fox resisted removal. They fought in northern Illinois and southern Wisconsin until they were finally beaten by the army.

Of the southeastern tribes, the Choctaw,

Indian land cessions increased greatly during Jackson's presidency. Tribes that depended on hunting, faced with a diminishing supply of game in the East, often gave little resistance to moving west. The Cherokee tribe, however, included prosperous farmers and merchants who fought removal through the courts. Many of the Cherokee read and wrote their language in an alphabet devised by Sequoyah *(right)*. The army's removal of the Cherokees to the West would have been unhappy even if well handled, but bureaucratic bungling and graft turned it into an atrocity. The Seminoles, living on a Florida reservation, fought removal *(left)*. Tribes on the western plains were forced to make way for the tribes from the East. Fort Laramie on the North Platte River *(below)* was a post for the fur trade. Indians who had been trapping and trading with whites moved west with the traders. These Indians battled with the plains tribes. The easterners, both non-Indian and Indian, brought diseases that began epidemics.

Chickasaw, and Creek were fairly easy to move to the new Indian Territory. The Cherokee and Seminole, however, refused to sign treaties with the government. When the state of Georgia tried to make the Cherokee subject to the state, the Cherokee took their case to the Supreme Court. Although the Court upheld the Cherokee position, Andrew Jackson did not. The President refused to execute the court's orders. He is reported to have said: "John Marshall has made his decision; now let him enforce it."

The state of Georgia, at Jackson's urging, harassed the Cherokee until some of them signed a removal treaty. The tribe was moved west in 1838 and 1839, after Jackson had left office. A fourth of the tribe died during the journey, which came to be called the Cherokee "Trail of Tears." Some of the Cherokee fled to the hills of North Carolina, where their descendants still live.

The Seminole, led by Osceola, fought the removal policy with guns. Refugee slaves often fled to Seminole settlements. They joined in fighting the Second Seminole War, which broke out in 1835. It lasted until 1842, when the United States Army gave up. Some of the Seminoles had surrendered and had been moved west. The holdouts settled in the Everglades of Florida. Their descendants did not sign a peace treaty with the United States until 1962.

SECTIONALISM

During Jackson's and Van Buren's terms as President, sectional feelings continued to intensify. The changes within the various regions of the United States in this period made the Northeast, Northwest, and South even more different from each other.

The Northeast

By the 1830's, textile manufacture—the spinning of thread and yarn and the weaving of cloth—had gone ahead of overseas commerce as the biggest business in New England. Most of the early factory workers came from farms. In many New England textile mills, whole families were hired. Children as young as four helped their parents tend the spindles and looms. Though far from ideal, this arrangement was better than some in England where orphans were bound over to mills and were overworked and exposed to all kinds of vice.

In Waltham and later in Lowell, Massachusetts, the mill owners wanted to avoid the evils of both the American and the British systems. The companies brought in farm women in their late teens and early twenties, put them up in boarding houses, and paid them reasonably well for the time. The idea

Yale University Art Gallery. The Mabel Brady Garvan Collection

was that after a few years the women would return home with their savings to marry and settle down. Many such women, however, went home to die, their health broken by the unhealthy working conditions.

Despite long hours—from sunup to sundown six days a week—which then were usual, the "Lowell girls" found time for some social and educational activities. They even wrote, edited, and published a literary magazine. More important, they tried to organize as a group to force the factory owners to improve working conditions. In 1845 the Lowell Female Labor Reform Association tried to get the Massachusetts legislature to pass a bill limiting the workday to ten hours. The lawmakers were, however, more impressed with the flower beds outside the mill than with the lack of ventilation inside it. The bill failed.

Most of the industrial workers in the United States worked long hours at low pay. For example, the men of the construction gangs performed backbreaking labor on turnpikes, canals, and railroads. An increasing number of them were Irish immigrants who got fifty cents to a dollar for a twelve- or fourteen-hour day, a low wage even then.

About 1840, Irish men and women began replacing the native farm families and farm women in the mills. The Lowell companies converted the boarding houses into overcrowded tenements. Piece rates replaced daily wages, and employees had to work harder in order to take home the same pay. In many mill towns, working and living conditions were worse in the 1840's than they had been in the 1820's and 1830's.

Bargaining Collectively

Some workers combined their efforts in order to bargain with their employers as a group, rather than as individuals. The worker combinations, which came to be known as unions, demanded shorter hours and higher pay. To back up their demands, the unions threatened to *strike*—that is, to quit work temporarily.

The first workers to organize themselves and bargain collectively were skilled artisans, such as printers, carpenters, masons, hatters, and shipbuilders. The cordwainers (shoemakers) of Philadelphia formed a union in 1792.

In each trade there were three levels of workers. A man began as an *apprentice,* or learner. He worked his way up to become a *journeyman* (originally he journeyed about for a time as a traveling worker). Finally, if he were able and lucky enough, he could become a *master craftsman.* The master was an employer as well as a laborer. He owned his own shop, hired apprentices and journeymen, and dealt with customers as a seller of goods or services. Journeymen, as well as masters, often owned farms or city homes.

As more and more products were made in factories, skilled workers began to feel that they were falling behind in the struggle for income and prestige. The cordwainers, for example, feared that they would get less money for the shoes they made if people could buy shoes that were made more cheaply by specialized workers under the putting-out system.

Children at work in a shoe factory. Many Americans viewed child labor as educational.

From colonial times, craftsmen had been organized in guilds. These regulated wages, working conditions, methods of production, and the price and quality of the products. The guilds failed as organizations for collective bargaining because they were dominated by the master craftsmen, who themselves were employers. As a result, many journeymen formed their own unions.

At first, the journeymen of one craft in one city acted alone. Thus, in 1825, six hundred journeymen carpenters in Boston struck, unsuccessfully, for a ten-hour day.

Later, the unions of various crafts cooperated in citywide federations. In 1835, the Philadelphia General Trades' Union, still seeking a ten-hour day, called a general strike of all the "workies" in the city. This strike also failed.

When it became apparent that conditions of labor in one city depended on conditions in other cities, labor leaders tried to set up intercity federations. In 1834, the leaders from six cities founded the National Trades Union. In 1836, the printers and the cordwainers set up national unions.

The early unions had few successes. They were handicapped by interpretations of the law. Whenever an employer took a labor dispute to court, the judge usually held that unions were illegal conspiracies. The unions were not strong enough to survive a period of widespread unemployment, and few survived the depression of 1837. Those that did helped persuade President Martin Van Buren to proclaim, in 1840, a ten-hour day for employees of the federal government.

Farming in the Northeast

Even before the depression of 1837 began, many farmers in the Northeast were suffering from hard times. They could not raise crops cheaply enough to compete with those from northwestern producers. More and more, the production of wheat, corn, cattle, sheep, and hogs was shifting to fresh lands in Ohio, Indiana, and Illinois.

The disadvantaged farmers of the Northeast could leave their farms, either moving westward and taking up new lands or going to the mill towns and getting factory jobs. Or they could remain where they were and produce special crops.

Thousands of northeastern farmers, especially in New England, abandoned their farms. Whole towns were practically deserted and the buildings left to fall in ruins.

In the Northeast as a whole, however, most farmers stayed put and took advantage of their nearness to the growing cities. They concentrated on producing items that could not easily be shipped in from a distance—milk, butter, cheese, potatoes, apples and other fruits, and hay.

The Northwest

The settlers who had started pushing into the Northwest in the 1820's were joined by many others in the 1830's. Most were still small farmers, buying their lands from the government or from land speculators.

A number of cities were developing, especially on the rivers and lakes. Cincinnati, on the Ohio, was the largest city, with a population of 40,000. St. Louis, on the Mississippi, was the second largest, with 10,000. Chicago had only a few hundred people in the 1830's but was growing fast.

The cities were centers for the storage, shipment, and processing of farm and forest products. The leading industries were lumbering, woodworking, flour milling, meat packing, whiskey distilling, and the manufacturing of leather products and farming equipment.

In the 1830's, most of the new settlers went to the northern parts of Ohio, Indiana, and Illinois and to Michigan and Wisconsin. Most were New Englanders, New Yorkers, or immigrants who had landed at Boston or New York. The southern parts of Ohio, Indiana, and Illinois had been settled earlier, often by people from Pennsylvania, Maryland, Virginia, North Carolina, Kentucky, and Tennessee.

New Approaches to Farming

The Northwest, with its huge level fields, was an area of grain crops and cattle farming. Much of the produce was shipped down the Ohio or Mississippi for export. The Great Lakes, tied in with canals, provided another route for exports.

New tools continued to have their greatest use in the Northwest. By 1830, iron plows were so much in demand that they were being mass-produced. Soon steel plows became available. They cut the soil cleanly and deeply and were more durable than those made of cast iron. These were especially useful in breaking up the tough prairie sod.

Index of American Design, National Gallery of Art, Washington, D.C.

Needlework arts like appliqué *(above)* were popular ways to pass the long winters in Vermont.

Cyrus H. McCormick demonstrated his reaper as early as 1831. With the McCormick machine, a crew of six or seven could harvest as much in a day as fifteen persons using the old-fashioned cradle scythe.

In years of prosperity many more people went west and many more acres of the public land were sold than in times of depression. During the early 1830's, annual sales rose to several times the highest previous level. Prices soared. Only about one-fourth of the land sold went directly to settlers. Most of it went to speculators, who bought large tracts and divided them into farms or town lots to be sold at a profit. When the depression struck in 1837, land sales and prices dropped. Thousands of overly optimistic buyers were left land-poor.

The South

For the South, the 1830's was a period of fantastic agricultural growth. In this decade, cotton finally became the principal crop in the region. More important, production in the Southwest surpassed that in the older tidewater section.

Both tobacco and cotton were hard on the soil. In the older states, the long-time cultivation of these crops had exhausted the natural supply of soil minerals. Heavy rains washed away much of the original topsoil and cut deep gullies in the hillsides. Many once-prosperous farms and plantations were ruined.

The more enterprising farmers and planters of the seaboard states reacted in one of two ways. Either they stayed on and attempted to restore the soil, or they moved west and began all over again.

Southern agricultural reform began in Maryland and Virginia. The greatest advocate of scientific farming was a Virginian, Edmund Ruffin. In his *Essay on Calcareous Manures* (1832) he recommended the application of calcium to exhausted soils.

Ruffin and other scientific farmers published farm journals, formed agricultural societies, and sponsored exhibits and fairs. Thus, they gave wide circulation to new ideas in farm management. As a result, some farmers and planters limited erosion, improved the quality of their cotton and livestock, diversified their crops, and learned better ways of using their slaves.

Nat Turner and his followers angrily plot a slave insurrection in Virginia in 1831.

Treatment of Slaves

Free the slaves or repress them? These were two of the choices that white southerners faced. Out of fear, habit, self-interest, and belief, they chose repression.

One reason for this choice was a slave revolt in Virginia. Nat Turner, a black preacher, led other slaves in an insurrection in 1831. They killed fifty-seven whites before they were captured. In the long chase by soldiers and sailors, perhaps as many as one hundred blacks were killed. Turner and twenty other blacks were tried and executed.

A shudder ran through the entire South, and afterward, white planters always wondered which slaves could be trusted. More than any other event, the Turner revolt led to the passage of a nightmarish series of laws, codes, and restrictions.

Every state with slaves had a slave code. This set up the legal position of the slave in relation to his or her master as well as to society. Most codes also prescribed minimum living conditions.

According to most codes, a slave was not to be away from the owner's land without a written pass. This pass had to be shown to any white who asked to see it. A slave could not preach, except to other slaves, and then only in the presence of a white. A slave could not own a gun, blow a horn, or beat drums. A gathering of five slaves or more was an unlawful assembly.

No one might teach a slave to read or write, and it was against the law to give books, pamphlets, newspapers, or other reading matter to slaves. A slave could not give drugs or medicine to whites.

In individual communities, the slave codes often included other rules. A curfew might be imposed. Some codes prohibited dancing or even any outward signs of joy.

The laws set up different standards for blacks than for whites. For example, in every southern state there was harsher punishment for blacks than for whites for the same offense. A crime that carried imprisonment for a white often carried a death penalty for a black.

The laws were, however, very harsh on any white who aided a slave. The stiffest penalties were given to those whites who hid a runaway or helped plan a rebellion. Death was the usual punishment.

The slave codes reflected a "closed society" in which any criticism of slavery could not be tolerated. Southerners who opposed slavery found it necessary to move north. Even in entertainment, such as plays, slaves had to be shown as servile.

Although there had been slave codes in colonial times, they had been relaxed during the first years of the new republic. The Turner revolt and the rising tide of abolitionist activity led to tighter controls.

THE ABOLITION MOVEMENT

In the early nineteenth century, there was a worldwide movement to abolish slavery. Britain ended slavery in Canada and the British West Indies in 1833. Argentina outlawed slavery in 1813, and Mexico abolished it in 1829. Reformers in the United States could claim no such victory.

The antislavery movement remained rather mild and weak in the United States until the 1830's. The largest antislavery organization was the American Colonization Society, set up in 1816. This society wanted to transport free blacks to Haiti or to West Africa. It founded the colony of Liberia on the African coast to receive them. The idea behind "colonization" was that owners would be more ready to free slaves if they could be sure that the blacks would be shipped out of the country. Prominent white southerners and northerners supported the program. Year after year, however, the society managed to transport only a few blacks out of the community.

Most blacks opposed the colonization idea. They felt that, as Americans, they should be granted the rights and privileges of citizens, not sent to a foreign land.

Free blacks played an important part in the antislavery movement. They held meetings and published newspapers and pamphlets to demand the abolition of slavery. Among the most influential blacks were David Walker and Frederick Douglass. Walker, a Boston clothing dealer, wrote a powerful tract, *Walker's Appeal* (1829). In it he advised slaves to use force if necessary to gain their freedom—"kill or be killed." Douglass, after escaping from a Maryland plantation, became a great orator. When white men and women joined the drive for abolition, most of the black abolitionists cooperated with them and joined the same societies.

Antislavery Societies

During the 1820's, the most active white crusader against slavery was Benjamin Lundy, a New Jersey Quaker. He organized societies in some southern states to cam-

This painting is the only one known to have been drawn belowdecks on a slave ship.

paign for manumission. He also edited an antislavery newspaper in Baltimore.

A young printer from Massachusetts, William Lloyd Garrison, worked on Lundy's paper. In 1831, Garrison started a paper of his own, *The Liberator,* in Boston. Garrison spearheaded a more militant phase of the antislavery movement. At one time, three-fourths of the subscribers to *The Liberator* were blacks.

In 1833, Garrison helped organize the American Anti-Slavery Society, which sent out agents to set up local societies. By 1840, nearly two thousand societies were scattered throughout the North. They had a total membership of perhaps as many as 200,000.

Though Garrison was the best-known leader, there were others equally important. Theodore Dwight Weld, for one, probably made more converts than Garrison did. A former revivalist, Weld usually lectured to church groups, reaching numerous audiences from Ohio to New York.

Many women were involved in the movement. Since they were not allowed to join the American Anti-Slavery Society, they formed their own groups. Two of the most important leaders were Sarah and Angelina Grimké, of Charleston, South Carolina. Their views made them unpopular in the South as well as within their own wealthy, slaveholding family. After Angelina wrote *An Appeal to the Christian Women of the South* (1836) asking women to fight slavery, she and Sarah were no longer welcome in Charleston.

They lectured throughout the North, at first only to women's church groups. In time, men joined the audiences. The sisters were the first American women to speak in public before male audiences, a shocking thing at the time. In July 1837, the Congregational ministers in Boston condemned this behavior, calling it "unnatural." The action by the ministry did not stop the sisters, but it did help tie abolitionism to a growing movement for women's rights.

In 1838, Angelina married Theodore Weld. She and Sarah then worked with Weld in compiling a collection of first-hand accounts into a powerful book, *American Slavery As It Is: Testimony of a Thousand Witnesses* (1839). Included in the book were southern newspaper advertisements for runaways, identifying them by scars and mutilations. These items gave proof of the brutality of slavery.

Garrison refused to have anything to do with the churches, for he thought they were against reform. He condemned the Constitution because it did not prohibit slavery, calling it "a covenant with death and an agreement with hell." A pacifist, he favored complete nonviolence and nonresistance. He also insisted that women be permitted to take an active part in the antislavery movement.

In 1840 those leaders who disagreed with Garrison formed a new organization, the American and Foreign Anti-Slavery Society. This division at the top did not slow down the movement. The local antislavery societies continued to grow.

Political Action

Most of the societies stated that "immediate emancipation" was their aim. The members did not really expect, however, to bring about emancipation soon. They realized that it would take many years. They explained that they hoped to have emancipation "promptly commenced" but "gradually accomplished."

At first, they appealed to the conscience of the slaveholder and tried to convince him or her that slaveholding was a sin. They made little headway this way, though a few slaveholders freed their slaves.

Later the societies turned their attention to the federal and state governments. Nearly all the antislavery people agreed that the federal government had no power over slavery in the states where it already existed. But they demanded that the federal government use its power to abolish slavery in the District of Columbia, prohibit it in the western territories, and bring an end to the interstate slave trade. In addition, they wanted to repeal the Fugitive Slave Act of 1793, which provided for the return of runaway slaves from one state to another.

Antislavery people often aided runaways directly. Along several routes from the slave states to the North and to British North America (Canada), friends of the slaves operated the "underground railroad." They hid the fugitives by day and moved them from one "station" to another by night. The most famous "conductor" was Harriet Tubman, a former slave who made many round trips, leading about 300 slaves to freedom.

In trying to influence the federal or state governments, the antislavery societies became pressure groups. They advised their members to vote for those political candidates who were the most favorable, or the least hostile, to the cause. The women's groups were especially active at collecting petitions to Congress. Since women were not allowed to vote, the only way they could make their views felt was by petition.

Unsympathetic Reactions

In the beginning, the antislavery people faced a great deal of hostility in the North as well as in the South. They were looked upon as troublemakers.

In 1833, for example, Prudence Crandall opened the first school for black girls in the nation in Canterbury, Connecticut. The townspeople broke windows, poured filth in the well, and tried to set fire to the building. For eighteen months the teacher and her pupils were besieged. Only after a mob broke into the building did they finally give up and move away.

Antislavery speakers were often pelted with stones or rotten eggs. Sometimes they were arrested and jailed. In 1837, the enemies of Elijah Lovejoy, an antislavery editor in Alton, Illinois, shot and killed him.

As time passed, the antislavery campaign received more sympathy from the northern public, even from people who cared nothing about slaves. This change in opinion resulted, in part, from the efforts of southerners to stop the antislavery movement.

In 1835, several southern legislatures appealed to northern legislatures to suppress the "incendiary" propaganda of the abolitionists. No northern legislature complied. In 1836, however, southerners succeeded in getting the national House of Representatives to adopt a "gag rule" for tabling all antislavery petitions and thus ignoring them. John Quincy Adams, once a President, then a congressman, led the fight against the gag rule. He finally secured its repeal in 1844. Such experiences as these convinced many northerners that antislavery people were telling the truth when they said there was a great slave-power conspiracy that would deprive all Americans of the right of free speech.

FOREIGN AFFAIRS

In Jackson's and Van Buren's terms as President, foreign policy took a back seat. Domestic affairs occupied far more time. The foreign concerns were mostly devoted to the neighbors of the United States.

British North America

There generally was peace between the United States and British North America (Canada). Americans and Canadians moved freely back and forth across the border. Many Americans settled in Canada, and many Canadians settled in the United States. Nevertheless, border conflicts occasionally broke out.

In 1837, some discontented Canadians rebelled against British rule. Aided by American sympathizers, the rebels hid on Navy Island on the Canadian side of the Niagara River. A United States steamboat, the *Caroline,* ferried supplies across the river from New York State to the rebels. This aid naturally angered both the Canadian loyalists and the British authorities. One night a band of Canadian soldiers attacked the *Caroline,* killed an American crewman, wounded others, and set fire to the boat. The boat soon sank, but Americans afterwards circulated pictures that showed the vessel going over Niagara Falls in flames, with screaming men aboard.

President Van Buren called upon all Americans to obey the neutrality laws. These forbade citizens to give military assistance to the enemies of nations with which the United States was at peace. Van Buren also sent an army to police the border and to keep American troublemakers at home. The British quickly put down the revolt, and quiet gradually returned to the border.

Trouble soon flared up in the Aroostook Valley, a disputed area between Maine and New Brunswick. Both the United States and Canada had land claims there. In 1839, militiamen from Maine and New Brunswick were sent to the scene, and the United States government began preparing for war. Before anyone was killed in the so-called Aroostook War, both sides agreed to a truce. Neither side abandoned its claim, however.

Eyes on Texas

After John Quincy Adams became President in 1825, he offered to buy Texas from Mexico, which had won its independence from Spain. Mexico refused to sell. President Jackson tried again in 1829, with no more success than Adams had had.

For Mexico, the outlying district of Texas was hard to defend or to develop. Nevertheless, the Mexicans understandably wished to keep such a large and fertile piece of land. In 1821 the Mexican government had begun making large grants of Texas land to Ameri-

The Treaty of New Echota

During the 1820's and 1830's, the federal government's policy toward Indians was complex. Tribes living within the United States often had treaties that recognized their independence, but the states, non-Indian people, and the national government did not always honor the treaties. The Cherokee provide a case in point.

The Cherokee were farmers, stock breeders, and traders. In 1825, members of the Cherokee Nation owned slaves, grist mills, sawmills, schools, and thousands of head of livestock. The tribe had a constitution modeled after that of the United States; officials were popularly elected.

Cherokee prosperity aroused the envy of many people of the United States. Throughout the 1820's, the state of Georgia attempted to find ways to get the Cherokee to give up their lands. After President Andrew Jackson took office in 1829, he advised the Georgians: "Build a fire under them. When it gets hot enough, they'll move."

A federal negotiator failed to win agreement on a removal treaty with John Ross, the official Cherokee leader. He turned to a faction of the tribe, led by Major Ridge, which represented only 350 members and was not authorized by law to make treaties. The Ridge group, worn out by white harassment, believed that removal was inevitable. They felt that the tribe would win better terms if it cooperated. In 1835, the Ridge group signed the Treaty of New Echota. According to the treaty, all the Cherokees were to leave the East within two years in return for western land and 5 million dollars.

Sixteen thousand Cherokees signed a petition saying that the treaty was illegal. Many political and military leaders in the United States protested that the document was a fraud; some even resigned in protest. But the Senate ratified the treaty by a one-vote margin.

The removal began in May 1838 and continued under miserable conditions through the summer, fall, and winter. In Indian Territory in July 1839, Ridge and two other signers of the treaty were "executed" by persons unknown. They had broken a Cherokee law, proposed by Major Ridge thirty-five years before, that provided a death penalty for any tribe member who illegally ceded tribal lands.

Seventeen tribes hold a council meeting in 1843 in Tahlequah, the Cherokee capital in Oklahoma.

cans. As things turned out, the Mexican government, so far as its own interests were concerned, was making a serious mistake.

By 1835, about 35,000 Americans were living in Texas, and they dominated that part of Mexico. Almost all were Protestants; most were southerners; many were slaveholders. Some were refugees from debt or jail.

The Texans who had come from the United States had difficulty in getting along with native Mexicans. The American settlers also found themselves in disagreement with the Mexican government. It passed laws to keep out additional slaves and immigrants from the United States and to revoke certain of the land grants that had been made. When Antonio López de Santa Anna became president in 1834, he tried to centralize the government and extend his personal control throughout Mexico. The Americans in Texas began to fear that the government might take away their lands, their slaves, and their political rights. These feelings caused the settlers to revolt.

In 1836, the Texans proclaimed their independence. A provisional government was set up, and Sam Houston was named commander of the army. The Texans received supplies and enlistments from sympathizers in the United States. Santa Anna advanced with a large army to put down the revolt. At the Alamo mission in San Antonio and at Goliad, the Mexicans defeated the Texans. Then, at San Jacinto, the main Texas army met the army of Santa Anna. The Texans, led by Houston, defeated the Mexican army and captured Santa Anna. They forced him, practically at the point of a bayonet, to sign a treaty that recognized the independence of Texas. The Republic of Texas then began a career of nine years as a sovereign nation.

Annexation Hopes

The leaders of Texas had not intended for it to remain independent. Most Texans were Americans who wanted Texas to be a part of the United States. Besides, they feared attacks from Mexico and from Indian tribes, and they looked upon membership in the Union as a means of protection. The first president of the new republic, Sam Houston, promptly asked the United States government to recognize Texan independence. This, he thought, would be a step toward annexation.

President Jackson hesitated, however, to grant recognition. The antislavery people of the North opposed having diplomatic relations with a new slaveholding nation. Just before leaving the presidency, Jackson opened diplomatic relations with Texas.

The Texas government then requested annexation. Jackson's successor, President Van Buren, was left to deal with the touchy subject. Annexation was popular in the South but unpopular in much of the North. The cautious Van Buren declined the offer.

Thus rebuffed, the Texans looked abroad, to Britain and France. They did not seek annexation but sought recognition, trade treaties, financial support, and protection against Mexico. Both the British and the French wished Texas to remain independent. An independent Texas would offer profitable trade without the interference of the United States tariff. Both the British and the French recognized Texas and made trade treaties with it.

ECONOMIC POLICY

The National Republicans (and later the Whigs) disagreed with the Democrats about the proper relationship between the government and the economy. The National Republicans favored much the same policies as Alexander Hamilton or Henry Clay. They thought that the federal government should encourage economic activity through protective tariffs, a national bank, and spending for

PRESIDENTIAL ELECTIONS: 1832-1844

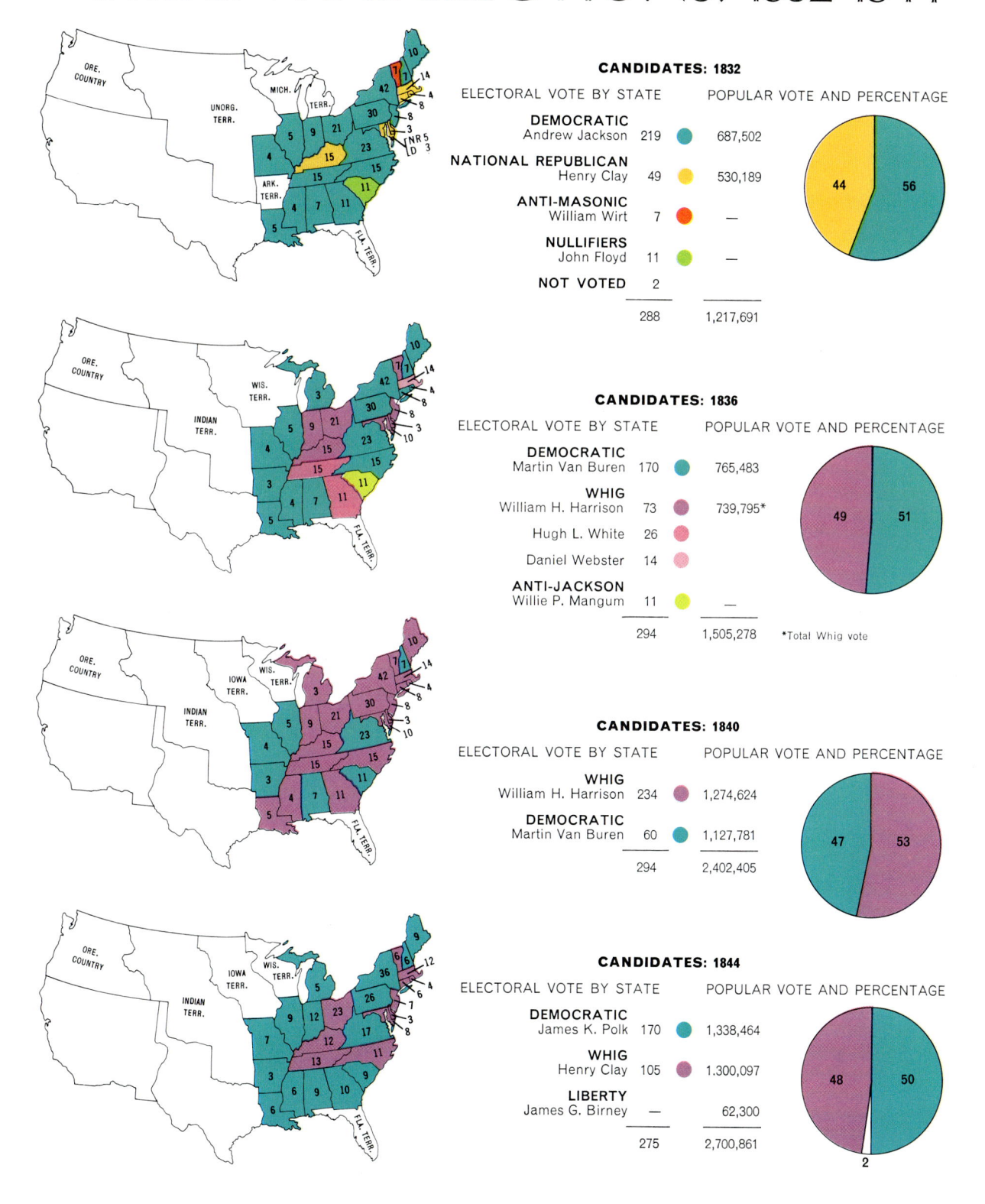

CANDIDATES: 1832

ELECTORAL VOTE BY STATE | POPULAR VOTE AND PERCENTAGE

DEMOCRATIC
Andrew Jackson   219   687,502

NATIONAL REPUBLICAN
Henry Clay   49   530,189

ANTI-MASONIC
William Wirt   7   —

NULLIFIERS
John Floyd   11   —

NOT VOTED   2

288   1,217,691

Pie chart: 44 / 56

CANDIDATES: 1836

ELECTORAL VOTE BY STATE | POPULAR VOTE AND PERCENTAGE

DEMOCRATIC
Martin Van Buren   170   765,483

WHIG
William H. Harrison   73   739,795*

Hugh L. White   26

Daniel Webster   14

ANTI-JACKSON
Willie P. Mangum   11   —

294   1,505,278   *Total Whig vote

Pie chart: 49 / 51

CANDIDATES: 1840

ELECTORAL VOTE BY STATE | POPULAR VOTE AND PERCENTAGE

WHIG
William H. Harrison   234   1,274,624

DEMOCRATIC
Martin Van Buren   60   1,127,781

294   2,402,405

Pie chart: 47 / 53

CANDIDATES: 1844

ELECTORAL VOTE BY STATE | POPULAR VOTE AND PERCENTAGE

DEMOCRATIC
James K. Polk   170   1,338,464

WHIG
Henry Clay   105   1,300,097

LIBERTY
James G. Birney   —   62,300

275   2,700,861

Pie chart: 48 / 50 / 2

transportation improvements.

The Democrats believed that such policies would help bankers, manufacturers, and some merchants but would hurt other merchants and nearly all farmers and planters. The Democrats wanted the government to stay out of economic affairs. They believed that the federal government should allow opportunity for all but should give favors to none. In open competition, they thought, individuals and companies would get ahead according to their own abilities.

The Bank War

The second Bank of the United States, chartered in 1816, served several important purposes. It handled the government's funds, made loans to businesses, and issued bank notes that were dependable currency.

Jackson and his followers disliked the Bank. They looked upon it as a dangerous monopoly, for it had an exclusive right to the federal government's banking business. Some also objected to it because they thought that only gold and silver coin should be used as money. Still others thought there should be even more paper money in circulation. These "soft money" people favored the banks chartered by the state governments. The Bank of the United States indirectly prevented these state banks from issuing notes as freely as they would have liked.

The Bank's charter was to expire in 1836. Fearing Jackson's opposition, the president of the Bank, Nicholas Biddle, made loans to some politicians and newspapermen in order to win their support. Henry Clay, a friend of Biddle's, suggested that it would be easier to get the Bank rechartered in 1832 than later on. Biddle applied for a new charter.

Congress passed a recharter bill in 1832, but President Jackson vetoed it. In the election that year, Clay ran against Jackson as a friend of the Bank. Both he and William Wirt, the Anti-Masonic candidate, were badly defeated. The Bank proved to be much less popular than Clay had realized.

Jackson now tried to weaken the Bank. He ordered the secretary of the treasury to stop depositing the government's money in it and to put the money in state banks instead. When the secretary refused because it would be against the law, Jackson appointed a new secretary. When this one also hesitated, Jackson appointed still another, who began to put the money in what Jackson's opponents called the administration's "pet banks."

Biddle responded by raising the Bank's interest rates and calling in some of its loans to businesses. He said he had to do this because the government had taken away so much of the Bank's deposits. Some companies were forced to close down. Many workers lost their jobs, especially in the Northeast.

Biddle blamed Jackson for the trouble. The Jacksonians blamed Biddle, saying he had deliberately brought on the "Biddle panic" in order to end the anti-Bank policy. If that was Biddle's aim, he failed. The government deposits were not restored to the Bank, and it ceased to exist in 1836.

The state banks began to issue loans and bank notes more freely than they had for many years. Prices rose and business boomed. Suddenly, in 1837, banks and businesses began to fail, and unemployment rapidly increased. This was much worse than the brief Biddle panic. It was the beginning of the worst depression the country had yet faced.

The Modern Business Cycle

Before the nineteenth century, hard times were generally due to wars, plagues, bad harvests, or other disasters. The troubles were usually limited to one region at a time, and they came and went irregularly.

During the nineteenth century, however, the periods of depression changed. The new

Detail from *Girls' Evening School*, M. and M. Karolik Collection, Museum of Fine Arts, Boston

depressions were periods of surpluses rather than of shortages. These depressions spread rapidly from one part of the nation to another and from one part of the world to another. They soon became general rather than local, and they followed a cycle.

The nineteenth-century business cycle had a typical pattern: panic, depression, recovery, and prosperity. The *panic* started with people rushing to the banks and trying to convert their bank notes into cash. Many banks closed down. Prices began to fall. With more goods on hand than they could profitably sell, many factories cut production or went out of business. Many workers lost their jobs. Prices of crops fell, and many farmers and planters found themselves unable to pay their debts. Mortgages were foreclosed. Soon the country was in the depths of a *depression*. After three or four

In the 1830's, many people were optimistic about the changes taking place in American society and technology. Many wanted to expand educational opportunity for both children and adults. *Above:* Women attend an evening school. The labor-saving "apparatus" *(below)* is an example of the new technology and "Yankee ingenuity" taken to extremes.

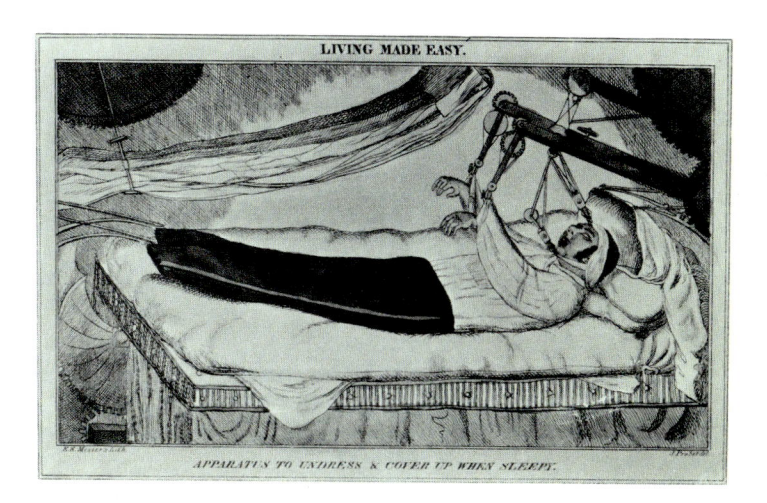

years, *recovery* began, and eventually the country enjoyed *prosperity* once more. During the nineteenth century, there was a panic leading to a depression about every twenty years—the first in 1819 and the second in 1837.

This business cycle resulted from the economic developments of the time. People were now producing for sale to others at a distance as well as for their own use. It was hard to predict how much could be profitably sold, and the tendency was to produce too much. Within the factory system, a longer time elapsed between the start of production and the final selling of the finished product. This made it still more difficult to match productivity to demand.

Organizing Corporations

Although the nation needed more and better money as a medium of exchange, it also needed money, or capital, for productive purposes. Much of the money backing transportation improvements came from the federal and state governments. Capital to set up the first factories came from merchants who had already collected profits in shipping and commerce. A large portion of the money for buying and developing farmland came from the farmers and planters, from individual savings, and from bank loans.

People who were looking for an easier way to raise capital became increasingly interested in the business *corporation*—a group of persons authorized by law to carry on a business together. At first, organizers of a company had had to get a special act from a state legislature in order to incorporate. Starting in 1837, the states passed general incorporation laws. These made it possible for a company to obtain a corporate charter merely by meeting the legal requirements.

The corporation had great advantages over individual firms or partnerships: It could raise money by selling shares of stock, and its life did not depend on one or two individuals. It could also borrow money by selling bonds.

The earliest corporations were set up for banking, insurance, and the construction and operation of toll bridges and turnpikes. Later, many companies were incorporated for railroad and manufacturing enterprises.

As more corporations appeared, regular markets developed for the purchase and sale of stocks and bonds. The largest by far of these marketplaces was in New York.

European investors furnished much of the capital for the early corporate growth in the United States. Even though governments, banks, and individuals provided large amounts of money, the financing of new enterprises remained difficult.

The Taney Court

While he was President, Jackson appointed seven new members to the Supreme Court, out of a total of nine. One of them was Roger B. Taney, who became chief justice upon the death of John Marshall.

There was no sharp break in constitutional interpretation between the Marshall court and the Taney court. There was, however, a change in emphasis. The new judicial spirit was seen in the case of *Charles River Bridge* v. *Warren Bridge* (1837).

The facts were these: Years earlier the Massachusetts legislature had given a company the right to build and operate a toll bridge across the Charles River. Later, the legislature authorized another company to build a free bridge. The first company brought suit to prevent the building of a new bridge, claiming it would deprive the company of its profits.

The constitutional question was the same as in the Dartmouth College case (1819). Could a state violate the terms of a charter it had granted to a private corporation? In the Dartmouth College case, Marshall had said no. In the Charles River Bridge case, how-

BUSINESS ACTIVITY 1800-1850

The chart of business activity in the United States *(below)* is based on major factors affecting the economy between 1800 and 1850. Those factors were commodity prices, imports, exports, government receipts and expenditures, shipbuilding, coal production, and iron exports. The green areas indicate periods of prosperity; the red areas indicate depression. Note that as the business cycle recurs, it varies in length and intensity. The detail of the chart *(right)* shows the four stages in the modern business cycle. The panic of 1819 began after a decline in foreign demand for American foodstuffs.

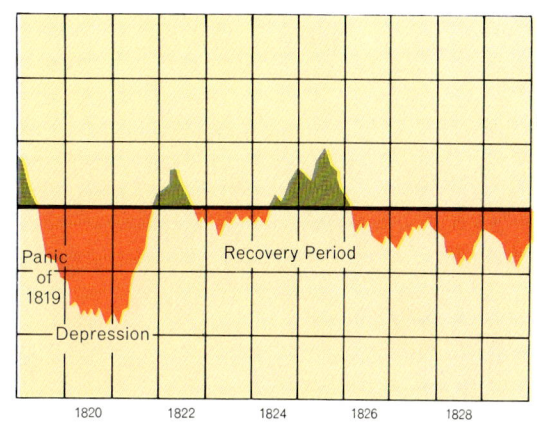

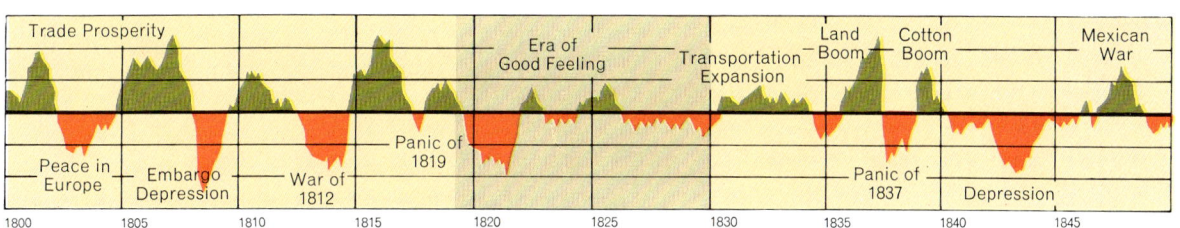

ever, Taney said yes. Taney held that the new bridge would aid transportation and commerce and would promote the general welfare. This, he said, was more important than the protection of property rights. This decision supported the Jacksonian principle that competition ought to be encouraged.

The Election of 1840

To most voters, the Whigs seemed to be the party of the rich and the Democrats the party of the common man. The Whig leaders began to realize that they could never elect a President until they changed the image of their party. They did so in 1840.

That year the Whigs nominated William Henry Harrison for the presidency. He was the victor of the Battle of Tippecanoe (1811). For the vice-presidency they nominated John Tyler, a Virginia Democrat who had turned against Jackson and was expected to attract the votes of some of Jackson's former followers. The Democrats renominated Van Buren.

In the campaign the Whigs turned the tables on the Democrats. The Whigs claimed that *they* were the friends and the Democrats were the enemies of the common man. A Democratic newspaper editor remarked that Harrison was a simple soul who would be happy just to live in a log cabin and guzzle hard cider. Immediately the Whigs took up the log cabin and the cider jug as symbols of their campaign. They said their candidate was indeed an unpretentious old soldier, a frontier fighter, a common man. They pictured Van Buren, on the other hand, as a snobbish easterner who lived in a mansion and ate with gold-plated spoons.

The Whigs in 1840 set a new pattern for political campaigns. Harrison was the first candidate to go out and make stump speeches for himself. Although electioneering by a presidential candidate did not become the accepted practice until after the Civil War, other Whig innovations were promptly adopted—huge mass meetings, parades of shouting marchers, campaign buttons and badges, campaign slogans and songs. The singing Whigs not only carried the election of 1840 but also stimulated more people to vote than ever before.

A Look at Specifics

1. Why did political parties become more organized as political activity in the states grew more democratic?

2. What reasons did members of the Democratic party offer for giving government jobs to party members?

3. Why was the Anti-Masonic party organized? What contribution did it make to American politics?

4. In what respect did President Jackson prove to be an advocate of nationalism? Of states' rights?

5. Why did Calhoun believe that a state could legally and constitutionally secede from the Union?

6. What were the goals of the American Colonization Society? Why were they generally opposed by black Americans?

7. What part did blacks play in the antislavery movement?

8. How did the "gag rule" influence northern opinion?

9. Why did Britain and France wish Texas to remain an independent republic?

10. What did the Whigs feel should be the proper relationship between the government and the economy? What did the Democrats believe it should be?

11. How did Biddle retaliate against Jackson's refusal to renew the charter of the second Bank? With what results?

12. What advantages did the corporation have over individual firms and partnerships?

13. What innovations did the Whigs make in the conduct of political campaigns?

A Review of Major Ideas

1. In what ways were state constitutions made more democratic?

2. What did political parties contribute toward making politics more democratic?

3. What were the causes of the nullification crisis in 1832?

4. What factors contributed to the growth of the Northwest into a section of small farms?

5. What changes took place in southern agriculture?

6. How did the growth of specialization and the widening of markets contribute to the ups and downs of the business cycle?

7. What measures did the Jacksonians take to promote economic opportunity?

For Independent Study

1. Calhoun believed that his nullification theory was based upon the same principles as the Kentucky and Virginia Resolutions (1798–1799) of Jefferson and Madison. Do you think Calhoun was justified in holding this position? Support your view.

2. How do you explain the fact that the spread of cotton cultivation in the South was not accompanied by a corresponding development of a southern textile industry?

3. Explain the paradox that overproduction often causes many people to suffer from poverty and hunger.

4. Reform agitation often has unintended effects. The antislavery crusade, for example, increased the sectionalism that eventually helped bring war. Discuss unintended effects arising from the following reforms: the failure to recharter the second Bank, the system of rotation in office, the lowering of property qualifications for voting.

Manifest Destiny

CHAPTER 8
1841–1850

Imperialism is often defined as the "policy of extending the rule or authority of one country over other countries and colonies." In 1845 the editor of a New York newspaper wrote that it is "our manifest destiny to overspread and to possess the whole of the continent which Providence has given us." Politicians soon picked up the phrase "manifest destiny" and used it to justify the expansion of the United States. The nation did not extend its boundaries to the equator and the North Pole, as some expansionists urged. But it did extend its control all the way to the Pacific. As you read this chapter, ask yourself: Was Manifest Destiny simply imperialism by another name?

SETTLING OLD BUSINESS

By the beginning of 1842, it seemed that a third war with Britain might begin soon. To the ill feeling resulting from the *Caroline* affair and the Aroostook War, another cause had been added. This was the *Creole* case (1841). On the *Creole,* an American slave ship, the blacks had mutinied, taken charge of the ship, and brought it into a British port in the Bahamas. There the slaves were set free by the British authorities. Just as northerners remembered the *Caroline,* so southerners remembered the *Creole* as a grievance against Britain.

There were, however, forces making for peace as well as for war. Britain was the best customer of the United States, buying much of the American wheat crop and most of the cotton crop. Likewise, the United States was Britain's best customer. Since the United States had not yet fully recovered from the Panic of 1837, any interruption of trade would delay the return of prosperity.

Government leaders in both countries were eager to settle their differences. Luckily the American secretary of state, Daniel Webster, admired the English, and they admired

A group of Mormons pauses on the way west.

him. The British government sent Lord Ashburton, who liked the United States, to negotiate with Webster.

Webster felt that the only way to settle the dispute concerning the northeastern boundary was to divide the disputed area. First, he had to get the consent of Maine and Massachusetts. He did so by means of his "red-line map." This was supposed to be a copy of the map that the peacemakers had used at Paris in 1783. It was marked with a red line, and this line upheld the British claim. Webster secretly showed the map to commissioners representing Maine and Massachusetts. They decided they had better give up part of the disputed land rather than risk losing all of it.

Webster-Ashburton Treaty

Webster now entered into conversations with Lord Ashburton, and, in 1842, the two drew up a treaty. It split the disputed area and awarded seven-twelfths of it to the United States. The Maine-New Brunswick boundary was set, and other provisions adjusted the boundary at the north of Vermont and New York and between Lake Superior and the Lake of the Woods. The British also gave up disputed territory at the head of the Connecticut River in New Hampshire. Nothing was said about the *Caroline* or the *Creole* in the treaty itself, but Lord Ashburton apologized for those incidents.

Democratic leaders, more anti-British than the Whigs, objected to the "sacrifice" of United States territory. Using secret funds of the state department, Webster paid newspapers to publish propaganda favorable to the treaty. The agreement was promptly ratified and proved quite popular.

On the whole, the Webster-Ashburton Treaty was a fair bargain. Though the United States lost some land on the northeast, it gained land elsewhere as a result of the other boundary adjustments. (Historians later discovered that Webster's red-line map had been wrong and that the true map, of which the British had a copy, really favored the American claim.) The area gained at the north of Vermont and New York was strategically important. The area gained at the west of Lake Superior contained rich deposits of iron ore, discovered many years later. More important at the time, the treaty assured peace. For the moment, in 1842, Anglo-American relations were better than they had been for years.

Texas Annexation

By 1844, the Lone Star Republic seemed about to become a British dependency. This possibility worried some prominent Americans. The Texans were told unofficially that the United States would welcome them if they would again ask for annexation. They submitted their request.

President Harrison had died one month after his inauguration. His Vice-President, John Tyler, had succeeded to the office of President, and he hoped to have the glory of annexing Texas before he left office. He saw that a treaty of annexation was quickly drawn up. Before the Senate had acted on it, however, John C. Calhoun became secretary of state, and he did something that ruined all chances for the treaty to pass the Senate. Calhoun wrote a letter accusing the British government of planning to abolish slavery in Texas. At great length he defended the institution of slavery as a good way of life for both slave and slaveholder. He said the institution would be endangered in the southern states if it should be abolished in Texas. Therefore, he argued, annexation was necessary as a means of protecting slavery.

Calhoun's letter aroused strong feelings among many northerners. They thought it proved that the abolitionists were right in saying that annexation was really a pro-slavery plot. The treaty did not obtain the necessary two-thirds majority in the Senate. Thus, in 1844, annexation failed again.

The Admission of Texas

Expansionism was the main issue in the presidential election of 1844. The Whig candidate was Henry Clay. The Whig platform made no mention of Texas, and Clay did not take a clear stand on the issue. He hoped to get votes from both annexationists and their opponents.

Van Buren had expected the Democratic nomination, but he ruined his chances by stating that Texas should not be annexed without the consent of Mexico. The Democrats instead nominated an unexpected candidate, the first such "dark horse." This was James K. Polk, the former Speaker of the House. He was a determined annexationist.

The Democratic platform called for "the re-occupation of Oregon and the re-annexation of Texas." By coupling Oregon with Texas, the Democrats hoped to appeal to northerners as well as to southerners. Using the terms "*re*-occupation" and "*re*-annexation" they tried to give the impression that Oregon and Texas had formerly belonged to the United States.

The Democratic campaign plan proved effective, for Polk defeated Clay. Despite a narrow victory, the Democrats claimed that they had a mandate from the people in favor of expansion.

President-elect Polk, however, would not take office for another four months. The Democrats did not want to wait that long to annex Texas, for the British were offering Texas a treaty guaranteeing independence. Though the Democrats did not have a two-thirds majority in the Senate, they had a simple majority in both houses of Congress. They could not get an annexation treaty ratified, but they could pass a joint resolution providing for annexation. This they did. On March 1, 1845, three days before he was to leave office, President Tyler signed the resolution into law.

Now the Texans had to act. They had a choice between the American offer of annexation and a British guarantee of independence. That summer they elected delegates to a special convention to consider the matter. The delegates voted overwhelmingly to add the Lone Star to the Stars and Stripes. In December 1845, Texas was admitted as a slaveholding state.

THE OREGON COUNTRY

The Oregon country extended from the Rocky Mountains to the Pacific Ocean and from the 42nd parallel northward to the latitude of 54°40' (the southern boundary of Russian America). At one time, four nations had claimed the territory. Now only the United States and Britain still had claims.

Neither the United States nor Britain really had a clear title to all of the Oregon country. The United States based its claim largely on exploration. Captain Robert Gray, an American, had sailed into a great river in 1792 and explored part of it. He named it after his ship, the *Columbia*. Lewis and Clark had later explored part of the same river. American fur traders and trappers had penetrated the region. But British explorers also had roamed through the Oregon country. A huge British monopoly, the Hudson's Bay Company, had come to control the fur trade there.

An arrangement of 1818, providing for joint occupation by the Americans and the British, had been intended to run for only ten years. In 1827, since the two governments still could not agree on a division of the territory, joint occupation was renewed for an indefinite period.

Oregon Fever

By the 1830's, a few Americans were in the Oregon country as traders and trappers or as missionaries to the Indians. A few others were beginning to arrive as settlers by way of the Oregon Trail. This route started at Independence, Missouri, and led two thousand miles across the Great Plains and the Rocky Mountains to Astoria, at the mouth of the Columbia River. The emigrants took several months to make the journey—if they succeeded in making it at all. Many died along the way from hunger, thirst, illness, or Indian attacks.

By 1841, there were five hundred Americans in the Oregon country. Year by year the numbers continued to grow. In 1845, an Independence newspaper editor described how the streets of that town were filled with "long trains of wagons" as travelers assembled to go west. The editor cheered them on:

TOTAL POPULATION GROWTH, 1790–1850

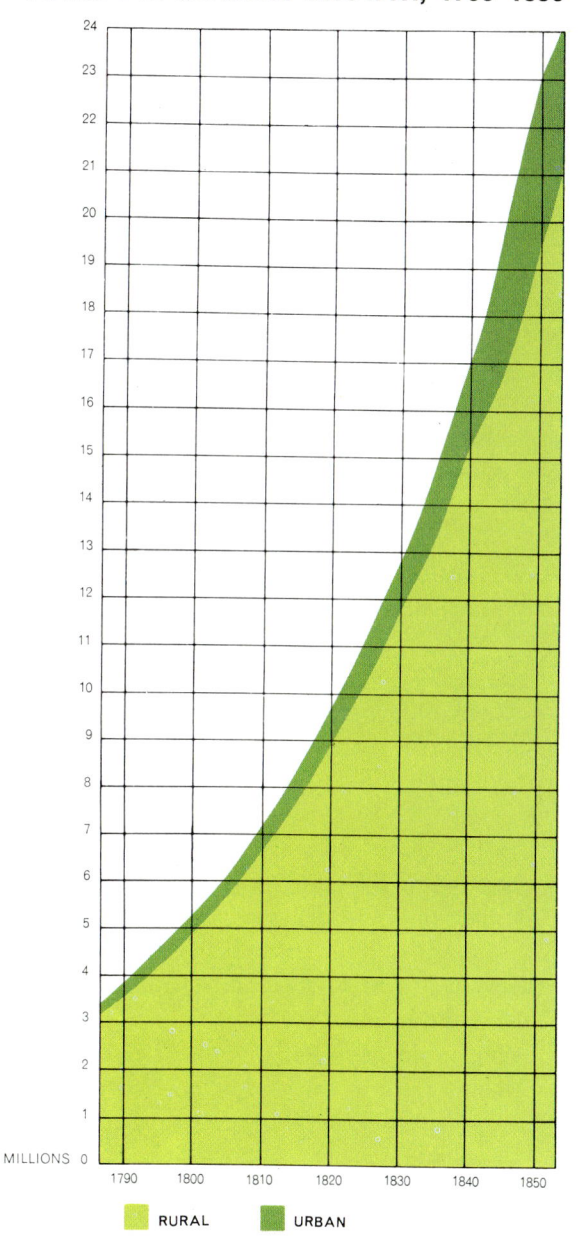

RURAL · URBAN

"Whoo ha! Go it boys! We're in a perfect *Oregon fever.*" Some three thousand people made the overland crossing that year.

A few were attracted to Oregon by the prospects of the fur trade or by the hope of converting Indians to Christianity. But most were drawn by news of the rich soil of the Willamette Valley, and they went as farmers. Other people were excited by reports of mar-

Many factors contributed to the increase in population between 1790 and 1850. The number of births continued high, and life expectancy increased as medical practices improved. Immigrants like those arriving in New York *(above left)* swelled the population in the 1830's and 1840's. The United States was becoming more cosmopolitan as immigration and trade involved all corners of the globe.

velous harbors on the Pacific coast. These harbors seemed important, both as ports for merchant ships and as naval bases.

Demands for Oregon

As the American population in the Oregon country increased, joint occupation became more and more unpopular. Expansionists demanded that the United States occupy all of the Oregon country, by force if need be.

The Democratic party took up this demand. In its platform of 1844, it claimed that the American title was "clear and unquestionable" and that "no portion" of the Oregon country "ought to be ceded to England or any other power."

In his first annual message to Congress, President Polk asked for authority to end the joint-occupation agreement and to extend the protection of federal laws over Americans in Oregon. When one congressman told the President that his policy might lead to war with Britain, Polk replied that "the only way to treat John Bull is to look him straight in the eye."

Most of the Whigs, in Congress and throughout the nation, did not think the American title was clear and unquestionable. Nor did they think that all of the Oregon country up to 54°40′, or any part of it, was worth fighting for.

Whig businessmen of the Northeast were interested only in the harbor possibilities of Puget Sound. These lay far to the south of 54°40′. Democratic farmers and planters in the South were more interested in Texas than in the Oregon country.

During the winter of 1845/46, Congress debated the Oregon question. Again, a third war with Britain seemed likely unless some compromise could be reached.

A Compromise

President Polk had spoken out for all of the Oregon country because his party had demanded it. Also, he wished to increase the nation's diplomatic bargaining power. But Polk did not really think the United States had a good claim to all of it, nor did he want a war with Britain. While publicly stating that the United States title was "clear and unquestionable," he privately offered to divide the territory at the 49th parallel.

Since 1818, in discussions between United States and British diplomats, the Americans had never seriously claimed anything north of 49°. The British had never insisted on anything south of the Columbia River. The United States wanted the line at 49° because it would give the nation access to Puget Sound. There were, in 1845, no settlers from the United States north of that line. To British diplomats the Columbia River seemed indispensable because the Hudson's Bay Company used it in the fur trade. The company carried on little or no activity, however, south of the river. Thus, the dispute really concerned only the area between the Columbia River and the 49th parallel.

When Polk first suggested a division of the territory, the British minister turned down the proposal without even referring it to his home government. Then Congress granted Polk authorization he had asked for. Polk notified the British government that in a year the United States would consider the joint-occupation agreement ended. At the same time, however, he expressed hope that this would lead to a friendly settlement.

A change in the British government and a change in the fur trade made such a settlement possible. In Britain the Whig party had come into power in 1845. The new British foreign secretary, Lord Aberdeen, believed that peace with the United States was worth more than the disputed portion of the Oregon country.

Already the fur trade was beginning to decline, partly because men were ceasing to wear beaver hats. As beaver pelts became

Many Indian trappers supplied fur traders *(above)* with animal pelts. Trappers and traders led rough, isolated lives. By the time the trade declined, it had stimulated foreign trade, displaced many Indians, and nearly exhausted a natural resource.

less salable, as beaver became scarcer, and as the danger of trouble with the Americans increased, the Hudson's Bay Company began withdrawing to the north. In 1845, it moved its headquarters to Vancouver Island.

In 1846, Lord Aberdeen sent President Polk the draft of a treaty placing the boundary at the 49th parallel from the Rockies to Puget Sound but leaving Vancouver Island to Britain. Polk, taking the advice of the Senate, accepted the treaty. Many in his own political party denounced him for the "surrender" of land they said rightfully belonged to the United States. In Britain many people accused their government of sacrificing British rights. Actually, both governments had finally arrived at a sound solution to a troublesome problem.

THE MEXICAN WAR

With the Oregon agreement, the United States avoided a war with Britain. By this time, however, the United States was at war with another nation—Mexico. The Mexican War (1846–1848) resulted from three subjects of dispute.

One dispute concerned Texas. The Mexican government refused to recognize Texas as independent. After the Battle of San Jacinto, Santa Anna had signed a treaty granting independence. The Mexican government denounced the treaty as illegal, because Santa Anna had been forced to sign it and the Mexican Congress had refused to approve it. When Texas joined the Union, Mexico broke off diplomatic relations with the United States.

In taking over Texas, the United States inherited a boundary dispute. Texas, according to the Mexican view, extended no farther to the southwest than the Nueces River. According to the Texan view, the state reached all the way to the Rio Grande and was almost twice as large as the Mexicans said. The United States government supported the Texans in their interpretation of the boundary with Mexico.

A second source of trouble between the two nations was a large debt owed by the Mexican government to United States citizens. Some Americans had provided loans or supplies to the Mexicans during their fight for independence from Spain in 1821. The Americans had never been repaid. Other Americans had lost property in Mexico as a result of revolutionary disorders following independence. All together, the Americans claimed that Mexico owed them about 5 million dollars. The Mexican government had acknowledged about 2 million dollars of the debt. It had promised to pay the debt over a period of twenty years but, since it was nearly bankrupt, had stopped paying.

A third cause of difficulty with Mexico was the desire of American expansionists for additional Mexican territory, especially California. War with Mexico might have been avoided if there had existed only the quarrels over Texas and over the money claims. War became inevitable, however, when President Polk tried to force the Mexican government to sell lands it did not want to give up.

The Lure of the West

To the west and northwest of Texas lay the Mexican provinces of New Mexico (much larger than the present state of New Mexico) and California. Both New Mexico and California were thinly settled by Mexicans and loosely held. Most of the people in these provinces were Indians. At one time as many as one-sixth of all the Indians in North America had lived in California. Few Indians lived in the Mexican settlements there.

The first Americans to visit California had arrived by sea. Even before 1800, New England shippers stopped along the coast to get sea otter pelts for the China trade. Later, Yankee whalers and, more important, buyers of cowhides and tallow visited California. Some remained to marry Mexican women and settle down as ranchers or merchants. Those who returned brought back reports of the fertile valleys, the pleasant climate, and the magnificent San Francisco Bay.

The first Americans to reach California overland were fur trappers and traders. One of these "mountain men," Jedediah S. Smith, arrived as early as 1826. In 1841 and after, landseekers began to turn off from the Oregon Trail and head southwest for California. The journey over the high Sierra was even more hazardous than the route to Oregon. By 1845, there were seven hundred of the newcomers in California. They had settled in the Sacramento Valley, and they did not get along with the native Californians as well as the earlier arrivals by sea had.

American interest in New Mexico arose from the Santa Fe trade, beginning in 1821. Year after year, traders gathered at Independence, Missouri, for the summer trip across the plains and back. The long wagon train carried manufactured goods to Santa Fe. It brought back gold, silver, furs, and mules. Except for a few traders who remained in Santa Fe, this "commerce of the prairies" did not lead to American settlement in New Mexico. But it called to the attention of expansionists another direction in which the United States might expand.

The first Americans to settle in New Mexico in considerable numbers were the Mormons, who began to arrive in 1846, after the Mexican War had started. They settled far to the northwest of Santa Fe, in the vicinity of the Great Salt Lake.

The Mormons belonged to the Church of Jesus Christ of Latter-day Saints, which had been founded by Joseph Smith in 1830 in New York State. The Mormons formed a closely knit community. From the beginning they faced the hostility of jealous and suspicious neighbors. Seeking a place of refuge, Smith had led his followers to Ohio, to Missouri, and then to Illinois. There he began to exert influence in state politics through his control of Mormon votes. In 1844 he was shot and killed by a member of an anti-Mormon mob.

Brigham Young then became the Mormon leader. He decided to start a new community outside the United States. He founded Deseret, as he called it, in the Salt Lake area of the Mexican territory. Thousands of Mormons crossed the plains and began to irrigate and cultivate the desert. They also started to sell supplies to non-Mormon emigrants going to the Oregon country or California.

Attempts to Get California

Some Americans assumed that the Mexican government would be glad to sell Cali-

Californians entertain guests *(above)*. After Mexico rebelled against Spain, huge land grants in California were given to the *Californios,* the Mexican settlers there. They continued the hide and tallow trade begun in the mission days. Mormons pulling handcarts *(below)* begin the journey to Great Salt Lake. Many people died walking the 1,000 miles from Illinois to Utah.

fornia. The native Californians, who were Mexicans, felt little loyalty toward the Mexican government. They frequently disobeyed and resisted the officials who were sent to rule them. It seemed that if Mexico should refuse to sell California, the Californians would eventually declare independence. Then Mexico would lose the territory without getting anything for it. Nevertheless, Mexico refused to sell California.

President Jackson, and later President Tyler, tried to buy the San Francisco Bay area, without success. President Polk was even more determined than they had been to acquire California, or at least a part of it. Polk justified his aim on the basis of Monroe's policy of 1823. Polk warned that if the United States failed to obtain California, the territory might fall under the control or even the ownership of Britain. Thus a European power would extend its influence, if not also its colonial possessions, in the American hemisphere.

Polk sent John Slidell to Mexico as the minister from the United States. Slidell took with him a price list for Mexican territory. If Mexico would agree to the Rio Grande as the Texas boundary, the United States would pay off its citizens who had claims against Mexico. For New Mexico, Slidell was to offer 5 million dollars, and for California, 25 million dollars more.

While thus trying to begin negotiations, Polk backed up his diplomacy with threats of military force. He ordered an army under General Zachary Taylor into the disputed area between the Nueces River and the Rio Grande. Polk sent warships to the Gulf coast of Mexico. He sent other warships to join the Pacific squadron, which had orders to seize San Francisco in case of war. Polk told a secret agent living in Monterey to encourage the Californians to separate from Mexico and join the United States. And he dispatched an explorer, Captain John C. Frémont, with a band of soldiers on a mysterious mission to northern California.

Santa Anna had been exiled from Mexico and was living in Cuba. A friend of his told Polk that Santa Anna was planning to return to Mexico and recover control of the government. Once back in power, the friend said, Santa Anna would gladly sell Polk at least a part of New Mexico and California. but no Mexican president would dare to sell the land unless it appeared to the Mexican people that he was forced to do so.

When Polk learned that the Mexican government had refused to deal with Slidell, he decided to use force. He prepared a message calling upon Congress for a declaration of war. Before he had delivered the message, news came that Mexican soldiers had crossed the Rio Grande into disputed territory and attacked Taylor's army, killing some Americans. Polk now revised his war message to say that Mexico had "invaded our territory and shed American blood upon the American soil." After receiving the message, Congress promptly declared war on Mexico on May 12, 1846.

Fighting the War

Polk did not expect a long or hard war. He thought the Mexicans had no chance to win and that they would be willing to make peace on his terms once they realized their weaknesses. Actually, the Mexican leaders were confident of victory. Their regular army was four times as large (32,000 soldiers) as the American army (8,000), and they expected aid from Britain and France.

This aid did not materialize. Moreover, with Americans volunteering by the thousands, the army of the United States rapidly grew to more than 100,000. The United States had a strong navy, and Mexico practically no navy at all. The United States had much greater industrial production. Also, Mexico was still being wracked by revolutions and had a very unstable government. Even so, the Mexican War proved to be a more difficult undertaking than Polk had thought.

Polk ordered General Taylor to cross the Rio Grande and invade Mexico from the northeast. After a hard battle, Taylor's troops took the city of Monterrey in September 1846. Between Monterrey and Mexico City, the capital, lay rough, mountainous land. Taylor knew that he would have trouble keeping up his supply lines if he were to try to move on southward. He instead settled down with his army to occupy northeastern Mexico.

Meanwhile, Polk dispatched a small army under Colonel Stephen Kearny to New Mexico and California. Kearny marched to Santa Fe and occupied the town. Then, with part of his force, he went to California. In California a revolt was already under way, resisted by the Mexicans there. With the aid of Frémont and his troops, American settlers had proclaimed independence from Mexico. Soldiers had landed from American ships, and they were carrying on a separate campaign. The situation was confused when Kearny arrived, but he took command of all the American forces. By the beginning of 1847, he had conquered California. He then attacked the Navaho and Pueblo tribes in New Mexico in order to assure control there.

Thus, after six months of fighting, the United States held California, New Mexico, and the northeastern part of Mexico. Yet the Mexican government refused to give up. Even after Santa Anna returned and resumed power, Mexico continued to resist.

Polk decided to carry the war to the heart of Mexico. With the general in chief of the army, Winfield Scott, he worked out a plan for taking the capital. The navy landed Scott's army at Veracruz, which it captured after a siege. Then the army advanced inland toward Mexico City, forcing the Mexicans to retreat. When, under Santa Anna, the Mexicans made a stand at Cerro Gordo, Scott once more pushed them back. They faced him in battle again just outside the capital. He forced his way into the city, capturing the fortress of Chapultepec on September 14, 1847. The fighting now was over, but peace was yet to come.

Making a Treaty

From the beginning, the Mexican War was controversial. Many Americans started demanding peace the same day that war was declared. The Whigs, though most of them in Congress had voted for the war declaration, called it a war of aggression. They said that Polk had brought on the war by sending Taylor's army across the Nueces River into territory that really belonged to Mexico. Many of them voted against the appropriations bills to carry on the war.

Antislavery people insisted that Polk was trying to get Mexican land in order to create new slave states. They and other opponents of the war supported the Wilmot Proviso, an amendment to Polk's peace bill that was introduced by David Wilmot of Pennsylvania. The amendment said that slavery must be excluded from any lands acquired from Mexico. The Proviso passed the House of Representatives but was voted down in the Senate.

Some of the Whigs, including Daniel Webster, opposed the acquisition of any Mexican territory. But many other Americans proposed that, when peace was finally made, the United States should take not only California and New Mexico but *all of Mexico*.

As Americans disagreed more and more—for permitting slavery or prohibiting it, for taking all of Mexico or none of it—Polk became more and more embarrassed. He himself wished to acquire California (including Lower California), New Mexico, and the Rio Grande boundary for Texas. He feared that Congress might never agree on

The Mexican War, 1846–1848

July 7, 1846–January 10, 1847 The campaign in California. The United States fleet (Commodore John D. Sloat) sailed from Mazatlán, Mexico, and took Monterey, California (July 7, 1846). Meanwhile, troops (Colonel Stephen Kearny) from Fort Leavenworth headed for California. They occupied Santa Fe (Aug. 18), set up a temporary government there, and moved on. They occupied San Diego Dec. 12. The fighting ended after the combined forces of the army (Kearny and Captain John C. Frémont) and navy (Commodore Robert Stockton, who had replaced Sloat) took Los Angeles (Jan. 10).

September 24, 1846–March 1, 1847 The campaign in northern Mexico. After some early skirmishing, the United States troops (General Zachary Taylor) attacked and captured Monterrey (Sept. 24). From Monterrey, the United States forces went to Saltillo, which they occupied (Nov. 13). Meanwhile, troops from San Antonio (General John Wool) had been sent to take Chihuahua. They won a battle at Monclova (Oct. 29) and then occupied Parras (Dec. 5). They joined Taylor's troops at Saltillo (Dec. 21). The combined forces captured Buena Vista (Feb. 27). Other United States troops (Colonel Alexander Doniphan) defeated the Mexicans at El Brazito (Dec. 25), El Paso (Dec. 27), and Sacramento (Feb. 28). Doniphan occupied Chihuahua (March 1).

March 9–September 14, 1847 Invasion of Mexico City. The deciding campaign of the war began with the landing of United States troops (General Winfield Scott) at Veracruz (March 9) and the capitulation of that city (March 27). United States forces routed the Mexicans at Cerro Gordo (April 18) and at Contreras (Aug. 19–20). The United States suffered heavy casualties at Churubusco (Aug. 20), but the Mexicans were forced to withdraw to Mexico City. The next United States move was aimed at Chapultepec. After a heavy bombardment and an assault, the Mexican defenders

were finally overcome (Sept. 14). United States forces entered Mexico City and occupied it. After several more days of fighting, the shooting war was finally over. The Treaty of Guadalupe Hidalgo (Feb. 2, 1848) formally ended the war.

The Capture of Mexico City by United States troops on September 14, 1847, marked the end of fighting in the Mexican War. *Above:* The Mexican army *(right foreground)* surrenders near the Cathedral of Mexico, while General Winfield Scott's men raise the United States flag over the Mexican National Palace. The Mexican cession *(right)* was later made into the states of California, Nevada, Utah, and Arizona and parts of Colorado and New Mexico.

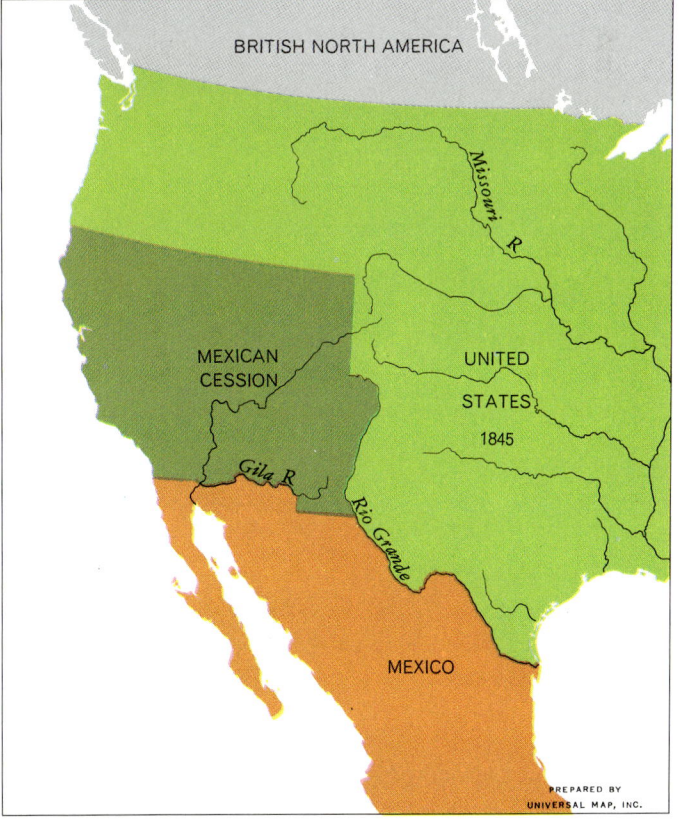

anything if the bickering continued. For one thing, the House had passed a resolution 85-81 that the war had been "unnecessarily and unconstitutionally begun by the President of the United States." By the time Scott's army was approaching Mexico City, Polk wanted to make a quick peace.

Accompanying Scott's army was a state department clerk named Nicholas P. Trist. He was instructed to make a treaty as Polk's personal representative. When, after the fall of Mexico City, Trist seemed unable to do what Polk wanted done, Polk ordered him to come home. But Trist stayed on and negotiated a peace treaty, which was finally signed in the Mexico City suburb of Guadalupe Hidalgo on February 2, 1848.

In the Treaty of Guadalupe Hidalgo, Mexico ceded California and New Mexico and recognized the Rio Grande as the Texas boundary. The United States agreed to pay 15 million dollars to Mexico and to take responsibility for paying the claims that United States citizens held against the Mexican government. It also guaranteed the Mexicans living in California and New Mexico certain rights, including that of having Spanish as the legal language.

When Polk received a draft of the treaty, he decided to accept it even though it did not

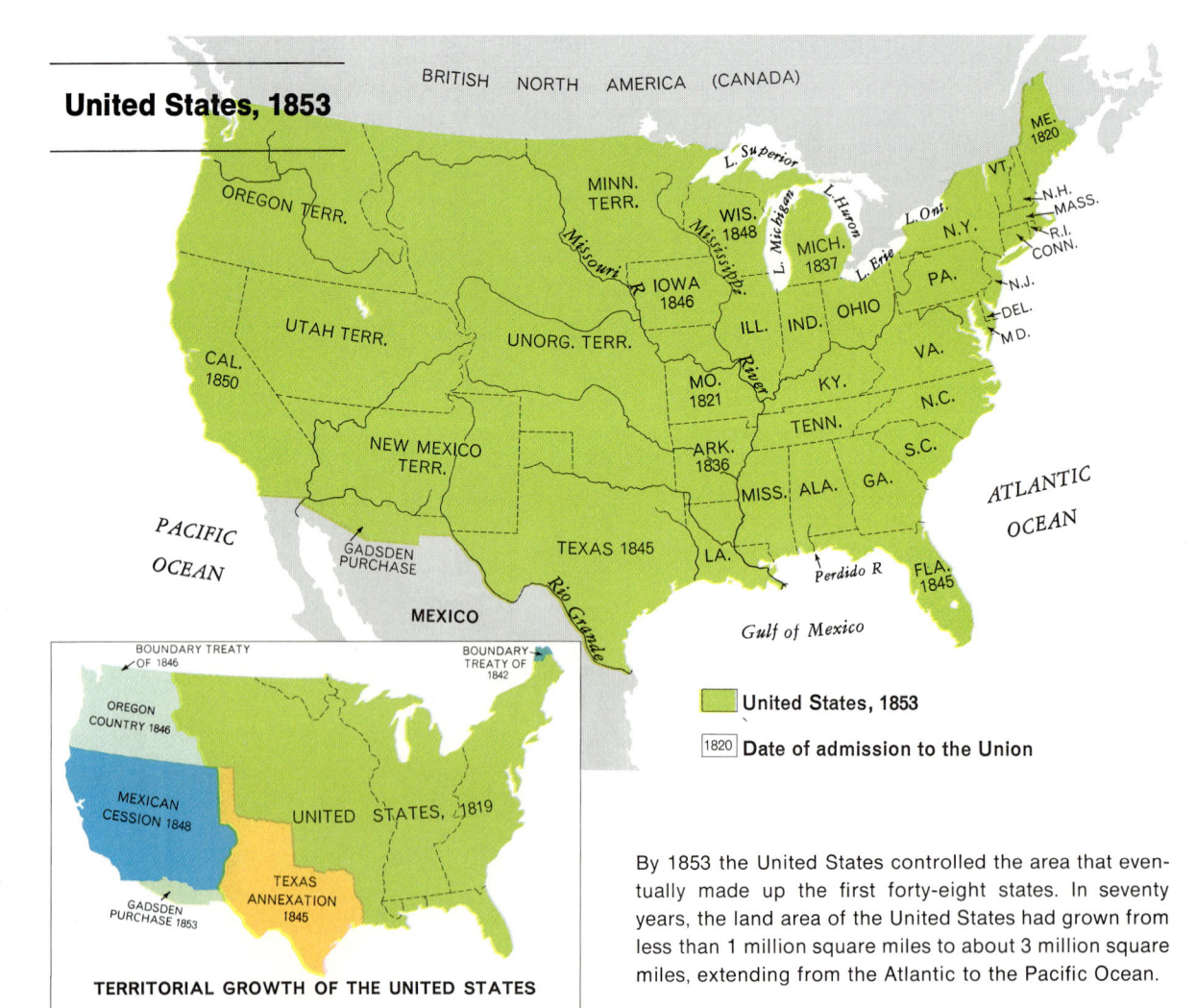

United States, 1853

By 1853 the United States controlled the area that eventually made up the first forty-eight states. In seventy years, the land area of the United States had grown from less than 1 million square miles to about 3 million square miles, extending from the Atlantic to the Pacific Ocean.

TERRITORIAL GROWTH OF THE UNITED STATES

include all he wanted. The Senate approved the treaty, and the House and the Senate appropriated the necessary money.

The War's Aftermath

Congress continued to argue over whether to allow slavery in any new territories. Although no one expected slavery to take root in Oregon, some southerners insisted that it be permitted there. They wanted to establish a principle that would later apply to the Mexican cession. Oregon was not organized as a free territory until August 1848.

For the time being, California and New Mexico did without regular territorial governments. California could not continue long without a government. Gold was discovered there in January 1848, while the Treaty of Guadalupe Hidalgo was being written. Soon the gold rush was on: a hundred thousand "forty-niners" swarmed into California in 1849, and they needed a government of their own.

The lands ceded in the Treaty of Guadalupe Hidalgo were not the last to be obtained from Mexico. In 1853, Santa Anna, again president of Mexico, needed money. Some railroad promoters in the United States desired a strip of land suitable for the construction of a railroad to California. By the Gadsden Purchase in 1853, the United States paid Santa Anna 10 million dollars for an area that now forms the southern parts of Arizona and New Mexico. This completed the conterminous territorial expansion of the United States.

Some of the consequences of expansion were not foreseen by those who favored it. One of these consequences was the Civil War. The war, of course, had many causes. But it would probably not have taken place without the acquisition of western territories. Even before the Mexican War had ended, the argument over slavery in the territories already was threatening to divide the nation.

By renewing and intensifying the slavery issue, the Mexican War helped bring on the Civil War.

The Mexican War was a forerunner of the Civil War in another way. The one war was a kind of unplanned rehearsal for the other. Ulysses S. Grant, Robert E. Lee, and most of the other generals, both Union and Confederate, gained battle experience in Mexico.

Miners like these in Spanish Flat worked hard sifting tons of California dirt, but few struck it rich. Stories of lucky strikes brought thousands of hopeful prospectors to the West.

REFORM MOVEMENTS

From the 1820's to the 1840's a number of social reform movements caught the public imagination. Americans formed organizations to fight all kinds of social evils, from drunkenness to slavery. They raised money, published newspapers and pamphlets, and drew up and submitted petitions to state legislatures or to Congress.

Some of the social reformers were Democrats, but most were Whigs. (In the case of political reformers, the reverse was true.) A few supporters were wealthy merchants who contributed thousands of dollars to various causes. Most leaders and members of reform societies, however, were middle-class people—farmers, shopkeepers, housewives, professionals. Few reformers were day laborers. A great many were women.

Some of the reformers came from the South, but the great majority were northerners. A large number were born or lived part of their lives in New England or upstate New York. While the reform agitation swept over the Northeast and the Northwest, it was less influential in the South.

Some reformers had no church connections or religious convictions. Most, however, belonged to one or another of the Protestant denominations. A great many were Quakers.

There was one thing that all the reformers had in common. That was a belief that human beings and their lives on earth could be made perfect or could at least be tremendously improved.

Changes in Religion

In colonial times most religious groups, especially the Puritans, had taken a pessimistic view of human potentialities, both in this life and in the next. The Puritans believed that people were born in sin and that only the "elect"—those God had foreordained to be saved—could escape eternal damnation. New religious movements in the early nineteenth century were more optimistic. These taught that salvation was open to all who would seek it. They implied that people could approach perfection not only in the next world but also in this one. As a result, the new doctrines encouraged social reform.

Many Congregational and Presbyterian churches remained conservative in both religious and social thought. They were, after all, basically Puritan or Calvinistic. In the early nineteenth century, these churches began to split into "Old Light" and "New Light" groups. The New Light people emphasized the idea of salvation.

Charles G. Finney preached in both Congregational and Presbyterian churches. He held revival meetings in New York and Ohio, from the 1820's on. In his sermons, Finney insisted that in order to be saved, people must rely on good works as well as on faith. Finney's preaching inspired a number of men and women to work for social reform.

Two new churches, the Unitarian and the Universalist, had been started earlier by former Congregationalists. The Unitarians and the Universalists believed that salvation was open to all. In 1832, a Boston Unitarian minister, Ralph Waldo Emerson, gave up the ministry and began to develop the philosophy of transcendentalism.

This was an optimistic philosophy. Its basic ideal was that of an "oversoul," which Emerson also called "truth" or "being." Every human soul was a part of this oversoul, a part of the reality that consisted of only the good and the true. By cultivating one's intuition, a person could "transcend" the limitations of his or her earthly nature and identify more and more fully with the universe.

Transcendentalism seemed mystical, yet it had practical consequences for its believers. It taught them to rely on themselves, to act with confidence, and to follow their hunches. "Nothing is at last sacred," Emerson wrote, "but the integrity of your own mind." Transcendentalism stimulated social reform by teaching that human beings could improve themselves and the world around them.

Concern over practical matters also caused new churches to appear. A great many churches faced battles over seating arrangements in racially mixed churches and over slavery.

Dissatisfied black Methodists in Philadelphia formed the Bethel Society in 1816. It later became the African Methodist Episcopal Church. In New York, a similar group, the Zion Society, became the African Methodist Episcopal Zion Church in 1821. In the 1840's, the Baptists, Methodists, and Presbyterians split into northern and southern branches because of disagreement over whether or not to oppose slavery.

The Catholic Church in America faced different problems. One of its biggest worries was the conflict between Catholics of different nationalities. The priests and church leaders were originally native Americans or French. They were often at odds with Catholic immigrants, most of whom came from Ireland or Germany. By 1850, about 1 million Catholics had emigrated to the United States. In the 1840's, the Irish began to have more influence in church affairs and took over much of the leadership. At about the same time, anti-Catholic feelings and actions on the part of Protestant Americans became a major problem.

European developments affected some religious groups. A reform movement among German Jews spread to the United States, which later became the world center of Reform Judaism. The first Reformed Society of Israelites was founded in 1824 in Charleston, South Carolina. Reform Jews changed many rituals and practices and reevaluated traditional beliefs and doctrines.

Public School Systems

Before the 1830's, a great many American children learned to read, write, and do simple arithmetic in private schools or at home. In a few cities and large towns the children attended public schools. As yet, however, no state had a system of public education, with full tax support and compulsory attendance. In the 1830's, reformers—especially labor leaders—began to demand such systems.

Geography and modern history were becoming school subjects in the mid-1800's.

The public school movement met strong opposition. Many people who had no children objected to paying taxes to educate other people's children. People who sent their children to parochial schools often considered it unfair to be taxed to support public schools for which they had no need.

Despite the opposition, Massachusetts and Pennsylvania soon began to set up statewide systems of elementary schools. Other states followed. By the 1850's, every state had such a system, at least on paper. In some parts of the country, especially in the West and the South, it was years before statewide school systems were actually set up. As late as 1860, only 15 percent of the children of elementary-school age in the country were actually going to school.

Under the leadership of such educators as Horace Mann of Massachusetts and Emma Hart Willard of New York, the quality of public education was gradually improved. The school year was lengthened from a few months to six months or more, barriers against education for girls were broken down, and special training was provided for teachers.

Most of the early teachers were men, many of whom taught for a few years after college and before going into the ministry, the law, or politics. Gradually, more and more women took up teaching, and it began to be looked upon as a career. In 1839, Massachusetts established the first state-supported teacher-training institution.

Only a few young people, most of them boys, were able to get a secondary education. By 1860 there were some tax-supported high schools, especially in Massachusetts and New York. In the country as a whole, however, there were twenty times as many private academies as public high schools.

In higher education, the principle of public support and control was slow to be adopted. By the time of the Civil War, twenty-one state universities were in operation. There were several times as many private colleges, most of them church-related. Many of them were larger and better equipped and staffed than the state schools.

The Women's Movement

As a group, women were barred from getting anything more than an elementary education. Job opportunities outside the home were limited. Women were not allowed to vote or hold office, and upon marriage, they lost all control of their property and earnings. Views on what was "ladylike" and "proper" made it impossible for them to speak in public, preach religion, or engage in sports.

Throughout the early nineteenth century, individual women started to break many of the customs that bound them. The large-scale movement for women's rights, however, was sparked by the abolition movement. When some American women were barred as delegates to a world conference on slavery in London in 1840, they decided that

A stern lecturer addresses a lyceum audience *(left)*. Lyceums were "mutual improvement" groups that sponsored lectures on current events, science, and the arts. They were intended to give working people some education. Between 1820 and 1860, about 3,000 such groups were started. The cartoon *(right)* is an antifeminist's dire prediction of the outcome of the women's movement.

they needed to work for their own freedom as well as freedom for the slaves.

In 1848, the same year that revolutions were rocking Europe, Elizabeth Cady Stanton and Lucretia Mott organized a meeting in Seneca Falls, New York, to discuss the rights of women. They placed a small announcement in the local paper. Much to their surprise, three hundred people jammed the meeting, some coming fifty miles in horse-drawn wagons. Nineteen-year-old Charlotte Woodward, who wanted to be a printer, explained why she went to the meeting:

We women did more than keep house, cook, sew, wash, spin and weave, and garden. Many of us were under the necessity of earning money besides. . . . We worked secretly . . . because all society was built on the theory that men, not women, earned money, and that men alone supported the family. . . . Most women accepted this condition of society as normal and God-ordained and therefore changeless. But I do not believe that there was any community anywhere in which the souls of some women were not beating their wings in rebellion. . . . I can say that every fibre of my being rebelled, although silently, all the hours that I sat and sewed gloves for a miserable pittance which, after it was earned, could never be mine. I wanted to work, but I wanted to choose my task and I wanted to collect my wages.

The people at Seneca Falls resolved that women should have the same opportunities as men in the trades, professions, and commerce. They said that all laws that treated women as inferior to men were a denial of human rights. The most controversial resolution said that women should be allowed to vote. (Of the 68 women and 32 men who signed the Declaration of Sentiments at the meeting, only Charlotte Woodward lived to see women get the vote in 1920.)

Attacks on Social Evils

Some reformers thought that poverty, crime, and other social evils were largely the fault of society itself. They hoped to eliminate these evils by improving society. Some of them planned communities that they expected would be models for others to follow. In these model communities, private ownership of land, homes, or means of production usually was prohibited, and everyone was expected to work for the common good.

Robert Owen, a textile manufacturer from Scotland, founded the community of New Harmony, Indiana, on the Wabash River. A number of New England intellectuals set up the community of Brook Farm, near Boston. Similar experiments in social planning were tried in various parts of the country. None of these experiments succeeded.

Most reformers, instead of trying to create new communities, directed their efforts toward correcting specific wrongs in society. Dorothea Dix, a Boston schoolteacher, devoted her life to improving conditions in jails and prisons. She also founded separate institutions for the mentally ill, who had usually been thrown in with convicts.

The American Society for the Promotion of Temperance, founded in 1826, worked to pass laws to prohibit liquor sales. Temperance crusaders persuaded Maine to adopt statewide prohibition in 1851. Other reformers believed that tobacco, coffee, and improper foods were as bad as strong drink in preventing people from realizing their full potentialities.

The American Peace Society, founded in 1828, campaigned for the elimination of war. The society's founder, William Ladd of Maine, drew up a plan for a congress of nations and a court of nations to preserve world peace. Nothing came of the plan. The peace movement was weakened by disagreements among its members. Some thought they ought to support wars of self-defense; others thought they ought to oppose all wars. Most of them denounced America's part in the Mexican War as aggression. But when the Civil War came, they were willing to fight or at least to support others who fought. They looked upon it as another war caused by the "slave power."

CULTURAL INDEPENDENCE

"America must be as independent in *literature* as she is in *politics,* as famous for *arts* as for *arms.*" Thus wrote Noah Webster, a young Revolutionary War veteran, in 1785. Though the United States was becoming commercially independent, Americans still looked to England and other European countries for their standards of literary and artistic excellence. Leaders of American thought continued to call upon the people to develop a culture of their own. "We have listened too long to the courtly muses of Europe," said Ralph Waldo Emerson in 1837. "We will walk on our own feet; we will work with our own hands; we will speak our own minds."

The United States was slow to achieve the literary and artistic originality that Webster and Emerson desired. Nevertheless, during the period from 1815 to 1850, some progress was made toward the development of a distinctively American literature.

European Impressions

As late as 1830, about 70 percent of the books sold in the United States were published in England. During the next decade, the American book industry grew rapidly, and by 1840 the proportions were reversed. Nevertheless, most of the books continued to be written by British authors.

A number of British visitors wrote travel accounts that upheld the view that the United States was a land with little culture. These accounts pictured American life as crude and dirty. The people were described as speaking a corrupted form of English, with a nasal twang. They were accused of bolting their food with a "gobble, gulp,"

Some reformers were more successful than others. In industrial boardinghouses *(above)*, as well as in poorhouses, many people lived in conditions of hunger, disease, and overcrowding. Change came slowly for them. The temperance movement, however, grew rapidly. By the 1830's, thousands of groups urged state controls on liquor. "Father Come Home" *(left)* illustrated temperance propaganda.

chewing tobacco and spitting the juice everywhere, gambling, dueling, beating slaves, and gouging out each other's eyes in free-for-all fights.

British critics were sure there could be no respect or encouragement for artistic creativity in a country where all the people were equal or thought they were. A young French visitor, however, took a different view. After touring most of the states in 1831 and 1832, Alexis de Tocqueville wrote two volumes on *Democracy in America* (1835 and 1840). He, too, believed that Americans lagged behind the English and other Europeans in science, literature, and art. But he did not think that democracy was to blame. Rather, he thought that Americans, because of their history and circumstances, were preoccupied with practical affairs and had little time for cultural and scientific pursuits.

American Themes

Despite the charge that there was no such thing as an American literature, a number of writers were beginning to take up native themes and treat them in an original way. The first American to be recognized abroad as a literary artist was a New Yorker, Washington Irving. Irving found material for stories in the Dutch folklore of the Hudson Valley. He used it in "Rip Van Winkle" and "The Legend of Sleepy Hollow," the most widely read of his many writings. Another New Yorker, James Fenimore Cooper, found inspiration for his Leatherstocking Tales in his boyhood on the New York frontier. Cooper turned out more than thirty novels between 1820 and 1850, most of them relating the adventures of Indians and pioneers.

Herman Melville, also a New Yorker, based some of his best novels on his experiences as a sailor. His *Moby Dick* (1851) was an adventure story, telling of the pursuit of a great white whale. It was also an allegory, full of symbols many readers could not understand. The novel was not very popular in Melville's lifetime, but it has come to be regarded as one of the greatest novels in the English language.

Edgar Allan Poe was a southerner who spent the last years of his life in New York. He invented the detective story, developed his own brand of horror tale, and originated a theory of poetry based on music and mathematics. He put his theory into practice in such poems as "Ulalume," "The Raven," and "Annabel Lee."

Walt Whitman called himself the poet of American democracy. The son of a Long Island carpenter, Whitman roamed the country, working at odd jobs. Since he could not persuade any publisher to take his poems, he paid a printer to put them into a small book, *Leaves of Grass* (1855). These poems, full of enthusiasm for the United States and its people, had no regular meter or rhyme. They struck many people as barbarous. Nevertheless, *Leaves of Grass* eventually was translated into many languages.

A "Flowering" of New England

At first, most of the outstanding writers were New Yorkers. In the 1840's, however, there was a "flowering" of literature in New England. One village, Concord, Massachusetts, almost outshone New York.

The leader of the Concord group was Ralph Waldo Emerson. Some people thought his mystical ideas were rather hard to understand, but many thousands could appreciate the practical part of his teachings. Though he borrowed ideas from a variety of thinkers, ancient and modern, he put his own stamp upon them. His philosophy was distinctively American in that it stressed optimism and individualism.

Henry David Thoreau, a friend of Emerson's, built a hut in the woods on Emerson's land and lived there for two years. In his book *Walden* (1854), Thoreau explained:

I went to the woods because I wished to live deliberately, to front only the essential facts of life, and see if I could not learn what it had to teach, and not, when I came to die, discover that I had not lived.

During the Mexican War, Thoreau refused to pay taxes because of his opposition to the war. He spent one night in jail, and then his friends paid his taxes for him. To justify his stand, Thoreau wrote *Resistance to Civil Government* (1849). This essay on "passive resistance" later influenced a number of social movements, including the civil rights movement of the 1960's.

Another member of the Concord group was Margaret Fuller, who edited *The Dial,* a transcendentalist magazine. She also spoke on women's rights, especially at the Boston home of another writer, Elizabeth Peabody. Fuller's talks were later published as *Woman in the Nineteenth Century* (1845). In 1844, she became literary critic of the New York *Tribune.*

Nathaniel Hawthorne, also a member of the Concord group, found themes for many of his stories in the Puritan past of New England. In *The Scarlet Letter* (1850) he examined the Puritan psychology of sin and evil. This book is still regarded as one of the finest American novels.

Popular Literature

While the Concord group was important in the development of American thought, its writings did not always capture the public imagination. The popular literature most often consisted of sentimental novels, books of moral uplift, escapist adventure tales and books of social instruction. These works rarely used symbolism and were generally easy to read (or at least easier than some transcendentalist works).

The best-seller list included books by Washington Irving, James Fenimore Cooper, and Richard Henry Dana, Jr., some of which are still enjoyed today. It also included such now-forgotten works as *Three Experiments of Living,* by Hannah Farnham Lee; *The Monks of Monk Hall,* by George Lippard; and *The Wide, Wide World,* by Susan Bogert Warner. Other popular authors of the day were Mrs. E. D. E. N. Southworth, Maria Susanna Cummins, and Mary Jane Holmes.

The reform novel came to the fore at the same time the reform movements started to flourish. The most important and most influential was *Uncle Tom's Cabin,* an antislavery novel by Harriet Beecher Stowe. Also popular was *Ten Nights in a Bar-Room and What I Saw There,* by Timothy Shay Arthur, which promoted temperance.

ECONOMIC LIFE

The 1840's were marked by changes in the banking system as well as in technology. Some of these changes would greatly affect the social system as well as the economic system.

The Bank Question

The failure to recharter the second Bank of the United States had left the government with a problem: How would it take care of public funds? The Democrats objected to establishing a new national bank, and the Whigs did not want to use "pet banks." President Van Buren proposed to "divorce" the government from all banks and to let the government handle its money.

Finally, in 1840, Congress took Van Buren's advice and set up the Independent Treasury system. The Independent Treasury kept tax revenues and other income in vaults in Washington, D.C., and in other large cities. The Independent Treasury did no banking business; it made no loans and issued no notes. From the time the money was collected to the time it was spent, it remained out of circulation.

The next year, when the Whigs were in power under President Tyler, they abolished the Independent Treasury. In 1846, however, the Democrats set it up again. It continued to be the repository for government funds until 1913.

Lowering the Tariff

Under the tariff law of 1833, the rates were lowered year by year. By 1842, the general level of duties was to be about where it had been in 1816. In 1842, however, the Whigs raised the tariff.

Although the Democrats did not oppose using tariffs to obtain revenue for the federal government, they were against using tariffs to protect United States producers from for-

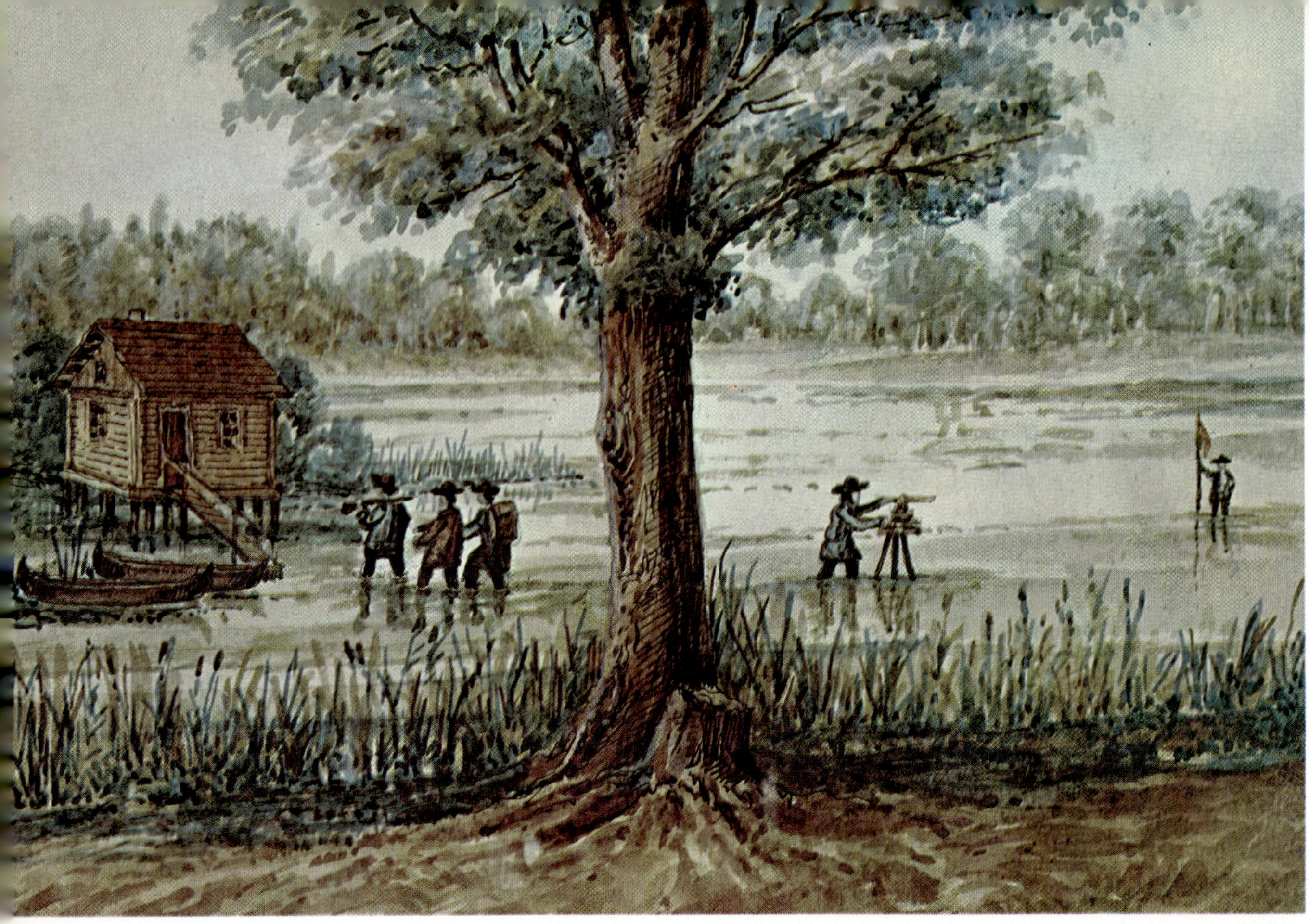

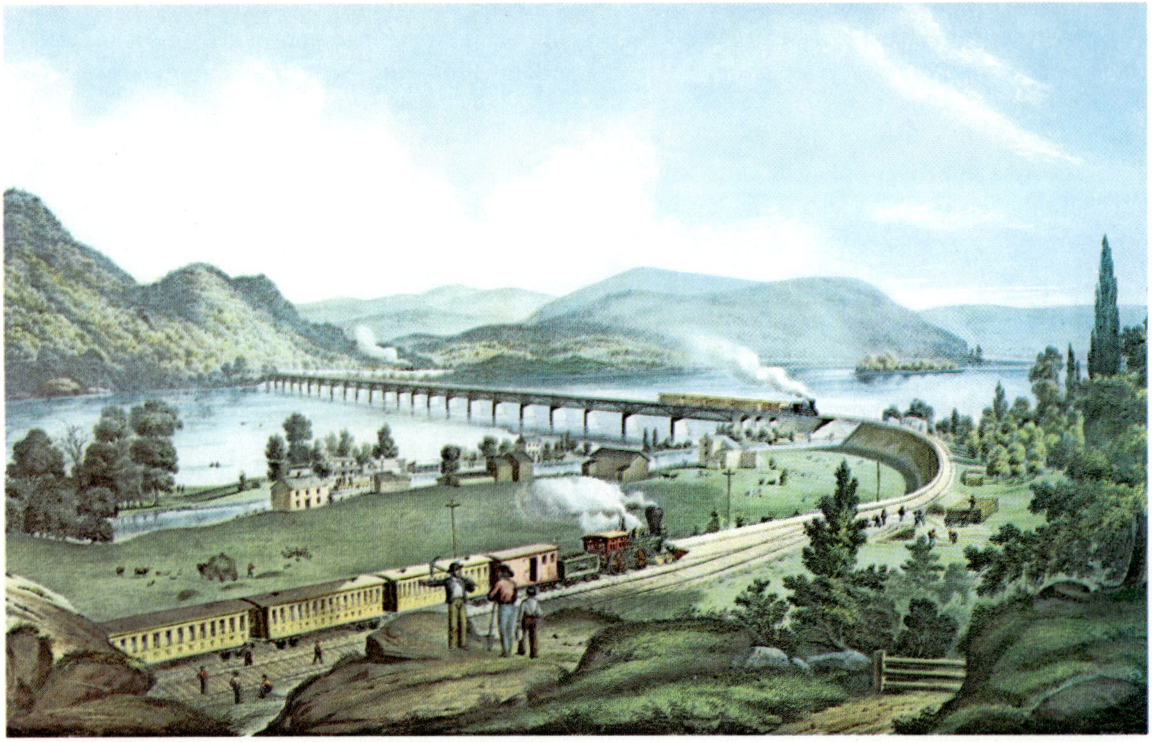

eign competition. Such protection, the Democrats argued, favored certain people at the expense of others.

In 1846, Democrats in Congress passed a bill to lower the rates, and President Polk gladly signed it. The main effect of this tariff was to provide revenue, not to keep competing goods out of the country.

In the continual debates over the tariff, clashes of economic interest were involved. There was a conflict between the manufacturers who demanded protective tariffs and most farmers and planters. But there was also a question of principle: Should the government aid certain groups or should it treat all of them alike? From the Democratic point of view, at least, the reduction of the tariff represented a gain for democracy.

Transportation

In the 1820's and 1830's, a great number of canals had been built. Even at best, canals had great disadvantages. Steamboats could not be used on canals, for the churning of propellers or paddle wheels would cause the banks to cave in. Canal boats, towed by horses or mules walking on a path along the side, were so slow that passengers could step off and stride ahead. Throughout the North, canals closed during winter freezes.

The canal age had hardly begun when its end was foreshadowed. A new means of transportation appeared, one that was much faster, more dependable, and so adaptable that it could be used almost anywhere—the railroad.

In 1826, a short rail line began to operate between two towns in England. The news stirred the interest of merchants in the United States, especially those in the seaboard cities who needed better access to the interior. By 1831, three short railroad lines were in operation. In 1836, the total trackage of American railroads was more than 1,000 miles; by 1850, it was more than 9,000 miles,

Railroads in Operation, 1850

By 1850, more than 9,000 miles of railroad track had been laid in the United States. Rail service was most extensive in the Northeast. Not for many years were the sections of the nation linked by railroads. Surveyors *(top)* plot a route across swampy land near Lake Huron. The early locomotives, unlike those in the scenic view of the Pennsylvania Railroad Bridge *(bottom)*, puffed clouds of cinder-filled smoke. Farmers complained that the trains scared their horses and lowered milk production by upsetting their cows.

with some in almost every state. There remained so many gaps between lines, however, that there was as yet no national railroad network.

Meanwhile, railroad equipment was being improved. A locomotive with two pairs of driving wheels, a cowcatcher, and a huge, flaring smokestack became standard. The American passenger car, at first a stagecoach on rails, developed into a long carriage with two rows of seats and a center aisle. The average speed of passenger trains rose to about thirty miles an hour.

These trains were noisy and uncomfortable. Accidents were frequent because of poor roadbeds. Yet the future belonged to the railroads, not the canals. Though rail travel and transport were more expensive, they were much quicker. To illustrate, in the 1850's the travel time from New York to Cleveland was 9 days by water and only 3 days by rail.

Communication Improvements

Samuel F. B. Morse, born in Massachusetts, studied art in England as a young man. On a voyage home from Europe, he learned that electric batteries could send a current over wire of almost any length. Immediately he thought of the possibility of sending messages long distances by wire. After several years' work on the idea at home, he applied for a patent on an electromagnetic telegraph (1837), but he needed money to develop and test his device. In 1843, Congress appropriated $30,000 to build an experimental telegraph line from Washington, D.C., to Baltimore, more than forty miles away. On May 24, 1844, Morse sent a message from Washington that his partner received perfectly in Baltimore: "What hath God wrought!"

By 1846, telegraph wires had been extended to New York City and, within a few years, to Chicago and New Orleans. Soon the wires reached out to most of the larger towns.

The telegraph was of great importance to the railroads, and most of the telegraph poles were put up along the railroads' rights of way. With the new invention, it was much easier than before to control the movement of trains. As a result, train service became safer and more regular.

The telegraph was also valuable to the newspaper business. Previously, publishers had gathered most of their out-of-town news from newspapers that came in the mail. Now the publishers could get their information immediately and directly by wire. Only weeks after Morse's great demonstration, a news report was sent over the original telegraph line that James K. Polk had won the Democratic nomination for the presidency at the convention in Baltimore.

A number of large newspaper firms joined in 1846 to form the Associated Press. In this organization the publishers cooperated in the gathering and the distribution of news by telegraph. That same year a new machine, the Hoe rotary-cylinder press, began to be used in the printing of newspapers. Now, news could be printed much more quickly. For the first time, people all over the country could, at a given moment, be reading and thinking about the same events within a day of their happening.

A Look at Specifics

1. How did Webster arrange a compromise in the boundary dispute between Maine and New Brunswick?

2. How was Texas annexed?

3. What was the basis of the American claim to the Oregon country? The British claim?

4. What were the subjects of dispute that led to the Mexican War?

5. Why did the Mormons found the settlement of Deseret?

6. Why did the Mexican leaders believe they could win a war with the United States? What military advantages did the United States have over Mexico?

7. What was the purpose of the Wilmot Proviso?

8. Why was the Gadsden Purchase made?

9. How did the acquisition of lands from Mexico help bring on the Civil War?

10. How did Charles G. Finney help change attitudes toward reform?

11. What was Emerson's philosophy of transcendentalism? How did it help the reform movement?

12. How did the women's movement get its start?

A Review of Major Ideas

1. Explain how domestic disagreements and international power struggles affected the annexation of Texas.

2. Describe the steps by which Oregon became part of the United States.

3. Explain how California and New Mexico became part of the United States.

4. Name some of the social reforms advocated between 1815 and 1850.

For Independent Study

1. Why did the feeling of a "manifest destiny" develop in the 1840's rather than in the 1830's?

2. Compare the expansion of the United States into lands claimed by other nations with that of a modern developing nation, for example, India or Indonesia. List (a) the motives for expanding, (b) the methods used, and (c) the rationale for the expansion.

3. The Monroe Doctrine included the idea that European nations should not establish colonies in the Western Hemisphere. Did it also intend that the United States should refrain from colonizing?

4. "Americans did not achieve artistic excellence because they placed too much value on equality and standardization and not enough on individual excellence." Defend or oppose this statement.

Unit Review
Examining the Times

1. How was the diplomacy of the United States between 1815 and 1850 influenced by the weaknesses and strengths of its neighbors? Was American diplomacy successful during this period?

2. Summarize briefly the changes that took place in economic development, political democracy, and territorial growth between 1815 and 1850.

3. What events or developments during the period from 1815 to 1850 tended to strengthen national unity? What tended to weaken it?

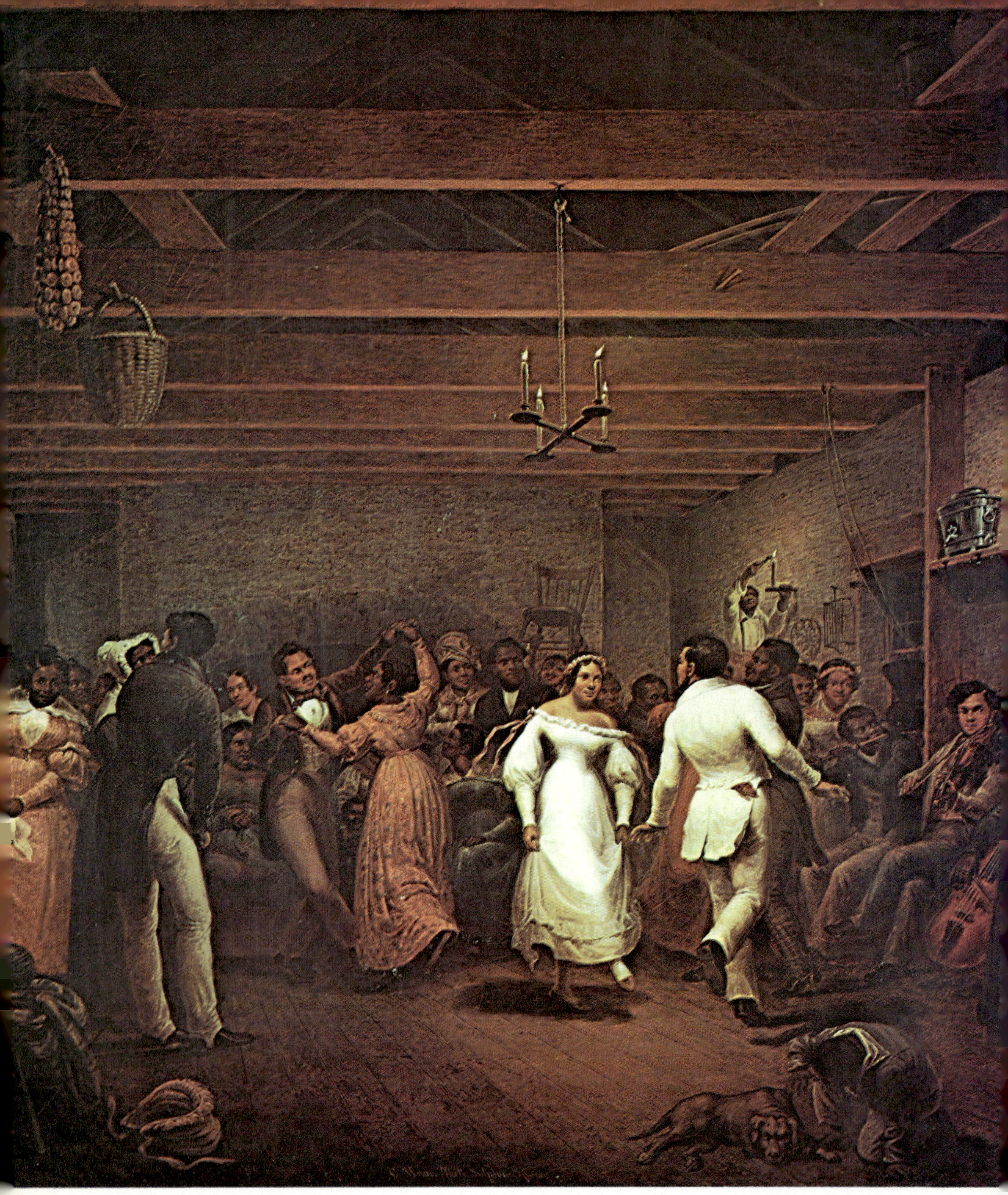

UNIT FOUR 1850–1877

Division and Reunion

Between 1850 and 1877, the American people quarreled among themselves, broke apart, fought a costly and bloody four-year civil war, and then gradually brought about peace and national unity. This—the division and reunion of the country—is the main theme of United States history during that period.

There was more to it than just division and reunion, however. By 1877, the United States was far different from what it had been in 1850. Not only did the nation have more people, bigger cities, and new kinds of machines. It also had millions of newly freed slaves. Above all, the United States had a much stronger national government. As late as 1850, the United States could still be described as a union of separate states. By 1877, it was well on the way to becoming a more unified and consolidated nation.

During this same period, there was conflict over national consolidation in other parts of the world. Small states combined to form bigger ones; loose groupings of people were brought together under more centralized governments; large and well-established nations remained large by defeating discontented elements that wanted to break away; some nations continued to enlarge their colonial empires.

In midcentury Europe, several fairly large, fairly old nations already existed: Britain, Spain, Russia, and France. The most industrialized was Britain, which was busily colonizing Asia and forcing its way into Africa. Spain, once great, was now in a decline. It had lost all of its colonies on the mainland of South America and was having difficulty holding on to its remaining colonies.

Russia soon underwent two experiences

similar to those the United States was undergoing—emancipation and rebellion. In 1861 the czar proclaimed freedom for the millions of Russian serfs. The next year he put down an uprising of his Polish subjects, who had hoped to create a nation of their own.

France, like Britain, was busy in Asia and Africa. It had begun its conquest of Indochina, capturing Saigon in 1858. After 1870, it joined other European nations in the scramble for African colonies. It began taking over parts of West Africa, setting up French colonies all along the Guinea coast.

The mid-nineteenth century was a time of widespread striving, in many places successful, to create larger or at least more highly unified nations. All this reflected the spirit of nationalism.

Nationalism is often defined as a mystic feeling that a people have that they belong together as a separate nation, with their own independent government. Usually these people have a common language, religion, and historical tradition. Nationalism does not necessarily make for bigger countries. For example, in the 1830's the new states in Latin America splintered into a number of relatively small nations. However, in the mid-nineteenth century, nationalism often led to efforts toward making countries bigger.

At the middle of the century, though it was common to speak of "Italy" and "Germany," these were as yet only geographical expressions, not designations of united countries with central governments. Italy then consisted of several independent states, and Germany consisted of dozens of kingdoms, principalities, and city republics. Parts of both Italy and Germany were included in the Hapsburg Empire. This empire also contained Austrians, Hungarians, and many other nationalities.

In 1848, revolutionary leaders in Hungary, Italy, and Germany attempted to set up new nations with representative governments. Americans generally cheered these efforts and made heroes of the leaders. The Hapsburg government, aided by Russian troops, crushed the Hungarian revolt. The German and Italian rebellions also failed.

Prussia and Austria were the largest and strongest German states. Prussia took the lead in German unification. Through wars with Schleswig-Holstein and Austria, Prussia was able in 1866 to set up the North German Confederation. Finally, in 1871, after winning the Franco-Prussian War, Prussia broadened the confederation to include the south German states (but not Austria) and converted it into the German Empire.

The Italian leaders took advantage of Prussia's wars in furthering Italian liberation and unification. By 1861, the Italians controlled all of the country except Venetia and the Papal States. That year, less than two weeks after Abraham Lincoln's inauguration as President of the United States, the Italians established the Kingdom of Italy. In 1866, the new kingdom joined Prussia in the war against Austria, and with Austria's defeat gained Venetia. In 1870, France withdrew its military forces from the Papal States, and Italy promptly took over these territories. The kingdom now included all of the Italian peninsula.

In 1867, the Austrian Empire was reorganized as the Austro-Hungarian Empire, with a separate parliament and cabinet for the Hungarians. The Austrian government had promised these concessions to the Hungarians in return for their support in the war against Prussia.

Thus, at about the time of the American Civil War, two new nations and a reorganized empire appeared in Europe.

In this same period an old nation re-emerged in Asia. Japan had been a hermit for more than two hundred years. Its rulers, believing that outsiders were causing many of the nation's troubles, had cut off contact with other nations. They refused to trade with foreigners, except for the Dutch, who were allowed to send one ship a year. For an even longer time the nation had been ruled by great landlord families. The leader of one of these families served as *shogun,* or military governor, acting in the name of the emperor, who actually had no power.

Americans played an important role in reopening Japan to the world. In 1853 and 1854, Commodore Matthew C. Perry paid official visits to Japan. The Japanese reluctantly agreed to a treaty permitting Americans to trade at certain ports. In 1860, the United States received the first delegation of diplomats sent abroad by Japan. After the United States established diplomatic relations with Japan, many European nations followed suit.

The reopening of Japan led to disturbances there. Some feudal lords objected to giving up the old policy of isolation. They refused to obey the shogun and from time to time attacked and killed foreigners. In 1864, an American warship joined with French, British, and Dutch warships to shell and destroy the fortifications of one feudal family that had been interfering with foreign shipping. Finally, in 1867, most of the influential Japanese agreed to the formation of a parliamentary government, with the emperor at the head of it. The new government was far more centralized than the old one. It maintained order throughout the country, which rapidly began to develop the railroads, shipping, industries, army and navy, and other features of industrialized nations.

During these years, China managed to preserve its national existence despite a terrible civil war, the Tai-ping Rebellion, which lasted fifteen years. The Chinese rebels, the Tai-pings, were influenced to some extent by ideas of nationalism that they learned from British traders and by notions of Christianity learned from American missionaries. But the British and the Americans in China, as well as their respective governments at home, supported the established government of the Manchu dynasty. The rebellion began in South China in 1850, spread over the Yangtze Valley, and kept the country torn and distracted until 1865.

Not only in Europe and Asia but also in parts of North America outside the United States, the trend toward centralization could be seen. By an act of the British Parliament in 1867, the formerly separate provinces of British North America were federated to form the Dominion of Canada, which remained a part of the British Empire.

Such large national units became feasible because of improvements in transportation and communication that enabled a government to keep in touch with people scattered over a wide area. But such improvements did not automatically bring about national unification. Wars were usually necessary.

The Civil War could be called the American war of national unification. The Union victory was in accord with the trend of the times. It did for the United States what contemporary struggles and victories did for such nations as Germany, Italy, and Japan. However, the Civil War did more than that. It gave a boost not only to strong, centralized government but also to democratic government—government of the people, by the people, for the people.

Two Ways of Life

CHAPTER 9
1850–1861

Shopping at the Canal Street Market, New Orleans.

By 1850 the North and the South were two very different sections. Although they were parts of the same nation, they were beginning to seem like two separate countries. The ties that held the sections together were, however, more important at the time than the forces that tended to divide them.

Both northerners and southerners were proud of the nation's achievements in industry, commerce, and agriculture. Both northerners and southerners looked to the West as the next great region of the country to be developed. Yet despite these agreements, there was growing hostility between the North and the South.

This antagonism was no mere accident. It was "an irrepressible conflict between opposing and enduring forces," as the New York political leader William H. Seward declared in 1858. It arose because the two sections had come to have such different ways of life, such different interests and ideals.

POPULATION CHANGES

Throughout the nineteenth century, the population of Britain and western Europe grew fast, but that of the United States grew even faster. Each new federal census showed the population to be about a third larger. In 1860 there were about eight times as many people in the United States as there had been in 1790. Most of this population growth resulted from the excess of births over deaths. But a considerable portion, especially after 1850, resulted from immigration.

Only a few immigrants had arrived during the period from the end of the Revolutionary War (1783) to the end of the War of 1812. After that, the number that came increased slowly and irregularly. Then, in the 1840's, partly because of conditions in Europe, a mass influx began. By 1860, nearly 4 million immigrants were living in the United States. One person in eight had been born abroad.

	1840		1850		1860	
1	New York, N.Y.	312,710	New York, N.Y.	515,547	New York, N.Y. (including Brooklyn)	805,658 1,092,791
2	Baltimore, Md.	102,313	Baltimore, Md.	169,054	Philadelphia, Pa.	565,529
3	New Orleans, La.	102,193	Boston, Mass.	136,881	Baltimore, Md.	212,418
4	Philadelphia, Pa.	93,665	Philadelphia, Pa.	121,376	Boston, Mass.	177,840
5	Boston, Mass.	93,383	New Orleans, La.	116,375	New Orleans, La.	168,675
6	Cincinnati, Ohio	46,338	Cincinnati, Ohio	115,435	Cincinnati, Ohio	161,044
7	Albany, N.Y.	33,721	St. Louis, Mo.	77,860	St. Louis, Mo.	160,773
8	Charleston, S.C.	29,261	Albany, N.Y.	50,763	Chicago, Ill.	112,172
9	Washington, D.C.	23,364	Pittsburgh, Pa.	46,601	Newark, N.J.	71,941
10	Providence, R.I.	23,171	Louisville, Ky.	43,194	Louisville, Ky.	68,033

Note: City population, exclusive of metropolitan areas

In 1840, the ten largest cities in the nation were in the Northeast and the South. But in the next two decades, as the Northeast became more industrialized, cities there grew faster than those in the South. The most spectacular population gains were recorded by new cities in the Northwest, including Chicago and St. Louis.

Differences in Growth

Not all parts of the nation were growing at the same rate. The Northeast gained less than the Northwest (which at this time included Ohio, Indiana, Illinois, Michigan, Wisconsin, and Iowa plus the Minnesota Territory). The Northwest gained less than the Far West. For example, the population of California quadrupled, jumping from 100,000 to 400,000 in the 1850's. The South gained even less than the Northeast.

The United States was still predominantly rural. In 1850, five times as many people were scattered over the countryside as were concentrated in towns and cities. For decades, however, the United States had been becoming more and more urban. The population of the cities was growing much faster than that of the farms.

The Northeast continued to be the most highly urbanized area. New York City together with Brooklyn had a population of more than a million by 1860. It continued to gain as the nation's leading port. Some of the cities farther west grew even faster. During the 1850's, St. Louis doubled in population, reaching 161,000, and Chicago tripled, reaching about 110,000.

The South had the second busiest port, New Orleans. Yet, on the whole, the South contained fewer cities, towns, and villages than the North. It was less densely settled. In 1860, the slave states had an average of about thirteen persons for each square mile; the free states, about twenty.

San Francisco, the biggest city in the Far West, was growing phenomenally. By 1860 its population was 56,000, double what it had been in 1848. California, Oregon, and New Mexico were still frontier areas. During the 1850's, some of the people who had come west to search for gold began to abandon the prospector's life. Many settled down to farm or to set up businesses. The Mormons in Deseret (Utah) had by the 1850's established a busy farming and trading community. Much of their prosperity was based on supplying the wagon trains bound for California or Oregon.

Growing Diversity

Immigrants hoped to make a better living in the United States than they had been able to earn at home. They learned about the United States from accounts, often exaggerated, that shipping companies and land dealers published in order to promote business. They also learned from "America letters" written by friends or relatives already in this country. "Now we get beef and pudding, tea and rum pretty regularly," an English immigrant wrote home; "to us who have been long half-starved in England, it appears like a continual feast."

No longer did Europeans cross the ocean as indentured servants, with a master paying the fare. Most could now pay their own way because transatlantic rates had been reduced several times by the shipping companies. Ships usually carried bulky exports, such as lumber, wheat, and cotton, from the United States to Europe and brought back compact imports, such as fine tools and machinery. On the return voyage there was, therefore, empty space. Shippers were glad to fill it with human cargo at almost any price.

The largest group of immigrants to come to the United States in the 1840's was Irish. Many people left Ireland because of the terrible famines of 1845 and 1846, when much of the potato crop rotted at harvest time. Even after the worst of the famines, people continued to leave Ireland rather than pay the rent increases that landlords continually imposed. Most of the Irish who came to the United States settled in New York City or in other cities in the Northeast. Few went inland to look for farms, since few of them had money enough to buy land or, for that matter, even a railroad ticket.

Germans made up the second largest group of foreign-born in the United States. A few former leaders of the German revolutionary movement of 1848 were in this group. Most of the Germans who came to the United States were peasants or farmers, though not so desperately poor as the Irish. Many brought money enough to buy farms,

German immigrants brought many of their national customs and celebrations to America. The parade forming in Weaverville, California *(left)* is a celebration of May Day. Music was an important part of these festivals. German people preserved their culture in other ways as well. They set up churches in new areas of settlement. German language newspapers were numerous by 1850. Some attempts were made to set up German schools, but most people took advantage of public education. German clubs and associations provided aid to immigrants. They also gave new settlers a way to participate in familiar social activities.

and while some chose to remain in eastern cities, others spread out to become a very large element of the population not only in New York and Pennsylvania but also in Ohio, Illinois, Wisconsin, and Missouri.

Other groups came to the United States in considerable numbers, too, especially the English, French, Swedes, and Norwegians. The Scandinavians in particular often settled on farms in the Midwest.

Few of the immigrants settled in the South. Most of them arrived at northern ports, especially New York, and remained there. Some immigrants landed at southern ports, especially New Orleans, but did not wish to remain in the South. Most of them disliked slavery on principle or wished to avoid the competition offered by slave labor. They went up the Mississippi River to look for homes in the Northwest or the Far West. As a result, the white population in the South remained fairly homogeneous while that in the North became more and more diversified.

Opposition to Immigrants

Many native Americans were alarmed by the influx of immigrants. Some of them believed that the newcomers threatened American society with an increase in poverty and crime. Others were alarmed because some immigrants were given fake citizenship papers soon after they landed and were led to the polls to vote for crooked politicians. And some Americans were afraid that they would lose their jobs to immigrants who were willing to accept lower pay. "Our public improvements, railroads, and canals are thronged with foreigners," a newspaper writer complained. "They fill our large cities, reduce the wages of labor, and increase the hardships of the old settler."

Most of the immigrants were Catholics (about half of the Germans and nearly all of the Irish). The prejudice against immigrants was greatly intensified because the nation was predominantly Protestant. Many anti-Catholic writers insisted that the immigrants were pawns in a gigantic plot to put the pope

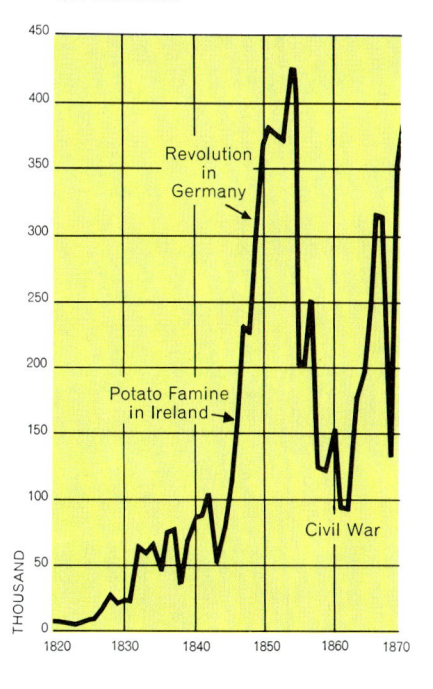

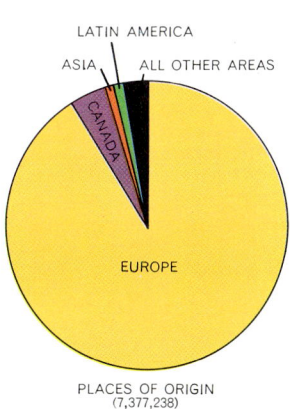

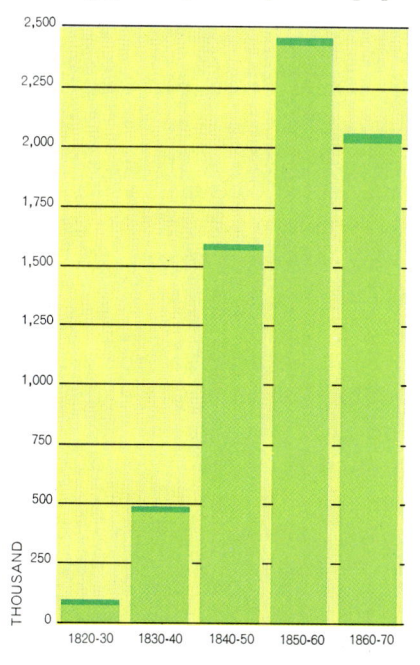

IMMIGRATION TO THE UNITED STATES 1820–1870

Northern and Central Europe
Britain, Ireland, Scandinavia, Belgium, Netherlands, France, Switzerland, Germany, Poland, Austria-Hungary

Eastern and Southern Europe
Russia and Baltic States, Romania, Bulgaria, Turkey, Greece, Italy, Spain, Portugal

In this 1856 cartoon, a wagon full of boisterous Know-Nothings rushes wildly down a Baltimore street. As part of their campaign to elect a Know-Nothing mayor, they have armed themselves to prevent the Irish and the Germans, particularly Catholics, from coming to the polls.

in control of the United States. They were being deliberately sent to this country, it was said, to prepare the way by extending the influence of the Roman Catholic Church through their votes.

Strict laws were demanded by many of the native Americans to discourage immigration and to limit the political activity of the foreign-born. One of the proposed laws would have stopped the immigration of Catholics. Another would have required aliens to reside in the United States for twenty-one years before they could be naturalized. Still another would have barred all the foreign-born from public office, even after they had become citizens. None of these restrictive laws was passed.

In 1850, a number of antiforeign groups combined to form a national secret society, the Order of the Star-spangled Banner. In 1854, they converted this into a political organization and named it the Native American party. Outsiders usually called it the Know-Nothing party because the members were instructed to say "I know nothing" whenever they were asked about the party's secrets.

Some southerners supported the Know-Nothing movement even though there were few immigrants in the South. They wished to limit immigration because they could see that it was doing little for their section while it was contributing a great deal to the economic and political strength of the North.

The Know-Nothings never had the support of a majority of the American people. A number of native citizens spoke out in defense of the immigrants. One said:

Laboring like slaves for us, they have built our cities and railroads; piercing the western wilds, they have caused them to blossom into gardens; taking part in our commerce and manufactures, they have helped to carry the triumphs of our arts to the remotest corners of the globe.

Another insisted that the "real American" was the person who gave both "mind and heart to the grand constituent ideas of the Republic," no matter where he or she had come from.

THE NORTH

Before 1850, there had been not one North but two—the Northeast and the Northwest. The Northwest had many economic ties with the South and carried on a large amount of trade by way of the Mississippi River and its tributaries.

During the 1850's, however, railroads, reaching from the Atlantic coast to the Mississippi Valley, made possible a growing east-west trade. The continued rise of industry in the Northeast and of agriculture in the Northwest provided an abundance of goods for this trade. Thus an economic basis was laid for a single, united North.

The Railroads

On a spring day in 1852, a train pulled into Chicago with passengers from as far away as New York. These people were the first to make so long a trip by rail. By 1860, Chicago had become a rail center, with fifteen lines radiating from it and with more than a hundred trains going and coming every day. Traveling at a speed of twenty to thirty miles an hour, the trains gave much faster service than stagecoaches or river boats.

In areas beyond the reach of railroads, stagecoaches continued to run. Congress encouraged fast freight by paying a stage line, the Overland Mail Company, for carrying letters and packages. The company's coaches took 25 days to travel the 2,700 miles of a route from Missouri to California.

For nearly two years, in 1860 and 1861, the Pony Express carried messages much faster. These relay riders covered the gap between two telegraph lines, one being constructed eastward from California and the other westward from Missouri. When the lines were joined, telegrams could be sent from New York across the continent to San Francisco.

River steamers became bigger, fancier, and busier than ever, but their business did not grow so fast as that of the railroads. Steamboaters feared the growing railroad competition. In 1855, a steamboat hit the new Rock Island railroad bridge across the Mississippi. Lawyers representing the steamboat companies tried to persuade an Illinois court to order the bridge removed as a nuisance to river traffic. Abraham Lincoln, as an attorney for the railroad, helped defeat the steamboat interests in this case.

New patterns of commerce were developing. The new east-west trade, brought about by the railroads, was becoming more important than the old north-south trade. Increasingly, the farmers of the upper Mississippi Valley looked to New York and other Atlantic seaboard cities, rather than to New Orleans, as a market for their crops.

International Communications

From the Atlantic seaports, especially New York, surplus products of the Northwest (and some of the cotton of the South) were exported to Europe. Improvements in overseas communications encouraged this commerce.

When a transatlantic cable was laid in 1858, telegrams could be sent from New York across the ocean to London. Soon after the first messages were exchanged, however, the cable went dead. (Another cable was laid in 1866, and it continued to work from that time on.)

During the 1850's, ocean shipping was speeded up. By paying a mail subsidy, the national government enabled the Collins Line, an American company operating passenger steamers, to compete temporarily with the famed British Cunard Line. A Collins Line steamship, the *Baltic,* set a record in August 1852 by going from Liverpool to New York in less than ten days.

Americans were most successful, however, with sailing vessels in the freight business. For this they often used swift clipper ships. The clipper had a slender, graceful hull and an abundance of square sails. When the winds were right, it could move almost as fast as the fastest steamer of the time. The clipper was originally designed for sailing from Atlantic ports around South America to California. It was also used for the India trade—for carrying ice cut from New England ponds to Asia—and for other trade in which speed was especially important. The United States was so successful with the clippers and other wooden sailing ships that, for a short time, its merchant marine was the largest and busiest in the world.

Farm Production

As the western population increased, so did the cultivation of wheat and corn. By 1850, Ohio and Indiana had surpassed New York and Pennsylvania in the production of these crops. By 1860, Illinois led all states, and Iowa and Missouri were close behind. On the black soil of the prairies, wheat and corn grew remarkably well. Total production increased, as well as production per acre and per worker.

In areas where the soil was less fertile, farmers found it hard to compete. Many whose farms lay close to city markets turned to truck farming—the growing of fruits and vegetables. Some farmers began to take better care of the land and to restore it with fertilizers. Interest in agricultural education grew. States and counties began to hold agricultural fairs, and several states provided for agricultural colleges. (The first state agricultural college was established in 1857 in Michigan.) More and more farmers demanded federal aid to agricultural colleges through the granting of public lands to the states. Meanwhile, the improvements in farming methods—learned through farmers' societies, newspapers, fairs, or colleges—added to the total output of northern farms.

On many small farms, farmers continued to use hand tools like hoes, spades, rakes, scythes, and flails. On an increasing number of farms, however, especially in the Northwest, there could be heard the clatter of horse-drawn machinery. Reapers in the fields had become a common sight. Mowing machines, hay rakes, corn planters, and other horse-drawn implements were coming into use. These enabled farmers to plant, cultivate, and harvest larger yields than they had been able to harvest previously. A person with a mowing machine, for instance, could cut an acre of hay three times as fast as someone with a scythe.

The horse was just beginning to become the most important draft animal of the northern farm. Before 1850, the ox was generally preferred because it was thought to have a stronger and steadier pull. Then, plowing and hauling contests at fairs demonstrated the horse's superiority. After 1860, horses became more numerous than oxen throughout the North.

Increased Manufacturing

Though the increase in farm production was great, the increase in the production of manufactured goods was even more remarkable. In 1850, the total value of manufactures was more than 1 billion dollars; in 1860, nearly 2 billion. That year, for the first time in history, the output of the factories, mills, shops, and mines of the United States was worth more than the output of all the farms and plantations in the nation.

Three northeastern states—New York, Massachusetts, and Pennsylvania—together produced more than half of the nation's total output of goods. But industrial centers were rising in the Northwest. Cyrus H. McCormick's decision to locate his reaper works in Chicago (1847) helped make that city a center for the manufacture of farm implements. With industrialization, the Northwest was acquiring a common interest with the Northeast in using tariffs to promote and protect manufactures. As for the South, it gained some new industries, especially cotton mills, but it still produced a small percentage of the nation's manufactures.

Numerous inventors designed machines or developed processes that helped increase American productivity. More than four times as many patents were issued in 1860 as in 1850. Charles Goodyear in 1839 discovered a method of vulcanizing rubber that kept it from becoming gummy when hot and brittle when cold. By the time he died in 1860, Goodyear had taken out sixty patents and had laid the foundation for a huge industry. In 1850, Elias Howe began to manufacture the sewing machine that he had invented. The next year, Isaac Singer patented a much improved model. Soon the Howe-Singer machine was being used to make large quantities of cheap, ready-to-wear clothing.

Various machines helped speed production and reduce costs. One of them shaped railroad spikes so rapidly that a plant with only

In the Northwest, farmers usually raised grain *(above)* for distant markets. In the Northeast *(below)*, they specialized in perishable crops for nearby cities.

Yale University Art Gallery. The Mabel Brady Garvan Collection

seven employees could produce five tons a day. Another took brass wire and formed it into pins so fast that a single factory had a daily output of 300,000. Samuel Colt improved upon the principles of mass production and eventually made his gun factory in Hartford, Connecticut, the largest in the world.

An American of the 1850's boasted that the United States offered

the best and cheapest farm implements, the best carpenters' tools, the best locks, fire-engines, nails, screws, and axes; the best firearms, the cheapest clocks, the fastest steamers and sailing vessels, the cheapest railroads, the lightest wagons, and many of the most useful labor-saving devices in every department of industry.

Until 1857, both the North and the South were unusually prosperous. Vast quantities of gold, coming from the mines of California, were being turned into coins. The abundance of money encouraged people to spend freely, thus stimulating business. The construction of railroads created thousands of new jobs. War in Europe (the Crimean War, 1854–1856) caused an abnormally large demand for the output of American farms, plantations, and factories. Ocean shipping as well as agriculture and industry thrived.

The boom suddenly ended with the Panic of 1857, which marked the beginning of the third great depression of the nineteenth century. The North, with far more industry than the South, was hit much harder by the depression. As a result, the economic progress of the North was temporarily slowed.

The Rich and the Poor

To an English visitor in the North, it seemed as if almost everyone was engaged in a scramble for wealth. Many people met with some degree of success. The great majority of northerners lived and worked on family-owned farms. Some became well-to-do, not so much by selling crops as by selling land

Skilled craftsmen like this northern wheelwright often worked fourteen-hour days and earned a bare living wage. Gradually, fewer people were attracted to craft apprenticeships, as factory-made goods began to replace individually made goods.

that had risen in value. But the wealthiest people got their money from commerce and manufacturers. Most of them lived in the cities and industrial towns, where the poorest people lived, too.

Most wage earners labored long hours—eleven or more for most of them. New England mill hands worked as many as fifteen hours a day. Unskilled workers received about a dollar a day, and skilled workers were seldom paid more than two dollars. Few laborers could earn more than $300 to $600 a year, even if lucky enough to have steady jobs. At any time, jobs were liable to disappear, temporarily or permanently. Slack business in particular industries, general depressions, or the introduction of labor-saving machinery ended many jobs. Poverty caused by industrialization became a special problem in manufacturing towns and cities.

Life was especially difficult for Irish immigrants and for blacks. The Irish lived in dark and dirty tenements and accepted whatever work they could get, usually the hardest and lowest paid. Many Irishmen swung pickaxes in construction gangs that laid railroad tracks and paved city streets. Irishwomen labored long hours as servants, janitors, or machine operators, earning scarcely enough to stay alive. Discouraging though conditions were, the newcomers from Ireland thought they could look forward to a better life for their children. Some of the children went to school, but most, like their parents, worked at menial jobs.

The blacks in northern towns and cities had even less to look forward to than the Irish. A very few black men became merchants, bankers, lawyers, and the like.

Others managed to get along fairly well as barbers or as servants in hotels or private houses. Most could get no work, however, except for the meanest of odd jobs. "Learn trades or starve!" the abolitionist leader and former slave Frederick Douglass advised. Those black men who did learn trades, such as masonry and carpentry, often could get no chance to practice them because of prejudicial treatment by employers.

Black women usually worked as servants, cooks, or janitors. Black children were rarely allowed to enroll in the schools. Most helped their parents at their work or did odd jobs.

As an English traveler observed, blacks in the North formed "a race apart, a strange people in a strange land." They were excluded from white neighborhoods, streetcars, eating places, and schools. Some whites did help blacks, especially in the field of education. In 1855, Senator Charles Sumner secured the admission of Negroes to the Boston public schools, with the argument that separate schools were necessarily unequal.

New labor unions were organized in the skilled trades, but unions did nothing for the great mass of unskilled laborers, whether black or white, native or foreign-born. Union members more and more frequently resorted to strikes. According to the common law, a strike was an illegal conspiracy. In 1842, however, a Massachusetts court held that strikes, if peaceably conducted, were permissible in certain cases. Courts in other states later agreed with this ruling.

Unemployed workers, most of whom had no union to represent them, took part in riots and mob demonstrations. The Panic of 1857 strengthened their fervor. "We want work!" "Work or bread!" mobs shouted in New York, Chicago, and other cities. City governments and private charities set up soup kitchens to feed the many jobless. Speakers on street corners and in city parks harangued the idle crowds and urged the workers to rise and take the government into their own hands.

THE SOUTH

Life in the slave states changed less rapidly than in the free states. People were less inclined to adopt new ideas, new ways of doing things. Railroads were built in the South, but less extensively than in the North. Some industries developed, but all of them together produced less than one-tenth of the nation's manufactures. The South's economy was based on agricultural production, especially of cotton. This in turn depended on the labor of black slaves.

Cotton was by far the most important of the many southern crops. It was the largest export of the United States and the greatest source of wealth for the South. It became far more than a valuable crop. It became a symbol of the southern way of life.

Cotton Is King was the title that David Christy gave to a book he published in 1855. "Cotton *is* king," southerners repeated over and over. A New Orleans newspaperman, James D. B. De Bow, explained: "To the slave-holding states, it is the great source of their power and their wealth, and the main security for their peculiar institution." By "peculiar institution," De Bow meant Negro slavery, which its defenders considered "peculiar" in the sense of "distinctive," not "odd." He went on:

Let us teach our children to hold the cotton plant in one hand and a sword in the other, ever ready to defend it as the source of commercial power abroad, and through that, of independence at home.

Southerners believed that King Cotton ruled the world. Certainly, it ruled their imaginations.

Farms and Plantations

Slavery was spread unevenly over the South, because of geographic conditions. Slaves were most numerous in the lowlands, which were best suited for the larger plantations. They were less numerous in the hilly or mountainous regions.

Crops varied from place to place throughout the South. Cotton was grown in a "cotton belt" that stretched in a great arc from North Carolina southward and westward to Texas and Arkansas. Tobacco was grown in a belt that extended northward from North Carolina to Virginia and Maryland and westward to Kentucky. Rice was produced along the coast of South Carolina, and sugar in the lowlands of Louisiana.

By 1850, the Southwest was producing nearly three-fourths of the total cotton crop. The cotton planters were located primarily in the "black belt" of central Alabama and Mississippi, a great treeless stretch of land with fertile black soil, and in the bottom lands of the Tennessee, Alabama, Mississippi, and other river valleys. When, in the 1840's, levees were built to control floods in the states of Mississippi and Louisiana, the wide, flat delta region of the Mississippi River became an extremely rich cotton-growing area.

Some novels and movies have painted a romanticized picture of the Old South—pillared mansions, vast fields of cane or cotton, grinning servants, singing field hands, and hospitable white gentlemen and ladies. This romanticized South contains only kindhearted masters and carefree slaves, except

The Know-Nothings

Between 1830 and 1860, more than 4 million immigrants entered the United States. Most came from Ireland and Germany, large numbers of them were Catholics, and many were poor.

In 1835, about half of those in poorhouses in New York, Boston, and New Orleans were immigrants. Growing numbers of native Americans believed that foreign paupers should be denied entry to the United States.

Many people in the United States also feared that the American system was endangered by the growing political power of the immigrants. Some German immigrants who had engaged in a revolt in their homeland were labeled as radicals and anarchists. The Irish were considered dangerous because their concentration in certain large cities made it possible for them to outnumber non-Irish voters on election day.

The mushrooming growth of the Catholic Church in the United States reinforced a long-standing distrust of Catholics on the part of Protestants. When Catholic immigrants began to run for office, many non-Catholics said that the church was trying to gain control of the American political process. In the 1840's, anti-Catholic riots erupted in many cities.

A number of antiforeign groups sprang up. The most notable was the American, or "Know-Nothing," party. Many voters were drawn to the party's "America for Americans" slogan and to its proposals to limit immigration.

Although the Know-Nothing party tried to promote national unity, it could not overcome sectional differences. The Know-Nothings of the South wanted to limit immigration in order to limit the growth and the votes of the North. They feared the antislavery sentiments of some immigrant groups. But many northern Know-Nothings were abolitionists. Their anti-immigrant feelings were often aimed at the Irish, who were usually antiabolitionist as well as Catholic. The Irish competed with blacks for jobs, and many favored slavery.

The slavery issue ultimately divided the Know-Nothings. It became the dominant political issue, and the Know-Nothing party faded.

Pat and Fritz, symbols of the Irish and the Germans, walk off with a ballot box.

The luxuries of grand plantation life idealized by writers and painters *(right)* were actually enjoyed by less than 1 percent of the white population. Small plantations with crude dwellings *(below)* were more typical. Their cotton and tobacco crops contributed to the economic growth of the North as well as to the South. Trading of southern crops boosted northern shipping, banking, and industry, and provided jobs for thousands of workers. Some southerners wanted more industry and shipping in order to increase prosperity and calm the growing sectional conflicts.

perhaps for an occasional "poor white" who appears briefly on the edges of the scene.

In the South of historical fact, most of the people were neither slaves nor slave owners. About 37 percent of the population was black. All except a very few of the blacks were slaves. Only one white in four was a slaveholder or a member of a slaveholding family. Of the nonslaveholders, only a tiny proportion could be classified into a special group known as "poor whites." Poor whites were more than just poor and white. They were sickly people who barely managed to keep alive on worn-out plantation lands or sandy, barren soils. Some other nonslaveholders were mountaineers living in rough and unproductive country. These highlanders were poor but vigorous and fiercely independent.

The great majority of white southerners were neither rich nor poor. They lived on family-owned farms and owned no slaves. Some hired a slave or two for extra help in busy seasons. In 1850, among the people who did own slaves, fewer than 2,000 in the entire South owned more than 100 slaves each. Half of all slaveholders had fewer than 10 each. Planters who owned vast fields and imposing mansions were rare.

Though the planters were a minority of the people, they (especially the cotton planters) controlled most of the wealth of the South. They dominated its politics, and they set the tone for its manners and its thought.

Slave Labor

On the plantation, the slaves did most of the work. Some labored as mechanics or artisans, a larger number as household servants, and the majority as field hands.

On a small plantation the slaves might work in the fields alongside members of the slave-owning family. On a large plantation, the owner usually hired an overseer, generally a white man, who divided the field workers into gangs. One of the male slaves was placed in charge of each gang. This slave, the "driver," carried a long whip that he used, if necessary, to keep the gang on the move.

The owner had a large investment in the slaves. It was in his or her interest to see to it that they were not worked too hard and were reasonably well fed and cared for. Slaves were seldom used for digging ditches in malarial swamps, for example, or for catching cotton bales by the chutes at boat landings. Irish immigrants, when available, were used for such dangerous or unhealthful work. If a slave died, the owner lost property worth as much as $1,000 or more. If a hired hand died, the employer lost nothing.

The owner's economic interest did not always assure good treatment for the slaves. The owner was not always guided by considerations of profit and loss. If kind, he or she would treat the slaves well. If cruel, he or she would find plenty of opportunity to vent this cruelty.

The overseer's interest in the slave differed from that of the owner. The larger the crop, the larger the overseer's pay. It was therefore to the overseer's advantage to get as much work as possible out of each and every slave.

The owner had almost absolute power over the slaves. True, an owner could not legally kill them—except in self-defense or, accidentally, in the course of punishment. If an owner were forced to justify a death, however, the courts would take his or her word about it. They would not listen to the testimony of slaves. This tyrannical authority of one person over another was the basic evil of slavery.

Slave women were encouraged to have as many children as possible, since each child that lived added to the supply of slaves. Slave men and women tried to maintain family relationships, but the laws did not recognize slave marriages. The slave owner might try to prevent the separation of couples or of parents and children, yet slave families often were broken up through sales, especially in settlement of estates after the owner's death.

Slaves had few ways of asserting themselves. They could resort to slowing down on the job, breaking or losing tools, or hiding out at busy times. Destruction of crops and property were also popular tactics. Slaves could run away, but unless they lived near the border of a free state, they had little chance of making good their escape. Captured slaves would be punished with the lash and sometimes the branding iron. Yet some ran off again and again. In newspaper advertisements, owners sometimes described fugitives as having not only physical but also psychological scars, such as a stutter or a nervous twitch.

Increased Need for Slaves

The newer states of the South—especially Alabama, Mississippi, Louisiana, and Texas—were growing much faster than the older ones. Planters continued to move southward and westward, taking their slaves with them. On the fresh and fertile lands of the newer states, there was a constant shortage of slaves. In the older states, the soil was worn out from long-time cultivation. The use of slave labor there was no longer very profitable, and there was a constant surplus of slaves.

An interstate slave trade had developed, and, in the 1850's, this trade thrived as never before. Slaves were taken to market by various routes. Some, chained together, were marched overland. Others were shipped from Chesapeake ports to ports on the Gulf of Mexico. Still others went by boat down the Mississippi (hence the expression "sold down the river").

At auctions, the slaves were sold to the highest bidder. Many prospective buyers gave the slaves in the market the same kind of inspection they would have given an animal, requiring them to walk back and forth as they were scrutinized for physical defects. The buyers were cautious, for the dealer often tried to cheat them by such tricks as blacking gray hair to make a slave look younger.

Most planters looked down upon the slave traders, both because of their sharp practices and because of the inhumane business itself. Though the planters seldom recognized or admitted it, the slave trader performed a service that was indispensable to the growth of slavery. Someone had to buy and sell slaves if the planters were to obtain enough slave labor to supply the demand.

A few southerners began to think that the interstate slave trade would not provide an adequate supply. They demanded the reopening of the foreign slave trade, which had been closed by federal law since 1808. Despite the law, a number of slaves were smuggled into the country every year. How large the number was, no one can say, but it was not large enough to have a noticeable effect on the supply or the price of slaves.

Many southerners, as well as many northerners, believed that slavery would need additional lands if it were to prosper or even survive. The assumption was that, because of soil exhaustion, slavery would eventually die out in the newer states, as it seemed to be doing in the older states.

Defending Slavery

At one time, leading southerners had questioned and criticized the enslavement of other human beings. As late as the 1830's, most southerners disliked slavery. They put up with it as something they had inherited and could not easily get rid of. By the 1850's, however, they no longer apologized for it as a necessary evil. They now boasted of it as "a good—a positive good."

Propaganda had helped convince the people, even those who owned no slaves, that slavery was a good thing. According to the proslavery argument, black people were by nature so primitive and childlike that they could not take care of themselves. Thanks to the slave owner, they were better off than northern free laborers, who had to worry about unemployment and old age. The people who favored slavery insisted that black slavery was good for southern whites, whether they owned slaves or not. It made the South prosperous, exempted it from strikes and other labor troubles, and enabled

Laws in southern states permitted slaveholders to treat their slaves as property. The poster *(above)* announces the raffle of a slave valued at $900. Fugitive slaves were considered to have robbed their owners by fleeing *(below)*.

the two races to live there in peace. Indeed, the "peculiar institution" of the South was good for everyone, everywhere, and it was in accord with the teachings of the Bible. So its defenders argued.

One proslavery enthusiast said that since slavery was such an ideal arrangement, it ought not to be used only on southern Negroes. It ought also to be tried on other workers, white as well as black, northern as well as southern.

Among nonslaveholders in the South, censorship silenced those whom propaganda failed to convince. The people seldom read or even received antislavery propaganda in the mails, for officials usually banned any books, pamphlets, or periodicals that criticized slavery. People were usually jailed when caught with such "incendiary" literature in their possession.

A North Carolina farmer, Hinton R. Helper, wrote a book to prove that slavery was harmful to nonslaveholders. Helper said it caused the South to lag behind the North in economic progress. He denied that cotton was king. "Hay is king," he maintained, pointing out that the northern hay crop was worth more than the southern cotton crop. He called his book *The Impending Crisis of the South.* In 1857, after he had moved to the North, he got it published in New York. In the South, few had a chance to buy or read his book. In the North, it became a best seller.

Propaganda and censorship, by themselves, did not fully account for the nonslaveholders' support of slavery. In many cases, propaganda only confirmed feelings the nonslaveholders already had. Censorship merely kept them from reading things like Helper's book, which might have caused them to question whether or not they were really better off because of slavery.

The nonslaveholders felt that under slavery, they had a chance to rise in the world, become slave owners themselves, and enjoy the delights of plantation life. Under emancipation, there would be millions of free blacks. Southern whites could not imagine themselves living safely or happily beside blacks. (In the North, prejudice was as strong or stronger, but blacks were vastly fewer. Northern whites were not as concerned about the consequences of emancipation because they expected that, once emancipated, most of the former slaves would remain in the South.)

Fewer nonslaveholders would have been proslavery if it had been feasible to send all of the blacks to western Africa. Many nonslaveholders would have been willing to let slavery disappear if they could have been sure that, at the same time, the blacks would also disappear.

DIFFERENT OUTLOOKS

Slavery and cotton in the South, free labor and industry in the North—these were the basic differences. Eventually they caused the two sections to differ also in economic interests, constitutional views, and social ideals.

Conflicting Economic Interests

Northern manufacturers desired high tariffs that would raise the price of competing goods that came into the United States from foreign nations. Thus the manufacturers would be able to sell larger quantities of their own products at higher prices.

Tariff advocates said that without such protection some mill owners might have to go out of business. Then workers would lose their jobs. After the Panic of 1857, a number of mills did close, and the production of others was cut back. Tariff protection then seemed more necessary than ever to manufacturers and their employees.

Northern shipowners wanted the government to aid them with mail contracts or other subsidies. They also wanted laws to keep foreign ships out of the coastal trade between American ports. Northern farmers wanted the government to aid them by providing free homesteads, supporting agricultural education, and helping finance the construction of railroads.

Some people in the North opposed such government aid, and some people in the South favored it. The sugar planters of Louisiana, for example, wanted tariff protection for their own product, since they wished to discourage the importation of Cuban sugar. Nevertheless, by 1860, a majority of northerners had come to favor one or more such measures, and a majority of southerners had come to oppose all of them.

Southerners argued that the North already had grown rich by exploiting them. In 1860, T. P. Kettell wrote *Southern Wealth and Northern Profits.* In this book he tried to prove that southerners produced more than their share of the nation's wealth but that the North took away a large part of it. Supposedly, through control of shipping, banking, and manufacturing, the North managed to get forty cents out of every dollar that southern cotton brought.

Year after year, delegates from southern states met in commercial conventions to discuss means of making the South's economy independent. These conventions accomplished little or nothing, largely because the delegates themselves disagreed as to what precisely should be done.

Though the planters opposed government aid to northern business, they demanded government support for their own labor system. Since they thought slavery had to expand in order to thrive, they wanted the government to guarantee its expansion. They wanted the government to make new territories available for the "peculiar institution" and to encourage and protect it within the territories.

ABOLITION OF SLAVERY, 1800–1865

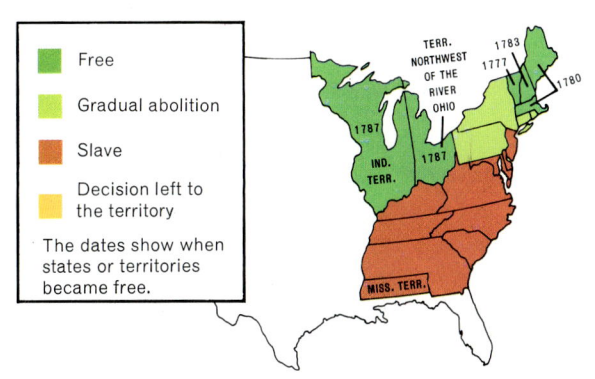

Legend:
- Free
- Gradual abolition
- Slave
- Decision left to the territory

The dates show when states or territories became free.

1800. The Northwest Territory was free from the start. By 1800, almost half of the states had taken some steps to abolish slavery.

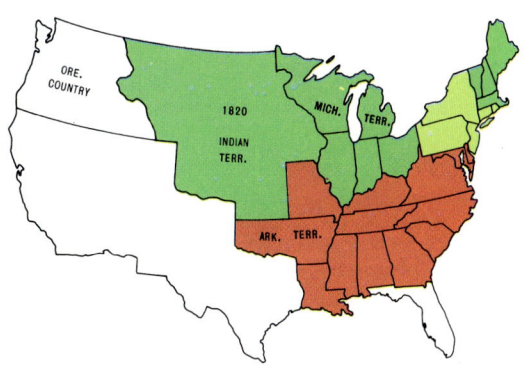

1820. The Missouri Compromise of 1820 prohibited slavery north of 36°30′ in the Louisiana Purchase territory, with the exception of Missouri.

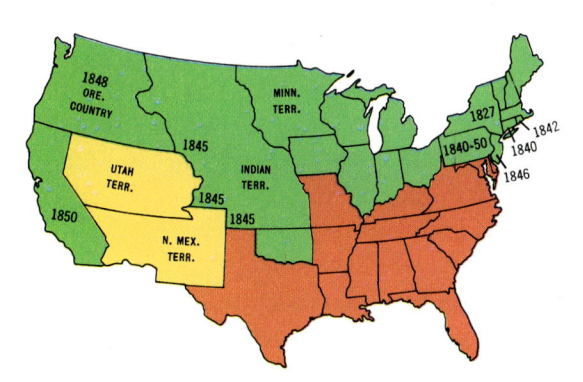

1850. Slavery was prohibited in Oregon Territory in 1848. The Compromise of 1850 admitted free California and allowed popular sovereignty in New Mexico and Utah.

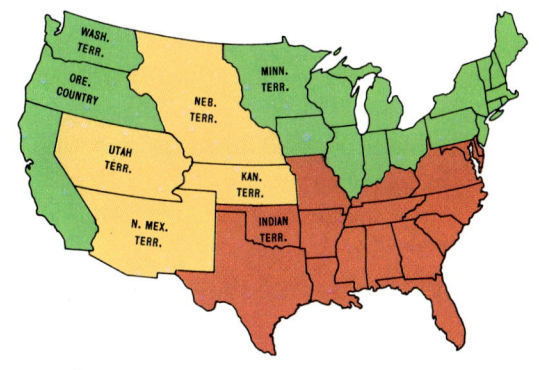

1854. Congress passed the Kansas-Nebraska Act, allowing popular sovereignty in the Nebraska and Kansas territories. In effect this law canceled part of the Missouri Compromise.

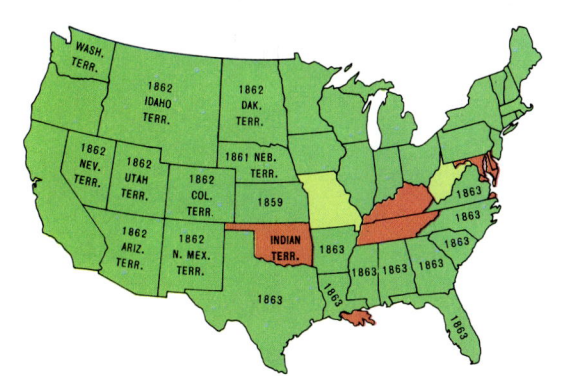

1863. In 1862, Congress forbade slavery in all organized territories. In 1863, the Emancipation Proclamation prohibited slavery in those parts of the Confederacy still in rebellion.

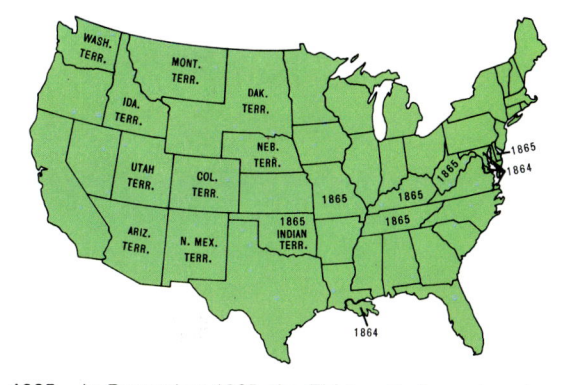

1865. In December 1865, the Thirteenth Amendment went into effect. It abolished slavery. Louisiana and Virginia had already freed the slaves in areas not covered by the Emancipation Proclamation.

Interpreting the Constitution

According to northern tariff advocates, the Constitution gave Congress the power to pass tariff laws. True, the Constitution said nothing about using tariffs to protect and encourage manufactures, but it did say that Congress could levy taxes and could regulate commerce with foreign nations. The tariff could be viewed either as a tax or as a measure for the regulation of commerce. Therefore, though not included in the specified powers, it would come within the "implied powers" of Congress. Southern opponents of the protective tariff insisted that Congress had no rightful powers except those specifically granted in the Constitution.

The question of who should control slavery and the slave trade also led to different constitutional interpretations. Both critics and defenders agreed that slavery in the southern states was a "domestic" institution that only the states themselves could abolish. Antislavery people in the North, however, said that since Congress had the specified power to regulate interstate commerce, it could abolish the interstate slave trade. They said also that Congress had the right to abolish slavery in the District of Columbia, since this area was under federal jurisdiction. According to defenders of slavery, Congress could not properly do so. They said that Maryland had ceded the area for the national capital with the understanding that slavery would continue to exist there.

Could Congress prohibit slavery in the territories? This became the most heatedly discussed constitutional question of the 1850's. The Constitution itself said:

> The Congress shall have Power to dispose of and make all needful Rules and Regulations respecting the Territory or other Property belonging to the United States; and nothing in this Constitution shall be so construed as to Prejudice any Claims of the United States, or of any particular State. *(Art. 4, sec. 3, para. 2)*

Wall Street bankers excitedly discuss business conditions in 1857. More than a billion dollars had been invested in manufacturing and a billion in railroads. Such heavy investments and a chronic shortage of cash helped bring on a bank panic.

According to most northerners, Congress could, indeed, legislate against slavery in the territories, since Congress could "make all needful Rules and Regulations" regarding them. Congress had, in fact, prohibited slavery in the Northwest Territory by repassing the Northwest Ordinance of 1787 (which was originally passed by the Confederation Congress before the adoption of the Constitution in 1789.)

According to most southerners, Congress could by no means legislate against slavery in the territories, since nothing in the Constitution was to be "so construed as to Prejudice any Claims . . . of any particular State." Each state had as much claim upon the territories as any other state. The people of any state should be able to move to any territory and take along their property, including slave property, with full assurance that it would be safe.

Southerners continued to discuss and interpret states' rights according to their particular needs and desires. Though they no longer mentioned nullification, they still insisted upon the right of secession. Some northerners also believed in states' rights, such as the right to resist federal laws that were designed for the recapture of fugitive slaves. Very few northerners, however, thought that any state had a right to secede.

Actually, the states' rights doctrine that evolved in the South had more to do with state *powers* than with state *rights*. It did more than assure self-government within the states and protect slavery against interference from the outside. It was essentially an aggressive doctrine. It asserted the power of the states to extend slavery beyond their own

ATLANTIC
MUTUAL
INS. CO.
MARINE
& INLAND
INSURANCE
SCRANTON
COAL
BROAD WAY

borders and into the territories. Many southerners maintained that in making territorial rules and regulations, Congress had no choice but to accept and approve the state laws in regard to slavery.

So far as the people of the territories were concerned, the states' rights doctrine of the South denied them the right of self-government. It denied the right of those people to exclude slavery, even if the great majority of them should wish to do so.

Social Ideals

In the North, democracy was a prevailing ideal, though not an accomplished fact. People continued to believe in the words of the Declaration of Independence that "all men are created equal" and are born with "certain unalienable Rights." Of course, people did not practice the ideal of equality. The rich and strong looked down upon the poor and weak. Whites treated blacks as inferiors. Women were second-class citizens. Nevertheless, some northerners became more and more convinced that blacks, as well as whites, possessed the basic rights of life, liberty, and the pursuit of happiness, and should be allowed to exercise them. People were inclined to feel guilty about the gap between the ideal and the reality in northern life.

In the South, many people were losing sight of democracy as an ideal. They questioned the revolutionary propositions regarding equality and liberty. Such political leaders as John C. Calhoun had ridiculed those propositions. He said they were as dangerous as they were ridiculous. They gave rise to fanatical movements like abolitionism, he explained, and unless these were checked, they might lead at last to civil war.

More and more, the slaveholders and even many nonslaveholders adopted aristocratic ideals. They came to believe that an upper class of gentlemen should run social and political affairs. In fact, this is what the planters did. Romantic novels, particularly those of Sir Walter Scott, were read and enjoyed by the would-be aristocrats of the South, who longed to be like the knights and ladies of old. The knights fought duels, and so did southern gentlemen, who were touchy on points of personal honor. The knights were brave, mannerly, and kind to ladies—so were southern gentlemen.

Southern "ladies" tried to act as they thought women behaved toward the knights. For example, it was considered stylish to be weak and helpless and to faint under the slightest stress. In actual fact, most southern aristocratic women were not the helpless damsels many of them pretended to be. Plantation households were almost small factories, and these women were the executives who ran them.

Even a Yankee visitor could admire the "high-toned gentleman" of the South. "The honesty and unstudied dignity of character, the generosity and the real nobleness of habitual impulses, and the well-bred manly courtesy which distinguish him," wrote Frederick Law Olmsted, "are sadly rare at the North." Still, Olmsted preferred the relatively democratic society of the North to the relatively aristocratic society of the South. He thought that northern men, as a whole, were "better, more gentlemanly even," than southern men, including all classes. This, of course, was only one observer's opinion, and a northerner's at that.

Thoughtful southerners knew that the North was surpassing their section in wealth as well as numbers. Inwardly, they grew concerned about the situation of the South, though outwardly they boasted of southern greatness. They feared the future and, so far as possible, clung to the past.

Yet, though the differences were many and deep, the similarities between the North and the South were even more numerous

Leisure

Farmers often combined pleasure with business. The flax-scutching bee *(above)*, like barn-raisings and corn-husking bees, was a time to get together with neighbors as well as to work. Horse racing was a popular feature of the country fair.

and fundamental. After all, both the northerners and the southerners were Americans, with a common heritage of many customs and beliefs.

Moreover, while northerners and southerners had conflicting interests, they also had interests in common. They benefited from trade with each other. They had ties of family and friendship, some northerners having been born in the South and some southerners in the North. They had ties of belief and membership that caused them to think of themselves not only as northerners or southerners, but also as Protestants or Catholics, as Whigs or Democrats.

Nevertheless, in recounting this period of United States history, it is necessary to emphasize the sectional differences rather than the similarities, the points of dispute rather than the areas of agreement. Eventually, the differences and disagreements prevailed. Only by paying close attention to these can it be understood how the United States came to be divided in two, and how Americans happened to begin a civil war against other Americans.

A Look at Specifics

1. In what areas of the country did most Irish immigrants settle? Most German immigrants? Why?

2. Why did few immigrants settle in the South?

3. What advances were made in agricultural education during the 1850's?

4. What problems were faced by the northern black during the 1850's? The Irish immigrant?

5. Why did southerners say that "Cotton is king"?

6. In what ways did geographical conditions affect the distribution of slaves?

7. What arguments did supporters of slavery use to justify their position?

8. How did the South control the spread of antislavery propaganda?

9. Why did many nonslaveholders support slavery?

10. Why were most southern cotton growers opposed to a tariff on manufactures?

A Review of Major Ideas

1. What changes took place in the nature and distribution of the population during the 1840's and 1850's?

2. What changes in the United States economy during the 1850's brought the Northeast and Northwest closer together?

3. How did the economy of the South differ from that of the North?

4. How did the different ways of life in the North and South contribute to different ways of thinking?

5. What interests did the North and South have in common?

For Independent Study

1. How do you account for the fact that the growth of cities between 1830 and 1860 was far slower in the South than in the North?

2. Many southerners claimed that the southern slaves were treated better and enjoyed a happier life than did the average northern industrial worker. Do you think that this was true? Explain.

A Divided Nation

CHAPTER 10
1850–1861

"I wouldn't vote for that idiot if you paid me. If he's elected, I'm leaving the country." So say many Americans during presidential election campaigns. Once the election is over, however, they usually remain in the country. Although they may still oppose the newly elected President, they know they have four years to work for that person's defeat.

The election of 1860 was different. After that election, one whole section of the nation tried to secede from the Union. Shortly after the new President was inaugurated, North and South began fighting a war that would last four long, bloody years. The question arises, "Why?" After all, the two sections had been part of the same nation for more than eighty years.

Separation and war came because of growing differences, real and imaginary, between the North and the South. The institution of slavery had disappeared in one of the sections, but not in the other, and industry was developing within each section at very different rates. Out of these differences grew the "irrepressible conflict."

A SECTIONAL COMPROMISE

Conflict does not necessarily mean *war,* nor does it necessarily lead to bloodshed. Within a democracy there are always clashes of opposing interests and opposing views. These are the stuff of which politics is made. Normally, politicians manage to smooth over the disputes. When conflicts go deep enough, however, politicians may intensify rather than relieve the conflicts.

It was possible for politicians to deal fairly well with sectional disagreements so long as the two political parties were organized on a national basis. It would become difficult if not impossible once the national parties had disappeared and sectional parties had taken their place.

The Banjo Lesson, by Henry Tanner. Courtesy The Hampton Institute

Long before the Civil War, in his Farewell Address, George Washington had said:

In contemplating the causes which may disturb our Union it occurs as a matter of serious concern that any ground should have been furnished for characterizing parties by *Geographical* discrimination, *Northern* and *Southern, Atlantic* and *Western;* whence designing men may endeavour to excite a belief that there is a real difference of local interests and views. One of the expedients of a party to acquire influence, within particular districts, is to misrepresent the opinions and aims of other districts.

In Washington's time it seemed that if the nation should ever divide, it would probably split into an East and a West. The Appalachian Mountains made a natural dividing line, and the Mississippi Valley formed a natural unit. By 1850, when the nation actually began to divide, the line of division cut across the natural barrier of the Appalachian Mountains and the natural unity of the Mississippi River Valley. The danger now was that northern and southern parties might emerge.

Long-Standing Issues

In 1850, the United States was facing a dangerous sectional crisis. Several issues concerning slavery needed to be settled.

One issue was the continued existence of slavery and the slave trade in the city of Washington. Here, close to the Capitol, were slave auctions and slave pens—sights the opponents of slavery considered shocking anywhere in the "land of the free." Members of antislavery societies continually petitioned Congress to rid the District of Columbia of both slavery and the slave trade.

This agitation offended and frightened many southerners. So did the northern opposition to the federal Fugitive Slave Act of 1793. In the case of *Prigg* v. *Pennsylvania* (1842), the Supreme Court had ruled that it was the duty of federal officials to capture and return fugitive slaves and that state authori-

"After the Sale: Slaves Going South from Richmond" vividly shows a frequent result of slave sales—the separation of families. The traders *(right foreground)* were despised for their work by both blacks and whites, even by those who were overseers or slaveholders.

ties were not required to help. Immediately the antislavery societies began urging the northern states to pass "personal liberty" laws, and several of the states did so. The personal liberty laws forbade state officials to assist in capturing or returning runaways. Thus, in the North, state laws partly nullified a federal act, but southerners denounced that kind of nullification.

The issue of slavery in the Louisiana Purchase territory had been settled by the Missouri Compromise (1820). That agreement prohibited slavery north of a certain line (36° 30'), except in Missouri. The line did not, however, apply to the newer territories of Oregon, California, and New Mexico.

Some people thought Congress ought to extend the line all the way to the Pacific Ocean. Others believed in "popular sovereignty"—that is, in allowing the settlers in each territory to decide for themselves whether or not to allow slavery. The extremists of the North opposed it and demanded "free soil" instead. That is, they insisted that Congress must exclude slavery from *all* the territories. Some southerners violently opposed this idea. They maintained that Congress must permit and protect slavery in all the territories.

In regard to New Mexico, there was a boundary dispute. Texas claimed all the land westward to the Rio Grande, and this claim included a large part of what New Mexico settlers thought was New Mexico. Northerners backed the New Mexicans, and southerners the Texans. If Texas should make good its claim, the area of slavery would be enlarged, for Texas was a slave state.

Threats of Secession

Zachary Taylor, elected in 1848, was the first professional military man to become President. Though honest and courageous, he lacked experience in government.

The Whigs had run Taylor for the presidency without a specific platform. Few people knew what he stood for. Southerners assumed that he would support proslavery policies, for he owned a Louisiana plantation with a hundred slaves. In fact, however, he had served on the frontier for so long that he no longer felt any particular attachment to the South. As President, he often listened to the advice of free-soil northerners, especially Senator William H. Seward of New York.

It seemed to President Taylor that California ought to become a state immediately, without going through the stages of territorial government. California needed strong agencies of law enforcement to maintain order in the wild mining camps, and it had a large enough population to qualify for statehood. Taylor suggested to some of the leading Californians that they frame a state constitution and apply for admission to the Union. They did so, framing a constitution (written in Spanish) that prohibited slavery. Then, late in 1849, Taylor suggested that Congress admit California as a free state.

Through the early months of 1850, southerners threatened that their own states would secede if California came into the Union. The legislature of Mississippi called a convention of southern states to meet in Nashville, Tennessee, in June. At this convention, some southern leaders expected to make plans for the slave states to secede as a group. The Mississippi legislature, when naming its delegate to the convention, also appropriated money for "necessary measures for protecting the state." Obviously, some southerners were thinking of the possibility of war.

A Compromise

While secession and war were threatening, Congress was discussing a compromise. Henry Clay, the aging senator from Kentucky, had presented a bill that dealt not only with California but also with other matters in dispute. Clay's "omnibus bill" had five main provisions:

(1) California would be admitted as a free state.

(2) In the rest of the area acquired from Mexico (that is, in New Mexico and Utah), territorial governments would be organized without any restriction on slavery. Presumably, these territories could adopt or reject slavery according to the principle of popular sovereignty. This would leave the way open for the creation of new slave states, which would counterbalance California and, later on, Oregon.

(3) Texas would give up its claim to a part of New Mexico, and, in return, the federal government would take over and pay the debts that Texas owed. (For the most part, this money was owed to people who had lent money to Texas when it was an independent republic.)

(4) The slave trade, but not slavery, would be abolished in the District of Columbia.

(5) A new fugitive slave act, with strict provisions for enforcement, would be passed.

Clay, a Kentucky slaveholder, spoke eloquently in favor of his bill. John C. Calhoun, a South Carolina slaveholder, now dying, condemned it. Calhoun argued that the South was not being given sufficient guarantees for its interests, especially slavery. He had in mind a constitutional amendment providing for two presidents, one from the North and the other from the South, each of them having a veto. Daniel Webster, of Massachusetts, defended Clay's compromise and pleaded for calm on both sides. William H. Seward opposed the bill on the ground that in opening territories to slavery it violated the "higher law," the law of God, which required devotion to the cause of freedom.

Clay's bill had no chance so long as Taylor remained in the presidency. Taylor insisted that California should be admitted at once, without regard to the settlement of other issues. If the bill had passed, he would have vetoed it.

On the Fourth of July, Taylor attended ceremonies at the Washington Monument. The sun was hot, and to cool off, he drank iced milk. He also ate quantities of fresh cherries. Soon he was sick. It was thought he had indigestion, but more likely he had cholera. In a few days he was dead.

Millard Fillmore, formerly Vice-President, was now President. A New York Whig, Fillmore soon proved himself to be far more ready to accept Clay's compromise than Taylor had been. The new President appointed Webster to the office of secretary of state and other procompromise men to lesser offices. Fillmore and his appointees encouraged votes for the compromise, which Congress finally passed.

An Unsettled Issue

In general, southerners felt that in the Compromise of 1850 the North had got the better of the bargain. Some of them still talked about secession. They looked forward to the Nashville convention, which had been postponed until November 1850. When it finally met, only about a third of the delegates arrived. They called for a new convention to represent the entire South. Most southerners, though, preferred to wait and see how well the compromise worked. Their feelings were summed up in the Georgia Platform, a series of resolutions passed by the Georgia legislature. These resolutions declared that the state would go along with the compromise—but only if the North lived up to all the terms, especially those regarding the return of fugitive slaves.

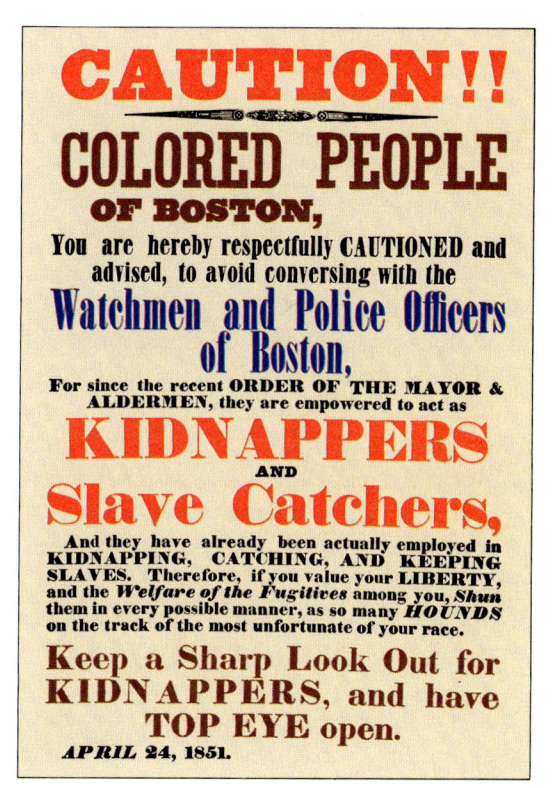

CAUTION!!
COLORED PEOPLE OF BOSTON,
You are hereby respectfully CAUTIONED and advised, to avoid conversing with the **Watchmen and Police Officers of Boston,** For since the recent ORDER OF THE MAYOR & ALDERMEN, they are empowered to act as **KIDNAPPERS AND Slave Catchers,** And they have already been actually employed in KIDNAPPING, CATCHING, AND KEEPING SLAVES. Therefore, if you value your LIBERTY, and the *Welfare of the Fugitives* among you, *Shun* them in every possible manner, as so many HOUNDS on the track of the most unfortunate of your race.
Keep a Sharp Look Out for KIDNAPPERS, and have TOP EYE open.
APRIL 24, 1851.

Handbills and posters were circulated in the North to warn black people that the Fugitive Slave Law posed a threat to their freedom.

Northerners generally approved the Compromise of 1850, except for the new Fugitive Slave Law. Most of them felt that this law was unfair. According to its provisions, a man pursuing blacks needed only to swear that they were his slaves. The blacks themselves could not testify, nor could they have a trial by jury. Thus free blacks would have no legal protection against a kidnaper trying to force them into slavery. Federal marshals were required to enforce the law, and citizens were supposed to help catch fugitives. Northerners protested that the law would make all the people "slave catchers."

Antislavery northerners made themselves slave rescuers instead. At various places throughout the North, opponents of the Fugitive Slave Law snatched fleeing blacks from the hands of federal officials and spirited them off to safe places. Each of these slave rescues, which got much attention in the newspapers, stirred up additional resentment of one kind in the North and of another kind in the South.

During the winter of 1851/52 the excitement over fugitive slaves was at its height. In this period a remarkable novel of "life among the lowly" appeared, chapter by chapter, in an antislavery periodical published in Washington, D.C. In 1852, the story was published as a book, and soon it was made into a play. This piece of fiction, one of the most influential works ever written, was *Uncle Tom's Cabin.*

Its author, Harriet Beecher Stowe, came from a famous Puritan family of New England. Her father, her seven brothers, and her husband were preachers, and she herself was deeply religious. While living in Cincinnati, she made occasional visits across the Ohio River to Kentucky, where she made some firsthand observations of slavery. In her story, she aimed to show that slavery brutalized the people who were connected with it, no matter what their sectional background. Therefore, she made the most hateful villain a Yankee from Vermont, Simon Legree.

Even though she made some of the most appealing characters southern ladies and gentlemen, the book infuriated southern whites. And northerners were increasingly outraged as they read this dramatic account of oppressed and hunted blacks.

A PERSISTENT QUARREL

The Compromise of 1850 proved to be no final settlement of the sectional issues. In a few years, the spirit of sectionalism was suddenly aroused again. The man who did the most to stir up new trouble was Stephen A. Douglas, a Democratic senator from Illinois.

The Collapse of the Whigs

For the election of 1852, the Democrats adopted a platform wholeheartedly endorsing the entire Compromise of 1850. They could not agree on which of their party leaders to nominate, so they chose a handsome, charming, but rather weak man from New Hampshire, Franklin Pierce. He was what antislavery northerners called a "doughface," that is, a northerner with southern principles. He made it clear that he would stand by his party's platform.

The Whigs were more divided. In their platform, they tried to evade the big issue, presenting only an ambiguous statement about the compromise. For their candidate, they bypassed the man already in office, Millard Fillmore—who everyone knew favored the compromise. They nominated the Mexican War hero Winfield Scott, whose views on the subject were vague.

Though a Virginian, Scott had the support of antislavery Whigs. They counted upon him to attract votes because of his military record. But he did not attract enough of them. On election day many southern Whigs, suspicious of Scott, either stayed home or voted for the Democratic candidate. Pierce won.

The Whig party was dividing into proslavery and antislavery factions, which in New England were known as Cotton Whigs and Conscience Whigs. Its old leaders, Clay and Webster, died in 1852, and no men of comparable stature were available to take their place. Scott's defeat came as a serious blow to the already disintegrating Whig party. It never recovered its old position as one of the two major parties.

A Transcontinental Railroad

Senator Stephen A. Douglas was a great orator. A native of Vermont, he had moved to Illinois as a young man. There he taught school, practiced law, and rose to leadership in the Democratic party. With good reason, he expected someday to be President. Douglas was ambitious, both for his country and for himself. He wanted the nation to remain united and hoped to see it grow ever bigger and stronger.

As chairman of the Senate Committee on the Territories, Douglas was in a position to promote national unity and growth. He had guided through Congress the Compromise of 1850. He also brought about a grant of federal lands to finance the construction of the Illinois Central Railroad. This line was to run southward through Illinois, one branch starting from Chicago and another from Galena. At the southern end, it was expected to connect with other lines that would reach to the Gulf of Mexico. Thus the Illinois Central would help tie together the North and the South.

Douglas hoped to see another railroad extended to the Pacific coast, to tie the Far West to the rest of the country. Such a line would require even more government aid than had been given to the Illinois Central. Douglas thought Chicago ought to be the eastern terminus of the transcontinental railroad. Other people in Illinois and the Northwest agreed with him.

But Chicago had rivals: St. Louis, Memphis, and New Orleans. Southerners insisted upon a southern route, preferably one having New Orleans as its starting point. A railroad along the route they favored would run through Texas and New Mexico—areas that already had state or territorial government.

Douglas's northern route would have to pass through unorganized territory west of Iowa and Missouri. That area would need local agencies of law and order before a railroad could safely be constructed through it. In 1854, therefore, Douglas turned to the task of providing the necessary territorial organization. He maneuvered to get and hold as much southern support as possible, both

Kansas territory became known as "Bleeding Kansas" because of its severe split on the slavery issue. Armed troublemakers touched off frequent skirmishes.

for his railroad plans and for his presidential ambitions.

The Kansas-Nebraska Act

At first, Douglas introduced a bill to set up a single new territory, to be known as Nebraska. This bill displeased southern whites, for all of the new territory would lie within that part of the Louisiana Purchase that the Missouri Compromise (1820) had closed to slavery.

To get southern support, Douglas repeatedly amended his bill. In its final form, it was known as the Kansas-Nebraska Act. It provided for not one but two new territories—Kansas and Nebraska. The people of each, through their territorial legislatures, would decide whether or not to permit slavery, according to the principle of popular sovereignty. Thus prohibition of slavery in this part of the Louisiana Purchase territory would be revoked and the voters would be allowed to choose slavery if they so wished.

Douglas assumed that Kansas would ultimately become a slave state and Nebraska a free state. He thought this balancing of the two ought to satisfy both the South and the North. In the spring of 1854, he managed to get enough southern as well as northern Democratic backing to secure passage of the act. But he provoked a much greater outcry than he had expected on the part of many northerners. They looked upon the Missouri Compromise, which had stood for thirty-four years, as almost sacred. Now it was being undone. More and more northerners began to believe those abolitionists who charged that there was a slave-power conspiracy to spread slavery, first over the free territories and then over the free states.

Anger Over Cuba Policy

Soon the suspicious northerners saw signs of a plot to acquire Cuba as additional land for slavery. There was in this suspicion a certain amount of truth, though not the whole truth.

Many Americans of the time believed in an acquisitive foreign policy. In particular, a group of Democrats, members of the "Young America" movement and supporters of Douglas for the presidency, demanded that the United States take a larger part in world affairs. Many of them called for the acquisition of nearby lands—particularly Canada and Cuba—the annexation of Hawaii, and the promotion of commerce in Asia. With respect to Europe, they favored assisting the cause of republics, even to the extent of encouraging revolutions to overthrow monarchies. These ideas attracted many Whigs as well as Democrats. The northern Whigs, but not the southern Democrats, were much more interested in obtaining Canada and Hawaii, which did not have slavery, than in obtaining Cuba, which did.

The Pierce administration pursued the interests of southern Democrats. William L. Marcy, the secretary of state, suggested to the United States ministers in Madrid, Paris, and London that they get together and advise him what to do about Cuba. The three met at the seaside resort of Ostend, Belgium, and drew up a statement in which they said: (1) the United States should try to purchase Cuba; (2) if Spain refused to sell and proved unable to keep order on the island, the United States should "wrest" it away.

In the fall of 1854, newspapers published this statement, the so-called Ostend Manifesto. It seemed to confirm the fears of many northerners that the Democratic party was devoting itself to the protection and promotion of slavery.

A NEW PARTY IN THE NORTH

As the Whig party disintegrated, the question arose: Who would take the place of the Whigs? For a time the Know-Nothings, with their antiforeigner and anti-Catholic program, hoped to do so. The Know-Nothing or American party grew rapidly, but soon it began to divide into northern and southern factions. The party eventually fell apart because of disagreements over the slavery issue, just as the Whig party had done.

In the South, the former Whigs had little choice except to combine with the Democrats. In the North, most of the former Whigs joined a new party—becoming Republicans. The modern Republican party arose because so many northerners thought the Democrats were proslavery and pro-South. The new party stood for northern interests and, in particular, for free soil.

Earlier Free-Soil Parties

As early as 1840, a group of politically inclined abolitionists set up the Liberty party. They ran James G. Birney, a reformed slaveholder from Kentucky, as their presidential candidate in 1840 and again in 1844. The Liberty party men did not expect to elect a President, but they hoped to draw so many votes away from the Whig and Democratic parties that one or both of them would adopt antislavery aims in order to get antislavery support. Birney obtained few votes, yet in 1844 he drew enough votes away from the Whig candidate Henry Clay to help elect the Democrat James K. Polk.

Strictly speaking, though the Liberty men were abolitionists, theirs was not an abolitionist party. Their platform did not call upon the federal government to abolish slavery in the South. It did call upon the federal government to prohibit the interstate slave trade and to prohibit slavery in the District of Columbia and the territories. Thus the Liberty party was essentially a free-soil party.

In 1848, the free-soil movement suddenly grew much larger as a result of a quarrel among the Democrats. Some northern Democrats thought President Polk too much a southerner. They particularly resented his veto, in 1846, of a bill that would have provided money for much-needed transportation improvements in the Northwest. The disgruntled Democrats combined with antislavery Whigs and men of the Liberty party to form the Free Soil Democratic party. In

PRESIDENTIAL ELECTIONS: 1848-1860

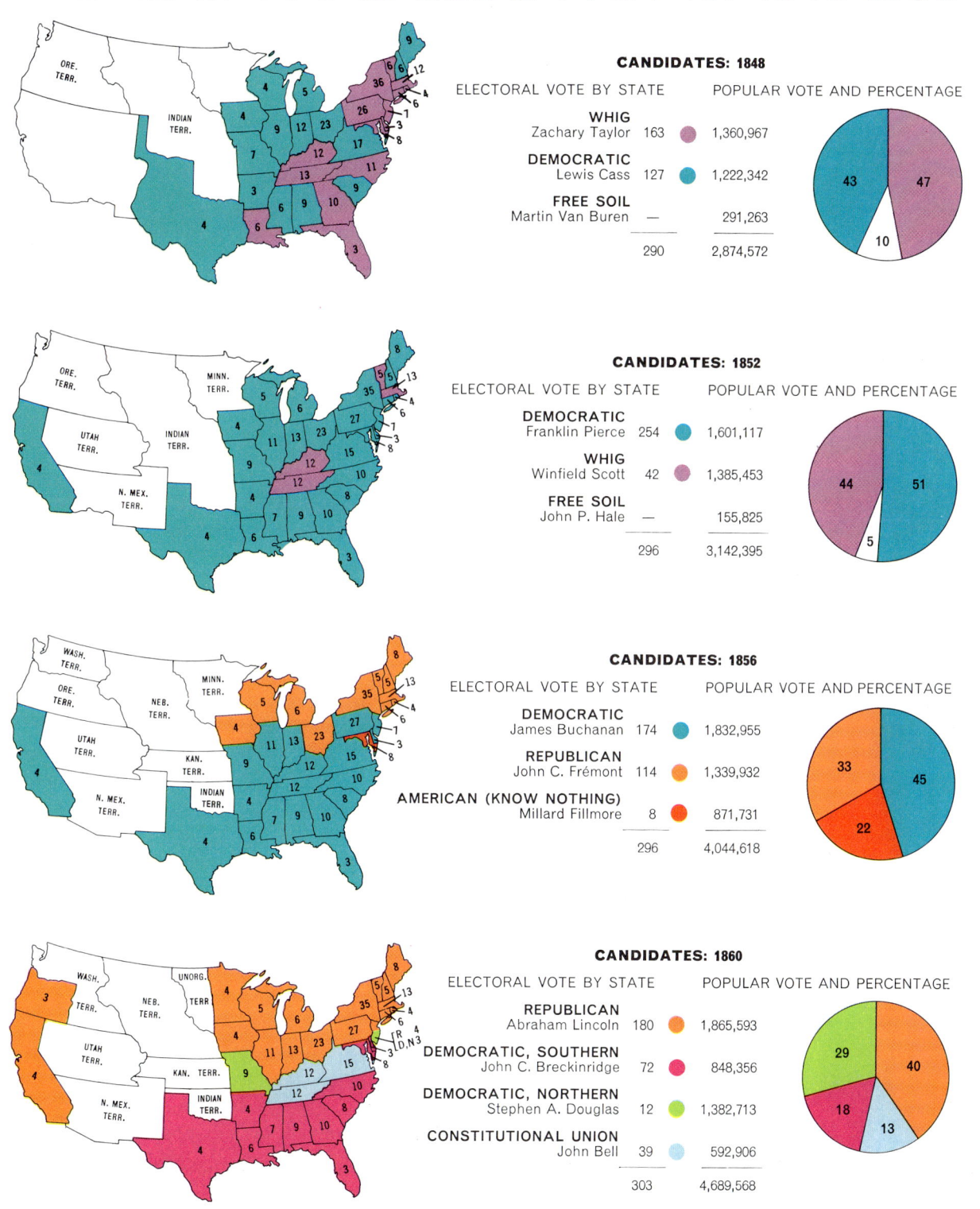

CANDIDATES: 1848

ELECTORAL VOTE BY STATE		POPULAR VOTE AND PERCENTAGE
WHIG Zachary Taylor	163	1,360,967
DEMOCRATIC Lewis Cass	127	1,222,342
FREE SOIL Martin Van Buren	—	291,263
	290	2,874,572

Pie chart: 47 / 43 / 10

CANDIDATES: 1852

ELECTORAL VOTE BY STATE		POPULAR VOTE AND PERCENTAGE
DEMOCRATIC Franklin Pierce	254	1,601,117
WHIG Winfield Scott	42	1,385,453
FREE SOIL John P. Hale	—	155,825
	296	3,142,395

Pie chart: 51 / 44 / 5

CANDIDATES: 1856

ELECTORAL VOTE BY STATE		POPULAR VOTE AND PERCENTAGE
DEMOCRATIC James Buchanan	174	1,832,955
REPUBLICAN John C. Frémont	114	1,339,932
AMERICAN (KNOW NOTHING) Millard Fillmore	8	871,731
	296	4,044,618

Pie chart: 45 / 33 / 22

CANDIDATES: 1860

ELECTORAL VOTE BY STATE		POPULAR VOTE AND PERCENTAGE
REPUBLICAN Abraham Lincoln	180	1,865,593
DEMOCRATIC, SOUTHERN John C. Breckinridge	72	848,356
DEMOCRATIC, NORTHERN Stephen A. Douglas	12	1,382,713
CONSTITUTIONAL UNION John Bell	39	592,906
	303	4,689,568

Pie chart: 40 / 29 / 18 / 13

1848 they nominated former President Martin Van Buren. He drew enough votes away from the regular Democratic candidate Lewis Cass to help elect the regular Whig Zachary Taylor.

In 1852, there was a Free Soil party in the running (not to be confused with the Free Soil Democratic party). John P. Hale of New Hampshire was its nominee. Many of the straying Democrats now went back to the regular fold. Hale received far less support than Van Buren had received in 1848.

Organizing the Republican Party

Throughout the Northwest in the spring of 1854, abolitionists, free-soilers, antislavery Whigs, and antiadministration Democrats met together to protest against the passage of the Kansas-Nebraska Act. For a time, they were known simply as "anti-Nebraska" men. Here and there they set up local organizations, cooperating against the party of Douglas and Pierce. Soon the anti-Nebraska men began to call themselves Republicans. In taking this name, they wished to emphasize that they, like the Jeffersonians, who also had been called Republicans, represented the interests of the common people.

At first, the Republican movement was most active in the Northwest and was mostly devoted to a single aim, that of keeping slavery out of the territories. Before long, however, the movement spread to the Northeast, and it took on additional aims: to raise the tariff, provide homesteads, and obtain federal money for railroads and other transportation improvements.

In the fall of 1854, the hastily organized Republicans amazed the country by winning many state and local elections. The Republicans won control of several northern states. Even more surprising, they came close to winning control of the House of Representatives. They could now look forward hopefully to 1856, a presidential election year.

"Bleeding Kansas"

By means of his Kansas-Nebraska Act, Douglas had hoped to remove from Congress the question of slavery in the territories. He intended to let the settlers themselves quietly decide the question. For the time being, few people migrated to Nebraska and that territory presented no problem. But large numbers moved to Kansas, and bloodshed soon followed. Talk of "bleeding Kansas" spread throughout the country. Things were not working out as Douglas had hoped.

Many of the people who went to Kansas were simply looking for new homes in a new territory, and much of the violence arose from the usual frontier lawlessness. Others went, however, with the deliberate purpose of making Kansas free—or slave. And at least part of the fighting was concerned with that issue.

The New England Emigrant Aid Company sent both men and guns to keep the soil of Kansas free. Armed bands of "border ruffians" rode from neighboring Missouri to fight the antislavery people and to vote for slavery. From the outset, the antislavery settlers outnumbered the proslavery people. Nevertheless, with the aid of the Missourians, the proslavery people got control of the territorial legislature in 1855 and passed laws making slavery legal. This legislature had the backing of the Pierce administration.

The free-soil majority set up a separate government, forbidding slavery, but this government had no official recognition. In 1856, with a proslavery federal marshal in the lead, a posse of about eight hundred men marched on Lawrence, arrested the free-soil leaders, and looted and burned the town.

An antislavery fanatic—John Brown—now appeared on the scene. Brown thought he was God's agent to avenge the attack on Lawrence. With a small band of followers, including a few of his sons, he struck one night at a settlement along Pottawatomie

SLAVERY: THREE VIEWS

JEFFERSON DAVIS
Senator from Mississippi and future president of the Confederacy

The slave trade ... so far as the African was concerned, was a blessing.... [Through] the portal of slavery alone, has the descendant of the graceless son of Noah ever entered the temple of civilization.... [Antislavery northerners] see that the slaves in their present condition in the South are comfortable and happy... they see our penitentiaries never filled, and our poor houses usually empty. Let them turn to the other hand, and they see the same race in a state of freedom at the North; but ... instead of being happy and useful, they are, with few exceptions, miserable, degraded, filling the penitentiaries and poorhouses, objects of scorn, excluded, in some places, from the schools, and deprived of many other privileges and benefits which attach to the white men among whom they live. And yet they insist that elsewhere an institution which has proved beneficial to this race shall be abolished.

STEPHEN A. DOUGLAS
Senator from Illinois

There is but one possible way in which slavery can be abolished, and that is by leaving a State ... perfectly free to form and regulate its institutions in its own way. That was the principle upon which this Republic was founded, and it is under the operation of that principle that we have been able to preserve the Union thus far. Under its operations, slavery disappeared from ... six of the twelve original slaveholding States; and this gradual system of emancipation went on quietly, peacefully and steadily, so long as we in the free States minded our own business.... But the moment the Abolition Societies were organized throughout the North, preaching a violent crusade against slavery in the Southern States, this combination necessarily caused a counter-combination in the South, and a sectional line was drawn which was a barrier to any further emancipation.

CHARLES SUMNER
Senator from Massachusetts

The slave is held simply *for the use of his master,* to whose behests, his life, liberty, and happiness, are devoted, and by whom he may be ... shipped as cargo, stored as goods,... knocked off at public auction, and even staked at the gaming table ... all according to law. ... He may be marked like a hog, branded like a mule ... and constantly beaten like a brute; all according to law. And should life itself be taken, what is the remedy? The Law of Slavery ... pronounces the incompetency of the whole African race—whether bond or free—to testify ... against a white man....

If the offense of Slavery were less extended; ... [all] would rise against it.... But what is wrong when done to one man cannot be right when done to many.... And yet this is denied by the barbarous logic of Slavery, which ... claims immunity because its usurpation ... cannot be safely attacked.

Creek. He calculated that five free-soilers had been killed in Lawrence, and so he murdered five supposedly proslavery men. This "Pottawatomie massacre" touched off a small-scale civil war in the territory.

In Washington, D.C., a Republican senator from Massachusetts gave a long speech on "the crime against Kansas." This senator, Charles Sumner, had in mind not the Pottawatomie massacre but the efforts to force slavery upon the territory. In this bitter speech against the South and slavery, Sumner ridiculed Andrew P. Butler, a proud senator from South Carolina. A few days later, as Sumner sat at his desk in the Senate chamber, a man came up to him and beat him about the head with a cane. Sumner collapsed. The assailant was Representative Preston Brooks of South Carolina, Butler's nephew.

Afterward, southerners applauded Brooks as a hero. Some gave him canes with such inscriptions as: "Use knockdown arguments." Northerners, however, referred to him as "bully Brooks," said he was typical of the southern gentleman, and looked upon Sumner as a martyr to the cause of liberty and decency. (Sumner only gradually recovered from the caning. He did not return to the Senate until 1859.) The very different reactions to the incident showed how far apart the North and the South were drifting.

In this atmosphere of bitterness, the election of 1856 was held. The Democrats endorsed popular sovereignty and nominated another doughface, James Buchanan of Pennsylvania. The Republicans chose John C. Frémont, a former senator from California, who was famous as an explorer of the Far West. They campaigned with the slogan: "Free Soil, Free Labor, Free Men, and Frémont." Another party, consisting of former Whigs and Know-Nothings, nominated former President Fillmore as its candidate.

Buchanan won the election, but Frémont and Fillmore together polled more popular votes than he did. The Republicans gained additional state and local offices and congressional seats. The election was, as one Republican said, a "victorious defeat" for them.

The Dred Scott Decision

In his inaugural address, on March 4, 1857, President Buchanan hinted that the Supreme Court was about to decide, once and for all, the standing of slavery in the territories. Two days later, the Court gave its decision in the Dred Scott case, but the decision did not put an end to the controversy. It only made it worse.

As the slave of an army surgeon, Dred Scott had lived at Fort Snelling in the Louisiana Purchase territory, at a time when slavery was illegal there because of the Missouri Compromise. Years later, after Scott's return to the slave state of Missouri, some abolitionists persuaded him to sue for his freedom. They said that he ought to be free because he had lived in a free territory. To bring the case before the Supreme Court, they arranged for a New Yorker to buy him. Thus Scott, in Missouri, would be suing his owner in New York. (The Constitution gives the Supreme Court authority to consider cases in which a citizen of one state has sued a citizen of another.)

In the Dred Scott decision, Chief Justice Taney, a former slave owner from Maryland, said that the Supreme Court did not really have jurisdiction over the case. Taney explained that by Missouri law no black could be a citizen of that state. He said, further, that no black could ever become a citizen of the United States. He might have left the matter at that.

Instead, Taney went on to say that if the Supreme Court had had jurisdiction, he would have had to deny freedom to Dred Scott. A slave was property, Taney argued, and the Fifth Amendment forbade Congress

After escaping from slavery, Harriet Tubman began work on the "underground railroad." During the Civil War, she aided the Union forces, planning and carrying out scouting operations and raids.

to deprive any person of property without "due process of law" (that is, without some kind of justifiable court proceedings). In adopting the Missouri Compromise, Congress was depriving persons of their slave property in the territories. Therefore, according to Taney's reasoning, the antislavery provision of the Missouri Compromise had been unconstitutional from the beginning.

The Dred Scott decision could be viewed as a severe blow to the Republican cause. In effect, the Supreme Court had declared unconstitutional the party's main principle—free soil. Certainly, the Republicans were angry at the seven justices (out of nine) who favored the decision. Yet the party was helped more than it was hurt by the decision. Here seemed to be one more piece of evidence to prove that a great slave-power conspiracy was at work. Alarmed northerners thought it urgent to back the new party that stood for free soil, and so the Republicans gained additional support.

THE RISE OF THE REPUBLICANS

Two other events in 1857 helped the Republican party. First, Congress again lowered the tariff, which was already quite low. Second, the Panic of 1857 began. Supporters of the protective tariff said that prosperity had been destroyed by the destruction of the tariff. They looked to the Republican party as a way to regain influence and raise the tariff rates.

As the Republican party gained support, it began to change in character. The party originally had represented the farmers of the Northwest. Now it began more and more to represent the industrialists of the Northeast as well. It became essentially an alliance of those two groups. Increasingly, it emphasized the economic aims of farmers and merchants, though it continued to oppose the extension of slavery into the territories.

Democratic Disagreements

Like President Pierce before him, President Buchanan favored the proslavery element in Kansas. He tried to persuade Congress to admit Kansas as a slave state, regardless of the real feelings of a majority of the voters in the territory.

The Buchanan policy meant something quite different from the kind of popular sovereignty that Senator Douglas had favored. Douglas had intended to give the settlers a real choice. Douglas now found himself in a dilemma. If he cooperated with Buchanan, he would have to violate his own principles. Besides, he would lose the support of many Democrats in the Northwest, where the Buchanan policy was unpopular. If he refused to cooperate with Buchanan, he would lose his support and also the support of most southerners. Either way, he would jeopardize his chances for the presidency.

Douglas came out for his own principles and opposed Buchanan's efforts to make Kansas a slave state. He and Buchanan broke all ties of political friendship. The Democratic party was now divided between the followers of the senator and the followers of the President.

Buchanan was determined to prevent Douglas's reelection to the Senate in 1858. When Douglas began his campaign in Illinois, therefore, he faced opposition from the regular Democrats, the "Buchaneers." They did not put up a candidate against him, but they did everything else they could to bring about his defeat. On the other side were the Republicans, who were running an old friend and rival of his, Abraham Lincoln.

Lincoln's Emergence

Lincoln had risen from poverty to become one of the most respected lawyers of Illinois. He was also one of the best-known politicians—the leading Whig and then the leading Republican of the state. As a politician, however, he had not done well. He had served a few terms in the state legislature and one term in the national Congress. That was all. He longed to be a United States senator from Illinois.

In Douglas, Lincoln saw a threat to his own ambitions. In popular sovereignty he

Having captured the arsenal at Harpers Ferry, John Brown and his eighteen followers attempt to hold off state and federal troops. In planning the raid, Brown thought that it would touch off a slave uprising and provide him with troops. However, the uprising never took place and the raid failed.

saw a threat to the Republican program for free soil. Some prominent Republicans of the Northeast talked of adopting Douglas as a Republican candidate because of his resistance to Buchanan. Lincoln and his friends undertook to head off the Republicans-for-Douglas movement. They induced the party to nominate Lincoln for senator and pledge its support to him.

When he accepted the Republican nomination, Lincoln made his famous "house divided" speech. "I believe this government cannot endure, permanently half *slave* and half *free,*" he said.

Either the *opponents* of slavery will arrest the further spread of it, and place it where the public mind shall rest in the belief that it is in course of ultimate extinction; or its *advocates* will push it forward, till it shall become alike lawful in *all* the States, *old* as well as *new*—*North* as well as *South*.

Besides making the usual separate campaign speeches, Lincoln and Douglas appeared together in seven formal debates, one in each congressional district in Illinois. Tremendous crowds came to these verbal duels between the tall, folksy Lincoln and the tiny, dignified Douglas.

In the debates, Lincoln stayed on the attack most of the time. He condemned Douglas as morally insensitive for saying, with regard to popular sovereignty, that he did not care whether slavery was "voted up or voted down." He maintained that the Douglas policy would encourage slavery to spread. He even accused Douglas of conspiring with Taney, Pierce, and Buchanan to fasten slavery upon the whole country.

Lincoln took advantage of the dilemma in

which circumstances had already put Douglas. Again and again he asked Douglas whether the people of a territory could lawfully keep slavery out. If Douglas answered "Yes," he would offend southern Democrats, who approved the Dred Scott decision. If he answered "No," he would offend those northern Democrats who believed in popular sovereignty.

Douglas avoided a yes-or-no reply. He said that, even though a territorial legislature could not pass laws *against* slavery, it could decline to pass laws *for* it. Then no slave owner would bring slaves in. "Slavery cannot exist a day, or an hour, anywhere," he explained, "unless it is supported by local police regulations." This reply did not satisfy many southerners. By harping on the question, Lincoln had helped widen the rift within the Democratic party.

Throughout the country, newspapers gave a great deal of space to the Lincoln-Douglas debates. The Republicans swept most of the northern elections, but they did not quite manage to get control in Illinois. Though Lincoln lost, Republicans began to talk of him as a possible President. He had not beaten Douglas in the senatorial contest, but he had prepared the way for beating him in the next presidential race.

John Brown's Raid

John Brown, the grim fanatic of the Kansas killings, still thought that God had commissioned him to free the slaves. Brown had worked out a plan. First he would capture the mountain town of Harpers Ferry, Virginia, and obtain guns and ammunition from the federal arsenal there. With Harpers Ferry as a base, he would raid plantations to set the slaves free. Then he would organize a black republic with its own army of freedmen. From further raiding, this republic would grow until, finally, it would be big and strong enough to force the South to give up the remaining slaves.

On an October night in 1859, Brown and eighteen followers descended on the town and got into the arsenal. From then on, nothing went as planned. Local militia companies trapped him and his men inside an arsenal building. A detachment of United States marines arrived. Brown was wounded and eight of his followers were killed. In the end, the marines broke in and took Brown prisoner along with the other survivors. Several weeks later, Brown and six other men were hanged for treason against the state of Virginia.

On the day of Brown's execution, the well-known writer Henry David Thoreau told a church meeting in Concord, Massachusetts: "He is not Old Brown any longer; he is an angel of light." Other prominent northerners also looked upon Brown as a martyr to a holy cause. Republican leaders like Lincoln and Seward disagreed. They thought Brown a well-meaning but misguided man, and they disapproved of his Harpers Ferry raid. The views of Brown's admirers were more newsworthy, however, and they gained the larger share of attention in the papers.

Southern whites were terrified, for the thing they most feared was a slave revolt. They looked upon Brown as a devil, not an angel. They got the impression that most northerners, at least most Republicans, sympathized with Brown. Southerners thought that if the Republicans should take over in Washington, they would set loose upon the South still more fanatics like him. Mississippi and other southern states prepared for self-defense. They started to enlarge their militia forces and to accumulate military supplies. Many southern students in northern colleges were called home.

The fear that beset southerners was real, even if it was irrational. It helps explain why they reacted so violently when the Republicans won the presidential election in 1860.

John Brown rides to his hanging seated on his own coffin. This painting was done by Horace Pippin from descriptions of the event by his grandmother, a slave. She had watched from the sidelines at the execution of Brown.

Lincoln's Election

When the Democrats met in Charleston, they had trouble agreeing on a platform. A majority of the delegates approved the "Douglas platform," which vaguely endorsed popular sovereignty and proposed that all questions regarding slavery in the territories be decided by the Supreme Court. Most of the southerners walked out of the convention, which then broke up. Later, the northern and southern Democrats had separate meetings and formed separate parties. The northerners chose Douglas; the southerners, John C. Breckinridge of Kentucky.

When the Republicans held their nominating convention in Chicago, their hopes ran high because of the Democratic split. Still, most of them thought the party should take no chances. They wanted a sure winner.

Seward, rather than Lincoln, was the most prominent of the party's leaders, and Seward was the preconvention favorite. But some of the delegates had doubts about him. They feared he would repel former Know-Nothings because, as governor of New York, he had given state aid to Catholic schools. They also feared he would frighten off conservative former Whigs because he had gained a reputation as an antislavery and antisouthern man. Many delegates thought that Lincoln, despite his "house divided" speech, would be a safer candidate, one who would lose fewer votes. On the first two ballots, Seward led but could not get a majority. On the third ballot, Lincoln was nominated.

Yet another party was in the field. The Constitutional Union party, consisting of remnants of the Whig and Know-Nothing parties, presented a platform that did little more than pledge loyalty to "the Constitution, the Union, and the laws." This party ran as its presidential candidate John Bell, a Tennessee Whig.

On election day, Lincoln received only about 40 in 100 of the popular votes throughout the country as a whole—and none at all in ten southern states. Yet he won all the electoral votes of every free state except New Jersey, and he had more than a majority of the electoral votes.

Not only was the Republican victory close, it was also incomplete. Though the Republicans had elected a President, they had failed to gain a majority in either the Senate or the House of Representatives.

SECESSION

During the campaign, southerners had threatened that their states would secede if the "black Republican" candidate should be elected. Republicans had dismissed the secession talk as bluff. Soon after the election, however, the secessionists began to carry out their threats. They did not wait to see what Lincoln would do after he was inaugurated as

President on March 4, 1861.

South Carolina, the home of Calhoun and his doctrines, appropriately led off the secession march. On December 20, 1860, a special convention in Charleston declared South Carolina an independent state. Other slave states soon held conventions to consider secession. The states also sent commissioners to one another to cooperate in seceding and in setting up a new confederacy.

Meanwhile, in the rest of the country, people discussed what to do about the disunion threat. Some said that secessionists should be hanged as traitors. Others said that they should be allowed to leave if they wanted to. Still others said that they should be encouraged, by means of a new compromise, to stay in the Union.

Compromise Efforts

President Buchanan favored compromise. A state had no right to secede, he told Congress, but the national government had no right to force a state to remain in the Union.

In the Senate, John J. Crittenden introduced a compromise plan. Crittenden, like Henry Clay, the Great Compromiser, came from Kentucky. Kentuckians felt that they were in the middle, between the North and the South. They had relatives, friends, and business connections on both sides. If war should come, it would make Kentucky a battleground and disrupt the ties of family, friendship, and business. Kentuckians were especially anxious for a peaceful settlement.

The Crittenden plan embodied a series of constitutional amendments. The two most important of these would have (1) guaranteed slavery forever in the states where it already existed, and (2) prohibited slavery north of the Missouri Compromise line—36° 30′—and permitted it south of that line in all present or *future* territories.

Republican leaders in the Senate and the House asked President-elect Lincoln for his advice. He had no objection to the first proposal. Congress adopted this one and sent it to the states for ratification. If the war had not intervened, three-fourths of them probably would have ratified. Then the Thirteenth Amendment would have guaranteed slavery instead of abolishing it!

But Lincoln objected to the proposal about slavery in the territories. Such an arrangement, he feared, would settle nothing. It would only lead slave owners to agitate for new territories south of the line—in Cuba, Mexico, or Central America. "Let there be no compromise on the question of *extending* slavery," he advised. "Have none of it. Stand firm. The tug has to come, & better now than any time hereafter." The Republicans stood firm, and this part of the Crittenden plan failed to pass.

Even if the proposal had passed, it would not have satisfied the extreme secessionists, the "fire-eaters." Possibly, though, it would have strengthened the southern Unionists and enabled them to prevent the secession of any more states. After the plan's defeat, six other states—Mississippi, Florida, Alabama, Georgia, Louisiana, and Texas—followed South Carolina's example and withdrew from the Union.

The Confederacy

On February 4, 1861, one month before Lincoln's inauguration, delegates from the seceded states met in Montgomery, Alabama, to form a government for the Confederate States of America.

The Montgomery convention, serving as a temporary congress, passed laws for the new nation. It appointed temporary officers and drew up a constitution for a permanent government. Months later, after this constitution had been ratified, senators and representatives were elected to a senate and house. Jefferson Davis was elected president and Alexander H. Stephens vice-president.

In most of its provisions, the Confederate constitution was simply a copy of the Constitution of the United States. There were a number of changes, most of them minor. For instance, the sovereignty of the separate states was now recognized, but not their right to secede from the Confederacy. The president and vice-president were given six-year terms and were limited to one term apiece. Cabinet members were allowed to sit in congress.

The important differences were those concerning slavery. In the Confederate constitution, congress was required to protect slavery throughout the Confederate territories. The Confederate congress was forbidden to abolish slavery anywhere. The states were not explicitly forbidden to abolish it, but they were required to recognize the right of a slave owner to travel and sojourn with his or her slaves. In fact, the states could not eliminate slavery from their own soil, even if they should wish to. Vice-President Stephens spoke truly when he said that slavery was the "corner-stone" of the new Confederate government.

Fort Sumter

As they seceded, the Confederate states took over forts, mints, custom houses, post offices, and other pieces of federal property. By the time Lincoln was inaugurated, the United States flag still flew at only four forts on soil the Confederacy claimed. The people North and South focused their attention on one—Fort Sumter, in Charleston harbor. Here, Major Robert Anderson remained at his post with only about seventy soldiers and with only enough food to last for six weeks or so. Before this time was up, Anderson would have to abandon the fort—unless he got supplies.

In his inaugural address, Lincoln made it clear that he intended to "hold, occupy, and possess" all the places belonging to the federal government. He vowed to preserve the Union and enforce the laws. Yet he insisted that if bloodshed were to come, the Confederates would have to start it. He would not. "In your hands, my dissatisfied fellow countrymen, and not in mine," he said, "is the momentous issue of civil war."

Jefferson Davis and all the top Confederates were determined to obtain Sumter and the other three forts—by diplomacy if possible, by force if necessary. Davis sent three commissioners to Washington to negotiate for a peaceful transfer. Lincoln refused to have anything to do with these men. (If he had dealt with them, he would have given the impression that he recognized the Confederacy as an independent nation.) Meanwhile, Davis pushed military preparations as fast as he could. He put General Pierre Beauregard in charge of the Confederate forces at Charleston. All around the harbor, Beauregard built up fortifications and batteries with big guns that pointed at Sumter.

When Anderson's supplies had almost run out, Lincoln decided on a relief expedition. He sent a messenger to Charleston who said an attempt would be made to "supply Fort Sumter with provisions only," and "if such an attempt be not resisted, no effort to throw in men, arms, or ammunition" would be made for the time being.

Without waiting for the expedition to arrive, Davis instructed Beauregard to demand Anderson's surrender and, if Anderson should refuse the demand, to open fire. Anderson did refuse it. Beauregard delayed as long as he could, for Anderson was an old friend and had been his professor at the military academy at West Point. At last, April 12, 1861, Beauregard ordered the firing to begin. Two days later, the fort a smoking ruin, Anderson surrendered.

Despite the heavy shelling, no one on either side had been killed. One of Anderson's men was fatally wounded by a gun

Confederate troops fire on Fort Sumter. The attack had a unifying effect on northern opinions about secession and enabled northerners to take the role of defenders of the Union.

explosion, however, when a salute was fired to honor the Stars and Stripes as the flag was taken down.

War!

The firing on the flag had an electric effect throughout the North. The section had been badly divided over the secession crisis. Democrats had been criticizing Republicans, and Republicans had been bickering among themselves. Some of the Democrats preferred Davis to Lincoln. The news from Sumter changed all this. "Every man must be for the United States or against it," declared the Democratic leader Douglas after a visit with Lincoln; "there can be no neutrals in this war—only patriots and traitors." When Lincoln called for 75,000 volunteers to put down the insurrection, men rushed to enlist, without regard to politics.

Lincoln's call for troops—on top of his effort to hold Sumter—had a similar unifying effect upon the South. Many of the people of the seven seceded states had never really favored secession. Now they became enthusiastically loyal to the Confederate cause. Soon four more states—Virginia, Tennessee, Arkansas, North Carolina—seceded from the Union and joined the Confederacy.

The Confederates had hoped to get all the slave states, including those of the border. Delaware had a few Confederate sympathizers, but Maryland, Kentucky, and Missouri had many. Only by a stern policy of military arrests did Lincoln manage to prevent Maryland from seceding. Kentuckians wanted to remain neutral, but the state finally sided with the Union. Missourians fought a civil war of their own before Missouri could be safely counted on the Union side.

Thus, as the Civil War got under way, the Confederacy numbered eleven states. (The Confederates claimed two more, Kentucky and Missouri, and the Confederate flag contained thirteen stars, but the Confederates did not really control either Missouri or Kentucky.) The Union had twenty-three. Fifty counties broke off from Virginia and combined in a new state, West Virginia. This, when admitted to the Union in 1863, made a total of twenty-four.

A Look at Specifics

1. Why did several northern states pass "personal liberty" laws?

2. How did Taylor's death make easier the passage of the Compromise of 1850?

3. Why was President Pierce called a "doughface" by antislavery northerners?

4. Why did Stephen A. Douglas introduce the Kansas-Nebraska bill? What were its major provisions?

5. What convinced northerners of the existence of a slave-power conspiracy?

6. What were the goals of the "Young America" Democrats?

7. What was the aim of the Liberty party? The free-soil parties? Why cannot these parties be considered "abolitionist" parties?

8. What events caused Kansas to become known as "bleeding Kansas"?

9. How did the North and South react to the caning of Senator Charles Sumner?

10. What arguments did Chief Justice Taney use to nullify the Missouri Compromise in the Dred Scott decision?

11. How did John Brown propose to free the slaves?

12. What was Lincoln's main objection to the Crittenden plan?

A Review of Major Ideas

1. What changes took place within the major political parties after 1850 that made it increasingly difficult to settle sectional differences?

2. How did the Compromise of 1850 help lessen sectional animosities?

3. What major issues and events contributed to a revival of sectional antagonisms between 1854 and 1861?

4. What circumstances contributed to Lincoln's rise to the presidency?

5. What events of 1860 and 1861 precipitated the Civil War?

For Independent Study

1. In 1858, William H. Seward noted that the systems of slave and free labor were coming into ever increasing contact because of the growth of population, the settlement of new lands, and the extension of a transportation network that increased commerce and travel between the sections. He believed that, as a result of these developments, friction between the two systems was unavoidable. "It is an irrepressible conflict," he said, "between opposing and enduring forces, and it means that the United States must and will sooner or later become either entirely a slave-holding nation or entirely a free-labor nation." Do you agree with his analysis of the reasons for the increased hostility between the sections? Do you agree that the friction was inevitable? Why?

2. Why did the Republican party, in contrast to the Liberty and free-soil parties, become a major party? How do you account for its rapid growth?

3. Do you believe that southern grievances in 1860 and 1861 justified secession? If not, under what circumstances would southerners have been justified in seceding from the Union?

The Civil War

CHAPTER 11
1861–1865

The shooting war—a heroic view.

Abraham Lincoln had little military experience. As a young man, he served briefly in the Black Hawk War (1832). Afterwards, he joked that he had seen no "live, fighting Indians" but had fought in "a good many bloody struggles with the mosquitoes."

Jefferson Davis, by contrast, was a professional soldier. A graduate of West Point, he had led troops on the frontier, fought in the Mexican War, and gained a reputation as a great war department head.

Thus it would seem that Davis, as president of the Confederate states, should have been a more successful war leader than Lincoln, as President of the United States. Yet Lincoln proved to be a much more effective war President. Indeed, Lincoln was one of the most valuable assets the Union had.

The Union also had other advantages. Its population outnumbered the free population of the Confederacy by more than three to one. Its mills and factories produced ten times as much as those of the Confederacy.

Why, given the odds against them, did the southerners risk a war with the North? The secession leaders believed the South had advantages that would offset the North's strength in men and materials. First, as these leaders saw it, the South would have better soldiers. Its people were supposedly more experienced at handling guns and horses, and they would fight harder and longer, since they would be fighting for independence and for the protection of their homes. Second, the rivers, swamps, and mountains of the region would serve as natural lines of defense. Third, the South would get help from abroad. Since Britain and France would need southern cotton in order to keep their factories going, both nations would step in to prevent the North from interfering with the cotton supply. Fourth, the South would not have to conquer the North but would only have to prevent its own defeat. Eventually, the northern people would

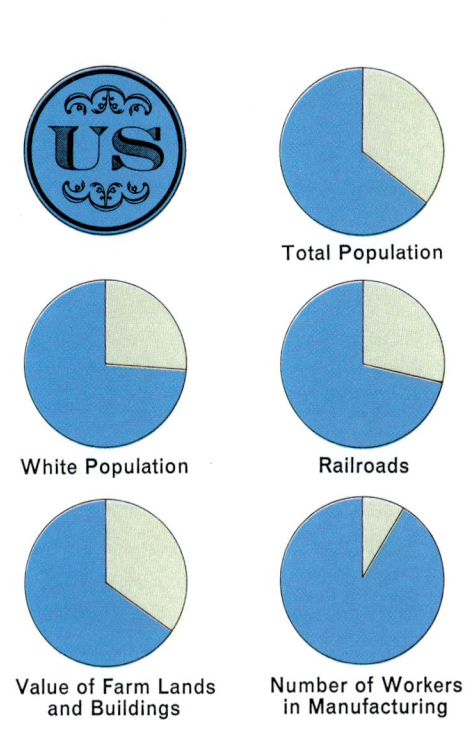

RESOURCES OF THE UNION AND THE CONFEDERACY: 1860

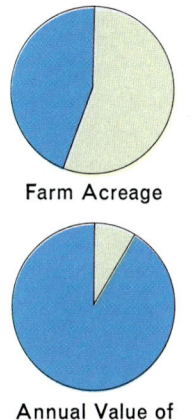

When the Civil War began, the Union had much greater resources than the Confederacy. It had more men to serve in its armies and an industrial system that could support both a large military and a civilian population. The Confederacy, in contrast, was forced to purchase much of its war materials in Europe. However, the North had to convert its factories to wartime production, and it took time for economic advantages to be felt.

divide and quarrel and grow weary of the war. Then they would quit and let the Confederacy alone. So it seemed to the hopeful Confederate leaders in 1861.

MOBILIZING UNION RESOURCES

When the war began in 1861, the North was not ready to fight. The United States Army had fewer than 17,000 officers and men, and most of them were scattered, guarding the western frontier. Only a few thousand state militiamen were trained, organized, and ready for combat. The United States Navy consisted of only ninety ships of all kinds, most of them either out of commission or stationed far from home.

The Union needed to build up its armed forces and its supplies of guns, ammunition, horses, wagons, and equipment of all kinds. The overwhelming wealth and population of the North could not by themselves bring about victory. They had to be converted into the means of military power and directed toward the Confederacy's defeat.

The Draft

The early rush to join the Union army did not last long. Soon it became necessary to attract more men than were volunteering. A soldier's pay ($11 a month until 1864 and then $16) was far below the wages a man could earn in civilian life. To make the service more attractive, city and state governments and the federal government paid bounties to recruits when they enlisted. By 1864, an enlistee could obtain as much as $1,000, altogether, in places where the state and local bounties were especially generous. These opportunities produced "bounty jumpers," who would enlist in one locality, collect the bounties, then would desert and reenlist in another locality.

When the call for volunteers was made, many free blacks in the North offered their services to the Union. President Lincoln refused to let them enlist, however, because he feared that such a move would anger the border states and perhaps affect the morale of Union soldiers. This policy was not changed until the fall of 1862, when the formation of all-black units was authorized.

The generous cash payments and the enlistment of black Americans failed to bring out as many men as the armed forces required. Therefore, in 1863, Congress passed the Conscription Act. This was something new. Though some of the states had resorted to the draft (conscription) in previous wars, the federal government had never done so.

According to the Conscription Act, each state was given a quota of troops to raise. If a state filled its quota with volunteers, there would be no draft in that state. If the state failed to raise its full quota, the balance would be made up by means of the federal draft. To be conscripted was to be disgraced, and the draft shamed many men into serving as volunteers.

If a man were drafted, he still did not necessarily have to go to war. By the terms of the Conscription Act he could either hire a substitute or buy exemption. At first, the price of a substitute was about the same as the price of exemption ($300). When the privilege of buying exemption was ended in 1864, the price of substitutes rose to heights that only the very rich could afford. A regular business developed in which "substitute brokers" provided men, usually immigrants who had just arrived, to take the place of wealthy draftees.

Many people thought it unfair that the rich could escape the draft. Many also thought it unfair that certain localities paid much higher bounties than others. The places that paid more drew many volunteers, and the poorer areas were left with unfilled quotas. Thus the draft sometimes hit hardest where able-bodied men were fewest. Criticism of the Conscription Act—and opposition to the war itself—in some places led people to resist the draft. The worst troubles occurred in New York City in July 1863. There, when names were drawn for the draft, a riot broke out and about five hundred persons were killed.

In this sketch of the main street of Knoxville, Tennessee, Union and Confederate armies recruit at opposite ends of town. Although Tennessee voted to secede, many people were outspoken Unionists, including the editor of the Knoxville paper. Other border states faced similar internal splits.

Despite its faults, the system of raising troops was successful. According to the best estimate, 1.5 million men served at one time or another in the Union armies.

Paying for the War

The Union had to find means to pay for the troops and materials that were required. Over the four years of fighting, the government resorted chiefly to borrowing by selling bonds. Some money was raised by taxation and by issuing paper money.

The banking firm of Jay Cooke and Company was the exclusive selling agent of war bonds. Cooke carried on a selling campaign by means of newspaper advertisements and door-to-door salesmen. Though he urged working people to put their savings into bonds, he was much more successful with people who had plenty of money to invest.

The government wished to create a still larger market for war bonds. This was one reason for the establishment of the National Banking System, by acts of 1863 and 1864. The government guaranteed the notes of banks that joined the system, but the banks were required to buy and deposit with the treasury department one dollar in bonds for every dollar in banknotes they issued. Thus the national banks helped the war effort by buying bonds and at the same time providing a new currency, the national banknotes.

The war taxes were heavy and were applied to almost everything that could be taxed. For the first time, a federal income tax was levied.

Paper money—"greenbacks"—was issued in large quantities and totaled nearly 450 million dollars. These bills were made legal tender. The government would not give gold in exchange for greenbacks, however, and the value of paper money fell whenever discouraging news came from the battlefronts. At its lowest, in 1864, a dollar in greenbacks was worth only about forty cents.

Helping Businesses and Farms

Congress repeatedly raised the tariff during the war. In 1864, "countervailing duties" were added to offset the excise taxes that American manufacturers, but not foreign manufacturers, had to pay. Manufacturers in the United States now had little to fear from foreign competition, for the tariff was higher than ever.

In 1862, Congress passed the Pacific Railroad Act. This gave generous loans and land grants for the construction of a transcontinental railroad. That same year Congress took steps to aid farmers by passing both the Homestead Act and the Morrill Land Grant Act. The Homestead Act made it possible for any citizen to register a claim to 160 acres of public land. After building on the tract and living on it for five years, the citizen could acquire outright ownership for a small fee. The Morrill Act provided for grants of land to the states. The proceeds from the sale of the land grants were to be used for education in agriculture, engineering, and military science. This act contributed to the development of the "land-grant" colleges and universities.

Businesses gained the most from the wartime boom. Not all business prospered, but war industries of all kinds thrived. New industries grew up, among them the ready-made clothing industry. Before the war, most clothes had been made by hand, at home or at a tailor's shop. Then, with the war, came the government's orders for tens of thousands of uniforms. Factories were set up, and thousands of women were hired to operate the cutting and sewing machines that could speedily fill the orders. After the war, many of these factories turned to the manufacture of civilian clothes.

A class of newly rich people appeared, particularly in large cities. Some had made their fortunes by honest effort together with considerable luck, but some had grown rich by profiteering. People often referred to the newly rich as the "shoddy aristocracy." *Shoddy* was a kind of reclaimed wool or cotton sometimes used in uniforms. Some of the shoddy uniforms, it was said, disintegrated the first time they were worn in the rain.

Wartime society had its ugly features, but these were only part of the picture. Most civilians throughout the North willingly labored and sacrificed to advance the war effort.

As in earlier wars, the bulk of the work usually done by men in farms and businesses was taken up by women and children. Women who were not employed elsewhere sewed or knitted clothing for soldiers at meetings of the ladies' aid societies. Both women and men contributed time and materials to fairs, held to raise money for the United States Sanitary Commission, a predecessor of the American Red Cross. The Commission was vitally important, for it often provided the only hospital and medical care the soldiers had.

Women make cartridges in a northern munitions factory. Both private industry and the government hired thousands of new workers to manufacture uniforms, fuses, shells, and other wartime products. The prosperity brought by the war caused expansion in mining, railroads, and other industries.

CHANGING WAR AIMS

Before the Civil War, almost no one thought that Congress or the President had the constitutional power to interfere with slavery in the southern states. At the outset of the war, the North's sole objective was to reunite the nation and restore the national authority over all of it.

Soon people began to disagree about the wisdom and justice of leaving the institution of slavery alone. Some thought that slave owners had forfeited all constitutional rights by rebelling against the government. They believed that slavery had not only caused the rebellion but also kept it going, for slaves tilled the southern fields and drove the teams and dug trenches at the front. The way for the North to win the war and bring peace, it seemed, was to liberate the slaves, enroll them as soldiers, and send them to fight against their former owners.

The Emancipation Proclamation

The slavery issue divided the Republican party into two factions. One group, the Radical Republicans, called for the use of emancipation as a means of prosecuting the war. The other faction, the Conservative Republicans, held back. So did the Democrats.

Before the end of 1861, the Radical Republicans had begun to pass laws directed against slavery. The enforcement of these laws was up to President Lincoln. Since he had doubts about their constitutionality, he did nothing to enforce these laws. Radical Republicans denounced him.

In 1862, replying to this criticism, Lincoln said: "My paramount object in this struggle *is* to save the Union, and is *not* either to save or destroy slavery." He added: "I intend no modification of my oft-expressed *personal wish* that all men everywhere could be free."

Lincoln looked upon slavery as a horrible wrong, but he doubted that he had constitutional power to act against it. Moreover, he wished to avoid antagonizing the white people of the border slave states, especially Kentucky, for those states might switch to the Confederate side. Then it would be even harder, if not impossible, to save the Union. He also worried about the social and economic problems that would result from a sudden change in the relationship of blacks to whites in the slave states.

Lincoln began working on an emancipation plan that would satisfy his own doubts. In his plan, the states would gradually free the slaves, providing compensation for slave owners. The federal government would assist by making loans to the states. The blacks, as they were freed, would be resettled in Africa, South America, or the West Indies, if they were willing to go. Lincoln hoped to start the process immediately in the loyal slave states and continue it after the war in the seceded states. He got nowhere, however, for the political leaders of the loyal slave states refused to try the plan.

Lincoln decided to approach the problem in a different way. He issued his Emancipation Proclamation, first in a preliminary form (September 22, 1862) and then in a final form (January 1, 1863). The Emancipation Proclamation did not apply to all the slaves—not to those in the loyal slave states nor to those in the parts of the Confederacy that the Union armies already had occupied. It applied only to the slaves in the areas that were still in rebellion. Critics ridiculed the proclamation. They said it applied only in places where Lincoln could not enforce it and not in places where he could. But Lincoln saw it as a war measure, a step he could constitutionally take only because of his authority as commander in chief of the army and the navy. He could justify a war measure only if he applied it exclusively to those areas where the war was still going on.

The Emancipation Proclamation brought

Seminoles fought on the Confederate side.

freedom to few slaves, perhaps to 200,000 (out of more than 3.5 million) by the end of the war. Many of the freed slaves were among the more than 150,000 blacks who served in the various Union armies. Since the proclamation was a war measure, even Lincoln did not know if it would give permanent freedom to anyone. Nevertheless, it was extremely important as a symbol. It indicated that henceforth the war was being fought for freedom as well as for reunion.

Stresses on the Union

During the war, many Americans questioned whether the United States should be one nation or a number of small republics. As the war dragged on, some people in the Northwest wanted to break away from the Union and set up a separate confederacy. Thus a delegation of leaders from Illinois visited Lincoln and asked him to ease the burden on his home state or face increasing opposition. In California, some of the people wanted their state to secede and set itself up as the Pacific Republic.

The Confederate government tried to win support in the Far West. New Mexico had been settled primarily by southerners, and there was some sentiment in that territory to join the Confederacy. The New Mexicans sided with the Union, however, in large part because the North had supported New Mexico's claim in its boundary dispute with Texas.

During the war there was an increase in fighting by the Indians on the Great Plains and in the western mountains and basins. Confederate agents told tribal leaders that if the North lost, the tribes could reclaim their eastern lands and perhaps set up a separate Indian nation. Indian attacks on northern settlements made it necessary for the Union to send troops from the eastern battlefronts to the frontier.

There was not any one tribal position in the war. Some tribes were completely neutral, and some fought against both sides. The Upper Creeks and some individuals supported the Union. The Cherokee were split, with some of them supporting the North and some the South. Many southern tribes—including the Kiowa, Comanche, Choctaw, Chickasaw, and Seminole—supported the Confederacy.

Lincoln's Reelection

For the North to win the war and achieve its aims, it was important for Lincoln and the Republican party to remain in power. Lincoln's first task was to hold his party together and maintain his leadership of it. This was difficult because of the two factions within the party.

In 1864, the Republicans renominated Lincoln, but some of them soon began trying to remove him as the party's candidate. They were convinced that Lincoln could not possibly win. At that time, the Union armies were winning no victories, and the war seemed more and more hopeless. Indeed, the Republicans renamed their party the Union party, hoping to thus win more votes.

The Democrats too were divided, though the prospects looked good for them. The War Democrats opposed the Lincoln administration but supported the war effort. The Peace Democrats—or Copperheads, as the Republicans called them—opposed both Lincoln and the war. The leading War Democrat was George B. McClellan, onetime general in chief of the Union armies. The most conspicuous Peace Democrat was Clement L. Vallandigham, a former Ohio congressman. He had been arrested in 1863 for making antiwar speeches, and Lincoln had banished him to the Confederacy. From there Vallandigham made his way to what is now Ontario in Canada and then back to the United States.

At the Democratic convention, McClellan got the nomination, but Vallandigham wrote the platform. The platform condemned the war as a failure and called for an immediate conference with Confederate leaders to make peace—without the abolition of slavery. The contradiction between the platform and the candidate, who favored fighting on to victory, hurt the Democrats. Their greatest handicap, however, was news of Union victories, especially General William Tecumseh Sherman's capture of Atlanta (September 2, 1864).

Lincoln was triumphantly reelected. More than ever, he was now master of his party.

The Thirteenth Amendment

The Thirteenth Amendment assured the end of slavery. Lincoln played an important part in bringing about the amendment, and for this he deserves his reputation as the Great Emancipator.

In 1864, the Radical Republicans had insisted upon a plank in the party's platform calling for an antislavery amendment. Lincoln approved. When the voters reelected him and increased the Republican majority in Congress, he believed they were showing their support for such an amendment. The Senate had passed the Thirteenth Amend-

Both sides destroyed miles of railroad track by heating rails over a fire of ties and bending them. Some Union advances were marked by "Sherman's hairpins," rails wrapped around trees.

ment in April 1864, but the House of Representatives had yet to vote on it.

The old Congress, meeting for its last session in the winter of 1864/65, contained too few Republicans to furnish the necessary two-thirds vote. The newly elected House, with its overwhelming Republican majority, would not meet until December 1865. Practically all of the Democrats in the old Congress had opposed the amendment.

Lincoln set to work to win over some of the Democrats. In his annual message to Congress, he urged them to consider the people's voice. Meeting with individual representatives, he brought all his powers of persuasion to bear. Finally, on January 31, 1865, enough Democrats voted with the Republicans to carry the proposal by more than two-thirds.

Lincoln rejoiced as the amendment went to the states for ratification. He rejoiced again as his own state of Illinois began and other states followed in acting favorably upon it. Lincoln did not, however, live to see its final adoption in December 1865.

THE CONFEDERACY

The South had fewer soldiers and smaller material resources than the North. It also faced serious handicaps in trying to make effective use of its resources. One handicap was the very idea of states' rights upon which the Confederacy had been based. Most secessionists disliked any centralization of governmental power. That was one reason they had led their states to secede. Yet a strong, centralized government was necessary for the most efficient development, organization, and application of the South's resources. The Confederate government was further handicapped because it was new.

The Armies

The Confederacy resorted to conscription in 1862, a year before the Union did so. At first, all able-bodied white men between the ages of 18 and 35 were subject to the draft (as compared with the ages of 20 to 45 in the North). Later, the age limits were extended, and men from 17 to 50 years of age were called up. Boys younger than 17 and men older than 50 served in state "home guards." The South raised a total of about 1 million troops.

The draft had unpopular features in the Confederacy as well as in the Union. The Confederate law did not provide for the purchase of exemption but did allow the sending of substitutes. The demand for substitutes grew so great that the price soon rose to $10,000 (in Confederate money). Even more unpopular were the provisions for exemption, especially the so-called twenty-Negro law, which exempted one white man for every twenty black persons on a plantation. This provision was included because it was feared that white families would not be safe if left without able-bodied white men to protect them from the slaves. But it caused men who owned small farms to feel that they were being forced to fight for the benefit of men who owned large plantations, men who could escape the draft. It was frequently said that the war was "a rich man's war and a poor man's fight."

Near the end of the war, the Confederacy needed additional troops so desperately that its congress passed a law for the enlisting and arming of slaves. The leading advocate of this measure was the Confederacy's greatest general, Robert E. Lee. He thought a plan of gradual emancipation should be worked out, for he considered it "neither just nor wise" to use black men as soldiers and still try to keep them as slaves. The Confederate congress never agreed to emancipation, and the war ended before any blacks actually served in the Confederate ranks.

Scarcities

The Confederacy was less successful than the Union in financing the war. It relied heavily on paper money rather than on borrowing and taxation. Southern banking facilities had always been inadequate, and the Confederacy lost its banking center when New Orleans was captured in the second year of the war.

The Confederate government as well as states, cities, banks, and corporations issued notes that passed as money. The amount of currency of all kinds circulating in the South increased ten or eleven times from 1861 to 1864. Prices rose sharply, eventually reach-

As the war continued, the supply of raw materials in the South diminished. The Confederacy issued an appeal to churches to turn in bronze bells for casting into cannon. This idealized drawing of a heroic contribution was used as propaganda.

ing an average more than a hundred times that of 1861. This price rise was due to the swelling of the money supply, the shrinking in the supply of goods, and the growing fear that the Confederacy would lose the war.

The South had been dependent upon the outside world for goods of many kinds. These became increasingly scarce as the Union tightened its blockade of southern ports. Southerners suffered from the worst inflation that any Americans had experienced since the War for Independence. They had to pay fantastic prices for scarce items. For example, a cup of coffee cost $5.00 in a Richmond restaurant in 1864. Most people used coffee substitutes. A favorite kind of "Confederate coffee" was made from peas and corn that were scorched and then ground together.

No substitutes could be found for some of the most essential items, such as salt. The South had imported most of its salt from Europe or the West Indies. When these sources were cut off, people began looking for new sources. Boiled seawater, salt mines, and salt springs eventually produced enough salt for most needs, though occasionally meat spoiled or cattle died for want of it.

Because of transportation difficulties, salt, grain, meat, and other goods seemed scarcer than they were. Often there was an abundance in certain localities but a shortage in others.

In some ways the Confederacy made excellent use of the inadequate railroads it had at the start of the war. For example, the Confederate army was the first to send reinforcements by rail to an army in the midst of battle. In other ways the Confederacy did less well. The Confederate government could not get enough skilled mechanics or enough materials and equipment to keep the rail lines in good repair. As tracks and trains wore out, the Confederacy became less and less able to wage defensive war.

The government tried to encourage manufacturing but used mostly indirect means. By manipulating the draft, for example, the government took workers from nonessential industries and spared them for essential ones. By controlling the railroads, it allowed raw materials to go to the most important factories and not to others.

To get scarce supplies, the government "impressed" them from farmers or merchants. That is, the government set its own price, then seized the goods it needed and paid for them at the set price. Farmers and merchants often hid their products, hoping to sell them later for much more than the Confederate government was paying. The more the goods were held back by such people, the more the prices rose. Thus, in some of its efforts to deal with inflation, the government only made matters worse.

As in the North, the women and children

carried on the family's work on small farms or in businesses. The southern people felt the impact of the war much more than the northern people. The fighting came much closer to home in the South. White families lost a higher proportion of their menfolk, and often they lost everything else—homes, crops, land. Southerners were too poor and their economic system was too badly organized to provide the same degree of soldier care and comfort that northerners provided.

Throughout the war most slaves carried on their life and work as usual. After the issuing of the Emancipation Proclamation, many slaves viewed the Union army as a liberating force. Some of the newly freed slaves left their homes on plantations to follow the Union army, working most often as cooks or servants.

Political Disputes

Political parties did not have enough time to develop in the Confederacy. Only one presidential election was held, and Jefferson Davis and Alexander H. Stephens ran unopposed. Though there were no organized parties, political opposition to the Davis administration soon arose. This opposition centered around the vice-president and two state governors.

Vice President Stephens, a former Whig, and Davis, always a Democrat, differed in their backgrounds. All of his life, except for congressional terms served in Washington, Stephens had lived in Georgia, one of the original thirteen states. He felt a deep sense of state pride. Davis, born in Kentucky and educated in New York, had made his home in the young state of Mississippi and had spent many years at frontier army posts as well as in Washington. He had no strong loyalty to a particular state.

The positions of the two men in the Confederate government also were quite different. As president, Davis held great respon-

The Union camp at City Point, Virginia, included a field hospital, munitions dump, and supply depot. With its wharves and extensive railroads, City Point made an ideal supply base for the Army of the Potomac during the last stages of the war.

sibilities; as vice-president, Stephens held none. Stephens could afford to indulge in fantasies about the high ideal of states' rights. Davis had to face the hard, practical realities of carrying on a war for national independence—a war that required the use of national powers. States' rights as opposed to national powers—this issue had already broken up the United States of America. Now it threatened to break up the Confederate States, too.

Stephens seldom appeared in the Confederate capital, which had been moved from Montgomery to Richmond in May 1861. He spent most of his time at his Georgia plantation home. There, in private meetings with other discontented leaders, he criticized almost everything that Davis did or tried to do.

The governors of Georgia and North Carolina refused to cooperate fully with Davis. Like Stephens, these men denounced the draft as unconstitutional, and they helped many of their citizens to evade it by appointing them to state offices. At times, Georgia's governor forbade Georgia soldiers to serve outside the state. The North Carolina governor objected to "foreigners"—men from other Confederate states—recruiting in North Carolina or serving as officers of North Carolina troops. He hoarded supplies for his state. While Lee's troops in Virginia were going ragged, warehouses in North Carolina were full of surplus uniforms.

As the Confederacy lost more and more ground, Davis's critics in the newspapers and in the congress put the blame increasingly upon him. He became the most unpopular man in the South. After the war the federal authorities imprisoned him for more than two years, thus making him seem a martyr. Only then did he become a southern hero again.

EUROPE'S POLICIES

Both the Union and the Confederacy directed their major diplomatic efforts at Britain, the European nation most able to affect the course of the war. The Confederate aim was positive: to induce Britain to recognize and help establish the independence of the Confederacy. The Union aim was negative: to prevent Britain from doing so. Britain never went far enough to please the South, yet it went too far to suit the North.

Cotton Diplomacy

At the beginning, southerners felt certain that cotton—or rather the lack of it—would help them achieve their purpose with Britain and with France as well. In 1861 they destroyed a large part of the crop and kept the rest from being shipped abroad. They thought that either the British and the French mill owners would have to close their mills or their governments would have to recognize the Confederacy.

It was true that the British and also the French had been buying most of their cotton from the American South. Even so, the southerners failed to get the kind of foreign help that they had counted on. There were several reasons for this.

First, the cotton shortage was slow to hit Britain. In 1861, British warehouses were bulging with cotton. The dealers were happy about the threat of scarcity, for they could get a high price for the stocks they had on hand. When the shortage finally became serious, in 1863, it hurt most the mill workers and their families.

Second, the British expected the shortage to be temporary, and they looked to other nations, particularly India and Brazil, for new sources of cotton.

Third, northern wheat proved to be as important as southern cotton. During the war, wheat exports took the place that cotton exports formerly had held in Anglo-American trade relations.

Fourth, in the beginning the British leaders thought the Confederates were going to win without British aid. Later, at the time the cotton shortage was beginning to be felt, the British could see that the war was going against the Confederacy. To enable the Confederacy to win, Britain would now have to provide a great deal of assistance. It would also have to risk a war with the United States, and Confederate independence scarcely seemed worth the probable cost.

Fifth, the European powers themselves were divided. None of them wanted to go ahead alone, get deeply committed in North America, and thus expose itself to possible attack in Europe.

Neutrality

Not long after the firing on Fort Sumter, Queen Victoria declared Britain's neutrality. Later, France and a few other nations also proclaimed theirs. This ought to have been satisfactory to President Lincoln and to the northern people, but actually it was not.

In their neutrality proclamations, Britain and the other nations said that a state of war existed in the United States, and they indicated that they would treat both sides alike. This meant that the Confederacy was recognized as a *belligerent,* that is, as an entity able to wage war, though not necessarily as an independent nation.

The queen issued her proclamation of neutrality in response to a proclamation of blockade that Lincoln had just issued. She took it for granted that the United States was actually carrying on a war and that the Confederacy was the enemy.

President Lincoln and Secretary of State Seward at first insisted that there was no war in the usual sense. They maintained that there was only a rebellion and a kind of police effort to put it down. Lincoln and Seward further claimed that the rebels were not entitled to the rights of foreign enemies under international law but deserved to be treated as traitors or pirates and executed when captured and convicted.

Lincoln never carried out such a policy. Early in the war, the Confederates took many prisoners and threatened to retaliate, man for man, if any Confederates were executed after being captured. The Union therefore treated prisoners as if they were foreign enemies.

The official attitude in the North finally recognized that there was both a rebellion and a war. It was officially called the War of the Rebellion. The Confederates could be looked upon as foreign enemies who were entitled to the benefits of international law. They could also be seen as domestic rebels who might be treated in some respects—in the confiscation of their property, for example—as if they were traitors.

Even so, Lincoln, Seward, and other northerners continued to complain because some foreign governments, particularly the

Union soldiers inflate an air corps balloon. Many leaders were slow to see the advantages of the balloons, which were eventually used for observing troop positions and directing artillery fire. Some were equipped to telegraph information to the ground.

British, had acted on the assumption that there really was a war. At the same time, Davis and other southerners were dissatisfied because European governments did not recognize Confederate independence.

Union Trouble with Britain

After Queen Victoria's proclamation of neutrality, trouble between the United States and Britain flared up on three occasions during the Civil War.

The first was the *Trent* affair, in 1861. The *Trent,* a British merchant ship, was bound for Britain with two Confederate commissioners, James M. Mason and John Slidell, aboard. The captain of a United States warship stopped the *Trent,* took off Mason and Slidell, and sent them as prisoners to Boston.

The British government protested against the capture. The British prime minister, Lord Palmerston, demanded that the United States release the two Confederates and apologize to Britain. To back up his demands, he began to make war preparations and sent 8,000 troops to Canada.

Finally, the United States government yielded. Though Seward did not apologize, he did let Mason and Slidell go. He pretended that the capture was similar to the old British practice of impressment and that, in protesting it, Britain had at last adopted the principles for which Americans had fought in the War of 1812.

In 1862, the British government came close to stepping in and trying to make peace. The cabinet considered an arrangement calling for a separation between the North and the South. One cabinet member, William E. Gladstone, said:

Jefferson Davis and other leaders of the South have made an army; they are making, it appears, a navy; and they have made what is more than either—they have made a nation.

In the Battle of Antietam (September 17, 1862), however, the Union army turned back a Confederate army and ended the first southern attempt to invade the North. When this news reached Britain, Palmerston and his colleagues felt less sure that Davis had created a nation that would endure. Never again did the British cabinet seriously discuss intervention.

In 1863, a crisis arose because British shipyards were building Confederate warships. The authorities had allowed several British-built cruisers to be sold to the Confederates, though this violated both British law and British neutrality. The United States minister in England, Charles Francis Adams, protested repeatedly but in vain. Besides new cruisers, some rams also were under construction. These vessels had iron prows designed for ramming and sinking the wooden ships in the Union blockade. Adams demanded that the British prevent the departure of the rams.

The cabinet finally did prevent their departure, as well as the departure of any more cruisers. British leaders had come to think it unwise to allow British-built ships to be used against a nation with which Britain was at peace. The leaders feared that, in the future, the United States might follow the British example and provide Britain's enemies with ships.

FIGHTING THE WAR

In comparison with previous wars, the Civil War seems very modern because of the many new devices that were used. Among these were the railroad, telegraph, armored ship, observation balloon, and repeating rifle. The Civil War also seems modern because it involved so fully the energies and resources of the opposing sides. It was fought by huge citizen armies and for all-out victory. It approached total war.

Overall Strategy

Lincoln and Davis, according to the terms of their respective constitutions, were commanders in chief of their armies and navies.

They were responsible for seeing that war plans were made and carried out. In this, Lincoln, for all his military inexperience, did better than Davis.

At first, Lincoln relied for advice on his general in chief, Winfield Scott. A veteran of the War of 1812, a hero of the Mexican War, Scott had been a great soldier. Now he was old, fat, and weak. He proposed that the Union forces merely blockade the southern ports, move down the Mississippi River to its mouth, and sit tight. Having cut the Confederacy in two, the Union forces would encircle the main part and deprive it of all outside supplies. Newspapers called this the Anaconda Plan, because it resembled the action of the giant snake that wraps itself around its prey.

Lincoln approved of Scott's plan as far as it went, but he wished to make it more active. He was convinced that the Union must throw its strength against the Confederacy, hitting several different points at the same time.

Lincoln had worked out his basic strategy. His next task was to find a general in chief who could successfully take charge of all the Union armies and carry out the plan. He dismissed Scott and tried George B. McClellan and then Henry W. Halleck, but neither of them measured up. At last, he found Ulysses S. Grant, the one Union general in the field who was consistently winning. During the final year of the war, Grant provided the kind of military leadership that Lincoln had been seeking.

Just as Lincoln tried to make the most of northern wealth and numbers, so Davis had to adapt his plans to the limited southern resources. Southern critics accused Davis of favoring a "dispersed defensive" strategy. They said he scattered the troops and kept them on the defensive when, instead, he should concentrate his forces, take the offensive, and constantly threaten the North. By

Confederate prisoners cook rats to supplement their rations in Point Lookout Prison. Prison life in the North was thought to be much better than that in the South. In 1864, the War Department retaliated by reducing prison rations to the southern level.

this kind of "offensive defensive," they argued, he could save the Confederacy.

Davis replied that the Confederacy lacked the means for keeping up such activity. "Without military stores, without the workshops to create them, without the power to import them," he explained, "necessity not choice has compelled us to occupy strong positions and everywhere to confront the enemy without reserves." Despite all the handicaps, Davis made use of the "offensive defensive" on several occasions. For example, he authorized Lee to invade Pennsylvania in the campaign that led to the Battle of Gettysburg.

Davis never worked out with General Robert E. Lee a command system comparable to the one that Lincoln formulated with Grant. Lee was a brilliant soldier with an outstanding record. Yet he served under Davis most of the time only as commander of the Army of Northern Virginia and had no authority over the rest of the Confederate armies. Davis preferred to act as his own general in chief. Not until 1865 did he appoint Lee to that position. Then it was too late for Lee to accomplish anything with his new authority.

The Union Blockade

At the war's beginning, the Union navy consisted of fewer than a hundred vessels. It grew to number nearly seven hundred by the end of the war. The navy's main task was to close off the commerce of the South, and this it did effectively. A blockading squadron was stationed at each major southern seaport. Once this was done, no regular ocean-going ship could get in or out.

Many small boats and low craft sneaked past the blockading squadrons. This was most often done at night. Some boats landed at lonely spots along the coast. These blockade-runners carried away cotton and brought back both military supplies and expensive luxuries to the South. At first, the great majority of the blockade-runners got through, but each year, more and more were captured. Blockade-running never made up for the regular trade that the South had lost.

Union naval and land forces filled gaps in the blockade by occupying southern coasts and seaports. During the first year of the war, these forces recovered most of the coastal area and off-shore islands of the Carolinas. Then they took the cities of New Orleans (1862), Mobile and Savannah (1864), and Wilmington (1865).

The Confederates made one dramatic attempt to break the blockade. They salvaged a warship, the *Merrimac,* which the Union navy had scuttled at Norfolk, and covered it with armor plate. On March 8, 1862, the clumsy *Merrimac* steamed into Hampton Roads, destroyed two of the wooden blockading vessels, and scattered the rest. That very night a brand-new and quite different ironclad vessel arrived—the Union's *Monitor.* It had a turret on a low, flat deck, like a tin can on a shingle. The next day the *Monitor* engaged the *Merrimac* in the first duel ever fought between armored warships. The duel ended in a draw, but the *Merrimac* never again threatened the blockade.

With its British-built cruisers, the Confederacy attempted a kind of counterblockade. These cruisers preyed upon northern shipping. The *Alabama,* the most famous of these cruisers, sank, burned, or captured 69 ships on the Atlantic in two years. The Union warship *Kearsarge* finally caught up with the *Alabama* on June 19, 1864, off Cherbourg, France, and sent it to the bottom. Though the Confederate raiders did serious damage to northern shipping, they had no significant effect upon the outcome of the war.

The Civil War, 1861–1865

Union strategy was threefold: (1) a blockade of the coast to starve the South; (2) an eastern campaign to capture Richmond, capital of the Confederacy; and (3) a western campaign to clear the Mississippi and Tennessee river valleys and split the Confederacy into several sections. In addition to defense, the Confederate strategy called for invasion of Maryland and central Pennsylvania in order to cut the Northeast off from the Northwest and force the Union to seek peace.

THE CAMPAIGN IN THE EAST

July 21, 1861 Battle of Bull Run. Confederate victory. Union troops (General Irvin McDowell) marching toward Richmond were defeated by the Confederates (Generals Joseph E. Johnston and Pierre G. T. Beauregard).

May 4–July 2, 1862 Peninsular campaign. Confederate victories. Union troops (General George McClellan) sailed down the Potomac from Washington and occupied Yorktown, Virginia (May 4). They were prevented from engaging the main part of the Confederate forces (Johnston) at Williamsburg (May 5) by a stubborn rearguard action. During an attack on McClellan's army at Fair Oaks (May 31), Johnston was wounded and replaced by General Robert E. Lee (June 1). Lee and McClellan engaged in the Seven Days' Battles (June 26–July 2). Union forces lost most of the encounters but finally held at Malvern Hill (July 1). Lee withdrew toward Richmond (July 2), but the Union troops had failed in their attempt to reach Richmond.

August 29–30, 1862 Second Bull Run. Confederate victory. After the failure of the Peninsular campaign, Union troops (General John Pope) tried again to reach Richmond but were defeated (Lee).

September 17, 1862 Antietam. A draw. McClellan caught Lee as he invaded Maryland but failed to break his lines. However, Lee retreated to Virginia.

December 13, 1862 Fredericksburg. Confederate victory. Union troops (General Ambrose Burnside) attempting to take Richmond by way of Fredericksburg suffered heavy losses at the hands of the Confederates (Lee).

May 2–4, 1863 Chancellorsville. Confederate victory. In another attempt to take Richmond, Union troops (General Joseph Hooker) failed to break Confederate lines at Chancellorsville.

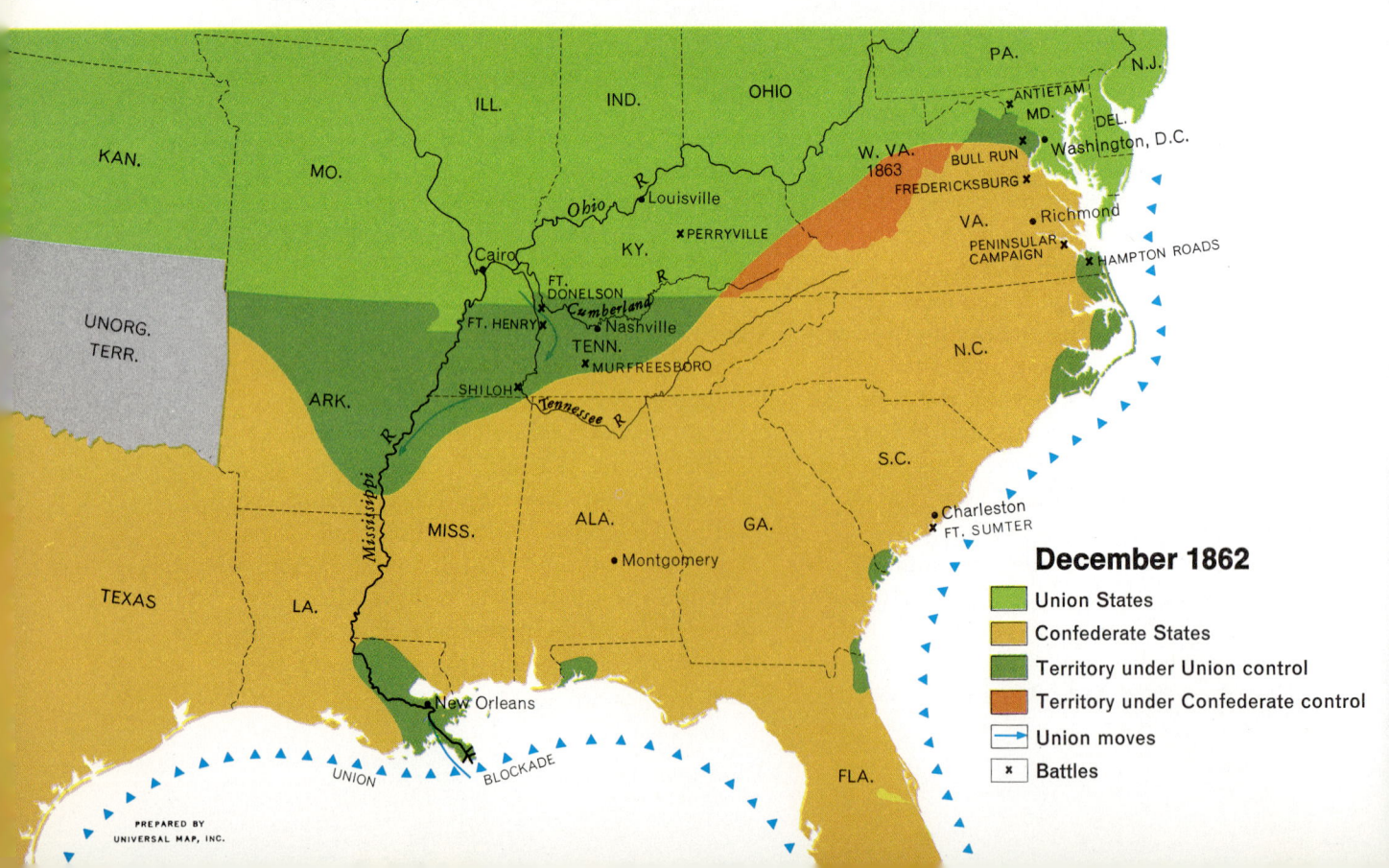

July 1–3, 1863 Gettysburg. Union victory. Lee, carrying the war to the North, was forced into battle at Gettysburg, Pennsylvania. After three days of bitter fighting, Lee retreated to Virginia.

THE CAMPAIGN IN THE WEST

February 6, 1862–January 3, 1863 Operations in Kentucky and Tennessee. Union victories. Combined Union forces (General Ulysses S. Grant and Commodore A. H. Foote) captured Fort Henry (Feb. 6) and Fort Donelson (Feb. 16). Grant marched to Shiloh (April 6–7). The Confederates (General Albert S. Johnston) caught Grant off guard. After a day of confused fighting, northern reinforcements arrived (Generals Don Carlos Buell and Lew Wallace) and the Union gained the upper hand. In the fall, the Confederates (General Braxton Bragg) tried to reach Louisville but were stopped by Buell at Perryville (Oct. 8). They were forced to withdraw from central Tennessee after a defeat at Murfreesboro (Dec. 31–Jan. 3) by Union troops (General William Rosecrans).

July 4, 1863 Vicksburg. Union victory. After many assaults on Vicksburg, Mississippi, Grant finally captured the city. The entire Mississippi River was in Union hands and the Confederacy was split.

September 19–20, 1863 Chickamauga. Confederate victory. Moving east, Union troops (Rosecrans) maneuvered the Confederates (Bragg) out of Chattanooga (Sept. 9) without a battle. Reinforcements were rushed to Bragg, and the Union line was broken at Chickamauga. The Union army retired to Chattanooga and Bragg besieged the city.

November 23–25, 1863 Chattanooga. Union victory. Grant, now in charge of the western campaign, attacked and routed Bragg's army. Union troops were now ready to divide the South by marching across Georgia.

THE FINAL SWEEP

May 7–September 2, 1864 Invasion of Georgia. Union victory. Union troops (General William T. Sherman) set out from Chattanooga and began invading Georgia. Confederate forces (General Joseph E. Johnston) fought a skillful series of defensive actions at Resaca (May 13–16), New Hope Church (May 25–28), and Kennesaw Mountain (June 27). Johnston was replaced by General John B. Hood, who twice attacked Sherman but was forced into Atlanta. He evacuated Atlanta (Sept. 1) and Sherman occupied it (Sept. 2).

November 14–December 22, 1864 The march to the sea. Union victory. Sherman left Atlanta and began the march across Georgia, destroying factories, warehouses, bridges, railroads, public buildings, and crops. He was virtually unopposed and occupied Savannah (Dec. 22).

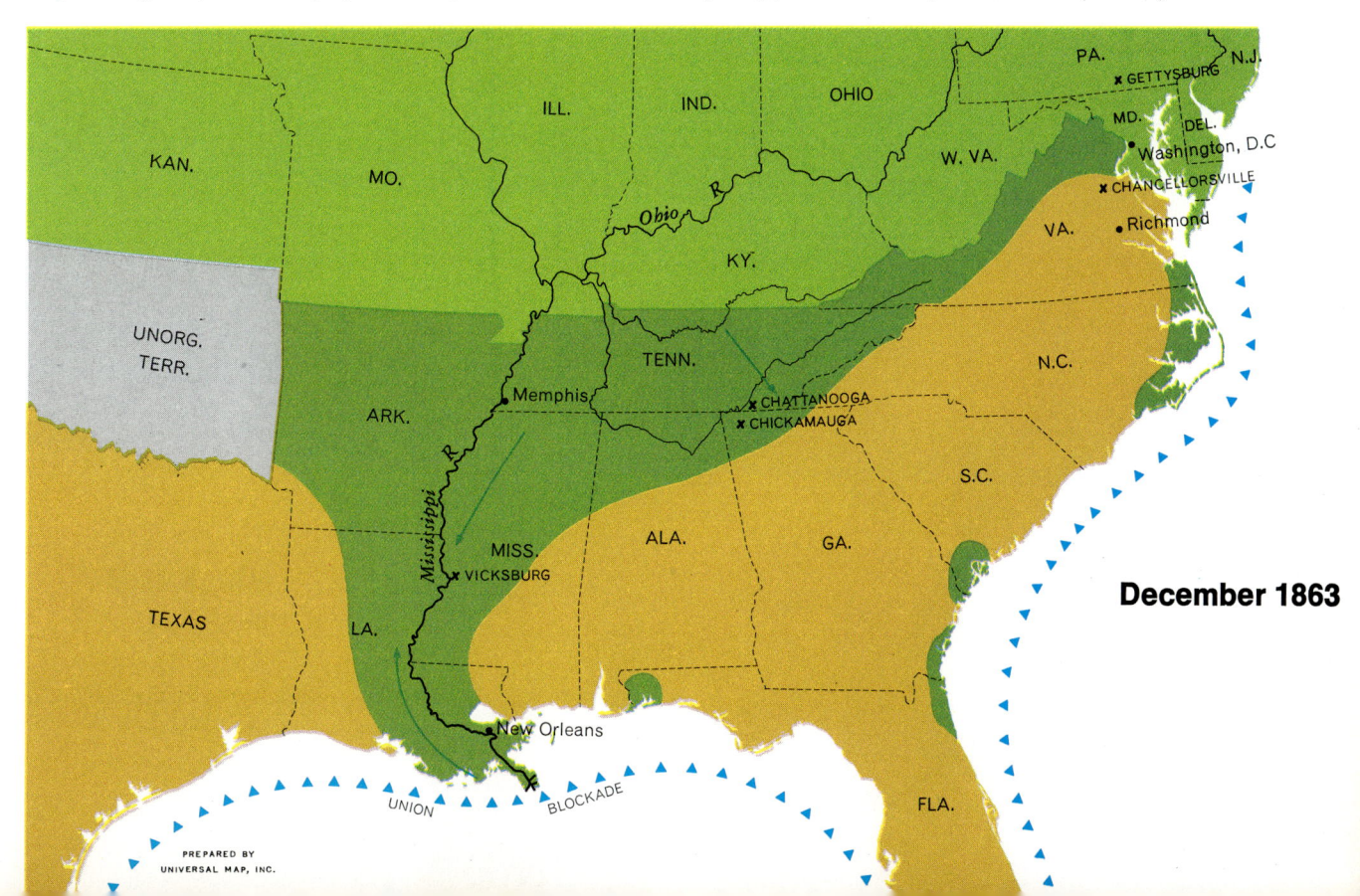

December 1863

December 15–16, 1864 Nashville. Union victory. While Sherman marched through Georgia, Confederate General Hood went after Union troops (General George H. Thomas) in Tennessee. Hood was repulsed at Franklin (Nov. 30) by General John Schofield, who then joined Thomas at Nashville. Hood's army was virtually destroyed there.

January 16–March 21, 1865 Invasion of the Carolinas. Sherman left Savannah and began a march that was even more destructive than the one through Georgia. The fall of Columbia (Feb. 17) led to the evacuation of Charleston (Feb. 18). Sherman moved into North Carolina, fought Joseph E. Johnston (again in command) at Bentonville (March 19–20). Union troops occupied Goldsboro (March 21). Johnston formally surrendered a week after the war ended.

May 5, 1864–April 2, 1865 The drive to Richmond. Union victory. With the Battle of the Wilderness (May 5–6) Grant began to hammer away at Lee's army. Despite heavy losses, Grant moved south. He failed to flank Lee at Spotsylvania (May 8–12). A frontal assault at Cold Harbor (June 3) failed, but Lee's army suffered heavy losses. Grant then decided to take Richmond from the rear. He moved his army to Petersburg but failed to take the city (June 15–18). He then began a siege that lasted nine months. Lee failed to break the siege at Fort Steadman (March 25) and at Five Forks (April 1). Lee evacuated Petersburg and Richmond (April 2).

April 9, 1865 The surrender at Appomattox Courthouse. After evacuating Petersburg and Richmond, Lee headed for Lynchburg, where he hoped to move by train to North Carolina and join forces with Johnston. Grant, however, won the race and blocked his path. Lee asked for terms and he met Grant at Appomattox (April 9).

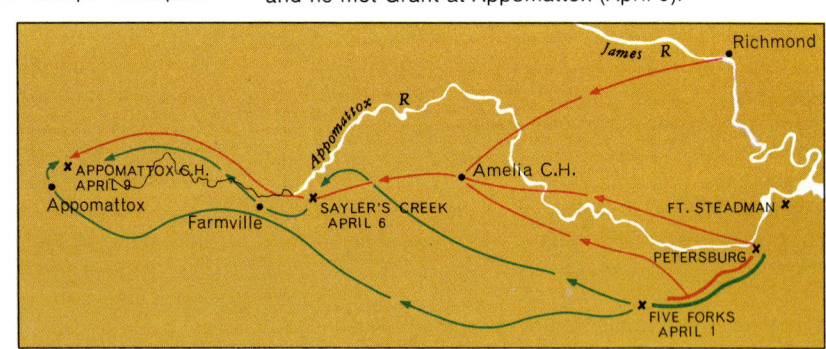

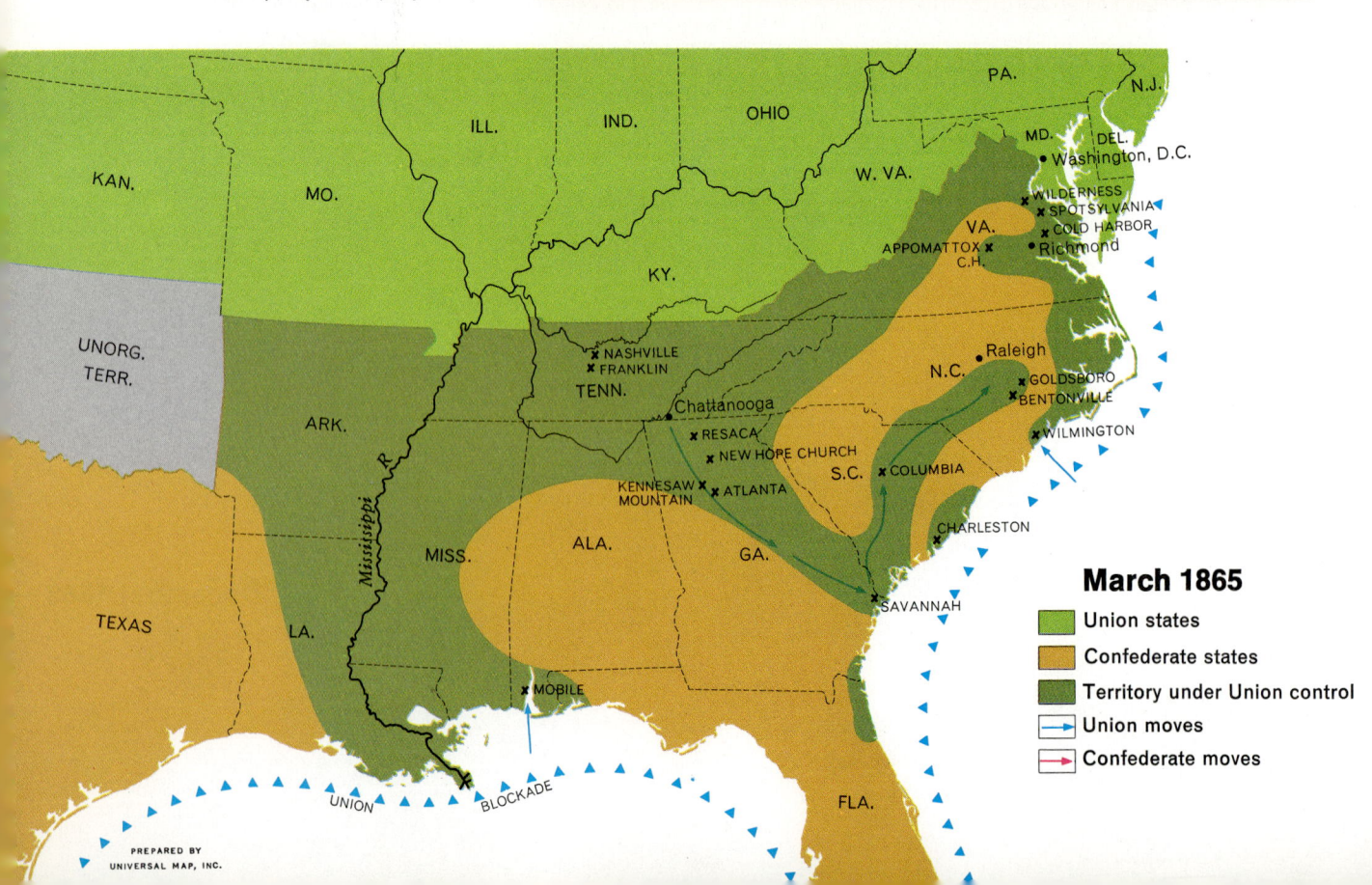

March 1865
- Union states
- Confederate states
- Territory under Union control
- Union moves
- Confederate moves

Lee's Hold on the East

Impatient to begin a land offensive, Lincoln ordered an inexperienced army to attack the Confederates in July 1861, at Manassas, Virginia, about thirty miles from Washington. In the war's first big battle, the Battle of Bull Run—southerners called it Manassas—the Confederates drove the Federals back in a rout.

From 1861 to 1863, the Union forces fighting on the Virginia front failed again and again to capture Richmond, the capital of the Confederacy. General Lee, who took command of the Army of Northern Virginia in 1862, successfully resisted a whole series of Union generals who commanded the Army of the Potomac.

George B. McClellan did an excellent job of training and equipping this army, but he hesitated to lead it into battle. The boastful John Pope replaced McClellan and held command long enough to be badly beaten by Lee and Thomas J. Jackson at the second Battle of Bull Run, or Manassas. Then McClellan got another chance. At the Battle of Antietam, or Sharpsburg, he managed to turn Lee back from Maryland but could not prevent his returning to Virginia.

Next appeared Ambrose E. Burnside, who feared he was unfit for high command. He proved it at Fredericksburg, when he sent wave after wave of bluecoats to fall before Lee's impregnable position on the heights above the town. Joseph Hooker fought no better when his turn came, for he failed at Chancellorsville.

When Lee again carried the war to the North, George Gordon Meade took over the Union troops in midcampaign. The two armies happened to come together at Gettysburg, Pennsylvania, and a three-day battle ensued (July 1–3, 1863). This time the Federals held the high, protected ground, and the Confederates wasted themselves with repeated assaults, ending in the slaughter known as "Pickett's charge." On July 4, Lee ordered the remnant of his army to withdraw. Once more he was able to get his men safely back south of the Potomac.

Grant's Victories in the West

The Battle of Gettysburg is generally thought to mark the "high tide of the Confederacy" and the turning point of the Civil War. It undoubtedly climaxed the fighting on the eastern front. But long before that battle, Union forces had begun to win important victories on the western front, in the Mississippi Valley.

As the year 1862 opened, there were two Union armies in Kentucky: the Army of the Tennessee under Grant and the Army of the Ohio under Don Carlos Buell. Opposing them were widely scattered Confederate forces under Albert Sidney Johnston. The two strongest points in the Confederates' long defensive line were Fort Henry on the Tennessee River and Fort Donelson on the Cumberland, in Tennessee. Grant took both of these forts, thus compelling the Confederates to pull far back to the south. The Confederates attempted to make a new and much shorter defensive line, abandoning half of Tennessee.

Then Grant moved south, with Buell following to give him support. Suddenly Johnston fell upon Grant in the hope of destroying his army before Buell could join it. Thus began the bloody Battle of Shiloh in southwestern Tennessee. For the North, it was a narrow victory. For the South, it was a serious defeat since Grant's and Buell's armies had been able to combine deep inside the Confederacy.

In an attempt to split the Confederacy, other Union forces, naval and land, were opening up the Mississippi River. By June 1862, they controlled most of the river except for a section of it around Vicksburg, Mississippi. This Confederate stronghold, high on

The Battle of the Crater was, as Grant said, "a stupendous failure" for Union forces. Misdirection of troops caused terrible losses.

a bluff, was assigned to Grant as his objective. Several times he tried and failed to get at the town by way of the rough, broken terrain to its north. In the spring of 1863, he by-passed Vicksburg by crossing into Louisiana. Then he recrossed the river and closed in upon Vicksburg from the rear, starting a siege of about six weeks. Vicksburg capitulated on the same day that Lee withdrew from Gettysburg (July 4, 1863).

While Grant was busy with the Vicksburg campaign, other Union troops were trying to get to Chattanooga, a strategic river port and railroad center in southeastern Tennessee. Now Grant came and took charge. The Battle of Chattanooga ended with Union soldiers rushing up the slope of Missionary Ridge to take the Confederate positions at the top.

The Union victory at Chattanooga ranks in importance with the decisive Union victories at Gettysburg and Vicksburg. The Union forces had gained control of most of Louisiana and Arkansas as well as Tennessee. They were now in a position to cut through Georgia and to split the Confederacy again.

Grant Versus Lee

Grant took command of all the Union armies on March 9, 1864. He chose to make his headquarters in the field rather than in Washington. He accompanied the Army of the Potomac, though Meade remained technically in charge of it. Grant planned two major campaigns for 1864. One was intended to bring Lee to a showdown in Virginia and the other to wear down the Confederate army in Georgia.

In Virginia, Grant headed into a rough, wooded area known as the Wilderness. Twice Lee struck savagely. Each time, Grant pushed on, instead of retiring and regrouping as the Union generals formerly had done. The third time he met Lee, at Cold Harbor, only a few miles from Richmond (June 3, 1864), Grant himself did the attacking, throwing his men against strong Confederate entrenchments. This month-long Wilderness campaign resulted in heavy casualties. Although Grant lost five men for every three that Lee lost, the campaign brought no decision.

Grant decided not to keep on slogging toward Richmond, but slipped away to the south in the direction of Petersburg. He tried to storm his way into Petersburg but failed and settled down to a siege. During the next eight months, he stretched his siege lines farther and farther around Richmond and Petersburg.

Meanwhile, William T. Sherman commanded the Union army in Georgia and Joseph E. Johnston the opposing Confederate army. When the two armies reached the outskirts of Atlanta, the Confederate leaders told Johnston to turn his command over to John B. Hood. Hood promptly made two attacks and suffered two defeats, then withdrew into Atlanta. Surrounding the city with his troops, Sherman forced Hood out and led the occupation of Atlanta (September 2, 1864).

Sherman now headed toward Savannah and the sea. Marching through Georgia, Sherman and his men met little resistance as they laid waste a strip of country sixty miles wide. His goal was to bring the war home to the southern people and destroy both their resources and their will to win. After taking Savannah, he turned northward and continued his march through the Carolinas.

By April 1865, Lee had concluded that he could no longer hold Richmond and Petersburg. He withdrew his army (April 2, 1865) and moved west. After a week's pursuit, Grant overtook him. On April 9, 1865, at Appomattox Courthouse, in Virginia, Lee surrendered.

A Look at Specifics

1. Why was the Conscription Act objectionable to many people in the North?

2. How did the Homestead Act give aid to farmers?

3. Why did Lincoln believe the Emancipation Proclamation was constitutional?

4. In what respects were the Democrats handicapped in the election of 1864?

5. What was the offensive-defensive strategy advocated by many southerners?

6. What was the purpose of the Union blockade?

7. Why were the battles of Vicksburg and Chattanooga crucial victories for the North?

A Review of Major Ideas

1. What advantages did the North have over the South in waging war? Why, in spite of their disadvantages, did many southern leaders think the Confederacy could win the war?

2. What influenced the issuance of the Emancipation Proclamation and the passage of the Thirteenth Amendment?

3. How was the South handicapped in its efforts to wage war?

4. Why were diplomatic relations strained between the Union and Britain during the war?

5. How did the Union's leadership and strategy contribute to its success in achieving military victory?

For Independent Study

1. The historian, David M. Potter, says: "If the Union and the Confederacy had exchanged presidents with one another, the Confederacy might have won its independence." Evaluate this statement.

2. In 1864, Lincoln said, "I claim not to have controlled events but confess plainly that events have controlled me." Do you think his judgment of himself could be applied to his emancipation policies? Explain your answer.

3. Was Sherman's march through Georgia an unjustifiable series of atrocities or was it a legitimate method for waging war? Can any limits be set on means of waging war?

Restoring The Union

CHAPTER 12
1865–1877

Former slaves outside their cabin in Richmond.

The Civil War had determined that no state could secede from the Union and that no person could own another as a slave. There remained questions, however, in regard to reconstructing the Union and reconstructing the southern states.

The South needed to be reconstructed physically as well as politically and socially. The war had left widespread desolation, especially along the route of Sherman's march through Georgia. There and elsewhere, the results of war and defeat were appalling: railroad tracks and bridges torn up, houses and barns burned or looted, fields left to grow up in weeds.

To rebuild would take money, but little coin was to be had, and Confederate money was worthless. So were the Confederate war bonds in which many southerners had invested their life savings. The slaves once valued at billions of dollars no longer could be counted as property at all. To rebuild also would take a great deal of labor, but the traditional labor system was gone.

The economic reconstruction of the South was delayed because of disputes over political and social reconstruction. The majority of white southerners thought their states ought to be readmitted to the Union promptly, with as little change as possible in society and government. The majority of northerners thought the states should not be admitted until important changes had been made.

RECONSTRUCTION PLANS

At the end of a war with a foreign nation, the President takes the lead in arranging peace terms. The Constitution provides that the President "shall have Power, by and with the Advice and Consent of the Senate, to make Treaties" *(Art. 2, sec. 2, para. 2).* At the end of the Civil War, however, there was no treaty of peace, for the Union government refused to recognize or deal with the

Confederate government. Yet a peace settlement had to be arranged somehow. The President and the Congress presumably should have worked together as peacemakers, each exercising the appropriate constitutional powers. Instead, a dispute arose over the proper roles of the President and the Congress.

Lincoln's Plan for Peace

In December 1863, President Lincoln had proposed a plan for restoring to the Union those southern states already under Union control. At that time he promised that he would pardon all Confederates (except the leaders and certain others) who would give up and take an oath of future loyalty to the United States and its laws, including the Emancipation Proclamation. He also announced that whenever 10 percent of the voters in a state had taken the oath, they could reestablish government in that state. He expressed the hope that the reorganized states would "recognize and declare" the permanent freedom of, and provide education for, those blacks who had already been freed.

Under the "10 percent plan," new constitutions and governments were formed in Arkansas, Tennessee, and Louisiana during 1864. Lincoln wrote to the first "free state" governor of Louisiana asking whether some blacks might not be allowed to vote, "especially those who have fought gallantly in our ranks." But Louisiana gave no blacks the vote at that time.

In Congress, most of Lincoln's fellow Republicans disapproved of his plan. They feared that the reconstructed states might continue to allow slavery, since the plan did not appear to require complete and permanent abolition (and the Thirteenth Amendment had not yet been passed). Republicans also feared that former secessionists, by taking Lincoln's loyalty oath, could recover control of the states. The majority in Congress, therefore, refused to recognize the states that were formed according to Lincoln's plan.

Congress supported, instead, a reconstruction plan sponsored by the Radical Republicans Benjamin F. Wade and Henry Davis, in 1864. According to the Wade-Davis bill, a majority of a state's voters, not just 10 percent, would have to take an oath of future loyalty. Only those who could also take an oath of past loyalty would be allowed to participate in forming a new government. They would have to swear that they had never willingly borne arms against the United States. The new states would be required to free all slaves, though not to give them the vote. When Congress passed the bill, Lincoln pocket-vetoed it. Its sponsors then bitterly denounced him in a public letter, the "Wade-Davis manifesto."

Thus, by the time of Lee's surrender, Lincoln was already at odds with Congress. In his last public address (April 11, 1865) he appealed to Congress to accept his "10 percent" government in Louisiana, though he did not insist that the same plan be followed in the other states. He and the Radical Republicans, however, were now farther apart than ever.

No one knows how well Lincoln would have done as a reconstruction President. He died on April 15, 1865, the victim of a madman's bullet. The assassin, John Wilkes Booth, was the mastermind of a plot aimed also at Vice-President Andrew Johnson and Secretary of State William Seward. Booth's accomplices were bunglers: Johnson was unharmed and Seward, though badly injured, managed to survive.

Shocked and horrified, many northerners believed the false rumor that leaders of the dying Confederacy were behind the plot. This belief added bitter feelings toward the South and increased the demands for a harsh peace. The Radical Republicans now gained

RECONSTRUCTION: TWO VIEWS

ANDREW JOHNSON
Seventeenth President
1865–1869

To me the process of restoration seems perfectly plain and simple. It consists merely in a faithful application of the Consitution and laws....

... [The] States lately in rebellion are still members of the National Union.

... If we admit now that ... [the ordinances of secession] were valid ... we sweep from under our feet the whole ground upon which we justified the war....

... I would be unfaithful to my duty if I did not recommend the repeal of the acts of Congress which place ten of the Southern States under ... military masters....

... The punitive justice of this age, and especially of this country, does not consist in stripping whole States of their liberties and reducing all their people, without distinction, to the condition of slavery. *(1867)*

THADDEUS STEVENS
Representative from Pa.
1849–1853, 1859–1868

Nearly six years ago a bloody war arose between different sections of the United States. Eleven States ... aimed to sever their connection with the Union.... On the result of the war depended the fate and ... condition of the contending parties....

The Federal arms triumphed. The confederate [States] ... surrendered unconditionally. The law of nations then fixed their condition. They were subject to the controlling power of the conquerors....

To reconstruct the nation ... to guaranty republican governments to old States are all legislative acts....

... Unless the rebel States ... should be made republican in spirit ... all our blood and treasure will have been spent in vain. *(1867)*

---

more popular support. They looked forward to taking charge of reconstruction under the presidency of Johnson, whom they considered a Radical like themselves.

Johnson's Reconstruction Plan

A southerner and a former slave owner, Johnson had never been a secessionist or a friend of the planter class. He was born (1808) into a poor family in North Carolina and, when a young man, moved to Tennessee. His wife, a schoolteacher, taught him to read and write. He worked as a tailor. As a Democratic congressman before the war, he advocated a homestead law, which most southern politicians opposed. When Tennessee seceded, Johnson, a senator, refused to go with his state. He remained in Congress, the only senator from a seceding state who did so. In 1862 he was appointed governor of conquered Tennessee. In 1864 he was nominated for the vice-presidency in order to make the Republican party seem to be a true "Union party," with a southern Democrat as well as a northern Republican on its national ticket.

Though Johnson at first agreed with the Radicals on the "crime" of secession, he disagreed with them on a number of important matters. He opposed economic policies favorable to northern business, which many of the Radical Republicans advocated. He sympathized much less than most of them did with the newly freed slaves. While the Radical Republicans emphasized national power, he thought it was his duty to protect the states in the proper exercise of their rights. It soon became apparent that he had more in

RECONSTRUCTION: TWO REACTIONS

HENRY C. DIBBLE
Louisiana Judge and Politician

No men in power ever designed more reforms and improvements, and accomplished less general good, than the Republicans who came into control of these State governments. . . . [The] nervous energy of these new rulers . . . found expression in elaborate schemes for . . . a new era for the South. . . . [But] a political party at war with the greater portion of the intelligence and wealth in the States, could not successfully execute plans for . . . public improvement. . . .

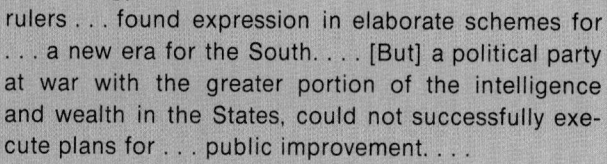

. . . [It] is unjust . . . to lose sight of the condition of public affairs throughout the country. It was an era of corruption. . . . The Republican ring at Washington, and the Democratic ring in New York, stole more than all the carpet-baggers, scallawags, and colored politicians in all the ten reconstructed States. *(1877)*

FREDERICK DOUGLASS
Black Journalist and Abolitionist

[To-day], in most of the Southern States, the fourteenth and fifteenth amendments are virtually nullified. . . . [The] newly enfranchised . . . [are] in a condition but little above that in which they were found before the rebellion. . . . [In] the eager desire to have the Union restored, there was more care for sublime superstructure of the republic than for the solid foundation upon which it could alone be upheld. . . .

. . . When the serfs of Russia were emancipated, they were given three acres of ground upon which they could . . . make a living. . . . [Our slaves] were sent away empty-handed, without money, without friends, and without a foot of land . . . . Old and young, sick and well, were turned loose to the open sky, naked to their enemies. *(1880)*

---

common with his fellow Democrats than with the Radical Republicans.

In Johnson's view, the southern states had never really left the Union. The state leaders had attempted to bring about secession and, in doing so, had temporarily resisted the national authority. These secessionists must be replaced by men from the same states who were loyal to the Union. The new leaders must come not from the aristocracy of planters but from the middle and lower class of white farmers. Thus white men's democracies would arise in the South.

In the spring of 1865, while Congress was not in session, Johnson launched his state-making program. He required the reorganized states to do three things: annul their ordinances of secession, abolish slavery, and repudiate their war debts. He proclaimed amnesty for all former rebels except the top leaders and the largest landowners, and he offered to pardon those people individually if they would apply to him in person.

During the summer of 1865, the southern states adopted new constitutions and elected state officers and national representatives and senators. Secession was annulled, slavery abolished, and war debts repudiated, but the old leadership was not overthrown. Most of the men elected were former Confederate leaders whom Johnson had pardoned so that they could take part in politics.

The kind of political revolution that Johnson had hoped for in the South had not taken place. Nevertheless, he concluded that reconstruction, or "restoration" as he preferred to call it, was now over. He was confident that when Congress met in December

1865, it would recognize the southern states and admit their congressmen.

When Congress met, however, the Republican majority refused to seat any representatives or senators from the South. The two houses then set up the Joint Committee on Reconstruction to consider what the southerners must do in order to be admitted.

Southern Attitudes

A prompt restoration of the southern states would seem to be justified if most white southerners accepted the consequences of the war, gave obedience to federal authority, and treated black Americans as truly free people. Otherwise, a delayed program of reinstatement with stricter requirements would seem to be called for.

Johnson received quite different reports from two men he had sent to investigate conditions in the South in the summer of 1865. "I am satisfied," General U. S. Grant told him, "that the mass of thinking men of the South accept the present situation of affairs in good faith." Carl Schurz, a leader in the Republican party, found that there was "among the Southern people an *utter absence of national feeling*" and that the Negro, "though no longer considered the property of the individual master," was "considered the slave of society."

Events in the South during 1865 and 1866 seemed to most northerners to confirm the Schurz report. The majority of southern whites, however, felt that they were doing the best that could be done, under the circumstances, to solve the postwar problems of the South.

The immediate concern was to make a living, and this was difficult for those farmers and planters who had depended on slave labor. Some thought blacks would work only as slaves, never as employees. Others began to experiment with hiring blacks, often their own former slaves. Many employers insisted upon labor contracts that required the blacks, if they were to be paid, to remain on the plantation until the harvest.

Another concern, as white southerners saw it, was to preserve order. They feared that blacks, without the bonds of slavery to confine them, would become vagrants and criminals. There were frequent rumors that the blacks were plotting an uprising against the whites.

After the war, soldiers of the United States Army, many of them black, continued to be stationed in the South. White southerners resented the presence of the army and especially of the black troops. Southerners protested that the army, instead of maintaining peace and order, would encourage the former slaves to make trouble.

The blacks also had urgent problems. With freedom, many blacks were displaced from their homes and lost all means of making a living. Though they generally were willing to work for wages, they would have preferred to work on land of their own.

They got some assistance from societies that northern churches and charitable groups had organized during the war. These societies provided food, medical care, schools, and teachers. An army agency, the Bureau of Freedmen, Refugees, and Abandoned Lands (created in March 1865), also provided some assistance. The Freedmen's Bureau undertook to resettle blacks on abandoned or confiscated lands. Not much land was available, however, for as President Johnson pardoned the former Confederates, they were able to reclaim their confiscated property. Besides providing education, transportation, and relief of various kinds, the bureau tried to safeguard Negroes in the making of labor contracts. The army stood ready to back up the agents of the bureau.

Most white southerners wanted to be left alone, to deal as they saw fit with the problems of the South. After the southern states had been reorganized on Johnson's plan, they passed laws, known as "black codes," to define the legal position of the former slaves. According to some of these codes, blacks were to be compelled to work for a white employer, and if they quit before the expiration of their contracted term of labor, they were subject to arrest. Those not employed could be arrested for vagrancy and could be assigned to the highest bidder to work out their fines. According to the Mississippi code, blacks could not own land to farm independently. These laws were similar to the slave codes that had existed before the war. They appeared to many northerners to reestablish slavery in disguise.

Blacks, southern white unionists, and northerners residing in the South said that they risked their lives whenever they tried to assert their rights, especially if they supported the Republican party. From time to time, blacks and their white sympathizers were beaten or murdered.

Johnson and Congress at Odds

The election of former Confederates to office, the passage of the black codes, and the mistreatment of blacks and white Republicans—all troubled the Republicans in Congress. They were convinced that they should require further changes in the southern states before allowing them to be represented in the Senate or the House.

At first, the Republicans disagreed among themselves over the changes. The Radical Republican leader in the Senate, Charles Sumner of Massachusetts, insisted upon black suffrage. The Radical Republican leader in the House, Thaddeus Stevens of Pennsylvania, demanded that plantations be confiscated and divided among the blacks. These Radical Republicans argued that no states, only territories, existed in the South. Sumner said the states had committed suicide by seceding, while Stevens said they had been reduced to "conquered provinces" through defeat in war. Therefore, Congress could do as it pleased with the South, without regard to states' rights. Most Republicans, however, refused to go along with the theories of Sumner and Stevens. The more moderate senators and representatives wished only to make sure that southern blacks were protected in their rights to life, liberty, and the pursuit of happiness.

To protect blacks, the Republicans passed a bill in February 1866 to enlarge the powers and prolong the life of the Freedmen's Bureau. Johnson vetoed the measure. In March, Congress passed a bill to make blacks citizens of the United States and to assure them the same civil rights as whites. Johnson vetoed the civil rights bill, but the Republicans repassed it over his veto. Later they passed, over his veto, an amended version of the Freedmen's Bureau bill.

In June, Congress approved and sent to the states for ratification a constitutional amendment, the Fourteenth. This reinforced the Civil Rights Act by putting guarantees of citizenship and civil rights for blacks into the Constitution. The amendment gave the states a choice of letting blacks vote or losing congressional representatives in a number proportional to the black population. It also disqualified most of the former Confederate leaders from holding either state or federal office.

This reconstruction plan went considerably beyond the Wade-Davis bill. No representatives or senators were to be accepted from a southern state until the state had ratified the Fourteenth Amendment. Johnson advised the states not to ratify it, and for the time being none of them did so except Tennessee, which Congress then (1866) readmitted to the Union.

As a result of his obstructionist stand, Johnson lost the sympathy of Republicans. Moderate Republicans had sponsored the civil rights and Freedmen's Bureau bills, and when he vetoed these, the moderates joined the Radical Republicans in opposing him. More and more, Johnson was forced to rely on the support of Democrats, northern and southern.

In the congressional elections of 1866, northern voters had an opportunity to choose between Johnson's position and the Republican policies. The voters overwhelmingly endorsed the Republicans, who consequently increased their majority in Congress. Henceforth they could easily override the President's veto.

REPUBLICANS IN CONTROL

After the war, the governments of the southern states went through a bewildering series of changes. These states were reconstructed first at the direction of President Johnson, then at the direction of Congress.

Radical Reconstruction

In a series of Reconstruction acts in 1867, the Radical Republicans presented their third congressional program for the defeated South. According to these acts, the South was to be divided into five districts, each under the command of an army officer, with troops to enforce his authority. Military rule was to continue until a new state government satisfactory to Congress had been formed. No one was to participate in constitution-making except those adult males, black or white, who could take an "ironclad oath" that they had never willingly supported the Confederacy. The states, thus reorganized again, had to ratify the Fourteenth Amendment and give voting and officeholding rights to black men.

Six states (Arkansas, North Carolina, South Carolina, Louisiana, Alabama, and Florida) complied with these requirements by the summer of 1868. Congress accepted the newly elected senators and representatives, and the military authorities allowed the newly elected state officials to take charge of the state governments.

The four other states (Mississippi, Virginia, Texas, and Georgia) failed to satisfy Congress in 1868. Congress imposed a fourth plan of reconstruction upon them. This included all the previous requirements and an additional one—ratification of the Fifteenth Amendment, which forbade the states to deny any person the vote on account of "race, color, or previous condition of servitude." Not until 1870 were these states readmitted to the Union and relieved of direct military rule.

Meanwhile, President Johnson had done his best to frustrate the congressional program by means of his appointments of civil and military officials and his orders to the ruling generals in the South. This was the primary reason that the Radical Republicans, in 1868, tried to remove him from office. They could do so, constitutionally, only by the process of impeachment, and only on the grounds of "high crimes and misdemeanors." When Johnson dismissed the secretary of war, Edwin M. Stanton, the Radicals charged that he had violated a law, the Tenure of Office Act. That law, passed in 1867, had been intended to prevent Johnson from removing high officials from office without the consent of the Senate.

Johnson was impeached and tried. No crimes were proven against him. While he was guilty of disagreeing with Congress, opposing its measures, and speaking disrespectfully of Radicals, these were not crimes in any sense of the word. Nevertheless, the Radicals demanded that all Republicans in the Senate vote for conviction out of loyalty to the party. If all but six Republicans had done so, he would have been convicted and removed. At the trial, seven Republicans and all the Democrats held him not guilty of impeachable offenses. He was saved by the margin of a single vote.

Republicans in the South

Through the Reconstruction acts, the Republicans in Congress intended to put members of their party in control of the South. Since there had been no Republican party in the South before the war, the party had to be organized as a new combination of political elements. It came to consist of black men and of two groups of white men, the so-called scalawags and carpetbaggers.

Black men made up the largest bloc of Republican voters in most of the states under Radical Reconstruction. Negroes served as state and local officials, legislators, and as United States representatives and senators, but they never held a majority of offices except in the South Carolina legislature. Although some attained state offices as high as lieutenant governor, none was ever elected governor. Many of the black officeholders had received no schooling and did not know how to read and write. Others, most of whom were free before the war, and some of whom had been born and reared in the North, were well educated. Several were eloquent speakers and effective leaders.

The *scalawags* were native white southerners who, temporarily at least, joined the Republican party. Some were farmers who had never owned slaves, who had long disliked the planter aristocracy, and who had given the Confederacy little or no support during the war. Others were wealthy or once wealthy planters and businessmen who had opposed secession but had "gone with their states" and had served in the Confederate army. Having once been Whigs, they did not feel quite at home as Democratics. They were willing to join once more with former Whigs (now Republicans) of the North. Moreover, they believed they could advance their own interests by cooperating with blacks and working to control black votes.

The southern white Republicans did not, of course, call themselves scalawags. They were called that by the Democrats, who viewed them as scoundrels. The Democrats held the same view of the *carpetbaggers*—northern Republicans who took part in southern politics after the war. The Democrats termed them carpetbaggers in order to give the impression that they were fortune-seekers who had gone south with all their possessions in a carpetbag (at that time a common kind of traveling bag).

Actually, the carpetbaggers included a variety of men from the North, well-off and poor, honest and dishonest. Nearly all were veterans of the Union army. Most of them came south during the war or within a year or two after its close. Some had arrived as Freedmen's Bureau agents or as federal officials. Others had come as planters, businessmen, or professional men who thought they saw a new frontier of economic opportunity in the postwar South. Though not numerous enough to be important as voters, the carpetbaggers were clever and courageous enough to be extremely influential as leaders. More willing than the scalawags to mingle socially with Negroes, the carpetbaggers were more successful in winning black confidence and support.

Under Radical Reconstruction, the old political order in the South seemed to be turned upside down, with recent slaves imposing laws upon their former masters. White Democrats complained of "Negro rule." Yet, in fact, Negroes alone never ran the southern states. For a time, they helped govern, but they did so in cooperation with white men, some from the North, a much larger number from the South.

Expanding State Activities

The Republican state governments did not change relations between blacks and whites as much as some people expected. For example, they refrained, except in a few cases, from legalizing interracial marriages or requiring integrated schools (in New Orleans, some of the schools were racially integrated for a brief period). Nevertheless, these governments were quite different from those that preceded them. The new ones undertook to do things that their predecessors had not done at all or had done only on a small scale.

One of these things was to provide education for masses of children, black as well as white. Before the war, every southern state had adopted some kind of public educational system, at least on paper. But none except North Carolina had actually established public schools throughout the state. In trying to educate hundreds of thousands of persons who had never been educated before, the Republican governments faced an expensive task. They had to build many schoolhouses. Most of the teachers had to be attracted from the North at high salaries.

The new state governments also tried to improve and expand the means of transportation. The Republicans—and many Democrats—believed that the South could prosper only if trade were encouraged by the construction of additional railroad lines. They believed that the states must give financial aid to railroad companies in order to encourage rapid expansion. Some of the governments under Johnsonian reconstruction had helped finance railroad construction, but the Republican governments did much more.

The states also borrowed money (by issuing bonds) for other purposes, such as the building of schools and the rebuilding of streets, roads, bridges, levees, and courthouses. Consequently, the state debts increased, some of them to a level several

Thomas Nast's cartoon (left) is a typical southern view of the carpetbagger. This unscrupulous fellow with his huge bag of southern spoils carries an empty one for further fleecing of the South. Black legislators were equally distrusted by most southern whites. Although many southern states had black legislators in

times as high as the prewar debts. Taxes also went up, both to pay interest on the debts and to meet increased running expenses.

Unfortunately, not all the money raised by taxing and borrowing was used for public improvement or the general welfare. Some of the money (no one can say how much) was wasted or diverted for private gain. Negroes, scalawags, and carpetbaggers were not the only ones involved. Black men were no more corrupt than white men, Republicans no more corrupt than Democrats, northerners no more corrupt than southerners. During the postwar years, political corruption was widespread throughout the nation. In the years after Reconstruction, however, the memory of corruption under the Reconstruction governments grew until it became the chief thing for which Reconstruction was remembered.

The Ku Klux Klan

In opposing the Republicans and their policies, the Democratic party in the South was handicapped by the political limitations imposed by Radical Reconstruction. Few of the most prominent Democrats could vote for, or serve as, delegates to the state constitutional conventions of 1867. Once the conventions had completed their work, however, the right to vote depended upon the provisions of the new constitutions. Only three states —Alabama, Arkansas, and Louisiana— disfranchised men because of their Confederate record. In all the other states, the former Confederate leaders were allowed to vote.

the earliest days of Reconstruction, only the South Carolina legislature *(center)* ever had a black majority. Black people of all ages began to attend school as soon as facilities were available *(right)*. Schools were set up by carpetbaggers, blacks, and the Freedmen's Bureau.

But the Fourteenth Amendment excluded Confederate leaders from either state or federal officeholding. President Johnson, despite his pardoning power, could not remove this disability; only Congress could do so. The new amendment kept about 100,000 to

150,000 white men from office, but there were about 650,000 whom it did not affect.

The former Confederate leaders still could exert a great deal of influence, both through the Democratic party and through secret societies like the Ku Klux Klan. The Klan's founder and first Grand Wizard was the Tennessean Nathan Bedford Forrest, a former slave trader, planter, and Confederate officer. Wearing white hoods and robes, Klansmen went on night rides to terrorize blacks and their scalawag or carpetbagger associates. Through floggings, lynchings, and torture, the Klansmen intimidated those who opposed them. The avowed aim of the night riders was to preserve order, protect white womanhood, and offset the activities of the Union Leagues. (The Union Leagues were Republican secret societies that enrolled Negroes and trained them in politics.) The Klan's actual effect was to lessen Republican influence in southern politics.

To check Klan terrorism, Congress in 1870 and 1871 passed three Enforcement (or Ku Klux) acts, which outlawed the Klan and authorized the use of the United States Army against it. In 1871, federal soldiers went to the assistance of Republican officials in the South on at least two hundred occasions. Martial law was declared in nine South Carolina counties. There and elsewhere, Klansmen were arrested, and some were convicted of crimes and imprisoned. After that, the Klan itself went to pieces, but "Ku Kluxism" (the use of terror to achieve political ends) continued.

TROUBLES UNDER GRANT

Radical Reconstruction helped the Republican party in national politics. The party could attract voters, in both the North and the South, by identifying itself with the ideals of union and freedom. Most of the Union veterans were Republicans, and many

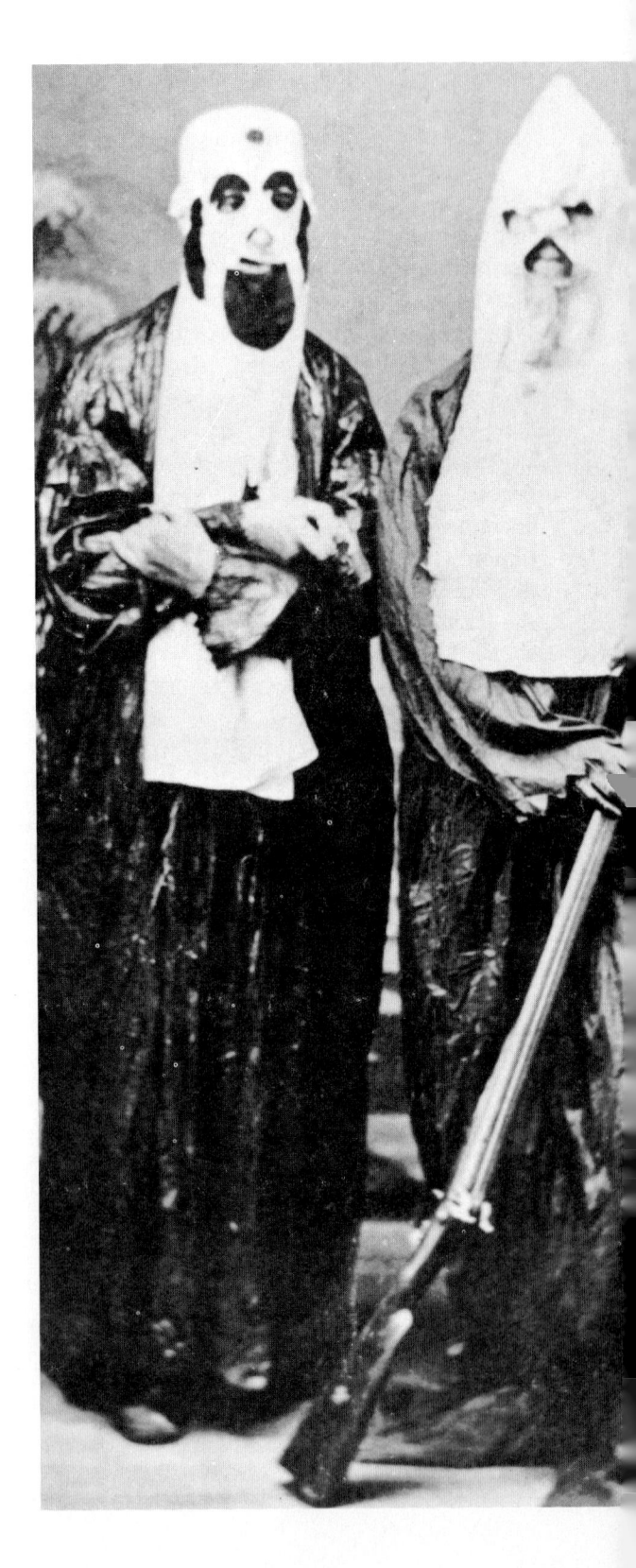

By 1866, the members of the Ku Klux Klan were actively waging a campaign of terror and intimidation. They wore hoods to conceal their identities as well as to appear frightening.

of them joined the Grand Army of the Republic (the G.A.R.), a veterans' organization that supported the party. In 1868, the party appealed to war memories and patriotic feelings—and won the presidential election—by running the popular hero Ulysses S. Grant.

Grant, a professional soldier, up to that time had shown little interest in politics and had had no experience in government. In the presidency, Grant showed the effects of his military background. He kept as official or unofficial advisers a number of old army cronies. Out of personal loyalty he supported them even after some of them had proved themselves dishonest or incompetent. Knowing little of politics, he deferred to certain party bosses. He took their advice in the distribution of the spoils of office and relied upon them and their subordinates to manage legislation in Congress. When he had decided upon a policy, he expected it to be carried out just as if it were an army order.

Scandals

Though Grant himself was honest, he failed to keep his administration free from political scandal. The first affair to be exposed was that of the Credit Mobilier, a construction company controlled by a group of Union Pacific Railroad stockholders. Some of them diverted government loans into their own pockets. To head off an investigation, the Credit Mobilier managers bribed a number of congressmen with company stock. Though all this had happened before Grant's presidency, the truth came to light during his first term. It seemed to disgrace his administration because his Vice-President, Schuyler Colfax, had been one of those congressmen who accepted bribes.

One scandal followed another during Grant's second term. In the case of the "Whiskey Ring," his private secretary and certain treasury officials cooperated with a group of distillers to make false sales reports and thus cheat the government out of taxes. Grant defended his private secretary and removed the head of the treasury department, who had discovered the fraud. In the Belknap case, the secretary of war was shown to have taken a bribe, and Grant again sided with the wrongdoer, who resigned to escape impeachment. Other cases, in the navy and treasury departments, involved officials who defrauded the government of money, which they used to enrich themselves and finance Republican political machines.

Before the end of his presidency, Grant openly confessed his political incompetence and apologized for the "mistakes" made under his administration.

The Liberal Republicans

Even before the end of Grant's first term, a number of important Republicans had become disgusted with what they called "Grantism." By this they meant the corruption, the spoils system, and other policies. They also meant Radical Reconstruction, which the administration was attempting to enforce, but which seemed to them to be producing more evil than good.

In 1872, these anti-Grant men decided not to support the President for reelection. Calling themselves Liberal Republicans, they organized a separate party and nominated as its presidential candidate the editor of the *New York Tribune,* Horace Greeley. They needed the votes of Democrats to elect him, but Greeley had a long record as an antislavery man and Republican extremist. Without much enthusiasm, the Democratic party gave him its nomination, too, but on election day a large number of Democrats stayed home. Grant won decisively.

An Economic Depression

At the time of Grant's second inauguration (1873), the nation seemed to be highly prosperous. Before the end of the year, however, a number of banks began to close their doors in order to forestall runs by depositors. The Panic of 1873 was on. It was followed by the longest and deepest depression the United States had yet known. It lasted for about six years and brought a drastic drop in agricultural prices, thousands of business failures, and unemployment of a half million people at a time.

Farmers suffered because their costs remained high while the prices of their crops fell. Farmers decided, for the first time, to organize on a large scale.

Before the panic, an organization known as the Patrons of Husbandry, or the National Grange, had been formed to bring together farm people for social and educational meetings. After the panic, the Grange attracted many more members, eventually a total of almost a million, and they took steps to improve their economic condition. The Grangers set up cooperatives for the purchase as well as the manufacture of farm machinery and other goods.

The Grangers also went into politics. They supported candidates, either Democratic or Republican, who favored state regulation of railroads. In Illinois, Wisconsin, Iowa, and Minnesota, the farmers and their friends secured the passage of "Granger laws" regulating railroad freight rates. The Supreme Court upheld these laws in the case of *Munn* v. *Illinois* (1877).

Hard times provoked farmers to organize but discouraged laborers from doing the same. Jobs were so scarce that workers hesitated to antagonize their employers and risk being fired. The number of union members fell from 300,000 in 1872 to 50,000 in 1878. Labor troubles became serious toward the end of the depression. A railroad strike in 1877 led to bloody rioting in Pittsburgh, Chicago, and St. Louis. Federal troops were called out to put down the violence.

Besides arousing farm and labor discontent, the depression caused many voters to turn away from the Republican party. In 1874, the Democrats won a majority of seats in the House of Representatives. The depression also intensified a public debate with regard to the national currency.

Paper Money

There were two kinds of paper money in circulation after the war. One consisted of the greenbacks printed during the war. The other consisted of various forms of currency, including the national banknotes issued by private banks belonging to the National Banking System and guaranteed by the United States Treasury. There was a big difference between the two kinds of money: the greenbacks could not be exchanged for gold. As a result, they fluctuated in value.

Some bankers and merchants, especially in New England, thought the government should get rid of the greenbacks. They wanted to rely only on "sound money," that is, coin or paper money that could be exchanged for coin. Other people, especially in the West and South, thought the government should keep the greenbacks in circulation, print more of them, and use them to pay off the war bonds as these fell due. The greenback advocates desired inflation, that is, an increase in the money supply and a rise in prices. They believed that rising prices would encourage business, provide jobs, and make it easier for farmers to pay their debts.

In 1875, Grant signed the Specie Resumption Act. This provided that more banknotes would be issued, that greenbacks would be kept in circulation, and that greenbacks as well as banknotes would be exchangeable for gold after 1879. The Specie Resumption Act was a compromise, and it did not satisfy all those who favored inflation. Some of them formed the Greenback party, which nominated a presidential candidate in 1876.

UNITED STATES DIPLOMACY

Neither Johnson's nor Grant's administration was very successful in dealing with domestic affairs. In foreign affairs, however, both administrations accomplished a great deal. This was largely the work of two of the ablest secretaries of state the nation has ever had—William H. Seward, who served under Johnson as well as under Lincoln, and Hamilton Fish, who served almost from the beginning of Grant's first term.

Seward's Policies

Seward favored an active foreign policy. He long had been an expansionist and had once said the United States flag ought someday to wave over all of North America. He also hoped, by diplomatic triumphs, to make the Johnson administration more popular than it was. He hoped to draw public attention away from the quarrel between Johnson and the Republicans.

As the Civil War came to an end, Seward's most urgent task was that of persuading the French to get out of Mexico. Napoleon III, the French emperor, had put Maximilian, a brother of the Austrian emperor, upon a golden throne as emperor of Mexico. Napoleon III was keeping Maximilian in power by using French troops against the Mexican people and army. This effort by a European power to dominate a Latin American nation was the most direct challenge to the Monroe Doctrine up to that time.

In dealing with France, Seward had to be cautious so long as the nation was still fighting the Civil War. As Union victory neared, he began to demand the withdrawal of the French troops. Finally, Napoleon III agreed to remove them, and in 1867 the last of them departed from Mexico. Maximilian stayed on and was shot by a Mexican firing squad. The Mexican republic was restored, and the Monroe Doctrine was upheld.

Seward took more interest in East Asia and the Pacific area than had any secretary of state before him. He cooperated with European powers in forcing Japan's feudal lords to develop trade. He negotiated the Burlingame Treaty (1868), which gave Americans additional rights of travel and residence in China and which permitted Chinese laborers to come and live in the United States. His most outstanding achievement, however, was the purchase of Alaska and the Aleutian Islands.

By 1867, Alaska was all that remained of Russian America. The czar of Russia, Alexander II knew there was gold in Alaska, and yet he wished to sell the territory. It was costly to hold, and he feared that if he did not dispose of it, sooner or later either the British or the Americans would take it over.

On a March evening in 1867, the Russian minister called on Seward at his Washington home. He said the czar was willing to sell and suggested that a treaty be drawn up. Seward suggested that they not wait. The men sat down and wrote the treaty, signing it at four o'clock in the morning.

The Senate promptly approved the treaty, but opposition to it arose in the House of Representatives. The House had to appropriate 7.2 million dollars to pay for the purchase. Opponents referred to Alaska as "Seward's Folly" or "Seward's Icebox" and argued that it was too far away and barren to be worth the price—less than two cents an acre. In July 1868, the appropriation bill finally was passed.

Fish's British Policies

Hamilton Fish proved to be much the best of all Grant's appointees. A wealthy New York lawyer, Fish had served as a member of the House of Representatives, governor, and a United States senator. He was not a party leader comparable to Seward, nor was he so daring and aggressive in his views of diplomacy. What the nation needed, however, was a calming influence in its foreign affairs, and this he provided.

Relations between Britain and the United States were bad at the end of the Civil War. Northerners still blamed the British government for having allowed cruisers to be built in British shipyards and sold to the Confederacy. These Americans demanded payment of the *Alabama* claims, that is, the claims for losses the various cruisers had caused to Union shipping. Charles Sumner, chairman of the Senate Foreign Relations Committee, argued that the claims should also include the cost of the war for its last two years. He said that British policy had prolonged the war by that much and he estimated these "indirect damages" at 2 billion dollars. He and others expected Britain to make payment by giving Canada to the United States.

Such talk worried the Canadians. They had a number of grievances against their neighbors to the south. There were disputes over the northwest water boundary, fishing rights, and Fenian activities. (The Fenian Brotherhood, an organization of Irish Americans, hoped to conquer Canada and thus compel Britain to grant independence to Ireland. Between 1866 and 1871 the Fenians made several raids across the border into Canada.) The troubles with the United States helped bring Canadians together in a federation of the provinces known as the Dominion of Canada (1867).

To deal with the disputes, Secretary Fish arranged for a joint commission of one Canadian, two Britishers, and three Americans to meet in Washington in 1871. They agreed to a treaty that settled, in one way or another, all the difficulties except the Canadian claim to damages for Fenian raids.

Under the treaty, an international court (with Swiss, Italian, Brazilian, American, and British judges) met in Geneva to decide on the *Alabama* claims. They awarded 15.5 million dollars to the United States. The German emperor arbitrated the boundary question. He decided in favor of the Americans, upholding their claim to the San Juan Islands in Puget Sound. Special Anglo-American commissions granted about 7.5 million dollars to Britain as compensation for losses suffered by British subjects during the war and as payment for American rights to fish in Canadian waters.

The Treaty of Washington of 1871 marked a turning point in the history of Anglo-American relations. Long traditional rivals, the United States and Britain began to draw together and become permanent friends.

RECONSTRUCTION'S END

Ten years after the passage of the Reconstruction acts, the national leaders of the Republican party stopped trying to enforce the reconstruction program. Even before that time, however, the program had been frustrated in most of the southern states.

Republican Losses in the South

Within a few years after the southern states had been readmitted to the Union, the Democrats recovered control in most of them. In Virginia, they were already in power when the state was readmitted in 1870. Where blacks were few, the task was comparatively simple for the Democrats. They had only to win over the votes of white men, including the scalawags. Most of the scalawags, losing all hope of controlling their black and carpetbagger allies, eventually deserted to the Democrats.

The southern Republicans faced increasing handicaps after 1872. They were weakened

PRESIDENTIAL ELECTIONS: 1864-1876

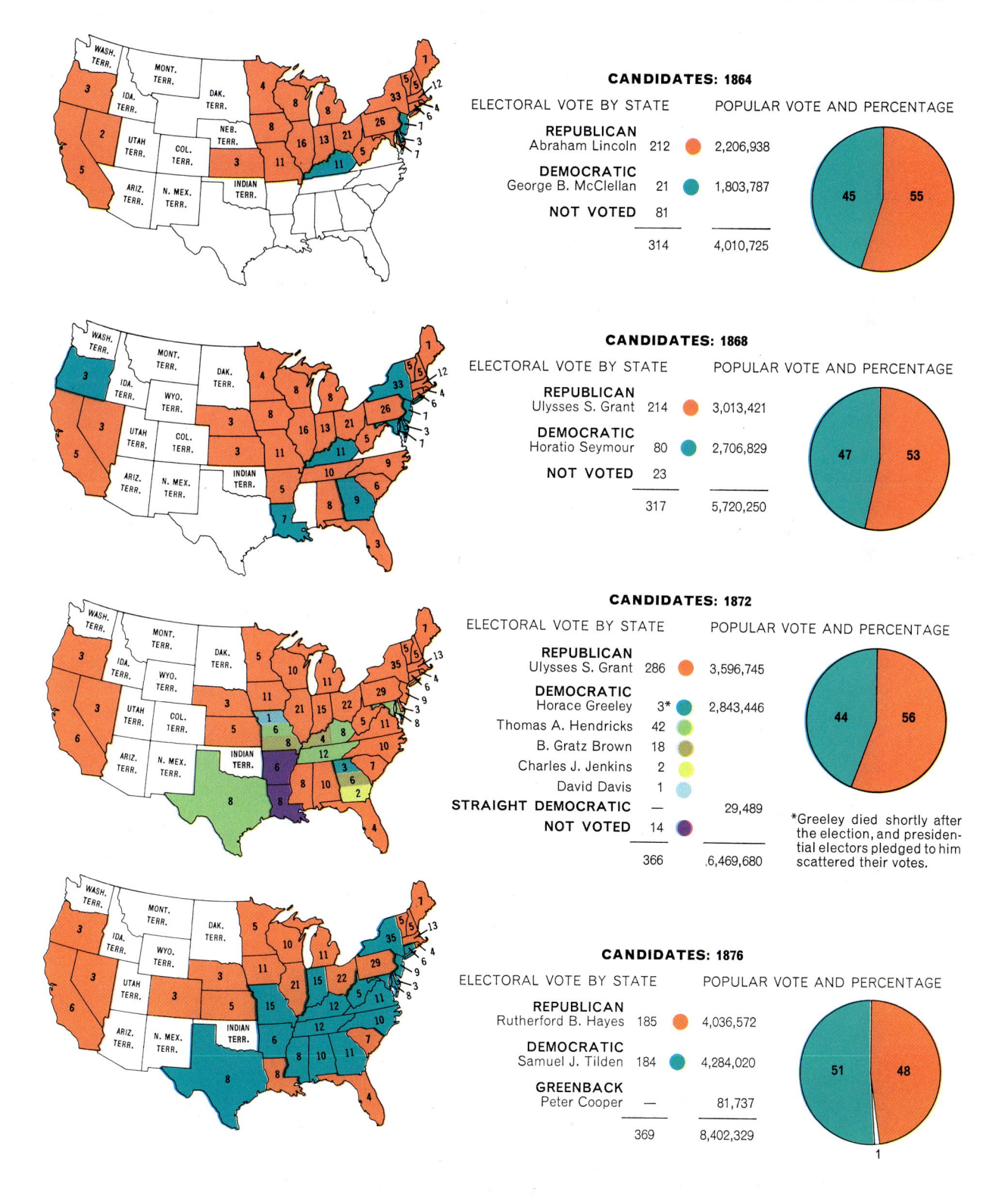

CANDIDATES: 1864

ELECTORAL VOTE BY STATE | POPULAR VOTE AND PERCENTAGE

REPUBLICAN
Abraham Lincoln 212   2,206,938

DEMOCRATIC
George B. McClellan 21   1,803,787

NOT VOTED 81

314   4,010,725

55 / 45

CANDIDATES: 1868

ELECTORAL VOTE BY STATE | POPULAR VOTE AND PERCENTAGE

REPUBLICAN
Ulysses S. Grant 214   3,013,421

DEMOCRATIC
Horatio Seymour 80   2,706,829

NOT VOTED 23

317   5,720,250

53 / 47

CANDIDATES: 1872

ELECTORAL VOTE BY STATE | POPULAR VOTE AND PERCENTAGE

REPUBLICAN
Ulysses S. Grant 286   3,596,745

DEMOCRATIC
Horace Greeley 3*   2,843,446
Thomas A. Hendricks 42
B. Gratz Brown 18
Charles J. Jenkins 2
David Davis 1

STRAIGHT DEMOCRATIC —   29,489
NOT VOTED 14

366   6,469,680

56 / 44

*Greeley died shortly after the election, and presidential electors pledged to him scattered their votes.

CANDIDATES: 1876

ELECTORAL VOTE BY STATE | POPULAR VOTE AND PERCENTAGE

REPUBLICAN
Rutherford B. Hayes 185   4,036,572

DEMOCRATIC
Samuel J. Tilden 184   4,284,020

GREENBACK
Peter Cooper —   81,737

369   8,402,329

48 / 51 / 1

by the party split, and some of them, as Liberal Republicans, cooperated with the Democrats. All but about five hundred Confederates were now relieved from the officeholding ban of the Fourteenth Amendment. Congress had lifted the ban in the Amnesty Act of 1872. In both the North and the South, the Democrats gained in popularity with the coming of the Panic of 1873 and with the news of political corruption. After the Democrats won control of the House of Representatives in 1874, the southern Republicans could no longer count on getting favorable legislation from Congress. Nor could they always depend on President Grant, who grew weary of their requests for army support.

By 1875, the Democrats held all but four of the former Confederate states: Mississippi, South Carolina, Louisiana, and Florida. In Mississippi and South Carolina, where blacks made up a very large part of the population, the Democrats tried to win elections by keeping them away from the polls. The Democrats carried Mississippi in 1875 by organizing mounted rifle companies that drilled openly and threatened all Republicans, black or white. Governor Adelbert Ames, a carpetbagger from Maine, dared not call out his Negro militia for fear of starting a race war.

In South Carolina, in 1876, the Democrats copied the "Mississippi plan." Armed men, wearing red shirts as their uniforms, rode into Republican meetings and broke them up. After the election, the Red Shirts claimed victory for their leader. The Republicans insisted that Governor D. H. Chamberlain, a carpetbagger from Massachusetts, had been reelected. Chamberlain continued to occupy the statehouse, and federal soldiers were stationed in and around it to protect him from the Red Shirts. If the troops should be removed, he would have to give up.

Similar situations existed at the same time in Louisiana and Florida. In these states, Republicans held on, but only with army support. The political future of these states depended on the outcome of the presidential election of 1876.

A Disputed Election

Both the Republican and the Democratic national conventions chose "reform" candidates in 1876. The Republicans nominated Rutherford B. Hayes of Ohio, a veteran of the Union army and a critic of the spoils system. The Democrats nominated Samuel J. Tilden of New York, a lawyer who had helped break up the Tweed Ring, a corrupt political machine in New York City.

On the morning after election day, the *New York Tribune* came out with the headline: "Tilden Elected." But Hayes and the Republican leaders refused to concede defeat. Republicans soon began to insist that the Democrats wrongly claimed one electoral vote from Oregon and all the electoral votes from South Carolina, Louisiana, and Florida.

In Oregon, the situation was this: One elector on the victorious Republican ticket had proved ineligible, since he already held a federal office. The Democrats insisted he should be replaced by the next highest candidate, a Democrat. The Republicans, however, succeeded in substituting another elector, and so Hayes kept the Oregon vote. Yet he still needed *all* the rest of the disputed votes in order to be elected.

In South Carolina, Louisiana, and Florida, the reconstructed governments had set up special "returning boards" to go over the election returns and throw out improper or fraudulent ballots. These boards threw out enough Democratic votes to carry the three states for the Hayes electors.

The Twelfth Amendment to the Constitution provides that if no presidential candidate gets a majority in the electoral college, the House of Representatives shall choose the President. The House had done so in 1824

The civil war and population dynamics

Death, birth, and migration are the principal means of population change. All were important forces in shaping the postwar nation.

Death or disability felled about the same proportion of troops in both the North and the South. But in terms of the total population, southern losses were much greater. About 5 percent of the southern white population, almost a generation of young men, was affected. Moreover, almost 38,000 casualties in the Union Army were southerners, mainly blacks.

When a great many young men die in battle, many young women do not marry, and the birth rate falls. The government did not keep records of the birth rate during the nineteenth century, but it did keep track of the ratio of young children to women of child-bearing age. This ratio fell more sharply in the South than in the North between 1860 and 1870. In all regions this ratio also fell as industrialization spread.

In-migration was more common to the North than to the South. The North's population grew rapidly as ship after ship from Europe unloaded its human cargo in northern ports. Few of the new immigrants went to the South because of the lack of job opportunities. At the same time, many southerners moved north.

Out-migration had its greatest impact on the South. In 1870 the percentage of northerners living in the South was 1.5, while that of southerners living in the North was 8.3. Some southern planters gave up trying to restore their lands and moved away, some as far as South America. Some black southerners moved west and north; thousands migrated to Kansas beginning in 1879. But as late as 1910, 90 percent of all blacks would still be in the South.

The population changes reflected the outcome of the war, but they also reflected the economic situation. Northern industries boomed after the Civil War, while southern industry limped along. Southern agriculture had suffered from neglect and depletion of livestock as well as from human losses. Cities like Richmond, Charleston, and Atlanta were in ruins, and many smaller towns were badly damaged.

when it elected John Quincy Adams, but the problem was quite different in 1876. This was not a case where none of the candidates had a majority. One of them did. The question was, which one? The answer depended on which set of returns from South Carolina, Louisiana, and Florida was counted—the Democratic or the Republican.

The dispute raged on into the winter of 1876/77, with the people in doubt as to who their next President was to be. Finally, Congress set up a special fifteen-member commission, chosen from the House, the Senate, and the Supreme Court. Eight of the fifteen were Republicans and seven, Democrats. By a vote of eight to seven, the commission ruled in favor of the Republican returns from the South.

Even so, the Democrats in Congress could have prevented the final approval of Hayes ("Old Eight to Seven," some called him) as President. As always, the official count of the electoral vote had to be made in the House of Representatives, and the Democrats were in the majority there. Some Democrats, northern and southern, talked of resisting and, if necessary, even waging a new civil war. But, the southern Democrats yielded and allowed Hayes to be counted in as President.

Republican leaders, acting in Hayes's behalf, had persuaded the southern Democrats by promising that Hayes would remove federal troops from the South, appoint a southern Democrat to his cabinet, and give other government jobs to southerners. In addition, the Republicans in Congress would approve federal expenditures for railroad construction and river and harbor improvements in the South.

These promises were made informally and unofficially, in an understanding among politicians. Yet the agreement was just as important as earlier sectional compromises (such as the Compromise of 1850) made by acts of Congress. Historians call this agreement the Compromise of 1877.

As a result of that compromise, the Republicans retained the presidency, but the Democrats took over all the southern states. Government policies favorable to northern business—such as the protective tariff and the national banking system—remained intact. Southern blacks were left somewhere between slavery and freedom. The Compromise of 1877 has been called a combination of "Reunion and Reaction." It appeased former Confederates and made them loyal to the Union again. But it did so at the expense of much of the idealism that the earlier antislavery movement and then the war itself had generated.

The Return of the Democrats

Soon after his inauguration, President Hayes ordered the federal troops out of the South. Immediately, the Republican governments in South Carolina, Louisiana, and Florida collapsed. Hayes hoped to reestablish Republican rule in the South by reorganizing the party. He wanted to base it on well-to-do and conservative southerners, especially former Whigs. But the Democrats, having gained control of all the southern states, prevented opposition from arising for a long time. They set up a one-party system and thus created the Solid South.

Democrats looked upon their own return to power as the restoration of "white supremacy" and the redemption of the South from "Negro rule." They did not, however, immediately put an end to black voting and officeholding. The complete disfranchisement of black men by state laws was not to come for twenty years or more.

After 1877, southern blacks had little political freedom and little economic independence. Very few of them had managed to acquire farms of their own. Most had become sharecroppers, as had many poor whites. Sharecroppers lived and worked on land that the owner had subdivided into a number of farms. The owner commonly furnished supplies and equipment as well as land. The tenants paid the owner not with cash but with a share of their crop. At the end of a season, their crop might not bring enough to pay all they owed. They went deeper and deeper into debt and were forbidden to leave the land until their debts were paid. So far as blacks were concerned, the sharecropping system developed as a kind of substitute for slavery.

A Look at Specifics

1. What constitutional justification did the President have for claiming the right to arrange peace terms with the Confederacy without the consent of Congress?

2. Following the war, what assistance did blacks receive from various northern groups?

3. How did the "black codes" control Negro labor?

4. What policies were promoted by the Grangers?

5. Why did Secretary of State Seward favor an active foreign policy?

6. Why did southern Republicans start losing political influence after 1872?

7. How did the "Mississippi plan" help reestablish white supremacy?

A Review of Major Ideas

1. In what ways was the dispute between the President and Congress over reconstruction policy affected by economic considerations? By interest in the welfare of the Negro? By different interpretations of the Constitution? By political considerations?

2. What were the differences between the first, second, third, and fourth congressional programs for reconstruction? How did these programs differ from Johnson's plan? From Lincoln's plan?

3. What problems plagued the administration of President Grant?

4. What significant diplomatic achievements were made during the Johnson and Grant administrations?

For Independent Study

1. To what extent was the impeachment of Johnson a threat to the basic structure of the federal system?

2. Do you feel that Radical Republican policies were *radical* in the sense of being extreme measures taken to meet postwar problems? Were their measures justified by existing conditions?

3. Many critics of Radical Reconstruction have criticized the Republicans for giving southern Negroes the vote so soon after they were emancipated. These critics claim that the Negroes were irresponsible and still too uneducated to be trusted with political power. Do you agree with this view? What standards, if any, should be set in a democracy for deciding who may vote? Explain your answers.

4. How effective was the work of the Freedmen's Bureau in helping to solve the problems of millions of emancipated people?

Unit Review
Examining the Times

1. What economic changes after 1850 gave the North a military advantage over the South?

2. What social, economic, and political features of the South in 1850 set it apart from the rest of the nation? To what extent had these features changed by 1877?

3. What major events between 1850 and 1860 led to increasing hostility between the North and South? What events led to hostility after the war?

4. Between 1850 and 1877, what changes took place in the lives of southern blacks? In what respects did conditions improve for them? In what respects did conditions become worse?

UNIT FIVE 1877–1900

Problems of an Industrial Nation

Technology—the art of using tools and machines—has developed gradually throughout human history. Its progress speeded up remarkably in the eighteenth century and still more in the nineteenth. Today it is going ahead faster than ever. Thus there has been a continuing and accelerating "industrial revolution" throughout modern history.

When historians refer to *the* Industrial Revolution, however, they have in mind a particular set of technological and economic changes. They are referring to the Industrial Revolution that started in England in the early eighteenth century and spread to other parts of the world in the eighteenth and nineteenth centuries. It has begun in yet other parts of the world in the twentieth century.

From the 1870's to about 1900, Britain, the United States, Germany, France, Italy, and Japan became important industrial nations, and many other nations were industrialized to some extent. Accompanying this so-called Industrial Revolution was a revolution in agriculture. In both industry and agriculture, scientific knowledge was being applied to methods of production.

Machines became more numerous and more complex, and to a greater and greater extent they were powered by steam engines instead of by people, animals, windmills, or water wheels. *Steam* power was an important characteristic of the nineteenth-century Industrial Revolution at its height. Other sources of power—*electricity, petroleum,* and *atomic energy*—have characterized the continuing industrial revolution of the twentieth century.

The Industrial Revolution and the accompanying agricultural revolution had far-reaching consequences. These consequences varied in detail from country to country, but all were felt in some way in the countries undergoing technological change. The most obvious and most direct result was a tremendous *increase in the production of material goods.* By 1900, for example, the textile machines of Britain were turning out billions of yards of cotton cloth a year. They produced many times as much as the people of that country could have made if all of them—men, women, and children—had been set to work with old-fashioned spinning wheels and hand looms.

The technological advances made possible great *population growth.* Britain, for example, had about three times as many people in 1900 as in 1815. The main reason for the increase was not that families had more children but that more babies survived and people in general lived longer. The death rate declined both because more food became available and because progress was made in the prevention and cure of disease. Medical science made its greatest single advance when, near the middle of the nineteenth century, a French professor of chemistry, Louis Pasteur, proved that many diseases were caused by bacteria.

At the same time, more and more people were crowding together in cities. That is to say, there was a great increase in *urbanization.* The new technology made large cities necessary, and it also made them possible. Large masses of labor were needed to operate the machines. The machines and hence the workers, together with shopkeepers to serve them, were concentrated in places where power and raw materials were readily available.

Another characteristic of the Industrial Revolution was the improvement of many different kinds of *transportation.* Steam locomotives and steamships could bring food from a distance to feed the people of the cities. Improved transportation also increased the mobility of large segments of the world's population, and emigration to other countries became common. Immigration to the United States from Europe and Asia increased greatly after the Civil War. A great deal of it was permanent, but some of it was seasonal. The speed of the transatlantic voyage, for instance, made it possible for some Europeans to come to the United States in the spring to work on farms and to return to their homes in Europe after the harvest was completed.

The technological and economic changes gave rise to a new kind of *industrial conflict,* that between corporations and unions. The owners of the industries came to consist largely of corporations. To offset the power of such companies, the employees formed unions. They resorted to strikes and boycotts and demanded that the companies improve working conditions, that the unions be recognized as bargaining agents, and that laws be passed to regulate industry.

The employers acquired social philosophies that opposed the union position. Many capitalists contended that government should not interfere with business. This idea, known as *laissez-faire,* had its origins in the writings of Adam Smith, an Englishman. He wrote in the late eighteenth century, when the Industrial Revolution was just starting to be felt in Britain. He demanded a free and open market, unregulated by government. In such a market, the price of everything would supposedly be determined by supply and demand.

The workers acquired two social philosophies that encouraged and justified them in their struggle against the employers. One of these philosophies was "scientific socialism," or *communism.* Its chief founder was Karl Marx, a German who came from a well-to-do family and received a good university education. According to Marx's economic theory, all wealth was created by and belonged to labor. Therefore the workers were being exploited when they failed to receive the whole value of what they produced—when part of it went to the employer-capitalists in the form of profits. According to Marx's philosophy of history, the class struggle was the main theme of all history. This struggle, Marx thought, was bound to end in victory for the *proletariat,* the working class. Marx's philosophy, with its prediction of a future working-class heaven on earth, served almost as a religion for many of his followers.

Another important doctrine was *anarchism,* as put forth by the Frenchman Pierre Joseph Proudhon. Government, he said, was the worst of evils, and people would never be truly free and happy until it was abolished. Proudhon and some of his followers were opposed to the use of violent force; indeed, they hated government because they thought it depended on brute force. But other followers, including several assassins, made use of violence.

In Europe, the working class gained the support of many people who were not communists or anarchists but who sympathized with the poor and supported legislation for improving conditions of life and work. The capitalists had the support of many people who were not themselves capitalists but who feared communism and anarchism. In the United States, similarly, politics involved reformers and anti-reformers and was by no means simply a contest between workers and capitalists. Though this contest was an important theme, there were also other conflicts, such as the conflict between farmers and businessmen and the one between blacks and whites. Communism and anarchism made far less headway in the United States than in Europe. Most American workers disliked thinking of themselves as permanent members of a working class. They hoped that they or their children could, individually, improve their economic and social standing.

Another important consequence of the Industrial Revolution was *imperialism,* a new movement for the acquisition of colonies. In earlier times, colonies had been desired mainly for purposes of trade. In the late nineteenth century, the industrialized nations began to seek colonies not only as markets for surplus goods but also as sources of raw materials and as places for the investment of excess funds. The new industrial system produced more goods than could be profitably sold in the home country, demanded more raw materials than could be obtained there, and yielded more profits than could be advantageously reinvested there. Hence European and Japanese business leaders looked for economic opportunities in the underdeveloped countries of Africa, Asia, and Latin America. These business leaders called upon their own governments to extend control over such countries in order to protect the economic interests that the businesses acquired there.

The governments themselves were eager to get additional territory for military or naval bases, and many of the people supported national expansion for reasons of patriotism. Between the 1870's and 1900, Britain enlarged its empire by one-third, France and Germany built up their empires from practically nothing to extensive overseas possessions, and Japan started making inroads on the Asian mainland. The United States joined the scramble for colonies and by 1900 had acquired a far-flung empire of its own.

The Rise of Industry

CHAPTER 13
1865–1900

Chinese immigrants labor on the western railroads.

Many Americans believe that when a war starts, all business picks up, and that when a war ends, the economy invariably suffers. Actually, while it is true that war-related industries prosper so long as the shooting continues, war generally is not good for most businesses.

The Civil War stimulated the growth of certain industries, such as meat packing, flour milling, and the manufacturing of shoes and cloth. But the war was not responsible for the development of the oil and steel industries, and it temporarily set back railroad and building construction.

The war was followed by a period of great industrial growth. Production had been increasing steadily until the start of the war, but the growth after the war was extraordinary. By 1900 the United States had become the greatest manufacturing nation in the world.

Technological skill, governmental policies, business leadership, natural resources, labor supply, mass market—all contributed to the rapid progress of the United States in industrial productivity. The kind of industrial transformation going on in the United States was also taking place in Britain, Germany, France, and Japan. The United States took the lead in industrial production because of its *combination* of advantages.

TRANSPORTATION AND COMMUNICATION

Improved transportation and communication made possible the rise of large-scale industry. Big business in the late nineteenth century depended upon the extension of railroad service and the development of the typewriter and the telephone.

A Rail Network

The most dramatic railroad construction took place in the West. The first transcontinental line, begun during the Civil War, was completed in 1869. One company, the

Union Pacific, laid tracks westward from Omaha while another, the Central Pacific, built eastward from Sacramento.

Immigrants were hired to do most of the heavy labor. Japanese, Chinese, and Mexican workers predominated in the building of the Central Pacific, and German, Irish, and Mexican laborers in the constructing of the Union Pacific. Both lines also employed a number of former slaves.

The work was difficult because of the tremendous distances and the deserts and mountains to be crossed. Workers with picks and shovels and horse-drawn scrapers prepared the roadbed. Other crews laid the rails by hand. Since the railroad lines brought settlers who did not always stay within the areas described in Indian treaties, Indians often fought the advance of the railroads. Armed guards were hired to fight off such attacks.

Later other rail lines were extended to the West Coast—the Southern Pacific; the Northern Pacific; the Great Northern; and the Atchison, Topeka, and Santa Fe. All except the Great Northern were built with government aid.

The federal government followed a generous policy toward these and other railroads. It provided millions of dollars in loans and millions of acres in land grants. The grants consisted of alternate one-mile-square sections on both sides of the right-of-way. The government retained every other section, and thus the granted and ungranted lands formed a checkerboard pattern. The government benefited from its policy because the value of the land it kept was increased by the construction of the railroads. Also, the railroads receiving the grants were required to carry mail, troops, and military supplies at less than the regular rates. State governments encouraged railroad construction by buying railroad stocks and bonds and by giving additional grants of land. Without this generous public help, most of the railroads in thinly settled areas would not have been built until much later, if at all.

The Great Northern, connecting Lake Superior with Puget Sound, was built by James J. Hill. Hill aimed to promote trade with East Asia and settlement on the Great Plains as well as to make money for himself. With no federal loans or lands, he paid for construction as he went along. As each stretch of track was completed, he gave free transportation to people taking up farms along the route. Then he sold them tools and machinery on easy credit. As farms developed, he made enough from the shipment of crops to pay for building his railroad farther west.

In the East the most important railroads were the New York Central, the Pennsylvania, the Erie, and the Baltimore & Ohio. By 1874, each of these had incorporated a number of relatively short lines to make a large system reaching from New York City, or its vicinity, to Chicago. The New York Central was developed by Cornelius Vanderbilt, who had made a fortune from the shipping business and from the stock market. He projected and carried out his great plan for connecting New York and Chicago by a "water-level route" along the Hudson and Mohawk rivers and the shore of Lake Erie.

In the South the first task of the railroads after the Civil War was to repair the war damage. Then new lines were constructed. By 1890, the South had six times as much trackage as in 1865. Finally, through consolidations, large systems were created—the Southern Railway, the Atlantic Coast Line, and the Illinois Central. Most of these railroads were financed by private investors, many of whom were British.

Improved Service

So many railroads were built that, especially in times of depression, there was not enough freight and passenger traffic to go around. Some investors temporarily received little or no return on their investment.

To get business, competing lines often cut their rates drastically. Then they would try to end the "rate wars" by agreements to stop the competition, put all their earnings into a common pool, and divide them up. Where no competing line existed, a railroad usually charged all that the traffic would bear. Thus a railroad would charge more for a short haul between two points served by only one line than for a long haul between two points served also by a competing line. Though rates varied from place to place and from one time to another, the average charge for a ton of freight in 1900 was half of what it had been in 1860.

The railroads were able to carry freight and passengers more economically and more rapidly because of technological improvements. Steel rails replaced iron ones. A uniform gauge was adopted, so that cars could be interchanged between one line and any other. More powerful coal-burning steam locomotives were introduced. High speeds were made safer by use of the air brake, which George Westinghouse invented in 1868, and by use of a signal system that was brought over from Britain. Even so, a number of terrible train wrecks took place, and accidents at road-crossings were common.

The growth of rail transportation in the United States led to the standardization of time. Before rail service was common, each locality followed its own "sun time," with noon corresponding to the zenith of the sun. The railroads began to base their schedules on "railroad time." This practice created confusion, for railroad time differed from sun time and from one rail line to another, even in the same area.

Finally, in 1883, the railroad owners of the United States and Canada agreed upon an arrangement for the standardization of time. They divided the continent into zones. Within each zone all railroad clocks were set alike; between each zone and the one to the east or west of it there was a time difference of one hour. Soon local communities and the states adopted standard time. Later, time zones were designated for the world, and almost all nations adopted standard time.

Other Transportation

As the railroad network spread, transportation by inland waterways became less important than it had been. An exception was traffic on the Great Lakes, which steadily increased. In 1881, the federal government took over the Soo Canal, which the state of Michigan had built to bypass the falls between Lake Superior and Lake Huron. During the months from April to November, when the canal was open, it was often the busiest waterway in the nation.

For many years, transportation by highways declined, except for local hauling to and from the nearest rail depot. Highways fell into disrepair until, by the 1890's, they were commonly worse than they had been a hundred years earlier. Then a "good roads" movement began, stimulated to a large extent by a new invention, the bicycle.

The bicycle of the 1880's had a large hard-rubber-tired wire wheel in front and a tiny one behind. The rider, sitting high over the front wheel, ran the risk of "taking a header" whenever the wheel hit a stone in the road. By 1890, this high-wheeler was being replaced by the "safety bicycle" with low wheels of equal size, air-filled tires, and a chain-and-sprocket drive. Almost anyone could ride the safety bicycle, and during the 1890's, millions of Americans did so.

A national organization of cyclists, the League of American Wheelmen, kept up a constant propaganda and lobbying activity to improve roads. By 1900, more than half the states had passed laws for better highway construction and maintenance.

Major Railroads in Operation, 1890

By bringing about road improvements, the bicycle helped prepare for the coming of the automobile. The bicycle's parts—chain-and-sprocket drive, wire wheels, tubular steel—were also used in making the first automobiles. Many of the early automobile builders had once been either bicycle repairmen, like Henry Ford, or bicycle manufacturers.

Communications Improvements

The postal service also was extended. Before the Civil War, a person had to pick up his or her own mail at the local post office. In 1863, Congress authorized free delivery of mail, and soon mail was being delivered in many cities. After 1896, with the beginning of rural free delivery, carriers made the rounds of farm homes. Meanwhile, the cost of postage was reduced.

Two other inventions that helped communication were the typewriter and the telephone. The first practical writing machine was developed by Christopher L. Sholes and his associates in Milwaukee between 1867 and 1872.

The typewriter made its way into practically every business office. It created thousands and eventually millions of new jobs for women. Neither business nor government could have grown as they did without the record keeping and rapid correspondence that the typewriter made possible.

Nor could business and government have done without the convenience of the telephone. This was chiefly the work of Alexander Graham Bell, a Scottish-born teacher of the deaf in Boston. Bell patented his invention in 1876 and exhibited it that year at the first world's fair in the United States, the Centennial Exposition in Philadelphia.

Within a few years, telephone exchanges were in operation in nearly all cities in the United States with more than 10,000 population. By 1889, it was possible to call long distance from Boston to Washington, D.C., or to Buffalo, New York, and by 1892, all the way to Chicago. Before the end of the century, telephone wires had been extended to most small towns and even to a few farms.

OLD INDUSTRIES AND NEW

After the Civil War, a number of old industries were so changed that they seemed almost like new ones. They now were carried on in larger plants, with a greater division of labor and with more complicated machinery. And they were more highly concentrated in one part of the country. Outstanding examples were meat packing and flour milling. While old industries were being transformed, some entirely new ones grew up. Three of the most important new businesses were oil, steel, and electric power.

Old Industries

Chicago became the great meat-packing center. It was well located in relation to the cattle-growing areas of the Great Plains and the hog-raising areas of the Middle West, and it had good rail connections. The refrigerator car, cooled by artificial ice, made it possible to ship fresh meat to more distant markets than before. Large-scale slaughtering by more efficient methods made it possible to undersell most local slaughterhouses. In the Chicago slaughterhouses an animal carcass was moved along on an overhead conveyor past a line of workers, each of whom cut off a part. This "disassembly line" inspired the assembly line that was later to be used in the making of many products.

Minneapolis became the flour-milling center. It was near the largest wheat-growing area, in the upper Mississippi Valley. The Minneapolis millers introduced iron rollers from Hungary that turned out a finer and whiter flour than did old-fashioned millstones. Small local mills and slaughterhouses did not disappear all at once, but a larger and larger share of the nation's flour, like its meat, came from the big processors.

Packinghouse workers slaughter hogs in a "disassembly" line. Although new butchering methods and refrigeration were great advances, improvements in sanitary and working conditions were still far off.

The Oil Business

The people in western Pennsylvania had known of petroleum or "rock oil" for years. They had noticed an oily film on the surface of springs and streams and had wondered what could be done with it. Some people bottled it and sold it as medicine. In 1855, a Yale professor reported that, when refined, it could be used for lights or lubrication. In 1859, Edwin L. Drake put down the first oil well, near Titusville, Pennsylvania. Though observers called it "Drake's folly," it soon was yielding 500 barrels of oil a month.

An oil boom followed in western Pennsylvania and later in Ohio and West Virginia. This was much like a gold rush, with fortune seekers flocking to the area. Year after year, production increased. In the 1870's the annual output came to 20 million barrels, and petroleum and petroleum products ranked fourth among the nation's exports.

From the start, it was hard to transport petroleum to the refineries. Boats or rafts carried it in barrels on inland waterways, or wagons hauled it over rough roads. But oil was being pumped out of the ground faster than it could be taken away. Eventually, railroads were extended to the oil fields. Refineries appeared throughout the oil region, especially in Pittsburgh and Cleveland.

In the early days it did not take much money to go into the oil business. As production increased, however, it became harder to make a profit. Producers and refiners competed madly, and prices sometimes fell below the costs of production. Finally a business organizer, John D. Rockefeller, brought order out of the chaos.

Rockefeller had been born on a modest New York farm. At nineteen, he became a partner in a Cleveland company that made huge profits selling produce to the government during the Civil War. At the end of the war he went into the oil-refining business in Cleveland. He proceeded to buy out other refineries, and in 1870 he formed the Standard Oil Company of Ohio.

The Standard Oil Company reduced the number of competitors by driving them out of business. It made arrangements with railroads for secret rebates on the charges for the oil it shipped. It engaged in price wars, and when these succeeded in forcing competitors to close down or sell out, it raised its prices again. It hired a large staff of salesmen who used high-pressure selling techniques. By the 1880's Rockefeller's company so dominated the oil industry that it could fix prices.

Nevertheless, prices were low enough to encourage people to use petroleum products. Kerosene took the place of whale oil, camphor, and other fuels for lanterns and lamps. Petroleum oil and grease took the place of animal fats as machine lubricants.

New Methods of Making Steel

The new age of machinery also depended on steel. In earlier times, steel was laboriously made from iron. Steel cost so much that it was used only for such things as swords, knives, and high-grade tools. After the Civil War, new steel-making methods were brought from Europe. The most important were the Bessemer and "open-hearth" processes. With these new methods, production increased, and the price fell so low that steel could be used in great amounts for rails, locomotives, and heavy machines.

Iron ore for the new steel furnaces came primarily from the Lake Superior region. By the 1890's, the Mesabi Range in Minnesota was becoming the greatest ore-producing region in the world. Meanwhile, other deposits were found near Birmingham, Alabama.

The ironworks of the prewar period had been rather small and had been scattered throughout the country, near local sources of ore and fuel. The huge new steel mills were concentrated in various places, sometimes at a great distance from the sources of raw materials. The Pittsburgh area was the greatest steel center, but other centers arose along Lake Erie and Lake Michigan. All of these places had easy access to iron ore brought by lake steamers and to coal brought by railroad cars from Pennsylvania, West Virginia, and the Middle West.

The greatest organizer of the steel industry was Andrew Carnegie. An immigrant from Scotland, Carnegie worked his way up from a job as bobbin boy in a Pennsylvania cotton mill to that of a partner in the Pennsylvania Railroad. In 1873 he opened a steel mill near Pittsburgh. Using much the same methods as Rockefeller, Carnegie ruined his competitors. He set out to control all stages of steel manufacture. His company leased part of the Mesabi Range, bought railroads and coal mines, and operated its own ore boats on the Great Lakes. Soon the Carnegie companies dominated the steel industry.

Electric Power

Batteries that produced electric current by chemical action had been in use since about 1800. The rather weak current from such batteries was enough to operate the telegraph

Workmen strain with a huge forging in the heat of an iron foundry. Most small ironworks rapidly disappeared after the development of new processes of making steel.

and the telephone. But a number of scientists thought it would be possible to create a much more powerful current by mechanical means—by generators or dynamos. In the late 1800's, the theory began to be put into practice by a number of inventors.

One of them was Thomas Alva Edison, a native of Milan, Ohio. Edison lost his hearing when he was young. His deafness allowed him to concentrate all the more on all kinds of mechanical and electrical problems that interested him. In 1876, he set up a laboratory at Menlo Park, New Jersey. Here Edison originated and worked out improvements upon many existing devices, such as the telegraph, the incandescent light, the electric motor, and the generator.

In 1877 he hit upon his most original production, the phonograph, while trying to find a way to record telegraph messages. He also devised a method for sending a number of messages at once over the same telegraph wire. In 1879 he succeeded in making the first practical electric light for indoor use. Later he opened a steam-operated electric-power plant in New York City. It sent current to 400 of his newly invented lamps in 59 neighboring buildings.

Edison's kind of power plant, however, produced only direct current, and this could be sent no farther than a mile or two. Alternating current, on the other hand, could be sent long distances. In 1886, George Westinghouse bought the French patents for an alternating-current generator and began to promote its use.

Edison's plan gave way to Westinghouse's, and alternating current eventually became the standard. By the end of the century, electricity was lighting many homes and factories and was beginning to power industrial machinery.

BIGGER AND BIGGER BUSINESS

While the total output of industry in the United States was increasing, the number of individual plants was decreasing. As plants grew fewer and on the average larger, so did the business firms that operated them. Before the Civil War, the typical firm had been owned and run by an individual or partners, though a number of corporations existed. After the war, corporations became larger and more numerous.

For the owners of a company, bigness had certain advantages. It enabled the company to lower its costs through mass purchasing and mass production. Often, bigness also meant the weakening or elimination of competitors, and thus it enabled the company to maintain or even to raise prices. For the public as a whole, big business was not necessarily so advantageous. To the extent that low costs led to low prices, the consumer benefited. But, according to the critics of big business, consumers did not benefit as much as they should have.

Trusts

There were several ways of forming larger business units. One was the *merger,* two or more corporations combining to form a single corporation. Another was the *pool,* an agreement by which several companies cooperated and acted pretty much as one organization, dividing the market and putting their profits into a common fund. Pooling agreements usually did not last long, for they were hard to enforce.

A third form of combination was the *trust.* In a trust, the stockholders (the owners) of two or more companies gave their shares of stock to a group of trustees to hold for them. In return, the owners received "trust certifi-

BUSINESS ACTIVITY   1850-1898

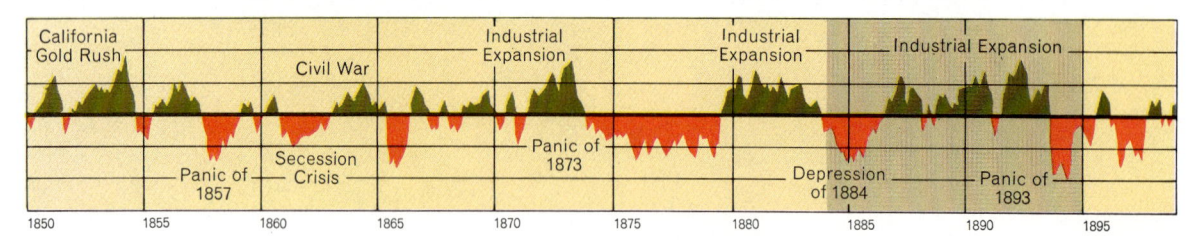

For the period from 1850 to 1898, the chart *(above)* is based on iron and cotton consumption; railroad and canal freight; coal, rail, and locomotive production; rail and ship construction; and blast furnace activity. Between 1877 and 1898, business activity fluctuated greatly. Many railroads were being built, and rail mileage far exceeded the needs of the people at the time. Overexpansion was also going on in other industries. Speculation in plants and equipment contributed to panics and depressions. Yet despite the economic instability, industrialization developed rapidly. As the detail *(right)* shows, periods of expansion were wedged between periods of depression, with sharp dips following peaks.

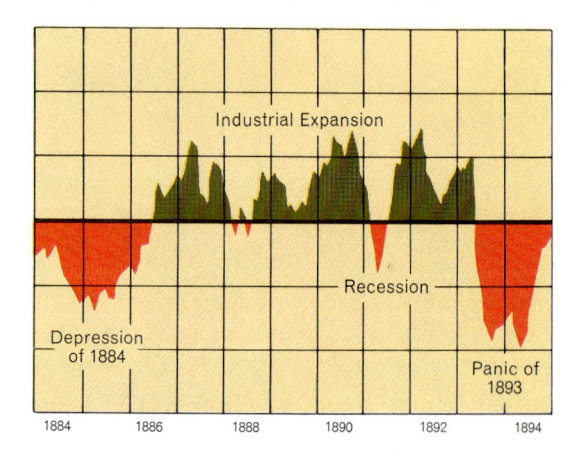

cates" that entitled them to their usual dividends. The trustees, however, exercised the voting rights of the stock. Controlling several companies in this way, the trustees could operate them as a single company.

A *holding company* was a corporation that owned the stock of other corporations. Obviously, it could control the others if it owned more than half of the stock in each. Often it could do so when it owned less than half, for the other shares might be scattered among many stockholders who could not easily cooperate against the holding company.

There was also the *interlocking directorate*. This existed whenever the same group of people served as directors in two or more companies. Although the companies might be separately owned and legally independent, the directors could operate them as if the companies were combined.

No matter which of these forms of consolidation was used, the general public called any large monopolistic or semimonopolistic business organization a *trust*. This term came into use when, in 1879, Rockefeller created the Standard Oil Trust to bring together refining companies in a number of states. The new organization owned or controlled nearly 90 percent of the refining business in the entire country. By the 1890's, trusts of one kind or another dominated many industries. The Carnegie Steel Company produced about one-fourth of the nation's steel. Other companies or combinations practically monopolized meat packing, sugar refining, tobacco processing, and the manufacture of such products as salt, whiskey, matches, wire, nails, and bicycles.

Finance Capitalism

Business leaders like Rockefeller and Carnegie gained wealth and power through skill in organizing industries. Such people are called "industrial capitalists." In the 1890's, investment bankers began to get control of many businesses. They provided the money needed to expand business operations and to make large companies still larger. Such bankers are known as "finance capitalists."

The most famous of them was J. Pierpont Morgan. Unlike Rockefeller or Carnegie, Morgan was reared with all the advantages of wealth. He had traveled widely and had been educated in Europe. He set up his banking firm on Wall Street in the 1870's. For more than thirty years, Morgan led in the financing of corporations.

Morgan and other investment bankers bought and sold corporation stocks and bonds. Since their professional reputations depended on the continuing value of these securities, bankers often required that their representatives be put on the board of directors of corporations with which they dealt. The bankers' representatives could then see to it that the corporation made a profit and paid dividends to stockholders. Thus the bankers came to control corporations by means of interlocking directorates.

In 1901, Morgan created the United States Steel Corporation. He bought the Carnegie Steel Company and merged it with ten other steel companies. The face value of the new stock he issued amounted to more than 1 billion dollars. Actually, the combined value of all the merged companies came to less than 700 million dollars. The difference represented *watered stock,* stock issued in excess of the real worth of the corporation.

By the end of the nineteenth century, the age of *industrial capitalism* was ending. The age of *finance capitalism* had begun.

Defenses and Criticisms

In 1892, there were more than 4,000 millionaires in the United States. Except for a few who had inherited fortunes, all had made their money since the Civil War, and most of them had made it in business.

Many of the people who got rich were understandably satisfied with the economic system. They had earned their money by being shrewd, industrious, and thrifty (as well as lucky). They believed that God rewarded their virtues and that most people were less well off because they were simple-minded, lazy, and wasteful.

Many of the wealthy believed in the philosophy of Social Darwinism. It was based on some of the ideas of Charles Darwin, an English scientist. According to Darwin, in nature there is a constant struggle for existence, and only the "fittest" survive long enough to reproduce. Thus, Darwin taught, living things had evolved through a process of natural selection.

Darwin was talking about biology, but the Social Darwinists applied his ideas to the business world and to society. They claimed that there was a struggle for existence among nations, business firms, and other groups. Those that got ahead were supposedly the fittest, the most deserving of success.

Some of the wealthy believed that God had given them their money to use in helping people who were less able and less fortunate. Carnegie gave away many millions of dollars, mostly to establish public libraries. Rockefeller and others also devoted part of their fortunes to charity.

Most of the people in the United States admired and envied the very rich but resented the practices of big business. *Trust* became a nasty word. Books denouncing the economic system were widely read.

Henry George's *Progress and Poverty* (1879) became a best-seller. George, an economist and reformer, thought that the monopolies, especially monopolies of land, were to blame for the unequal distribution of wealth. He proposed to eliminate both monopoly and poverty by means of the "single tax." This was to be a tax on the increase in land values that resulted from society's development rather than from the landowner's improvements of property. The tax was to be high enough to take away entirely this unearned increase in land value. It supposedly would make possible the repeal of all other taxes. Many of George's readers joined single-tax societies and, in 1886, his followers almost succeeded in electing him mayor of New York.

Another popular book was Edward Bellamy's *Looking Backward* (1888). In this novel a young man goes to sleep in 1887 and wakes up in the year 2000. He finds no one poor and everyone happy. The reason, he discovers, is that all trusts have at last given way to one big trust, which the people themselves own and operate. Soon after Bellamy's book had appeared, more than a hundred "Nationalist Clubs" were advocating the Bellamy brand of socialism.

Some American thinkers disagreed with Social Darwinism. One of them was Lester Frank Ward, a sociologist. In his book *Dynamic Sociology* (1883), he argued that it was wrong to compare human society with the animal world. He did not believe that a blind struggle for existence rigidly governed human behavior. Civilized society, he said, protected its citizens from the evils and uncertainties of raw nature. Ward believed that people could control their environment and could achieve progress through education and government.

LABOR'S GAINS AND LOSSES

The rise of industry made more goods available and it created additional jobs. However, it brought hardships as well as opportunities to a great many industrial workers.

The work day ranged from ten to fifteen hours, and there were six, sometimes seven, days in the work week. Conditions of labor were often disagreeable and dangerous. There were, as yet, practically no laws to require safe conditions or to provide compensation in case of injury or death on the job. During the period from 1865 to 1900, the wages of unskilled, nonfarm workers averaged no more than $1.50 a day. Over the years the cost of living fell somewhat, and so the purchasing power of people who were steadily employed rose, even though money wages remained about the same. Millions were unemployed from time to time, however, especially during the long depressions beginning in 1873 and 1893.

In earlier times, when most industrial workers were skilled artisans, they had enjoyed a good deal of independence. They were able to bargain with their employer on nearly equal terms, for the employer was either an individual or a partner, and skilled laborers were scarce. In the new industrial era, however, only a few of the workers in mines and mills were skilled, and the employer, usually a big and impersonal corporation, could fire anyone at will and hire another person. Most workers no longer had a feeling of importance and independence.

Many of the workers came to believe that if they were to get higher wages, shorter hours, and improved working conditions, they would have to organize and act together. Instead of each individual bargaining with his or her own employer separately, workers would have to form a union for *collective bargaining.*

Immigration

From 1860 to 1890, the population of the United States increased by about 31 million. During that time, more than 10 million immigrants entered the country. By 1900, in New England and the Middle Atlantic states, more than half of the people were either foreign-born or the offspring of foreign-born persons.

During the 1880's, nearly twice as many immigrants arrived as had come during the

The sad tale of the cities

Dirt and cities have always had an irresistible attraction for each other. (The country, even though its products come from the soil, is somehow always viewed as being clean.) In few places was this more evident than in the growing cities after the Civil War.

City transportation was based on the horse. Horse-drawn wagons, carriages, and carts jammed the streets. Horse droppings dirtied the pavements and attracted flies, and iron horseshoes and wagon wheels clattered on brick or cobblestone roads. During heat waves or epidemics of animal diseases, sickness or death of horses brought traffic to a standstill.

Sewer systems were at least as primitive as the transportation system. Many cities used open gutters for drainage, and coastal cities dumped their garbage in the sea. Cesspools and outhouses remained common. Until the flush toilet was perfected in the 1870's, sewer gas made indoor toilets obnoxious. But the toilet was a mixed blessing. Raw sewage from such toilets often emptied into sources of drinking water, and flushing strained water resources.

Changes in transportation helped improve city life. The first electric street railway opened in Richmond, Virginia, in 1888. By 1895 more than 800 cities had electric rail lines. Meanwhile, asphalt was coming into use as a paving material. It deadened street noises and was easier to clean than brick or cobblestone.

Water-supply systems, sometimes built and operated by private companies, were appearing in even the smaller cities. But few of the waterworks filtered or purified the water, and epidemics of typhoid were frequent. In the 1880's and 1890's several cities began to improve the purity of water supplies, and several state health boards began closer inspection of pollution and water.

If the street railway was the solution to the "horse problem," it didn't last long. Within a few years it was replaced by a new polluter, the automobile. And while filtration plants improved the quality of water used by humans, they did nothing to improve life for fish.

previous decade. While immigration was increasing as never before, its origin was changing. Before the 1880's, most immigrants had come from the British Isles or other parts of northwestern Europe. Then more and more began to come from eastern and southern Europe and from Asia. By the late 1890's, three of every five immigrants were coming from these areas.

The new immigrants—mainly Italians, Czechs, Slavs, Hungarians, Poles, and Russians in the East and Midwest, and Chinese and Japanese on the West Coast—were essentially like the earlier ones. They had left their homes, friends, and familiar ways of life because they had heard that America was a land of opportunity. Those who arrived in New York harbor were greeted by the Statue of Liberty, a gift from the people of France.

Once they had landed, however, the newcomers generally got an indifferent or hostile reception from native Americans. This was due in part to *nativism*, the feeling on the part of people born in the United States that they were somehow superior to the foreign-born.

Hostility toward immigrants also arose from competition for jobs. Peasants from eastern and southern Europe often were willing to accept pay that seemed good to them but that was unacceptable to native Americans, who were used to being paid more for their labor.

Working people generally supported demands that the federal government act to cut down immigration. Companies employing large numbers of workers opposed such demands. Although the government imposed a few restrictions, it did little to halt immigration to the United States. The Chinese Exclusion Act (1882) stopped any more Chinese from coming to the United States. Another act of Congress (1885) prohibited employers from bringing in immigrants and holding them to labor contracts made before the immigrants arrived. Still other laws forbade the

To many immigrants, the garment industry offered some hope of future independence from factory work. Some did piecework in their homes *(left)*, often after a day's work in a small, crowded factory. As more and more immigrants arrived, angry opposition to unlimited immigration grew. Hate-filled cartoons *(right)* and editorials began to appear regularly. Part of this opposition was based on the belief that native Americans were losing jobs to immigrants. In many cases, however, the influx of cheap immigrant labor enabled native Americans to move up more rapidly in expanding industries.

entry of paupers, lunatics, convicts, and people with certain kinds of diseases.

Forming Unions

Up until the Civil War, labor unions, when they existed at all, were usually local organizations. A few national unions were formed, but they were the exceptions. Immediately after the war, a number of national unions pledged their support for the National Labor Union, founded in 1866. It was never very strong nor was it truly "national." After the death of its leader, it collapsed.

In the 1870's, two other organizations tried to bring workers together on a large scale. One of these, the Noble Order of the Knights of Labor, reached its peak of strength and membership in 1886, then began to decline and finally disappeared. The other, the American Federation of Labor, was reorganized that same year and grew steadily from then on. The two were quite different.

The Knights hoped to create one big union that would include practically all kinds of workers, skilled and unskilled, male and female, white and black, native and foreign-born. The order aimed to improve not only the economic condition but also the social standing of its members. It wished to give them a sense of the "nobility" of labor. It encouraged worker education, started cooperative factories and stores, and supported the arbitration of disputes between employers and employees. At first it was secret, because many employers automatically fired union members.

The Knights' greatest leader was Terence V. Powderly, a Pennsylvania machinist. He had lost his job and had been *blacklisted*—barred from future employment in industry—because of union activities. As "Grand Master Workman" of the Knights, however, Powderly ended the rule of secrecy and saw the organization grow to 700,000 members. Although he disliked strikes and violence, he could not keep members from participating in them, and indeed the order grew largely because local leaders sponsored a series of successful railroad strikes.

Then came the Haymarket Riot. On May Day, 1886, workers throughout the country had gone on strike to dramatize their demand for an eight-hour day. On May 3, Chicago police killed several strikers near the McCormick Harvester Works. That evening a crowd met in Chicago's Haymarket Square to protest the brutality of the police. When mounted policemen tried to break up the meeting, someone threw a bomb. Seven policemen and four participants were killed and more than a hundred other persons were wounded.

Afterwards eight German immigrants were tried and convicted for their part in the riot. Four were hanged and one committed suicide. (Governor John P. Altgeld pardoned the other three in June 1893.) No evidence had been brought forth to connect any of the eight with the making or throwing of the bomb. All of them, however, were anarchists who had opposed all government.

Certainly the Knights of Labor had had nothing to do with the bombing. Yet, because they had taken a leading part in the May Day strikes, the Knights came to be viewed as dangerous radicals. This was one reason for the decline of the organization. A more important reason, however, was the Knights' continuing failure to attract many skilled workers.

The American Federation of Labor, on the other hand, was interested only in skilled craftsmen, such as carpenters, plumbers, and bricklayers. The AFL did not try to organize miners, steelworkers, or other unskilled laborers. It was not one big union but rather a federation of separate craft unions.

For nearly forty years the president of the AFL was Samuel Gompers, a cigar-maker. Under his shrewd leadership, the AFL con-

Eugene Debs delivers one of his many freightyard speeches to a crowd of workers. He wanted to organize a strong, all-inclusive rail union.

centrated on what he called "pure and simple" unionism, that is, the winning of higher wages bit by bit through direct bargaining with employers. Gompers favored strikes and boycotts to back up the workers' demands, but he managed to keep the AFL from taking part in any serious acts of violence. By 1900, about half a million men and a few thousand women belonged to the member unions.

Losing Battles

On several occasions industrial workers took part in strikes that became bloody when the employers used force against the strikers. Two of the worst cases were the Homestead strike of 1892 and the Pullman strike of 1894.

At the Homestead plant of the Carnegie Steel Company, the manager Henry Clay Frick decided to cut pay rates. The union, a branch of the Amalgamated Association of Iron and Steel Workers, refused to accept the wage cut. Frick closed the plant and hired 300 Pinkerton detectives to guard it. The strikers attacked the "Pinkertons," captured and disarmed them, and drove them out of town. Then Frick called upon the Pennsylvania governor for troops, and for five months the state militia guarded the plant. Public opinion supported the strikers until a young anarchist shot and wounded Frick. Finally, the workers had no choice but to accept the pay cut and go back to their jobs.

George M. Pullman, developer of the sleeping car, had set up the "model town" of Pullman, near Chicago, for his employees. During the Panic of 1893, the Pullman Company laid off a third of the workers and reduced the wages of the rest. But it did not lower the rent on company-owned houses nor lower the prices at the company-owned stores. Those workers who still had jobs left them in protest.

The American Railway Union came to the support of the Pullman strikers and saved them from starvation. Eugene V. Debs, founder and head of this union, thought all railroad workers ought to belong to a single organization. He had left the exclusive Brotherhood of Locomotive Firemen to form his own broad and inclusive union. Its members now refused to handle Pullman cars on trains. Railroad traffic was tied up between Chicago and New York, and many cars were looted and burned by tramps and angry workers without jobs.

At the request of the railroad companies, the federal government sent troops to Chicago to protect the mails, preserve order, and break the strike. Governor John P. Altgeld, who sympathized with the strikers, objected to this interference, saying that the local law-enforcement officials had the situation under control.

The railroad companies also obtained a federal *injunction,* a court order, prohibiting Debs from doing anything to support the strike. When he defied the order, he was sentenced to six months in jail. The strike soon collapsed.

In the conflicts at Homestead and Pullman, there were two major reasons for the strikers' failure. The employers could afford to hold out much longer than the strikers, and the employers had help from either the state or the federal government.

Converts to Marxian Socialism

Few of the important union leaders of the time wanted to overthrow the government or radically change the economic system. They directed their efforts mainly toward gaining a larger share of the benefits of capitalism for industrial workers. They looked upon anarchist and revolutionary activity as a hindrance rather than a help to their cause.

A few labor leaders, however, concluded that there could be no real hope for most workers until *capitalism,* the private ownership of the means of production and distribution, was replaced by *socialism,* public ownership. They adopted the revolutionary views of Karl Marx, a German writer whose ideas were expressed in the *Communist Manifesto* (1848) and *Das Kapital* (1867). Marx said that all history had essentially been a struggle between social classes. He predicted that the workers would become more and more numerous and more and more impoverished until, in desperation, they would revolt, take over both business and government, and create a peaceful, happy, classless society.

The most important American convert to Marxian socialism was the union leader Debs, who read Marx's writings while in jail. Later Debs founded, and for many years led, the American Socialist party. In 1912, he received about a million votes as his party's candidate for President. He and most of his followers believed that socialism could be introduced gradually and peacefully in the United States.

GROWING CITIES

With the rise of industry, cities were growing faster than ever. By 1900, one-third of the people in the United States lived in communities of 8,000 or more; a century earlier only one-thirtieth of the people had lived in communities of that size.

While the greatest growth was in the eastern port cities, communities in the West were growing phenomenally. With the extension of the rail system, cheap fares were available to Milwaukee, St. Louis, and Kansas City, as well as to Chicago and Cleveland. When a rate war between competing rail lines lowered the fare from Chicago to Los Angeles to $1.00, thousands of migrants streamed to southern California.

The cities drew population from the surrounding countryside and from Europe, Asia, and the Americas. Americans continued to leave the farms and small towns in such numbers that, as in earlier years, some rural counties in the United States actually lost population. Immigrants, most of whom remained in the cities after arriving, came very largely from rural villages.

The city had many attractions. Here were most of the rising industries that provided many job opportunities. Here were new comforts and conveniences, such as the telephone and the electric light. Here, too, were activity and excitement—an appealing contrast to the isolation and dullness of rural life. Although the city was alluring, it had its drawbacks. As the cities grew, so did their problems.

Physical Problems

The biggest problem that cities faced was that of coping with a large population when all of the facilities were built to handle a smaller population. The cities made some progress in providing means of transportation, street lighting, sewage disposal, water supply, and fire fighting. But more basic questions of how land could best be used were not adequately answered.

For transportation, individual horse-drawn carts gradually gave way to horse-drawn cars on street railways. As the cities expanded, they generally grew fastest along the railways as these were extended from the center of the city out to the suburbs. In more congested areas, the railways were built either above the ground or below it. New York and Chicago both had elevated railways that used first steam trains and then electric locomotives. Boston experimented with the nation's first subway.

Since the early nineteenth century, streets had been lighted by dim gas lamps. In the 1880's, these were supplemented with bright arc lights, which made the streets safer at night. With the coming of electric lights and telephones, however, the streets became cluttered with poles and wires.

Sewer and water systems were developed slowly. Science and technology eventually came up with systems that made tapwater safe and that carried sewage away from the

This drawing of tenement living appeared in a popular newspaper in 1865. Tenements contained as many as twenty-four "apartments" on each floor. An entire family squeezed into each two-room unit.

cities. In most cases, however, the solutions treated the symptoms rather than the causes. Water was often unsafe to drink or even to swim in. Epidemics of typhoid were fairly frequent.

Another common danger was fire. Many city houses were made of wood, and these and the brick tenements were often built so close together that any fire spread rapidly. Chicago in 1871 and Boston in 1872 suffered disastrous blazes. Most cities had only volunteer fire departments. Professional fire fighters appeared first in 1865 in New York City and Brooklyn.

Some effort was made at city planning. The gridiron plan, which had dominated American cities since William Penn devised it in the seventeenth century, began giving way to plans that called for parks and wide boulevards. Frederick Law Olmsted was the driving force behind the building of Central Park in New York City, in 1863. He inspired many people to try to build cities around master plans that provided adequate open space and physical facilities.

While the work of the city planners was important, most cities owed their appearance to land developers out to make a quick profit rather than to urban designers. In cities and suburbs, builders put up rowhouses, single homes, apartment houses, and tenements that served people's needs and pocketbooks. As the cities reached out to their borders, they often annexed the suburban areas that adjoined them. In the 1880's and 1890's many large cities doubled or tripled in size simply by annexing their outlying suburbs.

Social Problems

At least as serious as the physical problems of the city were the social problems. The worst of these arose from poverty. In the large cities the life of the wealthy few contrasted glaringly with the life of the impoverished many.

The very rich lived in imposing mansions like those that lined Fifth Avenue in New York. They were waited upon by servants and rode in fancy carriages. With money and time on their hands, some of these peo-

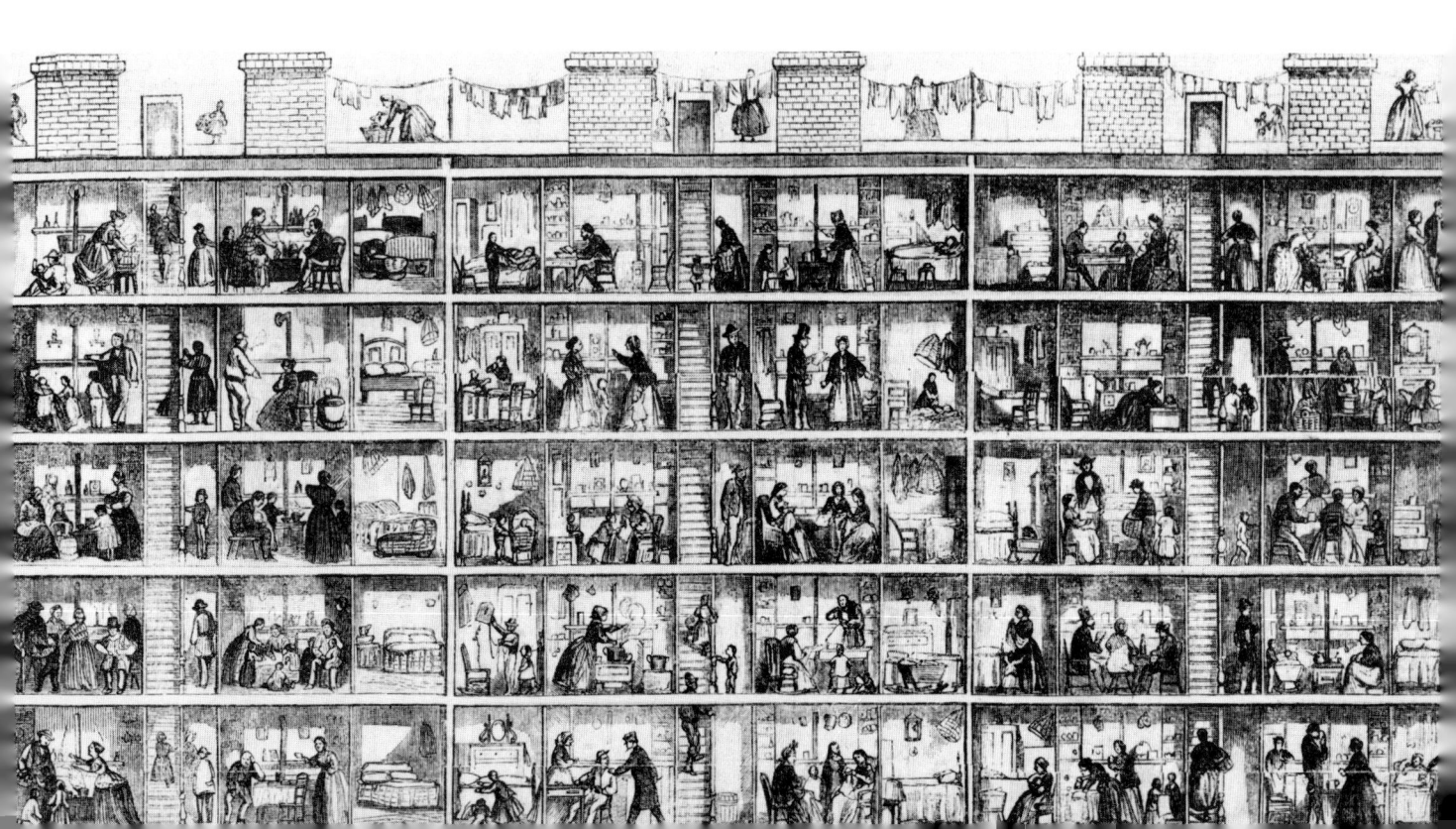

TOTAL POPULATION GROWTH, 1850–1900

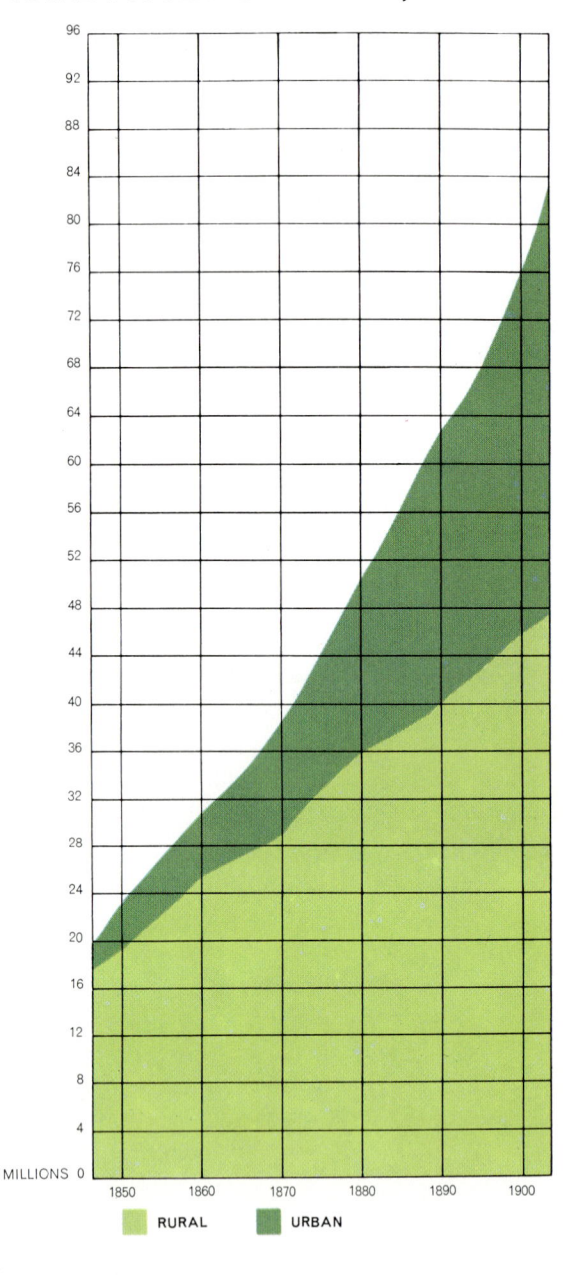

ple turned to extravagant amusements.

Only a few blocks from Fifth Avenue were rows of shanties in which poor Irish families lived and kept their goats. Elsewhere stood huge tenement houses honeycombed with rooms, many of them sunless and airless, into which whole families were jammed. More than half the people in New York City lived in such tenements.

Some people who were brought up in the slums took to crime. Robbery and murder were common in the slums, and street gangs menaced the people.

In the cities there was a middle class of shopkeepers, merchants, professional people, and skilled artisans. Some of these people, their consciences aroused, contributed to the support of charitable societies. The societies' agents took the view that poverty was due primarily to moral defects and only partly to misfortune. They tried to find and help the "deserving" poor.

More good was done by middle-class social workers like Jane Addams. After visiting London, Miss Addams borrowed the English idea of the "settlement house" and, in 1889, established Hull House in a slum district of Chicago. By 1900, there were more than fifty similar institutions in cities in the United States. The settlement houses often had club rooms, playgrounds, and libraries. They not only provided recreation and education for slum children but also gave experience to a growing profession of social workers.

Another social-service agency was the Salvation Army, which began its work in the United States in 1879, a year after it was founded in London. At first the uniformed men and women with their tambourines and brass bands concentrated upon religious revivals. Soon the army also turned its attention to the physical welfare of "slumdom."

Political Problems

The typical large city had a weak, inefficient, and corrupt government. Authority was divided among many officeholders—the mayor, councilmen, local judges, and other officials. Their authority was limited, however, by the state legislature, which could interfere in municipal affairs. No one person or group had clear responsibility.

This confusion of authority made possible, and perhaps made necessary, the rise of the political "boss" and "machine." The boss was the real ruler of the city, though he did not necessarily hold any official position. The machine was the party organization through which he controlled a majority of those who were in office. As a kind of "invisible government," he and his organization provided the centralized power that was lacking in the regular government.

The boss made money for himself and financed his machine through corruption. He often awarded contracts for the construction of streets, sewers, public buildings, and other projects at prices far above the real cost. He divided the surplus between himself and his friends. He also sold franchises for the operation of railways, waterworks, electric-power systems, and other utilities. He had the support of wealthy and important citizens who profited from their deals with him.

The boss also got the votes of the needy, many of whom were immigrants. They looked to him for help, and he furnished informal relief, such as coal for their stoves, a turkey at Thanksgiving, or a gift package at Christmas. He often stepped in to save them from punishment for petty crimes. Most important, he rewarded them with political jobs, with opportunities to rise in the party organization. In most cases the boss himself was of immigrant stock and had come up from poverty. Thus "boss rule" had its democratic aspects. It flourished because it took care of needs that no other institution of the time adequately met.

A Look at Specifics

1. In what ways did the policies of the federal government aid industrial development between 1865 and 1900?

2. What methods did the Standard Oil Company use to reduce the number of its competitors?

3. How did the typical form of business organization change after the Civil War?

4. Explain the following forms of business consolidation: mergers, pools, trusts, holding companies, interlocking directorates.

5. Why were bankers on the board of directors of many corporations?

6. Why did industrial workers of the late nineteenth century feel it was necessary to bargain collectively with their employers?

7. Why did many immigrants support political bosses?

A Review of Major Ideas

1. What factors accounted for the rapid industrial development in the United States after the Civil War?

2. In what ways did improved transportation and communication make possible the rise of large-scale industries?

3. How did industrial workers attempt to improve their lot? What successes did they achieve?

4. What problems arose as cities became larger? In the late nineteenth century, what attempts were made to solve the problems of the cities?

For Independent Study

1. Henry George's single tax theory was based on his observation that land values increased because of social accident. For example, an acre of land in the city was more valuable than one in rural areas only because of the concentration of people living in the city, not necessarily because the owner of city real estate had done any work to make the land more valuable. Thus George argued that rent on land ought to be paid to the state as a tax. Do you believe his ideas were valid? Explain your answer.

2. Some Americans think that today's big unions are as harmful as big businesses were considered in the nineteenth century. Do you agree? Why?

The Agricultural Revolution

CHAPTER 14
1865–1900

Harvesting machines work a field in the 1890's.

The agricultural revolution in the United States consisted of four great changes, all taking place at the same time. First, the Indians of the "Last West" were conquered and driven from much of their land. Most of the land that could be farmed was broken by the plow. Second, the South reorganized its agricultural system and started to recover from the economic setback caused by the Civil War. Third, scientific methods and machines were used more and more extensively in farming throughout the country. Fourth, agriculture became increasingly a business in which farmers produced materials for sale rather than for their own use, and the market in which they sold their products was widened to include the whole world.

None of these developments was entirely new. The closing of the last frontier was a continuation of the earlier westward movements. The "New South" grew out of the ante-bellum South. Machines and scientific methods had begun to be employed on farms in the United States long before the Civil War. Ever since colonial times, *commercial farming,* production for sale, gradually had been replacing *subsistence farming,* production for home consumption. In the 1870's, 1880's, and 1890's, however, these trends amounted to a revolution in agriculture because they now went so much faster and further than before.

THE LAST FRONTIER

As late as 1860, most of the western half of the United States had a population of less than two persons per square mile. A horseman riding west from Omaha—across plains, mountains, and deserts—would find Indians and plenty of buffalo, but he would find only a few non-Indian settlers until he reached Oregon or California. By 1900, this "last frontier" had disappeared.

In 1860, the only states that had been established in all the western territory were Texas, California, and Oregon. By 1900, most of the rest of the territory had been divided into states—Kansas in 1861; Nevada in 1864; Nebraska in 1867; Colorado in 1876; Washington, Montana, and North and South Dakota in 1889; Idaho and Wyoming in 1890; and Utah in 1896. The remaining territory later became the states of Oklahoma in 1907 and New Mexico and Arizona in 1912.

A Rush for Gold and Silver

When the California Gold Rush began in 1849, a few of the gold hunters "struck it rich" when they found gold nuggets in stream beds or near the surface of the ground. Before long, however, mines were being dug to reach gold ore, and mills were being built to refine it. All this was too expensive for most of the prospectors. Some of them stayed on as laborers in the mines or mills, or as farmers raising grain or fruit. Others left California to look for gold or silver elsewhere in the West.

A number of mining booms followed the one in California. The second one took place in what is now Colorado, in 1858. Some of the wagons then heading west bore the words "Pikes Peak or Bust"; some of them later returned east with those words crossed out and "Busted, by Gosh" painted in. In the 1870's, rich silver mines were opened near Leadville, and in the 1890's productive gold mines began operation in the vicinity of Cripple Creek. Also in the 1890's, gold was found in Alaska, and many prospectors headed for the Klondike.

Meanwhile, in 1859, the fabulous Comstock Lode was discovered in a part of the Utah Territory that later became the state of Nevada. In one year this lode was to yield more than 15 million dollars' worth of gold and silver. During the 1860's, other discoveries drew prospectors to the territories of Idaho, Montana, New Mexico, and Arizona.

A miner works in the King Mine along the Comstock Lode. In a twenty-year span, the lode yielded silver worth hundreds of millions of dollars.

In 1876, a mining boom developed in the Black Hills area in the southern part of the Dakota Territory.

Life in mining camps was crude and often violent. The miners slept in tents or shacks and spent their leisure time in the saloons, gambling-houses, and dance halls that lined the one, long, winding street in town. Women and children were few. Crimes were frequent. Gangs of outlaws preyed upon the stagecoaches that carried gold and silver from the mines to the nearest railroad stations. Miners sometimes "jumped," or took over, the claim that another had "staked out," and then a fight often would follow.

Local government was slow to develop in some parts of the mining country. As a result, worried citizens sometimes formed vigilance committees to deal with claim-jumpers, horse thieves, stagecoach robbers, and other criminals. The vigilantes, seeking to establish law and order, captured, tried, and hanged suspects. Even after a sheriff had been appointed, the vigilantes sometimes continued to ride in posses, taking the law into their own hands. Often it was hard to tell who represented the side of law and order—the vigilantes or the sheriff.

In the newer mining districts, the prospectors' hopes of making a fortune were soon dimmed. Gold and silver production, if it continued at all, became a big business. In the territories of Montana and Arizona, copper proved to be much more abundant than silver or gold. Its discovery laid the basis for a profitable and long-continuing copper industry. The gold and silver rushes usually resulted in the introduction of local agriculture and the establishment of stable family life. The mining towns provided a market at high prices for hay, fruit, and vegetables. In various parts of the West, as in California, some of the disappointed miners remained as farmers.

Government Policy Toward Indians

By the 1840's the policy of the federal government was to remove all Indians from their homes east of the Mississippi and resettle them in areas west of the Mississippi. Most of them were settled in the Indian Territory, west of Arkansas and Missouri. Since most Americans thought that the members of one tribe were like the members of any other tribe, the government did not usually ask the western Indians how they felt about having members of other tribes on their land. It simply divided the Territory into reservations and told the Indians where they were going to live. It then set up army posts to protect the Indians from each other and from white settlers.

When the great migration of non-Indians to the Far West began in the late 1840's, many of the tribes reacted violently. Wagon trains bound for California and Oregon were escorted through Indian country by the cavalry, which tried to protect the American settlers from the Indians and the Indians from the American settlers.

Epidemics cut the Indian population drastically. Four epidemics of smallpox swept the Great Plains between 1835 and 1860. In 1849 cholera was the big killer. More than half the Kiowas and Comanches perished from it, and other tribes on the plains also were hit severely.

In the early 1850's the government negotiated treaties with the Plains Indians at Fort Atkinson and Fort Laramie. In these treaties, the tribes set the boundaries of their territories and agreed to stop fighting, and the United States government promised to pay them annuities. In effect the Indians were setting up reservations, but their territory would eventually be nibbled away by further governmental action.

With the coming of the Civil War, most of the regular troops were withdrawn from the frontier posts for service against the Confederacy. Some of the Indians saw a chance to regain lost lands. They attacked white settlers as far east as Minnesota. The settlers took a fearful revenge. In Minnesota, for example, thirty-eight Sioux were hanged in 1862 for the murder of five settlers. In Colorado Territory, militiamen fell upon a peaceful camp of Arapaho and Cheyenne along Sand Creek and slaughtered more than a hundred men, women, and children.

After the Civil War, the federal government adopted a new Indian policy, intended to end the Indian resistance and bring permanent peace to the frontier. No longer would treaties be made with the various tribes as if they were more or less independent nations, nor would the tribes be allowed to roam over vast areas. Instead, the

Sioux Indians led by Sitting Bull surprise Custer's troops at Little Big Horn in this drawing by Amos Badheart Buffalo. Custer's men constituted only a small advance force of the United States Army.

Indians would be treated as "wards of the nation." They were to be confined on reservations, most of them in the Indian Territory, and supported by the government.

The Indians were understandably reluctant to give up their freedom to live as they desired. For years, units of the United States Army, transferred from the South to the West, were kept busy with efforts to enforce the new policy. The most important military campaigns were directed against the Sioux, the Nez Percés, and the Apaches.

The gold rush in the Black Hills brought thousands of prospectors into the reservation that had been set aside for the Sioux. The Sioux fled to the west, under the leadership of Sitting Bull and Crazy Horse. An army was sent out to bring them back. Moving ahead of the main army, the Civil War cavalry hero George A. Custer, with more than two hundred cavalrymen, intended to surprise the Sioux. Instead, the Sioux surprised him. Custer and all his men were killed in the Battle of the Little Big Horn in Montana Territory (1876). The rest of the army, however, later defeated the fleeing Sioux and brought them back to the reservation in the Dakota Territory, while Sitting Bull escaped to Canada.

After several years, Sitting Bull was persuaded to return to the reservation. In 1890, when the Sioux took part in new religious rites which featured a "ghost dance," the reservation authorities mistook their activities for a war dance. They ordered the arrest of Sitting Bull, and when he seemed to resist, he was shot and killed. Once more, the Sioux left the reservation. The United States Army pursued and surrounded them at Wounded Knee. About forty troops and three hundred Indians, including unarmed women and children, were killed.

Meanwhile, in 1877 the Nez Percés left their reservation in Idaho Territory and set

Sioux Indians gather at Standing Rock agency. The agents appointed by the government often cheated, robbed, or swindled the Indians whose rights they were supposed to protect.

out for Canada. Under one of their leaders, Chief Joseph, they eluded the army during a zigzag chase that covered more than a thousand miles before they were headed off. "I am tired of fighting," Chief Joseph said when he decided to surrender. "My heart is sick and sad. From where the sun now stands I will fight no more forever."

In the Southwest, the Apaches fought a fifteen-year war against being confined on reservations. In 1886 their most determined chief, Geronimo, finally surrendered.

In 1887 the reservation policy was modified. The Dawes Act gave individual parcels of reservation land to every man, woman, or child who was a member of a tribe. On receiving this allotment, an Indian became a citizen, but none gained outright ownership of the land until he or she had lived on it for twenty-five years. (All the previous years that Indians had lived on the land did not count toward individual ownership.) The Dawes Act was intended to break down tribal organization. But most of the Indians tried to hold on to their old customs in their new circumstances, and many lost their land.

The federal government also tried using education to change Indian culture. By 1899, the government ran 148 boarding schools, where young people were educated away from the influence of their families and tribes.

TAMING THE PLAINS

The Great Plains extend from approximately the 100th meridian on the east to the Rocky Mountains on the west, and from the Rio Grande to the delta of the Mackenzie River in Canada. The region is high and dry, ranging in altitude from 2,000 to more than 7,000 feet and averaging less than twenty inches of rainfall a year.

When first explored by Europeans, the Great Plains were covered with short, tough grass. A few trees could be found along the creeks and rivers. At that time, vast herds of buffalo roamed the plains.

As late as 1870, the buffalo numbered more than 5 million. Indians hunted the buffalo primarily for meat and hides. The Union Pacific Railroad divided the western buffalo into two main herds. Unlike the Indians, others began shooting the animals for sport. Using high-powered rifles, "sportsmen" rode in the trains and picked off the buffalo, leaving the carcasses to rot. This organized slaughter exterminated the southern herd by 1875.

In 1875, Congress passed a bill to protect the buffalo, but President Grant vetoed it. This was the first proposal that Congress passed to protect wildlife.

The northern herd was doomed by the completion of the Northern Pacific Railroad in 1880. By 1885, only about a thousand buffalo remained, in Yellowstone National Park and in Canada. The extermination of the buffalo deprived the Indians of a major source of food and of much-needed hides. It helped make possible the defeat of the Indians and their confinement on reservations.

Cattle Raising

At one time, the Great Plains served as a huge cow pasture. The short grass provided feed throughout the year, even during the winter, when it dried and turned into a kind of natural, uncut hay. As the Indians were brought under control, as the buffalo were killed off, as the railroads were pushed westward, great herds of cattle began to move over the plains, grazing on the open range.

The range-cattle industry began in Texas, where it developed from techniques that had been practiced in Mexico for centuries. At the end of the Civil War, Texas had a great many longhorn cattle. There was a problem in getting the cows to distant markets. In 1866, in the first of the "long drives," thousands of longhorn cattle were walked to Sedalia, Missouri, the nearest railhead. In later years, as the railroads were built farther west, the herds were directed to other "cow towns," among them Abilene and Dodge City, Kansas, and Cheyenne, Wyoming. From these places, the cattle were shipped to meat-packing centers like Kansas City and Chicago. Texas cattle were also driven north to start new herds on the northern plains, and the longhorns were crossed with other breeds to produce better beef.

The cattle grazed widely on public land, and they had to be branded so that each owner could identify his or her property. Each spring and fall the ranchers held a roundup at which the different herds were sorted out and each newborn calf was marked with the brand of its mother. The mavericks, or stray calves, were divided among the various owners in proportion to the number of cattle each owned.

In the days of the open range, a cattle owner needed very little land. He or she usually acquired a small ranch as a headquarters and access to streams or water holes in the vicinity of the ranch and along the route to the point of shipment. The pasturage was free. Thus, with a small investment, cattle owners could make a large profit. Not only individuals but also corporations went into the cattle business.

Cowboys were the hired hands of the cattle owners or the cattle companies. The largest number were white southerners, including many veterans of the Confederate army. The next largest number were black southerners. There were also some northerners, as well as Mexicans and other foreign-born workers. On their cow ponies (mostly mustangs, wild horses descended from stock developed by the Spaniards), these cowhands performed the chores of the roundup and the long drive. The cowhands' work was tedious, sometimes dangerous, and generally low-paid. In the saloons and gambling houses of the cow town at the end of the trail, they often spent their meager earnings in one wild, drunken spree.

The open range lasted about twenty years, from the 1860's to the 1880's. During this time, the cattle owners and cowboys had to deal with various enemies. Rustlers made off with many cattle, altered the brands, and sold them. Farmers, or "nesters," settled on much of the land and fenced in their farms, thus blocking the trails and the access to water. Sheepherders brought in large flocks of sheep that cropped the grass so short it died. At times (but not so often as depicted in movies), cattle owners and cowboys engaged in gunfights, not only with rustlers, but also with nesters and sheepherders.

The range-cattle industry began to disappear because, with increasing settlement, the open range itself was disappearing. Meanwhile, the range was being more and more heavily stocked with cattle. The range could support them only so long as the weather was favorable. The winter of 1885/86 was unusually cold on the plains. It was followed by a hot, dry summer, and then another bad winter, with terrible blizzards. Thousands and thousands of cattle starved or froze to death, and many cattle owners saw their businesses ruined.

After that, the range-cattle industry was abandoned in favor of the ranch-cattle industry. Some cattle continued to be raised on the open plains, but most were raised on ranches. Grazing lands were fenced, and shelter and supplementary feed were available in the winter.

New Farms

While some people were raising cattle on the plains, many more were moving in to take up family-size farms. These settlers included many Union Army veterans and many newly arrived immigrants, especially from the Scandinavian countries. Land seekers, rather than gold hunters or cattle raisers, accounted for most of the remarkable population growth of the plains area. The population of the best farming portion—Kansas, Nebraska, and the Dakota Territory—increased from about half a million in 1870 to 1.5 million in 1880 and 3 million in 1890.

Some of the newcomers got land directly from the federal government. Under the Preemption Act of 1841 (in effect until 1891), a settler could buy 160 acres of government land for as little as $1.25 an acre. Under the Homestead Act of 1862, a citizen of the United States or an alien who was over 21 and who had declared the intention of becoming a citizen could acquire 160 acres by paying a few dollars in fees and living on and improving the land for five years. Under a law of 1870, a Union veteran or his widow could count his years of army service; thus, if he had served four years, he or his widow could get a homestead by occupying it for only a year. Under the Timber Culture Act of 1873, a person could secure an additional 160 acres by agreeing to plant trees on part of that land.

Three million acres in Indian Territory (present-day Oklahoma), which had been set aside for Indians, were opened to homesteaders in 1889. On opening day, 50,000 people, who had been waiting on the border, raced into the territory on foot or horseback, on bicycles, in wagons or trains to stake out their claims. The sooner a person arrived, the better the chances of getting good land. Within a few hours, all the available land was taken up.

Throughout the West as a whole, however, individual homesteaders obtained far less of the public land than did companies. The railroads received tremendous government grants. Some of the mining, timber, and land companies acquired much of their land by fraud, by hiring men to take up homesteads for example, and then turning the land over to the company. More settlers bought their farms from the government or from a railroad or land company than tried to homestead. To hasten the sale of their land and also to increase traffic by encouraging settlement, the railroads often gave cheap and even free transportation to land seekers.

Families who began farming on the plains ran into difficulties because of the lack of timber for housing, fuel, and fencing. A sod house might shelter the members for a time.

Nebraska homesteaders sit in front of their first home, a tiny sod-walled dugout. They have done well enough to build a larger, fancier sod house, complete with windows. In contrast, the life of a cattle driver *(below)* was nomadic.

They would dig out a space in the ground, build low walls of mud bricks around it, and save their scarce and costly wood for the roof and for door and window frames. For fuel, the people commonly burned cow or buffalo "chips" (dried dung), sunflower stalks, corncobs, or twisted tufts of dry grass. For fencing they tried growing hedges but found nothing really satisfactory until the invention of barbed wire, which became available for use in 1874.

To deal with the scarcity of water, deep wells were drilled, and windmills to operate pumps were erected on derricks. In some of the river valleys, dams and ditches were constructed for irrigating the fields. Where irrigation was out of the question, farmers resorted to techniques of dry farming. Also, crops that were especially adapted to endure droughts were grown.

The forces of nature created problems that were especially troublesome to the farmers on the plains. There the farmers faced terrible droughts, cloudbursts and floods, hailstorms, tornadoes, and blizzards. Grasshoppers, often called locusts, swarmed every seven or eight years, arriving in a cloud that darkened the sky. Once they had landed on a growing field, they ate everything, leaving nothing but bare stalks.

Settlers were attracted to the plains in especially large numbers during the early 1880's, when there were unusually moist summers. These gave way to a series of extremely dry years, beginning in 1886. For a time, the westward movement was reversed, as some of the settlers abandoned the plains and turned back toward the East.

THE NEW SOUTH

After the Reconstruction period, some southerners hoped for a "New South" modeled on the North, with the same pattern of farms and factories, cities and trade. In 1886, the leading supporter of the New South, Henry W. Grady, editor of the Atlanta *Constitution,* proposed the creation of

a hundred farms for every plantation, fifty homes for every palace; and a diversified industry that meets the complex needs of this complex age.

To some extent, the South succeeded in expanding its industrial production, as Grady and others wished it to do. Yet, on the whole, the industries of the South grew less rapidly than those of the rest of the country. In 1900, the South actually possessed a smaller proportion of the nation's factories than it had in 1860.

The number of southern farms increased, and their average size fell. Agricultural production recovered, but not until 1878 did the cotton crop equal that of 1860. Still, the statistics regarding farms and farm output were misleading. The great majority of the southern farmers did not own the land they worked, nor did they share very largely in the benefits of its productivity.

A One-Crop Economy

Where a single plantation had stood in the Old South, a number of separate farms appeared after the Civil War. This division of plantations into farms helped increase the number and decrease the size of agricultural units. The *ownership* of the land, however, was not so widely distributed. Most of the land was still owned by the original planters or was acquired by others to add to already large holdings. The majority of the farms—about 70 percent by 1900—were occupied by tenants.

Some tenants were *renters,* who paid a set amount of cash or cotton for the use of the land. Others were *sharecroppers,* who gave a part of their crop (one-fourth to one-third or more of it) for the rent and also, in many cases, for the use of farm animals and equipment. The sharecroppers usually had no savings and owned practically nothing—no land, no livestock, no tools. Most black southerners could not afford to rent land, and so they became sharecroppers.

The farmer, whether a renter or a sharecropper, usually bought food and other supplies from a country store, which generally belonged to the landowner. The farmer bought on credit, hoping to pay the bill at the end of the growing season, when the crop was sold. The storekeeper, to ensure that the bill would be paid, took a lien on the crop. This lien was a legal form that gave the storekeeper the rights to enough of the harvest to cover the debt.

Often, especially in times of poor harvests or low prices, the farmer found that the proceeds from a crop were not enough to pay what he or she owed. Then it was necessary to go deeper into debt. So long as the debt remained, the tenant was compelled to go on working for the same landowner and trading at the same store. Thus he or she became the victim of a kind of *peonage,* or debt-slavery.

This system was obviously bad for the tenant. For groceries and other supplies, the sharecropper had to pay whatever was demanded, and this was often twice as much as cash customers paid. The typical southern tenant of that time had little or no education, could not do arithmetic, and thus could easily be cheated by a storekeeper.

On the other hand, the system did not necessarily benefit the landowners. Some of them made a good living, but others went into debt themselves, despite the high prices they charged at the store. The yield of the land in the South was not nearly so large as it ought to have been. The tenants had little incentive to work hard, increase output, or improve or even maintain the farms.

For these and other reasons, the system was harmful to the South as a whole. It caused southerners to depend very largely on one-crop agriculture, with cotton most often

that crop. The landowner insisted that the tenant plant cotton, since it was a staple cash crop—one that could always be sold at some price and could be stored for long periods. The landowner ordinarily forbade the tenants to raise hogs, corn, vegetables, or other foods for their own use, since this would take land and labor away from cotton and trade away from the store.

This kind of one-crop agriculture had seri-

Women and children in an Alabama cotton "factory" use outdated inefficient machinery. Cottage industry of this type was common both North and South.

ous consequences for the region. Many of the people were sickly. The insufficient diet of "meat, meal, and molasses" caused diseases like pellagra. Many people could not afford shoes and contracted hookworm while going barefoot. Much of the soil, already poor, was further worn out by the repeated cotton plantings without crop rotation or the regular use of fertilizers. Whenever the price of cotton dropped, those who depended directly or indirectly on it had nothing else to turn to for income. They became still poorer.

A One-Party System

In the South after Reconstruction, farmers in general and blacks in particular also had a number of social and political disadvantages. The so-called Solid South came into being, with the development of a one-party system in each of the southern states. The single party—known as the Democratic or the Conservative party—was dominated by the men with large landholdings and by the men who controlled big business. Hence it was difficult for small farmers to improve their economic condition through political action.

With the end of the Reconstruction period, southern blacks were abandoned by their former Republican friends in the North. Black southerners could no longer look to the federal government to guarantee the civil and political rights promised in the Fourteenth and Fifteenth amendments. Furthermore, the Supreme Court greatly weakened these amendments in a series of decisions concerning them.

Congress had provided in the Civil Rights Act of 1875 that all persons, regardless of race, were entitled to the "free and equal enjoyment" of public facilities like hotels, railroads, steamboats, and theaters and other places of amusement. In the Civil Rights Cases of 1883, however, the Supreme Court decided that the Fourteenth Amendment (with its phrases concerning "life, liberty, and property" and the "equal protection of the laws") applied only to the state governments and not to the people of the states. Thus, according to the Court, public officials and governments could not legally discriminate against blacks, but private individuals and corporations could.

In the case of *Plessy* v. *Ferguson* (1896), the Supreme Court went further and permitted the states themselves to discriminate. The Court now upheld a Louisiana law requiring the separation of white and black passengers on railroad trains. According to

George Washington Carver helps a chemistry student in a Tuskegee Institute laboratory. In fifteen years Tuskegee grew from a school with 30 students to a model institution with an enrollment of 1,600.

this decision, laws providing for "separate but equal" facilities for the two races were constitutional.

In the case of *Williams* v. *Mississippi* (1898), the Supreme Court approved of Mississippi's new voting requirements—a poll tax, a literacy test, and long residence in a particular precinct. These kept all but a few blacks in the state from casting ballots.

All the southern states passed laws to enforce the segregation of the races and to prevent blacks from voting. The enactment of these laws did not become widespread, however, until about 1900. Up to the 1880's, many blacks used the same public facilities, with the exception of schools, as whites; many blacks continued to vote; and a few even held offices.

The most important Negro leader of the time was Booker T. Washington, a former slave. In 1881 he became the head of the Tuskegee Institute of Alabama, an agricultural and industrial school for blacks. Washington advised blacks to concentrate on economic opportunities rather than social or political rights. He emphasized vocational training rather than academic training. He believed that blacks would get their rights not by agitation and demands for equality but by careful training, hard work, and self-improvement. "The opportunity to earn a dollar in a factory just now," he told a mixed white and black audience in 1895, "is worth infinitely more than the opportunity to spend a dollar in an opera house." Although whites praised these words, they ignored Washington's plea for economic cooperation between blacks and whites.

Those blacks who continued to vote were allowed to do so, for the most part, only so long as they cast their ballots for Democratic candidates. The landowners generally controlled the vote of their black tenants. Thus the Democratic leaders—commonly known as the Bourbons—added to their own political power. (They were called Bourbons because, like the Bourbon kings of France, who supposedly had learned nothing from the French Revolution, they were said to have learned nothing from the Civil War.)

The white farmers had many grievances against the landowners. It would have been to their advantage to join forces with blacks and resist the Bourbons in politics, but this was hard for white farmers to do. Whites held strong prejudices against blacks. The poor as well as the wealthy were in the habit of supporting the Democratic party. To form an effective new party, the white farmers would have to overcome their prejudices and change their political habits.

If the whites—landowners and tenants—should begin to oppose one another in separate parties, blacks might come to hold the balance of power between the two parties. Blacks would then be able to exert considerable influence in politics. The Bourbons constantly warned against the danger of "Negro domination."

SCIENCE AND MACHINERY

After the Civil War, agricultural production in the United States increased rapidly. In some places, production increased even when the number of people engaged in agriculture declined. There were two main reasons for the overall rise in productivity, both per acre and per person. One was the introduction of farm machinery on a larger scale, and the other was the development and spread of agricultural science.

The use of labor-saving machines was encouraged by the high cost of agricultural labor (except in the South). The use of scientific methods, on the other hand, had been discouraged by those same high labor costs. It was extremely expensive to undertake careful, intensive tillage. Careful farming also had been discouraged by the abundance of cheap and even free land. It was more profitable to deplete the soil than to preserve or to restore it. After the Civil War, as good, fresh land became scarcer and as exact knowledge grew and was made readily available, scientific methods began to be applied on American farms as never before, despite the continuing high cost of labor.

New Machines

Even before the Civil War, a number of improvements had been made in farm equipment. After the war, devices for planting, cultivating, and harvesting were further improved, sometimes dramatically, and they came into much wider use.

The steel plow of 1833 was far more efficient than wooden, iron-plated, or solid cast-iron plows, but it had a tendency to break. It was made more durable in 1868 when an outer surface of fine steel was combined with an inner core of soft iron. It was further improved, during the next thirty years, by the development of the riding plow. The way was now prepared for the gang plow, with which a single operator could make several furrows at once.

Exhibitions at fairs helped in the development and sale of improved farm implements. Rival manufacturers competed in plowing contests, and both they and the farmers learned the advantages and disadvantages of various new designs. Other improved devices coming into use were often shown at state and county fairs.

The most dramatic progress was made in the improvement of the reaper. Originally, the reaper had required a crew of six to ten persons, who could cut and bind from ten to twelve acres of grain in a day. One person drove the horses, and another raked the cut grain from a platform behind the cutting blades. The others followed along to pick up the grain and tie it in bundles. Later, the reaper was improved by the addition of a conveyor belt that brought the grain to a kind of table, where people could bind it while riding on the machine. Experiments were made with devices for binding the grain automatically, and in 1878 a successful "twine binder" was patented. With the new binder, one person could do as much as several workers had done with the old-fashioned reaper.

Horses generally pulled and powered the farm machines. The mechanical thresher was at first powered by horses walking on a treadmill. In the 1870's, steam-powered threshing machines came into general use. After 1900, gasoline engines began to replace steam engines on these machines. The reaper and thresher were eventually combined in a single machine called the combine. It performed the entire harvesting operation, from cutting the grain to bagging the kernels.

Farm machines were introduced more rapidly in some parts of the country than in others. Their use spread the fastest in the Central Valley of California and in Kansas, Nebraska, the Dakotas, Ohio, Indiana, Michigan, Illinois, Wisconsin, Minnesota, and Iowa. There the farms were large and level, farm wages were high, and the grain crops were suited to mechanical cultivation and (except for corn) harvesting. Machines were adopted most slowly in the South, where the farms were generally small, the incomes of the tenants low, and the cotton and tobacco crops not well suited to mechanical processes.

New Ideas in Agriculture

The federal and state governments promoted agricultural research and education. The Department of Agriculture, founded in 1862, became a full-fledged department in 1889. Its role was to acquire and spread information on agriculture and to find, test, and distribute among the people new seeds and plants. As Congress appropriated more and more money for it, the department developed into the nation's most important institution for agricultural research. It also coordinated the work of other institutions and brought together the results of their work.

Agricultural studies were also stimulated by the Morrill Act of 1862, which gave public lands to the states. According to the law, the states had to sell the land and invest the proceeds. They were to use the interest for assisting colleges that were primarily intended to teach "such branches of learning as are related to agriculture and the mechanic arts." Most of the states made very little from the sales, and for a time many of the land-grant schools struggled for existence.

The states handled the grants differently. Some—including Michigan, Iowa, and Indiana—set up "agricultural and mechanical" colleges separate from the state university. Others—including Ohio, Illinois, Wisconsin, and Minnesota—built the state university on part of the land grant.

As state appropriations for these schools increased, the training in agricultural sciences improved. Few graduates of the "A and M" colleges went into farming itself. Most of them looked for careers in teaching or research. Many practicing farmers, however, attended short courses that the colleges offered.

Agricultural experimentation was also encouraged by the Hatch Act of 1887, which gave federal support to an agricultural experiment station in each state and territory. These stations, some of them located on the campuses of land-grant colleges, were devoted to testing theories and discovering facts. In the beginning, they concentrated on immediate, practical problems. Later, they were authorized to carry on long-term projects of original research.

With the aid of the new research institutions, many improvements were made in breeds of cattle, hogs, and other livestock. The dairy industry was developed, particularly in Wisconsin. An agriculture professor at the University of Wisconsin, Stephen M. Babcock, invented the "Babcock tester," which measured the butterfat content of milk. By using this tester, farmers could tell which of their cows produced the richest milk and were most valuable for breeding good stock. Short courses at the university offered training in dairying and cheese-making. Largely through applied science, dairy farming was substituted for wheat farming in the state. By 1890, Wisconsin was on the way to becoming the leader in the production of milk and milk products.

Scientists successfully attacked animal diseases. In the 1880's, for example, researchers in the Department of Agriculture discovered that the Texas fever, which had hit the southwestern cattle herds, was carried by ticks. A dip was devised "to kill the ticks without killing the cattle," and the fever was brought under control.

Plants were improved. In a number of instances, new varieties were imported from abroad. Those that did well were publicized by the Department of Agriculture and the agricultural colleges. Mennonite farmers from Russia brought to Kansas a hard, red, winter wheat that eventually made Kansas the foremost wheat-producing state. A large part of California's agriculture was based on crops like plums, raisin grapes, and navel oranges, which were not native to the area. Sugar beets, previously grown in Germany, were tried in various states in response to Department of Agriculture propaganda. In the 1890's, beets became an important crop in Michigan, Colorado, California, and Utah.

To deal with insect pests, insecticides were developed. A kind of moth that threatened the orange groves of California was eliminated by a natural enemy, a beetle that was brought in from Australia for that purpose.

Methods of cultivation were made more effective after scientific discoveries regarding soils and plant life. The essential plant foods—nitrogen, potash, and phosphates—

California farmers harvest a large wheat crop in the 1870's. Scientific advances made such yields possible. Both domestic and foreign markets were eager to buy all the wheat that could be grown.

were combined in an artificial fertilizer for the first time in the 1870's. The use of this combination contributed enormously to the productivity of farms in the United States.

A LOSS OF INDEPENDENCE

At one time, most American farmers had been relatively independent in raising and marketing their crops. The whole family worked the farm, with occasional help from a hired hand or two. On market day, everyone would ride into town to the open market where they traded their produce. They would return home with calico, sugar, seeds, new farm implements, and perhaps a little cash.

By the 1890's, all this had changed. Farmers now sold their crops for money, and they sold them in markets that they never actually saw—the markets of the world. There, America's grain and meat competed with grain and meat from Canada, Australia, and Argentina; its cotton, with that from Egypt, India, and Brazil. The railroad and the steamship carried American produce everywhere, and the telephone, telegraph, and transatlantic cable kept sellers and buyers informed of the conditions of demand and supply and the resulting prices. No longer did farmers deal directly with the buyers. They now had to depend on warehouses, called elevators, to store and load their grain, on railroads to haul it away, and on other intermediaries to handle it and distribute it among the final buyers.

Unseen Forces in Control

To the farmer, it seemed that most merchants and manufacturers—and especially the manufacturers of farm machinery—were guilty of profiteering. American-made reapers often cost more in the United States than in foreign countries. Sales agencies received a high commission on every farm machine they sold.

To the manufacturer, however, the prices seemed reasonable enough. Cyrus Hall McCormick, whose Chicago factory was the largest farm-implement producer, pointed out that the sales agencies were necessary to assemble the machines from parts shipped from the factory. McCormick also explained that nearly two-thirds of his reapers were sold on credit, and he had to hire people to investigate credit ratings and to collect time payments.

Whether the price of farm machines was excessive or not, it was high in relation to the prices that farmers were receiving for their products. For most of the time between 1873 and 1893, the prices of cotton, wheat, and corn were falling. In some years, it cost more to produce a crop than the crop could be sold for. At that price, it was not worth the expense of picking the crop and hauling it to the railroads. Many farmers were burning corn for fuel.

These low prices were quoted on the leading exchanges, such as the Chicago Board of Trade and the New York Cotton Exchange. There dealers bought and sold *agricultural commodities*—farm products—in large quantities for immediate or future delivery. These dealers commonly speculated, that is, bought or sold commodities in the hope of making a profit from a rise or a fall in the price. A price decline, which necessarily meant losses to many farmers, brought gains to those speculators who had gambled on such a decline. To the farmers, such profiting from the misfortunes of others seemed downright wicked, especially since the farmers suspected the speculators of manipulating the market to cause the price to fall.

In any case, the price quoted on the exchanges was not the amount that farmers actually received. From the market price, several charges were deducted—the fee for storing and loading the crop, the freight, the insurance, and the commissions of merchants and brokers (the middlemen) who had taken part in a string of transactions through which the crop had finally reached the market.

Many farmers thought these charges, especially those of the grain elevators and the railroads, were exorbitant. Farmers often complained that it took one bushel of wheat or corn to pay the freight on another. Freight rates in the South and the West, where there was little competition among railroads, were from two to three times higher than those between Chicago and New York, where there were competing lines. Rates generally were higher for those who shipped small quantities of goods than for those who shipped large quantities; hence the rate was higher for the individual farmer than for the great manufacturing corporation.

Originally, many farmers had considered the railroad their best friend and had done all they could to encourage rail construction. From the 1870's on, they believed the railroad was their worst enemy.

A Growing Burden of Debt

In the plains area and in some of the older states of the Middle West, as in the South, most farmers had little or no savings of their own. They had to borrow money in order to farm. They needed both long-term loans, which were repayable in several years, and short-term loans, which were repayable in several months. The long-term loans were used to pay for land and equipment. Even the homesteaders, who needed practically no cash to get their land, had to have money for fences, buildings, and windmills and other machinery. Short-term loans were used to buy seed, livestock, and other supplies, and to pay for operating expenses during the growing season.

To obtain a long-term loan, a farmer could not depend on the banks. State banks hesitated to make loans on real estate, and national banks were forbidden by law to do so. The farmer usually borrowed from an individual moneylender or from an investment company. Investment companies sold bonds, which were secured by farm mortgages, in order to raise the money to lend. The bonds were bought mostly by easterners. The borrowing farmer was charged a high interest rate and other fees. If he or she could not raise the money to pay off the loan when it fell due, the mortgage might be foreclosed—which meant that the farm would be sold to pay the debt.

Nor could the farmer depend on the banks for short-term loans, since the banks would not accept as security crops or livestock that had not yet been raised. In much the same way that the southern farmer got credit from a country storekeeper, the western farmer usually obtained it from a local merchant. The interest for such credit often was 15 or 20 percent, and the price of the goods also was excessive.

The farmer's debt—the interest and the principal—represented a fixed cost. It remained the same and had to be paid off regardless of the amount or the price of the crops that the farmer sold. The farmer also had another fixed cost, the taxes on the land. This expense, too, bore no relation to one's ability to pay. In those days, there were no state income taxes; and only for a few years were there federal income taxes. State and local governments got almost all of their revenue by taxing real estate.

With interest, taxes, and other costs remaining high and the price of farm produce falling, farmers found it harder and harder to make ends meet. By the 1890's, nearly one-third of all the farms in the nation were mortgaged. In certain areas, even more were mortgaged—nearly half the farms in Wisconsin and Michigan, slightly more than half of those in Iowa, and much more than half of those in Minnesota, Kansas, Nebraska, and North and South Dakota.

With the disappearance of cheap or free farm lands in the West, it became more and more difficult to acquire land. With the growing burden of debt, many farm owners found it difficult or impossible to hold on to land they already had. Not only in the South but also in other parts of the nation, farm tenancy increased. In 1880, about one-fourth of all the farms in the nation were operated by tenants; by 1890, more than one-third.

Many of the farmers agreed on what they believed would remedy the problems they faced. As they saw it, the railroads and other handlers of the crop on its way to market should be strictly regulated. Tariffs should be lowered and monopolies broken up. Cheaper loans should be provided, and at least a part of the tax burden should be shifted—by means of an income tax—to those who could best afford to bear it.

To debtor farmers, it seemed that there was too little money in circulation. They thought that if more money were issued, the prices of farm products would rise. (This was probably true; for, as a rule, the more money there is in circulation, the higher prices in general will be.) The farmers believed that if agricultural prices rose high enough—and if other prices did not rise too high—they might be able to pay off their debts. Hence most of them were *inflationists,* or advocates of increasing the money supply.

All these things, however, would require strong action on the part of the government, especially the federal government. To get the government to act, the farmers would have to gain political power, and to do that, they would have to organize and work together. This was hard for them to do. They were individualists, accustomed to working alone. They had different political traditions; in the North, most of the farmers were Republicans, and in the South, most of them were Democrats. There were also racial and other differences among them. Nevertheless, the farmers eventually formed political combinations through which they could bring pressure to bear in state and national politics.

A Look at Specifics

1. How did the Dawes Act (1887) modify government policy in regard to the Indians?

2. How did federal legislation enable homesteaders to obtain land from the federal government?

3. Why did many southern farmers become victims of debt slavery?

4. How did the decisions of the Supreme Court in the Civil Rights Cases of 1883 allow southern individuals to discriminate against blacks? How did the Court's decision in *Plessy* v. *Ferguson* (1896) permit the states to discriminate against blacks?

5. Explain why white farmers did not unite with black farmers to resist domination by the Bourbons.

6. Before the 1890's, the farmers were relatively independent in raising and marketing their crops. How and why did this change?

7. Why did farmers, unlike manufacturers, have little control over the prices of their products?

A Review of Major Ideas

1. What difficulties did ranchers and farmers have in settling the Great Plains?

2. After the Civil War, why did farmers lose much of their former independence and their position in society?

For Independent Study

1. Farmers maintained that the railroads were unfair in setting higher rates for short hauls than for long hauls and in charging higher rates in the West and South than in the East. What arguments did railroad owners use to justify the unequal rates? In your opinion, who had the stronger case, the railroad owners or the farmers?

2. In 1903, W. E. B. Du Bois, a critic of Booker T. Washington, wrote that Washington was "striving nobly to make Negro artisans business men and property-owners; but it is utterly impossible, under modern competitive methods, for workingmen and property-owners to defend their rights and exist without the right of suffrage." Do you agree with Du Bois? Why?

3. The Dawes Act required that an Indian had to work on his or her allotment of land for twenty-five years before taking ownership of the land. The Homestead Act, however, required that white or black settlers on public lands need only work their tracts for five years in order to become the owners. For what reasons did Congress require a longer tenancy by Indians than by whites or blacks?

The Politics of Discontent

CHAPTER 15
1877–1900

A Granger view of farm-rail problems.

When a nation's economic and social systems are undergoing great changes, it almost invariably follows that its political systems are affected. In the United States the years between 1877 and 1900 made up a period of great change.

While Americans tried to adjust to living in an industrial society, government lagged behind. Many people were discontented, and they sought changes in the powers, actions, and make-up of their governments.

CIVIL SERVICE REFORMS

A large number of Americans were dissatisfied with the spoils system. They wanted to eliminate machine politics and make the government more responsive to the people. In trying to do so, they had to deal with the two major political parties.

Party Politics

The Republican party was basically an alliance between the industrialists of the Northeast and the more prosperous farmers of the Middle West. It also had the support of the Grand Army of the Republic, the Union veterans' organization. Republicans referred to their party as the party of Union and freedom, the party that had won the Civil War and freed the slaves. The Republicans made a practice of "waving the bloody shirt," that is, reminding the northern people that their former enemies had been Democrats.

The Democratic party was more varied than the Republican. It could count upon the Solid South after 1877, when control of the southern states was left to local Democrats. The party also depended upon the votes of workers, both native and foreign-born, in the big cities. Moreover, it had the support of many merchants and bankers in the North. It claimed, as it had before the war, to stand for the principle of states' rights.

On the whole, the Republican party contained a larger number of well-to-do persons, and the Democratic party a larger number of poor. Yet both parties included people of all economic levels and all economic interests. Both tried to appeal to as many voters as possible in order to win elections.

Under the spoils system, party bosses held their political machines together by rewarding their faithful followers with government jobs. The bosses then collected a portion of the salaries of these officeholders as campaign contributions. The machines also received money from individuals or corporations in payment for political favors, such as the passage of a desired law. Thus the spoils system contributed to governmental inefficiency, irresponsibility, and corruption.

Reformers demanded that the spoils system be replaced by a merit system. They wanted government jobs to go to the best-qualified applicants, regardless of their political views or party services.

Hayes and the Spoils System

There was nothing colorful about Rutherford B. Hayes, but he was honest and determined. When he became President in 1877, he intended to lead Congress and the country. In his inaugural address he declared that "he serves his party best who serves his country best," and "party leaders should have no more influence in appointments than other equally respectable citizens."

Congress, especially the Senate, was suspicious of any President who might try to limit its powers. Often called the "Millionaires' Club," the Senate had many rich members who headed state political machines and who really represented large corporations rather than the people. The leading senators, as one of them remarked, would have taken it as a "personal affront" if the President had asked them to pass a bill they did not like.

Thus Hayes ran into difficulties. Throughout his term, the Democrats controlled the House of Representatives, and during the last two years they also controlled the Senate. Many of the Republicans in Congress turned against him; at one time only three members of the Senate gave him their support. Nevertheless, Hayes made a little progress toward improving the civil service by executive action.

Hayes named a reformer, Carl Schurz, as secretary of the interior. Schurz then set up a merit system in his department. Hayes shocked Republican politicians when he issued his "Order Number 1." This forbade

Bosses of the Senate was one of many cartoons that helped spark public concern over the far-reaching powers of the trusts.

federal officeholders to "take part in the management of political organizations, caucuses, conventions, or election campaigns." If the order had been strictly obeyed, which it was not, it would have destroyed the spoils system at the federal level.

Hayes began his most important attack on the spoilsmen when he appointed a commis-

PRESIDENTIAL ELECTIONS: 1880-1888

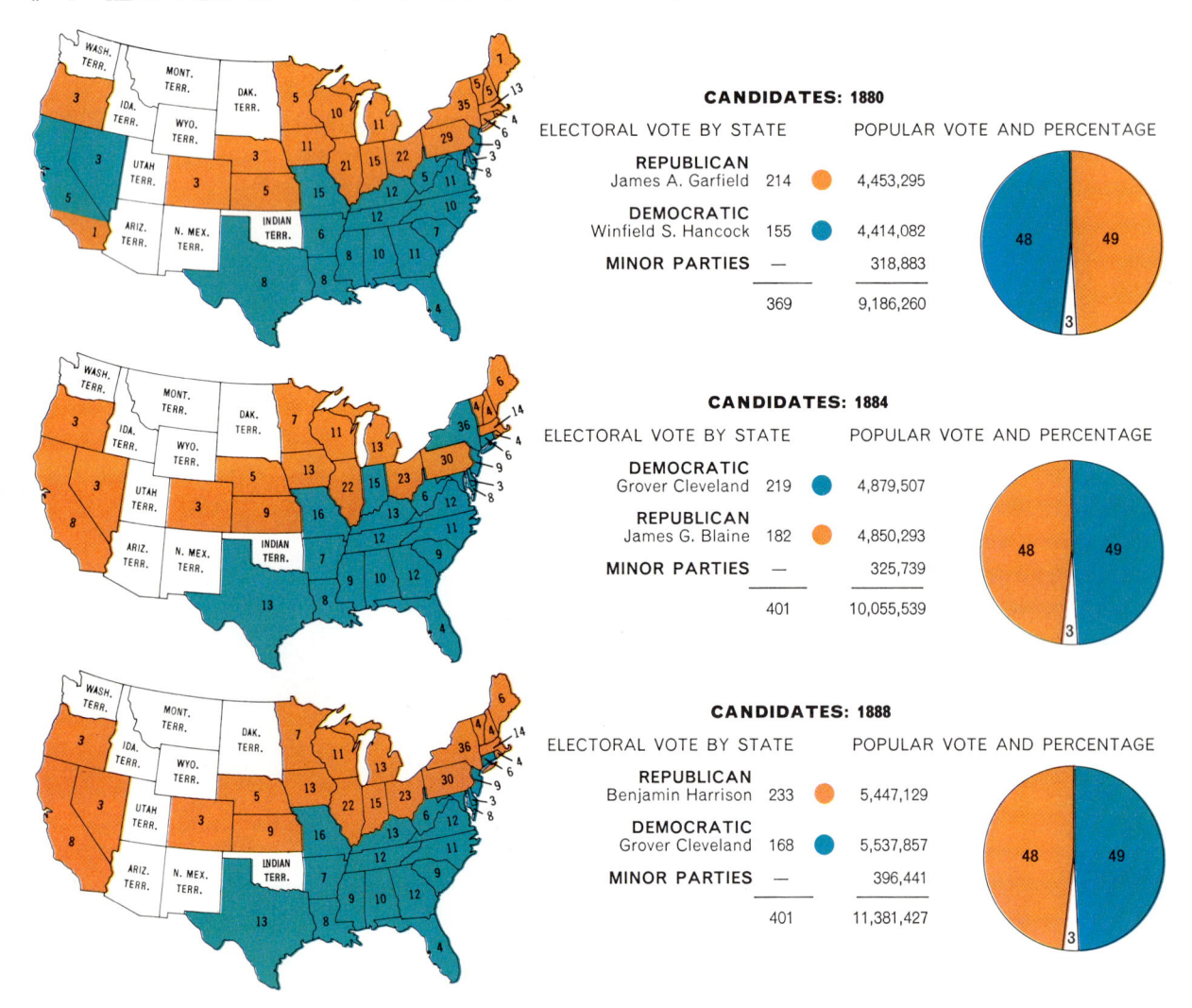

CANDIDATES: 1880

ELECTORAL VOTE BY STATE	POPULAR VOTE AND PERCENTAGE
REPUBLICAN James A. Garfield 214	4,453,295
DEMOCRATIC Winfield S. Hancock 155	4,414,082
MINOR PARTIES —	318,883
369	9,186,260

CANDIDATES: 1884

ELECTORAL VOTE BY STATE	POPULAR VOTE AND PERCENTAGE
DEMOCRATIC Grover Cleveland 219	4,879,507
REPUBLICAN James G. Blaine 182	4,850,293
MINOR PARTIES —	325,739
401	10,055,539

CANDIDATES: 1888

ELECTORAL VOTE BY STATE	POPULAR VOTE AND PERCENTAGE
REPUBLICAN Benjamin Harrison 233	5,447,129
DEMOCRATIC Grover Cleveland 168	5,537,857
MINOR PARTIES —	396,441
401	11,381,427

sion to investigate the New York custom house. This was the largest and busiest custom house. So many jobs existed there, and so much money was received in customs duties, that opportunities for patronage and graft abounded. It was said that whoever controlled the custom house controlled the state of New York. The investigating commission found that at least one-fifth of the employees were unnecessary, and that the place was full of "ignorance, inefficiency, and corruption."

After seeing the commission's report, Hayes boldly dismissed the collector and other major officeholders. All of them had been appointed on the advice of Senator Roscoe Conkling, the New York State boss. Conkling was angry. He persuaded the Senate to refuse to confirm Hayes's replacements for these officials. Hayes stood up to Conkling and kept on sending new appointments to the Senate until it finally approved his choices.

Though Hayes had won a battle, he did

not win the war against the spoils system. Throughout his term, Congress refused his request to revive the civil service commission that had been started under President Grant.

Garfield's Presidency

Before the end of Hayes's term, the Republican party had divided into factions. One group, the "Stalwarts," followed Senator Conkling. Another, the "Half-Breeds," followed Senator James G. Blaine of Maine. The Stalwarts included most of the state bosses and stood frankly for machine politics. The Half-Breeds pretended to favor reform but differed little from the Stalwarts. The two factions had arisen primarily because of the competition between Conkling and Blaine for control of the party. A third group, the Independents, tried to keep the party from breaking up, as it seemed about to do.

This split dominated the Republican convention in 1880. Hayes refused to run for reelection. The Stalwarts hoped to nominate Ulysses S. Grant for a third term. Most of the Half-Breeds supported Blaine. After many ballots the convention finally turned to a compromise candidate who had not been considered a contender, James A. Garfield. An Independent, Garfield was closer to the Half-Breeds than to the Stalwarts. To balance the ticket, the convention chose as the vice-presidential candidate a close friend of Conkling's, Chester A. Arthur, the former collector of the port of New York.

The Democrats nominated a former Union general, Winfield Scott Hancock. During the campaign, neither the Republicans nor the Democrats took a clear stand on any public issue. Both sides dealt in personalities. On election day, Garfield squeaked past Hancock and won the election.

Up to this time, Garfield's life had been a success story. He had been born in a log cabin, and he grew up to become president of Hiram College in Ohio and a congressman. He was handsome, athletic, genial, and well educated. It was said that he could write Greek with one hand and, at the same time, Latin with the other. But he often seemed indecisive, timid, and changeable. As President, he was soon overwhelmed by the demands that job seekers made upon him. "My God!" he once said. "What is there in this place that a man should ever want to get into it?"

Yielding to Blaine, Garfield awarded most of the patronage to the Half-Breeds. He gave Blaine the top cabinet position—secretary of state. Garfield showed his political independence, however, by naming a civil service reformer, Thomas L. James, as postmaster general. He also backed James when he began to expose some misdoings in the Post Office Department.

Many of Conkling's followers were bitterly disappointed when they did not get the jobs they wanted. One of them, the mentally unbalanced Charles J. Guiteau, had been refused a job in Paris by Garfield. On July 2, 1881, when the President was about to leave on a vacation trip, Guiteau stepped out of the crowd in the Washington, D.C., railroad station and fired two pistol shots at him. As Garfield fell, the assassin shouted: "I am a Stalwart and Arthur is President now!"

The Merit System

In fact, Chester A. Arthur was not yet President. Garfield lingered for eighty days with a bullet in his back and died on September 19, 1881. At this news, reformers were dismayed. They expected the worst from Arthur, who had a reputation as a spoilsman and a playboy. The challenge of the presidency, however, brought out his best qualities. He did not turn the patronage over to Conkling, as many had thought he would do. Instead, he took up the cause of reform.

The country was in a reformist mood.

Shortly before he was shot, Garfield had written in his diary: "Some civil service reform will come by necessity after the wearisome years of wasted Presidents have paved the way for it." These words proved to be prophetic.

The demand for reform was intensified by the exposure of scandals in the Post Office Department. Arthur followed the lead of Garfield in encouraging Postmaster General James's investigation.

In his first message to Congress, Arthur recommended the passage of legislation to reform the civil service. Both Republicans and Democrats were now eager to demonstrate their opposition to the spoils system. A Democratic senator from Ohio, George H. Pendleton, introduced a reform measure. It was passed by an overwhelming bipartisan majority in both houses of Congress early in 1883.

The Pendleton Act authorized the President to appoint a three-member bipartisan civil service commission. The commissioners were to arrange "open competitive examinations for testing the fitness of applicants for the public service now classified or to be classified." The law classified—that is, put under the competitive merit system—only a small number of lower offices. But the law provided that the President could add to the "classified list." The law also prohibited the enforced collection of campaign contributions from federal officeholders and protected from dismissal people who refused to make such party payments.

Arthur faithfully put the law into effect, appointing known civil service reformers to the new commission. At first, the commission had jurisdiction over about one-eighth of the federal offices. Each President who succeeded Arthur added to the classified list, and by 1900 the merit system covered two-fifths of all the federal offices.

Politics still played a part in federal appointments, even to jobs on the classified list. Usually the commission certified more than one candidate for a particular job. The appointing officer could usually find, among those who were certified, at least one person of the officer's own party. Nevertheless, the new procedure meant that a growing number of officeholders had some qualification, other than political, for their jobs.

Other consequences of civil service reform were less fortunate. As politicians lost some of their patronage, they had to find new sources of political support. More and more frequently they turned to wealthy business leaders who gave contributions in return for anticipated favors.

THE TARIFF QUESTION

Tariff reform was as badly needed as civil service reform, and it was even more difficult to bring about. During the Civil War, the general level of tariff rates had been raised to new heights. After the war, an overall reduction seemed nearly impossible. Protectionists claimed that if rates were reduced, cheap foreign goods would flood the country, resulting in ruin for American firms and unemployment for their workers. The protected industries supported one another, maintained powerful lobbies in Washington, D.C., and made friends among both Republicans and Democrats in Congress.

Many consumers complained that high duties led to overly high prices for manufactured goods. According to the critics, the tariff added excessive profits to manufacturing corporations and encouraged the growth of monopolies by preventing competition from abroad. Import and export merchants said that the tariff interfered with foreign trade. Most economists agreed that the existing rates were much too high for the good of the country. Nevertheless, no serious effort was made to deal with the tariff until more

SPECTACULAR SCENES AND SIGHTS DOWN ON THE JERSEY COAST

Leisure

Many people had increased free time in the new industrial era. "Bathing" in the ocean or lakes was a poor substitute for swimming, but it was all that was possible, given the dress of the time. Resort hotels along the beaches catered to vacationers. Such simple pleasures as watching a gory cockfight *(left)*, a bicycle race, or a vaudeville show were among the everyday forms of entertainment.

than twenty years after the end of the Civil War.

A Democratic President

In 1884, the Democrats won a presidential election for the first time since 1856. During the campaign, neither party had much to say about any significant subject. Each party simply tried to show that the other party's candidate was unfit for office.

The Republican candidate, James G. Blaine, was his party's most popular leader. Five times he had been a contender for the presidential nomination, but only this time did he get it. People loved him, but many did not trust him because he had been accused of using his influence in Congress to carry out an unethical deal.

The Democratic candidate, Grover Cleveland, had gained a reputation for honesty in public service as mayor of Buffalo and governor of New York. A number of reform-minded Republicans, the "Mugwumps," supported the Democratic ticket. Then, in mid-campaign, the newspapers published a story that Cleveland had once illegitimately fathered a child.

This put the Mugwumps in a dilemma, for Blaine had a spotless private life, and he was highly regarded as a model husband and father. But one of the Mugwumps found a way out of the dilemma. He told his fellow Republicans:

We should elect Mr. Cleveland to the public office he is so eminently qualified to fill and remand Mr. Blaine to the private life he is so eminently fitted to adorn.

This the voters did, by a narrow margin.

Among the Presidents from Lincoln to Theodore Roosevelt, Cleveland stands out as the ablest. Unimaginative and blunt, he charmed no one, but he had the courage to say no and the stubbornness to stand by his convictions.

The discontented farmer in this cartoon asks, "Here, gents, where do I fit in?" Seated at the banquet table, the nation's monopolists eat "trust roast" prepared in the "congressional kitchen."

The Republicans had a majority in the Senate, and Congress often disagreed with the President. Already known as a "veto governor," Cleveland set new records as a vetoing President. For example, he vetoed more than two hundred special pension bills for Civil War veterans. Congress passed these bills, often with no investigation or discussion, for individuals who did not qualify under the general pension laws. Cleveland signed many more than he vetoed, and despite his vetoes, pensions eventually cost far more than the war itself.

During every year of Cleveland's first term, the federal government took in about 100 million dollars more than it spent. This resulted in a treasury surplus, which was due mainly to the tariff, the main source of federal income at that time. Cleveland thought the surplus encouraged the extravagance of Congress. In 1887, he called for tariff reduction as a means of lessening government waste.

The Democratic majority in the House of Representatives approved a low-tariff bill in 1888. The Republican majority in the Senate, however, adopted a measure that maintained high duties. Neither house would accept the other's bill, and so the tariff question remained unsettled.

An Increased Tariff

In 1888, the Democratic party renominated Cleveland and made tariff reduction the key plank of the platform. The Republicans nominated Benjamin Harrison, the grandson of an earlier President. They pointed to Harrison's clean, though undistinguished, record. Harrison and his party took a protariff stand. Corporations desiring tariff protection contributed heavily to the Republican campaign fund, and the Republicans spent more money than any party had ever spent. Harrison was elected, but he won under unusual circumstances. Cleveland received 89,000 more popular votes than he, but Harrison carried enough of the large northern states to win a majority in the electoral college.

President Harrison lacked complete control over his administration. He was not really his party's leader, and he did not deal effectively with people. Harrison was as honest as Hayes or Cleveland, but he had far less personal force than either.

Without a strong President to restrain it, Congress handed out money more freely than ever. It made large appropriations for pensions, river and harbor improvements, government buildings, coast defenses, and other purposes.

With the Republicans now controlling both houses, Congress put together a tariff bill with higher duties on manufactured goods than the government ever before had levied. It even gave protection to industries that did not then exist in the United States.

The measure was expected to reduce the treasury surplus in two ways. First, its rates were so high that certain foreign products would be kept out entirely. Second, the bill removed the tariff on imported sugar and gave sugar producers in the United States a bounty of two cents a pound. The bounty would come out of the treasury. This measure became a law, the McKinley Tariff Act, in 1890.

In 1892 the Democrats won the presidency and a majority in both houses of Congress. The Wilson-Gorman Tariff Act, which Congress adopted in 1894, ended the bounty on sugar and restored the sugar duties. On the whole, the new law established rates lower than those of the McKinley Tariff, but not much lower.

After the Republicans had returned to power, they raised the level of duties again by passing the Dingley Tariff Act in 1897. The new rates were so high that imports and hence customs receipts fell off sharply.

ATTEMPTS TO REGULATE BUSINESS

Many discontented Americans demanded that Congress protect the public by passing laws regulating businesses. Congress responded in several ways. Sometimes it passed ineffective laws that were intended to stifle the demands without actually protecting the public. Sometimes, too, it passed effective laws that were then struck down by the Supreme Court.

Constitutional Problems

In the 1870's a farmers' organization, the Patrons of Husbandry (the National Grange) tried to get the state governments to regulate business. Several states set up commissions to supervise railroads and grain elevators and prevent them from charging unfair rates. By the 1880's, fifteen states and territories had passed antimonopoly laws. These regulatory efforts, however, were limited by decisions of the Supreme Court.

The Constitution gives Congress the power to regulate commerce among the states *(Art. 1, sec. 8)*. In 1877 the Supreme Court upheld the so-called Granger laws and granted that a state had the right to control a railroad's charges. In 1886, however, the Court said the state's regulations must apply only to traffic within the state, not to interstate commerce. Since this commerce made up about three-fourths of the railroads' business, the state commissions were left with little power.

The Constitution requires that each state give "full faith and credit" to the public acts of every other state *(Art. 4, sec. 1)*. The Supreme Court long had interpreted this to mean that a corporation chartered in one state could operate freely in any other. Thus a monopolistic company chartered in one state could also carry on business in states with antimonopoly laws.

The Fourteenth Amendment forbids every state to "deprive any person of life, liberty, or property, without due process of law." From 1886 on, the Supreme Court maintained that these words applied to corporations ("artificial persons") as well as to individuals. Thus the amendment prohibited a state from depriving companies of their property (that is, their profits) through laws interfering with their business. Therefore, if railroads were to be regulated and monopolies were to be prevented, the job was up to the federal government.

The Interstate Commerce Act

To provide for regulation of the railroads, Congress passed the Interstate Commerce Act in 1887. This stated that all railroad rates must be "reasonable and just." It forbade railroads to discriminate in favor of one shipper over another. It also outlawed *pooling* agreements and other common abuses.

The act provided for the appointment by the President of the Interstate Commerce Commission. But it failed to give the commissioners much power. They could investigate the management of railroads, require annual reports from railroads, and hear complaints from shippers. But they were not allowed to set rates or enforce any rulings. If the commissioners felt that the law was being violated, they could only sue the offending railroad. The federal courts would then decide what action was to be taken. Since the language of the law was vague, it was hard for either the commissioners or the judges to know whether the law was being broken. What, after all, were "reasonable and just" rates? Suits dragged on endlessly. When cases finally reached the Supreme Court, the decisions almost always favored the railroads.

The Sherman Antitrust Act

In the 1880's, more and more people were demanding that Congress do something to

The Rise of Jim Crow

In the Reconstruction era, the Fourteenth Amendment was passed to give blacks equal protection under the laws. To put the amendment into force, Congress passed the Civil Rights Act of 1875. It guaranteed use of public facilities, including those for transportation.

In the 1880's and 1890's, white Americans found ways to by-pass such laws. In 1883, in a series of Civil Rights Cases, the Supreme Court declared the Civil Rights Act of 1875 unconstitutional. The Court said that the Fourteenth Amendment applied only to acts by states. Congress therefore could not pass laws forcing private businesses to desegregate.

Despite this decision, some state legislatures passed segregation laws. Between 1887 and 1892, nine southern states passed laws requiring "equal but separate accommodations for the white and colored races." These were the first of a long series of "Jim Crow" laws. (Jim Crow was a slave character in a minstrel show.)

Blacks in a number of southern cities organized to protest these laws. They often had the backing of the streetcar companies, which favored integrated cars because of the expense of a dual system. Jim Crow streetcars were boycotted in New Orleans, Richmond, Charleston, and other cities. At best, these boycotts put only a temporary stop to segregation.

In Louisiana, a group of blacks formed the "Citizens' Committee to Test the Constitutionality of the Separate [Railroad] Car Laws." In 1892, with the support of the committee, Homer Plessy refused to move to a Jim Crow car. He was arrested and convicted. The Supreme Court agreed to hear his appeal and decide whether "separate but equal" facilities violated the Fourteenth Amendment. In *Plessy* v. *Ferguson* (1896), the Court ruled that the Louisiana car law was constitutional. Thus it provided a precedent for all succeeding Jim Crow laws.

Jim Crow laws were later passed to segregate schools, restaurants, and even telephone booths. In one state, courtrooms had separate Bibles for black witnesses; many states had different textbooks for blacks than for whites. Not until 1954 did the Supreme Court reverse the decision on separate but equal facilities.

White Leaguers guard the polls. By keeping blacks from voting, they stifled opposition to Jim Crow laws.

limit trusts. Others questioned whether Congress had the power to do so, since there is nothing in the Constitution about monopolies. Supporters of federal action pointed out that Congress has the power to regulate interstate commerce and that business combinations often restricted competition and blocked the free flow of such commerce.

Thus, in 1890, Congress passed the Sherman Antitrust Act. This law made illegal any combination that restrained "trade or commerce among the several states, or with foreign nations." In addition the law made it a misdemeanor to "combine or conspire" to monopolize such trade or commerce. The law set relatively light punishment for violators. Its toughest provision was that any person suffering a loss as the victim of an illegal combination might sue to recover three times the damages.

The Sherman Antitrust Act was as difficult to enforce as the Interstate Commerce Act. To break up a trust, the federal government had to sue the company or combination of companies, and the final decision was left to the Supreme Court. The President and the attorney general had to start the court action, and they would do so only if they were concerned about monopolies. Before 1901, the government brought in only eighteen antitrust suits, and it lost most of these cases.

In the case of *United States* v. *E. C. Knight Co.* (1895), the government charged that the Knight company controlled 98 percent of the country's sugar-refining business. The Supreme Court admitted this, but it concluded that the company's activities were perfectly legal. Sugar refining, the chief justice said, was not commerce. He said it was *manufacturing*. Even though the raw sugar came from many different places and the refined sugar was sold throughout the country, the Sherman Antitrust Act did not cover the situation. This decision made the law practically unenforceable against industrial monopolies.

THE POPULISTS

In the 1880's, the discontented farmers of the country demanded a number of national reforms. But these farmers were not organized to give effect to their demands. Although they still had a national organization, the National Grange, it was no longer a large crusading body. It had lost most of its members and had become essentially a fraternal and recreational society, whose leaders represented the more contented farmers. Supporters of reform began to develop new politically active organizations.

The Farmers' Alliances

Three large farm groups were formed in the 1880's. One was the National Farmers' Alliance of the Northwest, usually known as the Northern Alliance. It had its largest membership in the wheat-growing states of Kansas, Nebraska, Minnesota, and North and South Dakota. Another was the Farmers' Alliance and Industrial Union of the South, or Southern Alliance, with white members throughout the southern states. Affiliated with it was a separate organization for blacks, the National Colored Farmers' Alliance.

In their activities the Alliances at first were very similar to the old Grange. They carried on social and educational programs, set up cooperatives for buying and selling, and urged the passage of state laws to protect agricultural interests.

By 1890, however, the Alliance members had come to believe they ought to play a more active role in politics. The McKinley Tariff, which Congress had passed that year, antagonized the farmers and increased their discontent. They concluded that they could no longer rely on Republicans or Democrats who promised to help them.

In the western states, the farmers now began to support Alliance tickets in competition with the Republican and Democratic tickets. In the southern states, however, the white farmers hesitated to form a separate party. The Democratic party in the South stood for "white supremacy." If a new party should compete with it, one or both of the two might seek black support. And if blacks were thus encouraged to vote, they would probably hold the balance of power between the two parties. Fearing such a consequence, the southern white farmers tried to get members of the Alliance nominated on the Democratic ticket.

Alliance members were encouraged by the state and congressional elections of 1890. The Northern Alliance elected a number of state legislators and congressmen, and the Southern Alliance appeared to have done even better. Its candidates, running on the Democratic ticket, became governors of four states and gained control of the legislatures in eight.

The People's Party

Their successes in 1890 encouraged some of the Northern and Southern Alliance leaders to get together during the next two years and organize a national political party in time for the election of 1892. At meetings in Cincinnati and St. Louis in 1891, Alliance leaders made plans for a national organization and drew up a statement of grievances. The Alliance members named the new organization the People's party. From the Latin word for people, *populi,* came the related terms Populist and Populism.

The Populist leaders were mostly professional people rather than farmers. Unfortunately for the movement, few of them had much skill as practical politicians.

Ignatius Donnelly of Minnesota wrote books to prove that the mythical island of Atlantis had really existed, that Francis Bacon had written Shakespeare's plays, and that the oppressed poor would someday join a "brotherhood of destruction" and bring civilization to an end. Thomas E. Watson of Georgia at one time favored political cooperation of whites with blacks, but he later turned violently against Negroes and against Catholics and Jews. Jerry Simpson of Kansas, after making fun of an opposing candidate who wore silk socks, gained the title "Sockless Jerry, the Socrates of the prairies." Mary E. Lease, a fiery orator from Kansas, advised farmers to "raise less corn and more

A chapter of the Grange meets in an Illinois schoolhouse in the 1870's. At its peak, the Grange had 20,000 similar local units. As farmers got angrier, they began to organize into more militant groups to push for new legislation.

hell." The South Carolina leader Benjamin Tillman was known as "Pitchfork Ben" because he once threatened to tickle President Cleveland's ribs with a pitchfork.

The Populists hoped to make their organization a broad farmer-labor party. The large and growing American Federation of Labor, however, refused to join it. Only the Knights of Labor were willing to cooperate, and by this time that organization was almost extinct. Only the farmers in the West and South showed much interest, and in the South most of them continued to operate within the Democratic party.

Despite their handicaps, the Populists showed great enthusiasm as they gathered in 1892 for their first national nominating convention. They adopted a platform demanding a long list of radical reforms. Among these were the following:

(1) Inflation of the currency, either with new paper money or with additional silver coins.

(2) Government ownership and operation of the railroads and telegraph and telephone systems.

(3) A plan by which farmers could store surplus crops in government warehouses and could borrow money from the government in the form of special treasury notes.

(4) A federal income tax, to be "graduated" in such a way as to take a much higher proportion of large than of small incomes.

(5) The establishment of postal savings banks.

(6) A shorter work day in factories.

(7) The initiative and referendum. The *initiative* would enable the people, by petition, to introduce bills for the consideration of Congress or the state legislatures. The *referendum* would permit the people to vote on, and to defeat if they wished, bills that had already been passed.

(8) Election of United States senators by direct vote of the people.

(9) A single term for the President and the Vice-President.

After approving these planks, the Populists nominated James B. Weaver of Iowa for President. Weaver, a former Union general, had run on the Greenback ticket in 1880. For his running mate, the convention chose a former Confederate general, James G. Field of Virginia.

The Populist Legacy

In 1892 the Republicans nominated Benjamin Harrison for a second term. They still pushed for a high protective tariff, even though the McKinley Tariff had turned voters away from the party in the congressional elections of 1890. The Democrats again campaigned for tariff reduction, with former President Cleveland as their candidate. When the returns were in, Cleveland had a majority in the electoral college and a plurality of the popular votes.

More than 1 million popular votes went to Weaver. He also won electoral votes in six western states. The Populists that year also elected ten representatives, five senators, three governors, and about fifteen hundred state legislators.

The Populists took heart from these returns. They became even more optimistic of political success when, after the Panic of 1893, the worst business depression yet known began. As unemployment in the cities grew and incomes on the farms fell, the number of discontented Americans increased. So did the appeal of the Populist party. As a result, in the state and congressional elections of 1894, many more voters cast their ballots for the party's candidates than in 1892. Some Populist leaders thought these returns might mean that the party could capture the presidency in 1896.

The Populist party, however, soon suffered the same fate as a number of other third parties: One of the major parties stole its thunder. The most popular plank in the Populist platform of 1892 had been the demand for the additional coinage of silver. In 1896, the Democrats made the silver issue the main plank of their platform, and the Populists then supported the Democratic candidate. After that, the Populist party rapidly fell apart.

Nevertheless, the Populists left their mark on history. Many of the measures they favored were later enacted into law. The graduated income tax, the direct popular election of United States senators, the initiative and referendum, postal savings banks, a shortened work day, government loans to farmers—all came to pass. The results of the Populists' efforts show how important a third party may be, even when it does not gain control of the government.

The Populist movement also had other results. In the South, it helped bring about the passage of laws and state constitutional amendments to keep blacks from voting or holding office. Since the end of the Reconstruction period, most southern blacks had ceased to vote, for the dominant whites often used economic pressure or violence to keep them from the polls. A few Populists began to seek black support. Sometimes the Democrats managed to get blacks to vote for the Democratic instead of the Populist ticket. Each party usually blamed the blacks whenever its candidates were defeated. Both sides came to believe that blacks ought to be completely disfranchised.

The disfranchisement drive began in response to a bill that Representative Henry Cabot Lodge of Massachusetts introduced in Congress in 1890. Lodge's proposal provided for federal control of elections. Although it failed to pass, Lodge's bill alarmed many white southerners.

In 1890, the Mississippi constitution was amended in such a way that blacks could legally be kept from the polls. By 1910, similar laws or constitutional amendments had been adopted in all the former Confederate states and in Oklahoma. The new measures imposed poll taxes, literacy tests, or other requirements that could be used to disqualify blacks. The literacy tests did not prevent a white man from voting, no matter how illiterate he might be, since they contained a "grandfather clause" excusing from the test any man whose grandfather had been able to vote. Southern blacks could not be excused from the test, because their grandfathers had not been able to vote.

The Supreme Court upheld measures of this kind in the case of *Williams* v. *Mississippi* (1898). According to this decision, the measures did not violate the Fifteenth Amendment since (as judged by their language, at any rate) they did not disfranchise blacks because of "race, color, or previous condition of servitude."

Despite disfranchisement, blacks continued to serve in the federal government. Blacks were appointed to serve as ministers in Haiti, Liberia, and the Dominican Republic. They also worked in federal bureaus. After Blanche K. Bruce of Mississippi left the Senate in 1881, however, there would not be a black in the Senate for another eighty-six years. By 1900, the role of black Americans in politics was greatly diminished.

THE WOMEN'S MOVEMENT

Before the Civil War, people in the women's movement had concentrated on improving job opportunities, education, and the economic standing of women. After the war, their main thrust was directed toward getting the vote.

The movement's major goal became suffrage because women saw that they had no political power without the vote. As one politician said to a group of women seeking passage of a certain bill: "Well, you are no more than fifty thousand mice! How many votes can you deliver?"

Organization

For many years the antislavery movement and the women's rights movement had been linked, and the same people often belonged to both groups. After the Civil War, many feminists were dismayed to see that while the Fourteenth Amendment guaranteed equal rights for black men, it seemed to deny them to black women, and all other women as well. For the first time in the nation's history, the word "male" appeared in the Constitution. The amendment even seemed to imply that women were not citizens.

During the debate over the Fifteenth Amendment, many feminists tried, unsuccessfully, to get women included in its provisions. Members of the Equal Rights Association, the largest and most active feminist organization, were divided over this action. Some believed that women should push as hard as they could for their rights. Others felt that women should be silent during the "Negro's hour."

Bitterness over this disagreement led to the break-up of the Equal Rights Association. In 1868, Susan B. Anthony and Elizabeth Cady Stanton formed a new organization, the National Woman Suffrage Association. It favored pushing militantly for women's rights as well as for black rights. The following year, Lucy Stone and feminists in the less militant faction formed the American Woman Suffrage Association. Though the main goal of both organizations was the same, their styles of operating were different.

For the next few decades, the leaders of the NWSA fought for equality with men in many areas, including jobs, education, and legal rights. Because the group was involved in more than just getting the vote, it stirred up controversy and gained a reputation for radicalism. The leaders of NWSA pushed for a women's suffrage amendment to the Constitution.

The AWSA concentrated on the issue of suffrage, working to get state legislatures to pass suffrage bills. It also maintained a more respectable image than the NWSA. The two groups finally merged in 1890 to become the National American Woman Suffrage Association.

Tactics

There were three main approaches to gaining the vote—through court action, through state laws, and through a national constitutional amendment. The women's organizations used all three approaches.

In several elections between 1868 and 1872, women cast ballots in defiance of election laws. Some of them were trying to bring a test case before the Supreme Court to find out whether the provisions of the Fourteenth and Fifteenth Amendments applied to women. In 1872, Susan B. Anthony and sixteen other women registered and voted in the presidential election. Anthony was tried and convicted of illegal voting. Before her case could get any further, the Court ruled in the case of Virginia Minor.

In the Slaughter-House Cases in 1873, the Supreme Court had said that black men could not be denied the vote on account of race, because the Fourteenth Amendment had made them citizens. In the case of *Minor v. Happensatt* in 1874, the Court seemed to reverse itself. The Court ruled unanimously that women were citizens but that citizenship did not give them the right of the franchise. The Court's decision ended efforts to win the vote through court action. Feminist groups now turned to the state and national legislatures for women suffrage bills.

The efforts to persuade state legislatures to vote for women's suffrage were most successful in the West. Wyoming, Utah, Colorado, and Idaho gave women the vote before 1900. In many other states, the question of whether women should be allowed to vote was put before the voters in referendums but failed to be approved.

Opposition

Part of the opposition centered on beliefs about woman's "place." Women were seen as highly emotional, frail, childlike beings who would be corrupted by voting. (Since

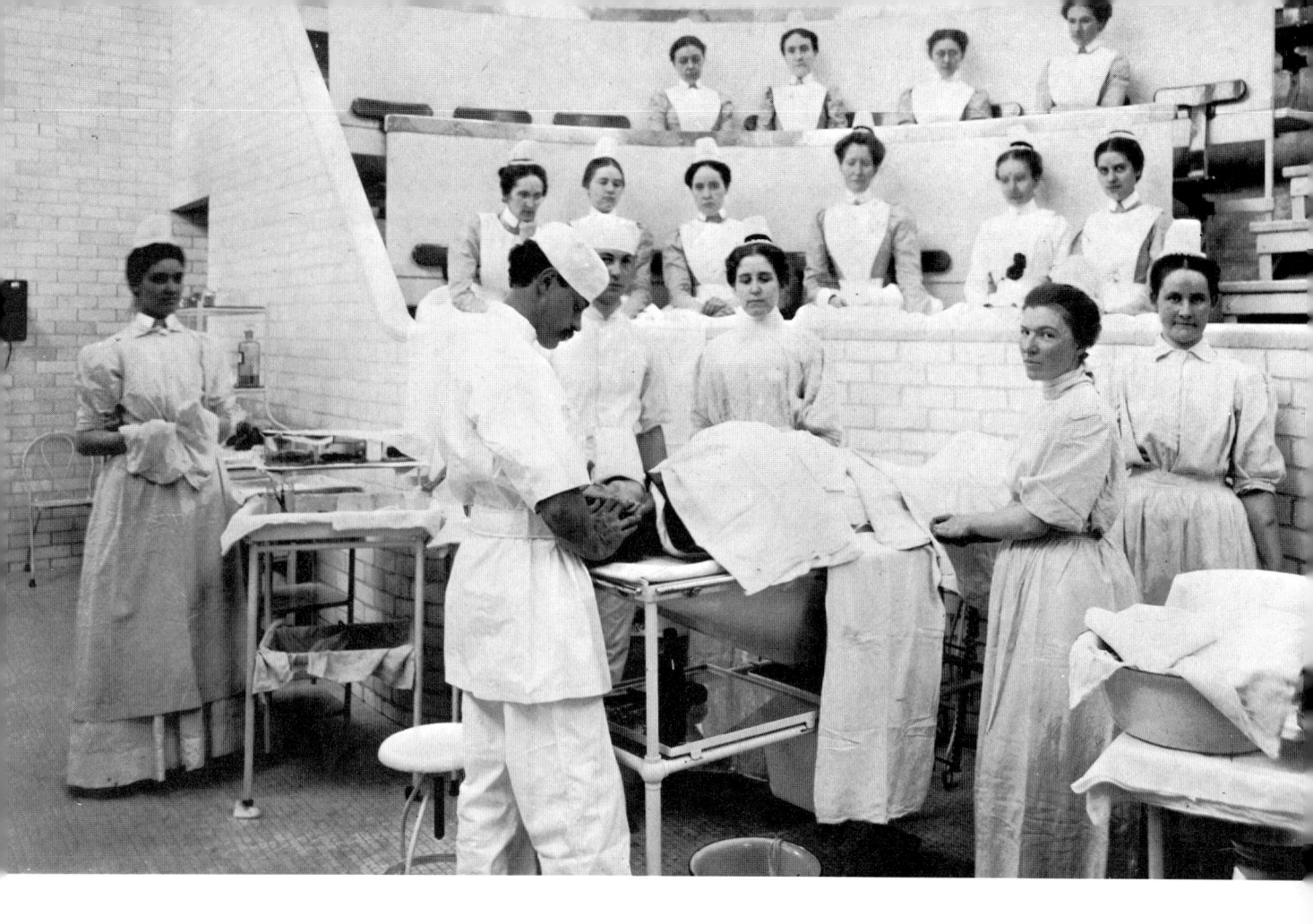

Technological advances and a growing demand for workers opened new jobs to women. Many began working in offices, stores, and hospitals. When the typewriter was introduced, women called "typewriters" demonstrated it. Employers were impressed by their work, and women and typewriters moved rapidly into the office. Employers increased production and saved on costs since "typewriters" could be hired for much lower wages than male clerks. *Right:* Women type in an insurance agency. *Above:* Nurses watch preparations for surgery.

the polling place in eighteenth- and nineteenth-century America bore a strong resemblance to a saloon, many of the men who voted against women's suffrage did so because they thought women didn't belong in such places.)

Notions of propriety were not, however, the sole basis for opposition to female voters. Many opponents were afraid that they would lose power if women were allowed to vote.

Highly organized opposition came from the liquor industry. The suffrage movement and the temperance movement had become linked in people's minds, if not in fact. Both groups were composed mainly of women, and Frances Willard, the outstanding leader of the Woman's Christian Temperance Union became an important spokeswoman for suffrage. She convinced many WCTU members that they should support votes for women. The conversion of thousands of temperance backers to the cause of suffrage aroused the worst fears of the liquor industry. Distillers used every means at their command, including the stealing of elections, to defeat women's suffrage.

Southern politicians who were in the process of disfranchising black male voters also opposed giving the vote to women. Although the southern wing of the suffrage movement was devoted to states' rights and white supremacy, it made no progress. Southern politicians feared the coming of a second Reconstruction. These fears were expressed in a pamphlet from Alabama:

Remember that *Woman Suffrage* means a reopening of the entire *Negro Suffrage* question; loss of State rights; and another period of reconstruction horrors, which will introduce a set of female carpet-baggers as bad as their male prototypes of the sixties.

Yet another group opposing women's suffrage was composed of factory owners in the industrial states. From their experience with female union members, many factory owners

The drinker in this 1874 cartoon drastically changes his attitudes after a mere four hours in a bar. Cartoons like this one were used to publicize the temperance movement. Public awareness of drunkenness increased as the nation became less rural.

were convinced that as voters women would support factory reform laws, and these would cut into profits.

The combined force of all these groups was enough to defeat most attempts at giving women the vote. Around 1900 the movement entered a slack period. Many of the old leaders were dying, and new leadership had not yet emerged. Activist women invested their time and energies in other social movements, including trade unions and settlement houses. The suffrage movement was not dead, however. It would rise again, and this time it would win.

THE "BATTLE OF THE STANDARDS"

During the 1890's, the American people fought the "battle of the standards" to decide what the basis of the nation's monetary system was to be. Both sides carried on the struggle with the zeal of religious crusaders. Both believed that the salvation of the country depended on the outcome.

The gold backers favored *monometallism,* a single gold standard, and the "silverites" insisted upon *bimetallism,* a combined gold-and-silver standard. The gold standard meant essentially that the dollar should be defined as a certain amount of gold, and that the government should exchange gold, on demand, for other forms of money. The bimetallic standard meant that the dollar should be defined as both a certain amount of gold and a certain amount of silver, and that the government should exchange either gold or silver for other forms of money.

The United States had been on a bimetallic standard since 1792. For many years, the dollar had been defined as a set quantity of gold and also as sixteen times that quantity of silver. In other words, the "mint ratio" between silver and gold was sixteen to one. If a person took sixteen ounces of silver to the mint, he or she could get one ounce of gold in exchange.

By 1873, however, nobody was taking any silver to the mint, for the price of silver had risen. A person could sell sixteen ounces of silver on the market for somewhat more than an ounce of gold. Since no silver was being brought to the government to be coined, Congress passed a law in 1873 to discontinue the coinage of silver.

Already, however, the price of silver had begun to drop. It did so because the supply was increasing and the demand decreasing. New silver mines were producing larger amounts than ever, and a number of foreign nations were abandoning silver as the basis of their monetary systems. Soon the price had fallen so low that the market ratio was more than sixteen to one. And the price of silver continued to fall.

The owners of silver mines now urged that the government start buying and coining silver again, at the old mint ratio of sixteen to one. If the government should buy all the silver they could produce, the mineowners would no longer have to worry about the market price.

If the producers alone had been interested in it, silver would never have become an engrossing issue. But the demand for "free silver" (the unlimited purchase and coinage at the old ratio) soon aroused the discontented farmers as well.

A Cry for "Free Silver"

Farmers suffering from debts and depressed prices for their products wanted the government to put more money into circulation. They felt, quite correctly, that an increase in the money supply would lead to a price rise and would make it easier for them to pay their debts. On the other hand, people with fixed incomes opposed such inflation, since they stood to lose from rising prices. Many others also opposed it on the grounds that a currency tied closely to gold was the only dependable one.

At first, the debtor farmers favored issuing more paper money (greenbacks), but from their point of view the coinage of large amounts of silver money would do just as well. They soon joined the mineowners in supporting the silver cause. To the silverites, it began to seem that Congress had done a deliberate wrong in passing the act of 1873 to discontinue silver coinage. They pushed for a new law to undo the evil they thought had been done. In 1890, they achieved a victory when Congress adopted the Sherman Silver Purchase Act. It required the government to buy an amount of silver approximately equal

William Jennings Bryan holds a rousing open-air rally during the campaign of 1896. In his speeches all over the West and South he made dramatic statements about free silver and the "tyranny" of railroad men and bankers in "enemy territory," the East.

to the output of all the mines in the United States.

These gains for the silver forces were lost, however, soon after Grover Cleveland took over the presidency for the second time, in 1893. Cleveland now faced a problem very different from the one he had encountered during his first term. By 1893, the treasury surplus had practically disappeared, and gold was flowing out of the government vaults at an alarming rate. Cleveland felt that he must maintain a large enough "gold reserve" to redeem all the paper and silver money that might be presented in exchange for gold. He asked Congress to repeal the Sherman Silver Purchase Act, which he blamed for much of the gold drain. After a bitter debate, Congress finally repealed the act in 1893.

Meanwhile, the start of a depression in 1893 had intensified the popular cry for inflation. Cleveland, like all the nineteenth-century Presidents, believed that the government had no responsibility for dealing with a depression and trying to promote recovery. He considered it his duty to protect the gold standard and maintain the government's credit, but that was all. The majority in Congress agreed with him. To the silverites, however, it seemed that the government should do something to bring prosperity. They believed that the government could bring it very easily—by merely restoring silver to its old place in the monetary system.

Bryan Versus McKinley

The election of 1896 proved to be the most exciting since 1860. So great was the popular interest in the money question that neither of the major parties could ignore the issue, though it threatened to split both of them.

When the Republicans convened, the silverites among them threatened to leave the party unless its platform contained a plank supporting free silver. The gold advocates held the upper hand, however. They adopted a plank that called for an international agreement with the leading commercial nations of the world in favor of free coinage of silver. But "until such agreement can be obtained the existing gold standard must be preserved."

Since the chances for an international agreement on bimetallism were slight, this statement amounted to a repudiation of silver. Thirty-four silverite Republicans walked out of the convention hall in protest.

The convention nominated William Mc-

Kinley, governor of Ohio, as the party's presidential candidate. McKinley had no reputation as a gold man; he had cooperated with the silverites in favoring the Sherman Silver Purchase Act. The Republicans nominated him because he was a dependable party man and a personal friend of Marcus Alonzo Hanna, the Ohio political boss.

When the Democrats met in Chicago a few weeks later, most of them thought they had a good chance to win the election by coming out unequivocally for silver. By doing so, they would upset President Cleveland and other "gold bugs" in the party, but they could gain the support of some Republicans and of silverites in general. Accordingly, the majority approved a plank calling for "the free and unlimited coinage of both silver and gold at the present legal ratio of sixteen to one without waiting for the aid or consent of any other nation."

In the debate on the platform, one man stood out. This speaker was thirty-six-year-old William Jennings Bryan, a former congressman from Nebraska. Bryan had written and spoken a great deal on the money question, and he was ready with a well-rehearsed speech to denounce the gold bugs and the Cleveland administration.

He made an emotional appeal, not a reasoned analysis of theories and facts. He drew a thunderous ovation when he concluded with the words: "You shall not press down upon the brow of labor this crown of thorns, you shall not crucify mankind upon a cross of gold." Before that speech, Bryan had not been considered a serious contender. Now, on the fifth ballot, he obtained the Democratic nomination.

Bryan, the "Boy Orator of the Platte," carried on a new kind of campaign. He was the first candidate to stump the whole country and tell the voters that he wanted to be President. Bryan traveled 18,000 miles and spoke to audiences totaling 5 million people.

McKinley did not try to match Bryan's style. He conducted a "front-porch" campaign. He stayed at home in Canton, Ohio, and greeted groups of visitors. Other Republican campaigners were busy, however. Corporations made even heavier contributions than in 1888. As election day approached, some employers told their employees that there would be no jobs for them, and some moneylenders told debtor farmers that their mortgages would not be renewed, if Bryan should win.

This campaign was much more than a personal contest between Bryan and McKinley. The nation was deeply divided. A majority of the people in the South and the West were lined up against the Northeast. Most farmers and laborers were opposed to the business interests.

In the late summer, it seemed that Bryan's chances were good. By November, however, the price of wheat had risen considerably. Many traditionally Republican farmers of the Middle West and Far West were now less willing to vote Democratic. On election day, McKinley scored a big victory over Bryan.

The Gold Standard

By 1897, when McKinley was inaugurated, prosperity was already returning. The recovery continued during his term, and this, together with McKinley's cheerful and gracious ways, made him a well-liked President. The improvement in economic conditions also seemed to demonstrate the wisdom of Republican policies.

McKinley delayed acting on the money question, to avoid antagonizing the silverites in his own party. He appointed a commission to look into the possibility of "international bimetallism" by agreement with foreign powers. To nobody's surprise, Britain refused to consider such an agreement.

Prospectors drag their equipment through the muddy street of an Alaska town in 1898. They are among the thousands who started off for the Klondike after major gold deposits were discovered there.

Finally, Congress disposed of the money problem by passing the Gold Standard Act in 1900. For many years, gold had been the actual basis for the currency, and this law made it the legal basis. Silver coins continued to be coined, but the dollar ceased to be defined in terms of silver. Hereafter, it had only a gold backing.

The adoption of the gold standard provoked little fuss. Agricultural prices were fairly high, and farm discontent was declining. The nation's money supply no longer seemed inadequate, even though there had been no large new issues of paper or silver currency.

The increase in the money supply had come about through a rise in the world's production of gold. By 1898, output was nearly two and a half times as large as it had been in 1890. This rise in productivity was due partly to the discovery of rich gold deposits in Alaska, Canada, Australia, and South Africa. It was due also to the introduction of a new method of gold refining that made it possible to extract much more metal from ore.

Bryan and the silverites had been right in saying the country needed more money, though they were wrong in thinking free silver would cure all the troubles of the time. The nation experienced a gold inflation, and this inflation was one reason for the prosperity in McKinley's time.

A Look at Specifics

1. How did the Supreme Court limit state regulation of railroads and monopolies?

2. What action could the Interstate Commerce Commission take against railroads that violated its rulings? Why was this action ineffective?

3. How did the Supreme Court decision in the case of *United States* v. *E. C. Knight Co.* (1895) weaken the power of the Sherman Antitrust Act?

4. Why were members of the Southern Alliance reluctant to form a third party?

5. What were the achievements of the Populists in the election of 1892?

6. How did the Supreme Court decision in the case of *Williams* v. *Mississippi* (1898) allow the southern states to disfranchise blacks?

7. What groups opposed women's suffrage?

8. Why did the United States abandon the coinage of silver in 1873? How did the changing price of silver lead to demands for a return to bimetallism?

A Review of Major Ideas

1. Between 1877 and 1900, which groups supported the Democrats? Which groups supported the Republicans?

2. Why did many people demand a lower tariff after the Civil War? Why was it difficult for advocates of a lower tariff to achieve their aim between 1877 and 1900?

3. Why was there pressure for the federal government to regulate railroads and other corporations? Why was regulatory legislation difficult to enforce?

4. What reforms were favored by farm groups in the 1880's and 1890's?

5. Why did reformers find it difficult to gain reform legislation between 1877 and 1900?

For Independent Study

1. What are the advantages and disadvantages of gold-standard currency? Why were many other countries switching to the gold standard?

2. Why has it always been difficult for third parties in the United States to become major parties?

The Gilded Age

CHAPTER 16
1877–1900

Fairgoers at the Columbian Exposition, Chicago, 1893.

Gilt is a coating of gold that is painted over a cheap base. Even though the gilt glitters, the ugliness it covers often shows through. In time, the gilt wears away, and the base material shows through. To the writer Mark Twain, "The Gilded Age" was the perfect term to describe American society in the period from the Civil War to the end of the century.

The nation had an outward appearance of well-being that hid the problems of a new industrial society. Sometimes, however, the problems showed on the surface. Many Americans tried to use scientific methods—the kind of "gilt" then popular—to cover these problems.

CULTURAL TRENDS

Machines brought a gradual increase in leisure time for a large number of Americans, including many of the industrial workers. These people could spend a little more time in self-improvement or recreation. Some advances were made in education. Popular entertainment began to be a big business. And newspapers and magazines gained greater circulation than ever.

New Challenges for Religion

In the realm of thought, as in the world of business, more and more stress was placed on the practical, the scientific. Even religion showed the influence of the scientific attitude. When a New Englander, Mary Baker Eddy, founded a new faith, she named it Christian Science. Mrs. Eddy stated her views in her book *Science and Health, with Key to the Scriptures* (1875). Healing through prayer is an important part of Christian Science. This faith rapidly gained believers among people of the rising business class, especially in the cities.

Many religious leaders were faced with the challenge of restating their faith in the light of new-found scientific knowledge and the problems created by an industrial society. An important development in the Protestant churches was the social gospel movement. It taught that the saving of society was necessary to the saving of souls. The poverty in the cities, the loss of church membership among the working people, and the wide acceptance of science caused religious leaders to rethink some of the concerns of their churches. Leaders of the social gospel movement said that much of the poverty in the industrial cities arose from conditions for which the individual could not be blamed.

The Catholic Church, too, felt the challenges of science and the industrial society. Its leaders took a conservative stand on the new scientific trends. In the United States some Catholic leaders opposed the social agitation of the 1880's and 1890's. But others believed that the workers and the poor—many of them Catholic immigrants—suffered from injustices caused by society and needed help from the church. In 1891, in a public letter called *Rerum Novarum,* Pope Leo XIII supported this view. He condemned the evils of the industrial system as "laying upon the shoulders of the working classes a yoke little better than slavery itself."

The Protestant and Jewish faiths were based primarily on biblical interpretation, while Catholicism concentrated on the sacraments. In the light of new knowledge, many Protestants and Jews applied scientific principles to biblical interpretation. The result was drastic change.

Within the Protestant sector, a number of heresy trials were held. One of two basic questions was usually at stake: Was the Bible to be interpreted literally or figuratively? Was Charles Darwin's theory of evolution correct? The resulting split between those who believed in a literal interpretation of the Bible and those who believed otherwise has not yet been resolved.

The application of scientific principles to religious beliefs took place at much the same time that a great number of Jews left Europe for America. Along with criticism of Talmudic writings came a concern for practical problems faced by American Jews. In the 1880's, Conservative Judaism was developed in the United States. Conservative Jews refused to go along with some of the changes promoted by Reform Jews but at the same time rejected some of the traditional practices of Orthodox Judaism.

The Catholic Church faced practical problems of nationality. By the 1880's the leaders of the church were mostly Americans of Irish descent. But the Catholic immigrants who streamed into the eastern ports were mostly Italian, Polish, or Slavic. They demanded, and eventually got, a few priests and nuns who spoke the same language. But several national churches splintered off from the Roman church.

Universities

A key date in the shift to a practical and scientific emphasis in universities was 1869. In that year a scientist became president of Harvard University, the nation's oldest institution of higher learning. He raised entrance requirements, enlarged the faculty, and introduced new courses. He also put the elective system into practice. Under this system, students were given wider freedom in choosing subjects. Harvard's changes had a great influence on other colleges.

The Johns Hopkins University, founded in Baltimore, Maryland, in 1876, set the pattern for advanced study in the United States. Unlike other universities, Johns Hopkins primarily offered graduate work. It stressed training in research through the use of laboratories and small seminars.

Scientific and practical trends made most rapid headway in several new private universities. Two of the most notable were Stanford University, founded in 1885 by railroad builder Leland Stanford, and the University of Chicago, created in 1891 and endowed by John D. Rockefeller.

State universities, too, responded to the new educational trends. Legislatures generally insisted that modern languages, modern history, and mechanical and agricultural sciences be included in the curriculum. Unlike the private colleges, most of the state universities admitted women undergraduates, but female students were few.

Women's education had received a big boost in the 1860's and 1870's with the opening of a number of women's colleges. The new institutions faced a lack of funds and of fully qualified students. The money problems were solved by greater endowments from generous individuals. The schools dealt with unqualified students by helping them to qualify for college work. Most of the new colleges—including Vassar and Wellesley—had preparatory departments, where young women could take concentrated courses that would prepare them for college-level work. By the 1880's, the general level of women's education had improved to such a point that the colleges began closing down their "prep" departments.

Writers

During the 1870's and 1880's, a number of writers revolted against *romanticism,* a fanciful and sentimental approach to literature. They tried to write fiction that would be true to human experience, that would portray men and women as they really behaved.

William Dean Howells, magazine editor, was the leader of the *realist* school. Howells recorded in his novels some of the problems of life in industrial America. His most widely read novel, *The Rise of Silas Lapham* (1885), dealt with a self-made businessman in a changing society.

Unlike Howells, Henry James found it hard to work in the United States, with its

Above: Young boys join in the excitement of a circus parade on Pennsylvania Avenue in Washington, D.C. *Opposite:* William and Caroline Astor and family pose for a portrait in their Fifth Avenue mansion. The ornate furniture and decoration were considered the height of expensive good taste.

materialistic atmosphere. He went to England and eventually became a British subject. His was a psychological realism. One of his finest novels, *The Portrait of a Lady* (1881), showed a naïve American girl caught in a decadent European society.

Mark Twain, whose real name was Samuel L. Clemens, was more successful than any other writer in capturing the tone, the values, and the attitudes of contemporary American society. His book *The Gilded Age* (1873), written with Charles Dudley Warner, ridiculed the materialism and the get-rich-quick spirit of the times. Twain based *The Adventures of Tom Sawyer* (1876) on his own boyhood in Hannibal, Missouri. He followed it with a sequel, *The Adventures of Huckleberry Finn* (1884). In this, his greatest novel, he exposed—through the sharp-witted but uneducated Huck Finn and his black friend, Jim—the brutality, greed, intolerance, and hypocrisy he found in the American society he knew.

The United States produced few important poets in the late nineteenth century, but Emily Dickinson stands out. Spending her life in seclusion, Dickinson wrote hundreds of gemlike bits of verse in which she expressed a vivid concern with humanity and nature. Her work remained virtually unknown until long after her death because she permitted only two of her poems to be published while she was alive.

Popular Culture

Most Americans ignored the works of these novelists and poets. The reading public, which grew larger as literacy and leisure spread, preferred stories of romance and adventure. One of the best-selling novels, General Lew Wallace's *Ben Hur* (1880), carried a religious message as well as an adventure theme. Poets like James Whitcomb Riley wrote sentimental verse about childhood and country life. Regional fiction like that of Sarah Orne Jewett was widely read.

Literature for children found a growing market. One of the earliest and most successful books for children was Louisa May Alcott's *Little Women* (1868). Also popular were the success stories of Horatio Alger, who wrote 135 books on a rags-to-riches theme between 1867 and 1899. Children also delighted in "dime novels," crude adventure tales that were published with cheap paper bindings.

Public libraries, as well as the writers of dime novels, catered to popular tastes. After the Civil War, hundreds of communities began using taxes to support lending libraries. Beginning in 1881, Andrew Carnegie paid for the building of libraries on the condition that towns supply the land and the maintenance. Carnegie helped set up more than 2,500 public libraries.

Adult education also became popular. The Chautauqua assembly gained the greatest attention. This assembly began in 1874 at Lake Chautauqua, New York, with a summer training program for Sunday-school teachers. Within a few years, other places had similar assemblies of their own or had programs sent out from the Chautauqua headquarters. Audiences throughout the country heard bands, singers, and speakers.

For entertainment, however, Americans turned to several sources. One was the traveling circus, the most famous of which was Phineas T. Barnum's "greatest show on earth." Vaudeville—traveling variety acts—became increasingly popular after 1885, when Benjamin F. Keith's theater in Boston introduced continuous performances at low prices. Especially important to small towns were "medicine shows." These toured the

Mark Twain sent this autographed picture *(above)* to a friend with a characteristic bit of advice: "Be good and you will be lonesome." *Opposite:* A young woman judges her appearance in a new dress and hat. As wages rose, more people could avail themselves of luxuries in dress and furnishings.

country, putting on brief performances to stir interest in the patent medicines they sold.

Spectator sports drew a larger and larger attendance. The first men's league of professional baseball teams was formed in 1876, and championship games began in 1883. College football developed rapidly after 1869. Basketball was invented in 1891. Boxing became more or less respectable in the 1880's, after the introduction (from England) of the Marquis of Queensberry rules.

In the late nineteenth century, it became more socially acceptable for women to engage in sports. Women still had to wear heavy clothing that hid their bodies but also restricted their breathing and movements.

Increasingly, they were able to engage in such sports as tennis, bicycling, swimming, and gymnastics.

The most interesting and enduring American music of the period came from the people—from gang laborers on the railroads, from women scrubbing clothes on washboards, from cowboys on the plains, from farmers in the Ozark Mountains, and especially from southern blacks. The spirituals, blues, and jazz of black Americans enriched the nation's music. By 1900, ragtime and jazz —which became the basis of much American popular music—were being played by white as well as black musicians in Mississippi River cities from New Orleans to St. Louis.

Newspapers and Magazines

With the introduction of the Linotype machine in 1886, printers no longer had to set type by hand. Newspapers therefore could be printed much more quickly and cheaply and could reach a much larger reading public.

The journalist who pioneered in making newspapers appeal to the people was Joseph Pulitzer, an immigrant from Hungary. In 1878, Pulitzer bought the bankrupt *St. Louis Dispatch* and made it a going concern. Five years later he bought the *New York World.* Under Pulitzer, the *World* crusaded for reforms. It also gave its readers sensational accounts of murders and other crimes, superior news coverage, and special features like the first comic strip in color.

Pulitzer's success attracted imitators. One of them was William Randolph Hearst, a wealthy young man from San Francisco. After buying the *New York Journal* in 1895, Hearst outdid Pulitzer in sensationalism, attempting to draw readers away from the *World.* Both papers used yellow ink in their comics, and their sensational, lurid, and cutthroat methods came to be known as "yellow journalism." As practiced by Pulitzer and Hearst, yellow journalism had redeeming qualities. Pulitzer made his paper generally public-spirited. Hearst, in his nationwide network of papers, attacked religious prejudice and appealed for social justice.

Many other newspapers followed the pattern set by Pulitzer and Hearst. Most of them tried to report the news accurately, though often sensationally. They broadened their coverage of foreign news and, through their influence on public opinion, sometimes affected United States diplomacy.

Like the newspapers, magazines reacted to social and cultural forces. They also catered to the thirst for knowledge among the people. In the 1880's and 1890's, a number of magazines, low in price but relatively high in literary quality, gained mass circulation. Among these were *Cosmopolitan, Collier's, National Geographic Magazine, Munsey's Magazine,* and the *Saturday Evening Post.* Most successful of all was the *Ladies' Home Journal,* founded in 1883. Many Americans found excitement and adventure as well as knowledge in the new magazines.

AN IMPERIALISTIC POLICY

By the 1890's, territorial expansion was already an old theme in the nation's history. Before the Civil War, the United States had enlarged its territory repeatedly. Other territories might have been added if the nation had not been divided by sectional controversy and the Civil War. In 1867, Alaska and the Midway Islands were obtained. But further expansion was delayed because the American people were busy with the reconstruction of the South, the conquest of the West, and the development of industry.

The New Expansionism

The American expansionism of the 1890's differed in important ways from that of earlier times. In the early nineteenth century the United States had been concerned with getting new territories that were (1) next to the existing territory of the United States, (2) sparsely populated and suitable for settlement by migrating Americans, and (3) suitable for organization as states. The new expansionism, on the other hand, was concerned with the winning of lands that were (1) separated from the United States by water, (2) densely populated or otherwise unsuitable for settlement by Americans, and (3) likely to remain indefinitely in a territorial or colonial condition.

"Whether they will or not, Americans must now begin to look outward," Alfred Thayer Mahan had declared in 1890. Mahan, an officer of the United States Navy, was the most important American backer of overseas expansion. He wrote a number of books and articles on the influence of sea power in history. Mahan believed that to be great, a nation must control ocean routes throughout the world. He therefore wanted the United States to build up its navy and merchant marine and set up naval bases and refueling stations in the islands of the Caribbean and Pacific. He also urged the building of a canal across the Isthmus of Panama.

Imperialism is the theme of this British cartoon of 1898. The United States dines on Cuba, "Porto" Rico, and the Philippines while other nations carve up China. England remarks, "We can't grudge him a light lunch while we are feasting."

Already, many Americans were beginning to "look outward." One reason for this was the rapid growth of American exports, which doubled between 1870 and 1890. Another was the imperialism of the European powers, which were dividing Africa into separate colonies and were threatening to do the same with China. This made it seem that the United States, for its own trade and its own defense, must acquire overseas territories.

In the minds of some American leaders, there was still another reason for adopting an imperialistic policy. The American people, many of them bitterly discontented, were quarreling among themselves. Some leaders thought that an active, dramatic foreign policy would divert the people from their domestic problems and would reunite the nation.

Hawaii and Samoa

The acquisition of California and, later, of Alaska had helped turn the attention of Americans to the Pacific. Long before that, United States ships had been trading with East Asia. The first of these entered Canton, China, shortly after the American Revolution. Trade with China grew steadily, and in 1830, the first American missionaries entered that country. American whalers soon began to roam the Pacific in search of whales, which were becoming scarce in the Atlantic. Commodore Matthew C. Perry opened the door to trade with Japan in 1854. Traders, fishermen, and naval officers put in at various Pacific islands to look for economic or strategic possibilities.

From the American point of view, the most important Pacific islands were those of the Hawaiian group. In 1820, some New England missionaries arrived there; they and their descendants remained to grow pineapples and sugar cane. In time, the Americans living in Hawaii had considerable influence with the native rulers. Most of the ships in Hawaiian ports were American, and most Hawaiian trade was with the United States. American business leaders and politicians were determined that the islands should fall to no other power. A treaty of annexation was drafted in 1854, but southerners opposed taking on free territory, and the treaty was never ratified.

Hawaii continued, however, to be drawn closer to the United States. In 1875, the islands became a United States *protectorate,* a nation whose nominal independence was protected and whose foreign policy was controlled by the United States. By the terms of a commercial treaty, Hawaiian sugar would enter the United States duty free, but the Hawaiian government agreed to make no economic or territorial concessions to other powers. In 1887, another treaty gave the United States the exclusive right to use Pearl Harbor as a naval base.

Trouble for the Americans began in 1891, when Queen Liliuokalani came to the Hawaiian throne. She intended to put an end to American influence. Two years later, the American residents in Hawaii rebelled. They had the help of the United States minister to Hawaii, who ordered United States Marines to be landed from a warship at Honolulu, supposedly to protect American life and property. The Americans overthrew the queen, set up a temporary government, and requested annexation.

A treaty of annexation was drawn up. Before the United States Senate had approved it, however, the administration of Benjamin Harrison ended, and Grover Cleveland returned to the presidency (1893). Cleveland thought it was improper for the marines to have taken part in the revolution. He withdrew the treaty from the Senate and tried to restore Queen Liliuokalani to her throne. But when she threatened to execute the revolutionists, Cleveland decided to let the matter drop. He recognized Hawaii as an independent republic but refused to annex it.

Annexation had to wait until William McKinley became President and a war drew attention to the strategic importance of Hawaii. Even so, McKinley doubted that two-thirds of the Senate would vote for an annexation treaty. Hence Hawaii was annexed, in 1898, by a joint resolution, which required only a simple majority in both houses of Congress.

The interest of the United States in the Samoan Islands led to conflict with European powers. American land and steamship companies had commercial plans for the Samoan Islands. The United States government was most attracted by the harbor of Pago Pago on the island of Tutuila. The almost landlocked harbor was an ideal spot for a naval base. In 1872, a Samoan king and a United States naval officer made a treaty giving the United States the use of the harbor. British and German firms, however, were also interested in Samoa, especially in its valuable coconut crop.

A three-way rivalry for the control of the Samoan Islands developed. In 1889, warships of the three nations almost came to blows. Suddenly, a hurricane struck, scattering or sinking most of the ships and ending the threat of a battle. That same year, the three powers agreed to a joint protectorate over the islands. But this resulted in renewed disputes. Finally, in 1899, Germany and the United States divided the islands between them. The United States retained Tutuila (American Samoa) with its valuable harbor at Pago Pago. Britain surrendered its claims in return for rights in West Africa and elsewhere in the Pacific.

Pan-Americanism

Pan-Americanism is the idea that the Latin American nations and the United States have important interests in common and should work together to further those interests. The United States had been invited to send two delegates to the first Pan-American conference, in Panama in 1825. But one delegate died on the way, and the other arrived after the meeting had ended. The United States played a leading role, however, at the next Pan-American conference, which met in Washington, D.C., in 1889. The person who did the most to revive Pan-Americanism was James G. Blaine, secretary of state under President Garfield (1881) and under President Harrison (1889–1892).

Blaine was upset because Britain controlled the bulk of the Latin American trade. He hoped to improve relations with the Latin American nations so that they would buy more manufactured goods from the United States. He planned a conference to discuss the settlement of disputes and the improvement of communications and commerce, with the United States taking the part of the "elder sister."

In 1889, delegates from seventeen Latin American nations arrived in Washington, D.C. First, they were taken by special train on a 6,000-mile tour of the nation's industrial centers. When the exhausted delegates returned to Washington, they accomplished three important things.

One was an agreement to reduce the tariffs on each other's goods. A second achievement was the formation of the International Bureau of American Republics (later called the Pan-American Union). It was intended to distribute information, encourage better understanding, and promote the peaceful settlement of disputes. The governing body of the Pan-American Union consisted of the Latin American diplomatic representatives in Washington and the United States secretary of state, who was the presiding officer. Third, the meeting set a precedent for further Pan-American, or Inter-American, conferences. These have been held every five or six years since 1889.

Strengthening the Monroe Doctrine

In the Monroe Doctrine (1823), the United States said that it opposed any effort on the part of a European power to extend its possessions or influence in the Americas. Since 1823, the doctrine had been invoked a number of times. In 1895–1896, the doctrine was restated in its broadest and most forceful terms yet. The occasion was a boundary dispute between Britain and Venezuela.

The boundary between British Guiana and Venezuela had never been definitely settled, and the quarrel over it grew worse when gold was discovered in the disputed area. By 1895, President Cleveland had begun to fear that Britain might use its power to force its interpretation of the boundary upon Venezuela. With Cleveland's approval, Secretary of State Richard T. Olney accused Britain of violating the Monroe Doctrine.

The British government, in its reply to Olney's note, refused to recognize the Monroe Doctrine as international law. It also said that the doctrine had no bearing on the boundary question. This angered Cleveland. He proposed to Congress that the United States take charge of the matter, send a commission to locate the true boundary, and be prepared to maintain this line by force.

Cleveland's message to Congress aroused a good deal of fighting spirit in Britain and in the United States. Although war preparations were begun on both sides of the Atlantic, cooler heads prevailed. A friendly petition from the House of Commons was sent to Washington. The English people did not want to go to war over a far-off tropical jungle, rich in gold though it might be. Besides, the British government was having troubles with Dutch settlers in South Africa and had no wish to add to its difficulties. Britain agreed to submit the Venezuela boundary to arbitration, as Cleveland and Olney had demanded. In the final settlement in 1899, the arbitrators gave Britain most of the land it had claimed in the first place.

By his stand on the Venezuela boundary, Cleveland successfully applied the Monroe

Doctrine against the greatest naval power in the world. The prestige of the doctrine was enhanced. At the same time, strangely enough, Anglo-American relations were greatly improved. Henceforth, war between the two great English-speaking nations seemed unthinkable.

A WAR WITH SPAIN

The Spanish-American War began with an effort by the United States to free Cuba from Spanish rule. Fighting took place not only in Cuba but also in other Spanish colonies—Puerto Rico and the Philippine Islands. The war ended with the United States dominating Cuba and taking over Puerto Rico, the Philippines, and Guam.

Ever since the time of Thomas Jefferson, Americans had been interested in Cuba, 90 miles from Florida. Before the Civil War, the United States government had tried to purchase the island. Some Americans had taken part in unauthorized military expeditions in attempts to liberate Cuba from Spain. The Cubans themselves fought an unsuccessful war for independence from 1868 to 1878. At that time, Americans generally sympathized with the Cuban rebels, and some Americans thought the United States government should step in and help them. But President Grant's secretary of state, Hamilton Fish, managed to prevent intervention.

When the Cubans rebelled in 1895, many more Americans demanded intervention. Americans now had a greater interest in Cuba than before. Some of them had invested large sums of money in Cuban mines, tobacco plantations, and sugar fields and mills. Certain political leaders were deeply impressed with the strategic importance of Cuba. They expected that a canal would eventually be built somewhere in Central America, and Cuba stood near the Atlantic approach to such a canal. A war to liberate Cuba could also seem like a glorious adventure. Since 1865, many people in the United States had forgotten the horrors of war, and a new generation had grown up that had never known them.

A squadron of six United States ships battles the Spanish in Manila Bay in the Philippines, May 1, 1898. After seven hours of fighting, all the Spanish ships were destroyed or captured. *Opposite:* Houses burn in Manila during the guerrilla war waged by Filipino nationalists against the American army. The Filipino uprising was ended in 1901.

A Catchy Slogan

The Cuban revolt of 1895 came about largely because of economic conditions on the island. These had grown worse with the coming of the worldwide depression in 1893, and still worse with the passage of the Wilson-Gorman tariff of 1894. That law put a high duty on Cuban sugar and thus cut down the sales to the United States. As unemployment and poverty spread, the rebels made conditions worse. Operating at night, bands of guerrillas burned sugar mills and ruined sugar plantations. They deliberately destroyed American property, for they wanted the United States government to intervene, stop the rebellion, and bring about Cuban independence.

The Spanish government sent General Valeriano Weyler to Cuba with reinforcements of troops. Weyler found it impossible to put down the revolt by regular military methods, for the rebels avoided open battle. They burned and destroyed property at night and became peaceful citizens in the daytime. Therefore, in the areas of greatest destruction, Weyler rounded up men, women, and children indiscriminately and put them in camps where he could watch them. Thousands of these people died of starvation and disease.

The American people were aroused by news of Weyler's activities. The *New York World* and the *New York Journal* made the most of their opportunity to sell papers by printing sensational news. These and other papers throughout the country gave much space to the doings of "Butcher" Weyler and to other cases of real or alleged Spanish cruelty. They seldom mentioned, however, the destruction and suffering that the Cuban guerrillas were causing. Representatives of the rebels were busy in cities in the United

States arousing sympathy and getting money and arms for the revolutionary effort.

In February 1898, two events excited people in the United States. First, the Hearst papers published a private letter written by the Spanish minister in Washington, Enrique Dupuy de Lôme. The letter had been stolen from the Cuban post office. In the letter, Dupuy de Lôme described President McKinley as a "would-be politician" who was "weak and a bidder for the admiration of the crowd." Hence, said Dupuy de Lôme, the United States would probably go to war with Spain, since McKinley could not or would not resist the demand for war. When this letter was published, Dupuy de Lôme resigned. The American people considered his words an insult to the President and to the nation.

Six days later, on February 15, 1898, the American battleship *Maine* blew up while anchored in Havana harbor. Some 260 members of the crew were killed. Many Americans jumped to the conclusion that the Spanish authorities had destroyed the ship. Actually, the Cubans had more reason for doing so, since they were eager to bring the United States into the war. The cause of the explosion has never been determined; it may have been accidental.

Nevertheless, the yellow journals attributed the disaster to Spanish agents and demanded United States intervention in Cuba. Soon Americans were repeating the slogan: "Remember the *Maine!*"

The United States government now insisted that the Spanish government grant home rule to the Cubans and restore peace on the island. Step by step, Spain moved toward accepting all of the American demands. Finally, on April 9, it suspended hostilities in Cuba.

Despite the Spanish action, two days later, President McKinley sent Congress a war message. He mentioned the latest Spanish concessions, but nevertheless asked Congress to authorize the use of the armed forces to force the Spanish out of Cuba. Congress passed the desired resolution on April 20, after adding the Teller Amendment. This amendment pledged that the United States would "leave the government and control of the Island to its people," after freeing and pacifying Cuba.

An American Victory

The war that followed was short. It lasted only 115 days and cost fewer than 3,000 American lives. Of these, more died from disease than from battle wounds.

Thanks partly to the assistant secretary of the navy, Theodore Roosevelt, the navy was an efficient fighting force. On February 28, 1898, Roosevelt had secretly ordered Commodore George Dewey to gather the Pacific fleet and be prepared to head for the Philippines in case of war. Following orders, Dewey steamed to Manila Bay after the war declaration. There, on May 1, he fought and

Theodore Roosevelt and the Rough Riders pose on San Juan Hill. Roosevelt was actually the commander of the charge up Kettle Hill, but he was billed in the news as the hero of San Juan. His unit received more publicity than any other in the army.

won the first battle of the war. He had no troops with which to take the city of Manila, and so he waited for reinforcements. Late in July, soldiers arrived, and on August 13 the city surrendered.

Meanwhile, the people living on the Atlantic coast of the United States were worried about the possibility of a Spanish attack. A fleet under Admiral William T. Sampson was sent out to intercept the Spanish ships led by Admiral Pascual Cervera, but Cervera slipped into Santiago harbor (May 19). Sampson then proceeded to blockade the harbor, thereby bottling up Cervera's fleet.

The United States Army was much less ready for war than the navy. Consisting of only 28,000 officers and men, the regular army was led by senior officers who had seen service in the Civil War. They were too old and physically unfit to lead troops into battle, particularly in the tropics. Commanding the troops sent to Cuba was General William R. Shafter, who was sixty-three years old and weighed three hundred pounds.

Congress authorized the calling of 125,000 volunteers. Roosevelt resigned his navy department position and helped organize a cavalry regiment known as the Rough Riders, an assortment of cowboys and college students. They were led by Colonel Leonard Wood and Roosevelt.

In May, the combined army began to assemble at Tampa, Florida. The congestion and confusion grew worse as more and more units arrived. Many of these lacked equipment and found no campsites ready to receive them. They were given heavy woolen uniforms, wholly unsuitable for the hot Cuban sun. Their rations included uneatable and sometimes spoiled canned meat, which they called "embalmed beef."

Despite the difficulties, part of the army sailed on June 14, and soon about 17,000 troops landed on the southern coast of Cuba. They were ordered to march to Santiago and approach the city from the land side. Spanish troops defending the city occupied positions on San Juan Hill. On July 1, with the aid of the Rough Riders, the American regulars captured the last of the Spanish positions. Although Roosevelt had a minor part in the battle, he was hailed in American newspapers as the hero of San Juan Hill.

Cervera, with his fleet in Santiago harbor, now could either surrender or try to escape. On July 3, the Spanish tried to run the American blockade. All of Cervera's ships were sunk or were forced aground. Two weeks later, on July 17, the Spanish army in Santiago surrendered.

General Nelson A. Miles landed a force on Puerto Rico on July 26. His troops moved rapidly across the island, receiving an enthusiastic welcome from the Puerto Ricans and very little opposition from the Spaniards. Only three Americans were killed in the entire Puerto Rican campaign.

New Overseas Territories

On August 12, 1898, Spain agreed to an armistice. Commissioners representing the United States and Spain met in Paris in October to make peace terms. Both sides readily agreed that Cuba should be given independence and that Puerto Rico and Guam should be ceded to the United States. The most difficult question the peacemakers faced was what to do with the Philippines.

Before the war, few Americans had known about these islands. There was, however, a small group of leaders, including Roosevelt and Mahan, who wished to get the Philippines for the United States. They were interested in Manila Bay as a naval base, and they valued the Philippines for economic reasons. The islands presumably would provide opportunities for trade and investment and would serve as stepping stones to the commerce of China. In the course of the war, many American business leaders had become aware of the economic possibilities of the islands.

When the war ended, President McKinley had not made up his mind what to do with the Philippines. He finally instructed the American peace commissioners in Paris to keep them. The Spaniards proved unwilling, however, to give up the islands. They agreed to do so only after the United States promised to pay 20 million dollars to Spain.

The Treaty of Paris (signed on December 10, 1898) was approved by the United States Senate (February 6, 1899) after a great debate and by the margin of a single vote. Thus the war, which had begun as a crusade to free a Spanish colony from Spain, ended with the transfer of other Spanish colonies to the United States.

By 1899, United States possessions dotted the Pacific. They formed a strategically valuable line of bases for shipping. In the Caribbean, possessions and protectorates were rapidly acquired. These became more important as interest grew in building a canal across the Isthmus of Panama.

ARGUING ABOUT IMPERIALISM

The armed forces of the United States had won quick victories on land and sea, and the American diplomats had got what they wanted at the peace conference in Paris. Nevertheless, a Yale professor, William Graham Sumner, afterwards wrote an article with the title "The Conquest of the United States by Spain." Professor Sumner claimed that Spain had really won the war, for its colonial policies were being adopted and continued by the United States. Thus, he said, Spanish ideas and practices were victorious.

There was an element of truth in what Professor Sumner wrote. In the Philippines and in Cuba, the United States found itself in a position similar to the one that Spain had been in before the war. In both places, however, the United States did more than Spain had done to promote the welfare of the people.

Cuba and the Philippines

Under General Leonard Wood as military governor (1899–1902), the United States occupation forces restored order to Cuba and set up an efficient government. Improvements were made in education, transportation, and particularly in public health. During an epidemic, Dr. Walter Reed, an army surgeon, proved that mosquitoes carried yellow fever. Acting on this information, American authorities made Havana entirely free from yellow fever by 1901.

In the Teller Amendment to the war resolution, Congress had promised that the United States would return control of the island to the Cubans. After the war, how-

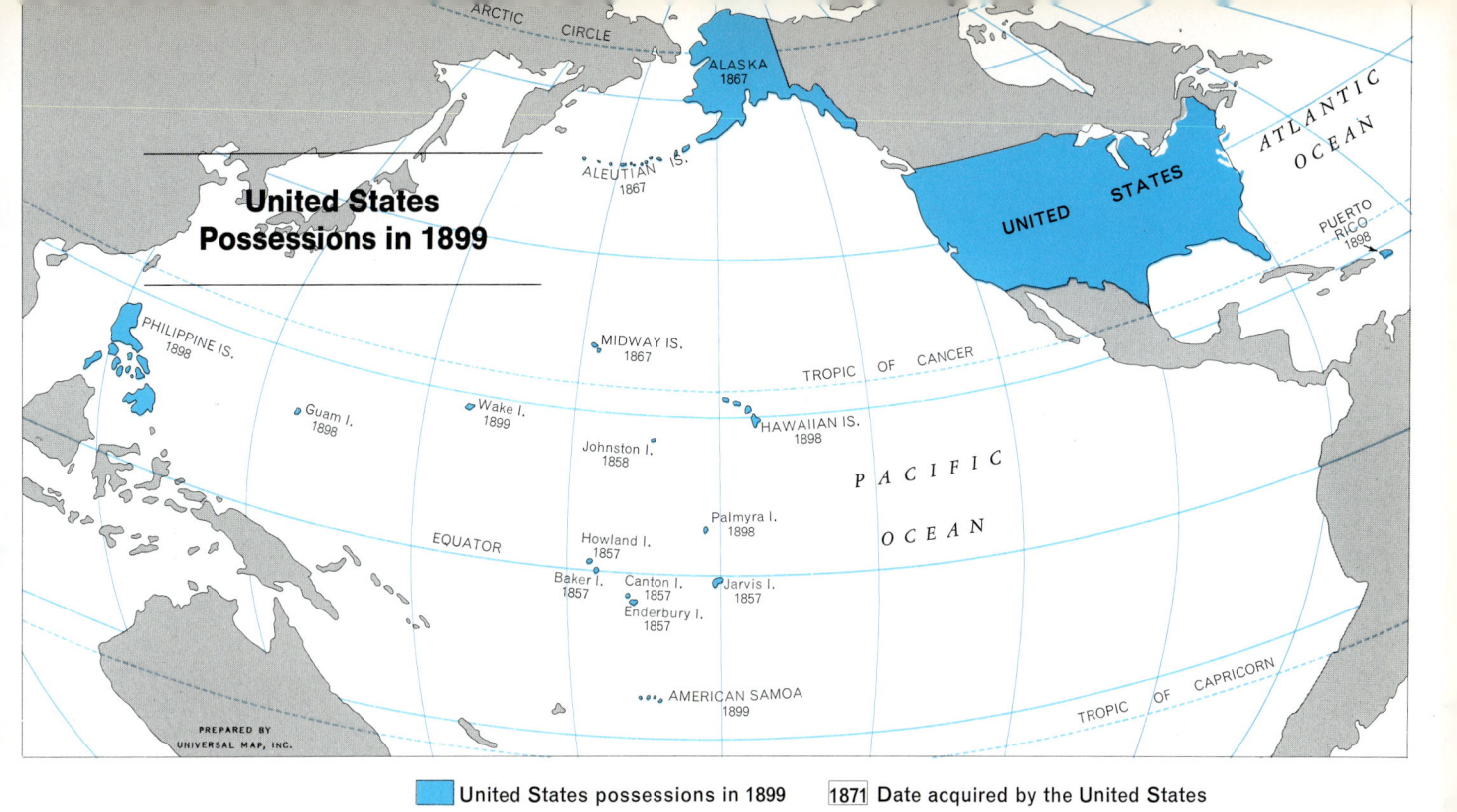

United States Possessions in 1899

■ United States possessions in 1899   [1871] Date acquired by the United States

ever, the fear arose that Cuba might come under the influence of Germany or some other power that could then use the island as a base for threatening the United States. Hence Congress adopted an amendment, introduced by Senator Orville Platt of Connecticut, to the army appropriation bill of 1901.

The Platt Amendment provided (1) that Cuba should make no treaties that might impair its independence and should allow no foreign power to control any part of the island, (2) that Cuba should contract no public debt too large to be paid from the island's own revenues, (3) that the United States should have the right to intervene in order to preserve Cuban independence or to maintain law and order, and (4) that the United States should be permitted to lease certain parts of the island for naval bases. These provisions had to be written into the Cuban constitution and into a treaty with the United States before the United States troops were removed from Cuba. In effect, Cuba had become a protectorate of the United States. Troops were withdrawn in 1902 but were sent back several times to put down unrest and restore order.

In taking over the Philippines, the United States became involved in a war that dragged on. Many of the Filipinos had no more desire to be ruled by the United States than to be ruled by Spain. They supported a government set up by the native leader Emilio Aguinaldo. On February 4, 1899, fighting broke out between Aguinaldo's forces and United States troops. Both sides resorted to savage methods of warfare and treated their prisoners cruelly. After trapping Aguinaldo, in March 1901, the Americans won over most of his followers by offering them pardons and food. This war cost more than 7,000 American casualties and 600 million dollars.

Already, the United States had begun a colonial policy that was intended to improve the general welfare of the Filipinos. In 1900, President McKinley sent a commission, headed by William Howard Taft, to the Philippines to help form a civil government. Taft served as the first American governor of the Philippines (1901–1904). In 1902, Congress authorized the establishment of a legislature with a lower house to be elected by Filipino voters and an upper house to consist of the United States commission and three appointed Filipinos.

Meanwhile, the American authorities in the Philippines helped build schools, roads, railroads, and telegraph lines, and improve sanitation. Illiteracy declined, infant mortality was greatly reduced, and smallpox and cholera were virtually wiped out. Under United States control, the Philippines soon enjoyed more prosperity than before, but the question of when the islands would gain independence was left unanswered.

Imperialists Versus Anti-imperialists

Throughout the country, from 1898 to 1900, the debate on imperialism was focused on one question: should the United States keep the Philippines? Most of the Republicans, including Senators Henry Cabot Lodge of Massachusetts and Albert J. Beveridge of Indiana, favored doing so. Lodge and Beveridge led the struggle for approving the peace treaty with Spain. The supporters of annexation used many arguments. They appealed to

United States troops guard captured Filipinos suspected of guerrilla activities. In the three-year war in the islands, American losses were estimated at 4,300 lives. Estimates of Filipino losses ranged from a low of 20,000 to a high of 600,000 lives.

national pride, saying it would be dishonorable to "haul down the flag" in the Philippines. They appealed to economic interests. And they appealed to the missionary spirit of the country. They claimed that Americans had a duty to teach the Filipinos democracy and Christianity (though a majority of the Filipinos were already Christians, having been converted by the Spaniards).

Some Republicans and most Democrats took the anti-imperialist side. The anti-imperialists claimed that it would be undemocratic as well as unconstitutional to hold people in subjection as colonists. Yet it would be impossible to provide democracy of the American type for peoples who were so different from Americans. To impose undemocratic government on colonies would weaken democracy at home, they said. Moreover, the control and protection of overseas possessions would require an increase in the army and the navy and, along with this, an increase in taxation. The anti-imperialists insisted that imperialism would involve the United States in entanglements and possibly in wars with European powers or with Japan. The Philippine insurrection, with all its cost in money and in blood, was proof enough of the evils of forcing American rule upon unwilling people, they said.

Opponents of the Philippine annexation organized the Anti-Imperialist League. Its membership included two former Presidents of the United States, Benjamin Harrison and Grover Cleveland, a number of college and university presidents, and such people as Carl Schurz, Jane Addams, Mark Twain, Andrew Carnegie, and Samuel Gompers.

The former Democratic presidential candidate William Jennings Bryan was a leading opponent of imperialism. He was, however, largely responsible for the Senate's approval of the peace treaty, with its provision for the transfer of the Philippines to the United States. The Senate at that time contained enough Democrats to defeat the treaty. Bryan advised the Democrats to vote for it. His aim, he later said, was to have the United States take the Philippines from Spain and then set them free. He hoped to win the election of 1900 by demanding independence for the Philippines.

The Campaign of 1900

As the election of 1900 approached, President McKinley was extremely popular, partly because of prosperity and partly because of his conduct of the war with Spain. He easily won renomination by the Republicans. The party platform endorsed prosperity, the gold standard, and expansion.

Since Vice-President Garret A. Hobart had died in 1899, the Republican convention had to choose someone for second place on the ticket. This gave the political boss of New York State a chance to get rid of the state's young governor, Theodore Roosevelt, the "hero" of San Juan Hill. Roosevelt was vigorously attacking corruption, promoting social legislation, and refusing to cooperate with the bosses. By making Roosevelt Vice-President, the bosses could get him out of the way.

McKinley went along with the idea, since Roosevelt, as a war hero, would bring glamour to the Republican ticket. But Roosevelt threatened to return to private life rather than be retired to the powerless position of Vice-President. Nevertheless, he accepted the nomination when it was offered to him. Mark Hanna, the Ohio political boss, who distrusted Roosevelt, told McKinley: "Your *duty* to the country is to *live* for four years from next March."

PRESIDENTIAL ELECTIONS: 1892-1900

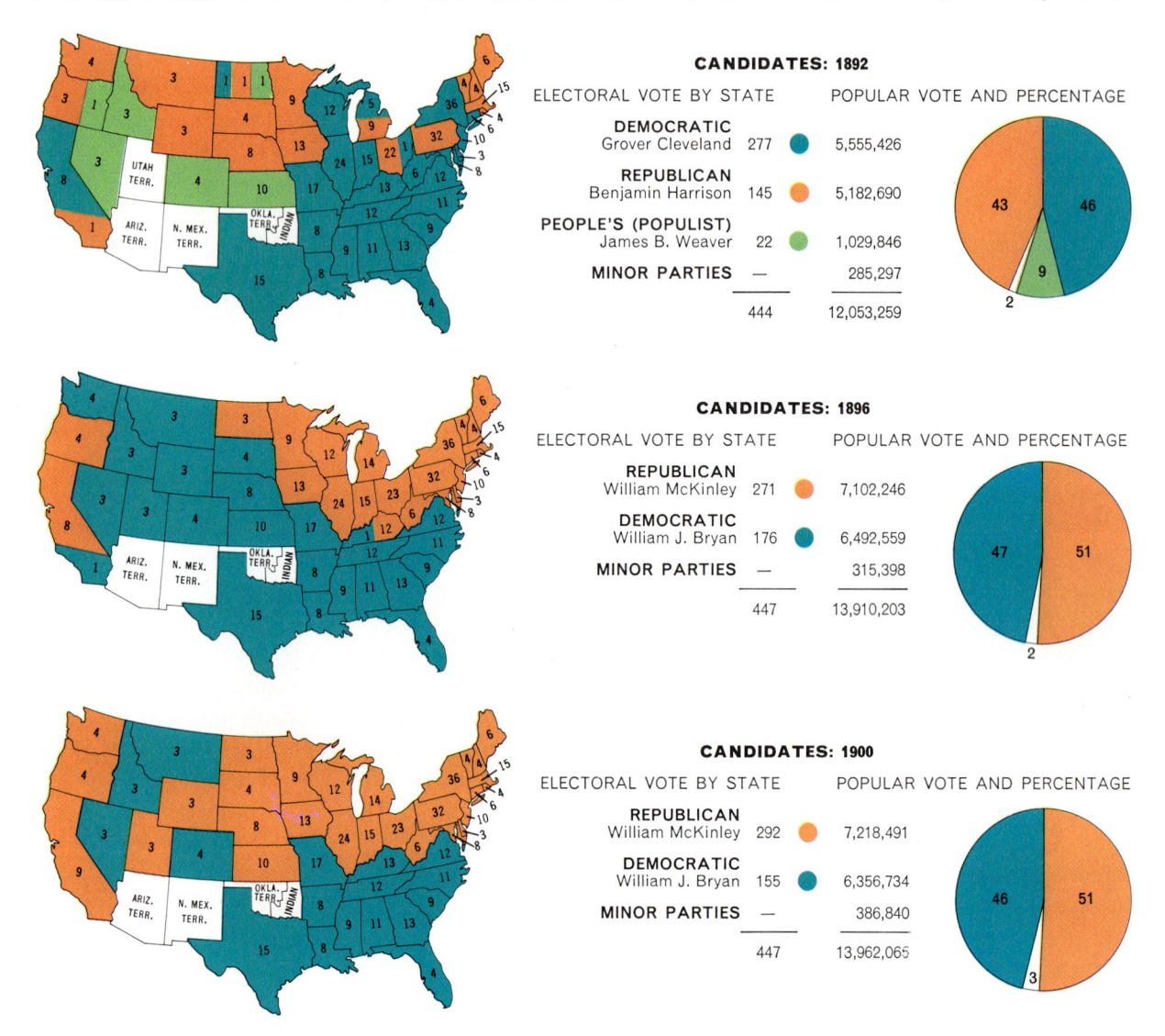

CANDIDATES: 1892

ELECTORAL VOTE BY STATE		POPULAR VOTE AND PERCENTAGE
DEMOCRATIC Grover Cleveland	277	5,555,426
REPUBLICAN Benjamin Harrison	145	5,182,690
PEOPLE'S (POPULIST) James B. Weaver	22	1,029,846
MINOR PARTIES	—	285,297
	444	12,053,259

Democratic 46, Republican 43, Populist 9, Minor 2

CANDIDATES: 1896

ELECTORAL VOTE BY STATE		POPULAR VOTE AND PERCENTAGE
REPUBLICAN William McKinley	271	7,102,246
DEMOCRATIC William J. Bryan	176	6,492,559
MINOR PARTIES	—	315,398
	447	13,910,203

Republican 51, Democratic 47, Minor 2

CANDIDATES: 1900

ELECTORAL VOTE BY STATE		POPULAR VOTE AND PERCENTAGE
REPUBLICAN William McKinley	292	7,218,491
DEMOCRATIC William J. Bryan	155	6,356,734
MINOR PARTIES	—	386,840
	447	13,962,065

Republican 51, Democratic 46, Minor 3

The Democrats nominated William Jennings Bryan as their presidential candidate. At his insistence, the Democratic platform demanded free silver and condemned Republican imperialism.

As in 1896, McKinley stayed home and conducted a "front porch" campaign. Republicans speaking in his behalf made the most of the nation's prosperity, repeating the party slogans: "The Full Dinner Pail" and "Let Well Enough Alone." Bryan again stumped the country, insisting this time that imperialism was the main issue. McKinley won by a larger margin than in 1896, receiving 51 percent of the votes. Some Republicans claimed that the returns meant a mandate for imperialism, but it is more likely that the voters had simply favored prosperity.

Six months after his second inauguration, McKinley went to Buffalo, New York, to give an address at the Pan-American Exposition. On the afternoon of September 6, 1901, he stood at the head of a reception line shaking hands with visitors. He stretched out his hand to greet a young man who had a handkerchief wrapped around his right hand. Two shots rang out, and McKinley slumped. An anarchist, Leon Czolgosz, had concealed a pistol beneath the handkerchief. On September 14, McKinley died and Roosevelt became President.

A Look at Specifics

1. How did the Chautauqua assembly further adult education in the United States?

2. How did Joseph Pulitzer influence the newspaper business?

3. Why did Alfred Thayer Mahan believe that the United States should develop a large navy and expand overseas?

4. Why did Cleveland oppose the annexation of Hawaii? How did the war with Spain help bring about Hawaiian annexation?

5. Why did many Americans believe that Cuba was of strategic importance to the United States?

6. Why did Cuba accept the Platt Amendment to its constitution?

7. How did the United States attempt to improve conditions in the Philippines?

8. Why was Theodore Roosevelt chosen as a candidate for Vice-President?

A Review of Major Ideas

1. How did American expansionism of the 1890's differ from that of the 1840's and 1850's?

2. Why did the United States pursue an active foreign policy in Hawaii, Samoa, Venezuela, and Cuba? Why did it attempt to improve relations with Latin America?

3. How did the United States become involved in a war with Spain? How did the victory over Spain lead to the development of an American empire? Did the Platt Amendment contradict the Teller Resolution?

4. How did economic developments in the United States between 1865 and 1900 lead to the growth of mass culture? How did they affect the foreign policy of the United States?

For Independent Study

1. If overseas colonies could increase the strength and prosperity of a nation by providing markets for its products and naval bases for its ships, should not the United States have made greater efforts to secure a larger overseas empire?

2. Why did the United States decide to make the Philippines a colony instead of granting them independence?

3. Why did the United States decide to go to war with Spain when the Spanish had shown their willingness to give in to American demands regarding Cuba?

Unit Review
Examining the Times

1. Between 1865 and 1900, how did American industry and agriculture change?

2. What reforms were promoted by farmers during this period? How did industrial workers attempt to improve their economic position?

3. What changes took place in American foreign policy during this period?

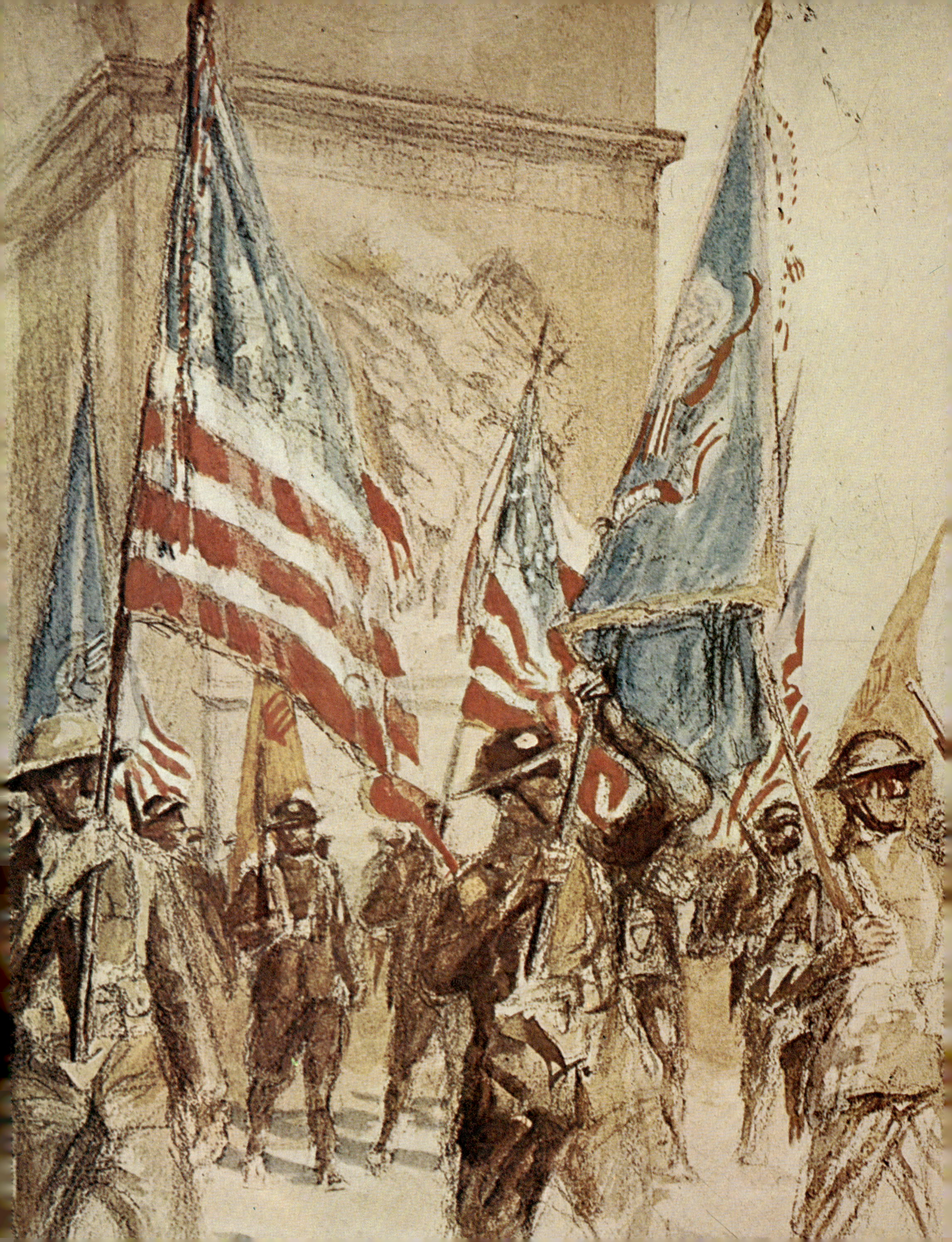

UNIT SIX   1900–1920

The Rise of a World Power

Imperialism and nationalism had contributed greatly to world tensions in the late nineteenth century. These forces continued to haunt international relations in the early twentieth century.

Imperialism created intense, often bitter, rivalries among the world powers. Sometimes the rivals went to war, as Russia and Japan did in 1904. Other times they teetered on the brink of war, as France and Germany did when they disagreed over Morocco in 1905 and 1911.

The causes of war are complex, but a major force leading to war early in the twentieth century was *jingoism,* extreme nationalism combined with a warlike foreign policy. Jingoes felt that their nation was superior to other nations and that war was necessary to prove national superiority.

In order to protect trade and colonies or to make their nations look strong in the eyes of the world, the great powers spent huge sums of money creating giant armies and navies. They built up their armed forces with the help of *conscription,* a compulsory draft of young men from the farms and factories. The officers usually came from aristocratic families. Professional soldiers on general staffs prepared careful strategies for war against possible enemy states. People had always fought wars, but now they had come up with something new—organized, professional, peacetime planning for war. Military planners of this era even worked out hour-by-hour schedules for the mobilization of the huge armies.

In the first dozen years of the twentieth century, a series of crises and limited wars, mainly in the Balkan countries of eastern Europe, threatened to trigger the mobilization of these armies. Full mobilization could lead to a major war because a system of alliances had divided Europe into two armed camps: the Triple Alliance of Germany, Austria-Hungary, and Italy, and the Triple *Entente* of Britain, France, and Russia. Since the rivals had interests, colonies, and allies all over the world, any clash would be likely to result in a world war, not just a war on the European continent.

In 1913, the French ambassador in Vienna reported that "the feeling that the nations are moving toward a conflict, urged by an irresistible force, grows day by day." In June of the following year, as the international tension continued, a Serbian terrorist killed the heir to the throne of Austria-Hungary. This act was the spark that touched off World War I, for it brought the alliance system into play.

So well planned was the mobilization of armies that in August 1914, the first month of the war, 15 million men were in uniform. Before the war ended, 70 million men, at one time or another, had engaged in the military discipline of making war. Thirty-one countries in six continents eventually entered the conflict. The two sides in the war became known as the Central powers and the Allied powers. As the war progressed, the line-up of nations on the two sides increased, and in some cases changed. The major Central powers included Germany, Austria-Hungary, and Turkey, while the major Allied powers included Britain, France, Italy, Russia, the United States, and Japan.

World War I lasted four years and drained Europe of blood and money. Like the fighting, the destruction was massive. The cost of the war has been estimated at 350 billion dollars. Ten million men, almost all of them young, died violently; 20 million others suffered physical or mental wounds. About 13 million civilian men, women, and children died from diseases, starvation, or injuries resulting from the war.

The Central powers went down in defeat. New states were formed from what were once the empires of Germany, Austria-Hungary, and Russia. The new Germany became a republic; the new Austria and Hungary became small, independent nations; the new Russia became a Communist dictatorship. Turkey, which had once ruled the vast Ottoman Empire in the Middle East, was reduced to a small republic. Though victorious, France was so devastated that recovery would take many years. Britain, like France, lost almost a whole generation of young men. Italy suffered great losses and became ripe for dictatorship.

The war overturned the old order. Colonies and spheres of influence all over the world were redistributed. Colonial peoples, as in India, intensified demands that they be allowed to govern themselves. Europe declined as a center of world power. The two nations that emerged from the war stronger than they had entered it were Japan and the United States.

Nationalistic motives were not limited to the world war. Efforts of peoples to gain independence, especially in pursuit of more democratic government, were evident many times in the first two decades of the century. A social revolution in Mexico, which began in 1910, led to the establishment of a government concerned with the welfare of the masses, the breaking up of large estates into smaller farms, the weakening of the Catholic Church, and the reduction of foreign ownership of Mexican resources and property.

In 1911, revolutionaries in China overthrew the Manchu dynasty. The revolt was led by Dr. Sun Yat-sen, who wanted to free China from foreign control, give the people a voice in the government, and raise the Chinese standard of living. Although these aims were thwarted by divisions within China during this period, they had important results for the future.

In Africa, many people increasingly resented the European colonists, and nationalistic movements grew, especially after World War I. In Europe, too, many nationality groups, including Czechs, Poles, and Irish, chafed under the rule of such imperial powers as Austria-Hungary, Russia, and Britain. Some of them succeeded in gaining their independence after the war. But political independence did not necessarily bring social reforms that benefited the masses of the people.

In the Middle East, the desire of Arabs to break away from the Ottoman Empire affected diplomacy during World War I. For example, in 1915–1916, the British promised the Arabs an independent state in exchange for Arab help in fighting the Turkish army. The boundaries of this proposed state were not defined at the time of the agreement. Many Arabs felt that the promises made to them were contradicted by the British-French Sykes-Picot agreement of 1916, which promised Syria to France and Iraq to Britain. The Arabs also felt betrayed by Britain's Balfour Declaration of 1917, which promised the establishment of a homeland in Palestine for the Jewish people.

Although the wars and revolutions from 1900 to 1920 dominated foreign affairs, forces were also working to achieve peace. Organized public and private efforts to maintain peace and to further international cooperation were especially apparent in the decade that preceded the start of World War I. At the Palace of Peace in The Hague in the Netherlands, conferences were held to discuss plans for the reduction of armaments and for the peaceful settlement of disputes. The use of arbitration had been greatly encouraged when the Permanent Court of Arbitration was established at The Hague in 1899. In *arbitration,* disputing countries agree to submit their claims or grievances to an impartial third party and to abide by the decision rendered. By 1914 the Court had made decisions in fourteen international disputes.

Many nations worked together cooperatively to establish trade agreements. For example, the Pan-American Union, established in the latter part of the nineteenth century, promoted trade among nations of the Western Hemisphere.

The greatest challenges to the talents of peacemakers, of course, came after World War I. In Paris in January 1919, the victorious states, representing Europe, America, Africa, Asia, and Oceania, held a peace conference. They wrote peace treaties that punished the losers. But they also set up the League of Nations, which they hoped would bring order and justice out of the chaos unleashed by the war. The League came into existence in January 1920, with headquarters in Geneva, Switzerland.

The Changing Society

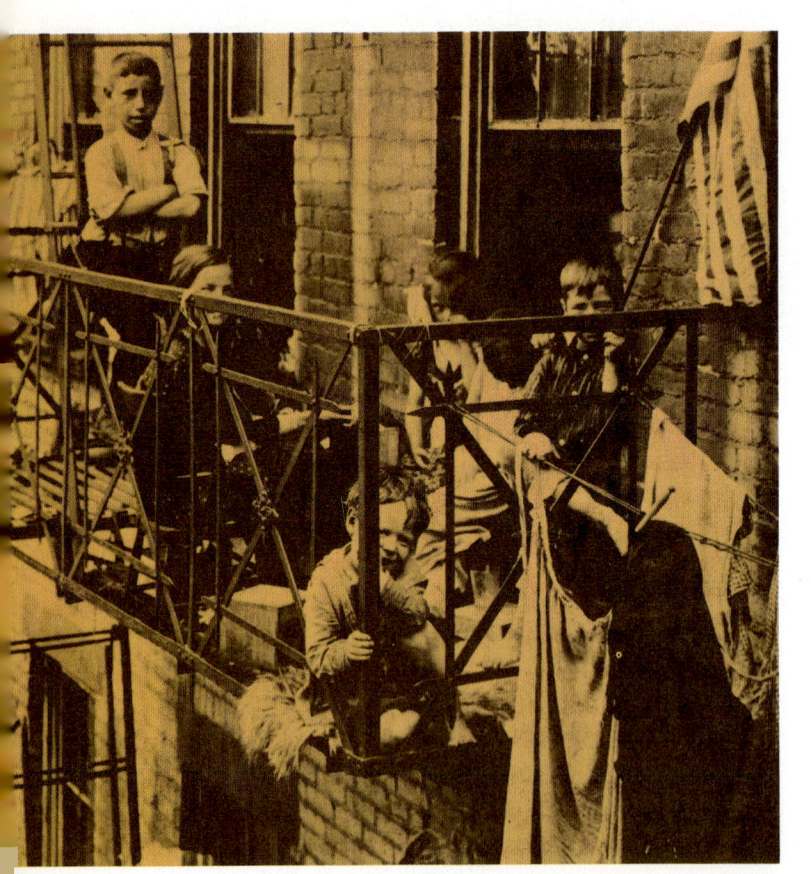

CHAPTER 17
1900–1915

An unplanned playground—the fire escape.

All countries, all peoples, are constantly changing. But many people are uncomfortable with change and try to resist it or slow it down. Americans, it has been said, are unique because they commit themselves to change as a normal part of life.

Between 1900 and 1920, the nature of the United States changed drastically. A rural nation became urban, the national origins and religions of Americans became more varied. As you read this chapter, ask yourself: Did the people of the United States embrace social change willingly, or did they, like people of other nations, show distrust for what was new and strange?

A CHANGING POPULATION

Two forces—immigration and urbanization—characterized the population changes from 1900 to 1920. About 15 million men, women, and children migrated to the United States in those years. Most of them went to live in cities. In this they were joined by growing numbers of native Americans.

Immigration

Of the immigrants who came to the United States after 1900, the great majority were from countries in eastern or southern Europe. The usual stepping-off point was New York City, but Boston, Philadelphia, Chicago, and San Francisco also received many immigrants.

Most of the European newcomers took jobs in the sweatshops of the eastern cities and crowded together in squalid tenements. Those who arrived on the West Coast also faced squalor and hard work. In California, many became farmers. Some immigrants, especially those from northern and western Europe, began farms in the Midwest.

A large number of immigrants came from Mexico. Not all were permanent; many were seasonal, migrant workers. Most Mexican immigrants took jobs working on the railroads. Instead of the squalor of the tenement, they faced the squalor of life in a boxcar. The least fortunate lived in tent cities on the edges of cotton fields in California and Texas or of beet fields in Michigan.

If the living conditions for immigrants were less than ideal, they were made bearable by the belief that life in the United States held a hope for the future that was not to be found in the old country. In the United States, the newcomers faced many obstacles. The problems were compounded because the immigrants usually settled in cities, often living in *ghettos*—areas where people of one nationality, race, or religion were concentrated. Earlier immigrants had seemed less noticeable because they had settled throughout the country.

The biggest problem was how to make a living in the face of overwhelming competition. In most immigrant families, everyone worked. The families might work both at home and outside the home. Whole families rolled cigars or sewed clothing by hand. Some school-age children might have after-school jobs, but many did not go to school, because their full-time pay was needed to help keep the family alive.

The immigrants faced prejudice and discrimination because of their religions and nationalities and because of the bigotry and racism of nativists. Great numbers of the immigrants were Jewish, Catholic, or members of Eastern Orthodox churches. These newcomers, nativists said, were "from beaten races, the worst failures in history" and did not have the pioneer virtues of earlier, northern European immigrants. Nativists said that the new immigrants would be difficult to assimilate, would not be loyal to democracy, and would produce more crime.

Like the immigrants who entered the country after the Civil War, those who came after 1900 met the opposition of organized labor. Native American workers and even fairly recent immigrants opposed allowing more people to enter the country. They felt that unlimited immigration pulled down the wages of all workers, for, with a huge supply of workers available, employers were able to get people to work for low wages.

Nativists talked about America's "unguarded gates" that were allowing "undesirables" into the country. A number of groups started asking Congress to pass laws limiting immigration.

On the West Coast, many people opposed the immigration of Chinese or Japanese laborers. This opposition had led to the Chinese Exclusion Act of 1882, which stopped immigration from China for twenty years. In 1902, Congress passed a new law that excluded Chinese immigration for an indefinite period.

The opposition to Japanese immigrants led to the "gentlemen's agreement" with Japan in 1906. In this agreement, President Theodore Roosevelt said that he would get San Franciscans to stop segregating Japanese-American schoolchildren if the Japanese government would limit the further emigration of Japanese laborers.

The Chinese Exclusion Act applied to Hawaii and other territories, but the "gentlemen's agreement" did not. The Oriental population in Hawaii was growing rapidly. The Chinese had begun coming in large numbers in the 1870's, the Japanese in the 1880's. These immigrants usually went to work on the sugar and pineapple plantations. By 1900, more than 50 percent of the people on the islands were Japanese or Chinese or of such descent. About 1910, Filipinos began entering Hawaii in large numbers.

In 1896, 1913, and 1915, Congress passed bills requiring a literacy test for immigrants. In each case, the President then in office vetoed the bill. Finally, in 1917, Congress passed such a law over President Wilson's

TOTAL POPULATION GROWTH, 1900–1920

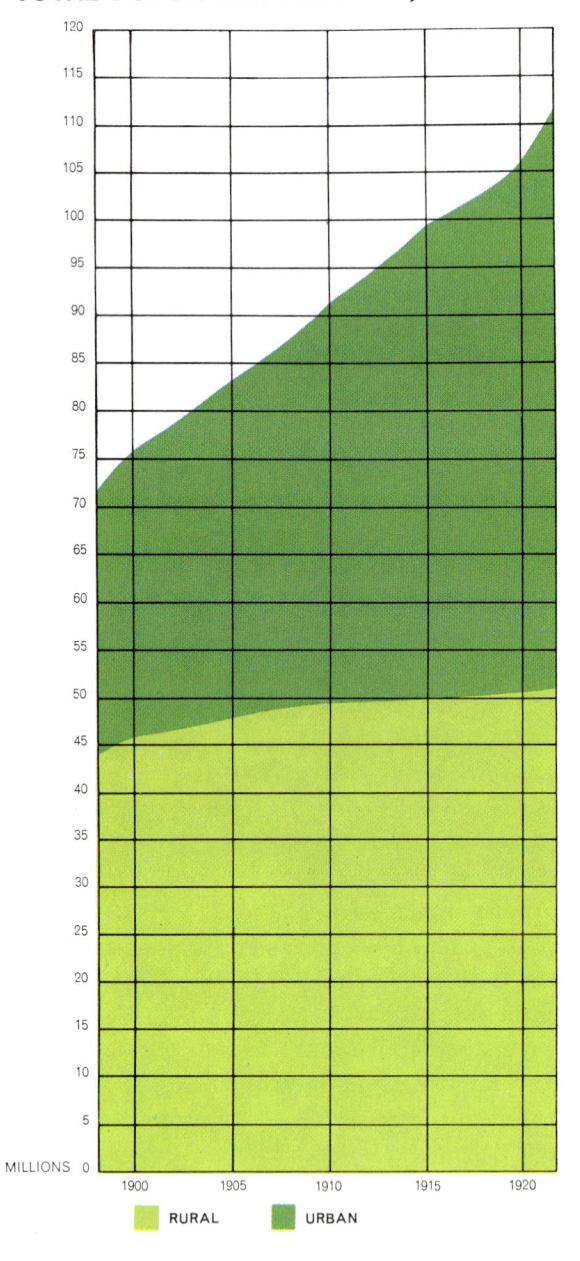

RURAL ■ URBAN

veto. The law provided that the literacy test could be taken in any language and that the immigrant had to be able to read only a paragraph or two. The test did not apply to those fleeing religious persecution or to illiterate members of the immediate family of an immigrant who had been admitted.

Right: Members of an immigrant family make artificial flowers. "Cottage industry" of this sort often involved the whole family. The family usually had to buy the materials from an agent and then hope that the agent would buy back the finished goods.

Urbanization

In 1800, only about 6 percent of the people in the United States lived in cities. In 1900, about 40 percent of the people lived in cities or towns, and by 1920, over 50 percent. Instead of being farmers or country people, as most of their parents and grandparents had been, Americans were becoming a nation of city dwellers.

The concentration of many people into small areas unavoidably changed American life. Some of the biggest changes were those in the family. On farms, a large family was a necessity. Everyone—from tiny children to elderly grandparents—was needed to perform chores so that the farm would produce a living. In the cities, however, many people began to think that a large family was a handicap. City families depended on wages, and wages were so low that they often were enough to support only one person. Even with both parents and all the school-age children working, life often was a struggle. Nonproductive children were a drain on the family's meager resources. Moreover, living quarters were small and difficult to find. A 3- or 4-room flat in the city was considered roomy, if not downright luxurious.

Trying to provide child care was a major problem. The family circle sometimes included an aunt, uncle, or grandparent who was willing to baby-sit while the parents worked. But some people left the children at home unattended. Others relied on such things as "Mother's Little Helper." This was a patent medicine, containing opium, that was given to a baby to make it sleep all day long so that its parents could leave it alone while they went out to work.

Lewis W. Hine, International Museum of Photography at George Eastman House, Rochester, N.Y.

The disadvantages of having a large family in a city contributed to a growing interest in limiting family size. Scientific discoveries had led to methods of family planning. In the 1870's and 1880's, however, a number of Protestant church leaders had persuaded some states to make it illegal to distribute information or devices to prevent conception. As a result, such people as Margaret Sanger, a public health nurse, were often jailed for distributing information about prevention of conception.

Family size was only one of the adjustments Americans faced in urban areas. They also had to get used to living in a *metropolitan area*—made up of a city, its suburbs, and outlying areas. Before the twentieth century, cities had grown by *annexing,* or taking over, the suburbs surrounding them. After about 1915, however, most cities stopped annexing. Although most suburban areas still depended on the city's facilities and prosperity, they did not come under the jurisdiction of the city government. Many now had their own local governments. As the number of governments increased, so did the difficulty of solving metropolitan problems.

CHANGES IN BUSINESS GROWTH

Soon after the new century opened, many Americans began viewing their nation's rapid economic growth with an uneasy concern. They became increasingly aware that although most of the people enjoyed a rising standard of living, many men, women, and children did not. As the United States became more industrialized, the evils seemed to spread.

Some Americans came to believe that poverty and ignorance lay at the root of these evils. But many people believed that the social, economic, and political difficulties were caused by the increasing concentration of the nation's economic power in fewer and fewer hands. This concentration of power had brought about one of the most important changes in the nation's history. A group of super corporations rather than a large number of small, competitive producers now dominated the economy.

The Super Corporation

The corporation was the most important development in American industry in the late nineteenth century. It replaced other forms of ownership as the chief means of bringing capital and labor together to produce goods. By 1899, 66 percent of all manufactured goods in the United States was turned out by incorporated businesses.

The first years of the twentieth century saw the rise of super corporations. Their ownership was spread among many stockholders. As the large corporation took shape, it produced a class of professional industrial managers. Although these managers supposedly were responsible to the stockholders, this class became in fact an independent center of economic power.

Another result of corporate growth was the rise of investment bankers to powerful positions. Most often these people gained power because they controlled vast sums of money, not because they had the special knowledge needed to operate a business. With ownership split among many stockholders, with investment bankers in control of finance, and with professional managers running the business, the modern corporation had come of age.

Various laws, but primarily a body of state law, made possible the growth of super corporations. New Jersey had taken the lead, in 1888, with laws that permitted industries to consolidate.

After 1895, court decisions helped promote the growth of super corporations. Before that time, laws of Congress and the states had slowed the first movement toward industrial concentration, the trust movement. But in 1895, the Supreme Court ruled that the federal antitrust law did not apply to combina-

Many of the new immigrants lived in overcrowded city tenements. Conditions in some areas were so bad that entire blocks were known as "tuberculosis blocks." Crime rates in these areas were often much higher than in other parts of the city.

tions in the field of manufacturing.

Another help for bankers was the increasing wealth of upper-class and middle-class Americans. Their money often went into banks and insurance companies, and it was used by investment bankers to expand into industrial and railroad enterprises.

Banker Control of Industry

By 1904, the two great financial empires in Wall Street were headed by J. P. Morgan and John D. Rockefeller. Around each of these empires were clustered a number of smaller financial houses. The Morgan and Rockefeller empires had competed for control of railroads and insurance companies.

In 1901 the two empires fought for control of the western railroads. The Morgan people controlled the Northern Pacific and the Great Northern; the Rockefeller group, the Union Pacific and the Southern Pacific. Both wanted to win control of the Burlington Railroad, which had tracks into Chicago. When the Burlington sold out to the Northern Pacific (Morgan), the Rockefeller group tried to gain control of the Northern Pacific on the open market. In the battle that followed, the price of Northern Pacific common stock jumped from $100 to more than $1,000 per share. The battle was so costly that both sides agreed to a truce. They joined in forming a new holding company—the Northern Securities Company—which controlled the Northern Pacific and Great Northern Railroads. Rockefeller's representatives sat on the boards of directors of these lines and of the Burlington. Now the two great financial empires controlled the major railroads west of the Mississippi River as well as a major rail line into Chicago.

Cliff Dwellers, by George Bellows, 1913. Los Angeles County Museum of Art, Los Angeles County Funds

The bankers' control of the railroads brought few benefits to most people. To assure profits, the railroads often charged excessive rates for poor service. The bankers did make money for themselves and for their stockholders. Some of the new managers even deliberately bankrupted their railroad properties in order to gain immediate profit.

A few years after the battle over the Burlington line, Morgan again showed his great financial power. In order to prevent the complete collapse of the stock market during the Panic of 1907, he brought together the resources of Wall Street bankers. After 1907 the Rockefeller group offered no further opposition to Morgan. In the next few years, the Morgan and Rockefeller groups formed what was, in effect, one huge financial empire that stopped competition and prevented industrial struggle.

In California, where economic opportunities for immigrants were greater than in the ghettos of the East, an unusual banking experiment got started. Amadeo Peter Giannini, born in San Jose of immigrant parents from Italy, started a bank that catered to the needs of Italian immigrants. The newcomers often distrusted banks run by Americans or could not obtain services or loans from them. With his Bank of Italy, which opened its first office in October 1904, Giannini brought branch banking to Italians in California. He gave them Italian-speaking tellers and performed various services, such as help with naturalization papers, free of charge. Ultimately, Giannini expanded the Bank of Italy beyond his ethnic group, changed the name to Bank of America, and made it the largest financial institution of its kind in the world.

SOCIAL AND EDUCATIONAL IDEAS

Material progress was one of the most striking features of the United States at the turn of the century. The very idea of progress became the center of philosophical and social discussions. Philosophers, educators, and social thinkers, became concerned with the practical measures needed to bring the benefits of material progress to the majority of the American people.

Attacks on Economic Theories

Professional economists attacked the ideas of Social Darwinism, laissez faire, and classical economics. They said that the assistance of the state in economic matters was necessary to human progress and that changing economic conditions had to be met by changing laws. Laissez faire, they said, was "unsafe in politics and unsound in morals."

One of the most original critics of industrial society was Thorstein B. Veblen, a midwestern economist. In his first two books, *The Theory of the Leisure Class* (1899) and *The Theory of Business Enterprise* (1904), he rejected the idea that the wealthy were more fit than others. He attacked the economic and social practices of the rich and the laws of the classical economist. His writings encouraged economists to be suspicious of theories that described economic life as being governed by simple, unchanging laws. He pointed out that much of the consumption in the United States was intended to increase the user's social standing but was wasteful and unnecessary.

Idealists Versus Pragmatists

Philosophers, too, were affected by Darwin's theories and by the problems of the industrial society. Those who believed that ideals were most important in the life of humans formed a school of philosophy called idealism. The idealists tried to reconcile Darwin's idea of change through evolution with the traditional Christian idea of an unchanging God.

The one major American philosopher who defended idealism was Josiah Royce of Harvard. Royce explained his beliefs in *The Philosophy of Loyalty* (1908). He believed that the quality in humans that raised them above the level of animals was loyalty, which included the ideals of devotion, unselfishness, and sacrifice.

Adult immigrants attend a naturalization class to prepare for the oral citizenship test. Most such classes emphasized reading and writing in English, for use of that language was considered a sign of "Americanness." People who believed in the melting-pot theory looked upon education as the flame under the pot. The benefits of education were sparingly extended to blacks and Indians.

Idealism was challenged at the turn of the century by pragmatism. Pragmatists taught that truth was governed by changing circumstances for each new generation and each society. They said that truth was not absolute and unchanging; it was relative.

The most important of the pragmatists was William James, a psychologist. James taught that the truth or value of an idea could be measured by how it worked or by what it did. His philosophy was one of individualism, for it required each person to establish his or her own truth, or practical values.

Another important pragmatist was John Dewey, a philosopher from Vermont. His deepest concern was society as a whole, rather than the individual. He sought to apply pragmatic thinking to the problems of society and to make it an instrument of social change. Dewey thought that philosophy could help the individual adjust to social change and could lead to a society that would serve the highest human purposes. In addition, Dewey believed that a new kind of education was needed that would prepare people for life in an industrial society.

Increased Opportunities for Education

Even before the age of industrialization, many Americans believed that everyone in a democratic society must be educated. A number of leaders laid the foundations for a public education system free of religious controls. By 1918, all states had passed compulsory education laws.

After 1870, it was clear that schools were slowly coming to the people. In 1870, 20 percent of the population above ten years of age could not write. By 1910, that figure had fallen to 7.7 percent. From 1890 to 1900, the number of children enrolled in all schools, public and private, had increased by 19.2 percent. But this progress was irregular. Northern children received an average of almost seven years of education in public schools; but southern children received an average of three years of schooling.

At the end of the nineteenth century, education, too, felt the effects of the new ideas in science and philosophy. Teachers began to show greater interest in the process by which people learn as well as in the information learned. They began to think of education as a part of life itself, not simply as a preparation for life.

Kindergarten, a system of preschool training, spread rapidly in the United States in the early years of the twentieth century. Two American innovations were the public junior college (1902) and the junior high school (1910). More important at the time was the expansion of the high school. In 1900, the United States had about 6,000 public high schools with a total enrollment of 500,000 pupils. Fourteen years later, the number of schools and students had doubled.

Higher Education

The earliest colleges trained students in religion, philosophy, mathematics, Latin, and Greek. By the beginning of the twentieth century, colleges and universities had increased their enrollments, expanded their course offerings, and responded to new ideas.

The changes were not great, however. Courses in science were few, and the only experiments that students usually saw were those demonstrated by the professor. Many colleges offered no work in modern languages, such as French and German. They also ignored modern history and other subjects that dealt with the social forces of the present and of the recent past. In effect, the American college had retained a course of instruction, taken from seventeenth-century England, that had little to do with current social and economic conditions. Change came with the demands of the industrial society for people who had technical knowledge.

In 1900, with the formation of the Association of American Universities, the nation's colleges and universities began a campaign to raise educational standards. Important improvements followed. State legislatures expanded their aid to universities, colleges, and junior colleges. Enrollments in state universities began to climb, and leading state universities, such as California, Michigan, Wisconsin, and Illinois, offered excellent opportunities for education. During the early 1900's, higher education in the United States acquired an excellence of its own.

Benefits for Blacks

Some groups did not benefit much from the changes going on. The social and economic standing of most blacks was worse than that of immigrants.

The Civil War and Reconstruction had not changed the determination of many people to keep blacks at the bottom of the social order. Slavery in the South, where most blacks lived, was replaced by a legal *caste system*—a system in which the law recognized blacks as a group and defined their place in society. Blacks were segregated from nonblacks in public schools, in restaurants, and in other establishments. Gradually, southern blacks were prevented from exercising the right to vote, which had been granted in the Fifteenth Amendment.

Basic educational opportunities were rarely available to black children. Yet there was some progress. From 1865 to 1900, illiteracy among blacks declined from 95 to 44.5 percent, and it went down further in the next decade. After 1900, some southern states recognized the need for public aid to black education. But as late as 1910, all the southern states, from Maryland to Texas, had only 141 black high schools, and these enrolled only slightly more than 8,000 pupils.

In these years of increasing discrimination, Booker T. Washington was the black person to whom whites listened in matters regarding race relations. Born a slave in Virginia, he managed to get an education at Hampton Institute, a vocational school. Washington believed that blacks could not gain social and political equality with nonblacks in one quick leap. He urged other

The staff of *The Crisis* prepares the next issue of the magazine. W. E. B. Du Bois *(standing right)* fought racism on many fronts. Du Bois worked especially hard to make whites aware that blacks still risked being lynched if they stood up for their rights.

blacks to put aside, for a time at least, demands for social and political recognition. He wanted them to concentrate on improving their economic standing. In 1881, he founded the Tuskegee Institute in Alabama, where blacks could learn a useful vocation. Although people all over the country praised Washington's doctrine, later many blacks would criticize what they called the Washington compromise.

Washington did much to train blacks for jobs in industry, but he encouraged blacks to stay on the farm. Migration to the cities was urged, however, by William E. B. Du Bois of Massachusetts, the first black to earn a doctorate in history from Harvard University. This was not the only point on which Du Bois disagreed with Washington. He also wanted blacks to press for political rights and higher education.

In June 1905, Du Bois met with a small group of blacks at Niagara Falls, Canada, where they adopted a program that called for full equality for blacks. Few whites paid attention to the Niagara Movement. Then in August 1908 a race riot broke out near Abraham Lincoln's home in Springfield, Illinois. Some white northerners began to pay more attention to black problems.

In February 1909, white educators, clergymen, and editors met with a group of blacks in New York City to organize the National Association for the Advancement of Colored People. This group adopted the principles of the Niagara Movement and worked to end racial segregation. During the NAACP's early years, Du Bois was the only black official of the organization. He also edited the group's magazine, *The Crisis.* Among black leaders the more militant views of Du Bois had greater influence in the twentieth century than the more passive course of action recommended by Booker T. Washington.

SCIENCE AND TECHNOLOGY

At the turn of the century, science and technology became more important to the growing power of the United States. Both profited from the expansion and improvement of the universities. Both also became important primarily because industry needed them. The support given to science and technology by people like John D. Rockefeller and Andrew Carnegie brought scientists a respect they had not previously known. Many people in the United States came to realize that technical knowledge and scientific investigation could be keys to a better life.

Advances

In the United States the period after the Civil War was a time of great technical achievement. Technical advances continued and increased in the twentieth century. In

An early biplane takes off. Air races and stunt flying drew huge crowds. Crashes were frequent but not always fatal.

December 1903, Orville Wright flew the motor-driven airplane that he and his brother Wilbur had invented. His flight in Kittyhawk, North Carolina, lasted for twelve seconds and covered a distance of 120 feet. Wright became the first person to fly a motorized, heavier-than-air machine.

The work of all American inventors had a number of things in common. All contributed to triumphs of people over their environment. All contributed to a revolution in the lives of the people of the United States.

The American way of life changed with the increasing use of new inventions.

Americans showed outstanding ability in applying mechanical knowledge to practical needs. In the field of pure science, however, Americans lagged behind Europeans. In this field, scholars may spend years patiently probing for new knowledge that might not have immediate practical application. Toward the end of the nineteenth century, however, Americans had begun their own researches in pure science.

In the field of *genetics,* which is the study of heredity, they showed that changes in a species could come suddenly rather than slowly over a long period of time. Albert A. Michelson made experiments in the field of physics that were more fully developed later. By the beginning of the twentieth century, American science was becoming the equal of American technology.

The Automobile

In the early 1900's, the automobile began to replace the bicycle as an important form of transportation. People had been intrigued by the idea of a "horseless" carriage for many years. Throughout the nineteenth century, inventors had experimented with engines driven by steam or electric power. By the 1870's, French, German, and Austrian designers had begun to develop the gasoline engines that soon replaced all other types. France took the lead in the early automobile industry, and from the French come such terms as *garage, chassis,* and the word *automobile* itself.

In the United States, the most important inventors were Charles and J. Frank Duryea, Ransom Olds, and Henry Ford. The first vehicle operated by a gasoline motor in the United States was built by the Duryea brothers in 1893. Three years later Ford produced the first of the cars that would bear his name. When Ransom Olds built 1,500 Olds-

Leisure

Elaborate amusement parks like Coney Island—with a variety of sideshows and rides—became popular. Then, as now, many Americans enjoyed the sinking feeling in the pit of the stomach brought on by a roller-coaster ride. Movies, shown in crude nickelodeon theaters *(left)*, were beginning to replace vaudeville. These early films were still silent, still black and white, but they "moved" and, in the process, entertained millions of Americans.

Movies, Five Cents, by John Sloan, 1907

The Immigrants

"There she lies, the great Melting-Pot—listen! Can't you hear the roaring and the bubbling? There gapes her mouth—the harbour where a thousand mammoth feeders come from the ends of the world to pour in their human freight. Ah, what a stirring and a seething! Celt and Latin, Slav and Teuton, Greek and Syrian, —black and yellow—"

In this way an English writer described the United States in 1910. Like many other people, he viewed America as a place where many cultures fused to become something distinctively American. This was the "melting-pot" theory.

A major idea in the melting-pot theory was that immigrants had come to the United States in search of freedom and jobs. Certainly, political and economic conditions caused great immigration between 1850 and 1920.

Many of the English, Swedish, and German immigrants were grain farmers who had been wiped out by competition from cheap American and Russian wheat. Others were skilled industrial workers put out of work by a depression. Thousands of Chinese emigrated during the Tai-ping Rebellion, which seriously disrupted their economy. Some Germans came to escape Prussian draft laws.

In Austria-Hungary, the breakup of large estates displaced many people who could not support themselves on small tracts of land. In the late 1880's, farm workers from southern Italy and Greece emigrated when fruit growing became unprofitable.

Some southern and eastern Europeans emigrated to escape religious persecution. Political unrest in Russia in the 1880's encouraged anti-Jewish riots and brought harsh restrictive laws. Finally, hundreds of thousands of Jews fled to escape death in the terrible pogroms of 1891 and 1905.

Far fewer of the later immigrants became farmers. They filled the need for industrial workers. Frequently, newcomers joined others of their nationality in rural or urban areas. Some immigrants tried to preserve their language and customs. But many factors encouraged them to drop their old language and to take on some new customs.

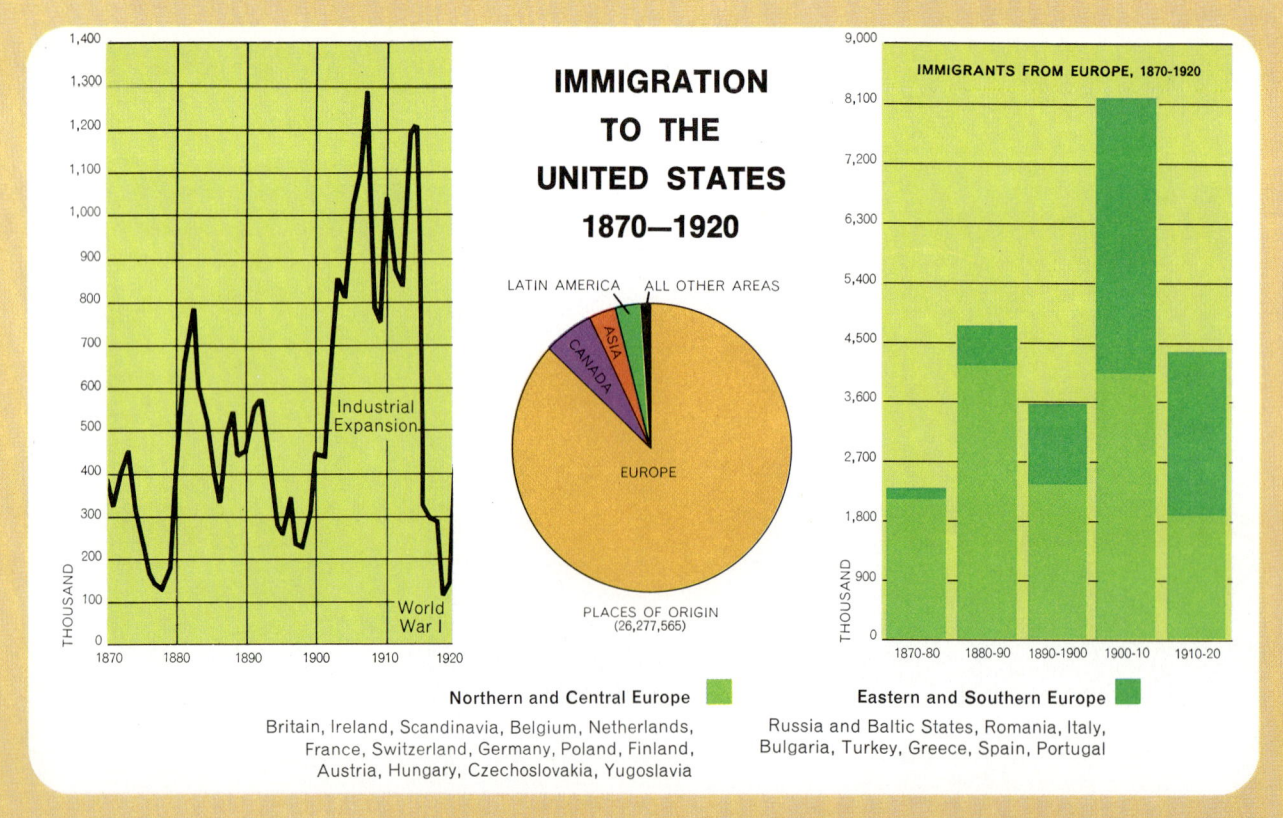

IMMIGRATION TO THE UNITED STATES 1870–1920

PLACES OF ORIGIN (26,277,565)

Northern and Central Europe
Britain, Ireland, Scandinavia, Belgium, Netherlands, France, Switzerland, Germany, Poland, Finland, Austria, Hungary, Czechoslovakia, Yugoslavia

Eastern and Southern Europe
Russia and Baltic States, Romania, Italy, Bulgaria, Turkey, Greece, Spain, Portugal

The sleekest cars of 1909 start their motors for the first race at the Indianapolis Speedway. Races like this one provided information about the workability of automobile parts.

mobiles in 1901, he became the first mass-producer of automobiles.

The production of automobiles gradually came to be centered at Detroit, Michigan. That city had skilled carriage builders, and it was close to supplies of iron ore and lumber. The automobile companies turned out more than 4,000 cars in 1900. Production did not immediately increase, for a number of reasons. Only 7 percent of the roads in the United States were suitable for automobile travel. In addition, the cost of manufacturing resulted in high car prices. When the producers turned to mass production, using a constantly moving assembly line, the automobile industry became one of the giants of the American economy. By 1909, the output of automobiles had increased 3,500 percent. The automobile had begun to transform many aspects of life in the United States. Modern, scientific road building began in 1912 and was given a big boost with the passage of the Federal Aid Road Act, in 1916.

Henry Ford became the leading figure in the automobile industry—the "flivver king." Although he was not the first to use mass production and interchangeable parts, he used these techniques more effectively than did many of his competitors. The Model T Ford, first built in 1909, was cheap, simple, and sturdy. It came out of the factory the same way year after year. A buyer could have a Model T in any color, Ford once said, so long as it was black.

CULTURAL ACTIVITIES

Societies with wealth and leisure often support art, music, literature, and other cultural activities. To some extent this was true of the United States in the late nineteenth century.

With their new wealth the families of the industrial leaders created a luxurious way of life modeled after that of the wealthy aristocracy of Europe. They also supported many philanthropies—orphanages, hospitals, and colleges—and became the recognized patrons of the arts. But the paintings and sculptures

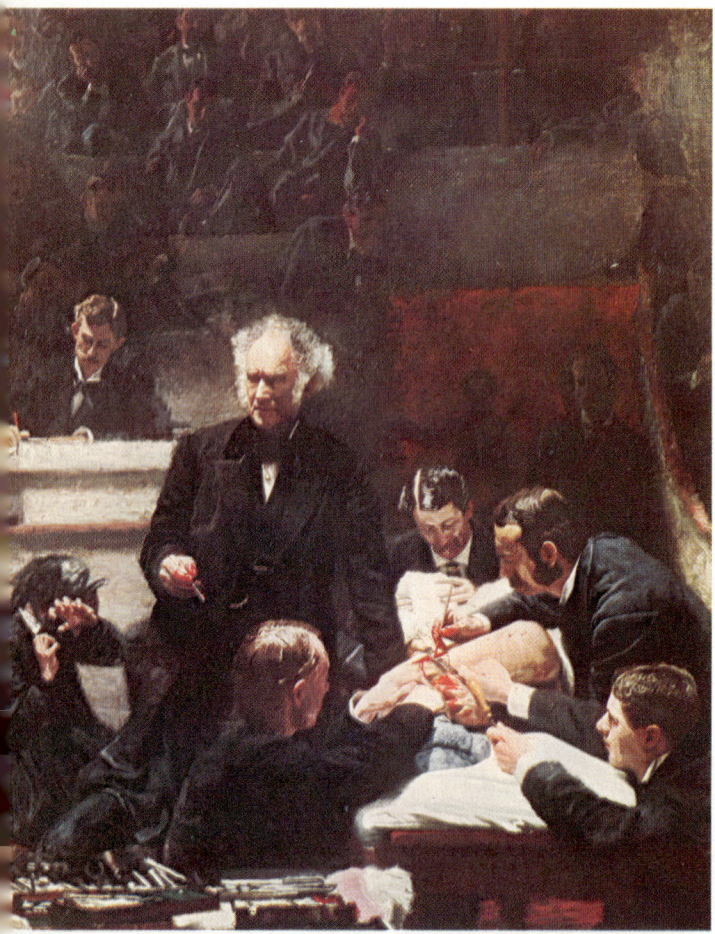

Gross Clinic, by Thomas Eakins, 1875

Mr. and Mrs. Isaac Newton Phelps Stokes, by John Singer Sargent, 1897

Sunday, Women Drying Their Hair, by John Sloan, 1912

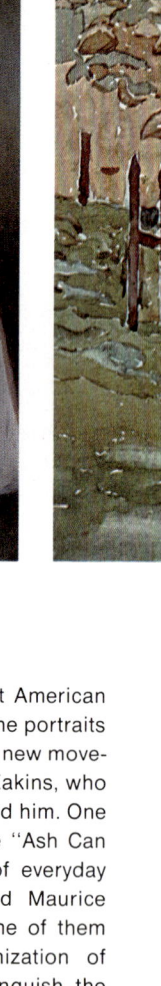

Up until the late nineteenth century, most American painters followed European ideas in art. The portraits by John Singer Sargent are in this class. A new movement toward realism was led by Thomas Eakins, who insisted on drawing scenes from life around him. One group of realistic painters was called the "Ash Can School," because they painted scenes of everyday city life. John Sloan, Robert Henri, and Maurice Prendergast were all in this school. Some of them painted in the abstract. Careful organization of shapes and bold splashes of color distinguish the impressionistic works of Maurice Prendergast.

The East River, by Maurice Prendergast, 1901. Collection, The Museum of Modern Art, New York. Gift of Abby Aldrich Rockefeller

Steelworkers' Noontime, by Thomas Anshutz, around 1890

they collected were of European origin or were copied from European models. The creative work done in the United States at that time often did not reflect what was vital in American society. One reason for this was that the United States was a land of varied cultural groups. Often there was little cultural exchange among these groups.

A New Literary Trend

Toward the end of the nineteenth century an important group of writers turned from realism and established a new literary school called naturalism. This school took its basic idea from the French writer Emile Zola. He said the writer must study human nature in the same way the biologist studies the animal world. The writer must describe life without applying moral judgments. Naturalists accepted the view of the Social Darwinists that life is an endless struggle against the blind forces of nature. They viewed society as harsh and impersonal.

Stephen Crane launched the American naturalist school in 1893, when he published *Maggie: A Girl of the Streets.* This was a tragic story of a young woman's struggle for existence in the slums of New York. Few read the book. Crane gained fame with his next novel, *The Red Badge of Courage* (1895). It described the ordeal of a young soldier during the Civil War. There was nothing romantic or noble about war in this novel. It depicted war as brutal and senseless.

Naturalism was treated in a direct, simple manner by two California writers, Frank Norris and Jack London. In his best-known works Norris concentrated on the theme of struggle and survival in industrial America. *The Octopus* (1901) dealt with a struggle between the Southern Pacific Railroad and wheat growers in California. It was followed by *The Pit* (1903), published after Norris's death, which told of struggle and turmoil among speculators in Chicago's wheat market. Jack London wrote about struggle in nature in *The Call of the Wild* (1903) and about struggle among men in *The Sea Wolf* (1904). He was the most widely read of the naturalists, primarily because he wrote exciting, action-filled stories.

The greatest of the naturalists was Theodore Dreiser. He, too, saw people as animals, but with ability to reason, driven by their instincts to struggle for survival. Dreiser also viewed environment as impersonal. Social forces, he suggested, drove people to violence. His first novel, *Sister Carrie* (1900), marked a turning point in American literary history. Naturalism and realism were found in all of Dreiser's novels, including *Jennie Gerhardt* (1911) and *An American Tragedy* (1925). Not all American writers joined the naturalist school, but by 1914 most young authors were trying to project naturalism through their works.

American Art, Architecture, and Music

After the Civil War most American painters studied in Europe and followed European traditions. Massachusetts-born James McNeill Whistler became a leading figure in London art society, never returning to the United States after he reached the age of 21. Mary Cassatt, member of a wealthy Philadelphia family, was better known in Paris than in the United States.

Three major American painters did not follow European traditions. Winslow Homer gave a rugged view of American themes and scenes, especially the New England seacoast. Albert Ryder, who lived as a hermit in New York, painted mystical scenes. Thomas Eakins of Pennsylvania insisted on factual presentation of his various subjects, usually drawn from life around him.

Almost every American town had a sculptured monument of some kind, but most of the statues were mediocre at best. The outstanding American sculptor of the period was

Augustus Saint-Gaudens. The hooded figure sometimes called *Grief* is an example of the rare beauty found in his sculptures.

American architecture, too, was based on European models. One of the first architects to successfully adapt the European tradition to American conditions was Henry Hobson Richardson. He developed an American Romanesque style.

After the Chicago fire in 1871, a group of architects, influenced by Richardson, developed the skyscraper. The construction of these tall and often graceful buildings was made possible by the new methods of steel production and by the perfection of the elevator. The most important architect of the Chicago group and of the time was Louis H. Sullivan. His guiding principle was that "form follows function"—a building's design should be based on the use to which the building is put.

The functional, steel-ribbed skyscraper brought a new appearance and a new way of life to great cities like Chicago and New York. Sullivan's ideas also influenced the most original American architect of the twentieth century, Frank Lloyd Wright. His "prairie house" was copied by other architects and led to today's "ranch style" house.

As in art, music had two strains—one European, one American. Music in the "classical," European tradition was supported mainly by the rich. They helped found many of the nation's great symphony orchestras during the Gilded Age. Americans who performed classical music often went to Germany or Italy for training.

American popular music drew from many sources. Variety show music and ragtime were being fused into something new by songwriters like George M. Cohan and Irving Berlin. Improvisational jazz was enjoying its heyday in the Storyville section of New Orleans. Black musicians like Charles "Buddy" Bolden and Freddie Keppard adapted the call-and-response chant of African religious music to the music of France, Spain, and other countries. In 1913, Storyville closed, and Dixieland musicians moved north.

A Look at Specifics

1. What arguments did nativists use in opposing immigration?

2. What were the objections to laissez faire?

3. What developments led to the formation of the National Association for the Advancement of Colored People?

4. What advances in the field of pure science were made by Americans at the turn of the century?

5. How did the ideas of Emile Zola influence American literature?

A Review of Major Ideas

1. In the late nineteenth century, what developments took place in the organization and control of United States industry? How did state and federal laws influence these developments?

2. How did new ideas in philosophy and economics lead to social reform movements and changes in education?

3. What important scientific and cultural trends were evident between 1895 and 1910?

For Independent Study

1. At the turn of the century, many members of the clergy tried to correct the injustices resulting from the new industrial era. Many others argued that it was not the function of the clergy to engage in social protest movements. With which position are you inclined to agree? Why?

2. Why has the philosophy of pragmatism been so widely accepted by Americans?

3. Social Darwinism was generally used in defense of laissez faire and the status quo. In what way might Social Darwinian arguments have been used to justify social reform?

The Progressives

CHAPTER 18

1900–1920

A young textile worker tends a spinning machine.

Lewis W. Hine, International Museum of Photography at George Eastman House, Rochester, N.Y.

"Progress" has been viewed by many Americans as one of the highest virtues. To be "progressive" has been to be in step with the times, perhaps even a little ahead of them.

In the first two decades of the twentieth century, a group of reformers appeared who called themselves "Progressives." The label was accurate, for they were certainly in step with the times. Just as business, religious, and cultural leaders were trying to apply the lessons of science and technology in their fields, the Progressives tried to apply these principles to government and society.

The Progressives did not, however, form one group. They included many different groups with many goals, some of which contradicted one another.

A GROWING MOVEMENT

The Progressive movement did not suddenly come to life as the new century began. It had its roots in the American past and in Europe. Ever since 1870, people had been writing about the problems that had come with industrial life. These people had demanded reforms. While many Americans read these protests, governments had not acted. After 1900, reformers were not content with talk. They entered politics in large numbers and achieved some practical results.

Origins of the Progressives

In many ways the Progressives' concern for the welfare of the people resembled the attitudes of the Populists of the 1890's. Progressives even took over many of the Populist proposals. But there were important differences between the two movements.

Populism had emerged in lean years among farmers in the West and South. Progressivism grew during years of prosperity and drew its support primarily from the middle classes in the towns and cities. The leaders in the Progressive movement often were bankers, lawyers, editors, prosperous farmers, or owners of small businesses. The rank and file, to a large extent, was made up of clerks, salespeople, and technicians who worked for city corporations or businesses. These people were often called white-collar workers because they wore white shirts, in contrast to laborers, who more often wore blue shirts.

Even though the Progressives were not united, they had some common goals. Most Progressives believed that all Americans could enjoy social and economic justice. The reformers wanted to do away with corrupt government and get more people actively involved in the government.

The Progressives did not always agree on ways to achieve their goals. Some of them insisted on economic reforms that would protect human beings from exploitation. Other Progressives insisted that clearing the city governments of corruption and freeing state governments from control by big business were of the first importance.

Unlike socialists and communists, Progressives accepted the capitalist system. Indeed, they looked with pride on the industrial strength of the United States. They hoped to use science and technology to eliminate poverty and other social ills.

Still, one reason that middle-class Americans became reformers was fear of the wealth and power of the great financiers. These reformers believed that the concentration of power would limit the economic and political opportunities for many Americans. Some Progressives also looked with alarm on the discontent of industrial workers. They disliked the growing strength of organized labor but, even more, they hated the increasing influence of socialism.

At the end of the nineteenth century, reformers had little influence in the federal government. William McKinley's election in 1896 had been a triumph for big business. With prosperity, few government leaders paid attention to the discontent of the workers. Progressive reforms, therefore, began in city and state governments but did not spread to the national government until McKinley's death.

The Muckrakers

Some of the people who were interested in reform worked for agencies in the federal and state governments. Although these people could not eliminate the evils they saw around them, they could make the ugly facts known. They hoped that an aroused public would bring about reforms.

The job of informing the public fell to a remarkable group of journalists called *muckrakers*. They gained their name from Theodore Roosevelt, who said they were so intent on raking muck that they could not see the better things above them.

McClure's Magazine started the muckraking trend in 1902 with a series of articles on the Standard Oil Company by Ida M. Tarbell. In her writings, Tarbell outlined the cutthroat practices of one of the super corporations. Another series of articles, by Lincoln Steffens, described a corrupt alliance between business leaders and city political bosses. A third muckraker, Ray Stannard Baker, attacked the malpractices of a union during a coal strike in Colorado.

Other magazines, such as *Collier's* and *Cosmopolitan*, began publishing muckraking articles by many of the nation's best-known authors. In addition, some muckraking articles were reprinted in newspapers and collected in books.

Three of the most sensational exposures appeared in 1906. In *The Bitter Cry of the Children*, John Spargo described in painful detail the exploitation of children working in factories. His writings encouraged the Progressives to seek laws to control the conditions of child labor. David G. Phillips published a book called *The Treason of the Senate.* Using exaggerated evidence, he charged that most of the senators had sold out to the corporations and had betrayed the people. The most important book of 1906 was probably Upton Sinclair's *The Jungle.* In it he described the dreadful conditions in Chicago's meat-packing plants.

By 1912, muckraking had passed from the scene. It lost its effectiveness because business had grown hostile to it and the people had grown tired of its exposures. The muckrakers, however, had given a push to the entire Progressive movement.

Reforming City Government

Some reformers began to attack the special problems of the cities, especially machine politics, in the 1890's. In 1894, for example, reform forces overthrew New York's political machine, Tammany Hall, which had been founded a century earlier.

One of the outstanding city reformers was Tom L. Johnson, a successful businessman who was mayor of Cleveland from 1901 to 1909. As mayor he attacked unfair taxes, self-serving public utilities, and graft. With his Progressive program, he earned for Cleveland the reputation of being the nation's best-governed city.

Progressives also created new forms of government for the cities. These were the commission and city-manager plans of government. Up until this time, cities usually had been governed by an elected mayor and council. The mayor was elected by all the voters in the city, and the council members by the people of their wards. Under the *commission plan* a group of administrators, each a specialist in one field, replaced the mayor and council. This plan was first used in Galveston, Texas, in 1900, after a tidal wave had devastated that city. The commission plan later was adopted in other cities.

Severe burns were among the hazards these boys faced while working in a glass factory. Many accidents came about through the workers' exhaustion.

In 1913, after a flood in Dayton, Ohio, the people adopted the *city-manager plan,* which was already in use in Staunton, Virginia. Commissioners, elected on a nonpartisan basis, made laws and policies. But they appointed a manager—usually an expert in city administration—to run the city's departments. This plan was adopted widely.

Progressives used these plans to break the grip of corporations and machine politicians upon city governments. But this was not enough. Many city political machines were allied to machines in state governments.

Progressive Control of State Governments

The Progressives also attacked the state political machines. Under the leadership of Robert M. La Follette, Wisconsin became a hotbed of reform. "Battling Bob" La Follette defeated the statewide Republican machine to be elected governor in 1900. In his three terms, La Follette pushed for laws that regulated railroads and public utilities, developed a fair tax system, conserved the state's natural resources, and gave some protection to industrial workers.

Other states, too, produced successful reform programs. Governor Hiram W. Johnson of California broke the Southern Pacific Railroad's grip on the state. He then went on to set up a nonpartisan government. It pioneered in the use of political devices that made government more responsive to the wishes of the people.

Progressive politicians often found that the state legislatures or city councils refused to enact their reform programs. The Progressives tried to get around the obstacles with new legal devices like the referendum, initiative, and recall. The *referendum* permitted the voters to accept or reject a law passed by

BUSINESS ACTIVITY 1898-1920

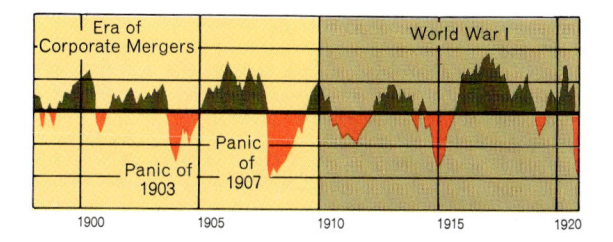

The chart *(above)* is based on manufacturing and mineral production. Upon the outbreak of a war, business prospects often become uncertain, and trade and industry are disturbed. Yet war production often stimulates, or even creates, prosperity. In the detail *(below)* the effect of World War I on the economy can be seen. In 1913, before the onset of the war, business activity in the United States seemed to be entering the first stages of a depression. The beginning of the war in Europe caused a further decline in prices and employment. But Europe's requirements for raw material, war supplies, and food forced the warring nations to turn to the United States. Before the end of 1915, European purchases turned the recession into a period of prosperity. With United States entry into the war in 1917, production demands were further increased. These demands touched off the greatest industrial effort in the nation's history. Reconversion to peacetime production brought only a temporary decrease in business activity. Industries that had been held back during the war quickly began great expansion. Prices soared until late 1920, when the boom ended and a depression began.

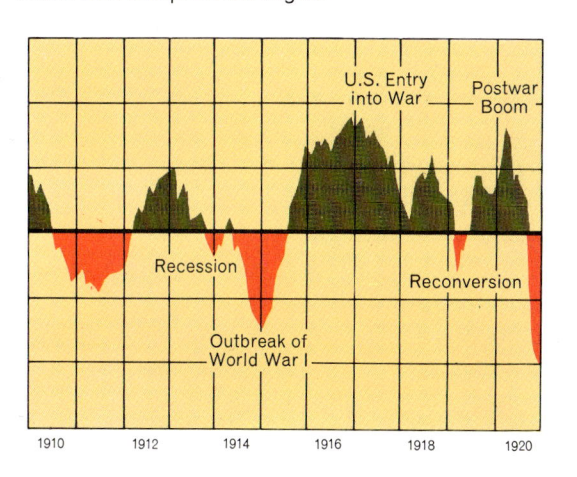

Trust Buster" such a popular President that Republican leaders did not dare drop him for a more conservative candidate. Roosevelt won his party's nomination. The Democrats nominated Judge Alton B. Parker, a conservative lawyer from New York.

The campaign was dull and the outcome never really in doubt. The people were impressed by "Teddy" and by his record, and he easily won the election.

Now that Roosevelt had been elected in his own right, he felt that he could carry out his own policies. He had promised business, labor, and the general public a "Square Deal," and he began his second administration with new attacks on the trusts.

Although dramatic, Teddy's "trust busting" did not halt the growth of giant corporations. Yet it did force the corporate financiers to proceed carefully. For the first time, the President effectively used the powers of government to curb big business.

Protecting the People

The Interstate Commerce Commission had proved ineffective in policing the railroads, primarily because the courts had limited its authority. Progressives wanted to strengthen the Interstate Commerce Commission. Roosevelt prodded Congress, and in June 1906, it passed the Hepburn Act. This proved to be the first truly effective law in regulating the railroads. It broadened the powers of the Interstate Commerce Commission by giving it authority over express companies and pipeline companies, as well as over the railroads. Most important, the new law gave the commission the power to set maximum rates.

During the struggle over the Hepburn Act, Roosevelt also used the power of the presidency to gain new laws to protect the people's health. Upton Sinclair's novel, *The Jungle*, had met with public outcry over such descriptions as these:

... There was never the least attention paid to what was cut up [in the hoppers] for sausage; there would come all the way back from Europe old sausage that had been rejected, and that was mouldy and white—it would be dosed with borax and glycerine, and dumped into the hoppers, and made over again for home consumption. There would be meat that had tumbled out on the floor, in the dirt and sawdust, where the workers had tramped and spit uncounted billions of [tuberculosis] germs. There would be meat stored in great piles in rooms; and the water from leaky roofs would drip over it, and thousands of rats would race about on it. It was too dark in these storage places to see well, but a man could run his hand over these piles of meat and sweep off handfuls of the dried dung of rats. These rats were nuisances, and the packers would put poisoned bread out for them. They would die, and then rats, bread, and meat would go into the hoppers together. This is no fairy story and no joke; the meat would be shoveled into carts, and the man who did the shoveling would not trouble to lift out a rat even when he saw one—there were things that went into the sausage in comparison with which a poisoned rat was a tidbit.

Roosevelt named a commission to look into conditions in the meat-packing industry. The investigators confirmed Sinclair's findings. Faced with this evidence and with an aroused public, Congress in June 1906 passed two important laws. The Pure Food and Drug Act barred the manufacture or sale of adulterated or mislabeled foods and drugs in interstate commerce. The Meat Inspection Act put some teeth into the existing sanitary regulations for meat-packing establishments and provided for federal inspection of companies preparing meat for interstate shipment.

The Conservation Crusade

In no area of reform did Roosevelt work longer or harder than in the conservation of the natural resources of the nation. He was particularly interested in preserving the wilderness areas. To gain support for his program, the President had to fight to change old practices.

Since the establishment of the United States, the federal government had followed a simple policy toward the natural resources it controlled. It had distributed public lands, mineral deposits, and other riches as quickly and as cheaply as possible to people who would develop them.

Roosevelt's first conservation victory came in June 1902, when he signed the National Reclamation Act (the Newlands Act). It allowed the federal government to construct and maintain large irrigation projects in western and southwestern states.

In his second term, Roosevelt put all the resources and power of his office into the conservation crusade. Through use of existing laws, he tried to stop the exploitation of the nation's forests. He also set aside millions of acres of phosphate and coal beds as national reserves, created five national parks, and set up more than fifty wildlife refuges. Although Roosevelt was unable to stop the looting of the national domain, he did slow it down. Equally important, he aroused national interest in conservation.

Uses of Presidential Power

Roosevelt believed that as President he could act unless a law or the Constitution specifically forbade him to do so. By applying his interpretation of presidential power, he advanced his programs. But he also came into conflict with business leaders and with Congress.

In the Panic of 1907, many business leaders claimed that the panic had been caused by Roosevelt's breaking up of the trusts. Roosevelt lashed back, saying that "certain malefactors of great wealth" had forced the crisis so that he would ease his attack on the corporations.

Regardless of the charges and countercharges, Roosevelt wanted to keep the panic from spreading. Some bankers convinced him that the panic would end if United States

The conservation movement

Theodore Roosevelt and John Muir visit Yosemite National Park.

Interest in conserving the natural resources of the United States dates far back in the nation's history. The earliest conservationists were usually more interested in saving the resources for use rather than for their scenic beauty. But as far back as the 1840's, Henry David Thoreau advocated setting aside natural preserves to protect wildlife.

After the Civil War, the federal government began acting to preserve resources. Congress set up Yellowstone, the nation's first national park, in 1872. It was a sanctuary for wildlife, including the few remaining buffalo. John Muir, a naturalist and writer, campaigned for forest conservation and organized the Sierra Club, which concerned itself with working to preserve the wilderness. In 1890, Muir helped persuade Congress to set aside land for Yosemite and Sequoia National Parks.

Muir and Gifford Pinchot helped sell President Theodore Roosevelt on conservation. Four-fifths of the nation's forests had been cut, and much that was left was in the hands of large lumber companies. Roosevelt put Pinchot in charge of all federal timberlands.

Pinchot used trained forest rangers to protect the woods and worked to educate the public on the need to save the forests. During Roosevelt's presidency, the federal government set aside 126 million acres of forest reserves. Earlier, Presidents Harrison, Cleveland, and McKinley had reserved a total of 47 million acres.

Roosevelt, Pinchot, and Muir also worked to promote scientific use and reclamation of resources. Under the Newlands Act, the government built great dams and many irrigation works. Thousands of acres of semidesert land in Arizona, California, Colorado, and Utah were opened to cultivation, much to the consternation of later ecologists.

In May 1908, Roosevelt held a White House conference of governors, federal officials, and business leaders to gain support for his policies. The meeting helped stir interest in important legislation. Roosevelt also appointed the National Conservation Commission to make a survey of the nation's mineral, forest, water, and soil resources.

Steel took over control of one of its competitors. He allowed the company to do so, even though that action might be a violation of the antitrust law.

This episode led Progressives to question Roosevelt's dedication to reform. But the incident also showed the power of the bankers over the economy. Roosevelt suggested a number of Progressive measures in 1907 and 1908 that would have increased government's influence over the economy. Congress considered his proposals too radical, however, and refused to enact them.

THE PROGRESSIVE REVOLT

On the night of his election to the presidency in 1904, Roosevelt had announced that the three-and-a-half years of McKinley's unexpired term he had served constituted his own first term. "The wise custom which limits the President to two terms regards the substance and not the form," he said, "and under no circumstances will I be a candidate for or accept another nomination."

Within the next four years this decision proved to be both painful and embarrassing. It pained Roosevelt because he really did not want to leave the White House. It embarrassed him because he was immensely popular and was under pressure to forget his pledge of 1904 and seek a third term. Roosevelt resisted the pressures, however, and stood by his promise.

A New President

Since Roosevelt was the leader of the Republican party, he chose the party's candidate. At the Republican convention, he arranged the nomination of William Howard Taft, secretary of war. Taft had been a staunch supporter of the President's policies, and he seemed to be committed to continuing them.

The Democrats nominated William Jennings Bryan for the third time. Both candidates expressed support for Progressive policies. Bryan attacked the trusts and promised to reduce the high Republican tariff. Taft promised to continue the Square Deal program and to revise the tariff.

After a dull campaign, Taft won the election. Shortly after Taft was inaugurated, Roosevelt left to hunt big game in Africa. Taft was on his own.

The new President had a long record of government service. He had been a federal judge, governor of the Philippine Islands, and secretary of war. Although Taft was conservative by temperament, he believed that the President should be more concerned with the public welfare than with the profits of giant corporations. Taft considered himself a Progressive.

Taft took office in troubled times. The old guard Republicans disliked Progressivism, and the party stood in danger of splitting. Only bold and clever leadership could prevent such a split. Taft could not offer such leadership.

One of the first disputes Taft faced was that over the tariff. For decades, Americans had disagreed about the tariff. By 1908, the pressure for action had become so great that the Republican platform came out for tariff revision, and Taft himself promised a reduction in rates.

Shortly after his inauguration, Taft called Congress into special session to revise the tariff. What emerged was the Payne-Aldrich bill, which lowered some rates but kept most of them high. A small group of midwestern senators, led by Wisconsin's La Follette, fought the bill. Although the Republican Progressives did not prevent passage of the bill, they amended it to include an income tax for corporations.

On the whole, the new tariff bill represented another victory for eastern manufacturers and old guard Republicans. Taft thought it contained a few worthwhile reductions, and so he signed it into law.

The Progressives attacked the Payne-Aldrich Tariff, and Taft decided to go to the people to defend his position. He showed poor political judgment in a number of instances. In one speech he said, "On the whole . . . the Payne bill is the best bill that the Republican Party has ever passed." Progressives suspected that he had repudiated his campaign pledge.

The Progressives and Taft also disagreed about conservation. The controversy began when the secretary of the interior, Richard Ballinger, reopened some water-power sites in Montana and Wyoming to development by private companies.

Ballinger was accused by the chief of the forest service, Gifford Pinchot, of having betrayed the conservation policies of Roosevelt. Taft investigated the matter in 1910 and decided that Ballinger had done nothing illegal. But Pinchot was dismissed. This action angered the Progressives.

A Divided Party

Taft also encountered trouble in the revolt of Progressives against Joseph G. Cannon, the speaker of the House of Representatives. Cannon had been a member of the House for almost fifty-five years when Taft became President. Cannon was skilled at political maneuvering; he ruled the House with an iron hand. Progressives disliked him because he was a friend of the corporations and because he used his power to block Progressive legislation.

As speaker, Cannon could recognize or refuse to recognize members who sought the floor and thereby control the issues brought before the House. He also appointed the members and chairmen of House committees. As chairman of the Committee on Rules, he could prevent any bill from leaving the committee to go to the House for debate.

In 1909, Progressive Republicans in the House made plans to limit Cannon's power. Speaker Cannon appealed to the President for help. Although Taft disliked Cannon, he thought he needed the support of the speaker. The President endorsed Cannon. When the revolt failed, some of the insurgents felt that Taft had betrayed them.

How many products of the 1970's could claim to destroy not only pain-causing demons but also a devil carrying a Confederate Stars and Bars flag?

In 1910 the Progressive Republicans again attacked Cannon. This time Republican insurgents worked closely with Democrats to gain enough backing to outvote the regular, or conservative, Republicans. A resolution to limit the power of the speaker of the House passed because more than forty insurgent Republicans voted with the Democrats. Under the new rules, the speaker could no longer rule the House but was merely the presiding officer.

Progressives did not capture control of the House. Cannon remained as speaker, and conservative Republicans continued to control the committees. But the Republican party was split. Since the President had not helped them, Progressives were convinced that he had sided with Cannon.

Taft had not favored Cannon, but in the elections of 1910, he worked with conservatives to defeat the midwestern insurgents. He had become convinced that the insurgents wanted to destroy his political career. Taft's action turned out to be disastrous. In the primary elections in states west of the Mississippi River, the Progressives defeated the regular Republicans.

In the November elections, the Republican party suffered a major defeat. The Democrats won control of the House. Republicans retained a weak grip on the Senate. These election results suggested that without the support of the Progressives, the Republican party was in danger. Many felt that Taft's blunders had split the party.

Taft or Roosevelt?

Progressives were harsh in their criticism of Taft. Yet he favored many Progressive objectives and continued many of Roosevelt's policies. For example, Taft started about twice as many suits for violations of the Sherman Antitrust Act as Roosevelt had started in seven-and-a-half years in office.

The Taft administration could also take

Taft tries to straighten out a tangled mess as a disgruntled Roosevelt looks on. Many Americans seemed to criticize Taft for not being Roosevelt.

some credit for Progressive legislation. But most of the measures passed primarily because Progressives pushed them.

While in Africa and Europe, Theodore Roosevelt heard rumors that his policies had been abandoned by the President. Roosevelt returned to the United States in 1910, during the peak of the controversy between Taft and the Progressives. At first he said nothing publicly about the quarreling within his party, but privately he felt that Taft had let him down. He was particularly upset because the strong party that he had built had fallen apart under Taft.

In January 1911, insurgent leaders formed the National Progressive Republican League. It sought to defeat Taft and gain the Republican nomination for Senator Robert La Follette, the nation's leading Progressive. When La Follette, exhausted and worried, delivered a rambling speech in February 1912, many insurgents deserted him. They turned to Roosevelt, who had changed his mind about a third term and was ready to fight for the Republican nomination. Roosevelt announced his candidacy, touching off a bitter primary campaign. Taft and Roosevelt had become opponents for their party's nomination for President.

A Democratic Triumph

In the thirteen states that held primary elections, Roosevelt won most of the delegates to the Republican National Convention. But most states chose their delegates in state conventions, which were usually controlled by conservative Republicans. Most of the delegates therefore went to Taft. In a dispute over the seating of delegates, Taft won almost all the seats. Angered, Roosevelt's delegates stormed out of the hall. Taft was renominated on the first ballot.

Roosevelt addressed his followers, shouting that he would fight for the presidency as the candidate of a third party. The reformers then organized the Progressive party. Its convention was held in August. Roosevelt was in fine spirits when he arrived, claiming he felt "as fit as a bull moose." That animal became the new party's symbol.

The convention adopted a platform that included most of the reforms that Progressives had long desired. Roosevelt, of course, was given the Progressive nomination.

The Democrats, too, had a battle between a Progressive candidate and a more conservative one. The opponents were Woodrow Wilson, the governor of New Jersey, and James "Champ" Clark, speaker of the House, from Missouri. After forty-six ballots, Wilson won the nomination. The platform called for reforms that Progressives had always wanted. But it did not go as far in its demands as did the "Bull Moose" platform.

Wilson and Roosevelt both campaigned as Progressives. This led Taft to remark, "I have no part to play but that of a conservative." Soon he practically dropped out of the running, and the struggle was narrowed to Wilson and Roosevelt.

Roosevelt campaigned for the "New Nationalism," a program of his Progressive ideas. During the campaign, an assassin shot Roosevelt but only wounded the candidate.

Wilson's program was called the "New

Above: Suffragists line up for a parade. Women's groups pointed out that in most states women had the same voting rights as lunatics, criminals, and feeble-minded men—none. *Below:* The Women's Christian Temperance Union urges law enforcement. Before passage of the prohibition amendment, many states outlawed the sale and manufacture of liquor.

Freedom." Wilson suggested that the New Freedom would free the people from the chains of big business.

When the ballots were counted and Wilson proclaimed the winner, it was clear that he had profited from the Republican split. He won about 42 percent of the vote, but that was enough for victory. The Democrats also won control of both houses of Congress. Although Wilson was a minority President, he did represent the majority will in the sense that the majority had voted for a Progressive government.

Women in Politics

From 1896 to 1910, the women's movement was in the doldrums. Its revitalization was sparked by Harriot Stanton Blatch, the daughter of Elizabeth Cady Stanton. Early in 1907, Mrs. Blatch helped set up the Equality League of Self-Supporting Women (later called the Women's Political Union). She felt that new methods of action were needed if women were ever to win the ballot and that suffragists needed to draw trade unionists, immigrants, and other working women into the fight for the vote.

Mrs. Blatch had been impressed by the militant suffrage campaign then taking place in England. The English feminists were using a number of tactics to attract attention to their cause—from smashing windows to pouring acid into mailboxes, from attacking government officials to staging hunger strikes in jail.

The League began using dramatic ways to call attention to its cause. It held demonstrations and worked to defeat antisuffrage legislators. It organized parades, a tactic that was soon being used by more conservative suffrage groups. Inspired by the vigor and success of the League, older suffrage groups revived, and new ones formed among all classes of women in the nation.

Results began coming in. In 1910, voters

WOMEN'S SUFFRAGE: THREE VIEWS

GEORGE G. VEST
Senator from Missouri

... [What] would be the result if suffrage were given to the women of the United States?

Women are essentially emotional. ... It is no more insulting to say that women are emotional than to say that they are delicately constructed physically and unfitted to become soldiers or workmen under the sterner, harder pursuits of life.

... [What] we need is to put more logic into public affairs and less feeling. ... There are kingdoms in which the heart should reign supreme. That kingdom belongs to women.

... It is said that the suffrage is to be given to enlarge the sphere of woman's influence. Mr. President, it would destroy her influence. It would take her down from that pedestal where she is today, influencing as a mother the minds of her offspring, influencing by her gentle and kindly caress the action of her husband toward the good and pure. *(1887)*

CARRIE CHAPMAN CATT
President, National American Woman Suffrage Association, 1900–1902, 1915–1920

Sex prejudice ... may be briefly stated as a belief that men were the units of the human race. They performed the real functions of the race; all the responsibilities and duties of working out the destiny of the race were theirs. Women were auxiliaries, or dependents ....

The whole aim of the woman movement has been to destroy the idea that obedience is necessary to women; to train women to such self-respect that they would not grant obedience and to train men to such comprehension of equity they would not exact it. ...

... The individual woman no longer obeys the individual man. ... The question now is ... [shall] the woman who enjoys the right of self-government in every other department of life be permitted the right of self-government in the State? ... It is no more right for men to govern women than it was for one man to govern other men. *(1902)*

ALICE DUER MILLER
Feminist poet and humorist, she listed "Our Own Twelve Anti-Suffragist Reasons"

1. Because no woman will leave her domestic duties to vote.
2. Because no woman who may vote will attend to her domestic duties.
3. Because it will make dissension between husband and wife.
4. Because every woman will vote as her husband tells her to.
5. Because bad women will corrupt politics.
6. Because bad politics will corrupt women.
7. Because women have no power of organization.
8. Because women will form a solid party and outvote men.
9. Because men and women are so different that they must stick to different duties.
10. Because men and women are so much alike that men, with one vote each, can represent their own views and ours too.
11. Because women cannot use force.
12. Because the militants did use force.

(1915)

in the state of Washington approved women's suffrage in a referendum. A massive campaign in California in 1911 won women the vote. In 1912, women's suffrage was approved in Arizona, Kansas, and Oregon; in 1913, in Illinois.

Success was limited, however. The closer victory seemed, the stronger the opposition became. In Michigan the election was stolen by the liquor interests. In Ohio and Wisconsin the liquor industry brought in the antisuffrage vote so heavily that outright theft was unnecessary. Many suffragists despaired of winning the vote state by state. In 1913 they turned their energies to getting an amendment to the Constitution.

They focused their activity on the Democratic party, which was then in control. They tried to force the party to support the national amendment. When this failed, they worked to defeat the party. Meanwhile, other groups continued the fight to win the vote through state referendums.

THE NEW FREEDOM

Woodrow Wilson was born in Virginia five years before the start of the Civil War. He was reared in Georgia and the Carolinas and studied law as a young man. Unsuccessful as a lawyer, he turned to graduate studies in political science and history, wrote a book on congressional government, and became a college professor.

In 1902, Wilson became president of Princeton University and began a number of educational reforms that brought him national attention. Wilson had always been interested in politics, and his office gave him an opportunity to speak out on political issues. At first his views were like those of many conservative southern Democrats. But gradually he joined the Progressives.

Two situations gave Wilson a chance to plunge into politics. Because of a disagreement at Princeton, in 1910 he was willing to resign his post. At this time, too, New Jersey's Democratic bosses were looking for a respected, educated, and cultured figurehead to run for governor. They offered Wilson the nomination. He accepted and went on to win the election. But as governor, Wilson was not a figurehead. He turned against the bosses and pushed a bold reform program through the state legislature. From that success he went on to win the presidency.

Lowering the Tariff, Again

Few men ever became President with a more carefully planned program than did Wilson. Basic in his plan was presidential leadership of Congress. Unlike Roosevelt, Wilson had the support of a party majority in Congress.

Wilson called Congress into special session to deal with the first objective of the New Freedom—the lowering of the tariff. Like many Democrats, Wilson believed the high tariff gave special favors to big business and helped build monopolies. When the special session met early in April, Wilson dramatically broke a precedent that had been followed by Presidents for over a hundred years. Instead of sending his messages to Congress by messengers, to be read by someone else, Wilson appeared before Congress to explain what he wanted. He pleaded his case for tariff reform.

The proposed Underwood Tariff passed easily in the House of Representatives in 1913. The bill called for duties that were low enough to bring European goods into competition with American products. This proposal alarmed industrialists, and their lobbyists put pressure on the Senate to raise the rates. The President stepped into the battle, acting as the lobbyist for the people. Public pressure became so strong that the Senate approved the bill with essentially the low rates the administration desired.

PRESIDENTIAL ELECTIONS: 1904-1916

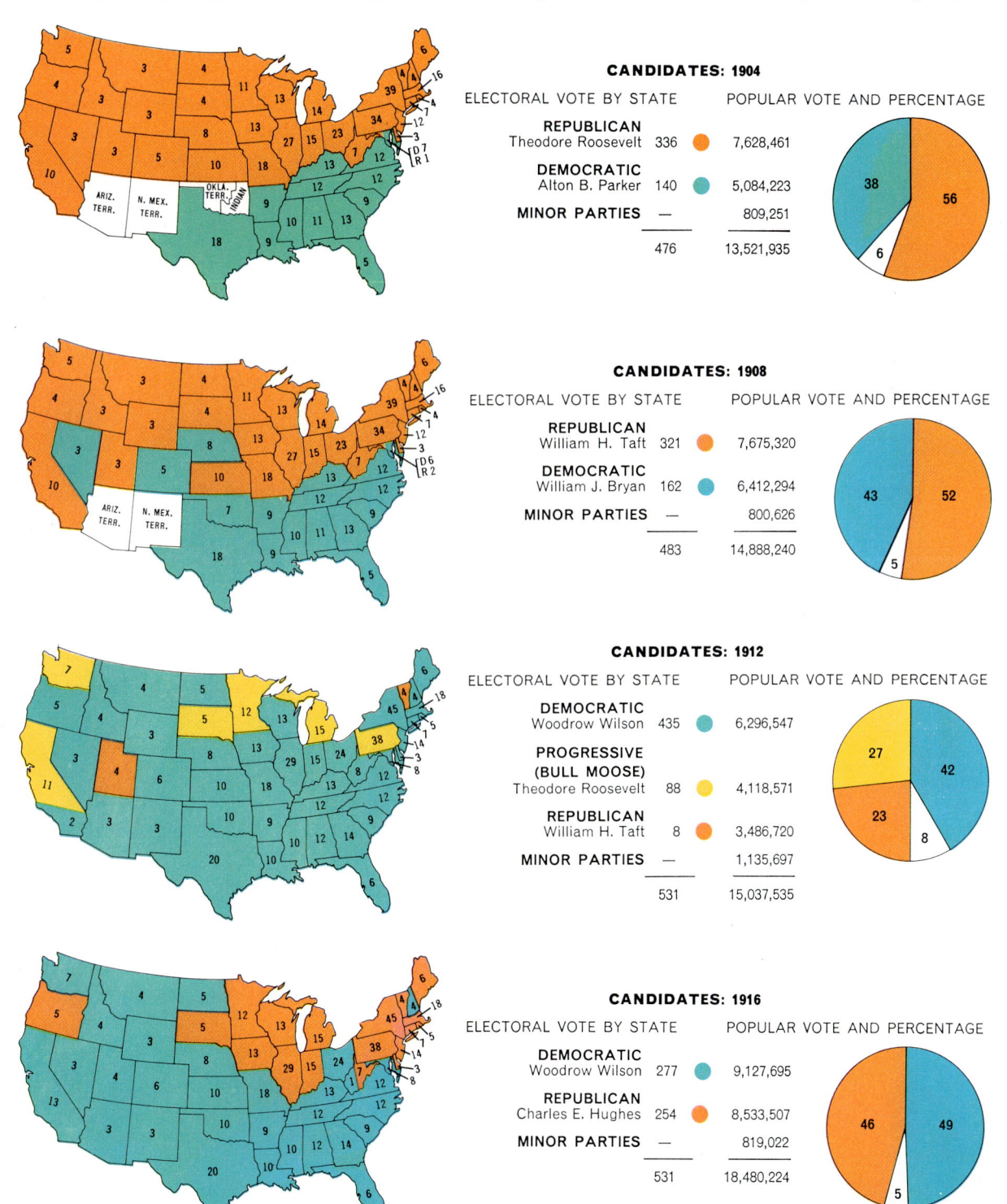

CANDIDATES: 1904

ELECTORAL VOTE BY STATE | POPULAR VOTE AND PERCENTAGE

REPUBLICAN
Theodore Roosevelt 336 — 7,628,461

DEMOCRATIC
Alton B. Parker 140 — 5,084,223

MINOR PARTIES — 809,251

476 — 13,521,935

Republican: 56, Democratic: 38, Minor: 6

CANDIDATES: 1908

ELECTORAL VOTE BY STATE | POPULAR VOTE AND PERCENTAGE

REPUBLICAN
William H. Taft 321 — 7,675,320

DEMOCRATIC
William J. Bryan 162 — 6,412,294

MINOR PARTIES — 800,626

483 — 14,888,240

Republican: 52, Democratic: 43, Minor: 5

CANDIDATES: 1912

ELECTORAL VOTE BY STATE | POPULAR VOTE AND PERCENTAGE

DEMOCRATIC
Woodrow Wilson 435 — 6,296,547

PROGRESSIVE (BULL MOOSE)
Theodore Roosevelt 88 — 4,118,571

REPUBLICAN
William H. Taft 8 — 3,486,720

MINOR PARTIES — 1,135,697

531 — 15,037,535

Democratic: 42, Progressive: 27, Republican: 23, Minor: 8

CANDIDATES: 1916

ELECTORAL VOTE BY STATE | POPULAR VOTE AND PERCENTAGE

DEMOCRATIC
Woodrow Wilson 277 — 9,127,695

REPUBLICAN
Charles E. Hughes 254 — 8,533,507

MINOR PARTIES — 819,022

531 — 18,480,224

Democratic: 49, Republican: 46, Minor: 5

To offset the expected loss of government revenue from the new tariff, a special section of the bill set up a graduated federal income tax. This measure marked the beginning of great change in the system of taxation in the United States.

The Federal Reserve System

Before the tariff issue had been settled, Wilson turned to the second part of his program—the reform of the nation's money and banking system. The Panic of 1907 had shown how serious the defects of the system were, and almost everyone agreed that it had to be changed.

In 1913 an investigating committee in the House of Representatives, led by Arsène Pujo of Louisiana, published a report. It showed that a few great investment bankers on Wall Street controlled much of the nation's wealth.

In June 1913, Wilson asked Congress for new banking laws that would not permit "the concentration anywhere in a few hands of the monetary resources of the country." Democrats differed among themselves over what the banking system should be. For a while the issue threatened to disrupt the party. Then the President and his advisers worked out a compromise bill that made its way through both houses of Congress and became the Federal Reserve Act of 1913.

The Federal Reserve System combined centralization with decentralization. While it left money and banking mostly in private hands, the government had an important voice in the system.

The Federal Reserve Act provided that the system would be supervised by a Board of Governors, with members serving fourteen-year terms. The members would be appointed by the President with the approval of the Senate. The board would help formulate the nation's monetary policy.

The law also divided the nation into twelve

From dawn to dusk the "breaker boys" separated coal from shale. The long hours and lack of fresh air sometimes stunted their growth. Many mine workers developed lung diseases from inhaling coal dust.

Federal Reserve Districts, each having one Federal Reserve Bank. Often called "bankers' banks," Federal Reserve Banks held the reserves of all public commercial banks that were members of the system. They also kept the depositories of the federal government and issued the paper currency—Federal Reserve notes. National banks were required to belong to the Federal Reserve System. State banks were allowed to join if they met certain federal requirements.

New Controls on Corporations

The President next tried to break up giant corporations. Many of them had continued to increase their power. Late in January 1914, he asked Congress for laws against holding companies and interlocking directorates and for a federal commission to supervise big business.

In September the President signed the Federal Trade Commission Act. This law set up a bipartisan commission that could investigate industries suspected of violating antitrust laws. It was empowered to issue "cease and desist" orders against those found guilty of using unfair methods of competition. If these orders were not obeyed, the commission could bring the accused corporation to court for trial.

The Clayton Antitrust Act, which became law in October 1914, was supposed to strengthen the Sherman Antitrust Act. It made interlocking directorates and other practices that lessened competition illegal. It also made corporation officers individually liable for violations of the antitrust laws.

The Federal Trade Commission and Clayton acts were passed just after war had broken out in Europe. It was a time of de-

Lewis W. Hine, International Museum of Photography at George Eastman House, Rochester, N.Y.

pression and unemployment, and Americans were uneasy. Although the depression was caused by conditions in Europe, business leaders in the United States blamed the Underwood Tariff and other New Freedom laws for it. The President tried to sooth the business leaders with mild applications of the new reform laws. When the United States was drawn into the war, the government suspended application of the antitrust laws.

Benefits for Workers and Farmers

For many years organized labor had suffered greater penalties under the antitrust laws than had the corporations. The courts had held that strikes and boycotts by labor and farm unions restrained trade and were punishable under the Sherman Antitrust Act. Since organized labor was not being helped by the Republicans, it turned to the Democrats. In 1912, Samuel Gompers and other leaders of the American Federation of Labor campaigned for Wilson. When Wilson was elected President, they assumed they had a friend in the White House.

The first test of Wilson's policy toward labor came with the Clayton Act. The law said that labor unions and farm organizations were not conspiracies in restraint of trade. It allowed strikes and peaceful picketing. It also prohibited the use of injunctions in labor disputes except when necessary to prevent "irreparable injury to property, or to a property right." Although the law seemed to grant labor's demands, the courts later interpreted it to make unions subject to prosecution under the antitrust laws.

In 1916, Congress passed an act that gave federal employees compensation during periods of disability. Wilson himself worked for passage that year of the Keating-Owen Act. It forbade the shipment in interstate commerce of goods manufactured by children. The Supreme Court, in the case of *Hammer v. Dagenhart* (1918), struck down the law as an invasion of states' rights. Nevertheless the act marked a beginning of federal control over such aspects of manufacturing. It also showed a greater concern for social justice than Wilson had previously exhibited.

The labor law that attracted greatest attention in 1916 came out of a dispute in which the railroad unions demanded an eight-hour day. The unions threatened a strike that would have paralyzed the nation's internal commerce. Wilson offered to mediate, but both sides turned down his offer. When he decided that the workers' basic demand was just, he asked Congress for a law that would prevent the strike. Congress passed the Adamson Act, which gave the railroad workers an eight-hour day at the rate previously paid for a ten-hour day. Business leaders were furious, but the law ended the threat of a strike.

Like the laborers, farmers expected special treatment from Wilson and the Democrats. In July 1916, the Federal Farm Loan Act was passed, setting up special banks in each of the Federal Reserve districts. Farmers could borrow money from these banks on a long-term basis at a low rate of interest. The farmers would use their land and improvements for security. The Federal Farm Loan Bank would watch over the whole system.

Farmers also benefited from two other laws passed during the Wilson administration. The Smith-Lever Act of May 1914 provided federal funds for rural education through the cooperation of the Department of Agriculture and the land-grant colleges. In February 1917 the Smith-Hughes Act provided federal money for vocational education in agriculture and the trades.

A Changing Program

In its first phase the New Freedom had not been much concerned with social justice. It had been a limited program of economic reform that tried to provide for free competition. In 1914 Wilson thought he had achieved this objective, and he called a halt to further reform. At first he opposed the bill for land banks to help farmers, refused to fight for a child-labor bill, and would not support women's suffrage. He also was a white supremacist. By executive action, he ended the integration of white and black workers in federal jobs, a policy that had been in effect since Reconstruction. His segregation policy alienated black voters from the Democratic party.

Progressive candidates lost everywhere in the congressional elections of 1914. The Republican party, united behind its candidates, greatly reduced the Democratic majority in the House of Representatives. Republicans also regained power in key eastern states and looked strong enough to win the presidency in the next election.

Early in 1916, Theodore Roosevelt said

that he would rejoin the Republican party and take his Progressive following with him. If this were to happen, the Democrats faced almost certain defeat. To prevent this, Wilson tried to lure Roosevelt Progressives into the Democratic party by showing that the party was committed to social reform. The first sign of this change was his appointment of Louis D. Brandeis, a labor lawyer, to the Supreme Court. Then followed the various reform laws. These laws passed Congress because most Democrats accepted Wilson's course as the best means of staying in power.

Wilson's record was not the only issue of the campaign. Foreign policy also became an issue. Speakers at the Democratic convention pointed out that Wilson had kept the United States at peace while the nations of Europe were fighting a great war. The Democrats renominated Wilson and adopted as a campaign slogan, "He kept us out of war."

Meeting in Chicago, the Republicans chose as their candidate Charles Evans Hughes, an associate justice of the Supreme

Workers showed their opposition to unsatisfactory conditions of labor in various ways. *Above:* Laundry workers in New York stage a sit-down strike. The International Workers of the World *(below)* sometimes resorted to violence. The I.W.W. members, or "Wobblies," were Marxist in their approach to social and economic problems. They attracted attention by singing as they marched. They issued *The Little Red Song Book*, which included such works as "Solidarity Forever," and "Joe Hill."

Court and former governor of New York. Hughes was acceptable to both factions of the party.

The Progressive party offered its nomination to Roosevelt. He refused it because he did not want to pull votes away from the Republicans, and he did want to see Wilson defeated. The Progressive party did not name another candidate. Many people who had voted for Roosevelt in 1912 now turned to the Democrats. The Woman's party, organized in June, campaigned in the twelve states where women had the vote to defeat Wilson and other Democratic candidates.

Wilson campaigned on two issues, Progressivism and peace. Hughes proved an unexciting campaigner. On most domestic issues he took a conservative position and on matters of foreign policy he seemed to favor intervention in the war. Roosevelt's support did not help, for he had abandoned Progressivism and was going around the country making speeches in favor of war.

Wilson was reelected and the Democrats retained control over both houses of Congress by a narrow margin. Progressivism, when fused with the peace issue, still seemed attractive enough to the voters to give victory to a minority Democratic party over a united Republican party. Wilson intended to continue on his course of Progressivism, but the war in Europe diverted him. By the time of Wilson's second inaugural in March 1917, Progressivism was dying.

A Look at Specifics

1. How did Progressivism differ from Populism? From socialism?

2. How did *The Jungle* influence reform?

3. Describe the new forms of city government developed in the Progressive era.

4. What were the functions of the initiative, the referendum, the recall, and the direct primary?

5. What steps did Roosevelt take to regulate big business?

6. What provisions of the Clayton Antitrust Act were intended to curb trusts?

A Review of Major Ideas

1. What reforms were made during the Progressive era?

2. In what ways was the role of the federal government broadened during the Progressive era?

3. Compare the roles of Roosevelt, Taft, and Wilson in promoting reforms.

For Independent Study

1. Roosevelt believed that the President could do anything that the Constitution did not specifically prohibit. Could this attitude lead to the development of a dictatorship? In your answer, consider the constitutional limitations on the President's power.

2. In the late nineteenth and early twentieth centuries, the tariff was often a major issue in election campaigns. Why is the tariff rarely a major issue any longer? What part has the income tax played in the declining importance of the tariff?

3. By instituting the city-manager and commission forms of city government, Progressives hoped to make city politics "nonpartisan." Do you think that political decisions can be "nonpartisan"? Discuss.

Foreign Involvement

CHAPTER 19
1900–1920

The United States victory in the war with Spain had cast the nation into two new roles—colonizer and world power. The people of the United States did not really know how they wanted the government to act in either situation. Nor were the nation's leaders equipped to handle these roles.

As you read this chapter, ask yourself: What misconceptions did the nation's leaders have about other governments and other peoples that affected their policies? Did the United States always consider its own self-interest first? Did American leaders view policies from a world perspective? In your opinion, how should a world power behave?

NEW AREAS OF INTEREST

In its role as a colonizer, the United States faced important constitutional questions. The nation also became more interested in other parts of the world than it had been.

A New Policy on Expansion

By 1900, the United States had acquired a colonial empire that stretched from the Caribbean Sea to distant places in the Pacific Ocean. That empire included Puerto Rico and Alaska as well as Hawaii, American Samoa, Guam, the Philippine Islands, and other islands in the Pacific.

When the United States had acquired new lands earlier in the nineteenth century, it had used a territorial system to govern them. The territories were treated as future parts of the Union, and the people in them were given the constitutional rights and privileges enjoyed by other United States citizens. In dealing with most of the new island possessions, however, the United States government did not follow this pattern. Instead, it set up a system of government that was very much like the system of colonial administration used in the British Empire.

The colonial system was based on the be-

American troops slog through a muddy field, July 1918.

lief that people in the colonies were not yet ready for self-government. But the Constitution guarantees rights of self-government to all United States citizens. Thus the administration of the dependencies raised a serious question: What were the constitutional rights of the people in the new colonies?

The Supreme Court provided an answer in the so-called Insular Cases between 1901 and 1922. The Court said that the Constitution did not apply in all places under United States control. In arriving at this decision, the Court made a vague distinction between "incorporated" and "unincorporated" territories. The Court held that people in the incorporated territories, such as Alaska and Hawaii, would enjoy the full rights guaranteed to United States citizens. But people in the unincorporated territories—dependencies like Puerto Rico, the Philippines, Guam, and American Samoa—were not entitled to all of the constitutional rights and privileges. Congress therefore could govern the colonies in almost any way it wished.

China Policy

When the United States gained an empire in the Pacific, it became directly involved in the politics of East Asia. Thus the government had to devise a policy for dealing with the nations of Asia and with the European nations with interests in that area.

Two developments greatly affected the nature of the American involvement. One was the continuing weakness of China, which had long been dominated by Europeans. The other was the rise of Japan to the standing of a great power. Japan had defeated China in 1895 in a war for control of Korea.

The British, who controlled about 80 percent of China's foreign trade, had supported the idea of equal commercial opportunity in China for all nations. In 1899, however, China's weakness led Britain, France, Russia, Germany, and Japan to demand more than privileges in trade and investment; they threatened to partition China, to carve it into colonies that they would control.

At first this threatened breakup did not alarm the United States, because trade with China had never been great. Some American business leaders, however, were concerned. They believed that China could be a huge market for trade in the future. If China were dismembered, each nation with a Chinese colony would probably discriminate against traders from other nations. The United States would then be frozen out of the Chinese market.

An American fighter shares his canteen with a wounded Japanese soldier during the Boxer Rebellion. The Boxers were opposed to all foreign intervention in China, whether by western or Asian nations.

In September and November 1899, Secretary of State John Hay sent notes to Britain, Germany, Russia, Japan, France, and Italy. In the notes he asked those nations to support the "Open Door"—equal commercial opportunity for all nations in China. All the replies were either qualified or evasive. Yet in March 1900, Hay announced that the powers had given him assurances.

In June a violent anticolonial uprising, the Boxer Rebellion, broke out in China. Powerful bands of Chinese nationalists, known as Boxers, overran the capital and besieged the foreign legations in the city. In August an international army of European, American, and Japanese troops finally rescued the trapped foreigners.

Secretary of State Hay feared that some of the powers would use the Boxer troubles as an excuse to take Chinese territory. In July 1900, at the height of the crisis, he restated his Open Door policy. He asked the other great powers to preserve China's territorial claims as well as freedom of trade.

The other powers did not pay much attention to Hay's policy. What saved China from dismemberment was the mutual jealousy of the powers. Nonetheless, Hay had made it clear that although the United States would not back the Open Door policy with force, it was concerned over China's fate.

The Russo-Japanese War

Russia used the Boxer troubles to gain control of Manchuria. Russia's moves aroused the Japanese, who also wished to take over Manchuria. Late in 1903, the two nations tried to reach an understanding about the future of Manchuria and Korea. When Russia would not accept Japan's terms, Japan broke off negotiations. In February 1904, the Japanese attacked the Russian fleet at Port Arthur, Manchuria. All the land fighting in the ensuing Russo-Japanese War took place on Chinese soil.

As soon as the war began, President Theodore Roosevelt reasserted the Open Door policy. He asked Japan and Russia to respect China's neutrality and independence, but neither did so.

Although the Japanese were winning victory after victory, the war was driving them to bankruptcy. In the spring of 1905, they asked Roosevelt to mediate. Russia agreed to peace negotiations at Portsmouth, New Hampshire. At the peace conference, Roosevelt helped arrange a compromise that led to the Treaty of Portsmouth (1905), ending the war. The compromise kept defeated Russia in East Asia and contributed to a balance of power between Russia and Japan.

Japanese Reactions

The Russo-Japanese War marked the first victory of a modern Asian nation over a major western power. It gave new life to nationalism in Asia, confirmed Japan as a world power, and made Japan the dominant power in Korea and southern Manchuria.

Almost everyone but the Japanese praised Roosevelt's peacemaking efforts. The Japanese people believed that the compromise arranged by Roosevelt had robbed their nation of the fruits of victory. Anti-American riots swept over Japan.

Developments within the United States increased tension with Japan. In October 1906, the San Francisco school board's segregation of Japanese children touched off an international crisis and started talk of war.

President Roosevelt was fond of quoting an old West African proverb, "Speak softly and carry a big stick." While he negotiated with the Japanese, he held his big stick—the navy—in reserve.

Roosevelt persuaded the San Franciscans to end their segregation. In return, the Japanese government promised to stop the immigration of Japanese laborers to mainland United States.

Dollar Diplomacy

When William Howard Taft became President, he would not accept the existing policy for Asia. He introduced the concept that became known as "dollar diplomacy." It was based on the idea that American money invested in China and Manchuria could undercut Japan's efforts to close the door there. At the same time, the investments would yield profits for Americans.

One of the first ventures in dollar diplomacy involved a loan agreement between the Chinese government and a group of British, French, and German bankers. Despite the resistance of the European bankers, President Taft intervened in 1910 to gain admittance to this *consortium,* or partnership, for American bankers.

Under Woodrow Wilson, relations with Japan continued to deteriorate. But they improved in April 1917, when the two nations tried to reach an agreement on China. In the Lansing-Ishii Agreement of November 1917, they reaffirmed their respect for the Open Door policy and China's independence. But the United States also said it recognized that Japan had a special position in China.

THE CARIBBEAN AREA

At the end of the Spanish-American War, the United States controlled Cuba and dominated the Caribbean Sea. In order to keep its dominance, the United States followed a policy of intervention that irritated the nations of Latin America. A prime example is its role in the building of the Panama Canal.

An Isthmian Canal

The idea of cutting a canal through Central America was an old one. French and American companies had tried to build interoceanic canals in the 1880's and 1890's but had failed. These failures had convinced the United States that any such canal would have to be constructed by the government. The United States government wanted to have full control over any canal it built, but the terms of an old treaty with Britain stood in the way. After long negotiations, the British agreed to the Hay-Pauncefote Treaty (1901). It permitted the United States not only to build a canal, but also to fortify and operate it.

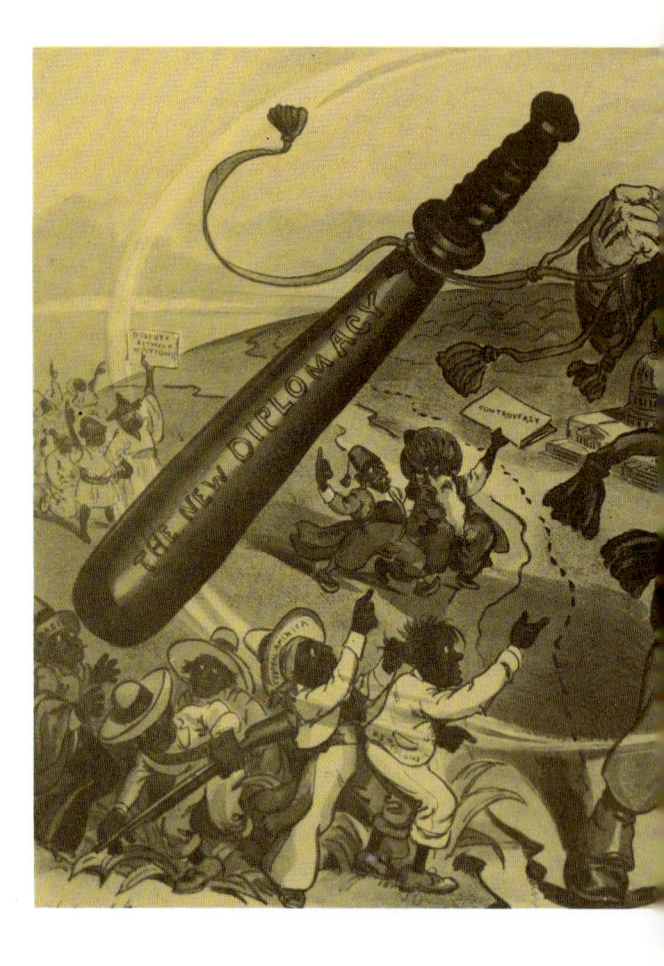

The United States now had to decide where to build the canal. After investigating two possible routes, one across the Isthmus of Panama and the other across Nicaragua, the United States chose the Panama route. At the time, Panama was part of Colombia.

In January 1903, a treaty was completed with the Colombian representative in Washington granting the United States control for 100 years or more of a strip of land 6 miles

Part troubleshooter, part bully, policeman Teddy swings his big stick as people in all parts of the world seek his aid in solving problems. Roosevelt's part in starting the Panama Canal aroused fear among many Latin Americans of Yankee imperialism.

wide across Panama. The United States would pay 10 million dollars in gold and an annual rent of $250,000. Despite a threat of retaliation by Hay if the treaty were not ratified, Colombia's government rejected the treaty. The Colombians wanted 40 million dollars.

The rejection angered President Roosevelt and alarmed many people in Panama. The people had long been discontented with Colombian rule, and many wanted the canal to be built. A group of them now prepared to secede from Colombia.

Philippe Bunau-Varilla was an engineer for the French company that had earlier tried to build a canal across Panama. In September 1903 he met with the conspirators and promised to support a revolution. In October he talked with Secretary of State Hay and President Roosevelt. Even though they made no promises, Bunau-Varilla deduced that the United States would not allow Colombian troops to suppress a revolt.

The revolt began on November 3. Soldiers from a United States warship kept Colombian troops from interfering. Panama declared its independence on November 4; and the United States recognized independent Panama on November 6. On November 18, Secretary Hay signed a canal treaty with Bunau-Varilla, who had made himself Panama's first minister to the United States. The treaty guaranteed the independence of Panama, granted the United States control of a 10-mile wide canal strip forever, and provided for a payment of 10 million dollars to Panama, plus $250,000 annually after nine years. The Senate approved the treaty in February 1904.

Roosevelt's "big stick" diplomacy had made Panama a United States protectorate. Many people in the United States and Latin America were upset by Roosevelt's ruthless action. To make amends, in 1921 the United States gave Colombia 25 million dollars as payment for its loss of Panama.

Policing the Caribbean

While Congress was considering rival canal routes, a dispute in Venezuela caused trouble for the United States. Venezuela's dictator, Cipriano Castro, had defaulted on some of the country's foreign debts. After futile negotiations, three of the creditor nations—Britain, Germany, and Italy—landed troops in Venezuela and blockaded its main ports (December 1902).

Workers prepare concrete forms for the Miraflores Lock in Panama. Epidemics of yellow fever had hampered earlier attempts to build a canal there.

At first President Roosevelt saw nothing wrong in this. Later, American public opinion became hostile toward Germany, which used the greatest force. Then Roosevelt put pressure on the creditor nations to arbitrate the dispute and get out of Venezuela. The powers did arbitrate, and in February 1903 they lifted the blockade.

This episode revealed a widespread sensitivity in the United States to any form of European intervention in Latin America. As a result, Roosevelt decided to add to the Monroe Doctrine.

The President expressed his corollary in his annual message to Congress in December 1904. He said that

in the Western Hemisphere the adherence of the United States to the Monroe Doctrine may force the United States, however reluctantly, in flagrant cases of . . . wrongdoing or impotence, to the exercise of an international police power.

In other words, to prevent any excuse for European intervention, the United States would intervene. Roosevelt applied the corollary first in the Dominican Republic.

Like Venezuela, the Dominican Republic had borrowed heavily from foreign nations. Early in 1904, the republic was bankrupt. It seemed likely that European creditors might use force to obtain payment of the Dominican Republic's debts.

In January 1905, the United States began collecting the customs receipts, making payments on debts, and keeping finances in order for the Dominican Republic. Most foreign debtors were satisfied with United States control, which continued for years, because it assured them a reasonable return on the debts. But Latin Americans disliked the intervention.

Intervention in Central America

President Taft's policy of dollar diplomacy, although begun for China, was most used for Central America. The United States tried to

Involvement With Mexico

The growth of the railroads and the rapid expansion of irrigation farming after 1900 brought great changes to the southwestern United States. The need for a labor force for growing, packing, and shipping crops encouraged large numbers of Mexicans to migrate into that region. Between 1901 and 1910, 49,000 Mexicans officially entered the United States; between 1911 and 1920, the number increased to 219,000; it continued to increase during the following decade. Thousands more were illegally brought in by labor contractors. Most of the Mexicans settled in Texas, Arizona, New Mexico, and California. Many had come to get away from the revolutions in Mexico.

Conflicts in Mexico occasionally spread into Texas and New Mexico. By 1911, when Porfirio Díaz fell from power in Mexico, there was continuous fighting in the border areas. Many of the raids into United States territory were followed by reprisals against Mexicans.

Díaz was replaced by several leaders in rapid succession. In 1915, President Wilson recognized the Mexican government led by Venustiano Carranza. As Carranza took over, one of his chief generals, Pancho Villa, broke away. Villa, who had led the revolutionary forces in the northern states of Mexico, hoped to force the United States to intervene in the revolution and help him gain enough popular support to defeat Carranza. He and his followers raided American towns in 1915 and 1916. These raids caused a wave of public anger. National guard regiments were called out to guard the border, and Woodrow Wilson sent a punitive expedition to Mexico to stop Villa's troops. The punitive expedition was unable to catch Villa, but its actions brought the United States to the brink of full-scale war with Mexico. Both the Mexican and United States governments wished to avoid war. In February 1917, Wilson withdrew United States troops from Mexico. Carranza's government adopted a formal constitution designed to bring democratic institutions to Mexico.

Pancho Villa leads his troops in a raid on the United States.

Europe, 1914

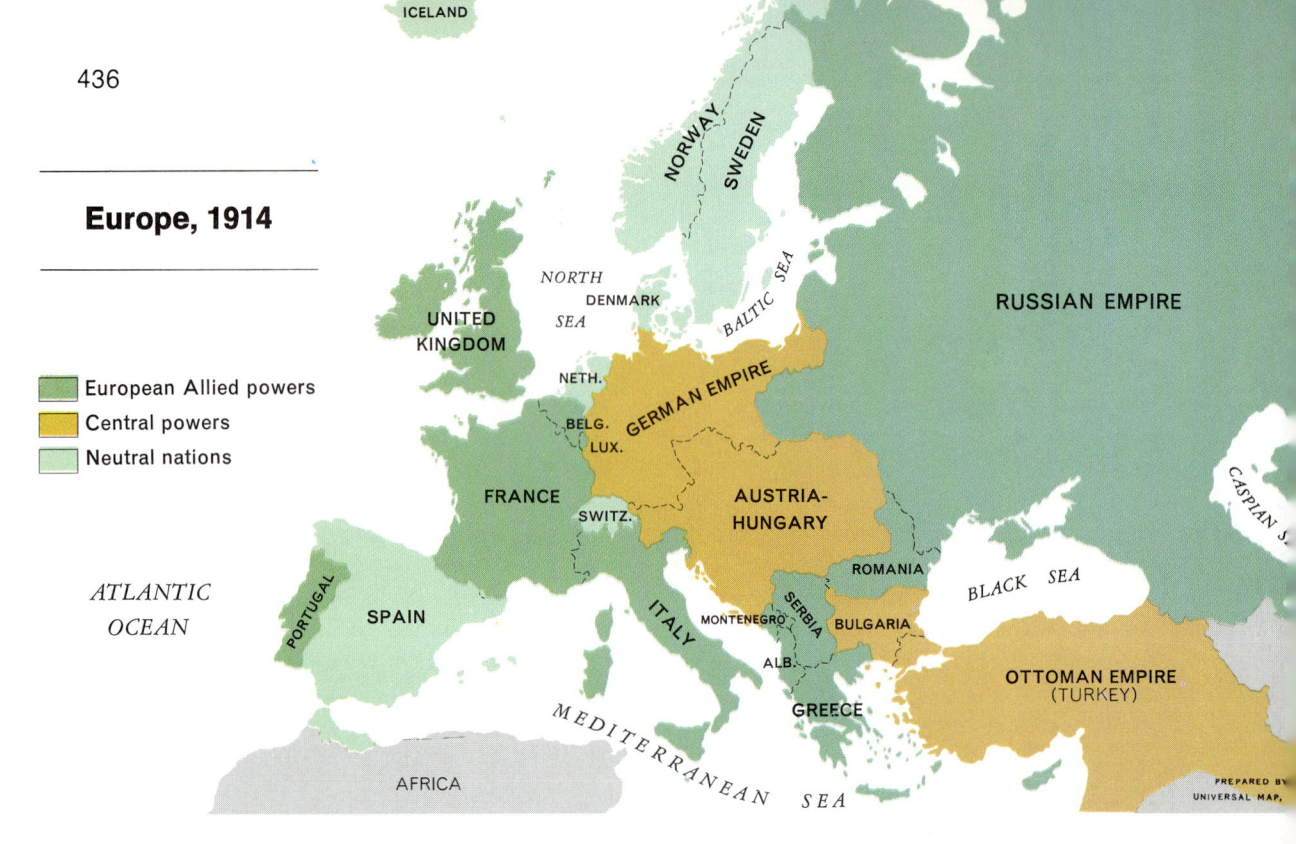

- European Allied powers
- Central powers
- Neutral nations

prevent European intervention in the Latin American nations by removing the excuse for intervention. Taft attempted to keep out new European investments and to force out European capital already there. With assurance of protection from the government, United States investments could then replace European investments. Taft's action in Nicaragua was the clearest example of dollar diplomacy.

Like other Caribbean republics, Nicaragua had borrowed from European investors. After a successful revolution in August 1910, Nicaragua turned to the United States for help in stabilizing its finances. In June 1911, Secretary of State Philander C. Knox worked out an agreement for a loan. Before the plan was completed, Nicaragua defaulted on its European debt. Encouraged by Taft, bankers in the United States loaned money to Nicaragua. According to the terms of the loan agreement, a United States Army officer took charge of Nicaragua's finances. When another revolution threatened the United States investments in July 1912, Taft sent more than 2,500 troops into Nicaragua and crushed the revolt. Then he stationed a warship and a military guard there to discourage future uprisings.

Woodrow Wilson continued Taft's policy in Nicaragua. In August 1914, the United States and Nicaragua signed the Bryan-Chamorro Treaty. In return for 3 million dollars to pay its debts, Nicaragua gave the United States the exclusive right to build and operate a canal and a naval base in Nicaragua. Thus Nicaragua also became a protectorate of the United States.

Missionary Diplomacy

Woodrow Wilson's interventions in Latin America grew out of a zeal to do what he thought was good. He and Secretary of State William Jennings Bryan wanted to save the peoples of Mexico and the Caribbean republics from internal anarchy and foreign dangers. This attitude, a kind of "missionary diplomacy," was behind Wilson's action in Nicaragua.

In the Dominican Republic, Wilson expanded the scale of control that Roosevelt had established. After an uprising in 1916, United States Marines occupied the nation, and an American military governor ruled as though he were the head of state.

Haiti, too, was continually racked by violence. In July 1915, after two rebellions within one year, Haiti's president, Vilbrun Guillaume Sam, brutally killed 167 political prisoners. This angered many people in the capital, Port-au-Prince. Sam fled to the French legation for safety, but a mob dragged him out and tore his body to pieces.

President Wilson then sent in marines to end the violence and to occupy the country. Using guerrilla tactics, the Haitians fought the occupation, but to no avail. In September the United States forced a treaty on Haiti that gave Americans tighter control of that nation than they had in any other Caribbean republic.

Trouble with Mexico

Wilson's missionary diplomacy faced its greatest difficulties in Mexico. In 1911, Francisco Madero, a young reformer, led a revolution that overthrew the long-time dictatorship of Porfirio Díaz. Madero dreamed of building a new democratic society for Mexico. But his leading general, Victoriano Huerta, seized power and apparently was involved in Madero's murder in February 1913.

When Wilson became President, he refused to recognize Huerta's government. He said the United States would not recognize governments that came to power by force and that did not represent the will of the people.

A civil war began in Mexico when General Venustiano Carranza, a follower of Madero's, opposed Huerta. President Wilson offered to mediate the Mexican civil war, but Huerta turned down Wilson's offer.

In April 1914, some American sailors who had gone ashore from a warship off Tampico were arrested and then released. Although Huerta's subordinate apologized, Huerta would not offer the kind of apology the American admiral demanded. Wilson then ordered battleships to Tampico.

Soon news reached Washington, D.C., that a German ship was headed for Veracruz loaded with guns for Huerta. Wilson ordered the navy to take Veracruz, rather than Tampico, to prevent the unloading of the guns. The Mexicans resisted. Before the city was occupied, 19 United States Marines and 126 Mexicans had been killed.

War was prevented when Argentina, Brazil, and Chile helped mediate the quarrel in a conference at Niagara Falls, Canada, in the summer of 1914. A short time later Huerta fled Mexico, and Carranza's forces took Mexico City. In October 1915, Wilson formally recognized Carranza's government.

SETTLING DISPUTES PEACEFULLY

Many people in the United States believed that as a world power the nation had an obligation to help maintain peace. The government therefore tried to settle disputes, even those that did not involve the United States, without resorting to force.

The Algeciras Conference

One of the most dramatic incidents concerned Morocco, in North Africa. The United States had no direct interest in that area, but Morocco had become a center of international controversy in which France and Germany were particularly concerned. For many years the French had been dominant in Morocco. In 1905, after gaining the support of Britain, France went ahead with plans to take over complete control of Morocco. Germany, which had built up some trade in the North African country, opposed the French plan. For a while it looked as if Germany's forceful opposition would touch off a war. Then President Roosevelt stepped in. He persuaded France and Britain to meet with Germany and other powers to discuss the Moroccan question. The conference opened in January 1906, in Algeciras, a small Spanish seaport across the Strait of Gibraltar from Morocco.

At the conference, Germany found itself almost alone in its demands for a share in the control of Morocco. Britain stood firmly by France, and even the United States favored the French position. Roosevelt finally worked out a compromise that was accepted by Germany. It preserved the principle of international control in Morocco but gave real power to France.

Critics in the United States attacked Roosevelt for participating in the diplomacy of the Moroccan crisis. They said he had violated the traditional United States policy of avoiding entanglements in European quarrels. Roosevelt replied that the crisis threatened world peace and that by intervening he had prevented war. Whether or not his actions had prevented war, Roosevelt had taken a significant step. He had used the power of the United States in a distant crisis on the theory that a threat to the peace of the world affected the United States.

Less dramatic but more important to the United States was the slow, steady development of friendship with Britain that took on the characteristics of an unwritten alliance. This did not mean that the United States and Britain managed to avoid disagreements. They had serious differences, but they were able to make peaceful adjustments.

Several of the most serious controversies with Britain grew out of Canada's relations with the United States. (Although Canada was in many ways independent, as a dominion in the British Empire its foreign affairs were handled by the British government.) The first of these disputes concerned the boundary between Alaska and Canada.

Two Canadian-American Problems

When gold was discovered in the region of Canada's Klondike River in 1896, thousands of people, most of them from the United States, rushed to the area. These prospectors usually landed at Skagway, crossed the Alaskan panhandle, and headed northward. Canada claimed a boundary between itself and Alaska that would have given Canada control of the access by sea to the Klondike gold fields.

President Roosevelt called the Canadian claim "an outrage pure and simple." Since the British feared the dispute might injure their friendship with the United States, they agreed in January 1903 to place the case in the hands of six judges. Three were chosen by Britain, and three by the United States. The decision, in October 1903, was almost entirely favorable to the United States. Many Canadians felt that their claim was just but that it had been sacrificed to the cause of Anglo-American friendship.

Another long-standing dispute between Britain and the United States still remained to be settled. The United States wanted broad privileges in the fishing grounds off the shores of Nova Scotia and Newfoundland. The Canadians wanted to restrict those fishing privileges or obtain concessions for them, such as the repeal of a United States tariff against Canadian fish.

In January 1909, Britain and the United States signed a general arbitration treaty, an agreement for peaceful settlement of differences. They submitted the fisheries dispute to the Permanent Court of Arbitration at The Hague. The decision, made in September 1910, was a compromise that allowed fishermen from the United States to continue their work in the disputed fishing grounds, subject, however, to local regulations. Although these terms were later changed, the longest dispute in the history of American foreign relations had thus been settled.

New Controversy

Canadian-American relations soon deteriorated, however. The Payne-Aldrich Tariff hit Canadian products quite hard, and Canada threatened to retaliate. To prevent a tariff war, President Taft and Prime Minister Sir Wilfrid Laurier of Canada concluded a commercial reciprocity agreement in January 1911. This meant that each nation would give special consideration to the goods of the other. Reciprocity was to go into effect through laws passed by the United States Congress and by the Canadian parliament.

Congress passed a reciprocity law in 1912. In urging its passage, however, the President and other supporters of reciprocity had given the impression that it would lead to the annexation of Canada. This attitude aroused Canadian nationalism, and the reciprocity bill in parliament went down to defeat.

Another law that caused trouble with British subjects was passed in August 1912. In that law Congress said that United States ships engaged in the coastwise trade from New York to California would not have to pay tolls when going through the Panama Canal. The British argued that this exemption violated the Hay-Pauncefote Treaty, which said the canal would be open on equal terms to the ships of all nations. If United States ships did not pay tolls, the British pointed out, then foreign ships would be charged higher tolls to make up the loss.

President Wilson became convinced that the British were right. He asked Congress to repeal the exemption on tolls, as a matter of friendship and national honor. Congress voted the repeal in June 1914. In August, the Panama Canal was officially opened on equal terms to all nations.

WORLD WAR I

In the summer of 1914, the forces that made for war were stronger than those that kept peace. The warlike forces included *extreme nationalism,* or an exaggerated patriotism that often led to hatred of other peoples; *imperialism,* a policy of extending the rule of one nation over another; *militarism,* an excessive reliance on arms and armies; and *international anarchy,* the lack of any true international means of controlling outbursts of violence among nations.

On June 28, 1914, in Sarajevo, Bosnia (a part of present-day Yugoslavia), a young Serbian nationalist assassinated the heir to the throne of Austria-Hungary, Archduke Francis Ferdinand. Austria-Hungary, determined to stamp out Serbian nationalism, gave an ultimatum to Serbia, which the Serbs rejected. Austria-Hungary then declared war, and its ally, Germany, joined in. Other declarations of war followed, for the nations of Europe were bound together by alliance systems that required them to aid their respective allies. Russia stood by Serbia, and France and Britain sided with Russia. By August 12, Germany and Austria-Hungary were formally at war with France, Britain, and Russia. An intricate system of mobilization schedules for huge armies now went into effect.

Germany and Austria-Hungary, later joined by Bulgaria and Turkey, were known as the Central powers. Opposing them were the Allied powers—France, Britain, and Russia, later joined by Japan and Italy.

Neutrality

President Wilson promptly issued declarations of neutrality and offered to mediate, but the warring nations refused the offer. Then he appealed to the people of the United States to be "impartial in thought as well as in action."

Most Americans were never impartial. Most probably sided with the Allies, because of ethnic, business, and cultural ties; but many favored the Central powers. German

World War I

Legend:
- Central powers
- Allied powers
- Neutral powers
- Area controlled by Central powers
- × Battles

Central Powers Strategy The Germans anticipated a two-front war, but they decided to concentrate a powerful offensive in the west. Under the Schlieffen plan, they wanted to invade France through Belgium, sweep around the main French defenses, and encircle Paris from the south. After France gave up, the Germans would reinforce the troops holding off the Russians on the eastern front.

Allied Strategy The Allied plan also called for an offensive. French troops were to invade Germany by way of Lorraine, ignoring the German threat on the Belgian border. The British were to sweep from the English Channel to Lorraine, and the Russians were to invade Germany on the eastern front.

WESTERN FRONT, 1914

August 4 Invasion of Belgium. Central powers victory. Well-prepared German troops sliced through Belgium, capturing Liège (Aug. 17) and Brussels (Aug. 20). By September, they had forced the Allies back to the Marne River, near Paris.

August 14–25 French offensive. Central powers victories. From the Ardennes Forest to the easternmost French provinces of Alsace and Lorraine, the French tried to invade Germany. They failed to dent the German lines.

EASTERN FRONT, 1914

August 17–September 15 Russian offensive in the north. Central powers victory. The Russians, at the request of France, had invaded East Prussia (Aug. 17) and pushed the Germans back to the Vistula River. But in a counteroffensive, the Germans routed the Russians at Tannenberg (Aug. 26–30) and the Masurian Lakes (Sept. 6–15), ending the Russian "steamroller" attack in East Prussia.

September Russian offensive in Austria. Allied victory. While the Russians were losing battles in the north, they scored successes farther south, against Austrian troops. On Sept. 12, the Russians captured Lemberg (present-day Lvov) and forced the Austrians to abandon their lines in the south.

Western Front 1914-1918

September 5–12, 1914 First Battle of the Marne. Allied victory. A French offensive (General Joseph Joffre) halted the Germans, who fell back to the Aisne River.

October 20–November 22, 1914 First Battle of Ypres. Allied victory. Allied and Central powers troops, racing to the English Channel, clashed at Ypres, in Flanders. The Allies held the town. The western front established by the end of 1914 did not change much during the next three years of fighting. All along a line from the English Channel to the French-Swiss border, both sides dug trench defenses.

April 22–May 25, 1915 Second Battle of Ypres. Central powers victory. Using chlorine gas (the first use of poison gas as a military weapon), German troops scattered Allied defenders but did not follow through. In May, the Germans moved some troops from the west to bolster the faltering Austrians. By September, Austro-German troops had crushed the Russian southern front. But a stalemate continued in France.

February–December 1916 Battle of Verdun. A draw. The Germans bombarded the forts around Verdun and captured them in some of the bloodiest battles of the war. French casualties numbered 460,000, while the Germans lost 300,000 soldiers. French troops began a counteroffensive in October and had recaptured the forts by December.

July–November 1916 Battle of the Somme. Allied victory. The British used a new weapon, the tank.

November 21–December 3, 1917 Battle of Cambrai. Allied victory. Using tanks in mass formation for the first time, British troops broke through German lines but were too exhausted to continue.

March 21–June 4, 1918 German spring offensive. Central powers victory. The Treaty of Brest-Litovsk (March 3, 1918) took Russia out of the war. The Germans brought most of their soldiers from the eastern front to the west. In three assaults—at the Somme River, the Lys River, and the Aisne River—the Germans smashed through Allied defenses. They were within 27 miles of Paris when American troops helped stop them at the Battle of Château-Thierry (June 4).

May 28, 1918 Battle of Cantigny. Allied victory. American troops (General John Pershing), who had arrived June 26, 1917, won their first victory.

June 6–July 1, 1918 Battle of Belleau Wood. Allied victory. In bloody fighting, American troops took a strategic German outpost.

July 15–August 7, 1918 Second Battle of the Marne. Allied victory. The Germans began another offensive aimed at Paris. French and American troops pushed the Germans back to the Vesle River. This marked a turning point in the war.

September 12–13, 1918 Battle of St. Mihiel. Allied victory. Supported by 1,400 combat planes (Colonel William Mitchell), American troops stormed and captured St. Mihiel.

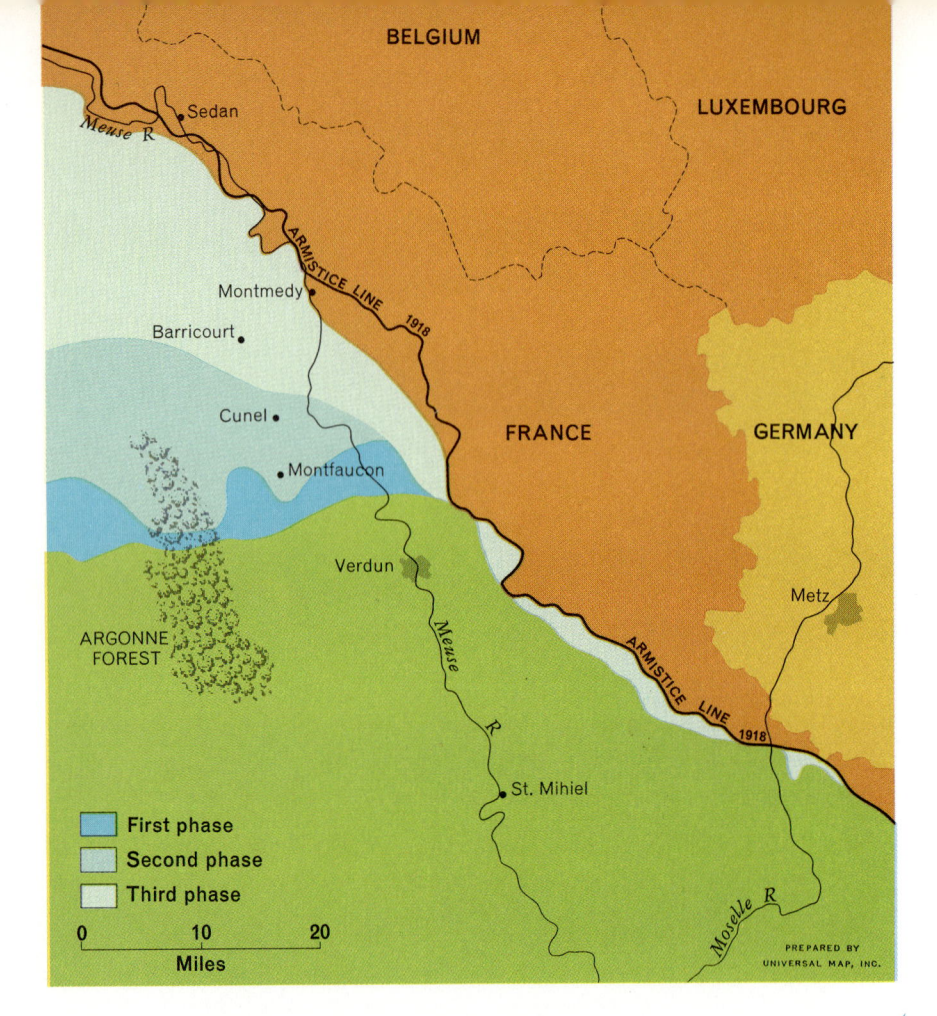

Meuse-Argonne

September 26–November 11, 1918
General Pershing planned a powerful frontal assault for a 20-mile wide zone between the Meuse River and the western edge of the Argonne Forest.

The defensive position was excellent: on the east were the heights of the Meuse River; on the west were heavy woods; in the center was a ridge with three heavily fortified positions: Montfaucon, Cunel, and Barricourt. Beyond this front line were three more German lines of defense, including strongly fortified points at woods and hills.

Pershing hoped to cut through all the defense lines without loss of momentum. The attack would continue until a breakthrough.

First phase: After a three-hour artillery barrage, the assault troops began to move (Sept. 26). By the end of the

---

Americans often were pro-German; some Irish Americans were anti-British; and some Jews and Poles were anti-Russian.

The first violations of neutral rights were made by Britain. The British navy was stronger than the German. Through its control of the seas, Britain could have access to the goods of most of the world while denying them to the Central powers. At first the British mainly stopped ships that were carrying *contraband*—implements of war such as guns—destined for Germany and neighboring nations. Later, they tried to stop all trade with Germany, whether or not it involved contraband. They even blockaded Denmark, the Netherlands, and Sweden, neighbors of Germany that imported goods by sea.

By the summer of 1915, the British navy had strangled most American trade with the Central powers and the neutral states of Europe. The United States protested these violations of its neutral rights, but it never used force to protect them. Moreover, the British did not push the United States too far in their violations because they were trying to retain its friendship.

Submarine Warfare

United States relations with the Central powers were relatively calm until Germany decided to use submarines in trying to break the Allied blockade. In February 1915, Germany proclaimed the seas around the British Isles a war zone. The German government announced that its submarines would attack on sight enemy ships within the zone. President Wilson immediately protested that this policy violated international law.

On May 7, 1915, a German submarine torpedoed the British passenger liner *Lusitania* off the Irish coast. Among the 1,198 persons who went down with the ship were 128

first day, the Americans had captured the forward German positions. Within the next few days, the first two defense lines were captured. The advance troops failed to break the third defense line, and the American attack was halted.

Second phase: On Oct. 4, the Americans began a drive through the third defense line. The Germans brought in fresh troops and fought stubbornly. Slowly, the Americans cleared the Argonne Forest of Germans and extended their attack east of the Meuse.

Third phase: On Nov. 1, the attack began again. The infantry moved forward and took the heights near Sedan (Nov. 7). Pershing then planned to attack Montmedy. As troops were moving into position for the attack, the armistice came (Nov. 11).

Right: A German submarine takes on supplies.

Americans. President Wilson demanded that Germany abandon the submarine campaign against passenger liners. The German government did not publicly give in to Wilson's demands, but it secretly told its submarine captains not to attack passenger liners.

During this period, Wilson had begun building up defenses. He had also tried to end the war through mediation, but the effort had failed.

In August 1916, Wilson signed a bill for the building of a huge navy as part of his preparedness program. After winning reelection, Wilson continued this program. He also tried again to bring about a negotiated peace, "a peace without victory." These efforts, too, were fruitless.

Early in 1917 the Germans decided to resume unrestricted submarine warfare. They gambled that the submarine could assure victory before the power of the United States could be brought into the war. The Germans told Wilson of their decision on January 31, 1917. Three days later, Wilson broke off diplomatic relations with Germany.

The President still hoped to avoid war. Then the British gave Wilson a message that they had intercepted. Alfred Zimmermann, the German foreign secretary, proposed that Mexico join an alliance with Germany if the United States went to war against the Central powers. Mexico's reward would be recovery of Arizona, New Mexico, and Texas. When the United States government published the note on March 1, strong anti-German feeling swept over the country.

On April 2, 1917, after several American ships had been sunk by German submarines, Wilson asked Congress for a declaration of war, saying that "the world must be made safe for democracy." Congress declared war on April 6.

Left: Women assemble bombs in a defense plant. Female workers moved into a number of areas previously reserved for men. They took jobs in manufacturing agricultural implements, airplane and automobile parts, high explosives, and steel plate, to name but a few. *Opposite:* Douglas Fairbanks, a popular movie star, urges a crowd in New York to buy Liberty Loan bonds. Rallies like this one raised huge amounts of money and also excited the people's support for the war effort.

Mobilizing the American People

United States involvement came at a crucial time. German submarines were sinking ships twice as fast as the Allies could replace them. On land the Allied cause had become shaky. Most of the fighting involved trench warfare in which huge numbers of soldiers were killed simply to move the front forward a few yards. French armies were weary, and some divisions had mutinied. The exhausted Russians, too, were tired of the war.

The United States Navy immediately joined the British in fighting the submarines and in tightening the blockade against the Central powers. To help the Allies, the United States mobilized for war. Instead of relying on volunteers, the government used a draft. Despite opposition from those who preferred a volunteer army, Congress passed the Selective Service Act on May 18, 1917. This law required all men between the ages of 21 and 30 to register for military service. Later, the limits were extended to include men between 18 and 45 years of age.

Congress gave the President almost dictatorial powers to speed the national mobilization. President Wilson set up six wartime agencies. One of the most important of these was the War Industries Board, directed by Bernard M. Baruch, a New York banker. It coordinated purchases, allocated raw materials, controlled production, and supervised labor relations.

Herbert C. Hoover, a mining engineer, became the director of the Food Administration. He worked to increase the production of food and to eliminate waste. The United States Shipping Board and the Emergency Fleet Corporation worked to provide desperately needed ships. The railroads, which had to carry goods, guns, and troops to the ships, were controlled by the government. The government also took over other means of transportation and communication, such as telephone and telegraph companies.

Laborers profited from the wartime boom but not as much as farmers and manufacturers. Thousands more women went into industry. Southern blacks in great numbers migrated north for jobs in the war industries. In 1918, the government set up the National War Labor Board to handle labor disputes.

To arouse patriotism, Congress created the Committee on Public Information. The committee staged bond rallies and pep talks. But it also scattered propaganda designed to show that Germans were evil and that Kaiser Wilhelm, the German monarch, had started the war. In the name of patriotism, hatred and intolerance were spread. Many German Americans anglicized their names to avoid prejudicial treatment. Anti-German hysteria was so strong that restaurant owners called *sauerkraut* "liberty cabbage," and *hamburger* became "Salisbury steak."

Two laws intended to crush disloyalty were passed. The Espionage Act of June 1917 provided a fine and imprisonment for anyone who interfered with the draft or encouraged disloyalty. The Sedition Act of May 1918 provided punishment for anyone who said or wrote anything "disloyal, profane, or scurrilous" about the government. More than fifteen hundred persons were convicted of violating these laws.

Fighting to Victory

The first troops from the United States arrived in France in June 1917, but they were only token forces intended to boost the sagging morale of Allied soldiers. These first "doughboys" went to quiet sectors of the battlefront as replacements in French and British units. Almost a year passed before a large American fighting force reached the battlefront.

Allied military losses created a pressing need for fresh troops. In October 1917, German and Austro-Hungarian forces attacked at Caporetto, in present-day Yugoslavia, and almost crushed an Italian army. With help hastily provided by the French and British, the Italians averted disaster. On the eastern front, Russian resistance was collapsing. Two revolutions swept over Russia, and in November, when the Bolsheviks (Communists) took control of the government, they offered the Germans peace.

On January 8, 1918, President Wilson outlined a peace program of fourteen points. The first five points dealt with general principles, such as freedom of the seas and reduction of armaments. The next eight points promised territorial adjustments, including German evacuation of Russia and Belgium, breakup of Austria-Hungary, and independence for Poland. The fourteenth point, which was Wilson's key for preventing future wars, offered an association of nations that would help keep world peace.

These fourteen points were widely published, but at first they did not make much of an impact on the Germans. In March 1918, the Germans forced the Bolsheviks to sign the Treaty of Brest-Litovsk, which gave Germany a great slice of eastern Europe and ended the war in the east.

The Russian collapse allowed the Germans to shift troops to the western front. In an effort to smash the Allies before many soldiers arrived from the United States, the Germans launched an offensive in March at

Motorized vehicles were replacing horse-drawn wagons *(opposite)*. Military aviation *(above)* was in its infancy. A terrible new weapon was poison gas. Chlorine, phosgene, and mustard gas killed or blinded thousands of people. Most of the fighting, however, was trench warfare *(right)*. To attack, the troops had to climb up and "go over the top."

the Somme River. In April, they aimed a second great blow at Flanders. These attacks nearly broke the Allied armies. The Allies pleaded for immediate reinforcements from the United States.

American troops had their first real taste of battle when 30,000 doughboys fought the Germans at Château-Thierry on the Marne River, only 27 miles from Paris. They helped blunt the German attack. In June, American troops cleared Belleau Wood and forced the Germans back across the Marne. By July 1, General John J. Pershing, commander of the American Expeditionary Force, had an army of 1 million men.

Two weeks later, the Germans launched their third great offensive toward Paris. This time 85,000 United States soldiers fought to throw back the attack. Shortly thereafter the

Allied commander, Marshal Ferdinand Foch, began a counteroffensive. The fresh American troops helped keep the Germans in steady retreat.

As part of this offensive, the American army attacked the Germans in the region of the Argonne Forest and the Meuse River. While this battle was going on, the German government appealed to Wilson for peace on the basis of the fourteen points. Meanwhile, Austria-Hungary collapsed and signed an armistice with Italy on November 3. Germany signed an armistice on November 11, 1918, that ended the war.

THE VERSAILLES TREATY

Some Americans wanted a surrender, not an armistice. Theodore Roosevelt and other

Members of the 23rd Infantry crawl through a barren forest during the Meuse-Argonne campaign. American troops fought only on the western front.

Republican leaders attacked the fourteen points as allowing peace terms that were too soft. These critics demanded a Republican victory in the congressional elections of November 1918.

Upset by these attacks, Wilson made a blanket appeal to the voters to elect Democrats to Congress. "The return of a Republican majority to either house of the Congress," he said, "would . . . be interpreted on the other side of the water as a repudiation of my leadership."

This appeal angered Republicans, many of whom had firmly supported Wilson's foreign policy. It also appeared to have little effect on the elections, for the voters gave the Republicans control of both houses of Congress by a narrow margin.

Wilson in Paris

In mid-November, Wilson announced that he would attend the peace conference in Paris. When he named the members of the American peace commission, Republicans were angered because he did not include a single important Republican.

Representatives from all the nations on the Allied side attended the opening of the peace conference on January 18, 1919. At first, the major responsibilities were handled by the five big powers—the United States, Britain, France, Italy, and Japan—meeting in a Council of Ten. When Japan dropped out, President Wilson, British Prime Minister David Lloyd George, French Premier Georges Clemenceau, and Italian Prime Minister Vittorio E. Orlando made the basic decisions at the conference. They were known as the "big four."

Although all wanted a lasting peace, these leaders quarreled over ways of achieving it. Wilson placed first importance on his plan for a league of nations. The French proposed that the peace treaties come first. The conference finally decided that a league of nations should be part of the peace treaty.

Wilson drew up the league's constitution, which he called a covenant. The league's two major bodies would be an assembly and a council. In the assembly, every member nation would have one vote. The council, or executive body, would be more powerful. The United States, Britain, France, Italy, and Japan would have permanent seats on the council and could deal with questions of war and peace.

The heart of the covenant was Article 10, which pledged all members to support the principle of *collective security.* This meant that the league would regard an attack on any one of its members as an attack on all of them and all would cooperate to defend the nation attacked.

After the conference had adopted the covenant of the League of Nations, the President returned to the United States to sign bills that Congress had passed during his absence. On the last day of the session, Republicans in Congress blocked the passage of vital bills. This would make it necessary for the President to call Congress into special session before summer to consider those bills. By that time the Republicans would be in control of the new Senate and would deal with the league.

A Losing Battle

In March, when Wilson returned to Paris to complete the peacemaking, he tried to amend the covenant to make it more acceptable to Americans. This led to bargaining in which the leaders of other Allied nations gained a number of concessions from him.

Germany lost about one-seventh of its territory. It agreed to pay a large reparations bill for war damages, to admit guilt for starting the war, and to recognize the new states in eastern Europe that were created when the Austro-Hungarian Empire broke up. These terms, plus the covenant of the League of Nations, were written into the Treaty of Versailles.

While the President was in Paris, Republicans in Congress planned to oppose the League of Nations. Led by Senator Henry Cabot Lodge of Massachusetts, they considered the covenant unsatisfactory, even as revised. William E. Borah of Idaho headed a small group of senators who were opposed to the league in any form. These senators, sometimes called "irreconcilables," were *isolationists,* people who believed the United States should avoid involvement in the politics of Europe.

Wilson called Congress into special session

Armistice Night, by George Luks, 1918. Collection Whitney Museum of American Art, New York. Anonymous gift

on May 19, 1919. The Republicans, who now had a majority of two in the Senate, quickly organized their forces. They chose Lodge as majority leader and as chairman of the Committee on Foreign Relations.

On July 10, Wilson asked the Senate to approve the Treaty of Versailles. He tried to stimulate public support for the treaty with a speaking tour of the West and Midwest. On September 25, 1919, after giving a speech in Pueblo, Colorado, Wilson collapsed from exhaustion. He returned to Washington. A few days later he suffered a stroke that incapacitated him for six months.

Lodge's committee, meanwhile, recommended approval of the treaty with reservations, or changes, to the league covenant. Most of the changes protected the right of the United States to act independently of the league. Since Wilson thought the Lodge reservations would destroy the league, he would not accept them. He urged the Democrats in the Senate to vote against the treaty with reservations.

The Democrats in the Senate voted as Wilson desired, but they did not have enough votes to gain approval of the treaty without changes. Most Republicans would have accepted the league with changes. Only the irreconcilables wanted complete defeat of the league. Perhaps some compromise could have been worked out, but Wilson and the Republican leaders distrusted each other. The Senate voted on the Treaty of Versailles twice, in November 1919 and in March 1920. Each time it was defeated.

The Election of 1920

Wilson could not believe that his own people would remain outside the league he had helped create. He thought that if the people understood what was at stake they would reverse the decision of the Senate. He believed that he could make the presidential election of 1920 a national referendum on the league.

This was unrealistic. Wilson had not been in close touch with events since his stroke, nor did he understand the mood of the

Europe, 1922

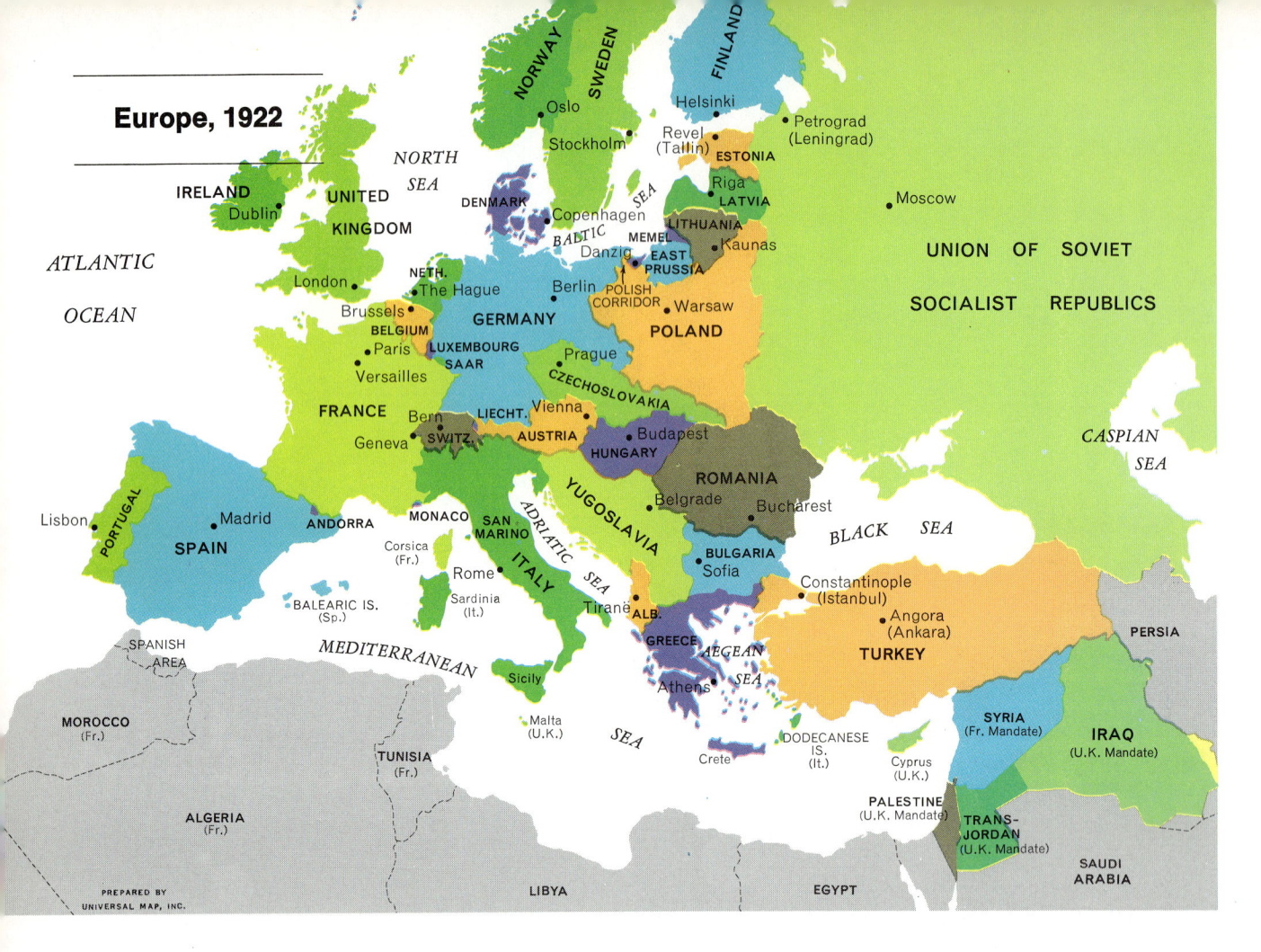

American people. The people were tired of squabbling over the league and were ready to express their resentment over domestic problems by voting against the party in power.

The Democratic convention ignored Wilson and chose James M. Cox, the governor of Ohio, as its candidate. The vice-presidential candidate was Assistant Secretary of the Navy Franklin D. Roosevelt. The party platform called for approval of the Treaty of Versailles, and Cox and Roosevelt spoke out for the league.

The platform approved by the Republicans promised higher tariff rates, lower taxes, and immigration restriction. It denounced Wilson's league, but promised an international agreement of some kind "to preserve the peace of the world." After two popular candidates had deadlocked, the convention nominated Senator Warren G. Harding of Ohio. Another conservative, Governor Calvin Coolidge of Massachusetts, was chosen to run for Vice-President.

During the campaign, Harding evaded practically all issues, but he did promise a return to "normalcy." Harding won the election, carrying every state outside the Solid South.

On July 2, 1921, the new Republican Congress declared by joint resolution that as far as the United States was concerned, the war was formally over. In August, President Harding negotiated separate peace treaties with Germany, Austria, and Hungary.

The rejection of the League of Nations did not mean that the United States could ignore the rest of the world. It was a world power. No matter how much some Americans yearned for a return to the less complicated days before 1898, that status could not be changed. But two crusades were over—one to reform society at home and the other to reform the world. Americans had entered an era of conservatism and isolationism.

Few people in the United States heeded the words of the dying Wilson in 1924. He said: "We had a chance to gain the leadership of the world. We have lost it, and soon we shall be witnessing the tragedy of it all."

A Look at Specifics

1. How did the Insular Cases (1901–1922) enable the United States to deny self-government to the inhabitants of American Samoa, Puerto Rico, and the Philippines?

2. How did the actions of the San Francisco school board cause tension between Japan and the United States?

3. What were the terms of the treaty of 1903 between the United States and Colombia? How did Colombia's rejection of the treaty lead to the Panamanian revolt?

4. Why did Wilson refuse to recognize Victoriano Huerta's government in Mexico?

5. What did the Zimmermann note propose? How did its publication affect public opinion?

6. How was the Committee on Public Information used to further the war effort?

7. How did Wilson anger many Republicans who were in favor of his foreign policy?

A Review of Major Ideas

1. How did Roosevelt, Taft, and Wilson promote the Open Door policy?

2. How and why did the United States establish a protectorate in each of the following: Panama, the Dominican Republic, Nicaragua, and Haiti?

3. Why did the United States enter World War I? How did it contribute to the Allied victory? To the terms of peace?

For Independent Study

1. Do you think the United States was justified in interfering with the sovereignty of Colombia, the Dominican Republic, Haiti, and Mexico?

2. The immediate cause of the United States entry into World War I was Germany's destruction of American ships. What other considerations do you think influenced the United States to declare war on Germany? Do you think the United States had sufficient cause for entering the war?

3. The historian Thomas A. Bailey has stated, "In the final analysis the treaty was slain in the house of its friends rather than in the house of its enemies. In the final analysis it was not the two-thirds rule, or the 'irreconcilables,' or Lodge, or the 'strong' and 'mild reservationists,' but Wilson and his docile following who delivered the fatal stab." Do you agree with Bailey's view of the defeat of the Treaty of Versailles?

4. Should the United States have granted the people of the Philippines, Puerto Rico, and American Samoa the same rights as were granted Americans who were living in the territories of Arizona, New Mexico, and Oklahoma?

Unit Review
Examining the Times

1. What new trends took place in philosophy, religion, art, literature, and journalism between 1900 and 1917?

2. During this period, what social, educational, economic, and political reforms were made?

3. What attempts did government make to control large corporations?

4. Between 1900 and 1920, what was the role of the United States in the affairs of Latin America, Asia, and Europe?

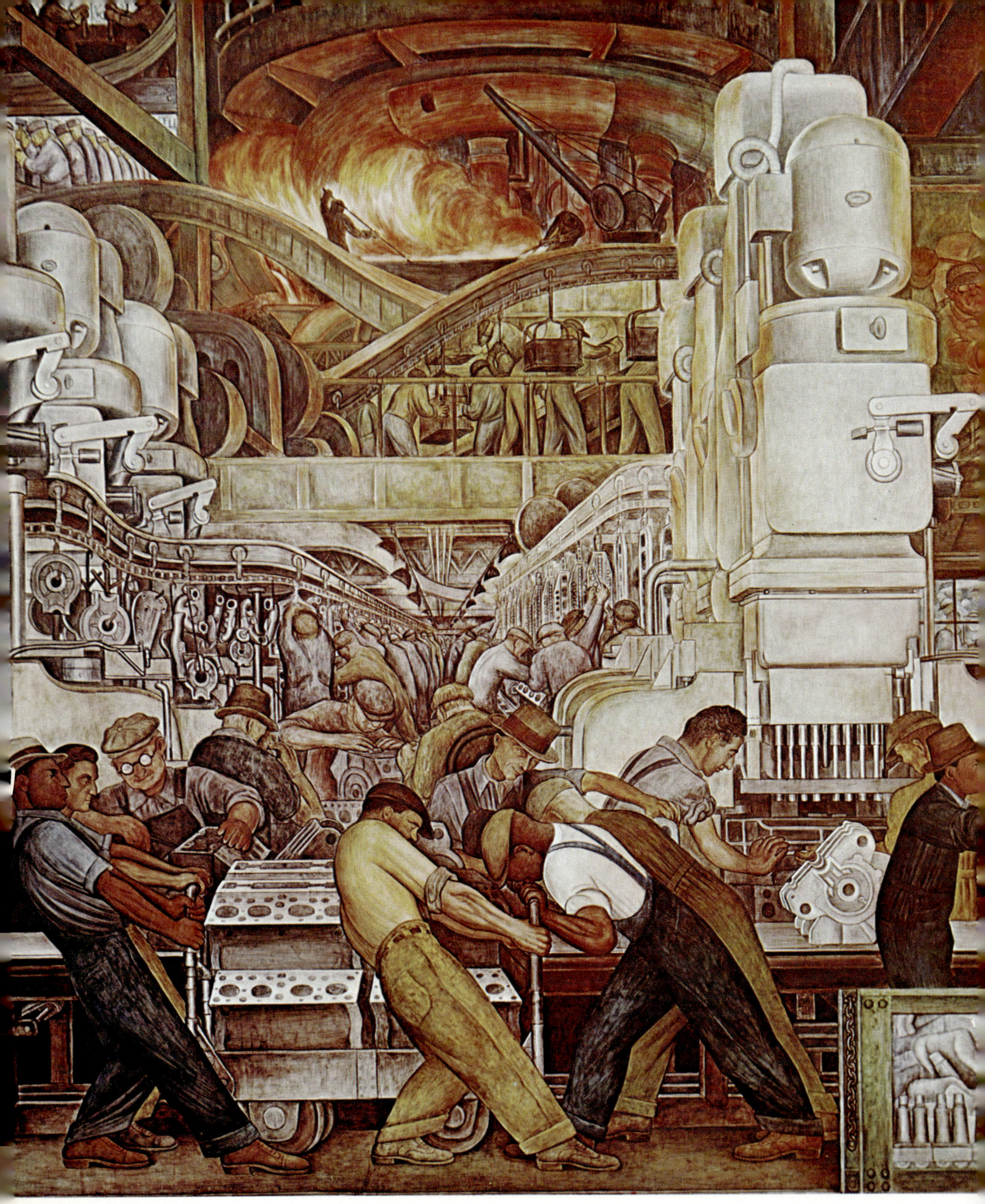

UNIT SEVEN 1920–1941

The Time Between the Wars

To many of the world's peoples, the collapse of the old empires after World War I was cause for hope. They saw it as the beginning of an era of freedom and as the triumph of democracy.

The leaders at the Paris Peace Conference, especially President Wilson, had attempted to create a new Europe based on the principle of self-determination of peoples. By this principle, each nationality group was to be free to set up its own independent nation or to join related nationality groups in forming a nation. Thus, the Poles set up their own nation, the Czechs and Slovaks joined in creating Czechoslovakia, and several groups of southern Slavs formed Yugoslavia.

Although it was impossible to create new nations in which each nationality group had equal power in the government, self-determination was achieved to a greater extent than before the war. Most of the new European nations set up republican forms of government.

In the 1920's and 1930's, fundamental changes were taking place in all parts of the globe. The Mexican revolution begun in 1910 had stirred other peoples in Latin America to demand political and social changes. Between 1919 and 1929, seven other Latin American nations adopted new constitutions.

In India, Mohandas K. Gandhi championed the cause of freedom from British rule. During the 1920's and 1930's, he used nonviolent resistance as a method of gaining his ends. In 1937, the British Parliament gave the Indian provinces self-government, and the British surrendered their power to Indian members of the legislature except in matters of defense and foreign affairs.

In China, Chiang Kai-shek, a forceful military leader, led his army northward in 1926 and succeeded in bringing limited unity to China. His Nationalist government in Nanking was recognized by the great western nations as the official government of China.

In his efforts to unite China, Chiang encountered growing opposition from Communist groups. He began a purge in which many Communists were executed. However, under the leadership of Mao Tse-tung, the Communists regrouped and waged guerrilla warfare against Chiang's Nationalist forces. After a series of military campaigns, Mao led his Communist followers on a 6,000-mile trek to settle in northwestern China. There the Communists set up a stronghold in 1935 and spent the next fourteen years working to gain control of China.

In the former German colonies in Africa and in the lands of the Middle East that had been freed from Turkish rule, independence movements were strong. Although some of these areas became independent immediately after World War I, most did not. Instead they came under the mandate system that was set up at the Paris Peace Conference.

Under the *mandate system,* native peoples were ruled by major powers but were protected by the League of Nations; some were assured that they would eventually be granted self-government. For example, Tanganyika (former German East Africa) was made a mandate of Britain. Syria and Lebanon were made mandates of France; Iraq, Palestine, and Transjordan, mandates of Britain; and the Marshall Islands, a mandate of Japan. Many of the native peoples opposed the mandates and pressed for complete independence.

The hopes of the world's peoples for peace, freedom, and prosperity were dashed by the start of the Great Depression. It began in 1929 in the United States with a crash in the stock market followed by a financial panic. Businesses could not sell their goods or obtain credit; wages dropped; and many people lost their jobs.

People everywhere felt the effect of the depression when Americans stopped buying goods from abroad, stopped investing, and withdrew money from Europe by selling their foreign investments. In Asia and in South America, people saw American markets and dollars slip away. With far more goods for sale than there were buyers, prices fell. Many people could not pay their debts.

In May 1931, the largest bank in Vienna, the *Kredit Anstalt,* failed. It had creditors, mainly other banks, in western Europe and in the United States. Since it had investments scattered all over central Europe, its collapse triggered many bankruptcies and business failures.

From the continent, like a disease, the economic crisis descended on Britain. As trade fell, unemployment rose and government tax revenues dwindled. In 1931, Britain went off the gold standard. This meant that the pound, long a symbol of stability in the world economy, had been cut in value and that foreigners could no longer obtain gold for their pounds sterling. Within two years, half the nations in the world, including the United States, went off the gold standard. Money could no longer cross borders and be easily converted to gold.

Almost everywhere the problem of finding jobs for able-bodied workers became so great that it resembled an epidemic. People who had lost their jobs and their life savings often lost hope for a stable, secure life. Many joined movements and political parties that preached violence and the overthrow of democratic institutions.

In Japan, antidemocratic military leaders took advantage of the hardships brought on by the world depression and seized more power. By late 1932 they were in control of the government. They murdered important leaders to crush opposition, and they glorified military force. They justified attacks on the Asian mainland with a "Japanese Monroe Doctrine." This policy promoted Asian rule in Asia and urged Europeans to give up their colonies in East Asia.

In other parts of the world, many desperate people turned to a form of dictatorship called *totalitarianism*. Such a dictatorship operated through a single political party that permitted no organized opposition. The totalitarian dictatorship crushed all opposition and subordinated the wishes of the people to the demands of the state.

The first of the totalitarian regimes began to emerge out of a great civil war in Russia in 1918–1922. The Communists, under the leadership of Vladimir Lenin, set up a socialist state based on a so-called dictatorship of the *proletariat,* the working class. This meant, in fact, a dictatorship by the leaders of the Communist party. No other party was allowed in the Union of Soviet Socialist Republics (the Soviet Union), Russia's official name from 1922 onward.

Lenin died in 1924 and was succeeded by Joseph Stalin, a dictator as brutal as any ruler Russia had known. Stalin introduced state economic planning and the idea of "building socialism in a single country." He covered the country with a network of secret police and spies who had unlimited power to arrest and exterminate critics.

The next nation to succumb to dictatorship was Italy. Out of the disorder and agitation of postwar Italian society emerged a new political movement called fascism. The name came from the Latin *fasces,* the bound bundle of rods that had symbolized the power of the ancient republic of Rome.

In October 1922, the fascists marched on Rome. The king installed their leader, Benito Mussolini, as premier. Mussolini later did away with the parliament and made the Fascist party the sole organ of government. Mussolini's dictatorship was based on the idea of the corporative state. The Fascists retained a capitalist system but placed the state in control of the nation's economic life.

Other countries also set up dictatorships that came to be called fascist. Germany established the most powerful, brutal, and frightening fascist state.

In the 1920's various political groups in Germany plotted for the day when they could take power. One of these groups, the National Socialist German Workers' (Nazi) party, attracted to it Adolf Hitler, a poorly educated man with shrewd intelligence and a frenzied speaking style. Hitler became the head of the Nazi party.

The depression brought greater economic blight to Germany than to almost any other industrial nation. The Nazis and the Communists, feeding upon popular discontent, made great gains. Finally, in January 1933, Hitler was named chancellor, the equivalent of prime minister.

Within a short time Hitler established a personal dictatorship. He did away with all parties except the Nazi party and governed through terror, brutality, and murder. A secret political police called the *Gestapo* rounded up opponents by the thousands and threw them into concentration camps. The Nazis unleashed a vicious campaign of persecution, torture, and murder against Jews and Slavs. Under Hitler the state demanded total obedience.

Besides having contempt for democracy, the fascist leaders glorified war. Many of the democratic nations continued to support efforts for peace, but the fascist and militaristic nations sought to expand by attacking other countries. Examples of this aggression included Japan's invasion of Manchuria in 1931, Italy's invasion of Ethiopia in 1935, and Germany's seizure of Austria and large areas of Czechoslovakia in 1938. The German invasion of Poland in 1939 was the incident that finally touched off World War II.

Postwar Politics

CHAPTER 20
1921–1932

Police in Philadelphia break up a crowd of strikers.

The 1920's are often regarded as a time of gaiety sandwiched in between a bloody war and a brutal depression. Called the "golden twenties" because many people experienced a prosperity they had never known before, the decade was also a time of bigotry and agricultural poverty.

The years will probably always be best remembered for their lighter side—the flagpole-sitting contests and the dance marathons, the easy money and the bathtub gin. But the serious events merit attention. People throughout the world struggled with problems of war and peace, of poverty and prosperity.

DEMOBILIZATION

In 1919 the people of the United States were eager to forget the war. Immediately after the armistice, the government began bringing American soldiers back from France. In addition, it gave relief to the starving people in Europe and prepared to end the war program at home.

The Esch-Cummins Transportation Act (1920) returned control of the railroads to their private owners. It also enlarged the powers of the Interstate Commerce Commission so that the government had control over rates, profits, and other aspects of operating the lines.

The General Leasing Act of 1920 reserved oil lands for the navy, beyond the reach of oil companies. It also permitted the government to lease oil and mineral lands on terms that safeguarded the public interest. The Water Power Act (1920) set up the Federal Power Commission. It was given authority to license the construction and operation of dams and hydroelectric plants on rivers in government lands. The commission was also authorized to regulate rates. The Merchant Marine Act (1920) allowed the government to sell some of its ships to private operators.

Striking Workers

During the war, the wage rates of many workers had been frozen. After the conflict, business interests in the United States were in no mood to meet labor's demands for higher wages without a fight. They wanted to run their businesses as they saw fit. Some leaders believed that the workers' struggle for higher wages was the first stage of the class revolution plotted by Communists. They persuaded other Americans to believe so as well.

Public hostility toward organized labor was apparent in the steel strike of September 1919. Working conditions in the steel industry, as in many others, were wretched. The average work week for the entire industry was just under sixty-nine hours. The American Federation of Labor had easily organized many of the workers. When the United States Steel Corporation refused to negotiate with the union, the workers went on strike.

The steel company succeeded in diverting public attention away from the real issues by claiming that the labor leaders were Communists. Popular opinion then became so hostile toward the strikers that they could not hope to win. Although the strike dragged on until January 1920, the company had won out earlier with the use of thousands of strikebreakers. The workers did not gain a single concession.

In November 1919, about 394,000 miners in the soft-coal industry left their jobs. They were led by John L. Lewis, president of the United Mine Workers. The miners went on strike even though Attorney General A. Mitchell Palmer had obtained an *injunction,* or court order, prohibiting leaders of the union from participating in the strike. Like many other industrial workers, the miners had major grievances. They had agreed not to strike during the war. For two years they had not received a wage increase, even though the cost of living had doubled.

When a second injunction was issued, Lewis finally canceled the strike. Many miners still refused to return to work. President Wilson stepped in and promised a wage increase as well as a commission to investigate the workers' demands. The coal strike ended, and the miners ultimately received a wage increase of 27 percent.

The Red Scare

The wartime demands for conformity in thought and the intolerance against foreigners spilled over into peacetime. One result was the hunt for radicals—called the Red Scare of 1919–1920.

Although the Red Scare was rooted in American problems, it was also connected with events in Russia after the Bolshevik Revolution of 1917. The Bolsheviks, or Communists, preached the idea of worldwide revolution by the proletariat, the working people. The Communists dedicated themselves to provoking class warfare in which workers would turn on their employers, seize private property, and take over the government.

Most Americans apparently were shocked by Bolshevik activities and the spread of communism. They were further upset when two Communist parties were formed in the United States in September 1919. The American Communists carried on an intensive propaganda campaign. They paraded, made speeches, distributed pamphlets, and demanded violent action to overthrow the capitalist system.

Many Americans denounced the Communists as foreigners and subversives. Business leaders and conservatives in general were alarmed, for they took seriously the threat of revolution. Strikes, bombings, and even the increasing inflation were seen as attacks by radicals on the foundations of American society.

In November 1919, Attorney General Palmer began a series of raids against Com-

Marcus Garvey *(left)* speaks to his followers from shipboard before being deported. Garvey urged Negroes to take pride in their blackness and their African heritage. *Right:* During the 1919 riot, Chicago policemen check the body of a black man who has just been killed by a mob of stone-throwing whites.

munists and other radicals. On January 2, 1920, agents of the Department of Justice, at Palmer's direction, raided Communist headquarters in thirty-three major cities in twenty-three states. In this one great roundup, more than 2,700 persons were hustled off to jails. Most of the people arrested during the Red Scare were released because they had committed no crime, but several hundred aliens were deported.

State officials, too, suppressed civil liberties. Many state legislatures passed restrictive laws designed to punish radicals. In April 1920, the New York legislature expelled five legally elected members because they were Socialists. After this act of intolerance, the Red Scare declined. Many Americans seemed to realize that the radical danger had been exaggerated.

Racial Violence

During World War I, hundreds of thousands of black people had left farms in the South for jobs in northern cities. Although they gained greater social and economic freedom than they had previously known, black people faced prejudice, stiff competition for jobs, and slum living as bad as or worse than that of immigrants. Some 400,000 blacks had served in the army, half of them in Europe. There they had experienced a social freedom they had not known in the United States.

After the war, blacks tried to break down some of the barriers that had kept them at the bottom of American society. The National Association for the Advancement of Colored People (NAACP) worked for a number of changes.

Many southern whites opposed this activity and tried to keep blacks in their old status. They revived the Ku Klux Klan. By 1919, it had grown from a small group to an organization with 100,000 members. In many southern communities, night-riding Klansmen terrorized victims, most of whom were black people. Lynchings of blacks increased and even included some men still in uniform.

In the North, as blacks moved closer to white neighborhoods, resentment exploded. Race riots broke out in twenty-six towns and cities, including Washington, D.C., and Chicago. Before 1919 was over, hundreds were dead or maimed from the riots, and millions of dollars' worth of property was destroyed.

During the war, a new leader had appeared who held out hope for a better life. Marcus Aurelius Garvey, a Jamaican immigrant, founded the Universal Negro Improvement Association. Working from the Harlem district of New York City, Garvey preached black nationalism and black pride. Follow me back to Africa, he said, and build a "free, redeemed and mighty nation."

By 1921, more than 4 million black people were paying dues to Garvey's organization.

Courtesy Chicago Historical Society

He gathered millions of dollars to buy ships to carry his followers to Africa, but the project never materialized. In 1923, a federal court convicted Garvey of using the mails to defraud. He was sent to prison and was later deported.

Victory of the Suffragists

During the war, the National American Woman Suffrage Association and other groups kept up the pressure for a federal women's suffrage amendment. In 1917, seven more states gave women the vote. Success bred more success as political leaders sensed that women's suffrage was inevitable and that they would be unwise to alienate future voters.

Finally in 1918, Congress agreed to consider the proposed amendment. The amendment passed in the House with exactly the number of votes needed to win. But it took another year and a half to get the measure through the Senate. Still the battle was not over, for the amendment had to be ratified by the states. Thousands of women poured their energies into struggles to get the state legislatures to pass the amendment. Finally, on August 26, 1920, Tennessee ratified the amendment, by a two-vote margin, and the battle was won.

In 1923, Carrie Chapman Catt, who had led the 2 million members of the National American Woman Suffrage Association, summed up the effort that it had taken to win the Nineteenth Amendment:

To get the word "male" in effect out of the Constitution cost the women of the country fifty-two years of pauseless campaign.... During that time they were forced to conduct fifty-six campaigns of referenda to male voters; 480 campaigns to get Legislatures to submit suffrage amendments to voters; 47 campaigns to get State constitutional conventions to write woman suffrage into state constitutions; 277 campaigns to get State party conventions to include woman suffrage planks; 30 campaigns to get presidential party conventions to adopt woman suffrage planks in party platforms, and 19 campaigns with 19 successive Congresses.

As the historian Eleanor Flexner comments, the forces against women's suffrage had "caused far more delay and difficulty than one would ever imagine from reading the usual phrase in the history books, announcing that American women were enfranchised after World War I."

Scandals in Government

President Warren G. Harding was kindly, friendly, and well liked by almost everybody who knew him, but he had no will power. Although he did not want to be President, he gave in to pressure from friends and political bosses to accept the Republican nomination. His administration was remembered as much for scandal as for any accomplishment.

Harding surrounded himself with old cronies, who became known as the "Ohio gang." They catered to his tastes but deceived him. He rewarded the leader of the Ohio gang, Harry M. Daugherty, with the post of attorney general. He gave another friend, Albert B. Fall of New Mexico, the job of secretary of the interior. Neither man was suited for his office.

Not all of Harding's appointments were bad, however. He had obtained three able and intelligent men in Charles Evans Hughes, secretary of state; Andrew Mellon, secretary of the treasury; and Herbert Hoover, secretary of commerce. They set the tone for the administration because Harding seldom made policy decisions on his own. He presided over government with outward dignity but left policy making to his cabinet members and to Congress.

Soon after Albert B. Fall took over as secretary of the interior, he persuaded the secretary of the navy to transfer to the Department of the Interior control over oil lands held in reserve to meet the future needs of the navy. Even though a few of the navy's oil experts protested, the President agreed to the transfer. Fall then secretly leased the reserve at Elk Hills, California, to Edward L. Doheny of the Pan American Petroleum Company, and the reserve at Teapot Dome, Wyoming, to Harry F. Sinclair of the Mammoth Oil Company. For these favors Sinclair gave Fall over $200,000 in government bonds, $85,000 in cash, and other presents. Doheny gave the secretary a "loan" of $100,000.

When Fall began spending this wealth, some senators became suspicious and investigated. Eventually the story was uncovered. In 1924, Doheny, Sinclair, and Fall were tried for conspiracy to defraud the government. All were acquitted. In 1929, Fall was convicted of taking a bribe, fined $100,000, and sentenced to a year in prison. Sinclair was fined $1,000 and served nine months in jail for tampering with the jury and for defying a Senate committee, but neither he nor Doheny was convicted of paying bribes.

Attorney General Daugherty also disgraced the Harding administration. Senate investigators in 1924 found that he had sold liquor permits and pardons. He was forced to resign from office and, in 1927, was brought to trial for fraud. In court, Daugherty refused to testify and implied that he chose to remain silent rather than make revelations that might injure Harding's reputation. The jury failed to agree on Daugherty's guilt or innocence, and he went free.

In June 1923, as rumors of corruption in government had begun to spread, Harding had begun a speaking tour of the West. He became ill while returning from an Alaska vacation. On August 2 he suffered a stroke and died. Not yet knowing of the scandals, the people of the nation mourned him for the kindly man he was and for the statesman they believed him to be.

Harding suspected that corruption had eaten into his administration. Before he started his trip he told a friend, "In this job I am not worried about my enemies. It is my friends that are keeping me awake nights." His friends had betrayed him to such an extent that his reputation was destroyed.

PROSPERITY AND PROBLEMS

On the night of Harding's death, Vice-President Calvin Coolidge was at his father's home near Plymouth, Vermont. In the little

The flivver: anatomy of a pollution cure

Something had to be done about the horse. It was definitely the city's worst polluter. The streetcar was fine for groups of city dwellers, but many people wanted individual means of transportation. They hailed the automobile as the ideal pollution cure. After World War I, automobile production rose greatly, and by 1928, was the largest industry in the United States.

Some historians describe city and suburban growth in terms of the type of transportation that was dominant or becoming important at the time growth took place. Thus, the oldest parts of many cities make up the "walking city"; parts that were built in the 1880's and 1890's are classified as the "streetcar city"; and parts built after the 1920's are the "automobile city." Most American cities are a mixture of walking, streetcar, and automobile cities. As each new form of transportation has become important, the people have changed or designed their cities to accommodate it.

Adjustments to the automobile were just beginning in the 1920's and 1930's. Most Americans then had no idea that their "flivvers" and "tin Lizzies" would transform the nation. In later decades, the narrow streets of the walking city would become one-way streets to accommodate the automobile. When streetcar tracks interfered with automobile driving, they would be dug up or paved over. The automobile city would be built with numerous parking facilities.

The use of the automobile changed the lifestyles of many people. Housing developments beyond the streetcar suburbs became possible. People with cars, irritated by traffic congestion and parking trouble in the walking and streetcar cities, often ceased to visit those areas.

While the automobile gave some Americans greater mobility, it also extracted a high price. More and more land was bulldozed and paved to make way for cars. Shops in the walking and streetcar cities often went out of business or moved to the automobile cities. Streetcar companies began losing customers as more and more people bought cars. Perhaps the most ironic price was pollution. By the 1960's, automobiles had become the major source of air pollution in the United States.

living room at 2:47 A.M., with his hand on the open family Bible, Coolidge took the presidential oath. His father, a notary public, administered the oath by the light of kerosene lamps.

This rural scene had tremendous appeal. To many people in the United States it suggested another chapter in the American dream. Another country boy had risen to occupy the White House.

Although Calvin Coolidge had not been poor, he had come from the country, and his career was that of a small-town politician who made good. Coolidge fitted the times. He was a conservative in almost everything. He favored legislation beneficial to big business because he believed business should run the country.

Coolidge was shy, and it was difficult for him to make friends. He spoke so seldom that he became known as "Silent Cal." Yet people liked his folksy virtues. He had the qualities the Ohio gang lacked, namely old-fashioned honesty and simplicity.

Business leaders controlled the Republican convention of 1924. They gave Coolidge the nomination and framed a platform that promised to continue things as they were.

The Democrats were badly divided. At their convention the urban and rural wings of the party could not agree on a presidential candidate. Finally, on the 103rd ballot, the Democrats nominated John W. Davis, a corporation lawyer who was as conservative as Coolidge.

Rebellious Republicans, labor leaders, and reformers organized a new Progressive party for the presidential campaign only. Their convention chose Robert M. La Follette to head the ticket. These Progressives gained most of their support from western farmers, organized labor, and socialists. La Follette received nearly 5 million votes, a substantial number for a third party, but he carried only the state of Wisconsin.

Farmers' Problems

During the war, many farmers had made money, and they had spent it as though their prosperity would continue. Their prosperity ended in 1920, when foreign countries cut down on their purchases of American wheat, meat, and other products, and the federal government withdrew support for the price of wheat. Farmers now had an output that exceeded demand. An agricultural depression began that summer in large areas of the country and lasted all during the 1920's.

Midwestern Republicans and southern Democrats formed a farm bloc in Congress to combat the economic crisis. The farm bloc helped gain high tariff protection for agricultural products. The Intermediate Credits Act of 1923 gave government loans to growers of livestock. Yet the farm distress persisted.

Beginning in 1924, farmers supported the McNary-Haugen bill, which included a plan for government aid to agriculture. This plan

Passage of the prohibition amendment did not end some people's thirst for alcoholic beverages. The sale of "bathtub gin" in "speakeasies"—illegal bars—flourished. Agents of the treasury department tried to break up illegal distilling operations and to shut down speakeasies. *Left:* Two male prohibition agents model their disguises. *Right:* John Held's cartoon "The Talkie" captures the busy mood of a Hollywood movie set.

would establish a system whereby farm products would be sold at two prices—a low world price and a higher price in the United States. The government would buy the farm surpluses at the American price, sell them abroad at the world price, and recover its losses through a special tax on farmers.

The McNary-Haugen bill was passed by Congress in revised form in 1927 and 1928. Coolidge vetoed it both times. Although organized farmers gained a number of benefits from the government, they failed to get their most important measure. They failed primarily because the President and big business interests in the East opposed the bill.

Restricting Immigration

Many Americans were no longer willing to allow unrestricted immigration into the United States. Organized labor wanted to shut off immigration in order to keep newcomers from competing for the available jobs. Many Protestants resented the influx of Catholics and Jews from southern and eastern Europe. Even employers now favored restrictions because they believed that many of the new immigrants were radicals.

Pressure from these groups led to the passage of the Emergency Quota Act in May 1921 and the National Origins Act of 1924. The 1921 law created a quota system by which the number of immigrants allowed from a given nation was based on the number of persons of that nationality living in the United States in the base year, 1910. The 1924 law changed the base year from 1910 to 1890. It favored northwestern Europeans over the southern and eastern, because a larger percentage of persons of northwestern European descent lived in the United States in 1890 than in 1910. Most Asians were completely barred, but immigrants from Latin America and Canada still had fairly free access to the United States.

The effect of the two immigration laws was that discrimination, as well as restriction of immigration, became a national policy.

Intolerance

Hostility toward foreigners and fear of radicals was also evident in a murder case that stirred deep emotions during most of the 1920's. In April 1920, two men in South Braintree, Massachusetts, killed and robbed a factory paymaster and his guard. Nicola Sacco, an employee in a shoe factory, and Bartolomeo Vanzetti, a fish peddler, were tried and convicted of the murder. Both men were Italian aliens and both were anarchists. Webster Thayer, the trial judge, publicly expressed contempt for anarchism. Since the evidence against Sacco and Vanzetti was circumstantial, many people believed that they had been judged guilty primarily because they were foreigners and radicals.

This belief, accompanied by protests all over the world against the decision, led to a special investigation of the case. The investigators said the judge had acted improperly, but they did not recommend a new trial. In August 1927, Sacco and Vanzetti died in the electric chair.

An even more sinister sign of bigotry in American life was the rapid growth of the Ku Klux Klan. After 1920, the Klan spread from the South to other parts of the country, particularly to the small towns of the Midwest and the Far West. By the end of 1924, it probably had 4 or 5 million members.

Proclaiming itself the protector of "Anglo-Saxon" Protestant America, the Klan waged illegal war on foreigners, blacks, Jews, and especially Roman Catholics. Its members wore their hoods and white sheets on brutal raids in which victims were beaten and sometimes murdered. The Klansmen announced their outrages by burning crosses.

In 1924, the political influence of the Klan was so great that it prevented the Democratic national convention from condemning its activities and caused a serious split in the party. In the following year a scandal exposed Indiana Klan leaders as immoral, dishonest, and corrupt. This disillusioned many of the rank-and-file members. By the end of the 1920's, this lawless organization had lost much of its influence.

The Election of 1928

Even though the Ku Klux Klan had declined, the spirit of intolerance remained. It affected the election of 1928. The difficulty began when the Democrats nominated Alfred E. "Al" Smith, four times governor of New York, for the presidency.

Smith represented something new in national politics. Never before had either of the two major parties nominated such a person. He was a Catholic with an immigrant background and a limited education. Reared on New York City's East Side, Smith was a "wet" who sought repeal of prohibition.

Calvin Coolidge could have had the Republican nomination, but he announced that he did not choose to run. The Republicans nominated Herbert Hoover, the secretary of commerce, who had served in the cabinet of the last two previous administrations.

Hoover campaigned on a conservative platform that avoided important issues and promised continuing prosperity. Three other issues also dominated the campaign—Smith's religion, his big-city background, and his opposition to prohibition. Everywhere, the people who feared Roman Catholicism attacked him. In the South the opposition to him became almost a crusade. Vile stories about him were whispered or circulated on crude handbills. In Oklahoma City, where Smith denounced the Ku Klux Klan, fiery crosses greeted him.

So great was the opposition to Smith that Hoover won by a landslide. He even broke the Solid South, the first Republican to do so

PRESIDENTIAL ELECTIONS: 1920-1932

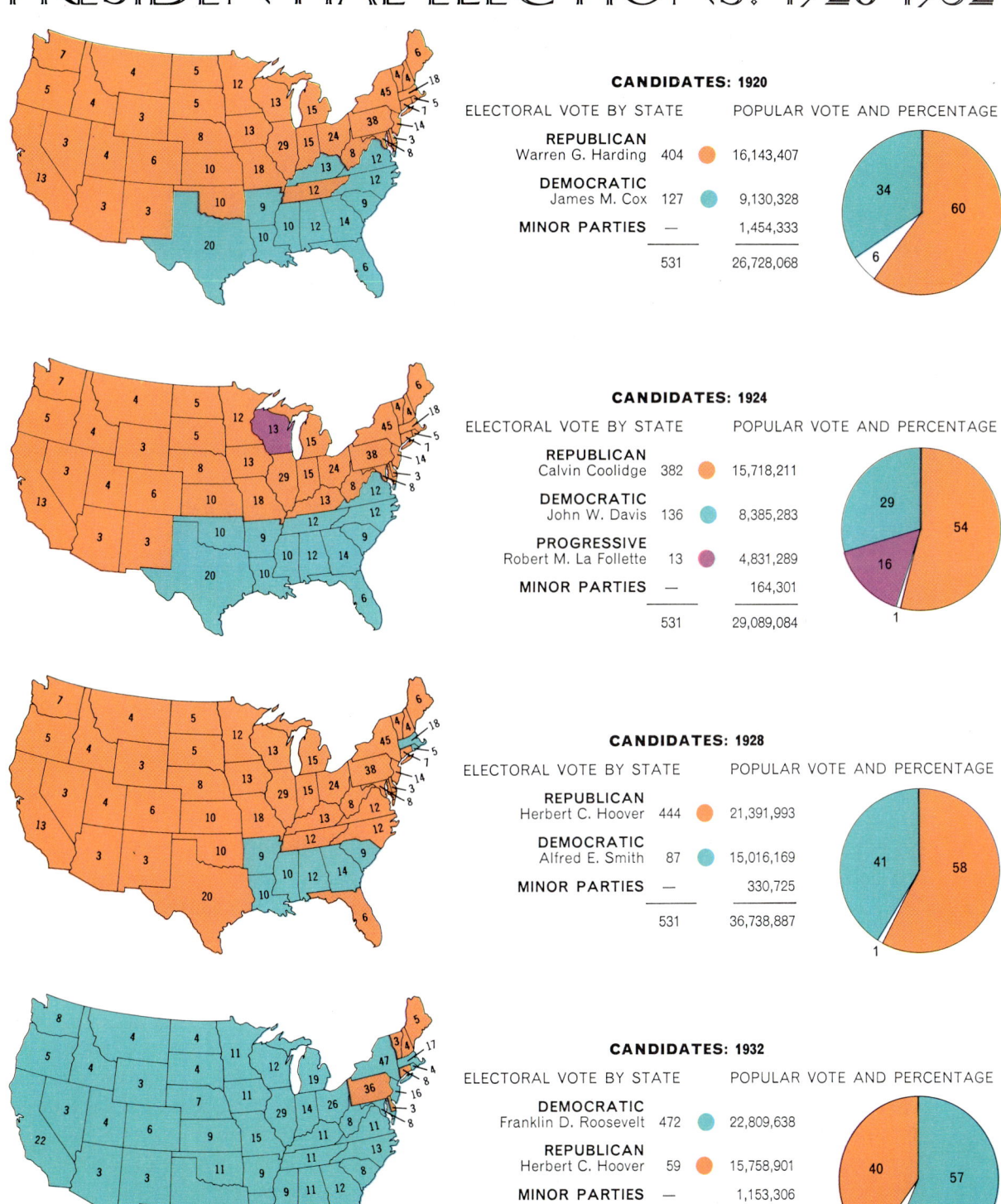

CANDIDATES: 1920

ELECTORAL VOTE BY STATE		POPULAR VOTE AND PERCENTAGE
REPUBLICAN Warren G. Harding	404	16,143,407
DEMOCRATIC James M. Cox	127	9,130,328
MINOR PARTIES	—	1,454,333
	531	26,728,068

Pie chart: 60, 34, 6

CANDIDATES: 1924

ELECTORAL VOTE BY STATE		POPULAR VOTE AND PERCENTAGE
REPUBLICAN Calvin Coolidge	382	15,718,211
DEMOCRATIC John W. Davis	136	8,385,283
PROGRESSIVE Robert M. La Follette	13	4,831,289
MINOR PARTIES	—	164,301
	531	29,089,084

Pie chart: 54, 29, 16, 1

CANDIDATES: 1928

ELECTORAL VOTE BY STATE		POPULAR VOTE AND PERCENTAGE
REPUBLICAN Herbert C. Hoover	444	21,391,993
DEMOCRATIC Alfred E. Smith	87	15,016,169
MINOR PARTIES	—	330,725
	531	36,738,887

Pie chart: 58, 41, 1

CANDIDATES: 1932

ELECTORAL VOTE BY STATE		POPULAR VOTE AND PERCENTAGE
DEMOCRATIC Franklin D. Roosevelt	472	22,809,638
REPUBLICAN Herbert C. Hoover	59	15,758,901
MINOR PARTIES	—	1,153,306
	531	39,721,845

Pie chart: 57, 40, 3

since the Reconstruction period. Probably no Democrat could have won, for the people were satisfied with Republican prosperity. Yet prejudice had marred the election and left an ugly wound in American society, one that would heal slowly.

HEADING FOR A FALL

As a poor orphan boy from the country who achieved wealth, fame, and power, Herbert Hoover seemed to fulfill the American dream. He was born in the small town of West Branch, Iowa, in 1874. He worked for his education at Stanford University and then became a mining engineer. His profession took him over most of the world—to Australia, Asia, Africa, and Europe. In 1914, he claimed that he was probably the wealthiest of American engineers. After wealth came fame, particularly as chairman of the Commission for Relief in Belgium, where he became known as a great humanitarian. Then followed his appointment as Wilson's food administrator and eight years as secretary of commerce.

Hoover believed in efficiency and service in government and strongly distrusted the spread of governmental power. The presidency was Hoover's first elective office, and he lacked political experience. He found it difficult to make the compromises demanded of a politician.

Prohibition

Prohibition had been a bitter issue in the election campaign. Protestant rural America favored it. Prohibitionists believed that drinking was a vice of immigrants and corrupt city dwellers. But many people who lived in the cities and industrial areas, where the drinking of liquor, wine, or beer was an accepted social custom, resented the Eighteenth Amendment as an invasion of their personal liberty.

Members of the Ku Klux Klan parade down a New Jersey street. The Klan, revived in 1915, recruited members North and South. Its antiforeigner stand appealed to isolationist Americans after World War I.

People who wanted to drink did so regardless of the Constitution. Bootleggers and rumrunners defied the law and furnished a steady supply of alcohol to the "wets." Criminals, many of them organized on a scale previously unknown, reaped untold profits from selling illegal liquor.

Enforcement of nationwide prohibition might have been possible if most people had supported it. But by law, the federal, state, and local governments were all responsible for enforcement. In "wet" areas the local authorities did nothing and left enforcement to the federal government. And Congress never appropriated enough money to do the job properly.

By 1928, enforcement of prohibition had become a joke. Shortly after Hoover entered the White House he appointed a commission, headed by former Attorney General George W. Wickersham, to investigate the problems of enforcement. Two years later, in January 1931, the Wickersham Commission gave its report. It documented what most Americans already knew—that prohibition was a failure. Yet the commission suggested no plan for attacking the problem.

Hoover strengthened the federal government's machinery for enforcement and did a better job than had Harding and Coolidge, but he too failed. His task actually became more difficult as opposition to prohibition grew. Finally, in August 1932, he announced that he favored repeal of the Eighteenth Amendment. Since the Democratic platform of that year had also come out for repeal, prohibition was doomed.

In February 1933, Congress submitted the repeal amendment to the states. In December, the Twenty-first Amendment, which repealed the Eighteenth Amendment, became law. The "noble experiment" was over.

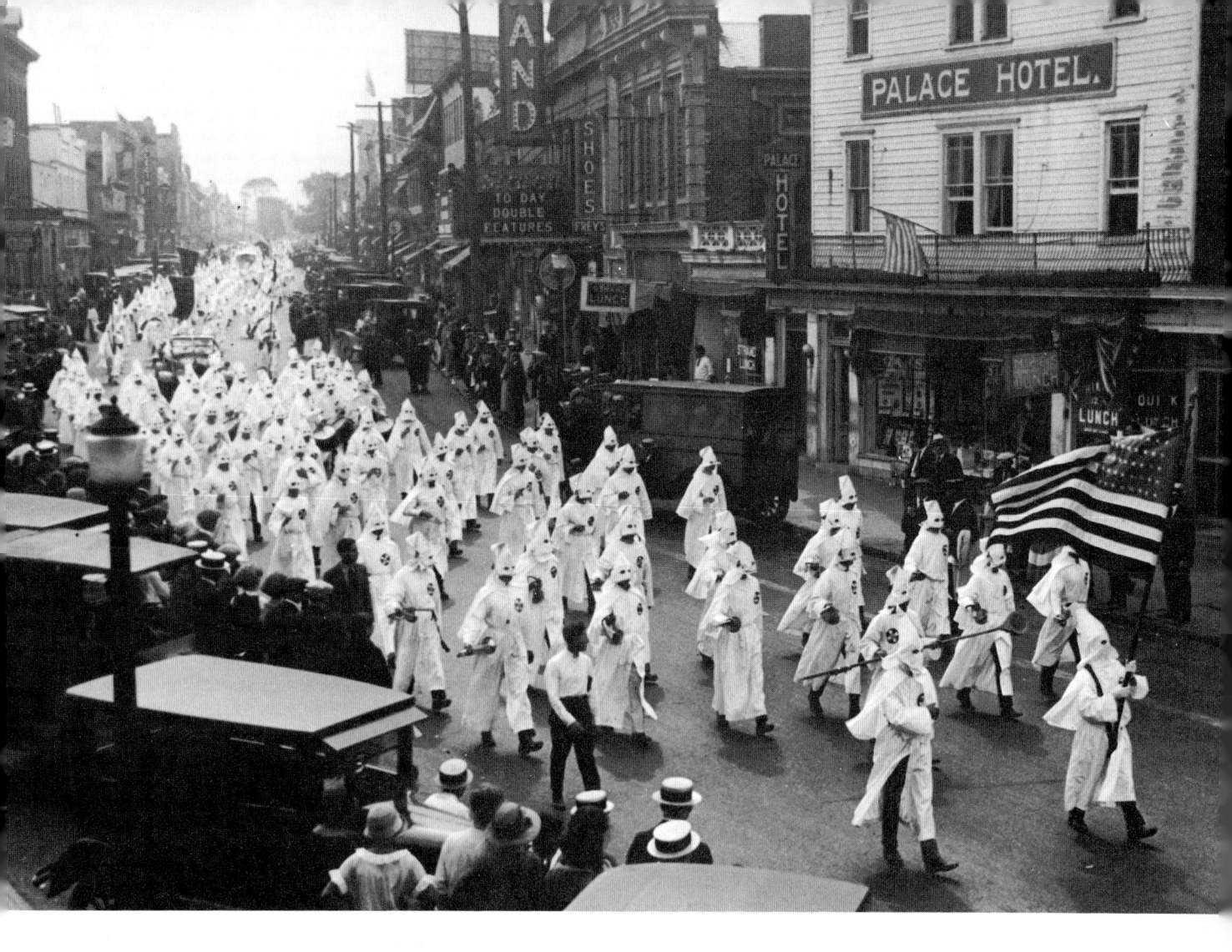

The Hawley-Smoot Tariff

When Hoover was inaugurated, many Americans were enjoying a booming prosperity. During the campaign, Hoover had promised help to the farmers, most of whom were not well off. To redeem his promise, Hoover called Congress into special session to pass laws to help farmers.

In June 1929, Congress passed the Agricultural Marketing Act to give aid to farmers through their own cooperative marketing organizations. This law set up the Federal Farm Board, which made loans to cooperative associations so that they could store and sell agricultural surpluses. In 1930, after the outbreak of a worldwide economic depression, the Farm Board created the Grain Stabilization Corporation and the Cotton Stabilization Corporation. These two agencies tried to keep prices stable by buying up surpluses, but prices fell drastically anyway. Hoover's farm experiment had failed.

Hoover also asked Congress to give farm products the same protection it had given to manufacturers by raising the tariff on agricultural products. The Hawley-Smoot Tariff bill, passed by Congress in June 1930, did raise the tariff on farm products. But it did not help farmers much because it also raised the rates on many manufactured goods that the farmers had to buy.

People everywhere pleaded with the President not to sign the bill. More than a thousand of the nation's professional economists said that it was economically unsound. Since business leaders and some farmers wanted the tariff, Hoover signed it.

The Hawley-Smoot Tariff Act, the highest peacetime tariff in the nation's history, failed to help farmers. They actually suffered because they were exporters. Within two years, other industrial nations retaliated with tariffs of their own against United States products. The Hawley-Smoot Tariff Act stimulated the growth of economic nationalism and helped deepen the depression.

A Mighty Crash

The depression in the United States was touched off by distress in the New York Stock Exchange. For several years the prices of stocks had been rising. People bought stocks because they thought they could get rich easily. They gambled on the stock market by buying on *margin,* that is, buying on credit from brokers. This kind of speculation was all right only so long as stock prices continued to climb, as nearly everybody expected they would.

Outside the market there were signs that prosperity was weakening. Much of the prosperity had been founded on the construction and automobile industries. In 1925, the construction of homes had reached a value of 5 billion dollars; in 1929, the value fell to 3 billion. By 1929, too, sales of automobiles and related products had declined. Some stock operators began to quietly dispose of their holdings. In September 1929, the stock market broke and then recovered. On October 24, called "Black Thursday," prices broke sharply, and many investors lost money. On the following day, President Hoover assured the people that what had happened was not very serious.

Then, on Tuesday, October 29, the big crash came. In a day of wild trading, a day that turned out to be the most devastating in

Bootleggers prepare to transport liquor. The gangs of criminals that organized during the Prohibition era later branched into other fields, both legal and illegal. The Purple Gang in Detroit, Solly Weissman in Kansas City, and Al Capone in Chicago dominated much of the illegal liquor trade.

the history of the Stock Exchange, nearly 16.5 million shares of stock exchanged hands. The frenzied selling went on for two weeks, until the value of the stocks on the Wall Street exchange had declined about 40 percent.

Leaders in government and business tried to bolster sagging spirits. When men and women everywhere were being wiped out financially, John D. Rockefeller, for example, came out with an optimistic statement. He said that the country was sound and added that "my son and I have for some days been purchasing sound common stocks." Many people applauded Rockefeller, but Eddie Cantor, a popular comedian, commented later, "Sure, who else had any money left?"

The mighty crash on Wall Street brought the prosperity of the twenties to a disastrous end. Although the crash was not the only cause of the Great Depression that followed, it was a contributing factor.

Fighting the Depression

When the depression struck, most people in business took the view that business cycles were inevitable and that, in time, prosperity would return. Some said the economy was sound, and that the only thing wrong was the people's lack of confidence.

No one could ignore the depression. It penetrated every aspect of life. A year after the crash, 6 million men and women in the United States walked the streets looking for jobs that did not exist. In 1931, unemployment in the nation rose to 9 million, and in 1932 it climbed to about 15 million. Thou-

Bootleggers, by Ben Shahn, around 1935

sands of banks failed, prices dropped, foreign trade shrank, and more businesses failed.

By the summer of 1932, steel plants were operating at 12 percent of capacity. Many factories had shut down completely. People lost their savings. When they could not make mortgage payments, they lost their homes. Charity soup kitchens opened in the cities, and long bread lines formed. The jobless slept where they could—on park benches or in the doorways of public buildings. Many suffered from cold and lack of food.

Hoover did not go along with those who advised him to do nothing. He used more of the resources of the government to fight the depression than did any previous President in an economic crisis. To increase business activity and help end unemployment, he stepped up federal construction of public buildings and roads.

Hoover would not go beyond this limited use of government spending. He was opposed to direct use of federal money for relief for the unemployed, believing that state and local governments and private charities should provide relief. He was afraid that Americans would lose their initiative and self-reliance if they became accustomed to turning to the federal government for aid during hard times. At first he relied on the voluntary cooperation of business, labor, and local government agencies to fight the depression. But these measures were not enough. State and local governments ran out of money, and private charities proved inadequate to care for the hungry and homeless.

Congress began to demand that Hoover abandon his reliance on voluntary measures and start some large-scale federal relief. Finally, after a panic in Europe made the depression in the United States worse, the President asked Congress to create the Reconstruction Finance Corporation (RFC) to lend money to banks, railroads, insurance companies, and other large businesses. Congress created the RFC in January 1932, and before the year was over, it had loaned 1.5 billion dollars to more than 5,000 business concerns.

Hoover followed this action with other measures, such as the Federal Home Loan Bank Act of July 1932, which saved home mortgages by giving help to building and loan associations. In the same month, however, he vetoed a bill for direct federal relief and a huge public works program. For this reason, many people believed that he was a heartless man who was willing to use government funds for big business but not for the relief of human suffering.

The President seemed to confirm that impression in his treatment of the "Bonus Army," which gathered in Washington in the spring of 1932. About 15,000 World War I veterans had come to demand immediate payment of a bonus that Congress had authorized in 1924. (The bonus was not due to be paid until 1945.) Congress voted down a bill for immediate payment, and over half of the bonus marchers left Washington. Several thousand remained. They had no jobs, no homes, and nowhere to go. The President ordered them evicted from government property. Finally, some units of the army, under the command of General Douglas MacArthur, drove the ragged veterans away with tanks and bayonets.

To many people it seemed as if both their business-trained President and capitalism had failed. While people went hungry, granaries spilled over with wheat that no one could sell. Some Americans began to read Karl Marx with increased interest, some began flirting with radical ideas, and many were ready for a change.

SHUNNING WORLD LEADERSHIP

When World War I ended, the United States was committed to a policy of isolation. Despite that commitment, the United States in the 1920's did not avoid all participation in world politics.

Female employees at work in an office. During and after World War I, the number of women in the paid work force increased greatly. Most, however, were employed in low-paying clerical or factory jobs.

Seeking Disarmament

In 1921, President Harding and Secretary of State Charles Evans Hughes, responding to the demands of Congress and the people, took steps to bring about naval disarmament among the world's sea powers. Nine nations—the United States, Britain, Japan, France, Italy, Belgium, the Netherlands, China, and Portugal—attended the Naval Disarmament Conference that opened in Washington in November 1921.

Resulting from this conference were three major agreements. In the Four-Power Pact, signed in December, the United States, Britain, Japan, and France agreed to respect each other's rights and territories in the Pacific. If any dispute arose among them, they agreed that they would discuss it in a conference. This agreement replaced an alliance between Britain and Japan.

Next the United States, Britain, Japan, France, and Italy worked on the Five-Power Naval Treaty, which they signed in February 1922. This agreement stopped the construction of large warships, such as battleships and battle cruisers, for ten years and called for the destruction of some of those ships that had already been built. It set up a ratio that allowed Japan nine ships, and France and Italy five ships, for every fifteen ships permitted the United States and Britain.

A third major agreement, the Nine-Power Open Door Treaty, was signed by all the delegates. It pledged all the powers to respect China's independence and territorial integrity and to uphold the principle of the Open Door.

Trying to Insure Peace

In the United States, public support for the Washington conference had come from a peace movement stronger than any in the past. Even though Americans had rejected membership in the League of Nations, the Republican administrations of the 1920's were willing to cooperate with other nations in disarmament conferences and peace pacts. In time, the Republican leaders even came to accept the League itself as being of some importance to United States foreign policy.

After spurning the League, the Harding administration cautiously began to cooperate with it in 1922 by sending "unofficial observers" to conferences sponsored by the

League. Coolidge and Hoover continued and expanded such cooperation.

In 1927, the failure of a disarmament conference in Geneva, Switzerland, contributed to a loss of public confidence in disarmament as a means of insuring peace. But the peace crusaders had turned to another idea—a movement to outlaw war.

Acting upon this idea, on August 27, 1928, the representatives of fifteen nations met in Paris to sign the Kellogg-Briand Pact. This treaty pledged the signers to renounce war "as an instrument of national policy" and to try to settle their disputes by peaceful means. In time, sixty-two nations signed the pact.

In April 1930, a naval conference in London produced the London Naval Treaty. It extended the "holiday" on naval shipbuilding agreed to in the Five-Power Naval Treaty. The London treaty also applied limitations to the building of smaller warships, such as cruisers, destroyers, and submarines. This treaty, most of which was accepted by the five major naval powers—the United States, Britain, Japan, France, and Italy—was the first in modern world history to limit all categories of ships.

A War in Asia

Although the United States and Japan had reached an accommodation on naval matters, tension between them had arisen again when Congress enacted the immigration law of 1924. While the act was under consideration, the Japanese had protested to the American government, saying that the new law would violate the "gentlemen's agreement," which they had carefully observed. Regardless of the Japanese protests, Congress went ahead with the law.

The bad feelings aroused by this law continued throughout the 1920's, but later in this period the area of Japanese-American disagreements shifted to the Chinese mainland. Beginning in 1925, the Chinese went through their second revolution of the twentieth century. The leader of this revolution was General Chiang Kai-shek, who had taken up the work of Sun Yat-sen, the founder of the Chinese Nationalist party.

Chiang clashed with both the Soviets and the Japanese. In 1929, when Chiang's Nationalists tried to take over the Soviet Union's holdings in northern Manchuria, Soviet troops invaded the province and defeated the Chinese. Secretary of State Henry L. Stimson tried to stop the fighting by invoking the Kellogg-Briand Pact, which both China and the Soviet Union had signed. The Soviets said the United States was not the enforcer of the pact and should mind its own business.

Japan was alarmed by Chiang's efforts to unify China and control Manchuria. Blaming the Chinese for a mysterious explosion on a Japanese railway near Mukden, Manchuria, late in 1931 the Japanese invaded southern Manchuria. Within a few months, Japan had conquered the province and set it up as a puppet state called Manchukuo.

Shortly after the Japanese invasion, China appealed to the United States, as sponsor of the Kellogg Pact, and to the League of Nations, under the covenant, to help keep the peace. Neither could do much. The League appointed a commission, which investigated the dispute and later condemned Japan as an aggressor. Secretary of State Stimson warned Japan that it was violating both the Kellogg-Briand Pact and the Nine-Power Open Door Treaty. Then on January 7, 1932, he announced what has become known as the Stimson Doctrine. It said the United States would not recognize Japan's gains made in violation of the Open Door principle and the Kellogg-Briand Pact.

Neither the League's condemnation nor Stimson's nonrecognition doctrine stopped the Japanese. Japan retained Manchuria and withdrew from the League.

Leisure

Mah-jongg, a game of Chinese origin, and crossword puzzles were leisure fads in the twenties. Ballroom dancing, especially in dance clubs, was extremely popular throughout the twenties and thirties. One craze was the dance marathon, in which contestants danced until they fell down from exhaustion.

Stomp, by Archibald Motley, 1927

Improved Relations with Latin America

Many Latin Americans were as hostile to the United States as were the Japanese. They feared that the United States wanted to exploit and dominate them. Continued occupation of Nicaragua, Haiti, and the Dominican Republic added to Latin America's distrust of the United States. So did friction with Mexico in the early 1920's. Under Coolidge, American troops also went into Honduras and Panama. In 1924, the United States exercised extensive control over the finances of most of the twenty Latin American republics and had troops stationed in six of them.

Coolidge carried on a "private war" in Nicaragua. He supported one faction there with arms and American troops, while Mexico gave assistance to another warring faction. His troubles with Mexico increased in January 1927 when the Mexicans put into effect two laws that restricted the rights of foreigners who owned oil property in Mexico. These laws, as well as laws against the Catholic Church, led many Americans to clamor once again for intervention in Mexico. Instead, Coolidge sent Dwight W. Morrow to Mexico as ambassador. Morrow turned out to be a fine diplomat, and he helped overcome the major difficulties. Then in January 1928, Coolidge delivered the opening speech at the Sixth Pan-American Conference in Havana. This was only the second time a President of the United States had ever set foot in a Latin American country. It indicated a new concern for relations with Latin America.

Hoover was more concerned about Latin America than was Coolidge. Late in 1928, as President-elect, Hoover made a good-will tour of eleven nations in Central and South America. He told the Latin Americans that he disapproved of intervention, and that he wanted the United States to be their good neighbor. Later, his administration issued a memorandum that repudiated the Roosevelt Corollary to the Monroe Doctrine.

Unlike his predecessors, Hoover did not start new interventions in Latin America. He denounced dollar diplomacy and began to end existing interventions. He removed marines from Nicaragua and began the evacuation of troops from Haiti. Although Latin Americans resented his signing of the Hawley-Smoot Tariff Act, which injured their trade, Hoover did improve relations with Latin America. His administration prepared the way for a stronger good neighbor policy.

Alienating Europe

Europeans also were upset by certain aspects of United States policy in the 1920's, particularly foreign economic policy. The nation's economic policy was of tremendous importance because the United States had emerged from World War I as the world's wealthiest power, greatest industrial nation, and most important market for raw materials and semifinished goods.

Between 1914 and 1919, the United States had also changed from a debtor to a creditor nation. European nations owed the United States about 10 billion dollars for war debts.

Many European leaders had thought the United States would consider the money it had loaned as part of its general contribution to the defeat of Germany and that it would cancel the debts. Congress and the American people, on the other hand, expected full payment. They considered repayment a matter of national honor. In the 1920's, the United States government negotiated agreements with the debtor countries that called for repayment over a period of years. These agreements usually cut the interest rate and hence reduced the debts.

The European debtors then began paying their American debts from reparations received from Germany. This system worked for a while because private American investors loaned money to German industries, and the Germans used most of this money to pay reparations. When the Great Depression struck, however, Americans stopped investing abroad. Germany halted its reparations payments, and the former Allies defaulted on their American debts.

These defaults caused anger in the United States, while Europeans were disappointed by the American insistence on payment. The Europeans felt that they had contributed far more blood on the battlefields of the war than had the United States and that the United States therefore should be glad to contribute dollars. Moreover, the money was loaned in the form of credits and goods sold at high wartime profits. The Europeans also resented America's high tariff policy, which they said prevented them from selling goods in the United States to earn dollars to pay the debts.

President Hoover tried to ease the debt crisis brought on by the depression. In June 1931, he announced that the United States would not demand payments on debts for one year if other nations would temporarily excuse German reparations and other debts. Hoover's action brought relief but did not get rid of the debt problem.

Early in 1933, Hoover started to renegotiate the debt agreements. Hoover wanted his successor, Franklin Delano Roosevelt, to agree to this debt policy. But Roosevelt refused to bind himself before taking office as President. Hoover left the White House with the debt structure crumbling about him. Some nations made token payments; then even those were stopped. Only Finland, with a small postwar loan, continued to meet its payments. The United States still has not forgiven these debts, and the European nations have never paid them.

A Look at Specifics

1. How were civil liberties threatened during the Red Scare?

2. In what way was the Harding administration involved in scandal?

3. Against which groups did the quota system of immigration discriminate?

4. Against which groups were the actions of the Ku Klux Klan directed in the 1920's?

5. Why was prohibition hard to enforce?

6. Why did Hoover oppose using federal money for the relief of the unemployed?

7. What attempts were made to bring about disarmament and an end to war during the 1920's and early 1930's?

8. Why did the issue of war debts lead to bad feelings between the United States and many European nations?

A Review of Major Ideas

1. In the years following World War I, how did workers attempt to improve their economic position?

2. What events and issues indicated a conflict between urban and rural Americans in the 1920's? How did ethnic divisions in American society aggravate this conflict?

3. What conditions led to the stock market crash in 1929? How did Hoover deal with the problems of the Great Depression?

4. In what ways did the United States participate in world affairs during the 1920's?

For Independent Study

1. In what ways did Hoover depart from tradition in his efforts to deal with the Great Depression? How did his commitment to tradition make it difficult for him to cope with the depression?

2. According to journalist Frank Simonds, the Kellogg-Briand Pact was "the high water mark of American endeavors for world peace which consisted in undertaking to combine the idea of political and military isolation with that of moral and material involvement." What events and issues would support this statement?

The New Deal

CHAPTER 21
1932–1941

Displaced Americans pause on the way west.

"There is a mysterious cycle in human events. To some generations much is given. Of other generations much is expected. This generation of Americans has a rendezvous with destiny." Thus spoke President Franklin Delano Roosevelt in June 1936.

The rendezvous with destiny he spoke of was the turmoil of two great crusades. First Americans had to struggle at home against starvation and despair. Then they had to fight in foreign lands against powerful and brutal dictatorships. They were tested as sorely as any Americans had ever been, but they prevailed and helped keep the American dream alive.

DEMOCRATS IN CONTROL

The actions taken by President Hoover to combat the depression were inadequate. By election time, the Democrats felt certain of victory. Their nominee for Vice-President, John Nance Garner, told Franklin Delano Roosevelt that to win "all you have to do is to stay alive until election day."

The Democratic Candidate

Franklin Delano Roosevelt was born in 1882 on an estate on the Hudson River, near Hyde Park, New York. After graduation from Harvard, he married a distant cousin, Anna Eleanor Roosevelt. The President of the United States, Theodore Roosevelt, who was the uncle of Eleanor and the fifth cousin of Franklin, gave the bride away.

In 1910, after practicing law in New York City for about three years, Franklin won a seat in the state senate. Three years later President Wilson appointed him assistant secretary of the navy. Franklin proved to be a capable administrator and a popular young Democrat. He was his party's nominee for the vice-presidency in 1920.

In August 1921, tragedy struck; he contracted poliomyelitis. Paralyzed in both legs,

Roosevelt taught himself to move about with the aid of crutches or the heavy steel braces that he had to wear for the rest of his life.

Roosevelt reentered politics in 1924, when he nominated Alfred E. Smith for the presidency at the Democratic National Convention. Four years later, at Smith's insistence, Roosevelt ran for governor of New York. Despite the Hoover landslide, he won. In 1930, he was easily reelected. Two years later he was ready to run for the presidency.

Friends and critics alike agreed that Roosevelt—a man of wit, optimism, and polished manners—had a magnetism that few could resist. Neither an intellectual nor a visionary, Roosevelt was a man with a warm personality that projected itself in a political appeal that became legendary.

After winning the Democratic nomination for President in 1932, Roosevelt immediately demonstrated that he would not let tradition bind him. He did not wait to be formally notified of his nomination. Instead, he quickly flew to Chicago and delivered his acceptance speech to the convention. "I pledge you, I pledge myself, to a new deal for the American people," he said. Thus, Roosevelt's program, which he had not yet constructed, got a name—the "New Deal."

The Election of 1932

Evidence was widespread that the people of the United States were unhappy with President Hoover, but the Republican party could not discard him. Hoover represented the best of the conservative kind of business leadership that had been widely admired in the 1920's. He had, moreover, within the limits of his own political beliefs, tried to cope with problems of the Great Depression. Early in June 1932, the Republicans renominated Hoover. The party adopted a platform that praised him and his efforts to fight the depression.

When the people went to the polls in November, they voted overwhelmingly for Roosevelt. The Democrats gained control of both houses of Congress. The people were tired of waiting for a prosperity that was "just around the corner." They were disillusioned with business leadership. Many turned to the New Deal, no matter how vague a program it was, because they found little else to turn to.

During the period between Roosevelt's election (November 8, 1932) and his inauguration (March 4, 1933), the "lame-duck" period, economic conditions grew worse. By the time Hoover was ready to leave the White House, the economy appeared to be grinding to a halt. It was difficult to foresee how Roosevelt and his promised New Deal would meet the crisis.

A Lame-Duck Government

While the people waited for the new administration to take office, more men and women became unemployed, prices dropped, and business activity decreased. Everywhere banks were failing, while others were on the brink of failure. Frightened depositors were even withdrawing their funds from sound banks. To halt the stream of withdrawals and to prevent damage to the whole banking system, authorities in state after state closed banks for short "bank holidays."

In this crisis, President Hoover and the lame-duck Congress seemed paralyzed. An outgoing President usually hesitates to act because he has little time to carry out new policies, and he usually does not wish to tie the hands of the new President with old policies. In the past, such inaction in the lame-duck period had not done much harm. But with the nation in an ever-deepening depression, inaction was adding to the crisis.

Hoover believed that he could not effectively deal with the situation without the cooperation of the President-elect. He appealed to Roosevelt to join him in an effort to restore public confidence. He wanted Roosevelt to accept his views on the depression, the bank panic, and a balanced budget.

Roosevelt refused to cooperate on President Hoover's terms; he had views of his own that he did not intend to abandon. Unlike Hoover, Roosevelt believed that the depression had domestic rather than international causes. He was convinced that the people had repudiated Hoover and his policies and that they demanded new policies, not a continuation of the old ones. Hoover admitted that if Roosevelt had accepted his proposals, it would have meant acceptance of the Republican program and "the abandonment of 90 percent of the so-called 'new deal.'"

As the worried and exhausted Hoover made preparations to leave the White House, the nation's economy seemed about to collapse. Thirty-eight states had closed their banks; in the other ten states, the banks were being operated on a restricted basis. Elsewhere, in commodity exchanges and stock exchanges, financial activity was severely crippled.

The Inauguration

During this period of drift, Roosevelt smiled, joked, and busied himself recruiting his cabinet. For secretary of state he chose Cordell Hull of Tennessee, a professional politician who was considered to be the most influential man in the Senate. The secretary of labor was Frances Perkins, a social worker from New York. She was the first woman appointed to a cabinet post. The secretaries of agriculture and the interior came from the ranks of Progressive Republicans from the Midwest. They were Henry A. Wallace of Iowa, publisher of a farm newspaper, and Harold L. Ickes of Chicago, former supporter of Theodore Roosevelt.

Roosevelt also gave positions in government agencies and on the White House staff to a group of men who became his unofficial advisers. A number of these advisers were professors, most of them from Columbia University. They came to be known as the "brain trust." The leader of the group was Raymond Moley, a political scientist. Members of the brain trust were to have a hand in drafting many New Deal measures.

Inauguration Day was misty, gloomy, and chilly, but Roosevelt was far from despondent. Defying the wretched weather and the widespread despair, the new President, his voice clear and ringing, announced that "This great Nation will endure as it has endured, will revive and will prosper . . . the only thing we have to fear is fear itself." Much needed to be done, he said, so that people could return to work, banks could reopen, and money could circulate. Roosevelt warned that if Congress failed to provide means for meeting the crisis, he would seek "broad Executive power to wage a war against the emergency, as great as the power that would be given to me if we were in fact invaded by a foreign foe."

Although Roosevelt had offered no new way out of the crisis, his words, the very tone of his voice, brought hope to millions of Americans listening around their radios. Within the next few days nearly half a million persons sent letters of support to him. The people did not know what Roosevelt was going to do, but they sensed that he would take some positive action.

ROOSEVELT'S PROGRAM

There was no need for Roosevelt to demand emergency powers. Members of Congress were so concerned about the economic crisis that they were willing to give him more power than any President had ever held in peacetime.

Roosevelt was dedicated to the traditional American ideals. He had faith in democratic government, and he favored private ownership of property, and the general principles of the capitalistic system. But he did not believe that the federal government should remain aloof from the problems of the people if it could do something to help them. Unlike Hoover, Roosevelt thought that the federal government should take direct action to im-

Many homeless Americans built shacks or put up tents in parks or vacant lots. Such shantytowns were called "Hoovervilles" by people who blamed President Hoover for not doing more to combat the depression. *Left:* The Bonus Army's Hooverville in Washington, D.C. *Center:* Long waits greeted those who tried to find work. *Right:* An evicted woman sits among her belongings on a Chicago sidewalk.

Collection, Whitney Museum of American Art, New York
Employment Agency, by Isaac Soyer, 1937.

Courtesy Chicago Historical Society

prove the day-to-day lives of the American people.

Roosevelt wasted no time. On his first day in office he ordered his advisers to act to avert a national economic collapse. On the following day he proclaimed a nationwide bank holiday, closing all banks in the United States for four days. He called Congress into special session, and it immediately began turning out laws to fight the depression. Congress remained at this task without letup from March 9 until June 16, 1933. This period, one of great cooperation between the executive and legislative branches of the government, has become known as the "hundred days."

New Laws

As the New Deal program unfolded, it could be seen that, despite the haste and experimentation, the objectives of immediate relief, prompt recovery, restoration of confidence, and long-range reform were there. The first measure of the hundred days was the Emergency Banking Relief Act of 1933. This law gave the President broad power to regulate banks and provided for the reopening of banks in sound condition. On the next day the President asked Congress for authority to cut government spending so that he could balance the budget. Within twenty-four hours, Congress responded with the Economy Act.

On the night of Sunday, March 12, Roosevelt gave the first of his "fireside chats." This was an informal report to the people given through a nationwide radio hookup. As an estimated 60 million Americans listened to their radios, he explained what his administration had done and assured the people that savings in the reorganized banks would be safe. The next day, when banks began to reopen, many people redeposited their money. The banking crisis was under control.

In June, long-range reform was brought to the banking system with the Banking Act of 1933. This law was designed to prevent bankers from speculating with depositors' money. To protect the depositor of small amounts of money, it created the Federal Deposit Insurance Corporation, which insured individual bank deposits up to $2,500. (By the early 1970's, accounts up to $20,000 were covered.) With the passage of this act, depositors were freed from the fear that a sudden bank failure could wipe out their savings accounts.

The Banking Act of 1935 completed Roosevelt's reform of banking and currency. It increased the federal government's control over the banking system, primarily through the Federal Reserve Board. That body could regulate interest rates on the money the reserve banks loaned to public banks.

Other laws protected stock investors. The Federal Securities Act of 1933 was designed to prevent fraud by requiring that information about new stocks be made public. The Securities Exchange Act (1934) created the Securities and Exchange Commission to regulate the stock market.

These reforms stabilized banking and investing and helped the investor who had limited funds. At the same time, the laws angered many people in business who resented government controls.

Experimenting with the Currency

Not all of Roosevelt's early reform measures were as successful as the banking laws. The President admitted that he expected some failures among his emergency measures. He told a radio audience: "I have no expectation of making a hit every time I come to bat." He certainly made no hit when he experimented with the gold content of the dollar.

Many of the President's advisers thought that a program of controlled inflation would stimulate recovery. They also believed that reducing the value of the dollar would lead to such inflation.

When Roosevelt became President, the nation was on the gold standard. This meant that the dollar was defined as a certain amount of gold and that anyone could exchange a paper dollar for that amount in gold. In April 1933, Roosevelt took the country off the gold standard. People could no longer convert their dollars into gold on demand. Soon, all debts that required payment in gold could be legally paid with paper money. When the United States went off the gold standard, the value of the American dollar dropped slightly.

Since the depression was worldwide, an international economic conference was called in London in June to try to bring some stability to money arrangements among countries. If an important nation like the United States experimented independently with its money, it seemed obvious that the conference could accomplish little. The delegates wondered what Roosevelt would do. In a message to the conference early in July, he gave his view on monetary collaboration; the message "fell upon it like a bombshell." He said, in effect, that the United States would experiment with its money as it saw fit. As a result of Roosevelt's stand on the matter, the conference was a failure.

After the end of the London conference, Roosevelt continued his policy of allowing the value of the dollar to go down in relation to gold and to other currencies. Finally, Congress passed the Gold Reserve Act, which gave the President full control over devaluation of the dollar. In January 1934, Roosevelt set the price of gold in the United States at $35 an ounce, thus making the dollar worth about 60 percent of what it had been worth in 1933.

Although prices rose slightly, Roosevelt's manipulation of the value of the dollar had little significant economic effect. But the de-

BUSINESS ACTIVITY 1920-1941

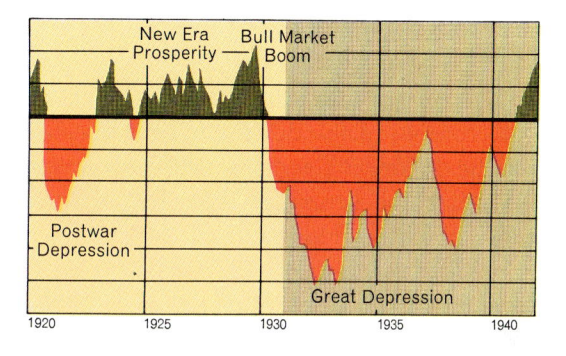

The chart *(above)* is based on the Federal Reserve index of industrial production. Unlike depressions in the nineteenth century, that of the thirties did not begin with a bank panic. It began with a crash on the stock market. This difference points up the increasing importance of corporations since the nineteenth century. By the late twenties, many Americans were no longer farmers or self-employed business people. They worked for corporations that were dependent on other corporations or on general prosperity. Severe farm problems coupled with overexpansion in the construction and automobile industries set off the crash. The effects of federal spending by the New Deal can be seen in the detail *(below)*.

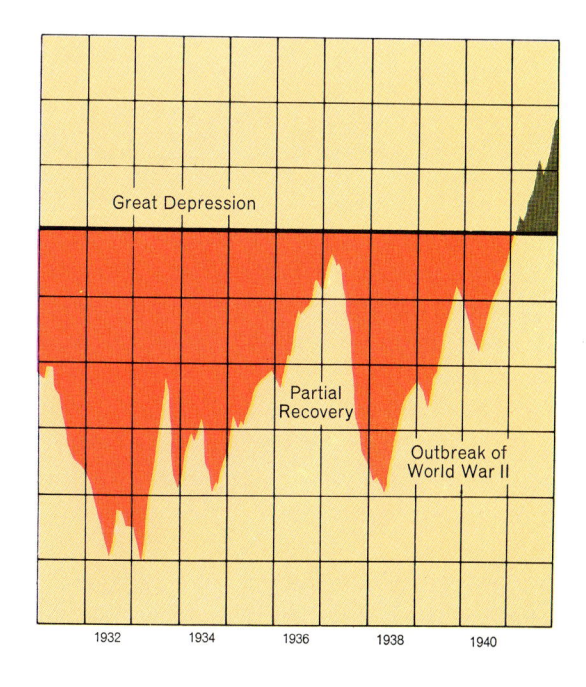

valuation alienated conservative Democrats and business people. Al Smith, for example, denounced the devalued currency as "baloney dollars."

Helping the Unemployed

All this concern about inflation and the gold content of the dollar had little meaning for the 15 million persons who were unemployed in the spring of 1933. For many of them, the only thing with real meaning was immediate economic relief to keep them from hunger or starvation.

One of the New Deal's first and most popular relief measures was the Civilian Conservation Corps (CCC), established in March 1933 and directed by the army. Young men who were between the ages of 18 and 25 and were unemployed could live in CCC camps and work on reforestation, road construction, flood control, and soil conservation projects, mainly in the West. As payment they would receive food, housing, and $30 a month, $25 of which had to be sent to their families. By 1941, when the program was ended, 2.7 million young men had served in the corps, and they had completed more than half of all the forest replanting that had been done in the nation up to that time.

Meanwhile, millions of other people were on relief, receiving subsistence payments from local or state government agencies. They faced hunger because the resources of relief agencies were exhausted. In May, Congress passed the Federal Emergency Relief Act. It appropriated 500 million dollars to be given to the states and towns for relief purposes. At the head of the Federal Emergency Relief Administration (FERA), Roosevelt placed Harry L. Hopkins, a social worker from New York.

Roosevelt regarded the FERA as a temporary measure to give people some support until recovery came. Even for this purpose, Hopkins told the President, the program

CCC members plant seedling trees in a national forest. Severe drought and dust storms in the early thirties ruined millions of acres of farmland and made the nation conservation-conscious.

could not do enough. In November, therefore, under powers authorized by the Federal Emergency Relief Act, Roosevelt authorized Hopkins to set up the Civil Works Administration (CWA). For the first time, the federal government did not channel relief through the states. Instead, it provided relief directly to the people by giving them, at minimum wages, jobs that would not compete with jobs already in existence. In all, the CWA project provided employment for more than 4.2 million persons, who did a wide variety of work, from repairing county roads to teaching adult art classes.

The CWA was costly, and it fell under criticism from people who considered it wasteful and radical. As a result, the CWA was closed down in the spring of 1934, and the main burden of relief fell on the FERA.

Helping Industry

While meeting some of the immediate needs of the unemployed, the New Deal also attempted to increase job opportunities and promote general recovery. The President proposed a sweeping program for industry and labor, the National Industrial Recovery Act (NIRA). Passed in June 1933, the NIRA tried to help industry by ending unfair competition and by limiting the production of goods to amounts actually needed. The New Dealers believed that limited production would raise prices and bring an increase in profits. Labor would benefit because the work week would be reduced and wages would rise. At the same time, reduced hours would require more workers to achieve at least the same level of production, and unemployment would decline.

The government hoped to reach these

goals through adoption of codes of "fair competition" by leaders in major industries. Since such agreements on prices and wages might violate the antitrust laws, the government suspended those laws. In section 7a of the NIRA, labor was given the specific right to organize and to bargain collectively with employers.

To carry out the law, Roosevelt established the National Recovery Administration (NRA). General Hugh Johnson, a gruff former cavalry officer with considerable administrative experience, was placed in charge. He was to supervise the drafting and enforcement of the various codes.

While the codes were being written, Johnson tried to drum up enthusiasm for the NRA. He sketched a blue eagle over the slogan "We Do Our Part," and this became the symbol of the NRA and the emblem for all who signed the fair competition codes. The blue eagle was displayed everywhere—on buttons, in factories, stores, books, elevators, and in NRA parades.

Johnson at first was successful. Within a matter of months he was able to get about 95 percent of the business interests of the country to adopt satisfactory codes. The codes were then approved by the President. They provided minimum-wage scales and maximum hours of work. They also gave each industry broad freedom to control production and prices.

To most Americans, the codes seemed invested with the full force of law. However, adherence to the codes was voluntary, and many people who accepted them later chose to ignore them. Soon some business people complained that the codes had been written by the giant corporations and offered few benefits to the small firms. Consumers complained about higher prices, and labor felt dissatisfied with its position under the codes. When business leaders who had at first supported the NRA also turned against it, failure seemed certain.

In May 1935, the Supreme Court declared the NIRA unconstitutional. In *Schechter Poultry Corporation* v. *United States,* known as the "Sick Chicken" case, the Court ruled that Congress could not "delegate legislative powers" to the President. The Court ruled, moreover, that Congress's control over interstate commerce, as in the poultry code of the NRA, did not apply to a local poultry business, such as that of the Schechter brothers in Brooklyn, who had brought the suit against the NIRA.

Until it was declared unconstitutional, the NIRA provided jobs for about 2 million people. Some of the jobs came from the Public Works Administration (PWA), a program established under the act and headed by Secretary of the Interior Harold L. Ickes.

Ickes carefully checked every proposal to make sure it would be useful. As a result, jobs were not created fast enough to help the economy. Ultimately, Ickes spent more than 4 billion dollars on some 34,000 government-sponsored projects. Many of these works, such as schools, dams, and highways, were of lasting benefit to the nation. But the PWA failed to provide the quick business recovery and unemployment relief needed at the time.

Aid to Farmers

To counteract the huge surpluses and low prices for farm products, the New Deal used the principle of limiting production. In May 1933, the Agricultural Adjustment Administration (AAA) was established under Secretary of Agriculture Henry A. Wallace.

The AAA sought to raise the income of farmers to a level equal to that between 1909 and 1914—a favorable period for agriculture. It tried to reach this goal by persuading farmers to cut production of crops like corn and cotton. In return, the government would give the farmers cash. In this way, surpluses would be reduced, and the farmers would receive higher prices for their products as well as cash from the government.

Money for the subsidies would come from taxes on processors, such as millers and operators of cotton gins. Since these processors would pass the increased cost on to the buyer, consumers would thus be subsidizing farmers' incomes.

Before the AAA could swing into action, the nation's farms had bumper crops. The government sent agents into the South and Southeast to urge farmers to uproot their cotton in return for benefit payments. To forestall a glut of pork in the nation's butcher shops, farm leaders convinced Wallace that it was necessary to order the slaughtering of more than 6 million pigs. This deliberate destruction of food when people were hungry aroused bitter comment, particularly from critics of the New Deal.

Despite its defects, the plan brought about a reduction in surpluses and a rise in farm prices. Then, in January 1936, when farm incomes were showing improvement, the Supreme Court declared unconstitutional the taxing and regulatory provisions of the Agricultural Adjustment Act. This decision ended the first AAA.

A severe drought between 1932 and 1936 had made farm problems more serious. In a vast area from the Texas Panhandle northward across the Great Plains to the Dakotas, farmers and sharecroppers were driven from their land by windstorms that blew away unanchored topsoil and left the land unfit for farming. These people, too, needed help.

The TVA

Another region that suffered from nature's destructive forces was the Tennessee Valley. The area was made up of about 40,000 square miles in seven states and contained some 2.5 million persons, many of them quite poor. For years, Progressives led by Senator George W. Norris of Nebraska had tried to obtain government operation of the Wilson Dam and power plant at Muscle Shoals, Alabama. Roosevelt not only went along with Norris's proposal, he had an even bigger plan. The President wanted to launch a huge regional experiment in social and economic planning. He wanted to transform the valley's eroded and wasted land into rich farms and change the lives of the people from poverty to abundance.

In April 1933, Roosevelt asked Congress to create the Tennessee Valley Authority

(TVA), an independent public corporation, to develop the valley's resources. Congress quickly responded and provided liberal appropriations for the task.

The TVA built dams to control floods and to generate cheap, plentiful hydroelectric power. The charges that it made for the electricity would be used as a "yardstick" for measuring the reasonableness of rates charged by private power companies. TVA also produced fertilizers, which were then distributed to the farmers of the region.

Within a few years, the TVA became one of the most noted and successful of the New Deal agencies. Its dams stopped floods in the Tennessee Valley, an area with one of the heaviest average annual rainfalls in the nation. Its conservation program reforested great sections, ended soil erosion, created lakes, and controlled malaria. The TVA also attracted industry to the region and brought the people improved recreational and educational facilities and other benefits.

Despite these accomplishments, the TVA had many critics. Private power companies resented the yardstick method of determining fair rates and brought suits to block the sale of TVA electric power. They said that the TVA could offer low rates primarily because it paid no taxes, and they argued that it was illegal for the government to sell electricity in competition with private companies.

Finally, in 1936, the Supreme Court ruled that all of TVA's activities were legal. In time, TVA became one of the nation's major producers of electric power. No other New Deal agency did so much to transform the economy, the lives, and the customs of an entire region.

THE SECOND NEW DEAL

Historians usually divide the New Deal into two phases. They talk about a first and a second New Deal, though they do not agree

While many people in cities went hungry, crops sometimes rotted in the fields because it cost more to pack and ship crops than farmers could get for the produce. *Above:* A father packs a bag of potatoes for his family at the Cleveland free food dump. *Below:* Farmers in Harvard, Illinois, pour milk on the ground. By destroying part of their crop, farmers hoped to drive the price up for the rest of the crop.

on the precise nature of the differences between the two. In any case, the first New Deal included the laws of 1933 and 1934, and it had the support of a loose alliance of business people, workers, and farmers. The second New Deal began in 1935, after this alliance fell apart.

In the 1934 congressional elections, the people of the United States gave Roosevelt and the Democratic party overwhelming support, even greater than they had given two years earlier. Poor and discontented voters wanted social and economic reforms to make more jobs available. Business and industrial leaders, however, turned more and more against the New Deal.

Organized Opposition

Organized opposition to the New Deal began to emerge in the summer of 1934, after the worst phase of the depression had passed. Business leaders believed that the New Deal had become too radical and that it was a threat to personal liberty. In August, a group led by executives of the Du Pont and General Motors corporations and conservative politicians from both parties formed the American Liberty League. This organization campaigned against New Deal agencies and reforms and emphasized the need to preserve states' rights.

The conservative revolt, however, did not have a large following. Roosevelt was more concerned about the growing opposition on the left. Many sharecroppers, unemployed people, old people, and others had begun to support agitators who called for drastic social change.

One of these agitators, Dr. Francis E. Townsend, made his home in Long Beach, California, where thousands of the elderly lived in impoverished retirement. Under his plan, the federal government would pay every nonworking citizen over sixty years of age a monthly pension of $200. The $200 had to be spent each month, thereby stimulating the economy. Thousands of Townsend Clubs were organized across the nation. By 1935, these clubs claimed about 5 million members, a sizable bloc of voters.

Charles E. Coughlin, a Roman Catholic priest from a parish in a Detroit suburb, had an even larger following than Townsend. Father Coughlin gained his following by combining persuasive sermons, delivered on nationwide radio, with comments on social and economic issues. At first, he had favored the New Deal but, by early 1935, he had become one of its harshest critics and promoted a vague program of "social justice." In 1934, he was reputed to be receiving more mail than anyone in the country, even more than the President. He was later silenced by his church superiors.

An anti–New Deal leader who seemed to pose the greatest threat to democratic government was a flamboyant, shrewd politician from Louisiana, Huey P. Long. People called him "Kingfish." First as governor and then as senator he set up a virtual dictatorship in Louisiana. When he said, "I am the law," nobody questioned him. Long gained a national following with his "Share-Our-Wealth" plan. He promised to make "every man a king" by confiscating large fortunes and giving every family a home, a car, a radio, and an annual income. His organization, it was said, had a mailing list of 7.5 million persons. Long was assassinated in September 1935, when he was at the height of his popularity.

Reform Laws, 1935

Roosevelt feared that the radical opposition might lure away his own following. He recognized that the New Deal had not yet solved many basic problems. In January 1935, he announced plans for a second New Deal and proposed a huge program of emergency employment on public projects. Con-

THE NEW DEAL: THREE VIEWS

ALFRED E. SMITH
Governor of New York, 1919–1920, 1923–1928. Democratic candidate for President, 1928

[The first danger from the New Deal to fundamental principles upon which this government was organized] is the arraignment of class against class. . . . The next . . . is the vast building up of new bureaus of government, draining the resources of our people, to pool and redistribute them, not by any process of law but by the whim of the bureaucratic autocracy. . . .

Just get the platform of the Democratic party and . . . the Socialist party and then study the record of the present administration . . . and you will have your hand on the Socialist platform. . . . [You] can't mix socialism or communism with . . . [a representative democracy]. . . .

I would suggest that . . . [the present administration] stop attacking all the forms . . . of our government without recourse to the people themselves, as provided in their own Constitution which really belongs to the people. *(1936)*

NORMAN M. THOMAS
Six times Socialist candidate for President

The reforms of the New Deal, while by no means negligible, were largely superficial. Perhaps the greatest contribution it made toward what we call recovery was that it suggested hope, confidence, action. . . .

. . . Impressive as the list of its efforts . . . may sound, there is nothing in it to warrant the argument that we have here a serious and successful attack upon the problem of poverty, insecurity, war, and the exploitation of workers. We have not had a reorganization of production and a redistribution of income to end near starvation in the midst of potential plenty. . . .

N.R.A. and A.A.A. were far removed from the old laissez-faire individualistic capitalism, but assuredly they were not socialism. The President . . . might talk much about the more abundant life, but they incarnated the inescapable capitalist doctrine that profit depends upon relative scarcity! *(1936)*

FRANCES PERKINS
Secretary of Labor, 1933–1945

[The] New Deal was not a plan, . . . and it was certainly not a plot. . . . Most of the programs . . . arose out of the emergency which Roosevelt faced when he took office. . . .

The NRA was a new, vigorous, and imaginative approach to the problem of reviving industry and overcoming unemployment. . . .

Those who . . . say that not enough consideration was given to these measures can hardly remember how gray and bleak and desperate were the people of this country. . . . It was a period of social danger. . . .

[Roosevelt] did not think we had discovered any panaceas. . . . [These] were temporary emergency measures. . . .

. . . The speedy enactment of the program . . . revived the faith of the people. It put us back on the upgrade. It gave us knowledge of industrial processes and complications which had never been in the possession of the government before. *(1946)*

gress, also frightened by the opposition, went along with the President. In April it voted for the Works Progress Administration (WPA) and other agencies. These programs gave jobs instead of relief to women and men who were unemployed but able to work.

Harry Hopkins, former head of the FERA, was put in charge of WPA. None of the jobs provided by WPA was supposed to compete with regular jobs provided by government or by private industry. As a result, many of the projects were in the nature of busywork that produced nothing of value.

Nonetheless, from 1935 until 1943, the WPA employed more than 8.5 million persons on 1.4 million projects. Many people of talent and education were unemployed, and Hopkins took the view that they should be given a chance to use their skills. Thus, WPA created jobs and paid the wages of musicians, artists, circus performers, writers, dance instructors, and actors. About 78 percent of the agency's money, however, went into the construction of hospitals, schools, and roads.

The New Dealers also experimented with reforms intended to root out rural poverty. In April 1935, Roosevelt created the Resettlement Administration and placed Rexford Guy Tugwell, a college professor, in charge. Tugwell tried to move poor farm families from worn-out lands to better farms. The RA also tried to provide such farmers with equipment and education. Congress opposed this program, and so it never got beyond the stage of experimentation.

Congress did support another reform agency, the Rural Electrification Administration (REA), set up by executive order in May 1935. The REA was to provide electricity for rural areas not served by private power companies. In 1935, nine out of ten farms in the United States had no electric power; in 1941, partly as a result of the REA efforts, four out of ten farms were electrified; and by 1950, nine out of ten were so equipped.

Congress also doubled funds for the Civilian Conservation Corps and, in June 1935, created the National Youth Administration (NYA). In seven years the NYA gave jobs of various kinds to more than 600,000 college students, 1.5 million high-school students, and 2.6 million young persons not in school.

Although the billions poured into WPA and other relief agencies did not lead to the lasting reforms desired by some, the works program overcame the despair of millions who had been unable to get any job.

One lasting reform was the Social Security Act (1935), which Roosevelt considered the New Deal's "supreme achievement." This law set up a system of old-age pensions; insurance for the unemployed; and government benefits for dependent mothers, children, and the crippled and the blind. Money for the program came from payroll taxes levied on both workers and their employers. With the passage of the Social Security Act, the federal government took on a permanent role in providing for the welfare of the people.

Labor's Gains

In July 1935, Congress passed the National Labor Relations Act, often called the Wagner Act. This law said that employers had to allow workers to join unions of their own choosing. Furthermore, employers were required to bargain collectively with union members who legally represented the workers. A nonpartisan National Labor Relations Board (NLRB) was created to enforce the law. In effect, the Wagner Act threw the weight of the federal government behind organized labor. It became the cornerstone of a revived, strong labor movement.

The American Federation of Labor was still basically an organization of craft unions. A group led by John L. Lewis of the United Mine Workers and Sidney Hillman of the

Home Relief Station, by Louis Ribak, 1935–36. Collection Whitney Museum of American Art, New York

Applying for relief was a shattering experience for many Americans. Private relief organizations were overwhelmed with requests for aid. Government programs often required some work from their recipients. *Above:* An old woman applies for aid from a home relief station. *Right:* Men dig a drainage ditch near Savannah, Georgia, as part of a malaria control program. President Roosevelt was opposed to racial discrimination in relief programs, but the local administrators of federal programs often followed their own inclinations rather than those of the President. Blacks received few white-collar jobs in federal projects.

Striking members of the United Auto Workers catch up on their reading. Although the idea of a sitdown strike was not new, the auto workers used it more successfully than did earlier strikers.

Amalgamated Clothing Workers demanded that the AFL work to unionize the mass-production industries, such as steel and automobiles. These leaders wanted the AFL to charter industry-wide unions for the task. Most AFL leaders, however, still wanted to rely on unions organized along craft lines. Hence, in November 1935, Lewis and other rebel leaders formed the Committee for Industrial Organization within the AFL. Three years later the CIO broke away from the AFL to form a new organization, called the Congress of Industrial Organizations.

Before breaking away from the AFL, the CIO tried to organize the steelworkers and gain union recognition from the steel industry. The first objective in 1936 was the United States Steel Corporation, which Lewis called "the crouching lion in the pathway of labor." To everyone's surprise, the corporation refused to endure a costly strike and recognized the steelworkers' union in March 1937. The CIO had won a great victory; "Big Steel" was at last organized.

CIO organizers expected the other steel companies, known as "Little Steel," to follow suit, but they were mistaken. Three of these companies fought back violently. In a skirmish known as the Memorial Day massacre of 1937, police killed ten strikers at the South Chicago plant of Republic Steel. Not until 1941, after the NLRB had compelled the companies to bargain collectively, did "Little Steel" admit defeat. The entire steel industry finally became unionized.

In December 1936, another CIO union called a strike against the General Motors Corporation in Flint, Michigan. The workers had a sit-down strike—they sat by their machines and refused to work or leave. In February 1937, General Motors recognized the United Automobile Workers and met most of the union's demands. Later that same year, other automobile companies also recognized the CIO union. However, the Ford Motor Company resisted until 1940.

By 1941, both skilled and unskilled workers in most of the nation's large industries had unions representing them. With the help of Roosevelt's New Deal, organized labor had become a giant.

TWILIGHT OF THE NEW DEAL

At the time the 1936 elections were held, the New Deal reforms were immensely popular. The economy seemed to be recovering; farm prices were up, employment had increased, and even the jobless were eating.

A New Deal for Indians

The quality of life for American Indians had grown steadily worse after passage of the Dawes Act of 1887. That law had divided tribal lands into allotments for individual Indians to farm. It did not, however, provide money for tools, livestock, or training. Moreover, much of the allotted land was not suitable for farming. Many Indians leased or sold their allotments at low prices. Of the 138 million acres held by Indians in 1887, all but 48 million had been taken over by non-Indians by 1934.

The Dawes Act had also granted citizenship to Indians, but "protective" legislation in 1906 withheld it. Citizenship was restored by the Snyder Act of 1924, passed to acknowledge Indian service during World War I.

By the 1920's, most Indians lived in extreme poverty, and their death rate was rising rapidly. Their condition began to attract public attention. In 1928, the Institute for Government Research proposed a reform program. Its report recommended changes in education and health care and suggested that many problems were rooted in the allotment policy.

In 1933, Roosevelt appointed a former officer of the American Indian Defense Organization, John Collier, to be Commissioner of Indian Affairs. Collier proposed that the allotment policy be ended and that allotted land be transferred to community ownership. These and other proposals were part of the Wheeler-Howard bill.

The reactions of Indians to the Wheeler-Howard bill were mixed. Some wanted to continue to assimilate on their own; others felt that reforms were too limited. Still others applauded it. The bill was modified; the result was the Indian Reorganization Act of 1934. The act provided for financial aid, training in land use, and greater participation by Indians in the Bureau of Indian Affairs. It had provisions for tribal constitutions and business corporations. Also, the new administration lifted bans on native religions and tribal customs.

Because of the new law, educational and medical facilities were upgraded. Improvements were made in Indian lands and herds. It was evident by 1940, however, that further reforms would be necessary.

A class on a reservation studies from visual aids. New Deal education policy deemphasized reading skills.

No Republican seemed capable of shaking Roosevelt's hold on the people. Jubilant Democrats renominated the President and endorsed everything he had done.

The Republicans denounced the New Deal and nominated Alfred M. Landon, the governor of Kansas. Landon was no match for FDR, and he carried only two states, Maine and Vermont.

The 1936 election also saw two important political developments. First, organized labor gave its united support to just one candidate, Roosevelt. Unions had traditionally divided their vote. Second, a Democrat gained a majority of the votes of blacks, who traditionally had voted Republican.

Roosevelt's Attacks on the Supreme Court

In his inaugural address—delivered on January 20, 1937, instead of March 4 because the Twentieth Amendment had gone into effect—Roosevelt promised more reform. He wanted to help the "one-third of a nation" that was "ill-housed, ill-clad, ill-nourished." In his view the Supreme Court stood in the way of giving the needed help. Because five of the nine judges were consistently hostile to New Deal measures, the Supreme Court had wiped out important New Deal laws.

Two weeks after his inauguration, therefore, Roosevelt asked Congress for a law enabling him to reorganize the Supreme Court. He wanted to be able to appoint a new justice for each one who failed to retire within six months after reaching his seventieth birthday. The total number of justices, however, could not exceed fifteen.

Roosevelt said that he wanted to enlarge the Court because it was behind in its work and needed new blood to catch up. Critics argued that what Roosevelt really wanted was a change in the Court so that it would support his reform program.

Although Roosevelt had expected opposition, he was stunned by the depth of feeling

Police break up a demonstration in Union Square in New York City. The depression increased the following for many political groups that offered easy cures for the nation's problems.

he aroused. Many Americans denounced his "court-packing" bill. They accused him of attempting to destroy the Constitution and trying to make himself a dictator. Roosevelt reluctantly abandoned the plan.

Very shortly thereafter the attitude of the Court changed. One of the conservative justices, Owen J. Roberts, switched sides. In a series of 5 to 4 decisions, he voted with the more liberal judges to uphold a number of reform laws. In April 1937, for example, the Court found the Wagner Act constitutional, and in May it upheld the Social Security Act.

Later, other justices either died or retired, and Roosevelt appointed liberals in their places. In decision after decision, the new Supreme Court upheld reform laws. By using a broad interpretation of the Constitution, the Court gave permanence to much of the New Deal legislation.

A Recession

The battle over the Supreme Court disrupted the unity of the Democratic party and gave new energy to conservatives in Congress. The angry and increasingly conservative Congress of 1937 refused to go along with some of Roosevelt's requests for reform, such as a law guaranteeing workers a minimum wage. Yet Congress did pass laws to help tenant farmers and to replace city slums with public housing.

The economic recovery of early 1937 had been built on government "pump-priming." This meant that the government had poured money into the economy to get it going, just as a little water is poured into a pump to start it flowing. In June, after Roosevelt had reduced expenditures for WPA and other agencies, a recession began. By August, the mood

Riot in Union Square, by Peter Hopkins, 1930

of Congress began to change.

The recession seemed to indicate to New Dealers that prosperity would not return without government spending. In October the President called Congress into special session to resume government spending and continue New Deal reforms. When Congress met in November, Roosevelt asked for laws to aid farmers, abolish child labor, set minimum wages, control monopolies, and reorganize the executive department.

Frightened by the recession, Congress went along with the President and once again primed the pump with additional governmental expenditures. Congress also passed the Agricultural Adjustment Act of February 1938. The new AAA was more comprehensive than that of 1933 and was acceptable to the Supreme Court. It gave subsidies to farmers in an attempt to assure them purchasing power equal to that in the period 1909–1914. That period was called the "parity" base. Thus the subsidies were termed *parity payments*. The AAA also restricted crops and provided for government purchase and storage of surpluses. Farm prices soon rose, but real prosperity did not return to agriculture until after 1941, when war conditions increased demands for food.

During the recession, Roosevelt succeeded in wringing from a reluctant Congress his last important reform, the Fair Labor Standards Act (June 1938). This measure set a minimum wage of 25 cents an hour, to be increased within eight years to 40 cents. It limited the work week to 44 hours, with a further reduction to 40 hours in three years. It also forbade the employment of children in

U.S. Highway 99, "broke—baby sick—car trouble," 1937. Many people sought to better their lives by moving elsewhere. California was a common choice, but that state, too, was hard hit by the depression.

the making of goods sold in interstate commerce. So many exemptions were written into the law that it protected relatively few working people. But it did strike a blow at sweatshops and exploiters of children.

Putting Reform Aside

As congressional support for the New Deal faded in 1938, Roosevelt decided to hit back at conservatives in his party who had fought his program. He openly campaigned against some of them in primary elections, mainly in the South. (Many white southerners opposed the New Deal for extending relief and reform measures to blacks.)

The President's "purge" failed, for conservative southerners usually won. Also, in the November elections the Republicans gained eighty seats in the House and seven in the Senate. For the first time since 1932, the Republicans were a strong force. Southern Democrats and Republicans, who were opposed to further New Deal reforms, could form a coalition to control Congress.

The President then decided that he could not further alienate the southern Democrats because he needed their support on foreign policy. Large-scale war threatened in Europe and Asia. Roosevelt felt that because of these threats the nation's foreign policy had to move away from isolationism.

Eastern Democrats were generally willing to support both an active foreign policy and domestic reforms. Southern Democrats tended to accept an active foreign policy but reject domestic reforms. Midwesterners usually favored domestic reforms and an isolationist foreign policy. Since Roosevelt now considered the foreign danger more important than domestic problems, he put aside reform partly to please southerners.

In his annual message of January 4, 1939, Roosevelt announced the end of the New Deal's "program of social reform." Then he talked about world affairs. But the needs of foreign policy and the growing opposition to the New Deal were not the only reasons for putting aside reform. The New Deal had reached most of its limited objectives.

An Analysis of the New Deal

In the view of most historians the New Deal had mixed successes and failures. It did not succeed in bringing full recovery. As late as 1941, 6 million Americans were still unemployed. The New Deal did help raise national income, but it did not increase business activity to any great extent. It did not find any lasting solution to farm problems, and the experiment in planning under the NRA was collapsing even before the Supreme Court declared it unconstitutional. The manipulation of the dollar brought no benefits, and the pump-priming did not go far enough to bring permanent recovery.

On the other hand, the achievements of the New Deal were greater in extent and impact than those of any previous period. New Deal laws reformed banking, regulated the stock exchanges, furthered vast regional development in the Tennessee Valley, enabled workers to organize unions, protected workers with a minimum-wage law, and helped many Americans through the social security system. Although no civil rights legislation was passed, Roosevelt took steps to see that reform measures could apply equally to blacks and whites. He also appointed more blacks to high offices than any previous President.

Critics were alarmed by the expansion of the power of the federal government, and many people in business opposed New Deal laws. Yet New Dealers could justifiably claim that their reforms blunted demands for more radical measures and saved the private enterprise system. The New Deal did not try to overturn the old social and economic system. Instead, without a planned design, it tried to rebuild a shattered economy and work toward a more just society.

The New Deal can be credited with many achievements in preserving and broadening democracy and in bringing a measure of justice to the exploited and underprivileged. Yet the New Deal left more unchanged than it changed. American society had only begun to deal with the problems faced by sharecroppers, minority groups, migrant workers, and urban dwellers.

A Look at Specifics

1. How did Roosevelt's beliefs about federal powers differ from Hoover's?

2. What was the purpose of the Federal Deposit Insurance Corporation?

3. What was the purpose of the NRA codes? Why did many people oppose them?

4. How did Dr. Townsend propose to aid the elderly and bring the nation out of the depression?

5. Why did the CIO split with the AFL?

A Review of Major Ideas

1. How did New Deal legislation reform the stock market and the banking system?

2. How did the New Deal attempt to promote industrial recovery before 1935? After 1935?

3. How did the New Deal legislation aid farmers and workers? The Indians?

4. What measures were passed to aid the unemployed?

5. Why was much New Deal legislation criticized? Why was the New Deal abandoned by 1939?

6. In what ways was New Deal legislation a failure? What were its achievements? In what ways was it a departure from the past?

For Independent Study

1. In what way did legislation passed during the New Deal resemble that of the Progressive era? Of Hoover's administration? In what way did New Deal laws and policies differ from those of the earlier periods?

2. In your opinion, was the National Recovery Administration a danger to democracy or an attempt to plan the economy on a nationwide scale without harsh controls over business? Explain your answer.

3. Should the government subsidize farmers if people working in other competitive industries are not subsidized? Why?

4. Historian Richard N. Hofstadter has stated, "The New Deal will never be understood by anyone who looks for a single thread of policy, a far-reaching, far-seeing plan. It was a series of improvisations, many adopted very suddenly, many contradictory. Such unity as it had was in political strategy, not economics." Do you agree or disagree? Explain your answer.

Years of Hope and Despair

CHAPTER 22
1920–1941

A Charleston contest in the mid-1920's.

The 1920's and 1930's are usually viewed as periods of contrast—one being an era of hope and promise, the other a time of despair. While the decades did greatly differ, in terms of the nation's culture they were more alike than they were different.

Culture is often defined as the customs, arts, and technology of a people. It rarely changes rapidly, for it usually builds on everything that has come earlier. Thus the customs, arts, and technology of the 1930's were little more than a continuation of those in the 1920's. The biggest differences were in tone, not substance.

PEOPLE AND THE ECONOMY

In both prosperity and depression, Americans tried to adjust to an economy based on the use of machines. Though machines made it possible to increase the production of all kinds of goods, they also threw many people out of work. In some regions, great numbers of people lost their jobs and had to seek work elsewhere.

Population Changes

During these decades, for the first time in three centuries, the rate of population growth declined. The birth rate began to fall in the 1920's, and it reached its lowest point in the 1930's. The new immigration laws also helped lower the growth rate by restricting the number of immigrants.

The census of 1920 showed that more than half the people in the United States now lived in towns and cities. A great number of the newest city dwellers were farm laborers who had been replaced by machines. Many of these workers were blacks who had moved from farms in the South to cities in the North or West.

Most of the western states registered great population gains, while states in the East and Midwest grew but little. Some states actually lost population, particularly those in the South and in areas of the country that suffered drought and dust storms.

For a few years during the depression, the trend toward urbanization reversed. Many people moved back to farms, where they knew they could grow food to keep alive, even if they could not make any money.

Business Growth

Business dominated most aspects of American life in the 1920's. The three Republican administrations cooperated closely with business leaders and followed policies favorable to big business. They practically ignored the antitrust laws, and many companies that were engaged in similar enterprises merged. In most industries, many small companies disappeared, and big ones grew bigger. At the same time, however, the variety of goods and the volume of business activity increased tremendously.

In the early 1900's, great industrialists had tried to gain a *monopoly,* exclusive control, of a product and in this way snuff out competition. In the Progressive era, antitrust suits broke up some monopolies.

In the 1920's, it became common for a few large companies—an *oligopoly*—to dominate and control an industry. Oligopoly often led to intense competition among companies within an industry. Some of this competition led to benefits for the people in the form of low prices for goods. For example, by 1929, mail-order houses and chain stores had come to control about 25 percent of the nation's retail business. Chain stores expanded into towns all over the United States, bringing the people a variety of quality goods at competitive prices. In so doing, they often destroyed the monopoly of the local merchant.

On the other hand, an oligopolistic situation could destroy or limit competition through price fixing. Frequently, the largest corporation in an industry would set policy

TOTAL POPULATION GROWTH, 1920–1940

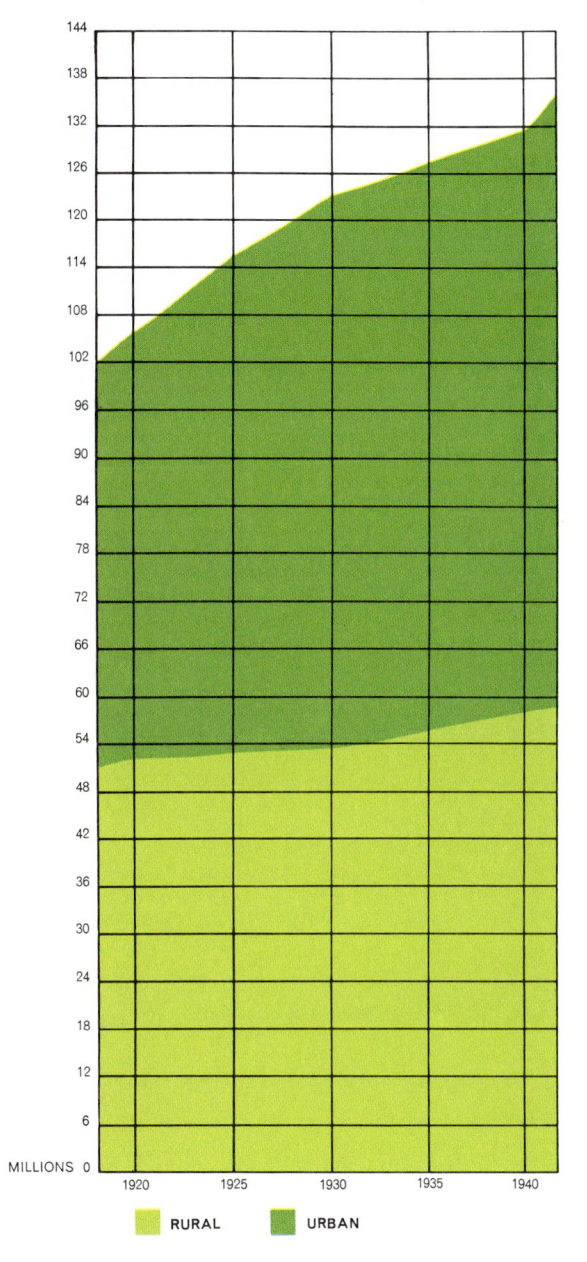

RURAL URBAN

on prices. Smaller rivals would follow suit. Competition would then shift from prices to improvements in quality or to increases in advertising.

Another device used to cut down competition was the *trade association*, a voluntary, cooperative, nonprofit organization made up of individuals (usually competitors) in a particular industry. Trade associations collected and distributed information on prices, shipping problems, advertising, and business practices. While many trade associations performed useful services, some engaged in price fixing or other unethical practices.

In 1920, only a small number of these trade associations were in operation. Harding, Coolidge, and especially Hoover encouraged their growth. By 1933, more than 2,000 trade associations were functioning. One of the most powerful was the National Association of Manufacturers.

The Managerial Class

In the 1920's, a new class of business leaders, the salaried executives, came to exercise great power over the economy. This new class had arisen as more and more corporations sold stock to the public and the management of business became separated from its ownership. Since many stockholders did not have the skill and knowledge to run the giant corporations, they left the making of important decisions to salaried executives.

At the same time, the continuing technological revolution vastly increased industrial output. New machines, new sources of power, and new techniques in production made it possible for each worker to produce more than ever before.

Most important in increasing production was industry's adoption of the assembly-line technique of mass production. For example, the use of a moving assembly line enabled Ford workers to reduce the time needed to make an automobile chassis from fourteen hours to less than two hours.

Even though industrial production in the 1930's was lower than in the 1920's, technological change continued. Using the same number of workers, industry produced 20 percent more goods and services in 1937 than it did in 1929.

Striking textile workers duck behind an overturned car during labor strife in Macon, Georgia. Employers and workers often clashed over unionization.

New Industries

New industries grew and existing industries expanded rapidly in the 1920's and 1930's. The most important of these were automobiles, electric power, aviation, motion pictures, and radio.

Of all the new products, the automobile had the greatest influence on American life and culture. It did much to supply the boom for the booming prosperity of the 1920's.

Use of the automobile led to vast road construction and maintenance programs and to growth in allied industries, such as petroleum. Automobile manufacturers became the most important buyers of rubber, plate glass, nickel, and lead. They used about 15 percent of the nation's steel production. In most towns, filling stations, garages, and motels were built. According to an estimate made in 1929, the use of the automobile gave employment, directly or indirectly, to 3.7 million persons in the United States.

The automobile also made possible the development of new suburbs and parts of cities that could be reached only by car, not by train. The automobile suburbs were often far from the center of the city.

Even during the depression years, when few people bought new cars, the family automobile took a good share of the people's incomes. During these years, it was said, Americans were the only people in history to ride to the poorhouse in automobiles.

After World War I, the electric power industry became one of the nation's industrial giants. In the 1920's, Americans used almost twice as much electric power as in all the years up to that time. Even in the 1930's, consumption continued to rise. At first, numerous small companies produced most of the power, but in the 1920's the industry became the chief area for mergers. By 1930, ten groups of holding companies controlled 72 percent of the country's electric power.

Aviation also became an important industry between 1920 and 1940. After the historic flight of Orville Wright in 1903, the airplane was used primarily for stunts and amusement. In World War I, airplanes were used in fighting and for other purposes. In 1924, government planes began regular transcontinental air-mail service from New York to San Francisco.

In May 1927, the first solo flight from New York to Paris captured worldwide interest. A young midwesterner, Charles A. Lindbergh, flew across the Atlantic in a single-engine plane, *The Spirit of St. Louis*. This feat brought Lindbergh a prize of $25,000 and world fame. Other historic flights followed. In 1932 Amelia Earhart became the first woman to fly across the Atlantic.

Scheduled airline passenger service began in 1926. By the end of the 1930's, flights connected Europe and the United States, and Americans could travel 200 miles an hour on coast-to-coast flights.

LITERATURE AND THE ARTS

In the 1920's, many artists and intellectuals rejected the business-centered society of America. Some isolated themselves in areas like New York City's Greenwich Village. Others fled to Europe. Writers attacked mechanization as a menace and criticized Americans for not paying as much attention to the quality of life as they did to business.

By the 1930's, many of these writers and artists had returned to the United States. During the depression, they rediscovered their country and began to write, paint, and talk about the nation's problems.

Novels

Novelists wrote on new themes in the 1920's and 1930's but continued to be influenced by the naturalists and realists of earlier days. Sherwood Anderson's *Winesburg, Ohio* (1919), a collection of stories about the frustrations of life in a small town, was written in a naturalistic style.

Sinclair Lewis was the first American author to win a Nobel Prize for literature. In *Main Street* (1920), Lewis described small-town America as narrow and mean. Lewis aroused controversy with *Babbitt* (1922), a satire on the life of a self-satisfied, unimaginative businessman in a bustling city.

F. Scott Fitzgerald became the symbol of the jazz age. He gained instant fame with *This Side of Paradise* (1920), a novel based on his life as a student. He also captured the excitement of his era in *Tales of the Jazz Age* (1922), *The Beautiful and the Damned* (1922), and *The Great Gatsby* (1925).

Ernest Hemingway, who lived among intellectual exiles in Paris, described them in *The Sun Also Rises* (1926). His simple style is best illustrated in *A Farewell to Arms* (1929), a novel that deals with the uselessness of modern war. His novel *For Whom the Bell Tolls* (1940) also dealt with this theme, centering on the Spanish Civil War.

John Dos Passos wrote *Three Soldiers* (1921), one of the first novels to debunk the glory often associated with war. His major work was a trilogy, *U.S.A.* In these three novels, he tried to capture the mood of life in the early twentieth century by using characters from many classes in American society.

Richard Wright, who wrote bitter novels about blacks, became a dominant literary figure in the 1930's. In *Uncle Tom's Children* (1938) and *Native Son* (1940), Wright described the lives of oppressed black laborers in the city. His autobiographical work *Black Boy* (1945) treated the same subject.

One of the finest writers of this period was William Faulkner, who wrote novels about life in his native Mississippi. In *The Sound and the Fury* (1929), he used the stream-of-consciousness writing technique, telling the story through the thoughts of characters. In some of his works, Faulkner explored relationships between whites and blacks as he wrote of the traditions of the South.

Faulkner was a naturalist, as were John Steinbeck, James T. Farrell, and Thomas Wolfe, other great novelists of the 1930's. Farrell wrote with brutal frankness about the lower-middle-class Irish in Chicago, his hometown. His best-known works made up the *Studs Lonigan* trilogy.

Steinbeck wrote about the dispossessed farmers and migratory workers of the depression era. His works included *Tortilla Flat* (1935), *In Dubious Battle* (1936), and *Of Mice and Men* (1937). In 1939, he published *The Grapes of Wrath,* which tells of a farm family driven from Oklahoma by dust storms and farm mechanization. This book was one of the most widely read novels of its time.

Like Farrell, Thomas Wolfe wrote in great detail about life as he had experienced it. The prose in his four huge novels is undisciplined but often beautiful.

Among many other fine novelists of this period was Willa Cather, who made use of realism in such novels as *One of Ours* (a Pulitzer Prize winner in 1922) and *Death Comes for the Archbishop* (1927). Pearl Buck drew on the experiences of her childhood in China in writing *The Good Earth* and other books. The best-selling novel in the 1930's was Margaret Mitchell's *Gone With the Wind* (1936), a panorama of southern life before, during, and after the Civil War.

Poetry

A renaissance in American poetry began shortly before World War I. Ezra Pound, who

After the Storyville section of New Orleans closed, jazz musicians moved north. In 1918, "King" Oliver started his Creole Jazz Band in Chicago. It played classic New Orleans jazz but eventually developed a new, "Chicago style." In 1922, a young cornetist, Louis Armstrong *(fourth from left)*, joined this group.

chose to live in Italy, was a key figure in this rebirth. He was one of the creators of a new school of poets called "imagists." The imagists broke with the poetic forms of the past. They believed that poets should use free-verse forms, write about any subject, and create concrete images. Amy Lowell succeeded Pound as the leader of the imagists in 1915.

Edward Arlington Robinson and Robert Frost also participated in the early years of this poetry revival. Robinson used nineteenth-century poetic forms to express pessimism about the lives of ordinary people. His first success came in 1916 with *The Man Against the Sky*. Some of his later poems, such as *Tristram* (1927), sold better than the popular novels of the time. Frost also used traditional poetic forms to write about familiar New England landscapes and people.

As the poetry revival gained momentum, poets continued to experiment with new forms and themes. Carl Sandburg voiced the feelings and experiences of people in everyday language in his first volume, *Chicago Poems* (1916). He used strong free-verse forms. Vachel Lindsay wrote poems on themes of American democracy, rural life, and folklore. He injected new life into these themes with the rhythms of religious revivals, political speeches, and jazz. Edgar Lee Masters used free-verse forms to expose the meanness and hypocrisy of a small town in *Spoon River Anthology* (1915).

The strongest poetic impact of these times was made by Thomas Stearns (T. S.) Eliot with the publication of "The Waste Land" in

1922. He believed that complex poetry was needed to explore a complex society. Both his poetry and his criticism greatly influenced younger poets. Eliot was awarded the Nobel Prize for literature in 1948.

During the 1920's, a group of black poets in Harlem were also experimenting with new forms and themes. They were leaders in the movement known as the "Harlem Renaissance." James Weldon Johnson, an older poet and essayist, encouraged such young writers as Langston Hughes, Countee Cullen, and Claude McKay. They used images of city life and African folklore, with the rhythms of jazz, to express both bitterness and racial pride. Langston Hughes spoke out against oppression in such poems as "Let America Be America Again," "As I Grew Older," and "Harlem." Countee Cullen sensitively explored human relationships in more traditional verse forms. His poem "Heritage" (1925) explored the relevance of African heritage to American blacks. Claude McKay wrote poems, novels, and short stories of protest. His poem "If We Must Die" is a militant call to fight back in the face of suffering.

Other important poets of the 1920's and 1930's were Marianne Moore, who wrote descriptive, detailed poems on unusual subjects; E. E. Cummings, who experimented with the sounds of poetry; and Stephen Vincent Benét, best known for his long narrative poem of the Civil War, *John Brown's Body* (1928). Archibald MacLeish wrote of personal discontent in the 1920's and of social injustices in the 1930's.

Edna St. Vincent Millay expressed light, youthful optimism in her earlier poetry; later she wrote poems of protest. She went on to develop a powerful style that she condensed into sonnet and lyric forms. Dorothy Parker was a popular poet, essayist, and short-story writer of this period. Her satirical poetry on the manners of the times is included in *Death and Taxes* (1936).

Although simple gospel meetings *(opposite)* were still held in the twenties, religious revivals became big business. Evangelists like Aimée Semple McPherson and Billy Sunday packed in huge crowds.

Music, Dance, and Drama

Music, dance, and drama underwent exciting changes in the twenties and thirties. Many of the trends in these fields matched developments in other arts.

In music, the improvisational jazz of prewar New Orleans gave way to formalized, written jazz. Large orchestras could not easily improvise; they needed written music. In big-band jazz, some spontaneity was lost but rich sounds were gained.

Fletcher Henderson and Edward "Duke" Ellington were the pioneers in formalizing jazz and making it suitable for dancing. By the 1930's, band leaders like Paul Whiteman had changed this music into swing—a slick commercialized form of jazz that was even better suited to ballroom dancing.

The music of musical comedy was gradually becoming integrated into the plot and story line of the show. Composers and lyricists like Jerome Kern, Cole Porter, Richard Rodgers, and Lorenz Hart were at work. Some of the most important developments, however, came from George Gershwin. He wrote not only the scores for musical comedies but also symphonic works based on American themes. His *Rhapsody in Blue* is an outstanding example of symphonic jazz. Gershwin's greatest work was *Porgy and Bess,* an opera, with lyrics by his brother Ira and libretto by DuBose Heyward.

Dance was affected by changes in music and by new ideas. Isadora Duncan, the leading prewar exponent of modern dance, fought for simple and natural dance. In the twenties and thirties, Ruth St. Denis and Ted Shawn took up where Duncan had left off, creating a training method.

A number of ballroom dancing fads swept

The Gospel Train, by John Steuart Curry

the country. Some of them had their origins in Harlem, where jazz spots and musical revues introduced white New Yorkers to black talent and black dances. The Charleston *was* the twenties. In the thirties, music and dances with Latin rhythms were becoming popular.

In the 1920's, drama became a vital form of literary expression in the United States. It was given a big boost by the little-theater movement, which began in 1915 in Provincetown, Massachusetts. There a group of young people founded the Wharf Theater as a place where playwrights could stage experimental dramas on serious themes.

The Provincetown group gave Eugene O'Neill his start. He often tried to explore human nature, not solely to entertain, in his plays. *The Emperor Jones* (1920), *Desire Under the Elms* (1924), and *Strange Interlude* (1928) are examples of his powerful dramas.

In the early 1920's, other fine playwrights appeared. *The Adding Machine* (1923) was a modern allegory by Elmer Rice. In *Street Scene* (1929), Rice turned to realism and social protest.

Social concern marked the early work of Maxwell Anderson. In 1924, with Laurence Stallings, he wrote an antiwar play, *What Price Glory?* Anderson also brought poetry back to the stage in plays about Elizabethan England and in *Winterset* (1935).

In the dramas *Our Town* (1938) and *The Skin of Our Teeth* (1942), Thornton Wilder explored the human condition. Robert E. Sherwood condemned decaying society in *The Petrified Forest* (1934); in *Idiot's Delight* (1936) he denounced war; and in *Abe Lincoln*

Early Sunday Morning, by Edward Hopper, 1930. Collection Whitney Museum of American Art, New York

Black Cross, New Mexico, by Georgia O'Keeffe, 1929

In the 1920's, abstract art gained a significant following. John Marin's imaginative interpretations of the Maine seacoast gave a new outlook to landscape painting. Georgia O'Keeffe was a pioneer in modern directions in art. She became famous for her portrayals of natural forms, such as rocks, flowers, and bones.

One trend in art in the 1930's was that of regional realism. John Steuart Curry, Grant Wood, and Thomas Hart Benton painted scenes of life in the Midwest. Edward Hopper did stark paintings of both urban and rural settings. Another trend in the thirties was social realism. Reginald Marsh, Ben Shahn, and Isaac Soyer were the natural successors to the Ash Can School. Their realistic views of urban life were often critical of American society. Their works reflected the spirit of the times, when many Americans were questioning the nation's goals and social structure.

Photography was coming into its own as an art form in the twenties and thirties. Edward Steichen, Dorothea Lange, Margaret Bourke-White, and Walker Evans were pioneers in making photographs that were works of art as well as valuable records of the times. During the depression, the federal government hired photographers to travel around the country taking pictures of the nation's people.

Stone City, by Grant Wood, 1930

Jack Curley's Dance Marathon, by Reginald Marsh, 1932

Maine Islands, by John Marin, 1922

in Illinois (1938) he praised democracy.

Acting techniques were changing. By the 1920's, the bent-knees, clasped-hands style of acting was being replaced by natural modes. Gone was the villain who swished his cape and twirled his mustache.

Art and Architecture

In the 1920's and 1930's many Americans expressed greater interest in the work of artists than they had in the past. Painting, sculpture, and art history were taught in high schools and colleges, and new art museums were set up in towns all over the country.

One of the events that had aroused public interest in art was the Armory Show, held in New York in February 1913. That exhibit, designed in part to show paintings of the Ash Can School, also introduced the public to modern art from Europe.

For the next several decades, two opposing ideas could be found in American painting. One was realism, which showed scenes from American life. The other was abstract art, which expressed the ideas and emotions of the artist through forms and color.

In 1929, a group of art collectors opened the Museum of Modern Art in New York City. In 1931, the Whitney Museum opened, the first museum devoted exclusively to American art. In the 1930's, the federal government tried to help artists suffering from the hardships of the depression by employing them to paint murals in post offices, schools, and courthouses.

A few sculptors experimented with abstract approaches, but realism was dominant in the sculpture of this period. Among the realistic sculptors was Gutzon Borglum, who is best known for his faces of the Presidents carved in the Black Hills of South Dakota.

Modernists were slow in influencing architecture in the United States. In the 1920's, traditional design continued, but in the 1930's, a modern style of straight, simple lines gained favor. This clean, uncluttered style was used in Rockefeller Center, a group of skyscrapers in New York City. The nation's most influential architect continued to be Frank Lloyd Wright. Whether designing homes or factories, Wright integrated the form, the function, and the materials of a building with its site.

THE CHALLENGE OF NEW IDEAS

The belief that ideas in all fields are interdependent influenced many intellectuals. Historians began probing the social, intellectual, and economic factors in history, not just the political. They also began studying world history in greater depth than before.

Sociologists, influenced by ideas from Europe, developed new techniques for the study of people and how they functioned in their environment. Economists became more concerned with how the economic system worked than with economic laws. In almost every field of study, new theories and ideas were challenging the old.

Psychology

Psychology was a relatively new social science, but in the 1920's it seemed to become a national craze. One of the most popular psychologists was Dr. John B. Watson. He said the mind is like an electric machine that receives signals and automatically sends out established responses. Watson said that environment and training are most important in shaping human conduct.

More important was Sigmund Freud, a Viennese physician who expressed the major ideas of his theory between 1914 and 1926. He developed a method—called *psychoanalysis*—for treating people who were emotionally disturbed. Freud claimed that many normal human drives are unconscious and irrational and that people became disturbed when their unconscious wishes are repressed.

If, as Freud said, the motives in human conduct are largely unconscious, then notions that people are self-reliant and capable of making intelligent choices are undermined. These implications troubled some people and inspired others. Freud's ideas influenced fiction, drama, history, political science, religion, and child-rearing.

A Tennessee Trial

By 1920, church leaders had resolved some of the conflicts between religion and science. Other disagreements, however, persisted. Some *fundamentalists,* who taught that the Bible is to be taken as literal historical record and prophecy, were especially upset by the theory of evolution. They wanted to prevent anyone from teaching this theory in the schools. Their crusade, led by William Jennings Bryan, was most successful in the South. In March 1925, the state legislature in Tennessee passed a law saying that the schools would not be allowed to teach any theory that denies the story of the divine creation of man as taught in the Bible and to teach instead that man has descended from a lower order of animals.

A few months later, John T. Scopes, a young high-school teacher in Dayton, Tennessee, was persuaded to test the validity of the law. He proceeded to discuss evolution in his classes. He was arrested and brought to trial, with Bryan serving on the staff of prosecuting attorneys. Clarence Darrow, the nation's most famous defense lawyer, represented Scopes.

The trial attracted worldwide attention, for it seemed to be a showdown between science and religion. Reporters, evangelists, and the curious jammed into Dayton, giving the events the atmosphere of a circus. Although the basic question concerned the limits of academic freedom, the trial developed into a verbal duel between Darrow and Bryan over the validity of the Bible and of the sciences. Scopes was found guilty, for he admitted

Angelo's Place, by Glenn O. Coleman, 1929. Collection, The Museum of Modern Art, New York. Gift of Abby Aldrich Rockefeller

As the United States became more and more urbanized, this change was reflected in the amusements and leisure activities of the people. The neighborhood pool hall, candy store, rib shack, or hot dog stand became familiar meeting places for young and old alike. The cracker barrel circles of rural general stores were gone.

breaking the law. He was fined $100, but the fine was later canceled. The anti-evolution campaign faded but later reappeared.

Church attendance was not hurt by the controversy. In the 1920's, attendance increased in Protestant and Catholic churches and in Jewish synagogues. But in the depression years of the 1930's, membership in all churches slumped.

Science

Conflict over scientific ideas was not limited to religious leaders. Scientists themselves were constantly discarding or modifying theories. New discoveries, particularly in physics and astronomy, led them to question the idea that the universe is governed by final and absolute laws. Using giant telescopes at observatories in California, astronomers discovered *galaxies,* huge clouds of stars. In 1930, at Lowell Observatory near Flagstaff, Arizona, Clyde Tombaugh discovered a ninth planet, Pluto. Scientists began to speak of an expanding universe.

These new ideas were accepted by American scientists, but most of the theoretical work was done by Europeans. Many of the ideas stemmed from the work of a brilliant German physicist, Albert Einstein. In 1905, he advanced a theory of relativity, which he refined in later years. According to this theory, only the speed of light is fixed or absolute. Everything else is relative to the motion and position of the observer. Part of this theory could be tested by the observations of astronomers.

Another part of Einstein's theory was later verified by experiments in physics. Einstein had said that when atoms split, they release energy. The amount of energy released could be determined by using the formula $E=mc^2$. This means that "E," or energy, equals "m," or mass, times "c^2," or the speed of light (186,000 miles a second) squared.

Scientists, primarily those in Europe, at first used Einstein's theories to unlock the atom. In England in the 1920's, Ernest Rutherford began exploring the uranium atom. In the 1930's, Enrico Fermi in Italy used information from England to conduct important experiments of his own with uranium. An Austrian physicist, Lise Meitner, developed the mathematical theory to explain the splitting of the uranium atom.

At the same time, American physicists began atomic experiments of increasing importance. In 1932, Ernest O. Lawrence, a young physicist at the University of California, Berkeley, built the first practical cyclotron. This powerful machine was designed to speed the movement of atoms so that scientists could study the nature of atoms.

In the 1930's many fine European scientists migrated to the United States to escape the tyranny of dictators. Einstein and Niels Bohr, a leading theorist from Denmark, went to the Institute for Advanced Study at Princeton, New Jersey. Fermi joined the faculty at Columbia University. These physicists and others, such as Leo Szilard from Hungary, worked to make the United States a great center of scientific research.

News reached Bohr in 1939 that scientists in Germany had split the uranium atom, which is capable of releasing an immense amount of energy. This alarmed some scientists, including Einstein. In August, Einstein wrote to President Roosevelt:

some recent work by E. Fermi and L. Szilard . . . leads me to expect that the element uranium may be turned into a new and important source of energy in the immediate future . . . [and] would also lead to the construction of bombs.

Einstein implied that scientists might soon be able to obtain a chain reaction among atoms as they split, releasing vast energy in a fraction of a second. By writing to Roosevelt, he hoped to ensure that the United States, not Germany, first developed the bomb potential of the splitting of the atom.

Highly publicized silliness gave the twenties the name of the "era of wonderful nonsense." Flagpole sitting, wearing pajamas in public, and goldfish swallowing were among the fads of the time. *Bottom right:* The repeal of the prohibition amendment was joyfully greeted in bars and saloons across the nation.

Education

The growth of scientific and scholarly research in the United States, much of it in the universities, was evidence of improvement in American education. By 1930, almost all Americans were literate. The ideal of a common school, supported by public taxes and open to all children, had become a reality. In the 1920's and 1930's, therefore, the primary concern of educators was to improve the schools.

Despite opposition from traditionalists, some educators set up progressive, or child-centered, schools. There children were encouraged to experiment and to participate in the learning process, rather than to memorize and drill. In the 1930's, the emphasis shifted to community-centered schools, in which students often studied social and economic problems.

High schools and colleges made the most significant progress. In earlier times, high schools offered only academic courses that prepared students mainly for college. Colleges, in turn, prepared students almost exclusively for professions. In the 1920's and 1930's, however, both high schools and colleges increasingly offered vocational courses. Employers began to insist on a high-school education for many jobs.

The establishment of junior colleges spread rapidly, especially in California and other western states. Professional training and higher research also expanded. Graduate schools in universities often grew more rapidly than undergraduate schools.

In the booming 1920's, schools expanded. In the 1930's, some schools closed for lack of funds, and many suffered from crowded rooms, shortened class periods, and lack of funds to pay teachers. But even during the depression, high-school and college enrollments increased. Since they could not find jobs, many young men and women stayed in school.

MASS ENTERTAINMENT

In the 1920's, many Americans had time for leisure and money to pay for entertainment. As a result, businesses that catered to leisure-time needs enjoyed a boom. Radios, movies, book clubs, and chain newspapers reached people all over the country with the same songs, jokes, stories, and ideas. The United States developed a nationwide popular culture.

Spectator Sports

For the promoters of organized sports, the 1920's were truly golden. Competitions drew huge crowds, and sports figures became national heroes. Gertrude Ederle was greeted by a ticker-tape parade in New York City after she swam the English Channel in 1926. Robert "Bobby" Jones was considered the greatest golfer of all time. He dominated golf and William T. Tilden dominated American tennis for a good part of the decade.

Knute Rockne, Notre Dame's football coach, was a hero to many. In 1925, Harold "Red" Grange, a football player at the University of Illinois, so captured the imagination of admirers that some of them circulated a petition seeking his nomination as a congressman, even though he was too young to hold office.

So great was the prowess of George "Babe" Ruth of the New York Yankees that his fame helped boost baseball to a peak of popularity. Known as the mighty "Sultan of Swat," he set new records for home runs. World Series crowds broke records for attendance and gate receipts.

Jack Dempsey, known as the "Manassa Mauler," drew overflow crowds to boxing matches in the 1920's. When Dempsey fought Gene Tunney in 1927 for the heavyweight championship, 145,000 spectators paid a record gate of more than 2.6 million dollars. An audience of 40 million heard a blow-by-blow account on the radio.

This craze for spectator sports lessened in the 1930's. Professional baseball, however, continued to hold the interest of the public. The big star of the thirties was "Joltin' Joe" DiMaggio of the Yankees. In boxing, the king was Joe Louis, the "Brown Bomber" from Detroit. Another black athlete, track star Jesse Owens, won four gold medals at the 1936 Olympic Games in Berlin.

An outstanding all-round athlete of the 1930's was Mildred "Babe" Didrikson. She won titles in all sports she was allowed to enter and was a track-and-field star in the 1932 Olympics. When she later took up golf, she won every amateur and professional title the sport offered.

Americans by the millions participated in sports, especially in the 1930's. The government encouraged such activities by building—often as relief work projects—camp grounds, ski jumps, swimming pools, tennis courts, and playgrounds.

The Printed Page

Between 1920 and 1941, publishing became a bigger business than ever. A trend toward newspaper mergers that had started earlier in the century continued. As a result, there were fewer newspapers, but those that survived had larger circulations than in the past.

Newspaper chains dominated the field. Since the head office usually made policy for an entire chain, member newspapers lost much of their former independence and individuality. They became increasingly standardized with news from press associations and with features gathered from a few central sources. The cable-car rider in San Francisco now often read the same press dispatch and the same feature column as did the subway passenger in New York.

The most important newspaper development in this period was the *tabloid*. It was a small, easy-to-handle newspaper, designed to appeal to the eye and to the emotions of the reading public. It used large splashy headlines and featured photographs, comic strips, and stories of violence and lust. The first American tabloid, the *New York Daily News,* was established in 1919. Five years later it had a circulation of 1.75 million, the largest in the country. Its success attracted numerous imitators.

Magazines, too, began to appeal to the eye by making greater use of pictures and short, simple narrative. Some magazines stopped publication during the thirties, but general-interest magazines like the *Saturday Evening Post, Woman's Home Companion,* and *Good Housekeeping* enjoyed a mass circulation. A new development came in 1923, when Henry Luce began publishing *Time,* a weekly digest of news. In 1936, Luce introduced a picture magazine called *Life.* The success of these journals produced vigorous rivals in *Newsweek* and *Look.*

Most bookstores operated in large urban areas. But book publishers wanted to find ways to reach people in other parts of the country. The Book-of-the-Month Club and the Literary Guild provided one method—book clubs. "Experts" picked books that were sent by mail to thousands of club members. In this way, a number of books had broad circulation. The clubs helped increase the number of book buyers. So did Pocket Books, which began publishing inexpensive paperbound books in 1939. Such paperbacks were sold from racks in drug stores, train stations, grocery stores, and other places with heavy foot traffic.

During the depression, the use of public libraries increased greatly. Millions of jobless people spent their days reading, and the libraries almost served as clubs for people with little or no money.

Movies

America's foremost commercial amusement in the 1920's and 1930's was the motion picture. It developed out of a device invented by Thomas A. Edison in 1896 called the *kinetoscope.* By peering into the kinetoscope, a person could see small figures move jerkily.

Gertrude Ederle prepares to swim the English Channel. Her skin has been covered with grease to help keep her warm during the 20-mile swim. She broke the existing men's record for the swim in 1926.

Rudolph Valentino and Agnes Ayres *(above)* starred in "The Sheik," the big hit of 1921. Many of the early movie stars lost their jobs when silent films gave way to sound flicks. Some of the greatest silent stars had squeaky voices or unchangeable accents. *Right:* "Gangbusters is on the air." Radio shows were broadcast live, right down to the sound effects.

In a short time, projectors were developed that threw flickering pictures on a screen. Soon crude theaters were set up all over the country. They were called *nickelodeons* because they charged a nickel for admission.

An important turning point for motion pictures came in 1915 when David W. Griffith produced *The Birth of a Nation.* This film about the Civil War and Reconstruction praised bigotry and did injustice to blacks. However, it introduced wide views of huge armies, battles, and mob scenes, as well as impressive closeups of the actors. It showed that movies could be a form of art. Others followed Griffith's techniques, and movies became immensely popular.

Hollywood, California, became the movie capital of the world, the source of a multimillion-dollar industry. By the middle of the 1920's, the movies ranked fourth in size among United States industries. By 1930, it was claimed that 100 million movie admissions were sold each week.

What the moviegoers usually got for their money was escape from reality into a land where everyone was rich, beautiful, and sophisticated and where good always triumphed over evil. Stars like Rudolph Valentino, Charlie Chaplin, Mary Pickford, and Douglas Fairbanks earned fabulous salaries, lived glamorously, and were popular idols.

The first full-length "all-talking, all-singing" movie, *The Jazz Singer,* was shown in

1928. Even though movie attendance decreased during the depression, the talkies helped the motion-picture industry weather the hard times.

Great elaborate movie theaters were built all over the country. Millions flocked to them to forget the depression for a few hours in the romances of such stars as Clark Gable, Claudette Colbert, and Dolores del Rio. A blonde, curly-haired child star, Shirley Temple, won the hearts of Americans.

In the 1930's, some movies dealt with social themes, but most offered pure entertainment. By 1935, full-color films were perfected, and attendance rose.

At its best, the motion picture brought art, fine dramas, and splendid acting to many people. At its worst it promoted intolerance and glorified a dream world. But most of the time it just brought entertainment.

Radio

A new invention, the radio, changed the daily living habits of more Americans in the 1920's and 1930's than either the newspapers or the movies. The first fully licensed broadcasting station, KDKA in East Pittsburgh, began operation in 1920.

Commercial radio came into existence when advertisers began sponsoring programs in 1922. Nationwide network broadcasting started in 1926, when the National Broadcasting Company transmitted programs coast-to-coast over telephone lines. By 1930, more than 12 million families had radios in their homes.

In 1927, Congress established the Federal Radio Commission to license stations, assign wavelengths, and establish hours for broadcasting. Seven years later the Federal Communications Commission took over the regulation of the radio industry.

Radio—through news, music, serial drama, comedy, and sportscasts—brought the outside world into the parlors of millions. News could be broadcast and heard simultaneously from coast to coast. The music of Fred Waring, Paul Whiteman, and Xavier Cugat became popular across the country. Comedians like Bob Hope, Jack Benny, and George Burns and Gracie Allen commanded huge loyal audiences. Some radio serials became so popular they were almost national institutions. Football and baseball games held the attention of millions of listeners.

Even the depression failed to halt the growth of radio. In the 1930's, the average household had a radio blaring about four and a half hours a day. By the beginning of 1940, 86 percent of the population had radios.

Radio, along with the automobile, the airplane, and the movies, helped break down the barrier between town and country. The culture of the United States was becoming the culture of the city. Literature, art, books, magazines, and even social attitudes spread outward from the city. Language, manners, customs, and dress had national standards, set by radio announcers, movie actors, and others in the public eye. This trend toward standardization in American culture was to continue in future decades.

A Look at Specifics

1. What techniques did business leaders use to control prices during the 1920's?

2. How did the federal government encourage the growth of the aviation industry?

3. Why were many American writers and artists of the 1920's critical of life in the United States?

4. How did the Great Depression influence American art and literature?

5. What did the Armory Show (1913) contribute to American art?

6. During the 1920's and 1930's, what changes took place in the study of history? In the study of economics? In the study of psychology?

7. How did newspapers become more and more standardized during this period?

8. Why did the culture of the United States become the "culture of the city"?

A Review of Major Ideas

1. What changes in population distribution took place in the 1920's and 1930's?

2. What trends were evident in United States industry during the 1920's and 1930's?

3. How did scientific achievements lead to new ideas in American thought?

For Independent Study

1. In what ways can the 1920's be considered conservative? In what ways can they be considered progressive?

2. During the 1920's, mass communication contributed to the development of a mass culture. What were the outward signs of this development?

From Isolation To War

CHAPTER 23
1933–1941

The 1930's were troubled years throughout the world, not just in the United States. The depression that threw millions of Americans out of work also struck elsewhere. It was especially severe in the industrial nations of Europe and in Japan.

Many discontented people, trying to erase the causes of their plight, followed leaders who promised simplistic solutions to their complex problems. The solution some of the leaders offered was war.

FOREIGN POLICY, 1933–1935

In his first years as President, Roosevelt was so engrossed in domestic problems that he more or less ignored world affairs. His major concerns in foreign policy were economic affairs and United States relations with Latin America. Nevertheless, events in Europe and East Asia eventually became so alarming that they commanded his attention.

Economic Policy

At the London International Economic Conference in June 1933, it became apparent that President Roosevelt favored economic nationalism. The announcement that the United States would manipulate its currency as it saw fit torpedoed the meeting. After the conference broke up, the nations of the world engaged in economic warfare. They raised tariffs on each other's goods and tried to solve economic problems by themselves.

Roosevelt's economic nationalism and the failure of the London conference were severe blows to Secretary of State Cordell Hull, who had devoted twenty-five years in Congress to a crusade for freer trade. Hull believed that increased international trade would help keep peace and that economic warfare would lead to real warfare.

When Hull went to London, he assumed that the President would support lower tariffs. But Roosevelt refused to cooperate.

Pearl Harbor, December 7, 1941.

Despite his disappointment, Hull did not give up his campaign. At his urging, Roosevelt asked Congress in March 1934 for authority to negotiate agreements with other nations for a mutual lowering of tariff duties.

Many people in business objected because they feared competition from foreign goods. Republican senators and representatives objected because the agreements would give the President greater power over foreign policy. The Democrats controlled both houses of Congress, however, and they followed the President's wishes. In June 1934, Congress passed the Reciprocal Trade Agreement Amendment to the Tariff Act of 1930.

This amendment permitted the President to make trade agreements with other nations without congressional approval. The new duties, however, could not vary from the existing ones by more than 50 percent. Also, any lowered tariff the United States granted to one nation would automatically extend to any other nation producing the item, if that nation had a trade treaty with the United States and did not discriminate against American goods.

By January 1940, the Roosevelt administration had made reciprocal-trade agreements with twenty-one countries. But the agreements never achieved what Hull had expected of them. They did not greatly increase American trade, nor did they help keep the peace. They did help, however, in overcoming the international ill will caused by the high Hawley-Smoot Tariff of 1930.

Recognition of the Soviet Union

Since 1917 every administration had refused to grant diplomatic recognition to the Soviet government in Russia. Soon after his inauguration, however, Roosevelt began to explore the possibility of recognizing the Soviet Union. Some business leaders wanted to trade with the Soviet Union. Also, Roosevelt wanted to maintain a balance of power between Japan and Russia in East Asia.

In November 1933, the United States formally recognized the Soviet Union. In return, the Soviet government promised to extend religious liberty to Americans in the Soviet Union, to curb revolutionary activity in the United States, and to negotiate a settlement of its debts owed to Americans.

Critics argued that recognition of the Soviet Union would open a Pandora's box of evils. Actually, no real trouble followed. On the other hand, few of the hoped-for benefits resulted. Trade with the Soviets increased very little; the Soviets continued their Communist propaganda; the debts were not settled; and no policy of cooperation against Japan was ever worked out during peacetime.

The Good Neighbor Policy

Roosevelt's Latin American policy was essentially an expansion of Hoover's Good

President Roosevelt greets the president of Uruguay with a friendly hug. Roosevelt's Good Neighbor policy included writing treaties in which the United States gave up the right to intervene in Latin America.

Neighbor policy. The United States government declared that it would treat Latin American nations as its equal in matters of common interest and that it would not intervene in their affairs.

Latin Americans were not impressed by the first practical application of the Good Neighbor policy. In August 1933, the Cuban army overthrew a brutal dictator named Gerardo Machado. A left-wing government led by a university professor, Dr. Ramón Grau San Martín, gained power. Roosevelt sent warships to Cuban waters to stand by in case the lives of Americans were endangered by the revolution, but he did not order troops to land. At the same time, he refused to recognize the regime of Grau San Martín. In January 1934, this regime was overthrown, and Roosevelt speedily recognized the conservative government that replaced it.

Many Latin Americans believed that the use of warships and nonrecognition were forms of intervention in Cuba. Roosevelt, on the other hand, thought that his failure to use force was consistent with the Good Neighbor policy. Later, in March 1934, he gave Latin Americans a more believable demonstration of the spirit of his Good Neighbor policy. He removed the Platt Amendment, which had given the United States the right to intervene in Cuban affairs. However, the United States held on to its naval base at Guantánamo Bay in Cuba.

The Good Neighbor policy met its most difficult test in Mexico. From 1933 to 1936, the Mexican government followed a policy of restricting the power of the Catholic Church and confiscating church lands. Some Catholics in the United States demanded intervention, but Roosevelt refused. Then, in 1938, President Lázaro Cárdenas took over most of the foreign-owned oil companies in Mexico. The American companies involved believed the Mexican government would never compensate them. They demanded intervention by the United States government to regain their investments.

The United States government refused to intervene. It accepted Mexico's right to expropriate foreign property but insisted upon fair and prompt payment for the property.

Finally, in November 1941, after long, bitter exchanges, the American and Mexican governments worked out a compromise settlement. Mexico agreed to make payment, but it paid the American oil companies far less than they had demanded.

Policy in East Asia

In Asia, as in Latin America, Roosevelt followed essentially the same policies as Herbert Hoover. He refused to recognize Japan's puppet state, Manchukuo (Manchuria), and he cooperated in a limited way with the League of Nations on Asian matters. Some of his advisers wanted him to do more—to actively oppose Japan's expansion.

In March 1933, Japan annexed to Manchukuo the Chinese province of Jehol. Then the Japanese forced harsh truce terms on the Chinese. Most Americans disliked Japan's aggressive program and sympathized with China. The administration, however, did nothing more than protest, partly because the American people were unwilling to support a stronger East Asian policy. They wanted to isolate themselves from the politics of Asia. The President also dealt cautiously with Japan because of his concern for the safety of the Philippine Islands and for other United States possessions in the Pacific Ocean.

The Philippines had long been a source of concern to American policymakers. At the turn of the century, many Americans considered the islands the key to increased trade with China and other East Asian nations. They had insisted that the United States keep possession of the Philippines. Since the hoped-for trade was never realized, by the 1930's many Americans were willing to allow the islands to become independent. In addition, it became increasingly evident that the islands could not be defended if Japan should decide to seize them.

In January 1933, Congress passed a law that offered independence to the Philippines after a ten-year period of transition. Farm and labor pressure groups had agitated for the act because they wanted to end competition from Filipino products and workers. The Philippine legislature rejected the offer, saying that the real aim of the act was not to free the Philippines.

In March 1934, Congress passed the Tydings-McDuffie Act. It was essentially the same as the earlier law, except that it called for eventual removal of United States military posts and for negotiations over United States naval bases in the Philippines. Since the Philippine legislature could not get better terms, it accepted the Tydings-McDuffie Act. In November 1935, the Commonwealth of the Philippines began to function as a semi-independent state.

Adolf Hitler reviews his troops. The soldiers carried shovels rather than guns during public drills because Germany was still barred from rearming by the Treaty of Versailles.

Militarists in Power

About a month before Roosevelt became President, Adolf Hitler became chancellor of Germany. He headed the National Socialist German Workers' party, popularly called the Nazi party. Hitler preached a doctrine that glorified hatred, war, and racism, inflaming the people of Germany to violence and murder. Basic to Nazism was the idea that Germans, especially blue-eyed, blond Germans, were a super race, and that Jews, Slavs, and certain nonwhites were inferior. Once in power the Nazis swept away the remains of a crumbled German democracy, made Hitler dictator, and established Nazism as the only permissible philosophy. Soon, Nazi storm troopers were beating up and humiliating Jewish men, women, and children in the streets of German cities while the police stood by and watched.

Since 1922, Italy had been controlled by a dictator, Benito Mussolini. Although Mussolini's Fascist party was not committed to racial hatred as were the Nazis, it also thrived on brutality and terror.

On the other side of the world, in Japan, military leaders aided by some business leaders were shaping their nation to their will. Although they did not force an absolute dictatorship on Japan, they, too, preached ideas of national glory through warfare. About a week before Roosevelt's inauguration in 1933, Japan defied world opposition to its conquest of Manchuria and pulled out of the League of Nations, never to return.

Of these three nations, Nazi Germany was the most warlike and the most powerful. Hence it was the most dangerous. The strongest nation in Europe, it had the resources to conquer any other nation, except perhaps the Soviet Union. Under the terms of the Treaty of Versailles, it was supposed to have been disarmed. But its leaders did not feel bound by paper obstacles. Hitler soon withdrew Germany from the League of Nations and began to rearm the nation and to rebuild the German armed forces.

At first most Americans saw no great danger to their own country in the rise of the dictatorships. They wanted to be left alone and to avoid involvement in the problems of other nations. In the early years of the New Deal, Roosevelt and many of his advisers shared this isolationist attitude. "Despite what happens in continents overseas," Roosevelt announced in October 1935, "the United States of America shall and must remain, as long ago the Father of our Country prayed that it might remain—unentangled and free."

ISOLATIONISM AT ITS HEIGHT

During the 1930's, most Americans were disappointed and disillusioned by the state of world affairs. Wilson's crusade to make the world safe for democracy had obviously failed. Democracies were crumbling or were on the defensive everywhere.

Writers and historians investigating the

causes of World War I concluded that considerable blame must be placed on the Allied side. They cast doubt on the idea that Americans had fought for worthy ideals.

Some people believed that financiers and munitions makers—"merchants of death"—had brought on the war for personal profit. Beginning in April 1934, a Senate committee headed by Gerald P. Nye, an isolationist from North Dakota, investigated the armaments industry. The Nye Committee tried to establish the "merchants of death" thesis.

Although there was no evidence that would indicate that war profiteers had tricked the nation into going to war, many Americans believed the charge and concluded that intervention in World War I had been a mistake. They thought that a similar error could be prevented if the United States isolated itself politically from the rest of the world, if the possibility of making a profit from war were removed, and if the President's power to decide matters of war and peace were curbed.

Neutrality Laws

Congress accepted the reasoning of the isolationists and passed laws designed to keep the nation from being dragged into a foreign war. The Neutrality Act of August 1935 provided for an embargo on arms to all belligerents as soon as the President proclaimed the existence of a state of war. The law also authorized the President to discourage Americans from traveling on belligerent ships by warning them they would do so at their own risk.

In October 1935, Mussolini's troops invaded the ancient empire of Ethiopia. Although Italy had not declared war, Roosevelt nonetheless proclaimed that a state of war existed. He applied the Neutrality Act to both sides. The League of Nations condemned Italy as an aggressor and voted to impose *economic sanctions* (an embargo) against Italy. Roosevelt and Secretary of State Hull then attempted a one-sided "moral embargo." They urged Americans to voluntarily stop selling oil, steel, and other supplies to Italy. The moral embargo and the League sanctions failed to stop the Fascist conquest of Ethiopia.

In February 1936, Congress passed the second Neutrality Act. It extended the embargo provisions to include materials other than arms, and it prohibited loans to belligerents. A week later Hitler sent troops into the demilitarized zones of the Rhineland in violation of the Treaty of Versailles. No one tried to stop the Germans, for most European countries were in no way ready or willing to go to war to uphold the treaty.

In July 1936, the Spanish army touched off a civil war in Spain. Since the neutrality law did not apply to civil wars, Roosevelt asked American exporters not to sell arms to either side in the Spanish war. When the voluntary embargo failed, Roosevelt asked Congress to extend the neutrality law to include civil wars. This Congress did in January 1937.

Liberals in the United States were disappointed by Roosevelt's policy. The Spanish Civil War had become a miniature international war. Italy and Germany gave aid to the rebelling army, led by General Francisco Franco. The Soviet Union gave limited assistance to the Loyalist government. Liberals charged that, by failing to distinguish between victim and aggressor, American policy helped the enemies of democracy.

The danger from fascism appeared greater when, in 1936, Italy and Germany signed a treaty establishing a Rome-Berlin Axis. In 1937, it was enlarged to include Japan. Although this Rome-Berlin-Tokyo Axis was supposedly directed against communism, it united three nations that opposed democracy and favored war.

At the same time, Congress made permanent the neutrality law, which was about to

Spanish refugees *(above)* flee the fighting in their homeland during the Spanish Civil War. They are heading for France and relative safety. The failure of the United States to take sides in the war in Spain was criticized by some Americans. *Right:* Italian troops march into northern Ethiopia. Mussolini sought a rich colony in Africa, and Ethiopia was a logical choice. Control of Ethiopia gave Italy a foothold on the Red Sea.

expire. The third Neutrality Act (May 1937) extended indefinitely most features of the old law and added two new provisions. It made illegal the travel of Americans on belligerent ships, and it permitted warring nations to buy goods in the United States only if they paid cash on delivery and carried those goods away in their own ships. This "cash and carry" provision was limited to two years.

Critics argued that the neutrality laws abandoned American rights at sea and, by making no distinction between friend and foe, actually endangered the security of the United States. Yet the laws were accepted by most of the people. Isolationist America looked upon these laws as safeguards against involvement in a great war.

Challenging the Isolationists

On the night of July 7, 1937, while tensions in Europe were still high, Japanese and Chinese troops clashed southwest of Peiping (Peking). A few weeks later Japanese soldiers invaded China, and war began. Japan refused to declare war, however, and referred to the conflict as the "China incident."

President Roosevelt, like most Americans, favored the Chinese. He deliberately did not recognize a state of war in China. As a result, he did not have to invoke the neutrality law. Americans continued, legally, to ship arms and other supplies to China.

Alarmed by Japan's aggressions and by the Rome-Berlin Axis, Roosevelt wanted to make Americans aware of the dangerous world situation. In a speech in Chicago on October 5, 1937, he warned Americans that no nation, not even the United States, was immune from attack. None could escape "through mere isolation or neutrality." He urged an international "quarantine" of the disease of lawlessness.

Those who believed in collective security were pleased, for they thought Roosevelt had broken with the isolationists. But important newspaper editors, isolationist leaders, and many other Americans reacted to the speech with anger. Some of the President's closest advisers warned him that he had gone too far in challenging the isolationists. Roosevelt himself was so shocked by the strength of the isolationist response that he gave up the idea of the quarantine.

As the President had warned, Americans were not immune from attack. In December 1937, Japanese planes bombed and sank the American gunboat *Panay*, while it was escorting oil tankers on the Yangtze River in China. Two Americans were killed and thirty were wounded. The Japanese government quickly apologized and offered to pay for the damage inflicted. Even though the attack was deliberate, most Americans took the matter calmly, and another of the crises in Japanese-American relations soon passed.

Fear that the crisis might lead to war speeded up action in Congress on a proposed amendment to the Constitution sponsored by Louis Ludlow, a representative from Indiana. The Ludlow amendment would have required a nationwide vote before the United States could go to war—except in case of an invasion of the United States or its territorial possessions. The amendment had wide support. Only intense pressure from Roosevelt prevented Congress from adopting the proposal, which would have limited the power of the President and of Congress to decide foreign policy.

THE DECLINE OF ISOLATIONISM

It became increasingly difficult for Americans to isolate themselves from the events in Europe. In March 1938, Adolf Hitler ordered his Nazi troops into Austria and annexed that nation to Germany. No one tried to stop him, not even the Austrians.

Dazed victims of a Japanese attack view their burning homes in Chucheng, China, in 1939. Japan wanted to make China, Indochina, and the East Indies part of its "Greater East Asia Co-Prosperity Sphere."

PRESIDENTIAL ELECTIONS: 1936-1940

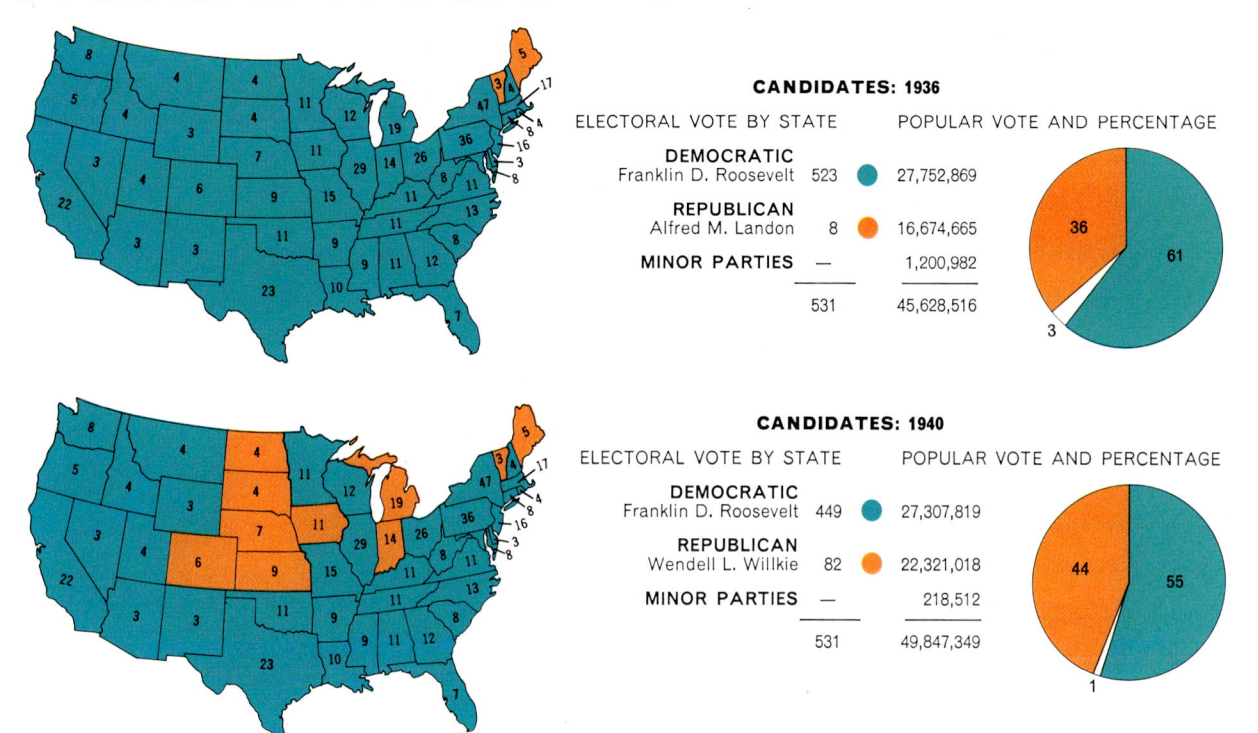

CANDIDATES: 1936

ELECTORAL VOTE BY STATE		POPULAR VOTE AND PERCENTAGE
DEMOCRATIC Franklin D. Roosevelt	523	27,752,869
REPUBLICAN Alfred M. Landon	8	16,674,665
MINOR PARTIES	—	1,200,982
	531	45,628,516

Democratic: 61 — Republican: 36 — Minor: 3

CANDIDATES: 1940

ELECTORAL VOTE BY STATE		POPULAR VOTE AND PERCENTAGE
DEMOCRATIC Franklin D. Roosevelt	449	27,307,819
REPUBLICAN Wendell L. Willkie	82	22,321,018
MINOR PARTIES	—	218,512
	531	49,847,349

Democratic: 55 — Republican: 44 — Minor: 1

The Munich Agreement

Hitler next threatened Czechoslovakia, saying that the Sudetenland, the western region of Czechoslovakia where some 3 million Germans lived, must become a part of Germany. The Czechs, who had defensive alliances with France and the Soviet Union, refused to give up the Sudetenland without a fight. Tension built up everywhere in Europe. In September 1938, Europe seemed ready to plunge into another great war.

Hitler delivered an ultimatum to the Czechs: They could either surrender to his demands or fight for the Sudetenland. Hitler finally agreed to a conference, held at Mu-

Eleanor Roosevelt shakes hands from the presidential train, 1935. Because the President was crippled, she made many fact-finding trips for him. The phrase "My Missus says" prefaced many of his comments.

nich on September 29 and 30, 1938. At that meeting Hitler, Mussolini, Prime Minister Neville Chamberlain of Britain, and Premier Edouard Daladier of France arranged the dismemberment of Czechoslovakia. The Sudetenland went to Germany, but Poland and Hungary also seized parts of the country. Hitler said that he had no further territorial ambitions in Europe. Although the western European democracies postponed war by appeasing Hitler, many of their leaders feared that they had not secured what Chamberlain called "peace in our time." They immediately accelerated their rearmament programs, for one reason they had allowed the dismemberment of Czechoslovakia was their lack of military might.

Most Americans thought the agreement at Munich meant peace. In November, Nazi brutality shattered the illusion. The Nazis, retaliating for the assassination of a German diplomat by a young Jew in Paris, attacked Jews throughout Germany and burned their homes, synagogues, and stores. Roosevelt was appalled; Americans were sickened. To indicate his strong disapproval, the President recalled the United States ambassador from Germany.

Europe at War

In October 1938, Roosevelt had announced that he was devoting a special sum of 300 million dollars to armaments. In his annual message to Congress, in January 1939, he clearly showed that he had given up any lingering attachment to isolationism. He told Congress that through "methods short of war" Americans might help in curbing the aggressors. He asked for repeal of the neutrality law so that American arms would be available to friendly nations.

The dictators proved that Roosevelt's fear was well founded. In March 1939, only six months after the Munich agreement, Hitler's troops invaded and overran what was left of Czechoslovakia. In April, Italy took over Albania. Next, Germany threatened Poland. Britain and France abandoned appeasement

American sailors prepare to abandon ship during the *Panay* incident. Their gunboat accompanied two Chinese oil tankers. Many of Japan's attacks were efforts to gain sources of crude oil, rubber, and scarce metal ores. *Opposite:* German troops battle snipers in Warsaw, September 1939. The Poles made a fruitless, last-ditch effort to ward off the Nazi invaders. Polish units outside the city rushed in to defend it, and civilians helped dig trenches and erect barriers.

and guaranteed Poland's boundaries.

Roosevelt denounced the dictators and refused to recognize their easy conquests. He asked the dictators to promise not to attack other nations. If they gave that pledge, he said, the United States would join other nations in efforts to ease international tensions. Hitler and Mussolini paid little attention to the President's appeal. On May 28, 1939, they concluded a military alliance. Roosevelt's diplomacy had accomplished nothing.

Meanwhile, Japan continued its assault on China and threatened French Indochina, the Philippines, and the Netherlands East Indies. Roosevelt had already registered his disapproval of Japan's actions by asking American manufacturers to place a voluntary embargo on war goods going to Japan. In July 1939, in response to pressure from Congress, he notified Japan that when its commercial treaty of 1911 with the United States expired in 1940, the United States would not renew it. This notice cleared the way for legal economic sanctions against Japan.

Roosevelt continued to ask Congress to repeal the neutrality law. Secretary of State Hull predicted war in Europe by the end of summer. He pleaded that France and Britain desperately needed supplies denied them by the law. But isolationist sentiment was still strong. Congress adjourned on August 4, 1939, without changing the neutrality law.

During this time the British and French were trying to persuade Joseph Stalin, the dictator of the Soviet Union, to join them in stopping Hitler. Stalin distrusted them because he feared they wanted Russia to take the full impact of a Nazi attack and because he had not been invited to the Munich conference. He wanted concessions from Poland that the French and British were unwilling to seek. On August 23, 1939, to the surprise of the world, Stalin concluded a non-aggression treaty with Nazi Germany. Hitler no longer had to fear a Soviet attack when he invaded Poland.

Hitler then demanded that Poland return territory that had once belonged to Germany. The Polish government refused and, on September 1, 1939, German soldiers smashed across the Polish frontier. Two days later, Britain and France declared war on Germany. World War II had begun.

The Revised Neutrality Act

Soon after the war broke out, President Roosevelt promised Americans that he would keep the United States out of the conflict. He then issued several proclamations of neutrality.

No one doubted the sentiments of the American people. Overwhelmingly, they blamed the Nazis for the war and wanted to see them defeated. But most Americans were also determined to stay out of the war.

Three weeks after Hitler attacked Poland, Congress was called into special session to consider Roosevelt's renewed request for a revision of the neutrality law. Isolationists put up a stiff resistance, but Roosevelt got what he wanted—a repeal of the embargo on arms. The new law, the Neutrality Act of November 1939, reestablished the "cash and carry" provision, which had expired under the old law. Now the Allies could at least buy American guns and other equipment, if they could carry away their own purchases.

Since this fourth neutrality act retained many parts of the old law, it still had some appeal for the isolationists. As one concession to the isolationists, the law designated certain areas as combat zones and prohibited American ships from going there. British and French ports were in the combat zones; the provision therefore assisted a German blockade of those ports.

This aspect of the law became clear after Germany crushed Poland in a *blitzkrieg,* a sudden, overpowering attack. After an almost immediate victory, Hitler divided Poland with Stalin, whose troops had moved in from the east. The Germans then began shifting their troops from Poland to confront the French and British in the west. During the winter of 1939/40, Germany tried to blockade Britain, which needed imports in order to survive. But goods from the United States in Allied ships were often blown up by German submarines and by mines planted in the entrances to British harbors.

Another attempt to protect and insulate the United States against the war came in September 1939. The first meeting of the Foreign Ministers of the American Republics, meeting in Panama, passed a resolution establishing sea safety zones for the Western Hemisphere. The Declaration of Panama said that the oceans south of Canada were off limits for fighting by the belligerent powers. This effort at insulation never worked, because the warring nations refused to accept the prohibition.

Violations of the neutrality zone by German and British warships disturbed many Americans late in 1939. They were even more disturbed by the Soviet Union's attack on Finland on November 30. The Finns put up a heroic resistance in the "winter war," but in March 1940 they were forced to surrender and meet Soviet demands. These demands included giving up some Finnish territory. Americans were able to give the Finns little more than sympathy.

Arming the United States

In April 1940, Nazi forces invaded Denmark and Norway and quickly occupied those nations. A month later German armored columns sliced into Belgium, the Netherlands, and Luxembourg, and then pierced France's defenses. Britain's new prime minister, Winston Churchill, and France's premier, Paul Reynaud, begged Roosevelt for help but, because of the neutrality law, the President could do little.

On June 10, 1940, Italy joined the war on Germany's side and invaded France from the south. Twelve days later, in the same rail-

Mothers opposed to the Lend-Lease bill *(below)* pray at the base of Capitol Hill in Washington, D.C. Many Americans feared that aid to Britain would pull the United States into the European war. The peacetime draft, approved in 1940, yielded many soldier trainees, but they lacked adequate equipment. Some had real guns *(above)*, but many were trained to fight using fake wooden guns.

road car in the Compiègne forest where Germany had agreed to the armistice in 1918, France signed an armistice with Hitler. Under the terms of the armistice, France north of the Loire River, as well as the entire Atlantic coast, would be occupied and administered by the Germans; the remainder, later called Vichy France, would have some self-government. The world was stunned by the tragic defeat of France and by the overwhelming victory of the Germans. Now only Britain stood between America and Hitler's well-armed troops.

During the blitzkrieg, Roosevelt had asked for huge appropriations to mechanize the army and to build a massive air force. Congress had responded quickly. After France fell, Roosevelt asked Congress for money to build a two-ocean navy, one that could meet both the Japanese and the German threats. Congress appropriated more than 5 billion dollars (4 billion dollars for the navy alone). Also in June, Roosevelt set up the National Defense Research Committee to work on new weapons. This group raced against time to build an atomic bomb, for members of the committee knew that the Germans were also trying to develop one.

In this same fateful June of 1940, a bill was introduced in Congress calling for compulsory military service. Despite bitter opposition from all over the nation, in September Congress passed the nation's first peacetime draft law.

The Roosevelt administration also took steps to defend the Western Hemisphere. In the second meeting of the Foreign Ministers of the American Republics, held in Havana in July, the United States agreed to cooperate with other nations in defending the hemisphere against outside attack.

In August 1940, Roosevelt met with the Canadian prime minister, William Mackenzie King, whose nation was already at war. The two leaders agreed to create the Permanent

The German-American Bund holds a rally in New York City on Germany Day in 1935. The Bund gained a reputation for being pro-Nazi.

Joint Board on Defense, which would coordinate defense efforts for the northern part of the Western Hemisphere.

Nonbelligerency

In dealing with crises in Japanese-American relations, Roosevelt had moved cautiously. When an old commercial treaty expired in January 1940, for instance, he did not impose economic sanctions on the Japanese. The United States needed time to build up its defenses. Then Hitler's smashing victories in Europe made the Japanese grow bolder. They stepped up their war in China and threatened British, French, and Dutch colonies in Asia.

In July 1940 Roosevelt ordered an embargo on airplane fuel and restrictions on the shipment of petroleum products and scrap metal. Japan protested because it needed these materials for its war effort. In August, Japanese troops advanced into French Indochina and took over some bases there. The United States responded in September with a complete embargo on the shipment of scrap iron and steel to Japan. The next day in Berlin, Japan's representative signed an alliance with Germany and Italy called the Tripartite Pact. The treaty was intended to keep the United States from stopping Japanese aggression. It pledged mutual political, economic, and military aid if the United States should attack any of the three nations signing the pact.

During this dangerous summer of 1940, the United States declared economic war against Germany and Italy, as well as against Japan. Public opinion polls showed that the American people approved these actions. Roosevelt switched from a policy of technical neutrality to one of *nonbelligerency;* that is, of helping friendly nations without actually declaring war. A powerful American pressure group, the Committee to Defend America by Aiding the Allies, helped make this view popular.

Winston Churchill hoped this policy would soon lead to United States intervention in the war on the side of Britain. Wave after wave of Nazi planes had been bombing British cities as a prelude to a German invasion of the British Isles.

In July 1940, Churchill made a desperate plea for some old American destroyers left over from World War I to replace British ships lost to Nazi planes. Roosevelt wanted to transfer the ships to Britain but doubted that he had the authority to do so. He was afraid that isolationists would block any move on his part to gain that authority from Congress. Finally, he by-passed Congress.

In September 1940, in exchange for eight air and naval bases on British possessions from Newfoundland to South America, Roosevelt transferred to the British fifty of the old destroyers—some of them barely seaworthy. He did this by executive agreement, so that he would not need the Senate's approval. In addition to the domestic problems involved, the destroyers-for-bases agreement violated international law and made the United States an ally of Britain.

Isolationists were so alarmed that the day after the President announced the destroyer deal they formed the America First Committee. It soon became the most powerful isolationist organization. But most Americans apparently approved of the agreement. Many believed it was possible to give Britain "all aid short of war" and still avoid direct involvement in the war.

TOTAL INVOLVEMENT

Roosevelt was so concerned over the course of the war that he had decided to challenge the tradition, set by George

Washington, that no person should serve more than two terms as President. He kept this decision to himself until after the Democratic convention had opened in July 1940. Then he was nominated by acclamation.

The battle for the Republican nomination was wide open. The Republicans finally decided on Wendell Willkie of Indiana, a political newcomer who, as the president of a utility company, had gained national attention fighting the Tennessee Valley Authority. Willkie favored aid to Britain.

Since both candidates were internationalists, isolationism was never a truly important issue in the campaign. But the campaign revealed a widespread fear that American entry into the war was imminent.

Willkie fought a tough campaign but failed to dislodge Roosevelt. The President had promised over and over again, "Your boys are not going to be sent into any foreign wars."

Lend-Lease

Well before the election results were in, it was obvious that Britain was almost bankrupt and nearly exhausted. After the election, Churchill asked Roosevelt for generous aid from the United States. The President was willing to give it. In December 1940, he told the people that the United States "must be the great arsenal of democracy" and give more help to Britain, even at the risk of war.

In working out a plan for large-scale aid, Roosevelt and his advisers wanted to prevent problems of postwar debt payments. They presented a plan, the Lend-Lease bill, to Congress in January 1941. This bill would permit the President to lend or lease arms and other goods to friends of the United States. After the war, in theory, the guns and tanks could be returned and no payment would be required.

Isolationist groups like the America First Committee did everything they could to de-

The battleship *West Virginia* goes up in flames during the Japanese attack on Pearl Harbor. The Tojo government gambled on destroying the bulk of the American fleet in the attack. Instead it won a stubborn opponent—the United States.

feat the measure, but they failed. It won approval in both houses of Congress and became law in March 1941. Lend-Lease allowed goods to go to any nation whose defense the President considered vital to the security of the United States. The program was another unofficial declaration of war against the Axis, and another link added to the unwritten alliance between the United States and Britain.

Before Lend-Lease could go into effect, hard-pressed Britain suffered further setbacks. Late in October 1940, Italian troops had invaded Greece but met humiliating defeats there as well as in North Africa against the British. Hitler came to the aid of his ally. In April 1941, German soldiers conquered Yugoslavia and Greece and mounted punishing attacks on British troops in North Africa.

At the same time, the Nazis stepped up their submarine attacks on British shipping in the Atlantic to break the flow of American supplies to Britain. The submarines attacked in swarms called "wolf packs" and sank ships much faster than the British could replace them. To help the British reduce their losses, Roosevelt ordered American naval vessels to help the British in antisubmarine patrols. This action led to clashes between United States destroyers and German submarines.

In April 1941, the President signed an agreement with Denmark. It temporarily placed Greenland, a Danish possession, under American control so that American ships could patrol the sea routes near there. Even though the Lend-Lease Act prohibited United States convoys, by the end of June 1941 the United States Navy was actively protecting the shipment of goods to Britain.

Undeclared Naval War

Roosevelt also took increasingly bold actions against the Japanese. Although he would not agree to an alliance with China and Britain to counterbalance the Tripartite Pact, he increased aid to China. The United States government applied economic sanctions against Japan bit by bit in the hope that the ever tightening restrictions would keep the Japanese from further expansion and yet not provoke immediate war. The government also built up defenses in the Philippines and Guam and made plans with the British and French for the defense of their colonial possessions in the Pacific.

Japan's leaders prepared for a showdown with the United States. In April 1941, Japan signed a neutrality treaty with the Soviet Union, thus protecting its northern frontiers in case of war with the United States and Britain. At the same time the Japanese ambassador in Washington, D.C., Kichisaburo Nomura, met with Secretary of State Hull in an apparent effort to avoid war.

These talks went on for months; by June 1941, they were stalemated. Basically, the United States wanted Japan to get out of China and to promise not to attack lands in the Southwest Pacific, such as the Netherlands East Indies. Japan wanted the United

States to end its economic sanctions and to recognize Japan's conquest in China.

At this point, a startling event changed the course of the war in Europe. On June 22, 1941, Hitler sent his armored columns roaring into the vast plains of the Soviet Union. Now that the scene of battle had shifted, American leaders no longer feared the immediate collapse of Britain from a Nazi assault. However, the Nazi invasion also increased the possibility of a Japanese attack against lands in the Southwest Pacific. The Japanese now were certain that the Soviet Union was too busy to threaten Japan from the north.

Roosevelt sent aid and lend-lease supplies to the Russians, who were putting up a stiff resistance against the Nazi invaders. In July 1941, United States troops were sent to Iceland. As a result, the United States Navy could protect British and American ships more than halfway across the sea.

In August, Prime Minister Churchill met secretly with Roosevelt on a warship off Newfoundland. There the two men arranged a convoy system for British and United States ships in the North Atlantic. They also issued a declaration of principles called the Atlantic Charter, which stated that both nations were opposed to aggression and would work for a better postwar world.

Roosevelt had to find some way to tell the people about the decision to use American ships to escort the convoys. His opportunity came on September 4, 1941, when a harassed German submarine fired on a United States destroyer, the *Greer,* near Iceland. On September 11, Roosevelt announced that he had ordered ships of the United States Navy to shoot on sight Axis ships that were operating in American "defensive areas."

In October, United States warships and Nazi submarines exchanged fire, and the shooting war began. In November 1941, Congress repealed, by a slim margin, the ineffective neutrality law. Armed United States merchant ships could now deliver guns and planes right to British and Soviet ports. The United States had entered a state of undeclared naval war in the Atlantic.

Pearl Harbor

After the Nazi invasion of the Soviet Union, Japan's militarists decided that the time had come to expand into the Southwest Pacific. Roosevelt and a few of his closest advisers were aware of this decision because American cryptographers had broken Japan's secret diplomatic code.

In July 1941, Japan demanded that France allow it to occupy southern French Indochina. Helpless, France's government at Vichy gave in. Next, Japan threatened the Netherlands East Indies, British Malaya, and the Philippines. Roosevelt, supported by the Netherlands and Britain, retaliated with drastic economic sanctions.

Japan was now cut off from oil and other supplies that it needed for its war machine. It had on reserve only a twelve to eighteen months' supply of oil for wartime use. Japan's leaders had to decide whether to stop their expansion now or to conquer lands that held the materials they needed.

In October, General Hideki Tojo became prime minister. Tojo and his advisers agreed that if the United States would not come to terms and lift the embargo within several weeks they would declare war. To stress the urgency of the crisis, Tojo sent a troubleshooter, Saburo Kurusu, to take part in the Hull-Nomura talks. At the same time Tojo's government made plans for an attack on American and British bases. American cryptographers learned of the Japanese plans but did not find out which bases would be the targets.

In Washington, D.C., the negotiators got nowhere. Step by step the Japanese war plan went into action. A group of aircraft carriers left the fog-enshrouded Kurile Islands and approached Hawaii undetected, as planes zoomed from carrier decks. Then, on Sunday morning, December 7, 1941, the first wave of Japanese bombers appeared over the United States fleet at Pearl Harbor and dropped their bombs; other waves quickly followed. The attack was a complete surprise. More than 2,400 servicemen were killed, practically every plane on the island of Oahu was destroyed, and six battleships—the heart of the American fleet—were sunk or disabled. Fortunately, three aircraft carriers outside the harbor were safe.

Japan also attacked the Philippines, Thailand, British Malaya, and other places. After its sneak attack, it declared war on the United States. The next day, Congress declared war against Japan. On December 11, Germany and Italy declared war on the United States. The attack on Pearl Harbor ended the great debate over isolationism and internationalism. It united Americans as they had never before been united.

A Look at Specifics

1. In what ways did Roosevelt intervene in the affairs of Cuba?
2. How did Roosevelt attempt to gain the good will of Mexico?
3. Why did many Americans believe the Philippines should be independent?
4. Why did many people charge that the United States neutrality laws aided Fascists in the Ethiopian and Spanish wars?
5. What methods did the United States use after July 1940 in an attempt to stop Japanese expansion?

A Review of Major Ideas

1. How did the United States use diplomatic means to increase its foreign trade?
2. How did the aftermath of World War I influence American attitudes toward foreign policy and international cooperation?
3. Between 1933 and 1939, how did the United States try to use legislation to keep itself out of foreign wars?
4. After the war broke out in Europe, what steps did the United States take to build up its defenses?
5. Before its entry into the war, how did the United States aid the British and the Soviet Union?
6. In what ways did Roosevelt by-pass Congress in order to aid the British?
7. What issues led to the involvement of the United States in a war with Germany? With Japan?

For Independent Study

1. How did Asian nations respond to the "Japanese Monroe Doctrine"? Was their response similar to that of Latin American nations to Monroe's announcement? Does any country have the right to say that an area outside its territory is off limits to the rest of the world?
2. Should an amendment be passed similar to the Ludlow amendment requiring a national referendum for a declaration of war except in time of invasion?
3. By placing an embargo on oil and metal exports to Japan, the United States placed Japan in the position of having to choose between abandoning the conquest of China and Southeast Asia or attempting a quick victory before its war supplies were depleted. Should the United States have compromised to avoid war?

Unit Review
Examining the Times

1. Compare the federal government's domestic and foreign policies of the 1930's with the policies of the 1920's.
2. What trends were evident in population distribution, industrial growth, literature, and mass communications during the 1920's and 1930's?

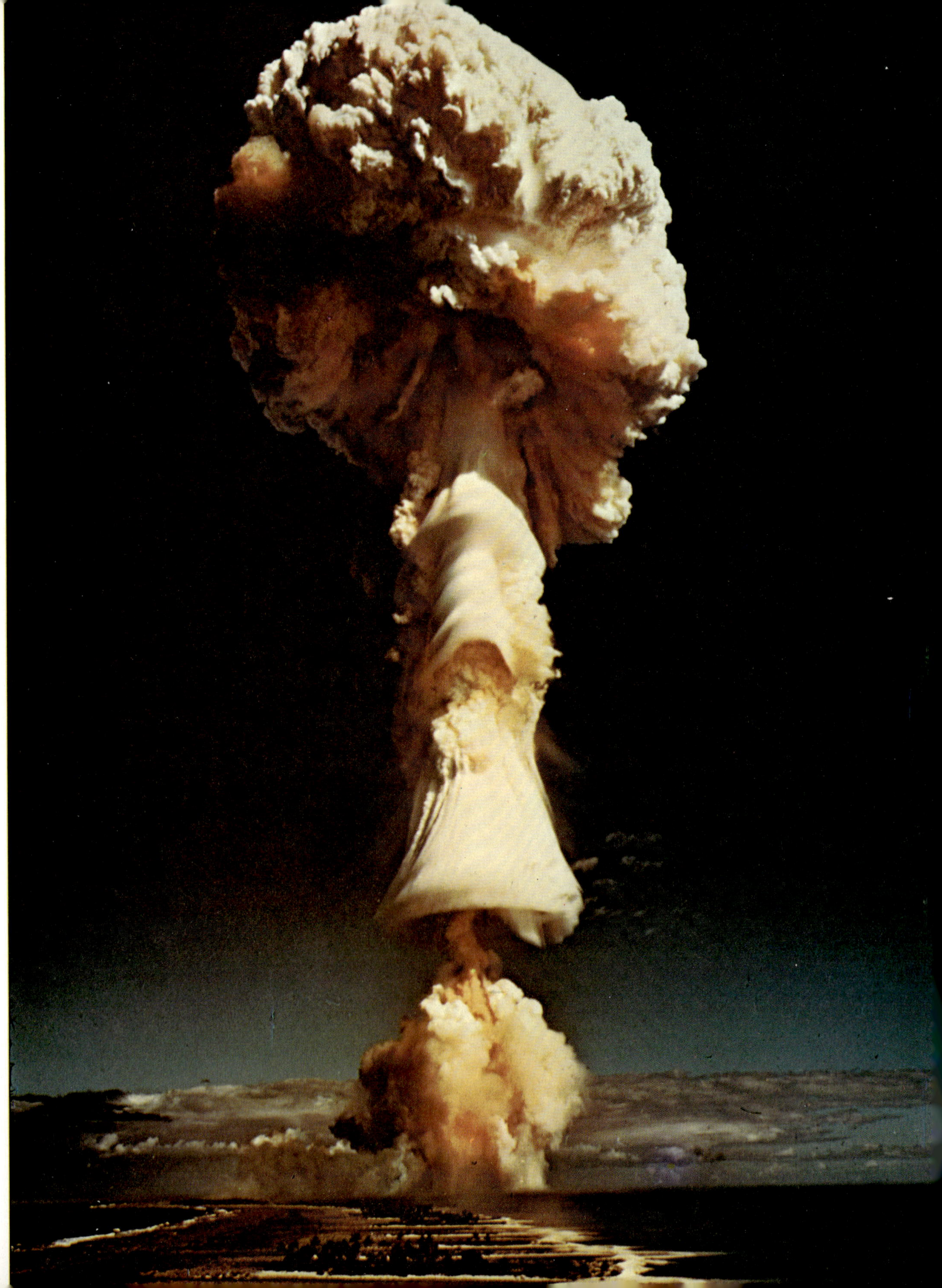

UNIT EIGHT   1941–1960

Hot and Cold Wars

On August 6, 1945, an American airplane dropped a single atomic bomb on Hiroshima, a city in central Japan. The bomb killed 250,000 persons and flattened 7 square miles of the city. Three days later another American plane dropped an atomic bomb on Nagasaki, one of Japan's important industrial cities. It caused similar devastation.

The world was stunned by these bombings. Except for a handful of scientists and high officials, no one had known it was possible to set off explosions of such power. The bombs were so effective and so destructive that almost immediately they revolutionized the thinking of military leaders on the nature of war. They had a similar effect on diplomats. Meanwhile, Japan surrendered, thus ending World War II.

Sole possession of the secret of making atomic bombs gave the United States a unique position in the postwar world. The United States used its possession of atomic secrets to awe its enemies and thereby protect its friends.

The period of America's monopoly lasted only four years. In September 1949, the Soviet Union exploded an atomic bomb. Now the attitude of the United States toward the U.S.S.R. changed. The United States began a race to build up a bigger stockpile of armaments—especially nuclear arms—than the Soviet Union. American leaders decided to work at full speed to develop a thermonuclear superbomb, or hydrogen bomb. After overcoming a number of obstacles, scientists developed such a weapon.

The first test of the hydrogen bomb took place on November 1, 1952, on a tiny coral spit in the Pacific Ocean. When the device was detonated, a bluish-white fireball lit up hundreds of miles of sky. The fireball itself was more than 3 miles in diameter. The bomb completely destroyed its target. All that remained was a cavity in the coral 1 mile wide and 175 feet deep.

The bomb used in this thermonuclear explosion was too big and bulky for military use. Early in 1954, American scientists produced a hydrogen bomb suitable for military use. Meanwhile, in August 1953, the Soviets had exploded their first hydrogen device. Now the United States and the Soviet Union stepped up the arms race.

The hydrogen bomb was as revolutionary in its impact on foreign relations as were the first atomic bombs. The difference in explosive power between a hydrogen bomb and an atomic bomb was about as great as that between an atomic bomb and a TNT "blockbuster" of World War II. Since the destructive force of the new thermonuclear weapons was discussed everywhere—in books, newspapers, magazines, and on television—many people knew that one superbomb was capable of destroying any large city in the world.

People now talked about war being outmoded. The superbombs, some said, were not truly weapons of war. They were instruments of terror, psychological weapons that could be used to terrorize whole populations.

The attitude of fright increased in many parts of the world after October 1957, when the Soviets flung *Sputnik I,* the world's first space satellite, into orbit. A rocket capable of putting *Sputnik* into orbit could carry a nuclear warhead 5,000 miles in about half an hour and deliver it to almost any place on the globe. Before this time the United States, as well as most of its allies, had been reasonably free from fear of sudden Soviet nuclear attack. Their sense of security shrank with the knowledge that the Soviets had a lead in long-range ballistic missiles.

People everywhere were horrified by the idea of a nuclear war. Even professional soldiers like General Douglas MacArthur insisted, "Global war . . . contains now only the germs of double suicide." But some other people maintained that after a nuclear war there would be survivors who would rebuild from the ruins of war as people always had done. Regardless of these differences, it was obvious that thermonuclear war would cripple civilization so badly that such a war would be folly.

Despite their horror of nuclear war, political leaders failed to provide ways to control the use of thermonuclear weapons. Yet in the fifteen years after the Hiroshima explosion it became clear that nuclear weapons had limitations as instruments of diplomacy. Unless willing to defy the feelings of the rest of the world, neither the United States nor the Soviet Union dared use its nuclear weapons in offensive war. Even if one nation threatened to use these weapons, it probably had to claim it was keeping an enemy from acting. In theory, a nation could not seek to destroy an opponent with atomic fire.

The power struggle between the United States and the Soviet Union, which came to be called the Cold War, affected the political makeup of the postwar world. At the end of World War II, the Soviet army occupied countries of eastern Europe. The Soviets set up Communist dictatorships in Poland, Bulgaria, Romania, Hungary, and Czechoslovakia. Although these countries were technically independent, the dictators of each had to answer to Stalin for any action taken. Only one Communist country, Yugoslavia, succeeded in remaining free of Moscow's control.

Most of the nations of western Europe were on the side of the United States in the Cold War. Defeated Germany was divided into two parts: West Germany, with a democratic government, and East Germany, with a Communist government. West Germany recovered rapidly from the war to become the most prosperous nation in Europe.

The great empires that France and Britain had built were almost totally dismembered after the war, and independent nations were created out of former colonies. Many of the new nations tried to avoid involvement in big-power politics by following a policy of neutralism or nonalignment.

As the developed nations made advances in science and technology, the economic gap between them and other, less developed nations widened. The developed nations sent aid in the form of money, machinery, and technical know-how to less developed nations. Even this aid became a part of the competition between the superpowers.

In 1945, the British agreed to give India full independence. Because of open hostility between Hindus and Muslims, however, former British India was partitioned in 1947 into two separate nations: India, which was mostly Hindu, and Pakistan, which was mainly Muslim. Partition did not end conflict between the two; they later fought several small wars.

Independence also came to several nations of Southeast Asia, including Burma, Cambodia, Indonesia, Laos, Malaysia, the Philippines, and Vietnam, all of which had been conquered by the Japanese during the war. When the Japanese surrendered, local leaders took control and proclaimed the independence of their nations.

The French tried to regain control of its former colony in Indochina and the Dutch tried to regain Indonesia, but armed conflict broke out. After nine years of fighting in Indochina, the French surrendered. The Dutch granted independence to Indonesia after four years of fighting.

In the Middle East, several new Arab states, including Syria, Lebanon, Iraq, and Jordan, won their independence during or after the war. From a large part of the British mandate of Palestine, the Jewish state of Israel was created. The refusal of Arab nations to recognize this new state led to armed conflict between Israelis and Arabs.

In East Asia, great changes shook China. The Chinese Nationalists and the Chinese Communists, who had joined forces to defeat Japan, resumed their civil war in 1945. The Communists emerged victorious and took over mainland China. In 1949, they set up the People's Republic of China, a totalitarian dictatorship led by Mao Tse-tung. Chiang Kai-shek and his Nationalist forces fled to the island of Taiwan, where they set up the Republic of China.

Defeated Japan, with American aid and guidance, changed from a militarist state to become the leading democratic country in East Asia. Manufacturing increased tremendously and the standard of living of the Japanese people rose steadily.

In Latin America, most of the nations made little progress in solving their social and economic problems. Changes in governments, often called "revolutions," were frequent. In these revolts, one military group usually would wrest control of the government from another military group without bringing needed reforms to the country.

Two exceptions to this pattern came in Mexico and Cuba. Mexico's 1910 revolution had led to major reforms in the country. Improvements in agriculture and advances in industry continued to raise the standard of living of the Mexican people.

In Cuba, a revolution in 1958 led to the establishment of a Communist dictatorship under the leadership of Fidel Castro. The presence of a Communist dictatorship so close to its borders created new problems for the United States. However, to many of the peoples of Latin America, Castro's regime posed as a model that other countries might seek to follow.

The Global War

CHAPTER 24
1941–1945

American tanks roll through Sicily, July 1943.

The Japanese raid on Pearl Harbor ended the bitter debate in the United States over foreign policy. With that attack on an American possession, World War II ceased to be a foreign war. Americans now had to fight to defend themselves, and they were united as never before.

The Axis powers seemed to be close to victory when the United States became a full belligerent. German armies were deep inside the Soviet Union. German submarines were sinking ships and cutting off supplies bound for Britain. Soon the Japanese were to overrun Dutch, British, and American territories in Asia and the Pacific.

Yet the outlook for those who were resisting the Axis powers was far from hopeless. The United States already had the beginnings of a large army as a result of the peacetime draft. It had industries and resources far greater than those available to the Axis. What the United States needed was time to develop its full war-making capacity.

MOBILIZING THE HOME FRONT

Modern warfare requires that a nation concentrate much of its industrial resources, workers, and scientific knowledge on defeating the enemy. Hence, during World War II the government had to take on broad powers affecting the lives of all Americans.

Few Americans actively opposed the war. The people of the United States assumed that they were fighting for survival. War was a grim but necessary business, and they wanted to end it as quickly as possible.

Industry

Industry had begun shifting from the production of civilian goods to the making of war materials in 1940, after the fall of France. In January 1942, President Roosevelt created the War Production Board and gave it authority to control industrial production.

American industry responded with remarkable results. For example, in 1940 Roosevelt had asked for 50,000 new planes a year, a demand that critics believed was impossible. In 1942, American factories turned out 47,000 planes, and in 1944, more than 96,000. Similar results were achieved in the manufacture of other war materials.

Despite the great demands of the war, civilians did not suffer any serious shortages in essential goods. Two-thirds of American industry continued to turn out goods for the civilian market.

All during the war, the United States functioned as a supply base for its allies. Without American trucks and tanks, for example, the Soviets probably could not have launched their successful offensives against the Germans. By the beginning of 1944, the output of American factories amounted to more than twice that of all the Axis nations.

The Work Force

Workers as well as machines made possible the miracle of wartime production. The armed forces had first choice of workers. Altogether, the fighting services enrolled 15 million men and 200,000 women. Men between the ages of 18 and 38 were subject to the draft. Women served voluntarily, working as nurses, air-traffic controllers, and mechanics, and in other noncombatant jobs. From 1940 to 1945, the civilian work force expanded from 46.5 million to 53 million persons. Many of the additional workers were women, elderly people, or very young people. Many defense plants encouraged the mothers of small children to take jobs by providing day-care centers where their children could be kept.

In April 1942, the government set up the War Manpower Commission to assure the best use of all workers. The commission could shift workers, on a voluntary basis, into areas with shortages or critical needs.

Labor unions cooperated faithfully in the war effort. In December 1941, the major unions pledged themselves not to strike during the war. The following month, the government set up the National War Labor Board. The NWLB ultimately had the power to set wages and hours for workers and to name the conditions for maintaining union membership.

Most union leaders kept the no-strike pledge, but as prices and profits rose, some strikes took place. Though strikes were usually brief, they were well publicized and widely criticized. The action of the United Mine Workers, led by John L. Lewis, particularly upset many Americans. In May 1943, when the mine operators refused to grant a wage increase, the miners went on strike. The following month, Congress passed the Smith-Connally Anti-Strike Act. Enacted over the President's veto, this law required unions to give thirty days' notice before striking. It also permitted the President to seize plants threatened by strikes.

Strikes affected only one-ninth of 1 percent of labor's working time during the war. Union membership increased from 10.5 million workers in 1942 to nearly 15 million employees in 1945.

More than a million black people migrated from the South to industrial areas in search of jobs. They continued to suffer from various kinds of discrimination, but they found work. In June 1941, President Roosevelt forbade, by executive order, racial discrimination in hiring and firing in plants with government contracts. The order set up the Fair Employment Practices Committee (FEPC) to investigate charges of racial discrimination.

Farmers enjoyed great wartime prosperity. From 1940 to 1945, farm prices doubled, and they would have gone higher if Roosevelt had not acted to stabilize them. Net cash income of farmers increased fourfold during World War II.

During the war, farm population dropped 17 percent, but each worker's output almost doubled. This increase resulted from greater use of machinery and from better fertilizers. American farms met the food needs of the armed forces, the domestic market, and many civilians in liberated areas overseas.

Curbing Inflation

Prosperity combined with a decrease in consumer goods produced inflation. Americans had plenty of money available for spending, but sellers had few goods for sale. As a result, the prices of available goods went up. The government wanted to control inflation, which could increase the cost of the war and cause discontent at home.

In January 1942, Congress passed the Emergency Price Control Act. This law made the Office of Price Administration (OPA) responsible for curbing inflation. When the OPA failed in this job, Congress passed an anti-inflation law that froze wages, rents, and food prices.

Another attack on inflation was the rationing of scarce goods. The government limited the purchase of automobile tires, gasoline, meat, canned food, sugar, coffee, butter, shoes, and other items. People could buy these things if they had stamps for them from ration books issued by the government. Some people cheated by going to "black markets," where goods were sold illegally at high prices. However, the economic controls of World War II assured most Americans a fairer share of available goods than had the less controlled economy of World War I.

The government sold war bonds and imposed new and higher taxes, both to fight inflation and to pay for the war. Everyone, from the factory worker to the millionaire, was encouraged to buy bonds. Eight war-bond drives brought more than 100 billion dollars into the treasury.

The government raised even more money through taxes, which were increased to drain off some of the people's buying power. As a result of the Revenue Act of October 1942, the income tax became a "mass tax." Millions of Americans who had never before filed an income tax return now had to do so. Some had incomes as low as $625 a year. To make collections simple and easy, Congress, in June 1943, passed a payroll deduction law that provided for the withholding of money for taxes when it was earned.

Restricting Civil Liberties

Violations of free speech and personal liberty were relatively few. Organized hate campaigns against Germans and Italians were rare. But an important exception to the government's good record on civil liberties was its treatment of Japanese Americans on the West Coast. In February 1942, Roosevelt authorized the army to exclude all persons of Japanese ancestry from "military areas" on the West Coast. Of the 112,000 persons affected by the order, 70,000 were American citizens born in the United States.

Later, the commanding general on the West Coast ordered the Japanese Americans to special camps surrounded by barbed wire and guarded by soldiers. Beginning in July 1942 some of the *Nisei,* citizens born in the United States of Japanese parents, were allowed to leave the camps to attend college, harvest crops, resettle in the Middle West, or volunteer for duty with the army. All first had to be cleared as loyal by the Federal Bureau of Investigation.

In December 1944, the Supreme Court ruled on two cases questioning the constitutionality of the evacuation. In one case, the Court said that the government's action was constitutional because it was prompted by "military necessity." In the other case, announced the same day, the Court said that the government could not keep a loyal citizen from returning to his or her home.

A Study in Hysteria

Anti-Japanese prejudice was nothing new in the United States. Immigrants from Japan (called *Issei*), unlike those from Europe, had never been allowed to become United States citizens. Their children, called *Nisei,* were citizens by birth.

The bombing of Pearl Harbor was followed by a period of anti-Japanese hysteria fostered in great measure by false rumors. Some newspapers on the West Coast hinted that Japanese Americans had helped the attackers. A wide range of groups in California—including farm, labor, veterans, fraternal, and political organizations—as well as major politicians, supported efforts to remove Japanese Americans from the West Coast. The opposition to removal was limited. The American Civil Liberties Union and Quaker groups were among the few working to oppose removal.

The Japanese Americans were first taken to assembly centers made from existing facilities, such as race track stables. They were later removed to eight camps in semidesert areas in the West and to two camps in Arkansas. They lived in tarpaper-covered barracks in which each family had a small room with thin walls.

The Japanese Americans in Hawaii did not suffer the same fate as mainlanders. Even though they lived in a more strategic area, they were allowed to stay in their homes and jobs.

As time passed, the falsity of the rumors became apparent. A year after the attack on Pearl Harbor, Bill Henry, a columnist for the *Los Angeles Times,* wrote: "The FBI chief says the yarns about the dead Jap flyers with McKinley High School (Honolulu) rings on their fingers, the stories of the arrows in the cane fields pointing toward Pearl Harbor, and the yarns about Jap vegetable trucks blocking the roadway to Pearl Harbor that day are all unadulterated hooey." Throughout the war, not one Japanese American was charged with committing a disloyal act.

In 1943 the army formed a segregated unit composed of Japanese American soldiers. The 442nd Regimental Combat Team fought in Italy, France, and Germany and won more decorations for bravery than any other American unit.

Military police load Japanese American evacuees onto buses in San Francisco.

The war did not stop some Americans from expressing their other traditional prejudices. The summer of 1943 brought riots directed against Mexican Americans in Los Angeles, other parts of the Southwest, and Chicago. Riots involving blacks and whites broke out in Detroit, New York, and other major cities. Although the rioting was sparked by various minor incidents, its root cause lay in resentment and frustration over social changes brought by the war.

Developing New Weapons

Like workers, farmers, and business people, scientists contributed their skills to the struggle against the Axis powers. Although the influence of science had grown greatly in the 1930's, the United States government had not done much to adapt scientific research to military uses. Germany, on the other hand, was using its scientists to produce new and powerful weapons.

Fear of German scientific developments led President Roosevelt to set up, in June 1941, the Office of Scientific Research and Development. This office organized scientists to develop and perfect weapons and supplies needed to win the war.

Allied scientists forged ahead in the use of an electronic instrument called "radar." This invention, perfected and put into use by the British, detected airplanes and ships by means of a radio beam. Radar could also guide shells against enemy craft.

The most devastating weapon of all was the atomic bomb. A major step in its creation came on December 2, 1942, when Enrico Fermi and other physicists working in Chicago achieved the first self-sustaining nuclear chain reaction. Under the direction of Dr. J. Robert Oppenheimer, other scientists at Los Alamos, New Mexico, harnessed the power of a chain reaction and built a bomb. At 5:30 A.M. on July 16, 1945, the world's first atomic bomb was detonated near Alamogordo, New Mexico. As Oppenheimer witnessed the blinding explosion and swelling poisonous cloud that spread over earth and sky, words from a sacred Hindu text flashed through his mind: "I am become Death, destroyer of the worlds." A new era of atomic wonders—and fears—had begun.

"Rosie the Riveter" was a symbol of American women during the war. Large numbers of women took jobs in defense plants, and many joined the military services.

EUROPE FIRST

As soon as the United States had declared war against the Axis powers, Britain's prime minister, Winston Churchill, crossed the Atlantic to talk to President Roosevelt about worldwide military strategy. Churchill knew that his exhausted nation could not continue alone the fight against the Nazis. Yet he feared that the sneak attack on Pearl Harbor might cause Americans to concentrate on the destruction of Japan rather than of Germany.

Roosevelt and his closest advisers agreed, however, that Germany was the more dangerous foe. Hitler controlled more people and greater resources than Japan, and Germany had a headstart on work to develop atomic bombs and guided missiles.

Roosevelt and Churchill decided to concentrate on defeating Germany first. They would give China only limited help and would try to keep the Japanese from advancing further rather than attempt to push them back. The Americans and British would pour most of their troops, guns, planes, and tanks into the European theater of war.

Submarine and Air Attacks

To defeat Germany, the United States had to get its guns, planes, and soldiers across the Atlantic. Hitler was determined to prevent that. Soon after the United States entered the war, Germany shifted its submarines across the Atlantic. Packs of these "U-boats" began sinking American and British merchant ships within sight of the American shore.

Allied shipping losses were staggering. During the first ten months of 1942, the Allies lost more than five hundred ships to submarines. Slowly, the United States Navy, cooperating with the British, was able to curb the submarine threat. The navy used a host of small ships, some of them converted yachts, to escort convoys along the coast. Radar and the sounding device called "sonar" proved especially effective in detecting submarines.

By the spring of 1943, the United States and British navies were destroying German submarines in large numbers. Allied shipyards were turning out merchant ships faster than they were being sunk. Convoys brought supplies and troops to Britain to prepare for an attack on the European continent.

The United States Army Air Force joined the British in August 1942 in the attempt to destroy German industrial might. The British bombed German cities at night; the Americans dropped bombs during the day.

Although these great air strikes did not destroy the German war machine, the constant bombing did lower German morale. In addition, the Allies eliminated the German *Luftwaffe* (air force) as an effective opponent and gained command of the skies over Europe. Without such control, no land assault on the continent could succeed.

Allied Invasions

In 1942 Stalin pleaded with the western Allies to invade Europe and lessen the pressure of German armies on the Russian front.

World War II

EUROPEAN THEATER, 1939-1942

September 1–27, 1939 Invasion of Poland. Axis victory. Germany's takeover of Poland began the war. As Warsaw fell, organized Polish resistance ended.

April 9–June 10, 1940 Invasion of Denmark and Norway. Axis victories. Denmark did not formally resist German troops. Official Norwegian resistance ended April 30, but some fighting continued until June 10.

May 10–June 4, 1940 Invasion of Belgium, Netherlands, and Luxembourg. Axis victories. The Germans occupied Luxembourg (May 10), the Netherlands fell (May 14), and Belgian resistance ended (May 26). British and French troops had rushed to the aid of Belgium. Trapped, the Anglo-French troops were evacuated from Dunkirk (May 28–June 4) with the help of an armada of small boats from England.

June 5–22, 1940 Fall of France. Axis victory. The Germans by-passed the Maginot Line fortifications (June 5). Italy joined in the attack (June 10). The Germans took Paris (June 14) and France fell (June 22). A puppet French government was set up in Vichy. The Free French organized in London.

August 8–October 31, 1940 Battle of Britain. Allied victory. German planes began bombing raids on British cities. The British won control in the skies; the Germans abandoned plans to invade Britain.

November 20, 1940–March 1, 1941 More nations joined the Axis: Hungary, Nov. 20; Romania, Nov. 23 (occupied by the Germans Oct. 8); and Bulgaria, March 1.

April 6–27, 1941 Invasion of Yugoslavia and Greece. Axis victories. Yugoslavia gave up April 17. Greece signed an armistice April 23. Underground movements formed to fight the German occupation.

June 22, 1941–September 14, 1942 Soviet Union campaign. Axis victories. The Germans attacked along an 1,800-mile front from the Baltic to the Black seas. In 1941, the Germans captured Riga (July 2), Kiev (Sept. 19), Odessa (Oct. 16), and Rostov (Nov. 22). Sieges began in Leningrad (Sept. 4), Moscow (late October), and Sevastopol (Nov. 15). The Soviets began a counteroffensive in the winter of 1941/42, but the Germans continued their advance the following summer. Sevastopol was taken (July 2, 1942). By Sept. 14, the Germans had begun to enter Stalingrad.

May 27–October 23, 1942 North African campaign. Since 1940, in battles between the British and Axis forces, cities like Bengasi and Tobruk had been taken and retaken by each side. The Germans began a new offensive in May 1942. They captured Tobruk (June 21) but were stopped near El Alamein. On Oct. 23, the British began a drive to regain lost territory.

November 8–13, 1942 Invasion of North Africa. Allied victory. American and British troops landed near Casablanca, Oran, and Algiers. The Vichy French in North Africa signed an armistice (Nov. 13).

But the American and British leaders felt that their forces were not yet strong enough. They decided instead to launch their first great offensive in a weakly protected region—French North Africa. The Vichy government of France held that area.

A fleet of more than eight hundred ships converged on the African shore on November 8, 1942. American and British soldiers splashed through the surf at Casablanca, Oran, and Algiers. They were under the overall command of the American general, Dwight D. Eisenhower. French resistance was slight, but the Germans reacted swiftly. They ferried troops to Tunisia from Sicily and flew others in from bases in Italy and France. These soldiers joined German and Italian armored forces in the *Afrika Korps*, led by the German field marshal, Erwin Rommel. His troops inflicted heavy losses on the inexperienced Americans.

For a while the battle of North Africa moved back and forth across the desert. Then, in May 1943, the battered Axis forces surrendered. In the campaign, the Axis powers lost 250,000 troops, valuable equipment, a foothold in Africa, and control of the Mediterranean.

The lengthy fighting in Africa had made an invasion of France in 1943 impossible, and so the Allies decided to strike at Sicily. On July 10, 1943, American and British forces swarmed over Sicily's beaches. They met only slight opposition from the Italians. German troops put up stiff rear-guard resistance, but after thirty-eight days of hard fighting, the Allies controlled the island.

The conquest of Sicily led to a crisis in the Italian government. King Victor Emmanuel III and some of his political advisers decided that the war was lost and that they must get rid of Mussolini. Mussolini appealed to Hitler for help against the Allies, but the German Führer offered little more than advice. The king overthrew Mussolini. The new government, headed by Marshal Pietro Badoglio, immediately sued for peace. Italy signed the document of unconditional surrender on September 3, 1943, and joined the fighting on the Allied side.

The surrender did not give the Allies control of Italy. Aware of the surrender maneuvers, the Nazis had swiftly moved troops into northern and central Italy. The British invaded the Italian peninsula from Sicily, and British and American troops struck at Salerno, south of Naples.

Allied leaders had assumed they could conquer Italy without great difficulty, but the country's hills and mountains gave the advantage to the defenders. With relatively few divisions, the Germans held back the American and British armies. The Allied forces did not enter Rome until June 4, 1944. Even then northern Italy was yet to be conquered.

Slogging to Victory

While weary American and British soldiers were marching toward Rome, the Allies brought together millions of troops and supplies in Britain for a direct assault on France. For six weeks in the spring of 1944, American and British bombers pounded airplane factories, oil refineries, bridges, roads, and railroads in France, Germany, and other Nazi-held areas.

The night of June 5, 1944, more than 100 gliders and 900 airplanes began leaving British airfields. Soon after they crossed the English Channel, they dropped thousands of troops behind the German lines in France. As dawn broke, the American and British air forces pounded the German defenses with thousands of tons of bombs. Shortly after dawn, a great armada, guarded by an umbrella of airplanes, moved across the English Channel. It deposited some 120,000 Allied soldiers on a sixty-mile strip of beach on the Normandy coast of France.

Allied forces ran into underwater obstacles, mines, barbed wire, deadly crossfire from pillboxes, tank traps, and shelling from protected German artillery. Slowly, the Allied soldiers overcame this opposition and built up their beachheads. After seven weeks of hard fighting along the beach areas, an American army broke through the German defenses around Saint-Lô, a transportation center that opened roads into the heart of France.

On August 15, 1944, an American army and a French army landed on the southern coast of France between Nice and Marseilles. This operation opened new lines of supply for the Allied forces. Ten days later, Paris fell to the Allies. By October, the Germans had been swept out of France.

On the eastern front, the Nazis were suffering even greater losses. After a great counteroffensive in 1943, which destroyed a German army at Stalingrad, the Soviet army had started moving west.

Throughout Europe the Allies were aided by resistance movements in the Nazi-held countries. The *Maquis* in France, the guerrillas in Poland, the *Chetniks* and partisans in Yugoslavia, the *Andartes* in Greece, the underground in Italy, Norway, Denmark, Belgium, Holland—all worked in secret to end Nazi rule. Despite the risk of torture and death should the Gestapo catch them, members of the resistance movements sabotaged industry, killed Nazi soldiers, hid Allied fliers, smuggled Jews to safe countries, and spread news of Allied victories.

With its armies falling back in both the east and the west, Germany's situation by 1944 seemed hopeless. Some of the German generals wanted to negotiate peace, but first they would have to overthrow Hitler, who insisted that the fighting go on. Hitler not only survived their attempt to kill him in July 1944 but also destroyed the generals involved in the plot against him.

In December 1944, the Allied advance in the west stalled. Hitler made a desperate gamble. At the front near Belgium and Luxembourg, where American troops were thinly spread, he began a counteroffensive designed to split the Allied armies. Nazi tanks broke through the defenses and created a "bulge" fifty miles deep in the Allied lines. It seemed for a while as if German armor might slice through to the center of France. Finally, American paratroopers at Bastogne stopped this last Nazi offensive.

In March 1945, the Americans captured a bridge across the Rhine River at Remagen. American troops quickly crossed the bridge into Germany and spread out. In April, near

The war was fought on many fronts, with a variety of climates. New kinds of weapons and equipment revolutionized warfare. For example, amphibious craft could be used on both land and water. Air power was critical. Planes were used to drop paratroopers as well as to bomb. *Above:* Troops wade ashore from their landing craft during the D-Day invasion of Normandy. *Right:* The 82nd Airborne Division slogs through snowy Belgium during the Battle of the Bulge. When the Americans were asked to surrender at Bastogne, General Anthony McAuliffe gave a one-word reply: "Nuts!"

Torgau, American and Soviet soldiers met for the first time. Allied victory was near.

In this hour of triumph the Allied soldiers uncovered evidence of a carefully planned and executed barbarism that hardly seemed believable. At Buchenwald, Bergen-Belsen, Dachau, and elsewhere, the Allies found concentration camps and slave labor camps in which the Nazis had systematically tortured and killed millions of people. The victims were an estimated 5.7 million Jews and 5 million Poles, Russians, Czechs, Yugoslavs, Gypsies, and political prisoners from occupied nations.

Though the existence of the death camps came as a shock to most Americans, Nazi beliefs had long been known. According to the Nazis, the Germanic peoples made up a master race. Throughout the 1930's, Hitler had preached that Jews were the cause of all Germany's problems and therefore must be eliminated. All other peoples, but especially Slavs, must be enslaved to serve the Germans. Hitler said on one occasion:

> What happens to a Russian and a Czech does not interest me in the slightest. . . . Whether nations live in prosperity or starve to death interests me only in so far as we need them as slaves for our *Kultur* [nation]: otherwise it is of no interest to me.

The death camps were Hitler's "final solution" to the "Jewish problem." The slave labor camps were the embodiment of his beliefs about non-Germanic peoples.

After the war, Nazi leaders were tried in Nuremberg for crimes against humanity. They were charged with the systematic slaughter of 10 million civilians and war prisoners. They were found guilty of burying and burning people alive, working slave laborers to death, starving and torturing people, performing ghastly "medical" experiments on living subjects, and mass shootings and gassings. Never before had a nation so sophisticated in science and technology

World War II
EUROPEAN THEATER, 1943-1945

January 24–May 13, 1943 North Africa campaign. Allied victory. American and British troops mounted a two-pronged drive to clear North Africa of Axis troops. British troops headed west from Egypt. The fall of Tripoli to the British (Jan. 24) was a major success. Eastbound American troops were caught by fierce fighting at Kasserine Pass (Feb. 14–23). Finally, the Axis troops were forced into a pocket on the Cape Bon Peninsula. They surrendered at Bizerte (May 7). The same day, the British captured Tunis. Axis troops in North Africa formally surrendered May 13.

July–November 1943 Soviet offensive. Allied victories. Allied bombs had severely hurt Germany's wartime production. Soviet production had greatly increased. The Soviets began an offensive in July and pushed the Germans back to the Dnieper River (October). Kiev was liberated Nov. 6.

July 10–August 17, 1943 Invasion of Sicily. Allied victory. An Anglo-American force (British General Bernard Montgomery and American General George Patton) overran the island of Sicily, with major victories at Palermo (July 24) and Messina (Aug. 17).

September 3, 1943–June 4, 1944 Invasion of Italy. Allied victory. British troops crossed into the Italian Peninsula from Messina (Sept. 3). American troops (General Mark Clark) landed at Salerno (Sept. 9) and met strong resistance from German troops. On Jan. 22, 1944, the Allies made an amphibious landing at Anzio, near Rome. Pushing into the interior, they captured a German stronghold at Cassino (May 18). Allied soldiers marched into Rome June 4.

January–May 1944 Soviet offensive. Allied victories. By Jan. 29, German troops had been expelled from the Moscow and Leningrad areas. The Soviets recaptured Odessa (April 10) and Sevastopol (May 9).

June 6, 1944 "D-Day" invasion of Normandy. Allied victory. Allied troops (General Eisenhower) stormed French beaches in Normandy province. After securing beachheads, the Allies took Cherbourg (June 27), Caen (July 9), and St. Lô (July 25). St. Lô opened important routes for the liberation of France. By July, about 1 million troops had landed in Normandy.

August 15, 1944 Invasion of southern France. Allied victory. Allied forces landed near Toulon and drove northward along the Rhone River. These forces joined the Normandy invaders at Dijon (Sept. 15).

August 25, 1944 Liberation of Paris. Allied victory. Sweeping across France, the Allies, including Free French forces, rode triumphantly into Paris.

October 20, 1944 Fall of Belgrade. Allied victory. While western Europe was being liberated, Soviet forces swept into eastern Europe. Aided by Yugoslav partisans, they captured Belgrade.

December 16–26, 1944 Battle of the Bulge. Allied victory. A surprise German offensive created a 50-mile bulge in the Allied lines at the Belgium-Luxembourg border. A stubborn stand by American troops at Bastogne robbed the Germans of a victory.

March 7, 1945 Crossing the Rhine. Allied victory. Allied troops crossed the Rhine River on the Remagen Bridge, which the Germans had hoped to destroy before the Allies arrived.

April 25, 1945 Meeting at the Elbe. Soviet troops had pushed eastward through Germany. They met United States forces near Torgau, southwest of Berlin.

May 1, 1945 Fall of Italy. Allied victory. One Allied column made its way north on the Italian Peninsula; another column came south from Germany. The two columns met at Brenner Pass, where German troops surrendered.

May 2, 1945 Fall of Berlin. Allied victory. Soviet forces won complete control of Berlin.

May 8, 1945 V-E Day. Allied victory. Fighting ceased, and the Allies celebrated victory in Europe.

When the Allies entered Bergen-Belsen, they found the bodies of thousands of dead prisoners stacked in heaps. Above: The British make Nazi officers carry the decaying bodies to mass graves.

used its knowledge to engage in such an orgy of brutality.

Facing defeat, some German leaders tried to destroy Germany rather than surrender. Inspired by Germanic legends of the *Gotterdammerung*, or twilight of the gods, Hitler had said that in defeat "we shall drag a world with us—a world in flames." On April 30, 1945, before Soviet troops reached his hideout in Berlin, Hitler committed suicide.

A day or so earlier, Italian partisans had captured and killed Mussolini. On May 7, one of Hitler's generals signed the document of unconditional surrender, and the next day the fighting in Europe stopped. The most devastating war that the continent had ever known was over.

WAR IN THE PACIFIC

Now the Allies mustered their strength to defeat Japan. Roosevelt and Churchill had stuck to their decision to concentrate first on the conquest of Europe, but they had not allowed Japan to advance. In fact, American strategy had shifted. Instead of merely holding off the Japanese, American military leaders had decided to wage an aggressive two-front war. The nature of the war in the Pacific made an offensive with limited resources possible. Japan's conquests, spread over vast distances of the Pacific Ocean, were vulnerable to naval and air attacks.

Fighting the Japanese

In the first few months of the war, the Japanese had made tremendous advances in the Pacific and Indian oceans. The attack on Pearl Harbor had left the American fleet badly mauled, and the United States Army was in even worse shape than the navy. Japanese torpedo planes and bombers had severely crippled the British navy in the Pacific. The Japanese had captured Wake Island, Guam, Singapore, Hong Kong, British Malaya, Burma, Thailand, and the Netherlands East Indies and had swarmed over the Philippine Islands.

The only source of inspiration in the gloomy winter of 1941/42 came from Bataan and Corregidor in the Philippine Islands. There, outnumbered American and Filipino

World War II

PACIFIC THEATER, 1941-1943

December 7, 1941 Raid on Pearl Harbor. Axis victory. In a surprise attack, Japanese bombers devastated the Pearl Harbor naval base in the Hawaiian Islands. During the two-hour raid, 19 American ships were sunk or disabled, 150 planes were destroyed, and 2,400 troops were killed. Simultaneously, the Japanese attacked Wake Island, the Philippines, Guam, and the Malay Peninsula.

January–May 1942 Attacks in the Pacific and Asia. Axis victories. Advancing on many fronts, the Japanese took British Malaya (Jan. 31), Singapore (Feb. 15), Burma (March 9), and Java (March 9). The Battle of the Java Sea (Feb. 27–Mar. 1) was a severe loss for the Allies.

May 6, 1942 Fall of the Philippines. Axis victory. American forces (General Douglas MacArthur) had retreated to Bataan Peninsula, where they were trapped. On President Roosevelt's orders, MacArthur was evacuated to Australia (March 17). The Japanese overran Bataan on April 9, leaving only the offshore island of Corregidor in American hands. The 72,500 Filipino and American troops on Bataan were forced to march 85 miles to prison camps; so many died that this event is remembered as the Bataan death march. Corregidor, with 61,000 soldiers, finally surrendered a month later (May 6).

May 7–8, 1942 Battle of the Coral Sea. Allied victory. Hoping to set up a base for an attack on Australia, a Japanese fleet headed toward Port Moresby in southern New Guinea. In a sea battle that involved only carrier-based planes, American pilots thwarted the Japanese plan.

June 3–6, 1942 Battle of Midway. Allied victory. A relatively small American force (Admiral Chester W. Nimitz) held off a major Japanese attack on the Midway Island naval base. The Japanese losses of planes, carriers, and trained pilots restored the balance of naval power in the Pacific.

August 7, 1942–February 9, 1943 Invasion of Guadalcanal. Allied victory. United States Marines landed on the island of Guadalcanal in the Solomon Islands and captured an airport. Allied military experts wanted to make Guadalcanal a base for an offensive in the Pacific. The naval Battle of Guadalcanal (Nov. 12–15) prevented the Japanese from landing reinforcements. The Japanese evacuated Guadalcanal Feb. 9, 1943.

defenders held off the Japanese for five months. The death tolls at Bataan and Corregidor were staggering. A great number of the troops were Mexican Americans who had been stationed in the Philippines because, like many Filipinos, they spoke Spanish. Although the troops were captured, their fighting spirit inspired Americans at home.

Another boost to American morale came from naval attacks on Japan. In April 1942 a squadron of army planes bombed targets in the Tokyo area. While the attacks had little strategic value, they had great psychological value. Many Americans, working on the home front to rebuild the navy and build up the army, viewed these raids as partial revenge for the attack on Pearl Harbor.

The importance of air power became apparent in two major battles in 1942. Early in the year, after easy conquests elsewhere, the Japanese decided to strike at southern New Guinea. Victory there would open the way to an attack on Australia. In May, a Japanese fleet moved southward into the Coral Sea toward Port Moresby. The United States Navy knew of the planned attack and sent two aircraft carriers and some cruisers against the invaders. Before anyone on the Japanese and American ships could see the ships of the other side, planes from the carrier decks of both sides struck.

Though both fleets suffered heavy damage, the Battle of the Coral Sea (May 7–8, 1942) ended as an American victory. The Japanese retreated without trying to land troops at Port Moresby. Australia was saved by the first sea battle in history in which all fighting was done by carrier-based planes.

Admiral Isoroku Yamamoto, the commander of Japan's combined fleet, decided to strike next at Midway Island. He hoped to use it as a stepping-stone in the capture of Hawaii and to destroy what remained of the

A convoy of aircraft carriers steams through the Pacific. Until these "floating islands" proved their worth in battle, some military leaders opposed using them. They feared the thin-decked carriers were too vulnerable and too slow.

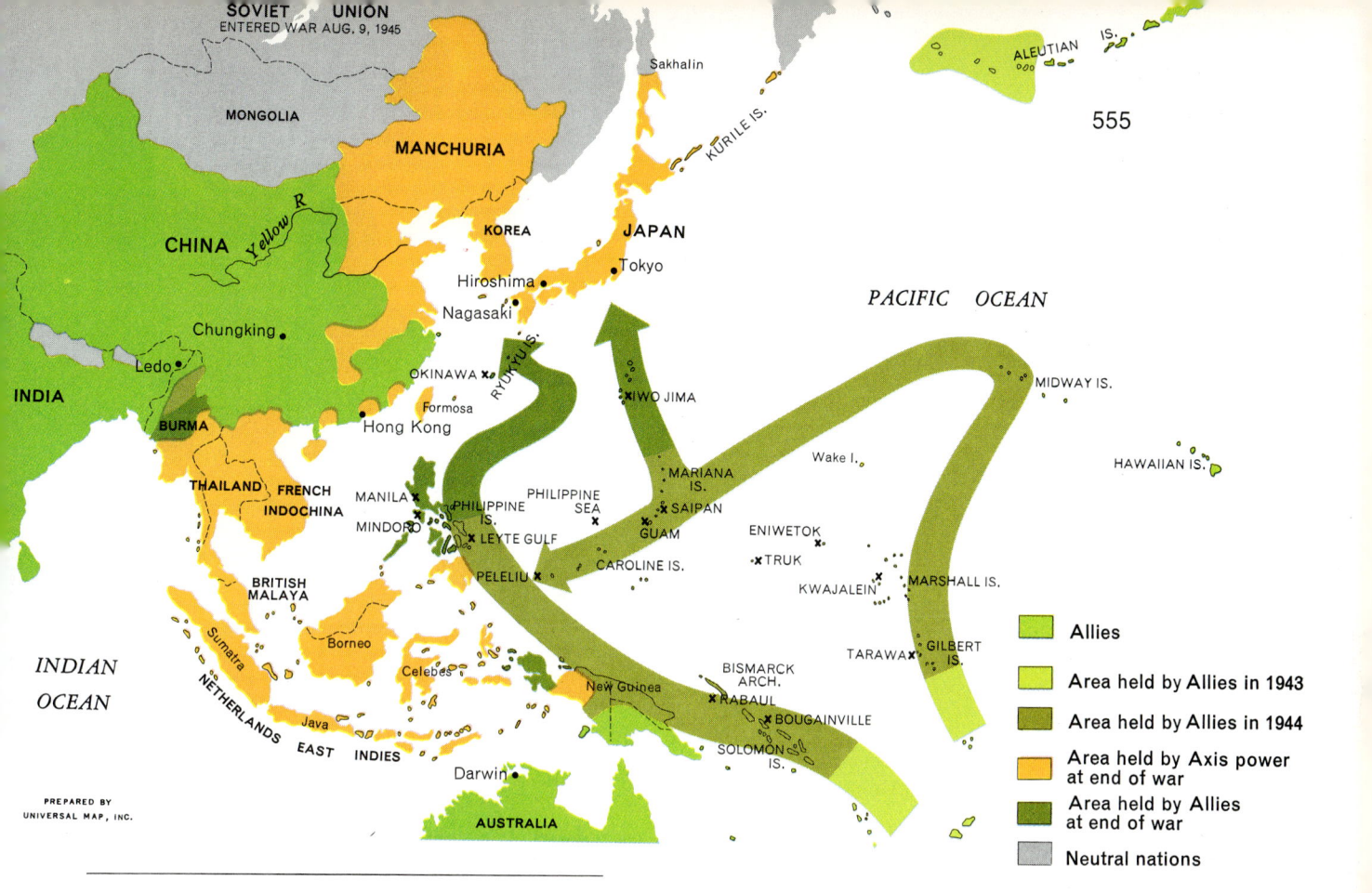

World War II
PACIFIC THEATER, 1943-1945

ALLIED STRATEGY

Japan's strategic island outposts were so far-flung that American military experts decided to attack the weakest islands and "leapfrog" toward the Philippines and Tokyo. The tactic was successful, and the United States won all the campaigns listed here.

July–November 1943 Solomon Islands campaign. After a series of naval encounters (July–October 1943) that cleared the waters around the central Solomon Islands, United States Marines landed at Bougainville (Nov. 1). From this base, MacArthur directed the conquest of the Solomons.

November 1943–September 1944 Central Pacific campaign. Admiral Chester Nimitz aimed at Japanese-held islands in the central Pacific. The Gilbert Islands fell (Nov. 24) after the bloody battle of Tarawa. Next the marines invaded the Marshall Islands, with significant battles at Kwajalein (Feb. 6) and Eniwetok (Feb. 17–22). The marines went on to the Mariana Islands, taking Saipan (June 15) and Guam (July 21). With the landing on Peleliu Island (Sept. 15), the central Pacific forces were ready to invade the Philippines.

January–September 1944 New Guinea campaign. MacArthur's forces inched along the northeast coast of New Guinea. Japanese resistance ended in September. MacArthur's troops joined Nimitz's forces to liberate the Philippines.

October 25, 1944–February 23, 1945 Liberation of the Philippines. The United States Navy virtually wiped out the Japanese fleet in the Battle for Leyte Gulf (Oct. 25). Landing on Mindoro Island (Dec. 15), American troops overcame Japanese resistance and took Manila, Feb. 23.

February 10–March 17, 1945 Battle of Iwo Jima. After many casualties, marines occupied this strategic island, only 660 nautical miles from Tokyo.

April 1–June 21, 1945 Invasion of the Ryukyu Islands. After almost three months of fighting, Americans occupied the main island of Okinawa.

August 15, 1945 V-J Day. Following atomic bomb attacks on Hiroshima (Aug. 6) and Nagasaki (Aug. 9) the Japanese government unconditionally surrendered. Americans celebrated victory over Japan.

Marines wade through the "main street" of their rest and recreation camp on Guadalcanal, 1944. During the rainy season in the jungles, equipment rusted, and mud slowed any attempts to advance.

United States fleet in the Pacific. Japan's armada in the Battle of Midway included four aircraft carriers and several battleships. Admiral Chester W. Nimitz, who commanded the American naval forces in the Pacific, knew an attack was coming at Midway and decided to take a gamble. Instead of taking battleships from the West Coast, thus leaving it unprotected, he concentrated on using aircraft carriers. The Americans had only three aircraft carriers, but they also had Midway Island, which they could use as an unsinkable carrier.

The Americans threw every plane they had into destroying Japanese air power. At the end of the battle, Japan's once magnificent fleet limped away, its four best carriers sunk or seriously damaged. Although this American victory was costly, it saved Hawaii and robbed the Japanese fleet of its offensive punch. Japan's advance across the central Pacific had been stopped.

In August, United States Marines landed at Guadalcanal. One of the Solomon Islands, it was used by Japan to protect its conquests. After six months of brutal, bloody fighting, the Japanese pulled their forces out of the southern Solomons. The United States had become the attacker.

In some of the bitterest fighting of the war, troops commanded by General Douglas MacArthur pushed northward from southern New Guinea. The army conquered New Guinea in September 1943, but the fighting in malarial jungle swamps took a heavy toll.

Leapfrogging Toward Tokyo

Japan's defenses were spread over thousands of miles and crisscrossed hundreds of small islands. American military leaders wanted to work out a strategy in which their forces would avoid fighting on every fortified island. They decided to "leapfrog" toward Tokyo by attacking some Japanese-held islands and by isolating others with American naval power.

Control of the skies and of the sea lanes made this strategy possible. Because the United States was short of aircraft carriers, the first leapfrog offensive did not start until November 1943. Then marines invaded Bougainville, the northernmost island in the Solomon chain. Within a few months a series of American victories in this area made it possible for planes and ships to encircle and neutralize Rabaul, Japan's stronghold in the Bismarck Archipelago. Meanwhile, far to the north in the central Pacific, American naval forces commanded by Admiral Nimitz struck at the Caroline Islands and captured the Gilbert Islands.

Late in January 1944, Admiral Nimitz unleashed the first large amphibious attacks in the Pacific theater against the Marshall Islands. By the end of February, the great Japanese naval base at Truk, in the Caroline Islands, had been neutralized. American conquests had cracked Japan's outer defense. The next attack hit the inner defenses. On June 15, marines invaded the beaches of Saipan, one of the largest of the Mariana Islands, only 1,600 miles from Tokyo.

The attack on Saipan forced the Japanese to bring out their rebuilt fleet. An American task force, under Admiral Raymond A. Spruance, was waiting. In the Battle of the Philippine Sea on June 19 and 20, 1944, Spruance's planes wiped out the Japanese carrier planes. United States long-range bombers from Saipan could now strike at the industries on Japan's home islands.

In October 1944, the American navy and army invaded Leyte, a central island in the Philippines. The Japanese decided to commit their entire fleet to the destruction of the invaders and their ships. In the Battle of Leyte Gulf, the Americans destroyed the Japanese navy. In the following months, the United States Army proceeded to conquer the Philippines, while the navy blasted its way toward Tokyo.

The power of one atomic bomb did this damage and more. The number of civilian deaths at Hiroshima was much greater than American leaders had anticipated. Many people in the target area did not seek shelter when they saw only two bombers approaching.

A Japanese Surrender

Only on the Asian mainland were the Japanese able to hold on to much of their conquered territory. Japanese forces had isolated China from its allies. With an army of Chinese, Indians, and a few Americans, the United States General Joseph W. Stilwell fought his way through northern Burma in 1943. His army built the Ledo Road, which went into operation in January 1945 and provided a route into China. Despite Stilwell's efforts, China remained outside the main struggle against Japan.

While the fighting went on in China, Burma, and the Philippines, United States Marines landed at Iwo Jima, an island about 750 miles from Tokyo. In March 1945, after weeks of tough fighting, the marines captured the island. This conquest gave the Americans airfields for fighter planes to protect the huge bombers sent to raid Japan.

On April 1, soldiers and marines invaded Okinawa, the largest of the Ryukyu Islands, only 370 miles from Japan. The battle for Okinawa lasted until June 22 and took a frightful toll of men and ships. The Japanese ordered pilots of the *Kamikaze* Corps to crash into American ships and sink them. The suicidal Kamikaze attacks were so effective that by the time the battle ended, the Kamikaze pilots had sunk thirty-six ships and seriously damaged several hundred.

The deadly resistance at Okinawa convinced United States military planners that a direct assault on Japan's main islands would be long and costly. Although Japan now had almost no ships and only a few planes capable of defending Japanese cities, it still had 2 million soldiers and a force of 5,000 planes for Kamikaze attacks. Moreover, its military leaders seemed determined to continue the fighting.

In July 1945, Allied leaders demanded that Japan surrender or face destruction. The emperor, the premier, and other civilian leaders were willing to seek peace, but Japan's military leaders rejected the ultimatum. The United States met this refusal with an awesome weapon. On August 6 an American plane flew over the city of Hiroshima and released a single bomb. Fifty seconds later came a blinding flash, an earsplitting roar, and a huge mushroom cloud. The first atomic bomb used in war had just destroyed every building within a four-mile radius and had killed an estimated 250,000 persons.

On August 9, the Soviet Union declared war on Japan and attacked Manchuria. That same day, an American atomic bomb leveled Nagasaki and killed tens of thousands of persons. On August 14, after rapid negotiations, the Japanese agreed to surrender, and the fighting stopped. Japan signed the final terms of surrender on September 2, 1945.

THE POLITICAL FRONT

During wartime, a nation's leaders must decide the extent to which long-term political considerations should influence their military strategy. In World War II, American leaders often gave immediate military success top priority in their diplomatic dealings.

The other major Allies, however, had important political goals in fighting the war. Britain wanted to preserve its influence in the Mediterranean; the Soviet Union sought territory in central Europe and in Asia. American leaders tried to delay the settlement of political issues until the Axis powers were defeated.

A Grand Alliance

On New Year's Day, 1942, President Roosevelt, Prime Minister Churchill, Ambassador Maxim Litvinov of the Soviet Union, and representatives of twenty-three other nations at war with the Axis powers signed the Declaration of the United Nations. This agreement formed a grand alliance against the Axis. The signers pledged to uphold the principles of the Atlantic Charter and agreed not to make a separate armistice or peace with the enemies.

Almost immediately it became clear that the alliance would not work smoothly. Before Hitler's invasion of the Soviet Union, the Soviets had absorbed the three small Baltic states of Lithuania, Latvia, and Estonia, as well as portions of Poland, Finland, and Romania. The Soviets announced that they intended to keep these territories, but Roosevelt and Churchill refused to recognize these conquests.

Military strategy also became a source of friction between the Soviet Union and its Anglo-American allies. In 1942 the three major Allied powers had to decide where to attack the Axis. The Soviets wanted an invasion of Europe, while the Americans wanted cooperation against Japan. Since one or another of the Allies did not feel strong enough to pursue either of these proposals, the Americans and the British decided to invade North Africa.

In January 1943, Roosevelt and Churchill met in Casablanca to discuss war strategy.

By this time the Allies had crushed most of the Axis resistance in North Africa. At this meeting, Roosevelt accepted the British proposal to invade Sicily. The British accepted an American proposal to demand unconditional surrender by the Axis enemies. Later, Stalin also accepted the policy of unconditional surrender.

Late in November 1943, Roosevelt met in Cairo with Churchill and Chiang Kai-shek, China's leader. The most important result of this conference was the Declaration of Cairo, announced on December 1 after the Soviets had approved. It said that the Allies would strip Japan of its possessions and would restore to the Chinese all of the territories that Japan had taken. Korea would eventually be independent.

President Roosevelt had long wanted to talk to Stalin. After the surrender of Italy, the President urged a meeting of the Big Three—Roosevelt, Churchill, and Stalin—to discuss worldwide strategy. Stalin refused to travel far from the Soviet Union, and Roosevelt reluctantly agreed to go to Teheran, Iran, for the meeting in November 1943.

In the Declaration of Teheran, released on December 1, Roosevelt and Churchill promised that the long-awaited invasion of France would come in the spring. Stalin again promised that the Soviet Union would join the war against Japan after Germany's defeat. The Big Three also discussed the possible division of Germany and the nature of a postwar system of collective security. They parted with Roosevelt believing that victory would come soon and that Allied cooperation would continue after the war. The Teheran meeting marked the high point of cooperation with the Soviets.

The Wartime Election

In September 1944, Roosevelt met with Churchill in Quebec. They agreed on plans for final victory in Europe and Asia and for

Roosevelt *(right)* meets with King Ibn-Saud of Saudi Arabia on a naval cruiser in 1945. The President sought to win nonbelligerents over to the Allied side. The nations of the Middle East were crucial because they controlled vast supplies of oil.

the future control of Germany. Churchill wanted another Big Three conference right after the Quebec meeting. He was alarmed by the actions of the Soviet Union. He feared that as Soviet armies occupied areas formerly held by the Nazis, the Soviets would make the occupied countries into Communist satellites. Roosevelt, however, refused to leave the Western Hemisphere during his campaign for reelection.

The wartime election campaign had started in June 1944, a few weeks after the Allies had begun their invasion of France. The Republicans had nominated Governor Thomas E. Dewey of New York for President. Dewey favored a foreign policy of international cooperation. The vice-presidential candidate, Governor John W. Bricker of Ohio, was an isolationist.

Three weeks later, Roosevelt received his fourth nomination from the Democrats. Since he was aging and ill, considerable interest centered on the choice of a running mate. The convention by-passed the incumbent Vice-President, Henry A. Wallace, who was unacceptable to major groups within the party. The Democrats chose a senator from Missouri, Harry S Truman, as a compromise candidate.

Both of the party platforms promised international leadership in the future. Although Dewey conducted a vigorous campaign, he could not shake the people's confidence in Roosevelt. The President won decisively.

Yalta

After the election, Roosevelt agreed to another meeting of the Big Three. He conferred with Churchill and Stalin from February 4 to

11, 1945, at Yalta, a Soviet resort on the Black Sea. Disagreement threatened to split the grand alliance.

The Yalta conference, the most controversial and important of the war, covered four main topics: the problems of Asia, the government of Poland and of other eastern European nations, the future of Germany, and the basis for a new league of nations.

In return for his renewed promise to bring the Soviet Union into the war against Japan, Stalin obtained promises from Roosevelt and Churchill. They agreed that the Soviet Union could have possession of Japan's Kurile Islands, control over Outer Mongolia, return of the southern half of Sakhalin Island, and recovery of privileges in Manchuria that had been lost in the Russo-Japanese War (1905).

This agreement was kept secret because the Soviet Union was officially still at peace with Japan.

Roosevelt and Churchill also reluctantly agreed that the Soviet Union could keep a part of eastern Poland. As compensation for this loss, the Poles were to receive territory carved from eastern Germany. Roosevelt and Churchill refused to give definite approval to Poland's new western frontier. They also refused to recognize the Polish government that the Soviets had set up in Lublin, in eastern Poland. In the end, the western leaders accepted a compromise. They agreed that the Lublin (Communist) government would be reorganized to include non-Communist Poles and that free elections would be held in Poland after the war.

The Big Three worked out a division of Germany into four zones. The Soviet Union, the United States, Britain, and France each would occupy a zone in Germany and in Berlin. All agreed to try Nazi leaders as war criminals. But the Big Three disagreed on the matter of reparations. The United States asked for none, and the British mainly sought some German equipment with which to repair war damage. The Soviets demanded that the Germans pay a total reparations bill of 20 billion dollars, of which the Soviet Union would receive half. Roosevelt and Churchill would not agree to this amount. They did, however, accept the Soviet terms as a basis for future discussion of the issue of reparations.

Although Stalin was unenthusiastic about the United Nations Organization that Roosevelt hoped to set up after the war, he agreed that the Soviet Union would be a part of it. He also accepted voting and membership policies for the organization that the Soviets had previously opposed.

Roosevelt returned home believing the Big Three had laid a firm foundation for peace. He said that the Yalta conference was a turning point in history. It proved to be a turning point, but not the kind he had in mind.

Stalin did not honor his pledges, and disillusionment over the diplomacy at Yalta quickly followed. Most Americans afterward felt that Roosevelt's concessions, when measured against Stalin's unkept promises, were unwise. Roosevelt had probably counted too much on Soviet good faith. Yet, except for the Kurile Islands, he and Churchill had not promised more than the Soviet army was in a position to take on its own. The decisions at Yalta reflected the strength of the Soviet Union in a new balance of power.

A New President

Franklin D. Roosevelt never experienced the disillusionment over Yalta. On the afternoon of April 12, 1945, while in Warm Springs, Georgia, he died of a cerebral hemorrhage. Roosevelt's death struck millions of Americans with the force of a personal loss. To millions, Roosevelt had been a symbol of hope in an era of despair.

Harry S Truman quickly took the presidential oath of office. The next day he told reporters:

Boys, if you ever pray, pray for me now . . . when they told me yesterday what had happened, I felt like the moon, the stars, and all the planets had fallen on me.

Truman had cause to be worried. As Vice-President he had not been kept informed of Roosevelt's decisions. He had not been prepared to take over the responsibility of ending the war and guiding the diplomacy that could affect the course of events in the postwar world. He had not even been told of the work being done to develop an atomic bomb.

Truman's education did not go much beyond high school. He had served in the artillery in World War I, and shortly after the war he entered politics, working closely with the Democratic boss of Kansas City, Tom Pendergast. The smell of corruption surrounded Pendergast, but Truman was known for his honesty. In 1934, the people of Missouri elected Truman to the United States Senate, where he consistently supported the New Deal. He gained the attention of President Roosevelt through his work as chairman of a special committee that investigated war production. Truman's reputation for political moderation and his popularity in Congress made him a logical compromise choice for Vice-President in 1944.

Potsdam

On taking office as President, Truman bent his efforts to learn all that he could about his new job in as short a time as possible. Truman assured everyone that he would continue Roosevelt's policies and carry out his wartime agreements.

Churchill was worried about the increasing friction between the Soviet Union and the Anglo-American allies. He urged another meeting of the Big Three to discuss mutual problems, and Truman agreed. This last of the high-level wartime conferences took place in Potsdam, Germany, from July 17 to August 2, 1945. The meeting began with Truman, Churchill, and Stalin present. During the conference, however, Clement Attlee replaced Churchill, whose party had just lost the parliamentary election in Britain.

Though the formalities seemed pleasant, uneasiness lurked beneath the surface politeness at Potsdam. The Big Three squabbled over reparations from Italy and Germany and over the Yalta agreements on eastern and central Europe. They agreed on details for occupying and governing Germany and on a compromise for handling reparations. But they could not agree on Poland's western boundary, and so they put that issue aside. Germany's easternmost provinces remained under Polish control. The Big Three also agreed to establish a council of foreign ministers, representing their nations and France, to prepare peace treaties for Italy, Hungary, Bulgaria, Romania, and Finland. Truman and Attlee sponsored the Potsdam Declaration, the ultimatum that demanded Japan's surrender.

A Look at Specifics

1. How did the government promote the efficiency of the industrial labor force during the war?

2. Why did the government ration many items during the war?

3. Why did the United States decide to concentrate on defeating Germany before defeating Japan?

4. How did World War II change the international balance of power?

5. What rulings did the Supreme Court make about the government's removal of Japanese Americans from the West Coast?

A Review of Major Ideas

1. How did the government mobilize the economy to support the war?

2. How were civil liberties in the United States affected by the war?

3. What strategy enabled American forces to defeat Japan?

4. What decisions were made at the following diplomatic conferences: Casablanca, Cairo, Teheran, Yalta, Potsdam?

For Independent Study

1. What military advantages does a dictatorship have over a democratic state of similar size and resources? What are its disadvantages? How can a democratic nation maintain a balance of power with autocratic nations and still remain democratic?

2. To what extent did Germany's decision to attack the Soviet Union and Japan's decision to attack the United States make possible the defeat of the Axis? Could the Axis powers have been victorious without those decisions? Explain.

Period of Adjustment

CHAPTER 25
1945–1952

New Yorkers celebrate V-J Day, Aug. 14, 1945.

Americans greeted the end of the war with joy. The knowledge that families would be reunited and that friends would be coming home was cause enough for celebration. But elation over the defeat of the Axis soon gave way to concern.

The war had brought great changes in American life—greater changes than most people realized at the time. Now came a period of adjustment, as the economy shifted to peacetime conditions, as military personnel became civilians, and as families became reacquainted. Perhaps the biggest change was that of the role of the United States, now more powerful than any country had ever been. The nation's leaders faced many problems in trying to adjust to this role.

THE PEACETIME SOCIETY

World War I had been followed by recessions and then a great depression. Many people feared that similar conditions would appear after World War II. These fears proved to be unfounded, for although the economy did lag for a few months during the reconversion period, it soon began to boom.

The Veterans

After the war ended, the government used every available ship to return soldiers, sailors, and marines to the United States. In all, 12 million servicemen and women returned to civilian life.

The Servicemen's Readjustment Act, known as the G.I. Bill of Rights, helped the returning veterans adjust to the peacetime economy. (The letters *G.I.* stood for "government issue." During the war, American soldiers had called themselves G.I.'s, and the veterans had retained that name.) Under the G.I. Bill, any man or woman who had served in the armed forces for ninety days or more and who was honorably discharged could get help from the government in securing a job, in acquiring an education, or in buying a house, farm, or business.

Veterans were particularly attracted to the educational benefits. By the summer of 1956, when the educational provisions of the G.I. Bill ended, more than 7.8 million veterans had received some form of education at government expense. Of these, some 2.2 million had jammed into college and university classrooms.

In the late 1940's and early 1950's, makeshift dormitories and temporary or crowded classrooms were common sights on most campuses. Married college students had been rare before the war, but they became typical after it. People whose plans for the future had been interrupted by four years of war did not want to wait until they had finished their schooling to get married and have children.

Although many veterans found that their prewar jobs had been filled by other people, most were able to find work without great difficulty. Some job openings appeared when women quit; in other cases, women were laid off to make room in industry for returning male veterans. The demand for consumer goods also created a demand for workers to produce them.

Economic Legislation

Most Americans had agreed on ways to help the veterans. But Americans could not agree on ways to return the economy to peacetime production. Congress paid little attention to President Truman's recommendations. In a message to Congress in September 1945, he outlined what he later called his "Fair Deal." His program, he explained, would expand "the progressive and humane principles of the New Deal." Conservative Republicans and southern Democrats had had enough of New Deal experiments. They planned to block Truman's programs.

The government lifted most of the controls that it had imposed on the economy. Most Americans apparently were pleased to see the end of rationing. But they wanted to end all controls that prevented them from spending their money as they wished. Few agreed with the government economists who advised continued controls over wages and prices to curb inflation. Business leaders argued that the best weapon against inflation was an increase in production. When supplies met the demand, they said, prices would become stable.

In 1946, Congress agreed to continue price controls for another year, but it limited the power of the Office of Price Administration. Truman had asked for tight controls, but Congress followed the wishes of business leaders who wanted the OPA limited. The lawmakers also wanted to deflate the President's swollen wartime powers to the peacetime norm. With weak price controls, inflation soared.

Americans went on a buying spree, bidding for scarce refrigerators, stoves, and other appliances. The housing shortage that plagued the postwar years was not helped by the removal of most rent controls. Rents rose phenomenally. Other prices continued to rise unchecked, and inflation remained a major problem.

Since many Americans still feared another depression, Congress did not block all economic legislation. Most important was the Employment Act of 1946, which stated that it was the responsibility of the federal government "to promote maximum employment, production, and purchasing power." The law also set up the three-member Council of Economic Advisers, composed of professional economists. The Council's job was to help the President "formulate and recommend economic policy." Americans could now expect the government to regulate economic activity in order to prevent unemployment.

Congress had heated debates over the use and development of atomic energy. The

The rapid return of veterans accentuated the housing shortage. Some 1,500 quonset huts were set up in Griffith Park in Los Angeles *(below)* as emergency housing for veterans. California grew phenomenally after the war. Huge numbers of suburban tract houses were built. *Opposite:* Moving vans jam a Los Angeles street on moving day in 1952. Many businesses geared their output to the postwar "baby boom." *Right:* Infants race to the finish line of a "Diaper Derby" in New Jersey, in 1946.

issue of whether to place peacetime control of atomic energy in military or civilian hands aroused the most controversy. The Atomic Energy Act of 1946 placed complete control of atomic research and production in the hands of the Atomic Energy Commission. Under this law, only the President could order the use of atomic bombs in a war.

Labor Problems

Inflation made life a struggle for many of the nation's people. Many workers found their buying power sharply reduced by the loss of overtime pay and by the shrinking value of the dollars they took home. They asked for wage increases, but industrialists often resisted these demands. The economy was caught in an upward "wage-price spiral." Each time workers got a raise, prices of goods had to be raised in order to cover the increased cost of production. Then workers asked for pay raises to cover the increased cost of goods.

Strikes by union members tied up various parts of the economy. The strike that posed the greatest threat to the nation's economy involved the railroad unions. In May 1946 they threatened to stop all rail traffic, for the first time in the nation's history.

In order to keep the trains running, President Truman seized control of the railroads. Then the government offered labor and management a compromise settlement. All but two of the railroad unions accepted the government offer. The two unyielding unions went on strike, ignoring the President's pleas to return to work. Truman threatened to draft "all workers who are on strike against their government" and to use the army to run the trains. After he asked a joint session of Congress for emergency legislation to cope with the strike, the two unions accepted the government's proposal, and their members returned to work.

Many Americans were angered by this strike. Some felt that the Wagner Act of 1935 encouraged unions to stick stubbornly to their demands. These critics, especially Republicans and conservative Democrats, urged that the law be revised to limit the power of unions.

The Eightieth Congress

In the congressional campaigns of 1946, Republicans promised that if elected they would limit the power of organized labor. Using the slogan "Had Enough? Vote Republican," they capitalized on various dissatisfactions with the Truman administration. For the first time since 1931, the Republicans won majorities in both houses of Congress.

A strike by the United Mine Workers in November 1946 made it easier for Republicans in the Eightieth Congress to carry out their campaign pledge for a new labor law. The miners defied a court order against a strike and closed the mines for seventeen days. They did not return to work until after a federal judge had fined their leader, John L. Lewis, and the union.

Convinced that labor was abusing its power, Congress passed the Taft-Hartley Labor-Management Relations Act in June 1947. This law, repassed over President Truman's veto, banned the closed shop but allowed the union shop. (In a *closed shop,* a person must be a union member before being hired; in a *union shop,* he or she must join the union after being hired.) The law made unions liable to damage suits and required them to publish annual financial statements. It also provided that the President could seek a court order to delay for eighty days any strike that might be against the national interest.

Bitter quarrels characterized the relationship between the President and the Eightieth Congress. Truman's opponent in most instances was the most influential Republican in Congress, Senator Robert A. Taft of Ohio. The son of a former President, Taft opposed many of the progressive social reforms of the New Deal and the Fair Deal.

Taft and his fellow Republicans had promised to cut the high wartime taxes. They passed two tax bills, but Truman vetoed them, claiming the reductions would help the rich and promote inflation. Congress then enacted a third tax-reduction bill into law over his veto in April 1948.

Truman and Congress also disagreed over the need for civil rights legislation. Late in 1946, Truman had appointed the Committee on Civil Rights to investigate "all areas of racial and religious discrimination." The committee called for laws that would provide everyone with an equal opportunity to get a job, buy a home, and go to a decent school. In February 1948, Truman asked Congress to pass such laws. Congress ignored his request, but Truman used his executive powers to attack discrimination. He ended racial segregation in the armed forces by executive order. He also asked the Department of Justice to help individuals in civil rights cases.

Many Americans were concerned about the breaking of the tradition that limited a President to two terms in office. Franklin D. Roosevelt had broken with precedent when he was elected to a third and then a fourth term. In March 1947, Congress adopted a proposal to prevent any person—except Truman—from serving more than two terms in the presidency. In February 1951, this proposal became the Twenty-second Amendment to the Constitution.

As a result of problems encountered during the war, Congress passed the National Security Act in July 1947. The new law created the National Security Council, which would try to coordinate military and foreign policy. It also set up the National Military Establishment, later called the Department of Defense, to unify the armed forces. All of the services—army, navy, and air force—were placed under the control of the secretary of defense, which was made a cabinet position.

The National Security Act also created the Central Intelligence Agency (CIA). The CIA was responsible for the collection, analysis, coordination, and interpretation of secret information from all over the world. The National Security Council and the President could use CIA information when determining policy.

Upset by foreign affairs, some Americans believed that Communists had infiltrated the executive branch of the government. As a result, in 1947 President Truman ordered the Federal Bureau of Investigation and the Civil Service Commission to check the loyalty of all persons employed in the executive departments. These probes led to the dismissal of a small number of employees whose loyalty seemed doubtful.

Meanwhile, the House Committee on Un-American Activities was trying to uncover evidence of Communist subversion and espionage. The committee won great publicity when Whittaker Chambers, a former Communist, testified before it in August 1948. He accused Alger Hiss, a former official in the Department of State, of being a Communist agent and of passing secret government documents to the Soviets in 1938. Hiss denied the charges, but Chambers produced some stolen secret documents from a scooped-out pumpkin on his farm and linked them to Hiss. After two trials for perjury (the statute of limitations on espionage had run out), Hiss was found guilty in January 1950 and sentenced to five years in a federal prison.

IN SEARCH OF PEACE

Well before the end of World War II, the United States government had begun planning a new international organization to keep peace. In 1942, Secretary of State Cordell Hull set up a committee to guide the President as he worked with Allied leaders on plans for the postwar period. President Roosevelt and Secretary Hull wanted to avoid the mistakes made by Woodrow Wilson in 1919. Thus they included Republicans as well as Democrats on the committee. They sought and received support in their planning from leaders of the Republican party and from Congress.

Roosevelt's Hopes

Franklin D. Roosevelt believed that a lasting peace would be possible if the wartime cooperation of the Allies would continue into the postwar era. In any new international organization, he wanted the Big Four—the United States, Britain, the Soviet Union, and China—to have control over all important matters, such as decisions of war and peace. Roosevelt thought he could count on the support of the British and the Chinese. What he needed to win was the cooperation of the Soviets.

The Soviets, however, cooperated only grudgingly. In a conference in 1944 they demanded sixteen votes in any new international organization, one for each of the republics within the Soviet Union. They also insisted on the right of an absolute veto.

The United States refused to accept these demands. But by the end of the conference, the Big Four had agreed on a tentative charter for a proposed permanent international organization to maintain world peace. The new organization ultimately became known as the United Nations.

The voting rights and veto privileges of members were finally agreed to at Yalta. There, Stalin accepted the American view that the veto in the United Nations would apply only on big issues, not in "procedural matters."

An awkward compromise settled the voting problem. In the General Assembly (one of the branches of the new organization), the Soviet Union got three votes—one for itself and one each for the Ukraine and Byelorussia (White Russia).

At Yalta the Big Three also agreed to a method to draw up the final United Nations charter. Invitations were sent to the other governments then at war with the Axis. Their representatives met in San Francisco on April 25, 1945, for the United Nations Conference on International Organization.

The United Nations Charter

Roosevelt died before the opening of the San Francisco conference, but President Truman carried out the late President's plans. Hopes grew in all parts of the world that the conference would create an organization that would maintain peace.

The conference sessions did little to encourage these hopes. From the beginning, the United States and the Soviet delegates bickered. Finally, on June 26, 1945, after many compromises, the fifty allied nations signed the charter of the United Nations.

The United Nations Charter differed little from the old League of Nations Covenant. All members of the United Nations were represented in the central body, the General Assembly. There, each nation's representative could discuss any matter within the jurisdiction of the United Nations. The General Assembly could not make decisions that would legally bind its members. It did not have the authority to enforce its decisions.

The Security Council, composed of fifteen members, had greater power. Five of these members—the United States, the Soviet Union, Britain, France, and China—held permanent seats and had the power to veto. The other ten were elected by the General Assembly for two-year terms. The Security Council could make decisions, even on matters of war and peace, binding on all members of the United Nations. But, because of the veto power, important decisions could be made only if all of the Big Five powers agreed. Within the broad structure of the United Nations, there were several other important bodies, but these often did not deal with political issues.

This time the Senate and the people gave overwhelming approval to United States participation in the worldwide organization. The United States was the first nation to accept the charter. The Senate gave its consent on July 28, 1945, by a lopsided vote of eighty-nine to two.

Congress passed a joint resolution inviting the United Nations to make its permanent headquarters in the United States. The world organization later accepted the invitation and chose New York City for its center.

The Peace Treaties

Although peace was the basic objective of the United Nations, the organization was not responsible for writing the peace treaties after the war. The great powers entrusted this work to the Council of Foreign Ministers (from the United States, Britain, the Soviet Union, France, and China).

As the Big Three had decided at Potsdam, Germany was divided and occupied by the United States, the Soviet Union, Britain, and France. By the beginning of 1947, cooperation among the four Allies had broken down, and Germany was split into two hostile

Europe, 1952

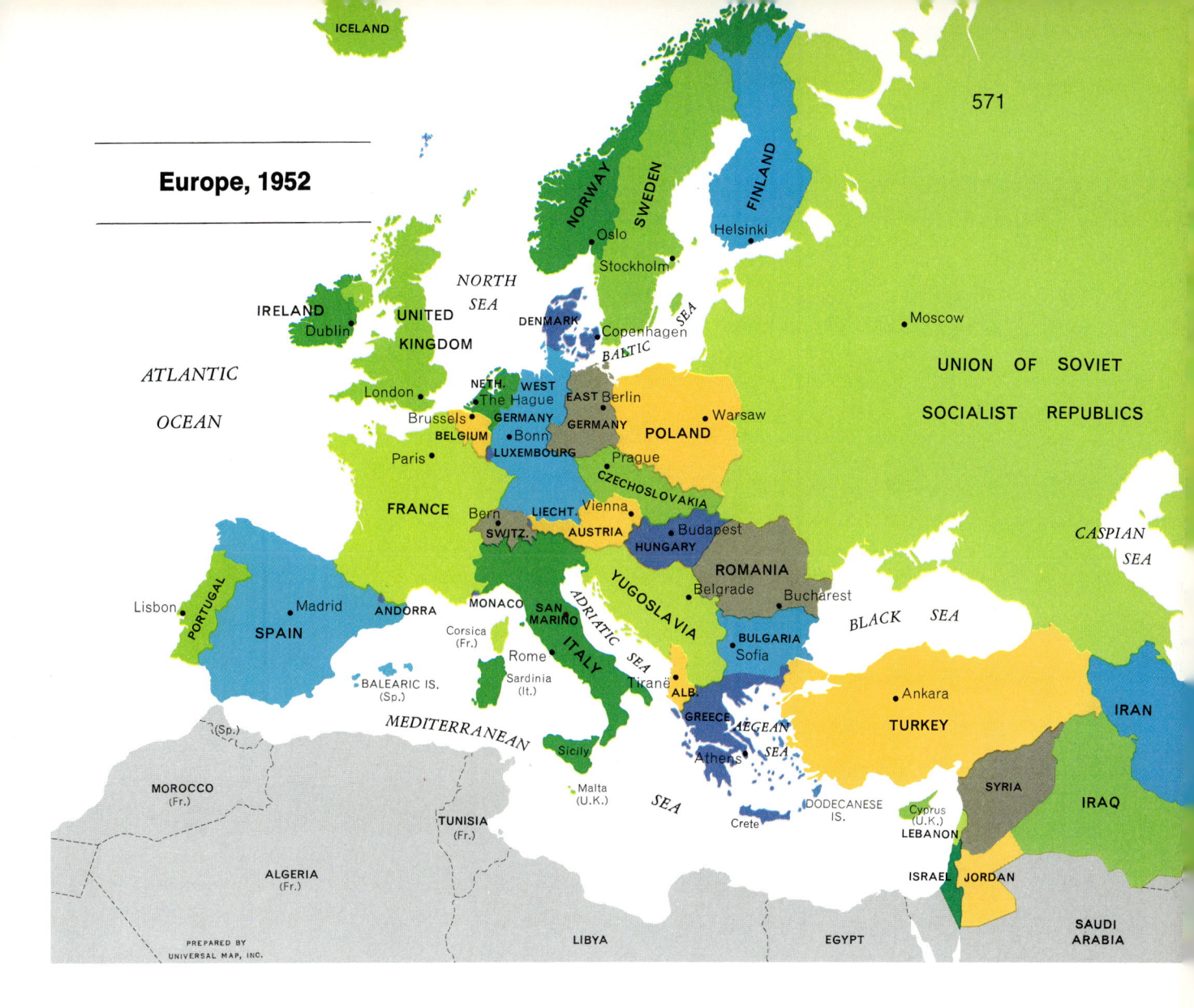

areas. Three of the Allies held western Germany, and the Soviet Union controlled eastern Germany.

Austria, too, was divided and occupied by the former Allies. The Soviet Union blocked the United States efforts to make a peace treaty. For ten years after the war, Austria remained occupied because no agreement on a peace treaty could be reached.

For the five other European nations that had been allied with Germany—Italy, Hungary, Romania, Bulgaria, and Finland—peacemaking proved difficult. The United States and its friends wanted these states to be independent democratic nations. The Soviets wanted them to be Communist nations that they could control, especially in eastern Europe. In general, the Soviets got what they wanted.

The treaties were finished in 1947. Four of them—those with Hungary, Romania, Bulgaria, and Finland—assured Soviet control of eastern Europe. The treaty with Italy was more complicated. It stripped Italy of all its colonies and its fleet, gave small strips of Italian territory to France and Yugoslavia, and awarded 100 million dollars in reparations to the Soviet Union. Although aware that the treaties contained flaws, the Senate finally approved them in June 1947.

THE COLD WAR

In March 1946, Winston Churchill made a speech in which he described the situation in Europe. An "iron curtain," he said, had been drawn across the continent by the Communists. All those behind the curtain in the east had no freedom; they were controlled from Moscow. Churchill thought the United States should follow a "get-tough" policy toward the Soviet Union. Others feared that such a policy would wreck the United Nations and lead to war.

President Truman's basic goal was "containment," preventing the Soviet Union from expanding further. The United States began a program of military and economic aid to enemies of communism. This program led to conflict with the Soviets, but it was fought with political and diplomatic weapons rather than with guns. The conflict was called the "Cold War."

East-West Tensions

The destruction caused by the atomic bomb led to efforts to place tight international controls on the manufacture of nuclear weapons. In January 1946, with Soviet agreement, the General Assembly created the United Nations Atomic Energy Commission. Bernard M. Baruch, the American member of the commission, offered a plan to place all control over atomic activities in an international agency. Eventually no more atomic bombs would be made, and all atomic weapons in existence would be destroyed. The agency was to have power to search any country for violations of the international ban on atomic weapons.

The Soviets regarded the plan as a device for keeping the atomic bomb secrets solely in America. Since the Soviets would not allow inspection of their land, the Baruch plan failed. Meanwhile, the Soviets worked feverishly to build their own atomic bomb. On September 23, 1949, President Truman announced that the Soviets had exploded an atomic device and that America's nuclear monopoly had ended.

Even before the efforts to control nuclear weapons had failed, the United States had quarreled with the Soviet Union over Iran, Turkey, and Greece.

During the war, the Soviet Union and Britain had occupied Iran. After the war, the British withdrew their troops, but the Soviets increased their forces. They threatened to take over Iran and make it another Communist satellite.

At the first United Nations Security Council meeting in January 1946, the Iranians charged the Soviets with intervention in Iran. The Iranians also appealed to the United States for help. President Truman took a strong stand against the Soviets. Faced with American firmness and hostile world opinion, the Soviets, in May, withdrew their forces.

From Turkey the Soviets demanded two provinces near the Soviet border and control over the Bosporus and Dardanelles. With American and British support the Turks defied the Russians.

In Greece the situation was more complicated because a civil war raged there. Communists in neighboring Yugoslavia, Albania, and Bulgaria supported the Greek Communists, who were trying to destroy the Greek monarchy. The king's forces were supported by British troops. In February 1947, the British decided that they could no longer afford this aid to Greece, nor the help they were giving to Turkey. If Britain withdrew, Greece and Turkey appeared certain to fall to communism.

Dock workers bag American wheat at the port of Kavalla, Greece. The United States postwar aid program concentrated first on temporary measures to keep people alive, then on reconstruction.

President Truman decided that the United States should help Greece and Turkey. On March 12, 1947, he told Congress that "it must be the policy of the United States to support free peoples who are resisting attempted subjugation by armed minorities or by outside pressures." This policy later became known as the Truman Doctrine. Congress approved the President's request for 400 million dollars' worth of aid to Greece and Turkey. It also gave him the authority to send civilian and military advisers there.

Marshall Plan

Many people in Europe were desperate in the cold winter of 1947. Throughout western Europe, but particularly in Italy and France, Communist parties were becoming stronger. The President and his advisers decided that the people of Europe needed more than fuel and food. They needed money, machinery, and farm equipment to make a sound economic recovery from the destruction of war. That recovery, it was felt, would itself contain the spread of communism in Europe.

The President and his advisers wanted to help Europe as a whole. They decided that the European nations should get together and work out a recovery program that cut across national boundaries. Then they should present their needs to the United States. Secretary of State George C. Marshall made this idea the theme of a speech he gave in June 1947. Thus it became known as the Marshall Plan.

The Soviet Union and the nations of the Communist bloc refused to participate in the Marshall program. Spain—because of its Fascist government—was not invited to participate. The other sixteen nations of western Europe quickly accepted Marshall's offer. Congress passed the European Recovery Act

Berliners wave at an American plane in "Operation Vittles," the airlift bringing food and fuel to Berlin despite a Soviet blockade. Western planes flew in all kinds of weather, 24 hours a day.

with an appropriation of 17 billion dollars in March 1948. Later, Congress voted additional billions for aid to Europe.

European countries rebuilt their economies on sound foundations. Four years later, their farms and factories were producing more than before the war. Communists lost voting strength, especially in Italy and France. With American help western Europeans had contained communism.

Western Germany, which had been included in the Marshall Plan, also recovered some of its prewar strength. Since it had factories and skilled workers, western Germany would make a valuable ally in the Cold War. In June 1948 the United States, Britain, and France therefore agreed to establish a West German government by uniting their zones of occupation.

This plan angered the Soviets. They retaliated by throwing a land blockade around Berlin, which was occupied by American, British, French, and Soviet troops, even though it was 110 miles within the Soviet zone. The western zone of Berlin depended on shipments of food and fuel from western Germany. Faced with the prospect that the Soviets might start shooting if westerners forced their way into Berlin, the Americans and British organized a massive airlift. For almost a year, until May 1949, supplies came to West Berlin through the blockade.

In May 1949, the West Germans proclaimed the German Federal Republic, and the East Germans proclaimed the German Democratic Republic. As a result, there were now two German states, one democratic and the other Communist. The Soviets ended the Berlin blockade.

At about this time, Yugoslavia had a disagreement with the Soviet Union and withdrew support from the Greek Communists. The Greek national army then crushed the rebels. By October 1949, the Marshall Plan and the Truman Doctrine had helped in containing communism in western Europe and in the eastern Mediterranean.

The North Atlantic Treaty

The Truman administration wanted to strengthen containment with a system of military alliances in western Europe. In April 1949, the foreign ministers of twelve nations met in Washington, D.C., and signed the North Atlantic Treaty. The heart of the treaty said that an attack against any one of the allies would be considered an attack against all. Other nations later joined this alliance, but the original members were Belgium, Canada, Denmark, France, Britain, Iceland, Italy, Luxembourg, the Netherlands, Norway, Portugal, and the United States.

The Senate approved the treaty in July 1949. For the first time since the French alliance of 1778, the United States had entered a formal alliance with Europeans.

Latin America

Latin America had always been an area of concern to the United States. During the war, all the Latin American nations except Argentina supported the Allies against the Axis. In March 1945, Argentina declared war on Germany and Japan, but this action brought only temporary unity to the Western Hemisphere. In 1946, the United States interfered in Argentina's presidential election, attempting to defeat Colonel Juan D. Perón, a right-wing military strongman. He won the election, and the United States lost some of the good will that the Good Neighbor policy had created.

In the following year the Truman administration adopted a less hostile attitude toward Argentina. In September 1947, representatives from the United States and nineteen other American republics signed a permanent defensive military alliance, usually known as the Rio Pact. This alliance was the first regional defense arrangement made under the charter of the United Nations.

In April 1948, representatives of the American republics met in Bogotá, Colombia, to create the Charter of the Organization of American States. The Organization of American States (OAS) established a permanent body to help bring peace and security within the Western Hemisphere.

The Middle East

Another change in United States foreign policy in the postwar years was a growing concern for the Middle East. The region became important to Americans because of its vast oil fields and its strategic importance in the policy of containment.

United States policy first encountered difficulty in the Middle East because of the bitter rivalry between Arabs and Jews in Palestine. Jews had long dreamed of restoring their nation in Palestine, their original homeland. Affected by the rise of nationalism in Europe and by constant persecution, they worked for Jewish national independence, a concept known as Zionism. In

1917, the British, who controlled Palestine, promised that the Jews would be allowed to rebuild their nation. At the same time, the British promised independence to Arabs in British-controlled areas, including Palestine.

In the 1930's and 1940's, many Jews went to Palestine to escape Nazi brutalities. Arabs in the mandate of Palestine protested the increasing immigration and attacked Jewish settlements. When the British restricted Jewish immigration, the Jews fought the British and the Arabs.

Dr. Ralph J. Bunche *(center)*, acting UN mediator for Palestine, talks with the chief military observer in Haifa, 1948. For his work on the Arab-Israeli settlement, Bunche received the Nobel Peace Prize in 1950.

The United States became deeply involved because, since World War II, it had been the center of the world Zionist movement. Jews in Palestine got most of their money and other support from people in the United States. President Truman, as did most national politicians, supported the idea of a Jewish state in Palestine as a means of containing Soviet expansion in the Middle East.

The British found themselves unable to govern Palestine without assistance. In February 1947, they turned the Palestine problem over to the United Nations. After deliberation, the United Nations recommended the partition of Palestine into an Arab state and a Jewish state. This recommendation angered the Arabs, who looked upon Palestine as theirs. They began guerrilla warfare against the Jews.

In May 1948, when the British withdrew the last troops from Palestine, the Jews proclaimed the independent state of Israel. The Arabs immediately launched a full-scale war. Eleven minutes after Israel came into existence, Truman officially recognized it. The Soviet Union also quickly recognized Israel, in hopes that it would become anti-British and align itself with the Soviets.

The Jews defeated the Arabs in a war that lasted until July 1949. Then Dr. Ralph J. Bunche, an American diplomat employed by the United Nations, worked out a truce. In the following year the United States, Britain, and France agreed to guarantee the armistice between Israel and the Arab nations.

THE FAIR DEAL

The election of 1948 seemed to carry a forecast of great changes. Encouraged by the results of the congressional races in 1946, the Republicans were confident of victory. They were sure that they would end sixteen years of Democratic rule.

The 1948 Election

When the Republicans convened in June 1948, they nominated Thomas E. Dewey of New York for President and Governor Earl Warren of California for Vice-President.

The gloomy Democrats met in July, and nearly all of them seemed resigned to defeat. The exception was Harry Truman, who received the presidential nomination. The vice-presidential nomination went to Alben W. Barkley, a seventy-one-year-old senator from Kentucky.

A major battle broke out over the party platform. The civil rights plank called for federal laws to prevent discrimination in employment, to penalize lynching, and to end poll taxes. When the majority approved the plank, a number of southerners walked out of the convention. They formed the States' Rights Democratic (Dixiecrat) party and chose Governor J. Strom Thurmond of South Carolina as their presidential candidate.

Another defection was that of former Vice-President Henry A. Wallace, who had disagreed with Truman on foreign policy. He headed the ticket of a new Progressive party that tried to attract unhappy former New Dealers, pacifists, and left-wingers.

Public opinion polls, newspaper accounts, and politicians' prophecies apparently convinced Dewey that he would win in a landslide. He carried on a conservative, confident campaign and limited his speeches to vague general statements.

The odds against Truman were great. His party did not have much money in its campaign war chest; moreover, a divided party rarely wins. Truman ignored the odds and launched a slashing campaign against the record of the Republicans in Congress. The President stumped the country by rail. At practically every "whistle stop," he made earthy, twangy speeches denouncing the "do-nothing Eightieth Congress."

Election day came, and the prophets were stunned. Truman won, and the Democrats captured control of both houses of Congress. Truman had scored the biggest political upset in the nation's history.

Social Reforms

Despite the Democratic victory at the polls, only a small part of Truman's "Fair Deal" was enacted. A group of Republicans and southern Democrats who opposed social and economic changes still formed a coalition that controlled Congress.

In July 1949, Congress passed the National Housing Act. It set aside large sums to help cities clear slums and build low-cost public housing. (This law seemed to expand certain powers of the cities, and many cities delayed using its provisions until 1954, when the courts ruled that the law was constitutional.) Congress also raised the minimum wage from 40 to 75 cents an hour. In 1950 and 1952, Congress amended the Social Security Act to include an additional 10.5 million persons. People already receiving social security benefits were given increased payments to meet the higher cost of living.

Truman's farm program, proposed by Secretary of Agriculture Charles F. Brannan, failed to win approval from Congress. The Brannan Plan emphasized high income for farmers through direct federal payments. People engaged in large-scale farming, and others as well, called the plan "socialistic." Truman instead accepted the Agricultural Act of October 1949, which set up a system of high price supports.

In 1947, Truman had appointed a committee, headed by former President Herbert Hoover. to study the executive branch of government and recommend ways to simplify its structure. In June 1949, Congress acted upon the Hoover reports and passed the Reorganization Act. Truman carried out more than half the Hoover recommendations.

The Anti-Communist Crusade

The Hiss case had made the nation acutely aware of Communist subversion and had set off an anti-Communist crusade. In the campaign of 1948, some Republicans charged the Democratic party with being "soft on communism." But the person who most exploited and abused the Communist issue was Joseph R. McCarthy, a Republican senator from Wisconsin. His actions introduced a new word into the American language: *McCarthyism,* the making of indiscriminate and irresponsible charges of political disloyalty.

McCarthyism first appeared in February 1950, when the senator claimed that the State Department was "thoroughly infested with Communists." As chairman of the Permanent Subcommittee on Investigations, McCarthy accused and frightened many people over a period of four years. But he never proved his charges. Because of his unscrupulous methods and careless accusations, McCarthy caused much controversy.

The courts rendered some decisions that made it easier to prosecute Communists. In 1940, Congress had passed the Smith Act, which prohibited the advocacy of the violent overthrow of the government. In 1949 eleven leaders of the Communist party were convicted of violating the Smith Act. The Supreme Court upheld the convictions in 1951 and held the law to be constitutional.

At the same time, the government struck at Soviet spies. A trial in England in 1950 revealed that Dr. Klaus Fuchs, a physicist who had worked on the American atomic bomb project, had slipped nuclear secrets to the Russians. Fuchs's conviction led to the arrest of several spies in the United States. The case of Ethel and Julius Rosenberg created the greatest stir. The Rosenbergs were convicted of espionage in 1951 and given the death penalty.

Congress reacted to the spy trials and the Communist exposures by passing the McCarran-Nixon Internal Security Act of 1950. This complex law required all Communist and Communist-linked organizations to register with the government. It also made it unlawful for anyone to conspire to perform any act that would "substantially contribute" to the establishment of a dictatorship in the United States. "In a free country," Truman said when he vetoed the bill, "we punish men for the crimes they commit, but never for the opinions they have." Congress overrode his veto.

Two years later, Congress overrode another of Truman's vetoes to pass the McCarran-Walter Immigration and Nationality Act of 1952. This new law ended the total exclusion of Asians. It gave them a small quota and allowed them to become citizens through naturalization. Yet it continued the discriminatory features of the old quota system against southern and eastern Europeans. It even tightened some of the restrictions in order to prevent Communists from emigrating to the United States.

EVENTS IN ASIA

During the immediate postwar years, no part of the world had greater discontent and unrest than Asia. There, strong nationalist movements sought independence from foreign control.

The Philippines

Both Franklin D. Roosevelt and Harry S Truman sympathized with some of these movements. Their attitude toward the Philippines reflected United States friendliness toward Asian nationalism.

In 1934, the Americans had promised the Philippines independence ten years hence. During the war—to strengthen Filipino resistance to the Japanese—President Roosevelt promised that once Japan was defeated, a fully independent Republic of the Philippines would be established.

President Truman carried out this pledge. On July 4, 1946, when the Republic of the Philippines was proclaimed, the United States surrendered control over its former colony. Special defense treaties bound the United States and the Philippines, but the Filipinos ran their own government.

Oh strange new world

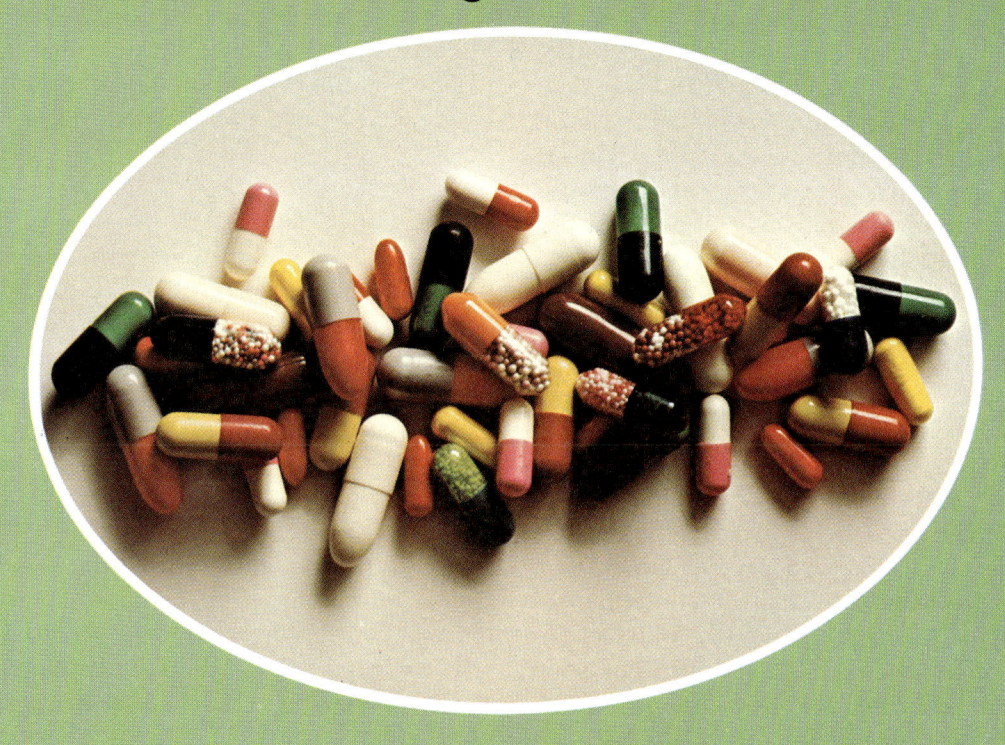

The causes of some postwar environmental problems were obvious. After all, bomb craters do not easily revert to farmland. But many of the war's effects were so subtle that they were not yet recognized as causes of problems.

The testing of nuclear weapons in the atmosphere was known to be dangerous even at the time of the first tests, before the bomb was dropped on Hiroshima. *Fallout*, the radioactive dust from a nuclear bomb, could cause radiation poisoning if it fell in concentrated doses. Despite the dangers, the world powers carried on a number of nuclear tests in the Pacific after the war.

One of the war's subtle effects was a postwar population "explosion." Some of the population increase was delayed growth that would normally have taken place during the four to six years that the war was fought. But much of the growth could be chalked up to wartime advances in medicine. Wonder drugs like sulfa and penicillin dramatically lowered the death rate. In many nations a high death rate had balanced a high birth rate to produce a more or less stable rate of growth. Now, with fewer deaths and a continuing high number of births, the world's population grew incredibly. By the late 1950's, a number of nations would seek government policies of limiting births.

In the postwar United States, the "baby boom" was a boon to manufacturing. So were two new ideas: built-in obsolescence and disposability. Products were made in such a way that they would be obsolete and require replacement in a few years. They were also built so that repair would not be worthwhile. Many of the new products were made of plastics that had been developed just before the war. Plastics were made from coal tar or the wastes of petroleum distillation. They were so cheap that they competed with glass, paper, and wood as packaging material. Like aluminum, which also came into wide use during the war, plastics do not decompose rapidly. The disposal of plastics and aluminum eventually produced monumental garbage problems.

China

Soon after Japan surrendered, American planes moved Nationalist Chinese troops into major cities like Shanghai and Nanking in order to help Chiang Kai-shek stay in power. In the north, however, the Chinese Communists conquered farms and villages. They seized Japanese guns and other equipment, particularly in Manchuria, where the Soviets were in control.

President Truman recognized the Nationalist regime as "the only legal government in China." Yet in December 1945, President Truman sent General George C. Marshall to China to try to mediate the quarrel between the Nationalists and the Communists. Marshall tried to persuade Chiang Kai-shek to broaden his Nationalist government so that it would represent all political groups in China, including Communists. Marshall arranged a truce, but his basic mission failed. By the end of 1946, when he was called home, civil war had broken out in China.

Despite great quantities of military equipment and money from the United States, the Nationalists could not stop the Communist drive. Opponents of the Truman administration's policy demanded massive intervention against the Chinese Communists. Truman refused to go beyond his aid program. He and his advisers insisted that containment could not work in a country as large and populous as China.

The Communists, headed by Mao Tse-tung, defeated the Nationalists and, on October 1, 1949, proclaimed the People's Republic of China (Red China). In December, Chiang Kai-shek fled to the island of Taiwan (Formosa) and set up his Nationalist government there. Many nations, including Britain, recognized the Communist government of China. The United States refused to recognize Red China and blocked its efforts to get into the United Nations.

In February 1950, the Soviet Union and Red China signed a thirty-year alliance and mutual assistance agreement. Since both nations were hostile to the United States, the United States turned to Japan, its recent enemy, as its major ally in Asia.

Japan

General Douglas MacArthur, Supreme Commander for the Allied powers, headed the occupation forces in Japan. Under his direction, Japan carried out extensive programs of political, economic, and social reform. In a new constitution the Japanese people agreed to renounce war.

The United States would not call a conference in which the Soviets would help write a peace treaty for Japan. The Soviet Union wanted to keep Japan weak. After Mao Tse-tung took control of China in 1949, the United States concentrated on making Japan an ally in the Cold War. The United States urged the Japanese to rebuild their industries and gave them aid.

To further strengthen the Japanese position in East Asia, American policy makers wanted to end the enemy status of Japan. First, to overcome fears of danger from a revived Japan, the United States signed a defense treaty with the Philippines and another one with Australia and New Zealand. Then, on September 4, 1951, President Truman opened a peace conference in San Francisco with representatives from fifty-two nations. The conference met to accept or reject the terms of a treaty already worked out by representatives of the United States and Japan. All but the Soviet Union and two of its satellite nations accepted it.

Although the treaty stripped Japan of all territory except the home islands, it was generous. It set no reparations and put no restrictions on the Japanese economy. At the same time, the United States and Japan signed a treaty that gave the United States the right to maintain armed forces in Japan.

War in Korea

As the Cold War became increasingly intense, the United States and the Soviet Union found it more difficult to settle their differences. In Korea, a former colony of Japan, the political conflict finally turned into a shooting war.

In 1945, the United States and the Soviet Union had stationed occupation troops in Korea. They divided the nation along the 38th parallel, the Soviets occupying the northern part, the United States the southern part. Soon, this line became a zone of tension, and the United States and the Soviet Union put aside efforts to unify Korea.

To break the deadlock, the United States asked the United Nations to supervise Korean unification. The Russians refused to go along with the plans of the United Nations for elections to choose a new government. Elections were therefore held only in South Korea. In August 1948, the South Koreans set up the Republic of Korea. The North Koreans then established the Democratic People's Republic of Korea, a Communist state. Within a year the Soviet Union and the United States withdrew their occupying forces.

The president of South Korea had said he would try to unify the entire nation by force. Since the United States did not want him to start a war, it only equipped his army with light weapons. The Russians, on the other hand, trained the North Korean soldiers and gave them heavy equipment.

Early on June 25, 1950, the well-drilled North Korean army smashed across the 38th parallel. The surprised and lightly armed South Koreans retreated in panic.

As soon as news of the Communist attack reached New York, the Security Council of the United Nations went into emergency session. The Soviet Union was boycotting the United Nations at the time, and thus could not use its veto. The Council declared the North Korean attack "a breach of the peace" and ordered the North Koreans to cease fire and withdraw their troops. Then, in response to a South Korean plea, President Truman sent naval and air assistance to the South Koreans. When the Security Council urged members of the United Nations to help South Korea, the United States sent ground troops.

Another resolution of the Security Council authorized the use of the blue United Nations flag in Korea and permitted President Truman to name General MacArthur the commander of United Nations forces. Although sixteen United Nations members eventually sent some forces to Korea, Americans and South Koreans did most of the fighting. But the United States never declared war on North Korea.

At first, the fighting went badly for the United Nations. The raw, untrained recruits, rushed from occupation duty in Japan, could not stop the Communists. In August 1950, the United Nations forces stopped retreating and established a line on the southeastern tip of Korea, near the port city of Pusan. On September 15, General MacArthur surprised the Communists with an amphibious attack at Inchon, far behind North Korean lines. This attack trapped thousands of North Koreans and caused others to flee north.

Pleased by the impressive victory, American policy makers permitted MacArthur's forces to cross the 38th parallel and attempt to unite Korea. As the United Nations troops approached the banks of the Yalu River, the border between Red China and Korea, the Chinese became increasingly alarmed. In November 1950, Red Chinese troops, which had been secretly entering Korea, crashed through MacArthur's lines. In their offensive the Red Chinese pushed the United Nations troops far south of the 38th parallel.

MacArthur wanted to launch attacks on China, but the President and his advisers

Map Legend

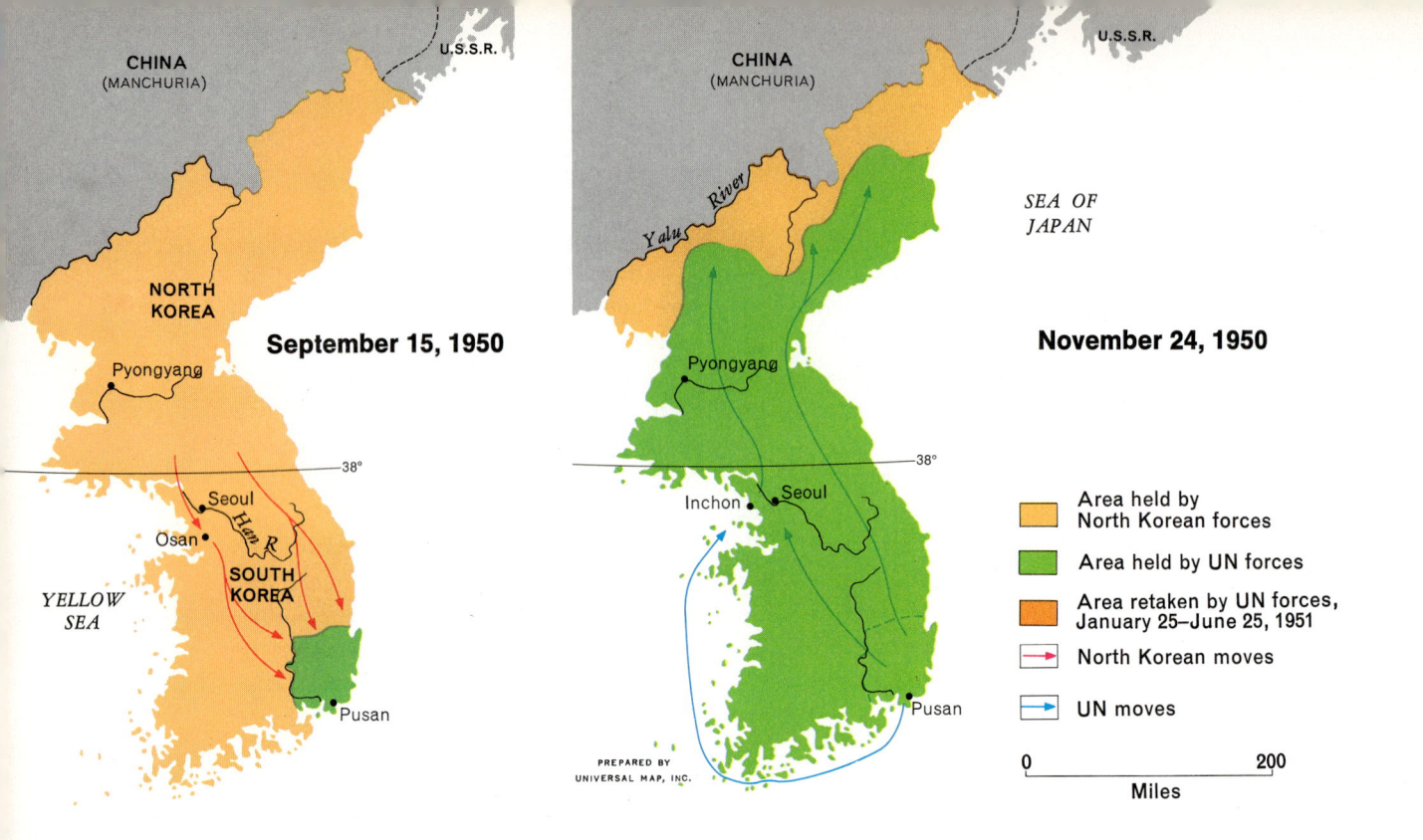

- Area held by North Korean forces
- Area held by UN forces
- Area retaken by UN forces, January 25–June 25, 1951
- North Korean moves
- UN moves

0 — 200 Miles

Korean War, 1950-1953

June 25, 1950 Invasion of South Korea. Communist victory. A North Korean army crossed the 38th parallel. Three days later the troops entered Seoul, the South Korean capital. The South Korean army hastily retreated, leaving most of its equipment behind. The use of United States troops to help the South Koreans was authorized on June 30. On July 2, a few Americans were sent to Osan to fight a delaying action until more troops could be brought in. A unified United Nations command was set up in late July under General Douglas MacArthur.

August 5–September 15, 1950 Battle of the Pusan Beachhead. United Nations victory. By August, American and South Korean troops were cornered in the southeast tip of Korea. They made a final stand along a 140-mile perimeter around Pusan. The North Koreans hammered at the thinly held line for more than six weeks but failed to break it. Meanwhile, troops from other nations came to South Korea, and MacArthur began arranging a counterattack.

September 15–November 24, 1950 Inchon landing. United Nations victory. UN troops made an amphibious landing at Inchon (Sept. 15). The same day, UN troops broke out of the Pusan perimeter. They moved north while the Inchon invaders swept east. Seoul was recaptured Sept. 26. The North Korean capital, Pyongyang, fell Oct. 20 as the UN army headed toward the Yalu River on the Manchurian border. An end-the-war offensive began Nov. 24.

November 26, 1950–January 1951 Chinese intervention. Communist victory. Small numbers of Chinese soldiers had crossed into Korea as early as Oct. 26, but the Chinese waited until Nov. 26 to begin a massive attack. Caught unprepared, UN forces retreated. They abandoned Pyongyang (Dec. 5), fell back to the 38th parallel, and finally held a line south of Seoul.

January 25–June 25, 1951 United Nations offensive. United Nations victory. Moving north, UN troops recaptured Seoul. By March 19, they held a line that divided Korea near the 38th parallel, but UN troops were not allowed to penetrate North Korea. During two years of off-and-on peace talks, limited but fierce fighting continued for strategic ridges and hills.

July 27, 1953 Armistice. The main issue that delayed an armistice was repatriation of war prisoners. The North Koreans insisted that all captured Communists must be returned to them. However, many Communist prisoners did not want to return, and the United Nations command refused to force them to do so. Finally, it was agreed that both sides would have a chance to convince their captured men to return home. The armistice was signed at Panmunjon July 27.

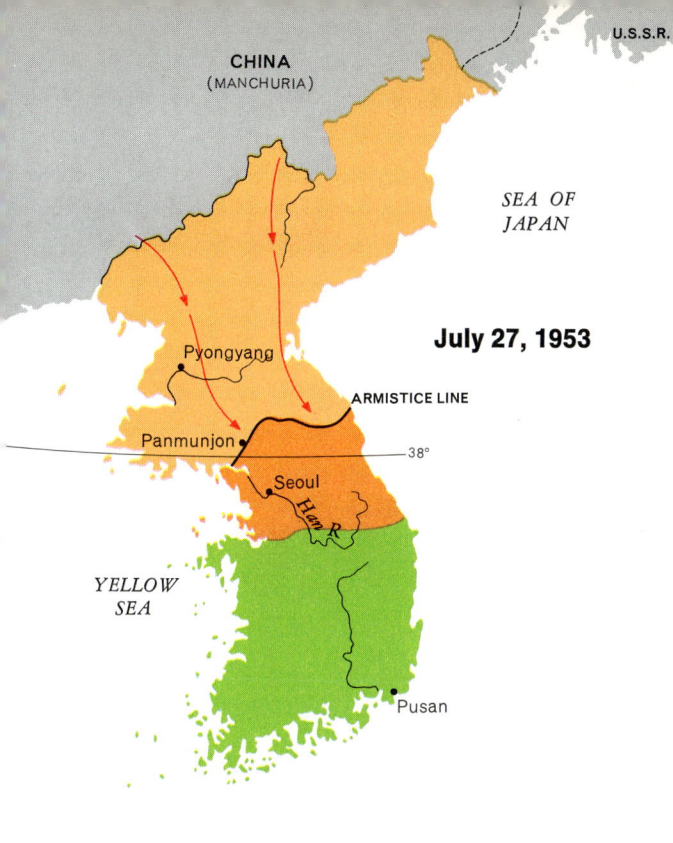

American troops *(above)* fire at snipers in Seoul during the Inchon offensive. Paratroopers *(below)* were important in attacks behind enemy lines. The Korean War brought the first widespread use by the United States of racially integrated military units.

opposed this course. They feared that it would bring the Soviet Union into the conflict and touch off a world war. In April 1951, after MacArthur had publicly criticized the administration's policy, Truman dismissed him for insubordination. The dismissal created a political furor. When MacArthur returned to the United States, he was given a hero's welcome and a chance to defend his views before Congress. But Truman's Korean policy and the principle of civilian supremacy in government remained unchanged.

On the battlefield, meanwhile, the war had settled into a stalemate. Chinese and American armies slugged at each other in the hills north of the 38th parallel. The Americans and the Communists began truce talks that dragged on for two years. Finally on July 27, 1953, after American policy makers implied that the United States might use tactical atomic bombs if necessary, the Communist negotiators agreed to an armistice.

Neither side could claim victory. The demilitarized zone, dividing North and South Korea, was still in the vicinity of the 38th parallel. Yet, for the first time, no matter how limited the commitment, the United Nations had tried to use force on a large scale. Americans could at least say that they had contained communism in Korea without bringing on a third world war.

A Look at Specifics

1. What policy was announced in the Truman Doctrine?
2. Why did the Soviet Union blockade Berlin in 1948? How did the Americans and British respond to the blockade?
3. Why did the United States want to strengthen Japan?
4. Why, despite the Soviet Union's membership on the Security Council, was the United Nations able to vote to send troops into Korea?
5. How did the government aid returning veterans? How did veterans' benefits affect higher education?
6. Why did Congress pass the Taft-Hartley Act?
7. Why was the campaign of 1948 a difficult one for the Democrats?

A Review of Major Ideas

1. How did American participation in world affairs after World War II differ from American participation after World War I?
2. What efforts did the United States make to contain communism during the Truman administration?
3. What social and economic problems did the United States experience during the Truman administration? What efforts did the President and Congress make to solve these problems? What successes did they achieve? In what areas did they fail?

For Independent Study

1. Why did the United States restrict the freedom of political parties that advocate the overthrow of the government by force? Should such parties be outlawed or should they be given the same opportunity to voice their opinions as have other political parties?
2. "Having suffered greater loss and devastation than any other country during the war, the Soviet Union was exceedingly sensitive about its safety as a nation. It tried to protect its frontiers by controlling neighboring countries and by maintaining big armies. American policy makers, however, perceived the Soviet actions as part of a worldwide Communist plot. Their get-tough policy resulted in the Cold War." Oppose or defend this view.

The Eisenhower Years

CHAPTER 26
1952–1960

The 1950's are often pictured as a bland decade in which nothing exciting happened. A fatherly general occupied the White House; businessmen in gray flannel suits dominated the government. Moderation was the ideal; extremism was the exception.

The bland image is deceptive, however. The fatherly military man seemed to face a new international crisis every week. The businesslike secretary of state's policy was one of "brinkmanship"—bringing the nation to the brink of war without slipping over the edge. And despite all the talk of moderation, many Americans began working for social and economic reforms that had once been considered extreme.

A REPUBLICAN VICTORY

By 1952, many Americans were ready for a change. Discontent over the Korean War, fear of communism, and disgust with some scandals in the executive branch suggested that the Democrats would have difficulty in the 1952 elections. Moreover, some Americans felt that if the Republicans did not end twenty years of Democratic rule, the two-party system would be dead.

Changing the Guard

As the time for their party convention grew near, the Republicans were divided. One group, composed of conservatives and party faithfuls, supported Robert A. Taft, "Mr. Republican." But the other faction, Republicans with internationalist leanings, believed Taft was still an isolationist. They rallied behind General Dwight D. Eisenhower, who battled the Taft forces and won the presidential nomination. Eisenhower tried to please Taft's followers by choosing a young conservative, Senator Richard M. Nixon of California, as his running mate.

Truman had decided not to run again. The Democrats drafted Adlai E. Stevenson, the

Bulky television sets roll off the assembly line.

governor of Illinois, as their candidate. A man of wit, intelligence, and eloquence, Stevenson had great appeal for intellectuals and liberals. He campaigned on a platform that endorsed the Truman policies.

Eisenhower denounced corruption and "creeping socialism" at home and promised to end the war in Korea. He won in a landslide, and the Republicans gained narrow majorities in Congress.

The New President

Dwight D. Eisenhower was born on a farm and grew up in the Middle West. After graduation from the military academy at West Point in 1915, he spent most of his life in military service. The exception was a brief period when he was president of Columbia University.

Eisenhower became well known in 1943, after President Roosevelt named him commander of the Allied forces in North Africa. Successes in battle brought Eisenhower the supreme command of Allied forces in Europe. Long before the war ended, Eisenhower had become a national hero. Millions of Americans knew him as "Ike." In 1950, at President Truman's request, he took command of the NATO forces in Europe. He resigned in 1952 to run for President.

Before the campaign, Eisenhower had had no civilian political experience, yet he had definite views on government. In domestic affairs, he was conservative. He believed that the government should not place controls over the lives of the people, particularly in economic matters. In foreign affairs, Eisenhower was an internationalist and a supporter of the United Nations. He considered isolationism outdated and dangerous.

The President relied heavily on the cabinet for advice and gave each department head considerable power. Most of Eisenhower's cabinet officers had been executives in big business. Secretary of State John Foster Dulles, a lawyer from New York, became the most powerful member of the cabinet. He usually shaped foreign policy.

When Eisenhower entered the White House, he held the view that the powers of the President had become swollen under Roosevelt and Truman. He wanted to restore the balance to the three branches by limiting his own power and by encouraging Congress to make policy.

The new President and his close advisers felt that government should act decisively, but with the least possible expense, in three main areas: to ensure a stable dollar, to balance the budget, and to maintain the nation's defenses. Eisenhower believed that this moderate program, which he called "modern Republicanism," reflected the views of millions of Americans.

Lowering Taxes

Republican campaigners had promised the voters prosperity and stable prices, brought about by balancing the budget, lowering federal taxes, and removing government restrictions on the economy.

Through executive orders in February 1953, President Eisenhower ended the weak controls that had been placed on rents, wages, and prices during the Korean War. He decided to try to stop inflation by curbing credit rather than by controlling wages and prices. The Federal Reserve System helped establish a tight-money policy, in which money became more difficult to get because the cost of borrowing it went up.

In an effort to balance the budget, Eisenhower tried to cut government spending. But almost two-thirds of the budget was allotted to national defense, and the President would not let the drive for economy endanger national security. Thus Eisenhower's first budget showed a deficit of 3.1 billion dollars.

Nevertheless, Republicans in Congress wanted to reduce taxes. At first, the Pres-

PRESIDENTIAL ELECTIONS: 1944-1956

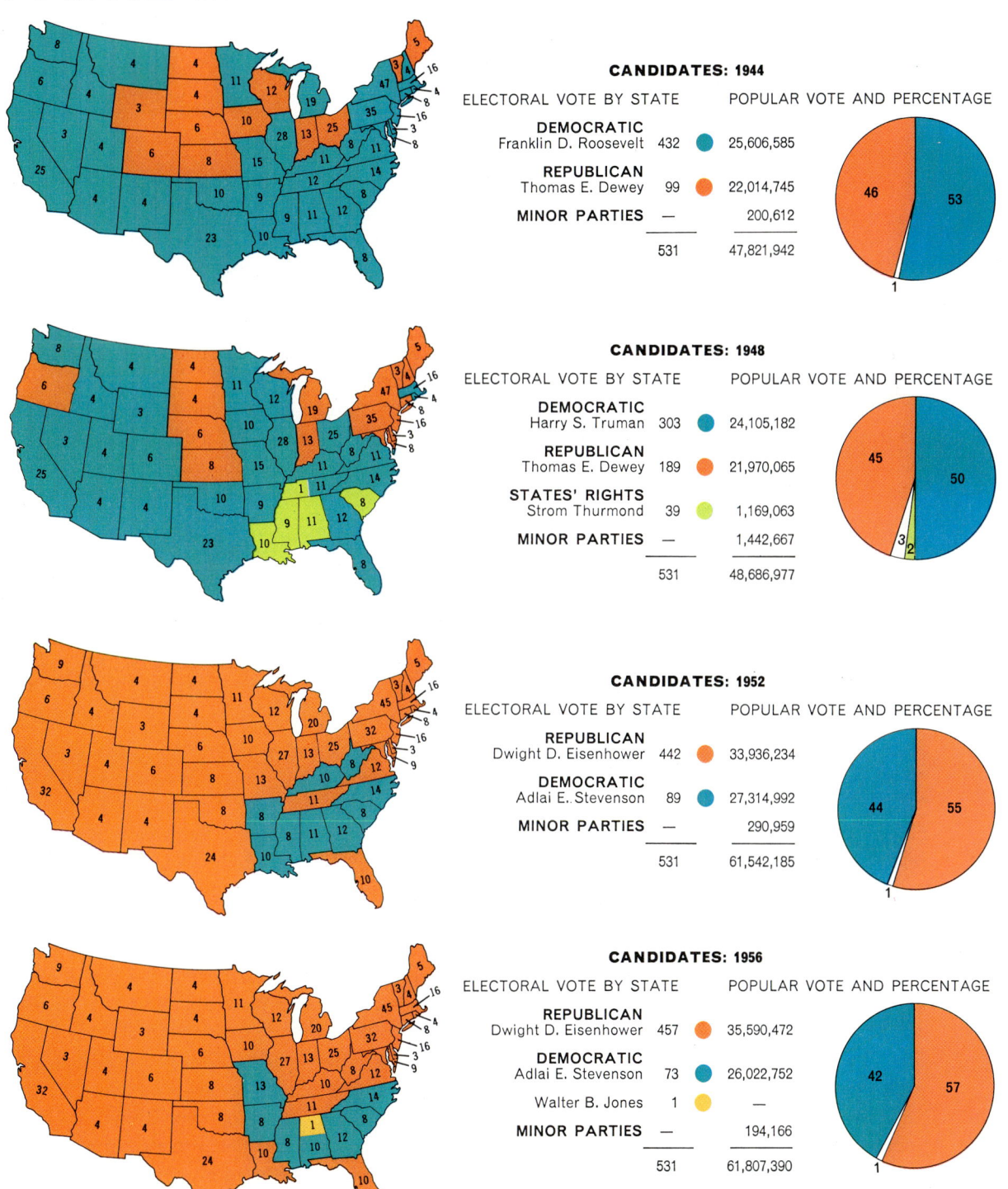

CANDIDATES: 1944

ELECTORAL VOTE BY STATE			POPULAR VOTE AND PERCENTAGE
DEMOCRATIC Franklin D. Roosevelt	432	🟦	25,606,585
REPUBLICAN Thomas E. Dewey	99	🟧	22,014,745
MINOR PARTIES	—		200,612
	531		47,821,942

Pie chart: 53 / 46 / 1

CANDIDATES: 1948

ELECTORAL VOTE BY STATE			POPULAR VOTE AND PERCENTAGE
DEMOCRATIC Harry S. Truman	303	🟦	24,105,182
REPUBLICAN Thomas E. Dewey	189	🟧	21,970,065
STATES' RIGHTS Strom Thurmond	39	🟨	1,169,063
MINOR PARTIES	—		1,442,667
	531		48,686,977

Pie chart: 50 / 45 / 3 / 2

CANDIDATES: 1952

ELECTORAL VOTE BY STATE			POPULAR VOTE AND PERCENTAGE
REPUBLICAN Dwight D. Eisenhower	442	🟧	33,936,234
DEMOCRATIC Adlai E. Stevenson	89	🟦	27,314,992
MINOR PARTIES	—		290,959
	531		61,542,185

Pie chart: 55 / 44 / 1

CANDIDATES: 1956

ELECTORAL VOTE BY STATE			POPULAR VOTE AND PERCENTAGE
REPUBLICAN Dwight D. Eisenhower	457	🟧	35,590,472
DEMOCRATIC Adlai E. Stevenson	73	🟦	26,022,752
Walter B. Jones	1	🟡	—
MINOR PARTIES	—		194,166
	531		61,807,390

Pie chart: 57 / 42 / 1

ident refused to put a tax cut ahead of a balanced budget, but in 1953–1954, the nation experienced a recession. Fearing that a depression might follow, Eisenhower eased the tight-money policy and changed his stand on a tax cut.

In the summer of 1954, Congress responded with the Internal Revenue Act, a major revision of the tax laws. The law reduced taxes for farmers, business owners, and investors. Another law lowered many excise taxes. Although the tax cuts amounted to 7.4 billion dollars, critics charged that they primarily benefited people with relatively high incomes.

Farm Policy

Farmers demanded more than tax relief. Even during the prosperity of the early 1950's, the prices of their products fell while the prices of other goods rose.

The secretary of agriculture, Ezra Taft Benson, was convinced that government price supports encouraged farmers to overproduce and that the farm surplus kept prices down. He proposed replacing high, rigid price supports with flexible supports on a sliding scale. He hoped to lower the supports gradually so that farm prices would eventually be based on supply and demand.

Many farmers expressed alarm over the plan. They feared it would lower their already declining incomes. Nonetheless, in August, Congress passed the Agricultural Act of 1954, which established the program Benson wanted. Congress also passed the Agricultural Trade Development and Assistance Act. It allowed the government to send surplus agricultural products to foreign countries in exchange for goods of strategic value to the American economy.

These laws were of some help to the farmers, but basically Benson's plan did not work. In 1955, the surplus was still huge; farm income continued to decline; and the

Joseph McCarthy *(standing)* badgers Joseph N. Welch at a Senate hearing into McCarthy's charges that Communists had infiltrated the army. As the lawyer for the army, Welch effectively deflated McCarthy.

cost of government subsidies rose by about 1.5 billion dollars.

Eisenhower then tried to attack the farm problem with another scheme. Under the new plan, the government would pay farmers if they would voluntarily not grow certain crops. This plan also included the *soil bank,* a plan for taking some farm land out of production. Two agricultural acts passed in 1956 and 1957 gave subsidies to farmers who reduced their crops.

Even though farm income rose in 1958, no plan, Eisenhower admitted, "really got at the roots of the farm problem." The agricultural surplus continued to grow, and the cost of price supports continued to rise.

Encouraging Free Enterprise

Eisenhower's position on the use of the nation's natural resources reflected his belief that the government should avoid regulating the economy. Soon after he took office, he had to decide if oil resources in tidelands should be developed by the federal government, as the property of the nation. In May 1953, he turned the tidelands over to the states for development by private oil companies. He considered this an act against the expansionism of the federal government.

The President also wanted to stop the expansion of federal power projects like the Tennessee Valley Authority. Yet Eisenhower did not favor complete abandonment of federal help. If private or local groups could not finance a power plant, he was willing to use government money for such a project. But he preferred to do so in partnership with a local unit of government or a private corporation.

The Eisenhower administration used the partnership idea to break the government's monopoly over nuclear power. The Atomic Energy Act of 1954 permitted private utility companies, under license from the Atomic Energy Commission, to own and operate atomic reactors for the production and commercial use of electricity. By 1960, several privately owned and operated nuclear-power plants were in operation.

Decline of McCarthyism

Eisenhower's beliefs often differed from those of many members of his party. In his policies on civil liberties he tried to avoid splitting the party. Although Eisenhower disliked Senator Joseph McCarthy's methods, he tried to placate the senator. He stepped up the hunt for subversives in government and fired employees who were viewed as security risks. In August 1954, Congress passed the Communist Control Act. It outlawed the Communist party.

Many people criticized the Eisenhower administration for some of its security policies. But some extreme conservatives—particularly McCarthy—claimed the administration did not go far enough. McCarthy even accused Eisenhower's choice as ambassador to the Soviet Union of being a "security risk." In December 1953, McCarthy accused the secretary of the army of shielding Communists in the army.

Later the army accused McCarthy of seeking special treatment for an assistant who had been drafted. In April 1954, Congress held hearings on the charges made by McCarthy and by the army. For more than a month the hearings were broadcast on nationwide television. Millions of Americans watched McCarthy bully and insult witnesses, among them high-ranking officers.

McCarthy began to lose his hold on the public, and in December 1954, the Republican-controlled Senate turned against him. It condemned him, by a vote of 67 to 22, for conduct unbecoming a senator. Eisenhower publicly expressed satisfaction with this blow at McCarthyism. The senator's influence dropped abruptly, never to return.

Other politicians tried to use anticommunism to attract votes, but the issue had lost much of its effectiveness. In the 1954 congressional election campaign, Vice-President Nixon stumped the country proclaiming that the Democrats were "soft on communism" and should not be elected. Despite his efforts, the Republicans lost control of both houses of Congress.

Social Legislation

Although basically conservative, Eisenhower did not attempt to erase the welfare laws of the Democratic past. He signed into law a boost in the minimum wage. He established a new Department of Health, Education, and Welfare and chose Mrs. Oveta Culp Hobby to head it. During Eisenhower's administration, social security benefits were increased for millions of Americans.

Congress passed a number of laws to help communities build public housing and to help people buy their own homes. The policies of the Federal Housing Authority favored massive urban renewal in which decaying low-rise buildings were torn down and replaced by tall, high-density structures. This policy, coupled with FHA's backing for development housing in the suburbs, accentuated the split between city and suburbs and aggravated many social problems.

In June 1956, Congress passed the Federal Aid Highway Act, the largest road-building project in the nation's history. It provided for the construction of a 41,000-mile interstate highway system. The cost, spread over thirteen years, was estimated at nearly 33.5 billion dollars and was to be shared by the federal government and the states.

The birth rate had risen sharply after World War II. The "baby boom" of the late 1940's led to overcrowded and understaffed schools in the 1950's. Since state and local

California was gaining enough children each day to fill a school. Students in one town attended class in tents. Nationally, the baby boom of the forties caused overcrowded schools in the fifties.

governments were running out of money to build schools, most educators wanted federal aid for elementary and high schools. But many conservatives resisted the idea, and President Eisenhower did not try to overcome the resistance.

Only after the Soviets had launched a space satellite did Congress act to help education. The National Defense Education Act, passed in 1958, gave federal aid to colleges and universities to improve the teaching of science, mathematics, and foreign languages and to provide loans and graduate fellowships for students preparing for college teaching careers. It did nothing, however, about eliminating classroom shortages.

Conservatives offered even greater resistance to a federal health-care program. Millions of people living on middle or low incomes could not afford the high costs of hospital and medical care. The partnership Medical Care Act of September 1960 offered federal assistance to the states to meet some of the needs of the elderly but did not meet the health-care needs of other Americans.

The 1956 Campaign

Although Eisenhower had suffered a heart attack and had undergone major surgery in the last year, in 1956 he ran for a second term. Richard M. Nixon again was the nominee for Vice-President. The party platform praised four years of Republican peace, progress, and prosperity, and promised more of the same for the future.

The Democrats once again chose Adlai E. Stevenson to head their ticket. As in 1952, Eisenhower's personality and immense popularity dominated the campaign. Eisenhower won a smashing victory, the greatest since that of Franklin D. Roosevelt in 1936.

The President was much more popular than his party; the Democrats retained control of both houses of Congress. Two years later the Democrats increased their margin of control in Congress and won many state offices. Throughout his second term, Eisenhower had a Democratic Congress.

FOREIGN POLICY

During the 1952 presidential campaign, the Republicans had denounced the policy of containment and had promised a new, positive foreign policy. Once in office, however, the Republicans continued containment instead of abandoning it. Eisenhower gave much responsibility for initiating foreign policy to his secretary of state, John Foster Dulles, who was strongly anti-Communist.

Like Truman before him, Eisenhower struggled with two major forces in Asia and Africa—anticolonial nationalism and communism. Although most Americans disliked colonialism on principle, they often opposed nationalist causes that seemed to be pro-Communist.

Indochina

Efforts to distinguish the nationalists from the Communists were especially difficult in Indochina. That French colony had been occupied by the Japanese during World War II. In fighting the Japanese, the United States had given aid to a number of nationalist groups in Indochina. One of them was the Viet Minh, led by Ho Chi Minh, a Soviet-trained Communist.

Once the war was over, the United States faced a dilemma: Should it help the French regain their colony, thus violating American anticolonial beliefs, or should it continue to help the Viet Minh, thereby aiding nationalists who might also be Communists? When a war broke out in 1946 between the Viet Minh and the French, the United States at first tried to remain neutral. It did not help the French or the Viet Minh. In 1949, the way was opened for American aid when the French set up an "independent" State of Vietnam. This government, headed by Bao Dai, was an anti-Communist front for the French. In 1950, Ho Chi Minh, apparently aided by the Chinese Communists, stepped up his attacks. The French lost important strongholds, and United States leaders became more concerned. They decided to take steps to oppose the Viet Minh.

Truman recognized the State of Vietnam, the regime that was headed by Bao Dai. During the Korean War, the United States sent economic and military aid to the French and to the Bao Dai government.

When Eisenhower became President, he increased this aid. He took the view that if Indochina fell to the Communists, all the states of Southeast Asia, like a row of dominoes, would fall to them. This was known as the "domino theory."

Despite American help, the French suffered a series of defeats. In the spring of 1954, the Viet Minh trapped a large French force in Dien Bien Phu, a remote northern fortress. The French pleaded for United States intervention to relieve the fortress. Eisenhower and most of his advisers were willing to intervene, but the President would not do so without support from Congress and from allies like Britain. Since Britain refused support and congressional leaders in the United States were hostile, the idea of intervention collapsed.

In April 1954, a few weeks before Dien Bien Phu finally fell, the French attended a peace conference in Geneva to discuss Indochina. The Soviet Union and Red China represented the Communist world, and France and Britain negotiated for the western nations. The Geneva Accords provided for a cease-fire and divided Vietnam at the 17th parallel, in anticipation of national elections. Vietnam had two governments, and each claimed to represent the same national territory. The Democratic Republic of Vietnam, led by Ho Chi Minh, controlled the northern part; the State of Vietnam, led by Bao Dai, controlled the southern section. Laos and Cambodia became independent kingdoms.

France now withdrew its troops, its former colonists, and its economic aid from Vietnam. The United States, however, increased its aid, especially after Ngo Dinh Diem overthrew Bao Dai's government in July and proclaimed a republic. Diem refused to honor the Geneva Accords, because the South Vietnamese government had not signed them. When the national elections promised for 1956 were not held, anti-Diem guerrillas in

Pro-French Vietnamese dig in during the Battle of Dien Bien Phu. France's defeat in this fight persuaded the French government to pull its forces out of Indochina. The Viet Minh then seemed ready to take over the country.

the south began terrorist activities. Throughout Eisenhower's second term, the United States increased economic and military aid to Diem. Eisenhower did not send troops, but he did send military advisers.

Eisenhower's deepest Asian involvement came in Laos. The President sent economic and military aid in 1959 and 1960 to the kingdom of Laos. The Pathet Lao, a nationalist movement that received Communist support, fought this conservative government. The Pathet Lao claimed to represent the people of Laos and accused the United States of opposing national self-determination. Although the Pathet Lao was winning the civil war, the Eisenhower administration would not send United States troops to Laos. Eisenhower did not want to risk a war with Communist China, which supported the Pathet Lao.

Alliance or Neutralism?

Eisenhower did not carry out his anti-Communist policy solely through aid. He also tried to prevent the expansion of communism in Asia through a loose alliance. In September 1954, representatives of Australia, France, Britain, New Zealand, Pakistan, the Philippines, Thailand, and the United States signed an agreement to consult each other in case of a Communist threat. This alliance developed into a regional organization called the Southeast Asia Treaty Organization (SEATO).

Unlike NATO, this alliance had little power, partly because few important Asian nations were members. Burma, Ceylon, India, and Indonesia refused to join. India, the most important of these Asian nations, set the lead in following a policy of "neutralism." In the Cold War, it sided with neither the Soviet Union nor the United States. More often than not, Indian statesmen opposed United States policies in Asia.

India's attitude began to change after two incidents in 1959. Communist China brutally suppressed a rebellion in Tibet, and Chinese soldiers clashed with Indian soldiers on Tibet's borderlands. President Eisenhower tried to further improve relations with India by visiting Asia in December 1959.

China

Throughout his terms in office, Eisenhower followed the policy that the Nationalist government in Taiwan was the legitimate government of China. He refused to recognize the People's Republic of China, the Communist government that controlled the mainland.

Eisenhower's biggest problems with China involved deciding how much help to give the Nationalist regime. Shortly after he took office, the President "unleashed" General Chiang Kai-shek from restrictions on American military aid that kept Chiang's forces tied to Taiwan. Since the Nationalists proved to be too weak to attack China's mainland, nothing happened.

In September 1954, however, the Chinese Communists shelled and threatened to invade small islands along the China coast, most of which were held by Chiang's Nationalist troops. Dulles signed an alliance with the Nationalist government in December 1954 in which the United States promised to come to the aid of Nationalist China, if the Reds attacked it. This pledge did not, however, apply to the islands along the Chinese mainland. In this crisis, and in a similar one in August 1958, the United States persuaded the Nationalists to pull out of several of the coastal islands.

The Western Hemisphere

Anti-Yankee feeling was a common manifestation of nationalism in Latin America. The early actions of Eisenhower's administration only increased the hostility.

When Colonel Jacobo Arbenz Guzmán became president of Guatemala in 1951, Communists gained important posts in the government. The Guatemalan's confiscation of United States property irritated many Americans. His purchase of arms from Communist Czechoslovakia in May 1954 finally provoked action. Dulles announced that "Communist colonialism" had taken over in Guatemala and endangered the peace of the Western Hemisphere. The United States sent arms to Nicaragua and Honduras and made them available to Colonel Carlos Castillo Armas, an exiled Guatemalan army officer. In June, Castillo Armas invaded Guatemala from Honduras, overthrew Arbenz Guzmán, and established a conservative regime.

Many Latin Americans denounced Eisenhower's aid to Castillo Armas as intervention in Guatemala's internal affairs and as a revival of "big stick" diplomacy. Anti-Yankee feeling intensified in many parts of Latin America.

After the furor over the Guatemala affair had died down, Eisenhower tried to improve relations with the Latin American countries. He asked them to join the United States in an inter-American partnership, called the "good partner policy."

Eisenhower sent Vice-President Richard M. Nixon on a good-will tour of eight South American nations in 1958. From the beginning, Nixon encountered hostile demonstrations. Everywhere, Nixon bore the brunt of an exploding anti-Americanism. Bitter students swore at and spat on the Vice-President. Finally, in Caracas, Venezuela, a mob attacked him in his car.

Upon his return home, Nixon suggested that the United States pay more attention to Latin America and increase economic aid. Eisenhower and Secretary of State Dulles agreed. In 1959, the United States joined an inter-American development bank to provide credit and other financial help for Latin American nations.

To the north, Eisenhower faced difficulties with Canada. The building of a seaway from the Gulf of St. Lawrence to inland ports on the Great Lakes had long been wanted by many Americans and Canadians. But political problems had always blocked the project.

In May 1954, Eisenhower persuaded Congress to set up a corporation to finance, construct, and operate the United States portion of such a seaway. The St. Lawrence Seaway and the St. Lawrence power project were completed in partnership with Canada in April 1959. Besides strengthening the bonds of friendship between the two nations, the Seaway increased government revenues.

Cuba

A yearning for economic and social reform was common among many Latin Americans. That yearning led to revolution in Cuba. In January 1959, after five years of plotting and fighting, a revolutionary movement led by Fidel Castro overthrew the conservative dictatorship. At first, many Americans were sympathetic toward Castro's efforts. When Castro began confiscating United States property and establishing a left-wing dictatorship, however, public opinion in the United States turned against him.

After Castro made a deal to sell Cuban sugar to the Soviet Union, Eisenhower became truly alarmed. With the approval of Congress, he put an embargo on Cuban sugar imports. In October 1960 he broadened the embargo to include everything but the export of food and medical supplies. By that time, Castro had recognized Red China, announced his acceptance of the Soviet Union's protection, and imported Soviet arms.

Earlier, in February 1960, Eisenhower had toured Argentina, Brazil, Chile, and Uruguay. He found little evidence of the violent anti-American sentiment experienced by Nixon two years earlier. Yet his good partner policy had not been successful. Castro's Cuba had brought Latin America into the politics of the Cold War.

Europe

The thrust of Eisenhower's policy in Europe was to support political and economic union. Eisenhower also wanted a common defense policy for Europe. He committed the United States to rely primarily on its atomic "deterrent" rather than on land armies for defense of western Europe. This policy, as well as a relaxation of tension after the death of Stalin, in March 1953, led many Europeans to desire "peaceful coexistence" with the Soviets.

A treaty of October 1954, signed by Europe's leading NATO nations and West Germany, created the Western European Union. It provided for the defense of Europe through the use of national armies and a system of interrelated alliances. Separate agreements ended the Allied occupation of West Germany and admitted that nation to membership in NATO. In May 1955, in answer to

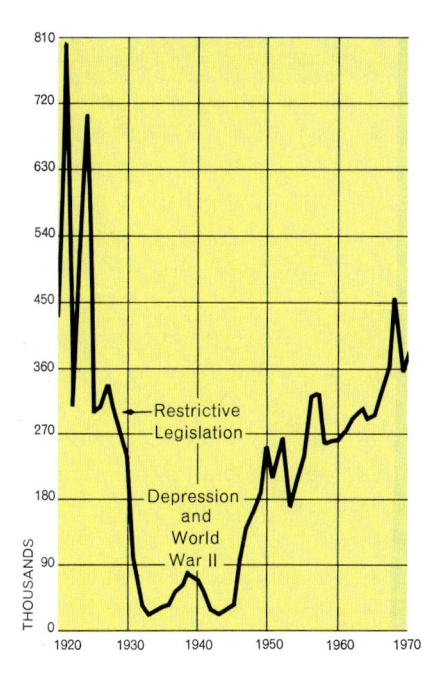

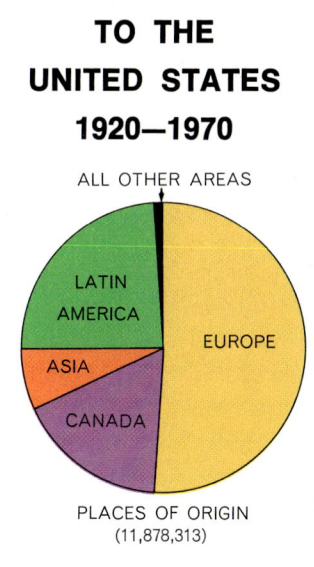

IMMIGRATION TO THE UNITED STATES 1920–1970

IMMIGRANTS FROM EUROPE, 1920-1970

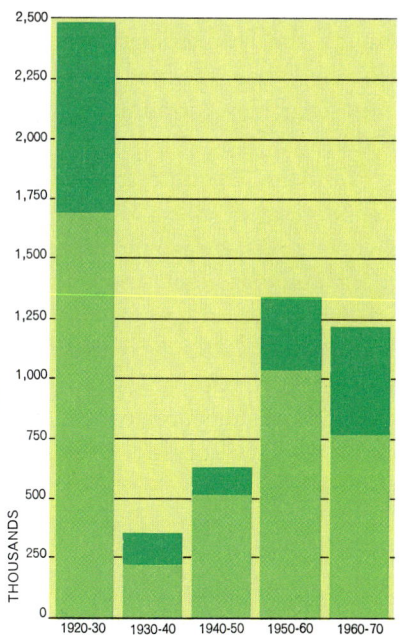

PLACES OF ORIGIN (11,878,313)

Northern and Central Europe
Britain, Ireland, Norway, Sweden, Finland, Denmark, Netherlands, Belgium, Luxembourg, France, Switzerland, Czechoslovakia, Germany, Austria, Yugoslavia, Hungary, Poland

Eastern and Southern Europe
U.S.S.R., Lithuania, Latvia, Estonia, Romania, Bulgaria, Turkey, Albania, Greece, Italy, Spain, Portugal

Hungarian rebels burn pro-Communist books during the 1956 revolt. Some of the rebels were nationalists who wanted to keep communism but end Soviet control of their country.

western alliances, the Soviets signed the Warsaw Pact, an alliance with Europe's Communist nations.

One aspect of Eisenhower's early views of international affairs had pleased many conservative Americans: He had announced that his administration would replace "containment" with a policy of "liberation" of the peoples behind the iron curtain.

In Hungary, in October 1956, students rioted against their Communist rulers. Soon others, including units from Hungary's Communist army, joined the revolt. The rebels demanded the end of Communist rule, denounced the Warsaw Pact, and tried to take Hungary out of the Communist bloc. This effort at self-liberation brought in the Soviet army with heavy tanks and big guns. Although the Hungarians fought for Budapest block by block, the Soviets crushed them and imposed a new Communist government on Hungary.

President Eisenhower had pleaded with the Soviets to allow Hungary to decide its own fate. But he would not intervene to aid the Hungarian rebels for fear of starting a nuclear war. Hungarians were bitterly disappointed because they received no help from the West. Critics charged Eisenhower and Dulles with encouraging captive peoples to revolt against hopeless odds, a charge both men denied.

Suez Crisis

During the Hungarian revolt, a crisis arose in the Middle East. The difficulties grew out of Egypt's policy of anticolonialism and its desire to become the leader of the Arab world.

In 1951, the United States and its western allies had worked out a plan for an organization in the Middle East to protect the region against a Communist attack. Egypt refused to participate and demanded that British troops guarding the Suez Canal zone get out. In July 1952, a bloodless revolution swept Egypt, and corrupt King Farouk was overthrown. Ultimately, Gamal Abdel Nasser, a nationalistic young colonel, came to power. In October 1954, Nasser made an agreement with Britain that led to the withdrawal of its troops from the Suez.

Egypt still refused to join the new Middle East alliance. This alliance, known later as the Middle Eastern Treaty Organization (METO), included Turkey, Iraq, Britain, Pakistan, and Iran. The United States sponsored the pact but did not join it.

In December 1955, the United States and

Britain agreed to help build a high dam at Aswân on the Nile River, about 800 miles south of Cairo. Nasser delayed accepting these offers to help finance the dam, apparently in hope of getting better terms from the Soviet Union. In July 1956, Dulles withdrew the American offer, and the British withdrew theirs. Nasser then seized the Suez Canal (owned primarily by British and French stockholders) and announced that he would use the canal tolls to help pay for dam construction. The outraged French and British threatened to retake control of the canal by force.

Their opportunity came in October. The Israelis, alarmed by Nasser's threats, attempted to end terrorist raids from Egypt by invading the Gaza Strip and the Sinai Peninsula. Within a few days British and French forces occupied Port Said at the western end of the canal. The Egyptians retaliated by sinking ships to block the canal. Elsewhere Arabs blew up oil pipelines, forcing western Europeans to ration oil.

Eisenhower was surprised and shocked by the assault on Egypt. He joined the Soviets in condemning the attack. Through the United Nations, he asked for a cease-fire and withdrawal of foreign troops from Egypt. The Soviet Union threatened to use missiles against England and France to help Egypt, but the United States said it would block such interference. Faced with the opposition of their major ally, of the Soviet Union, and of the United Nations, the British and French withdrew from Egypt. The Israelis withdrew after being assured of their right to use international waterways. In April 1957, the Suez Canal was reopened to traffic, after it had been cleared by a United Nations salvage operation.

The Eisenhower stand in the Suez crisis won favor among Arabs and anticolonialists everywhere. It also revealed a gulf between the United States and its two major allies, Britain and France.

The Eisenhower Doctrine

After the Suez crisis, the Soviets moved into the Middle East with enhanced prestige. They seemed able to fill the power vacuum left by the retreat of Britain and France. To counter the Soviet moves, the President issued a warning, known as the Eisenhower Doctrine, which said that the United States would help defend the nations of the Middle East threatened by Communist aggression.

In March 1957, at the President's request, Congress approved by joint resolution the Eisenhower Doctrine. It also provided 200 million dollars for economic and military aid to nations in the Middle East.

Various crises in the Middle East kept the United States Sixth Fleet on the alert in the eastern Mediterranean. The crisis that led the administration to invoke the Eisenhower Doctrine, however, grew out of a civil war in Lebanon. Lebanon's ruler, Camille Chamoun, charged President Nasser of the United Arab Republic (a union of Egypt and Syria) with stirring up a revolt.

Nasser had flooded Iraq with Arab nationalist propaganda just before a group of army officers overthrew Iraq's monarchy. Fearing a similar *coup,* Lebanon's President Chamoun appealed to the United States government for help. Eisenhower sent 5,000 marines to Beirut, Lebanon's chief port, and soon increased the force to 14,000.

Despite the protests of Nasser and Soviet leaders, the United States kept troops in Lebanon until October 1958. Then United Nations observation teams began patrolling the borders to prevent infiltration by Communists and other political extremists.

The Continuing Cold War

Eisenhower's opposition to the Suez war had badly shaken Britain and France. In 1957, United States and European diplomats worked to mend the North Atlantic alliance. The need for strengthening the alliance seemed urgent because of the Soviet Union's demonstrated ability to launch long-range missiles with nuclear warheads.

Eisenhower had increased defense spending to help end the brief recessions of the 1950's. To save money, he and his advisers cut down expenditures for conventional weapons for the army, navy, and air force. They made nuclear weapons the nation's main line of defense. Such weapons, they said, could be used in "massive retaliation" against a foe and cost less than the support of huge armies and navies.

Some military and political leaders criticized this defense policy. They argued that the United States should maintain a balanced military force, one that could quickly fight a limited war with conventional weapons or a major war with nuclear weapons.

Other critics charged that the government was delaying the development of guided missiles. In October 1957, the Soviets launched *Sputnik,* the first space satellite. As a result, during Eisenhower's second term, Americans debated whether or not the United States had to overcome a "missile gap" to catch up with the Soviets.

In November 1958, the Soviet Union threatened the Allied foothold in Berlin. Premier Nikita Khrushchev demanded that the United States, Britain, and France get out of West Berlin within six months. The Allies had about 10,000 troops in Berlin, which they refused to withdraw. Khrushchev finally removed the six-month deadline but asked for a meeting with Eisenhower and other heads of state to discuss the status of Berlin.

Secretary of State Dulles opposed diplomatic conferences by heads of state—the so-called summit meetings. After Dulles's death in May 1959, Eisenhower began to take a more direct part in diplomacy. In July, he invited Khrushchev to the United States "to melt a little of the ice" of the Cold War.

The Soviet premier arrived in September and made a whirlwind trip across the United States. In conversations with Eisenhower, Khrushchev removed any threat of a time limit for negotiations over Berlin. Eisenhower then agreed to a summit meeting of the Big Four—the heads of state from the United States, the Soviet Union, Britain, and France. The summit meeting was scheduled for May 16, 1960, in Paris.

On May 1, a United States plane, with only the pilot aboard, was forced down over Sverdlovsk, an industrial city about 1,200 miles inside the Soviet Union. The aircraft was a U-2 reconnaissance plane, equipped with sensitive photographic equipment. This plane and others like it had been making reconnaissance flights over the Soviet Union for almost four years, usually flying so high that they could not be intercepted.

At first, the United States government denied that the U-2 plane had been engaged in spying activities. But when the Russians announced that they were holding a U-2 pilot captive, the President acknowledged that he had authorized the flight. Khrushchev then used the U-2 incident to disrupt the Paris summit meeting. He withdrew his invitation to Eisenhower to visit the Soviet Union. "The Russian people would say I was mad," he explained, "to welcome a man who sends spy planes over here." Thus Eisenhower's effort to ease the tensions of the Cold War had been thwarted.

Africa

In Africa in the 1950's, many colonies of European countries were being prepared for independence. Most of the new nations were committed to ending all foreign control over their continent. The Soviets and the Chinese claimed to be anticolonial, and they tried to win the African nations to their side in the Cold War. The United States wanted African support in the Cold War but did not want to offend allies like Britain and France by committing itself to an anticolonial policy.

The first open struggle between the Soviets and the Americans for the allegiance of an African nation occurred in the Belgian Congo. Belgium abruptly gave the colony its independence in June 1960, without going through a transition period to place the Congolese in charge of the government. Almost immediately, the Congolese army began slaughtering white officers and Belgian settlers. Belgian forces intervened. When the Soviets threatened a counterintervention, the United States warned that it would block Soviet troops if they attempted to enter the Congo. Finally, the United Nations sent in troops to try and bring order to the young Republic of the Congo.

THE DOMESTIC SCENE

A number of social movements caught the public eye in the 1950's. Some were revivals of old movements, while others met new situations in postwar America. The most important was that concerned with civil rights.

School Integration

Southern states had long enforced segregation of blacks and whites in trains, buses, restaurants, schools, and other public places. An 1896 Supreme Court decision was the legal basis for this practice

After World War II, the Supreme Court heard a number of cases that challenged the "separate but equal" doctrine. The most important was that of *Brown* v. *Board of Education of Topeka.* In May 1954 the justices ruled unanimously that separate facilities in public education were by their nature unequal and kept blacks from enjoying educational rights on terms equal with whites. A year later, the Supreme Court required the southern states to integrate their schools "with all deliberate speed."

In the border states and in some of the large cities, authorities began admitting black and white children to the same schools. But in most of the South the decision met with bitter resistance that finally led to crisis.

In September 1957, Governor Orval Faubus of Arkansas challenged the authority of the federal government. He used all available means to keep black students out of Central High School, an all-white school in Little Rock. When local authorities did not control rioting there, President Eisenhower ordered paratroopers to Little Rock to protect the black students and to enforce the federal court's order. "Mob rule," he told the nation, "cannot be allowed to override the decisions of our courts."

Despite the President's use of the army, desegregation of schools in Arkansas was

Armed troops escort black students into Central High School in Little Rock, Arkansas *(left)*. The end of the Montgomery bus boycott also marked the end of legally required racial segregation on public buses. *Opposite:* Ralph Abernathy, Dr. Martin Luther King, Jr., and two other leaders of the boycott celebrate with a bus ride after the Supreme Court's decision in the case.

delayed for several years. Other southern states followed a policy of "token desegregation," allowing only a few blacks to enter white schools. By the beginning of 1961, a small percentage of the 3 million black children in the South were attending integrated classes, but no legal doctrine blocked further integration.

Nonviolent Protest

School integration was but one of the issues. In the North, as well as in the South, black leaders began attacking discrimination in housing, employment, and other areas of life. They used their political power in the North and their rising economic power in the South to secure some changes.

As Truman before him had done, Eisenhower ordered the armed forces to operate on the principle of racial equality. He also appointed blacks to several important positions in the government and ordered administration officials to end racial discrimination in hiring. Eisenhower asked Congress for a civil rights law to put the power of the federal government behind the right of black Americans to vote.

The Civil Rights Act of 1957 marked a turning point in the struggle for civil rights. It permitted federal judges to punish state and local officials who interfered with the right of blacks to vote. This section of the law led to some openings in the barrier against black political activity in the South, but the law was not strictly enforced.

This slow action against racial discrimination did not satisfy many blacks, particularly the young leaders. Some of them used a strategy of nonviolent protest to fight segregation. They refused to obey city and state laws that they believed violated the Constitution by requiring racial discrimination. The outstanding leader of the nonviolent protest movement was Dr. Martin Luther King, Jr., a young, black clergyman from Montgomery, Alabama.

He made headlines in December 1955 when he attacked segregation on buses. Authorities in Montgomery had arrested and fined a black woman, Rosa Parks, for refusing to move from the white to the black section of a bus. King helped organize a peaceful boycott of the bus company to end that discrimination. He urged blacks to walk or to ride in car pools rather than to use segregated buses. The boycott, which lasted more than a year, ended late in 1956 when the Supreme Court ruled that bus segregation was illegal.

Dr. King headed an alliance of church groups, the Southern Christian Leadership Conference (SCLC), which decided after the success in Montgomery to conduct protests in other cities. Other organizations, such as the Congress of Racial Equality (CORE), also adopted the strategy of nonviolence.

The Labor Supply

There was nothing new about machines being developed to do the work of humans. But the 1950's brought *automation,* in which machines were developed to operate other machinery. Automation wiped out the jobs of large numbers of unskilled workers. The economy now demanded refined skills and high levels of education.

Automation also had a decided impact on labor organizations. The source of their membership was shrinking, and in time their power would also decline. In December 1955, the labor leaders ended old rivalries. The American Federation of Labor and the Congress of Industrial Organizations merged to form a new organization, the AFL-CIO, with George Meany as president. Like other union leaders, Meany was concerned about the economic slumps of the 1950's. Each slump increased the number of unemployed people in industrial centers.

During the recession of 1957, which lasted nine months, industrial production decreased 14.3 percent and unemployment increased by about 4.6 percent. In some parts of the country, even after economic recovery, unemployment remained high. Labor leaders urged the government to establish a public works program to create jobs, but the Eisenhower administration refused to do so.

Many congressmen were hostile to certain labor unions because congressional investigations had uncovered corruption among union leaders. In 1959, Congress enacted the Landrum-Griffin Labor-Management Reporting and Disclosure Law to clean up the internal affairs of unions and to outlaw abuses by union officials.

Automation affected more than just industrial centers. The factory farms that had grown up in World War II were becoming increasingly machine oriented. This was especially true in California, where the terrain and corporate land ownership suited the large-scale use of farm machinery. César Chavez, director of a community organization, led a fight in the 1950's to end the use of *braceros*—contract farm laborers from foreign countries—when local farm workers were unemployed. His major goal was to find jobs for fellow Mexican Americans.

The seeds of a revival of the women's movement were being sown in the 1950's. Many of the women who had left jobs in industry after World War II now began looking for employment outside the home. But when women took paying jobs, they usually were given lower salaries than men doing the same work and they had fewer chances for advancement.

Many women felt that such policies violated their rights. Some sought help from the government in the form of laws. A new push began for passage of the Equal Rights Amendment, which had been proposed in every session of Congress since 1923. In the 1950's Martha Griffiths, a newly elected congresswoman from Michigan, became chief sponsor of the proposed amendment.

Internal Changes

Pressure to pass statehood bills for Alaska and Hawaii had grown in the 1940's. Many Alaskans wanted to rid themselves of restrictive territorial laws and get more help in developing the area's resources. After years of congressional debate, the state of Alaska was admitted to the Union in 1959. Action on Hawaii's bid for statehood had been deferred when the Korean War began. Then Congress stalled because of party arguments. Statehood was finally achieved in 1959.

Indian policies were also debated during the 1950's. Some lawmakers felt that the Indian Reorganization Act was not improving conditions for Indians; others were concerned about its cost. The Hoover Commission recommended policies that would encourage Indians to leave the reservations and suggested the transfer of Indian assistance programs to the states. This policy of "termination" of both tribal unity and tribal ties to the federal government was favored by the Commissioner of Indian Affairs. Congress quickly shifted responsibility for Indian programs to the states.

In the late 1950's, termination policies faced criticism as it became obvious that not enough planning for protection of Indian rights was included: Indians were urged to relocate in cities without adequate job opportunities; government services were withdrawn when no adequate substitutes existed. Congress therefore began reconsidering termination policies.

CULTURE IN THE FORTIES AND FIFTIES

The performing arts—music, dance, and drama—dominated the culture of the 1940's and 1950's. Much of the time these arts were

Transforming Puerto Rico

Ever since the United States acquired Puerto Rico in the Spanish-American War (1898), the island's status in relation to the mainland has been a question. At first, self-government was limited; most political control was exercised from Washington, D.C. In the 1940's and 1950's, however, Puerto Rico was transformed.

First came economic change, promoted by Operation Bootstrap (*"Fomento"*), a program to industrialize the island. Under the leadership of Rexford Guy Tugwell, who was appointed governor by President Roosevelt, the island government began building industries to serve local needs. Although many projects failed, Tugwell had laid important groundwork.

Equally important were political changes. Since 1917, Puerto Rico had been governed under provisions of the Jones Act. That law had given Puerto Rico a two-house legislature elected by universal male suffrage and had granted United States citizenship to the people of Puerto Rico. In 1947, Congress passed a law providing for an elected governor. Luis Muñoz Marín was elected in 1948. Muñoz sought to end the questions about the island's status by making Puerto Rico an independent commonwealth, somewhere between statehood and independence, in 1952. As a commonwealth, the island government controls internal affairs; the United States government, foreign relations. The people remain United States citizens.

Under Muñoz, Operation Bootstrap took on a new look. Teodoro Moscoso, who headed *Fomento* from 1942 to 1961, suggested that Puerto Rico encourage investments from the mainland. Unlike Tugwell, Muñoz agreed. With the incentive of tax-free status, many industries began moving to Puerto Rico. Moscoso also promoted tourism.

By the mid-1950's, Puerto Rico was no longer primarily agricultural. The growing industries had brought many people to cities. At the same time, low air fares were encouraging migration to the mainland. During the fifties alone, half a million Puerto Ricans moved to the mainland. Most of them settled in New York City. Like earlier migrants from Puerto Rico, many of them intended to stay on the mainland only long enough to raise capital to start a new life on their home island.

Puerto Ricans in New York City transformed East Harlem into Spanish Harlem, "El Barrio."

The forties and fifties brought a new diversity of themes and styles in art. Abstract expressionism became important in painting. Jackson Pollack, Willem de Kooning, and Arshile Gorky sought free expression in the act of creating. But realism still had many followers. Andrew Wyeth, probably the most popular painter of these decades, painted both rural and urban scenes in a realistic, detailed style. Other artists adopted a technique called "surrealism," in which realistic objects were combined or depicted in startling ways. A "primitive" style characterized the works of Anna "Grandma" Moses, who did nostalgic rural scenes. Painters like Horace Pippin portrayed subjects from American folklore. In sculpture, abstract pieces came to the fore. Experiments with such metals as aluminum and steel yielded works unlike traditional bronze statuary. Alexander Calder produced hanging, moving structures called "mobiles." Richard Hunt did linear metallic figures. Irene Pereira experimented with glass and various metals to create designs of changing planes and shapes.

Water of the Flowery Mill, by Arshile Gorky, 1944

Young America, by Andrew Wyeth, 1950

Ready-to-wear, by Stuart Davis, 1955

Domino Players, by Horace Pippin, 1943

The Subway, by George Tooker, 1950. Collection, Whitney Museum of American Art, New York. Juliana Force purchase

expressed through electronic media—radio, television, motion pictures, and recordings.

Drama, Dance, and Music

New themes were characteristic of work in the American theater. Tennessee Williams dealt with human decay and degeneracy in *The Glass Menagerie* (1944) and *A Streetcar Named Desire* (1947). In plays like *Death of a Salesman* (1949), Arthur Miller examined the behavior of people who were overwhelmed and defeated by circumstances and personal weakness. One of the most promising of the young American playwrights of the fifties was Lorraine Hansberry. She died at the age of thirty-five after the success of *A Raisin in the Sun* (1959), a drama of black family life.

Musical plays were usually more successful than serious drama. In the 1940's, musicals began to develop believable plots and characterization. Choreographers like Agnes de Mille, George Balanchine, and Jerome Robbins brought new kinds of dance to musical comedy. They combined the traditions of ballet with the ideas of jazz and modern dance to produce dramatic dance.

Richard Rodgers and Oscar Hammerstein II collaborated for the first time to create the musical *Oklahoma!* They integrated music and dance into the plot. They continued their success with *Carousel* and *South Pacific*. After the initial success of Rodgers and Hammerstein, older composers like Cole Porter and Irving Berlin, and younger ones like Alan Jay Lerner and Frederick Lowe created such famous musicals as *Annie Get Your Gun* (1946), *Kiss Me, Kate* (1948), and *Brigadoon* (1947). These musicals provided many of the popular songs of the forties. The most successful musical of the fifties was Lerner and Lowe's *My Fair Lady,* which ran for more than six years on Broadway.

The 1940's became known as the era of the "big bands." Count Basie, Duke Ellington, Benny Goodman, and Glenn Miller led bands that played swing. People who danced to swing music were known as "jitterbugs," for their wild, gymnastic footwork. Improvisational jazz enjoyed a revival in the late 1940's. Charlie Parker, Thelonius Monk, and Dizzy Gillespie sparked an interest in "abstract" sound.

With the decline of the big bands, singers like Nat "King" Cole, Frank Sinatra, Peggy Lee, and Perry Como became more important. The subdued music of these mood singers remained popular when "rock'n'roll," a raucous mixture of country-western music and black rhythm and blues, appeared. Elvis Presley brought rock'n'roll into the public eye. He sold millions of records and was imitated by dozens of young performers.

American themes were popular in the symphonic music of the forties and fifties. Aaron Copland's ballets *Billy the Kid, Rodeo,* and *Appalachian Spring* drew from folklore and folk music. New patterns in sound were characteristic of many works. As a result, Charles Ives, who had composed most of his major works before 1920, won belated recognition. In compositions like *Fourth of July* (1913) he wove bits of popular songs, marches, hymns, patriotic songs, and country dances into complex and original patterns. Gian-Carlo Menotti wrote operas on American themes to be sung in English.

Motion Pictures, Television, and Radio

American films made in the forties were popular all over the world. They consisted of a large proportion of musicals, as well as comedies, westerns, thrillers, and animated cartoons. Some dealt directly with the themes of war, and many contained anti-Nazi and anti-Japanese propaganda.

Filmmakers often explored society's problems, including anti-Semitism, racism, and postwar problems of veterans. Adaptations of best-selling books became popular, including *All the King's Men* (1949), the story of a politician's rise to power. Westerns like *High Noon* (1952), musicals, and Alfred Hitchcock thrillers remained popular.

As movie audiences declined due to the expansion of television, some studios tried to capture public interest by producing expensive movies on grand scales. Most of these "spectaculars" were made by Cecil B. deMille, and some of them paid off for the studios. Among his famous screen epics were *Samson and Delilah, The Greatest Show on Earth,* and *The Ten Commandments.* The most enduring stars of the forties and fifties included Clark Gable, Bette Davis, Humphrey Bogart, Marilyn Monroe, and the cartoon characters of Walt Disney.

Television had been invented in the 1920's, but it did not gain a mass audience until 1947. Then it became the rage. By 1949, Americans were buying 100,000 television sets each week. Three years later, there were TV sets in 3.1 million American homes.

For the most part, Americans were watching their favorite radio stars who had switched to the new medium. Many radio stars were unsuccessful on TV, which required a different kind of show. The early fifties are remembered as the "golden age" of television. New shows created especially for TV reached the public. Political activities like the national party conventions also drew millions of television viewers. Many watched the hearings of the Special Committee to Investigate Organized Crime, headed by Senator Estes Kefauver of Tennessee.

The fifties also brought numerous situation comedies and quiz shows, the first "talk shows," and the news commentary of Edward R. Murrow. By 1955, there were television sets in 32 million American homes.

The rise of TV had a great impact on radio and movies. Radio became a medium of talk, music, and news. The movie studios fell on hard times and fought off bankruptcy by turning to production of TV shows.

A Look at Specifics

1. What was Eisenhower's "partnership idea" regarding nuclear power plants? How did he put this idea into practice?
2. How did SEATO differ from NATO?
3. What was the policy of "massive retaliation"? How did it affect defense strategy?
4. How did the Civil Rights Act of 1957 attempt to protect voting rights for blacks?
5. How did blacks use the strategy of nonviolent protest to combat segregation?

A Review of Major Ideas

1. In what ways did Eisenhower continue to support domestic, foreign, and military policies of the Roosevelt and Truman administrations? In what ways did it depart from Democratic precedents?
2. What did the Eisenhower administration do to prevent Communist take-overs of nations in the Middle East, Latin America, and East Asia? How did the United States promote the defense of western Europe?
3. During the Eisenhower administration, what efforts were made to eliminate racial segregation and restore civil rights to blacks? What successes were achieved?

For Independent Study

1. Does the fear of Communist take-overs in foreign countries justify United States intervention in the internal affairs of foreign governments?
2. "The policy of termination has been a disaster for most Indians." Oppose or defend this statement.

Unit Review
Examining the Times

1. In what ways did Truman and Eisenhower continue to promote domestic reforms begun during the New Deal? In what ways did they go beyond these reforms?
2. After World War II, what new demands on American foreign policy appeared?

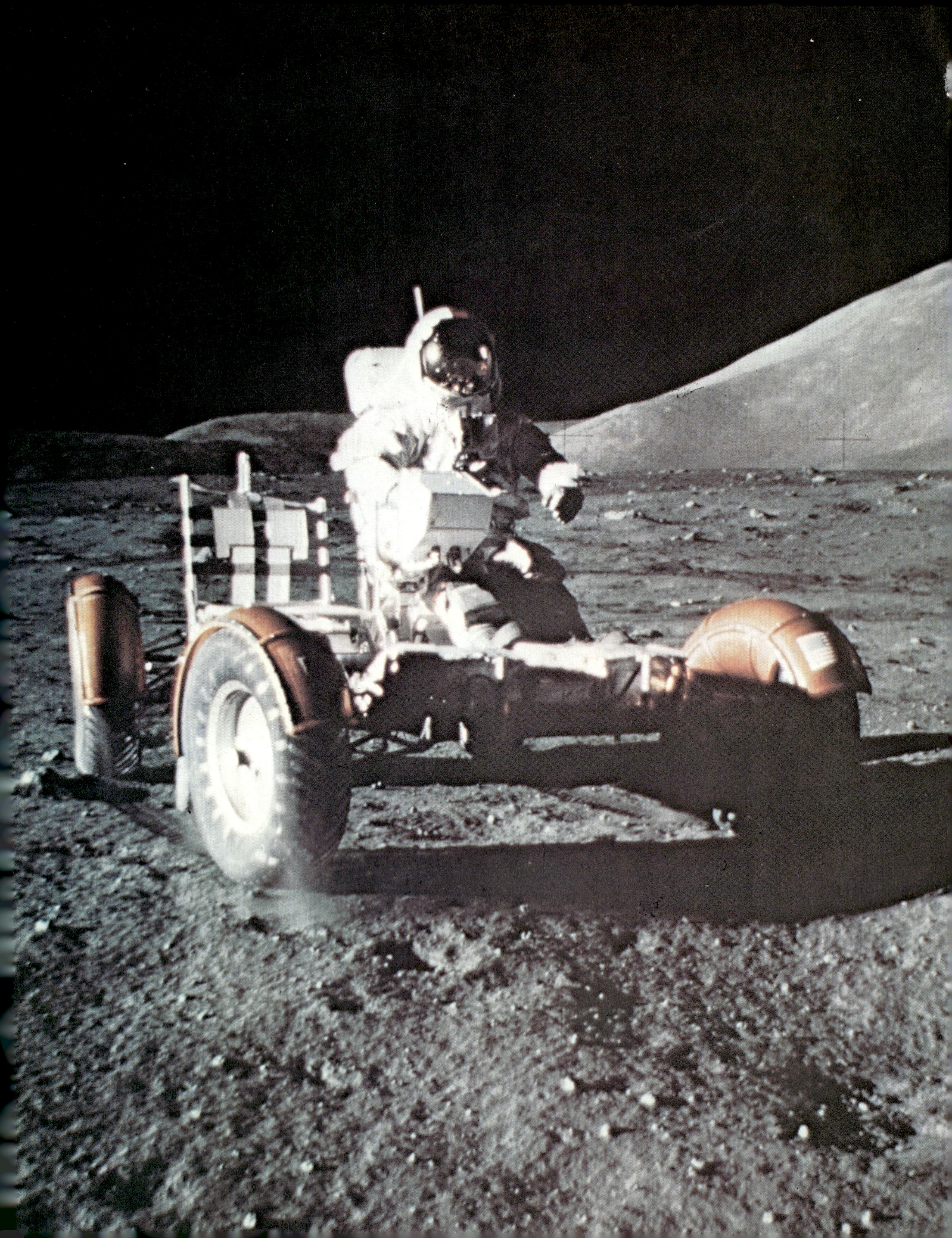

UNIT NINE 1960–1972

Challenges of the Space Age

On July 10, 1969, an American astronaut stepped out of a lunar lander and walked on the surface of the moon. Watching on television, millions of people all over the world saw his achievement, which came midway in the flight of *Apollo 11.*

Since 1961, when a Soviet cosmonaut made a space flight, the Soviet Union and the United States had been engaged in a race to be first to land people on the moon. The space race was an outgrowth of the arms race. But it also represented a yearning on the part of many Americans for national prestige.

Nationalism had remained the dominant force in international relations for most of the world, and in the sixties it gained new strength. The great colonial empires relinquished control over the last of their large holdings, and new nations emerged from the old colonies. The British Empire was reduced to a few island possessions, but it kept special trade privileges among former colonies through its Commonwealth of Nations. France lost all but a few tiny islands.

Nationalism also weakened regional defense alliances. France pulled its troops out of the North Atlantic Treaty Organization in 1966 but remained a member of the alliance.

This weakening of the alliance system also reflected the diminishing Cold War. The United States and the Soviet Union remained antagonists but pursued policies designed to bring "peaceful coexistence."

International cooperation in economic matters became more important than ever, for technology and finance ignored national boundaries. Belgium, France, Italy, Luxembourg, the Netherlands, and West Germany formed the European Economic Community, or Common Market, in 1958. The EEC got rid of tariffs and other economic barriers among its members and set up common tariffs for nonmembers. By 1962 the

Common Market had become the largest trading bloc in the world.

In October 1961, Britain had applied for membership in the EEC. President Charles de Gaulle of France disliked Britain's close ties to the United States, and in January 1963 he vetoed Britain's admission.

De Gaulle and other French leaders resented various aspects of American policy. Since the United States refused to share nuclear secrets with France, an ally, the French developed their own nuclear weapons. American policy makers viewed this nuclear build-up and De Gaulle's insistence on an independent policy for France as unfriendly. De Gaulle insisted that he was a true friend of the United States but wanted to free France, and Europe, of American domination. When De Gaulle retired from office in 1969, France's relations with the United States were improving.

Although prosperity continued into the seventies, Europe also experienced minor recessions and inflation. European unity grew stronger in the 1970's, and Britain, Ireland, and Denmark joined the Common Market in January 1973.

Many Americans were used to thinking of the world as being divided into two camps, one democratic and one Communist. The fifties and sixties saw the rise of a "third world," affiliated with neither group and composed of nations in Asia, Africa, Oceania, and Latin America. Most of the people in the third world were nonwhites whose nations were struggling to become industrialized, to become "developed."

The third-world countries contained an overwhelming majority of the earth's people but had only a small percentage of the earth's industrial might. They also had more than their share of the world's problems. Throughout the sixties, the third world was rocked by riots, revolutions, and wars.

Both the democratic and Soviet blocs attempted to aid the developing nations with loans, advisers, and technical experts. The Peace Corps set up by the United States was one such effort. Peace Corps volunteers received brief, intensive training before being sent to countries in Asia, Africa, Latin America, and Oceania. There they served as teachers, engineers, medical personnel, and agricultural experts.

Just as Europe had been the great battleground around the turn of the century, Asia was the soldier's arena in the mid-twentieth century. The United States had become involved in some of the fighting. Since 1941 it had fought major wars against Japan and North Korea and had sent aid and advisers to fight Communist guerrillas in the Philippines, China, and Indochina. While the United States fought in Korea, the British fought Communists in the Malay Peninsula, the future Malaysia. During the sixties, the United States all-consuming involvement was Vietnam.

India and Pakistan made some economic progress during the 1960's. Both nations were held back by open warfare, particularly over Kashmir, an area north of India that each nation claimed. Further tensions between India and Pakistan arose when the people of East Pakistan tried to break away from West Pakistan to form their own country. A civil war erupted in which India finally intervened, sending troops against the Pakistani army. In December 1971 the Pakistani forces surrendered, and the new independent state of Bangla Desh was created out of East Pakistan.

Pressures to admit Communist China to the United Nations became irresistible. In October 1971 the UN General Assembly voted to seat Communist China and to oust Nationalist China (Taiwan). In November, the People's Republic of China took Nationalist China's seat as a permanent member of the Security Council.

Japan's prosperity continued into the 1960's and 1970's. Long the wealthiest nation in East Asia, within twenty years after World War II, Japan had become a great industrial power. It competed with both the United States and the Common Market.

During the 1960's and into the 1970's, the Middle East continued to be a trouble spot. In 1967, Arabs and Israelis fought the Six-Day war. Victorious Israel took over some former Arab lands, including the Sinai Peninsula. After the war, the Soviet Union provided new arms to Arab forces, especially to Egypt. In 1969 the United States sold warplanes to Israel.

In the Middle East, the United States government avoided making the kind of commitment it had made in Vietnam. The United States supported Israel's right to exist, but it did not supply troops to aid the Israelis in their fight for survival. The Arab countries controlled much of the world's oil supply, and the United States did not want to cut itself off from major energy sources. Nevertheless, American aid to Israel often served to alienate Arab countries.

The most outstanding development in Africa in the 1960's was the end of most colonial rule. In 1950, only Ethiopia, Liberia, Egypt, and the Union of South Africa were independent states. In the next decade, Libya, Sudan, Morocco, Tunisia, Ghana, and Guinea ceased to be colonies. But 1960 was the big year for independence celebrations; seventeen new nations came into being in Africa that year.

The new African states faced incredible problems. The nations in the arid north depended on the petroleum industry. They had few resources other than oil. Arable land was scarce and overcrowded. The tropical west coast of Africa was ill suited to mechanized agriculture and was sorely lacking in energy or mineral resources. Only in East Africa and the Cape region had nature been generous.

The leaders of the new nations also had to wrestle with the legacy of their colonial past. The boundaries of colonies had been based on the interests and military prowess of the colonizing powers. They did not necessarily follow the lines separating one tribe or language group from another tribe or language group. Tribal ties often crossed national boundaries, and tribalism contributed to the instability of governments in newly independent nations of Africa.

The most publicized conflicts emerged in the Congo and in Nigeria. Near civil war broke out in the Congo shortly after Belgium ended colonial rule there in 1960. The fighting was finally ended by United Nations forces. Nigeria, too, had gained its independence in 1960. A civil war broke out in 1967 that was basically a tribal conflict. Despite such divisions, most black Africans were united in their opposition to European rule. "Africa for Africans" was one slogan of guerrillas who sought to end European rule in Mozambique, Rhodesia, and South Africa.

In Latin America, economic and social progress remained slow in most areas. As in the past, military dictatorships held power in many of the countries. In some countries—including Peru, Chile, and Venezuela—democratic governments struggled against heavy odds. In Mexico, the military had neither the desire nor the capability to gain control of the government. Communists tried but made few gains in Latin America in the 1960's and early 1970's.

In the first ten years after World War II, it had seemed that the Soviet Union and Communist China posed the greatest threat to the United States. But by the 1970's, it appeared that conflicts between China and the U.S.S.R.—and the eagerness of both nations to get the friendship of the United States—might make possible a world balance of power, which in turn might lessen the danger of all-out nuclear war.

New Hopes and Old Realities

CHAPTER 27
1960–1972

A political party holds its national convention.

The 1960's began with a surge of reform similar to that of the New Deal in the 1930's. For a while the nation seemed committed to ending poverty and securing equal opportunity for all Americans. Yet hopes soon bumped into realities, and much of the ferment for reform faded.

POLITICS

Throughout the sixties, the nation's political parties seemed to be in the process of realigning themselves. The Democratic party preserved the Roosevelt coalition of labor, northern blacks, and southern whites in the elections of 1960 and 1964. But by 1968, many union members and southern whites had departed from traditional party ties. They had become "swing" voters who could decide the outcome of presidential elections.

Regardless of how they voted in the presidential race, most Americans continued to choose Democrats to represent them in Congress. But the party itself was not united; it was composed of many groups, each of which had its own viewpoints and goals.

The 1960 Election

Worldwide turmoil, cold war tension, and fear of depression provided the background for the presidential election of 1960. Although still popular, Eisenhower was barred by the Twenty-second Amendment from running for a third term.

At the Democratic convention, Senator John F. Kennedy of Massachusetts won the presidential nomination on the first ballot. For his running mate, he chose his most powerful rival, Lyndon B. Johnson of Texas, the majority leader of the Senate. The platform criticized Eisenhower's domestic policies and promised a program of social welfare measures.

The Republicans nominated Eisenhower's Vice-President, Richard M. Nixon, for President. He selected Henry Cabot Lodge, Jr., of Massachusetts, the ambassador to the United Nations, for the vice-presidential spot. The Republican platform defended Eisenhower's record, called for "businesslike methods" in government, and supported "internationalism" in foreign policy.

Nationwide television emphasized the differences between the candidates. Nixon and Kennedy held four "debates," which some 65 to 75 million Americans saw and heard. These debates worked to Kennedy's advantage because they made him as well known as Nixon.

An important underlying concern in the campaign was religion. Kennedy tried to overcome the prejudices against having a Catholic as President by bringing the issue into the open.

The election results were close. Out of 68.8 million votes, Kennedy obtained only 118,550 more than Nixon. Both houses of Congress remained in Democratic hands, but conservative southern Democrats held most of the key committee posts.

Although the youngest man ever to have been elected President, Kennedy brought considerable political experience to the presidency. His father and both his grandfathers had been active in politics, and Kennedy had learned much by watching these men in action. A graduate of private preparatory schools and Harvard University, Kennedy had commanded a torpedo boat during World War II. Right after the war, he won election to Congress from the state of Massachusetts. In 1952, with the concerted help of his large and wealthy family, he defeated Henry Cabot Lodge, Jr., to become senator from Massachusetts. After winning reelection in 1958, he carefully planned the campaign that eventually brought him into the White House.

Kennedy's election gave the nation its first Catholic President. The slogan "New Frontier," which had been used to describe Kennedy's campaign, became the name of his administrative and legislative programs.

Kennedy saw the New Frontier as a continuation of the ideas of the New Deal and the Fair Deal. In his inaugural address, he asked his fellow Americans to work with him on the New Frontier to "explore the stars, conquer the deserts, eradicate disease, tap the ocean depths, and encourage the arts and commerce."

During the congressional elections of 1962, Kennedy campaigned vigorously for those Democrats who had supported his program. For the first time since 1934, the party in power did not lose strength in Congress in the midterm elections. The Democrats lost two seats in the House but picked up four in the Senate.

A New President

Like every President, Kennedy was loved by some Americans and hated by others. His policies on civil rights and on coexistence with the Soviet Union made him especially unpopular in the South. Late in 1963, he decided to visit Texas, the largest southern state, to try to strengthen his position and that of his party for the 1964 election.

On November 22, 1963, the President flew to Dallas. As the presidential motorcade moved from the airport through the city, shots rang out from a building along the route. Bullets struck Kennedy and Governor John B. Connally, Jr., of Texas. Both men were rushed to a hospital, where the President died.

Later, Dallas police captured Lee Harvey Oswald, a self-proclaimed Communist, and charged that he was the assassin. Two days later, a Dallas night-club owner, Jack Ruby, shot and killed Oswald as he was being transferred from one jail to another.

When Kennedy was shot, Vice-President Johnson was riding just two cars behind.

Under heavy security guard, he was rushed to the airport. There, in the presidential airplane, Johnson took the oath of office.

President Johnson promised to continue Kennedy's policies. He asked all of Kennedy's cabinet and staff members to remain on the job and assist him in running the government. Unlike Harry Truman, who as Vice-President had not been kept informed, Johnson knew what resources he could command as President. Kennedy had kept him fully informed of what he was doing.

Johnson was a man of action and tremendous energy. His background stood in sharp contrast to Kennedy's. He had been born and reared near the small village of Stonewall, in central Texas. After graduation from high school at age sixteen, Johnson roamed for two years, taking various jobs. He returned home, he said, with "empty hands and empty pockets." In 1926, he entered Southwest State Teachers College in San Marcos, Texas, and after graduation, he taught school.

In 1931, he worked in the campaign of a victorious candidate for Congress. Johnson went to Washington as the congressman's secretary. In 1935, President Roosevelt put Johnson in charge of the Texas office of the National Youth Administration. Politics had begun to fascinate Johnson, and in 1937, he sought and won a seat in the House of Representatives.

In 1948, Johnson won a seat in the Senate. Five years later, he became minority leader in the Senate. In 1954, he was reelected and became majority leader. In this position, he was the outstanding legislative leader of his time.

In 1960, Johnson surprised almost everyone by accepting the vice-presidential nomination. He was a tireless campaigner. Without Johnson on the ticket, the Democrats might have lost the South and, with it, the presidential election.

A Democratic Landslide

Within the Republican party, many conservatives had long been discontented with the course of United States politics. They claimed that Republican moderates like Wendell Willkie, Thomas Dewey, and Dwight Eisenhower had not offered the voters a clear alternative to the Democratic candidates. They argued that a true conservative candidate would not only win election but would also save the nation from the evils of big government and Communist subversion.

At the Republican convention in 1964, the conservatives took command and nominated Senator Barry M. Goldwater of Arizona for President. The vice-presidential candidate was Representative William E. Miller from upstate New York. The platform reflected Goldwater's conservative views. Goldwater went to the people offering "a choice not an echo." He claimed that the federal government had invaded the rights of the states. In foreign affairs he called for a more aggressive policy against communism.

The Democrats nominated Johnson. They also accepted his choice for Vice-President, Senator Hubert H. Humphrey of Minnesota. The platform warmly endorsed the Kennedy-Johnson policies and promised more of the same.

Johnson made few specific campaign promises. He pledged to continue the program that he had taken over, which he called "the Great Society." It set the goals of "abundance and liberty for all."

Goldwater confused and frightened many voters. Many people thought he opposed government participation in social welfare programs and was willing to risk nuclear war with the Soviet Union. The result of the campaign was a rout. Johnson won in a landslide, and many Democratic candidates for lower offices held on to his "coattails" to win election. The Democratic majority in Congress and in the statehouses increased.

PRESIDENTIAL ELECTIONS: 1960-1972

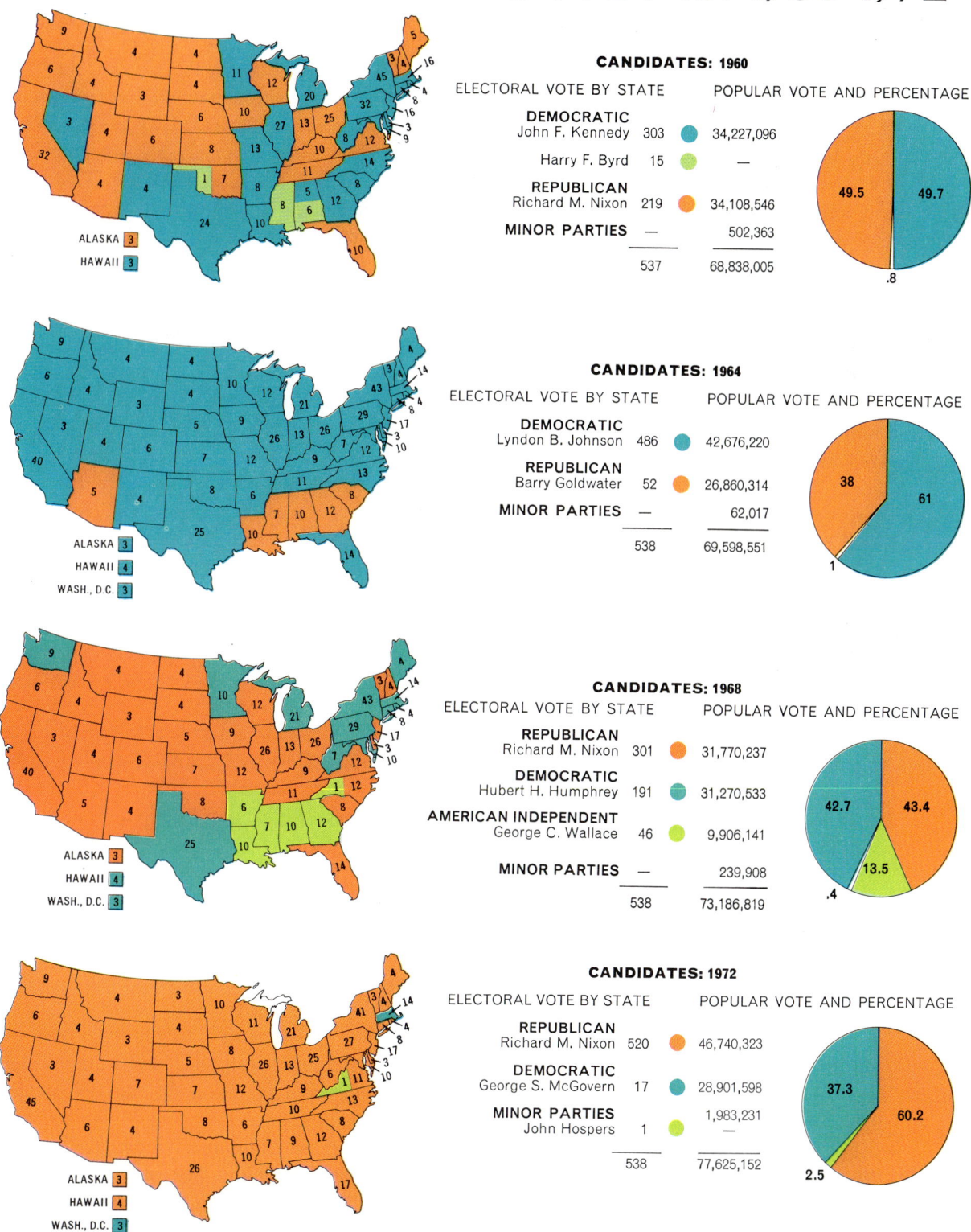

CANDIDATES: 1960

ELECTORAL VOTE BY STATE

DEMOCRATIC
John F. Kennedy — 303

Harry F. Byrd — 15

REPUBLICAN
Richard M. Nixon — 219

MINOR PARTIES — —

Total: 537

POPULAR VOTE AND PERCENTAGE

- 34,227,096
- —
- 34,108,546
- 502,363

Total: 68,838,005

Percentages: 49.7 / 49.5 / .8

CANDIDATES: 1964

ELECTORAL VOTE BY STATE

DEMOCRATIC
Lyndon B. Johnson — 486

REPUBLICAN
Barry Goldwater — 52

MINOR PARTIES — —

Total: 538

POPULAR VOTE AND PERCENTAGE

- 42,676,220
- 26,860,314
- 62,017

Total: 69,598,551

Percentages: 61 / 38 / 1

CANDIDATES: 1968

ELECTORAL VOTE BY STATE

REPUBLICAN
Richard M. Nixon — 301

DEMOCRATIC
Hubert H. Humphrey — 191

AMERICAN INDEPENDENT
George C. Wallace — 46

MINOR PARTIES — —

Total: 538

POPULAR VOTE AND PERCENTAGE

- 31,770,237
- 31,270,533
- 9,906,141
- 239,908

Total: 73,186,819

Percentages: 43.4 / 42.7 / 13.5 / .4

CANDIDATES: 1972

ELECTORAL VOTE BY STATE

REPUBLICAN
Richard M. Nixon — 520

DEMOCRATIC
George S. McGovern — 17

MINOR PARTIES
John Hospers — 1

Total: 538

POPULAR VOTE AND PERCENTAGE

- 46,740,323
- 28,901,598
- 1,983,231

Total: 77,625,152

Percentages: 60.2 / 37.3 / 2.5

615

The glow of Johnson's victory, the greatest in American history, did not last long. Friction and disagreement over a number of issues led to a slight Democratic loss in the 1966 congressional elections.

A Divided Party

By 1968, American involvement in the war in Vietnam had become the nation's most important political issue. Those who opposed the war were called "doves," while those who supported it were called "hawks." Eugene J. McCarthy, a Democratic senator from Minnesota and a dove, decided to oppose Johnson in the election. Surprisingly, his campaign, supported mainly by students and antiwar activists, caught on. In the New Hampshire presidential primary in March 1968 he made a strong showing. Within a week, Senator Robert F. Kennedy of New York entered the Democratic race as an antiwar candidate.

On March 31, 1968, President Johnson stunned the nation by announcing that he would not run for reelection. Johnson said that he had decided not to run in the hope that by removing himself from the political arena he would speed the coming of peace.

Even with Johnson's withdrawal, the war remained the basic issue in the campaign. Vice-President Hubert H. Humphrey immediately entered the race as a supporter of Johnson's Vietnam policies. While Humphrey received the backing of most of the party regulars, Kennedy and McCarthy fought in the primaries. Kennedy seemed to be pulling ahead in the race. Then, on June 6, 1968, just after Kennedy won the California primary, a young Arab immigrant murdered him in Los Angeles.

The front-running Republican candidate was again Richard M. Nixon, a Vietnam hawk of long standing. Since Johnson's war policy seemed to be driving him from the White House, Nixon played down his own hawkish attitudes. He gained the Republican nomination on the first ballot. He chose as his running mate the governor of Maryland, Spiro T. Agnew.

Later in August the Democrats met in a Chicago convention hall that was fenced by barbed wire and guarded by police. When the convention opened, it was practically torn apart by the Vietnam issue. The Humphrey-Johnson forces defeated a McCarthy peace plank and gave Humphrey the nomination on the first ballot. Humphrey chose Senator Edmund S. Muskie of Maine as his running mate. Meanwhile, outside the hall, antiwar demonstrators clashed with the police. The violence brought hundreds of arrests and injuries and provided yet another issue in the campaign.

Many people, especially Democratic segregationists, did not like either Humphrey or Nixon. A number of them rallied behind Governor George C. Wallace of Alabama. He became the presidential candidate of the American Independent Party, with General Curtis E. Le May as his running mate. Both were extreme hawks.

People who were opposed to the war were bitterly disappointed by the party conventions. All the major candidates supported the war. The Democratic and Republican platforms came out for an honorable peace and supported Johnson's Vietnam war policy. Nixon said that he had a secret plan to end the war but revealed nothing specific.

The election results were close. Nixon received 43.4 percent of the popular vote; Humphrey, 42.7 percent; Wallace, 13.5 percent. The Democrats retained control of both houses of Congress.

The newly elected President, an ambitious and energetic man, had won the nation's highest office against great odds. Nixon had been born and reared in small-town southern California. He attended Whittier College and Duke University Law School.

Leisure

During the sixties, Americans rediscovered the joys of the "bike." In some years, more bicycles than cars were sold. The reshuffling of national holidays to provide occasional three-day weekends resulted in a number of short vacation periods. Sometimes they were used for bike trips or camping expeditions. Amusement parks like Disney World *(below)* presented a live-in fantasy land for vacationers.

After service in the navy in World War II, Nixon returned to California and entered politics. He won a seat in the House of Representatives and gained national attention during his first term by his campaign against Communists in government. In 1950, Nixon won a Senate seat. Two years later, Eisenhower chose him as his running mate.

After his 1960 defeat by Kennedy, Nixon returned to California. In 1962 he ran for governor but lost. He returned to the practice of law, first in California, then in New York. But he could not stay out of politics. In 1964 and 1966 he worked for Republican candidates all over the country and won the gratitude of his party. He easily won the presidential nomination in 1968.

The midterm elections of 1970 produced mixed results. The Democrats increased their majority in the House by eleven but lost two seats in the Senate. In the statehouses, however, they increased their hold, gaining eleven governorships.

The 1972 Election

The results of the midterm elections encouraged the Democrats. Eleven of them entered the primaries for their party's presidential nomination in 1972. The early front runner was Edmund Muskie. He faced stiff competition from Hubert Humphrey and from George Wallace, again a Democrat.

A gunshot once more changed the course of a presidential campaign. At a political rally in Laurel, Maryland, in May 1972, a 21-year-old bus boy shot Wallace, paralyzing him. Wallace was knocked out of the race.

Meanwhile, a new front runner was emerging. Senator George S. McGovern of South Dakota, the earliest-announced candidate, surged ahead and won the Democratic nomination on the first ballot. For his running mate he chose Thomas F. Eagleton, a young senator from Missouri. A month later, Eagleton was forced off the ticket after it was disclosed that he had been hospitalized three times for severe depression. McGovern replaced him with R. Sargent Shriver, a former director of the Peace Corps.

Nixon and Agnew were renominated by the Republicans. Nixon did little campaigning. He controlled the machinery of government and used it to keep himself before the public as President, not as a politician.

McGovern tried to make Vietnam policy the central issue of the campaign. But Nixon outflanked him. Twelve days before the election the President's chief foreign-policy adviser, who had been negotiating an end to the war, announced that "peace is at hand." Deprived of his main issue and beset by fighting within his party, McGovern didn't stand a chance. Nixon won in a landslide, receiving more than 60 percent of the vote. But the Democrats increased their margin in the Senate and in the statehouses and lost only a few seats in the House.

One incident from the campaign would later haunt Nixon. In June 1972, burglars were caught breaking into Democratic party offices in the Watergate Hotel in Washington. They were later unmasked as spys for the Committee to Re-Elect the President. The "Watergate affair" had little effect on the election but became a major scandal in 1973.

CIVIL RIGHTS

In the 1960's, the most explosive domestic issue was the fight for civil rights. Many blacks began a crusade to win a full measure of their rights. They sought equal protection under the laws, an end to racial discrimination in employment, increased educational opportunities, improved housing, and recognition of their cultural uniqueness. By the end of the decade, their successes had prompted other groups—especially Puerto Ricans, Mexican Americans, and American Indians—to organize for power.

Backers of Shirley Chisholm in Georgia urge the election of a delegate pledged to their candidate. Under new party rules, many of the delegates to the 1972 Democratic National Convention were chosen by voters rather than by state party conventions.

Organization

Historically, blacks had been concentrated in the South. There, white leaders had set up legal barriers which, along with customs of the region, kept blacks at the bottom of the social and economic ladder. In the past, blacks who had attempted to stand up for their rights had faced increased repression. Many of them were among the millions of blacks who migrated to the North and the West. After 1940, the black population outside the South more than tripled, while that of the South held steady or declined.

When blacks moved to the North or West, they discovered no promised land. They found the *de facto,* or actual, segregation imposed by custom rather than the legal segregation imposed by "Jim Crow" laws. But in the North and West, blacks were allowed to vote. As their numbers increased in those regions and as they became concentrated in urban areas, blacks elected persons of their own race to local, state, and national offices. Perhaps as important as these victories, many blacks began organizing for power.

The oldest organization working to protect the civil rights of black people was the National Association for the Advancement of Colored People (NAACP), founded in 1909. It had concentrated on securing black rights by appealing to the courts. Almost as old was the Urban League, which worked to break down employment barriers.

In the 1950's and 1960's, blacks formed a number of new organizations that used a variety of tactics. The Southern Christian Leadership Conference was a coalition of southern church leaders. Its strategy was based on nonviolent protest, often using large numbers of peaceful marchers. Other groups devoted to nonviolent demonstrations were the Student Non-Violent Coordinating Committee (SNCC) and the Congress of Racial Equality (CORE). All had white members as well as black. All urged their members not to strike back when attacked.

The civil rights crusade was not, however, unified. Many blacks disagreed with the leaders, goals, and tactics of these organizations. Some thought they were too radical, while others thought they were too conservative. These groups worked to promote racial integration, but some blacks thought that they should work for black nationalism or black separatism.

The oldest of the black nationalist movements, the Black Muslims, combined religion—Islam—with race consciousness. This movement dated back to 1930 but experienced its greatest growth in the fifties and sixties, under the leadership of Elijah Muhammad. In 1964, the movement was split when Malcolm X, the second-ranking leader, pulled out to form his own Black Nationalist group. Another separatist group was the Black Panther party, which began as a political party but became increasingly radical.

Tactics

The integrationists did not abandon old tactics, such as seeking court decisions to extend voting rights and to end school segregation. But they did gain attention and sympathy for their cause by using new tactics.

In February 1960, four students from a Negro college challenged a practice of long standing in the South. They sat on stools reserved for whites at a lunch counter in a Greensboro, North Carolina, dime store. No one would serve them, yet the blacks had

The march from Selma, Alabama, gets under way. The marchers included a large number of clergy. Some of the demonstrators carried United Nations flags and sought international backing for their cause.

made their point. They were refusing to accept traditional discrimination.

The Greensboro "sit-in" inspired similar demonstrations throughout the South. Usually, the local authorities arrested the protesters for breaking the peace or trespassing on private property. These sit-ins, along with court action and nationwide boycotts of chain stores that practiced discrimination in their southern outlets, finally ended segregation at most lunch counters.

In May 1961, blacks and whites, under the sponsorship of the Congress of Racial Equality (CORE), rode buses from the North into the South. They wanted to test the effectiveness of federal laws against segregation in interstate buses and stations. In Alabama, mobs severely beat several "freedom riders" and destroyed one of the buses with a firebomb. In the face of more violence, Attorney General Robert F. Kennedy ordered federal marshals into Montgomery, Alabama, to protect the freedom riders. He also ordered federal enforcement of nonsegregation of all interstate travel facilities.

In 1963, the one-hundredth anniversary of the Emancipation Proclamation, the civil rights crusade picked up in intensity. On August 28, about 200,000 persons gathered in Washington, D.C., and staged the largest civil rights demonstration ever seen. Demanding jobs, justice, equality, and freedom, they marched from the Washington Monument to the Lincoln Memorial. No violence disturbed this massive march. Elsewhere in the nation, however, rising racial tension, violence, and bloodshed accompanied the civil rights crusade.

To help blacks obtain the right to vote in the South, civil rights leaders plunged into the stronghold of segregationists. In the summer of 1964 they brought hundreds of volunteers into Mississippi to register and educate blacks as voters. Three of the civil rights workers, two white and one black, were murdered. Despite such bitter resistance, the drive continued.

In March 1965 more than 25,000 blacks and whites, singing "We Shall Overcome," staged a "freedom march." Led by Dr. Martin Luther King, Jr., they walked fifty-four miles from Selma to Montgomery, Alabama. Out of this march came another murder. Ku Klux Klan members shot Viola Gregg Liuzzo, a white civil rights worker from Detroit.

Government Reactions

During the first two years of his administration, President Kennedy tried to improve conditions for blacks through executive action rather than by new legislation. In March 1961 he established the Committee on Equal Employment Opportunity. Headed by Vice-President Johnson, this committee sought to persuade firms holding government contracts to provide equal job opportunities for all employees. Kennedy also appointed many blacks to high offices.

Early in 1962, Kennedy urged Congress to pass laws that would end the use of literacy tests and poll taxes as means of preventing blacks from voting. Congress responded by passing a constitutional amendment that prohibited any state from requiring a citizen to pay a poll tax in order to vote in a federal election. In January 1964, it became the Twenty-fourth Amendment.

In September 1962, Kennedy had to uphold federal authority in what was probably the most serious clash with state authority since the Civil War. The Supreme Court had ordered the all-white University of Mississippi to admit a qualified black resident of that state, James H. Meredith. When Meredith arrived at the campus accompanied by federal marshals, Governor Ross R. Barnett personally blocked his registration at the university. Anticipating more defiance, Kennedy sent federal marshals to the campus.

Rioting broke out. Two men were shot and killed by rioters, and two hundred persons were injured. To restore order, the President sent federal troops to the campus and federalized the Mississippi National Guard to remove it from the governor's control. The troops protected Meredith as he registered and attended classes.

In November 1962, the President issued a long-awaited executive order on housing. It banned racial discrimination in housing financed with federal funds.

In a June 1963 television appearance the President asked all Americans to accept the civil rights crusade and help make it constructive and peaceful. That month he also sent to Congress a comprehensive civil rights bill. Action on it was slow. It was not passed until the "Freedom Summer" of 1964. The Civil Rights Act of 1964 was the most sweeping legislation of its kind since Reconstruction. It prohibited discrimination and segregation in schools, voting, public facilities, and jobs. It authorized the attorney general to bring suit in federal court against those who practiced discrimination.

The Selma march of 1965 made a great impression. It prodded Congress into passing the Voting Rights Act of 1965. This law abolished literacy tests for voters and authorized federal officials to register voters in precincts where less than 50 percent of the people of voting age were registered.

Escalating Violence

In some areas of the South, extremists and members of racist organizations bombed the homes and churches of blacks. Police used dogs and high-pressure water hoses against demonstrators. In other places, whites and blacks fought in the streets. But racial violence was by no means limited to the South.

Widespread violence erupted in the ghettos of northern cities in "the long hot summer" of 1964. Trouble began in New York City after an off-duty policeman killed a black youth. Blacks immediately denounced "police brutality." In Harlem, the nation's largest black community, and in the Bedford-Stuyvesant section of Brooklyn, blacks smashed windows, looted, and ransacked stores. Other cities had similar outbreaks.

The next summer was even "hotter." In August 1965, a highway patrolman arrested a young black man for drunken driving in Watts, a black community in Los Angeles. Immediately, rumors of "police brutality" spread through Watts. Almost a week of rioting, looting, burning, and shooting followed. Expressing hatred for whites, angry blacks set fire to hundreds of buildings.

Using tear gas, bayonets, rifles, and machine guns, national guardsmen finally suppressed the riot. The toll was high. Thirty-six were dead—most of them blacks—and about 900 persons were injured. About 4,000 were arrested, and damage was estimated at 47 million dollars. The same week, black riots broke out elsewhere.

Most of the rioters were bitter, unemployed blacks who had not benefited from the civil rights crusade. They rebelled against the conditions that trapped them, and many blacks became increasingly militant.

Groups like the Black Muslims called for a separate black community within America's larger white society. The Muslims urged blacks to strike back when attacked but did not advocate black aggression. The Black Panther party, however, accepted violence and class struggle as means of enhancing the status of blacks.

Whether violent or nonviolent, the militant black nationalists changed the character of the civil rights crusade. They took up the

Right: Directed by the police, Birmingham firemen use high-pressure hoses to break up a sit-in demonstration. The use of hoses and dogs to break up nonviolent protests was highly publicized and helped win many white Americans over to the side of the civil rights crusaders. In the next few years, blacks who were angry and disillusioned by the lack of progress rioted in major northern cities. The riots increased white opposition to the civil rights struggle, and efforts to win equal rights were stalled. *Above:* Firemen arrive to fight a fire set by rioters in Detroit during the "long, hot summer" of 1967.

slogan "black power," which was interpreted differently by almost every person who heard it or used it. Some Americans thought it meant "black supremacy," while others thought it simply meant that blacks should have more power over their own lives.

Some Americans believed that the philosophy of the black nationalists contributed to the riots in cities. In 1966, black unrest was again evident across the nation. The summer of 1967 brought the worst riots yet. In July, rioters in Detroit went on a week's rampage, looting, burning, and killing. Entire blocks went up in flames. Only the power of federal troops put down the disorders. In the rioting, forty-three persons were killed, 2,000 were injured, 5,000 were made homeless, 5,000 were arrested. Damage was estimated at more than 200 million dollars.

President Johnson appointed the National Advisory Commission on Civil Disorders to investigate the black unrest. The commission published its findings early in 1968. It blamed the racist attitudes of the country's white majority for the repeated summer riots. "Our nation," the report concluded, "is moving toward two societies, one black, one white—separate and unequal."

Within a few months, events dramatized this assessment. On April 4, 1968, a white man in Memphis, Tennessee, assassinated Dr. Martin Luther King, Jr. That murder set off shock waves of riots in more than fifty cities. In Washington, D.C., President Johnson had to call in troops to restore order.

The whole nation mourned King's death. More than 150,000 persons, including some of the nation's leaders, attended the funeral, and millions watched the events on television. No person who had not held high public office had ever been so honored in death.

King's murder gave a final boost to more civil rights legislation. The Civil Rights Act of 1968 outlawed discrimination in the sale and rental of most real estate.

A Shift of Focus

While black militancy persisted, widespread violence subsided in the next few years. Blacks concentrated on fighting their battles in the political arena. By 1972, black political leaders had formed blocs of their own. In 1960, there had been four blacks in Congress; by 1973, there were fifteen. At least eight cities had black mayors.

Nevertheless, blacks still had a higher rate of unemployment than did whites, and black children usually had to attend segregated schools. President Nixon was less responsive to black demands than Kennedy and Johnson had been. In 1971, in *Swann* v. *Charlotte-Mecklenburg Board of Education* and four companion cases, federal courts ruled that the busing of children from their neighborhoods to schools at a distance for purposes of integration was proper. This ruling met with violent opposition from many whites and became an issue in the presidential election in 1972. Nixon said that he did "not believe that busing to achieve racial balance is in the interest of better education."

Ethnic Consciousness

Many groups had a stake in the civil rights crusade. Puerto Ricans, Chicanos (Mexican Americans), and American Indians challenged white control of American society with increasing militancy. Chinese, Japanese, and Filipino Americans also worked to protect their rights.

In several instances, Puerto Ricans in New York and New Jersey and Chicanos in Los Angeles rioted. They suffered from high unemployment, bias in education, and continuing discrimination in housing.

In October 1971, Spanish-speaking civil rights leaders filed suit against four federal agencies for discrimination in employment. They noted that Spanish-speaking people made up 7 percent of the population but held only 2.9 percent of the federal jobs.

A New Look at the Melting Pot

By the 1960's, it had become obvious that the melting-pot theory had flaws. America has many cultures, not just one. The civil rights struggle led to renewed pride in their heritages for blacks, Puerto Ricans, Indians, and many other ethnic groups.

Improvement in the education of Spanish-speaking children posed a special problem. Many people thought that bilingual instruction might offer a solution, but it would require a change in the basic social philosophy of American public education. In the United States the use of English alone had been compulsory, and it had been viewed as the means of "Americanizing" immigrants.

A number of Indian leaders asked for changes in the government policy toward tribespeople. Some wanted payment for land that had been taken from their ancestors. In May 1969, the Indian Claims Commission awarded 12.3 million dollars to the Seminoles for land that United States military forces seized in the nineteenth century.

The most persistent demand by Indians (or Native Americans, as some preferred to be called) was for control over their own destinies. Some Indians, seeking to change government policy, had formed national intertribal organizations. Eight such groups sponsored the "Trail of Broken Treaties," a cross-country trek to Washington, D.C., in October 1972. Arriving at the nation's capital on November 2, they occupied the offices of the Bureau of Indian Affairs.

They sought government approval of a twenty-point proposal. Their basic demands were for recognition of treaties, revocation of termination laws, and abolition of the BIA by 1976. Similar demands arose from an even more dramatic event, the Indian occupation and battle at Wounded Knee, South Dakota, in the spring of 1973.

THE ECONOMY

Many economists had predicted that there would be a serious depression after World War II. Yet for more than twenty-five years after the war, this prediction had not come true. The nation had experienced only a few short recessions within the longest boom of prosperity in modern history. Industry in the United States had grown rapidly to keep up with the demand for consumer goods. This tremendous production brought wealth that promoted technological development and the creation of still more wealth.

Automation and Jobs

The use of automated machinery accounted for much of the increase in production. The most sophisticated machine was the computer, which could be programmed to do the work of many men or women. But only one, two, or three persons were needed to operate one. Computers could be used to control machines that made automobiles, refrigerators, and other complex products. This use of computers to run productive machinery has been called *cybernation.*

For the business owner a cybernated industry had many advantages. It swiftly produced goods of uniform quality at low cost. It reduced the work force, thereby reducing labor costs, and it eliminated many human errors. For the economy, it meant increased power to produce goods and services. For workers, however, cybernation meant not the loss of an occasional job, but of many jobs.

The technological society required skilled workers; thus unskilled workers were in decreasing demand. In 1900, some 11 million common laborers had jobs. By 1950, despite a huge increase in population, only 6 million were at work. In the 1960's the number of nonfarm unskilled laborers rose but their percentage within the work force declined.

Automation and cybernation accounted in large part for the decreasing number of jobs for unskilled laborers. But in the sixties and early seventies, both processes also displaced skilled and professional workers. Leaders of organized labor became alarmed. Unions often tried to meet the thrust of automation with *featherbedding,* forcing employers to keep people in jobs that were no longer of any use. Featherbedding delayed the impact of the new technology but did not prevent it.

Business Mergers

American industry had long been growing bigger and bigger. Changes in technology stimulated the trend toward industrial concentration. In 1903 the Wright brothers had been able to assemble an airplane in a bicycle shop. In the sixties, the construction of jet airplanes required armies of skilled technicians and billions of dollars. Few corporations commanded the resources necessary for such projects.

In the fifties and sixties, *conglomerate* mergers became popular. In a conglomerate, firms that handled or made different kinds of products or services were merged into one giant corporation. For example, one conglomerate included a major league baseball team, a radio and television network, a publishing company, and several manufacturing companies.

The conglomerate seemed to have many advantages for business. During boom years, the giant corporations were able to pay for expansion and for new equipment from their own funds. They no longer needed credit from bankers and other financiers. During lean years, the profits from one division of the conglomerate supposedly could be used to prop up or expand other divisions.

The proportion of manufacturing assets owned by the nation's 200 largest firms had been less than 50 percent in 1948, but by 1969 it was about 60 percent. Under such conditions, critics claimed, competition could scarcely survive.

Many Americans feared concentration of ownership in conglomerates. In 1969 the Department of Justice cited the antitrust laws in filing suits against some conglomerate mergers. The lawsuits and the recession of 1970 slowed the conglomerate trend.

The Changing Face of Unionism

As automation eroded the labor force in blue-collar industries like steel, automobiles, railroads, mining, and meat packing, labor unions lost strength. In 1945 about 14.5 million workers, almost 36 percent of the labor force, were union members. In 1962, the 16.5 million union members made up less than 30 percent of the work force.

In order to help the American labor movement keep pace with changing technology, some union leaders began to step up recruiting among white-collar workers. These workers had become an increasingly large part of the nation's work force, and many were frightened by automation and uneasy about their jobs. In the sixties, union organizers made notable headway among government employees.

In the 1920's, attempts to organize government employees had met violent opposition. By the 1950's, however, trade unionism had become an accepted institution in American life. Organized labor had suffered some embarrassment through exposures of graft, corruption, and racketeering in a few unions. But many leaders worked to keep a reputation for responsible behavior that would appeal to the public. For instance, in 1957 the AFL-CIO expelled the Teamsters Union on charges of corruption. The fifties and early sixties saw few violent strikes.

Government unionism was also promoted by President Kennedy's Executive Order 10988 in January 1962. It encouraged unionism in federal service and had a contagious effect on workers in state and local service.

Since 20 to 25 percent of all local and state employees were teachers, unions made a special effort to recruit among them. In the middle sixties the American Federation of Teachers, an affiliate of the AFL-CIO, won bargaining rights for teachers in New York, Chicago, Detroit, and elsewhere. The National Education Association also sought to bargain for teachers. In the late sixties, as teachers, policemen, firemen, postal workers, and others felt the pinch of inflation and recession, they joined unions. Strikes by other government workers had once been novelties. Now they became common.

The unionization of its employees involved the government more and more in labor disputes. In March 1970, for the first time in the nation's history, postal workers went on strike. At its height, the strike involved more than 200,000 workers. President Nixon declared a state of national emergency and sent troops to New York City to try to move the mail. The strike was settled after the government offered pay raises and a reorganization of the postal system.

Some Americans expressed alarm over the vulnerability of vital services to what they called a "misuse of union power." Generally, when a major labor dispute threatened the national economy, national security, or the political situation, the government stepped in to work for a settlement. Government treated labor policy as a part of national economic policy.

One of the most widely publicized labor disputes of the sixties was that of grape pickers in California. The people involved were mostly Mexican American farm workers. Migrant farm workers were not covered by federal labor laws and had been largely unorganized. The strike began in 1965, but it did not gain momentum until César E. Chávez, a leader of the United Farm Workers Organizing Committee, made it more than a labor dispute. Led by Chávez, it became *"La Causa,"* almost a religious movement.

In 1968, Chávez called for a consumer boycott of California table grapes. Publicized by news of Chávez's hunger strikes and supported by national unions, the boycott caught on. Housewives and students picketed supermarkets, and bumper stickers asked Americans not to eat grapes. Sales of

Striking farm workers march in California. "Agribusiness," large corporations, ran many of the huge farms in that state. *La Causa* was backed with religious fervor by workers who sought better pay, improved working conditions, and union recognition.

table grapes fell. In July 1970 the grape growers signed an agreement with Chávez's union, and the strike ended. Public sympathy helped bring victory, but it was not a lasting victory.

Kennedy's Economic Policy

When Eisenhower left office, the nation was in the midst of a recession that struck some sections hard but barely touched others. With 8.1 percent of the labor force out of jobs, unemployment was much too high.

Two weeks after his inauguration, President Kennedy asked Congress for an extension of insurance payments to the unemployed, an increase in the minimum-wage rate, a boost in social security payments, and a program to clear slums and build public housing. Congress turned these requests into law. It also passed the Area Redevelopment Act, which made federal aid available to bring industries into areas with chronic unemployment. In 1962, Congress supplemented this law with the first broad public works program since the New Deal.

Before the end of 1961, the economy began to perk up. Kennedy could not, however, get Congress to back his program of long-range economic reform. The old coalition of southern Democrats and conservative Republicans that controlled key positions in Congress also opposed much of Kennedy's program.

Kennedy felt that economic reform would be hurt by inflation. In 1962 he had a showdown with leaders of the steel industry over policies that he believed were inflationary.

Kennedy had asked the steel companies to keep prices down and had urged the unions to hold their wage demands in line with increases in productivity. The industry and the union agreed upon benefits and raises that did not seem inflationary. After the last major wage contract had been signed, the United States Steel Corporation told Kennedy that it was going to raise the price of steel. But the price increase would be four times as great as the wage increase. The next day, five other steel companies raised prices.

Kennedy felt that the steel executives had acted in bad faith. He denounced the "tiny handful of steel executives" for placing profit above public responsibility.

Several smaller steel companies had held out against the price increase. Kennedy told government agencies to shift their purchases of steel to such companies. This action forced United States Steel and others to bring their prices down to meet the competition. Within a few days all the major steel companies canceled their price increases.

The Pressured Economy

When Kennedy died, some of the bills he most wanted were stalled in Congress. Five days after taking over, President Johnson asked a special session of Congress to act on the programs of the New Frontier. Johnson guided a tax-reduction bill through both houses of Congress; it became law in Febru-

BUSINESS ACTIVITY 1941–1971

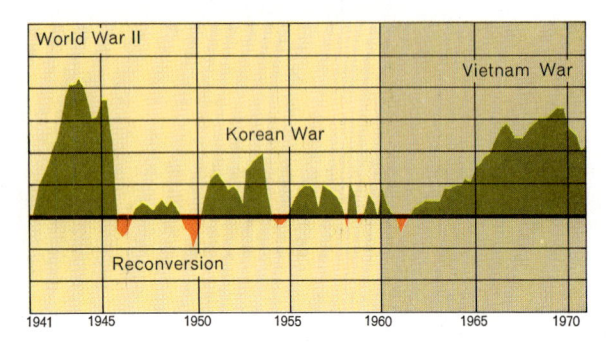

The thirty years after the United States entered World War II were the most prosperous in the nation's history. The chart *(above)* of the Federal Reserve index of industrial production and utilities shows that recessions were short and relatively mild. Nevertheless, trying to find jobs for the unemployed remained a problem. Mechanization of agriculture and automation of industry demanded new skills of job seekers. The impact of the Vietnam war on the economy can be seen in the detail *(below)*. As involvement in the war increased and decreased, so did industrial production. But industrial output did not tell the total story of the nation's economy. Services were becoming a bigger part of the economy, and they were dependent on general prosperity.

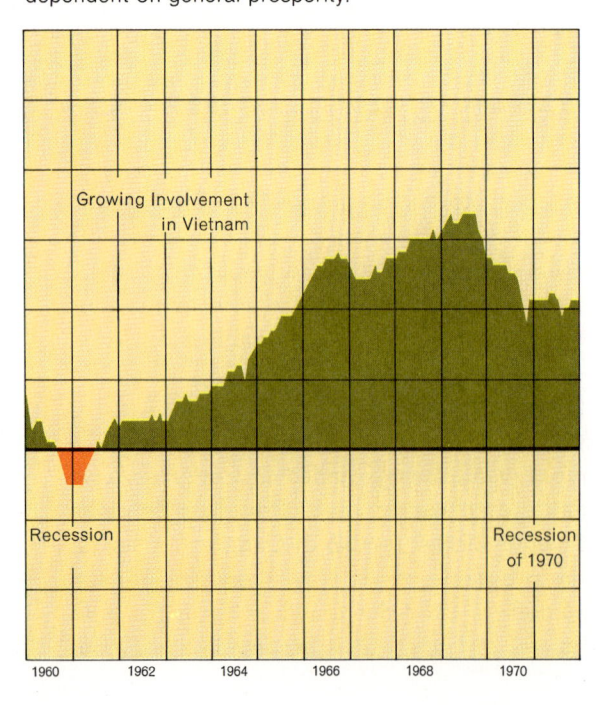

ary 1964. Johnson hoped it would stimulate the economy by allowing taxpayers greater take-home pay to spend, save, or invest.

President Johnson also proposed to fight a "war on poverty," to help the millions of Americans who struggled to get along on incomes below or near the poverty level. In August, Congress passed the first major piece of legislation in this battle—the Economic Opportunity Act of 1964. This law set up a number of agencies. One was the Job Corps, in which school drop-outs were taken out of their usual environment and paid while they trained for jobs. Another was VISTA (Volunteers in Service to America), which used volunteers to teach new skills in ghettos, Indian reservations, and depressed areas.

Yet unemployment among blacks, teenagers, Mexican Americans, and people in depressed areas remained high. Congress passed a number of other laws to fight poverty and unemployment within these groups. In the Appalachian Regional Development Act of 1965, Congress set aside 1.1 billion dollars for economic improvements in the eleven-state Appalachian region. The Public Work and Economic Development Act of 1965 authorized the spending of 3.3 billion dollars to help depressed areas.

Social programs of this kind were expensive. They could be best accomplished when the economy was strong. To keep the economic boom going, Johnson continued the policy of budget deficits and tax cuts. He wanted to stimulate the economy and reduce unemployment. But as unemployment declined and as factories functioned near capacity, pressure developed to raise prices and wages. Fearing runaway inflation, President Johnson asked industry not to increase prices and labor not to seek wage increases above a 3.2 percent guideline.

By February 1966, a long-standing aim of both Kennedy and Johnson became a reality.

Unemployment fell to 4 percent of the labor force. The President's economic advisers looked upon this figure as signifying, for all practical purposes, full employment.

At the same time, however, the nation was unable to absorb the financial demands of the expanding war in Vietnam and the costs of services at home. Economic growth slowed down. Despite government efforts, the pressure for inflation mounted. In March 1966, the government was forced to reinstate some of the excise taxes that had been cut in the previous year. But the government refused to meet rising costs with higher taxes. Inflation stepped up, and Americans were caught in an upward wage-price spiral. Although the unemployment rate fell below 4 percent, the cost of living zoomed. The poor and those on fixed incomes suffered most.

Industrial production continued upward, but by the end of 1969, real economic growth in the United States had practically stopped. The rate of inflation reached 4.5 percent, the worst since the Korean War.

Recession

In 1970 a recession set in. By the end of the year, 6 percent of the nation's work force was unemployed. This recession was unusual in that the rising unemployment was accompanied by rising prices. Usually, the burden of inflation is made more bearable by high employment and overtime pay.

Worry over the economy spread. In June 1970 the Penn Central Transportation Company failed; it owned the nation's largest railroad. The Lockheed Aircraft Corporation, the nation's largest defense contractor, also found itself on the verge of collapse. Only a 250-million-dollar loan from the government in 1971 kept it going. Rumors said that other major corporations were almost bankrupt.

At first President Nixon insisted that the government would not tamper with the economy. Then in August 1971, as unemployment increased and inflation surged ahead, he announced a change in policies. He unfolded a program to freeze wages and prices for ninety days and to stimulate the economy with corporate tax cuts. He also decided to place an extra tax on imports. Under the President's new economic program, unveiled in October, he replaced the wage-price freeze with government controls over wages, prices, and services. In January 1973, he removed controls but announced that a review board of labor and business leaders would suggest wage-price guidelines.

A Look at Specifics

1. What were the major issues in the election of 1960? 1964? 1968? 1972?

2. In what way was the recession of the early 1970's unusual?

3. Why did labor unions fail to grow in proportion to the expanding work force?

A Review of Major Ideas

1. What was the role of the Kennedy, Johnson, and Nixon administrations in securing equal civil rights for all Americans?

2. What effect did the black civil rights movement have on other groups that experienced discrimination?

3. How did the conglomerate mergers affect competition among companies?

For Independent Study

1. Many people think that political parties should align ideologically, conservatives with conservatives, liberals with liberals. Others believe that a party should represent a broad spectrum of opinion. What are the advantages and disadvantages of each system? Which do you think you would prefer?

2. What effect did mass communications have on the civil rights movement?

3. How might public employees get pay increases without harming the public interest? Give evidence to support your view.

Global Turmoil

CHAPTER 28
1960–1972

Historically, United States foreign policy has been directed more toward events in Europe or Latin America than toward problems in other parts of the world. In the 1960's and early 1970's, however, problems elsewhere dominated American foreign policy.

In the early sixties, the United States and the Soviet Union had several showdowns, and these were followed by a relaxation of tensions between the superpowers. The United States then spent most of a decade working to resolve conflicts in Asia.

THAWING THE COLD WAR

The efforts of Kennedy, Johnson, and Nixon to preserve peace and end the Cold War were most successful in European nations. All three Presidents also made some progress toward nuclear disarmament.

The Search for Peace

In September 1961, with the approval of Congress, President Kennedy set up the Arms Control and Disarmament Agency. It was the first government body concerned full-time with planning for peace and disarmament.

The United States also continued to participate in a disarmament conference sponsored by the United Nations in Geneva, Switzerland. At this conference, the Soviets demanded the abolition of all armies and weapons over a period of four years. The United States urged gradual disarmament over a longer period, with inspection by an international commission of the arms retained by each nation. Since the Soviets and Americans were unable to reach an agreement, disarmament remained only a hope.

President Kennedy worried that someone might accidentally set off a nuclear war. Moreover, people all over the world were afraid of contamination by radioactive fallout. Kennedy wanted to lessen these dangers through nuclear disarmament. Therefore, he sought a treaty to prohibit the testing of nuclear weapons in the atmosphere.

In September 1961, the Soviets broke an unofficial moratorium on nuclear testing in the air. In two months they exploded about fifty nuclear devices and increased radioactive contamination of the atmosphere. Negotiations for a test-ban treaty broke off. The United States resumed nuclear testing in April 1962.

President Kennedy, joined by Prime Minister Harold Macmillan of Britain, urged the Soviets to negotiate a test-ban treaty. In June 1963, Soviet Premier Nikita Khrushchev finally agreed to discuss such an agreement. On July 25, American, Soviet, and British negotiators signed a treaty that prohibited nuclear testing in the air, in space, and underwater, but not underground. More than one hundred other nations signed the same pledge, but Communist China, France, and Cuba refused to sign.

Like Kennedy, President Johnson worried about the dangers of nuclear weapons. He wanted an agreement among nuclear powers to limit the spreading manufacture of such weapons. Events in the Communist world served to further Johnson's goal.

In October 1964, Khrushchev was suddenly removed from power. He was replaced by two other Soviet leaders—Aleksei N. Kosygin as premier and Leonid Brezhnev as first secretary of the Communist party. That same week, Communist China exploded its first atomic device, thus becoming the world's fifth nuclear power.

The new Soviet rulers quarreled bitterly with Chinese leaders over the goals of the Communist world. In time, the Soviets came to feel that something must be done to stop the spread of nuclear arms.

In July 1968 the United States, the Soviet Union, Britain, and fifty-six other nations signed the Nonproliferation Treaty. It prohibited the spread of nuclear arms and of weapons technology. France and Red China did not sign the agreement. Since the treaty did not bar continued development of nuclear weapons by nations that already had them, it did not stop the arms race. It only kept other countries from entering the race.

The arms race had one basic feature: Each side tried to keep up with the other by creating bigger and more expensive weapons. In October 1969, American and Soviet leaders decided to talk directly about this costly race of death. In November, American and Soviet delegates began Strategic Arms Limitation Talks (SALT) in Helsinki, Finland.

Two of the agreements reached in these talks were signed in May 1972, when President Nixon visited the Soviet Union. The Treaty on Anti-Ballistics Missile Systems prohibited each country from building more than two modest ABM systems. The Interim Agreement on Limitation of Strategic Offensive Arms froze the building of offensive missile launchers for five years. These treaties were the first that placed any kind of limit on the manufacture of nuclear weapons. They were the crowning achievement of Nixon's trip.

The Berlin Question

Shortly after Kennedy became President, he and Soviet Premier Khrushchev agreed to meet in Vienna to discuss important differences between their two countries. At the two-day meeting in June 1961, Khrushchev revived the crisis over divided Berlin. He demanded an immediate settlement of the status of the city on Soviet terms. Khrushchev claimed that the Soviets were prepared to risk war to gain this end.

Kennedy replied that the United States and its allies would defend their right to be in Berlin at any cost. He called reserve units into active service and built up United States combat forces in Europe.

This crisis sent a flow of East German refugees into West Berlin. By early August, more than 2,000 persons were streaming across the border each day. To stop this exodus, the Communists began sealing off their sector of the city, first with barbed wire and then with a concrete-block wall 28 miles long. The wall, which was guarded day and night, stopped the flow of refugees. Khrushchev then retreated from his maximum demands. On October 17, he withdrew his six-month deadline for a showdown, and the crisis ended. But a deadlock continued over the question of German unification.

LATIN AMERICA AND AFRICA

As the decade of the sixties began, American foreign policy met tremendous challenges in Latin America and Africa. Strong anti-Yankee feeling in the Americas and violent anticolonialism in Africa created a series of crises.

The Bay of Pigs Fiasco

President Kennedy had long been interested in Latin America, where continuing poverty and unrest encouraged Communist agitators to seek a foothold. When he entered the White House, the most pressing Latin American problem centered on Cuba.

Two weeks before Kennedy took office, President Eisenhower had broken off diplomatic relations with Fidel Castro's regime. Upon becoming President, Kennedy had to decide if he should continue support for a plan devised by the Eisenhower administration. It called for Cuban exiles to invade their homeland and overthrow Castro's government. Some members of Kennedy's staff advised him to drop the idea, but others encouraged him to support this plan, believing that an invasion would trigger a large-scale Cuban rebellion.

In April, Kennedy took his first decisive step against Castro's Cuba. The Department of State issued a statement of policy denouncing Castro as a threat to peace in the Americas.

Then, on April 17, an invasion force of about 1,400 Cuban exiles landed in the Bay of

American *(foreground)* and Soviet tanks line up on either side of "Checkpoint Charlie" on Friedrichstrasse, a crossing point in the wall between East and West Berlin. War threatened in 1961.

Pigs, on Cuba's southern coast. The brigade of exiles lacked adequate air cover or naval support. Though they fought bravely, the exiles were no match for Castro's force of about 20,000. Within seventy-two hours, all the invaders had been killed or captured.

The Kennedy administration at first denied involvement, but it soon became clear that the exile volunteers had been trained, armed, transported, and directed by the Central Intelligence Agency (CIA) of the United States. At the United Nations, Castro charged the United States with aggression. The leaders of many other countries severely criticized United States participation. President Kennedy ultimately took full responsibility for the fiasco.

On May 1, 1961, Castro proclaimed Cuba a socialist state. Later he admitted that he was a Communist, and he became the leader of "Fidelismo," a movement designed to bring socialist revolutions to other parts of Latin America.

The Alliance for Progress

Kennedy tried to contain Castro's Communist revolution in Cuba and to build up aid to the rest of Latin America. In March 1961 he had announced a broad program of economic aid, which he called the Alliance for Progress. In August, economic experts from the Latin American republics met for the first conference on the Alliance for Progress.

All of the Latin American nations except Cuba signed the charter of the Alliance. A minimum of 20 billion dollars was to be spent over a ten-year period to fight poverty, disease, illiteracy, and unemployment. More than half of this money was to come from the United States government; the remainder, from private investors.

Johnson continued support for the Alliance, but after about 1966, the main focus of his foreign policy was elsewhere. When Nixon took office, the Alliance for Progress was dying, and he did not try to keep it alive.

Nixon instead talked about "Partners in Progress." He made an effort to conciliate people in Latin America by sending Governor Nelson Rockefeller of New York on four fact-finding trips to twenty South American countries in 1969. In his report, Rockefeller urged that policies be changed to give certain trade advantages to nations of the Western Hemisphere. Nixon did not accept the scope of Rockefeller's recommendations.

In October 1969, Nixon gave the Alliance a new slogan: "Action for Progress in the Americas." He also made it clear that United States aid and support would no longer require a democratic regime in another country. "If our partnership is to thrive, or even to survive," he said, "we must recognize that the nations of Latin America must go forward in their own way, under their own leadership." Aid to Latin America was drastically reduced.

The Missile Crisis in Cuba

The Alliance for Progress had excluded Cuba. During the Kennedy administration, the United States continued an embargo on trade with Cuba. The embargo was not effective then or later because Castro had committed his nation to economic cooperation with the Communist nations.

In the fall of 1962, President Kennedy learned from photographs taken by American planes that Soviet technicians were installing missile bases on Cuba. From such bases, missiles with nuclear warheads could destroy major cities in the United States.

On October 22, in a nationwide television address, the President announced a limited naval blockade to prevent shipments of missiles from reaching Cuba. He warned the Soviet Union that if missiles were launched from Cuba against any nation in the Western Hemisphere, the United States would immediately retaliate against the Soviet Union.

Kennedy also said that if the Soviets did not dismantle the bases on Cuba, United States planes would bomb the installations. The European allies of the United States, as well as the Organization of American States, supported this position.

United States and Soviet armed forces went into combat readiness, and people everywhere waited uneasily for the Soviet response to Kennedy's challenge. United States planes observed Soviet ships, loaded with weapons, steaming toward Cuba with submarine escorts. But instead of testing the blockade, the Soviet ships turned back. In an exchange of letters with Kennedy, Premier Khrushchev promised to remove offensive weapons from Cuba and to permit inspection by the United Nations to verify the removal. In return, he asked the United States to lift its blockade and to refrain from invading Cuba. Kennedy agreed.

The Soviets withdrew their missiles and bombers and dismantled the launching sites, but Castro refused to permit inspectors on Cuban soil. The United States carried out its own inspection by air. On November 22, Kennedy lifted the blockade.

An improvement in Soviet-American relations began after the Cuban missile crisis. Diplomats call this kind of relaxation of tension a *détente*. In April 1963, the Soviet Union and the United States agreed to establish a direct and uninterrupted teletype communication—a "hot line"—between Moscow and Washington. The purpose was to help reduce the possibility of either nation accidentally setting off a nuclear war.

Trouble in Panama

Johnson's first crisis in foreign policy came seven weeks after he became President. Early in January 1964, a group of United States high-school students raised a United States flag over their school in the Canal Zone. Panamanian students demonstrated in protest. In the riots that followed, twenty-one Panamanians and four United States soldiers were killed.

The Republic of Panama broke off diplomatic relations and demanded renegotiation of the 1903 treaty that had given the United States special rights in the Canal Zone. After a period of bitter exchange, President Johnson agreed to negotiate.

In September 1965, both nations declared that the treaty of 1903 would be canceled and that a new treaty would recognize Panama's sovereignty over the Canal Zone. In June 1967, they announced agreement on three new treaties. Although the draft treaties provided that Panama would eventually operate the canal, in September 1970 the Panamanian government rejected them.

In June 1971 the United States and Panama resumed negotiations, this time over the construction of a new sea-level canal ten miles west of the old one. Since aircraft carriers and huge tankers could not squeeze through the old Panama Canal's locks, the United States wanted a new, wider canal.

The Dominican Crisis

President Johnson's next crisis in Latin America involved the Dominican Republic. In 1961, the dictatorship of Rafael Leonidas Trujillo had ended after 31 years. The next year the Dominicans had elected as their president a social reformer with leftist leanings, Juan Bosch. After seven months, he was overthrown, and a *junta*—a group of military officers—ruled the nation. In April 1965, Bosch's followers tried to bring him back into power with a mass uprising.

After announcing that the fighting endangered Americans in the capital city of Santo Domingo, President Johnson dispatched 400 marines to protect American lives and United States property. Then he sent in paratroopers and other soldiers, ultimately building up the United States forces there to about 30,000. On May 2, he said on nationwide television that "a band of Communist conspirators" had taken over the rebel movement in Santo Domingo. He asserted that another Communist government must not be established in the Western Hemisphere.

Bosch and others denied Johnson's charge. Many Latin Americans considered Johnson's intervention hasty and ill advised. Some criticized the United States for violating the charter of the Organization of American States, which forbade intervention in the internal affairs of a member.

The OAS relieved the United States of some embarrassment by voting to establish the Inter-American Peace Force to maintain order in Santo Domingo. That force included a few units from Latin American nations. In March 1966, the intervention was continued with a force of 8,000 soldiers, three-fourths of them from the United States. After negotiating with leaders of different factions, OAS mediators established a provisional government.

In June, the Dominicans held national elections. Joaquín Balaguer, a conservative, defeated Bosch to become president of the Dominican Republic. After Balaguer was inaugurated on July 1, United States troops began leaving the country. The intervention officially ended in September. It did not, however, dispel anti-Yankee feeling throughout the Americas. Johnson's use of force had damaged the Alliance for Progress and revived Latin American fears of United States imperialism.

United States troops distribute food supplies to refugees in the Dominican Republic. Many Latin American nations protested the United States intervention on the Caribbean island.

Policy in the Congo

The Kennedy administration followed a policy of supporting the anticolonialism of new nations in Africa. The Congo, however, presented special problems. The United States backed efforts to keep the country united as well as independent.

Maintaining unity proved difficult. In February 1961, some Congolese murdered Patrice Lumumba, a popular young revolutionary who had been displaced as premier by military officers. The nation teetered on the brink of civil war. Several provinces threatened secession. Moise Tshombe led the province of Katanga on an independent course. Since that province was rich in minerals, its secession threatened the economic base of the Congo. The United Nations used troops to combat the secession.

When, in December 1961, the UN forces carried out an offensive against Tshombe, the United States helped with money and equipment. This aid from the United States angered the British, French, Belgian, and Portuguese governments, which favored Tshombe. Nevertheless, the Kennedy administration persisted in its policy. Finally, the UN forces ended Katanga's secession.

Some exiled Congolese, with support from Communist China, organized the Committee for National Liberation. In 1963 this committee led a revolt against the central government. The United States aided the government with arms and military advisers, but the rebels kept on gaining territory. In July 1964, Moise Tshombe, who had been in exile, was named premier. Using hired troops and American equipment, he quashed the rebellion early in 1965. But he was unable to form a lasting government. In November General Joseph Mobutu staged a bloodless coup and proclaimed himself president. After that the Congo enjoyed relatively stable government. In 1971 the Congo changed its name to the Republic of Zaïre.

Other Problems in Africa

Political instability and violence were common in many of the new African nations. This instability made the white rulers in South Africa, Southern Rhodesia, Angola, and Mozambique determined to hang on. They resisted the demands of black African nationalists for self-rule. American leaders said they favored the aspirations of the African nationalists, but the United States would not back up this statement with force. For example, the United States did not join in imposing sanctions against South Africa, which had a policy of *apartheid,* strict segregation of blacks and whites.

In Southern Rhodesia, 200,000 whites ruled 3.7 million blacks who had no political privileges. In 1965, Southern Rhodesia's white minority proclaimed their colony's independence from Britain. In 1970 they made Rhodesia a republic. Since the new government of Rhodesia discriminated against blacks, Britain refused to recognize the act of independence. The United Nations called for economic sanctions against Rhodesia. The United States supported these measures, but the sanctions failed to bring political rights to black Rhodesians.

American policy makers were also concerned about the civil war that broke out in May 1967 in Nigeria, Africa's most populous nation. The Ibo people in the east proclaimed a republic called Biafra. The central government, controlled mainly by members of the Hausa tribe, tried to crush the secession. The United States did not take sides in the struggle. It embargoed the sale of arms to both sides but maintained formal relations with the legal central government. Nonetheless, the Hausa government became angry at the United States. It resented the efforts of American humanitarian organizations, and of a pro-Biafra lobby, to break its blockade of Biafra. The American groups wanted to bring medical supplies and food to starving Biafrans. In January 1970, Biafra gave up. In time, United States relations with reunited Nigeria became friendly.

SOUTHEAST ASIA

In the mid-sixties, the people of the United States quarreled bitterly over the nation's role in Southeast Asia. Involvement in the Vietnam war became the overriding issue in American politics.

Laos

In Laos, President Kennedy abandoned the Eisenhower policy of helping pro-Western regimes in anti-Communist wars. Kennedy accepted a British plan for a cease-fire in the civil war in Laos and for a neutralist government that would be neither pro-Western nor Communist.

The Soviets, too, accepted this plan. In May 1962, however, it looked as if Communists might overrun the nation. President Kennedy reacted with a show of strength. He ordered the Seventh Fleet into the waters next to Laos and stationed more than 5,000 combat troops in neighboring Thailand. The Communist offensive ceased. In June, fourteen nations signed agreements guaranteeing independence and neutrality for Laos.

The Rise of the Viet Cong

Across the border in South Vietnam, the anti-Communist position was even shakier. In the late 1950's, the *Viet Cong,* a group of pro-Communist South Vietnamese, had stepped up guerrilla warfare against Ngo Dinh Diem's government. In March 1960, the Viet Cong established the National Liberation Front, which called for the liberation of South Vietnam from United States "imperialism." The Communists of North Vietnam supported this movement. Recruitment of guerrillas for the Viet Cong spread over the countryside. In October 1961, the Viet Cong began a series of attacks on the large towns and cities of South Vietnam.

United States leaders were divided over the proper policy to take in South Vietnam. Some wanted to step in with extensive military aid, including troops, against the Viet Cong. Others believed that South Vietnam's president, Ngo Dinh Diem, ought to liberalize his dictatorial regime in order to gain popular support against the Communists.

As a holding action, the United States government increased the size of its military mission, which was used mainly to advise and train Diem's army. When Kennedy became President, 2,000 United States military advisers were in South Vietnam. By the end of 1963, about 16,000 troops, including combat units, were stationed there.

The Diem regime had continued to resist reform. Early in November 1963, some young generals seized the government and assassinated Diem. This coup failed to bring stability to the strife-ridden land.

Increased Involvement

In 1964, Viet Cong forces stepped up their attacks against the South Vietnamese army. By May, the Viet Cong seemed to be on the verge of taking over the country. President Johnson and his advisers feared that if the Viet Cong were successful, all of Southeast Asia would fall into Communist hands. Johnson therefore increased aid to South Vietnam and built up the concentration of United States troops there.

In August, Johnson claimed that torpedo boats from North Vietnam had attacked American destroyers on patrol in the Gulf of Tonkin. He said that he had ordered jet bombers to strike at gunboat bases and oil storage tanks in North Vietnam. On August 7, Congress overwhelmingly passed the Gulf of Tonkin resolution. It gave the President support for "all necessary measures" to repel the attacks and to "prevent further aggression." During the election campaign that fall, the President said that he had no intention of broadening the war by turning it into an attack on North Vietnam.

Early in 1965, Johnson and his advisers concluded that the Viet Cong could not be stopped without greater United States involvement. Up to this time, American troops were supposedly serving as advisers. They were pledged not to shoot unless they were attacked. Johnson sent more troops to South Vietnam for the purpose of fighting full-scale battles. In February, he ordered American planes to bomb bridges, military installations, and other objectives in North Vietnam. He explained that his aim was to force the Communists to negotiate a settlement. He said that he was willing to open "unconditional discussions" with any powers that could end hostilities. The Soviet Union, Communist China, and North Vietnam rejected his terms.

People all over the world criticized Johnson's policy. At home, opposition to American involvement in the Vietnam war came mainly from colleges and universities and from some members of Congress. But most members of Congress and most Americans apparently supported Johnson's policy.

The protest grew louder in June 1966.

The constant bombing of Indochina *(left)* was a much-criticized aspect of American military policy. Vietnamese villagers often took to the rivers *(above)* to escape bombardment. Many Vietnamese hid from ground troops by submerging and breathing through reeds. Helicopters were the workhorses of the war. They landed troops *(opposite)* and dropped supplies. They were invaluable in picking up the wounded and rapidly getting them to field hospitals.

President Johnson, in an attempt to halt North Vietnamese aid to the Viet Cong, ordered air strikes against oil depots around Hanoi and Haiphong, North Vietnam's major cities. Despite objections, Johnson increased American combat strength.

To pay for the war the government cut back on its domestic programs. Johnson tried, unsuccessfully, to raise taxes. Inflation mounted, and the casualty lists became longer. Opposition to the war spread to all parts of American life. By the beginning of 1967, according to public-opinion polls, Johnson's war policy had lost the approval of the majority of Americans.

Critics condemned the war as illegal because Congress had not declared it. They denounced it as immoral because a big, powerful nation was killing the civilians of a small, poor country. Supporters of the war argued that it was legal because the President as commander in chief could use the armed forces wherever he wished. They said that in modern wars, civilians always suffer and that American action in Vietnam was no more immoral than that of the Viet Cong.

Regardless of who was right or wrong, by the end of 1967 most Americans were tired of the war. By that time, the United States had more than 500,000 troops in Vietnam. In

January 1968, the Viet Cong launched a surprise offensive throughout South Vietnam. The Viet Cong captured many cities and for a short time held the American embassy compound building in Saigon. Criticism of Johnson's war policy intensified. The President announced that he would not run for reelection in 1968 so that he could spend more time on peace-making efforts.

The war was the major issue of the campaign. The bombings of North Vietnam received especially strong criticism. In October, hoping to help his party's candidates as well as to encourage North Vietnam to negotiate, Johnson halted the bombings.

Nixon's Policy in Vietnam

When he took office, President Nixon did not change Johnson's basic Vietnam policy. Nor did he reveal the "peace plan" he had talked about in his campaign.

In July and August 1969, Nixon visited six Asian countries. On the island of Guam he announced the Nixon Doctrine, saying that America's allies in Asia must defend themselves. The United States would give them aid but not troops. He also said that he would "Vietnamize" the war, turn the fighting over to the South Vietnamese. Then he could remove American ground troops.

He began to withdraw American soldiers in August, but many doves denounced the slow pace of troop withdrawals. In October and November, protesters staged antiwar demonstrations across the nation.

Late in 1969 many people were shocked by revelations of American brutality. In 1968 an American infantry unit had massacred about 500 men, women, and children in the Vietnamese village of My Lai. Critics used this as evidence that the war was dehumanizing American soldiers.

Nixon nonetheless persisted in his Vietnam policy and asked the "great silent majority" of Americans to support it. In April 1970, in an effort to destroy Communist sanctuaries, he launched an invasion of Cambodia, which was technically neutral. This expansion of the war touched off new protests, riots, and demonstrations.

In Congress, doves tried to curb the President's war-making powers. The Senate in June 1970 managed to repeal the Gulf of Tonkin resolution. Nixon defended the Cambodian invasion and refused to retreat from his war policy.

During the next two years the President drastically reduced draft calls and regularly pulled American troops out of Vietnam. American casualties steadily declined. But peace on his terms eluded Nixon.

In March 1972 the Viet Cong and North Vietnamese launched a massive ground offensive that made a shambles of Vietnamization. South Vietnam was threatened with collapse. Nixon resumed the systematic bombing of North Vietnam, the first such air strikes in four years. Still the Communist forces rolled on.

Nixon ordered American pilots to mine Haiphong harbor and other ports and to bomb rail lines, highways, and installations around Hanoi. In effect, he established a land and sea blockade of North Vietnam. At the same time, he offered to withdraw all United States forces from Vietnam in four months once North Vietnam returned the American prisoners it held and agreed to a cease-fire throughout Indochina. The Communists spurned the offer. They wanted complete American withdrawal with few strings attached.

Nixon's stepped-up air war set off another wave of antiwar protests. Many people

Top: A returning prisoner of war waves joyously from his stretcher as he arrives in the Philippines. More than 500 American POW's were returned, but many troops were missing in action. *Bottom:* An American nurse treats a napalm burn on a Vietnamese woman.

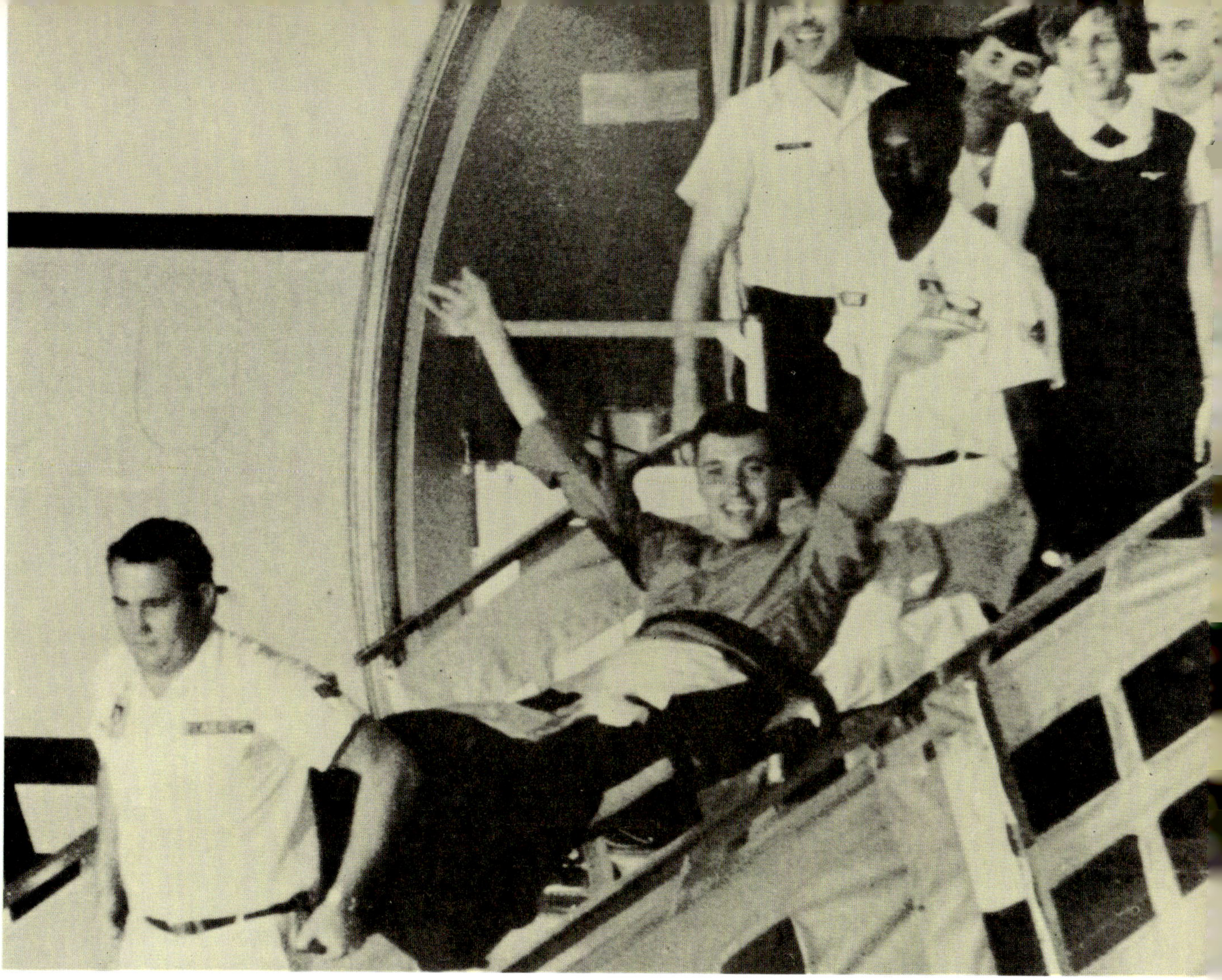

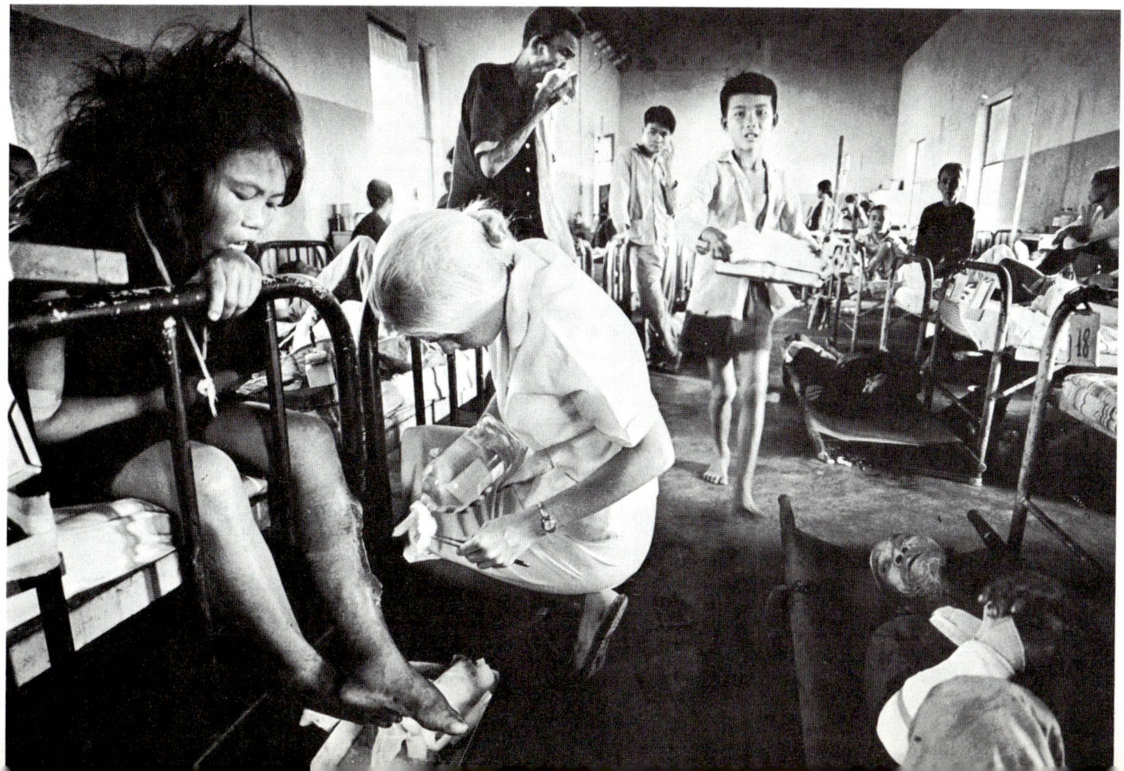

feared that the blockade would provoke the Chinese or the Soviets into war. But neither the Soviet Union nor Communist China took up the challenge. Despite criticism from around the world, the President stuck to his new policy.

This new policy kept the United States deeply involved in the war. But it substituted air power for soldiers and Vietnamese deaths for American. By September 1972, all American ground troops had been removed from combat in South Vietnam. Nixon's reduction of ground troops to fewer than 40,000 pleased great numbers of Americans and weakened the antiwar movement in the United States.

The Paris Peace Talks

In March 1968, President Johnson had urged the North Vietnamese to negotiate a peace. He called a halt to the bombing of all but a small section of North Vietnam. In May, the North Vietnamese agreed to meet in Paris to discuss peace.

After the 1968 election the talks were expanded to include the South Vietnamese government and the Viet Cong. But the talks, and the war, dragged on. Some humorists suggested that if the talks were held outdoors in Antarctica rather than in the charming confines of Paris, peace would break out overnight. In fact, however, it took another election year to prompt some action.

President Nixon's chief national security assistant was Henry M. Kissinger, a former college professor who had also advised Kennedy and Johnson. In January 1972, Kissinger disclosed that he had begun secret peace talks with the North Vietnamese.

Certain issues were basic to the discussions. The United States was most concerned with arranging a cease-fire and the release of American prisoners of war held by the North Vietnamese and the Viet Cong. The Vietnamese most wanted to settle questions about their country's political status: Was Vietnam one nation or two? If it were one nation, which was the legitimate government—the Democratic Republic of Vietnam (North) or the Republic of Vietnam (South)? If it were two nations, which was the legitimate government in the South—the Provisional Revolutionary Government of South Vietnam (the Viet Cong) or the Republic of Vietnam?

In October, Kissinger announced that "peace is at hand," but his statement proved to be premature. Not until January 27, 1973, did the United States, North Vietnam, South Vietnam, and the Viet Cong sign a peace agreement.

It provided for an immediate cease-fire, withdrawal of all American troops from Vietnam within sixty days, the release of American prisoners within sixty days, and an international commission to supervise the cease-fire and troop withdrawals. It left unanswered the questions about Vietnam's political status. All sides agreed to recognize a provisional demilitarized zone at the 17th parallel. They also set the long-range goal of reunification of North and South into one country. But reunification was to be achieved through negotiations by the two Vietnams, not by outsiders.

The agreement came after thirty years of fighting, the United States having been deeply involved for the last eleven of those years. President Nixon called it "a peace, however fragile, which we have hopes will endure." But Nguyen Van Thieu, South Vietnam's president, said when he announced the cease-fire agreement, "There is no guarantee that the forthcoming peace will be an ideal and lasting peace."

Israeli military forces head across the Sinai Peninsula. The Arab-Israeli dispute constantly flared up. Some Arab terrorists carried on a worldwide campaign of plane hijackings, letter bombings, and kidnapings.

ELSEWHERE IN ASIA

Though Vietnam issues dominated foreign policy, conflicts in other parts of Asia also troubled the United States.

Southwest Asia: The Middle East

Nationalism, friction between Arab states, and Arab-Israeli hostility continued to keep the Middle East in turmoil. Since the United States stood by Israel, Arab leaders like Egypt's Gamal Abdel Nasser turned to the Soviet Union for help.

When the Soviets began giving Egypt and Syria modern weapons, Israel's leaders asked the United States for an alliance guaranteeing their nation's independence. President Kennedy refused. But in May 1963 he said that the United States would oppose aggression anywhere in the Middle East.

After the Sinai War of 1956, President Eisenhower had persuaded the Israelis to withdraw from Sharm el-Sheikh, a base that commanded the Strait of Tiran, the entrance to the Gulf of Aqaba. He had promised that the United States would uphold Israel's right to use the gulf.

In May 1967, that promise was challenged. Nasser asked the United Nations to withdraw its peacekeeping emergency force from Egyptian soil. For ten years that force had guarded the armistice line between Egypt and Israel, from the Gaza Strip to Sharm el-Sheikh. When United Nations soldiers withdrew, the Egyptians moved their troops in. Nasser then closed the Strait of Tiran to Israeli shipping.

President Johnson condemned the closing of the strait as illegal. He asked Nasser to allow Israel free passage through the gulf. Nasser rejected Johnson's appeal.

After Egypt, Syria, and Jordan massed troops on Israel's border, Israel attacked. In one morning's fight, Israeli planes destroyed most of the Egyptian air force on the ground.

At first the United States feared that the Soviets would send troops and planes to aid the Arab nations. Then President Johnson and Soviet Premier Kosygin agreed over the "hot line" that they would keep their countries out of the conflict. This lessened the danger that the war would spread.

Israel quickly defeated the armies of the Egyptians, Syrians, and Jordanians. Israeli forces took control of the Sinai Peninsula and other strategic areas. The warring countries accepted the demand for a cease-fire by June 10, and the fighting ended. They could not, however, agree on a peace settlement.

The United Nations demanded that Israel give back to the Arabs lands that it had conquered. The Israelis refused, calling instead for direct peace negotiations with the Arab governments. But the Arab states said that they would not talk peace until the Israelis had withdrawn from the occupied lands. The Soviets backed the Arabs. American policy makers supported Israel.

Almost immediately the Soviets sent new arms, as well as technicians and military advisers, to Egypt and other Arab states. In the late 1960's and early 1970's the Soviet battle fleet cruised the Mediterranean, using Arab ports. To the dismay of American policy makers, the Soviets had gained an important foothold in the Arab world.

Japan

Another nation of special concern to the United States was Japan. Through foreign trade it had become one of the world's economic giants. As the postwar period of adjustment ended, Japan sought to regain control of the Bonin and Ryukyu Islands, held by the United States since the end of World War II.

In 1968 the United States returned the Bonins to Japan. Four years later the United States gave up control of the Ryukyu Islands, the home of about a million Japanese. The United States retained military bases on Okinawa, the largest of the Ryukyus.

India and Pakistan

In 1947, former British India was split into two nations—India and Pakistan—one Hindu and the other Muslim. The new Islamic nation of Pakistan was composed of two parts, West and East, on either side of India. This partition ended a large-scale war of religions, but fighting broke out from time to time over Kashmir, a province that both India and Pakistan wanted.

In 1962, when India and Red China fought a small war on their mountain frontier, the United States aided India with arms. This aid angered Pakistan, which turned to Red China for support. In 1965 when India and Pakistan again fought for control of Kashmir, the United States remained neutral. But the United States promised aid to India if China should intervene.

In December 1971, India and Pakistan went to war again. This time the issue was the freedom of the Bengali province of East Pakistan. The government of Pakistan, controlled by West Pakistanis, had crushed a rebellion by the Bengalis. India sided with the Bengalis and went to war against Pakistan. Within two weeks, India gained a complete victory over the Pakistanis in the east. The Pakistani forces surrendered, and their government accepted India's terms for a cease-fire. East Pakistan then proclaimed its independence as the state of Bangla Desh.

President Nixon did not intervene in the conflict, but he openly sided with Pakistan. When war broke out he suspended 87.6 million dollars in aid to India. Many Americans were dismayed by the President's support of Pakistan, ruled by a military dictatorship. Nixon's policy alienated India and did little to save Pakistan from dismemberment.

China

Kennedy, Johnson, and Nixon continued the long-standing policy of refusing to recognize the People's Republic of China (Communist) as the legitimate government of China. In July 1971, however, President Nixon stunned the world by announcing that he would visit Communist China.

Nixon flew to China in February 1972 and stayed for a week. He met and talked with

President and Mrs. Nixon and their entourage visit the Great Wall of China. The 1972 trip to the Asian mainland rekindled American interest in Chinese culture and helped reopen trade channels.

Premier Chou En-lai and Communist Party Chairman Mao Tse-tung. This first visit by an American president was a great spectacle, witnessed by millions through television. Nixon called it a "journey for peace." Its main direct result was an agreement that the two countries should increase contacts, especially in the area of trade.

SOCIAL TURMOIL

The sixties witnessed more social protests than any period since the Great Depression. Group after group organized to point out society's wrongs and to propose possible corrections. Some of the most vocal protesters were quite young, and they received so much publicity that it seemed as if all the protesters were college students.

Student Activism

One of the distinctive developments of the 1960's was the emergence of organized activist youth. More than half the population was under 25 years of age, and young people were aware of the power of their numbers as never before.

Not all young Americans were rebels. Most of them cherished the traditional values and tried to work within the system, even when they were trying to change it. Rebellious youth, however, questioned almost everything and attacked what they considered to be society's fundamental evils.

The organized youth rebellion began in February 1960 with the black student sit-ins in the South. Students from the North, white and black, joined the civil rights crusade. Many of the young people who entered the civil rights battle were idealists. Their experiences changed them, and some returned to their college campuses as radicals.

Radical youth was especially well entrenched on the Berkeley campus of the University of California. In the fall of 1964 the radicals there applied their experience in the civil rights crusade to a student protest known as the free-speech movement. For the first time, students made a large-scale attack on the impersonal authority of the modern giant university. Widely publicized, the Berkeley rebellion gripped public attention as had no other student uprising. It stimulated youthful agitation in favor of educational, political, and social reform.

Hippies

The style setters of the sixties were the hippies. They were the spiritual descendants of the Beat Generation of the late 1940's and 1950's. "Beatniks" rejected materialism and dabbled in mysticism. In the late 1950's, some of the beatniks moved to the Haight-Ashbury district of San Francisco, a neighborhood of Victorian houses. Members of a new generation were attracted to the area and took up some of the beatnik characteristics while rejecting others. These were "hippies," sometimes called flower children.

Hippies rejected some aspects of materialism—such as pursuing a career—while embracing other aspects—such as working long enough to buy a stereo set or a car. Pursuing a philosophy that stressed love and sharing, some hippies lived together in communal apartments and houses. Many smoked marijuana and experimented with other drugs. The hippies' hair flowed long and often uncombed; men were bearded; men and women wore patched jeans and army or navy surplus jackets.

Although the hippie movement attracted only a small minority of youth, its impact was great. Young people everywhere took up the dress and hair styles, if not the drug attitudes and philosophy, of the flower children. Young people dressing and acting as hippies could be seen hitchhiking on highways to San Francisco, Big Sur, Chicago, New York, and elsewhere. Often they would be packed into a camper painted with flowers or exotic designs. Typically, they would have a dog or two and a guitar. These were America's gypsy children.

Many nonhippies took to drugs. Like the hippies, they believed that marijuana was less dangerous than the alcohol their parents' generation drank. The use of marijuana became widespread. Drug users became younger and younger, and drugs of all kinds were widely used by high-school and college students.

The Antiwar Movement

As American involvement in the Vietnam war escalated, so did opposition to that war. The antiwar movement was not supported solely by the young. It drew strength from the clergy, women, veterans, and many other groups who looked on the war as an immoral, unnecessary bloodbath. Protest by young people was especially directed against the draft.

Those who opposed the draft and the war usually used nonviolent protest to express their opposition. Some young men burned

Peace advocates hold a protest march. The Vietnam war provoked more antiwar demonstrations in the United States than any war in the twentieth century. Groups that favored the war also demonstrated.

their draft cards. One group, led by a priest, broke into a government office in Maryland and poured animal blood on draft records and other contents of the filing cabinets.

Antiwar activists were conspicuous among those working to defeat Lyndon B. Johnson in 1968. They contributed greatly to Eugene J. McCarthy's remarkable showing in the Democratic primary in New Hampshire. Various peace groups, notably the National Mobilization Committee to End the War in Vietnam, planned massive antiadministration demonstrations for the Democratic National Convention in Chicago. The dissenters succeeded in disrupting the convention and making it one of the most unruly in the nation's history.

The noisy and continuing opposition to the draft influenced government. Congress changed the draft laws to end student deferments and to put the system on a lottery basis. Then the Department of Defense began working out plans for an all-volunteer army. By 1973, the draft was all but ended.

Offshoots

As with every social movement, the antiwar movement was not united. Some of the protesters objected to the war as a violation of religious principles. They usually used nonviolent or symbolic means to protest. Others saw the antiwar movement as a means to overthrow the government and promote revolution. They seized university buildings, destroyed property, set fires in public buildings, planted bombs, and battled police and national guard units.

A significant student uprising took place at Columbia University in April 1968. In a protest over plans to build a gymnasium in a park next to the campus, radicals used force to wrench concessions from the university.

That fall, at San Francisco State College, black students supported by white militants threatened violence if their "nonnegotiable demands" were not met by the administration.

The youthful turmoil stirred a deep uneasiness in lawmakers and the general public. "Law and order" was a major issue in the 1968 election. In March 1969 a Gallup Poll claimed that campus violence had replaced the Vietnam war as the primary concern of most adult Americans. Other public-opinion polls indicated that the public favored strong measures to stop agitators.

Some form of organized dissent, according to a report by the Carnegie Commission on Higher Education, had surfaced at 57 percent of the nation's colleges and universities. In 1970 legislators in thirty-two states passed laws to curb youthful agitators.

President Nixon's orders to the army to invade Cambodia brought youthful unrest to a dreadful climax. At Kent State University in Ohio in May 1970, national guardsmen fired point-blank on student protesters. Four unarmed youths were killed. The same day, two antiwar protesters at Jackson State College in Mississippi were killed.

In 1971, campuses quieted down, for many reasons. The ground war in Vietnam was winding down, the draft laws had been changed, and the recession limited the job market. Also, college and civil authorities were firmer in putting down agitation, and many young people were becoming disillusioned with the limited achievements of violent protest.

Youth did, however, gain a greater voice in government. In December 1970 the Supreme Court ruled that 18-year-olds must be allowed to vote in federal elections but could be excluded from local elections. This ruling created administrative confusion in most states, and Congress hurriedly passed the Twenty-sixth Amendment to the Constitution. It permitted persons 18 and over to vote in any election in the United States. The amendment, which became law on June 30, 1971, placed 11 million Americans between 18 and 21 on the voting rolls.

A Look at Specifics

1. What measures did the United States take to stop the Soviet establishment of missile bases in Cuba?
2. What agreements were made to control nuclear weapons?
3. Why did American troops invade the Dominican Republic in 1965?
4. Why did the United States become involved in the Vietnam war?
5. What was an important practical gain of the youth movement?

A Review of Major Ideas

1. What was the role of the Kennedy, Johnson, and Nixon administrations in lessening the danger of nuclear war and in improving relations with the Soviet Union and Communist China?
2. How did Kennedy, Johnson, and Nixon each modify the Vietnam policy of his immediate predecessor?

For Independent Study

1. In World War II, in Korea, and in Vietnam, many Americans disagreed over the nation's goals in fighting. Some said that the United States should seek unconditional surrender, "total victory." Others said that the United States should fight limited wars for limited goals. What are the arguments for and against each of these positions?
2. About what did the United States and Communist China disagree?

People or Machines?

CHAPTER 29
1960–1972

When President Eisenhower left office, he made a farewell address in which he warned against the growth of "a permanent armaments industry of vast proportions." He urged Americans not to allow generals and business executives, leaders of the "military-industrial complex," to control government and upset the idea of balanced government.

Throughout the sixties and early seventies, Americans wrestled with a "guns-or-butter" dilemma: If the government concentrated on building up military defenses, it would not be able to afford programs designed to ease social problems. Yet a nation's social condition is its first line of defense, and if the United States ignored its social problems, its defenses would be weak.

POPULATION PRESSURES

Government finances were affected by the distribution of population. The United States had more old people and more young people than at any other time in its history. Most of them were not major taxpayers. The cost of supporting government programs therefore hit hard at the people in the middle.

Population Characteristics

In the 1940's the birth rate skyrocketed and continued to do so through most of the 1950's, though it then began to decline steadily. By 1972 the birth rate was the lowest since full record-keeping began in 1917.

Improvements in medicine, nutrition, and sanitation had made possible a longer life for the average American. A baby born in 1900 was expected to live 49 years; in 1950, 68 years; and in 1970, almost 71 years. The postwar baby boom and the longer life expectancy resulted in a population consisting of a higher proportion than in the past of both the very young and the very old.

Since the increase in population had come without much immigration, the proportion of

Hippies have a songfest in a Berkeley coffeehouse.

foreign-born to native Americans dropped. The white population in the 1960's and 1970's became more homogeneous.

The nonwhite population also increased. According to the census of 1970, nonwhites numbered 25.5 million, of which 22.6 million were black. The majority of blacks no longer lived in the South. In 1940 the eleven states of the old Confederate South contained 69 percent of the nation's black people; in 1970, only 45 percent. Blacks usually went to cities in New York, California, Michigan, Illinois, and New Jersey. In 1970, New York had the largest black population of any city, but Washington, Gary, Newark, Atlanta, and other smaller cities had black majorities.

Americans continued the long-term pattern of moving from country to cities and from cities to suburbs. During the 1960's the proportion of Americans living in rural areas dropped from 30.1 percent to 26.5 percent. By 1970 there were 53.6 million rural residents, 9.7 million living on farms. The number of farm people had decreased by almost 6 million. Americans left the farms for many reasons, but mechanization of agriculture was probably the most common.

In the forties, fifties, and sixties, newer cities in the West and Southwest showed the most growth. But the population of all cities did not keep pace with the growth of population in the suburbs that surrounded them. People were becoming concentrated in great metropolitan areas, such as New York City and its suburbs or Los Angeles and its neighboring communities. By 1970, suburbanites numbered 74.9 million and made up the largest single bloc of the population.

Medical Care

President Johnson had interpreted his victory in 1964 as an endorsement of his pro-

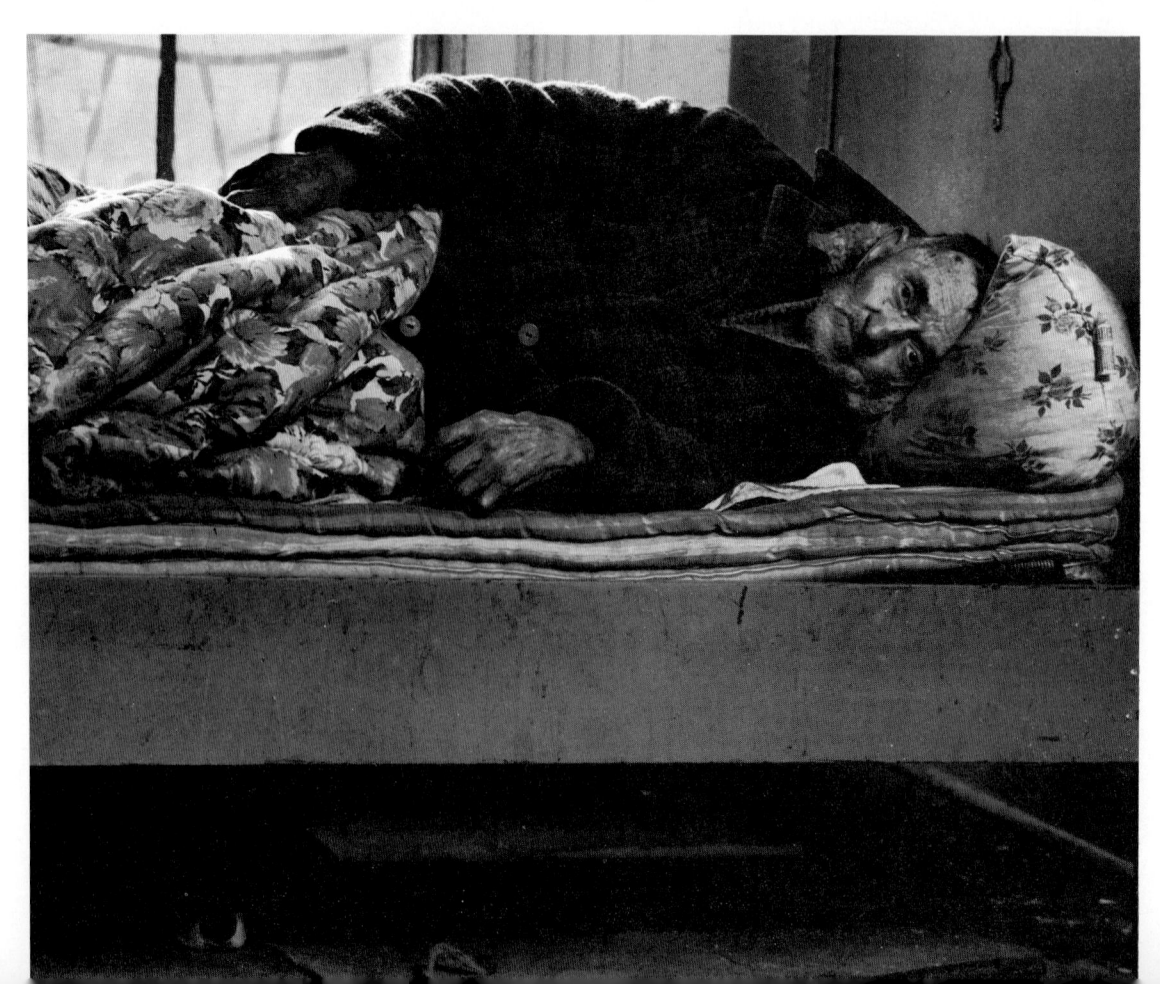

TOTAL POPULATION GROWTH, 1940–1970

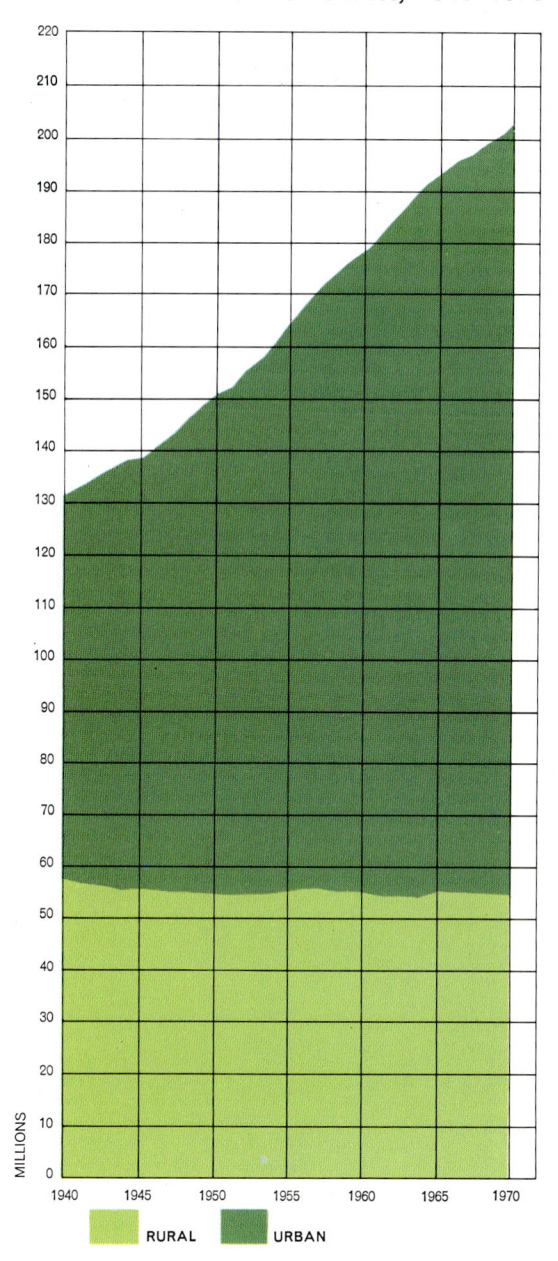

The conditions of life for the elderly *(opposite)* in the United States aroused public interest from time to time. Relatively few old people lived with their grown sons and daughters. Most lived in nursing homes, old peoples' homes, retirement villages, and the least expensive parts of urban areas.

posals for social legislation. When Congress convened in January 1965, he asked for laws that would move the nation toward the Great Society. Congress responded quickly. One of the most important measures it enacted dealt with medical care for old people.

Specialization in science and medicine had made health services better but increasingly expensive. In the 1960's the cost of health services in the United States rose three times faster than the prices of goods and other services, placing medical help beyond the reach of many. Some Americans relied on private health insurance to meet their medical needs, but more and more people thought the federal government should take responsibility for health care.

The Social Security Amendments of July 1965 established Medicare and Medicaid programs. Medicare provided limited hospital care and medical insurance to persons over 65, who usually could not get private health insurance. Medicaid, with money from federal and state governments, paid part of the medical bills for the poor.

The battle for these programs had been long and intense. Many old people and labor unions had favored them, but the American Medical Association and private insurance companies had fought them as first steps toward "socialized" medicine. Still, these programs did not fully meet the needs of the old and the poor.

In a sense the health-care crisis was worldwide. But every major industrialized nation except the United States had some kind of national health program to help people obtain medical services. In the early seventies, American lawmakers were discussing more than a dozen proposals for some kind of national health insurance.

Education

The American system of mass public education was one of the most successful in the world. Yet in the decades after World War II, many Americans were dissatisfied with the schools.

Education had become increasingly important as machines had become more and more complicated. The technological society demanded highly trained, literate men and women to run its machines. College degrees were required for many jobs, and graduate degrees were needed for most professions.

In the late sixties, more than one-fourth of all Americans were enrolled in some program of formal education. Administrators had difficulty in keeping standards high while expanding their schools.

Teachers' salaries were low, and school buildings were overcrowded and inadequate in many parts of the country. The richest states could afford well-equipped schools and good salaries for teachers. But poorer states could not spend nearly so much, even though some of these states spent a larger part of their income on education.

Many people felt that the quality of education could be improved and the soaring costs cut through the use of teaching machines, television, audio-visual aids, and computers. Attempts to develop such materials forced educators to study the learning process more carefully than before. By the seventies, the use of teaching machines had stalled.

The most pressing problem was that of providing education for poor people, many of whom were black or Spanish-speaking. To help improve education, Congress passed the Elementary and Secondary Education Act of 1965. It provided billions of dollars in federal funds for the nation's classrooms.

One of the most highly publicized programs sponsored by the federal government was called Head Start. It tried to prepare disadvantaged children for school before they entered first grade. It was hoped that these children could then compete successfully with middle-class children.

An important nationwide educational experiment began in November 1969, when the Corporation for Public Broadcasting launched a series called "Sesame Street." This was the most intensive effort ever made to use television to reach and teach young children. It used cartoons, skits, and other techniques to gain and hold the attention of preschool children while explaining concepts, words, and numbers. Broadcast over hundreds of stations, "Sesame Street" won the acclaim of children, educators, and critics.

Special programs and education in general were expensive. In the late sixties and early seventies, taxpayers throughout the country rebelled. In many areas, they voted down bond issues and property tax increases for supporting schools. Expansion slowed.

Colleges and universities followed a similar pattern. They too went through a cycle of explosive expansion and then cutbacks in the seventies. They too felt the sting of criticism. Critics charged that higher education had become so narrow and specialized it had lost touch with students as human beings.

In June 1972, President Nixon signed into law the Education Aid Bill. It provided, for the first time, federal money that colleges and universities could use as they wished. Through scholarships, grants, and loans, the federal government would also provide financial help for college students who needed it. But in 1973 only a small amount of federal money actually reached the colleges.

Immigration Laws

Since 1921, the United States had followed a policy of setting quotas for immigrants on the basis of national origin. Many Americans felt that the immigration laws were racist and should be changed.

Congress had occasionally passed special laws to allow particular groups into the country. For instance, after the Hungarian revolution of 1956, the United States had granted refuge to thousands of "freedom fighters." Likewise, it had aided Cubans fleeing from Castro's regime. But it had not changed the basic policy. Both Kennedy and Johnson proposed revisions.

In October 1965, President Johnson signed into law far-reaching immigration and nationality bills. The new standards gave preference to close relatives of residents in the United States and to people with special talents, such as artists, professional people, and skilled workers. It set an annual quota of 170,000 on immigrants from all nations outside the Western Hemisphere. Immigration from nations of the Western Hemisphere, previously unlimited, was to be held to 120,000 annually after 1968.

Urban Crisis

By 1970, more than 70 percent of the people of the United States lived in urban areas, in either city or suburb. In general, suburbs had a higher proportion of upper- and middle-income Americans than did the cities, and their residents usually sought to maintain this situation.

Racial integration was uncommon in the suburbs, and fear (which is not the same thing as hatred) of blacks was a common reason that whites moved to the suburbs. During the sixties, about 2.5 million whites moved to the suburbs while about 3 million blacks moved from rural areas to cities. Cities also gained other groups, such as Mexican Americans, Puerto Ricans, and Indians.

Both cities and suburbs suffered from these shifts in population. With the concentration of low-income people in cities, some neighborhoods became known for high crime rates, slum housing, alcoholism, drug abuse, and personal violence. Many middle-class Americans, both white and black, came to feel that the cities had become "places of terror" where people lived in constant fear.

The suburbs, however, were not the beds

The closely packed areas of the streetcar city *(foreground)* contrast with widely spaced lots in the automobile city *(background)*. "Urban sprawl" raised important questions about land-use policy.

of roses their promoters pictured. Nonexistent or poorly enforced building and housing codes, haphazard zoning laws, as well as the prospects of profits, had encouraged developers to build in the suburbs. Many had thrown together communities that lacked adequate water supplies, fire protection, sewers, transportation, and schools. All of these facilities then had to be built and paid for by the taxpayers in the new developments. Even in communities that had been thoughtfully planned and built, population often grew so rapidly that public facilities were strained.

Since most local governments depended on property taxes to pay for their services, they sought to increase the tax base by increasing industrial and commercial development within the community boundaries. Cities and suburbs engaged in a giant tug-of-war, the cities attempting to keep industries and the suburbs trying to lure them away.

In 1965, Congress created the Department of Housing and Urban Development. It brought together under one administrator a number of agencies. The first secretary of HUD was Robert C. Weaver, who was also the first black cabinet member.

In 1966 President Johnson persuaded Congress to pass the Model Cities Program. It tried to make life in the cities better by rebuilding homes, schools, parks, and other facilities.

In urban areas all over the United States, people questioned whether or not the modern city, and the economic and social system on which it was based, could survive. They pointed out that the urban crisis was worldwide. Urban areas everywhere were suffering from pollution, overcrowding, and wide differences between rich and poor.

Those who speculated on the future of the American metropolitan areas were pessimistic. Under existing social and economic conditions, neither cities nor suburbs were able to cope with the crisis.

Law and Order

Critics of growth pointed out that as the density of population rises, so do violence and crime. What happened in the United States in the 1960's seemed to bear out the generalization. Reports by the Federal Bureau of Investigation showed that crimes of all kinds rose steadily throughout the decade. The student disorders, black riots, and political assassinations aroused fears that lawlessness had gotten out of control.

These concerns made "law and order" a big issue in the presidential campaign of 1968 and stimulated federal action. President Johnson created the National Commission on the Causes and Prevention of Violence. In 1970, this commission reported that violence was "corroding the central political process" of American society.

Shortly after taking office, President Nixon proposed a national war on crime. In 1970, Congress passed the Omnibus Crime Control Act, which strengthened the power of federal law-enforcement agencies to deal with organized and unorganized violence.

Despite public concern, the crime rates, especially of young people, continued to rise. Women, too, became more involved in crime. From 1960 through 1970, arrests of men for serious crimes rose by 73 percent while arrests of women rose by more than 200 percent. Assaults on police became common and aroused national concern.

Drugs

In the early 1970's, concern over drug use and the crimes associated with drugs became almost a national hysteria. Although there had always been drug users in the United States, until the 1950's large-scale consumption of drugs other than alcohol had been rare. Then the quantity and variety of drugs increased steadily.

In 1970, according to various estimates, some 20 million Americans used or experimented with marijuana. Heroin, once used mainly by poor whites and blacks, found numerous users in the armed forces and among upper- and middle-class whites. People of every class popped pills for some kind of release, relief, or stimulation.

In June 1971 President Nixon centered within his executive office federal efforts to solve the drug and narcotics problem. He called drug abuse a disease that affected not only the "crime-prone heroin addict" but also "the suburban housewife dependent on tranquilizers and diet pills" and "the student leaning on amphetamines to help him cram for exams."

Drug use, however, continued to flourish. The United States had become the world's greatest market for drugs. Since addicts needed a great deal of money to support their drug habits, many turned to crime. Muggings, assaults, breaking and entering, and other crimes were often blamed on drug addicts. Some of the opposition to the Vietnam war was based on reports that large numbers of Americans were becoming addicts in Vietnam and that highly placed members of the South Vietnamese government were trafficking in heroin.

The Judicial Crunch

Social analysts believed that laws alone would not curb crime. The system of dispensing justice had to be improved. Courts were crowded, and trials dragged on for years. Law and its enforcement did not match the pace of the world of the 1970's. Critics also pointed out that the poor and underprivileged could have no confidence in "law and order" when they saw it as a slogan for the privileged. They saw wealthy lawbreakers going free while the poor were jailed for minor crimes.

The quality of justice reached beyond the courtroom to the prison. In the 1960's America's prisons were affected by the social turmoil outside their walls. There were many outbursts of violence, but the bloodiest took place in September 1971 at the Attica Correctional Facility in New York State. The Attica inmates rebelled and held the prison for more than four days. Then 1,500 state troopers and law officers stormed the prison and overwhelmed the 1,200 unarmed inmates. Thirty-four prisoners and nine guards and civilian employees died.

This tragedy accented what many people already knew: Most "correctional" institutions did not correct; they bred more crime than they controlled. Yet in the early seventies, money for a thorough reformation of prisons and jails was not forthcoming. Most states were cutting rather than increasing such funds.

Welfare

The high costs of public welfare and of social services strained the resources of most states. Many taxpayers resisted efforts to expand welfare benefits. States reduced social services and tightened eligibility for those welfare benefits still available. The federal government acted to take on much of the welfare burden. Bills were prepared in Congress that would provide a nationally uniform system of minimum payments to poor families.

Poverty was part of the urban crisis. As more and more businesses moved to the suburbs, many of the lowest-paid people were unable to keep their jobs. They were neither able to afford to live in the suburbs nor to buy the automobiles necessary to carry them to their jobs. Many of them went on welfare.

In 1970 the poverty level was defined as a yearly income of $3,968 for an urban family of four. On this basis, 25.5 million Americans were poor. Poor whites outnumbered poor blacks, 17.5 million to 7.7 million. But one black in three lived in poverty in comparison to one white in ten.

SCIENCE AND TECHNOLOGY

In the years following World War II scientific and technological accomplishments were spectacular. The universities, with their laboratories and skilled researchers, were the breeding grounds for scientific development. They trained young scientists and carried out experiments.

Government, industry, and private foundations gave large sums of money to universities to support research. In 1950 the government set up the National Science Foundation to coordinate its activities in scientific research and education.

Nuclear Energy

Nuclear physicists, with their work on the atom, had great success. They developed nuclear bombs, but they also found peaceful uses for atomic energy. Such energy came to be used in the treatment of cancer, in supplying electricity, and in powering ships.

In the late 1960's and early 1970's the United States faced a shortage of electricity. Scientists showed that nuclear power could cheaply produce electricity. Although many people looked on this as a great breakthrough, in 1970 the nuclear-power industry began experiencing setbacks. Critics charged that radiation from nuclear-power plants was far more hazardous to life and the environment than the public had realized. They said that danger from cancer and leukemia as a result of atomic radiation was twenty times greater than scientists had thought only ten years earlier.

Some state and local governments passed laws prohibiting the operation of nuclear-power plants. Yet if Americans wanted to experience the comforts of the electronic era, the nation needed more electricity. Nuclear power, despite its dangers, seemed to be a logical source. Efforts to find safe ways to operate such plants continued.

Electronic Revolution

Some of science's greatest advances came from the "quiet revolution" in electronics. This revolution in one way or another touched the lives of all the people. The computer industry benefited most from the new developments in electronics. The demands of this industry in turn stimulated new accomplishments in electronics.

The computer is an electronic machine that can rapidly perform routine or complex tasks. It can also interpret information, make decisions, and even correct its own mistakes. The first electric computers were big and cumbersome. They carried their electricity through vacuum tubes. In 1948, scientists at Bell Telephone Laboratories invented the transistor. This device, about the size of the tip of a ball-point pen, performed efficiently most of the functions of a vacuum tube. It

Machines like these computers could replace hundreds of clerical workers. Despite jokes about massive computer errors, such machines were usually faster and more accurate than people.

made possible smaller, genuinely functional computers.

The next stage in the "quiet revolution" came in 1967 with the introduction of *integrated circuits.* These were chips of silicon with chemical deposits that formed complete electrical circuits. Integrated circuits reduced the size of computers and cut the costs of producing electronic equipment.

No other nation used as many computers as the United States. Americans used computers in industry, communications, weather prediction, and police work. Computers moved shipping, railroad trains, and subway cars. They handled bank accounts, school enrollments, and bills.

The public became especially interested in computers as *data banks,* which stored large amounts of information in a small amount of space. Credit agencies used data banks to check the references of people who had applied for loans or for jobs. Police could store records, fingerprints, and photographs and retrieve such information with a computer in five minutes.

Many Americans worried that data banks invaded their privacy. People who worked in the area of civil liberties were concerned because computers could not discriminate between users, and no one was safe from probings into his or her life.

Police used other electronic devices on a large scale to spy on suspected criminals. Such "bugging" devices could pick up conversations in a closed room. Electronic devices could trace telephone calls and scan fingerprint files automatically. In the seventies, lawmakers were studying ways to provide the people with safeguards against improper use of information accumulated by bugging devices and stored by data banks.

Space Exploration

For over a decade no feat of the scientists and engineers gripped people's imaginations as did the exploration of space. The "space age" began on October 4, 1957, when the Soviet Union launched *Sputnik 1* into orbit around the earth. In January 1958 the United States sent up its first satellite, *Explorer 1.*

Many Americans were upset by the Soviet lead in space technology. The Soviets had gained their advantage after World War II by concentrating research on engines that could boost heavy rockets. The United States did not begin serious work on space rockets until after it had developed lightweight nuclear weapons. In July 1958, Congress created the National Aeronautics and Space Administration (NASA) and gave it responsibility for the scientific investigation of space.

For several years the Soviet space accomplishments outshone those of the United States. In April 1961 the Soviets launched *Voskhod 1.* Inside was Yuri A. Gagarin, the first human to orbit the earth and return safely. In February 1962 the United States sent an astronaut, Lieutenant Colonel John Glenn, Jr., into orbit around the earth. Americans were thrilled. They now felt that their scientists could win the space race.

Both the Soviets and the Americans flung larger capsules into space for longer periods. Through television, millions of people shared the excitement and fears of each American flight into space.

America's greatest triumph came in 1969 when *Apollo 11,* with three astronauts aboard, streaked for the moon. On July 20, 1969, Neil A. Armstrong became the first human to touch the lunar surface. As he stepped onto the moon he said, "That's one small step for a man, one giant leap for mankind." He and another astronaut, Edwin E. Aldrin, Jr., spent more than twenty-one hours on the moon and then returned to Earth.

After that the United States landed several other missions on the moon. Each one brought back rock and soil samples and hundreds of photographs. Through science and technology, humans had made outer space a laboratory.

In 1972, the United States launched its last lunar mission. Many Americans felt that the United States should use its resources to improve the quality of life on Earth rather than to continue with vast expenditures in space. The government decided to put aside its development of rockets that could only be used once. It backed plans for space-shuttle vehicles that could travel back and forth from Earth to stations in space. These space laboratories would remain in orbit for long periods, collecting information.

Medicine

Researchers made great advances in the biological sciences and in medicine. Many diseases that people had long dreaded, such as typhoid fever and malaria, were brought under control with drugs and vaccines.

One of the most dramatic scientific struggles against disease was fought against poliomyelitis, long a crippler. Dr. Jonas Salk discovered a killed-virus vaccine, and Dr. Albert B. Sabin developed a live-virus vaccine. By the early 1960's, these vaccines had almost wiped out polio.

Improved technology made possible better care for those who suffered heart attacks. Electrocardiograms recorded the activity of the heart, and electronic pacemakers regulated the heartbeats of those who suffered from heart disease. In the early 1970's, nuclear-powered pacemakers were successfully implanted in patients.

In these years, medical scientists stressed the danger of cigarette smoking to health. Their research showed that smoking produced many diseases. A number of groups conducted nationwide campaigns against tobacco. They succeeded in getting cigarettes labeled as dangerous to health and in banishing cigarette commercials from television and radio. For a while, tobacco consumption in the United States dropped, but it began to rise again in 1970.

Americans took a new look at alcoholism and concluded that it should be treated as a disease. This view was reflected in a law of 1971 that set up the National Institute on Alcohol Abuse and Alcoholism.

More than ever, Americans became concerned with the health of the mind. Community health centers opened in many places to treat mental diseases. In the 1960's and early 1970's, psychiatry concerned itself more and more with social problems. Psychiatrists tried to treat groups, such as drug users, as well as individuals.

Transportation: Short-Haul

In the forties, fifties, and sixties, automobile ownership expanded tremendously. The United States became a nation on wheels, with many families owning two, even three, cars. Since many city and suburban areas had been built that could be reached only by car, automobiles became necessities for millions of Americans.

The automobile had an impact on every phase of American social and economic life. Millions of Americans had jobs manufacturing or servicing automobiles or working in related industries. State and federal governments poured billions of dollars into road-building efforts to provide highways for the avalanche of cars. The automobile dictated the layout of metropolitan areas. Demands made by the automobile never seemed to end. Roads, parking areas, and servicing facilities could not be built fast enough to keep ahead of demand.

Important though the automobile had become, it was but one part of a complex system of moving people and goods. Urban transit—the moving of people by train, trolley, bus, and subways—had been a vital part of community growth for over a century. But public transportation had not been expanded to reach many areas. Subway, trolley, bus, and train systems were losing money or collapsing. Those that survived often offered facilities that were dirty, uncomfortable, run down, and unreliable.

As late as the 1940's most urban mass-transit systems were privately owned, but as profits disappeared these companies collapsed. In the fifties, sixties, and seventies, local governments took over subways, bus systems, and trolleys. By default, public ownership became the standard.

In the sixties the federal government began offering assistance to communities with transportation problems. In 1964 Congress passed the Urban Mass Transportation Act to help stimulate a revival of mass transit. In 1966 Congress established the Department of Transportation, to handle all kinds of transportation problems.

A rapid-transit train heads up a hill in the midst of a rush-hour traffic jam. In the sixties and early seventies, a number of major cities tried to extend such service into areas served only by automobiles.

Transportation: Long-Haul

The railroads, too, were in trouble. Commuter trains faced chronic deficits. The officers of privately owned railroads said that they could not offer commuter service without great loss. Wherever they could, they ended such service. But losses on long-haul passenger service were even greater.

Critics charged that railroad managers were interested only in the highly profitable freight business and that they deliberately drove passengers away with poor service and dirty trains. Clean, high-speed trains, they said, would attract passengers, reduce automobile traffic, and cut down jams at airports.

In 1970, Congress created the National Railroad Passenger Corporation, known eventually as Amtrak. Amtrak began operation in May 1971 as a single public system that handled most intercity passenger rail service. It was hoped that this system would end the long-term deterioration of rail service in the United States.

Although the basic cause of the passenger railroad's difficulties was competition from automobiles, airplanes too competed. The airlines industry dated from the 1930's, and each year more passengers flew on newer and faster planes. Rapid growth created problems that the airlines could not easily solve. Jet planes crowded the airports with dangerous traffic jams. On the ground, scarce land and complaints of noise pollution made airline expansion difficult.

In 1970 the first generation of superjets entered service. But in March 1971 Congress voted against supporting plans for a supersonic transport (SST). Critics said it would bring more noise pollution and congestion.

The gravest problem facing the airlines was skyjacking—piracy in the air. In the late sixties, public outcry against air piracy became so great that government acted. In 1970, President Nixon ordered federal "sky marshals" on all major flights. In 1973, the government required inspection of all passengers for guns or other weapons before planes could be loaded.

Prosperity stimulated tourist travel for ordinary Americans. Each year, millions of Americans took vacations, most of them in automobiles in the United States. They spent billions on food, lodgings, fuel, camping equipment, and other needs.

As in the past, Europe attracted more tourists from the United States than any other part of the world. In the sixties, more than a million Americans visited Europe each year. They were attracted by special economy flights, vacation package deals, low-cost charter flights, and special youth fares.

Passenger service at sea under the American flag virtually disappeared. By the early seventies there were no scheduled American passenger ships sailing the once-popular Atlantic run to Europe. A few ships flying the American flag still sailed the Pacific, but mostly in leisurely cruise service.

SOCIAL MOVEMENTS

The sixties formed a decade of turmoil, in which many different groups sought changes in the social order. Three of the most important social movements dealt with feminism, ecology, and consumerism.

The Women's Movement

In the 1960's, feminism emerged as a major movement. Activists in the movement challenged the laws, customs, and traditions that made woman's position in American society secondary to that of man. Feminists sought legal, political, and social reforms to ensure equal treatment for both sexes.

In a sense, Betty Friedan's book *The Feminine Mystique* (1963) launched the "women's liberation" movement. Friedan struck a responsive chord in thousands of readers when she wrote of the problems that American women faced. In 1967 the National Organization for Women (NOW) held its first national convention. Within five years it stood out as the best-known and largest feminist group, with 20,000 members.

The changes that feminists sought reflected a wide range of opinions on woman's "place" in society. The main thrust of organized groups was directed toward economic issues. Limited job opportunities and unequal pay

Feminists parade in New York City in 1970. Many feminists argued that the changes they sought would benefit men as well as women. For example, they said that men would be freed from customs which demanded that they "prove" their masculinity by acting tough or by beating their brains out in business.

were attacked by many groups.

The Civil Rights Act of 1964 had made job discrimination on the basis of sex illegal. Yet the federal government did not enforce this law until pressured to do so by feminists. As late as the early 1970's, women's salaries in the United States averaged about 42 percent below those of men.

While most feminist groups concentrated on economics, they did not ignore other issues. Many were concerned with revising popular notions of masculinity and femininity. They noted that both men and women were sometimes discouraged from following their individual interests because of such notions. Many feminists also sought to have men take a more active role in child-rearing and the home. They pointed out that most girls are trained from birth to be wives and mothers but that few boys are trained to be husbands and fathers.

The feminists met organized opposition to some of their goals. Some women's groups whose members believed "woman's place is in the home" worked to prevent Congress and state legislatures from passing laws supported by the feminists. Some men in positions of power also thwarted the feminists.

Nevertheless, the feminists had made an impact. They stimulated a general awareness of women's problems with a flood of books, articles, and television programs. Feminist activity led to the establishment of numerous day-care centers for children, to commitments from employers throughout the country to make special efforts to hire and promote women, and to increased and prominent roles in political parties.

Political lobbying was an important activity of the women's movement. The National Woman's party, led by Alice Paul, had begun lobbying for an equal-rights amendment to the Constitution in 1923. However, during the thirties, forties, and fifties, feminist organizations were largely inactive. New groups took up intensive lobbying in the sixties. In March 1972, Congress passed the amendment by large majorities and sent it to the states for ratification. The Equal Rights Amendment prohibited discrimination based on sex by any law or action of federal, state, or local government.

Ecology

Some Americans had long been concerned about the quality of the environment in the United States. But not until the 1960's did they attract much attention. *Ecology*—the study of the interrelationship of living things and the environment—became popular.

In 1962 Rachel Carson, a biologist, published a disturbing book called *Silent Spring*. This book warned that indiscriminate use of the products of technology was upsetting the balance of nature and hideously transforming the environment. Organized environmentalists and conservationists—the Sierra Club Foundation, the Audubon Society, and Friends of the Earth—took up the cause. They said that people must stop spoiling the earth or the earth would die.

At the core of the problem was modern technology. Industries and machines produced so much waste that air, water, and earth could no longer absorb it. The problem was worldwide, but American technology produced the greatest waste and the worst environmental crisis.

Increased automobile traffic contributed greatly to air pollution. New York, Los Angeles, and other cities for days and weeks at a time were covered with poisonous smog that made eyes water and throats rasp. "Tomorrow morning when you get up," New York environmentalists said in 1967, "take a deep breath. It'll make you feel rotten."

Americans had long polluted their environment. They dumped debris into rivers, lakes, and oceans; littered cities, towns, and countryside with refuse; and bulldozed wildernesses and wildlife. Americans sprayed, dusted, or dumped millions of pounds of long-lasting poisons into the environment.

The growth in population also caused problems. Unspoiled land was disappearing. Americans were using up water and some forms of energy so fast that none would be left for future generations. Ecological problems were multiplying faster than society could handle them.

Americans took a few steps to protect their surroundings. First the federal government gave its protection to open spaces with the Wilderness Act of 1964. Then came measures, supported unanimously in Congress, for a national cleanup of water through use of federal funds.

Since the automobile was one of the major contributors to air pollution, environmentalists and others attacked those who were building urban expressways. Urban dwellers also opposed the expansion of airports because jet aircraft were a major source of noise and air pollution. People living near airports demanded cleaner, less noisy planes.

Pollution of another kind became big news in January 1969. At that time, oil drilling off the shore of Santa Barbara, California, produced a leak that coated beautiful beaches with millions of gallons of crude oil. Television, newspapers, and magazines showed pictures of the ruined coast and of dying, oil-smeared birds. The ecological movement took on the qualities of a crusade.

Partly in response to this movement, the government in 1970 set up two agencies to help protect the environment. These were the Council on Environmental Quality and the Environmental Protection Agency.

Americans started campaigns to recycle cans, newspapers, and other waste. They celebrated Earth Day, first observed on April 22, 1970, to keep the nation aware of the dangers of pollution. Communities and groups brought lawsuits against polluters, whether in industry or government. Environmentalists used technology to try to find new, nonpolluting sources of energy. But the efforts to curb pollution and consumption required international, not merely national, action. In June 1972, delegates to the UN-sponsored World Conference on the Human Environment endorsed a declaration of principles favoring an international campaign against pollution.

Consumers' Revolt

Much of the American economy was based on consumption. Advertising was used to stimulate purchase of the huge quantities of goods produced by industry. Another stimulant was credit. Credit buying had long been a significant part of American life, but now it seemed essential to prosperity. Credit cards replaced currency in consumer transactions involving billions of dollars annually.

While buying increased and prices rose, the quality of many products declined.

Students spread straw to pick up oil from the waters of San Francisco Bay. Oil spills in the oceans drew worldwide attention. Although the United States government set up some standards to improve the quality of the environment, standards often were relaxed when critics said they interfered with business.

American consumers grumbled with dissatisfaction over what their money bought. Even for simple gadgets, people had difficulty getting repairs. Properly trained repairmen were hard to find, and repairs sometimes cost more than the price of the item.

In the past the consumer had been able to judge the quality of what was bought. In the technological society the consumer had to depend on confusing labels, guarantees, and advertising claims. Reformers wanted government controls that would protect the consumer against fraud. Since some products were unsafe or injurious to health, reformers also demanded impartial agencies to test and certify them.

A big surge in consumer-protection agitation came in the early 1960's, when President Kennedy formed the Consumer Advisory Council. Lyndon B. Johnson continued the support for consumerism by creating the President's Committee on Consumer Interests in 1964. It cooperated with numerous national but private consumer organizations.

Stimulated by the federal government, consumer organizations sprang up in many states. To coordinate the work of these groups, the Consumer Federation of America was formed in 1968. In 1972 it claimed to speak for some 30 million consumers.

Ralph Nader, a young lawyer who had become famous by challenging the safety of General Motors' cars, emerged as the most effective agitator for consumer protection. He often testified before congressional committees on behalf of consumer interests. He and his assistants, known as "Nader's Raiders," regularly publicized studies of products and commercial practices.

This consumer reawakening led to the passage of an impressive number of laws on behalf of buyer protection. These laws, however, were not adequately enforced. For example, the Food and Drug Administration did not receive enough money to enforce the Fair Packing Act, and so the law was largely ineffective.

Consumer-protection advocates did not quit. They demanded a permanent Office of Consumer Affairs in the Executive Office of the President or a Department of the Consumer within the President's cabinet. In this way, they believed, the consumer's interest would be represented on the highest level of government. In February 1971, President Nixon responded by setting up the Office of Consumer Affairs.

The consumer movement had an impact beyond government. Some industries became more safety- and label-conscious, and some grocery stores dated perishable goods so that consumers could judge their freshness. Many companies set up special procedures to control the quality of their products. Everywhere producers seemed to become more responsive to consumer complaints.

Community Organization

Another significant development in the sixties was a growing willingness on the part of city dwellers to organize to give themselves a greater voice in deciding the fate of their neighborhoods. The demands for community control did not constitute a social movement in the same sense that feminism or consumerism did. Community organizations did not have national programs.

Community organizations were given a boost by provisions of some legislation. Laws providing for federal funding of urban renewal, highway construction, and hospital or university expansion also provided that the plan should have the approval of the neighboring community. Although these provisions were often quietly ignored, in some areas they were employed to the fullest.

The growing interest in community organization was also engendered in part by the legal separateness of the suburbs. City dwellers often felt that they were nameless, faceless masses ignored by city hall. People who lived in suburbs were represented in a government that was smaller and closer to home. Community organizations gave city dwellers an opportunity to be heard.

Some city governments attempted to decentralize their functions to make them more responsive to the people. For example, in 1968 New York City experimented with giv-

The earth as guinea pig

What will Earth's fate be? This was a question that plagued average Americans as well as scientists during the 1960's and early 1970's. For every prophet of doom, there was a corresponding prophet of bliss. As time passed, however, several things became clear.

First, it was obvious that no easy solutions would be found for Earth's environmental problems. Scientists cannot study the environment in the same way they study a chemical reaction in a test tube. Earth is too big, and too many uncontrollable (and often invisible or unnoticed) forces are at work to make such study possible.

Second, every solution produces a new set of problems. The automobile may have eliminated horse droppings and dead horses from city streets, but it also increased the possibility that city dwellers would contract lead poisoning or respiratory diseases. It also seriously affected land and energy resources.

Third, even when likely solutions appear, there are few ways to make people accept them. Most ecologists believe that limiting population growth is the most important step in solving Earth's environmental problems. But many economists believe that growth is necessary. Moreover, among many of the world's peoples, babies are looked upon as a form of wealth. People with these beliefs are not likely to support efforts to limit births.

Fourth, concern for the environment cannot end at national boundaries. Earth, like a spaceship, has only limited resources that must be recovered, recycled, and reused. If only one country passes tough pollution-control laws, industries may move to where the laws are less strict. This might improve the economic situation of the people in the newly industrialized country, but it would only shift the pollution problem. The United States, with less than 6 percent of the world's population, produces more than 60 percent of the world's pollution. If the other 94 percent of Earth's people became equally industrialized and equally wasteful, the prophets of doom would have their day.

Two new painting styles, op and pop, drew attention in the 1960's. The geometric patterns of "op art" gave the optical illusion of movement on the painting's surface. "Pop art," popularized by Andy Warhol and Roy Lichtenstein, glorified common objects—soup cans, soap boxes, comic strips. A fresh new look in abstract art was found in the works of Corita Kent. Some artists began using real objects, such as machines or moving lights, in their paintings. Sculptors like Larry Rivers, Louise Nevelson, and George Segal also used everyday objects in their constructions. Wall paintings beautified cities and often expressed ethnic pride or anger. Leading painters in this medium were William Walker and Sachio Yamashita.

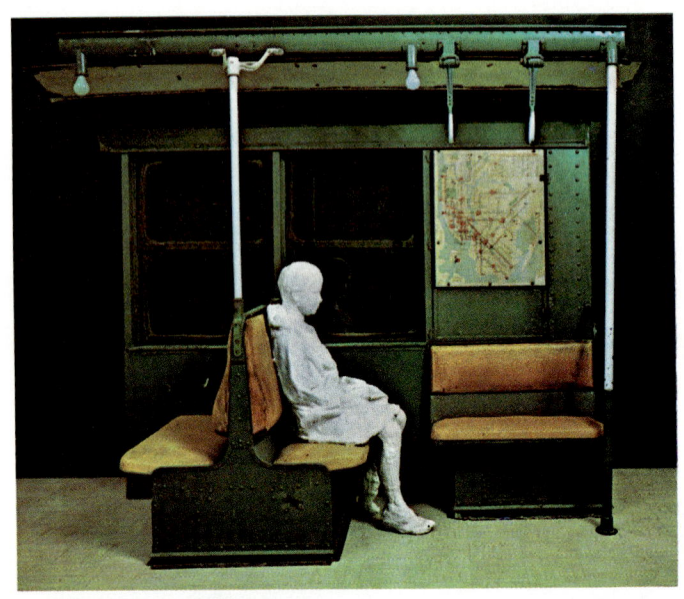

The Subway, by George Segal, 1968
Wall of Black Love, by William Walker

Spiral Illusion, by Tom Strobel, 1965

The Map, by Roy Schnackenberg, 1964

ing community control to two school districts within the city. The course of study and teachers were supposed to be subject to community approval. In other cities, community organizations were sometimes allowed to plan urban renewal programs.

POPULAR CULTURE

During the sixties and seventies, popular culture reflected the urban nature of the American people. Culture was also affected by the mobility of the people.

Spiritual Values

For millions of Americans the church continued to be the center of cultural life. About two-thirds of the people were church-goers, and about 123 million Americans were church members. However, in the late sixties, membership began to decline. Public-opinion polls, based on nationwide surveys of clergy and lay people, indicated that religion was losing influence on Americans.

Within the churches, social activism and changes in rituals were evident. Church leaders of all faiths showed an increasingly vocal concern about poverty, racial oppression, and the brutalities of war. Protestants and Catholics worked toward Christian unity. The rank and file in both groups often supported the movement.

Christian and Jewish clergy frequently cooperated and tried to overcome old prejudices. Neither anti-Catholicism nor anti-Semitism disappeared, but never before had the relationship between diverse religious leaders been so cordial.

One of the foremost concerns of American church leaders was to overcome the racism evident in many of their churches. They sought ways to break down the separation between white and black churches.

Some Americans became interested in mysticism, Buddhism, and Hinduism. The

A rock group, Moby Grape, performs. Rock music came in many flavors: folk, acid, hard. Many of the new sounds in rock were started by the Beatles, a British group. The sixties also saw the rise of "soul" music, a mixture of jazz, rock, and rhythm and blues.

Native American Church gained members who were attracted to its support for traditional American Indian values.

The Printed Word

Newspaper circulation rose as the population increased. Some major newspapers merged; others were bought by large corporations. Between 1960 and 1970, however, more than 150 daily newspapers went out of business, usually in cities. In the same period, more than 160 daily papers were founded, especially in rapidly growing sections of the country.

The late 1960's brought a marked increase in the publication of "underground" newspapers. Most of these were small weekly or monthly papers published by special-interest groups. Others were published by individuals to present political views or subjects considered unacceptable by large newspapers.

Magazines also gained readers. *Reader's Digest* continued as the circulation leader. *Ladies' Home Journal, National Geographic,* and *Time* continued to number their readers in the millions. Specialized magazines like *Psychology Today* also did well.

Many magazines lost sizable advertising revenues to television. Others felt the effects of rising costs, especially for postage. Among the 160 magazines that ceased regular publication were the 148-year-old *Saturday Evening Post* and Henry Luce's magazine of photojournalism, *Life*.

The demand for American books was worldwide. Paperback books improved in quality and enjoyed good sales. Americans read new fiction by William Faulkner, Eudora Welty, Saul Bellow, Flannery O'Connor, and Norman Mailer. Science fiction was widely read. Also, fiction written in a humorous but heavily ironic tone became popular in the early sixties. Joseph Heller, Philip Roth, and Kurt Vonnegut, Jr., used satirical techniques to bring out the humor in such bleak subjects as war and madness.

Many writers of these years did not fit a particular category of theme or style. John Updike dealt with themes of adolescence, marriage, and middle-class family life in his novels, including *Rabbit, Run* and *The Centaur.* John Barth explored ideas about fiction and the task of the writer in *The Sot-Weed Factor* (1960) and *Lost in the Funhouse* (1968). Joyce Carol Oates emerged as a leading novelist and short-story writer. Unlike much of contemporary fiction, her writing was sharply realistic and often violent. Oates was awarded the National Book Award in 1970 for her novel *them.*

An increasing number of writers from minority groups also became important. One of the best-known was James Baldwin, who wrote of black urban life in *Another Country* (1962) and *Tell Me How Long the Train's Been Gone* (1968). Bernard Malamud wrote of the lives of Jewish city dwellers in his novels and stories. He won a National Book Award for *The Fixer* (1966). N. Scott Momaday, a Kiowa Indian noted for his fiction and poetry, was awarded the Pulitzer Prize in 1969 for his novel *House Made of Dawn.*

The diversity of fiction at this time was matched in nonfiction. Many biographies of political, literary, and entertainment figures were published and enjoyed great popularity. Works by black-power advocates, feminists, American Indians, and others involved in social protest caught the attention of the public. The revival of interest in handicrafts caused a great demand for books.

The works of poets in the sixties and seventies reflected the belief that all aspects of life can be explored in poetry. They continued to experiment with form. Many dealt with social and moral issues like the Vietnam war and racism. Some of the best-known poets of this time were Mona van Duyn, Robert Hayden, John Berryman, Denise Levertov, and Anne Sexton.

A new group of black poets emerged who continued the tradition of protest begun in the Harlem Renaissance. Their outlook and goals, however, were different from those of their predecessors. LeRoi Jones (Imamu Amiri Baraka) was perhaps the best-known of the poets of the "black consciousness." Others were Mari Evans, David Henderson, and Nikki Giovanni.

Sports

Spectator sports continued to draw huge crowds. Baseball drew the biggest audiences, but its hold on the American spectator was challenged by professional football, basketball, and hockey.

Racial segregation on professional teams had begun to disappear in the late forties. Jackie Robinson had broken the color line in baseball in 1947. By the sixties, black and Puerto Rican players were among the top players in both major leagues. Blacks were also prominent in football, basketball, and track and field competitions.

Television contributed to public awareness of sports. A great variety of competitions, from figure skating to weight lifting, from demolition derbies to golf, were televised.

The sixties and early seventies saw a rising interest in professional sports for women. Tennis and golf tournaments with female players began drawing large audiences. At the amateur level, many high schools began interschool competitions for girls.

A Look at Specifics

1. What changes were made to increase the number of people who would benefit from the advances in medical science?

2. How did the Johnson administration reform immigration laws?

3. What factors contributed to the urban crisis?

4. What peaceful uses of atomic energy were developed after World War II?

5. Why did consumers need more help and protection than they had in earlier days?

6. What problems did transportation companies face during the sixties and seventies?

7. What were the major developments in the newspaper and magazine industries?

8. What did the feminist movement accomplish in the early 1970's?

A Review of Major Ideas

1. How did developments in technology affect health care? The environment?

2. Why did interest in education increase so much in the fifties and sixties?

For Independent Study

1. Until about 1915, as suburbs became more urban, they were usually incorporated into the major city they adjoined. Since then, they have usually remained legally independent no matter how much a part of the city they have in other ways become. What factors might account for this change?

2. "The efforts of urban dwellers to stop government from building superhighways through their neighborhoods are similar to the efforts of Indians to prevent the building of the transcontinental railroads through their territory in the 1860's." Oppose or defend this statement. Give evidence to support your view.

Unit Review
Examining the Times

1. How were the civil rights, antiwar, and feminist movements related?

2. How did the Vietnam war affect the economy? Presidential politics? The American people? The Vietnamese people?

Reference Section

Atlas of the Modern World
   The World   674–675
     North America   676
     South America   677
     Europe   678
     Asia   679
     Africa   680
     Oceania   681
     United States
       Relief   682
       Political   683
       Alaska and Hawaii   684
The Declaration of Independence   685
The Constitution of the United States of America   687
Presidents, Vice-Presidents, and Secretaries of State   708–709
Bibliographies   710
Acknowledgments   716
Index   720

The World

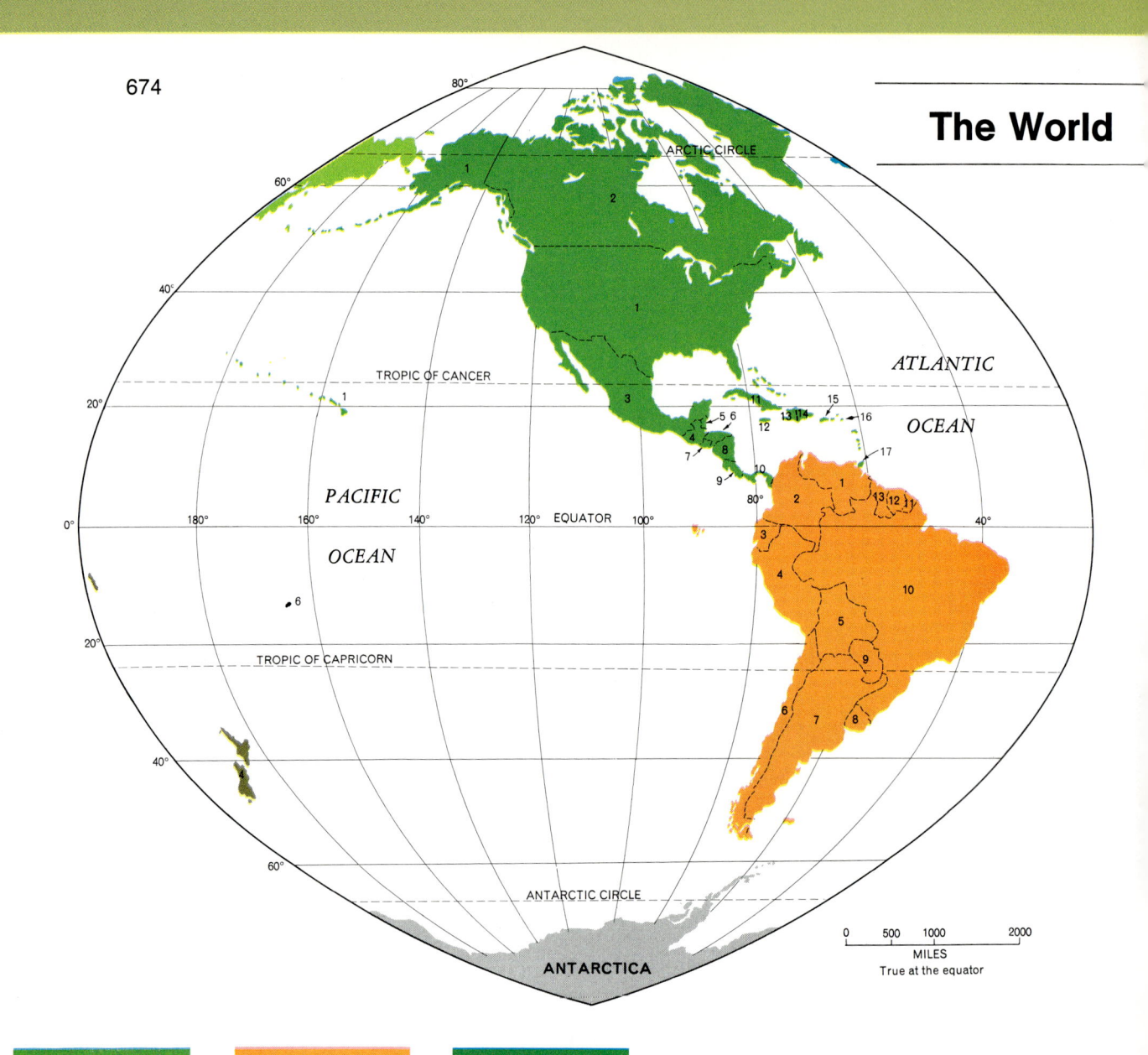

NORTH AMERICA

1. UNITED STATES
   ALASKA
   HAWAII
2. CANADA
3. MEXICO
4. GUATEMALA
5. BRITISH HONDURAS
6. HONDURAS
7. EL SALVADOR
8. NICARAGUA
9. COSTA RICA
10. PANAMA
11. CUBA
12. JAMAICA
13. HAITI
14. DOMINICAN REPUBLIC
15. PUERTO RICO (U.S.A.)
16. VIRGIN ISLANDS (U.S.A.)
17. TRINIDAD AND TOBAGO

SOUTH AMERICA

1. VENEZUELA
2. COLOMBIA
3. ECUADOR
4. PERU
5. BOLIVIA
6. CHILE
7. ARGENTINA
8. URUGUAY
9. PARAGUAY
10. BRAZIL
11. FRENCH GUIANA
12. SURINAM (Neth.)
13. GUYANA

AFRICA

1. ALGERIA
2. MOROCCO
3. SPANISH SAHARA
4. MAURITANIA
5. SENEGAL
6. GAMBIA
7. PORTUGUESE GUINEA
8. GUINEA
9. SIERRA LEONE
10. LIBERIA
11. IVORY COAST
12. MALI
13. UPPER VOLTA
14. GHANA
15. TOGO
16. DAHOMEY
17. NIGERIA
18. NIGER
19. CHAD
20. CENTRAL AFRICAN REPUBLIC
21. CAMEROON
22. EQUATORIAL GUINEA
23. GABON
24. CONGO REPUBLIC
25. ZAIRE
26. ANGOLA (Port.)
26. arrow. CABINDA (Angola)
27. NAMIBIA (SOUTH-WEST AFRICA)
28. SOUTH AFRICA
29. LESOTHO
30. SWAZILAND
31. BOTSWANA
32. MALAGASY REPUBLIC
33. MOZAMBIQUE (Port.)
34. RHODESIA
35. ZAMBIA
36. MALAWI
37. TANZANIA
38. BURUNDI
39. RWANDA
40. UGANDA
41. KENYA
42. SOMALI REPUBLIC
43. FRENCH TERRITORY OF AFARS AND ISSAS
44. ETHIOPIA
45. SUDAN
46. UNITED ARAB REPUBLIC (EGYPT)*
47. LIBYA*
48. TUNISIA

Data correct as of March 1, 1973

*Future union proposed

EUROPE		ASIA			OCEANIA
1. ICELAND	19. AUSTRIA	1. TURKEY	19. SRI LANKA (CEYLON)		1. TERRITORY OF NEW GUINEA (Australia)
2. NORWAY	20. CZECHOSLOVAKIA	2. CYPRUS	20. NEPAL		2. TERRITORY OF PAPUA (Australia)
3. SWEDEN	21. HUNGARY	3. SYRIA	21. SIKKIM		3. AUSTRALIA
4. FINLAND	22. YUGOSLAVIA	4. LEBANON	22. BHUTAN		4. NEW ZEALAND
5. UNION OF SOVIET SOCIALIST REPUBLICS	23. ALBANIA	5. ISRAEL	23. BANGLA DESH		5. GUAM (U.S.A.)
6. POLAND	24. GREECE	6. JORDAN	24. BURMA		6. TUTUILA (U.S.A.)
7. EAST GERMANY	25. BULGARIA	7. SAUDI ARABIA	25. THAILAND		
8. WEST GERMANY	26. ROMANIA	8. YEMEN**	26. CAMBODIA		
9. DENMARK		9. SOUTHERN YEMEN**	27. LAOS		
10. NETHERLANDS		10. OMAN	28. SOUTH VIETNAM		
11. BELGIUM		11. UNITED ARAB EMIRATES	29. NORTH VIETNAM		
12. UNITED KINGDOM		12. QATAR	30. CHINA		
13. IRELAND		13. KUWAIT	31. MONGOLIA		
14. PORTUGAL		14. IRAQ	32. NORTH KOREA		
15. SPAIN		15. IRAN	33. SOUTH KOREA		
16. FRANCE		16. AFGHANISTAN	34. JAPAN		
17. SWITZERLAND		17. PAKISTAN	35. TAIWAN		
18. ITALY		18. INDIA	36. PHILIPPINES		
			37. MALAYSIA		
			38. BRUNEI		
			39. INDONESIA		

**Future union proposed

In 1972, the United Arab Republic and Libya announced that they had reached an agreement to unite their nations in several years. Yemen and Southern Yemen also agreed to unite in the near future.

Data correct as of March 1, 1973

South America

Data correct as of March 1, 1973

Europe

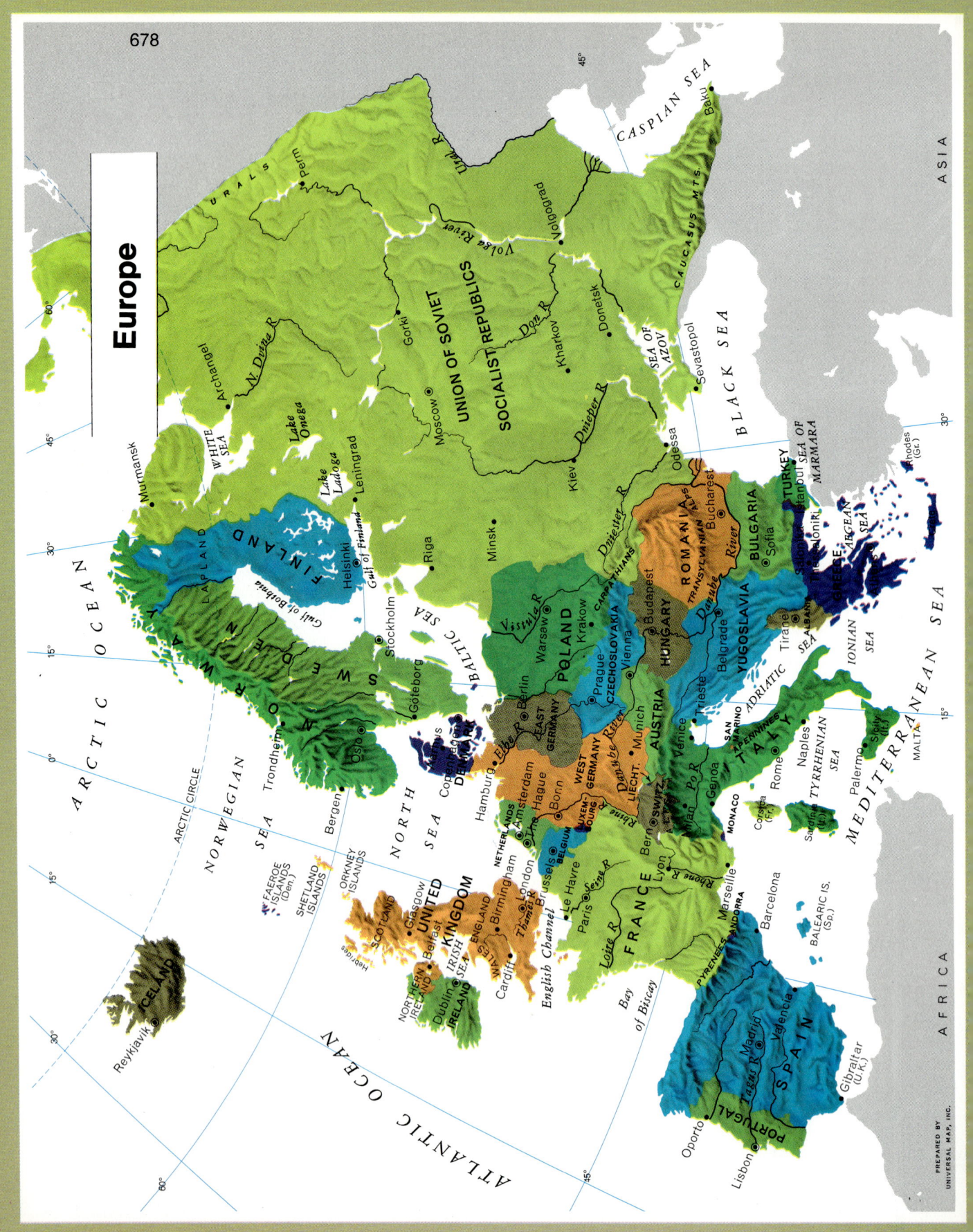

Data correct as of March 1, 1973

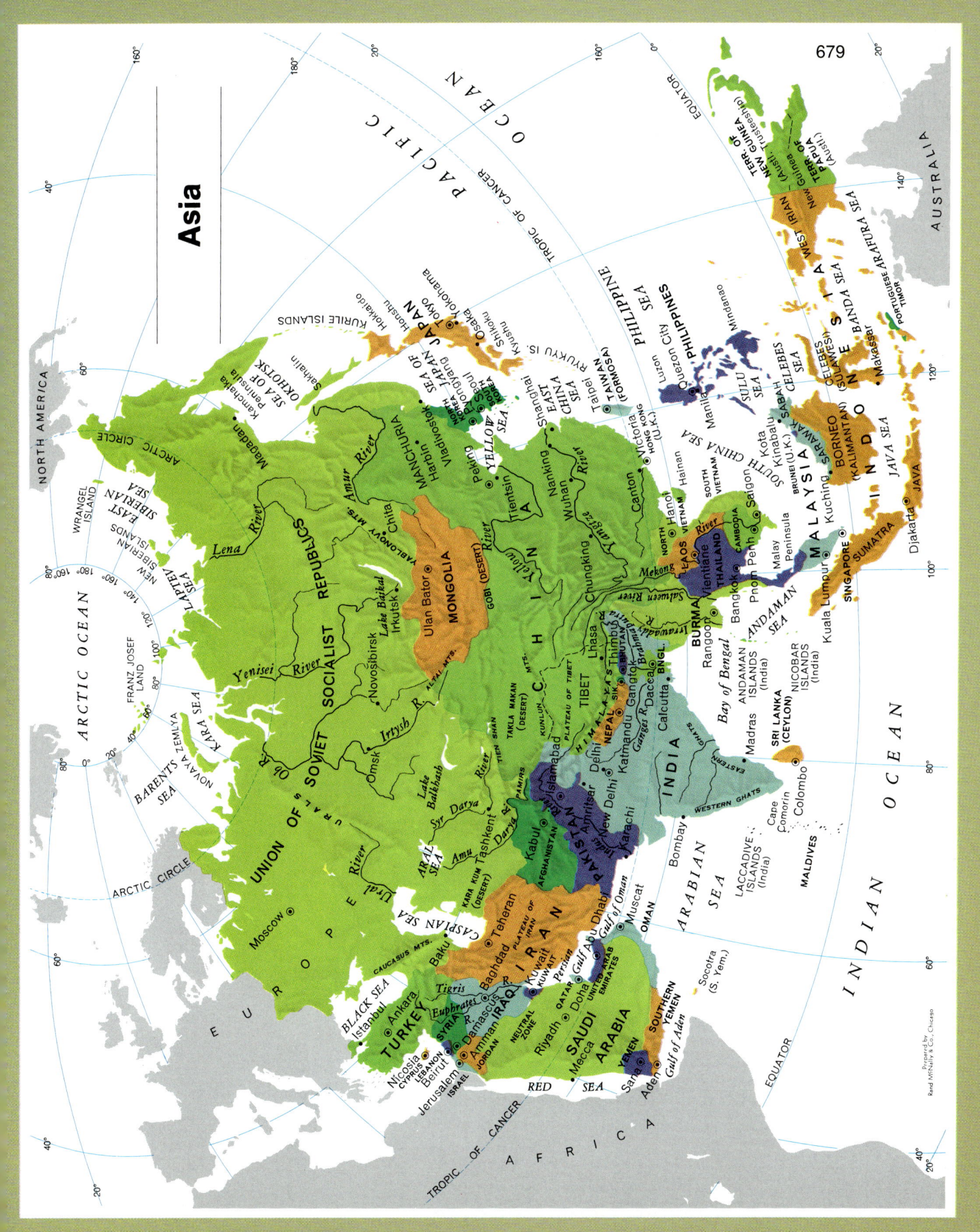

Data correct as of March 1, 1973

Africa

Data correct as of March 1, 1973

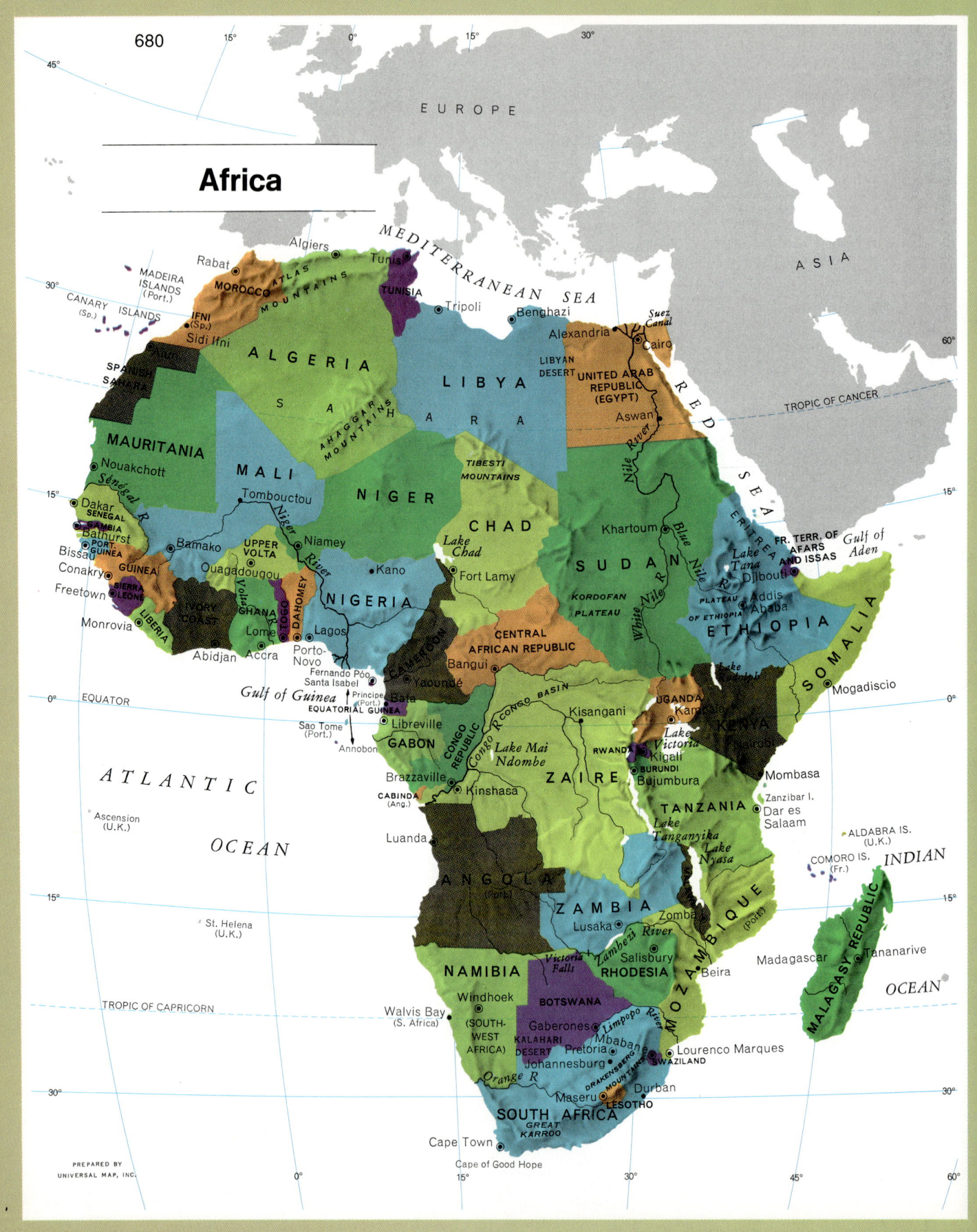

Oceania

Data correct as of March 1, 1973

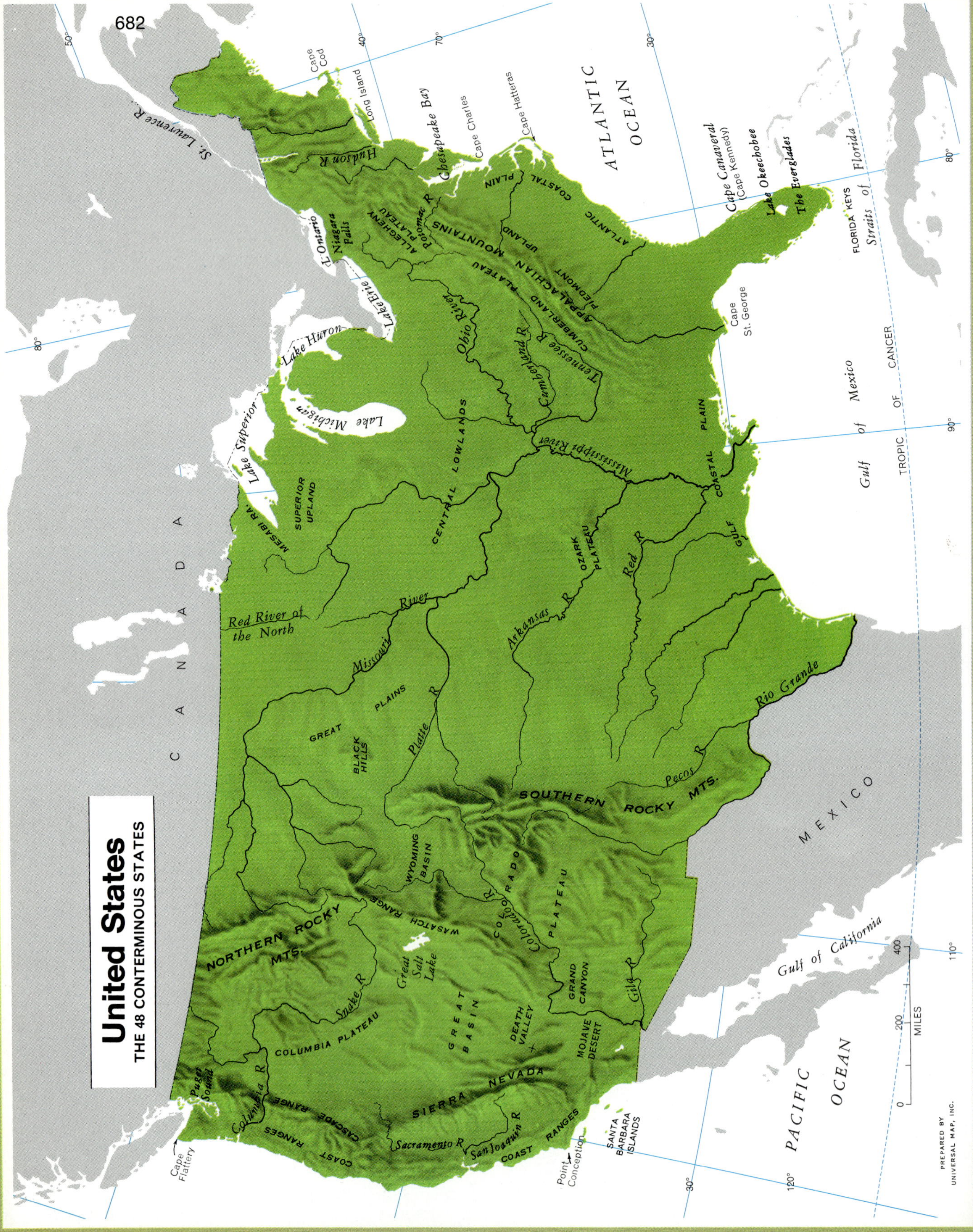
United States
THE 48 CONTERMINOUS STATES
C A N A D A
M E X I C O
ATLANTIC OCEAN
PACIFIC OCEAN
Gulf of Mexico
Gulf of California
Straits of Florida
FLORIDA KEYS
TROPIC OF CANCER
St. Lawrence R.
Cape Cod
Long Island
Chesapeake Bay
Cape Charles
Cape Hatteras
Cape Canaveral
(Cape Kennedy)
Lake Okeechobee
The Everglades
Cape St. George
Hudson R.
L. Ontario
Niagara Falls
Lake Erie
Lake Huron
Lake Michigan
Lake Superior
ALLEGHENY PLATEAU
Potomac R.
APPALACHIAN MOUNTAINS
UPLAND
PIEDMONT
ATLANTIC COASTAL PLAIN
CUMBERLAND PLATEAU
Ohio River
Cumberland R.
Tennessee R.
Mississippi River
CENTRAL LOWLANDS
SUPERIOR UPLAND
MESABI RA.
GULF COASTAL PLAIN
OZARK PLATEAU
Red R.
Arkansas R.
Red River of the North
Missouri River
GREAT PLAINS
BLACK HILLS
Platte R.
Rio Grande
Pecos R.
SOUTHERN ROCKY MTS.
WYOMING BASIN
COLORADO PLATEAU
Colorado R.
WASATCH RANGE
NORTHERN ROCKY MTS.
Great Salt Lake
Snake R.
GRAND CANYON
Gila R.
GREAT BASIN
DEATH VALLEY
MOJAVE DESERT
COLUMBIA PLATEAU
Columbia R.
Puget Sound
CASCADE RANGE
SIERRA NEVADA
COAST RANGES
Sacramento R.
San Joaquin R.
Cape Flattery
Point Conception
SANTA BARBARA ISLANDS
50°
40°
30°
80°
70°
90°
110°
120°
0
200
400
MILES
PREPARED BY UNIVERSAL MAP, INC.

Data correct as of March 1, 1973

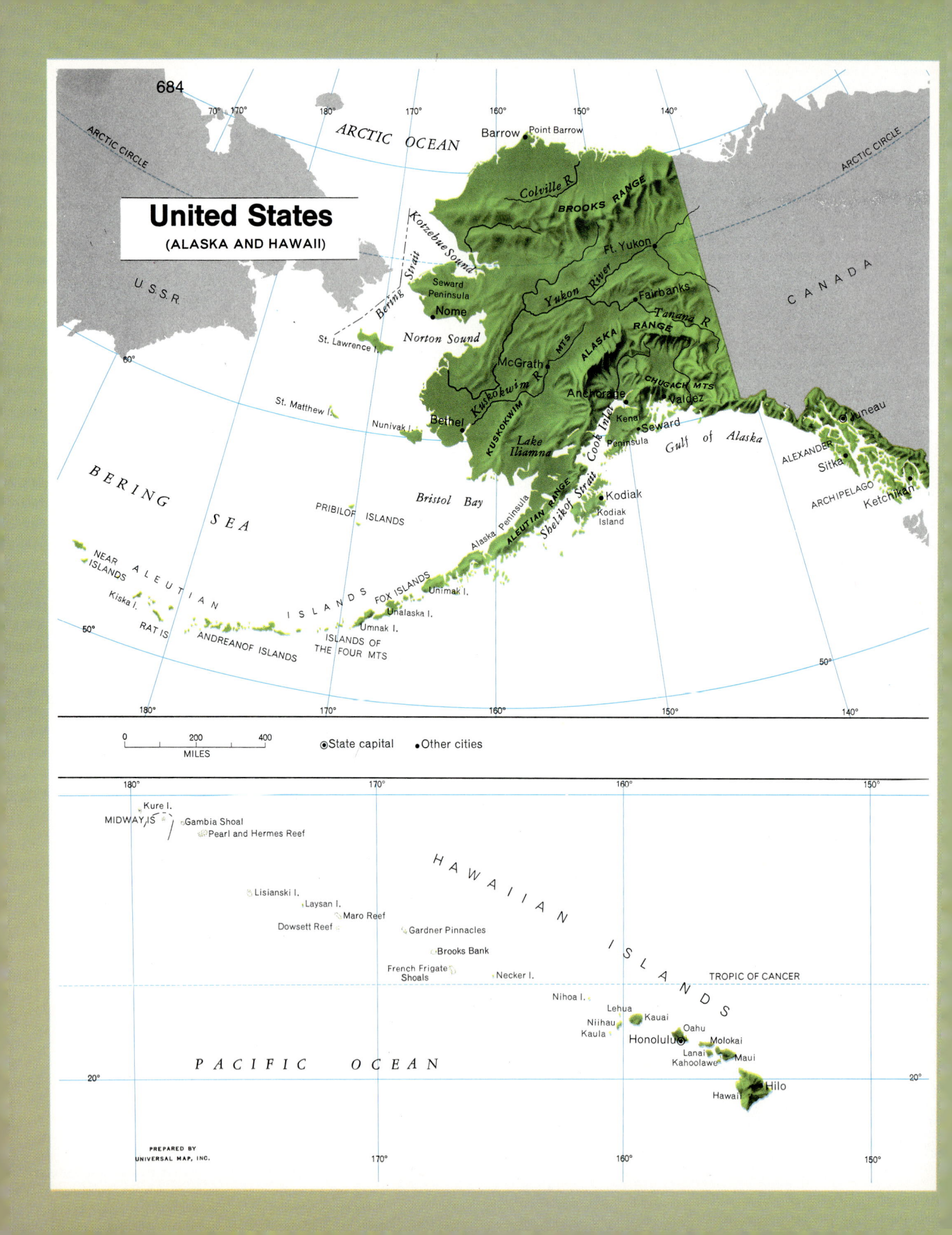

United States
(ALASKA AND HAWAII)

The Declaration of Independence

in Congress, July 4, 1776

THE UNANIMOUS DECLARATION OF THE THIRTEEN UNITED STATES OF AMERICA,

When in the Course of human events, it becomes necessary for one people to dissolve the political bands which have connected them with another, and to assume among the powers of the earth, the separate and equal station to which the Laws of Nature and of Nature's God entitle them, a decent respect to the opinions of mankind requires that they should declare the causes which impel them to the separation.—We hold these truths to be self-evident, that all men are created equal, that they are endowed by their Creator with certain unalienable Rights, that among these are Life, Liberty and the pursuit of Happiness.—That to secure these rights, Governments are instituted among Men, deriving their just powers from the consent of the governed,—That whenever any Form of Government becomes destructive of these ends, it is the Right of the People to alter or to abolish it, and to institute new Government, laying its foundation on such principles and organizing its powers in such form, as to them shall seem most likely to effect their Safety and Happiness. Prudence, indeed, will dictate that Governments long established should not be changed for light and transient causes; and accordingly all experience hath shewn, that mankind are more disposed to suffer, while evils are sufferable, than to right themselves by abolishing the forms to which they are accustomed. But when a long train of abuses and usurpations, pursuing invariably the same Object evinces a design to reduce them under absolute Despotism, it is their right, it is their duty, to throw off such Government, and to provide new Guards for their future security.—Such has been the patient sufferance of these Colonies; and such is now the necessity which constrains them to alter their former Systems of Government. The history of the present King of Great Britain is a history of repeated injuries and usurpations, all having in direct object the establishment of an absolute Tyranny over these States. To prove this, let Facts be submitted to a candid world.—He has refused his Assent to Laws, the most wholesome and necessary for the public good.—He has forbidden his Governors to pass Laws of immediate and pressing importance, unless suspended in their operation till his Assent should be obtained; and when so suspended, he has utterly neglected to attend to them.—He has refused to pass other Laws for the accommodation of large districts of people, unless those people would relinquish the right of Representation in the Legislature, a right inestimable to them and formidable to tyrants only.—He has called together legislative bodies at places unusual, uncomfortable, and distant from the depository of their public Records, for the sole purpose of fatiguing them into compliance with his measures.—He has dissolved Representative Houses repeatedly, for opposing with manly firmness his invasions on the rights of the people.—He has refused for a long time, after such dissolutions, to cause others to be elected; whereby the Legislative powers, incapable of Annihilation, have returned to the People at large for their exercise; the State remaining in the mean time exposed to all the dangers of invasion from without, and convulsions within.—He has endeavoured to prevent the population of these States; for that purpose obstructing the Laws for Naturalization of Foreigners; refusing to pass others to encourage their migration hither, and raising the conditions of new Appropriations of Lands.—He has obstructed the Administration of Justice, by refusing his Assent to Laws for establishing Judiciary powers.—He has made Judges dependent on his Will alone, for the tenure of their offices, and the amount and payment of their salaries.—He has erected a multitude of New Offices, and sent hither swarms of Officers to harass our people, and eat out their substance.—He has kept among us, in times of peace, Standing Armies without the Consent of our legislatures.—He has affected to render the Military independent of and superior to the Civil power.—He has combined with others to subject us to a jurisdiction foreign to our constitution, and unacknowledged by our laws; giving his Assent to their Acts of pretended Legislation:—For quartering large bodies of armed troops among us:—For protecting them, by a mock Trial, from punishment for any Murders which they should commit on the Inhabitants of these States:—For cutting off our Trade with all parts of the world:—For imposing Taxes on us without our Consent:—For depriving us in many cases, of the benefits of Trial by jury:—For transporting us beyond Seas to be tried for pretended offenses:—For abolishing the free System of English Laws in a neighbouring Province, establishing therein an Arbitrary government, and enlarging its Boundaries so as to render it at once an example and fit instrument for introducing the same absolute rule into these Colonies:—For taking away our Charters, abolishing our most valuable Laws, and altering fundamentally the Forms of our Governments:—For suspending our own Legislatures, and declaring themselves invested with power to legislate for us in all cases whatsoever.—He has abdicated Government here, by declaring us out of his Protection and waging War against us.—He has plundered our seas, ravaged our Coasts, burnt our towns, and destroyed the lives of our people.—He is at this time transporting large Armies of foreign Mercenaries to compleat the works of death, desolation and tyranny, already begun with circumstances of Cruelty & perfidy scarcely paralleled in the most barbarous ages, and totally unworthy the Head of a civilized nation.—He has constrained our fellow Citizens taken Captive on the high Seas to bear Arms against their Country, to become the executioners of their friends and Brethren, or to fall themselves by their Hands.—He has excited domestic insurrections amongst us, and has endeavoured to bring on the inhabitants of our frontiers, the merciless Indian Savages, whose known rule of warfare, is an undistinguished destruction of all ages, sexes and conditions. In every stage of these Oppressions We have Petitioned for Redress in the most humble terms: Our repeated Petitions have been answered only by repeated injury. A Prince, whose character is thus marked by every act which may define a Tyrant, is unfit to be the ruler of a free people. Nor have We been wanting in attentions to our British brethren. We have warned them from time to time of attempts by their legislature to extend an unwarrantable jurisdiction over us. We have reminded them of the circumstances of our emigration and settlement here. We have appealed to their native justice and magnanimity, and we have conjured them by the ties of our common kindred to disavow these usurpations, which, would inevitably interrupt our connections and correspondence. They too have been deaf to the voice of justice and of consanguinity. We must, therefore, acquiesce in the necessity, which denounces our Separation, and hold them, as we hold the rest of mankind, Enemies in War, in Peace Friends.—

WE, THEREFORE, THE REPRESENTATIVES OF THE UNITED STATES OF AMERICA, in General Congress, Assembled, appealing to the Supreme Judge of the world for the rectitude of our intentions, do, in the Name, and by authority of the good People of these Colonies, solemnly publish and declare, That these United Colonies are, and of Right ought to be FREE AND INDEPENDENT STATES; that they are Absolved from all Allegiance to the British Crown, and that all political connection between them and the State of Great Britain, is and ought to be totally dissolved; and that as Free and Independent States, they have full Power to levy War, conclude Peace, contract Alliances, establish Commerce, and to do all other Acts and Things which Independent States may of right do.—And for the support of this Declaration, with a firm reliance on the protection of divine Providence, we mutually pledge to each other our Lives, our Fortunes and our Sacred Honor.

John Hancock

Button Gwinnett
Lyman Hall
Geo Walton.
W[m] Hooper
Joseph Hewes.
John Penn
Edward Rutledge.
Tho[s] Heyward Jun[r].
Thomas Lynch Jun[r].
Arthur Middleton
Samuel Chase

W[m]. Paca
Tho[s]. Stone
Charles Carroll of Carrollton
George Wythe
Richard Henry Lee.
Th Jefferson
Benj[a] Harrison
Tho[s] Nelson Jr.
Francis Lightfoot Lee
Carter Braxton

Rob[t] Morris
Benjamin Rush
Benj[a]. Franklin
John Morton
Geo Clymer
Ja[s]. Smith
Geo. Taylor
James Wilson
Geo. Ross
Caesar Rodney
Geo Read
Tho M: Kean

W[m] Floyd
Phil. Livingston
Fran[s]. Lewis
Lewis Morris
Rich[d]. Stockton
Jn[o] Witherspoon
Fra[s]. Hopkinson
John Hart
Abra Clark
Josiah Bartlett
W[m]. Whipple

Sam[l] Adams
John Adams
Rob[t] Treat Payne
Elbridge Gerry
Step Hopkins
William Ellery
Roger Sherman
Sam[el] Huntington
W[m]. Williams
Oliver Wolcott
Matthew Thornton

687

The text of the Constitution is printed in black. Portions of the text within brackets [. . . . . .] are no longer in force. An explanation of the Constitution is printed in color. The explanation and the headings are not a part of the Constitution.

Constitution of the United States of America

WE THE PEOPLE of the United States, in order to form a more perfect Union, establish justice, insure domestic tranquility, provide for the common defence, promote the general welfare, and secure the blessings of liberty to ourselves and our posterity, do ordain and establish this Constitution for the United States of America.

We citizens of the United States adopt this Constitution because we want to:

Form a better union of our states than we had under the Articles of Confederation,

Give fair treatment to everybody,

Secure peace in all our states,

Defend ourselves and our country against any enemies,

Enjoy good living conditions,

Possess liberty for ourselves and for future generations of Americans.

ARTICLE 1 • LEGISLATIVE BRANCH

Congress

Sec. 1. All legislative powers herein granted shall be vested in a Congress of the United States, which shall consist of a Senate and House of Representatives.

Laws for the United States are made by Congress. Congress is made up of two "houses," a Senate and a House of Representatives.

Composition of the House

Sec. 2, para. 1. The House of Representatives shall be composed of members chosen every second year by the people of the several states, and the electors in each state shall have the qualifications requisite for electors of the most numerous branch of the state legislature.

Representatives have two-year terms and are elected by the voters of each state. Citizens who are allowed to vote for state representatives are also qualified to vote for a representative in the national House of Representatives. This section recognizes the right of each state to make laws about voting. Several amendments have extended voting rights.

Qualifications of Representatives

Sec. 2, para. 2. No person shall be a representative who shall not have attained to the age of twenty-five years, and been seven years a citizen of the United States, and who shall not, when elected, be an inhabitant of that state in which he shall be chosen.

A representative must be at least twenty-five years old, a United States citizen for at least seven years, and a resident of the state from which he or she has been elected. The Constitution does not require a representative to live in the district that he or she serves, but custom does.

Basis of Representation

Sec. 2, para. 3. Representatives [and direct taxes] shall be apportioned among the several states which may be included within this Union, according to their respective numbers, [which shall be determined by adding to the whole number of free persons, including those bound to service for a term of years, and excluding Indians not taxed, three-fifths of all other persons]. The actual enumeration shall be made within three years after the first meeting of the Congress of the United States, and within every subsequent term of ten years, in such manner as they shall by law direct. The number of representatives shall not exceed one for every thirty thousand, but each state shall have at least one representative; [and until such enumeration shall be made, the state of New Hampshire shall be entitled to chuse three, Massachusetts eight, Rhode Island and Providence Plantations one, Connecticut five, New-York six, New Jersey four, Pennsylvania eight, Delaware one, Maryland six, Virginia ten, North Carolina five, South Carolina five, and Georgia three].

This paragraph is part of the Great Compromise made at the Constitutional Convention. It provided that the number of representatives a state has and the amount of direct taxes the state pays would be based on the number of people in the state. Each slave was to be counted as three-fifths of a free person; untaxed Indians were not to be counted at all. Since the abolition of slavery and property qualifications for voting, all Americans are counted in the same way. Provisions for direct taxes were changed by the Sixteenth Amendment. Besides requiring a census every ten years, this section requires Congress to decide how the count shall be made and the number of representatives from each state, except that the number of people may not be fewer than 30,000 for each representative. Each state has at least one representative even if its population is less than 30,000. Congress later set the total number of representatives at 435. By 1970, each member of the House represented about 465,000 persons.

Filling Vacancies

Sec. 2, para. 4. When vacancies happen in the representation from any state, the executive authority thereof shall issue writs of election to fill such vacancies.

If a state does not have its full number of representatives, the governor of the state is supposed to call an election to fill any vacancy.

Organizing the House • Impeachment

Sec. 2, para. 5. The House of Representatives shall chuse their speaker and other officers; and shall have the sole power of impeachment.

The House of Representatives selects its speaker (presiding officer) and other officers. The speaker has always been a member of the House. The House of Representatives alone has the power to *impeach,* to sit as a grand jury and decide whether or not high executives and judicial officers should be tried for misbehavior in office.

Composition of the Senate

Sec. 3, para. 1. The Senate of the United States shall be composed of two senators from each state, chosen [by the legislature thereof,] for six years; and each senator shall have one vote.

The Senate is made up of two senators from each state. Up until 1913, senators were chosen by the state legislatures; the Seventeenth Amendment changed this provision. Each senator is elected for a six-year term and has one vote in the Senate.

Choosing Senators

Sec. 3, para. 2. [Immediately after they shall be assembled in consequence of the first election, they shall be divided as equally as may be into three classes. The seats of the senators of the first class shall be vacated at the expiration of the second year, of the second class at the expiration of the fourth year, and of the third class at the expiration of the sixth year, so that one third may be chosen every second year; and] if vacancies happen by resignation, or otherwise, [during the recess of the legislature of any state,] the executive thereof may make temporary appointments [until the next meeting of the legislature, which shall then fill such vacancies].

The terms of senators in the first Congress were arranged so that one-third of the senators would be elected every two years. When a vacancy appears, the governor of the state arranges to hold an election, but if state laws permit, the governor may appoint a temporary senator.

Qualifications of Senators

Sec. 3, para. 3. No person shall be a senator who shall not have attained to the age of thirty years, and been nine years a citizen of the United States, and who shall not, when elected, be an inhabitant of that state for which he shall be chosen.

A senator must be at least thirty years old, a United States citizen for at least nine years, and a resident of the state that he or she represents.

Officers of the Senate

Sec. 3, para. 4. The Vice-President of the United States shall be president of the Senate, but shall have no vote, unless they be equally divided.

Sec. 3, para. 5. The Senate shall chuse their other officers, and also a president pro tempore, in the absence of the Vice-President, or when he shall exercise the office of President of the United States.

The Vice-President presides at Senate meetings but votes only when there is a tie.

The Senate chooses its other officers and may select a presiding officer to serve when the Vice-President is absent.

Impeachment Trials

Sec. 3, para. 6. The Senate shall have the sole power to try all impeachments. When sitting for that purpose, they shall be on oath or affirmation. When the President of the United States is tried, the Chief Justice shall preside: And no person shall be convicted without the concurrence of two-thirds of the members present.

Sec. 3, para. 7. Judgment in cases of impeachment shall not extend further than to removal from office, and disqualification to hold and enjoy any office of honor, trust or profit under the United States: but the party convicted shall nevertheless be liable and subject to indictment, trial, judgment and punishment, according to law.

The Senate is given the power to try officials who are impeached by the House of Representatives. The senators must take an oath to try the case fairly. If the President is tried, the Chief Justice presides over the Senate at the trial, but in other cases the Vice-President presides. To convict an official, two-thirds of the senators present must vote guilty.

The penalty for the convicted official shall not be more than the loss of office and of the right ever to hold another United States government office. But he or she may still be tried in the regular courts for any crimes that caused the loss of office and be punished if found guilty.

Congressional Elections

Sec. 4, para. 1. The times, places and manner of holding elections for senators and representatives, shall be prescribed in each state by the legislature thereof; but the Congress may at any time by law make or alter such regulations, except as to the places of chusing senators.

The states may make laws about when, where, and how elections for senators and representatives are held. But Congress may change the state laws. Congress, for example, has fixed the first Tuesday after the first Monday in November of even-numbered years as the date for election of senators and representatives. Representatives must be elected from districts by secret ballot. Senators are now elected at the same voting places as other officials.

Meetings of Congress

Sec. 4, para. 2. The Congress shall assemble at least once in every year, [and such meeting shall be on the first Monday in December, unless they shall by law appoint a different day].

Congress must meet at least once a year. The date of regular meeting is now fixed by the Twentieth Amendment at January 3.

Qualifications • Quorum

Sec. 5, para. 1. Each house shall be the judge of the elections, returns and qualifications of its own members, and a majority of each shall constitute a quorum to do business; but a smaller number may adjourn from day to day, and may be authorized to compel the attendance of absent members, in such manner, and under such penalties as each house may provide.

The House of Representatives and the Senate each may decide if its own members are entitled to be in Congress. Both have kept out members who met the qualifications of the Constitution but who were thought by more than half the House or Senate to be undesirable persons. Neither House nor Senate can hold meetings for business unless more than half the members are present, but the absence of a quorum often is not noticed. The Senate and the House of Representatives can each make rules and fix penalties for not attending meetings.

Rules

Sec. 5, para. 2. Each house may determine the rules of its proceedings, punish its members for disorderly behaviour, and, with the concurrence of two-thirds, expel a member.

The House and the Senate may each make its own rules for conducting its business and may punish its own members for not following these rules. In either the House or the Senate, two-thirds of the members present must agree if they wish to expel a member. In practice, it has been easier to keep a member out of Congress than to put one out.

Journal

Sec. 5, para. 3. Each house shall keep a journal of its proceedings, and from time to time publish the same, excepting such parts as may in their judgment require secrecy; and the yeas and nays of the members of either house on any question shall, at the desire of one-fifth of those present, be entered on the journal.

The House of Representatives and the Senate must each keep a record of what is done at its meetings. Not only are proceedings recorded, but most of what is said and much that is not said is printed in the big *Congressional Record*. The record is to be printed unless the members decide to keep some matters secret. If one-fifth of the members present wish, the record must show how each member voted on any question.

Adjournment

Sec. 5, para. 4. Neither house, during the session of congress, shall, without the consent of the other, adjourn for more than three days, nor to any other place than that in which the two houses shall be sitting.

While Congress is meeting, neither the House nor the Senate shall let three days pass without holding a meeting, unless the other agrees. Both must meet in the same city.

Congressional Privileges

Sec. 6, para. 1. The senators and representatives shall receive a compensation for their services, to be ascertained by law, and paid out of the treasury of the United States. They shall in all cases, except treason, felony and breach of the peace, be privileged from arrest during their attendance at the session of their respective houses, and in going to and returning from the same; and for any speech or debate in either house, they shall not be questioned in any other place.

Senators and representatives shall be paid out of the United States treasury according to the law that fixes their salaries (now $42,500 a year).

Members of Congress attending meetings of Congress, or going to and from meetings, shall not be arrested except for treason, serious crime, or breaking the peace. This protects them from interference in doing their duty. They cannot be held responsible for anything they say in their meetings, no matter how criminal it may be, except by the house to which they belong.

Congressional Restrictions

Sec. 6, para. 2. No senator or representative shall, during the time for which he was elected, be appointed to any civil office under the authority of the United States, which shall have been created, or the emoluments whereof shall have been increased during such time; and no person holding any office under the United States, shall be a member of either house during his continuance in office.

Senators and representatives cannot hold other United States government offices while they are members of Congress. During the time for which they have been elected, they cannot take any government position that has been created during that time nor any position for which the salary has been increased during that time.

Origin of Money Bills

Sec. 7, para. 1. All bills for raising revenue shall originate in the House of Representatives; but the Senate may propose or concur with amendments as on other bills.

Only members of the House of Representatives may propose bills that levy taxes. But the Senate may amend such bills and always does. In fact, the Senate often substitutes an entirely different bill.

Overriding a President's Veto

Sec. 7, para. 2. Every bill which shall have passed the House of Representatives and the Senate, shall, before it becomes a law, be presented to the President of the United States; If he approve he shall sign it, but if not he shall return it, with his objections to that house in which it shall have originated, who shall enter the objections at large on their journal, and proceed to reconsider it. If after such reconsideration two-thirds of that house shall agree to pass the bill, it shall be sent, together with the objections, to the other house, by which it shall likewise be reconsidered, and if approved by two-thirds of that house, it shall become a law. But in all such cases the votes of both houses shall be determined by yeas and nays, and the names of the persons voting for and against the bill shall be entered on the journal of each house respectively. If any bill shall not be returned by the President within ten days (Sundays excepted) after it shall have been presented to him, the same shall be a law, in like manner as if he had signed it, unless the Congress by their adjournment prevent its return, in which case it shall not be a law.

A bill that has passed both the House of Representatives and the Senate shall be sent to the President. If the President signs it, the bill becomes law. If the President does not approve the bill, he or she sends it back, without signing it, to the house that first passed it. The President has to give reasons for not approving it, and these reasons must be put in the record of proceedings. The members of that house must vote on the bill again. If two-thirds of the members present agree to pass the bill, it is sent, together with the President's objections, to the other house. If two-thirds of that house favor the bill, it becomes a law without the President's approval. The records of Congress must show how each member voted.

The President has ten days, not counting Sundays, after receiving a bill to consider it. If he or she keeps it longer, it becomes a law without being signed. But if Congress has adjourned, the unsigned bill does not become a law. (This is called the "pocket" veto.)

Need for President's Consent

Sec. 7, para. 3. Every order, resolution, or vote to which the concurrence of the Senate and House of Representatives may be necessary (except on a question of adjournment) shall be presented to the President of the United States; and before the same shall take effect, shall be approved by him, or being disapproved by him, shall be repassed by two-thirds of the Senate and House of Representatives, according to the rules and limitations prescribed in the case of a bill.

This clause prevents Congress from making laws without the consent of the President. If either the House of Representatives or the Senate takes action that needs mutual agreement, the matter must be sent to the President for approval. If the President agrees, it takes effect. If the President does not agree, both houses must pass the measure again by a two-thirds vote before it takes effect.

Powers of Congress • Taxing

Sec. 8, para. 1. The Congress shall have power
To lay and collect taxes, duties, imposts and excises, to pay the debts and provide for the common defence and general welfare of the United States; but all duties, imposts and excises shall be uniform throughout the United States.

Congress has the power to get money by taxing. Such income can be used (1) to pay the debts of the national government, (2) to defend the country, and (3) to provide services for the good of all the people. All national taxes in the form of import duties or excise taxes must be the same in all parts of the country.

Borrowing Money

Sec. 8, para. 2. To borrow money on the credit of the United States;

Congress has the power to borrow money for the government to use. There is no constitutional limit to the amount.

Regulating Commerce

Sec. 8, para. 3. To regulate commerce with foreign nations, and among the several states, and with the Indian tribes;

Congress has the power to make laws to control trade, transportation, communication, and related transactions with other countries, among the states, and with the Indian tribes.

Naturalization • Bankruptcies

Sec. 8, para. 4. To establish an uniform rule of naturalization, and uniform laws on the subject of bankruptcies throughout the United States;

Congress has the power to say how people born in other countries can become citizens of the United States. Congress has the power to set up a national bankruptcy law.

Money • Weights and Measures

Sec. 8, para. 5. To coin money, regulate the value thereof, and of foreign coin, and fix the standard of weights and measures;

Congress has the power to coin money and say how much it is worth and to put a value on foreign money. Combined with the power to borrow money, this power enables Congress to issue paper money and make it legal in payment of all debts. Congress has the power to define weights and measures so that they will be the same throughout the nation.

Punishing Counterfeiters

Sec. 8, para. 6. To provide for the punishment of counterfeiting the securities and current coin of the United States;

Congress has the power to make laws to punish persons who make imitation government bonds, stamps, or money.

Postal Services

Sec. 8, para. 7. To establish post offices and post roads;

Congress has the power to provide post offices and roads.

Copyrights and Patents

Sec. 8, para. 8. To promote the progress of science and useful arts, by securing for limited times to authors and inventors the exclusive right to their respective writings and discoveries;

Congress has the power to help science, industry, and the arts by making laws under which inventors, writers, and artists may receive patents and copyrights on their work.

Lower Courts

Sec. 8, para. 9. To constitute tribunals inferior to the Supreme Court;

Congress has the power to set up national courts that are lower in authority than the Supreme Court of the United States.

Piracy • International Law

Sec. 8, para. 10. To define and punish piracies and felonies committed on the high seas, and offences against the law of nations;

Congress has the power to make laws about crimes committed on the seas or oceans. Congress also has the power to make laws to punish those who break laws that are recognized by all nations (international law).

Declaring War

Sec. 8, para. 11. To declare war, grant letters of marque and reprisal, and make rules concerning captures on land and water;

Congress has the power to declare war, to permit persons to capture or destroy ships and goods of enemy nations without being guilty of piracy (this power given up in 1856), and to make rules about seizing enemy property on land or sea.

Military Forces

Sec. 8, para. 12. To raise and support armies, but no appropriation of money to that use shall be for a longer term than two years;

Sec. 8, para. 13. To provide and maintain a navy;

Sec. 8, para. 14. To make rules for the government and regulation of the land and naval forces;

Congress has the power to raise armed forces and supply them by any means and to any extent necessary. But Congress may not provide money for the army for more than two years at a time. No time limit was put on appropriations for the navy because the navy was not considered as dangerous to liberty as a permanent army. Congress also has the power to make rules for the organization and control of the armed services.

The Militia

Sec. 8, para. 15. To provide for calling forth the militia to execute the laws of the Union, suppress insurrections and repel invasions;

Sec. 8, para. 16. To provide for organizing, arming, and disciplining, the militia, and for governing such part of them as may be employed in the service of the United States, reserving to the states respectively, the appointment of the officers, and the authority of training the militia according to the discipline prescribed by Congress;

Congress has the power to call out able-bodied Americans organized as militia to (1) enforce the national laws, (2) put down rebellion, and (3) drive out invading enemies.

Congress has the power to provide ways and means for states to have civilian soldiers and to make rules for using these soldiers for the whole country. But the states have the right to select the officers of the militia and to see that the militia is trained according to rules made by Congress. The organized militia is the national guard.

The Federal District

Sec. 8, para. 17. To exercise exclusive legislation in all cases whatsoever, over such district (not exceeding ten miles square) as may, by cession of particular states, and the acceptance of Congress, become the seat of the government of the United States, and to exercise like authority over all places purchased by the consent of the legislature of the state in which the same shall be, for the erection of forts, magazines, arsenals, dock-yards, and other needful buildings;

Congress has the power to make all laws for the District of Columbia, which includes the national capital (Washington, D.C.). Congress governs all places bought from the states for use as forts, arsenals, navy yards, and public buildings.

The "Elastic Clause"

Sec. 8, para. 18. And to make all laws which shall be necessary and proper for carrying into execution the foregoing powers, and all other powers vested by this Constitution in the government of the United States, or in any department or officer thereof.

This paragraph—the "elastic clause"—is basic to a broad interpretation of the Constitution. It gives Congress power to make any laws that may be needed to carry out the specific powers granted in the first seventeen paragraphs of Section 8 and in the rest of the Constitution. It does not, however, give Congress the power to do whatever it chooses. Congress must act within the framework of the specified powers.

Slave Trade

Sec. 9, para. 1. The migration or importation of such persons as any of the states now existing shall think proper to admit, shall not be prohibited by the Congress prior to the year one thousand eight hundred and eight, but a tax or duty may be imposed on such importation, not exceeding ten dollars for each person.

Congress could not forbid the bringing in of slaves before 1808. It could, however, levy a tax as high as $10 on each one brought in.

Habeas Corpus

Sec. 9, para. 2. The privilege of the writ of habeas corpus shall not be suspended, unless when in cases of rebellion or invasion the public safety may require it.

Only when the country is in danger from rebellion or invasion can Congress stop the courts from issuing papers called "writs of habeas corpus." A writ of habeas corpus forces a jailer or other person to bring a prisoner into court so that the prisoner can have a judge decide if he or she is being held lawfully.

Bill of Attainder • Ex Post Facto

Sec. 9, para. 3. No bill of attainder or ex post facto law shall be passed.

Congress cannot pass a law convicting or punishing a particular person. Congress cannot pass a law that makes unlawful something that was not illegal at the time it was done.

Direct Taxes

Sec. 9, para. 4. No capitation, [or other direct,] tax shall be laid, unless in proportion to the census or enumeration herein before directed to be taken.

Congress cannot levy "head" taxes or poll taxes unless all persons (men, women, and children) in the United States are taxed the same. Other direct taxes (except on incomes, according to the Sixteenth Amendment) also must be based on population instead of value, size, or any other factor.

Prohibition of Export Duties

Sec. 9, para. 5. No tax or duty shall be laid on articles exported from any state.

Congress cannot tax goods or products for being sent out of any state.

Equal Treatment to All States

Sec. 9, para. 6. No preference shall be given by any regulation of commerce or revenue to the ports of one state over those of another: nor shall vessels bound to, or from, one state, be obliged to enter, clear, or pay duties in another.

Congress cannot make any laws that favor one state or one city more than another in matters of trade or commerce. Ships from any state may enter the ports of any other state without paying charges.

Care of Public Money

Sec. 9, para. 7. No money shall be drawn from the treasury, but in consequence of appropriations made by law; and a regular statement and account of the receipts and expenditures of all public money shall be published from time to time.

Government money can be spent only if Congress passes a bill for that purpose. An account of money taken in and spent must be made public.

Titles of Nobility

Sec. 9, para. 8. No title of nobility shall be granted by the United States: and no person holding any office of profit or trust under them, shall, without the consent of the Congress, accept of any present, emolument, office, or title, of any kind whatever, from any king, prince, or foreign state.

The United States government cannot give a noble title (such as count, duchess, earl) to anyone. No one in the service of the United States can accept a title, a present, or a position from another country without permission of Congress. This prevents foreign governments from corrupting our officials.

Prohibitions on the States

Sec. 10, para. 1. No state shall enter into any treaty, alliance, or confederation; grant letters of marque and reprisal; coin money; emit bills of credit; make any thing but gold and silver coin a tender in payment of debts; pass any bill of attainder, ex post facto law, or law impairing the obligation of contracts, or grant any title of nobility.

States cannot make treaties with foreign countries. States cannot give private citizens permission to fight other countries. States cannot coin their own money or issue paper money. States cannot pass laws that allow materials other than gold and silver to be used as money. States cannot pass laws declaring a particular person guilty of a stated offense and describing the punishment. States cannot pass laws that would punish a person for something that was not against the law when it was done. States cannot pass laws that excuse people from carrying out lawful agreements. States cannot give titles of nobility.

Sec. 10, para. 2. No state shall, without the consent of the Congress, lay any imposts or duties on imports or exports, except what may be absolutely necessary for executing its inspection laws: and the net produce of all duties and imposts, laid by any state on imports or exports, shall be for the use of the treasury of the United States; and all such laws shall be subject to the revision and control of the Congress.

Sec. 10, para. 3. No state shall, without the consent of Congress, lay any duty of tonnage, keep troops or ships of war in time of peace, enter into any agreement or compact with another state, or with a foreign power, or engage in war, unless actually invaded, or in such imminent danger as will not admit of delay.

States cannot tax goods entering or leaving a state unless Congress agrees. But states may charge an inspection fee if necessary. Any profit from state import or export taxes approved by Congress must go into the United States treasury, and these state tax laws may be changed by Congress. Unless Congress provides otherwise, states may not tax ships, or keep troops (except civilian soldiers—militia) or warships in time of peace. States cannot make alliances with other states or with foreign countries unless Congress agrees. States cannot go to war without the consent of Congress unless they have been invaded or are in such great danger that delay would be disastrous.

ARTICLE 2 • EXECUTIVE BRANCH

The Presidency

Sec. 1, para. 1. The executive power shall be vested in a President of the United States of America. He shall hold his office during the term of four years, and, together with the Vice-President, chosen for the same term, be elected as follows

The leader and manager of the national government is the President, who has a four-year term of office. The Vice-President is elected to the same term of office.

Electoral College

Sec. 1, para. 2. Each state shall appoint, in such manner as the legislature thereof may direct, a number of electors, equal to the whole number of senators and representatives to which the state may be entitled in the Congress: but no senator or representative, or person holding an office of trust or profit under the United States, shall be appointed an elector.

The President is elected by electors chosen by each state in the way the state legislature decides. Each state chooses as many electors as it has representatives and senators. No senator or representative in Congress or anyone holding a national government position may be an elector.

Original Election Method

Sec. 1, para. 3. [The electors shall meet in their respective states, and vote by ballot for two persons, of whom one at least shall not be an inhabitant of the same state with themselves. And they shall make a list of all the persons voted for, and of the number of votes for each; which list they shall sign and certify, and transmit sealed to the seat of government of the United States, directed to the president of the Senate. The president of the Senate shall, in the presence of the Senate and House of Representatives, open all the certificates, and the votes shall then be counted. The person having the greatest number of votes shall be the President, if such number be a majority of the whole number of electors appointed; and if there be more than one who have such majority, and have an equal number of votes, then the House of Representatives shall immediately chuse by ballot one of them for President; and if no person have a majority, then from the five highest on the list the said house shall in like manner chuse the President. But in chusing the President, the votes shall be taken by states, the representation from each state having one vote; a quorum for this purpose shall consist of a member or members from two-thirds of the states, and a majority of all the states shall be necessary to a choice. In every case, after the choice of the President, the person having the greatest number of votes of the electors shall be the Vice-President. But if there should remain two or more who have equal votes, the Senate shall chuse from them by ballot the Vice-President.]

This paragraph was changed by the Twelfth Amendment. See that amendment to find out how electors now choose the President and Vice-President.

Date of Elections

Sec. 1, para. 4. The Congress may determine the time of chusing the electors, and the day on which they shall give their votes; which day shall be the same throughout the United States.

Congress has the power to set the day for choosing electors and the day when the electors vote. The date set for choosing electors, Election Day, is the first Tuesday after the first Monday in November in every fourth year. The President is not actually elected until the electors cast their votes on the first Monday after the second Wednesday in December.

Qualifications for President

Sec. 1, para. 5. No person except a natural-born citizen, or a citizen of the United States, at the time of the adoption of this Constitution, shall be eligible to the office of President; neither shall any person be eligible to that office who shall not have attained to the age of thirty-five years, and been fourteen years a resident within the United States.

To be President, a person must have been born in the United States or been born of parents who were citizens of the United States at the time of the birth. Such a person must be at least thirty-five years old and must have lived in the United States at least fourteen years. (Foreign-born persons who were citizens at the time the Constitution was adopted were also eligible to be President.)

Succession to the Presidency

Sec. 1, para. 6. [In case of the removal of the President from office, or of his death, resignation, or inability to discharge the powers and duties of the said office, the same shall devolve on the Vice-President, and the Congress may by law provide for the case of removal, death, resignation or inability, both of the President and Vice-President declaring what officer shall then act as President, and such officer shall act accordingly, until the disability be removed, or a President shall be elected.]

This part has been changed by the Twenty-fifth Amendment.

Salary

Sec. 1, para. 7. The President shall, at stated times, receive for his services, a compensation, which shall neither be encreased nor diminished during the period for which he shall have been elected, and he shall not receive within that period any other emolument from the United States, or any of them.

The President is paid a salary, which cannot be raised or lowered during the term of office. While in office, the President cannot receive any other salary from the national government or from any state. The salary is now $200,000 a year.

Oath of Office

Before he enter on the execution of his office, he shall take the following oath or affirmation:—"I do solemnly swear (or affirm) that I will faithfully execute the office of President of the United States, and will to the best of my ability, preserve, protect and defend the Constitution of the United States."

Before taking the office of President, the person elected must promise to faithfully carry on the duties of the job and make sure that the Constitution is obeyed.

Military and Civil Powers

Sec. 2, para. 1. The President shall be commander in chief of the army and navy of the United States, and of the militia of the several states, when called into the actual service of the United States; he may require the opinion, in writing, of the principal officer in each of the executive departments, upon any subject relating to the duties of their respective offices, and he shall have power to grant reprieves and pardons for offences against the United States, except in cases of impeachment.

The President is the head of the country's armed forces, including the state militia when it is called into national service. The President may ask for reports from the cabinet officers and other important leaders charged with executing the laws. The President may pardon or postpone the sentences of those convicted in the national courts but cannot interfere in cases of impeachment.

Treaty and Appointment Powers

Sec. 2, para. 2. He shall have power, by and with the advice and consent of the Senate, to make treaties, provided two-thirds of the senators present concur; and he shall nominate, and by and with the advice and consent of the Senate, shall appoint ambassadors, other public ministers and consuls, judges of the Supreme Court, and all other officers of the United States, whose appointments are not herein otherwise provided for, and which shall be established by law: but the Congress may by law vest the appointment of such inferior officers, as they think proper, in the President alone, in the courts of law, or in the heads of departments.

Sec. 2, para. 3. The President shall have power to fill up all vacancies that may happen during the recess of the Senate, by granting commissions which shall expire at the end of their next session.

The President has the power to make treaties with other countries, but the Senate must approve the treaties by a two-thirds vote of those present.

The President has the power to appoint persons to represent the United States in other countries, but the Senate must approve the choices by a simple majority vote. The President also has the power to appoint, with the Senate's approval, the justices of the Supreme Court and other government officials, unless the Constitution provides a different way.

Congress may pass laws giving the President, the courts, or heads of government departments the right to select people for certain government positions.

The President may appoint persons to fill vacancies that appear in the executive department when the Senate is not meeting. These appointments hold good until the end of the next meeting of the Senate.

Other Presidential Powers

Sec. 3. He shall from time to time give to the Congress information of the state of the Union, and recommend to their consideration such measures as he shall judge necessary and expedient; he may, on extraordinary occasions, convene both houses, or either of them, and in case of disagreement between them, with respect to the time of adjournment, he may adjourn them to such time as he shall think proper; he shall receive ambassadors and other public ministers; he shall take care that the laws be faithfully executed, and shall commission all the officers of the United States.

The President informs Congress about the nation's condition (this is the State of the Union message the President gives at the beginning of each session of Congress). The President recommends necessary laws and advises Congress about desirable changes in the government.

In emergencies the President calls meetings of the House of Representatives, the Senate, or both.

If the two houses of Congress disagree about ending their meetings, the President may end them. (This has not yet happened.)

The President deals with representatives of other countries.

It is the President's duty to see that the laws of the country are followed.

The President must sign the papers that show the right of officers to hold their positions.

Impeachment

Sec. 4. The President, Vice-President and all civil officers of the United States, shall be removed from office on impeachment for, and conviction of, treason, bribery, or other high crimes and misdemeanors.

The President, Vice-President, and other officers of the national government (except congressmen and military officers) can be removed from office after being accused by the House of Representatives and then convicted by the Senate of treason (aiding the nation's enemies), of taking bribes, or of committing other serious crimes.

ARTICLE 3 • JUDICIAL BRANCH

Courts and Judges

Sec. 1. The judicial power of the United States, shall be vested in one Supreme Court, and in such inferior courts as the Congress may from time to time ordain and establish. The judges, both of the supreme and inferior courts, shall hold their offices during good behaviour, and shall, at stated times, receive for their services, a compensation which shall not be diminished during their continuance in office.

The power to judge is given to the Supreme Court and to whatever lower courts Congress sets up. Judges of all national courts hold office for life or until they are proved guilty of wrongful acts. They are paid a salary that cannot be lowered while they hold office.

Power of National Courts

Sec. 2, para. 1. The judicial power shall extend to all cases, in law and equity, arising under this Constitution, the laws of the United States, and treaties made, or which shall be made, under their authority;—to all cases affecting ambassadors, other public ministers and consuls;—to all cases of admiralty and maritime jurisdiction;—to controversies to which the United States shall be a party;—to controversies between two or more states;—[between a state and citizens of another state;]—between citizens of different states,—between citizens of the same state claiming lands under grants of different states, and between a state, or the citizens thereof, and foreign states, citizens or subjects.

The national courts settle disputes that have to do with the Constitution, with laws of the United States, with treaties, and with laws about ships and shipping. These courts also settle disputes in which representatives of foreign countries, the national government, or two or more state governments are interested.

National courts may also settle disputes between people of different states, disputes in which people of the same state claim lands in other states, and disputes between a state or citizens of a state and a foreign country or citizens of a foreign country. The Eleventh Amendment took away the power of national courts to settle disputes between a state and citizens of another state.

Original and Appellate Jurisdiction

Sec. 2, para. 2. In all cases affecting ambassadors, other public ministers and consuls, and those in which a state shall be party, the Supreme Court shall have original jurisdiction. In all the other cases before mentioned, the Supreme Court shall have appellate jurisdiction, both as to law and fact, with such exceptions, and under such regulations as the Congress shall make.

If the representative of a foreign country is in the dispute, or if a state is in the dispute, the trial is heard directly by the Supreme Court. All other disputes are tried in a lower national court first. Decisions in such cases may be appealed to the Supreme Court. Congress has the power to make further rules about these cases.

Trial by Jury

Sec. 2, para. 3. The trial of all crimes, except in cases of impeachment, shall be by jury; and such trial shall be held in the state where the said crimes shall have been committed; but when not committed within any state, the trial shall be at such place or places as the Congress may by law have directed.

With the exception of an impeached official, anyone accused of a crime against the national government has a right to a trial by jury. The trial is held in the state where the crime was committed. If the crime was not done in any state (for example, a crime done at sea), the trial is held in a place Congress has chosen by law.

Treason

Sec. 3. Treason against the United States, shall consist only in levying war against them, or in adhering to their enemies, giving them aid and comfort. No person shall be convicted of treason unless on the testimony of two witnesses to the same overt act, or on confession in open court.

The Congress shall have power to declare the punishment of treason, but no attainder of treason shall work corruption of blood, or forfeiture except during the life of the person attainted.

Treason is defined as carrying on war against the United States or helping the enemies of the United States. No one can be punished for treason unless he or she confesses in court or unless at least two witnesses testify that the accused person committed a treasonable act.

Congress has the power to set the punishment for treason. Congress cannot punish the family of a person guilty of treason for his or her crime.

ARTICLE 4 • THE STATES

Full Faith and Credit

Sec. 1. Full faith and credit shall be given in each state to the public acts, records, and judicial proceedings of every other state. And the Congress may by general laws prescribe the manner in which such acts, records and proceedings shall be proved, and the effect thereof.

All states must accept as legal and binding the laws, records, and court decisions of other states. Congress has the power to make laws that say how these laws, records, and decisions must be presented for acceptance.

Privileges and Immunities

Sec. 2, para. 1. The citizens of each state shall be entitled to all privileges and immunities of citizens in the several states.

Sec. 2, para. 2. A person charged in any state with treason, felony, or other crime, who shall flee from justice, and be found in another state, shall on demand of the executive authority of the state from which he fled, be delivered up, to be removed to the state having jurisdiction of the crime.

Sec. 2, para. 3. [No person held to service or labour in one state, under the laws thereof, escaping into another, shall, in consequence of any law or regulation therein, be discharged from such service or labour, but shall be delivered up on claim of the party to whom such service or labour may be due.]

A citizen from another state has the same rights as the citizens of the state where he or she happens to be.

Anyone accused of crime who is found in another state shall be sent back for trial, if the governor of the state where the crime was committed requests it. But there is no legal way to force a governor to return such a person.

Slaves did not become free by escaping to a free state but had to be sent back to their owners.

New States

Sec. 3, para. 1. New states may be admitted by the Congress into this union; but no new state shall be formed or erected within the jurisdiction of any other state; nor any state be formed by the junction of two or more states, or parts of states, without the consent of the legislatures of the states concerned as well as of the Congress.

Congress has the right to add new states to the United States. No way is provided for a state to leave the Union.

No state can be divided to make another state without the consent of the original state and Congress. Two such states have been formed from existing states: Maine from Massachusetts in 1820; and West Virginia from Virginia in 1863. The law admitting Texas to the Union provided that it could later be divided into five states.

A new state cannot be made from parts of two or more states without the agreement of the legislatures of the states and of Congress. None has been formed this way.

Territories

Sec. 3, para. 2. The Congress shall have power to dispose of and make all needful rules and regulations respecting the territory or other property belonging to the United States; and nothing in this Constitution shall be so construed as to prejudice any claims of the United States, or of any particular state.

Congress has the power to make rules about all government lands and property. The government of territories before they become states is determined by Congress.

Guarantees to the States

Sec. 4. The United States shall guarantee to every state in this union a republican form of government, and shall protect each of them against invasion; and on application of the legislature, or of the executive (when the legislature cannot be convened) against domestic violence.

The national government must make sure that every state has a government in which the people rule and that each state is protected from invasion. Help must be sent a state to put down riots if the state legislature asks it, or if the governor asks when the legislature is not meeting. The President can also send troops into a state without the request of state officials if necessary to enforce national law and maintain peace.

ARTICLE 5 • AMENDING PROCEDURES

The Congress, whenever two-thirds of both houses shall deem it necessary, shall propose amendments to this Constitution, or, on the application of the legislatures of two-thirds of the several states, shall call a convention for proposing amendments, which, in either case, shall be valid to all intents and purposes, as part of this constitution, when ratified by the legislatures of three-fourths of the several states, or by conventions in three-fourths thereof, as the one or the other mode of ratification may be proposed by the Congress; provided [that no amendment which may be made prior to the year one thousand eight hundred and eight shall in any manner affect the first and fourth clauses in the ninth Section of the first Article; and] that no state, without its consent, shall be deprived of its equal suffrage in the Senate.

The Constitution provides two ways of suggesting amendments to the Constitution. One way is for two-thirds of the Senate and two-thirds of the House of Representatives to suggest amendments. The other way is for the legislatures of two-thirds of the states to ask Congress to call a meeting of specially elected persons to suggest amendments. Amendments proposed in either of these ways must then be ratified. They become a part of the Constitution if legislatures of three-fourths of the states agree, or if three-fourths of the states have special meetings that agree to the amendments. Congress may decide which of these two ways of ratifying amendments is to be used.

No amendment could be made before 1808 that would stop the slave trade or allow direct taxes without distributing the burden according to the population of the states. No amendment can take away a state's right to have the same number of senators as other states, unless the particular state agrees to this change.

ARTICLE 6 • NATIONAL SUPREMACY

All debts contracted and engagements entered into, before the adoption of this constitution, shall be as valid against the United States under this Constitution, as under the Confederation.

This Constitution, and the laws of the United States which shall be made in pursuance thereof; and all treaties made or which shall be made, under the authority of the United States, shall be the supreme law of the land; and the judges in every state shall be bound thereby, any thing in the constitution or laws of any state to the contrary notwithstanding.

The senators and representatives before mentioned, and the members of the several state legislatures, and all executive and judicial officers, both of the United States and of the several states, shall be bound by oath or affirmation, to support this Constitution; but no religious test shall ever be required as a qualification to any office or public trust under the United States.

Promises to repay borrowed money and agreements made by Congress before the adoption of the Constitution shall be as binding on the United States as they were before this Constitution was put into effect.

This Constitution, the laws made by Congress as permitted under this Constitution, and treaties made by the United States shall be the highest law of the United States. Judges must follow this law, even if state laws contradict it. This is the "supremacy clause."

All national government and state government officials must promise to follow this Constitution.

Officials and employees of the national government cannot be required to take any kind of religious test in order to hold office.

ARTICLE 7 • RATIFICATION

The ratification of the conventions of nine states, shall be sufficient for the establishment of this Constitution between the states so ratifying the same. Done in convention by the unanimous consent of the states present the seventeenth day of September in the year of our Lord one thousand seven hundred and eighty seven and of the independence of the United States of America the twelfth. In witness whereof we have hereunto subscribed our names.

When nine states have held meetings and agreed to this Constitution, government under the Constitution shall begin in the states that have agreed to it. This method of changing the form of government differed from the existing Articles of Confederation, which required consent of all thirteen states. Within a year, nine states had ratified the new Constitution.

The states represented in the Constitutional Convention on September 17, 1787, agreed to the Constitution as a plan of government to be proposed. Rhode Island had refused to take part in the convention. The other twelve states selected sixty-five men to go to the convention; and fifty-five of them attended meetings. Forty-two were present the day the Constitution was signed, but only thirty-nine signed it. The signers were:

George Washington—President and deputy from Virginia

New Hampshire
John Langdon
Nicholas Gilman

Connecticut
William Samuel Johnson
Roger Sherman

New York
Alexander Hamilton

New Jersey
William Livingston
David Brearley
William Paterson
Jonathan Dayton

Pennsylvania
Benjamin Franklin
Thomas Mifflin
Robert Morris
George Clymer
Thomas FitzSimons
Jared Ingersoll
James Wilson
Gouverneur Morris

Delaware
George Read
Gunning Bedford, Junior
John Dickinson
Richard Bassett
Jacob Broom

Massachusetts
Nathaniel Gorham
Rufus King

Maryland
James McHenry
Daniel of St. Thomas Jenifer
Daniel Carroll

Virginia
John Blair
James Madison, Junior

North Carolina
William Blount
Richard Dobbs Spaight
Hugh Williamson

South Carolina
John Rutledge
Charles Cotesworth Pinckney
Charles Pinckney
Pierce Butler

Georgia
William Few
Abraham Baldwin

Attest WILLIAM JACKSON Secretary

AMENDMENTS TO THE CONSTITUTION

AMENDMENT 1 (1791)
RELIGIOUS AND POLITICAL FREEDOM

Congress shall make no law respecting an establishment of religion, or prohibiting the free exercise thereof; or abridging the freedom of speech, or of the press; or the right of the people peaceably to assemble, and to petition the government for a redress of grievances.

Congress cannot pass laws that make any religion the official religion of the country, nor can it make laws that prevent people from following their own religion; or laws that prevent people from speaking and printing what they wish (if it is not slanderous or seditious); or laws that prevent people from meeting peaceably so that they may ask the government to right any wrong.

AMENDMENT 2 (1791)
RIGHT TO BEAR ARMS

A well regulated militia, being necessary to the security of a free state, the right of the people to keep and bear arms, shall not be infringed.

Because people have a right to protect themselves with armed citizens (militia), Congress cannot pass any laws that prevent people from keeping and carrying firearms for military purposes. Congress can and has restricted the possession of sawed-off shotguns and concealed weapons for private purposes.

AMENDMENT 3 (1791)
QUARTERING OF SOLDIERS

No soldier shall, in time of peace be quartered in any house, without the consent of the owner, nor in time of war, but in a manner to be prescribed by law.

In peacetime, citizens cannot be forced to give either room or board to soldiers in their homes. In wartime, this may be done if Congress passes a law providing for it.

AMENDMENT 4 (1791)
SEARCH AND SEIZURE

The right of the people to be secure in their persons, houses, papers, and effects, against unreasonable searches and seizures, shall not be violated, and no warrants shall issue, but upon probable cause, supported by oath or affirmation, and particularly describing the place to be searched, and the persons or things to be seized.

A person's house cannot be searched and his or her property or papers taken except in ways that are according to law. Courts cannot issue search warrants unless convinced there is good reason for doing so. Whoever asks for a search warrant must give the reasons and explain exactly where the search is to be made and what is to be taken. This amendment was intended to prevent the use of "writs of assistance," which were general warrants used by the British chiefly to catch smugglers.

AMENDMENT 5 (1791)
LIFE, LIBERTY, AND PROPERTY

No person shall be held to answer for a capital, or otherwise infamous crime, unless on a presentment or indictment of a grand jury, except in cases arising in the land or naval forces, or in the militia, when in actual service in time of war or public danger; nor shall any person be subject for the same offence to be twice put in jeopardy of life or limb; nor shall be compelled in any criminal case to be a witness against himself, nor be deprived of life, liberty, or property, without due process of law; nor shall private property be taken for public use, without just compensation.

No one can be tried in a national court for a serious crime unless a grand jury makes an accusation. But this rule does not cover members of the armed forces in times of war or public danger.

No one who has been found innocent of committing a crime can be tried again for the same offense. But if the offense is a crime under state law, the person can be tried again in a state court. Or if the offense hurts someone, the person can be made to pay for damages.

No one can be forced to say anything in a national court that would help convict himself or herself of a crime. (This provision was intended to prevent the use of torture in extracting confessions.)

The government cannot take a person's life, freedom, or property except in the exact ways laid down by law. The Fourteenth Amendment applies this rule to the states, too.

The government cannot take a person's property without paying a fair price for it and then only if it is to be used for the benefit of everybody.

AMENDMENT 6 (1791)
RIGHTS OF THE ACCUSED

In all criminal prosecutions, the accused shall enjoy the right to a speedy and public trial, by an impartial jury of the state and district wherein the crime shall have been committed, which district shall have been previously ascertained by law, and to be informed of the nature and cause of the accusation; to be confronted with the witnesses against him; to have compulsory process for obtaining witnesses in his favor, and to have the assistance of counsel for his defence.

A person accused of committing a crime must be given prompt trial in public. Guilt or innocence must be decided by a jury chosen from the state and the district where the crime was committed. The accused must be told what he or she is being tried for. The accused must be present when witnesses speak in court. The accused can have witnesses called to testify for him or her. The accused can have a lawyer to defend him or her. This amendment applies only to national courts, but the states follow nearly the same rules.

AMENDMENT 7 (1791)
RIGHT TO JURY TRIAL

In suits at common law, where the value in controversy shall exceed twenty dollars, the right of trial by jury shall be preserved, and no fact tried by a jury, shall be otherwise reexamined by any court of the United States than according to the rules of the common law.

In disputes over property worth more than twenty dollars, either party to the dispute can insist on having a jury trial, or both can agree not to have a jury. After a jury's decision, no questions of fact can be brought up again in a higher court unless before a jury.

AMENDMENT 8 (1791)
BAIL AND PUNISHMENT

Excessive bail shall not be required, nor excessive fines imposed, nor cruel and unusual punishments inflicted.

People who are accused of crimes may be allowed out of jail on bail while they are awaiting trial. *Bail* is the sum of money or property that the accused person gives the court to hold as a guarantee that he or she will show up for the trial. The Eighth Amendment forbids the courts to require an unusually large bail.

Courts cannot fine persons too much for the crime done or punish convicts in cruel or unusual ways (such as branding with a hot iron). On June 29, 1972, in the case of *Furman* v. *Georgia,* the Supreme Court ruled that the death penalty was cruel and unusual punishment.

AMENDMENT 9 (1791)
ALL OTHER RIGHTS

The enumeration in the Constitution of certain rights, shall not be construed to deny or disparage others retained by the people.

The mention of certain rights in the Constitution does not mean that these are the only rights that people have or does not make other rights less important. (These unnamed rights probably meant those like "pursuit of happiness"—rights so vague that they cannot be legally defined.)

AMENDMENT 10 (1791)
RIGHTS OF STATES AND THE PEOPLE

The powers not delegated to the United States by the Constitution, nor prohibited by it to the states, are reserved to the states respectively, or to the people.

All powers not given by the Constitution to the national government, and all powers not denied to the states by the Constitution are kept by the states or by the people of the states. This guarantees states' rights but not state supremacy.

This amendment and the other nine ratified in 1791 are called the Bill of Rights.

AMENDMENT 11 (1798)
SUITS AGAINST A STATE

The judicial power of the United States shall not be construed to extend to any suit in law or equity, commenced or prosecuted against one of the United States by citizens of another state, or by citizens or subjects of any foreign state.

Citizens of other states or of foreign countries cannot sue a state in the national courts.

AMENDMENT 12 (1804)
ELECTION OF EXECUTIVE

The electors shall meet in their respective states and vote by ballot for President and Vice-President, one of whom, at least, shall not be an inhabitant of the same state with themselves; they shall name in their ballots the person voted for as President, and in distinct ballots the person voted for as Vice-President, and they shall make distinct lists of all persons voted for as President, and of all persons voted for as Vice-President, and of the number of votes for each, which list they shall sign and certify, and transmit sealed to the seat of the government of the United States, directed to the president of the Senate;—The president of the Senate shall, in the presence of the Senate and House of Representatives, open all the certificates and the votes shall then be counted;—The person having the greatest number of votes for President, shall be the President, if such number be a majority of the whole number of electors appointed; and if no person have such majority, then from the persons having the highest number not exceeding three on the list of those voted for as President, the House of Representatives shall choose immediately, by ballot, the President. But in choosing the President, the votes shall be taken by states, the representation from each state having one vote; a quorum for this purpose shall consist of a member or members from two-thirds of the states, and a majority of all the states shall be necessary to a choice. [And if the House of Representatives shall not choose a President whenever the right of choice shall develop upon them, before the fourth day of March next following, then the Vice-President shall act as President, as in the case of the death or other constitutional disability of the President.] The person having the greatest number of votes as Vice-President, shall be the Vice-President, if such number be a majority of the whole number of electors appointed, and if no person have a majority, then from the two highest numbers on the list, the Senate shall choose the Vice-President; a quorum for the purpose shall consist of two-thirds of the whole number of senators, and a majority of the whole number shall be necessary to a choice. But no person constitutionally ineligible to the office of the President shall be eligible to that of Vice-President of the United States.

In the election of 1800, it became apparent that the provisions for electing a President needed to be made clearer. This amendment was passed so that the Vice-President would no longer be the person who came in second in the presidential election but would be elected on his or her own. Under the amendment's provisions, the electors meet in their own states and cast separate ballots for President and Vice-President. At least one of the candidates they vote for must live in another state. After the vote, the electors make a list of the persons voted for as President and another list of the persons voted for as Vice-President. On each list they write the total votes cast for each person and then sign their names, seal the lists, and send them to the president of the Senate in Washington.

In a meeting of all members of Congress, the president of the Senate opens the lists from all the states, and the votes are counted. The person having the most votes for President is President, provided the number of votes received is more than half of the total number of all electors. (Now 270 or more.) If no person has such a majority, the House of Representatives selects the President from the candidates who have the highest number of electoral votes, but no more than the three highest can be considered. Each state has one vote, no matter how many representatives it has. Two-thirds of the states must be represented when this vote is cast. The candidate who receives a majority of the votes of the states is President.

If the House of Representatives does not elect a President before the date set for the new President to take office, the Vice-President acts as President.

The person who receives the most electoral votes for Vice-President becomes Vice-President, but he or she must get more than half the electoral votes. If no person has more than half, the Senate chooses a Vice-President from the two highest on the list of candidates. Two-thirds of all the senators must be present when the vote is taken. To be elected Vice-President, the candidate must receive the votes of more than half (51 or more) of all the senators.

A person who does not have the qualifications for President of the United States cannot be Vice-President. (This addition corrected an oversight in the original Constitution.)

AMENDMENT 13 (1865)
ABOLITION OF SLAVERY

Sec. 1. Neither slavery nor involuntary servitude, except as a punishment for crime whereof the party shall have been duly convicted, shall exist within the United States, or any place subject to their jurisdiction.

Sec. 2. Congress shall have power to enforce this article by appropriate legislation.

Slavery is not allowed in the United States or in any lands under its control. No one may be forced to work unless a court has given that punishment for committing a crime.

Congress has the power to make laws that will put this amendment into effect.

AMENDMENT 14 (1868)
CIVIL RIGHTS IN THE STATES

Sec. 1. All persons born or naturalized in the United States, and subject to the jurisdiction thereof, are citizens of the United States and of the state wherein they reside. No state shall make or enforce any law which shall abridge the privileges or immunities of citizens of the United States; nor shall any state deprive any person of life, liberty, or property, without due process of law; nor deny to any person within its jurisdiction the equal protection of the laws.

Sec. 2. Representatives shall be apportioned among the several states according to their respective numbers, counting the whole number of persons in each state, excluding Indians not taxed. But when the right to vote at any election for the choice of electors for President and Vice-President of the United States, representatives in Congress, the executive and judicial officers of a state, or the members of the legislature thereof, is denied to any of the male inhabitants of such state, being twenty-one years of age, and citizens of the United States, or in any way abridged, except for participation in rebellion, or other crime, the basis of representation therein shall be reduced in the proportion which the number of such male citizens shall bear to the whole number of male citizens twenty-one years of age in such state.

Sec. 3. No person shall be a senator or representative in Congress, or elector of President or Vice-President, or hold any office, civil or military, under the United States, or under any state, who, having previously taken an oath, as a member of Congress, or as any officer of the United States, or as a member of any state legislature, or as an executive or judicial officer of any state, to support the Constitution of the United States, shall have engaged in insurrection or rebellion against the same, or given aid or comfort to the enemies thereof. But Congress may by a vote of two-thirds of each house, remove such disability.

Sec. 4. The validity of the public debt of the United States, authorized by law, including debts incurred for payment of pensions and bounties for services in suppressing insurrection or rebellion shall not be questioned. But neither the United States nor any state shall assume or pay any debt or obligation incurred in aid of insurrection or rebellion against the United States, or any claim for the loss or emancipation of any slave; but all such debts, obligations and claims shall be held illegal and void.

Sec. 5. The Congress shall have power to enforce, by appropriate legislation, the provisions of this article.

The Fourteenth Amendment did several things.

It gave citizenship to former slaves, provided ways to protect their rights, punished Confederate officers, and canceled Confederate debts.

The first section defines a citizen as someone born or naturalized in the United States who is subject to the country's laws. Such a person is a citizen of the state in which he or she resides as well as of the United States. By defining state citizenship, the amendment removed the means for states to set up their own citizenship requirements that would keep blacks from being state citizens. The section also extended some of the protections of the Bill of Rights (the first ten amendments). Thus it says that states cannot make or enforce laws that prevent any citizen from enjoying his or her rights. States cannot take anyone's life, liberty, or property except in ways that the courts say are legal and proper. Anyone living in any state is entitled to that state's protection and the benefit of its laws.

The second section canceled the "three-fifths clause" (Article 1, Section 2, para. 3) by providing that all people, except untaxed Indians, are counted in order to determine how many representatives in Congress each state is to have. The section also provided that a state's representation in Congress would be decreased if it kept male citizens, who were twenty-one and over and who had not committed crimes, from voting. This provision was intended to force states to allow black men to vote; it has never been enforced.

The third section barred certain Confederate leaders from voting and holding office. Congress worded the amendment so that only those Confederate leaders who had previously held national or state office were affected. This included most of the top leaders of the Confederacy. Congress removed this barrier on June 6, 1898.

The fourth section barred the states or the national government from paying any part of the Confederate debt. At the same time, it provided that the payment of the Union debt would not be questioned.

Congress was given the power to make laws that would put this amendment into effect.

AMENDMENT 15 (1870)
BLACK SUFFRAGE

Sec. 1. The right of citizens of the United States to vote shall not be denied or abridged by the United States or by any state on account of race, color, or previous condition of servitude.

Sec. 2. The Congress shall have power to enforce this article by appropriate legislation.

Neither the United States nor any state has the right to keep citizens from voting because of their race or color or because they were once slaves.

Congress has the power to make laws that will put this amendment into effect.

AMENDMENT 16 (1913)
INCOME TAX

The Congress shall have power to lay and collect taxes on incomes, from whatever source derived, without apportionment among the several states, and without regard to any census or enumeration.

Congress has the power to levy and collect income taxes from the people. In levying such a tax, Congress does not have to apportion it among the states or divide the taxes according to the population. The provision "from whatever source derived" has been used to prosecute top criminals for income-tax evasion when no other crimes could be proved.

AMENDMENT 17 (1913)
DIRECT ELECTION OF SENATORS

The Senate of the United States shall be composed of two senators from each state, elected by the people thereof, for six years; and each senator shall have one vote. The electors in each state shall have the qualifications requisite for electors of the most numerous branch of the state legislatures.

When vacancies happen in the representation of any state in the Senate, the executive authority of such state shall issue writs of election to fill such vacancies: *Provided,* That the legislature of any state may empower the executive thereof to make temporary appointments until the people fill the vacancies by election as the legislature may direct.

This amendment shall not be so construed as to affect the election or term of any senator chosen before it becomes valid as part of the Constitution.

The Senate is made up of two senators from each state, elected by the people of the state (not by the state legislature) for six-year terms. Each senator has one vote. Citizens entitled to vote for representatives in the state legislatures may vote for senators.

The governor of a state calls an election to fill a vacancy among that state's senators. But the state legislature may allow the governor to appoint someone to fill the Senate vacancy until the election is held.

This amendment did not affect any election that had been held or the term of office of any senator in the Senate at the time the amendment was adopted.

AMENDMENT 18 (1919)
NATIONAL PROHIBITION

Sec. 1. After one year from the ratification of this article the manufacture, sale, or transportation of intoxicating liquors within, the importation thereof into, or the exportation thereof from the United States and all territory subject to the jurisdiction thereof for beverage purposes is hereby prohibited.

Sec. 2. The Congress and the several states shall have concurrent power to enforce this article by appropriate legislation.

Sec. 3. This article shall be inoperative unless it shall have been ratified as an amendment to the Constitution by the legislatures of the several states, as provided in the Constitution, within seven years from the date of the submission hereof to the states by the Congress.

One year after this amendment was ratified it became illegal to make, sell, or carry in the United States and its territories intoxicating liquors for drinking purposes. It became illegal to send such liquors out of the country and its territories or to bring such liquors into them. This amendment was declared in force on January 29, 1919.

Congress passed the Volstead Act to make this amendment effective. It defined the percentage of alcohol in intoxicating liquors and provided penalties for violations. The states and the national government were to share enforcement duties.

This amendment would not have become a part of the Constitution unless ratified by the legislatures of the states within seven years. The need for ratification within seven years was written into this and later amendments so that the government would not have many partially ratified amendments on the books.

AMENDMENT 19 (1920)
WOMEN'S SUFFRAGE

The right of citizens of the United States to vote shall not be denied or abridged by the United States or by any state on account of sex.

Congress shall have power to enforce this article by appropriate legislation.

Neither the United States nor any state has the right to keep a citizen from voting because she is a woman.

Congress has the power to make laws that will make this amendment effective.

AMENDMENT 20 (1933)
THE "LAME-DUCK" AMENDMENT

Sec. 1. The terms of the President and Vice-President shall end at noon on the twentieth day of January, and the terms of senators and representatives at noon on the third day of January, of the years in which such terms would have ended if this article had not been ratified; and the terms of their successors shall then begin.

Sec. 2. The Congress shall assemble at least once in every year, and such meeting shall begin at noon on the third day of January, unless they shall by law appoint a different day.

Sec. 3. If, at the time fixed for the beginning of the term of the President, the President-elect shall have died, the Vice-President-elect shall become President. If a President shall not have been chosen before the time fixed for the beginning of his term, or if the President-elect shall have failed to qualify, then the Vice-President-elect shall act as President until a President shall have qualified; and the Congress may by law provide for the case wherein neither a President-elect nor a Vice-President-elect shall have qualified, declaring who shall then act as President, or the manner in which one who is to act shall be selected, and such person shall act accordingly until a President or Vice-President shall have qualified.

Sec. 4. The Congress may by law provide for the case of the death of any of the persons from whom the House of Representatives may choose a President whenever the right of choice shall have devolved upon them, and for the case of the death of any of the persons from whom the Senate may choose a Vice-President whenever the right of choice shall have devolved upon them.

Sec. 5. Sections 1 and 2 shall take effect on the fifteenth day of October following the ratification of this article.

Sec. 6. This article shall be inoperative unless it shall have been ratified as an amendment to the Constitution by the legislatures of three-fourths of the several states within seven years from the date of its submission.

This amendment shortened the "lame-duck" period—the time between election and inauguration. The terms of office of President and Vice-President end at noon, January 20 (instead of March 4). The terms of office of senators and representatives end at noon, January 3, of the same years they would have ended if this amendment had not been made.

Congress must meet at least once a year. The meeting must begin at noon, January 3, unless another date is selected by law. The former date was the first Monday in December; this meant that new members of Congress would not normally meet until thirteen months after election.

If the person elected President dies before inauguration day, the person elected Vice-President becomes President. If a President has not been chosen by January 3, or if the person chosen is not qualified to be President, then the person elected Vice-President acts as President until a President has qualified. Congress may pass a law to determine who shall act as President if neither the person elected President nor the one elected Vice-President qualifies for the position. Congress may decide how this person shall be chosen.

Congress has the power to make a law that tells the House of Representatives what to do in case it must select a President and one of the candidates has died. Congress also has the power to make a law that tells the Senate what to do in case it must select a Vice-President and one of the candidates has died. (See Amendment 12.)

Sections 1 and 2 of this amendment became law on October 15 after three-fourths of the states had agreed to this amendment. This amendment was declared to be ratified on February 6, 1933.

AMENDMENT 21 (1933)
REPEAL OF PROHIBITION

Sec. 1. The eighteenth article of amendment to the Constitution of the United States is hereby repealed.

Sec. 2. The transportation or importation into any state, territory, or possession of the United States for delivery or use therein of intoxicating liquors, in violation of the laws thereof, is hereby prohibited.

Sec. 3. This article shall be inoperative unless it shall have been ratified as an amendment to the Constitution by conventions in the several states, as provided in the Constitution, within seven years from the date of the submission hereof to the states by the Congress.

This amendment repealed the Eighteenth Amendment. The national government could no longer prohibit the manufacture, sale, or transportation of intoxicating liquor. But if a state forbids bringing liquor for drinking purposes across its boundaries for use in that state, such carrying of liquor is a crime against the United States as well as against the state.

Congress required this amendment to be ratified by assemblies specially elected for that purpose. It is the only amendment adopted in this way. It was ratified on December 5, 1933.

AMENDMENT 22 (1951)
PRESIDENTIAL TERM OF OFFICE

Sec. 1. No person shall be elected to the office of the President more than twice, and no person who has held the office of President, or acted as President, for more than two years of a term to which some other person was elected President shall be elected to the office of the President more than once. But this article shall not apply to any person holding the office of President when this article was proposed by the Congress, and shall not prevent any person who may be holding the office of President, or acting as President, during the term within which this article becomes operative from holding the office of President or acting as President during the remainder of such term.

Sec. 2. This article shall be inoperative unless it shall have been ratified as an amendment to the Constitution by the legislatures of three-fourths of the several states within seven years from the date of its submission to the states by the Congress.

No person can have more than two terms as President. Holding the office of President, or acting as President, for more than two years will be considered as one full term. This article did not apply to Harry Truman, who was President at the time this amendment was proposed by Congress and ratified by the states.

AMENDMENT 23 (1961)
VOTING IN THE DISTRICT OF COLUMBIA

Sec. 1. The district constituting the seat of government of the United States shall appoint in such manner as the Congress may direct:

A number of electors of President and Vice-President equal to the whole number of senators and representatives in Congress to which the District would be entitled if it were a state, but in no event more than the least populous state; they shall be in addition to those appointed by the states, but they shall be considered, for the purposes of the election of President and Vice-President, to be electors appointed by a state; and they shall meet in the district and perform such duties as provided by the twelfth article of amendment.

Sec. 2. The Congress shall have power to enforce this article by appropriate legislation.

This amendment gave the District of Columbia the right to take part in the election of the President and Vice-President of the United States. Congress enacted legislation that provided for the direct election of electors by residents of the district. The number of electors was limited to no more than the number of electors from the state with the smallest population. In this way, the district was given three votes in the electoral college.

This amendment did not provide for representation in Congress or for a system of home-rule municipal government for the district.

AMENDMENT 24 (1964)
ABOLITION OF POLL TAXES

Sec. 1. The right of citizens of the United States to vote in any primary or other election for President or Vice-President, for electors for President or Vice-President, or for senator or representative in Congress, shall not be denied or abridged by the United States or any state by reason of failure to pay any poll tax or other tax.

Sec. 2. The Congress shall have the power to enforce this article by appropriate legislation.

This amendment prohibits any national or state law making the payment of a poll tax or any other tax a requirement for voting in a primary or general election of national officers, namely, President, Vice-President, electors of these, senators, and representatives in Congress.

AMENDMENT 25 (1967)
PRESIDENTIAL DISABILITY AND SUCCESSION

Sec. 1. In case of the removal of the President from office or his death or resignation, the Vice-President shall become President.

Sec. 2. Whenever there is a vacancy in the office of the Vice-President, the President shall nominate a Vice-President who shall take office upon confirmation by a majority vote of both houses of Congress.

Sec. 3. Whenever the President transmits to the president pro tempore of the Senate and the speaker of the House of Representatives his written declaration that he is unable to discharge the powers and duties of his office, and until he transmits to them a written declaration to the contrary, such powers and duties shall be discharged by the Vice-President as Acting President.

Sec. 4. Whenever the Vice-President and a majority of either the principal officers of the executive departments or of such other body as Congress may by law provide, transmit to the president pro tempore of the Senate and the speaker of the House of Representatives their written declaration that the President is unable to discharge the powers and duties of his office the Vice-President shall immediately assume the powers and duties of the office as Acting President.

Thereafter, when the President transmits to the president pro tempore of the Senate and the speaker of the House of Representatives his written declaration that no inability exists, he shall resume the powers and duties of his office unless the Vice-President and a majority of either the principal officers of the executive departments or of such other body as Congress may by law provide, transmit within four days to the president pro tempore of the Senate and the speaker of the House of Representatives their written declaration that the President is unable to discharge the powers and duties of his office. Thereupon Congress shall decide the issue, assembling within forty-eight hours for that purpose if not in session. If the Congress, within twenty-one days after receipt of the latter written declaration, or, if Congress is not in session, within twenty-one days after Congress is required to assemble, determines by two-thirds vote of both houses that the President is unable to discharge the powers and duties of his office, the Vice-President shall continue to discharge the same as Acting President; otherwise, the President shall resume the powers and duties of his office.

This amendment fills two gaps in the original Constitution: (1) It provides for filling the office of Vice-President in case of a vacancy in that office; the President is allowed to appoint a Vice-President, subject to confirmation by a vote of Congress. (2) It determines the existence and duration of the inability of the President to fulfill the powers and duties of office.

It provides that the President is to notify Congress if he or she is unable to perform official duties. Thereupon the Vice-President takes over and serves as Acting President. If a disabled President is unable or unwilling to notify Congress of his or her incapacity, the Vice-President, with approval of a majority of the Cabinet, makes such a declaration and becomes Acting President.

When the President recovers from a disability, he or she may so notify Congress and resume the powers and duties of office.

If the President's recovery appears doubtful, then the Vice-President with approval of a majority of the Cabinet (or of some other body designated by Congress) may challenge the President's declaration. The issue then goes to Congress. If two-thirds or more of each house votes against the President, the Vice-President continues to serve as Acting President; otherwise, the President resumes office.

AMENDMENT 26 (1971)
EIGHTEEN-YEAR-OLD VOTE

Sec. 1. The right of citizens of the United States, who are eighteen years of age or older, to vote shall not be denied or abridged by the United States or by any state on account of age.

Sec. 2. The Congress shall have power to enforce this article by appropriate legislation.

This amendment was hurriedly passed and ratified after the Supreme Court had held that eighteen-year-olds could not be barred from voting for national officers. The amendment extended the Court's ruling to all elections. Had this amendment not been passed, polling places would have had to have had separate ballots and voting lists for persons between eighteen and twenty-one and for those twenty-one and older.

Presidents, Vice-Presidents, and Secretaries of State

PRESIDENT	PARTY	STATE[2]	BORN	DIED	TERM OF OFFICE	VICE-PRESIDENT	SECRETARY OF STATE
George Washington	None	Virginia	1732	1799	1789–1797	John Adams	Thomas Jefferson Edmund Randolph Timothy Pickering
John Adams	Fed.	Massachusetts	1735	1826	1797–1801	Thomas Jefferson	Timothy Pickering John Marshall
Thomas Jefferson	Rep.[1]	Virginia	1743	1826	1801–1809	Aaron Burr George Clinton	James Madison
James Madison	Rep.[1]	Virginia	1751	1836	1809–1817	George Clinton Elbridge Gerry	Robert Smith James Monroe
James Monroe	Rep.[1]	Virginia	1758	1831	1817–1825	Daniel D. Tompkins	John Quincy Adams
John Quincy Adams	Rep.[1]	Massachusetts	1767	1848	1825–1829	John C. Calhoun	Henry Clay
Andrew Jackson	Dem.	Tennessee (S.C.)	1767	1845	1829–1837	John C. Calhoun Martin Van Buren	Martin Van Buren Edward Livingston Louis McLane John Forsyth
Martin Van Buren	Dem.	New York	1782	1862	1837–1841	Richard M. Johnson	John Forsyth
William Henry Harrison	Whig	Ohio (Va.)	1773	1841	1841	John Tyler	Daniel Webster
John Tyler	Whig[3]	Virginia	1790	1862	1841–1845	———	Daniel Webster Abel P. Upshur John C. Calhoun
James K. Polk	Dem.	Tennessee (N.C.)	1795	1849	1845–1849	George M. Dallas	John C. Calhoun James Buchanan
Zachary Taylor	Whig	Louisiana (Va.)	1784	1850	1849–1850	Millard Fillmore	John M. Clayton
Millard Fillmore	Whig	New York	1800	1874	1850–1853	———	Daniel Webster Edward Everett
Franklin Pierce	Dem.	New Hampshire	1804	1869	1853–1857	William R. King	William L. Marcy
James Buchanan	Dem.	Pennsylvania	1791	1868	1857–1861	John C. Breckinridge	Lewis Cass Jeremiah S. Black
Abraham Lincoln	Rep.	Illinois (Ky.)	1809	1865	1861–1865	Hannibal Hamlin Andrew Johnson	William H. Seward
Andrew Johnson	Rep.[4]	Tennessee (N.C.)	1808	1875	1865–1869	———	William H. Seward
Ulysses S. Grant	Rep.	Illinois (Ohio)	1822	1885	1869–1877	Schuyler Colfax Henry Wilson	Elihu Washburne Hamilton Fish

PRESIDENT	PARTY	STATE[2]	BORN	DIED	TERM OF OFFICE	VICE-PRESIDENT	SECRETARY OF STATE
Rutherford B. Hayes	Rep.	Ohio	1822	1893	1877–1881	William A. Wheeler	William M. Evarts
James A. Garfield	Rep.	Ohio	1831	1881	1881	Chester A. Arthur	James G. Blaine
Chester A. Arthur	Rep.	New York (Vt.)	1829	1886	1881–1885	——	James G. Blaine Frederick T. Frelinghuysen
Grover Cleveland	Dem.	New York (N.J.)	1837	1908	1885–1889	Thomas A. Hendricks	Thomas F. Bayard
Benjamin Harrison	Rep.	Indiana (Ohio)	1833	1901	1889–1893	Levi P. Morton	James G. Blaine John W. Foster
Grover Cleveland	Dem.	New York (N.J.)	1837	1908	1893–1897	Adlai E. Stevenson	Walter Q. Gresham Richard Olney
William McKinley	Rep.	Ohio	1843	1901	1897–1901	Garret A. Hobart Theodore Roosevelt	John Sherman William R. Day John Hay
Theodore Roosevelt	Rep.	New York	1858	1919	1901–1909	—— Charles Warren Fairbanks	John Hay Elihu Root Robert Bacon
William H. Taft	Rep.	Ohio	1857	1930	1909–1913	James S. Sherman	Philander C. Knox
Woodrow Wilson	Dem.	New Jersey (Va.)	1856	1924	1913–1921	Thomas R. Marshall	William Jennings Bryan Robert Lansing Bainbridge Colby
Warren G. Harding	Rep.	Ohio	1865	1923	1921–1923	Calvin Coolidge	Charles Evans Hughes
Calvin Coolidge	Rep.	Massachusetts (Vt.)	1872	1933	1923–1929	—— Charles G. Dawes	Charles Evans Hughes Frank B. Kellogg
Herbert C. Hoover	Rep.	California (Iowa)	1874	1964	1929–1933	Charles Curtis	Henry L. Stimson
Franklin D. Roosevelt	Dem.	New York	1882	1945	1933–1945	John N. Garner Henry A. Wallace Harry S Truman	Cordell Hull Edward R. Stettinius
Harry S Truman	Dem.	Missouri	1884	1972	1945–1953	—— Alben W. Barkley	Edward R. Stettinius James F. Byrnes George C. Marshall Dean G. Acheson
Dwight D. Eisenhower	Rep.	New York (Tex.) Pennsylvania	1890	1969	1953–1961	Richard M. Nixon	John Foster Dulles Christian A. Herter
John F. Kennedy	Dem.	Massachusetts	1917	1963	1961–1963	Lyndon B. Johnson	Dean Rusk
Lyndon B. Johnson	Dem.	Texas	1908	1973	1963–1969	—— Hubert H. Humphrey	Dean Rusk
Richard M. Nixon	Rep.	New York (Calif.)	1913		1969–	Spiro T. Agnew	William P. Rogers

[1] The Jeffersonians called themselves Republicans. The party is often called the Democratic-Republican party because in the 1820's it became the Democratic party.
[2] State of residence at time of election. If state of birth is different, it is shown in parentheses.
[3] Democrat but elected on Whig ticket
[4] Democrat but elected on the ticket of the National Union party, which was the name of Republican party during the Civil War.

Bibliographies

An asterisk * indicates a paperbound book.

**UNIT ONE
THE PATH TO INDEPENDENCE 1492–1783**

Adams, James Truslow. *The Founding of New England.* Peter Smith. Little, Brown.*

———. *Provincial Society: 1690–1763* (A History of American Life, vol. 3). Quadrangle.*

The American Heritage Book of the Revolution. Bruce Catton (ed.). Simon & Schuster. Dell.*

Boorstin, Daniel J. *The Americans: The Colonial Experience.* Random House, 1958. Random House.*

Bradford, William (ed.). *Of Plymouth Plantation: The Pilgrims in America.* Abridged ed. G. P. Putnam's.*

Cooper, James Fenimore. *The Last of the Mohicans.* New American Library.*

De Voto, Bernard. *The Course of Empire.* Houghton Mifflin, 1952. Houghton Mifflin.*

Franklin, Benjamin. *The Autobiography, and Other Writings of Benjamin Franklin.* Russel B. Nye (ed.). Houghton Mifflin, 1963.

Gallman, Robert E. *Developing the American Colonies: 1607–1783* (Economic Forces in American History series). Scott, Foresman, 1964.*

Jefferson, Thomas. *Notes on the State of Virginia.* William Peden (ed.). W. W. Norton, 1972.*

Morgan, Edmund S. *The Birth of the Republic: 1763–1789.* University of Chicago Press, 1956. University of Chicago Press.*

Morison, Samuel Eliot. *The Story of the "Old Colony" of New Plymouth: 1620–1692.* Alfred A. Knopf, 1956.

Morris, Richard B. *The New World: Prehistory to 1774* (The Life History of the United States, vol. 1). Time-Life Books, 1963.

The Parkman Reader. Samuel Eliot Morison (ed.). Little, Brown, 1955. Little, Brown.*

Peckham, Howard H. *The War for Independence: A Military History.* University of Chicago Press, 1958. University of Chicago Press.*

Scheer, George F., and Hugh F. Rankin (eds.). *Rebels and Redcoats.* World Publishing, 1957. New American Library.*

Smith, Bradford. *Captain John Smith.* J. B. Lippincott, 1953.

Van Alstyne, Richard. *Empire and Independence: International History of the American Revolution.* John Wiley, 1965. John Wiley.*

Vaughan, Alden T. *New England Frontier: Indians and Puritans, 1620–1675.* Little, Brown, 1965.*

Wahlke, John C. (ed.). *The Causes of the American Revolution.* Rev. ed. D. C. Heath, 1962.*

Wright, Louis B. *The Cultural Life of the American Colonies: 1607–1763.* Harper & Row, 1957. Harper & Row.*

———. *Everyday Life in Colonial America.* G. P. Putnam's, 1966.

**UNIT TWO
ESTABLISHING A NEW NATION 1783–1815**

Brown, Stuart Gerry. *Thomas Jefferson* (Great American Thinkers series). Twayne.

Corwin, Edward S. *The Constitution and What It Means Today.* Atheneum, 1963.*

Cunningham, Noble E., Jr. (ed.). *The Making of the American Party System: 1789–1809.* Prentice-Hall, 1965.*

DeConde, Alexander. *The Quasi-War: The Politics and Diplomacy of the Undeclared War with France, 1797–1801.* Charles Scribner's, 1966.

Dos Passos, John. *Men Who Made the Nation.* Doubleday, 1957.

Forester, C. S. *The Age of Fighting Sail.* Doubleday, 1956.

Jefferson, Thomas. *The Autobiography of Thomas Jefferson.* G. P. Putnam's, 1959.*

Miller, John C. *Crisis in Freedom: The Alien and Sedition Acts.* Little, Brown, 1964.*

Padover, Saul K. *The Living United States Constitution.* Rev. ed. New American Library.*

Perkins, Bradford (ed.). *The Causes of the War of 1812: National Honor or National Interest?* Holt, Rinehart & Winston, 1962.*

Rutland, Robert A. *Birth of the Bill of Rights: 1776–1791.* University of North Carolina Press, 1955. Macmillan.*

———. *The Ordeal of the Constitution: The Antifederalists and the Ratification Struggle of 1787–1788.* University of Oklahoma Press, 1966.

Tomkins, Calvin. *The Lewis and Clark Trail.* Harper & Row, 1965.

Van Every, Dale. *Ark of Empire: The American Frontier, 1784–1803.* New American Library.*

White, Patrick C. *A Nation on Trial: America and the War of 1812.* John Wiley, 1965. John Wiley.*

UNIT THREE
LIFE IN A GROWING NATION   1815–1850

Bristow, Gwen. *Jubilee Trail.* Thomas Y. Crowell, 1969. Popular Library.*

Burt, Jesse, and Robert B. Ferguson. *Indians of the Southeast: Then and Now.* Abingdon, 1973.

Commager, Henry Steele. *The Era of Reform: 1830–1860.* Van Nostrand Reinhold, 1960.*

Current, Richard N. *Daniel Webster and the Rise of National Conservatism* (The Library of American Biography). Little, Brown, 1962.*

———. *John C. Calhoun* (Great American Thinkers series). Twayne.*

Dana, Richard Henry. *Two Years Before the Mast.* Dodd, Mead. New American Library.*

De Voto, Bernard. *Across the Wide Missouri.* Houghton Mifflin, 1947. Houghton Mifflin.*

———. *The Year of Decision: 1846.* Houghton Mifflin, 1950. Houghton Mifflin.*

Guthrie, A. B., Jr. *The Big Sky.* Houghton Mifflin, 1947. Houghton Mifflin.*

Hawkins, Hugh (ed.). *The Abolitionists: Immediatism and the Questioning of Means* (Problems in American Civilization series). D. C. Heath, 1964.*

Henry, Robert Selph. *The Story of the Mexican War* (American Classics series). Frederick Ungar, 1960.

James, Marquis. *The Raven: A Biography of Sam Houston.* Paperback Library, 1971.*

Jayne, Mitchell F. *Old Fish Hawk.* J. B. Lippincott, 1970. Pocket Books.*

Johnson, Gerald W. *The Congress.* William Morrow, 1963.

———. *The Supreme Court.* William Morrow, 1962.

Johnson, William Weber. *The Birth of Texas.* Houghton Mifflin, 1960.

Lavender, David. *Westward Vision: The Story of the Oregon Trail* (American Trails Library series). A. B. Guthrie, Jr. (ed.). McGraw-Hill, 1963.*

Monaghan, Jay (ed.). *The Book of the American West.* Simon & Schuster, 1963.*

Parkman, Francis. *The Oregon Trail.* Dodd, Mead. New American Library.*

Perkins, Dexter. *A History of the Monroe Doctrine.* Rev. ed. Little, Brown, 1955. Little, Brown.*

Remini, Robert V. *The Election of Andrew Jackson* (Critical Periods of History series). J. B. Lippincott, 1963.*

Ruiz, Ramón Eduardo (ed.). *The Mexican War: Was It Manifest Destiny?* Holt, Rinehart & Winston, 1963.*

Schlesinger, Arthur M., Jr. *The Age of Jackson.* Little, Brown, 1945. Little, Brown.*

Sellers, Charles. *Andrew Jackson, Nullification, and the State-Rights Tradition.* Rand McNally, 1963.*

Sinclair, Andrew. *The Emancipation of the American Woman* (original title, *The Better Half*). Harper & Row, 1965. Harper & Row.*

Stegner, Wallace. *The Gathering of Zion: The Story of the Mormon Trail* (American Trails Library series). McGraw-Hill, 1964. McGraw-Hill.*

Tinkle, Lon. *The Alamo.* New American Library, 1967.*

Turner, Frederick Jackson. *The Frontier in American History.* Holt, Rinehart & Winston.*

Van Every, Dale. *The Final Challenge: The American Frontier, 1804–1845.* William Morrow, 1964.

Weisberger, Bernard A. *Abolitionism: Disrupter of the Democratic System or Agent of Progress?* (Berkeley Readings in American History series, vol. 8). Rand McNally, 1963.*

UNIT FOUR
DIVISION AND REUNION   1850–1877

The American Heritage Picture History of the Civil War. Narrative by Bruce Catton. American Heritage, 1960.

Bishop, Jim. *The Day Lincoln Was Shot.* Harper & Row, 1955. Harper & Row.*

Buckmaster, Henrietta. *Freedom Bound: A Handbook of Negro Liberty.* Macmillan, 1965. Macmillan.*

Catton, Bruce. *The Coming Fury* (Centennial History of the Civil War, vol. 1); *Terrible Swift Sword* (vol. 2); *Never Call Retreat* (vol. 3). Doubleday, 1961. Pocket Books.*

———. *A Stillness at Appomattox.* Doubleday, 1953. Pocket Books.*

———. *This Hallowed Ground: The Story of the Union Side of the Civil War.* Doubleday. Pocket Books.*

Commager, Henry Steele. *The Defeat of the Confederacy.* Van Nostrand Reinhold, 1964.*

Cramer, Kenyon C. *The Causes of War: The American Revolution, the Civil War, and World War I* (Scott Foresman Problems in American History). Scott, Foresman, 1965.*

Crane, Stephen. *The Red Badge of Courage.* Modern Library.*

Current, Richard N. *Lincoln and the First Shot* (Critical Periods of History series). J. B. Lippincott, 1964.*

Donovan, Frank. *Mister Lincoln's Proclamation: The Story Behind the Emancipation Proclamation.* Dodd, Mead, 1964.

Franklin, John Hope. *Reconstruction after the Civil War.* University of Chicago Press, 1961.*

Freeman, Douglas Southall. *Lee of Virginia.* Charles Scribner's, 1958.

Greeley, Horace. *An Overland Journey from New York to San Francisco* (American Past series). Charles T. Duncan (ed.). Alfred A. Knopf. Ballantine Books.*

Leech, Margaret. *Reveille in Washington.* Grosset & Dunlap.*

McKitrick, Eric L. (ed.). *Slavery Defended: Views of the Old South.* Prentice-Hall, 1963.*

McPherson, James (ed.). *The Negroes' Civil War: How American Negroes Felt and Acted.* Random House.*

McWhiney, Grady. *Reconstruction and the Freedmen* (Berkeley Readings in American History series). Rand McNally, 1963.*

Mitchell, Margaret. *Gone With the Wind.* Macmillan, 1936. Pocket Books.*

Momaday, N. Scott. *The Way to Rainy Mountain.* University of New Mexico Press, 1969.

Nevins, Allan. *The War for the Union* (Ordeal of the Union, vols. 4–8). Charles Scribner's, 1959–1960, and 1971.

Parrish, Anne. *A Clouded Star.* Harper & Row, 1948.

Quarles, Benjamin (ed.). *Narrative of the Life of Frederick Douglass, An American Slave.* Harvard University Press, 1960. New American Library.*

Roland, Charles P. *The Confederacy.* University of Chicago Press, 1960.*

Rozwenc, Edwin C. *Slavery As a Cause of the Civil War* (Problems in American Civilization series). Rev. ed. D. C. Heath, 1963.*

———. *Reconstruction in the South* (Problems in American Civilization series). D. C. Heath, 1952.*

Sandburg, Carl. *Abraham Lincoln: The Prairie Years and the War Years.* Harcourt Brace Jovanovich. Dell.*

Scott, Anne Firor. *The Southern Lady: From Pedestal to Politics, 1830–1930.* University of Chicago Press, 1970.*

Stampp, Kenneth M. *Era of Reconstruction: 1865–1877.* Alfred A. Knopf, 1965. Random House.*

——— (ed.). *The Causes of the Civil War.* Rev. ed. Prentice-Hall, 1965.*

———. *The Peculiar Institution.* Alfred A. Knopf, 1956. Random House.*

Stowe, Harriet Beecher. *Uncle Tom's Cabin.* Harper & Row.*

Wiley, Bell Irvin. *The Plain People of the Confederacy.* Quadrangle.*

Williams, T. Harry. *The Union Sundered* (The Life History of the United States, vol. 5). Time-Life Books, 1963.

UNIT FIVE
PROBLEMS OF AN INDUSTRIAL NATION 1877–1900

Adams, Andy. *The Log of a Cowboy.* University of Nebraska Press.*

Addams, Jane. *Twenty Years at Hull-House.* New American Library.*

Aldrich, Bess Streeter. *A Lantern in Her Hand.* Grosset & Dunlap, 1928. Grosset & Dunlap.*

Bellamy, Edward. *Looking Backward.* New American Library.*

Billington, Ray A. *The Far Western Frontier: 1830–1860.* Harper & Row, 1956. Harper & Row.*

Black Elk Speaks. As told through John G. Neihardt. University of Nebraska Press, 1961. Pocket Books.*

Bontemps, Arna. *One Hundred Years of Negro Freedom.* Dodd, Mead, 1961. Apollo Editions.*

Cather, Willa. *My Antonia.* Houghton Mifflin, 1918. Houghton Mifflin.*

Davis, Lance E. *The Growth of Industrial Enterprise: 1860–1914* (Economic Forces in American History series). Scott, Foresman, 1964.*

Fanning, Leonard M. *Titans of Business.* J. B. Lippincott, 1964.

Ferber, Edna. *Cimarron.* Doubleday, 1951. Fawcett World.*

Flexner, Eleanor. *Century of Struggle: The Woman's Rights Movement in the United States.* Harvard University Press, 1968. Atheneum.*

Green, Constance. *The Rise of Urban America.* Harper & Row, 1965. Harper & Row.*

Greene, Theodore P. (ed.). *American Imperialism in 1898* (Problems in American Civilization series). D. C. Heath, 1955.*

Hagan, William T. *American Indians.* University of Chicago Press, 1961. University of Chicago Press.*

Handlin, Oscar. *The Uprooted.* Little, Brown, 1951. Grosset & Dunlap.*

Hawkins, Hugh (ed.). *Booker T. Washington and His Critics: The Problem of Negro Leadership* (Problems in American Civilization series). D. C. Heath, 1962.*

Hoogenboom, Ari. *Spoilsmen and Reformers* (Berkeley Readings in American History series). Rand McNally, 1963.*

Iman, Raymond S., and Thomas W. Koch. *Labor in American Society* (Scott Foresman Problems in American History). Scott, Foresman, 1965.*

Josephson, Matthew. *The Robber Barons.* Harcourt Brace Jovanovich.*

Kennedy, Gail (ed.). *Democracy and the Gospel of Wealth* (Problems in American Civilization series). D. C. Heath, 1949.*

Lewis, Arthur H. *Lament for the Molly Maguires.* Harcourt Brace Jovanovich, 1964. Pocket Books.*

Meier, August and Elliott Rudwick (eds.). *The Making of Black America* (Studies in American Life series). Atheneum, 1969.*

Riis, Jacob. *How the Other Half Lives: Studies Among the Tenements of New York.* Hill & Wang.*

Rölvaag, Ole Edvart. *Giants in the Earth: A Saga of the Prairie.* Harper & Row, 1927. Harper & Row.*

Taylor, George Rogers. *The Turner Thesis Concerning the Role of the Frontier in American History* (Problems in American Civilization series). D. C. Heath.*

Webb, Walter Prescott. *The Great Plains.* Grossett & Dunlap, 1957.*

Wister, Owen. *The Virginian.* Macmillan, 1925. Pocket Books.*

Woodward, C. Vann. *The Strange Career of Jim Crow.* Oxford University Press, 1955.

UNIT SIX
THE RISE OF A WORLD POWER 1900–1920

Aaron, Daniel. *Men of Good Hope: A Story of American Progressives.* Oxford University Press, 1951. Oxford University Press.*

Adams, Henry. *The Education of Henry Adams: An Autobiography.* Houghton Mifflin. Houghton Mifflin.*

Allen, Frederick Lewis. *The Great Pierpont Morgan.* Harper & Row.*

Baldwin, Hanson W. *World War I.* Grove Press, 1963.

Beale, Howard K. *Theodore Roosevelt and the Rise of America to World Power.* Macmillan, 1966.*

Dos Passos, John. *Mister Wilson's War.* Doubleday, 1962.

Faulkner, Harold U. *The Quest for Social Justice: 1898–1914.* Quadrangle.*

Hofstadter, Richard. *The Age of Reform: From Bryan to F.D.R.* Random House.*

———. *The Progressive Movement: 1900–1915.* Prentice-Hall, 1964.*

Iman, Raymond S., and Thomas W. Koch. *Labor in American Society* (Scott Foresman Problems in American History). Scott, Foresman, 1965.*

Leech, Margaret. *In the Days of McKinley.* Harper & Row, 1959.

Leuchtenburg, William E. *The Perils of Prosperity: 1914–1932.* University of Chicago Press.*

Link, Arthur S. *Woodrow Wilson and the Progressive Era: 1910–1917.* Harper & Row, 1954. Harper & Row.*

Lord, Walter. *The Good Years.* Harper & Row, 1960. Bantam.*

Lyons, Thomas T. *Realism and Idealism in Wilson's Peace Program.* D. C. Heath, 1965.*

May, Ernest R. *Progressive Era* (The Life History of the United States, vol. 9). Time-Life Books, 1964.

Meltzer, Milton (ed.). *In Their Own Words: A History of the American Negro, 1865–1916.* Thomas Y. Crowell, 1965.

Norris, Frank. *The Octopus.* Doubleday. Bantam.*

Remarque, Erich Maria. *All Quiet on the Western Front.* Little, Brown, 1929. Fawcett World.*

Sinclair, Andrew. *Era of Excess: A Social History of the Prohibition Movment.* Harper & Row.*

Sinclair, Upton. *The Jungle.* New American Library.*

Steffens, Lincoln. *The Autobiography of Lincoln Steffens.* Harcourt Brace Jovanovich. Harcourt Brace Jovanovich.*

———. *The Shame of the Cities.* Hill & Wang.*

Sullivan, Mark. *Our Times, the United States, 1900–1925.* 3 volumes. Charles Scribner's, 1926–1935. Charles Scribner's.*

Tuchman, Barbara. *The Guns of August.* Macmillan, 1962. Dell.*

———. *The Proud Tower.* Macmillan, 1966. Bantam.*

Washington, Booker T. *Up From Slavery.* Bantam.*

Wheeler, Thomas C. (ed.). *The Immigrant Experience.* Dial Press, 1971.

UNIT SEVEN
THE TIME BETWEEN THE WARS 1920–1941

Allen, Frederick Lewis. *Only Yesterday.* Harper & Row. Harper & Row.*

———. *Since Yesterday: The 1930's in America.* Harper & Row.*

———. *The Big Change, 1900–1950.* Bantam.*

Bird, Caroline. *The Invisible Scar.* David McKay, 1965. McKay.*

Burns, James M. *Roosevelt: The Lion and the Fox.* Harcourt Brace Jovanovich. Harcourt Brace Jovanovich.*

Congdon, Don (ed.). *The Thirties: A Time to Remember.* Simon & Schuster, 1970.*

Cronon, E. David (ed.). *Labor and the New Deal.* Rand McNally, 1963.*

Dos Passos, John. *U.S.A.* Houghton Mifflin. Houghton Mifflin.*

Freidel, Frank (ed.). *The New Deal and the American People.* Prentice-Hall, 1964.*

Handlin, Oscar. *Al Smith and His America.* Little, Brown, 1958. Little, Brown.*

Keller, Morton (ed.). *The New Deal: What Was It?* Holt, Rinehart & Winston, 1963.*

Lash, Joseph P. *Eleanor and Franklin.* W. W. Norton, 1971. New American Library.*

Lawrence, Jerome, and Robert E. Lee. *Inherit the Wind.* Bantam.*

Leuchtenburg, William E. *Franklin D. Roosevelt and the New Deal, 1932–1940.* Harper & Row, 1963. Harper & Row.*

Lewis, Sinclair. *Babbitt.* Harcourt Brace Jovanovich. New American Library.*

———. *Main Street.* Harcourt Brace Jovanovich. New American Library.*

Lindbergh, Charles A. *The Spirit of St. Louis.* Charles Scribner's. Charles Scribner's.*

May, Ernest R. *War, Boom and Bust: 1917–1932* (The Life History of the United States series, vol. 10). Time-Life Books, 1964.

McDougall, Duncan. *World Power and New Problems, 1914–1930* (Economic Forces in American History). Scott, Foresman, 1964.*

Merrill, Edward H. *Responses to Economic Collapse: The Great Depression of the 1930's.* D. C. Heath, 1964.*

Mowry, George E. (ed.). *The Twenties: Fords, Flappers, and Fanatics.* Prentice-Hall, 1963.*

Schlesinger, Arthur M., Jr. *The Crisis of the Old Order: 1919–1933* (The Age of Roosevelt, vol. 1); *The Coming of the New Deal* (vol. 2); *The Politics of Upheaval* (vol. 3). Houghton Mifflin, 1957, 1959, 1960. Houghton Mifflin.*

Smolensky, Eugene. *Adjustments to Depression and War, 1930–1945* (Economic Forces in American History). Scott, Foresman, 1964.*

Steinbeck, John. *The Grapes of Wrath.* Viking Press, 1939. Viking Press.*

Waller, George M. (ed.). *Pearl Harbor: Roosevelt and the Coming of the War* (Problems in American Civilization series). Rev. ed. D. C. Heath, 1965.*

UNIT EIGHT
HOT AND COLD WARS 1941–1960

Baruch, Bernard. *Baruch: My Own Story.* Holt, Rinehart & Winston, 1957.

Bradley, Omar N. *A Soldier's Story.* Popular Library.*

Buchanan, A. Russell. *The United States and World War II* (New American Nation series). 2 vols. Harper & Row, 1964. Harper & Row.*

Donovan, Robert J. *PT-109, John F. Kennedy in World War II.* McGraw-Hill, 1961. Fawcett World.*

Eisenhower, Dwight D. *Crusade in Europe.* Doubleday, 1948.

———. *The White House Years: Mandate for Change, 1953–1956.* Doubleday. New American Library.*

———. *The White House Years: Waging Peace, 1956–1961.* Doubleday.

Faber, Harold. *Soldier and Statesman: General George C. Marshall.* Farrar, Straus & Giroux, 1964.

Forester, C. S. *Sink the Bismarck!* Bantam.*

Goldman, Eric F. *The Crucial Decade and After: America 1945–1960.* Random House.*

Graebner, Norman A. *Cold War Diplomacy: American Foreign Policy, 1945–1960.* Van Nostrand Reinhold, 1962.*

Hersey, John R. *Hiroshima.* Alfred A. Knopf. Bantam.*

Hine, Al, and S. L. A. Marshall. *D-Day: The Invasion of Europe* (American Heritage Adventures in History series). American Heritage, 1962.

Lamont, Lansing. *Day of Trinity.* Atheneum, 1965.

Lord, Walter. *Day of Infamy.* Holt, Rinehart & Winston, 1957. Bantam.*

MacArthur, Douglas. *Reminiscenses.* McGraw-Hill, 1964.

Morison, Samuel Eliot. *The Two-Ocean War: A Short History of the United States Navy in the Second World War.* Little, Brown, 1963. Ballantine.*

Newcomb, Richard F. *Iwo Jima.* Holt, Rinehart & Winston, 1965.

Potter, Charles E. *Days of Shame.* New American Library, 1971.*

Rovere, Richard. *Senator Joe McCarthy.* World Publishing.*

Ryan, Cornelius. *The Longest Day: June 6, 1944.* Simon & Schuster, 1959. Fawcett World.*

Snyder, Louis L. *The War: A Concise History, 1939–1945.* Simon & Schuster, 1960.

Söderberg, Sten. *Hammarskjöld: A Pictorial Biography.* Viking Press, 1962.

Toland, John. *But Not in Shame: The Six Months After Pearl Harbor.* Random House, 1961. New American Library.*

Truman, Margaret. *Harry S. Truman.* William Morrow, 1973.

Whyte, William H., Jr. *The Organization Man.* Simon & Schuster, 1956. Doubleday.*

UNIT NINE
CHALLENGES OF THE SPACE AGE 1960-1972

Abel, Elie. *The Missile Crisis.* J. B. Lippincott, 1966. Bantam.*

Bird, Caroline. *Born Female.* David McKay, 1968. Pocket Books.*

Drucker, Peter. *The Age of Discontinuity.* Harper & Row, 1969.

Farmer, James. *Freedom—When?* Random House, 1966.

Ford, Gerald, and John R. Stiles. *Portrait of the Assassin.* Simon & Schuster, 1965.

Galbraith, John Kenneth. *The New Industrial State.* Houghton Mifflin, 1967. Houghton Mifflin.*

Halberstam, David. *The Best and The Brightest.* Random House, 1972. Random House.*

Hunter, Sam. *American Painting of the Twentieth Century.* Harry N. Abrams, 1972.

Kennedy, John F. *The Burden and the Glory.* Edited by Allan Nevins. Harper & Row, 1964.

King, Martin Luther, Jr. *Where Do We Go From Here: Chaos or Community?* Harper & Row, 1967. Beacon Press.*

———. *Why We Can't Wait.* Harper & Row, 1964. New American Library.*

Lewis, Oscar. *La Vida: A Puerto Rican Family in the Culture of Poverty—San Juan and New York.* Random House, 1965.

Malcolm X with Alex Haley. *Autobiography of Malcolm X.* Grove Press, 1965. Grove Press.*

McLuhan, Marshall. *Understanding Media.* New American Library, 1971.*

Nader, Ralph. *Unsafe at Any Speed.* Rev. ed. Grossman Publishers, 1972.

Packard, Vance. *The Hidden Persuaders.* Pocket Books.*

———. *The Waste Makers.* Pocket Books.*

Schlesinger, Arthur M., Jr. *A Thousand Days: John F. Kennedy in the White House.* Houghton Mifflin, 1965. Fawcett World.*

Silberman, Charles E. *Crisis in Black and White.* Random House, 1964.

Sorensen, Theodore C. *Decision-Making in the White House.* Columbia University Press, 1963.*

Toffler, Alvin. *Future Shock.* Random House, 1970. Bantam.*

Udall, Stewart L. *The Quiet Crisis.* Holt, Rinehart & Winston, 1963. Avon.*

The U.S. Overseas: Puerto Rico and the Territories. The Editors, Time-Life Library of America. Time-Life Books, 1969.

Walsh, William B. *A Ship Called "Hope."* E. P. Dutton, 1964.

Ward, Barbara. *The Rich Nations and the Poor Nations.* W. W. Norton, 1962. W. W. Norton.*

———, and René Dubos. *Only One Earth.* W. W. Norton, 1972.

Warren Commission. *Concise Compendium of the Warren Commission Report on the Assassination of John F. Kennedy.* Popular Library.*

Acknowledgments

COVER AND TITLE PAGE

The pictures on the cover and title page spell out the words WE THE PEOPLE. Credits for the letters of those words are as follows:

W Philadelphia Museum of Art: Given by John T. Morris. **E** *The Hunting Party,* artist unknown. Courtesy Mr. and Mrs. Samuel Schwartz. **TH** *Wall Street, 1857,* by James H. Cafferty and Charles G. Rosenberg. Courtesy Museum of the City of New York. **E** Denver Public Library. **P** Jan Nacio Brown, BBM Associates. **EO** *Steelworkers Noontime,* by Thomas P. Anshutz. Courtesy of Kennedy Galleries, Inc. **P** *Mrs. Mayer and Daughter,* by Ammi Phillips. Courtesy St. Louis Art Museum. **L** Photo Researchers. **E** NASA.

The following list shows the sources from which other illustrations were obtained. Positions are indicated thus: (t) top, (c) center, (b) bottom, (l) left, (r) right.

UNIT ONE
12 *The Manner of Their Fishing* by John White, around 1585, Courtesy of the Trustees, The British Museum. **14** Library of Congress.

Chapter 1
18 Scenes of Life in Secoton, a North Carolina Village, by Theodore deBry, 1590. From: *Narrative of the First Plantation of Virginia,* by Thomas Hariot, 1588. Rare Book Division, The New York Public Library. Astor, Lenox, and Tilden Foundations. **19** Map of Mexico and Pacific from Guillaume LeTestu, *Cosmographie Universelle,* 1555. Bibliothèque du Ministère des Armées, Paris, photo Giraudon. **23** Trappers of Davis Strait. From *Orbis Habitabilis,* Carolus Allaro. Rare Book Division, The New York Public Library. Astor, Lenox, and Tilden Foundations. **24** *The Studthuy of New York in 1679.* Courtesy of the New-York Historical Society, New York City. **27** Martyn, *Reasons for Establishing the Colony of Georgia,* 1733. Courtesy of The Newberry Library, Chicago. **28** Library of Congress. **31** Chandler Wedding Tapestry, American Antiquarian Society. **33** "Early to Bed and Early to Rise," *Poor Richard Illustrated.* Yale University Library. **35** Engraving in John Trumbull, *M'Fingal,* 1795. Library of Congress. **37** "One of the Mississippi Bubbles," John Law's Concession at New Biloxi, 1720. Drawing by Jean Baptiste Michel Le Bouteux. The Newberry Library, Chicago. E. E. Ayer Collection.

Chapter 2
40 Library of Congress. **42** From the Pennsylvania *Journal,* 1765, The Colonial Williamsburg Collection. **43** (t) The John Work Garrett Library of The Johns Hopkins University. **43** (b) *The Fishing Lady,* 18th-century needlepoint, Courtesy Museum of Fine Arts, Boston. **44** From the *Boston Gazette & Country Journal,* March 12, 1770, The Newberry Library, Chicago. **45** Culver Pictures. **46** Library of Congress. **48** *Minuteman Preparing For War,* around 1776. *Family Album for Americans,* Ridge Press, Inc. **49** (t) *The Battle of Lexington,* by Amos Doolittle, 1775, The Connecticut Historical Society. **49** (c) *The Battle of Lexington,* by Pendleton, 1830, The Lexington Historical Society. **49** (b) *The Dawn of Liberty,* by Henry Sandham, 1866, The Lexington Historical Society. **53** *Mrs. Philip Schuyler Setting Grain Fields on Fire,* Courtesy *American History Illustrated.* **57** *Francis Marion's (Swamp Fox) Partisans Crossing the Pee Dee River,* by William Ranney. Collection of Mrs. Preston Davie. **61** National Maritime Museum.

UNIT TWO
64 *Fourth of July Celebration,* by Krimmel. The Historical Society of Pennsylvania.

Chapter 3
68 *Early American Court,* by Lewis Miller, 1804. Collection of The Historical Society of York County in York, Pennsylvania. **69** Birth Certificate (detail), 1789, The Metropolitan Museum of Art, Gift of Mrs. Robert W. deForest, 1933. Photograph by Robert S. Crandall. **71** *Farm Scene, 18th Century,* by Edward Hicks, 1845. Abby Aldrich Rockefeller Folk Art Collection. **72–73** T. Astley, *A New and General Collection of Voyages,* Vol. 3, 1745–47. Courtesy of The Newberry Library, Chicago. **76** An American Log-House, Victor Collot, *Voyage Dans L'Amerique . . . , 1826.* Rare Book Division, The New York Public Library. Astor, Lenox, and Tilden Foundations. **79** Indians at Carmel's Mission, with Franciscan friars, to welcome the Comte de la Perouse's visiting French scientific expedition. Museo Naval, Madrid. **81** *Hotel Cook Baking Bread,* by Lewis Miller, 1800. Collection of The Historical Society of York County in York, Pennsylvania. **89** Brown Brothers.

Chapter 4
91 *Pennington Mills,* Baltimore, by Francis Guy, 1804. Collection of Peabody Institute of the City of Baltimore. **93** *A Newgate Convict,* Brunton, The Connecticut Historical Society. **96** *Christening the Baby,* by Lewis Miller, 1799. Collection of The Historical Society of York County in York, Pennsylvania. **97** *Inside the Old Lutheran Church in 1800, York, Pennsylvania,* by Lewis Miller. Collection of The Historical Society of York County in York, Pennsylvania. **100–101** *The Old Plantation,* artist unknown, 1800. Abby Aldrich Rockefeller Folk Art Collection. **105** *Frigate Constellation,* 1799, Franklin D. Roosevelt Library, Hyde Park, New York. **109** *Wooden Tape Loom (dyer),* Lewis Miller. Collection of The Historical Society of York County in York, Pennsylvania. **110** *A Tollgate On the Baltimore-Reisterstown Road,* by Francis Blackwell Mayer. The Metropolitan Museum of Art.

Chapter 5
112 "Mad Tom (Jefferson) in a Rage," around 1802. This item is reproduced by permission of The Henry Huntington Library, San Marino, California. **115** *Night Life in Philadelphia,* by Pavel Petrovich, 1793. The Metropolitan Museum of Art. Photograph

by Robert S. Crandall. **119** *The Water Color Class,* 19th century, anonymous American. Courtesy of The Art Institute of Chicago. **121** *Passenger Pigeon,* Audubon. Courtesy of The New-York Historical Society, New York City. **122–123** *Death of Tecumseh,* H. M. Brackenridge. History of the Late War between the United States and Great Britain, 1818. Courtesy of The Newberry Library, Chicago. **125** *Negroes in Front of the Bank of Pennsylvania,* by Paul Svinin. The Metropolitan Museum of Art, Rogers Fund, 1942. **127** (t) *The Balloon Almanac,* printed by John Steele, Philadelphia, 1786. American Antiquarian Society. **127** (b) *Entertainment at the Yearly Market,* by Lewis Miller, 1801. Collection of The Historical Society of York County in York, Pennsylvania. **128–129** *Mission San Carlos Del Rio Carmelo,* by Oriana Day. Published by permission of the M. H. de Young Memorial Museum, San Francisco.

UNIT THREE
132 *War News from Mexico,* by Caton Woodville, around 1846. National Academy of Design.

Chapter 6
136 *City of Washington from Beyond the Navy Yard,* by W. J. Bennett, 1833. I. N. Phelps Stokes Collection, Prints Division, The New York Public Library. Astor, Lenox, and Tilden Foundations. **137** *The Book Bindery,* anonymous American, mid-19th century. M. and M. Karolik Collection, Museum of Fine Arts, Boston. **138** Glenbow-Alberta Institute. **139** (t) *American Log-House, Snake Fence,* by John Hackett, 1822. The Hudson's Bay Company. **139** (b) *Sowing Grain at Bishop Hill (Illinois),* by Olaf Krans. Department of Conservation, Bishop Hill, Illinois. **141** (t) *The Plantation,* artist unknown, around 1825. The Metropolitan Museum of Art, Gift of Edgar William and Bernice Chrysler Garbisch, 1963. **141** (bl) Old Dartmouth Historical Society, Whaling Museum, New Bedford, Massachusetts. **141** (br) *Capturing a Sperm Whale.* Courtesy of The New-York Historical Society, New York City. **143** *The Yankee Pedlar,* 19th century. Collection of the IBM Corporation, courtesy American Heritage Publishing Company. **145** *Junction of the Erie and Northern Canals,* by J. Hill, around 1830–1832. Courtesy of The New-York Historical Society, New York City. **149** Soil Conservation Service Photo. **151** Library of Congress.

Chapter 7
158 *An Election Scene During the Harrison-Van Buren Campaign, 1840,* by Francis H. Schell. The Franklin D. Roosevelt Library, Hyde Park, New York. **161** *Rural Court Scene,* by A. Wighe, 1849. Museum of Art, Rhode Island School of Design. **163** (l) *Preacher,* Kentucky, 1850's. Courtesy of The Art Institute of Chicago. **163** (r) *The Firemasters and Officers of the Volunteer Fire Companies of Charleston,* by Christian Meyr, 1840. City Council Chambers, Charleston, S.C. **164** Library of Congress. **165** (t) Courtesy of the American Museum of Natural History. **165** (b) *Fort Laramie on the North Platte River in Wyoming,* by Alfred Jacob Miller, 1837. The Walters Art Gallery. **166–167** Barfoot, *Progress of Cotton: No. 6, Spinning.* Yale University Art Gallery. The Mabel Brady Garvan Collection. **168** The Bettmann Archive. **169** Appliqué picture of women chatting, 19th century, by Eunice Cook, Vermont. Index of American Design, National Gallery of Art, Washington, D.C. **171** Culver Pictures. **172–173** Slave Deck of the Ship *Albany.* National Maritime Museum, London. **175** From *American Anti-Slavery Almanac,* 1839. Courtesy of The Newberry Library, Chicago. **177** International Cherokee Indian Council, by John M. Stanley, Smithsonian Institution. **181** (t) *Girls' Evening School* (detail), anonymous American. M. and M. Karolik Collection, Museum of Fine Arts, Boston. **181** (b) American Antiquarian Society.

Chapter 8
185 Denver Public Library, Western Collection. **188–189** *Immigrants Debarking at the Battery,* by Samuel B. Waugh, around 1855. Museum of the City of New York. **191** *The Trappers,* by Alfred Jacob Miller, 1837. The Walters Art Gallery. **193** (t) *San Maxymo at Xibara,* by William H. Meyers, around 1838. Manuscripts and Archives Division, The New York Public Library. Astor, Lenox, and Tilden Foundations. **193** (b) *Handcart,* painting by C. C. A. Christensen. The Church of Jesus Christ of Latter-Day Saints. **197** *General Scott's Entrance into Mexico, 1847,* by George Wilkins Kendall in *The War Between the United States and Mexico,* 1851. Courtesy of The Newberry Library, Chicago. **199** Courtesy California State Library. **201** *Geography Lesson,* 1844. Courtesy of Kenneth M. Newman, The Old Print Shop, New York City. **202** *A Lyceum Lecture,* artist unknown, around 1841. The Museum of the City of New York. **203** Library of Congress. **205** (t) Culver Pictures. **205** (b) "Father Come Home," from the first edition of Timothy Shay Arthur's *Ten Nights in a Barroom,* 1854. *KL The New York Public Library. **208** (t) Glenbow-Alberta Institute. **208** (b) *View of Pennsylvania Railroad Bridge,* by Herline and Hensel, around 1850. Courtesy Kenneth M. Newman, The Old Print Shop, New York City.

UNIT FOUR
212 *Kitchen Ball at White Sulphur Springs,* by Christian Mayr, North Carolina Museum of Art, Raleigh.

Chapter 9
216 *Canal Street Market, 1860* (detail), by Henry Mosler. The Cincinnati Historical Society. **218** California Historical Society. **220–221** Maryland Historical Society. **223** (t) *Corn Husking,* by Eastman Johnson, 1860. Everson Museum of Art, Syracuse, New York. **223** (b) *Preparing for Market,* L. Maurer, published by Nathaniel Currier. Yale University Art Gallery, The Mabel Brady Garvan Collection. **225** *A Wheelwright Works at His Trade,* by E. T. Billings, mid-1800's. Collection of E. F. Fisher, Brighton, Michigan. Photograph by Joe Clark. **227** Cartoon by John H. Goater. Courtesy of The New York Public Library. Astor, Lenox, and Tilden Foundations. **228** William Bollaert, *Observations on the Geography of Texas,* 1850. Courtesy of The Newberry Library, Chicago. **229** (l) *Right and Left,* by William Sidney Mount, 1850. Courtesy of The Suffolk Museum and Carriage House at Stony Brook, New York. **229** (r) *A Plantation on the Mississippi,* by Currier and Ives, 1868. The Harry T. Peters Collection, Museum of the City of New York. **231** (t) Library of Congress. **231** (b) Culver Pictures. **235** *Wall Street, 1857,* by James H. Cafferty and Charles G. Rosenberg. Museum of the City of New York. **237** (t) *Flax Scutching Bee,* by Linton Park, around 1860. National Gallery of Art, Washington, D.C. Gift of Edgar William and Bernice Chrysler Garbisch. **237** (b) *Peytona and Fashion's Great Match.* Smithsonian Institution, Photo #48674–D.

Chapter 10
239 *The Banjo Lesson,* by Henry O. Tanner. Original is the property of Hampton Institute. **241** *After the Sale: Slaves Going South from Richmond,* by Eyre Crowe. Courtesy Chicago Histor-

ical Society. **243** From *The Outlook,* September 1898. **245** Culver Pictures. **251** Library of Congress. **253** The New York Public Library. **255** *John Brown Going to His Hanging,* by Horace Pippin. Pennsylvania Academy of Fine Arts. **258** Library of Congress.

Chapter 11
260 Library of Congress. **263** *Simultaneous Recruiting for the Confederate and Union Armies, Knoxville, Tennessee, 1861,* by Samuel Bell Palmer. Collection of Herman Warner Williams, Corcoran Gallery of Art, Washington, D.C. **264** The Bettmann Archive. **266** *Chief Billy Bowlegs (Holatamico),* by Charles F. Wimar, 1861. The St. Louis Art Museum. **267** L & N Collection, National Archives. Louisville and Nashville Railroad. **269** Courtesy Dr. William Spinelli. **270** Association of American Railroads. **273** National Archives. **275** John Omenhausser drawing from *True Sketches and Sayings of Rebel Characters in the Point Lookout Prison, Maryland.* Maryland Historical Society, Baltimore. **280** *Battle of the Crater,* by John Elder. Commonwealth Club, Richmond.

Chapter 12
282 Courtesy Chicago Historical Society. **284** (l) Brown Brothers. **284** (r) Culver Pictures. **285** (l) Culver Pictures. **285** (r) Brown Brothers. **290** (l) *Harper's Weekly,* November 9, 1872. **290** (r) The Bettmann Archive. **291** Library of Congress. **292** Library of Congress. **299** Library of Congress.

UNIT FIVE
302 Courtesy of The New-York Historical Society, New York City.

Chapter 13
306 Courtesy of Southern Pacific. **310–311** Library of Congress. **313** *Forging the Shaft: A Welding Heat,* by John Ferguson Weir. The Metropolitan Museum of Art, Gift of Lyman G. Bloomingdale, 1901. **315** Library of Congress. **318** Library of Congress. **319** Library of Congress. **321** Brown Brothers. **323** *Frank Leslie's Illustrated Newspaper,* July 1, 1865.

Chapter 14
326 *Harper's Weekly,* August 29, 1891. **327** Library of Congress. **329** *The Battle of the Little Big Horn,* by Amos Badheart Buffalo. University of Nebraska Press. **330–331** James D. Horan, Western Americana Collection. **333** (t) Nebraska Historical Society. **333** (b) Copyright Charles J. Belden. Courtesy Whitney Gallery of Western Art. Cody, Wyoming. **335** Smithsonian Institution, Neg. #22760. **337** Library of Congress. **341** *California Wheat Harvest,* by Virgil Williams. Progressive Farmer Co. Photo courtesy Time-Life Publishing Company.

Chapter 15
344 Culver Pictures. **345** Library of Congress. **349** (t) Library of Congress. **349** (b) *Nearing the Issue at the Cockpit,* by Horace Bonham, around 1870. Corcoran Gallery of Art. **351** *Puck,* April 4, 1888. **353** The New York Public Library. **355** *Frank Leslie's Illustrated Newspaper,* January 31, 1874. **359** (t) Library of Congress. **359** (b) Courtesy Metropolitan Life Insurance Company. **360** Library of Congress. **363** Brown Brothers. **364** Library of Congress.

Chapter 16
366 Library of Congress. **368** *Portrait of William Astor Family,* by L. Rossi, 1875. Collection of Mrs. Vincent Astor. **369** Lightfoot Collection. **370** Emily Driscoll. **371** *Their Pride,* by Thomas Hovenden. The Union League Club, New York City. Photograph by Robert S. Crandall. **373** Culver Pictures. **376** Library of Congress. **377** Library of Congress. **378–379** Library of Congress. **382** Library of Congress.

UNIT SIX
386 *Troupes Americaines sous l'Arc de Triomphe,* by Charles Fouqueray. Musée de la Guerre, Paris. Courtesy American Heritage.

Chapter 17
390 Amalgamated Clothing Workers of America. **393** Lewis W. Hine, International Museum of Photography at George Eastman House, Rochester, N.Y. **395** *Cliff Dwellers,* by George Bellows, 1913. Los Angeles County Museum of Art, Los Angeles County Funds. **397** Library of Congress. **399** Underwood & Underwood. **400** Culver Pictures. **401** (t) *Steeplechase Park, Coney Island, New York,* around 1903. Museum of the City of New York. **401** (b) *Movies, Five Cents,* by John Sloan, 1907. Herbert A. Goldstone. **402** Culver Pictures. **403** Motor Vehicle Manufacturers Association. **404** (tl) *Gross Clinic,* by Thomas Eakins, 1875. Courtesy of Jefferson Medical College of Philadelphia, photographed by the Philadelphia Museum of Art. **404** (tr) *Mr. and Mrs. Isaac Newton Phelps Stokes,* by John Singer Sargent, 1897. The Metropolitan Museum of Art, Bequest of Edith Minturn Stokes, 1938. **404** (b) *Sunday, Women Drying Their Hair,* by John Sloan, 1912. The Addison Gallery of American Art, Phillips Academy, Andover, Massachusetts. **405** (t) *The East River,* by Maurice Prendergast, 1901. Collection The Museum of Modern Art, New York City. Gift of Abby Aldrich Rockefeller. **405** (b) *Steelworkers' Noontime,* by Thomas Anshutz, around 1890. Courtesy of Kennedy Galleries, Inc.

Chapter 18
408 Lewis W. Hine, International Museum of Photography at George Eastman House, Rochester, N.Y. **411** Lewis W. Hine, National Child Labor Committee. **415** Culver Pictures. **417** Library of Congress. **419** *Puck,* June 22, 1910. General Research and Humanities Division, The New York Public Library. Astor, Lenox, and Tilden Foundations. **420** (t) Brown Brothers. **420** (b) Courtesy The Women's Christian Temperance Union. Evanston, Illinois. **421** (l, r) Culver Pictures. **421** (c) The Bettmann Archive. **425** Lewis W. Hine, International Museum of Photography at George Eastman House, Rochester, N.Y. **427** (t) Historical Pictures Service. **427** (b) The Archives of Labor History and Urban Affairs, Wayne State University.

Chapter 19
429 U.S. Signal Corps Photo, National Archives. **430** Keystone View Company. **432–433** *Judge,* January 7, 1905. Culver Pictures. **434** National Archives. **435** FPG-Photoworld. **443** United Press International. **444** U.S. Army Signal Corps Photo, National Archives. **445** Culver Pictures. **446** Photo #111–SC27652, U.S. Army Signal Corps, National Archives. **447** (t) Photo #111–SC11886, U.S. Army Signal Corps, National Archives. **447** (b) Imperial War Museum, London. **448** Photo #111–SC94980, U.S. Army Signal Corps, National Archives. **450–451** *Armistice Night,* by George Luks, 1918. Collection Whitney Museum of American Art. Anonymous gift.

UNIT SEVEN

454 *Part Production and Assembly of Motors.* Detail from mural by Diego Rivera, 1933. The Detroit Institute of Arts. Gift of Edsel B. Ford.

Chapter 20
458 Culver Pictures. **460** A. P. Bedou photograph, courtesy E. David Cronen. **461** Courtesy Chicago Historical Society. **463** Culver Pictures. **464** Underwood & Underwood. **465** Courtesy Mrs. John Held, Jr. **469** Brown Brothers. **471** *Bootleggers,* by Ben Shahn, around 1935. Museum of the City of New York. **473** No acknowledgment. **475** (t) FPG-Photoworld. **475** (b) *Stomp,* by Archibald Motley, 1927. Artist's private collection.

Chapter 21
478 Dorothea Lange, Library of Congress. **480** Photo # 111-SC97522, U.S. Army Signal Corps, National Archives. **481** (l) *Employment Agency,* by Isaac Soyer, 1937. Collection Whitney Museum of American Art, New York City. **481** (r) Courtesy Chicago Historical Society. **485** U.S. Forest Service Photo. **487** (both) United Press International. **489** (l, c) Culver Pictures. **489** (r) Brown Brothers. **491** (t) *Home Relief Station,* by Louis Ribak, 1935–36. Collection Whitney Museum of American Art. **491** (b) Photo #69–N–1398, National Archives. **492** Library of Congress. **493** Wide World Photos. **495** *Riot in Union Square,* by Peter Hopkins, 1930. Museum of the City of New York. **496** Library of Congress.

Chapter 22
498 Missouri Historical Society. **501** The Archives of Labor History and Urban Affairs, Wayne State University. **503** Culver Pictures. **505** *The Gospel Train,* by John Steuart Curry. Syracuse University Art Collection. **506** (t) *Early Sunday Morning,* by Edward Hopper, 1930. Collection Whitney Museum of American Art, New York City. **506** (b) *Black Cross, New Mexico,* by Georgia O'Keeffe, 1929. The Art Institute of Chicago. **507** (t) *Stone City,* by Grant Wood, 1930. Collection of the Joslyn Art Museum, Omaha, Nebraska. **506** (bl) *Jack Curley's Dance Marathon,* by Reginald Marsh, 1932. Everson Museum of Art, Syracuse, N.Y. **507** (br) *Maine Islands,* by John Marin, 1922. The Phillips Collection. **509** *Angelo's Place,* by Glenn O. Coleman, 1929. Collection, The Museum of Modern Art, New York. Gift of Abby Aldrich Rockefeller. **511** (both) Brown Brothers. **513** United Press International. **514–515** (both) Culver Pictures.

Chapter 23
517 U.S. Navy Photo, National Archives. **518–519** Wide World Photos. **521** Wide World Photos. **523** (t) Acme Photos, United Press International. **523** (b) Wide World Photos. **524** United Press International. **525** United Press International. **526** Wide World Photos. **527** U.S. Navy Picture, courtesy American Heritage Publishing Company. **529** (both) Wide World Photos. **531** Underwood & Underwood. **533** Wide World Photos.

UNIT EIGHT

536 Hydrogen bomb, South Pacific, island of Mururoa. Rapho Guillumette Pictures, Inc.

Chapter 24
540 U.S. Army Photograph. **543** (t) U.S. Coast Guard. **543** (b) U.S. Army Photograph. **552** World Federation of Bergen-Belsen Associations. **554** Navy Department, Photo #80–G–301351, National Archives. **556–557** U.S. Marine Corps. **558–559** U.S. Army Photo. **561** United Press International.

Chapter 25
564 Wide World Photos. **566** (t) Cornell Capa, LIFE Magazine © 1958 Time, Inc. **566** (b) Wide World Photos. **567** J. R. Eyerman, © 1954 Time, Inc. **573** Wide World Photos. **574–575** Fenno Jacobs from Black Star. **576** Official United Nations Photo, Department of Public Information. **579** Ralph Cowan. **583** (both) U.S. Army Photos.

Chapter 26
585 Monkmeyer Press Photo Service. **589** Robert Phillips, LIFE Magazine, © 1972 Time, Inc. **591** Allan Grant © Time, Inc. **592–593** H. Roger Viollet. **596–597** Erich Lessing, Magnum Photos. **600** Burt Glinn, Magnum Photos. **601** Wide World Photos. **603** Steve Shapiro, Black Star. **604** (t) *Water of the Flowery Mill,* by Arshile Gorky, 1944. The Metropolitan Museum of Art, George A. Hearn Fund, 1956. **604** (bl) *Young America,* by Andrew Wyeth, 1950. The Pennsylvania Academy of the Fine Arts, Courtesy American Heritage Publishing Co. **604** (br) *Ready-to-wear,* by Stuart Davis, 1955. The Art Institute of Chicago, Gift of Edgar Kaufmann, Jr. **605** (t) *Domino Players,* by Horace Pippin, 1943. The Phillips Collection. **605** (b) *The Subway,* by George Tooker, 1950. Collection Whitney Museum of American Art, New York City. Juliana Force purchase.

UNIT NINE

608 A ride on the moon, *Apollo 17.* NASA.

Chapter 27
612 Bill Stanton, Magnum Photos. **617** (t) Schwinn Bicycle Company. **617** (b) Walt Disney Productions. **619** Ron Sherman, Nancy Palmer Agency. **620** N. McNamara, Nancy Palmer Agency. **623** (t) Declan Haun, Black Star. **623** (b) Charles Moore, Black Star. **625** (tl) Nacio Jan Brown, BBM Associates. **625** (tr) Photo Researchers. **625** (b) Bob Mader, Tom Stack and Associates. **629** Gerhard Gscheidle, Jeroboam.

Chapter 28
632 LOOK Collection, Library of Congress. Copyright © Cowles Communication Inc., 1970. **634** Wide World Photos. **636–637** Keystone Press. **640–641** (all) United Press International. **643** (t) Wide World Photos. **643** (b) Philip Jones Griffiths, Magnum Photos. **645** Cornell Capa, Magnum Photos. **647** Wide World Photos. **649** Paul Sequeira.

Chapter 29
651 Howard Harrison, Jeroboam. **652** Bruce Davidson, Magnum Photos. **655** Elihu Blotnick, BBM Associates. **658–659** Charles Gatewood, Magnum Photos. **661** Paul Sequeira. **663** Leslie Leon, Keystone Press. **665** Howard Harrison, Jeroboam. **668** (t) *The Subway,* by George Segal, 1968. Collection of Mr. and Mrs. Robert B. Mayer. **668–669** *Wall of Black Love,* by William Walker. Courtesy Amalgamated Meatcutters and Butcher Workmen of North America. **669** (l) *Spiral Illusion,* by Tom Strobel, 1965. Devorah Sherman Gallery, Chicago. **669** (r) *The Map,* by Roy Schnackenberg, 1964. Main Street Galleries, Chicago. **671** Elliot Landy, Magnum Photos.

Index

Abolition movement, 171–176, 227, 240, 245–248, 250; and blacks, 172, 174, 175; and women, 172, 175, 179; reaction to, 175–176; antislavery societies, 240
Adams, John, 50, 52, 58, 61, 78, 90, 99, 104, 105, 108, 118; election of 1796, 102; and undeclared naval war, 102, 104; and election of 1800, 106, 108
Adams, John Quincy, 151, 160, 176; and Monroe Doctrine, 154; election of 1824, 156, 160; election of 1828, 156–157, 160
Adams, Samuel, 42, 44–48
Addams, Jane, 324, 383
Advertising, 665
Africa, 13, 72–73, 121, 134, 305, 373, 389, 456, 599, 611. *See also names of individual nations*
African Methodist Episcopal Church, 201
African Methodist Episcopal Zion Church, 201
Agnew, Spiro T., 616, 618
Agricultural commodities, 341
Agriculture, 18, 27, pre Civil War period, 137–138, 140, 149, 168–170, 223, 226–228; post Civil War period, 326, 332–335, 337–343; and education, 338; and Hatch Act of 1887, 339; and world markets, 340; Populists, 355–357, 408; and financing, 342–343; Federal Farm Loan Act, 426; irrigation, 435; and World War I, 445; depression in 1920's, 464–465; McNary-Haugen Bill, 464–465; tariff protection, 464, 469–470; Agricultural Marketing Act of 1929, 469; Agricultural Adjustment Act of 1933, 486; drought of 1932–1936, 486; Tennessee Valley Authority, 486–487; in 1930's, 486, 487, 495; Resettlement Administration, 490; Rural Electrification Administration, 490; Agricultural Adjustment Act of 1938, 495; and World War II, 541; Truman administration, 577; Eisenhower administration, 588; effects of automation, 602, 652; unionization of farm workers, 602, 628. *See also* Farming
Agriculture, Department of, 338, 339

Aguinaldo, Emilio, 381
Aircraft carriers, 554
Alabama, 138, 226, 230, 256, 291
Alabama claims, 275–276
Alamance, battle of, 45
Alamo mission, 178
Alaska, 153, 295, 327, 365, 372, 430, 438
Albany Plan of Union, 36
Alcott, Louisa May, 370
Aldrin, Edwin E., Jr., 660
Aleutian Islands, 295
Aleut Indians, 153
Alger, Horatio, 370
Alien and Sedition Acts, 104, 106
Allen, Gracie, 516
Alliance for Progress, 635, 637
Altgeld, John P., 320, 321
Alvarado, Luis de Moscoso de, 17
America First Committee, 531–532
American Colonization Society, 172
American Federation of Labor, 319–320, 355, 426, 459, 490, 601, 627. *See also* Labor
American Independent party, 616
American Liberty League, 488
American party. *See* Know-Nothing party
American Peace Society, 204
American Railway Union, 321
American Red Cross, 264
American Revolution, 40–66; military strategy maps, 51, 55, 59; American and British resources, 53, 54; and Loyalists, 53, 54, 58; and blacks, 54; and women, 54; and Indians, 54; and France, 56–57, 60–62; and Spain, 60, 62; peace treaty, 61–62; impact on France, 65–66; and social distinctions, 70–71; effect on population, 103
American Socialist party, 322
American Woman Suffrage Association, 358
Amnesty Act of 1872, 298
Anarchism, 305, 320
Anderson, Maxwell, 505
Anderson, Robert, 257
Anderson, Sherwood, 502
Anglican Church, 20, 22, 30, 43
Anthony, Susan B., 358
Antietam (Sharpsburg), battle of, 273, 275
Antifederalists, 87–89
Anti-Masonic party, 160–161, 180
Antiwar movement, 648–650
Apaches, 13, 329, 330
Apartheid *(def.)*, 638
Appalachian Regional Development Act of 1965, 630
Appomattox, 281
Apprentices, 28; *(def.)*, 167
Arabs, 389, 539, 575–576, 597

Arapahos, 328
Arbitration *(def.)*, 389
Architecture, 407, 508
Argentina, 153, 172, 575, 595
Arizona, 199, 327, 328, 415, 422, 435
Arkansas, 226, 258, 280, 283, 288, 291
Arms Control and Disarmament Agency, 632
Arms race, 537–538
Armstrong, Louis, 502
Armstrong, Neil A., 660
Aroostook War, 176
Art, during 1890's and early 1900's, 406–407; during 1920's and 1930's, 506–507; during 1940's and 1950's, 604–605; during 1960's and 1970's, 668–669
Arthur, Chester A., 347–348
Arthur, Timothy Shay, 207
Articles of Confederation, 69–70, 84; ratification of, 70; and Indians, 70; and foreign affairs, 77–80; criticism of, 80–82
Assembly lines, 310, 403, 500
Aswan Dam, 597
Atlantic Charter, 534, 559
Atomic bomb, 537, 544, 558
Atomic energy, 303, 510, 530, 565–566, 579, 589, 658
Attucks, Crispus, 44
Audubon Society, 664
Austin, Stephen, 152
Australia, 365, 554, 574, 580, 593
Austria, 524, 571
Austria-Hungary, 133, 135, 153, 214, 388, 389; in World War I, 439, 440, 446, 448
Automation *(def.)*, 601
Automobiles, 317; invention of, 400; growth of industry, 403, 500, 661, 664; impact on society, 403
Aviation industry, 400, 500–501, 662, 664–665
Axis powers, 544, 546–548, 559; formation of, 522; industrial production of, 541
Ayres, Agnes, 514

Babcock, Stephen M., 339
Baker, Ray Stannard, 409
Balanchine, George, 606
Baldwin, James, 671
Ballinger, Richard, 417
Ballooning, 127, 272
Baltimore, Lord, 30
Bangla Desh, 610, 646
Banking, 95, 130, 140, 142, 148, 180, 207, 262–263, 294–295, 342; and Jackson, 180; and Confederacy, 268–269; investment banking, 394–395; Federal Reserve System,

425; crisis of 1933, 479–480; and New Deal, 482
Bank of America, 396
Bank of the United States, First, 95, 130; Second, 142, 148, 180
Bao Dai, 592
Baptists, 30, 82, 96
Barbary pirates, 67
Barbed wire, 334
Barkley, Alben W., 577
Barnett, Ross R., 622
Barnum, Phineas T., 370
Barth, John, 671
Bartram, John, 121
Baruch, Bernard M., 444, 572
Basie, Count, 606
Bay of Pigs invasion, 634–635
Beauregard, Pierre, 257, 276
Belgium, 446, 528, 575, 609, 611
Bell, Alexander Graham, 309
Bell, John, 255
Bellamy, Edward, 316
Belligerent (def.), 272
Bellow, Saul, 670
Benét, Stephen Vincent, 504
Benny, Jack, 516
Benson, Ezra Taft, 588
Benton, Thomas Hart, 506
Bering Strait, 13
Berlin, Irving, 407, 606
Berryman, John, 672
Bessemer process, 312
Bethel Society, 201
Biafra, 638–639
Bicycles, 308, 617
Biddle, Nicholas, 180
"Big stick" diplomacy, 431–433
Bill of Rights, 88, 92, 700–701
Biloxi, colony of, 37
Bimetallism *(def.),* 361; 364
Birney, James G., 246
Black codes, 287
Black Hawk, 164
Blacklisting (def.), 319
Black Muslims, 620, 622
Black Panther party, 620, 622
Blacks, 17, 25, 77, 86, 122, 130, 150, 158–159, 170, 201, 224–225, 236, 283, 296, 354–355; education, 32, 336, 396, 398–399; slave trade, 67; and slavery, 25–26, 72–73, 226, 228–232; in Revolutionary War, 54; Haiti, 66; voting rights, 69, 159, 336–337, 357, 621–622; free, 29, 69, 146, 150, 172, 243, 261; and trades, 225, women, 225, 229; children, 225; and Compromise of 1850, 242–243; and Fugitive Slave Law of 1850, 243; and Dred Scott decision, 250–251; and emancipation, 265; and Civil War, 261–262, 265–266, 268, 270; and Reconstruction, 286–292; and Republican party, 289; legislators, 290; migration, 299, 498; status after 1877, 300–301; and cattle industry, 331; and Civil Rights Cases of 1883, 336; and *Plessy* v. *Ferguson,* 336; and Jim Crow laws, 353; and Democratic party, 426; in World War I, 460; race riots of 1919, 460; nationalism of, 460–461, 620, 622–624; attacked by Ku Klux Klan, 287, 466; and New Deal, 494, 497; and literature, 504, 671–672; in World War II, 544; during Truman administration, 568, 577; civil rights movement, 599–601, 618–624, 648; riots of 1960's, 622, 624; black power, 624; population in 1970, 652; in cities, 652, 655, 657; in sports, 672
Blaine, James G., 347, 350, 375
Blatch, Harriot Stanton, 420
Blitzkrieg (def.), 528
Bogart, Humphrey, 607
Bohr, Niels, 510
Bolden, Charles "Buddy," 407
Bolsheviks. *See* Communists
Bonus Army, 472, 481
Booth, John Wilkes, 283
Borah, William E., 449
Borglum, Gutzon, 508
Boston, Massachusetts, 32, 42, 46, 50–51, 140, 168, 174, 225, 227, 322, 370, 390
Boston Massacre, 40, 44
Boston Tea Party, 46
Bourke-White, Margaret, 506
Boxer Rebellion, 430–431
Braceros (def.), 602
Braddock, Edward, 38
Bragg, Braxton, 277
Brandeis, Louis D., 427
Brazil, 20, 30, 271, 595
Breckinridge, John C., 254
Bricker, John W., 560
Brinkmanship (def.), 585
Britain, 13, 17, 20, 28, 98, 108, 213, 303, 305; and colonies, 13, 14, 37, 134; and Spain, 20, 36; government of, 22, 33–34, 35; and France, 36, 38; and French and Indian War, 38–39; colonial policy after 1763, 40–53; in Revolutionary War, 50–63; and slavery, 72, 171–172; Confederation and government, 78; and Jay's Treaty, 99–100; and relations with Jefferson, 118–120; relations with Madison, 120–128; War of 1812, 123–130; and Rush-Bagot Agreement, 152; and Cuba, 154; and Monroe Doctrine, 154, 375–376; and Canadian-American problems, 176, 185–186, 438–439; and Creole case, 185; and Texas, 186–187; and Oregon country, 190–191; colonizing Asia and Africa, 213; and Civil War, 260, 271–273; and *Alabama* claims, 296; and Treaty of Washington (1871), 296; and international bimetallism, 364; and Samoa, 374; Sykes-Picot agreement, 389; Balfour Declaration, 389; and Open Door policy, 430–431; and Hay-Pauncefote Treaty, 432; and Venezuela, 433; Algeciras conference, 438; in World War I, 440, 442, 446; Versailles Treaty, 448–449; mandates after World War I, 456; at Munich, 526; aided by U.S., 528, 531–532, 534; and Yalta agreements, 562; and World War II peace treaties, 570–571; aid to Greece and Turkey, 572; governing Palestine, 576; joins SEATO, 593; and Middle East, 596–597; entry into Common Market, 610; and test-ban treaty, 633; and Rhodesia, 638
British North America. *See* Canada
Brook Farm, 204
Brooklyn, New York, 323
Brooks, Preston, 250
Brown, John, 248, 250, 253–255
Bruce, Blanche K., 357
Bryan, William Jennings, 362–364, 383–384, 416, 436, 509
Buchanan, James, 250, 251–252, 256
Buck, Pearl, 502
Buell, Don Carlos, 277, 279
Buffalo, 330, 415
Bulgaria, 439, 538, 563, 571
"Bull Moose" party. *See* Progressive party
Bunau-Varilla, Philippe, 433
Bunche, Ralph J., 576
Bureau of Indian Affairs, 164, 493, 626
Burnside, Ambrose, 276, 279
Burr, Aaron, 106–108, 117
Business. *See* Economy; Industry
Butler, Andrew P., 250

Cabeza de Vaca, Alvar Núñez, 17
Cabot, John, 17
Cabot, Sebastian, 17
Cabrillo, Juan Rodriguez, 17
Calder, Alexander, 604
Calhoun, John C., 162–163, 186–187, 236, 242
California, 79, 192, 194–195, 199, 217, 240–242, 266, 338–339, 396, 410, 415, 422, 435, 543
Californios (def.), 193
Calvinists, 30, 32
Cambodia, 539, 592, 642, 650

Canada, 17, 36, 123, 152, 175, 176, 215, 246, 272, 296, 329, 331, 365, 575; invasion during War of 1812, 124; relations with U.S., 176, 185–186, 438, 439; unification of, 215; Alaskan boundary, 438; coordination of defenses with U.S., 530; and St. Lawrence Seaway, 594
Canals, 110, 144, 209, 314
Canning, George, 154
Cannon, Joseph G., 417
Capitalism *(def.)*, 321
Carlos III, King of Spain, 37, 79
Carnegie, Andrew, 312, 315, 370, 383, 400
Carnegie Steel Company, 314–315, 320
Carolinas, 23, 138
Carpetbaggers, 289–292
Carson, Rachel, 664
Cartier, Jacques, 17
Carver, George Washington, 336
Cassatt, Mary, 406
Cass, Lewis, 248
Caste system *(def.)*, 398
Castro, Fidel, 539, 594, 634–636
Cather, Willa, 502
Catholics, religious conflicts, 20, 22; and immigration, 25, 30, 219, 227, 367, 391; in colonial period, 30, 32, 73; prejudice against, 32, 201, 219–220, 227, 466, 468; and Quebec Act of 1774, 46; political restrictions, 69, 158; and freedom of religion, 73; and Indians, 79; conflicts between, 201; and science, 367; and social reform, 367; and Mexican government, 388, 519; and Ku Klux Klan, 466; in 1920's and 1930's, 510; and election of 1960, 613; and Christian unity, 670
Catt, Carrie Chapman, 421, 461
Cattle industry, 331–332
Caucuses *(def.)*, 156
Central Intelligence Agency (CIA), 569, 635
Cervera, Pascual, 379
Chamberlain, Neville, 526
Chambers, Whittaker, 569
Champlain, Samuel de, 17
Chaplin, Charlie, 514
Chautauqua assembly, 370
Chávez, César, 602, 628
Checks and balances, 85–86, 117–118
Cherokees, 21, 75, 129, 165–166, 177, 266
Cheyennes, 328
Chiang Kai-shek, 455–456, 474, 539, 560, 580, 593
Chicago, Illinois, 144, 169, 217, 221, 223, 244, 254, 307, 310, 320, 322, 324, 331, 394, 407, 410

Chicanos. *See* Mexican Americans
Chickasaws, 21, 166, 266
Children, in colonial period, 29–30; as workers, 168, 225, 229, 409–410, 416; and city life, 392
Chile, 153, 595, 611
China, 215, 293, 373, 380, 389, 544; and trade, 67; and Opium War, 134; and Tai-ping Rebellion, 215; and Open Door policy, 430–431; Boxer Rebellion, 430–431; Russo-Japanese War, 431, 474; civil wars, 455–456, 539; attacked by Japan, 474, 520, 523–524, 527; in World War II, 558, 560. *See also* Taiwan; China, People's Republic of
China, Nationalist. *See* Taiwan
China, People's Republic of, 611; Communists gain control, 580; and Korean War, 584; and Indochina, 592–593, 640; and India, 593, 646; Eisenhower's policies toward, 593–594; admission to U.N., 610; building of atomic weapons, 633; and Nixon's visit, 646–647
Chinese, 307, 318, 391, 402
Chinese Exclusion Act, 318, 391
Choctaws, 21, 164, 266
Chou En-lai, 647
Christian Science, 366
Churchill, Winston, 528, 532, 534, 544, 552, 559–563, 572
Church of England. *See* Anglican Church
Church of Jesus Christ of Latter-day Saints. *See* Mormons
Cincinnati, Ohio, 169
Cities, 322–325; and transportation, 317, 322, 463; government, 324–325, 393, 410; family life, 391–392; and annexation, 393; reform of government in, 410; and air pollution, 463; in 1960's and 1970's, 655, 657; organizations in, 666, 670. *See also* Urbanization
City-manager plan *(def.)*, 410
Civilian Conservation Corps (CCC), 484, 489–490
Civil rights, laws, 287, 336, 353, 600, 622–624; Civil Rights Cases of 1883, 336, 353; during Truman administration, 568; as theme in campaign of 1948, 577; end of "separate but equal" doctrine, 599; Little Rock crisis, 599–600; degree of integration, 600–601; and women, 663
Civil rights movement, 618–624; black organizations in, 619–620; and legislation, 622; in 1960's, 648
Civil service, 344–348
Civil War, 215, 258–281; Confederate and Union resources, 260–263, 268–269; recruitment, 261–262; and blacks, 261–262, 265–266, 268, 270; internal splits, 262; taxes, 262; northern business and agriculture, 263–264; and slavery, 265–266; and Indians, 266; and railroads, 267; propaganda, 269; and family life, 269–270; and women, 269–270; effects on South, 270; and European neutrality, 271–272; prisoners, 272, 274–275; and technology, 272–273; strategy, 273–274, 276–278; major battles, 273–281; surrender, 281; casualties, 299. *See also* Confederacy; Union
Clark, James "Champ," 419
Clay, Henry, 140, 156, 163, 178, 180, 187, 242, 244, 246; and Missouri Compromise, 146–147
Clayton Antitrust Act, 424, 426
Clemenceau, Georges, 449
Cleveland, Grover, 375, 383, 415; election of 1884, 350; and Congress, 350; election of 1892, 356; second term, 362
Clinton, DeWitt, 124, 144
Clinton, George, 117
Clinton, Sir Henry, 57
Closed shop *(def.)*, 568
Cohan, George M., 407
Colbert, Claudette, 515
Cold War, 538–539, 598–599, 609; beginning of, 572; limiting nuclear weapons in, 632–633; *détente*, 636
Cole, Nat "King," 606
Colfax, Schuyler, 293
Collective security *(def.)*, 449
Colleges and universities, 202, 367–368; colonial, 32; private, 74, 368; state agricultural, 222; land-grant, 263, 339, 426; agricultural and mechanical, 339; curriculum, 368, 398; and women, 368; junior, 398; state aid, 398; and student unrest, 647–650
Collier, John, 493
Colombia, 66, 153, 432–433
Colonies, English, 14–15, 23–24, 37, 103; Spanish, 14, 20, 36–37; French, 14–15, 36, 38, 58; and Europe, 18, 20, 22–23; and trade, 20, 22, 24, 28, 34, 35, 47–48, 52, 62; southern, 24; New England, 24; middle, 24; population, 24–26; social classes in, 29; religion in, 30; intellectual development in, 32; and English government, 33–34, 39; corporate, proprietary, and royal, 34; and currency, 34; and Indian wars, 35; voting qualifications in, 35; Dutch, 36; French

and Indian War, 38; British policy after 1763, 40–50; and taxes, 41–42, 44–45; Stamp Act Congress, 42; and nonimportation, 42–43, 47–48; tea boycott, 46. *See also* American Revolution
Colonists, 14–15, 30; African, 14, 24–25, 29–30; English, 14, 24, 30, 47; French, 14–15, 25–26, 35–36, 47; Spanish, 14, 37; Finnish, 15; Polish, 15; Swedish, 15; German, 15, 25, 30; Scotch-Irish, 15, 26; Scottish, 15, 30; Dutch, 15, 30, 36; Italian, 15, 37; Irish, 25–26; Pennsylvania German, 26; social origins of, 29–30; Greek, 37
Colorado, 327, 339, 358, 415
Colt, Samuel, 224
Columbus, Christopher, 17–18, 20
Comanches, 226, 328
Comic strips, 372
Commission plan *(def.)*, 410
Committee on Public Information, 445
Committees of correspondence, 47
Common Market, 609–611
Common Sense, 52
Communications, 210, 306, 309–310, 515–516
Communism, 538; *(def.)*, 304–305; in Russia, 457, 459; in U.S., 459; in France and Italy, 573; in Cold War, 591; in Indochina, 591–592. *See also* Communist party; Communists
Communist Manifesto, 321
Communist party, 459; outlawed in U.S., 589; as political issue, 590
Communists, 446; raids against, 459–460; and Truman administration, 569, 577–578; laws relating to, 578; and Vietnam war, 639–644
Compromise of 1850, 233, 242–244
Compromise of 1877, 300
Computers, 626, 658–659
Comstock Lode, 327
Concord, Massachusetts, 50, 206
Confederacy, 233, 256–258, 265, 267–271; constitution, 257; resources of, 260–261; armies, 268; arming of slaves, 268; finances, 268–269; conscription, 268, 270; scarcities, 268–270; and railroads, 269; political disputes, 270–271; and European neutrality, 271–272; war strategy, 273–274; prisons, 274; battles, 276–281
Conglomerate *(def.)*, 627
Congo, 611, 638
Congregational Church, 30, 73, 200
Congress of Industrial Organizations (CIO), 492, 601
Congress of Racial Equality (CORE), 601, 620–621

Congress, United States, 84, 233, 263, 265, 293, 352, 354, 375, 381–382, 541; during Confederation period, 69–70; powers of, 86, 234, 236; "implied powers" of, 234; and slavery, 234, 236; and Compromise of 1850, 242–243; and Dred Scott decision, 250–251; and Reconstruction, 283–284, 287–289; and Treaty of Versailles, 449–451; and "hundred days," 482. *See also* Continental Congress
Conkling, Roscoe, 346, 347
Connally, John B., Jr., 613
Connecticut, 24, 30, 35, 45, 84, 89
Conscription *(def.)*, 387
Conscription Act of 1863, 262
Conservation, 410, 414–415, 417, 487. *See also* Ecology
Consortium *(def.)*, 432
Constitutional Convention, 80–86
Constitutional Union party, 254
Constitutions, state, 68–69
Constitution, U.S., 82–84, 87, 687–707; and three-fifths clause, 84, 145; and slavery, 84, 174, 234; government structure, 85; separation of powers, 85; checks and balances, 85, 86–87; and executive branch, 85, 91; and Supreme Court, 86–87, 147–148, 150, 250; "necessary and proper" clause, 86, 88, 95, 148; amending process, 87; ratification, 87–90; "elastic clause," 95; and commerce, 148, 352; and electoral college, 159; implied powers, 234; and Reconstruction, 282. *See also* Bill of Rights; *individual amendments*
Consumerism, 665–666
Containment, 572, 591
Continental Congress, First, 47–49; Second, 50–54, 68–72
Cooke, Jay, 262
Coolidge, Calvin, 500; election of 1920, 452; becomes President, 462, 464; election of 1924, 464; foreign policy of, 474, 476
Cooper, James Fenimore, 206–207
Copland, Aaron, 606
Cornwallis, Lord, 58–59
Coronado, Francisco Vásquez de, 17
Corporation for Public Broadcasting, 654
Corporations, 182, 394, 483; and banking, 394–396; changes in 1920's and 1930's, 499–501; in 1960's, 627
Cotton industry, 109, 170, 226, 335
Coughlin, Charles E., 488
Council of Economic Advisers, 565
Courts, under Articles of Confederation, 70; and U.S. Constitution, 86, 92. *See also* Supreme Court

Cowboys, 331
Cox, James M., 452
Crandall, Prudence, 175
Crane, Stephen, 406
Crawford, William H., 156
Crazy Horse, 329
Credit cards, 665
Crédit Mobilier, 293
Creeks, 21, 129, 166, 266
Creoles, 130
Crèvecoeur, Michel Guillaume Jean de, 15
Crozat, Antoine, 37
Cuba, 37, 154, 245–246, 256, 376–381, 432; revolt against Spain, 377; and Teller Amendment, 378; and Good Neighbor policy, 519; revolution in, 539, 594–595; U.S. embargo, 595; Bay of Pigs invasion, 634–635; missile crisis, 635–636; and test-ban treaty, 633. *See also* Spanish-American War
Cuban Americans, 655
Cugat, Xavier, 516
Cullen, Countee, 504
Culture *(def.)*, 498
Cumberland Road, 142–143, 162
Cummings, E. E., 504
Cummins, Maria Susanna, 207
Currency, 28, 34, 41, 80, 95, 180, 262–263, 294, 343, 356, 361–365, 424; colonial, 41; during Revolutionary War, 53; scarcity of, 142; Confederate, 268–269, 282; Sherman Silver Purchase Act, 361–363; Gold Standard Act, 365; and New Deal, 482–484. *See also* Economy
Curry, John Steuart, 506
Custer, George A., 328–329
Cybernation *(def.)*, 626
Czechoslovakia, 455, 525–526, 538
Czechs, 318
Czolgosz, Leon, 385

Dakota Territory, 332
Dana, Richard Henry, Jr., 207
Dance, 475, 504, 602, 606
Darrow, Clarence, 509
Darwin, Charles, 315, 367
Das Kapital, 321
Daugherty, Harry M., 462
Daughters of Liberty, 46
Davis, Bette, 607
Davis, Henry, 283
Davis, Jefferson, 256–257, 260, 270–271; views on slavery, 249; and Civil War strategy, 273–274
Davis, Stuart, 604
Dawes Act, 330, 493
Dayton, Ohio, 410
De Bow, James D. B., 226
Debs, Eugene V., 282, 320, 321

Declaration of Independence, 50–53, 56, 66, 685–686
De facto segregation *(def.)*, 619
Defense, Department of, 569
De Grasse, François, 58
De Kooning, Willem, 604
Delaware, 23, 24, 88
Del Rio, Dolores, 515
Deloria, Vine, Jr., 13
De Mille, Agnes, 606
De Mille, Cecil B., 607
Democratic party, 112, 157, 180, 200, 207, 209, 246, 251–254, 258, 265, 284, 288, 294, 296, 298, 300, 336, 344–345; and congressional elections of 1910, 418; 1918, 448–449; in South, 298; and farmers' alliances, 355; and imperialism, 383; and Progressives, 418; and women's suffrage, 422; and blacks, 426, 494; and League of Nations, 450–451; and Ku Klux Klan, 466; trends in 1960's, 612, 616. *See also* Elections
Democratic radicalism, 133–134
Democratic-Republican party, 157. *See also* Democratic party; Republican (Jeffersonian) party
Dempsey, Jack, 512
Denmark, 442, 528, 532, 575, 610
Depressions, 120, 145, 224, 314, 356, 362, 402, 413, 456; *(def.)*, 181–182; of 1783, 80; of 1837, 168, 180; in agriculture, 1920's, 464–465; unemployment in 1930's, 470–472, 479, 489, 490, 492, 496; of 1929, 483, 494, 496, 506; 1936 recession, 494; recession of 1957, 602; recession of 1970, 627, 631. *See also* Economy; Panic
Deseret, 192, 217
De Soto, Hernando, 17
Détente (def.), 636
Detroit, Michigan, 403
Dewey, George, 378
Dewey, John, 397
Dewey, Thomas E., 560, 576–577
Dibble, Henry C., 285
Dickinson, Emily, 369
Dickinson, John, 44, 69
Didrikson, Mildred "Babe," 512
Dien Bien Phu, battle of, 592
DiMaggio, Joe, 512
Disney, Walt, 607
District of Columbia, 175, 240, 242, 246
Dix, Dorothea, 204
Doheny, Edward L., 462
Dominican Republic, 357, 434, 436–437, 637
Domino theory *(def.)*, 592
Doniphan, Alexander, 196
Donnelly, Ignatius, 355
Dos Passos, John, 502

Douglas, Stephen A., 243–245, 248–249, 252–254
Douglass, Frederick, 172, 225, 285
Draft, 387; during Revolutionary War, 53–54; in Civil War, 261–262, 268, 270–271; Selective Service Act of 1917, 444; during World War II, 529, 540, 541; during Vietnam war, 649–650
Drake, Edwin L., 310
Drake, Sir Francis, 17
Dreiser, Theodore, 406
Drugs, 648, 656–657
Du Bois, William E. B., 399
Due process of law *(def.)*, 251
Dulles, John Foster, 586, 591, 594, 597–598
Duncan, Isadora, 504
Dupuy de Lôme, Enrique, 378
Duryea brothers, 400
Dutch, 15, 30, 36
Dutch Reformed Church, 30

Eagleton, Thomas F., 618
Eakins, Thomas, 404, 406
Earhart, Amelia, 501
East India Company, 45
Ecology *(def.)*, 664; during colonial period, 26–27; during 1790's, 121, 149; after World War II, 579; during 1960's and 1970's, 664–665, 667. *See also* Conservation
Economic sanctions *(def.)*, 522
Economy, 343; growth of, 80; modern business cycle, 183; in North and South, 228; investments, 234; trusts, 314; and business cycle, 335; and super corporations, 393–394; and banking, 393–394; during 1920's, 470, 499–501; in 1930's, 470–472; bank holiday, 482; New Deal programs, 482–497; World War II inflation, 542; war bonds, 542; end of World War II controls, 565; after Korean War, 586; tax cuts in 1959, 588; and automation, 601–602; in 1960's and 1970's, 626–631; advertising and credit cards, 665; consumerism, 665–666. *See also* Agriculture; Currency; Depressions; Industry; Inflation; Labor; Railroads
Eddy, Mary Baker, 366
Ederle, Gertrude, 512, 513
Edison, Thomas Alva, 312, 513
Education, colonial, 30–33; of Indians, 32, 330, 493; of women, 32, 181, 202, 368; of slaves, 32; origins of public education, 74, 201–202; in South, 290; during Reconstruction, 291; Chautauqua assemblies, 370; of immigrants, 396;

John Dewey and, 397; high schools, 398; and blacks, 398–399; rural and vocational, 426; during 1920's and 1930's, 511–512; of World War II GI's, 564–565; during Eisenhower administration, 590; since 1945, 653–654
Egypt, 596–598, 611, 645
Eighteenth Amendment, 468, 704
Einstein, Albert, 510
Eisenhower, Dwight D., 546, 612; in campaign of 1952, 585–586; economic policies of, 586–589, 590; in campaign of 1956, 590–591; foreign policies of, 591–599, 634, 635; and civil rights, 599–600
Elections, of 1789, 90; of 1792, 98–99; of 1796, 102; of 1800, 106–107; of 1804, 117; of 1808, 120; of 1812, 129; of 1816, 130; of 1820, 156; of 1824, 156, 160; of 1828, 156–157, 160; of 1832, 161; of 1836, 160; of 1840, 183–184; of 1842, 244; of 1844, 187, 190; of 1848, 241, 248; of 1852, 244; of 1854, 248, 249; of 1856, 250; of 1860, 239, 254–255; of 1864, 266–267; of 1866, 288; of 1868, 293; of 1872, 293; of 1874, 294, 298; of 1876, 298, 300; of 1880, 347; of 1884, 350; of 1888, 350–351; of 1892, 351, 356; of 1894, 356; of 1896, 356, 362–364; of 1900, 383–384; direct primary *(def.)*, 411; of 1904, 413; of 1908, 416; of 1912, 418–420; of 1916, 426–428; of 1920, 451–452; of 1924, 464; of 1928, 466–467; of 1932, 479; of 1934, 488; of 1936, 494; of 1938, 496; of 1940, 532; of 1944, 560; of 1946, 568; of 1948, 576–577; of 1952, 585–586; of 1954, 590; of 1956, 590–591; of 1960, 612–613; of 1964, 614; of 1968, 616, 649, 650, 656; of 1972, 618; *charts*, 107, 155, 179, 247, 297, 346, 384, 423, 467, 525, 587, 615
Electoral college, 86, 298
Electric power, 303, 312–313; and railways, 317, 322; industry, 500–501
Eliot, Thomas Stearns, 503–504
Elizabeth I, Queen of England, 20
Ellington, Edward "Duke," 504, 606
Emancipation Proclamation, 233, 265–266, 270, 283
Emerson, Ralph Waldo, 200, 204
Employment Act of 1946, 565
England. *See* Britain
English, 14, 24, 30, 47, 219, 402
Equal Employment Opportunity, Committee on, 621
Equal Rights Amendment, 602, 664
Equal Rights Association, 358

Era of Good Feelings, 136–157, 160
Eric the Red, 17
Ericson, Leif, 17, 18
Erie Canal, 137, 144–145
Estavanico, 17
Estonia, 559
Ethiopia, 522–523, 611
Europe, migration to America, 14; 1783–1815, 65–66; 1850's, 213–215; effects of Great Depression, 456, 477, 517; World War I debts, 476–477; 1950's, 595–596, 598; European Economic Community, 610. *See also* names of individual countries
Evans, Mari, 672
Evans, Walker, 506
Evolution, theory of, 367, 396
Expansionism, 372; in Pacific, 373–374; and Spanish-American War, 376, 380; and election of 1900, 383; and Insular Cases, 430. *See also* Imperialism
Exploration, 18, 20; of North America by Europeans, 14, 16–17; during Jefferson's administration, 114, 116–117; of Alaska, 153

Factory system, 108–109, 134–135, 137
Fairbanks, Douglas, 444, 514
Fair Deal, 565, 577
Fair Employment Practices Committee (FEPC), 541
Fall, Albert B., 462
Fallen Timbers, battle of, 100
Fallout *(def.)*, 579
Family life, 26, 29, 103; of slaves, 229; of immigrants, 391; in cities, 392, 393; and child care, 392
Farming, 26, 169, 222, 334–335, 340, 435; in colonial period, 26, 68; Indian, 27; in Northwest, 137–138; in South, 138, 140; scientific, 149, 170, 326, 334, 337–341, 435; subsistence *(def.)*, 326; commercial *(def.)*, 326; problems, 464–465. *See also* Agriculture
Farrell, James T., 502
Fascism *(def.)*, 457
Faubus, Orval, 599
Faulkner, William, 502
Featherbedding *(def.)*, 626–627
Federal Aid Highway Act of 1956, 590
Federal Aid Road Act, 403
Federal Bureau of Investigation (FBI), 542, 656
Federal Communications Commission (FCC), 516
Federal Deposit Insurance Corporation (FDIC), 482

Federal Housing Authority (FHA), 590
Federalist, The, 88
Federalists, 87–89, 92, 98–108, 112–114, 117, 123, 130, 136, 146, 156
Federal Power Commission, 458
Federal Radio Commission, 516
Federal Reserve System, 424, 482, 586
Feminine Mystique, The, 662
Fermi, Enrico, 510, 544
Ferrelo, Bartolomeo, 17
Field, James G., 356
Fifteenth Amendment, 288, 336, 357–358, 398, 703–704
Fifth Amendment, 250, 700
Filipinos, 391, 624
Fillmore, Millard, 242, 244, 250
Finance capitalism *(def.)*, 315
Finland, 528, 559, 563, 571
Finney, Charles G., 200
Finns, 15
Fish, Hamilton, 295, 376
Fitzgerald, F. Scott, 502
"Five Civilized Tribes," 21
Flexner, Eleanor, 461
Florida, 17, 36, 67, 78, 150–152, 288
Foch, Ferdinand, 448
Foote, A. H., 277
Ford, Henry, 309, 400, 403
Foreign affairs, Confederation period, 77–80; Jeffersonian Republicans, 98; under Federalists, 98–104; under John Adams, 105–106; effects of War of 1812, 130; 1800–1824, 150–154, 156; 1825–1840, 176–178; 1840–1860, 185–199; during Civil War, 271–273; *Trent* affair, 272; 1865–1876, 295–296; dollar diplomacy, 432, 476; during 1920's, 472–477; Good Neighbor policy, 517–535; and nuclear weapons, 538; 1945–1960, 570–576; formation of NATO, 574–575; in 1960's and 1970's, 609–611; relations with Soviet Union, 632–634; relations with Latin America, 634–637; relations with new African nations, 638–644; and Middle East, 611, 645–646; relations with People's Republic of China, 646–647. *See also* Cold War; World War I; World War II; names of individual countries
Fort Laramie, 165, 328
Fort Sumter, 257–258
Fort Ticonderoga, 51, 55, 56
Fourteenth Amendment, 288, 291, 298, 336, 352–353, 357–358, 702–703
France, 25, 101, 123, 133–134, 145, 153, 214, 303, 305, 387, 388; and colonies, 13, 14, 37, 134; and England, 36, 38; and French and Indian War, 38–39; in Revolutionary War, 53, 56–58, 60–62; Revolution, 65–66, 98, 99; and U.S., 99, 101, 118–119, 271, 609; and "XYZ" affair, 102; and undeclared naval war, 102, 104–106; and Louisiana Purchase, 113–114; revolutions of 1830 and 1848, 135; colonizing Asia and Africa, 214; and Confederacy, 260; and Mexico, 295; Sykes-Picot agreement, 389; and Open Door policy, 431; Isthmian canal, 432; Moroccan crisis, 437–438; and World War I strategies, 440; Versailles Treaty, 449; at Munich conference, 526; defeated by Germany and Italy, 528, 530; and Japan, 534; independence of Indochina, 539; Vichy government, 546; Allied invasion, 547; and Yalta agreements, 562; and World War II peace treaties, 570–571; joins SEATO, 593; and Middle East, 597; and NATO, 609; and test-ban treaty, 633
Francis I, King of France, 17
Francis Ferdinand, 439
Franco, Francisco, 522
Franklin, Benjamin, 33, 36, 47, 52, 57, 60–62, 82, 84
Freedmen's Bureau, 286–287, 289
"Free silver," 361–362, 365, 384
Free-soil movement, 246–248
Frémont, John C., 194, 196, 250
French and Indian War, 37–40, 54, 114
French Canadians, 124
French, 14, 25, 26, 35, 36, 47, 219
Frick, Henry Clay, 320
Friedan, Betty, 662
Friends of the Earth, 664
Frost, Robert, 503
Fuchs, Klaus, 578
Fugitive Slave Law, of 1793, 175, 240; of 1850, 243
Fuller, Margaret, 206
Fulton, Robert, 143–144, 148
Fundamentalists *(def.)*, 509
Fur trade, 17, 23, 26, 35–36, 165, 187, 190–191

Gable, Clark, 515, 607
Gadsden Purchase, 199
Gallatin, Albert, 113, 130
Galloway, Joseph, 47
Galveston, Texas, 410
Garfield, James A., 347
Garment industry, 264, 318, 319
Garner, John Nance, 478
Garrison, William Lloyd, 174
Garvey, Marcus Aurelius, 460–461

Genêt, Edmond C., 99
Genetics *(def.)*, 400
Geneva Accords, 592
George III, King of England, 40, 48, 52, 58, 121, 147
George, Henry, 315
Georgia, 24, 25, 72, 89, 118, 138, 166, 177, 271, 288
German Federal Republic. *See* Germany, West
Germans, 15, 25, 26, 30, 218-219, 227, 307, 402
Germany, 25, 30, 214, 226, 303, 381, 387, 388, 538, 550-551, 561; and Samoa, 374; and Open Door, 431; and Venezuela, 433-434; Moroccan crisis, 437-438; and World War I strategies, 440; and U.S. neutrality, 442-443; and armistice, 448; World War I reparations, 449; treaty with U.S., 452; Nazis gain power, 457, 520; relations with U.S., 521, 524, 526-528, 530-532, 534-535; prelude to World War II, 522, 524, 525, 526-530, 532, 534, 535; and weaponry, 544-545; and Yalta agreements, 562; division after World War II, 570-571; unification of West, 574; treaties signed with, 595; Berlin crisis of 1958, 598
Germany, East, 538; refugees, 634
Germany, West, 538, 609; Berlin blockade, 574; Berlin crisis of 1961, 633-634
Geronimo, 330
Gerry, Elbridge, 102
Gershwin, George, 504
Gershwin, Ira, 504
Gestapo, 457, 548
Ghettos *(def.)*, 391
"Ghost dance," 329
Giannini, Amadeo Peter, 396
G.I. Bill, 564
Gillespie, Dizzy, 606
Giovanni, Nikki, 672
Glenn, John, Jr., 660
Gold rush, 199, 327, 329, 438
Goldwater, Barry M., 614
Goliad, battle of, 178
Gompers, Samuel, 320, 383, 425
Goodman, Benny, 606
Goodyear, Charles, 223
Gorky, Arshile, 604
Grady, Henry W., 334
Grand Army of the Republic, 293, 344
Grandfather clause, 357
Grange, Harold "Red," 512
Grange, 294, 344, 354-355
Granger laws, 294, 352
Grant, Ulysses S., 199, 277, 347; in Civil War, 277, 280-281; as President, 293-295, 350; election of 1868, 293; election of 1872, 293; and southern Republicans, 298
Graves, Thomas, 59
Gray, Robert, 187
Great Awakening, 32
Great Plains, 307, 310, 330, 331
Great Society, 614, 653
Greece, 133, 532, 572-573
Greeks, 37, 402
Greeley, Horace, 293
Greenbacks, 262-263, 294-295, 361
Greene, Catharine, 109
Greene, Nathanael, 56, 58
Greenland, 17, 532
Griffith, David W., 514
Griffiths, Martha, 602
Grimké, Angelina, 174
Grimké, Sarah, 174
Guam, 376, 380, 430, 552
Guantánamo Bay, 519
Guatemala, 594
Guinea, 611
Guiteau, Charles J., 347
Gulf of Tonkin resolution, 639, 642

Hague, The, 389, 438
Haiti, 66, 172, 357, 437
Hale, John P., 248
Halleck, Henry W., 274
Hamilton, Alexander, 67, 88, 93-97, 100, 104-106, 108, 117, 178; economic program, 93-96; Report on Manufactures, 95, 130; and the British, 99
Hammerstein, Oscar, II, 606
Hampton Institute, 398
Hancock, Winfield Scott, 347
Hanna, Marcus Alonzo, 363, 383
Hansberry, Lorraine, 606
Harding, Warren G., 500; election of 1920, 452; scandals, 462; death of, 462; foreign policy of, 473-474
Harlem Renaissance, 504, 672
Harpers Ferry, Virginia, 253-254
Harrison, Benjamin, 375, 383, 415; election of 1888, 350-351; and Congress, 351; election of 1892, 356
Harrison, William Henry, 122, 126, 160; election of 1840, 183-184
Hart, Lorenz, 504
Hartford Convention, 124
Hawaii, 152, 246, 373-374, 391, 430, 543, 602
Hawthorne, Nathaniel, 207
Hay, John, 431, 433
Hayes, Rutherford B., 298, 300, 345
Haymarket Riot, 320
Health, Education, and Welfare (HEW), Department of, 590
Hearst, William Randolph, 372, 378
Held, John, 472

Heller, Joseph, 671
Helper, Hinton R., 231
Hemingway, Ernest, 502
Henderson, David, 672
Henderson, Fletcher, 504
Henri, Robert, 404
Henry, Patrick, 42, 47
Hessians, 56
Heyward, DuBose, 504
Hill, James J., 307
Hillman, Sidney, 490
Hippies, 648
Hiroshima, bombing of, 537, 558
Hiss, Alger, 569, 577
Hitchcock, Alfred, 607
Hitler, Adolf, 457, 520, 544, 548, 550, 552
Hobart, Garret A., 383
Hobby, Oveta Culp, 590
Ho Chi Minh, 591-592
Holding companies *(def.)*, 314; 424
Holmes, Mary Jane, 207
Homer, Winslow, 406
Homestead Act of 1862, 263, 332
Hood, John B., 278, 281
Hooker, Joseph, 276, 279
Hoover, Herbert, 444, 468, 481, 500, 577; secretary of commerce, 462; election of 1928, 466–467; domestic policies, 468, 472; foreign policy, 474, 476–477
Hope, Bob, 516
Hopis, 21
Hopkins, Harry L., 484, 490
Hopper, Edward, 506
Horseshoe Bend, battle of, 129
House Committee on Un-American Activities, 569
House of Burgesses, 34, 41, 159
Housing, pioneer, 76, 139; in industrial towns, 167, 224, in cities, 323–324, 392, 577, 656; on Great Plains, 333–334
Housing and Urban Development (HUD), Department of, 656
Houston, Sam, 178
Howe, Elias, 223
Howe, William, 56–57
Howells, William Dean, 368
Hudson, Henry, 17
Hudson's Bay Company, 152, 187, 190–191
Hughes, Charles Evans, 427–428, 462, 473
Hughes, Langston, 504
Hull, Cordell, 480, 517–518, 522, 527, 533, 569
Hull, William, 124
Humanitarianism, 133–134
Humphrey, Hubert H., 614, 616, 618
Hungarians, 318
Hungary, 388, 538, 563, 571, 596
Hunt, Richard, 604
Hydrogen bombs, 537–538

Iceland, 575, 610
Ickes, Harold L., 480, 486
Idaho, 327, 358
Idealism *(def.)*, 396–397
Illinois, 137, 168–169, 219, 222, 253, 268, 422
Immigrants, 150, 169, 189, 304, 391–392; Irish, 218, 224, 227, 307; German, 218–219, 227, 307, 402; French, 219; Norwegian, 219; English, 219, 402; Swedish, 219, 402; Catholic, 227, 367, 391; and railroads, 307; Japanese, 307, 318, 391; Chinese, 307, 318, 391, 402; Mexican, 307, 390–391, 435; Italian, 318, 396, 402; Czech, 318; Hungarian, 318; Polish, 318; Russian, 318; and nativism, 318–319, 391; in Haymarket Riot, 320; and "boss rule," 325; and sweatshops, 390; families, 391; Filipino, 391; Jewish, 391, 402; and banking, 396; Greek, 402
Immigration, 26, 103, 216, 218–220, 304, 316, 318, 390; in colonial period, 15, 25–26; "America letters," 218; opposition to, 219–220, 227, 318, 465; 1830–1860, 227; restrictions on, 318–319, 391–392, 431, 465; and cities, 391; and melting-pot theory, 402; U.S. policies in 1920's, 465, 474; effects of laws, 498; under McCarran-Walter Act, 578; decline, 651–652; revised laws, 654–655. *See also* Colonists; Immigrants
Imperialism, *(defs.)*, 185, 305, 439; in Japan, 373; in Philippines, 380–383; in Cuba, 380–381; and economic interests, 383; opposition to, 383; and election of 1900, 384; and international rivalries, 387; U.S. colonies, 429; and China, 430–431; and Panama Canal, 432–433; and Dominican Republic, 434, 437; and Haiti, 437
Impressment, 119–120, 122–123, 126, 128
Indentured servants, 24–26, 29, 218
Independent Treasury System, 207
India, 13, 38, 222, 271, 388, 455, 539, 593; and war with Pakistan over Kashmir, 610, 646
Indiana, 168–169, 222, 338
Indian Claims Commission, 626
Indian Reorganization Act, 493
Indians, 13, 27; relations with colonists, 14–15, 24; culture areas, 21; and colonial wars, 24, 35–36; land cessions, 24, 62, 75, 122, 137, 164–166, 177, 332; and education, 32, 330, 493; Pontiac's Rebellion, 40–41; in Revolutionary War, 54, 56; and treaties, 62, 99–100, 128, 177; and voting rights, 69; and Articles of Confederation, 77; and Spanish missions, 79; and exploration, 114; and War of 1812, 129–130; and Andrew Jackson, 129, 164, 166; Cherokee removal, 166, 177; and Mexican War, 195; and Civil War, 266, 328; and railroads, 307; government policy, 328–330, 493, 602, 626; and termination, 602; civil rights struggle, 618, 624, 626; Native American Church, 670. *See also specific tribes*
Individualism *(def.)*, 397
Indochina, 214, 527, 530, 534, 591–593, 610
Indonesia, 539, 593
Industrial Revolution, 134, 303–305
Industry, colonial, 24, 34; craftworkers, 26, 28; "putting out" system, 108–110, 168; expansion during War of 1812, 130; in Northeast, 136–137, 166–168; in South, 140; during 1850's, 223–226; development of transportation network, 306–309; growth of communications, 309–310; growth after Civil War, 310–313; formation of trusts, 313–319; and finance capitalism, 314–316; banker control of, 394–395; and New Deal, 484–485; in 1920's and 1930's, 498, 500–501; during World War II, 540–541; and conglomerates, 627
Inflation, 262–263, 294, 343, 361–362, 364–365; during World War II, 542; Emergency Price Control Act, 542; and rationing, 542; post-World War II rise in, 566–567; during 1960's, 630–631
Initiative *(defs.)*, 356, 411
Injunction *(defs.)*, 321, 458
Interior, Department of, 462
Interlocking directorates, 314–315, 424; *(def.)*, 314
Interstate Commerce Commission (ICC), 352, 413, 458
Intolerable Acts of 1774, 46–48, 57
Inventions, 18, 109–110, 181, 210, 223, 303–304, 308–310, 312–313, 334, 338, 544–545
Iowa, 222, 338
Iran, 560, 596
Iraq, 389, 456, 539, 596, 598
Ireland, 25–26, 135, 218, 227, 610
Irish, 15, 25, 26, 218, 219, 224, 227, 307
Iroquois, League of the, 21, 35–36, 62
Irving, Washington, 206–207
Isabella, Queen of Castile, 20
Isolationists, 449–451, 453, 472, 521–524, 527–528, 531–532, 535
Israel, 539, 576, 597, 611, 645–646

Issei (def.), 543
Italians, 15, 37, 318, 402
Italy, 135, 214, 303, 388, 396, 563, 575, 609; and Open Door policy, 431; and Venezuela, 433; and World War I, 439, 448; Versailles Treaty, 449; relations during 1930's, 521–522, 524, 527, 530, 535; Fascists gain power, 457, 520; invades Ethiopia, 522; joins Axis, 522; in World War II, 526, 528, 532, 535; Allied invasion, 547; surrender, 547; World War II treaty, 571
Ives, Charles, 606

Jackson, Andrew, in War of 1812, 129–130; and Indians, 129, 150, 164–166; on Florida frontier, 150–152; election of 1824, 156, 160; election of 1828, 156–157, 160; domestic policies, 161–166; foreign policies, 176–178; and Bank War, 180
Jackson, Thomas J., 279
James, Henry, 368
James, Thomas L., 347
James, William, 397
Jamestown, 25, 34, 36
Japan, 214, 295, 303, 305, 383, 387–388, 537, 539, 544, 610; reopening of, 215, 373; and "gentleman's agreement," 391; and Open Door policy, 430–431; Russo-Japanese War, 431; Lansing-Ishii Agreement, 432; Versailles Treaty, 449; and U.S., 474, 518, 520, 524, 527, 530, 533–535; invades Manchuria, 474; withdraws from League of Nations, 474, 521; attacks on China, 520, 523–524, 527, 530, 533–534; joins Axis, 522; economic sanctions, 530, 534; and bombing of Pearl Harbor, 534–535; in World War II, 552–558; surrender, 558–559; peace treaty, 580; as industrial power, 611; return of Japanese territory, 646
Japanese, 307, 318, 391, 624; restrictions on civil liberties, 542–543
Jay, John, 60–61, 88, 100
Jazz, 407, 606
Jefferson, Thomas, 73, 94, 102, 108, 121, 149, 150; and Declaration of Independence, 52–53; and education, 74; opposition to Hamiltonians, 97–98; and democracy, 98, 112–113; and French Revolution, 99; and nullification, 104, 106; election of 1800, 106–107; first administration, 112–118; and Louisiana Purchase, 113–114; election

of 1804, 117; second administration, 118–120; and Supreme Court, 118; foreign policy, 119–120; and livestock breeding, 121
Jeffersonians, 112–113
Jewett, Sarah Orne, 370
Jews, 510; in colonies, 30, 32, 73; settlements in New Amsterdam and Rhode Island, 30; immigrants, 30, 367, 391, 402; prejudice against, 32, 466; political restrictions, 69, 158; and religious freedom, 73; Reform Judaism, 201; and biblical interpretation, 367; Conservative Judaism, 367; persecution by Nazis, 457, 520, 526; attacked by Ku Klux Klan, 466; in World War II, 548; in Nazi death camps, 550, 552; and Palestine, 576; cooperation with Christians, 670. *See also* Israel
"Jim Crow" laws, 353, 619
Jingoism *(def.)*, 387
Job Corps, 630
Johnson, Andrew, accession to office, 283; Reconstruction plans, 284–286, 291; disagreements with Congress, 287–288; impeachment of, 288–289
Johnson, Hiram W., 410
Johnson, Hugh, 485
Johnson, James Weldon, 504
Johnson, Lyndon B., election of 1960, 612; accession to office, 613–614; election of 1964, 614; in 1968 election, 616; civil rights policies, 621, 624; foreign policies of, 633, 635–637, 639–642, 644–646; domestic policies of, 652–656, 666
Johnson, Tom L., 410
Johnston, Albert Sidney, 277, 279
Johnston, Joseph E., 276–277, 281
Joliet, Louis, 17
Jones, LeRoi, (Imamu Amiri Baraka), 672
Jones, Robert "Bobby," 512
Jones Act of 1917, 603
Jordan, 539, 645
Joseph, Chief of Nez Percés, 330
Journeyman *(def.)*, 167
Judicial review, 85, 117
Judicial system, development of, 91–92, 118
Junta (def.), 637

Kalm, Peter, 36
Kansas, 245, 248, 250, 251, 327, 332, 338, 354, 422
Kansas City, 331
Kansas-Nebraska Act, 233, 244, 248
Kearny, Stephen, 195, 196

Kefauver, Estes, 607
Keith, Benjamin F., 370
Kennedy, John F., election of 1960, 612–613; assassination, 613; civil rights policies, 621–622; economic policies, 627–629; foreign policy, 631–636, 645–646; and disarmament, 632–633; and Cuban missile crisis, 635–636; domestic policies, 655, 666
Kennedy, Robert F., 616, 618
Kent, Corita, 668
Kentucky, 138, 226, 258
Kentucky and Virginia resolutions, 104–105
Keppard, Freddie, 407
Kern, Jerome, 504
Kettell, T. P., 232
Key, Francis Scott, 126
Khrushchev, Nikita, 598, 599, 633–634, 636
King, Martin Luther, Jr., 600–601, 624
King, Rufus, 130
King, William Mackenzie, 530
King George's War, 38
King Philip. *See* Metacomet
King Philip's War, 35
King William's War, 38
Kiowa, 266, 328
Kissinger, Henry M., 644
Klondike, 327, 364, 438
Knights of Labor, 319–320, 355
Know-Nothing party, 220, 227, 246, 254; election of 1856, 250
Knox, Philander, 436
Korea, 430, 431, 560, 581
Korea, North, 581, 610
Korea, South, 581
Korean War, 581, 584, 586
Kosygin, Aleksei N., 633, 645
Ku Klux Klan, 291–292, 294, 468, 621; and Enforcement Acts, 292; revival after World War I, 460, 466; in election of 1928, 466
Kurusu, Saburo, 534

Labor, 167–168, 316, 318–322; colonial, 24–26, 28, 45; and children, 168, 409–410, 416; and immigrants, 224–226, 390–391, 435; and industrial growth, 316; unskilled, 316, 626; and collective bargaining, 316, 485; and unions, 319–321; skilled, 320; and nativism, 391; government policy, 412, 426; and antitrust laws, 425; during World War I, 445; and public opinion, 459; against immigration, 465; and New Deal, 490, 492, 497; Wagner Act (1935), 490, 494, 568; formation of CIO, 492; Fair Labor Standards Act, 495–496; in World War II, 541; after World War II, 566–568; Taft-Hartley Act, 568; featherbedding, 626–627; effects of automation, 627; white-collar workers, 627–628; farm workers, 629. *See also* Unions; Strikes
Ladd, William, 204
Lafayette, Marquis de, 59
La Follette, Robert M., 410, 416, 418
Laissez-faire *(def.)*, 304
Land policy, 23, 118; ordinances of 1785 and 1787, 74–77; speculators, 74–75, 79, 94; law of 1820, 145; and railroads, 307
Landon, Alfred M., 494
Lange, Dorothea, 506
Lansing-Ishii Agreement, 432
Laos, 539, 592–593, 639
La Salle, Robert René Cavelier, 17
Lasuen, Fermin Francisco de, 79
Latin America, colonies in, 66–67; and Monroe Doctrine, 153–154, 156; and trade with U.S., 375; effects of Great Depression, 456; relations with U.S., 476, 517–519, 575, 594, 634–637; political and social changes, 455; during World War II, 530; revolutions in, 539; during 1960's, 611, 634–637. *See also names of individual countries*
Latvia, 559
"Law and order," 650, 656–657
Lawrence, Ernest O., 510
Lawrence, Kansas, 248, 250
Leadville, Colorado, 327
League of Nations, 389, 449–452, 473–474, 520–522; withdrawal of Japan, 474, 521; withdrawal of Germany, 521
Lease, Mary E., 355
Lebanon, 456, 539, 598
Lee, Hannah Farnham, 207
Lee, Peggy, 606
Lee, Richard Henry, 88
Lee, Robert E., 199, 268, 274, 276, 280–281
Legal tender *(defs.)*, 80, 142
Leisure, 127, 349, 366, 401, 475, 498, 509, 617. *See also* Sports
Le May, Curtis E., 616
Lend-Lease, 529, 532
Lenin, Vladimir, 457
Lerner, Alan Jay, 606
Letters from an American Farmer, 15
Letters of a Federal Farmer, 88
Levertov, Denise, 672
Lewis, John L., 459, 490, 541, 568
Lewis, Sinclair, 502
Lewis and Clark expedition, 116, 187
Lexington, battle of, 49–51

Liberia, 172, 357, 611
Liberty party, 246
Libraries, 370
Lichtenstein, Roy, 668
Liliuokalani, Queen of Hawaiian Islands, 374
Lincoln, Abraham, 221, 256, 260, 271–273, 279; "house divided" speech, 252, 254; election of 1860, 254–255; first inaugural address, 257; and Emancipation Proclamation, 265–266; election of 1864, 266–267; Civil War strategy, 273–274; Reconstruction plans, 282–283; assassination, 283
Lincoln-Douglas debates, 252–253
Lindbergh, Charles A., 501
Lindsay, Vachel, 503
Lippard, George, 207
Literacy tests, 357, 392
Literature, U.S., early nineteenth century, 204–207; late nineteenth century, 368–370; in 1920's and 1930's, 501–505, 508; in 1940's and 1950's, 602, 606; in 1960's and 1970's, 670–672. *See also individual authors*
Lithuania, 559
Liuzzo, Viola Gregg, 621
Livingston, Robert, 148
Lloyd George, David, 449
Locke, John, 52
Lodge, Henry Cabot, 357, 382, 449–450
Lodge, Henry Cabot, Jr., 613
London, Jack, 406
London International Economic Conference of 1933, 483, 517
Long, Huey P., 488
Los Alamos, New Mexico, 544
Louis, Joe, 512
Louisiana, 105, 114, 117, 138, 226, 256, 283, 288, 291, 336
Louisiana Purchase, 67, 113–114, 116, 152, 233
Lovejoy, Elijah, 175
Lowe, Frederick, 606
Lowell, Amy, 503
"Lowell girls," 166–167
Loyalists, 51, 53, 62, 71–72, 78, 103
Luce, Henry, 513
Ludlow amendment, 524
Lundy, Benjamin, 172, 174
Lutherans, 30
Luxembourg, 528, 575, 609
Lyceums *(def.)*, 203
Lynchburg, Virginia, 278

MacArthur, Douglas, 472, 538, 556, 580–581, 584
McCarran-Nixon Internal Security Act of 1950, 578

McCarthy, Eugene J., 616, 649
McCarthy, Joseph, 577–578, 589–590
McClellan, George B., 267, 274, 276, 279
McCormick, Cyrus Hall, 169, 223, 340
McGovern, George S., 618
"Machine" government, 325, 410
McKay, Claude, 504
McKinley, William, 374, 409, 415; election of 1896, 362–364; and money question, 364–365; and Spanish-American War, 378; and Philippines, 380–381; election of 1900, 383–384; assassination of, 385
MacLeish, Archibald, 504
Macon's Bill No. 2, 120, 122
McPherson, Aimee Semple, 504
Madison, James, 73, 83, 88, 92, 95, 98, 104, 107, 113, 118, 154; election of 1808, 120; first administration, 120–124; and War of 1812, 123–128; election of 1812, 124; second administration, 124–128
Magazines, 32, 372, 670
Magna Charta, 33
Mahan, Alfred Thayer, 372, 380
Mailer, Norman, 670
Maine, 176, 186, 204
Malcolm X, 620
Manchuria, 431–432, 474, 520, 559, 562
Mandans, 116
Mandate system *(def.)*, 456
Manifest Destiny, 185–199
Manila Bay, 378–379, 380
Mann, Horace, 202
Manumission *(def.)*, 73
Mao Tse-tung, 456, 539, 580, 647
Marcy, William L., 246
Margin *(def.)*, 470
Mariana Islands, 557
Marijuana, 657
Marin, John, 506
Marion, Francis, 56
Marne, battles of the, 441
Marquette, Jacques, 17
Marsh, Reginald, 506
Marshall, George C., 573, 580
Marshall, John, 102, 117–118, 147–148, 150, 166
Marshall Plan, 573–574
Marx, Karl, 304–305, 321–322, 472
Maryland, 23, 26, 30, 70, 82, 89, 126, 226, 258
Mason, James M., 272
Mason-Dixon Line, 147
Masons, 161
Massachusetts, 34, 72, 81, 89, 146, 159, 167, 201, 202
Mass production, 224, 403
Mass transit, 661
Master craftsman *(def.)*, 167–168

Masters, Edgar Lee, 503
Maximilian, 295
Meade, George Gordon, 279–280
Meany, George, 601
Meat Inspection Act, 414
Medicine, 304, 392, 579, 652–653, 660
Meitner, Lise, 510
Mellon, Andrew, 462
Melting-pot theory, 396, 402, 625
Melville, Herman, 206
Mennonites, 339
Menotti, Gian-Carlo, 606
Mercantilism *(def.)*, 33
Merchant Marine Act of 1920, 458
Meredith, James, 621–622
Merger *(def.)*, 313
Merit system, 347–348
Metacomet, 35
Methodist Church, 96
Metropolitan area *(def.)*, 393
Mexican Americans, immigrants, 307, 390–391, 435; cowboys, 332; in World War II, 544, 554; and César Chávez, 602, 628; civil rights struggle, 618, 624; strike of farm workers, 628
Mexican War, 191–199
Mexico, acquires California, 79; and slavery, 172; and Texas, 176, 178; war with U.S., 191–199; Treaty of Guadalupe Hidalgo, 198–199; and Maximilian, 295; revolution in, 388, 435, 437, 455, 539; World War I, 443; relations with, 476, 519
Miami Indians, 77, 100
Michelson, Albert A., 400
Michigan, 169, 222, 338–339
Middle East, 388–389, 539, 575–576, 596–597, 611, 645–646. *See also names of individual countries*
Middle West, 310, 312, 498
Midway, 372; battle of, 553–554, 556
Miles, Nelson A., 379
Militarism *(def.)*, 439
Millay, Edna St. Vincent, 504
Miller, Alice Duer, 421
Miller, Arthur, 606
Miller, Glenn, 606
Miller, William E., 614
Mining, 327–328; labor disputes, 412; coal, 424; automation, 627
Minnesota, 294, 338
"Missionary diplomacy," 436
Missions, Spanish, 79, 128–129
Mississippi, 226, 241, 288, 357
Mississippi plan, 298
Missouri, 146, 222, 248, 258
Missouri Compromise, 146–147, 233, 240, 244, 250
Mitchell, John, 412
Mitchell, Margaret, 502
Mitchell, William, 440

Mohawks, 21
Moley, Raymond, 480
Momaday, N. Scott, 671
Monitor and *Merrimac,* battle of, 275
Monk, Thelonius, 606
Monometallism *(def.),* 361
Monopoly, 315, 352; *(def.),* 499
Monroe, James, 114, 123, 128, 130, 136, 150–152
Monroe, Marilyn, 607
Monroe Doctrine, 152, 295, 375, 434, 476
Montana, 327–328
Montcalm, Marquis de, 38
Monterrey, California, 195–196
Montgomery, Alabama, 256, 270
Moore, Marianne, 504
Moratorium *(def.),* 81
Moravians, 30
Morgan, J. Pierpont, 315, 394–396, 412
Morgan, William, 161
Mormons, 192–193, 217
Morocco, 387, 437–438, 611
Morrill Land Grant Act of 1862, 263, 339
Morrow, Dwight W., 476
Morse, Samuel F. B., 210
Moscoso, Teodoro, 603
Moses, Anna "Grandma," 604
Motion picture industry, 500, 513–515, 606–607
Mott, Lucretia, 203
"Mugwumps," 350
Muhammad, Elijah, 620
Muir, John, 415
Munich agreement, 525–526
Muñoz Marín, Luís, 603
Murrow, Edward R., 607
Music, 371, 407, 504–505, 602, 606, 671
Muskie, Edmund S., 616, 618
Mussolini, Benito, 457, 520, 523, 547
My Lai massacre, 642

Nader, Ralph, 666
Nagasaki, bombing of, 537, 559
Napoleon Bonaparte, 65–66, 105, 114, 119, 122–124, 126, 133
Napoleon III, 295
Narváez, Panfilo de, 17
Nashville Convention, 241–242
Nast, Thomas, 280
National Aeronautics and Space Administration (NASA), 659
National American Woman Suffrage Association, 358, 461
National Association for the Advancement of Colored People (NAACP), 399, 460, 619–620

National Broadcasting Company (NBC), 516
National Colored Farmers' Alliance, 354
National Education Association (NEA), 627–628
National Industrial Recovery Act of 1933 (NIRA), 484
National Labor Relations Board (NLRB), 490
National Labor Union, 319
National Liberation Front (NLF), 639
National Mobilization Committee to End the War in Vietnam, 649
National Organization for Women (NOW), 662
National Recovery Administration (NRA), 485
National Security Council, 569
National Trades Union, 168
National War Labor Board, 445, 541
National Woman Suffrage Association, 358
National Youth Administration (NYA), 490, 614
Nationalism, 66, 130, 136, 387–388; *(def.),* 213; in U.S., 67; in 1950's, 609
Native American Church, 670
Native Americans. *See* Indians
Nativism, *(def.),* 318–319; 391
Navahos, 195
Navigation Acts, 34
Nazis, 457, 520, 526, 548, 562
Nebraska, 245, 248, 327, 338
Neutralism, 539; *(def.),* 593
Neutrality, Proclamation of 1793, 99; Act of 1794, 99; before World War II, 522–523, 526, 528
Nevada, 327
Nevelson, Louise, 668
New Deal, 479–497, 562
New England, 206, 244; and King Philip's War, 35; in Revolutionary War, 50–51; and northern confederacy, 117; and War of 1812, 126; industry, 136–137, 166; reformers, 200, 204; literature, 206–207
New Hampshire, 30, 89
New Harmony, Indiana, 204
New Jersey, 69, 88, 117, 394
New Mexico, 192, 199, 266, 327, 435
New Netherland, 36
New Orleans, Louisiana, 37, 114, 129, 140, 144, 210, 215, 217, 219, 221, 227, 244, 268, 275, 290, 407; battle of, 129, 130, 275
Newspapers, 32, 210, 372, 670
New York City, 144, 210, 217, 262, 322, 390, 399
New York State, 24, 30, 36, 44, 89, 106, 126, 144, 159, 202, 222

New Zealand, 580, 593
Nez Percés, 329–330
Ngo Dinh Diem, 592, 639
Nicaragua, 432, 436, 476, 594
Nickelodeons *(def.),* 514
Nigeria, 611, 638–639
Nimitz, Chester W., 556–557
Nineteenth Amendment, 461, 704–705
Ninth Amendment, 92, 701
Nisei (def.), 542
Nixon, Richard M., as Vice-President, 585, 590, 594; election of 1960, 612–613; election of 1968, 616, 618; election of 1972, 618; Watergate affair, 618; domestic policies of, 631, 654, 656–657, 662, 665–666; foreign policy of, 633–635, 646–647, 650; and Vietnam war, 642–644
Nonbelligerency *(def.),* 530–531
Nonintercourse Act of 1808, 120
Normandy, invasion of, 548
Norris, Frank, 406
Norris, George W., 486
North, 219, 220–226, 232, 236, 238, 246, 248, 250–252, 256, 258, 260; and Compromise of 1850, 242; Fugitive Slave Law of 1850, 243
North Africa, 545–547, 560
North Atlantic Treaty Organization (NATO), 598, 609; formation of, 574–575
North Carolina, 26, 89, 90, 226, 258, 271, 288, 290
North Dakota, 327, 338
Northeast, 200, 217, 219, 223, 248, 251–252; description of, 136–137, 166–169
Northern Alliance, 354–355
Northern Securities Company, 394, 412
Northwest, 200, 217, 223, 248, 251–252, 266; description of, 137–138, 169–170
Northwest Ordinance of 1787, 76–77, 234
Northwest Territory, 74; and Indians, 77–78; and slavery, 146, 234
Norway, 528, 575
Norwegians, 219
Nuclear disarmament, 632–633
Nuclear weapons, 537–538, 572, 579
Nullification, theory of, 104, 106, 162–163
Nuremberg trials, 550
Nye, Gerald P., 522

Oates, Joyce Carol, 671
O'Connor, Flannery, 670
Office of Price Administration, 542, 565

Ohio, 159, 168–169, 222, 338
Ohio Company, 74–75
Ohwachiras (def.), 21
O'Keeffe, Georgia, 506
Okinawa, 646; battle of, 558
Oklahoma, 327, 332
Olds, Ransom, 400, 403
Oligopoly *(def.),* 499
Oliver, "King," 502
Olmsted, Frederick Law, 236, 323
Olney, Richard T., 375
Oneidas, 21
O'Neill, Eugene, 505
Onondagas, 21
Open Door policy *(def.),* 431–432
Open hearth process, 312
Operation Bootstrap, 603
Oppenheimer, J. Robert, 544
Oregon, 199, 327, 422
Oregon country, 152, 187–191
Oregon Trail, 188, 192
Organization of American States (OAS), 575, 636–637
Osceola, 166
Ostend Manifesto, 246
Oswald, Lee Harvey, 613
Owen, Robert, 204
Owens, Jesse, 512

Pago Pago, 374
Paine, Thomas, 52
Pakenham, Sir Edward, 129–130
Pakistan, 593, 596, 610, 646
Palestine, 389, 456, 575–576
Palmer, A. Mitchell, 459–460
Palmerston, Lord Henry, 272–273
Panama, 372, 432–433
Panama, Declaration of, 528
Panama Canal, 380, 432–433, 439
Pan-American Conference of 1928, 476
Pan-Americanism *(def.),* 374–375
Pan-American Union, 375, 389
Panay incident, 526
Panic *(def.),* 181; of 1819, 183; of 1837, 185; of 1857, 224, 232, 251; of 1873, 294, 298; of 1893, 320, 356; of 1907, 395, 414, 424
Parity payments *(def.),* 495
Parker, Alton B., 413
Parker, Charlie, 606
Parker, Dorothy, 504
Parks, Rosa, 601
Park system, national, 414–415
Paul, Alice, 664
Peabody, Elizabeth, 207
Peace Corps, 610
Peddlers, 142–143
Penn, William, 323
Pennsylvania, 23, 26, 45, 72, 88, 159, 201, 222, 287, 310
Pennsylvania Germans, 26

Peonage *(def.),* 335
People's party. *See* Populists
People's Republic of China. *See* China, People's Republic of
Pereira, Irene, 604
Perkins, Frances, 480, 489
Permanent Court of Arbitration, 389, 438
Perón, Juan D., 575
Perry, Matthew C., 215, 373
Perry, Oliver Hazard, 126
Pershing, John J., 440, 442, 447
Personal liberty laws, 240
Peru, 66, 153, 611
Petersburg, battle of, 281
Petroleum industry, 310–311, 500, 588, 611, 665
Philadelphia, Pennsylvania, 56, 140, 142
Philadelphia General Trades' Union, 168
Philippine Islands, 376, 378, 380, 430, 539, 552, 554, 558, 610; war with U.S., 381; aid from U.S., 382; annexation treaty, 382–383; become semi-independent, 520; attacked by Japan, 527, 532, 534–535; achieve independence, 578; join SEATO, 593
Phillips, David G., 410
Photography, 506
Pickford, Mary, 514
Pierce, Franklin, 244–245, 248, 252
Pike, Zebulon, 116–117
Pinchot, Gifford, 415, 417
Pinckney, Charles C., 102
Pippin, Horace, 604–605
Pitt, William, 38
Pittsburgh, Pennsylvania, 312
Plastics, 579
Platt Amendment, 381, 519
Poe, Edgar Allan, 206
Poison gas, 447
Poland, attacked by Germany and Soviet Union, 526–528; and Yalta, 562; Lublin government, 562; and Potsdam, 563
Poles, 15, 318
Political liberalism *(def.),* 133–134
Political parties, 93, 97–98, 156, 160–161. *See also* Elections; *names of individual parties*
Polk, James K., and Texas, 187; election of 1844, 187, 246; and Oregon country, 190–191; and Mexican War, 192–199; and California, 192, 194; and tariff, 209
Pollack, Jackson, 604
Pollution, 149, 317, 463. *See also* Ecology
Ponce de León, Juan, 17
Pontiac's Rebellion, 40
Pony Express, 221
Pool *(def.),* 313

Pope, John, 276, 279
Popular sovereignty, *(def.),* 240; 242, 245, 250, 252, 254
Population, Indian, 21, 79; colonial, 26, 38; growth, 74, 103, 189, 324, 392, 499, 651–653; national origins and religions, 103; internal migration, 138; in cities, 217, 392, 652; and Civil War, 299; and Industrial Revolution, 304; postwar "baby boom," 566, 579
Populists, 355–357, 408
Porter, Cole, 504, 606
Portugal, 20, 72–73, 575
Postal service, 35, 309
Potawatomis, 100
Potsdam Declaration, 563, 570
Pound, Ezra, 502–503
Powderly, Terence V., 319
Presidio (def.), 128
Pragmatism *(def.),* 397
Prendergast, Maurice, 404
Presley, Elvis, 606
Prisons, 93, 657
Proclamation of 1763, 40–41, 54
Progressive party, 419, 426–428, 464, 577
Progressivism, 408–420; goals, 409; and muckraking, 409–410; and local government, 409–410; and state government, 410–411; and Robert La Follette, 410, 416, 418; and women's suffrage, 411; Taft's policies, 416–418
Prohibition, 420, 468–470, 472, 511
Proletariat *(defs.),* 305, 457
Protectorate *(def.),* 374
Protestants, Protestant Reformation, 20; dissenters from Anglican Church, 22; in English colonies, 30, 32; Great Awakening, 32; and rivalries between French and British colonies, 36; and separation of church and state, 73; "Old Light" and "New Light" groups, 200; and anti-Catholicism, 227; social gospel movement, 367; and biblical interpretation, 367; during 1920's and 1930's, 510. *See also names of individual churches*
Psychoanalysis, 508
Public domain, 144
Public Works Administration (PWA), 486
Publishing industry, 371–372, 512–513, 670–672
Pueblos, 195
Puerto Ricans, migration to mainland, 603; in civil rights movement, 618, 624; in sports, 672
Puerto Rico, in Spanish-American War, 376, 379–380; becomes U.S. colony, 376, 380; and the Insular Cases, 430; under Operation

Bootstrap, 603; becomes commonwealth, 603
Pujo, Arsène, 424
Pure Food and Drug Act, 414
Puritans, 22, 30, 32, 200

Quakers, 22, 30, 158, 200, 543
Quartering Act of 1765, 41, 44
Quebec Act of 1774, 46–47
Queen Anne's War, 38

Radar, 544
Radical Republicans, 265, 267, 283–285, 287–291
Radio industry, 500, 514–516, 606–607
Railroads, 221, 263, 395, 435; beginnings of, 209–210; and Stephen A. Douglas, 244–245; in Civil War, 267, 269; and Reconstruction, 290; growth of, 306–308; in 1890, 309; freight, 314; and farmers, 341–342; and interstate commerce, 352; and immigrants, 391; and Hepburn Act, 413; and Adamson Act, 426; and World War I, 444; automation in, 627; in 1970's, 661–662. *See also* Transportation
Randolph, Edmund, 83
Reaper, 169, 338
Recall *(def.)*, 411
Reconstruction, 282–292; acts of 1867, 288; and Republican losses, 296, 298; and Solid South, 300–301
Reconstruction Finance Corporation (RFC), 472
Red scare, 459–460
Red Shirts, 298
Reed, Walter, 380
Referendum *(defs.)*, 356, 410
Reform movement, 1820–1850, 199–204
Relativity, theory of, 510
Religion, 30, 32, 200–201, 366–367, 509–510, 670; and state laws, 69; separation of church and state, 73; freedom of, 73; Christian Science, 366; and science, 366–367; social gospel movement, 367. *See also* Catholics; Jews; Protestants; *names of individual denominations*
Republican (Jeffersonian) party, 98–101, 104–106, 107, 108, 112–113, 117, 123–124, 130, 156, 157. *See also* Democratic party
Republican party, 246, 251, 252–256, 258, 286, 287, 294, 300, 344–345, 418, 426, 427, 429; organization of, 248; and Dred Scott decision, 251; in the South, 289; and blacks, 289; and Ku Klux Klan, 292; and imperialism, 382; and Progressives, 416–418; and Wilson, 448–450; and Paris peace conference, 449; and League of Nations, 449–451; and Vietnam war, 616; congressional elections of 1910, 418; 1918, 448–449; 1946, 568. *See also* Elections; Radical Republicans; *names of individual candidates*
Resistance movements, European in World War II, 548
Revere, Paul, 44
Rhode Island, 24, 44, 87, 90
Rhodesia, 611, 638
Rice, Elmer, 505
Richardson, Henry Hobson, 407
Richmond, Virginia, 207, 317
Ridge, Major, 177
Riley, James Whitcomb, 370
Rio Pact, 575
Rivers, Larry, 668
Robbins, Jerome, 606
Roberts, Owen J., 494
Robinson, Edwin Arlington, 503
Robinson, Jackie, 672
Rochambeau, Jean Baptiste de, 58
Rockefeller, John D., 315, 368, 394–396, 400, 470
Rockefeller, Nelson, 635
Rockne, Knute, 512
Rodgers, Richard, 504, 606
Romania, 538, 559, 563, 571
Roosevelt, Anna Eleanor, 478, 525
Roosevelt, Franklin D., 478–479, 552; and election of 1920, 452; and war debts, 477; foreign policy of, 483, 496, 517–535, 560; election of 1932, 479; New Deal, 479–497; and "brain trust," 480; and the Supreme Court, 494; election of 1936, 494; and isolationists, 527–528; and aid to Britain, 531; election of 1940, 532; and Fair Employment Practices Commission, 541; and agriculture, 541; diplomacy, 559–562; election of 1944, 560; postwar plans of, 569
Roosevelt, Theodore, 391, 411, 418, 478; and Spanish-American War, 378–379; and expansionism, 380; and election of 1900, 383; accession to presidency, 385; and immigration policy, 391; and organized labor, 412; and election of 1904, 413; and trusts, 412–414; conservation efforts, 414–415; relations with Congress, 414, 416; and Taft, 418–419; and election of 1916, 426–428; and Russo-Japanese War, 431; and Panama Canal, 433; and "big stick" diplomacy, 431, 433; Roosevelt corollary, 434, 476; and Moroccan crisis, 438
Rosecrans, William, 277
Rosenberg, Ethel and Julius, 578
Ross, John, 177
Royce, Josiah, 396
Ruby, Jack, 613
Ruffin, Edmund, 149, 170
Rural Electrification Administration (REA), 490
Rush, Richard, 154
Rush-Bagot Agreement of 1817, 152
Russia, 17, 79, 133, 153, 213–214, 387–389; and the U.S., 152–154; and Alaska, 153–154, 295; and Hawaii, 154; and Open Door policy, 430–431; Russo-Japanese War, 431, 562; and eastern front, 440; and Allied powers strategy, 440; and World War I, 439, 444, 446; Bolshevik revolution, 446. *See also* Soviet Union
Russian America, 295
Russians, 318
Ruth, George "Babe," 512
Rutherford, Ernest, 510
Ryder, Albert, 406
Ryukyu Islands, 558, 646

Sabin, Albert B., 660
Sacajawea, 116
Sacco, Nicola, 466
St. Denis, Ruth, 504
Saint-Gaudens, Augustus, 407
St. Lawrence Seaway, 594
St. Louis, Missouri, 144, 169, 217, 244, 294, 322
Salk, Jonas, 660
Salutary neglect, *(def.)*, 34; 39
Salvation Army, 324
Samoa, 373–374, 430
Sampson, William T., 379
Sandburg, Carl, 503
Sand Creek massacre, 328
San Francisco, California, 217, 431
Sanger, Margaret, 393
Santa Anna, Antonio López de, 178, 194, 199
Santa Fe trade, 192
Sarajevo, Bosnia, 439
Saratoga, battle of, 55–57
Sargent, John Singer, 404
Sauk and Fox, 164
Scalawags, *(def.)*, 289; 291–292, 296
Schnackenberg, Roy, 669
Schofield, John, 277
Schurz, Carl, 286, 345, 383
Science fiction, 670
Scopes, John T., 509
Scotch-Irish, 15, 26
Scott, Winfield, 195, 197, 244, 274

Scottish, 15, 30
Secession, 234, 241, 255–259
Secret ballot, 411
Sectionalism, 136, 145, 148, 150, 162–164, 166–171, 216–243; and Know-Nothings, 227
Securities and Exchange Commission (SEC), 482
Sedition Act of 1918, 445
Segal, George, 668
Seminoles, 21, 150, 165–166, 266, 626; removal of, 165
Seneca Falls Convention, 203
Senecas, 21
Sequoia National Park, 415
Sequoyah, 165
Serra, Father Junípero, 79
Servicemen's Readjustment Act, 564
Seward, William H., 216, 241–242, 254, 272, 283, 295
Sexton, Anne, 672
Shafter, William R., 379
Shahn, Ben, 506
Sharecroppers, 300–301, 334–335; (def.), 334
"Share-Our-Wealth" plan, 488
Shawn, Ted, 504
Shawnees, 77, 100, 122
Shays's Rebellion, 80–81
Sherman Antitrust Act of 1890, 354, 412, 418, 424, 425
Sherman, William Tecumseh, 267, 277, 281
Sherwood, Robert E., 505
Shiloh, battle of, 279
Shipbuilding, 24, 26, 130, 141, 314
Shoemaking, 108–109
Sholes, Christopher L., 309
Shoshones, 21, 116
Shriver, R. Sargent, 618
Sicily, invasion of, 546–547, 560
Sierra Club, 415, 664
Silent Spring, 664
Silver, Comstock Lode, 327; free silver question, 361–365
Simpson, Jerry, 355
Sinatra, Frank, 606
Sinclair, Harry F., 462
Sinclair, Upton, 410, 413
Sioux, 13, 328–330
Sitting Bull, 328–329
Skyjacking, 662
Slater, Samuel, 108
Slaughter-House Cases, 358
Slave revolts, in Haiti, 114; Nat Turner, 170; southern fears of, 170, 254
Slavery, in Spanish colonies, 14; in English colonies, 25; and Thomas Jefferson, 52; abolition by states, 72; during Confederation, 72–73; barred in Northwest Territory, 77, 146; and cotton, 110, 138, 140, 226; and Missouri Compromise, 146–147; slave codes, 150, 170–171; fugitive slave laws, 175, 242–243; territories, 195, 199, 234, 236; and religion, 201; and European immigrants, 219; extent of in South, 226, 228; and Know-Nothings, 227; and women, 229; and the family, 229; defense of, 230–232; and censorship, 231; and "popular sovereignty" (def.), 240; and Compromise of 1850, 242–243; *Uncle Tom's Cabin*, 243; and "free soil," 240, 246; and Kansas-Nebraska Act, 245; and "bleeding Kansas," 248, 250; and Dred Scott decision, 250–251; and Abraham Lincoln, 252–253, 256, 265–268, 283; and Crittenden plan, 256; and Confederate constitution, 257; and Civil War, 265–266, 268, 270; and Thirteenth Amendment, 267–268. *See also* Slave revolts; Slaves; Slave trade
Slaves, in colonies, 25–26, 29–30; and Revolutionary War, 54; and three-fifths clause, 84, 145; and "underground railroad," 175; fugitive, 175, 229–230; plantation life, 228–230; legal status, 229; Emancipation Proclamation, 265–266. *See also* Slave revolts; Slave trade; Slavery
Slave trade, in colonial period, 28; "middle passage," 28; traders, 72, 230; prohibition of, 72, 242; after Revolutionary War, 67, 103; interstate, 230; and constitutional interpretation, 234; in Washington, D.C., 240; and Liberty party, 246
Slidell, John, 194, 272
Sloan, John, 506
Sloat, John D., 196
Smith, Adam, 304
Smith, Alfred E., 466, 479, 484, 489
Smith, Jedediah S., 192
Smith, Joseph, 192
Smith Act of 1940, 578
Social classes, 29–30, 70–71, 94
Social Darwinism, 315–316, 396
Social gospel movement, 367
Socialism, (def.), 133–134; 321–322, 409, 412
Social Security, 490, 494, 577, 590, 653
Soil bank (def.), 588
Sons of Liberty, 42, 44, 47
Soo Canal, 308
South, 24, 73, 135, 163, 219, 226–232, 234, 236, 238, 241, 334–337; population, 25, 299, 499; Revolutionary War, 56, 58; description, 138, 140, 170–171; and cotton, 138, 140; and industry, 140; growth of, 217; and Compromise of 1850, 242; and Fugitive Slave Law of 1850, 243; and Dred Scott decision, 250; and Harpers Ferry raid, 253–254; and secession, 256–257; and Fort Sumter, 257–258; and Reconstruction plans, 282–288; and Republican control, 288–290; and Ku Klux Klan, 291–296; and railroads, 307; and agriculture, 334–335. *See also* Agriculture; Blacks; Civil War; Cotton industry; Slavery
South Carolina, 25–26, 72, 89, 159, 163, 226, 256, 288
South Dakota, 327, 338
Southeast Asia Treaty Organization (SEATO), 593
Southern Alliance, 354–355
Southern Christian Leadership Conference (SCLC), 601, 620
Southworth, Mrs. E. D. E. N., 207
Sovereignty (def.), 69
Soviet Union, 457; in Manchuria, 474; and U.S., 518, 534, 609; and Spanish Civil War, 522; pact with Nazi Germany, 527; attack on Finland, 528; pact with Japan, 533; attacked by Germany, 534; and arms race, 537–538, 572; and World War II, 540, 545, 559; Yalta agreements, 561–562; and U.N., 570; peace treaties, 570–571; and Iran, Turkey, and Greece, 572–573; opposes Marshall Plan, 573; and Berlin, 574, 598; and Mideast, 576, 597, 611; and China, 580; and Korean War, 581; and Indochina, 592; and Warsaw Pact, 596; and Hungarian revolution, 596; in Congo, 599; aid to developing nations, 610; and disarmament, 632–633; and Vietnam war, 640. *See also* Russia
Soyer, Isaac, 506
Space exploration, 609, 659–660
Spain, 38, 60–62; and colonies, 14, 36–37, 133; and England, 20, 36; and Confederation government, 78–80; and Pinckney's Treaty, 100–101; and the Louisiana Purchase, 113–114; and Florida, 150–152; and Latin America, 153; and Cuba, 246, 376; civil war in, 522–523
Spanish-American War, 376–380
Spanish colonists, 14, 37
Spanish missions, 79, 128
Spargo, John, 409
Special Committee to Investigate Organized Crime, 607
Spoils system, 160, 293, 344–347
Sports, from 1870 to 1900, 370–371; in 1920's and 1930's, 512, 516; in 1960's and 1970's, 672

Sputnik, 538, 598, 659
"Square Deal," 413, 416
Stalin, Joseph, 457, 527, 545, 560–563, 570, 595
Stallings, Laurence, 505
Stamp Act Congress, 42, 47
Stamp Act of 1765, 41–42, 48
Standard Oil Company, 314, 409
Stanford, Leland, 368
Stanton, Edwin M., 288
Stanton, Elizabeth Cady, 203, 358, 420
States, legislatures of, 69; powers of, 70, 86, 95–96, 104, 117; constitutions of, 71; state courts, 92; and voting rights, 158–159
States' rights, and Tenth Amendment, 92; and secession, 234; and Confederacy, 270
States' Rights Democratic (Dixiecrat) party, 577
Statue of Liberty, 13, 318
Statute of Religious Liberty, 73
Steamboats, 143–144, 148, 221
Steam power, 303
Steel industry, 311–312, 314, 627–629
Steelworkers union, 320, 459, 492
Steffens, Lincoln, 409
Steichen, Edward, 506
Steinbeck, John, 502
Stephens, Alexander H., 256–257, 270
Stevens, Thaddeus, 284, 287
Stevenson, Adlai E., 585–586, 590
Stilwell, Joseph W., 558
Stockton, Robert, 196
Stone, Lucy, 358
Stowe, Harriet Beecher, 207, 243
Strategic Arms Limitation Talks (SALT), 633
Strikes *(def.),* 167; carpenters (1825), 168; court rulings on, 225–226; railroad (1877), 294; and Haymarket Riot, 320; Homestead, 320; Pullman, 320–321; coal miners, 412, 459; and antitrust laws, 425–426; railroads, 426; steel strike of 1919, 459; Memorial Day massacre, 492; sit-down strikes, 492; textile workers, 500; Smith-Connally Anti-Strike Act, 541; after World War II, 567–568; postal workers, 628; farm workers, 628
Student activism, 647–650
Student Non-Violent Coordinating Committee (SNCC), 620
Suburbs, 323, 393, 652, 655–657
Subways, 322
Suffolk Resolves, 47
Sullivan, Louis H., 407
Sumner, Charles, 225, 249–250, 287, 296

Sumner, William Graham, 380
Sunday, Billy, 504
Supreme Court, and Constitution, 86–87, 92; powers of, 87; and John Marshall, 147–148, 158; and Roger Taney, 182–183; and corporations, 352, 354, 394, 412; and civil rights, 353; and women, 358; and New Deal programs, 485–487, 494; attacked by Roosevelt, 494; and Japanese internment, 542; and civil rights, 601, 621; and eighteen-year-old vote, 650
Supreme Court decisions, *Marbury* v. *Madison,* 85, 117–118; *Fletcher* v. *Peck,* 118, 147–148; *Dartmouth College* v. *Woodward,* 147; *McCulloch* v. *Maryland,* 148; *Gibbons* v. *Ogden,* 148, 150; Cherokee removal decision, 166; *Charles River Bridge* v. *Warren Bridge,* 182–183; *Prigg* v. *Pennsylvania,* 240; Dred Scott decision, 250–251, 253; *Munn* v. *Illinois,* 294; *Plessy* v. *Ferguson,* 336, 353; *Williams* v. *Mississippi,* 336, 357; Civil Rights Cases of 1883, 353; *United States* v. *E. C. Knight Co.,* 354; Slaughter-House Cases, 358; *Minor* v. *Happensatt,* 358; *Hammer* v. *Dagenhart,* 426; Insular Cases, 430; *Schechter Poultry Corp.* v. *United States,* 485; *Brown* v. *Board of Education of Topeka,* 599; *Swann* v. *Charlotte-Mecklenburg Board of Education,* 624; *Furman* v. *Georgia,* 701
Swedes, 15, 219, 402
Syria, 389, 456, 539, 645
Szilard, Leo, 510

Tabloids *(def.),* 513
Taft, Robert A., 568, 585
Taft, William Howard, 381; election of 1908, 416; tariff policy, 416–417; and Progressives, 417–418; and election of 1912, 418–419; antitrust activities, 418; and dollar diplomacy, 432, 434–436; reciprocity agreement, 439
Taft-Hartley Act, 568
Taiwan, 580, 593, 610. *See also* China
Talleyrand-Périgord, Charles Maurice de, 102, 105
Tammany Hall, 410
Taney, Roger B., 182–183, 250–252
Tarbell, Ida M., 409
Tariffs, 232, 234, 350–351; and Hamilton, 95–96; of 1816, 130, 140; of 1828, 162; of 1832, 162; of 1833, 207; of 1846, 209; of 1857,

251; reform, 348–350; Dingley, 351; McKinley, 351, 354; Wilson-Gorman, 351, 377; and Latin America, 375; of 1894, 377; Payne-Aldrich, 416–417, 439; Underwood, 422, 425; Hawley-Smoot, 469–470, 477, 518; Reciprocal Trade Agreement Amendment of 1934, 518
Taxes, colonial, 41–42, 44–47, 53; and Shays's Rebellion, 81; and Constitution, 84, 86; excise, 95; federal income, 262, 356, 424; Revenue Act of 1942, 542; Internal Revenue Act of 1954, 588; tax-reduction bill of 1964, 629–630
Taylor, John, 149
Taylor, Zachary, 194, 196, 242, 248; and election of 1848, 241, 248; and Compromise of 1850, 241–242
Tea Act of 1773, 45–46
Teapot Dome scandal, 462
Tecumseh, 122–123, 126
Telegraph, 210, 221, 312, 340
Telephone, 306, 309–310, 320, 340
Television industry, 607, 654
Teller Amendment, 378, 380
Temperance movement, 204, 360
Temple, Shirley, 515
Tenant farming, 334–335, 342
Tennessee, 258, 287
Tennessee Valley Authority (TVA), 486, 588
Ten Nights in a Bar-Room and What I Saw There, 207
Tenskwatawa, 122
Tenth Amendment, 92, 701
Tenure of Office Act, 288
Texas, 152, 176, 178, 186–187, 191, 226, 240, 242, 256, 288, 327
Textile industry, 166–167
Thayer, Webster, 466
Thirteenth Amendment, 233, 267–268, 283, 702
Thomas, George H., 278
Thomas, Norman M., 489
Thoreau, Henry David, 206, 254, 415
Thurmond, J. Strom, 577
Tilden, Samuel J., 298
Tilden, William T., 512
Tillman, Benjamin, 355
Timber Culture Act of 1873, 332
Time zones, 308
Tocqueville, Alexis de, 205
Tojo, Hideki, 534
Tombaugh, Clyde, 510
Tooker, George, 605
Totalitarianism *(def.),* 457
Town meetings, 35, 46
Townsend Clubs, 488
Townshend duties of 1767, 42, 44–45, 48
Townships, 74; *(def.),* 76

Trade associations *(def.)*, 499–500
Trail of Broken Treaties, 626
"Trail of Tears," 166
Transatlantic cable, 222
Transcendentalism, 200
Transistors, 658–659
Transportation, before 1800, 110–111; 1800–1830, 140, 142–144; 1830–1850, 209–210; 1865–1900, 306–309; impact on city growth, 317, 322, 463; 1960–1973, 661–662
Transportation, Department of, 661
Treaties, with Indians, 24, 75, 77, 164, 166; Paris, 1783, 62; Jay's, 99–102; Greenville, 100; Pinckney's, 100–101, 151; Mortefontaine, 105–106; Ghent, 128; Adams-Onís, 152–153; Rush-Bagot Agreement, 152; New Echota, 177; Guadalupe Hidalgo, 1848, 196, 198–199; Burlingame, 295; Washington, 296; Paris, 1898, 380; Portsmouth, 431; Hay-Pauncefote, 432; Panama Canal, 432–433; Bryan-Chamorro, 436; Brest-Litovsk, 441, 446; Versailles, 449–452, 521; Four-Power Pact, Five-Power Naval Treaty, and Nine-Power Open Door Treaty, 473; Kellogg-Briand Pact, 474; after World War II, 570–571, 580; on Anti-Ballistics Missile Systems, 633; Nonproliferation, 633
Triangular trade, 28
Tripartite Pact, 530, 533
Trist, Nicholas P., 198
Truman, Harry S, election of 1944, 561; Potsdam conference, 563; domestic policies of, 565–569, 577–578; economic policies, 565–568; civil rights policies, 568; foreign policies of, 570–576, 578, 580–581, 584, 592; election of 1948, 576–577; and dismissal of MacArthur, 584
Trusts, 394; *(def.)*, 313–314; regulation of, 352–353, 485; and Theodore Roosevelt, 412–414; suits against, 627. *See also* Monopoly
Tubman, Harriet, 175, 251
Tugwell, Rexford Guy, 490, 603
Tunisia, 546, 611
Tunney, Gene, 512
Turkey, 439, 572–573
Turnbull, Andrew, 37
Turner, Nat, 170
Turnpikes, 110–111, 142–143
Tuscaroras, 21
Tuskegee Institute, 336, 399
Tutuila, 374
Twain, Mark, 366, 369–370, 383
Tweed Ring, 298
Twelfth Amendment, 108, 298, 701–702

Twentieth Amendment, 494, 705
Twenty-first Amendment, 468–469, 705–706
Twenty-fourth Amendment, 621, 706
Twenty-Negro law, 268
Twenty-second Amendment, 569, 612, 706
Twenty-sixth Amendment, 650, 707
Tydings-McDuffie Act of 1934, 520
Tyler, John, 183, 186, 194, 207
Typewriter, 306, 309, 359

U-2 incident, 599
U-boats, 545
Uncle Tom's Cabin, 207, 243
Underground Railroad, 175
Union Leagues, 292
Union party. *See* Republican party
Union, 261–268; war finances, 262; agriculture, 262–264; business, 263–274; slavery, 265–266, 267; blockades, 269, 273, 274–275; problems with Britain, 272–273; Anaconda Plan, 274; war in the East, 279, 280–281; war in the West, 279–280; casualties, 299. *See also* Civil War
Unions, before 1850, 167–168, 225; origins of AFL, 319–320; Knights of Labor, 319–320; Clayton Act, 426; union shop *(def.)*, 568; merger of AFL-CIO, 601. *See also* Labor; Strikes
Unitarian Church, 200
United Auto Workers, 492
United Farm Workers Organization Committee, 628
United Mine Workers of America, 412, 459, 541, 568
United Nations, formation of, 562, 569–570; Korean War, 581, 584; in Egypt, 597–598; admission of Communist China, 610; in Congo, 611; disarmament conference, 632
United Nations, Declaration of, 559
United States Steel Corporation, 315, 459, 629
Universalist Church, 200
Universal Negro Improvement Association, 460
Updike, John, 671
Urbanization, in 1850, 217; 1900–1920, 304, 322–323, 392–393; in 1920's and 1930's, 498–499; by 1970's, 652, 657. *See also* Cities; Suburbs
Urban League, 620
U.S.S.R. *See* Soviet Union
Utah, 327, 339, 358, 415
Utes, 13

Valentino, Rudolph, 514
Vallandigham, Clement L., 267
Valley Forge, 56
Van Buren, Martin, election of 1836, 160; domestic policies, 168, 207; foreign policies, 176, 178; election of 1840, 183; election of 1848, 248
Vanderbilt, Cornelius, 307
Van Duyn, Mona, 672
Vanzetti, Bartolomeo, 466
Vaudeville, 349, 370, 401
Veblen, Thorstein B., 396
Venezuela, 66, 375, 433–434, 611
Verdun, battle of, 441
Vermont, 72
Verrazano, Giovanni da, 17
Versailles, Treaty of, 449–452, 521
Vesey, Denmark, 150
Vest, George G., 421
Vicksburg, battle of, 279–280
Victor Emmanuel III, 547
Viet Cong, 639–644
Viet Minh, 591–592
Vietnam, 539, 610
Vietnam, North, 592, 639, 640–642, 644
Vietnam, South, 592, 639–644
Vietnam war, 639–644; in 1968 election, 616; in 1972 election, 618; Viet Cong, 639–644; Gulf of Tonkin Resolution, 639–642; public opinion on, 640–641, 648–650; peace talks, 644
Vigilantes, 327–328
Villa, Pancho, 435
Virginia, 23, 26, 45, 73, 82, 89, 94, 159, 226, 258, 280, 288
Volunteers in Service to America (VISTA), 630
Vonnegut, Kurt, Jr., 671
Vulcanization, 223

Wade, Benjamin F., 283
Wade-Davis bill, 283, 287
Walker, David, 172
Walker, William, 668
Wallace, George C., 616, 618
Wallace, Henry A., 486, 560, 577
Wallace, Lew, 277, 370
Wampanoags, 35
Ward, Lester Frank, 316
War hawks, 122–124
Warhol, Andy, 668
Waring, Fred, 516
Warner, Charles Dudley, 369
War of 1812, 123–130, 133, 150
War on poverty, 630
Warren, Earl, 576
Warsaw Pact, 596
Washington, 327, 422
Washington, Booker T., 336, 399

Washington, D.C., 126, 144
Washington, George, in Revolutionary War, 54, 56–59, 62; Farewell Address, 67, 101–102, 240; and slavery, 73; and Constitution, 82–83; election of 1789, 90; and Whiskey Rebellion, 97; and reelection, 98–99
Watered stock *(def.)*, 315
Watergate affair, 618
Water power, 110, 149, 458
Watson, John B., 508
Watson, Thomas E., 355
Weaver, James B., 356
Weaver, Robert C., 656
Webster, Daniel, 147, 159, 160, 185–186, 195, 242, 244
Webster, Noah, 204
Weld, Theodore Dwight, 174
Welty, Eudora, 670
West, 216, 306; growth of, 217; population gains, 498
West Florida, 101
West Indies, 38, 41, 61, 104–105
Westinghouse, George, 308, 312
West Virginia, 259
Weyler, Valeriano, 377
Wheeler-Howard bill, 493, 602
Whigs, 156, 160–161, 289; philosophy of government and economics, 178; election of 1840, 183–184; and Webster-Ashburton Treaty, 186; election of 1844, 187, 190; and Mexican War, 195; and bank question, 207; and tariff, 207; Cotton and Conscience Whigs, 242; election of 1852, 244; disintegration, 246
Whiskey Rebellion, 96–97, 113
Whiskey Ring, 293
Whistler, James McNeill, 406
White, Hugh L., 160
Whiteman, Paul, 504, 516
Whitman, Walt, 206
Whitney, Eli, 109
Wickersham Commission, 468
Wilder, Thornton, 505
Willard, Emma Hart, 202
Willard, Frances, 360
Williams, Tennessee, 606
Willkie, Wendell, 532
Wilmot Proviso, 195

Wilson, Woodrow, election of 1912, 419–420; early career, 422; domestic policies, 422–426; election of 1916, 427–428; Lansing-Ishii Agreement, 432; relations with Latin America, 435–437; Panama Canal, 439; and U.S. neutrality, 439, 442; Fourteen Points, 446; Paris peace conference, 449; Treaty of Versailles, 450–451; relations with Congress, 449–450; League of Nations, 449–451; election of 1920, 451–453
Wirt, William, 180
Wisconsin, 169, 338
Wolfe, James, 38
Wolfe, Thomas, 502
Woman's Christian Temperance Union (WCTU), 360, 420
Woman's party, 428, 664
Women, 14, 43, 119, 327; Indian, 21; in colonies, 26, 29; education of, 32, 181, 202, 368; denied voting rights, 35, 66, 69, 77, 158, 357–358, 360, 411; in American Revolution, 46, 54; as workers, 137, 224–225, 309, 359, 565, 602; abolitionists, 174–175; in reform movements, 200, 202–204; before Civil War, 202–203, 236; during Civil War, 264, 269–270; in gold rush, 364; in sports, 370–371, 672; in Progressive movement, 411, 428; in World War I, 445; in World War II, 541; and crime rate, 656; in 1960's and 1970's, 662–664. *See also* Women's rights movements
Women's Political Union, 420
Women's rights movements, in 1830's, 174, 202–203; Seneca Falls Convention, 203; suffrage, 357–358, 360, 420–422, 461; in 1960's and 1970's, 662–664
Wood, Grant, 506
Woodward, Charlotte, 203
Wool, John, 196
Works Progress Administration (WPA), 490, 494
World War I, outbreak, 388, 439; effects, 388, 455; battles, 440–443; 445–448; submarine warfare, 442–443; U.S. in, 443–445; propaganda, 445; and technological advances, 447; armistice, 448; peace conference, 449; reparations, 449; U.S. treaties, 452; aftermath, 458
World War II, outbreak, 528; France surrenders, 528, 530; Lend-Lease, 532; German invasion of U.S.S.R., 534; attack on Pearl Harbor, 534–535; Japanese internment, 542–543; atomic bomb, 544, 558–559; technological advances, 544, 549, 558–559; war in Europe, 544–552; death camps, 550, 552; Nuremberg trials, 550; German surrender, 552; war in Pacific, 552–559; Japanese surrender, 559; Allied diplomacy, 559–563; reparations, 562–563; peace treaties, 570–571
Wounded Knee, South Dakota, 329, 626
Wright, Frank Lloyd, 407, 508
Wright, Orville, 400, 501
Wright, Richard, 502
Wright, Wilbur, 400
Wyandots, 77
Wyeth, Andrew, 604
Wyoming, 327, 358

"XYZ" affair, 102

Yakimas, 13
Yalta conference, 561–562, 570
Yamashita, Sachio, 668
Yellow journalism, 372
Yorktown, battle of, 57–58
Young, Brigham, 192
Young America movement, 245–246
Yugoslavia, 538, 574

Zaïre. *See* Congo
Zimmermann, Alfred, 443
Zionism *(def.)*, 575
Zion Society, 201
Zuñis, 21